THE HISTORY OF
THE BRITISH COAL INDUSTRY

VOLUME 3

1830–1913: VICTORIAN PRE-EMINENCE

THE HISTORY OF
THE BRITISH COAL
INDUSTRY

VOLUME 3、

1830–1913: Victorian Pre-eminence

BY

ROY CHURCH

with the assistance of

ALAN HALL and JOHN KANEFSKY

CLARENDON PRESS · OXFORD
1986

Oxford University Press, Walton Street, Oxford OX2 6DP
Oxford New York Toronto
Delhi Bombay Calcutta Madras Karachi
Kuala Lumpur Singapore Hong Kong Tokyo
Nairobi Dar es Salaam Cape Town
Melbourne Auckland
and associated companies in
Beirut Berlin Ibadan Nicosia

Oxford is a trade mark of Oxford University Press

Pubished in the United States
by Oxford University Press, New York

British Library Cataloguing in Publication Data
Church, Roy
The History of the British coal industry.
Vol. 3: 1830-1913
1. Coal mines and mining–Great Britain–History
I. Title
388.2' 724' 0941   HD9551.5
ISBN 0-19-828284-2

Set by Joshua Associates Ltd
Printed in Great Britain by
Biddles Ltd,
Guildford and King's Lynn

Acknowledgements

Only an extreme optimist would expect to succeed in writing a comprehensive history of the coal industry from 1830 to 1913, yet that was the brief accepted by the author. While the study attempts to be comprehensive, including in its compass social and political as well as economic dimensions, it claims to be neither exhaustive nor definitive. Far too much primary material lies unused in the various record repositories throughout the country to justify any such pretence, though almost all of this material has been sifted by examining the detailed listings, where they existed, and by sampling. The general strategy in the use of archives, largely dictated by the sources, though which can be justified on other grounds, has been to concentrate on those relating to large and medium-sized colliery enterprises, particularly where together with relatively lengthy series of data which have survived descriptive materials have been found which facilitate evaluation and interpretation.

The voluminous published literature, theses, parliamentary sources, and business and estate archives, necessitated the appointment of two research assistants. For a combined total of seven man years Drs Alan Hall and John Kanefsky collaborated fully in the location, evaluation, and interpretation of these materials. This process took us to libraries, record offices, estate muniment rooms, and business premises throughout the country, and our regular meetings to exchange ideas and indulge in mutual criticism were crucial to the progress of an integrated research strategy. The penultimate draft was subjected to the critical scrutiny of Drs Hall and Kanefsky, who gave generously of their time even though their contracts had ended and each was in full-time employment. My thanks are due to them, therefore, for their expertise and unflagging commitment throughout the project.

It is inevitable that in a project which involves research in archives and libraries in all the coal mining regions as well as in the major national repositories, indebtedness to archivists and librarians is similarly widespread. To mention all who were helpful would produce an impossibly long list, yet to thank only some would be invidious. Thanks are extended, therefore, to them all for the assistance which has always been offered willingly and for the patience they have shown when presented with requests to consult items in bulk and in store. The staff of Hobart House Library have shown special indulgence in the sheer volume of loans they were willing to make in order to expedite the research. By kind permission of Mr R. F. Childs of the Clay Cross Company, and of Mr Seagrave of Powell Duffryn, Stanhope Gate, London, uncatalogued business records relating to these two companies were consulted *in situ*. Throughout the project Prof. Peter Mathias has been a source of encouragement and advice, with beneficial effects on the final typescript. The discussion of problems in common and the reconciliation of some basic statistical series with the authors and researchers engaged on volumes 2 and 4 was advanced by Prof. Barry Supple, Stephanie Tailby and Dr Nick Tiratsoo, Dr David Stoker, and the late Prof. Michael Flinn whose untimely death before his own volume was published deprived co-authors of other volumes of a respected critic and colleague.

Thanks are also due to the drawing department at Hobart House for their work in preparing figures in the text. I am grateful to the editors of the Scottish Dictionary of Business Biography, Prof. Anthony Slaven and Dr Sheila Hamilton, for making available certain data assembled in the course of that project. Dr David Jeremy was also helpful affording advice from his work in preparing the *Dictionary of Business Biography*. I am indebted to Dr B. R. Mitchell, who kindly allowed me to read a draft of his book, *The Economic Development of the British Coal Industry, 1800-1914* (Cambridge, 1984) which was eventually published while the typescript of this volume was already with the OUP.

I would also like to acknowledge the assistance, in various ways, of Mr Dudley Baines, Dr Roger Burt, Prof. Lance Davis, Prof. Michael Edelstein, Dr Ben Fine, Dr A. R. Griffin, Dr C. P. Griffin, Dr Valerie Hall, Dr Roy Hay, Prof. Leslie Hannah, Mrs Christine Hiskey, Dr M. Kirby, Dr Joseph Melling, Mr Michael Morris, Mr Steve Moseley, Dr Michael Moss, Prof. Ashok Parikh, Prof. Sidney Pollard, Dr W. D. Rubinstein, Prof. A. J. Taylor, Dr Rhodri Walters, Mrs J. C. White, and Mr John Woodhurst. Virtually all of the typing in the preparation of this book was undertaken by Mrs Carol Haines, a task requiring enormous patience and perseverance, and which was performed with exceptional accuracy and good humour. Miss Judith Sparks provided further skilled secretarial support. To all I record my thanks, and to the ESRC Economic and Social History Committee which awarded a pesonal research grant to relieve me of teaching and administrative duties—for six months in 1982/3. The incidence of the opportunity costs of research-ing and writing this book has fallen heavily upon Wendy, to whom my debt is the greatest, and upon Benjamin, Joseph, Thomas, and Naomi, who wondered when it would end.

R.A.C.

December, 1984

Contents

Illustrations

Tables

Figures

References to Sources in Footnotes

Manuscript sources. A list of collections used and the location of the record offices in which they are housed are given in the appropriate section of the Bibliography. Abbreviations of record offices are given in 'Abbreviations in Notes and Bibliography'. In the footnotes the abbreviation of a record office is followed normally by the name of the collection, its reference number (where one has been allocated), and a page or folio number where relevant: thus, 'NuRO Armstrong 725/B4/125', meaning the Armstrong papers in the Northumberland County Record Office numbered 725 in their catalogue, document B4, folio 125. In the manuscript collection of the North of England Institute of Mining and Mechanical Engineers in Newcastle-upon-Tyne the name of the collection is followed by two or three numbers for shelf (in the basement room where all the manuscript collections are housed on consecutively numbered shelves) and volume number on that shelf, with a page or folio number where relevant: thus, 'NEI Forster 53/8/3', meaning the Forster collection on shelf 53 volume number 8, folio 3.

Printed books and articles. This section includes those secondary works used in the preparation of this book which are also referred to only by author's name and date of publication in the notes. It excludes detailed local works and many items which though relevant are not mainly concerned with the coal industry and do not appear in the comprehensive bibliography by Benson, Neville, and Thompson 1981. Books and articles in both categories are referred to with full references in the notes. London is the place of publication unless otherwise indicated. For abbreviations of articles, see the following list.

Unpublished theses. The full references for all these theses are set out in the thesis section of the Bibliography. They are cited in notes in author's name only (followed by the word 'thesis' to indicate the section of the Bibliography in which the full references may be found) with date and page numbers where relevant.

Parliamentary papers. References in notes to the principal parliamentary papers used have abbreviated titles which may be easily identified with the full references in the appropriate section of the Bibliography or in Benson, Neville, and Thompson 1981. Select Committee is abbreviated as SC, Royal Commission as RC, and House of Commons as HC. References to other papers are given in full in the notes.

Abbreviations in Notes and Bibliography

AA	*Archaeologia Aeliana*
BH	*Business History*
BJIR	*British Journal of Industrial Relations*
BL	British Library
BPL	Birmingham Public Library
BRO	Bristol City Record Office
BroLU	Brotherton Library, Leeds University
BSCEMRRC	British Steel Corporation East Midland Region Record Centre, Irlhlingborough
BSCNRRC	British Steel Corporation Northern Region Record Centre, Middlesborough
BSSLH	*Bulletin of the Society for the Study of Labour History*
BUL	Birmingham University Library
CG	*Colliery Guardian*
CJ	*Commons' Journal*
ClRO	Clwyd County Record Office
CoRO	Coventry Record Office
CuRO	Cumbria Record Office
DeRO	Derbyshire County Record Office
DUJ	*Durham University Journal*
DuRO	Durham County Record Office
EDCC	Economic Development and Cultural Change
EEH	*Explorations in Economic History*
EH	*Economic History* (Supplement to *Economic Journal*)
EHR	*Economic History Review*
GlaRO	Glamorgan Record Office
GLMR	Guildhall Library and Muniment Room
GPL	Gateshead Public Library
GRO	Gloucestershire County Record Office
HJ	*Historical Journal*
HMC	*Historical Manuscripts Commission*
IA	*Industrial Archaeology*
IAR	*Industrial Archaeology Review*
IRSH	*International Review of Social History*
JBSMS	*Journal of the British Society of Mining Students*
JEAH	*Journal of Education and Administration and History*
JEH	*Journal of Economic History*
JIH	*Journal of Interdisciplinary History*

JRL	John Rylands Library, University of Manchester
JRSS	*Journal of the Royal Statistical Society*
JTH	*Journal of Transport History*
KM	Kirkcaldy Museum
LaRO	Lancashire County Record Office
LCA	Leeds City Archives Department
LEA	Lambton Estate Archives
MH	*Midland History*
MJ	*Mining Journal*
NCL	Newcastle City Library
NCRO	Nottingham City Record Office
NEI	North of England Institute of Mining and Mechanical Engineers
NeUL	Newcastle University Library
NH	*Northern History*
NLS	National Library of Scotland
NLW	National Library of Wales
NoRO	Nottingham County Record Office
NPL	Newcastle Public Library
NUL	Nottingham University Library
NuRO	Northumberland County Record Office
OEP	Oxford Economic Papers
PICE	*Proceedings of the Institute of Civil Engineers*
PP	*Parliamentary Papers*
PPres	*Past and Present*
RC	Royal Commission
RMS	*Renaissance and Modern Studies*
SC	Select Committee
SCL	Sheffield City Library
SHR	*Scottish Historical Review*
ScRO	Scottish Record Office
ShRO	Shropshire County Record Office
SoRO	Somerset County Record Office
StRO	Staffordshire County Record Office
TCandWAAS	*Transactions of the Cumberland and Westmorland Antiquarian and Archaeological Society*
TFIME	*Transactions of the Federated Institute of Mining Engineers*
TH	*Transport History*
THSLandC	*Transactions of the Historic Society of Lancashire and Cheshire*
TLandCAS	*Transactions of the Lancashire and Cheshire Antiquarian Society*
TIME	*Transactions of the Institute of Mining Engineers*
TMIME	*Transactions of the Midland Institute of Mining Engineers*
TNEIME	*Transactions of the North of England Institute of Mining Engineers*
TNS	*Transactions of the Newcomen Society*
TNSIMME	*Transactions of the North Staffordshire Institute of Mining and Mechanical Engineers*

TSSEWIME	*Transactions of the South Staffordshire and East Worcestershire Institute of Mining Engineers*
TTS	*Transactions of the Thoroton Society*
TWRO	Tyne and Wear County Record Office
UBHJ	*University of Birmingham Historical Journal*
UCNW	Library of the University College of North Wales
VCH	*Victoria County Histories*
WaRO	Warwickshire County Record Office
WiRO	Wigan Record Office
WMDL	Wakefield Metropolitan District Library
YBESR	*Yorkshire Bulletin of Economic and Social Research*

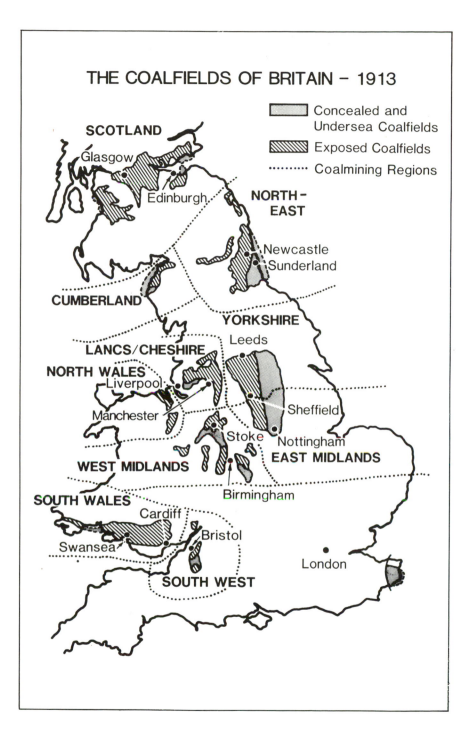

THE COALFIELDS OF BRITAIN – 1913

Concealed and Undersea Coalfields

Exposed Coalfields

Coalmining Regions

SCOTLAND

Glasgow

Edinburgh

NORTH-EAST

Newcastle
Sunderland

CUMBERLAND

YORKSHIRE

Leeds

LANCS/CHESHIRE

NORTH WALES

Liverpool

Manchester

Sheffield

Stoke

Nottingham

WEST MIDLANDS

EAST MIDLANDS

Birmingham

SOUTH WALES

Cardiff

Swansea

Bristol

London

SOUTH WEST

CHAPTER I

The Rise of the Coal Economy: Output and Demand

i. Resources and production: trends, limits and location

Attempts to classify this or that age, as contemporaries and historians have often been tempted to do, contribute little to an analytical appreciation of the dynamics of change during a particular period. It is nevertheless interesting that whereas Clapham labelled the second quarter of the nineteenth century as 'The Railway Age' Britain's leading locomotive engineer who played a vital role in it, George Stephenson, had remarked that 'the strength of Britain lies in her iron and coal beds ... The Lord Chancellor now sits upon a bag of wool; but wool has long since ceased to be emblematical of the staple commodity of England. He ought rather to sit upon a bag of coal.'[1] Stephenson's belief in the future for coal was demonstrated by deeds. In 1833 George and Robert Stephenson were brought to Leicestershire to build railways linking collieries with the market in Leicester. The consequences demonstrated in two ways the economic potential and the social effects of coal-mining expansion. Transport improvements stimulated the development of collieries in four parishes, which together formed the rapidly growing mining town which, with literal symbolism, was given the name Coalville.[2] The Stephensons played an even more direct role when they purchased the Snibston Estate to set up their own colliery company, a step which was repeated on a much larger scale in 1837 when, following the unexpected exposure of coal seams cut through in the course of constructing the Midland Railway near Chesterfield, George Stephenson formed the Clay Cross Colliery Company.[3] Thirty years later the distinguished academic statistician, W. Stanley Jevons, was as explicit as Stephenson had been in claiming for coal a central significance in Britain's economic supremacy: 'Coal alone can command in sufficient

[1] Quoted in Samuel Smiles, *Lives of the Engineers, The Locomotive, George and Robert Stephenson* (London, 1879), 276.
[2] Dennis Baker, *Coalville, The First Seventy-five Years 1833-1908* (Leicester, 1983), 94.
[3] Smiles, 1879, 275-8.

abundance either the iron or the steam; and coal, therefore, commands this age—the Age of Coal'.[1] By 1907 the value of coal output accounted for approximately 5 per cent of UK national income and employed nearly one million people—almost 6 per cent of the employed population and representing 8 per cent of male employment. National coal production in 1913 was 287 million tons.

Historians have disagreed over output levels before 1872, when the Coal Mines Regulation Act marked the beginning of a reliable output series. The difficulty of estimating production during the early to mid-nineteenth century stems from the lack of interest among contemporaries in national, or even regional, figures. Consequently historians have been compelled to try to reconstruct a statistical picture of the industry from data gathered for various specific purposes, mainly price and output regulation, tolls, customs, and taxation, most of it assembled at local or district levels, and differing in scope and comprehensiveness. Data from these various sources have been assembled to show new estimates of national production from 1830. National series, however, are inadequate as a basis for the history of an industry characterized by such intense regional diversity, and consequently output series have been estimated for ten mining regions (some of which contained several clearly separated coalfields) as follows: Scotland, the North-east, Cumberland, Lancashire and Cheshire, North Wales, Yorkshire, East Midlands, West Midlands, South Wales, and the South-west. The revised national estimates summarized in Table 1.1 exceed all previous figures, including the recent and most accurate 'new estimates' presented by Pollard for the years before 1854, from which date historians have used Robert Hunt's uncorrected *Mineral Statistics*.

The justification for revising these, by using Hunt's own amendments made retrospectively, is explained in Appendix 1.1. The effect of the revised estimates is to reveal a pattern of growth which differs from that identified hitherto. For the fitting of a straight line and of a growth curve suggests that a deceleration in the secular trend occurred not in the 1880s as is generally believed, but from around 1860; the cyclical annual growth rates presented in Table 1.1 point to the probability that the cycle of 1854–66 marked the beginnings of this break in trend—though absolute increments to annual output continued to grow. As a result of these revisions, conventional accounts of the course of labour productivity will also require critical re-examination in Chapter 7. The main

---

[1] W. S. Jevons 1865, vii–viii.

Table 1.1. *Estimates of UK coal production, 1830-1913, by mining region*
(million tons, average per annum per quinquennium)

	1830–4	1835–9	1840–4	1845–9	1850–5	1855–9	1860–4	1865–9	1870–4	1875–9	1880–4	1885–9	1890–4	1895–9	1900–4	1905–9	1910–13
Scotland	3.2	3.8	4.6	6.1	8.1	9.9	12.0	13.9	15.9	18.4	20.4	21.7	24.8	29.6	34.1	38.6	41.3
North-east	7.1	8.4	10.0	12.0	15.2	17.4	20.9	25.8	35.2	31.0	36.1	36.2	38.8	43.3	46.8	53.1	54.2
Cumberland	0.6	0.7	0.8	0.8	0.9	0.9	1.3	1.4	1.2	1.4	1.8	1.7	1.7	2.0	2.1	2.2	1.8
Lancashire and Cheshire	4.2	4.9	6.0	7.5	9.6	11.2	12.8	13.7	15.8	18.6	20.3	21.6	21.9	24.0	24.8	24.9	23.9
North Wales	0.6	0.7	0.7	1.0	1.4	1.6	1.8	2.2	2.5	2.3	2.6	2.6	2.9	3.0	3.1	3.3	3.4
Yorkshire	3.0	3.5	4.4	5.4	6.7	8.5	9.2	9.9	13.6	15.7	18.6	20.1	21.5	24.7	28.1	33.7	33.9
East Midlands	1.8	2.0	2.4	2.9	3.4	4.4	6.0	7.2	9.7	12.1	14.5	16.3	18.5	21.6	25.9	30.1	31.2
West Midlands	5.9	6.9	7.8	9.2	10.9	11.5	13.0	15.2	16.8	15.6	16.6	16.4	17.0	17.5	18.1	19.4	20.3
South Wales	4.8	6.0	7.1	8.7	10.6	13.2	14.3	15.1	16.5	16.7	23.4	26.0	30.8	33.9	41.1	48.2	51.5
South-west	0.8	0.9	1.0	1.1	1.4	1.3	1.8	2.0	2.0	1.9	2.1	2.2	2.1	2.3	2.5	2.6	2.7
Total (tons)[a]	32.0	37.8	44.7	55.9	68.4	80	92.5	106.4	123.3	133.6	156.4	165.2	180.3	201.9	227.4	256.1	271.0
(tonnes)	32.5	38.4	45.4	56.8	69.5	81.3	94.0	108.2	125.3	136.3	158.9	167.8	183.2	205.1	231.0	260.2	275.3

Annual compounded rate of growth (%)

(1815–30)	(1831–37)	(1837–47)	(1847–54)	(1854–66)	(1866–73)	(1873–83)	(1883–90)	(1890–1900)	(1900–7)	(1907–13)
2.1	3.2	3.6	4.8	2.8	2.9	2.5	1.5	2.2	2.0	1.8

[a] Including Ireland.
Sources See Appendix 1.1.

difference between our regional output estimates and those presented by Pollard is the tendency of the latter to underestimate output in the West Midlands (which cannot be accounted for by different definitions of the region), though in other respects too our regional distribution differs somewhat. Figure 1.1 shows the convergence of our national estimates with others by the 1860s, the most striking difference being the variations in growth rates between 1840 and the mid-1860s. Appendix 1.1, which contains Table 1.12 showing annual estimates of UK coal production also explains the sources and methods employed in compiling these and the revised regional estimates.

By 1830 the coal industry was already one of Britain's major industries and was growing rapidly. While extraction of coal at the face was achieved by miners' muscle power, aided by pick, hammer, and wedge, as it had been in 1700, the widespread adoption of steam engines and the safety lamp had together contributed towards a solution of some of the problems of drainage, ventilation, and lighting presented by the deeper mining which became necessary to expand output to meet demand. The substitution of horse for human power in the haulage of coal, together with other improvements in transport underground, and the application of steam power to the winding of coal to the surface rendered possible the movement of ever-growing quantities of coal without

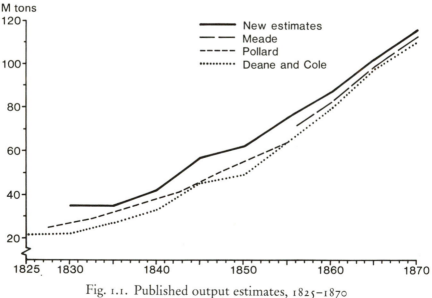

Fig. 1.1. Published output estimates, 1825–1870
Sources: See Appendix 1.1.

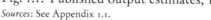

increasing pithead prices. Comparable improvements in the transport of coal between pithead and consumer contributed further to this achievement, notably the wrought-iron wagonway rail and latterly the substitution of steam for horse traction on colliery wagonways, and of steam locomotives on the wagonways of some of the larger collieries. More modest and difficult to measure before 1830 were the contributions from improved mine design and extraction methods. The accumulation of knowledge and experience by the industry's major viewers (managers and management consultants) in the North-east by 1830 makes it possible to refer to a body of professionals whose skills and advice were an important asset to an industry faced with inherent problems of supply and diminishing returns in the context of rapidly increasing demand. By 1830 industrial consumers had overtaken domestic purchasers as the greatest source of demand for coal. Already iron had established itself as the largest industrial category, while the transformation to coal-based sources of energy was well advanced also in cotton, non-ferrous metal smelting, pottery, flour-milling, and brewing.

The consequences for coal demand of the application of steam to transport on land and sea were also immense. With a per-capita domestic consumption of nearly two tons in 1830 (a level which approached that obtaining 150 years later) it is clear that the secular boom in coal production which culminated in the peak of 1913 had already begun by 1830, so the problem which faced Victorian coal-owners of how to sustain ever-increasing output levels was not new, though the dimensions of expanding demand were quite unprecedented.[1] One consequence of the change in scale and patterns of demand was the redistribution of production between and within coalfields, a development which changes in knowledge and technology affecting the winning and working of collieries and the transport of coal rendered possible.

Both supply and demand factors, therefore, explain the diverse histories of the relative size and rates of growth in the various regions. On the supply side the ultimate determinants were those relating to the geology of the coalfields: the extent of exposed seams which cropped out at the surface or which could be worked by sinking pits at no greater depth. As output grew the more easily worked seams were exhausted, further expansion depending upon the more intensive working of existing

[1] This survey of the industry in 1830 is based on Flinn 1984, 422–57; Dunn 1844, 1–10; Galloway 1898, 1–16.

fields and the development of new, more difficult, more risky, and more dangerous concealed coalfields. Thus, in the principal major coal-mining region after the outcrops and shallow seams had been worked out along the rivers Tyne and Wear and to the north of Newcastle as far as Ashington in Northumberland, deep mining of coal through the Permian formation beneath the magnesium limestone began in eastern Durham from the 1820s. As a result, coals were raised for the first time at Monkwearmouth in 1831, followed by Hetton, Haswell, Murton, Shotton, Castle Eden, and Trimdon, the effect of which was to transform the output capacity of the district within a dozen years. In addition to this intensive form of exploitation of minerals at collieries within easy reach of river, coast, or canal, the advent of improved railway transport facilitated extensive development to the south and west of the county between Durham and Bishop Auckland.[1]

While the abundant and comparatively accessible coal of the North-east enabled the latter to retain its lead in levels of production to 1913, at the other extreme the output share of the West Midlands, with the second largest output in 1830, began to be overtaken by other regions from the 1870s as a consequence of the virtual exhaustion of safely workable reserves in the Thick, or Ten Yard, coal found less than sixty metres from the surface in south Staffordshire and east Worcestershire. Outputs in these districts plummeted, as inundation rendered even more problematical the raising of coal from the numerous tiny mines characteristic of the area. Against this, beginning in the 1850s, but especially from the 1860s, deeper sinkings led to the discovery of thick coal to the north of Birmingham around Cannock Chase, and the rising production from much deeper mines in north Staffordshire and in Warwickshire restored the position of the West Midlands as a sizeable producer of coal, though much diminished in comparison with the second quarter of the century.[2]

The development of the north Staffordshire mines was contingent upon the solution of serious problems associated with deep mining in a district where seams were frequently faulted, pitching steeply, and where gas and water problems complicated operations. These were features characteristic, too, of Lancashire and Cheshire. By mid-century the output from drifts and shallow workings in the outcrops to the north-east of the latter region were becoming inadequate to meet a

[1] Dunn 1844, 112–19; H. S. Jevons 1915, 59–64; D. J. Rowe 1971, 126–8.
[2] Dunn 1844, 138–9; H. S. Jevons 1915, 88–92; A. J. Taylor 1967, 68–107; E. Taylor Thesis 1974, 11, 209.

rapidly growing demand for coal, and a shift occurred towards the mining of the deeply concealed seams in the south-west of Lancashire, centred upon Wigan. As in the West Midlands, however, while mining the less accessible coal enabled output to expand, it could not prevent the relative decline in the region's importance as a coal producer.[1]

Of the other major coalmining regions, the resources of South Wales proved to be the most responsive to rapid exploitation and had already carried this region to third position by 1830. Although mining was initially located on the south-western and north-eastern perimeters of the coalfield, the developments of the area between saw the emergence of Monmouthshire and east Glamorgan as the major producing districts, following the increased accessibility provided by dock and rail transport facilities. Improvement in deep mining techniques enabled the industry to spread from the Aberdare Valley to the Rhondda, beginning in 1851 with the first sinkings to reach the Upper Four Feet Seam at 114 metres, followed by the deeper minings in the Rhondda Fawr and the Rhondda Fach in the 1870s. By 1900 the Rhondda dominated coal production in South Wales.[2]

In comparison with the benign geological characteristics and resource endowments of South Wales, the Scottish achievement of expansion, sustained throughout most of our period, occurred despite extensive faulting in the eastern area. In the early years this was the result mainly of development in the west, especially of Ayrshire and Lanarkshire following the discovery of the famous blackband measures and the construction of rail links from inland coal deposits to the major Scottish markets. Whereas until the 1870s Scottish coal supplies were drawn from the shallower fields, development in the late nineteenth century was the result of deep mining, particularly in the hitherto virgin areas of Hamilton to the south-east of Glasgow, where the seven-foot Ell coal contributed to the rapid expansion of the 1880s and 1890s.[3]

Producing an output of similar size to that of Scotland by 1913, Yorkshire was one of the three fastest growing regions from the late nineteenth century. At the beginning of the period, when Yorkshire ranked fifth, the outcrops of West Yorkshire in the vicinity of Bradford, Halifax, and Huddersfield had supplied the major proportion of output from the county, where until the 1840s sufficient shallow seams offered easy working without encountering the technical problems already

[1] Dunn 1844, 128–34; H. S. Jevons 1915, 72–4; Challinor 1972, 258.
[2] Morris and Williams 1958, 1–10, 91–8, 113–15; Walters 1977, 2–7, 49–50.
[3] Dunn 1844, 119–28; H. S. Jevons 1915, 82–6, 143–9.

facing coalowners in the deeper fields of Lancashire and the North-east. Exhaustion of shallow workings in the west, however, was one of the factors which from the 1850s led to the rising relative importance of South Yorkshire, as coal was raised from the Silkstone and, at increasing depths, from the Barnsley Bed, the two major seams on the exposed coalfield. After the Oaks Colliery, won at a depth of 262 metres in 1838, and Denaby Main Colliery in 1866 sunk to 382 metres to the south-west of Doncaster, the first important exploitation of the concealed coalfield to the east occurred in 1892 with the Cadeby sinking to 715 metres. By that time south Yorkshire had outstripped West Yorkshire in coal production.[1]

Comparable to the course and chronology of development in Yorkshire was the expansion of mining in the East Midlands, which from 1830 was the smallest of the major regions, and even in 1870 ranked only seventh. Acceleration in output well above average from the 1850s, however, carried the region to fourth place by 1913. Outcrop mining characterized the early nineteenth century in each of the East Midland counties, and in Warwickshire between Tamworth and Atherstone. In Leicestershire development centred on the districts of Coleorton and Swannington, while in the exposed coalfield of Nottinghamshire and Derbyshire, an area running to the west of a line between Nottingham and Chesterfield in the Erewash Valley formed the principal source of coal supply. The 1860s and 1870s saw the sinking of a series of new collieries in the Leen Valley to the south of Nottingham which heralded the beginnings of concealed coalfield exploitation at Shireoaks, Hucknall, Bulwell, Annesley, Bestwood, Linby, Watnall, and Newstead. Other sinkings in the Sutton in Ashfield district north of Nottingham were also on the edge of the concealed coalfield. In the 1890s the Top Hard seam was tapped by more new pits spreading out from Mansfield and to the east of Chesterfield, and included Bolsover, Creswell, Markham, and Shirebrook.[2]

So rapid was the growth in UK output that in one after another region coalowners found themselves under pressure to sink below the Permian formation, a decision which involved commitment of greater amounts of capital to increasingly high-risk investment in the uncharted areas where the concealed coalfields were believed to be. Yet, although for the future of geology as an inductive science Lyell's *Principles of Geology*, published in 1830, was important and led to the inauguration

---

[1] Dunn 1844, 134; Hopkinson thesis, 230; Evison thesis, 5–12.
[2] Williams 1962, 175–7; A. R. Griffin 1971, 97, 160.

of the Geological Survey, many years were to elapse before the details of coalfield structures were incorporated in the surveys. In the 1830s local maps were published of Monmouthshire and of the Forest of Dean, but not until 1853 did the Geological Survey issue a special coalfield memoir—significantly on the south Staffordshire coalfield where resource exhaustion appeared to be imminent.[1] The coal reserves of the East and West Midlands were charted on one-inch maps in 1860, while the publication in the same year of the Lancashire coalfield survey on a six-inch scale set the standard for future memoirs produced by the Survey. A dozen years later the concealed coalfields were still inadequately charted, only Yorkshire and certain areas within the Scottish region having joined Lancashire and Cheshire as areas for which six-inch memoirs were complete.[2] Much of the boring carried out, therefore, continued to be literally exploratory and, although considerable progress was made in mapping after the *Report of the Coal Supply Commission* in 1871, even in 1900 mapping was incomplete and for some regions outdated.

The early geological surveys were the responsibility of Professor Edward Hull, who in 1861 was the author of *The Coal Fields of Great Britain* in which for the first time serious attention was given to the possibility of the exhaustion of British coal reserves. His conclusions were optimistic, yet two years later Sir William Armstrong, the leading engineering tycoon, startled his audience when in the course of his presidential address to the British Association he alluded to the distinct probability that the principal coal seams of the North-east faced exhaustion within two hundred years. In the introduction to *The Coal Question* published two years later, Professor W. S. Jevons endorsed Sir William's fears of the consequences of 'the rapid exhaustion of our most valuable seams . . . everywhere taking place.'[3] Despite subsequent disclaimers, Jevons's remarks were widely misinterpreted as a gloomy prediction of crisis in the nation's coal supply, which on Hull's evidence might be within little more than two hundred years. Concern first expressed in Parliament by John S. Mill was echoed by Gladstone in his budget speech of 1865; a lengthy debate on the subject in 1866 ended when Hussey Vivian, a prominent South Wales coalowner, persuaded the House to agree to set up the Coal Supply Commission to investigate.[4]

[1] Sir John Smith Flett, *The First Hundred Years of the Geological Survey of Great Britain* (London, 1937), 11–55.
[2] Ibid., 63–177.   [3] W. S. Jevons 1865, 19.
[4] R. Nelson Boyd, 'Collieries and Colliery Engineering', CG 10 Nov. 1893, 820; D. A. Thomas 1903, 462.

The ensuing report, issued in 1871, reckoned that on the worst assumptions concerning the growth in consumption coal reserves could be expected to last at the minimum nearly three hundred years, an estimate based on calculations of resources in known coalfields to a depth of approximately 1,230 metres. Experts guessed that seams lying below the Permian and other formations might increase the estimates by more than 60 per cent.[1] The Commission accepted Sir Roderick Murchison's view that concealed measures probably existed at workable depths in the South of England, a conclusion which in 1872 led the British Association to form the Sub Wealden Exploration Committee which marked the beginning of the long search for coal in Kent. The fears expressed in the 1860s, coincident with a deceleration of output, were thus dispelled by the Commission, whose findings were found subsequently to have vastly underestimated the country's coal reserves, not least in those areas which by 1913 were challenging the North-east for first place.

The extent of this redistribution is revealed in Table 1.2, which also revises other historians' ranking of regions in the early nineteenth century. Thus, the continuing importance of the West Midland region in 1830, then second (18 per cent) after the North-east (23 per cent) and

Table 1.2. *Estimates, 1830-1913, by mining regions,*
as percentages of total output

Mining Region	1830	1850	1870	1890	1913
Scotland	9.8	11.8	12.9	13.4	14.8
North-east	22.6	22.4	24.2	21.9	19.6
Cumberland	2.0	1.4	1.2	0.9	0.8
Lancashire and Cheshire	13.1	13.8	12.7	12.6	8.6
North Wales	2.0	1.9	2.0	1.7	1.2
Yorkshire	9.2	9.8	9.2	12.3	15.2
East Midlands	5.6	5.1	6.8	10.4	11.7
West Midlands	18.4	16.0	14.9	9.4	7.2
South Wales	14.4	15.5	14.3	16.2	19.8
South-west	2.6	2.1	1.7	1.3	1.0

Source: See Appendix 1.1.

[1] *Coal Supply* 1871, XVIII.

overtaken by South Wales only in the 1850s, underlines the rapid deterioration of the industry in this region during the third quarter of the century. Lancashire and Cheshire (13 per cent), in 1830 below the North-east, the West Midlands, and South Wales (14 per cent), conceded its position more gradually. Scotland was the fifth largest, producing 10 per cent of UK output in 1830. The newly expanding regions beginning to assume major coalfield status were Yorkshire and the East Midlands, though their outputs remained well below the other large producing regions until the end of the century. The most striking development before that time was the emergence of South Wales as the second largest producing region in the 1870s and which by 1913 was equal with the North-east. For most of the forty years before 1913 Scotland ranked third, but from the late 1880s Yorkshire followed by the East Midlands gained rapidly on Scotland; in 1913 Yorkshire took third place. At that time the East Midlands (12 per cent) ranked fifth after South Wales (20 per cent), the North-east (20 per cent), Yorkshire (15 per cent), Scotland (15 per cent), Lancashire and Cheshire (9 per cent), and the West Midlands (7 per cent). Rarely differing in output by as much as a million tons, the three minor regions, Cumberland, North Wales, and the South-west, remained at similar levels in relative decline throughout the period.

Measures of average percentage annual increases and percentage annual growth rates both show that the regions where the UK rate was exceeded most frequently were Scotland, South Wales, Yorkshire, and the East Midlands. It is hardly surprising that none of the older and longer-worked coalfields which were also the largest in 1830, the North-east, the West Midlands, and Lancashire and Cheshire should have appeared as pace-setters in the industry's expansion; neither is it so surprising that Yorkshire and the East Midlands, both expanding from a low base in 1830, should have experienced above-average rates of growth consistently from the 1850s. More remarkable is the relatively sustained rate of increase in output from Scotland and South Wales, for the latter was already by 1830 among the four largest coalmining regions, while Scotland, though a long-established coal producer, was quicker to exhaust the large reserves in exposed seams.

The supply of coal depended not only upon geological factors, but ultimately upon the decisions of landowners acting either as colliery proprietors or as the owners of coal and potential lessors. For except in the Forest of Dean, where minerals were the property of 'free miners' subject to a Crown royalty, in Britain minerals and the associated rights to exploitation belonged to the owners of land, rather than to the state as was customary in the rest of Europe.[1]

The exploitation of coal seams directly by landowners was not the norm in 1830. Large landowning colliery proprietors continued to exist (and to dominate production in certain districts), but the rapidity with which new enterprises sprang up to sink new collieries resulted in the relative decline in importance of the established landed producers. For this reason, and because landowners were withdrawing from active mining enterprise, even by the 1830s perhaps not more than 10 to 15 per cent of coal production came from collieries worked by landed proprietors, a share which was probably half that figure by the 1870s and fell to a negligible proportion by 1913.[2] Several factors contributed to this trend away from landed enterprise: an increase in the capital requirements of large-scale mining operations; greater complexity of organization, and the prospect of conceding greater powers and influence to the growing number of viewers, agents and managers possessing the technical and legal knowledge necessary to minimize risks and maximize gains.[3] When companies commenced coal production they did so usually without acquiring possession of the land; few colliery companies worked freehold coal.[4] Consequently, it was by negotiating leases and fixing royalty payments in terms which might help either to promote or to hinder the pace and efficiency of mineral exploitation that landowners in the nineteenth century played a major role, for theoretically landowners might have exercized their monopoly powers to prevent the working of coal reserves, either by insisting upon excessive rents and royalties or by refusing to make leases available.

Leases were not framed to the exclusive benefit of landowners, most leases containing clauses which allowed for arbitration by viewers to be appointed to judge the workability and profitability of coal on lease, though occasionally such safeguards were insufficient to prevent bankruptcy for the lessee. Some leases included 'breaks' at periodic intervals,

[1] *RC Mining Royalties* 1893, XLI, 334–5; see also Sorley 1889, 64.

[2] These percentages are guesses based on evidence from the 1842 *Children's Employment Commission*, XVI–XVIII; the *Lists of Mines* 1854–1913, and secondary sources relating to particular regions and/or collieries; Hassan thesis, 178 ff; Spring 1971, 16–62; John Davies thesis, 495–502; Challinor 1972, 261–2; Ward 1963, 61–74; A. R. Griffin 1971, 28, 110–11; R. W. Sturgess 1971, 173–204; Morris and Williams 1958, 118–8; C. G. Down and A. J. Warrington, *The History of the Somerset Coalfield* (Newton Abbott, 1971), 162; A. Dodd, *The Industrial Revolution in North Wales* (Cardiff, 1933), 189–97; *CG* 17 Feb. 1888; Ward, 'Some West Cumberland Landowners and Industry', *IA* 9 (1972), 341–62.   [3] Ward 1971, 72–4.

[4] *Sankey Commission* 1919, XII, Q 27437, ev. of Sir Richard Redmayne; *RC Mining Royalties* 1893, XLI QQ 61824.

actual termination requiring perhaps a year's notice. The duration of a lease depended upon the balance of interests between the landlord, in whose interest it was to secure rapid but thorough working of his minerals, and the lessee whose preference normally was for a long lease offering flexibility in working with the option of discontinuous mining operations.[1] The length of leases, therefore, varied considerably, though there is some reason to believe that until the final quarter of the century leases may have become shorter in some regions. Up to that time most English leases fell within a range between twenty-one and sixty-three years, and in Scotland between twenty-one and thirty-one years.[2] There is no evidence to suggest reasons why leases became shorter, and it is impossible to indicate whether the trend affected regions other than South Wales, Lancashire, and Cheshire. One possible explanation is that landowners came to recognize the value of minerals in newly exploited and rapidly expanding coalfields. The explanation for the reverse trend during the later nineteenth century, however, was clearly associated with increasing mine depths accompanied by the greater capital expenditure necessary for deep mining operations, developments which led colliery companies to insist upon leases of sufficient duration to justify the heavier capital investment associated with long-term mining development.

The general framework of mineral leases tended to be similar, but within which was to be found immense variation. Most leases normally included a fixed, or certain, 'dead' rent; a royalty or payment per ton of mineral worked; and in some cases, notably in Durham, Northumberland, South Wales, and to a lesser extent Yorkshire, provision was made for instroke, outstroke, shaft, and wayleaves, which were, in effect, payments, usually on a pro rata basis, for facilities for access to, or the removal of, coal through or over land not always owned by the lessor but adjacent to the coal on lease.[3] Royalties were usually assessed on the basis of acreage of coal worked and calculated not only on the area of coal leased, the location, thickness, and quality of the seams, but also took into account factors affecting underground and surface transport, access to markets, and the trading outlook at the time when leases were negotiated.[4] An incentive towards sustained mineral extraction was also

[1] Sorley 1889, 65–6; Hassan thesis, 147; C. P. Griffin thesis, 246–8.
[2] *RC Mining Royalties* 1893, XLI, 351–4.
[3] For an enumeration of general clauses inserted in colliery leases see Dunn 1852, 33–5; *RC Mining Royalties* 1893, XLI, 312.
[4] Fordyce 1860, 50–3; *RC Mining Royalties* 1893, XLI, 352.

provided by the minimum or dead rent. Minimum rents merged with
royalty payments, for under normal trading conditions (considerations
which helped to determine the minimum rent level initially) the fixed
rent would cover the royalty payment. When working or trading conditions were adverse the coal raised might fall below the amount required
to meet the minimum rent, which nevertheless was payable to the
lessor.[1] However, leases typically contained a clause which took account
of such deficiencies, or 'shorts', to be worked in succeeding years without liability for additional royalties, most commonly within five years.
Royalties thus protected the landlord against rapid mineral exhaustion,
while the dead rent offered protection against undue delay in working.
The lessee was often afforded protection against crippling financial
burdens in the early stages by inclusion in the lease of a clause postponing rent until the mine had been opened up, working begun, and coal
won, and in many instances payments were graduated to take account
of this gestation period.[2]

Flexibility in leasing arrangements, especially from the 1880s, had a
counterpart in the decline in wayleaves, enabling a lessee to carry coals
beneath, or across, property belonging to neighbouring landowners.
Wayleaves, customarily charged by the ton, applied mostly to mining
roads and wagonways, both underground and especially on the surface,
and were designed to compensate a landowner for damage or maintenance costs resulting from the use of his land to bring out coal from a
neighbouring royalty.[3] In 1830 colliery owners who wished to build
wagonways were compelled to negotiate with the landowners in order
to secure access across his land. In the North-east, where many collieries
in close proximity were located on land belonging to owners who were
experienced in the economics of coal mining, considerable scope existed
for bargaining over wayleaves. The Grand Allies, the extensive monopolistic partnership composed of coalowners in the North-east, were
especially adept at exploiting and acquiring control of wayleaves for the
express purpose of frustrating competitors by denying them access to
markets. In coalfields where mines were few and scattered, access for
wagonways probably created few serious problems even before 1830.
Thereafter, the advent of public railways had the effect of diminishing
the need to negotiate rights of way.[4] By 1890, outside the North-east,
where relatively lengthy private wayleave lines which had preceded

[1] Sorley 1889, 65–6.
[2] Ibid., 66; *RC Mining Royalties* 1893, XLI, 353; *Sankey Commission* 1919, XII, 658.
[3] Sorley 1889, 65–8.   [4] Flinn 1984, 160–1.

public railways continued to offer cost effective service to colliery owners and merchants, only a small proportion of coal output was subject to wayleaves. The figure for Durham was above one-third, for Northumberland and South Wales about one-third, and one-quarter for Yorkshire; elsewhere wayleaves were exceptional.[1]

In so far as we are concerned with the material influence of royalties on the development of industry, then even had royalties been abolished completely our discussion of the elasticity of demand for coal in the context of the tax on coal exports,[2] the most rapidly growing sector after 1880, suggests that the long-term consequences would have been unlikely to have afforded an appreciable stimulus to the industry, either by increasing the volume of mineral extracted or by expanding the supply of capital. After assessing the considerable volume of evidence before it in 1893 the Royal Commission on Royalties found that the development of mineral resources had not been impeded in any important respect.[3] The supply of minerals available for commercial exploitation had increased with demand, while wastage—attributable mainly to difficulties arising from the separation of mineral from surface land-ownership—were small. The fundamental explanation for the unhindered development of mineral resources was explained in 1893: 'The interest of a landed proprietor is that they should be worked so as to bring him a return from his property'.[4] The Duke of Portland added a moral gloss to the justification for this coincidence of private gain and public interest when he remarked that while he had no particular wish to see even a model colliery so near to Welbeck, as an owner of minerals he felt he had 'no right to lock up the mainspring of England's wealth and prosperity'.[5]

Twenty years later the conclusion of the 1919 Acquisition and Valuation of Land Committee was that 'freedom of contract with its incentive for commercial profit has, in the main, been the best system for developing the mineral resources of this country'.[6] None the less, the report listed fourteen factors associated with landownership and leasing arrangements which were regarded as having contributed to loss or waste of mineral resources, evidence later employed in the Sankey Commission Report in support of the nationalization of royalties. Even so, two categories only were regarded as important sources of minerals

[1] *RC Mining Royalties* 1893, XLI, 336–7.   [2] See below 65–6.
[3] *RC Mining Royalties* 1893, XLI, para 53.   [4] Ibid.
[5] Quoted by B. P. Broomhead, *RC Mining Royalties* 1890, XXII, Q 1905.
[6] *Acquisition and Valuation of Land Committee of the Ministry of Reconstruction* 1919, XXIX, 56–7.

lost to the nation. One was that resulting from the need to leave coal for the support of buildings and railways belonging to adjoining property owners. The other major category of waste was coal left to form barriers to separate adjacent mines in order to prevent water flowing between the two.[1] Yet in 1903–5 the Coal Commission had estimated a total loss of only 9.5 million tons as attributable to these combined factors.[2] Representing less than 5 per cent of coal output, this does not suggest that before 1914 a fundamental revision of the royalty system was urgent. The various reports between 1889 and 1919 did indicate, however, that the subdivision of property and the separation of surface and mineral ownership was becoming a matter of increasing concern, from the standpoint of optimal resource development and the need for greater co-ordination and national control of the search for and extraction of minerals.[3]

Until the twentieth century, however, delay rather than prevention was probably the most common consequence of such a division of ownership, an eventuality acknowledged by managers—who planned business strategy accordingly. For example, when the Staveley Coal and Iron Company was formed as a limited company in 1864 the directors commissioned the leading viewer from Newcastle, William Armstrong, to examine the firm's resource position. The result was his plan to acquire extensive leases on coal bearing land in the Midlands, which became the basis of company policy patiently pursued for some twenty years through tedious and protracted negotiations with a handful of landowners.[4] The time spent upon, and the importance attached to, securing agreements is suggested in a letter from William Armstrong to Staveley's managing director, Charles Markham, in 1870, shortly before the successful completion of six years of negotiation for the Barlborough steam coal. The value of the lease lay not only in the quality of coal but in the access the land offered to several smaller holdings: 'By every contrivance and solicitation, by every artifice fair and unfair towards your wily competitor for the Portland Coalfield and who has acted most unrighteously throughout, I would beg your perpetual and persistent effort to circumvent his intrigue and if possible attach this very valuable coalfield to the Staveley collieries.'[5] The incentive for so doing was the secular increase in the demand for coal and the growing

---

[1] Ibid., 56–7, 66, 71, 73.   [2] *RC Coal Resources* 1905, XVI, 45–171.
[3] Ibid.; *Coal Conservation Committee* 1918, VII, 673–4. In 1918 coal left in the form of barriers was estimated at between 3.5m. and 4m. tons.
[4] Chapman 1981, 76–7.   [5] NuRO Armstrong 725/B7.

tendency among consumers to discriminate between coals varying in price and quality.

ii. Patterns of consumption

In his account of *The British Coal Trade*, published in 1915, Professor H. Stanley Jevons supposed that to the unitiated 'coal' meant something pretty definite, 'but to the dealer in coal it is only the name of a whole class of substances, and . . . means about as much as the words "cloth" or "paper".'[1] This observation underlines the enormous differentiation in coal as a commercial product that took place in the course of the nineteenth century, a result of novel forms of consumption, refined methods of coal utilization, and, underlying the process of product improvement, the intensification of competition. Differentiation developed on the basis of three distinct uses of coal: for burning, for distillation to produce coke, gas, and later other by-products including patent fuels and chemicals, and for application to smelting iron and other metals when it was mixed with the molten metal in the furnace. The changing relative importance of the regions is largely explicable by the markets available to them, which were determined partly by the qualities of the coal produced in the coalfields and partly by the state of communications. Explanations of differential regional growth, however, must be preceded by the construction of estimates which reveal the variations in the patterns of coal consumption.

During the course of the nineteenth century important changes occurred both in the level of composition of demand neither of which is easy to quantify, for whereas the existence of mineral statistics, beginning with those of Robert Hunt in 1854, provided an increasingly reliable basis for calculating both regional and national production figures, no such series detailing coal consumption, either at county or regional levels, are available. For this reason, an attempt to obtain a precision for regional markets comparable to that attaching to our output figures after 1854, or even to the less dependable but nevertheless robust estimates for the earlier years, has not been made. Official statistics are available for exports and coastwise trade throughout the period, as are figures for canal and railway distribution and the annual volume of coal delivered to the London market. It is nevertheless impossible in

[1] H. S. Jevons 1915, 31.

many cases to identify the destination of coal distributed outside London, or to ascertain precisely the geographical origins of coal consumed in the London market.

We are in a better position to identify the sources of demand in the iron-producing regions, for the Coal Supply Commission presented estimates for coal consumed in pig iron in various districts in 1869,[1] a practice adopted by Hunt and published by Meade in the 1870s, which thereafter appeared annually as part of the official *Mineral Statistics*. In some regions the geographical origin of the coal consumed in the iron industry is quite clear, but with the coming of the railways and increasing inter-regional competition assumptions have to be made about traffic flows and resource utilization which render increasingly dubious the estimates which might be made even for the end of our period. A further difficulty arises from the lack of information on the amount and sources of coal used in the manufacture of finished iron (for which official figures do not exist), and the same applies to coal consumed in other industries and for domestic use by households. Nonetheless, Table 1.3 presents figures and estimates of UK coal consumption by use between 1830 and 1913.

The sources and methods used to produce consumption estimates before and after 1869 are discussed in detail in Appendix 1.1; they should be regarded as indicators of trends in relative magnitudes, but nothing more precise before 1880. The largest category of demand in 1830 was domestic consumption, estimated at 12 million tons and accounting for 38 per cent; although the volume was twice that in 1830, as a proportion of domestic consumption it had declined to 12 per cent by 1913 when 35 million tons were burnt, principally in British homes. Throughout the period London's consumers took roughly 7 per cent of total production, but the sources of its coal supply, almost exclusively North-eastern before 1830, altered considerably.

Beginning in 1851, the Great Northern Railway Company began to carry small amounts of railborne coal direct to London from South Yorkshire, and by 1860 the London and North Western, the Great Western, and the Midland Railway Companies were all competing in the London market.[2] The main beneficiaries of this transport revolution, however, were the coalmining counties of Derbyshire and, in the later 1890s, Leicestershire and Warwickshire. These counties were geographically the nearest to London, the mines in these areas raising highly

---

[1] *Coal Supply* 1871, XII, Appendix to the Report of Committee E, 1244–85.
[2] *CG* 2 Apr. 1896, 655.

Table 1.3. *Estimated distribution of coal consumption by use, 1830–1913*
(million tons, and percentages of total consumption)

	1830		1840		1855		1869		1887		1903		1913	
	m. tons	%	m. tons	%	m. tons	%	m. tons	%	m. tons	%	m. tons	%	m. tons	%
Iron and steel	5.65	18.5	9.60	22.5	19.0	24.9	27.0	24.3	27.3	16.8	30.3	13.2	33.4	11.6
Other industries	8.60	28.2	12.10	28.3	23.0	30.1	33.4	30.3	48.4	29.9	61.7	26.8	65.9	22.9
Railways	—	—	0.30	0.7	2.4	3.1	3.2	2.9	6.5	4.0	13.0	5.6	15.0	5.2
Coastal bunkers	—	—	0.20	0.5	0.6	0.8	1.2	1.1	1.5	0.9	2.1	0.9	2.4	0.8
Gas	0.50	1.6	0.90	2.1	1.7	2.2	3.7	3.3	5.5	3.4	8.5	3.7	10.2	3.5
Electricity	—	—	—	—	—	—	—	—	—	—	3.0	1.3	5.0	1.7
Domestic	11.65	38.2	12.65	29.6	16.0	20.9	20.0	18.0	28.3	17.5	32.0	13.9	35.0	12.2
Collieries and mines	1.50	4.9	2.50	5.9	5.0	6.5	7.5	6.8	10.9	6.7	16.0	7.0	20.5	7.1
Waste	2.15	7.0	2.70	6.3	3.0	3.9	2.0	1.8	2.0	1.2	2.0	0.9	2.0	0.7
UK consumption	30.0	98.4	40.95	95.9	70.7	92.5	97.8	88.2	130.4	80.4	166.6	73.3	189.4	65.9
Exports	0.50	1.6	1.60	3.8	5.2	6.8	10.9	9.8	24.8	15.3	46.9	20.4	77.0	26.8
Foreign bunkers	—	—	0.15	0.4	0.5	0.7	2.2	2.0	6.9	4.3	16.8	7.3	21.0	7.3
Total production	30.5	100	42.7	100	76.4	100	110.9	100	162.1	100	230.2	100	287.4	100

Source: Appendix 1.1.

Table 1.4. *Net coal consumption in London showing method of delivery, 1830-1913*
(million tons, figures in brackets are estimates)

| | Delivered in London | | Less re-exports and bunkers equals net London consumption (m. tons) |
	Sea (m. tons)	Inland (m. tons)	
1830	2.079	(0.008)	(2.030)
1850	3.553	0.086	(3.420)
1870	3.011	3.775	(6.100)
1889	4.843	7.896	(11.640)
1913	9.061	8.305	15.649

Sources: *Coal Supply,* Cttee E 45, 155; *Annual Statements of Trade*; *Mineral Statistics*, 1927 *Colliery Yearbook*, 693.

bituminous household coal for domestic purposes besides supplying coal for the manufacture of gas. Improved communications intensified inter-regional competition in the domestic trade, and while all coal-producing regions could supply coal at least adequate for household use within the region, and held an advantage in price by avoiding substantial transport costs, fierce competition ensued outside the coalmining areas, especially in the South-east and South-west, the South Midlands and East Anglia. The importance of internal trade for domestic consumption to the growth of coal production in the East Midlands is shown by the dispatch in 1870 of 50 per cent (and 30 per cent in 1913) of its coal outside the region, mostly for household consumption.[1]

As inland trade expanded from the 1850s the coastwise trade to London and to other ports stagnated, falling as a percentage of UK production from 20 per cent in 1830 to 8 per cent by the late 1880s. The North-east continued to dominate the trade, but coal shipped from British Channel ports, mainly originating from South Wales, remained second in importance at less than half that level, followed by the North-west whence coal from Cumberland, Lancashire, and Cheshire was dispatched to Ireland. The levels of coastal shipments from Scotland

[1] Mitchell thesis, 69–82.

Table 1.5. *Coastwise shipments of coal (excluding bunkers) 1830-1913*
(million tons)

	Bristol Channel	North-west	North-east	East	Scotland	Total (inc. minor)
1835	1.097	0.452	3.875	0.129	0.557	6.118
1850	1.589	0.840	6.296	0.166	0.465	9.368
1870	2.735	1.299	5.804	0.187	1.063	11.129
1890	3.080	1.533	7.183	0.639	1.671	14.375
1913	3.739	3.132	8.055	2.722	2.821	20.522

Bristol Channel: Bristol → Milford
North-west: Chester → Carlisle
North-east: Berwick → Middlesborough
East: Humber → Thames Estuary
Sources: *Annual Statements of Trade; Mineral Statistics.*

were similar to those from the North-west but greater than those originating from Yorkshire through the east coast ports, which before 1900 was a million tons annually. Except for South Wales each of the regions increased coastwise shipments after 1890, the coastal trade to London continuing to be the largest coastwise market at between 75 and 82 per cent before 1870. After two decades during which inland deliveries had exceeded coastal shipments by a wide margin, the 1890s saw a rapid growth in the coastwise coal trade to London, and after 1900 this once more exceeded land supplies (Table 1.6). This must have been due in part to greater price competitiveness: traders complained against the railway companies' concerted rise in rates in 1893, and there was therefore an incentive to switch freight, where it was feasible, from rail to sea transport.[1] However, Vamplew has presented evidence on Scottish companies to suggest that the upward shift in receipts per ton were short-lived and that by 1895 the majority of coal traders were probably paying lower rates than in 1890.[2] Moreover, interpretations placed on the Railway and Canal Traffic Act of 1894 thereafter made it difficult for railway companies to raise their rates, which from the traders' standpoint had beneficial effects from the mid-1890s, when the downward trend of prices went into reverse. The short-term advantage arising from

[1] P. Cain, 'The Genesis of the Railway and Canal Traffic Act of 1894', *JTH*, NS II (1973), 72–4.
[2] Vamplew thesis, 369.

Table 1.6. *Coastwise coal-receiving ports, 1830-1913* (million tons)

	1830	1835	1840	1845	1850	1855
London	1.972	3.011	3.726	5.277	7.999	9.061
Kent and Sussex	0.397	1.051	1.045	1.203	1.154	1.223
Hants and Dorset	0.208	0.630	0.651	0.787	1.178	1.802
Devon and Cornwall	0.311	1.025	0.977	1.329	1.332	1.679
Somerset and Glos.	0.031	0.590	0.690	0.506	0.492	0.580
South Wales	0.016	0.017	0.017	0.030	0.090	0.045
N. Wales and IOM	0.111	0.167	0.156	0.172	0.152	0.148
Lancs and Cumb	0.003	0.199	0.050	0.183	0.394	0.389
North-east	—	0.010	0.011	0.005	0.004	0.018
Yorks and lincs	0.067	0.045	0.047	0.044	0.013	0.028
East Anglia	0.004	0.015	0.049	0.058	0.061	0.197
East Scotland	0.004	0.015	0.049	0.058	0.061	0.197
S.W. Scotland	0.056	0.078	0.112	0.106	0.108	0.185
	4.441	8.121	7.912	10.728	13.219	16.765
Ireland	0.778	2.568	2.863	3.403	3.895	4.747
Total	5.219	10.689	10.775	14.131	17.114	21.512

* The figures for 1828 include coke, and from 1870-1913 also include patent fuel.
Sources: SC Lords Coal Trade *1830*, App. 2; *Annual Statements of Trade*; *Mineral Statistics.*

alterations in railway rates is, therefore, insufficient to account for the remarkable recovery in coastal coal traffic. Probably a more important reason for this change lay in the rising efficiency of sea transport, a result of the introduction of faster, larger colliers, the improvement of unloading facilities in London, and the growth in coal traffic for industrial use.

Steamers dominated bulk trade in coal for industrial use, for bunkering in the Port of London and, of increasing importance, for bulk deliveries to gas companies. Shippers benefited from the growth in the use of coal for ships and the spread of industrial enterprises along the banks of the Thames.[1] The railways, on the other hand, had the advantage in the delivery of household coal, which was deposited in and distributed from central points inland; for they were able to avoid the additional costs involved in breaking bulk, requiring payment for unloading and screening on arrival at the point of delivery, either to the nearest port of shipment or to the local coal depot in the town to which

[1] *RC Canals and Inland Navigation 1910*, XII, paras 293-4; Smith 1961, 339-40.

the load was consigned. A comparison of crude freights by sea and rail from Yorkshire to London shows that by the end of the century shipping costs of between 3s. and 5s. per ton compared with between 7s. and 7s.9d. by rail, the latter offsetting the apparent cost advantage of the former because of differences in non-transit transfer costs.[1]

The supply of coal for domestic household consumption, and increasingly in the later period for the directly related manufacture of gas, was important for all producing regions, but especially to those which dispatched either by ship or rail to other regions, notably the North-east during the first half of our period, the East Midlands, parts of the West Midlands, and in later years Yorkshire. But domestic consumption was also a sizeable element in Lancashire and Scotland, regions where dense local populations absorbed supplies, although Lancashire also imported coal from Yorkshire. In all regions the rise of other markets explains a fall in the relative importance of local domestic demand.

We have alluded to the growing, if minor, significance of gas as a component of consumption in relation to domestic demand. Street lighting and illumination of public buildings generated most of the demand before 1850; later, gas lighting in private homes, and from the 1880s gas for heating and cooking, swelled the demand for coal, and gas came to be used in industry too.[2] Nevertheless, the overall impact of coal was small. From barely a million tons in the early 1840s (2 per cent of UK production), the figure for gas consumption rose steadily to 10 million tons (3.5 per cent) by 1913. Until the late 1880s this demand affected principally the owners of those high quality bituminous coal seams in the North-east more easily accessible to London via the coast-wise trade. Even more highly prized, in the London markets especially, was the cannel coal mined in the Lothians and in Lancashire. Scottish gas coals, however, lost favour with the gas companies from the 1860s, partly due to dwindling reserves and rising costs, but also because coke produced from Lothian coals as a by-product of gas manufacture was commercially unattractive, for it tended to spoil the coke of other coals when mixed for carbonization.[3] Alternative lower quality coals came to be substituted after 1887, when the invention of the Welsbach incandescent gas mantle used in conjunction with Bunsen's non-luminous flame burner replaced naked flame lamps.

[1] *Coal Merchant and Shipper*, 27 Oct. 1900, 161.
[2] M. Falkus, 'The British Gas Industry before 1850', *EHR* 2nd ser., XX (1967), 500–2.
[3] Hassan thesis, 100–4, 111.

Domestic and gas consumption together represented a relatively stable component of demand, growing as the urban population increased. Much less stable was the demand for coal for industrial purposes, iron and steel production throughout our period forming the largest single component of UK industrial consumption, and one exhibiting a high degree of instability. The characteristics of coal required in the furnaces consisted of a mineral bituminous in type, possessing a high gas and low sulphur content which caked well to yield a hard coke; it also needed to be sufficiently strong to withstand the weight and the grinding action to which it was exposed in the furnace, yet of such a structure as to produce the high temperatures required in the course of ore production.[1] Prior to the introduction of the hot blast which permitted the burning of raw coal, coke was necessary for the furnace and provided the basis for the growth of the coked coal industry of south Durham in the 1840s. Based on the coking of small coal in beehive ovens, partly initially to supply railway demand, south Durham collieries also came to deliver coke to iron producers as far distant as south Staffordshire and South Wales, until the diffusion of the hot blast removed this particular market for coke.[2]

Coal used in the production of iron and iron manufactures probably reached almost 6 million tons (amounting to nearly 19 per cent of UK production) by 1830. A continuing rise in iron output raised this proportion to a peak of 25 per cent in the 1850s and 1860s, after which total consumption grew only slowly, precipitating a decline in the proportion of coal output burnt in furnaces. Unlike coal produced for domestic consumption, the production of coal for ironworks was a highly localized activity, the location of which depended much upon the state of blast furnace technology and the character of the resource base. By this criterion our period falls roughly into two parts, separated by the introduction of the steel-making innovations of the 1850s and 1860s.

In 1830 the West Midland region and South Wales each produced an estimated 41 per cent of pig iron output, generating demands for coal which comprised 47 per cent of the coal output of the West Midlands and 43 per cent of that produced in South Wales.[3]

---

[1] H. S. Jevons 1915, 37–8; Bulman 1920, 126–7.

[2] Samuel Bailey, 'On the advantages and necessity of the introduction of power for the purpose of underground conveyance in the coal and ironstone mines of South Staffordshire', *TNEIME* X (1961), 25–39; Mott and Greenfield 1936, 31–3, 44–8.

[3] Riden 1980, Table 3.2.

Iron, therefore, was the single major component of consumption, which placed the West Midlands output (18 per cent of the national total) in second place to the North-east (23 per cent) in size, followed by South Wales (15 per cent). By 1840, however, pig iron production in South Wales had outstripped that in the West Midlands where output was actually in decline. By 1870 the West Midlands produced only 10 per cent of the country's pig iron. Coal consumed in ironworks in the West Midlands is estimated at around 25 per cent of the regional total output by 1880, a figure which reflects the growth of the finished iron trades based on the use of cheaper imported pig iron.[1] By 1913 the figure was closer to 16 per cent. In South Wales iron-induced coal production also diminished as a proportion of the region's output. From 43 per cent in 1830 the figure fell to 24 per cent by 1869, 12 per cent in the 1880s, and below 10 per cent thereafter. From 1870 a falling share in a static market meant an absolute reduction in the iron-based coal demand in South Wales.

While the West Midlands, and especially South Wales, depended upon the growth of iron to generate high, and for South Wales accelerating, levels of demand for coal before 1860, even more spectacular rates of growth in coal production were achieved by Scotland which is only partly explicable by the lower base for the region in 1830. In two of the four decades between 1830 and 1870 South Wales exceeded national growth rates in coal production; Scotland achieved this in each decade before 1880. From a 6 per cent share in pig iron production in 1830 the Scottish share rose rapidly to 17 per cent within a decade and at its peak in the early 1850s stood at 29 per cent. This was the result of J. B. Neilson's hot blast, introduced in 1828, which made possible the utilization of the Lanarkshire 'splint' coal and the valuable 'blackband' ironstone; the consequent improved fuel consumption between 1840 and 1870 reduced the amount of coal required per ton of pig iron by more than one-half where best furnace practice was in use.[2] Fourteen per cent of Scottish coal production was for ironmaking in 1830, rising to perhaps 30 per cent by 1850 and falling from 1870 to 11 per cent by 1913. Unlike the West Midlands (and to a lesser extent South Wales) where the effects of fuel economies were cushioned, Scotland lacked a sizeable foundry and forge sector to provide a market for coal with which to transform pig into finished metal.[3]

[1] Mitchell thesis, 46–8, 96–8, 100.
[2] R. H. Campbell, *Scotland since 1707: The Rise of an Industrial Society* (Oxford, 1965), 119, 238–9.
[3] A. L. Slaven, *The Development of the West of Scotland* (London, 1975), 121–2.

Another reason for the declining importance of iron in the coal markets of South Wales and Scotland was the shift of iron and steel production away from the ironstone measures on the coalfields to the non-coal measure ones of the North-east, notably in the Cleveland district, the North-west, in the area of Cumberland and Furness, and later to the Jurassic belt in Lincolnshire and Northamptonshire.[1] Vastly improved railway communications and innovations in blast furnace construction and operation lay behind this important relocation of iron and steel production, which by 1875 had increased the North-west's share to 17 per cent, compared with only 3 per cent in 1855. During the same period the North-east's share rose from 9 per cent to 32 per cent.[2]

The implications for relocation differed between regions and over time. Until the 1860s the coalfields of Northumberland and Durham supplied coal for the Teeside iron and steel industries and for those in the West Riding, Lancashire, and Lincolnshire, as they had earlier to the small but vigorous iron industry of south Durham. Thereafter, from the 1860s the adoption of the practice in Yorkshire of coking small coal from the Barnsley seam enabled the Yorkshire coalowners to oust at least the lower quality Durham coke from most of these markets, the demand from which was enlarged later by the growth of the iron industry in Northamptonshire.[3] On the assumption that by 1881 Yorkshire supplied 75 per cent of the iron and steel coal requirements of Lincolnshire and Northamptonshire in addition to the blast furnaces of the West Riding and some in Lancashire, then the iron industry of the North-east probably consumed more than 25 per cent of the region's coal output. Ten years later the share was probably closer to 15 per cent; 12 per cent by 1913.[4]

The rise of iron and steel production in Yorkshire and the ability of Yorkshire colliers to supply the needs of other new iron- and steel-producing districts which lacked a coal resource base enabled Yorkshire, too, to move against the national trend, and in a similar fashion to the North-east found iron and steel providing an expanding market for coal. One estimate has put Yorkshire's coal consumption relative to ironworks at 6 per cent in 1870, and 16 per cent ten years later, at which level it continued until 1913 when the figure was 14 per cent. Of the remaining regions, the small coal output from the East Midlands in

---

[1] Alan Birch, *The Economic History of the British Iron and Steel Industry, 1784-1879* (London, 1967), Ch. 9; W. K. V. Gale, *The Black Country Iron Industry: A Technical Industry* (Newton Abbot 1966), 4–5.   [2] Riden 1980, Table 3.2.

[3] Meade 1882, 556, 572.   [4] Mitchell thesis, 67–8, 72, 76.

the 1850s depended upon local ironworks to a greater degree than in later decades at perhaps 16 per cent, falling to a relatively stable 10 per cent share between 1870 and 1913.[1] The coalfields of Lancashire and Cheshire and Cumberland depended least for their markets upon ironworks. Lancashire possessed a small iron industry but it was partly supplied with metallurgical coke from Durham. The Cumberland industry, which developed during the last quarter of the nineteenth century, came also within cost-effective distance of Durham collieries.[2] As well as providing the key to the relative importance of the patterns of regional coal production, until the 1870s movements in the demand for coal associated with iron also constituted the major determinant of fluctuations in coal output and to a lesser extent prices, the outstanding example occurring in the boom of 1872–3.

The absolute amount of coal consumed under the general category 'other industries' (excluding collieries and mines) represented the largest component of consumption, account for about 36 per cent of national output until the 1880s. Thereafter, an acceleration of export growth depressed industrial coal consumption to 23 per cent in 1913. Within this general industrial category are elements which were common to all regions and possessed a long history of coal utilization even before the application of steam power. Coal for heating was used by brewers, bakers, brick and tile makers, and tanners, who were almost ubiquitous in 1830 wherever populous towns or cities existed, but the major growth point was the consumption of coal for steam-powered production in factories and workshops.[3]

Because of fuel costs, however, even until 1870 water power was significantly cheaper than steam power where both were available. In all but very exceptional circumstances accessibility to water power was limited for an increasing proportion of manufacturing activity. Rapid expansion of the coal, iron and urban textile trades, and to a lesser extent of copper and lead production, all depended on the availability and versatility of steam power. Von Tunzelmann's figure of 240,000 total nominal horsepower in 1838 seriously underestimates the volume of power in mines and grain mills, and undoubtedly Kanefsky's estimate of 400,000 horsepower is closer to the correct figure. Kanefsky also attributes half the total fixed horsepower in Britain to steam by the late

[1] Ibid., 81–3.
[2] Ibid., 62..
[3] A. E. Musson, 'Industrial Motive Power in the United Kingdom, 1800–70', *EHR* 2nd ser., XXIX (1976), 3–39; Kanefsky thesis, 363–75.

1830s, rising to 90 per cent by 1870, by which time possibly 30 per cent of UK coal production was consumed by steam engines.[1]

Steam power spread most rapidly, of course, in Lancashire and Cheshire which ranked among the major coal-producing regions throughout the nineteenth century, though dropping from fourth in 1830 to sixth by 1900. Steam-powered mechanization in the cotton textile industry enabled this region to achieve a higher than average annual UK growth rate in the 1840s of roughly 5 per cent, exceeded only by Scotland, though only in the 1870s was the Lancashire and Cheshire region to find itself among the leaders in this respect. The textile industries were the basis of much of the local coal market, for demand was generated by dye and bleach works, and textile-related engineering workshops, but glass and paper factories, salt and sugar refineries, and chemical and alkali works also provided significant markets.[2] As the region lacked a sizeable iron and steel industry or an appreciable export trade, the slowing down in the growth of manufacturing production at the end of the century was inevitably accompanied by a relative decline in the region's position as a coal producer.

Such a fate would also have befallen Yorkshire had 'other industries' formed a comparably large proportion of the markets supplied by the region's colliery owners after 1860, but iron and steel production and a growing export trade together prevented a similar decline. In 1830 the Yorkshire region resembled Lancashire and Cheshire in industrial structure in so far as the iron industry was small but possessed a coal-consuming textile base, which was smaller but similar in kind to that of the North-west. Dependent upon woollen and worsted, rather than cotton, manufacture to generate local multiplier effects, and deriving coal demand from the small metal trades of south Yorkshire centred upon Sheffield, the growth of steam power in industry in this region lagged behind that in Lancashire and Cheshire.[3]

Textiles of many kinds also provided the basis for much of the Scottish non-domestic coal consumption in 1830, to which distilleries, glass factories, saltworks, chemical and soap factories, and engineering workshops added further demands. Even in 1830, however, hot blast iron-making was increasing rapidly in Scotland and generated possibly one-half of the industrial market for coal. In the long run, however, the relatively broad base of Scottish industry provided a major component

[1] Kanefsky thesis, 172–5, 337–8, 348–9, 350 fn 2.
[2] *Coal Supply* 1871, VIII, Appendix to the Report of Committee E, 1251–6.
[3] Ibid., 1271–2.

of demand before 1870, larger in proportion compared with other major regions. This broad demand was an offsetting factor from the 1870s, when iron and steel declined in relative importance and helped Scotland to remain the third largest coal-producing region until after 1900 even without the very large export trade which bolstered the positions of South Wales and the North-east. The minimal consumption of English coals in Scotland (which is evident in the tables presented by Committee E of the Coal Supply Commission in 1871) was largely because of the insulation afforded by distance and cost from inter-regional competition. True, the construction of Anglo-Scottish routes in the 1840s offered access to the triangle encompassing the industrial regions of the Western Lowlands and to the Lothians and Edinburgh market, but the elaboration of the Scottish railway system had the effect of intensifying intra-regional competition, and with the exception of a trade in special coals and coke and in certain locations, notably Aberdeen, protected the Scottish market from appreciable penetration by Welsh or English coal, either by rail or sea.[1]

The East Midlands, lacking either a sizeable iron industry or access to export markets, depended much upon local industries for coal demand, and in 1830 collieries in this region probably produced about 5 per cent of total UK output, exceeding only the South-west, North Wales, and Cumberland in size. By 1900, however, the East Midlands had also overtaken the West Midlands and Lancashire and Cheshire. Development was slow, reflecting the pace of steam-powered growth of local industries, mainly hosiery, lace, and beginning in the third quarter of the century leather and engineering, which by 1869 altogether accounted for perhaps one-fifth of the demand for coal within the region, rising possibly to a half by 1913.[2] Expansion in production depended also upon the sale of coal for household use, gas manufacture, and railway consumption, supplemented by a modest fillip toward the end of the period by exports from the east coast ports.

Industrial demand from the inland coalfields grew rapidly, the extension of the railways themselves contributing to the market for coal which in the earliest years had been burnt raw in the boiler. The smoke and cinders emitted from the Stockton and Darlington's engines were alleged to frighten cattle and people, which led to the incorporation in the Liverpool and Manchester Railway Bill of 1830 of a clause requiring

[1] Vamplew thesis, 358–62, 366.
[2] Mitchell thesis, 88.

locomotives to consume their own smoke, though later Acts specified coke as the required fuel. In fact the greater steam-raising power of coke per unit of weight justified its use on efficiency criteria, as Nicholas Wood, a leading colliery viewer, was quick to emphasize.[1] This development afforded a stimulus to the north-eastern coalfields, especially in south Durham which for a time was undisputed leader in the market for high quality coke for railway consumption. The Marley Hill colliery belonging to John Bowes and Partners was the largest producer of coke in the 1840s, more than four hundred ovens supplying English and Scottish consumers. Writing to John Bowes in 1848, another partner, William Hutt, MP, described how nearly all the railways in Scotland dispatched wagons to Marley to be loaded with coke: '. . . We shall be the *primum mobile* of Scotland, we are pretty sure to act in the same way for Ireland . . .'.[2]

Hutt's optimism was ill-founded, for the prospects for a large growth in the demand for railway coke encouraged efforts to substitute raw coal for coke, though the immediate motives which lay behind the innovations required to achieve this successfully differed. Thus, whereas the celebrated experiments carried out by Charles Markham in the 1850s, when he was a member of the engineering staff of the Midland Railway Company at Derby,[3] had intended to secure lower fuel costs, modification to a locomotive fire box in South Wales in 1857 followed a strike of colliers in the Rhondda, which disrupted coke supplies to the Taff Vale Railway. For this reason the company resorted to the use of steam coal on fire bars which were protected from damage from rapid burning by covering them with fire brick.[4] Cheaper than coke, steam coal soon became the preferred fuel on all railways, which by 1869 were consuming three million tons, about 3 per cent of UK production, rising to 15 million tons (5 per cent) by 1913.

The substitution of steam coal for coke widened the possible sources of fuel supply, but with the exception of the North-east and Scotland (one negative the other positive), in absolute terms redistribution can have had little effect on the relative importance of railway demand in the various regions. While the East Midland (and to a lesser extent Yorkshire) suppliers dominated railway contracts in the London South-east, and Midland areas, the outlying regions of Scotland, South Wales, and the North-east met railway demand mainly from local suppliers.[5]

[1] Nicholas Wood, *Treatise on Railroads* (London, 1838), 530–42.
[2] Mountford thesis, ix–x, quoted 61.   [3] Chapman 1981, 73.
[4] Morris and Williams 1958, 47.   [5] *CG* 2 Apr. 1896, 655; Mitchell thesis, 84.

The amount of coal used for colliery purposes varied considerably; since most was used for feeding the boilers of pumping and winding engines, the depth and volume of the pumping load determined demand. In those regions where before 1870 coal consumed in this way was virtually all slack and otherwise unsaleable, particularly in the North-east and the West Midlands, colliery managers are likely to have been prodigal in fuel consumption, as contemporary estimates indicate. Indeed, there was every incentive to burn slack wastefully in this period in order to reduce the problem of waste disposal. On the basis of steam power employed, colliery consumption is estimated to have increased from perhaps 5 per cent in 1830 to 7 per cent by 1913. Only in the North-east was there a small decrease, which in part reflected a rise in steam engine fuel efficiency.[1] Additionally, however, one other trend may have offset growth in colliery consumption after 1870, especially in the North-east. For the changing relative prices of large coal and slack effectively reversed the pre-existing incentive to maximize the burning of slack, simultaneously stimulating fuel economy.[2] More productive utilization of resources, especially of small coal, was also the motivation behind the transition, accelerating in the 1880s, from slow and wasteful carbonization in coke heaps to comparatively rapid carbonization in coking plant. The latter also offered the advantage of facilitating the recovery of by-products from a much wider range of coals than the friable and strongly swelling coals of Durham. From these origins emerged a supply-initiated demand for coal chemicals, from the carbonization of 33 million tons of coal in 1905, when figures are first available, rising to 37 million by 1913. Yielding by-products of ammonium sulphate, benzole, and coal tar, for industrial use, these provided a vital ingredient in the production of dye stuffs, pigments, perfumes, medicines, disinfectants, explosives, and photographic materials.[3] Patent fuel, another new product in search of a market, possessed a long history but demand was slow to develop; barely two million tons were produced annually by 1913. Anthracite also found a limited market, reaching an output of five million tons for the first time in 1913 (1.8 per cent of all UK coal products) supplied from mines in South Wales.[4]

As a percentage of UK production in 1913 exports were the largest single category at nearly 27 per cent, though including coal supplied to foreign bunkers this rose to 34 per cent, which amounted to 98 million

[1] Liefchild 1854, 114–21; Kanefsky thesis, 370.
[2] *CG* 29 May 1885, 855.   [3] Bulman 1920, 131–2.
[4] E. F. Methy, 'The Anthracite Coal of Swansea', *TNEIME*, XXI (1881–2), 184–7; John thesis.

tons leaving British ports; in 1830 fewer than one million tons had been shipped overseas, barely 2 per cent of UK production (Table 1.7). The basis of this development was the rise of the trade in 'steam coal' (a category which did not exist before 1830) mainly from South Wales, where the exceptional quality of bituminous coals was almost unique as a component of British mineral resource endowment (though Northumberland coalowners contested this claim). The combination of rapid ignition, a burning intensity which avoided caking, producing minimal clinker, and the production of an exceedingly hot and smokeless fire rendered raking unnecessary, thereby economizing on labour for stoking.[1]

Table 1.7. *British coal exports, 1830-1913*
(net, million tons)

Year	Coal	Coke (coal in)	Pat. fuel (coal in)	Total exports	Bunkers	Total shipments
1830	0.5	inc.	—	0.5	—	0.5
1850	3.2	0.3	—	3.5	0.5	4.0
1870	11.2	0.6	0.2	11.9	2.2	14.1
1890	28.7	1.2	0.6	30.6	8.1	38.7
1913	73.4	1.7	1.9	77.0	21.0	98.0

Sources: (i) Coal: *Annual Statements of Trade*; *Mineral Statistics.* The coke yield from coal was taken to be 55 per cent to 1865, rising to 65 per cent in 1905–13. The comparable figures for patent fuel were 90 per cent to 1900, and thereafter 92 per cent. (ii) Bunkers: Estimates to 1870, thereafter *Mineral Statistics.*

Before 1830 some of the coking coal used in ironworks was that which later became known as 'smokeless steam coal': since 1830 when the first consignment of 'Merthyr' coal was conveyed from the Thomas's colliery *via* the Glamorganshire Canal to George Insole, a London merchant.[2] Until the 1860s, however, the bituminous coal of the North-east dominated Britain's relatively small export trade, which supplied household, industrial, and railway coal mainly to northern Europe and to North America. Out of a total 3.5 million tons in 1850, which represented nearly 5.5 per cent of UK output, about 65 per cent was shipped ports in the North-east, and only 12.5 per cent from the Bristol Channel ports.

[1] H. S. Jevons 1915, 37–40.   [2] Morris and Williams 1958, 19–20.

Changes in the market for 'smokeless' best steam coal had begun to take place with the introduction of iron steamships, indeed its appearance was quickly followed by small but influential orders from the Admiralty, hitherto accustomed to the high quality Northumberland coals. South Wales coalowners, individually and in unison, challenged the assumption that North-eastern coals were superior for raising steam and emerged as unqualified victors from a series of public trials held between 1846 and 1851, which were financed by the Admiralty and conducted by Sir Henry de la Bèche and Dr Lyon Playfair.[1] Comparable in the high calorific content to steam coal from the North-east, the major advantages of Welsh steam coal included swift ignition and clinker-free burning, but of clinching commercial importance was that because of its density Welsh steam coal occupied less bunker space per unit of energy output, was more resistant to weathering, and afforded smaller risks of spontaneous combustion.[2] Welsh success provoked the Steam Colliers' Association of Northumberland to offer a prize of £500 for the best smokeless coal primarily intended for use in steam boilers, an award made this time by judges from the North-east who in 1858 pronounced Northumberland Hartley coal to be the best.[3] Nonetheless, the following decades saw the northern coalfield conceding markets to steam coalowners of South Wales, whose superior port facilities and more direct rail access offered important economic advantages.[4]

Such advantages were to be exploited fully beginning in the 1860s with the introduction of compound, followed a year later by marine, engines which transformed merchant shipping; by 1885 the gross tonnage of UK steam shipping exceeded sail. One of the effects was to reduce fuel consumption by half in the best and most efficient engine between 1865 and 1872, but from the standpoint of coal sales this fuel-saving effect was more than offset by the increasing cargo space which resulted, coupled with greater speed. These changes had important consequences for the growth in carrying capacity; the concomitant lower shipping costs stimulated an expansion of the carrying trade and with it the increasing amount of coal burnt in ship's bunkers, and the growth of shipments to coaling stations.[5]

When official statistics were first recorded in 1872 bunker coal amounted to 3.3 million tons, rising to 21 million tons by 1913, but these

[1] Ibid., 34–6.
[2] A. W. Kircaldy, *British Shipping, Its History, Organisation and Importance* (London, 1919), 611, Appendix XII.   [3] *CG* 23 Jan. 1858, 58–60.
[4] *CG* 5 Feb. 1886, 227.   [5] See the discussion by Palmer 1970, 337–8.

figures were excluded from exports—unlike coal shipped to coaling stations for which no separate figures exist. Witnesses giving evidence before the Coal Supply Commission in 1905 thought these amounts were substantial; one coal exporter said that 'not less than' five million tons were supplied to foreign coaling stations, of which about half was for use in British ships; this was in addition to the 17 million tons of coal shipped as bunkers from Britain.[1] The most dependable estimate, based on consular evidence, has been put at 10 million tons, equivalent to one fifth of the total coal exports shipped for bunkers overseas.[2] In 1903, when official statistics first distinguished between coal supplied for manufacturing other than steam raising, only 4 per cent of exports were so classified, underlining the extent to which the UK had become not so much an exporter of coal as of steam coal. Before World War I coal continued to fuel a very large proportion of the entire motive power of the world's merchant fleet, though by 1913 the Admiralty had switched decisively to oil burning vessels, a portent for British steam coalowners.[3]

More than 75 per cent of British coal exports went to Europe, of which in excess of half were destined for northern Europe. The reasons for British dominance of European markets were referred to in a French official's report issued in 1859: superiority in the extent and richness of British coalfields, excellent quality of coal, and favourable circumstances for low-cost shipping trade. The report concluded, 'any attempt at competition would necessarily be followed by defeat'.[4] Outside Europe exports were distributed between many scattered destinations, with the exception before the 1870s of North America which until then took up to 12 per cent of British coal exports. Thereafter, Europe's share did not fall below 80 per cent. By volume, British coal exports, including bunkers, rose at an annual average rate of 6 per cent between 1870 and 1880, and never less than 4 per cent down to 1913. In 1913 coal exports were five times the level they had been in 1870, which represented a rise from roughly 12 to 34 per cent of output. Dominance in the long-distance trade in coal stemmed from the lower freight rates shippers were able to charge because coal provided a bulk commodity. One of the very few such cargoes in north-western Europe, coal left British shores in large and regular volume to overseas ports, filling space in steamers bringing food and raw materials back to Britain.[5] As carrying

[1] *RC Coal Resources* 1905, XVI, QQ 21591–8.
[2] Palmer 1970, 337–8.   [3] Fletcher 1975, 7.
[4] D. A. Thomas 1903, 458.   [5] Fletcher 1975, 4.

Table 1.8. *Destination and origin of British coal exports, 1830-1913*
(per cent of total exports)

	1830	1850	1870	1890	1913
Destination					
Russia	5.3	7.0	7.2	5.0	8.0
Scandinavia	1.7	3.1	5.6	7.7	9.6
Denmark	19.8	8.8	6.1	4.5	4.3
Germany	18.7	17.1	13.9	11.1	11.7
Holland and Belgium	4.5	4.8	4.6	3.7	5.3
France	10.3	18.3	18.1	16.9	17.2
Iberia	2.8	7.7	6.8	10.0	7.4
Mediterranean	2.5	9.7	6.7	18.2	17.5
Africa	1.2	2.4	4.5	8.2	7.9
North America	22.0	10.3	7.4	2.1	0.3
South America	0.7	4.5	5.6	6.5	9.9
Asia/Australasia	0.5	4.5	5.8	5.7	1.1
Origin					
Scotland	9.3	10.0	11.4	14.4	13.9
North-east	68.8	64.9	47.2	31.4	30.6
East Coast	1.5	2.0	4.3	7.9	12.3
South Coast	4.5	2.4	0.6	0.2	0.4
Bristol Channel	2.6	12.5	31.6	44.0	41.8
North-west	13.9	8.0	4.9	2.1	1.0

Sources: Annual Statements of Trade; Mineral Statistics.

capacity on the outward voyage tended to be in surplus, and vessels were left in ballast in the absence of cargo to fill bottoms, British ship-owners chose to carry coal at low freights for sale at low prices, so that in 1850, for example, English coal was selling more cheaply in New-foundland than coal from Nova Scotia. Ballast rates expanded the export market for coal in the mid-nineteenth century, as the existence in the 1860s of marked differences in freight rates on outward bound and homeward journeys from such far-flung ports as Calcutta, Shanghai, Havana, and Rio de Janiero, indicate.[1]

Expansion and greater efficiency in the operation of steam shipping after 1870, together with the alteration in international trade-route

[1] Palmer 1970, 341-3.

patterns consequent upon the opening of the Suez Canal, led to a 'wonderfull fall of freight rates'[1] and to a narrowing of differences between individual quotations. Except in trade to particular destinations where the absence of homeward cargo could be important in highly competitive conditions, coal could be shipped cheaply without the benefit of high back rates,[2] and the differences of rates attributable to such a factor, which before 1870 could be measured in shillings, could be calculated in pence by 1900.[3] By this time the main factor influencing the level of coal freights, though not in proportion, was the length of voyage. One result of this development was the decline in tonnage taken by the more distant markets, South America remaining the only remote destination of any significance by 1900.[4] This had the effect of increasing the share of UK trade accounted for by exports to Europe, rising from about three-quarters in the 1870s to more than four-fifths by 1913.[5] Altogether, the British share of the world's seaborne trade in coal amounted to about 70 per cent shortly before 1913, though this concealed a fall from a·peak of 85 per cent in 1900, a sign that Britain's virtual monopoly of the overseas trade in coal had ended.[6]

As in the pre-1870 period the South Wales region was the major contributor to this trend in exports, the share rising from 32 per cent to 42 per cent; whereas the North-east's share fell from 47 per cent to 31 per cent in 1913. Scotland increased its share from 11 to 14 per cent, as did exports from the east coast ports, principally from collieries in Yorkshire and the East Midlands, from 4 to 12 per cent. Ports in the North-west dispatched only 5 per cent of exports in 1870, falling to only one per cent in 1913. Trade with northern Europe was dominated by ports in Scotland and the North-east, whereas South Wales was dominant in southern Europe, including France which from 1850 overtook Germany as the major importer of British coals. South Wales was also the largest supplier to the remoter destinations, an indication of that region's critical role as the world's greatest source of best steam coal.[7]

Whereas in 1850 coal exports as a proportion of production in South Wales was 4 per cent, twenty years later the figure was 23 per cent, rising to 46 per cent in 1890 and 57 per cent by 1913. Moreover, these figures take no account of bunker coal, the origins of which cannot be identified

[1] H. S. Jevons 1915, 691.
[2] Palmer 1970, 344.
[3] W. S. Jevons 1865, 307.
[4] H. S. Jevons 1915, 685–6.
[5] Palmer 1970, 335–6.
[6] H. S. Jevons 1915, 681–2.
[7] Fletcher 1975, 5–7.

before 1896 when they amounted to 2.5 million tons; their all-time high was 5.2 million tons in 1913. The role of the export trade from the North-east followed this pattern to a lesser, but still very marked, degree. From 16 per cent in 1850 exports as a percentage of the region's output rose to 20 per cent in 1870, 24 per cent in 1890, and by 1913 reached 42 per cent. Vulnerable from fluctuations in the demand for iron before 1880, South Wales was even more dependent upon a highly volatile export sector thereafter. As for the North-east, ironworks demand, which had been relatively large during the 1860s and 1870s, similarly gave way later to the primacy of exports. In Scotland, exports and ironworks which reinforced instability in combination accounted for approximately 40 per cent of the region's coal production between 1870 and 1890, falling to 30 per cent, with exports dominant, by 1913. Thus, from the 1870s exports replaced iron as the principal determinant of the growth and fluctuation of coal production, a transformation which held important implications for economic and social development in the regions. Throughout the period imports were negligible, only once exceeding 50,000 tons, which was during the national stoppage of 1912.

iii. Access to markets: the transport of coal

Access to markets was of critical importance in influencing the differential rates of resource development in the coalfields, both over time and by comparison between regions. Increasing population and industrial growth generated unprecedented levels of demand for coal, first in the UK, followed by Continental Europe and the United States; but in many instances the desire to link supply to a potential or existing demand was the dominant motive which lay behind investments in improved communications. Between 1830 and 1913 the three major developments were the railways which opened up the inland coalfields, steam-powered iron ships which underpinned the huge expansion in the export trade in coal, and the provision of improved dock and harbour facilities, important pre-conditions for the unhindered growth of all shipping trade.

In 1830 the leadership of the North-east coalfield rested not only upon the excellence of mineral resources but critically upon the three navigable rivers, the Tyne, Wear, and Tees. Supplemented by rail and wagonways conveying coals to riverside staithes, fleets of small sailing ships, known as keels, carried the cargoes from the staithes to the larger collier ships moored at Newcastle or Sunderland. The greater cost of land carriage and the relative absence of canals in south-eastern and western England enabled coalowners on the Tyne, and increasingly, too, those on the Wear and the Tees, virtually to monopolize those markets for household coal until the 1850s.[1]

In the North-east the unanticipated development of a coal-shipping trade on the river Tees, following the opening of the Stockton and Darlington Railway in 1825, led to the construction of staithes, docks, and harbours linked by railways to the coalfield of south-west Durham and the Wear district. When total shipments from the North-east doubled between 1830 and 1850 a key factor was the series of major improvements in local port facilities necessary to accommodate expansion on this scale.[2] During that time more than forty acres of wet dock came into existence, serving coal trains brought to the docks on high-level railways to the drops which substituted gravity for manual labour in the transfer of coal to ship's hold.[3] Significantly, the Marquis of Londonderry, the largest coalowner in the North-east, built the first dock, at Seaham, for the shipment of coal from his collieries at Rainton, a project which when completed in 1831 heralded a new era in dock and harbour investment. Even more important for the development of the Tees coal trade was the construction, beginning in 1832, of a dock at Hartlepool for the shipment of coal from the neighbouring collieries of Haswell, Thornley, and Littletown and which by 1840 was linked by railway to the coal of south-west Durham. The third successful major enterprise was the dock built at Middlesbrough as a response to the threat of competition from the Hartlepool Dock. When it was opened in 1842 the Stockton and Darlington Railway Company agreed to ship all company coal brought beyond Stockton through this dock.

Simultaneously, the navigability of the Tees and Wear was also significantly improved, with the most spectacular results for the Tees shipping trade. The 1840s and 1850s brought comparable developments. West Hartlepool was completed in 1847, extended to cope with expansion in 1850; in Sunderland, a new dock opened in 1850, likewise equipped to provide easily accessible accommodation for traffic on the Wear, and when the South Dock was opened in 1856 it afforded direct access from dock to sea. The Tyne, too, had a long history of river traffic, but major improvements lagged behind those on the Tees and

---

[1] Flinn 1984, 216.
[2] The following paragraphs rely heavily on Kenwood 1971–2, 72–3.
[3] W. Laird, *Letters on the Export Coal Trade* (Liverpool, 1850), 42–7.

Wear. Groynes and jetties provided amelioration, but not until 1857 when the Northumberland Dock was opened were facilities transformed. The Tyne acquired its second dock two years later with the completion of the North Eastern Railway Company's private dock. The second dock to be built by the Improvement Commissioners, the 'Albert Edward', was opened in 1884, by which time the North Eastern had completed Middlesbrough's second dock. Sunderland's docks were improved in 1880 and greatly enlarged over the succeeding twenty years.[1] These late-nineteenth-century developments were related increasingly to the exploitation of export possibilities, whereas the coastal shipping trade, which had provided the stimulus to dock and harbour investment and the use of steam tugs, before the 1850s stagnated.

Railway building and port development were interdependent, the railway companies filling a prominent role in the provision of additional shipping facilities, as indeed did some private dock companies.[2] In 1850 Braithwaite Poole, goods manager of the London and North Western Railway, remarked with admiration upon the intermeshing railway, wagonway, and dock networks of the North-east 'where the operation of loading a ship with coal occupies as many *hours* as it would require *days* in Liverpool'.[3] Leading colliery viewers in Lancashire continued to envy the superior facilities for the coal trade of the North-east—and South Wales—following their campaign in 1850 (which failed) to persuade the Liverpool Corporation Dock Committee to concede the Stanley Dock entirely for the coal trade. Competing claims from other industrial interests prevented such a development, and although the Dock Committee erected high-level railways on two of the quays the bulk of the coal shipped was taken to vessels by canal boats from which transhipment occurred 'by the most primitive contrivances'.[4] An observer noted, however, that the main consumers of coal purchased in south Lancashire were local and that only when supply exceeded demand did coalowners press for outlets to reach other markets.

The superiority of the North-east, in particular during the pre-export period, gained not only from better dock facilities: another advantage of the shipping trade to the south was that in ballast colliers returned with white clay from Devon and Cornwall, with Cheshire salt from Humber, and chalk and limestone from the Thames and even from French ports. Not until the introduction of twin-hulled vessels and water ballast from the 1840s did the comparative advantage of long-distance shipping begin

[1] Owen 1939, 109–21, 143–58.   [2] Kenwood 1971–2, 69, 78.
[3] Quoted in *MJ* 10 Aug. 1850, 352.   [4] *CG* 6 Mar. 1858, 145, 147.

to lose in competition with the greatly reduced costs of railway carriage from the inland coalfields close to London.[1]

In South Wales by 1840 the combination of dock and railway was beginning to effect that transformation in coal transport which was to carry the region to the forefront of the export trade, where Cardiff was the metropolis.[2] The initiative of the Marquis of Bute in building (ahead of traffic) the West Dock, opened in 1839, and the action taken by a group of iron-masters who controlled the Taff Vale Railway Company in securing the completion of a line to Merthyr from the coast, finally removed the canal company's hold on the region's transport system, thereby freeing the movement and stimulating the extraction of coal. In 1846 the rebuilding of the railway at a high level, in order to ship coal from self-acting drops specially designed to cope with large Welsh coal, reduced costs, and by speeding up the transport process greatly enhanced shipping capacity.[3] Extension of the Taff Vale Railway up the Rhondda Valley in 1855 had an impact upon the growth of the steam coal trade of Cardiff which it is difficult to exaggerate. Shortly afterwards, the canal monopolies at Newport and Swansea were finally destroyed by a series of major dock developments, while between 1855 and 1874 nearly a hundred acres of dock accommodation was added at Cardiff, most of which was owned by the Bute interest.

Scotland's favourable river configuration, supplemented by canals, meant that dock development occurred later and played a minor role by comparison with the North-east and South Wales. Apart from docks built at Leith beginning in 1865 and later at Bo'ness, Alloa, and Burntishead, the largest development occurred at what became the London and North Eastern Railway Company's principal coal-shipping port at Methil, where docks were opened in 1887, 1897, and 1913.[4] Elsewhere, the most important docks affecting the coal trade were those on the Humber, following the formation of the Hull and Barnsley Railway in 1880 to serve the small, but growing, export trade in coal originating from Yorkshire. In close proximity to the East Midlands, was Immingham Dock, five miles from Grimsby, was opened in 1912, complete with cranage and coaling appliances,[5] to assist the coal export trade of the inland coalfields.

---

[1] Rowe 1971, 129.

[2] This paragraph relies heavily on Daunton 1977, 18–36.

[3] W. Laird, *Letters on the Export Coal Trade* (Liverpool, 1850), 48–9.

[4] R. H. Campbell, *Scotland Since 1707: The Rise of an Industrial Society* (Oxford, 1965), 287, 307–8, 313–16.   [5] Owen 1939, 92, 97–9, 104–5.

Important though exports became after 1870, it was the inland coal trade which continued to form by far the largest category of consumption, and consequently from the 1840s the development of all coalfields depended to some extent upon the expansion of the railways. In the North-east, where river transport played an important role, the railways played a less critical role in the early years, as is suggested by the continued use of keels to transport river-borne coal after 1850.[1] Already in 1830 the region possessed an extensive wagonway system, often consisting of a combination of horse, fixed engines, inclined planes, and iron rails, which traversed the districts around the Tyne and Wear. Although the Stockton and Darlington Railway was initially conceived as a means of carrying coals for landsale, in general railway building in the North-east in the 1830s was concerned almost exclusively with promoting the local carriage of coal from the collieries of west and south-west Durham to ports on the east coast. With the exception of the Darlington to Berwick railways and part of the main line linking London with Edinburgh, most of the 472 route miles opened before 1850 were intra-regional, including the Stockton and Hartlepool which connected the port of Hartlepool to the south-west Durham coalfield and the Wear Valley.[2] None the less, by 1844 it was possible (though not as yet economic) to carry coals from the Tyne to London by rail.

In Scotland, railways were instrumental in opening up the landlocked coafields *via* branch line construction, stimulating competition in the low-cost carriage of cheap coal to a market which until 1870 was almost entirely within Scotland.[3] In South Wales, as in Scotland, the dominance of the iron industry in regional coal consumption was accompanied by the development of integrated coal and iron-producing companies, for which transport other than short-haul wagonways was unimportant in 1830. It is significant that the first in the principality to use a locomotive for low-cost haulage was Thomas Powell, a seasale colliery owner, though not until 1837 was the first Welsh mineral railway constructed. The major period for railway development came after 1860, when 'a prodigality of construction' arising from the disparity in mineral resources between valleys saw railway companies penetrating further to the east in order to secure traffic at the docks.[4]

Coal-related railway develpoment in other coalfields was rapid from the 1830s; even by 1835 no fewer than thirty-one separate railways

[1] Rowe 1971, 129.   [2] Kenwood 1971–2, 72.
[3] Vamplew thesis, 366; J. A. Hassan, 'The Coal Industry and the Transport Revolution in the Lothians, 1780–1880', *JTH* 11 (1980), 212–5.   [4] Morris and Williams 1958, 89–98.

served as feeders to the Erewash and Nottingham Canals[1] and by 1845 the Midlands and Yorkshire were served by a basic network which, with few additions, carried a rising proportion of coal consumed in Britain.[2]

Crucial to the expansion of the inland coalfields were the links with London, where until 1850 Euston had been the single point of arrival. Beginning in 1852, with the opening of King's Cross, the Great Northern Railway began to carry large quantities of coal to London from the new main line through from Doncaster, a policy adopted during the next few years by the London and North Western, the Great Western, and the Midland Railway Companies. Until 1858 the coal trains of the Midland entered London *via* the North Western's lines from the junction at Rugby, discharging their loads at Camden where a coal depot had been opened in 1854. Six years later the Midland constructed a depot at Kings Cross and by 1862 could boast of a coal traffic which already exceeded all except that carried by the North Eastern. The coal brought from the East Midlands competed on even terms with that originating from South Yorkshire and delivered in London by the Great Northern. Aggressive rate-fixing by the Midland saw the Derbyshire coal trade to the metropolis double during a period when the tonnage of coal from South Yorkshire to London fell, a development to which the opening of the Midland's extension of the line from Bedford to London, culminating in the opening of the St Pancras terminus in 1868, contributed much. For several months in 1870 the coal-rate war intensified, to the extent that rates were halved before a *modus vivendi* was reached between the Midland and the Great Northern. Thereafter, the Midland's St Pancras terminus, the largest in London, enabled that company to dominate the supply of coal to London and the South-east, a factor which was instrumental in the rapid expansion of coal production in the East Midlands.[3]

This brief survey of the main railway developments affecting the coal trade suggests several general conclusions. The early mineral railways were built because growth in the demand for coal began to put increasing pressure upon the limited capacity of canals, with the result that rates and carriage costs increased; or, in those instances where canals were owned by coal interests, because the bottlenecks which resulted threatened the sheer physical ability of coalowners to meet rising levels

[1] Herbert Green, 'The Southern Portion of the Nottinghamshire and Derbyshire Coalfield and the Development of Transport before 1850', *Derbyshire Archaeol. and Natural History Society Journal* 9 (1936), 65–8.

[2] F. S. Williams, *The Midland Railway* (London, 1876), 3–6; Hopkinson thesis, 133, 366.

[3] *CG* 2 Apr. 1896, 655.

of demand. The Monkland and Kirkintilloch Railway in Scotland is an example of the first, as is the Taff Vale Railway designed to compete with the Glamorganshire Canal, while the Newport to Pontypool line built by the Monmouth Canal Company, was a desperate recapitulation to railways in 1850 after years of resistance to the coal-based railway pressure groups. The Swannington to Leicester line also resulted from the desire of coalowning interests to break out of the Erewash Valley canal monopoly.

Lancashire, specifically the Worsley Collieries of the Duke of Bridgewater, provides an extreme instance where coal transport was checked by physician limitation imposed by the canal and river system. This occurred in what was probably the largest and most elaborate waterway system built in the UK, the Bridgewater Canal, which incorporated a surface canal conveying coals to Manchester and underground canals operating at different levels. By 1846 the extended system covered a distance of about 46 miles, but rising demand presented both greater opportunities and increasing burdens: '... we could sell a much larger quantity [of coals] if we had the means of getting them', the general manager observed, 'but our levels are nearly choked up with boats, and indeed, we are short of boats'.[1] A few years later the manager for the Bridgewater Trustees underlined the cost advantage of railways, in that coal could be lowered directly from wagon into cart, dispensing with the need to shovel from boat bottom, a laborious and lengthy process. The solution lay neither in tramways nor overland cartage, but in the construction by the Trustees of their own mineral railways which during the 1860s linked pits with canal and in due course connected directly with London and North Western Railway's lines, when the Eccles, Tyldesley and Wigan line through Worsley was completed in 1864.[2]

Elsewhere, too, the effects of railway communication in bringing competition into markets hitherto monopolized by intra-regional supplies stimulated further interest in railway provision. Exacerbating the physical supply difficulties was the dramatic effect upon profitability. In 1844 Lord Francis Egerton reported that his colliery income had fallen by two-thirds owing to 'the opening of the sources of supply by new railroads'.[3] One mining engineer linked profitability indirectly with cost when he remarked that 'the only obstacle to the fuller working of the (south Yorkshire) coalfield is the want of a good railway communication', a view shared not only by directors of the several railway

[1] Quoted by Mather 1970, 317–18.
[2] Ibid., 319–20.   [3] Quoted by Spring 1971, 36.

companies seeking routes into the south Yorkshire coalfield, but also by local coalowners who were active in railway promotion in the 1840s and 1850s.[1] Durham coal in transit by rail to markets in the Humber basin appeared as one threat to the trade, while the coal of south Yorkshire was for a time priced out of markets which it had long monopolized along the River Ouse and the Derwent Navigation. J. D. Charlesworth, partner in one of the largest collieries in the West Riding, declared in 1846 that 'the North Country coals beat us out';[2] in south Yorkshire in the 1840s Earl Fitzwilliam found irksome the sight of coke railed from Durham travelling past his collieries at Parkgate on its way to foundries in the Midlands.[3] However, further railway development in Yorkshire and the Midlands was to alter that situation, and within a decade the achievement of through routes obviating transhipment and facilitating through rates increased the competitiveness of collieries in these regions. Thereafter, coalowners' associations spent increasing amounts of time considering the structure of rates as they affected coal prices and sales from different regions differentially.[4]

Canals survived either by drastic reductions in charges or by turning themselves into railway companies; either way the effect was to reduce transport costs, though by how much (between 30 and 50 per cent perhaps) it is difficult to decide, especially as delivery to inland consumers not situated by river or canal faced road as well as canal charges.[5] Vamplew's examination of the relation between coal prices and rail costs in Scotland suggests that railway charges were generally less than one-third of road haulage costs, which for producers located some distance from waterborne traffic represented a considerable economy. He quotes examples of coal price reductions consequent upon railways of more than 20 and 30 per cent.[6] The advent of railways, therefore, allowed only the most favourably located canals, hauling minerals direct from colliery to large industrial consumer, to survive competition. Outside London railways quickly captured inland coal traffic during the 1840s and 1850s.[7]

The growth of the railway system helped to promote increasingly complex mineral flows between the regions, which also reflected discrimination among consumers between the increasingly differentiated

[1] Hopkinson thesis, 126–7, 130.   [2] Quoted in Hopkinson thesis, 371.
[3] Ibid.   [4] CG 4 Feb. 1881, 185, 21 Sept. 1894, 527.
[5] See the discussions in G. R. Hawke, *Railways and Economic Growth in England and Wales 1840-1870* (Oxford, 1970), 62, 178–80; T. R. Gourvish, *Railways and the British Economy 1830-1914* (London, 1980), 30, 34.   [6] Vamplew thesis, 372–3.
[7] Hawke 1970, 162.

coal types, qualities, and condition cultivated by coalowners who were becoming increasingly sensitive to market potential and the need to satisfy customers.[1] Railborne coal into London and the South-east, however, while increasing rapidly during the 1850s and 1860s, found difficulty in capturing this important market: mainly because whereas the long established coastal trade from the North-east was direct, the failure of competing railway companies to reach agreements before 1863 meant that through rates were denied to some of the more remote rail-linked collieries. Uncertainty over rates to London, and in the case of Yorkshire coalowners the disincentive of discriminatory freight rates which favoured Derbyshire coalowners, may also have hindered trade.[2] Most collieries were grouped by the railway companies for the purpose of charging common rates irrespective of distance from destination, though most of the North-eastern mineral railways did operate on a basis of mileage rates charged for shorter distances to reflect the costs of working traffic.[3]

Nevertheless, the rate of increase in total coal freight carried by rail had grown steadily from 1845, the Derbyshire coalowners setting the pace. After 1863, however, South Yorkshire coalowners also became competitors after benefiting from the withdrawal by the directors of the Great Northern from an entrepreneurial role in the coal trade; their new policy was to carry coal as freight, conceding the use of sidings to merchants and producers.[4] By 1870, when railborne coal supplied to London first exceeded that arriving by sea, the East Midlands accounted for more than 50 per cent of this railborne traffic; a further 20 per cent was from Yorkshire; less than 10 per cent originated from the North-east. A decade later, more than 60 per cent of London's coal arrived by rail.[5]

This expansion in the railway's share of the coal trade was the consequence of the cost-reducing effects of rail which tilted the balance away from the shipping trade. But the rating policies of the railway companies in the 1880s, when allegations of excessive charges were abundant, prompted serious consideration of ways to reduce the comparative cost of shipping.[6] The most spectacular outcome of such deliberations was the construction of the Manchester Ship Canal, built

[1] Ibid., 163–6; see also *Coal Supply*, Appendix to the Report of Committee E, 920–9, 960–9.
[2] *CG* 25 Nov. 1870, 580, 21 July 1871, 68, 28 July 1871, 83–97; Hopkinson thesis, Chap. III.
[3] *CG* 4 Feb. 1881, 185.
[4] *CG* 25 May 1888, 743, 15 Feb. 1889, 235; Smith 1961, 283–4; Williams 1962, 46.
[5] Hawke 1970, 169.   [6] *CG* 25 May 188, 743.

to accommodate sea-going vessels and which on completion in 1894 was over thirty-five miles in length. Increasing export opportunities contributed something to the reawakening interest in water transport, but contemporary accounts of the justification for turning to the sea were presented by reference to the comparative costs of wagon and ship.[1] The tide in favour of railways began to turn back in favour of shipping; by 1900 sea shipments to London once again exceeded inland shipments for the first time since 1866, and retained the lead until 1913.

The coincidence of this development with coalowners' criticism of the railway companies suggests that the latters' pricing policies may have been important contributory factors. They were criticized (especially in the 1880s) for discriminating unfairly against certain trades and for maintaining rate levels in periods of falling prices, causing the real burden to rise. For several years after 1890 falling coal prices provided the context in which such criticisms from coalmasters intensified, especially from January 1893 following the railway companies' decision to substitute new maximum charges for the special rates so fiercely condemned hitherto.[2] Moreover, the 'heavy' lines, which had carried large volumes of goods traffic at special rates, secured significant increases in revenue from higher charges to customers. Yet even by the mid-1890s coal traders were beginning to pay lower charges than in 1890; for under the new rates legislation of 1892, as coal prices began to move upwards after 1895 the railway companies found it difficult to raise their rates, whereas for the traders, 'what had been a curse became something of a blessing'.[3] Coal prices remained well above the lowest levels of the early 1890s for most years to 1913. The picture is one of lower real costs of inland transport from the mid 1890s, so the relative decline in inland, compared with coastal, deliveries to London during that period should not be blamed on the freight-rate policies of the railways.

The explanation, which also accounts for the beginning of diminishing comparative advantage in the 1870s and 1880s, is to be found in those innovations which reduced the costs of waterborne traffic, a repetition of the sequence of events which explains such resilience in coastal shipping during the 1850s and 1860s. In that period steam shipping was the most important of these, the launching of the 'Bedlington', built especially for the Bedlington Coal Company and which worked out of

---

[1] Ibid.
[2] Cain 1973, 67–8, 72; Vamplew thesis, 369.   [3] Cain 1973, 80.

the port of Blyth betwen 1841 and 1854, marking an historic development in the coal trade of the North-east.[1] One contemporary observer
reckoned that even before taking into account time saved through
greater speed or the lessened risk of cargo deterioration, screw steamers
reduced transport costs by 12.5 per cent.[2] So convinced of the
economies to be gained by this innovation were the Palmer brothers,
George and Charles, the latter a partner in the large Durham colliery
enterprise of John Bowes and Partners, that they formed the firm of
Palmer Brothers in Jarrow to design the first iron screw collier. On its
maiden voyage in 1852 the 'John Bowes' completed a round trip to
London in 120 hours, including 24 hours for unloading, and delivered
530 tons of coal. The equivalent payload would have required two
sailing colliers each spending a month or more to deliver. Furthermore,
dependence on weather conditions meant that sailing vessels usually
managed less than a dozen voyages annually whereas screw vessels
could make more than thirty journeys in a year.[3] By 1864 screw colliers
carried some 30 per cent of all coal shipped into London and ten years
later nearly all seaborne coal was carried in steam vessels.

In coastal districts steamers continued to compete with rail, for
example carrying Scottish coal to the south of the industrial coalfields as
well as to the north, forcing railway rates down as a result.[4] The appearance of screw colliers on the Thames hastened advances in the type and
speed of unloading machinery because of the need for rapid turn-round
of the heavy capital investment which they represented. For this reason
the 1860s saw the introduction of hydraulic cranes, automatic weighing
machines, and floating derricks to facilitate the simultaneous unloading
of two steam colliers.[5] External economies consequent upon this innovation arose from the reduction in river congestion and improved general organization of the Pool of London. As a result of these various
developments it is not surprising to find that the 1872 Select Committee
on Railways reported that sea competition influenced some rates at no
fewer than 60 per cent of all railway stations.[6] Until the 1880s such
improvements had slowed down (but could not prevent) the capture by
the railways of nearly two-thirds of London's coal trade. Thereafter, the
trend was reversed, and by 1900 more than half London's coal again

---

[1] Stephen B. Martin and Norman McCord, 'The Steamship Bedlington, 1841–54', *Maritime History* 1 (1971), 46–64.

[2] *CG* 27 Feb. 1858, 136.   [3] Mountford thesis, 74–5; Smith 1961, 285.

[4] Vamplew thesis, 526.   [5] Smith 1961, 290–1.

[6] T. C. Barker and C. I. Savage, *An Economic History of Transport in Britain* (Leicester, 1974), 72.

arrived by sea, at round about which level the modes distribution stabilized until 1913.

iv. Prices

(a) Trends and fluctuations — demand and elasticity

We have already drawn attention to the increasing heterogeneity of coal for sale from the 1870s, which destroys the notion of a single price for coal. Both between, and even within, different varieties of the major kinds of coal—house, manufacturing (including steam), coking, and gas—prices varied according to quality and between and within different regions. Price complexity was characteristic of the industry even in 1830, as the daily prices of coal quoted on the London market and recorded by the Coal Factors' Society demonstrate, for even in the case of the house-coal category differences were to be found in the prices of coal hewn from the same seam in the same district yet raised from pits at different collieries.[1]

Best house coal from the North-east fetched the highest prices for most of the nineteenth century, but the spectacular rise in the prices of best steam coal from the 1850s, when it first became clearly distinguishable from general manufacturing coal, is clearly reflected in the high prices paid for the coal of South Wales. From that time Welsh coal prices were higher than in any other region where coal was raised for purposes other than domestic use. This relationship may be illustrated by noting that whereas after the price boom of 1872–3 until 1913 the price index for coal exports (1900 = 100) fluctuated between 80 and 103, Welsh large coal prices rose from 107 to 195. The ratio of best steam coal prices to best household coal sold in London rose from less than 50 per cent in the late 1870s to more than 70 per cent (exceeding 80 per cent in some years) by 1913.[2]

Throughout the century the price of Wallsend best quality ranked above most other household coal, some collieries in Yorkshire and North Staffordshire using the description 'Wallsend' for their best qualities; but by 1913 gold medal winning 'Derby brights', originating from the Clay Cross collieries in the 1840s, were probably the largest category to be sold on the London Coal Exchange, though this included

---

[1] Dunn 1844, 36; GLMR, Coal Factors' Society, 'Prices of Coal at the Coal Market, 1932–6', 5 vols; NuRO 1073/1–83 Coal Market Lists.

[2] Walters 1977, 327–9, and Appendix B for f.o.b. Cardiff prices of large coal; the prices of Best Wallsend Hetton Coal delivered in London are given in Mitchell and Deane 1962, 483.

'brights' from Nottinghamshire, too.[1] That nomenclature was an important asset in selling coal is demonstrated by the litigation to which the Marquis of Londonderry resorted in 1886, when he made an unsuccessful attempt to restrain a merchant at King's Cross who for several years had been selling coal under the name of 'Londonderry Wallsend' yet which did not originate from the Londonderry collieries.[2] The category 'selected' comprised very hard close-grained Silkstone seam coal from Yorkshire, while 'Best Silkstone' included best Black-shale seam coal from north Derbyshire and best north Staffordshire coal; 'New Silkstone' was second quality and was in decline. Lower qualities, or 'kitchen coal', were much more diverse in character, carrying labels which varied from one locality to another. Cobbles and nuts were descriptive terms relating to size, most of those supplied to the London market by the late nineteenth century originating princi-pally from Leicestershire and Warwickshire.[3]

Within these quality classifications individual collieries showed increasing concern to cultivate a colliery or company identity, which explains why when it launched a determined attack on the London market in the 1850s the south Yorkshire firm of Newton Chambers persuaded the Great Northern to alter its policy of accepting only general categorizations such as 'Silkstone Coal'.[4] Thereafter, collieries began to advertise in London newspapers and in trade journals, refer-ring to their coal by seam, by colliery, and by class of coal; for example, 'best', 'common', 'forge coals', 'inferior', 'best slack', 'fine slack', and regional variants upon these categories, though competition also encouraged comparative descriptions too.[5] In 1851 proprietors of Ince Hall Coal and Cannell Coal pits in Wigan arranged with the London and North Western to supply coals to the metropolis. After advertising the qualities of Ince Hall coals for domestic and industrial use, claims were made that they possessed 'all the qualities of the best Durham, New-castle and Harecastle coal', stressing the freedom from sulphur and white ash when burned in domestic hearths, and claiming that when used in furnace ovens did not produce clinker. The advertisement ended by listing customers willing to endorse these claims.[6] The importance which a colliery attached to maintaining a good reputation was demon-strated by the advice offered by the Scottish viewer, Thomas Robertson, to the owners of Fordell Colliery in 1853. It was agreed that future

[1] *The Times* 1 Dec. 1913, 26.   [2] *CG* 25 June 1886, 102.
[3] *The Times* 1 Dec. 1913, 26.   [4] *CG* 6 Mar. 1858, 153.
[5] *Coal Supply* 1871, XVIII, Q 2198.   [6] *MJ* 31 May 1851, 266.

expansion was feasible only by working the second-class seams, but he recommended that at the same time a moderate supply of the main splint coal should be raised 'by any passable means', on the assumption that the colliery's general standing in the market was determined by the best quality coal the colliery produced.[1]

The third quarter of the century saw colliery owners paying increasing attention to the preparation of small coal, introducing screens and washing plants to offer cleaner coal, more uniform in size and quality. Such developments were explained partly by the greater use of small coal for coking and supply to iron and steel producers, partly to a growth in export demand for small coal, and partly to expanding production of patent fuel, though this was relatively small before 1913.[2] It has proved impossible to quantify this trend for data are scarce and in any case difficult to interpret; the marketing process was intended to improve the product and consequently bedevils the construction of a single price series for 'small' coal. George Elliot, Powell Duffryn's chief executive, traced the beginning of this trend to the boom of 1870-3,[3] when exceptionally high prices stimulated the substitution of small for large coal among industrial and commercial users.[4] This process was facilitated by improvements in the design of engines, furnaces, and coke ovens to exploit the coking properties of small coal more fully, developments which rendered it economic for collieries where small had been stacked below ground to bring it to the surface for crushing, washing, and coking prior to sale. When Horace Walker, chairman and managing director of the Wharncliffe Silkstone Coal Company, introduced such a policy in 1869 he also drew attention to the added advantage of coking coal's saleability throughout the year,[5] which reduced seasonal influences on price.

Most of our information on market prices relates to the London trade and to exports, which until steam shipping came to predominate were seasonally affected by weather, but we may infer that coal of any variety which depended for delivery upon water transport was similarly affected to some degree before 1870. Favourable trade winds and brisk trade went together, as did short-time working, fog, ice, and gales in the winter months, and as these various factors influenced supply and

---

[1] ScRO GD 172/888/1.   [2] CG 29 May 1885, 855.

[3] SC Dearness and Scarcity 1873, X, Q 7582.

[4] CG 18 Mar. 1910, 515–17, 'The small coal question'. The only actual price series discovered relating to small and round (large) coal are for Broomhill Colliery in Northumberland, NuRO Broomhill BR/Box 24, royalty tentale acount 1873–1913.

[5] SCL Wharncliffe Silkstone NCB 1429/1, 17 Apr. 1869.

demand coal prices tended to be higher in the winter than in the summer. After the 1870s, by which time steam ships and railways dominated coal transport, only the more extreme weather conditions appear to have affected market prices. The effect was to reduce the significance of seasonal climatic variations for coal prices, except in the case of household coal which continued to show the characteristics of a product in seasonal demand: prices rising in the months preceding winter, declining in the spring.[1] It seems likely that prices in markets which were remote from the ports were also affected in this way, especially as the railways extended the influence of prices determined in the major centres of distribution.

The trend towards a decline in the amplitude of seasonal fluctuations was only in part due to changing methods of transport, for another stabilizing influence was the early growth in long-term contractual arrangements between buyers and sellers, especially in the markets for railway, gas, and manufacturing coal, both at home and overseas.[2] However, sometimes pressure exercized by very large purchasers in order to depress prices in the run up to the autumnal contract season tended to intensify fluctuations. In the South Wales coal trade bearing tactics of this kind were frequently successful from the 1870s, especially at times when the market was fundamentally weak.[3]

Fluctuating freight rates were another destabilizing influence in their effects upon prices fixed in the course of spot transactions in overseas trade. They also affected the timing of shipments under forward selling, for many coal exporters looked to the speculative gains that could be made on freight transactions as much as to the gains to be derived from a normal merchanting profit on the coal dispatched. The sources of such freight-rate fluctuations were various; they included the state of fruit and grain harvests in overseas countries, which influenced the potential for ballast in the form of coal; war and rumours of war, which affected expectations of a coal scarcity; and strikes or strike threats.[4] Except in particular years and in certain regions, however, none of these various short-term influences were sufficiently powerful to affect annual as well as monthly price fluctuations.

Complexity characterized markets for coal as they influenced prices,

[1] GLMR, Coal Factors' Society, 'Prices of Coal at the Coal Market', (1932–6) 5 vols; NuRO Misc Company records 1073/1–83, Coal Market lists 1830–96; See the discussion in Walters 1977, 338–9.
[2] Mather 1970, 311; NuRO NCBI/SC 607(18); BSCEMRRC Stanton and Staveley 2034/7/2, MB 24 April 1869; Chapman 1981, 45.
[3] Walters 1977, 334–5. [4] Ibid., 331–9.

and any attempt to simplify for the purposes of a sustained analysis is constrained by the price data available, which even at the level of the individual colliery are usually available, if at all, in the form of averages of coal prices rather than in a series relating to specific varieties of coal. Three main long-run prices may be used: those of best London coals, declared average f.o.b. values of coal exports (which are also available for the major ports) and pithead prices published in the *Mineral Statistics* from 1882. To these existing series we have added estimates of pithead prices, based on price (though often average value) data taken from the records of several collieries and averaged to provide a national pithead price series back to 1830. The later estimates which link with the published data in 1882 are more reliable than those for earlier years, because the later series is based on data derived from several collieries from all major regions whereas estimates for the period before the 1860s have been constructed on weaker foundations. The alternative to devising these estimates would have been to extrapolate backwards for fifty years, or to proceed on the untested and implausible assumption that before the 1880s pithead prices were identical in their relationship with export or London prices as they were after 1882, even though few regions were involved to a large extent either in the export or London trade.

Beginning with the most reliable figures certain observations can be made with confidence. The movements of the three series presented in Figure 1.2 and Table 1.9 exhibit several trends. The London figures comprise two overlapping runs of prices, but follow each other closely during overlap (1873–89) and may be regarded in practice as a unified series. They moved downwards until roughly 1880, thereafter remaining stable or rising slightly though they fluctuated more widely than the other two series. The export price series, based on quantities and declared value of exports, may be divided into five phases: almost stationary at roughly 7s. 6d. until 1852; again stationary at just under 10s. after a jump in 1853–4; moving upwards rapidly from 1871 to the peak of 21s. in 1873, and down as quickly to slightly below 9s. until 1889; then upwards about wider annual fluctuations until 1913.

The relative decline in the importance of the London market and the minimal size of the export market until the later nineteenth century justifies concentration upon pithead coal prices in a comparison with general price movements in the economy. The fall in coal prices in the 1830s and 1840s was sharper on the London market than the movements indicated by our pithead price index, which displays fluctuations

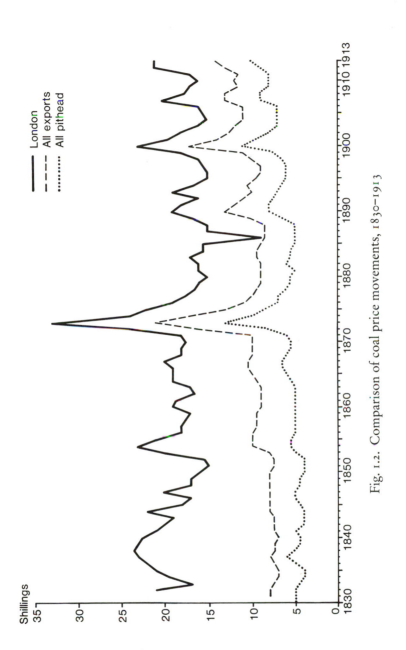

Fig. 1.2. Comparison of coal price movements, 1830–1913

Table 1.9. *Index of pithead coal price estimates, 1830-1913*
(1900 = 100)

1830	48.5	1851	37.7	1872	75.4	1893	63.1
1831	49.2	1852	35.4	1873	119.2	1894	60.8
1832	43.8	1853	43.1	1874	103.1	1895	55.4
1833	41.5	1854	49.2	1875	78.5	1896	53.8
1834	39.2	1855	49.2	1876	68.5	1897	54.6
1835	39.2	1856	48.5	1877	60.8	1898	58.5
1836	48.5	1857	46.9	1878	54.6	1899	70.0
1837	52.3	1858	43.3	1879	50.8	1900	100
1838	46.2	1859	44.6	1880	50.0	1901	86.2
1839	40.0	1860	46.9	1881	48.5	1902	76.2
1840	40.0	1861	48.5	1882	52.3	1903	61.5
1841	42.3	1862	45.4	1883	51.5	1904	66.9
1842	38.5	1863	44.6	1884	50.0	1905	63.8
1843	39.2	1864	48.5	1885	47.7	1906	64.6
1844	39.2	1865	53.8	1886	44.6	1907	83.8
1845	42.3	1866	59.2	1887	44.6	1908	82.3
1846	46.9	1867	57.7	1888	46.9	1909	72.8
1847	47.7	1868	54.6	1889	58.5	1910	75.4
1848	42.3	1869	50.0	1890	76.2	1911	75.4
1849	40.0	1870	50.0	1891	73.8	1912	83.8
1850	38.5	1871	52.3	1892	66.9	1913	93.1

Sources: Before 1843 the pithead price series consists of an average of fewer than six separate series; between 1856 and 1865 the average is eight, rising to twelve between 1866 and 1881. Some are actual average prices, others are average receipts.

Midleton Colliery 1830–59, LCA, MC 70–74 Middleton Colliery Journals 1830–60. for the period 1830–9 the series differs from that given by Rimmer ('Middleton Colliery Near leeds, 1770–1830', *YBESR* 7 (1955), 41–57), since the latter calculates prices on the basis of total sales rather than output.

Stella Coal Company 1839–71, DuRO, NCB I/SC/98–108, balance sheets and abstracts of accounts.

Elphinstone colliery 1830–72, *SC Dearness and Scarcity* 1873, X 328.

Grangemouth Colliery 1843–85, ScRO 240/7, abstract of royalty payments.

Newbattle Colliery 1838–80, ScRO, Lothian MSS GD 40/94–11

Staveley Coal and Iron company 1856–85, BSC EMRRC 2034/2/22–3, detailed balance sheets.

Wyken Colliery 1858–82, CoRO, 285/24/1–3; fortnightly cost sheets refer to No 1 pit to 1864, thereafter to the Main Pit.

Wharncliffe Silkstone 1857–74, SCL, NCB 1280/1429/1, balance sheet and accounts.

Lochgelly Iron and Coal Company 1867–85, ScRO, CB2/115–123, 218.

Cannock Chase Colliery Company 1866–85, BUL, uncatalogued accounts and papers.

Oakthorpe Colliery 1866–85, C. P. Griffin thesis, 277.

Clay Cross Company 1868–85, balance sheets at Clay Cross, Chesterfield.

Londonderry Collieries 1869–85 (f.o.b. Seaham, gas coals) DuRO, B134–175.

Sources: to Table 1.9 (cont.)

Durham Coal, all types, 1871–85, C. E. Mountford thesis, Appendix D.

Engine coal delivered in Manchester 1830–85, John Knowles 'The Coal Trade', *Manchester Geological Society*, Pt II, XX (1888) 49.

Reliable pithead price data are available from the official *Mineral Statistics*, beginning in 1882, which provided the basis for adjusting our pithead price series for the period 1830 to 1881. A comparison of the mineral statistics series and our crude average for the period 1882–90 revealed our series to be roughly 20 per cent higher than the official series. A similar comparison of the crude average series between 1830 and 1865 with that for 1866 to 1880 showed a further 5 per cent upward price difference. Explanations for the distortion in our crude series is the inclusion, in the search for coverage, of delivered price series, and the probability that pithead prices and average receipts recorded in some of the colliery sources refer to large coal only. In order to reconcile the official with our computed price series we have applied a 20 per cent deflator in 1866–81 and a 25 per cent deflator in 1830–65.

around a relatively stable trend. Following the brief rise between 1852 and 1854, which was also revealed in prices of exported coal, pithead prices gradually moved upwards on trend until the colossal price inflation of 1872–4, greater in amplitude in the export price series. The absolute levels of pithead prices were higher in the 1850s and 1860s than in preceding decades, higher still in the 1870s, falling back to pre-1870 levels in the following decade. From the 1890s price levels were higher than in all previous decades.

In a comparison between coal and general price movements, shown by the intercyclical changes in price indexes, the 1870s emerges as a turn-

Table 1.10. *Intercyclical comparisons of coal prices, 1832-1913*
(by average indices)

		Rousseaux general index	Sauerbeck–Statist index	Board of Trade index	Pithead coal price index
1832/7	−1838/47	+2.1			−1.9
1838/47	−1848/54	−13.9			−2.1
1848/54	−1855/66	+17.8	+17.4		+8.2
1855/66	−1867/73	−2.1	+0.7		+17.3
1867/73	−1874/83	−10.9	−12.2		−3.7
1874/83	−1884/90		−18.3	−17.1	−9.2
1884/90	−1891/1900		−5.0	−9.5	+13.0
1891/1900	−1901/7		+6.1	+3.4	+6.2
1901/7	−1908/13		+6.8	+10.4	+8.7

Sources: Calculated from Mitchell and Deane, *Abstract*, 470–8, and Table 1.9 above.

ing point. Except for the early 1850s, the forty years before the 1870s boom saw pithead coal prices tending to fall relative to those included in the Rousseaux General Index (confirmed for the period 1848–66 by the Sauerbeck–Statist Index). Thereafter, coal prices tended to increase relative to general prices, marking a fundamental change in the industry's position *vis-à-vis* all energy users, a trend which was of some importance to British industry as a whole.

Any attempt to proceed beyond analysis at the national level encounters considerable difficulties. The regional estimates of pithead prices from 1883, published in the *Mineral Statistics*, though not completely reliable, do suggest wide regional variations which none the less moved in the same directions of the overall trend and for the most part at the same time (Table 1.11). Prices in Somerset and in other geographically isolated regions tended to be well above average, as did those in Glamorgan, which were pushed up by the high rates paid for anthracite and steam coal. Scottish prices were generally below the national average by around a shilling, as were those in Northumberland by a smaller amount. Yorkshire coal fetched slightly more than the average in the 1890s, but below it after 1900. Prices in other areas were bunched closely around the mean.

While long-term trends in exports and pithead prices are similar, our pithead price series reveals a considerably greater susceptibility to fluctuation than do export prices before the 1880s, from which time pithead and export prices moved much more closely together. The explanation is to be found in the changing relative importance of home and export demand, for until after the boom of 1870–3 the market for, and price of, iron were closely correlated with the price of coal.

In the early period coal prices rose because iron masters demanded more coal to enlarge their production of iron and because those who supplied their own furnaces with coal compounded the shortage by checking coal sales to others made hitherto from surplus output.[1] William Menelaus, manager of Dowlais, justified the increasingly common practice in South Wales whereby as a matter of policy iron masters raised coal for sale in addition to furnace coal for internal use: 'In good times if the master refuses to accede to the demands of the colliers, which are frequently unreasonable, they attempt to gain their

---

[1] For example, in 1860–1 the proportion of coal for furnace consumption raised by William Baird's collieries at Gartsherrie was 75 per cent; twenty years later that figure was 36 per cent. Corrins thesis, 225.

ends by keeping the works short of coal, preventing the master making quantity when he would be able to realize large profits'.[1] Intra-regional competition for labour between coal-producing iron masters and coal-owners contributed to the upward pressure on prices in sale-coal markets. In 1861 William Alexander, Inspector of Coal Mines in Scotland, described the process thus: '... the ironmaster who, under a drooping market, finds it hard to advance the wages of his workmen has to compete in the labour market with his neighbour, who under ordinary circumstances, when he requires to advance the wages of his workmen, makes also a corresponding advance in the price of coal.'[2] Just as the connections between coal-raising iron masters and sale coal masters transmitted a rise in iron prices to the price of coal, in periods of low activity in the iron trade the coal which under normal trading conditions would have been consumed in the ironworks was sold on the market, the effect being to depress sale-coal prices.[3]

George Elliot, formerly pit lad, viewer, and leading colliery owner with extensive experience of the coal trade in the North-east and South Wales and whose knowledge of the industry was rivalled by few of his contemporaries, discerned influences on coal prices which were unrelated to the 'real' foundations of price inflation. Describing the events of 1872, he explained the peculiarity of the coal trade: '... if there is a scarcity of coal you are on your beam ends; you know not what to do; you must have it at any price. And the very apprehension of such a possibility was ... one of the great reasons for the rise.' Elliot pointed to two 'real' factors the coincidence of which upset the coal markets: the thirteen-week strike by miners in South Wales and the expansion in demand for coal from the burgeoning iron industry of Middlesbrough. But Elliot suggested that of possibly even greater significance in precipitating the unprecedented rise in prices was 'the panic which the public got into that there was going to be this scarcity, and persons who had their large fleet of ships, others who had their large companies and large businesses altogether depending upon the supply of coal took alarm ...'.[4] The fact that output increased by only 10 per cent between 1870 and 1873 compared with a doubling of prices suggests that while supply inelasticity was a key influence, Elliot's stress on the psychological or irrational determinants of price should not be disregarded. It

---

[1] Quoted by Morris and Williams 1958, 82, 88.
[2] *Inspector's Report* 1862, XXII, 320.
[3] John R. Leifchild, *Our Coal at Home and Abroad* (London 1873), 6–7, 137.
[4] *SC Dearness and Scarcity* 1873, Q 7531–3.

Table 1.11. *Regional pithead coal prices, 1882-1913*

	Scotland	North-east	Cumb.	Lancs. and Ches.	North Wales	Yorks.	East Mid	West Mid	South Wales	South-west
	s. d.	s. d.	s. d.	s. d.	s. d.	s. d.	s. d.	s. d.	s. d.	s. d.
1882	4 5	4 9	5 6	5 10	5 3	6 6	6 0	7 1	5 10	7 0
1883	4 3	5 0	5 6	6 0	5 4	5 7	5 6	6 1	6 3	7 0
1884	4 7	4 9	5 2	5 10	5 4	5 4	5 3	6 2	6 3	7 0
1885	4 6	4 7	4 9	5 6	5 2	5 0	5 2	5 10	5 10	6 7
1886	4 0	4 6	4 7	5 3	5 0	4 9	5 0	5 7	5 1	6 3
1887	4 0	4 6	4 9	5 2	4 11	4 9	4 9	5 5	5 4	6 4
1888	4 2	4 5	4 11	5 5	5 4	5 1	5 4	5 6	5 10	7 7
1889	5 2	5 2	5 9	6 6	6 3	6 3	7 5	6 6	7 0	8 6
1890	6 11	7 5	7 7	8 2	8 3	8 9	8 8	7 6	10 4	10 1
1891	6 5	7 1	7 1	8 1	8 0	8 3	8 4	7 5	10 3	10 1
1892	5 9	6 4	6 7	7 5	7 0	7 9	7 10	7 3	8 9	9 2
1893	5 9	5 8	6 2	7 6	6 10	7 2	7 11	7 8	7 6	9 7
1894	6 0	5 9	6 0	6 11	6 5	7 4	6 5	6 10	7 7	8 7
1895	5 4	5 1	5 6	6 5	6 2	6 5	5 8	6 2	7 2	7 7

Year										
1896	5 1	5 1	5 5	6 3	6 2	6 5	5 7	5 10	6 0	7 7
1897	5 3	5 4	5 7	6 0	5 9	6 7	5 7	6 0	6 9	7 7
1898	6 1	5 11	5 10	6 6	6 9	7 0	5 11	6 1	7 1	7 7
1899	7 6	7 0	6 9	7 5	7 9	7 8	7 1	6 10	8 10	10 7
1900	10 11	10 4	9 3	10 9	11 6	10 1	10 8	10 2	12 1	13 1
1901	7 11	8 7	8 2	9 8	9 3	8 7	9 7	9 1	11 8	11 4
1902	6 8	7 4	7 3	8 4	8 6	8 1	8 4	8 0	10 6	10 11
1903	6 3	7 1	6 10	7 9	7 7	7 6	7 9	7 7	9 5	10 9
1904	5 11	6 5	6 7	7 5	7 5	7 1	7 1	7 3	9 1	10 0
1905	5 9	6 4	6 6	7 4	7 5	6 8	6 5	6 11	8 9	9 5
1906	6 5	6 11	6 6	7 6	7 5	6 9	6 6	6 9	9 4	9 3
1907	8 10	8 9	8 0	8 6	7 11	8 1	8 0	7 8	11 10	10 4
1908	7 9	8 8	7 9	9 1	8 5	8 5	8 2	8 3	11 1	10 10
1909	6 8	7 6	7 2	8 5	8 0	7 6	7 0	7 8	10 9	10 3
1910	6 10	7 11	7 3	8 6	8 2	7 8	7 2	7 3	11 0	9 11
1911	6 8	7 5	7 2	8 7	8 4	7 6	7 4	7 3	11 2	9 11
1912	8 5	9 1	9 0	9 3	8 11	8 4	7 8	8 3	11 2	10 3
1913	9 8	10 6	9 4	10 3	10 0	9 5	8 9	8 11	10 11	10 9

Source: Mineral Statistics

seems likely that such factors helped to precipitate the slightly lower price peak of 1900, but whereas the 1873 peak was induced by the state of the market for iron, in 1900 a boom in exports and enlarged bunker-coal demand were the 'real' elements which underlay the rise, a reflection of the changing balance of iron and exports as constituents in the market for coal.

All three national price series for the most part share identical peaks in 1837, 1847, 1854, 1873, 1890, 1900, 1907, and 1913, though price fluctuations exhibited greater amplitude and volatility compared with other industrial prices. Cyclical price movements also reveal a regular pattern in which a rapid rise was followed by a somewhat slower fall and fluctuation, a sequence explicable fundamentally in terms of the economics of colliery working explored in Chapter 6.

It is tempting to try to relate the course of output and prices in an attempt to unravel the matrix of supply, demand, and price, and in particular to explore the significance of price elasticity to the growth of the industry. It will be apparent, however, that serious problems are associated with any attempt to measure elasticity: the deficiencies of the data, the complications introduced by increasing product differentiation, the fragmentation of markets based on quality differences, and massive shifts in consumption patterns. What can be said is that assuming insignificant stocking practices (for which at least from 1860 there is some evidence for Scotland, South Wales, the West Midlands and Lancashire)[1] we might accept output as representing the level of demand for foreign and domestic consumers, which increased most rapidly between 1830 and 1860. This coincided with a relatively stable, or slightly downward, price trend in the 1830s and 1840s (a fall in real terms when compared with other commodities),[2] followed by violent fluctuations in the 1850s. The growth of output measured by deviations from the trend was greatest during the price boom of the early 1850s and immediately following, falling to a lower level in the 1860s. The same applied in the boom of 1872–3. Thereafter, the low and falling prices of the 1880s were also accompanied by a large expansion in output, in fact the largest deviation from trend to occur during the entire period between 1830 and 1913. From the late 1880s growth in output was at a

---

[1] Youngson Brown thesis, 123; *SC Dearness and Scarcity* 1873, X, QQ 227, 327, 485. One report suggested that the extra expense involved in cartage, conveyance to heaps, and recarting for subsequent sale might be 3*d*. per ton (equivalent to perhaps 5 or 6 per cent of working costs), *Children's Employment Commission* 1842, XVI, para 29.

[2] Contrary to the conclusion drawn by W. S. Jevons 1865, 57–67.

maximum when coal prices rose relative to others, a trend which marked a fundamental change in the relation of coal to industrial prices in general.[1] Over the long term, and excluding the years of strikes in 1893 and 1912, output actually fell on only nine occasions: in 1858, 1874, 1878, 1884 to 1886, 1892, 1901, and 1908, each simultaneous either with a fall from a price peak or with a prolonged collapse of prices.

There are reasons for supposing that the demand for coal was affected relatively little by price; certainly several knowledgeable members of the coal trade during the early nineteenth century thought as much. Thus in 1846 T. J. Taylor, a northern coalowner possessing lengthy experience of the London trade, remarked on the absence of cheaper substitutes for coal even at the unprecedentedly high prices then prevailing: 'a regulation price is maintained without any aggregate sacrifice of quantity'.[2] Even by 1830 coal was a producers' good and Taylor made the point that 'the large producer, with given plant and equipment, has definite requirements which do not depend on the price at all; while when it comes to opening new plants, larger considerations than the price of coal govern such decisions'.[3] A large proportion of the coal used in industry was used in blast furnaces, and the proximate explanation for the rise in coal consumption in this sector was the new-found ability of the iron masters to utilize lower priced fuel, following the introduction of Neilson's hot blast process, rather than a response to movements in the price of coal *per se*, though the demand for cheap iron, of course, was the ultimate determinant of coal demand.

Railways and steamships were also significant consumers of coal, but as a proportion of total costs of operation coal prices could not have been a serious consideration in influencing investment decisions nor, therefore, in affecting the rate of growth in coal demand. Between relatively expensive coke and raw coal, however, there was scope for substitution. As in the use of the hot blast, this was a matter of the elasticity of demand *between* types of coal. In the production of gas, coal was the only raw material, the price of which, therefore, in theory might have influenced the rate of growth of the gas industry and indirectly of coal demand, especially as the demand for gas in the nineteenth century was sensitive to price.

The major factors contributing to falling gas prices, however, were the rise in the efficiency of manufacturing apparatus and gas-burning

[1] G. C. Allen, *British Industries and their Organisation* (London 1933), 51.
[2] Sweezy 1938, 81 fn. 6.
[3] Ibid., 83.

equipment and competition. By the 1880s the by-product coke yield of gas coal was influencing decisions on the choices between different qualities of gas coals, as were relative prices.[1] The other major, though somewhat mixed, category of industrial consumption was similarly affected only marginally by movements in coal prices.[2] There is no convincing reason for the supposition that in these years price elasticity was operative. This was a period during which the large investment boom of the 1870s sparked off by the price rise of the early 1870s completed a period of gestation, when new, enlarged, deeper, and more capital-intensive pits disgorged supplies onto a market in which prices had stabilized at levels below those current in the 1850s and 1860s. The last forty years of the period saw export demand increasing in relative importance which was explained by the dominant position held by British suppliers of steam coal and which remained unchallenged until 1900. The course of output and price fluctuations provide a further clue to the price-demand mechanism. Output variations measured as differences from the trend were relatively small, within the 3 per cent range on either side before 1870, increasing to 6 per cent deviation above and below thereafter. However, we have seen that price fluctuations were very large. This relationship again suggests the interaction of a relatively inelastic supply within a highly volatile market in which first iron and later exports were the primary sources of fluctuations.

(b) Monopoly, competition, and taxation

Ultimately, of course, production costs formed a price floor below which the continued existence of a colliery enterprise could be jeopardized, but there were other important elements contained in the market price which arose from the structure and organization of the coal trade, both at the industry and firm level: taxation and the role of government. A report issued in the late 1830s commented on excessive hindrance to the conduct of trade in coal, which was affected by nearly two hundred regulations and Acts of Parliament, 'most of them utterly inconsistent with every just principle of political economy'.[3] While aimed at abuses and monopolistic practices in the coal trade, these regulations which were designed to check combination among sellers and to limit prices were not, on the whole, enforced. This was in contrast to the taxation of the trade in coal, which government had every incentive to ensure was

---

[1] M. Falkus, 'The British Gas Industry before 1850', *EHR* 2nd ser., XX (1967), 501–2; Hassan thesis, 104.   [2] Kanefsky thesis, 172–5.

[3] Quoted in Flinn 1984, 280.

effective, and was the object of more sustained and widespread criticism during the 1820s, culminating in the Lords' Committee inquiry in 1830. As a result of their recommendations some of the elements tending to inflate the price of coal disappeared.

The Act of 1831 for regulating the Vend (by which the highly organized coal trade between producers in the North-east and London factors was organized) and for regulating the delivery of coals in London and the home counties went some way to reduce corruption.

The Crown tax was also abolished in 1831, but the City of London Dues, despite rationalization, continued to be levied at the rate of 1s. per ton on all seasale coal entering London, adding roughly 4 per cent to the delivered price on best London coals. This was the price for substituting sale of coal by weight for sale by measure within a radius of twenty-five miles of London, a clause in the Act which abolished the office of meter and a variety of petty time-wasting formalities. The London Coal Duties Abolition Act of 1889 finally brought to an end the Chartered and Statutory Duties levied by the Corporation, at which time they represented some 7 per cent of the average price of London coals, 4 per cent on the delivered price of best coal.[1]

Information on the costs of distribution is sparse, and that which is available is not strictly comparable. None the less, it is possible to deduce orders of magnitude of the principal components and the changes that occurred between 1830 and 1913. In 1830 the Marquis of Londonderry reckoned that the wholesale selling cost of best household coal in the Port of London was roughly twice that of the pithead price, though the final price to the consumer was raised by about 50 per cent by the duties and charges of various kinds.[2] Buddle's 1830 estimates endorsed this picture of onerous on-cost burdens.[3] In 1873 leading coal merchant Richard Cory estimated costs of delivery from barge to consumer at between one-fifth and one-third of the London price, excluding additional costs incurred for lighterage, leading, cartage, and allowance for loss by standing over. This evidence suggests a fall in the cost of distribution from about two-thirds of market price in 1830 to perhaps one-third to one-half.[4] In 1914 best coal sold for about twice the pithead price.[5]

---

[1] T. W. Bunning, *Account of the Duties on Coal* (Newcastle 1883); Smith 1961, 336.

[2] Buxton 1978, 46.

[3] *SC Lords* 1830, VIII, 307–8. This figure is also consistent with the ratio of pithead prices to London shipside prices of the Stella Coal Company's coal in the 1840s. In the 1860s the ratio was about 75 per cent of shipside prices. DuRO Stella NCB 1/SC 105A 623–7.

[4] *SC Dearness and Scarcity* 1873, X, QQ 7122, 7128, 7182.

[5] *The Colliery Yearbook and Coal Trades Directory* 1927, 680.

Comparisons containing greater detail of distribution costs of Derbyshire coal are instructive of the changing relative importance of various cost–price components. When in 1836 the agent of the Derbyshire estate belonging to the Duke of Chatsworth was estimating the profitability of selling coal in London, he reckoned on an average pithead price of 5s. per ton to which he added 12s. 9½d. to meet canal charges, sea freight, handling, and agency charges.[1] A similar ratio of pithead price of 5s. per ton, to which he added 12s. 9½d. to meet canal Stephenson and Co., later to become the Clay Cross Coal Company and one of the largest suppliers of high quality household coal to London. Pithead price was 37 per cent of the London market price, and city dues were nearly 8 per cent.[2] In 1914 an overall ratio quoted in an analysis of distribution costs showed pithead price as 47 per cent of the selling price to the consumer, before allowing 8 per cent profit on pithead price.[3] In 1847 Clay Cross Coal paid 2s. 4d. per ton mile, or 2s. 9½d. to central London; the Derbyshire figure for 1914 was fractionally more. However, whereas in 1847 railway freight was one-third greater than pithead price, by 1914 the rail costs added only 55 per cent to coal prices at the pithead, though this difference is possibly distorted by the contrasting coal price levels in 1847 and 1914, the former at a trough, the latter at a peak.

While transport costs and taxes were thus diminishing as a proportion of selling price, the increasing complexity of an expanding market saw the development of commercial organization which involved higher, rather than lower, costs. Wagon hire (11 per cent of the Clay Cross market price in 1847 and 4 per cent of the Derbyshire figure in 1914) continued to figure in sales costs, as did wharfage which by 1914 included rent for sidings, weighbridge charge, demurrage, and wharf rent, although these together accounted for less than one per cent of the sale price. The other major miscellaneous category embraced a whole range of loading and picking, screening, cartage, and stabling costs, which in the 1840s did not figure at all, yet which in 1914 absorbed about 8 per cent of the sale price before profit. It is likely, however, that the 'establishment charges' and clerical salaries recorded in 1914, together comprising about 10 per cent, were merely excluded from the Clay Cross figures for 1847 as a difference in accounting practice, for although the firm's sales organization was undoubtedly small at that

---

[1] Chapman 1981, 35.   [2] Ibid., 66.
[3] *The Colliery Yearbook and Coal Trades Directory* 1927, 680.

time it did exist and presumably increased in importance in subsequent years.

Even supposing these charges to have amounted to 5 per cent of the net sale price in 1847, reducing somewhat the relative contribution of pithead price and rail freight, none the less, as in 1914, these two categories together amounted to between 70 and 75 per cent of the net sale price, the burden of London dues having been replaced since their abolition in 1889 by rising costs of commercial organization. These were doubtless the result of intense competition between coal companies in the 1870s and 1880s, when demand was insufficient to support remunerative prices, the period when many iron companies who found themselves in financial difficulties turned to the sale-coal market for compensating revenue. A further factor inflating distribution costs in the form of establishment charges was the increasing importance of the export trade, which could involve a greater number of intermediaries and larger administrative expense.

A similar comparison made between 1901 to 1905 and 1914 would have revealed another item under costs, for in 1901 government revived taxation on coal exports. Until 1831 this had been substantial, but in that year duties were consolidated and reduced, as they were again three years later when a single *ad valorem* duty of 10 per cent applied to all coal, culm, and cinders in British bottoms, and to a flat 4s. per ton upon cargo in foreign ships. In 1842 large coal exports in British ships were charged 2s. per ton and small coal 1s. per ton, but all duties were repealed in 1845, excepting those applicable to foreign shipping which remained in force until 1850.[1]

The relaxation of export duties coincided with an increase in the volume of exports, particularly of small coal. But the advanced state of British coal mining, especially in the North-east, the high reputation of British coals, both from the North-east and increasingly from South Wales, the lack of comparable alternative supplies in industrializing Europe, and freight-factor advantages for coal exports to distant markets, together offer a more plausible explanation for the growth in exports, for the upward trend pre-dated the abolition of duties, albeit from a small base of fewer than one million tons before 1835. An export tax was re-introduced in 1900 of 1s. per ton, representing less than 2 per cent of the average price of coal exported between 1901 and 1905, the period during which the tax was operative. Predictably, the *Colliery Guardian* condemned the tax as detrimental to the trade. It is doubtful,

[1] D. A. Thomas 1903, 444–5.

however, whether the very modest advance in price which the coal tax may have occasioned was the cause of export trends during this period, though a differential effect on trade may have resulted. It is true that exports from the Humber ports increased most following the removal of the tax at the beginning of 1906, and the presumption was that the previously depressed trade was due to the ability of German coal producers to provide import replacements from their own resources, which were acknowledged by that time to be comparable in quality and price with the coal shipped from English and Scottish east coast ports. Exports of anthracite and best smokeless steam coal from South Wales did not falter, either between 1901 and 1906, or after the tax was removed, demonstrating a continued ability to exploit the unrivalled quality of Welsh coal at higher prices.[1]

The hypothesis that the east coast shippers were adversely affected by the tax while the lower price elasticity of Welsh coal enabled shippers from that region to escape the effects seems to be a plausible one; yet a similar relationship between trends in South Wales and the Humber ports can be identified in the pre-tax period of 1896 to 1900 and also between 1904 and 1907. Differences in the conditions of overseas markets and cyclical fluctuations in prices appear to have affected industrial demand for coal much more than did the tax on exports. Moreover, during the operation of the tax colliery owners sent smudge, or refuse coal, to market which sold at prices sufficiently low to escape the export tax.[2]

Price competition was characteristic of the industry for most of our period with the exception of the seasale coal trade of the North-east before 1845, where for many years the vend coal sold to shipowners was regulated in order to support prices in London and other markets along the coast.[3] Each 'regulation' was preceded by meetings of the committees of coalowners on the Tyne and the Wear when, on a proportional allocation of usually three-fifths of the total output for collieries on the Tyne and the remainder for those on the Wear, each committee ranked collieries and allocated a share, an individual 'vend', on that basis. During the course of the regulation period market conditions formed the basis on which the committees calculated the actual quantity to be sold by each colliery month by month, applying sanc-

---

[1] H. S. Jevons 1909, 6–8.   [2] Ibid.; *US Consular Report* 316 (1907), 59.
[3] The following paragraphs draw heavily on Sweezy 1938; A. J. Taylor 1953; D. Large, 'The Third Marquess of Londonderry and the end of the Regulation 1844–5', *DUJ* new ser. XX (1958–9), 1–9; Hiskey 1983, 1–9.

tions on coalowners who exceeded their allocation (who were required to compensate others) and allowing those whose sales fell short to make up later, decisions which involved a system of abritration.

Both the rules and practice were complex, but could operate reasonably well so long as no dramatic changes occurred to affect the relative importance of producers, whether they were members of the vend committee or were outside the Tyne and Wear cartel. As changes of this kind did occur during the second quarter of the century the cohesion necessary to sustain permanent regulation was absent, and the temporary control achieved was acknowledged by the participants to be effective only for so long as trading conditions and the negotiating position of committee members remained largely unaltered. For brief periods, however, limitation by coal factors did affect prices, which during the regulation of 1836, according to the evidence of shipowner James Thompson, added at least 2s. a ton to the price of coal,[1] or about 10 per cent. The success of sales control depended critically upon the interpretation of conditions and events by the coalowners and agents of the three major coal producers, the Lords Londonderry and Lambton, and the Hetton Coal Company led by Arthur Mowbray. In 1829 the United Committee representing collieries on Tyne and Wear had declared trade open to competition, the 'fighting trade' that ensued following Londonderry's reaction against Lord Durham's refusal to abide by the committee's reference, or adjudication, that he should cease over-vending.

When regulation was renewed it was not long before Londonderry found himself under attack for a similar reason. This occurred because on completion of Seaham harbour Londonderry was anxious to secure an enlarged vend commensurate with his greater capacity for shipment. Thus, in 1832 he adopted a tactic hitherto associated especially with the Hetton Coal Company and attempted to force the issue by over-vending to establish a case for receiving a larger allocation. Lord Durham reacted by adopting a similar course, with the result that within months the regulation was discontinued. John Buddle, the leading viewer until his death in 1843, eventually succeeded in persuading Londonderry, by whom Buddle was retained as a consultant, to co-operate in a further regulation only because his finances were too weak to enable him to 'contend against the whole body of the coalowners'. In fact by the 1830s Buddle acknowledged that regulation on a permanent basis was quite impossible: '. . . The trade is constantly fluctuating and changing . . . We might as well talk about controlling the winds and the waves as of

[1] *SC Regulating the Vend and Delivery of Coals* 1837-8, XV QQ 339–40.

making anything like a permanent regulation.'¹The longest period of regulation he regarded as feasible was two or three years; and so it proved, until the final collapse occurred in 1844.

The proliferation of new collieries and the connivance of signatories to the agreements secured by the United Committee, by exceeding quotas, failing to submit accurate returns, or trimming prices by allowing customers over-measure, led to a general feeling, even among those most anxious to secure effective control, '. . . that . . . the maintaining of prices and obtaining adequate vends appears to be utterly impracticable',² a view expressed by the clerk to the committee in 1843. Adding regulated collieries to those outside the regulation, Matthias Dunn estimated that between 1829 and 1836 the number of seasale collieries in the North-east rose from 73 to 94 and by 1843 had reached 155, including several large-scale winnings. 'Since the year 1836 the successive exploitation of new coalfields has proceeded with the greatest vigour; the public railways have continued to open more extensively the western districts of the Wear, the Derwent, the Tyne, and the Tees, and a succession of winnings have been completed in the deep coal districts . . .';³ reinforcing these developments were the improved dock and harbour facilities. Signs that competition originating outside the region might eventually threaten the North-east's monopoly of the London trade were also in evidence, the railways linking the East Midlands with London heralding a new phase of competition between inland and sea-borne coal. In 1840 the Clay Cross Company dispatched its first load of coal to London, by rail to Rugby and thence by canal; four years later Clay Cross became the first to send coal by rail direct to the metropolis; though in fact serious competition with the North-east was slow to develop.⁴

It was against this background of growing intra-regional and inter-regional competition that in 1844 the event which precipitated the disintegration of the vend occurred. During the pitmen's strike in 1844 Lord Londonderry decided to minimize losses by selling in excess of his quota, a policy already adopted by other colliery-owners. He refused to pay the £8,600 penalty imposed under the rules of regulation, declining, as he put it, to remain 'faithful to the faithless'.⁵ In 1851 regulation was attempted yet again, the new vend committee distinguishing between

---

¹ Quoted in Hiskey 1983, 9. On John Buddle see Flinn 1984, 59–60.
² NEI Johnson 4/9/314.   ³ Dunn 1844, 202–3.
⁴ *Over a Hundred Years of Enterprise: Centenary Supplement of the Clay Cross Company Ltd, 1837-1959* (privately printed n.d.), 12.   ⁵ Quoted by Sweezy 1938, 127.

household, gas, coking, and steam coal collieries.[1] In 1867 two branches
of the Household Collieries Association were reported to have had a
'very languid existence for some years past',[2] and achievements in other
sections of the trade may be assumed to have been similarly limited. In
1867 members of the Association resolved formally to relinquish
responsibility for regulatory activities, and to confine attention to
industrial relations, legislation, and the general interests of the trade.[3]
Henceforward, coalowners in the North-east became almost obsessed
with the need for wage parity within the coalfield, which can be interpreted as a limited form of minimum price-control, an approach which
coincided with the increasing interest shown by miners' trade unions in
price fixing as a method of raising or protecting wages.

   Collusion in pricing survived longest in the North-east, and the
combined effects of intra- and inter-regional competition in the London
market stimulated by the transport revolution was the fundamental
reason for its disappearance. However, the collapse of the vend is less
surprising than its survival for so long after the market conditions
necessary for regulation had vanished. Elsewhere, price-fixing combinations were fewer, less extensive, and only temporarily effective.[4]

   An article in the *Colliery Guardian* in 1858 highlighted changes which
had transformed the general climate for price fixing:

We allude to the reckless opening of new collieries to an extent altogether
beyond the legitimate demands of the trade. The intersection of the country in
all directions by railways has brought almost every estate in the coal districts
within reach of a market, and there is a natural desire on the part of the owners
to make their mineral wealth to some extent available. The openings thus
afforded have been rapidly filled by men of enterprise and capital, and we have
seen during the last twenty years that the trade has undergone a prodigious,
and as we conceive, unwarranted, expansion.[5]

   During the remainder of the century occasional tacit agreements
among producers superseded formal efforts to establish orderly trading,
and associations came to focus attention almost entirely upon wage-
rather than price-fixing agreements. There were two exceptions. The
first occurred in 1871–2, when for twelve months the South Wales
Steam Collieries' Association operated a Sale of Coal Committee to
prevent over-supply following a strike, though without sanctions it is
difficult to believe that the Committee succeeded in stabilizing prices at

---

[1] *CG* 30 Jan. 1858, 72; A. J. Taylor 1953, 29–30.
[2] *CG* 3 Aug. 1867, 93.   [3] Ibid.
[4] See Chapter 8.   [5] *CG* 13 Feb. 1858, 99.

a time of unprecedented fluctuation in 1871 and 1872.[1] Twenty years later a period of low prices revived aspirations for more regulation. Members of the South Yorkshire Steam Coalowners' Association fixed contract prices for steam and locomotive coal; associations in the East Midlands and Yorkshire shared an 'understanding' on prices in the London market and sold exclusively to certain agents;[2] the Durham and Northumberland Coal Association was formed in 1894 with the intention of controlling (i.e. raising) the prices of all kinds of coal and coke, particularly by discouraging very long-term contracts and the consignment of coals on speculation;[3] a ring of Monmouthshire coal companies, members of the Monmouthshire and South Wales Coalowners' Association, failed in their attempts to regulate output between 1890 and 1893, as did Lancashire owners, and in 1905 an initiative by Yorkshire coalowners with similar aims came to nothing.[4]

The failure to control prices meant that competition was the principal price-determining factor, individual colliery owners or their representatives fixing prices in accordance with expectations of market demand and competition. Except for local sales, especially in the remoter producing localities, for most producers after 1850 this implied price-taking in a highly competitive context. Large coalowners preserved some degree of manoeuvre for negotiating prices of gas, coking, and steam coals, most of which were sold under contracts to merchants, railway, gas, or steamship companies, but the scope for departing from market prices was, in the view of Griff Colliery's manager, E. E. Melly, extremely limited. His experience, from the 1880s until shortly before 1913, in selling coal by various types of contract was the basis for his judgement that not even the very best salesman or selling organization could secure selling prices of $3d.$ per ton above that obtainable under the worst and most casual arrangements; 'the cost side is really the test of good management, while the selling price is to a very great extent beyond one's control'.[5] He did, however, acknowledge the potential effectiveness of marketing initiatives to increase sales volume; greater efficiency and lower costs of distribution providing further opportunities for successful competition. This was not an unrepresentative view, evidence of which is to be seen in the changes that occurred in commercial organization during the second half of the century.

[1] A. Dalziell, *The Colliers' Strike in South Wales: Its Causes, Progress and Settlement* (Cardiff, 1872), 171–2.

[2] *CG* 12 Dec. 1890, 970.   [3] *CG* 29 Feb. 1894, 363.

[4] Walters 1977, 341; H. S. Jevons 1915, 317; GLA UGD 161–2.

[5] WaRO CR/1169/22–208.

v. Commercial organization and marketing

Concluding his report on nine collieries owned by the directors of the West Hartlepool Railway and Harbour Company in 1863, viewer William Armstrong offered his prescription, often repeated in other reports, for ensuring success in colliery enterprise: 'The question of what profit these collieries shall make is one which is peculiarly governed by the Fitting Office ... the capacity to sell is a more important power than to work cheap for the latter depends wholly upon the former.'[1] Successful colliery enterprise was a matter of marketing as well as of engineering and investment, and the intensification of competition within and between regions brought about changes in the structure and organization of the coal trade.

The legislation of 1831 freed the organization of the coal trade of London and the South from the ossified, antiquated differences of commercial function embodied in the coal code since the eighteenth century; this removal of the legal impediments to change was reinforced in the mid-1840s with the breakdown of the vend on the North-east coast. The long-standing arrangement in 1830 was such that typically the entire supply of a colliery's household coal was consigned to coal factors working on commission who transferred the cargo to the shipowner. At that stage, in return for a high discount to avoid the risk of bad debts, the coalowner received guaranteed payment. Factors representing shipowners then sold the coal to coal merchants, the largest of whom kept wharves and owned barges and who could unload coal direct from colliers in the Pool of London. Most of London's domestic fuel, however, was purchased by lesser merchants and dealers.[2]

The effect of sporadic periods of price competition which in the 1830s and 1840s intervened between periods when the vend was effective tended to promote 'freighting', whereby coal proprietors dispatched coal to London at their own risk instead of leaving the risks of buying and reselling to a shipmaster. Already by 1836 about 10 per cent of coal entering London, chiefly from Scotland and South Wales, did so outside the control of factors.[3] In 1850 one-third of the coal sold from the Lambton estate consisted of sales direct from colliery to merchant.[4] Even those proprietors who still preferred to minimize risks by retaining factor distribution began to alter the precise arrangements. In 1863

[1] NuRO Armstrong 725/B5/580-1.
[2] MJ 24 Jan 1846, 39; CG 23 Mar. 1861, 189; Smith 1961, 276-7.
[3] SC Coal Trade 1836, XI, Q 587.   [4] LEA, Morton to Lord Durham 25 Sept. 1851.

William Armstrong condemned the high factor charges paid by the Londonderry Collieries and recommended a rearrangement of contracts in such a way as to relate renumeration of factors to prices rather than to tonnage, a practice already adopted successfully by several other large colliery owners in the North-east and considered to have spurred factors' efforts to maximize prices and sales.[1] But he also advocated the appointment of a salaried coal agent, whose sole function would be to hold on to the coastal trade in competition with coal from the other regions and to develop the Continental trade,

I should advertise his salary, a small fixed payment and by commission upon all the cash received, and he should be fully authorized on the spot to contract for the sale of any coals he may have upon his list . . . in these days of keen competition it becomes essential to have a representative at the chief coasting ports who would be cognisant of the operations of the colliery owners and would be there to meet any case of difficulty and afford any explanation . . . .. I do not approve of the Fitter's absence, he is better at home and besides his visits are intermittent and his proper place is in his own office . . . .. I feel persuaded that with an active salesman a much larger tonnage at a price higher than the average of the London sales throughout the year can be effected in the Coasting Markets.[2]

Coal came to be shipped by, or on behalf of, the coalowners, on whose behalf factors, acting as their agents, sold to merchants on the London Coal Exchange. The independent factor's role, however, diminished, for not only did the volume of coastal trade begin to stagnate by 1870, but an increasing proportion of sales consisted of bulk deliveries to industrial users in London and the South-east, especially to gas companies, either via a merchant or, especially after 1870, direct from coalowner to consumer.[3] Some large coalowners dropped both factors and shipowners. From South Wales, Thomas Powell's Duffryn coal was sold through the firm's sole agent in London in the 1840s, but from vessels owned by Thomas Powell.[4] In the 1850s John Nixon, Cardiff coalowner, Hugh Taylor, chairman of the London Coal Exchange, William Cory, leading coal merchant, and a handful of other merchants prominent in the London trade contracted for the construction of the steamship 'William Cory' to carry 500,000 tons of coal a year to the Thames. In the North-east, meanwhile, the Hetton Coal Company and the John Bowes partnership jointly with Lord Ravensworth and partners had become

[1] NuRO Armstrong 725/B5/199–200.
[2] NuRO Armstrong 725/B5/364–5, 535–6.
[3] Fraser-Stephen 1952, 30–1.   [4] Morris and Williams 1958, 29, 164.

steamship owners, their first iron screw collier having been launched at Jarrow in 1852.[1] The elimination of intermediaries between coalowner and consumer in the London trade culminated in 1896 with the amalgamation of eight London firms of coal merchants and factors, lightermen, and steam-collier owners, to form William Cory and Son Ltd. Handling over one-third of all coal shipped to London, including more than 70 per cent of the seaborne trade, the merger marked the final disappearance of any real distinction, except perhaps in size, between factor and wholesale merchant.[2]

On the London Coal Exchange coalowners fixed prices through negotiations between merchant and colliery agent paid either by commission on pithead prices or on tonnage. Railway, gas, and steamship company contracts were settled increasingly through tenders invited direct from the coal companies. Normally the contract required the buyers, especially railway companies, to provide wagons, and asked for a price delivered into wagons at the pithead or some suitable junction, conditions which offered every incentive for the coalowner to tender direct.[3] At least from the 1870s gas company managers either issued printed circulars or advertised publicly, inviting suppliers to tender for contracts. First, the tenders were ranked in terms of price, quantity of gas per ton, illuminating power, ash per cent of coke, and other qualities; second, experiments were conducted with mixtures, samples being subjected to practical burning trials under laboratory conditions, the reports on which formed the basis for a comprehensive annotated list for the directors' consideration. After rigorous procedures of this kind some of the largest gas companies entered into contracts for periods of up to three years, which for other customers was quite unusual at this time.[4]

The growing importance of railborne coal supplies to London contributed further to the diminishing importance of factors, for railway companies sought to promote traffic by making depots and 'drops' in London available to coalowners for rent, and offered storage space for merchants and dealers. Charges for such facilities were subsequently discontinued in preference for a guaranteed minimum volume of annual traffic in return for unloading accommodation.[5] Both inside and outside London, from the 1850s railway companies also

[1] CG 2 Jan. 1858, 5, 16 Jan. 1858, 40.
[2] Coal Merchant and Shipper 27 Oct. 1900, 161; Smith 1961, 343-5.
[3] Ibid.; Morris and Williams 1958, 165.   [4] CG 31 Jan. 1890, 167, 1 Aug. 1890, 178.
[5] SC Dearness and Scarcity 1873, X, QQ 7112-3, 7195-8; The Times 1 Dec. 1913, 26; Smith 1961, 284.

advertised the benefits of purchasing coal from railway depots, where quality and (of equal importance in an age of higgling over price) correct weight could be guaranteed.[1] By 1908 the companies maintained no fewer than 155 depots situated throughout the metropolitan area alone, enabling merchants to deliver with minimum cartage and to keep truck-loads in store from which they could offer customers a variety of coals.[2]

From the 1880s an increasing volume of coal was sold by the wagon-load to customers possessing private sidings and transport for delivery. Factors seldom possessed depots, horses, and vans, usually confining their activities to ordering truckloads of coal 'to wait order sidings' for replacement after sales to merchants and country dealers; however, where factors were able to extend credit to the smaller merchants they often effectively monopolized supplies to particular stations outside London. Coal merchants in London took coal direct to their own depots and wharves for delivery, and it was their transactions which determined the advertised London prices.[3] Dealers, generally small tradesmen who drew a ton at a time from the depots at 'dealers prices', retailed coal in one- or two-hundred weight sacks, a practice which had spread to Scotland by 1870; 'trolley men' were traders who made regular weekly rounds of poor neighbourhoods, hawking coal in tiny quanti-ties.[4] At this local level of distribution practices differed little in London from those in the provinces, where higgling dealers who evaded weights and measures regulations none the less after 1900 found themselves under increasing pressure, threatened by the succes of the Co-operative Societies' bag trade plus dividend.[5]

The organization of the wholesale trade outside London was less complicated, in part for historical reasons. In London the statute and customs which had for so long regulated the commerce in coal between the North-east and London had spawned a complex network of factors, merchants, and other intermediaries which did not exist elsewhere. For those used to the risk-averting advantages of such a system its absence might sometimes pose problems. For example, in 1840 Lord Bute explained that the reason why he refused to sell coal from his Glamorgan estates while continuing to do so from his estates in the North-east was the absence in the newly developing South Wales trade of similar intermediaries to perform comparable functions. Indigenous

[1] Vamplew thesis, 365.   [2] Smith 1961, 340.
[3] *The Times* 1 Dec. 1913, 26; Fraser-Stephens 1952, 106–11.
[4] John A. Hassan, 'The Supply of Coal to Edinburgh 1790–1850', *TH* 5 (1972), 216; *The Times* 1 Dec. 1913, 26.   [5] *Sankey Commission* 1919, XII, QQ 24840–24886.

commercial enterprise, often integrating backwards into production, solved this particular problem when the shipping trade, coastal and export, increased in importance after 1850.[1]

The development of the inland coal trade was free from historical encumbrances; furthermore, inland coal was more economical to handle and for that reason did not require large numbers of intermediaries. There were no lighterage charges, and the risk of losses on small coal through breakage in loading and unloading were relatively small. The practice of sale by consignment, a relic of the seaborne trade in coal, was adopted from the beginning in the 1850s, but the increasingly competitive character of the trade undermined the orderliness of traditional consignment trading; in 1873 a committee of inquiry failed to substantiate rumours circulating within the trade of a price-fixing ring of inland coal dealers.[2] The growth of direct sales pushed by companies' agents and later by salaried salesmen ensured the existence of price competition.

The way in which railway and colliery companies co-operated in developing the inland trade is illustrated by the opening up of south Yorkshire as a supplier of coal to London. It began with Edward Dennison MP, chairman of the Great Northern, encouraging Samuel Plimsoll, formerly a solicitor's clerk in Sheffield, to pursue his scheme for securing cheaper coal supplies from Barnsley to Sheffield via the South Yorkshire Railway, thence on the Great Northern's line to London. After the line between Sheffield and Barnsley was completed in 1853, Plimsoll was so encouraged by the interest shown by local coal owners that he set up as a coal merchant to handle their supplies to London.[3] After bankruptcy following a dispute with the general manager of the Great Northern, Plimsoll opened another London office, one year after his marriage into the Chambers family, co-proprietors of Newton Chambers' collieries at Thorncliffe near Sheffield, a firm which employed a salaried, though also profit sharing, agent in London. Improved relations with the Great Northern enabled Samuel to obtain alterations in the sidings at King's Cross so as to improve unloading facilities for the greatly enlarged traffic he anticipated. Next, he invited two hundred London coal merchants and officials of gas and water companies to visit the Yorkshire pits to inspect the coal seams. In 1859 a special train carried a large number of the

---

[1] Morris and Williams 1958, 113–15, 164–5.
[2] Nor was there evidence of effecting collusion on pricing by producers. *SC Dearness and Scarcity* 1873, X, 9–10. [3] George H. Peters, *The Plimsoll Line* (London 1975), 11–24.

visitors from King's Cross, collecting mine-owners and officials at Doncaster prior to a tour of the Lund, Edmunds, and Oaks pits, culminating in a dinner at the Barnsley Corn Exchange. Contracts immediately followed this public relations exercise, which was described in the *Colliery Guardian* as the most important marketing initiative since the opening of the Great Northern.[1]

Other colliery owners responded quickly. Wharncliffe Silkstone's London agents informed the partners of the Great Northern's concession to allow coal from individual collieries to be clearly identified, a response to Newton Chambers's new policy of advertising the company's coal by name. Wharncliffe Silkstone's managing director, Horace Walker, urged his co-directors to respond with greater exertions in the sale of coal to London. The result was the establishment of a joint agency with the neighbouring Silkstone and Elsecar owners, which in the 1860s operated from offices at the London Exchange and King's Cross, and from London depots.[2] At the same time, Walker attempted to negotiate exclusive agency arrangements with provincial merchants. Continuing difficulties in competing with other collieries supplying Silkstone coal, principally due to relatively high getting costs and inferior quality coal, led Walker to bid for a growth in sales by appointing a travelling salesman to spend two or three days each week visiting stations along the Great Northern's line to the south of Peterborough, though he decided to rely on local agents for sales in the eastern region in the hope of loosening the grip which four large merchants virtually monopolized.[3]

Another example of marketing initiative by coal merchants is provided by George Lockett, a London brewer who also sold coal. Regarding the coal trade of the North-east as too well organized, from pithead to Exchange, to allow scope for new enterprise, George Lockett and another merchant named Duke travelled to South Wales with the intention of bringing cheaper coals to London on a regular basis. After witnessing the exceptional burning quality of Welsh coal in 1844 they contracted for 100,000 tons from Anthony Hill. Lockett and Duke arranging to transport it by rail to the wharves, and thence by chartered ships to the Thames.[4] In a similar fashion commission merchants took on sales agencies for those coal producers lacking in capital or com-

[1] *CG* 16 Jan. 1858, 41.
[2] SCL Wharncliffe Silkstone NCB 1429/1 16 June 1859, 21 Jan. 1864, 4 Mar. 1865.
[3] Ibid., 15 Oct. 1858, 14 Apr. 1858, 31 Oct. 1868, 6 Mar. 1869, 16 Apr. 1870.
[4] Fraser-Stephen 1952, 50-2.

mercial enterprise, though most coalowners appointed salaried agents who operated from dockside offices as sole sale representatives. For example, the Powell Duffryn Steam Coal Company possessed two such offices, one at Newport specializing in house-coal sales while the Cardiff office handled the export trade.[1]

The eastern region was opened up by Thomas Coote, originally a corn merchant who had commenced coal sales to farmers' wagons as a return load from the port at King's Lynn. After he had been approached by the Great Northern for advice on the location of a distribution centre for the eastern counties, Coote left the corn trade to become the first merchant to bring trucks of inland coal into the region. In 1857 he signed an agreement with the Great Northern and the North Eastern Railway Companies, by which he undertook to deliver daily a full train-load of empty coal wagons at the Great Northern's Peterborough station prior to dispatch to Yorkshire collieries. Simultaneously, the manager of the Eastern Counties Railway received an undertaking from four large merchants, including Coote, operating in the eastern counties, to develop the inland coal trade at stations on lines yet to be opened as part of the Eastern Railway Company's plan to extend lines adjacent to London. This marked the beginning of Coote's trade with the metropolis in which, because Coote had become sales agent for the Butterley Company of Derbyshire, the latter played an important role. So highly valued was Coote's effectiveness in this respect that Butterley took shares in the Coote partnership.[2]

Even closer association between production and marketing occurred when the Cannock Chase Colliery Company was formed in 1859, for John Robinson McClean, the founder, not only leased minerals to the Company but was lessor, too, of the South Staffordshire Railway which monopolized coal supplies to the market.[3] When McClean died in 1875 the company also took over the agencies which he had established through his Cannock Chase Railway Company, in London, Birmingham, Cambridge, Stafford, and elsewhere, proceeding to conduct both the production and distribution of coal. A travelling sales-man was appointed to assist the agent resident in London who also spent two days each week at the Birmingham office and attended quarterly conferences with the managers in Stafford.[4] Connections were of vital importance in commercial tactics. Staveley's directors praised

[1] Walters 1977, 167–9, 172–3.
[2] Fraser-Stephens 1952, 79–80.   [3] NuRO Armstrong 725/B5/296.
[4] BUL, BR 14/ii–iii/Cannock Chase Colliery, MB. 8 Mar. 1975, 17 Oct. 1887, 29 Jan 1891.

their managing director, Charles Markham, formerly of the Midland Railway Company, for securing orders 'in consequence of his intimacy with those who had them to give'.[1] The advantage of appointing agents in possession of knowledge of particular markets also became clear at the Sheepbridge Coal and Iron Company, when in 1869 the managing director appointed Alfred New, hitherto company secretary of one of the company's major customers, and allotted to him the task of establishing a London agency for Sheepbridge which was then poised to enter the London market. After visiting the collieries of the Derbyshire firm his recommendations for improving the picking and sorting of coal elicited praise from his Sheepbridge employers, and before long a second appointment was added to the London sales staff.[2]

The lengths to which some companies were prepared to go in order to eliminate intermediaries' profits is illustrated by the entry of Staveley's sales agent into the London retail trade, for which purpose in 1866 he was instructed to purchase three vans at the company's expense. With the support of a bookkeeper in the London office and advertisements on selected London railway stations, the company's London agent was urged to concentrate on expanding coal sales. By the mid-1870s this was being done from seven depots, the administration of which posed difficulties of financial control. Nevertheless, manager Charles Markham decided to continue retail sales as a more profitable outlet for surplus quantities of coal than could be obtained through merchants, who then handled one-third of the company's London sales.[3] In 1870 coalowners formed the South Yorkshire Steam Collieries Association for the purpose of shipping coal direct from Hull and Grimsby without the intervention of merchant or middleman.[4]

The growing practice of negotiating contracts directly provided greater incentives to appoint not only agents but travelling salesmen, a policy adopted by many of the large colliery companies, including Newton Chambers and Staveley in the 1880s.[5] When in 1900 the Staveley managers discovered that their Chesterfield agent had been

---

[1] BSCEMRRC Stanton and Staveley 2034/2/9 MB. 6 Sept. 1869.

[2] BSCEMRRC Stanton and Staveley 2034/7/2 MB 24 Apr., 10 May 1869, 2034/7/4, MB 18 Mar. 1882.

[3] BSCEMRRC Stanton and Staveley 2034/2/13 MB 19 Feb. 1866, 17 June 1867, 17 Feb. 1868, 2034/2/14 29 May 1876.

[4] CG 30 Dec. 1870, 714.

[5] Newton Chambers Co. Ltd., Staindrop. Typescript, Directors' Minutes 27 Nov. 1882, 28 Jan., 25 Feb., 28 Apr. 1884; 27 Apr. 1885; 4 Jan. 1886; 4 Mar. 1910.

buying quantities of coal from other collieries a decision was taken to sell direct from the station depot.[1] When Consett turned to coal sales in the 1890s commercial manager William Jenkins avoided the concentration of sales in the hands of a few agents and looked for direct contract sales.[2]

The trend towards direct sales diminished, but did not destroy, the London Coal Exchange. By 1913 rooms were allocated not only to the Coal Factors' Society and to the London Coal Merchants, but also to colliery companies. Owners and representatives of Midland and Yorkshire collieries met together with principal coal merchants to conclude bargains, each settled twenty days after transactions were recorded.[3] Coal exchanges were also formed in several towns and cities outside London beginning in the 1870s. In Manchester, Leeds, Birmingham, Glasgow, Middlesbrough, Hull, and Cardiff independent markets were established where trade terms and usages were peculiar to the region each one served. After the London Coal Exchange the second most important exchange was at Manchester, first formed in 1878, where the bulk of the trade was for domestic and industrial consumption within Lancashire and Cheshire; the Cardiff Exchange, opened in 1886, became the centre of the South Wales export coal trade.[4]

An important impetus in the formation of these exchanges was the increasing refinement in the varieties of coal coming to market and a concomitant concern within the regions for accurate specification and the maintenance of standards. Thus, in order to enhance the reputation of coals from Yorkshire and the East Midlands exported through the Humber ports, Hull municipal corporation appointed an official coal inspector whose services were available, at a fee, to owners and merchants. This safeguard offered to the buyer was in addition to the certificate issued by the South Yorkshire Steam Coal Owners' Association, which stated the true quantity delivered in each cargo. Checks were carried out by the Association's inspectors, who, free of charge, certified for the purchaser that the coal mentioned in the colliery certificate was actually on board the vessel.[5]

Trends we have identified in the coastal and inland trade are also to be found, though in modified forms, in the export trade. Some companies disposed of a part of their output to customers under f.o.b. contracts,

[1] BSCEMRRC Stanton and Staveley 2034/2/15 MB 27 Mar. 1900.
[2] A. S. Wilson thesis, 120–2.   [3] *The Times* 1 Dec. 1913, 26.
[4] Ibid.; *The Coal Merchant and Shipper*, 29 Sept. 1900, 16–17; Daunton 1977, 53.
[5] *The Times* 1 Dec. 1913, 26.

while others also arranged c.i.f. transactions, for customers or for their own depots abroad. Some colliery companies owned ships or, more commonly, established links with, and occasionally integrated into ship-owning firms, thereby securing control over each stage of delivery from coal face to customers' yards or bunkers.[1] Following the screw collier pioneers of the 1850s and 1860s, Henry Briggs and Son formed the Yorkshire Coal and Steamship Company in 1873 to promote exports to Europe through Goole; the Ashington Coal Company, the leading Northumberland exporter, owned two steamship companies, whose contribution in reducing transport costs aided trade development with Russia; and when in 1896 Sir James Joicey acquired Lambton Collieries the size of the shipping fleet at his company's command rose to fifty. In South Wales the Main Colliery Company and Lord North's Navigation Collieries were also directly involved in shipping coal for export.[2]

None the less, because of the greater risks relating to freight rates and price movements in foreign markets, middlemen continued to play a central role in the export trade; in general, most colliery owners owned neither ships, nor agencies, nor depots, preferring to sell f.o.b. It was left to merchants to undertake the financial risks contingent upon freight fluctuations and the mode of c.i.f. payment, to familiarize themselves with the requirements of the various markets, to supervise the mixing of coals at the docks, and to undertake arrangements for chartering ships, loading, and for discharge at points of delivery. Depots required organ-ization in their main function which was to service and supply passing shipping, for this involved tugs, lighters, and stock control, while some coal exporters supervised the selling of coal from depots.

The Cory brothers of Cardiff, who after beginning as shipbrokers and exporters in 1844 and became colliery owners in 1869, assumed this function from the 1870s, eventually extending to more than eighty agencies and establishing no fewer than twenty-three depots to provide bunkering services in the Mediterranean, West and East Africa, the Indian Ocean, India, South America, and the West Indies, and occasion-ally undertaking the disposal of a colliery's entire output on a com-mission basis.[3] Other large exporting merchants operated in a similar fashion, though few owned their own ships.[4]

Morris and Williams reckoned that even by 1875 probably the major

[1] Walters 1977, 299, 305–6.

[2] BroLU Special Collections MS 160, Briggs MB 25 Aug. 1873; NuRO Ashington Coal Co ZMD/54/2–4; Jevons 1915, 318.

[3] Morris and Williams 1958, 165–6.   [4] Walters 1977, 310–11.

proportion of coal from South Wales was sold without the intervention
of middlemen, a trend which intensified with rapid growth in sales to
the Admiralty, to the large steam-shipping lines, and to merchants overseas, each representing sections of the market requiring the highest
standards of service.[1] Such was the character of transactions which
dominated the export business of Powell Duffryn, and in Scotland of the
Fife Coal Company, each owners of foreign depots by 1913 and
contracting direct with customers.[2] Middlemen also took contracts, but
middlemen were in decline, as owners sought to control them through
acquisition and elimination. Such were the motives which lay behind the
amalgamation of the Ocean Coal Company with the depot-owning firm
of Wilson and Sons; the same was true of the formation of the Cambrian
Combine, a merger between coalowner Samuel Thomas and Cardiff
merchants J. O. and O. H. Riches.[3] In 1907 D. A. Thomas, Samuel's son,
bought out other producers while at the same time creating several merchanting concerns; this was a policy which he predicted would 'eliminate the speculative middlemen but not . . . interfere with the *bona fide*
merchant, to whose enterprise in the development of foreign markets
. . . colliery owners owe so much.'[4] By that time scope for speculative
middlemen was limited to the purchase and resale of job lots surplus to
contract requirements. Taking bigger risks than those regarded as being
'legitimate' middlemen, who usually dealt in guaranteed sales on contract at moderate profit, it was still possible for the relatively few large
speculative middlemen in operation after 1900 to make a killing, though
that depended upon their knowledge of markets and their ability to
organize finance.[5]

Profits secured from sales at spot prices were by no means the
monopoly of middlemen. In 1893, for example, the chairman of the
Main Coal Company criticized the commercial director for a failure to
effect sufficient spot sales (he had recommended between one-third and
one-half) to take advantage of rising prices, a formula he regarded as
essential to maximize profits.[6] How widely such a view was held,
however, we do not know. By World War I, H. S. Jevons reckoned that
in the Main Coal Company's region (South Wales), the proportion sold
on contract was usually between 60 and 75 per cent, occasionally rising

[1] Morris and Williams 1958, 167–8.

[2] Walters 1977, 301; Augustus Muir, *The Fife Coal Company Limited: A Short History* (Leven,
1954), 7, 12–13; H. S. Jevons 1915, 293–4. [3] Daunton 1977, 60–1.

[4] Quoted in Daunton 1977, 61. [5] Ibid.

[6] GlaRO Main D/DMC MB 13 Dec. 1893.

to 85 per cent, whereas in the Midlands and Yorkshire, which were both less export-oriented, the figure was probably below 50 per cent and was, he thought, around the average figure for all coalfields.[1] Here spot sales may have been higher than in South Wales.

Market fluctuations, particularly marked in export markets, also raised supply problems for those more dependent upon rail than water transport, for almost invariably periods of high demand were accompanied by shortages of wagons to move coal from pithead to ports or to inland delivery points. From their beginning early railway companies had built lines ahead of trade to stimulate coal traffic, and the construction of mineral tracks, coal drops, and dock facilities was a policy which, while aiming to promote new investment producing greater traffic, at the same time reduced the fixed capital required by coalowners to transport coal from pithead to market. The early railway companies also built wagons to carry this traffic, though by the early 1850s some had begun to introduce hire charges as an incentive to coalowners to provide their own. This was a policy which the companies found difficult to sustain for fear of losing traffic. Colliery owners, in turn, encouraged buyers, particularly the large ones, to take delivery in their own wagons.[2]

The management of wagon stock, whether owned by railway company or colliery owner, held important commercial implications, for prices quoted for contracts were based on estimates of pithead costs and costs of transporting coal to the port or other place of delivery. Whereas railway charges were predictable wagon costs were variable, and in dealing with a given annual output depended largely upon the number of return journeys made by each wagon. Moreover, at the peak the demand for wagons inevitably exceeded aggregate supplies. At these times ownership and control of wagons was a major advantage in competition with collieries dependent upon the railway companies for wagon supply. Among the most spectacular gains from shrewd forward purchase of wagons were those achieved by the Derbyshire coalowner, Alfred Barnes, whose acquisition of 350 wagons for the relatively small Grassmoor Colliery prior to the boom of 1872–3 brought huge profits deriving from a superior capacity to transport coal to customers during the coal 'famine'.[3] This was the reason why, after selling railways, sidings, and locomotive engines to the Midland Railway Company in 1864,

[1] H. S. Jevons 1915, 293.
[2] Kenwood thesis, 87–8; Vamplew thesis, 375, 378; Morris and Williams 1958, 170–1.
[3] Stephens thesis, 195.

Staveley's wagons were built in the company's own workshops, though the railway company continued to allow the Derbyshire firm to use some of their wagons at no charge for moving coal for internal purposes between the collieries and the ironworks; none the less, wagon supplies continued to cause difficulties in peak trading years, so long as the company was partly dependent on others for wagon supplies.[1]

When in 1865 Robert Baxter, a non-executive partner in the Wharncliffe Silkstone Coal Company, enquired of the reasons for under-production and an apparent lack of market development, he was told by the chairman that under-production was due to a shortage of wagons supplied by the railway companies for coal delivery to Wharncliffe Silkstone's major customers—the Great Northern itself and the gas companies at Hull and Grimsby. Wagon shortage, which occasionally compelled the short-term stocking of coal, and the difficulty of securing hiring agreements from wagon suppliers for a period of less than seven years, explained why sales efforts had been concentrated within the Sheffield region, thereby minimizing truck miles per ton sales.[2] Baxter regarded such a policy, in part a reflection on financial limitations, as short-sighted, and persuaded his co-directors to launch a more ambitious marketing policy; this necessitated the hire of many more wagons from suppliers on a seven-year lease leading to ownership. In the short term, merchants were offered price reductions on coal dispatched in wagons sent to the company's pits, but several hundred wagons were acquired on lease in subsequent years.[3]

During the 1872–3 boom coalowners complained that an acute wagon shortage had caused prices to rise even more, and blamed the railway companies for inadequate investment.[4] Coal companies responded by acquiring, and in some cases building, their own wagons,[5] a trend which for two reasons intensified again from the 1890s. Most important was the expansion in trade and the growth in production from new collieries which were often distant from the main flow of traffic. The chairman of Dalton Main Colliery Company reckoned that the increased capital cost and inconvenience was more than offset by the uncertainty of the ability

[1] BSCEMRRC Stanton and Staveley 2034/2/13 MB 24 Oct., 23 Dec. 1864, 2034/2/15, 22 Feb. 1909.

[2] SCL Wharncliffe Silkstone NCB 1429/1 29 Sept., 19 Nov. 1864, 4 Feb., 18 Mar. 1865.

[3] Ibid., 26 Feb. 1870, 13 Aug. 1871, 25 Jan. 1873, 23 Dec. 1887, 28 Nov. 1899.

[4] SC Dearness and Scarcity 1873, X, QQ 1769, 1869, 4799, 4803; Vamplew thesis 375–6.

[5] BSCEMRRC Stanton and Staveley 2034/7/2 MB 24 Apr. 1869; 2034/7/3 MB 1 Sept. 1870, 2034/7/4 MB 18 Mar. 1882; 2034/7/5 MB 28 Nov. 1889, 2034/7/7 MB 1 Mar. 1909; NoRO New Hucknall, NCB 1/40–1.

of railway companies to supply enough wagons when trade conditions required[1]—which explains why, by the early twentieth century, Staveley owned 90 per cent of the rolling stock the company needed, all built in the company's workshops.[2] The other reason which encouraged wagon ownership was the agreement of the railway companies, still the major wagon owners by far, upon a common policy to enforce wagon hire charges upon merchants, whose failure to load or discharge wagons within the time allowed had led to under-utilization of rolling stock.[3] In 1896 a railway company brought a successful legal action for demurrage against a coal merchant, an event which the Griff Colliery Company's manager regarded as an important victory for wagon owners, whose rental income would benefit.[4]

Encouraged, no doubt, by the profitable opportunities in an industry in which fluctuating demand for coal and transport posed perpetual problems, from the 1860s specialist wagon companies were formed to construct wagons for sale or for hire. Wagon companies experienced similar problems to those of the railway companies, however, for the economics of the trade did not justify the stocking of wagons in sufficient quantities to meet peak demand. Those wagon firms which did flourish tended to be those which offered some form of credit to colliery owners who either lacked the facilities or inclination to maintain their own rolling stock, and to others who favoured current rather than capital outlay.[5] It has been suggested that the growth in private wagon supplies led to overcrowding of sidings and depots, increasing the volume of shunting and marshalling and lengthening delays in delivery: private interests may have thereby reduced the efficiency of the inland coal transport system overall.[6] Less than optimal wagon utilization was a weakness which the Dowlais Coal and Iron Company sought to minimize by contracting to sell part of its output at the pithead into wagons provided by the buyers, and also by keeping waiting wagons filled with coal.[7]

A further criticism aimed at the coal companies, for which there is some evidence, was that they hindered the introduction of large wagons by the railway companies through an unwillingness to reorganize and

[1] *RC Coal Supplies* 1904, XXIII, Q 1557.

[2] BSCEMRRC Stanton and Staveley 2034/2/8 MB 27 Mar. 1900, 2034/2/9 MB 26 July 1904, 21 Feb. 1905. The Wigan Coal and Iron Company owned 5,300 wagons in 1886. *CG* 19 March 1886, 469.   [3] Vamplew thesis, 376–7.

[4] WaRO CR/1169/22–71.   [5] Walters 1977, 133–4.

[6] Vamplew thesis, 378–80.   [7] Morris and Williams 1958, 132–4.

re-equip surface colliery facilities, which determined the layout of loading and transport systems in each colliery.[1] The case of Staveley is of interest because the company was sinking new pits in the late nineteenth century and well placed to innovate in respect of wagon size. The offer was made to replace the company's small wagons with thirty-ton steel wagons, but only on condition that the Midland Railway Company agreed to charge a reduced rate per mile. When this proposal was turned down, Staveley's managers decided to use the ten-ton wagons already introduced for colliery to works traffic, because they were cheaper to build in threes than a single large wagon made of steel. Fifteen-ton wagons were constructed from 1903 but none larger for the facilities for dealing with shipping wagons at Grimsby were not adapted to accommodate them, though it was noted that 'the railway companies will doubtless in time lay themselves out to deal with them'.[2] It would seem, therefore, that railway companies must share some of the responsibility with coal companies for the relatively slow introduction of larger wagons, a process much affected by the inter-relatedness of the two industries, yet whose separate interests hindered the achievement of maximum efficiency in the supply of coal.

Appendix 1.1: Estimates of coal output and consumption

(a) Output

Beginning with the Coal Mines Regulation Act of 1872, increasingly reliable output series are available in the *Mineral Statistics*, both on a national and regional basis. Before that time revisions are needed of all existing estimates. The measurement of coal production is complicated by an ambiguity in the working definition adopted by colliery owners themselves, some of whom excluded coal which was too small to justify bringing to bank at the surface, and commonly called 'waste'. Most of the coal got, filled, and screened but remaining underground (a declining proportion as the century progressed) was abandoned as unmarketable, though some slack was consumed underground by ventilation furnaces and engines. It is impossible to estimate the volume so used, but in comparison to waste is likely to have been small; consequently, while coal burnt for those purposes should be included with colliery consumption it has been excluded from output altogether. Output,

---

[1] *RC Coal Resources* 1904, XXIII, Q 15424.
[2] BSCEMRRC Stanton and Staveley 2034/2/9 MB 27 Sept. 1903.

Table 1.12. *Annual estimates of UK coal production, 1830-1913*

1830	30.5	1851	65.2	1872	125.1	1893	164.4
1831	31.5	1852	68.3	1873	128.0	1894	188.4
1832	32.1	1853	71.2	1874	127.2	1895	189.8
1833	32.9	1854	75.1	1875	133.4	1896	195.4
1834	33.8	1855	76.4	1876	134.2	1897	202.2
1835	35.2	1856	79.0	1877	134.2	1898	202.1
1836	36.4	1857	81.9	1878	132.7	1899	220.2
1837	37.8	1858	80.3	1879	133.8	1900	225.3
1838	39.3	1859	82.8	1880	147.1	1901	219.1
1839	40.8	1860	87.9	1881	154.3	1902	227.2
1840	42.6	1861	89.2	1882	156.6	1903	230.4
1841	43.8	1862	91.1	1883	163.8	1904	232.5
1842	44.2	1863	95.7	1884	160.9	1905	236.2
1843	46.0	1864	99.1	1885	159.5	1906	251.2
1844	47.6	1865	102.3	1886	157.6	1907	267.9
1845	51.1	1866	104.9	1887	162.2	1908	261.6
1846	53.1	1867	106.4	1888	170.0	1909	263.9
1847	54.0	1868	108.2	1889	177.0	1910	264.5
1848	56.6	1869	110.9	1890	181.7	1911	272.0
1849	59.3	1870	115.5	1891	185.6	1912	260.5
1850	62.5	1871	121.4	1892	181.9	1913	287.5

therefore, is defined as all coal brought to bank, and is consistent with the definition adopted by Pollard.[1]

His recent estimates of British coal production between 1830 and 1850 are by far the best hitherto published, and supercede those of Deane and Cole whose figures Pollard revealed to have been under-estimates. The validity of Pollard's estimates depend, however, upon his critical assumption of the accuracy of Robert Hunt's *Mineral Statistics*, for this semi-official source provided Pollard with a seemingly reliable 'fixed point' in 1854, to which the end of his series is anchored; similarly, the alteration of Deane and Cole's figure for 1855, made by Mitchell for the series in *Abstract of European Historical Statistics*, was justified by reference to Hunt's work.[2] But this anchorage is less than firm, and the

[1] Sidney Pollard, 'A New Estimate of British Coal Production, 1750–1850', *EHR* 2nd ser., XXXIII (1980), 220.
[2] Compare Phyllis Deane and W. A. Cole, *British Economic Growth 1688-1959* (Cambridge, 2nd edn., 1969), 216; B. R. Mitchell, *Abstract of European Historical Statistics* (London, 1975).

defects of Hunt's initial figures suggest that all previous estimates are too low. One of the reasons why the early *Mineral Statistics* are not reliable is the lack of any compulsion for colliery owners to complete and return the circulars issued to them by Hunt.[1] Partly because the response rate rose by 1868 the estimates were based on returns from two-thirds of all colliery owners,[2] and the availability of additional information from the Mines Inspector's Reports and Returns[3] compiled from 1864 (and for some regions even from 1856) did much to improve accuracy. Throughout the entire period Hunt further supplemented his intelligence by making his own enquiries in the coalfields, in order to record statistics of production much more accurate than any previous contemporary estimates; and so meticulous was his research that in subsequent years he drew attention to his own past errors and revised the inaccurate figures retrospectively, revisions which historians have overlooked.

Careful scrutiny of the year-by-year estimates and a close reading of Hunt's introduction to the *Mineral Statistics* reveal that from 1859 he began to rectify errors due to simple under-recording (2.5 million tons before 1858 in Lancashire);[4] or caused by ignoring or understating colliery coal consumption and waste, particularly in the North-east (4 million tons before 1860);[5] or resulting from a misinterpretation of local measurements, for example the weight of a Staffordshire 'boat load' (2 million tons) discovered in 1864.[6] When such amendments are incorporated in the totals for previous years the output rises from 64.5 million tons in 1854 (Pollard's estimate) to 73.1 million tons, though adjusted on a pro-rata basis the 1854 figure is closer to 71.5 million tons. In addition, 3.1 million tons of coal raised in South Wales was completely overlooked by Hunt. It seems probable that two major factors were responsible for this oversight. The first is that output was calculated customarily in 'lease weight', which ranged from 1.125 to 1.2 tons and for which Hunt made no adjustments.[7] The second explanation for consistent underestimates is that in common with most of the *Mineral Statistics* data prior to 1864 the figures refer to sales rather than to output. It is

---

[1] Robert Hunt, *Mineral Statistics of the United Kingdom of Great Britain and Ireland for 1853 and 1854* (Museum of Practical Geology, 1855) and annually thereafter until 1882.

[2] For a detailed discussion see Roger Burt, 'The Mineral Statistics of the United Kingdom: An Analysis of the Accuracy of the Copper and Tin Returns for Cornwall and Devon', *Journal of the Trevithic Society* 8 (1981), 31–6.   [3] *Inspectors' Reports*.

[4] *Mineral Statistics* (1859), xiii, (1860), 113.   [5] *Mineral Statistics* (1860), xii–xiii.

[6] *Mineral Statistics* (1864), viii.   [7] J. Davies thesis, 570.

possible to derive an alternative series by applying an approximate multiplier to pig iron output,[1] adding the figures of coal shipments from South Wales[2] together with an estimate of demand generated by other sectors. Such a formula, imprecise though it is, yields an estimate approximately 3 million tons greater than that presented by Hunt, bringing our own revised estimate to 75 million tons in 1854, compared with the Hunt (Pollard) total of 64.5, a difference of 8.5 per cent. This higher figure provided our point of departure in estimating output in the pre-statistical period.

(b) Consumption estimates, 1830-1873

In the absence of reliable estimates of coal production before 1854 it is necessary first to try to calculate the probable consumption of coal, an exercise fraught with difficulties even for the comparatively well documented North-east which is the obvious starting point. The usually well-informed John Buddle offered evidence to the Lords Committee in 1829 to the effect that manufacture, household consumption, and coastwise trade together accounted for 15.9 million tons in England and Wales,[3] a figure which grossly underestimated coal consumed in iron production and which fell far short of total consumption by excluding colliery consumption, miners' coal and waste, exports, and the Irish trade, and at the same time ignoring over-measure on the vend. Scotland was also omitted from his calculations. After revising this figure by re-examining Buddle's estimates, and by supplementing his omissions, a revised estimate for the North-east of 6.9 million tons is arrived at.[4] The next step was to examine each of the other regions, paying particular attention to population and per capita coal consumption, shipments, and the growth of major local industries, especially the iron industry; then proceeding to construct consumption and output estimates for 1830 and 1854, and finally converting these into an annual series by interpolation on the basis of changes in trends and structure of the component consumption and output variables.

In view of the impossibility of building upon contemporary estimates of extremely doubtful validity, it becomes necessary to adopt the first reasonably reliable set of national consumption estimates for 1869, compiled for the Coal Supply Commission,[5] and which, after some

---

[1] From Mitchell and Deane 1962, 131-2.
[2] From the Annual Statements of Trade in Parliamentary Papers.
[3] SC Lords Coal Trade 1830, VIII, 71.   [4] See Flinn 1984, 29-33.
[5] Especially the Appendix to the Report of Committee E, Coal Supply 1871, XVIII, 1244-85.

modification, serve as one of our fixed points in estimating consumption between 1854 and 1869.

Deane and Cole extrapolated backwards from the 1869 breakdown of consumption on the basis of broad assumptions concerning trends in population, alterations in industrial structure, and changes in coal-fuel technology, to which the addition of the export and London import series available throughout the period provided a degree of certainty.[1] Some of the shares they attribute to various sectors are open to challenge, notably the 3 per cent share attributed to colliery consumption,[2] but to advance alternative figures on a national basis in this way would be unlikely to yield estimates of greater reliability than those which they have suggested. Pollard also rejected this method, which for the early nineteenth century would require even greater flights of hypothetical fancy. He adopted the only feasible alternative, which was to take a regional approach, offering the advantage of exploiting the relatively rich historical sources for the North-eastern region (and to a lesser extent some others) and highlighting the differential growth rates in the various coal-producing areas.

The reason for also presenting estimates for 1873 is the wealth of material contained in the Report and evidence of the Dearness and Scarcity Committee; when combined with the *Mineral Statistics* and Meade's data (in evidence to the Dearness and Scarcity Committee) these provided the basis for the first reasonably reliable estimates. Those for 1887 were derived from Richard Price Williams, and from the *Mineral Statistics*; those for 1903 are interpolations from totals for 1887 and 1913, for which year the Samuel Commission gives reliable figures. The *Mineral Statistics*, combined with the *Final Report of the Royal Commission on Coal Resources*, were used for the 1903 interpolation.[3]

Having disputed Hunt's 1854 figure for coal production, our consumption estimates are necessarily also at variance with those of Pollard. Before explaining the methods and sources used in our revision of his figures and those of others after 1854, it is worthwhile drawing attention to the principal discrepancies and their origins. Differences in the volume of coal consumed in manufactures of all kinds explains most of the disagreement. New estimates of pig iron production indicate that

[1] Deane and Cole, *British Economic Growth 1688-1959* (Cambridge, 1967), 215–16, 219.
[2] See below.
[3] *Coal Supply* 1871, XVIII, Appendix to the Report of Committee E, 1244–85; *Samuel Commission* 1926, II, Part A; Williams 1899, 1–46; J. H. Jones, 'The Present Position of the British Coal Trade', *JRSS* XCII (1930), 1–62; *RC Coal Supplies* 1905, XVI; *Annual Statements of Trade*.

his allowances for coal per ton pig and bar iron are too low[1]—the consequences of an underestimation of coal for blast engines as well as that used in calcining ore, and of understating the amounts needed for processing into bars. The use of 'long ton' measurements has magnified the resulting degree of underestimation.

After 1830, fuel economy improved dramatically following the introduction of the hot blast, coupled with better furnace design and improvements in engine and coking technology, though the diffusion took time. Multipliers applied for coal consumption in several other industries also appeared to be too low. A further source of disagreement hinges upon the hundredweight equivalent of the chaldron in South Wales, which was 30 cwt. and not 25.5 cwt., a correction which raises both the consumption estimates for the region and the volume of coastwise shipments.[2]

The detailed estimates are explained in detail by categories:

(1) *Coastal and export trades.* Known as the 'vend' and regulated by the Joint Coalowners Association at the two main ports, Newcastle and Sunderland, the administration of control involved the accumulation of a considerable body of data, to which we may add results of the parliamentary inquiries into its operation. Pollard correctly indicated that the lengthy series of coal shipments recorded are valuable but none the less fall short of the total output of coal in the North-east, for in addition were shipments from the Blyth and Tees collieries. Both these and the vend figures were almost certainly understatements, due to the practice of coalowners supplying over-measure, either through oversight, or, more frequently, as a deliberate policy of making allowances to consumers against breakages and losses in transit, and as an incentive for fitters and shipowners to favour their collieries in competition with others. Over-measure was thus a form of non-price competition in a system of sales control which was better equipped to detect and deal with price cutting than with discrepant keel loads. Estimation of the amount accounted for by over-measure relies upon occasional contemporary statements. We have assumed that by 1830, as a proportion of seasale coal the figure was less than 10 per cent and was declining, as the effectiveness of control diminished. In 1825 the North-eastern ports contributed 79.5 per cent of the nation's coastal trade.[3] Thereafter,

---

[1] Riden, 'The Output of the British Iron Industry to 1850', *Econ. Hist. Rev.* 2nd Series, XXX (1977), 442–9, 455.   [2] J. Davies thesis, 510.
[3] Flinn 1984, 30, 216.

annual *Statements of Trade* and the *Mineral Statistics* contain data on coastal and export trades, though these need to be adjusted for coal to make coke (a 58 per cent yield by 1869), and 90 per cent for patent fuel.

(2) *Waste*. This is a particularly difficult category of coal 'consumption', for which sources referring to the North-east are the most suggestive. For 1830 our estimates depend upon guesswork based upon Buddle's evidence to the *S C Lords Coal Trade* in 1829, (between 10 and 20 per cent), estimates in the *Edinburgh Encyclopaedia* in 1827 and 1829 (about 10 per cent), and Mines Inspectors' *Reports* on the region in the early 1860s. The amount of coal burnt or wasted in 1830 in the North-east was a particularly large proportion compared with most other regions. The existence of literally wasted coal dust and slack is attributable to the relatively high prices obtained for large coal in the London market, which explains why seasale collieries screened out all coal less than $\frac{3}{4}$ inches in diameter from that vended. However, concessions on export duties on small coals since 1866 had led to double screening in order to separate coals of between $\frac{1}{2}$ and $\frac{3}{4}$ inches, which were sold for industrial use in overseas markets.[1] Even so, coal stowed underground was not the only waste in 1830, for other unusable fragments and dust remaining after double screening was suitable for no other uses than road-making, wagonway ballast, stacking in heaps, or burning. The *Coal Supply* evidence in Committee B (on Waste in Working) was that perhaps 5 to 8 per cent of all coal rasied was waste, compared with an implied 14 or 15 per cent in the North-east less than ten years before.[2] For the end of the period the Conservation Committee's estimate was 7 per cent.[3]

(3) *Colliery consumption*. For the amount of coal consumed in domestic heating and for cooking purposes there is indirect evidence from contemporary sources. Important distinctions must be made between per capita consumption in rural and urban areas, and between non-mining and mining communities where miners' free coal allowance influenced consumption levels. Amounts of coal consumed in collieries, principally for feeding the boilers of pumping and winding engines, were in direct relationship to the depth and volume of the pumping load. The coal used was almost entirely slack, for which neither

[1] Ibid., 31, 106–7; *Children's Employment Commission* 1842, XVI, 154–5.
[2] *Coal Supply* 1871, VIII, Committee E, Q 1598; Robert Hunt, *Mineral Statistics* 1860, xii, 99; 1861, viii, 93. [3] *Coal Conservation Committee* 1918, VII, 668.

alternative use was available nor incentive to economize in consumption. Prodigal use of this small coal, therefore, justifies calculation on the basis of steam horsepower employed.

Estimates for colliery consumption in the North-east in 1830 are based upon an intermediate figure between the colliery data, which implied a figure of 14 per cent of seasale or 6.8 per cent of coal output,[1] and a calculation based on horsepower per ton of coal employed in that region as revealed in contemporary sources,[2] which suggested a figure of 8.8 per cent. As the North-east employed power more intensively than any other coalfield in 1830, a national average of 4.9 per cent (1.5m. tons) was adopted (implying that in other regions the average figure was around 4 per cent).

The figures for 1840 and 1855 are interpolations between the estimates for 1830 and for 1869 included in the Report of Committee E of the Coal Supply Commission. These were based on about two thousand colliery returns which yield individual estimates of colliery consumption at 6.7m. tons or 6.25 per cent of output:[3] a total mine consumption of 7.2m. tons yields a ratio of 6.7 per cent of output. Hunt's 1873 *Mineral Statistics* showed total coal consumption in collieries and mines at 9.5m. tons,[4] the 9m. tons consumed in collieries representing roughly 7.1 per cent, which suggested that the 1869 estimate was too low. Accordingly, the 1869 figure has been raised from 7.2m. tons to 7.5m. tons, implying a ratio of 6.3 per cent for colliery consumption.

The interpolations between 1869 and 1913 (1887 and 1903) are based on the figures presented by Jones and those contained in the 1918 Conservation Committee's report.[5] These two sources differ in that Jones puts colliery consumption at 18m. tons (6.26 per cent), compared with a 6.8 per cent ratio implied by figures reported by the 1918 Committee; regional variations were considerable, ranging from 5 per cent in the North-east to 9.4 per cent in Scotland. Grossing up to total output and allowing for metal mines and quarries yields a figure of 20.5m. tons.

(4) *Domestic consumption*.   Domestic consumption must be largely a residual category for even very crude estimates for per capita consumption for domestic heating and cooking are sparse, even in the North-

---

[1] Flinn 1984, 35.   [2] Kanefsky 1979, 370.
[3] *Coal Supply* 1871, VIII, Committee E, 993.   [4] *Mineral Statistics* (1873), xvi.
[5] Jones 1930, 1–62; *Coal Conservation Committee* 1918, VII, 668.

east. A figure of approximately one ton per head for rural Northumberland in 1829 is not inconsistent with coal imports in excess of 2m. tons to supply roughly that number of people, for not only was the amount consumed by London manufacturers in 1830 unlikely to have been great, but domestic consumption in London is also likely to have been less than elsewhere, as all the coal supplied to that market at this time was large coal and up to three times the price of that available in the North-east (where in any case miners received free coal allowances).[1] We have adopted figures of 0.66 ton per capita consumption, except in mining districts where we allow 1.25 tons. The Dearness and Scarcity Committee reckoned on 14 cwt. per head for domestic purposes, but this applied to all counties and included miners whose coal allowances were included under colliery consumption.[2] Per capita consumption in London, after excluding coal used in manufacturing, can be calculated at 12 cwt.[3] After including estimates of miners' allowance coal by region[4] and deducting an estimated 1.2m. tons of Irish output, our best per capita coal consumption estimate for 1869 is 14.5 cwt., adopting a figure of 13 cwt. for 1855.

(5) *Consumption by the iron industry.* As the distinction between iron as a producer good and as a consumer good is imprecise, so any estimates of coal consumed in iron and steel production must also suffer from imprecision, especially as changing technology complicates the formulation of a definition which is appropriate for both the beginning and end of our period. Our definition of iron and steel includes castings produced by smelting firms, but excludes those made at foundries distant from ironworks using pig iron bought in from suppliers. All coal used in the processes of smelting iron and refining it for use by other industries is included in our estimates, except that consumed in mining the raw material and transporting it to the works. And also included is all wrought iron, all puddled, hammered, and rolled metal (whether girders, bars, rails, etc.), since even rails may be regarded as an intermediate product. Items which are the product of further fabrication, such as shipbuilding, engineering, and tinplate manufacture are

[1] *SC Lords Coal Trade* 1830, VIII, 71. Compare the average per capita consumption implied of 6 tons annually in the Stockton and Darlington area. NEI, Prospectus, Report of the Darlington and Stockton Railway, 1821.

[2] *SC Dearness and Scarcity* 1873, X, QQ 60–70.

[3] Ibid., 74–93.

[4] Ibid., 2193, 4244, 2583–4, 6529–31, 6740–3; Alexander Smith, *The Allowance Coal Question*, (privately printed, Dudley, 1875).

excluded. Beginning with the detailed statistics contained in the Dearness and Scarcity report, the increasing accuracy of the *Mineral Statistics* and the careful research and analysis by Meade[1] affords some confidence in the reliability of our series for the amount of coal consumed in the manufacture of pig iron after about 1870. Before 1870, however, considerable problems arise in estimating consumption in the industry, especially due to the diversity of measures employed in different regions[2] and the difficulty in assessing the typicality of individually quoted figures and of reconciling best with average practice.

The amount of coal used in the smelting of iron in the period before 1873 and the fact that small coal and otherwise useless slack was often without commercial value meant that coal used in calcining iron ore, in fuelling and heating the blast, or consumed in donkey engines for a variety of purposes, often went unrecorded. Recent studies of the introduction of the hot blast process, and William Truran's excellent treatise published in 1855,[3] however, provide some indications of the extent of such secondary fuel consumption and also permit a fairly accurate assessment of the timing of fuel-saving innovations between 1830 and 1855. Despite inter- and intra-regional variations in fuel efficiency, therefore, we may be reasonably confident in presenting regional and national figures for coal consumed in pig iron production even before 1870; after which date, with some small modifications, the official series may be adopted.

More difficult is the estimation of coal consumed in processing pig iron into bar iron, which Hyde's research indicates accounted for around two-thirds of all pig iron produced between 1830 and the mid-1860s, after which steel output accelerated.[4] Truran enables us to identify a range of between 4.5 and 10 cwt. needed in the refining furnaces, depending upon coal quality, iron composition, and the heat already in the pig.[5] Puddling wasted 25 or 30 per cent of the iron in 1830, falling to a loss of between 10 and 15 per cent by 1870. Coal consumption ranged from 11 cwts to one ton when refined iron was used, 15 to 24 cwt. if raw pig was used, and presumably more before 1855 when Truran offered these observations. Our 1840 estimate depends

---

[1] Meade 1882, Chapter XXV, especially 813–20.

[2] See above.   [3] William Truran 1855, 175–6.

[4] Charles K. Hyde, 'The Adoption of the Hot Blast by the British Iron Industry: A Reinterpretation', *EEH* X (1972–3), 281–93; Charles K. Hyde, *Technological Change and the British Iron Industry 1700-1870* (Princeton, 1978), 140–2, 154–8.

[5] William Truran 1855, 14–15, 53–7, 85–7, 136–171.

mainly upon extrapolation of 1830 data in order to modify Jessop's 1840 list,[1] in which the figures are plainly too low in the light of data revealed in sources relating to the period between 1830 and 1855.[2]

Between 1860 and 1885 the *Mineral Statistics* provide details of the number of puddling furnaces and rolling mills in each region; when considered in conjunction with Meade's data on furnace output and fuel consumption and Hyde's figures for bar iron production, these enable us to estimate coal utilization. Meade's estimates of fuel consumption for most iron-making regions in 1873 and 1880 are low by comparison with the Coal Supply Commission's 1869 estimates.[3] Evidence presented to the Dearness and Scarcity Committee in 1873,[4] together with formulae for processing taken from Truran and Meade, suggest that neither is accurate; therefore a middle estimate was chosen. Castings, which required relatively small amounts of coal, were made by many firms excluded from our definition of iron producers; nevertheless, our totals (based on 10 cwt. per ton of coal on average) are augmented by a half million tons or more above the published figures for 1869, and appropriate amounts are included in our estimates for earlier years. Steel produced by the cementation process before 1860 justified a very small addition to the estimates, but thereafter Bessemer steel output grew rapidly, augmented by open hearth production in the early 1870s. Steel output caught up with puddled iron, each recording 1.9m. tons by 1885. In 1913 an output of 1.2m. tons of puddled iron compared with 7.7m. tons of steel, which required considerably less coal per ton of output than did bar iron and precipitated a steady fall in coal consumption, to 1.2m. tons per ton by 1913.

(6) *Industrial consumption.* The sources for other industries before 1887 rest heavily on data from the Coal Supply Commission 1871, Committee E, which, where no earlier contemporary fuel conversion formulae or estimates exist (the case for the majority of industries), have been used as a basis for extrapolation backwards. The most valuable sources before 1871 include John Holland, *Fossil Fuel* (1835) in which

[1] Jessop's list is to be found in Meade 1882, 836.

[2] In addition to those referred to above see: R. D. Corrins, 'The Great Hot Blast Affair', *Industrial Archaeology* VI (1970), 223–63; Thomas Smith, *The Miners' Guide* (Birmingham and London, 1836), 87; Trevor Raybould, *The Emergence of the Black Country: A Study of the Dudley Estate* (Newton Abbott, 1973), 135–145; Barrie Trinder, *The Industrial Revolution in Shropshire* (Chichester, 1973), 233–48.

[3] *Coal Supply* 1871, VIII, Report of Committee E, 998.

[4] *SC Dearness and Scarcity* 1873, QQ 19–41.

coal consumption equations are given for potteries, glasshouses, and gasworks. Thus, our coal consumption estimates used in brickmaking, brewing, malting, distilling, paper manufacture, and the production of non-ferrous metals depend upon the Coal Supply Commission 1871 Committee E, and output figures from Mitchell and Deane, *Abstract*, supplemented by the relevant customs data where necessary. Coal consumption in chemicals and alkali works, tanneries, waterworks, and miscellaneous manufacture, are essentially guesses, but were of minor importance in comparison with other categories before 1870. In three important categories, textiles, steamships, and railways, data on the amount of steampower employed in 1869 as shown in Committee E provided a starting point, against which earlier estimates were compared to form a basis for 1855, 1840, and 1830. The bunker coal recorded by the Coal Supply Commission data also offered a continuous series of all coal consumed by steamships trading abroad after 1872; earlier figures are estimated from data on shipping tonnages. For railways we have used Hawke's series for England and Wales for 1840,[1] multiplied by 1.14 to produce a British total; for 1855, Hawke's figure is adjusted from 0.7 to 0.6 tons of coke per ton of coal; Hawke's 1869 figure, which comes from the Coal Supply Commission and incorporated in Mitchell's *European Historical Statistics*, is shown by the 1873 Dearness and Scarcity figures to have been much too low, which is why we have substituted a figure of 3m. instead of 2m. tons for 1869.

(c) Consumption estimates, 1873-1913

The estimates for 1873, 1887, 1903, and 1913 rely on the same sources as those for coal consumed in iron production, though there are some differences. In 1887 Price Williams's figures for gas consumption are gross, whereas we have deducted coke sold by gasworks (as in our earlier figures) to show net coal consumption in gas manufacture. This approach explains the difference also between the estimates for the 'miscellaneous industry' category, and the slight discrepancy between the official export and our revised figures. Price Williams admitted a large exaggeration in the amount of coal he attributed to consumption in coastal bunkers, which has been corrected from the *Mineral Statistics* and other sources. He completely ignored waste, which we have estimated on the basis of information contained in the Coal Supply inquiry and the *Mineral Statistics* for 1912.

[1] G. R. Hawke, *Railways and Economic Growth in England and Wales, 1840-1870* (Oxford, 1970), 296-7.

The inclusion of waste accounts for differences between our estimates compared with those presented by the Coal Resources Commission of 1905, and with those published by Jones in 1913; as is our inclusion of net, instead of gross, coal consumption in gas manufacture, which also affects the miscellaneous residual industrial estimates. Coal consumed in collieries and mines, also shown in the Coal Resources Commission report, has been estimated at a higher level after taking into account the evidence for fuel economies referred to in the Coal Conservation Committee's proceedings in 1918. Our 'collieries and mines' category differs from that of Jones, which refer to collieries only. For coal consumed in coastal bunkers we have used the official figures. Otherwise, differences are negligible and are due to rounding.

CHAPTER 2

Capital Formation and Finance

i. Definitions and dimensions

The vast expansion of coal production, which involved the growth in the number, size, and depth of mines, inevitably required the accumulation of capital and its mobilization. Before we can assess the difficulties of capital supply, by what means growth was financed, and by whom, it will be necessary to attempt to measure the industry's reproducible and historic capital stock and the flow of capital formation. This is an exercise which is fraught with theoretical and practical problems, and because of the nature of the statistical evidence and the difficulties of interpretation associated with it can yield only estimates which, particularly for the early period, inevitably rest upon slender evidence combined with informed judgement. Furthermore, our capital estimates are averages, which cannot reflect the variety of operational features characteristic of the industry. Mines of diverse size and layout were sunk under very different conditions and costs, shafts varying in width and depth, and systems of underground and surface transport designed to meet the peculiar requirements which differed from one location to another. In this the coal industry did not differ much from manufacturing industries, though it seems unlikely, because the amount of capital required to produce a ton of coal differed so widely between collieries, that such a variety of capital–output ratios typical of colliery enterprise was also characteristic outside mining. The explanation for this, of course, is the critical influence of geological conditions on the ease of extraction, the basis of the economics of the industry.

Since both capital costs and capital–output ratios tended to be higher in the early stages of operation, during and immediately following sinking when typically production was small, at any given time the industry consisted of several thousands of individual units possessing a wide spectrum of capital structures and capital costs per ton of output. At the coal face, seam thickness, roof conditions, method of working, and type of coal extracted were also important in affecting, directly or indirectly, capitalization in any given colliery.[1]

Not surprisingly, therefore, even well-informed contemporary observers could offer only broad estimates of the volume of capital employed in the industry at various dates. Moreover, until the twentieth century the failure to explain the methods of calculation, a lack of precision in definition, or the adoption of dubious assumptions, render such general estimates unsuitable for the purpose of constructing national or regional figures.[2] In the absence of reliable national estimates for the nineteenth century, an alternative approach might be to exploit the large number of specific estimates of the amount of capital required to produce a ton of coal in a given colliery or locality and to utilize actual observations relating capital to the realized output of mines and collieries which are to be found in viewers' report books and colliery archives and which provide numerous such estimates.[3] But the immense variety of the industry is such that the resulting pattern displayed by the many observations available (which nevertheless represent a small fraction of colliery investment) is highly ambiguous. An additional difficulty arises from the use of capital estimates derived from business archives, for they rarely reveal the rates of depreciation so critical in the evaluation of capital at historic cost, conceal differences in definitions, and frequently treat the increments of net investment required to develop new workings in existing pits in order to replace those exhausted as current rather than capital expenditure.[4] To assess the

---

[1] Dunn 1852, 58–73; Bidder 1894, 807–8.

[2] Nineteenth century estimates include those by John R. Leifchild, *SC Children's Employment Commission* 1842, XVI, para. 204; Braithwaite Poole, *Statistics of British Commerce* (London 1852), 70; T. Y. Hall, 'The Extent and Probable Duration of the Northern Coalfield with remarks on the Coal Trade in Northumberland and Durham', *TNEIME*, II (1854–5), 195–6; William Fordyce, *A History of Coal, Coke, Coalfields* (London 1860), 44, 47; G. C. Greenwell, 'The Rating of Coalmines', *TNEIME*, XIV (1865), 95; J. Simpson Bell, *Capital and Labour in Coalmining* (Newcastle, 1900), 10–11.

[3] For example, Brown and Adams, 'Deep Winning of Coal in South Wales', PICE LXIV (1880–1), 81, 95–6; 'Notes on a Visit to Collieries in the South Wales Coalfield', *JBSMS*, XIV (1891–2), 176–80; Arthur Sopwith, 'Depreciation of Colliery Plant', *TSSWIME* 9 (1883), 133, 144; *SC Lords Coal Trade* 1830, Buddle's evidence, 52. Observations found in archival sources include NuRO Armstrong 725/B.20/95–101; NEI Shelf 4, vol. 9, 88, Johnson's View Book; NuRO Johnson ZWI/5 view books 564–9, 619–20; NuRO Wallsend and Hebburn Collieries 1439/1, reports to directors.

[4] Fixed mining capital output ratios were calculated for various years for thirteen colliery firms between 1860 and 1913, but apart from an increase in ratios caused by the early 1870s boom and a subsequent post-boom fall, the most striking feature was the diversity between collieries over time. Variations in definition help in explaining this, but the key factor is the varying ages of mines; those sunk recently exhibited high capital–output ratios compared with others, in part

historic costs of colliery capital formation from such sources, therefore, would be an impossible task, involving an analysis of thousands of individual units with unique levels of capital endowment at various rates of depreciation. Colliery archives can, however, provide clues to the detailed composition of colliery capital in the form of tangible or physical assets, and reveal information which the 'conventional' capital–output ratios exclude, but which none the less are important.

While disregarding the national estimates of gross capital formation at historic cost presented by contemporaries, which are inevitably little more than guesses, those provided by colliery owners and statisticians in the early twentieth century deserve serious consideration, for their independent estimates have received general agreement as to the general orders of magnitude. Although they are insufficient by themselves as a basis for extrapolation backwards beyond 1900, nevertheless they do provide a rough check upon the figures arrived at by our own preferred method of measurement. That method, which is not new, derives from estimates made by nineteenth-century observers who themselves employed capital–output ratios as the basis for estimation.[1]

Such an approach enables us to use the observations made by colliery owners, viewers, managers, directors, engineers, and statisticians concerning the probable amount of capital required (under 'normal' conditions) to create a specified output capacity. Relating to various years throughout our period, these data form the most reliable single body of material on capital–output and changes in average capital–output ratios over time, and commands confidence inasmuch that it represents a consensus of contemporary expert opinion on the subject of capital requirements.

Since estimates, of whatever kind, are more abundant and gain in reliability as the century progresses, estimates made towards the end of the period provided the starting point. Moreover, since capital–output estimates are both more numerous and possess greater precision than estimates of capital stock, the former were employed in order to calculate the latter. The impossibility of adopting a colliery-by-colliery method of assessing historic costs of capital formation has been indicated, and although ultimately historic cost estimates are needed, it is necessary to proceed first to attempt to estimate capital and capital

explained by the exclusion of underground roadways from these capital estimates. When average capital–output ratios were calculated for seven companies for which data have survived continuously for at least twenty-five years they fell between 7s. and 12s. per ton.

[1] More recently it has been employed by Mitchell (thesis, Chap. 2), and by Feinstein, 1978, 42, 57.

formation at replacement cost, using the capital–output estimates available. The result is a measure of the costs of replacing existing capital at current prices by plant and machinery of similar type and age, though not necessarily similar in capacity. Use of this concept is dictated by the limitations of the data and initially allows no deduction for wear and tear or for obsolescence, and excludes certain categories of tangible assets. None the less, depreciation (and certain physical assets, omitted from our definition) justifies separate consideration. Specifically, gross fixed capital costs are defined here as all costs incurred in the sinking, equipping, and initial opening-out of collieries, including the value of shafts and all surface arrangements which assist in the production, preparation, and transport of coal. In adopting such a definition we are influenced both by practical considerations and by conventional colliery accounting practice which usually assigned underground road-ways driven to the coal to working costs, along with stores and materials. Variations in colliery accounts meant that minor items of moveable plant, such as mechanical cutters and conveyors, for example, were often attributed to working costs, as occasionally were major items of capital expenditure; none the less, when placed in the context of the enormous volume of aggregate capital employed in the industry, over-laps such as these may reasonably be regarded as relatively insignificant and the variety of estimates available may be regarded as a kind of control in dealing with the problem presented by discrepant definitions.

Capital–output ratios were influenced by a variety of factors and it is not a simple matter to identify and measure those which exercized the greatest influence. The differential age structure of collieries and the extent of new sinkings clearly influenced capital–output ratios, but since ageing collieries tended to be associated with falling rates of growth in output (as in Lancashire for example) the deflationary effect on capital formation is sufficient to obviate adjustment to the ratios, for at this stage we are concerned only with replacement cost. Unlike the value at historic costs, the replacement value of colliery shafts and plant is not materially affected by the age of the collieries in question, since the definition depends upon the replacement of existing plant by machinery of comparable type and age but possibly of different capacity.[1] There are several reasons to explain why the capital costs of replacement (at constant prices) would not have altered markedly over time. Width of seam was an undoubtedly important factor for output potential, but its

---

[1] See the discussion of the definition of capital at replacement cost in J. C. Carrington and G. T. Edwards, *Financing Industrial Investment* (London 1979), 52–3.

Table 2.1. *Estimate of mining capital at constant prices, 1826-1913*
(1900 = 100)

	1 Length of cycle post-peak to peak	2 Detrended output	3 Capital-output ratio	4 Productive capital	5 Annual capital formation	6 Investment lag	7 Unproductive capital	8 Total replacement capital	9 Capital-output ratio inc. unproductive capital	10 Increase in historic capital	11 Total historic capital	12 Historic capital-output ratio	13 Annual depreciation	14 Total depreciation
	(years)	(m. tons)	(£/ton)	(£ m.)	(£ m.)	(years)	(£ m.)	(£ m.)	(£/ton)	(£ m.)	(£ m.)	(£/ton)	(pence/ton)	(£ m.)
1826		28.0	0.34	9.52			(0.3)	(9.82)	0.35		6.00	0.21	(0.86)	
1831	5	31.5	0.35	11.03	0.32	2	0.64	11.67	0.37	1.55	7.55	0.24	0.96	1.35
1837	6	38.0	0.37	14.06	0.55	2.25	1.23	15.29	0.40	2.93	10.48	0.28	1.10	2.15
1847	10	55.2	0.39	21.53	0.80	2.5	2.00	23.53	0.43	7.31	17.79	0.32	1.29	5.57
1854	7	72.8	0.40	29.12	1.03	2.75	2.83	31.95	0.44	7.78	25.57	0.35	1.40	6.03
1866	12	104.0	0.43	44.72	1.17	3.25	3.80	48.52	0.47	13.92	39.49	0.38	1.52	15.49
1873	7	124.5	0.44	54.78	1.30	3.75	4.88	59.66	0.48	10.00	49.49	0.40	1.59	12.44
1883	10	154.3	0.46	70.98	1.41	4.5	6.36	76.34	0.495	14.89	64.38	0.42	2.09	25.65
1890	7	176.7	0.47	83.05	1.73	5.25	9.10	92.15	0.52	13.16	77.54	0.44	2.19	24.79
1900	10	217.0	0.50	108.50	2.25	6.0	13.48	121.98	0.55	23.66	101.20	0.47	2.33	44.49
1907	7	253.1	0.52	131.61	2.32	6.5	15.08	146.69	0.58	20.01	121.21	0.48	2.38	38.75
1913	6	(275)	0.54	148.5	2.40	6.5	15.60	164.10	0.60	10.97	132.18	0.48	2.41	37.95

Sources: See text and Appendix 2.2.

significance for capital–output ratios was probably marginal. Once sunk a colliery had to produce sufficient output to justify the capital investment undertaken. The working of thinner seams over time simply dictated a policy of developing larger working areas and more faces to compensate than would have been the case for collieries with thicker seams. The consequences of thinner seams thus affected working costs (and labour productivity) rather than capital investment. The size and especially depths of mines were clearly the most powerful determinants of capital–output ratios.[1]

Because we must deal with capital–output ratios—which relate to capacity rather than to output—we need to avoid the effects of demand fluctuations upon the capital estimates by isolating the years when production was at maximum capacity, for the capital–output ratios available assume optimum conditions of production. For this reason adjustments have been made to those contemporary capital–output ratios which do not refer to the peak year in each cycle. The transformation of current into constant prices was consequent upon the construction and application of an index of colliery opening-out costs, which was intended to yield capital–output ratios at constant prices—an essential

Table 2.2. *Estimated mining capital at current prices, 1826-1913*

	3 Replacement capital–output ratio (£/ton)	4 Productive capital replacement (£ m.)	8 Total replacement capital (£ m.)	9 Total replacement capital–output	11 Historic capital (£ m.)	12 Historic capital–output ratio (£/ton)
1826	0.25	6.85	7.07	0.25	4.32	0.15
1831	0.25	7.78	8.23	0.26	5.32	0.17
1837	0.29	11.08	12.05	0.32	8.26	0.22
1847	0.29	16.00	17.48	0.32	13.22	0.24
1854	0.28	20.09	22.05	0.30	17.64	0.24
1866	0.35	36.63	39.74	0.38	32.34	0.31
1873	0.48	59.93	65.27	0.53	54.14	0.43
1883	0.35	54.44	58.55	0.38	49.38	0.32
1890	0.41	73.17	81.18	0.46	68.31	0.39
1900	0.50	108.50	121.98	0.56	101.20	0.47
1907	0.54	136.67	152.32	0.60	122.04	0.48
1913	0.56	154.00	170.18	0.62	134.62	0.50

Sources: See text and Appendix 2.2.

[1] See below 104-5.

prerequisite for the assessment of capital costs at constant prices, capital stock, and capital formation over time. The index and an account of its construction is presented in Appendix 2.1.

The capital–output ratios which appear in column 3 of Table 2.2 were constructed by working backwards from the most reliable contemporary estimates, which are those referring to the period between 1890 and 1913.

Before multiplying capital–output ratios for peak years by coal production figures to estimate replacement cost, we need to consider the implicit assumption underlying this procedure, that all capital invested in the industry was productive capital. For whereas initially such an assumption may seem plausible, on reflection it seems unlikely that cyclical peaks coincided with production at full capacity, for that would imply that all new construction was undertaken at post-boom periods and completed before the ensuing peaks. Chronological dispersion was the feature to emerge from our examination of the investment patterns of thirteen colliery companies between 1860 and 1913, as might have been expected in an industry in which the gestation period was relatively lengthy and increased over time.[1] A proportion of current capital formation was devoted to new and as yet unproductive mining, and this needs to be estimated and added to the estimates calculated above which refer only to productive capital. All contemporary accounts refer to the fact that the sinking and opening out of a new colliery was often a lengthy process, depending upon colliery size and the depth of sinking. The *Colliery Guardian's* detailed 1871 survey, for example, reported that average sinking time might vary from 10 to 38 months (dependent on depth) for dry sinking, and from 18 to 40 months where water-bearing strata were involved.[2] Neither of these estimates included the time taken to erect surface plant (a process not necessarily concurrent with sinking) or the opening-out process underground (taking 12 to 18 months), which could only begin once the shafts were completed. Later in the century between five and ten years elapsed before full scale production was reached.[3] At any time, therefore, the industry required a considerable volume of capital which was temporarily unproductive, contributing nothing to current output. The size of this capital (which must be offset against previous lagged investment,

---

[1] The companies were Ashington, Bell Brothers, Briggs, Butterley, Cannock Chase, Carlton Main, Consett, Fife, Lochgelly, Main, Powell Duffryn, and Staveley.

[2] *CG* 2 June 1871, 586–8.

[3] NuRO Armstrong 725/B12–278–9, 379–80, 879–83; Brown and Adams 1881, 81.

unproductive at the preceding peak but productive at the current one) may be estimated if it is possible to devise estimates of gestation periods for each cycle. There is sufficient evidence to suggest that the length of time taken to sink and open out a new colliery increased gradually during the century, as the size, depth, and complexity of mining operations increased.[1]

The crucial factor influencing capital–output ratios was not the size of mines—for especially during the early nineteenth century sizeable drift mines could be operated without the need for costly winning—but their depth. For so long as coal-getting remained unmechanized the capital-intensive aspects of mining were those related to sinking, haulage, pumping, and ventilation, each of which was related to the depth (and size consequent upon depth) of mines. Sufficient, though far from satisfactory, information is available on mine depths for the mid-nineteenth century and at the end of our period to enable us to construct a mine depth index.[2] The weakness of the estimates in the intervening period is unavoidable, and requires interpolation in order to obtain a basis for estimating probable investment lags between 1830 and 1913. The details are explained in Appendix 2.2.

The next step was to make a judgement, for the lack of other evidence and the character of our data precluded doing more, of average production lags at the beginning and end of our period; that the average duration of lagged capital investment during the cycle 1827–8 was two years, rising to six and a half years by 1907–13. The lags for the intermediate cycles were then interpolated in accordance with our information on the depth of mining modified by the known trends in technology and investment. Finally, in conjunction with a formula in which the net product of earlier lagged investment and current investment was assessed, it was possible to ascribe values to the additional capital required (at constant prices) to allow for the unproductive portion in each cycle. When added to the capital formation figures it becomes feasible to attempt a calculation of aggregate national capital stock and capital formation over each cycle; though at this stage,

---

[1] Compare the times quoted for the deep winnings referred to in the previous footnote, and others described in the *Colliery Guardian* (for example at Hamstead, *CG* 12 May 1893, 675; Ashton Moss, *CG* 5 Aug. 1892, 235–6; Maypole, 20 May 1898, 881; Worsley, 4 May 1861, 278) with particularly difficult and very deep winnings; Edward Potter, 'On Murton Winning in the County of Durham', *TNEIME* 1856–7, V, 45–61; Dunn 1852, 64–71.

[2] See the detailed analysis containing comparisons of capital-cost implications of size, depth, seam thickness, in dry and water-bearing strata in *CG* 2 June 1871, 586–8, and the valuable data presented in the *Samuel Commission* III, 188–93. See also Appendix 2.2.

because of regional differences in the extent of coking plant, the latter is excluded from the capital measurements in Tables 2.1 and 2.2. These national estimates necessarily rest upon complex and (at least for the early period) highly conjectural component estimates, in the construction of which the many statistical gaps have been filled by extrapolations and informed guesses. In view of the even greater difficulties involved in the construction of regional estimates it has been decided that to attempt to do so would risk transforming a tolerable heroism into culpable heresy.

The most recent estimates of capital in the industry are those made by Feinstein.[1] They refer to gross replacement capital at current cost, and while making some general allowance for changing capital–output ratios seem to disregard what we have described as unproductive capital and production lags. Furthermore, as all calculations of capital stock by this approach depended upon an output multiplier it is not surprising that because the coal production figures he used have been superseded by higher, new estimates, our 1830 estimates for total replacement capital (when expressed in 1851–61 prices to compare with Feinstein's capital estimates for mining and quarrying) should almost double his figure. By 1860 the new output estimates are much closer to those employed by Feinstein, exceeding his by less than 5 per cent. Our figures thus suggest a considerably greater rate of growth in the industry's gross stock of reproducible fixed capital occurring between 1830 and 1860. Such comparisons are not without interest, but it is questionable whether such an abstract concept of capital at reproducible cost is of more than limited use in what it can reveal to historians about the stock and flow of capital formation over time.

The formula employed in calculating capital at replacement cost requires the assumption that investment replaces depreciated plant at original levels of technology; also implicit in the concept as applied to the coal industry is the assumption that all increased capacity comes from 'new' mines, i.e. mines opened out at current levels of capital output. Together, these assumptions ensure that figures for replacement cost overstate the actual investment at any point in time. However, the calculation of capital at replacement cost is a necessary prerequisite for the estimation of capital at historic cost, which is what we need in order to enable us to obtain a more realistic estimate of actual demand for capital over time, of the effective flow of investment into the industry,

---

[1] Feinstein 1978, 42, 57.

and of the rate of return on assets; all of which are meaningless in relation to capital at replacement cost.

While the transformation of replacement into historic costs at constant and current prices is not an unduly complicated exercise, and is completed in Table 2.2, two key components which are necessary for estimating required detailed source-based justification, for upon these depend the credibility of the results. The calculations are cumulative, adding the net increments to capital formed during the course of a cycle to that of the previous cycle, and while it is possible to use replacement costs as a proxy for capital increments over a cycle, the initial historical-cost figure forms the critical foundation. It is derived from Buddle's evaluation of the amount of capital invested in the collieries of the Tyne and Wear,[1] enlarged to take into account capital associated with the mining of landsale coal at Blyth and along the Tees, and revised in accordance with our definition of capital (based on subsequent colliery accounting practice) which excludes underground tramways. The capital–output ratio resulting from these figures relating to the North-east was applied to the index generated from depth and output estimates previously employed in the calculation of production lags to obtain national estimates of capital and capital–output ratios. The other prob-lematical decision was the choice of depreciation rates, which detailed analysis of practices within the industry suggested a 5 per cent figure to be the correct order of magnitude for the forty years after 1873, and 4 per cent before that time.[2]

The resulting figures for gross and net capital formation at historic cost (expressed in current and constant prices) are, of course, estimates only, and one cannot infer from the figures for total gross expenditure that the total indicated in Table 2.1 was actually spent. Rather, the figures suggest that had full depreciation been made then the sums

[1] Buddle's 1929 estimate for capital invested in those collieries shipping coal on the Tyne was £1.5m., and on the Wear £0.6–0.7m. SC Lords Coal Trade 1830, VIII, 34, 52. To this needs to be added about £0.2m. which probably would have been employed in raising coal from the Blyth and Tees collieries for landsale, increasing Buddle's figure to £2.3 or £2.4m. Because the method adopted in estimating capital allows only estimates over the cycle an initial estimate is required for 1826, the beginning of our first cycle; in accordance with price trends a reasonable figure for capital stock in that year is £2.1m., from which has been deducted 10 per cent as an approximate figure representing capital in underground tramways, in order to conform to our definition of capital stock in mining. The figure of £1.9m. yields a capital–output ratio of 0.3, which when applied to the depth and output estimates employed in the calculation of logs gives a national total of £4.32m. at current prices—£6m. at constant (1900) prices.

[2] See below 533. Calculating capital using rates of depreciation of one per cent above or below these figures makes very little difference.

expended over the entire period would have been of the order of £341m. at 1900 prices, of which £127m. would have been invested in net increases in productive capacity charged at current cost, and the remainder in repairs and replacements of the capital stock. Assuming full depreciation expenditure, before 1873 net investments to create new capacity would have exceeded depreciation in each cycle. The boom of the early 1870s brought about a reversal of the relationship. Thereafter, increases in net investment fell far below the depreciation required to maintain and renew productive capacity in a vastly expanded industry, in which the scale and capital intensity of operations increased while output grew at a decelerating rate. For the same reasons, increases in historic capital were at their highest during the cycles of 1837–47 and 1847–54, when they rose from 5.6 per cent per annum during the previous cycle, 1831–7, to exceed 7 per cent. After falling to 3.7 per cent in 1854–66 the rate of capital formation remained below 3 per cent in each cycle until 1907, when the figure dropped to 1.6 per cent. As the basis and detail of our capital estimates differ substantially from those presented by Feinstein, it is not possible to compare growth rates, though his figure for the annual rate of growth of the stock of capital in all sectors of 2.3 per cent between 1831 and 1860 suggests that during its peak expansion phase the coal industry was probably exercizing a considerably heavier demand on the nation's financial resources than most other sectors.

ii. Composition of capital: asset structures and estimates

The fixed capital we have attempted to measure so far includes the value of all colliery plant which directly relates to the production of coal; it includes sinking and opening-out costs, all surface and underground plant, transport facilities (horses, stables, wagons, engines, railways), and office facilities. However, these fixed assets employed in winning and preparing coal, what we shall term *mining assets* comprising *mining capital*, exclude coke works, which in some regions at some periods were integral to mining activity in the nineteenth century (but the capital investment in which is less susceptible to measurement by formulae). They also exclude capital invested in fixed assets, land, houses, farm buildings, and farms, which while falling outside the strict definition of mining capital were none the less regarded by many colliery owners as complimentary to successful colliery operations. When all these elements are estimated and combined with mining capital we shall refer to the total as *colliery capital*, comprised of *colliery assets*. Coke works will be included as a mining asset. The argument for so doing rests on the fact that while coke may be regarded as a different product, produced independently of coal by a separate work force often under separate management, in some areas the entire *raison d'être* of the collieries was to produce coke, the survival or profitability of a colliery enterprise depending upon it. This was the case at the beginning of the period for many collieries in west Durham, the major coke-producing region then and until 1913. By that time south Yorkshire and the Monmouth–Glamorgan border had become major coke-making areas, though substantial quantities were also produced at collieries in Cumberland, Derbyshire, Lancashire, Staffordshire, Lanarkshire, and Stirlingshire to supply local blast furnaces.[1] However, as beehive ovens closed down and were replaced by recovery plants, from about 1900 coke plant tended to be built at the ironworks.[2]

Before 1840 the volume of capital tied up in coke making was very small, though we can only infer this from knowledge of the technology of coke production and estimates of capital–output ratios. In 1830 the requirements for coke production consisted of a brick chimney to remove gases and provide a draught to the large open heaps of coal, and tubs or trucks for transport. Probably less than £0.2m. at current prices was invested in coking plant in 1830.[3] The 1840s saw the rapid adoption of beehive ovens, especially in the coking collieries of west Durham. Dunn's figures provide the basis for a capital estimate of £0.35m. at replacement cost in 1850, while Meade's data yield an estimate of between £2.5m. and £2.7m. for 1882.[4] After 1900 the sources permit a systematic and more reliable assessment of capital in a period which brought the widespread introduction of modern capital-intensive recovery ovens. A detailed breakdown of beehive, by-product and retort ovens differing in capital costs, together with reliable output data from the *Sankey Commission*, justifies an estimate of £7m. embodied in by-product ovens in 1913 and £2m. in beehives,[5] though perhaps 10 per cent of the £9m. was invested in coking plant at steelworks, bringing the colliery coking figure down to around £8m. These various calculations

[1] Dunn 1852, 73, 372; Meade 1882, 13–15; *Mineral Statistics*, 1913; Mountford thesis, Appendix F.

[2] *Samuel Commission*, II, part B, 842–62.

[3] Galloway 1898, 363–4; *SC Children's Employment Commission* 1842, XVI, 357–8.

[4] Dunn 1852, 73; Meade 1882, 15.

[5] Mountford thesis, Appendix F; *Samuel Commission* II, Part B, 842–62.

suggest that to mining capital at replacement cost should be added some 2 per cent in the 1840s, rising to 5 per cent by the 1880s.

A combination of assumptions and formulae enabled us to estimate coal mining and coking capital, because these processes resulted in a measurable output. Specific capital goods involved in their production, however—colliery plant, railways, and wagons—present difficulties in measurement, as do brick works and horses, neither of which can be estimated by devising formulae, for brick works were not always an accompaniment to mining, while horses and ponies were substitutes for manual labour in the early period and later became alternatives to machinery; perhaps the most problematical, however, is estimating the shaft component in mining capital. The difficulties and the methods adopted in an attempt to overcome them are explained in Appendix 2.3, and while the deficiencies of the resulting estimates dictate the formulation of conclusions in a subjunctive mode, without such an exercise an analysis of the structure of mining assets could not proceed beyond the episodic or individual company level.

The assets of the industry may be examined in three ways: mining assets (including all 'fixed' assets used in winning and preparing coal—colliery plant, railways, wagons, coke works, brick works, and horses); colliery assets (mining assets plus other 'fixed' items—land, houses, farm buildings, and farms); and *company assets*, which incorporate the remaining items in asset structure. From all the business archives examined only nine provide data suitable for detailed analysis of this kind.[1] In 1913 their combined output amounted to 5 per cent of national production, though each of the major regions is represented, with the exception of Lancashire and Cheshire. The firms were middling to large, seven of them each producing more than a million tons in 1913. The data refer almost entirely to the period after 1870. Three of the firms did not coke coal and a further two possessed no brickworks. At most, therefore, our sample firms enable us to learn something about the asset structure of middle- to large-scale colliery enterprises. Yet there are no obvious reasons why the mass of smaller middle-sized firms, with outputs measured in hundreds of thousands, rather than millions of tons, should have possessed a noticeably different asset structure so far as mining assets are concerned; for the equipment needed to mine coal was (at least within broad divisions from the standpoint of mining technology) homogeneous to a considerable degree. There is, therefore, some

---

[1] Ashington, Briggs, Carlton Main, Consett, Hamstead, Lochgelly, New Hucknall, Powell Duffruyn, and Walsall Wood.

justification for regarding the averages derived from our nine companies as sufficiently representative of the type of firms from which the bulk of national production came—and to proceed further.

While it is fairly clear that colliery plant, railways, and wagons were assets common to all colliery companies, they were not always separately distinguished in the accounts; consequently we have been compelled to hypothesize a capital structure for those companies where the accounts lacked detailed definition. At the same time, however, an attempt has been made to preserve the individuality and basic variety of the evidence from sampled firms presented in Appendix 2.3. With regard to brick works, coke works, and horses, for which numerous gaps exist, it seems preferable to refer to averages, not for collieries as a whole but of *averages for collieries where such assets existed* (or were valued separately). The figures which result indicate three-quarters of mining assets to have comprised colliery plant, 11 per cent railways, 5.5 per cent wagons, 4 per cent coke works, 3.5 per cent brick works, and horses roughly one per cent.

Colliery plant, by far the largest item, was itself a composite category in which some companies (not only those in the sample) included such items as 'pits' or 'sinking pits', or that of land, houses, and farm buildings, with the consequence that even when we have adjusted the figures for plant to take into account railways, wagons, coke works, and horses, 'colliery plant' might still incorporate at least part of the value of the mine or shafts themselves. Evidence from certain company accounts and from contemporary mining engineers and technical experts show that while capital costs of shafts might vary, most observations fall within the range of 40 to 48 per cent.[1] The evidence does not point to changes over time; colliery plant became more sophisticated and more expensive as the average depth of colliery sinkings increased, consequently shaft costs seem to have risen in roughly equal proportion. In fact there was a clear tendency for company accounts to undervalue shafts and therefore to undercapitalize assets, probably by this amount. Therefore, if railways, wagons, coke works, brick works, and horses are put at 25 per cent of mining assets, the remaining 75 per cent in 'colliery plant' should then be reallocated in such a way that 40 per cent of the total is attributed to shafts as implied in the technical literature; the effect of which is to reduce colliery plant to 35 per cent of total mining

[1] Redmayne 1914, 189–90; Brown and Adams 1881, 95–6; BSCEMRRC Stanton and Staveley 2034/3/12 Staveley, New Hollingwood, Seymour, and Markham colliery-sinking accounts. Recalculation of capital costs for Merthyr Vale Colliery in 1869–75 from Walters 1977, 245.

assets. The revised formula requires adjustment as shown in Table 2.3. The tentative character of this exercize cannot be overemphasized; the variety of the estimates found in the company data and technical literature indicate clearly that at any single point in time differences between collieries tend to swamp changes over time in 'average' ratios.

Our structural breakdown of mining capital still excludes houses, farms, farm buildings, and land, items which are usually combined in colliery accounts. In certain regions, the North-east, Scotland, and later the East Midlands, it was common practice for viewers and colliery engineers to include housing as a component in their estimates for opening a new colliery or enlarging an existing one, adopting a ratio of output to hewers to houses at current building costs. For this reason the category of assets comprised of land, farms, houses, and non-mining buildings has been combined with mining capital to form colliery assets, or colliery capital. The effect of broadening the definition reveals the very considerable importance of this category of capital asset, and while it needs to be emphasized that our estimates refer to large- and medium-sized colliery companies, nevertheless it is of interest to note that such firms as Ashington, Briggs, Consett, Staveley, New Hucknall, and (exceptional in its extensive landownership) Hamstead owned considerable amounts of land and/or large numbers of workers' houses. On the basis of our company asset data, adjusted for the shaft-sinking component which is taken to be 40 per cent of mining assets, the component of colliery capital is calculated as follows: value of shafts 33.6 per cent; colliery plant 29.4 per cent; railways 9.2 per cent; wagons 4.6 per cent; coke works 3.4 per cent; brick works 2.9 per cent; horses 0.8 per cent; land, farms, farm buildings, and houses 16 per cent (Table 2.3).

Table 2.3. *The composition of mining capital in 1870-1913*

	per cent
Value of shafts	40
Colliery plant	35
Railways	11
Wagons	5
Coke works	4
Brick works	4
Horses	1

Table 2.4. *The composition of colliery assets in 1870-1913*
(percentages)

	Colliery plant	Railways	Wagons	Coke works	Brick works	Horses	Land, farms, houses, and buildings
Lochgelly	50	16	7	5	3	1	19
Carlton Main	71	8	10	5		1	7
Briggs	65		3	5	2	1	18
Consett	58	11	3	5		1	24
Ashington	58	14	3		3	1	22
Hamstead	36	4			2	1	58
Walsall Wood	70	8	10		12	1	
New Hucknall	58	6	4	6	3	1	24
Powell Duffryn	77	7	7	6	3	1	
Mean	60	9	5	4	3	1	19

Sources: See text and Appendix 2.3.

It should be possible to transform our static analysis of the structure of mining assets into a dynamic formulation of the growth of mining assets over time. This is a consequence of the identical definitions of mining assets incorporating the value of shafts with that employed in our earlier analysis of capital–output and capital formation, and which as a result is embodied in our UK capital estimates. By applying our mining asset proportions, representing separate items of plant, to the UK capital estimates it should be possible to arrive at figures for disaggregated mining investment. There are, however, difficulties in doing so, not least because the many caveats made regarding the sources for analysis of capital, even for the period 1870–1913, apply much more to the preceding years. None the less, taking into account changing technology and developments in mining practice, we have extrapolated backwards in order to obtain a crude chronological profile of mining and colliery assets from the mid-nineteenth century. Assumptions of shallower shafts in the period before 1870, and proportionately higher labour-to-capital costs in sinking more primitive shafts and driving shafts are unquestionable. Since, however, capital endowments were less sophisticated and involved lower expenditure, the case for adjusting the shaft–plant ratio is not compelling. Railway capital was undoubtedly a major element in colliery enterprise before 1850, but we have no adequate data from colliery accounts in that period. Some increase in the capital costs of railways between 1847 and 1870 (compared with 1870–1913), at least that borne by coalmining firms themselves, does appear to be justified in view of the degree of regional dispersion of coal production prior to 1870. An assumption of a growing proportion of capital attributed to wagons between 1873 and 1913 takes account of an increasing trend towards wagon ownership referred to in Chapter 1.

The railway companies' initial policy had been to provide only track and haulage, leaving users to provide their own wagons, except for those supplying railway coal in the coalmining regions. Elsewhere, practically all traffic handled by the railway companies was handled in wagons owned by the railways, a situation which still obtained in the North-east in 1913. None the less, the leasing of wagons from wagon companies, which was the preferred arrangement until the 1870s, was replaced by private ownership. By 1925 the Samuel Commission reported 520,000 out of 700,000 wagons for coal transport were privately owned.[1] Coking facilities, too, were less extensive in 1873 than in 1913, and likewise before 1873 were even less capital intensive. The proportion of capital in brick works was almost certainly as large before as after 1873, though it is possible that it may have been even higher in view of a greater level of company housebuilding in this earlier period, when a less well-developed domestic construction industry existed.[2] Horses as a capital element were almost certainly more important in 1854 than in 1873, for the intervening period brought about considerable progress in the mechanization of haulage and winding.[3] Our very crude independent estimate for horse capital during the pre-war period suggests a figure of about one per cent of capital at current prices. After all adjustments, the final proportional estimates of mining-asset structure at five of the cycle peaks between the 1850s and 1913 is seen in Table 2.5, though the apparent precision suggested by the figures presented should be seen in the context of the reservations made concerning the weakness of the data on which they are based. None the less, the relative importance of the constituent assets may be accepted as broadly accurate, at least for the later period.

The calculation of colliery assets including capital in houses, land, and buildings is even more problematical when attempting to advance beyond a single ratio for the 1873–1913 period based on company data. Undoubtedly the major element in this category was housing, the cost

[1] *Samuel Commission* I, 114.   [2] See below 599–600.
[3] Hughes 1892, 189–90; Pamely 1904, 495–500; Kerr 1904, 377–82.

Table 2.5. *The composition of mining assets including shafts, 1854-1913*
(percentages)

	Shafts	Colliery plant	Railways	Wagons	Coke works	Brick works	Horses
Average from company sample	40	35	11	5.5	4	3.5	1
Adjusted peak year estimates							
1854	40	36	11.5	4.5	2	4	2
1873	40	36	11	5	3	3.5	1.5
1890	39.5	35.5	11	5.5	4	3.5	1.5
1900	39.5	35.5	11	5.5	4	3.5	1.5
1913	39	34.5	11	6	5	3.5	1

Sources: See text and Appendix 2.3.

of which increased dramatically during those forty years, at a time when the cost of new houses at constant prices more than doubled—largely because housing standards and expectations rose dramatically.[1] Off-setting this trend was the decline in the number of houses built by colliery companies, as the relative importance of those regions where traditionally colliery-owned houses and been the norm (notably in the North-east and Scotland) diminished. Taking these factors into account, we have assumed that land, farms, farm buildings and houses repre-sented $18\frac{1}{2}$ per cent of all fixed colliery capital in 1913 and $13\frac{1}{2}$ per cent in 1873; extrapolating backwards, our starting figure for 1854 was $12\frac{1}{2}$ per cent.[2]

Independent calculations of colliery housing capital in 1913 produce a figure (at replacement cost) which is 81 per cent of the total estimated category including other buildings and land, a figure which confirms the

[1] Estimating replacement capital for miners' housing depends upon evidence of varying quality, and the results are tentative in the extreme. The *Samuel Commission* data, especially in III, appendix 18, Table 37, 247–9, was the starting point; the revised employment data were the basis for extrapolation backwards; price information was taken from *Reports of the Commissioners on the State of the Mining Districts* 1844, XV, i, 1845, XXII, 197, 1846, XXIV, 383, 1848, XXVI, 233; *SC Dearness and Scarcity*, 1873, X, i; *RC Labour* 1892, XXXIV, 313 and XXXVI, 5; *Eight Hours Committee* 1907, XIV, 525 and XV, i.

[2] By assuming that 13.5 per cent of colliery assets in 1873 rose to 18.5 per cent in 1913, thus averaging the 16 per cent (company-based) figure over the period as a whole, it is possible to calculate the capital which this might have represented by taking the remainder (86.5 to 81.5 per cent depends on the date) as equivalent to the value of total mining assets in each peak year.

general magnitude of our asset estimates and which may also be taken as
an indication of housing's relative share; for earlier years that proportion is likely to have been lower.[1] These figures also suggest the relative importance of social overhead capital in colliery asset structure.
Our estimates of the distribution of capital between the different categories of colliery assets between 1854 and 1913 are shown in Table 2.6.

The explanation for the relative size of the components of asset
structure over time have already been rehearsed in the course of forming
our estimates and require no further elaboration. In the context of establishing the sources of capital supply, however, it is relevant to note that
while our overall estimates of mining and colliery capital almost
certainly understate their value by the omission of underground roadways, construction of the latter was financed for the most part over time
from working capital in the form of payments for wages and materials.
Our estimates of disaggregated colliery capital presented in Tables 2.7
and 2.8 are derived by applying the proportional distribution of the
components to our national estimates of colliery capital shown in Table
2.6.

Assets in the form of stores and materials have been estimated on the
basis of sixteen observations from eleven firms which provide sufficient
detail to identify their relative contribution to total working costs.[2]
One-half fall within the 9 to 12 per cent range and with one exception all
register between 6 and 14 per cent, a spread of observations which is not
surprising in view of the problems of achieving a common definition of
the term 'stores'. When data on average working costs[3] in the industry
are combined with detrended output, the 9 to 12 per cent range yield
figures for annual historic costs in the industry as a whole and add
between 5 and 7 per cent to colliery capital (6 to 10 per cent to mining
capital).

The overwhelming importance of fixed capital, however defined,
is indisputable: as a proportion of total assets of a dozen colliery

---

[1] The highly tentative estimates derived from the sources listed in the last footnote but one of
the replacement value of company-owned houses are £12.7m. in 1890, £9.3m. in 1883, and £6.1m.
in 1873.

[2] The firms are: Bridgewater Collieries, Bell Brothers (3), Briggs, Cannock Chase, Carlton
Main, Consett (3), Govan, Middleton, Mitchell Main (2), and Staveley. The figures for Briggs
differ from those quoted for the individual seams analysed in detail by Hodges. Differing defini-
tions from the main company accounts (which have been used here) is the likely explanation. I.
Hodges, 'Increase of Working Costs in Coal Mines during the past Half Century, the Rate of
Increase and the Causes Thereof', *TFIME*, 40 (1910–11), 172.

[3] See below Table 6.5.

Table 2.6. *Colliery asset structure, 1854–1913*

	Shafts %	Colliery plant %	Railways %	Wagons %	Coke works %	Brick works %	Horses %	Land, buildings, houses %	Fixed colliery capital (replacement) £ m.	Fixed colliery capital (historic)
1854	35.0	31.2	10.1	3.9	2.2	3.3	1.8	12.5	36.5	29.2
1866	34.8	31.3	9.8	4.1	2.4	3.1	1.5	13.0	55.8	45.4
1873	34.7	31.2	9.5	4.3	2.6	3.0	1.3	13.5	68.8	57.2
1883	34.2	30.4	9.4	4.3	3.0	3.0	1.3	14.5	89.3	75.3
1890	33.3	29.8	9.3	4.6	3.4	3.0	1.1	15.5	109.1	91.8
1900	32.8	29.6	9.2	4.6	3.3	2.9	1.0	16.5	145.3	120.9
1907	32.2	28.9	9.1	4.9	3.7	2.9	0.8	17.5	176.9	146.8
1913	31.8	28.1	9.0	4.9	4.1	2.9	0.8	18.5	200.4	163.5

Sources: See text and Appendix 2.3.

Table 2.7. *Disaggregated estimates of historic colliery capital at constant (1900 = 100) prices, 1854-1913* (£ m.)

	Fixed colliery capital (replacement cost) £ m.	Fixed colliery capital (historic cost) constant prices	Shafts	Colliery plant	Railways	Wagons	Coke works	Brick works	Horses	Land, buildings, houses
1854	36.5	29.2	10.23	9.14	2.94	1.15	0.64	0.96	0.51	3.65
1866	55.8	45.4	15.80	14.22	4.44	1.88	1.09	1.38	0.69	5.90
1873	68.8	57.2	19.80	17.82	5.44	2.47	1.48	1.73	0.74	7.72
1883	89.3	75.3	25.75	22.85	7.08	3.22	2.25	2.25	0.97	10.92
1890	109.1	91.8	30.63	27.33	8.53	4.27	3.10	2.71	0.97	14.22
1900	145.3	120.9	39.66	35.86	11.11	5.55	4.04	3.53	1.26	19.96
1907	176.9	146.8	47.18	42.34	13.32	7.24	5.43	4.22	1.21	25.67
1913	200.4	163.5	51.99	45.99	14.66	7.99	6.65	4.66	1.33	30.27

Sources: See text and Appendix 2.3.

Table 2.8. *Disaggregated estimates of historic colliery capital at current prices, 1854–1913* (£ m.)

	Shafts	Colliery plant	Railways	Wagons	Coke works	Brick works	Horses	Land buildings, houses	Colliery capital
1854	7.06	6.31	2.03	0.79	0.44	0.66	0.35	2.52	20.16
1866	12.94	11.64	3.64	1.54	0.89	1.13	0.57	4.83	37.18
1873	21.66	19.49	5.96	2.71	1.62	2.24	0.81	8.45	62.94
1883	19.75	17.53	5.43	2.47	1.73	1.73	0.74	8.37	57.75
1890	26.98	24.08	7.51	3.76	2.73	2.40	0.85	12.53	80.84
1900	39.64	35.85	1.11	5.55	4.04	3.53	1.26	19.96	110.94
1907	44.92	40.32	12.67	6.91	5.20	4.03	1.15	24.43	139.63
1913	54.09	47.85	15.26	8.32	6.93	4.85	1.39	31.48	170.17

Sources: See text and Appendix 2-3.

companies fixed assets fell within a range of 66 to 87 per cent, with one explicable exception.[1] Colliery investment, therefore, was different from almost all other types of industrial investment because of the relative size of fixed capital requirements, the gestation period necessitating relatively long-term commitment, and the uncertainty associated with mining, given the state of the art. While it is impossible to be precise on this matter, we may deduce from our knowledge of asset structure and our discussion of the determinants of capital costs that as the century progressed more collieries needed to raise greater financial resources for longer periods, though regional and local differences were important influences upon the chronology and extent of these trends.

The timing of investment seems to have been influenced more by non-cyclical than cyclical factors, for analysis of detailed company data for the period 1860–1914 shows capital to have been invested at various stages of the cycle, no single phase appearing to be more significant than another.[2] The rationale for this is apparent in a report to the Londonderry Collieries written by the viewer John Daglish in 1866. He criticized the cutback in capital expenditure that had occurred during the depression of 1861 and 1862, to which he attributed the difficulty of expanding output when trading conditions subsequently improved:

time is an important element in mining operations especially at large collieries: the effect of any attempt to curtail the winning charges is not visible at once in reducing the quantity, in fact several years will elapse before, on the one hand the injury is accomplished, but on the other hand, still longer time is required to restore the mine to its proper condition. The effect of 'reducing expenses' in 1861 and 1862 was not felt in its worst until 1865, at the very time when coals were selling at high prices, and although immediately on my entering on the charge of the Londonderry Collieries in the Autumn of 1864 the necessary winning drifts etc. were commenced and have continued without intermission until now, still it is only in 1866 that any benefit has been derived from them.[3]

---

[1] The firms are: Butterley, Cannock Chase, Carlton Main, Fife, Lochgelly, Main, Powell Duffryn, Staveley, Wigan Iron and Coal, and Briggs which was the exception. This is explained by the very high level of the firm's external investments, amounting to one-third of total assets.

[2] In addition to the colliery companies listed in the previous footnote, the chronology of capital expenditure was analysed for Ashington, Bell Brothers, Consett (coal only), and Main.

[3] DuRO Londonderry LO/B/318 Daglish Reports. A similar conclusion appeared in the manager's annual report on the Newbattle Colliery in 1868. ScRO Newbattle GD 40/V/110. Thirty years later, mining engineers Liddell and Smith recommended the Dudley Trustees to sink new pit shafts when wages were low, which coincided with periods of slack trade, in order to exploit rising coal prices in the boom. Raybould thesis, 122.

He estimated the opportunity cost to have amounted to a gross loss of £50,000. On the basis of company data the only possible generalization is that investment was least likely to be made in the immediate pre-peak period, but even this assertion is weak and contradicted in several instances, and consequently the conclusion must be that companies invested at all stages of the cycle.

iii. Proprietorships and partnerships to 1855

The implications of our capital estimates for the demand for finance are not immediately obvious, partly because of their limitations, especially for the pre-company era, and partly because the statistical information on colliery sizes before 1894 is unsatisfactory and probably unreliable before 1860. It is unsatisfactory because before 1894 it is possible only to calculate average figures. However, if we accept the averages as no more than a crude indicator of mine, and by implication before 1860 (except for the North-east) for the most part colliery, size,[1] then the relevant capital–output ratio implies an average fixed-capital requirement of less than £7,000 in the 1860s, and lower for preceding years.

Such figures are irrelevant, of course, to most units of mining production, though even in aggregate the smallest mines probably produced a relatively small proportion of total coal output. Outside the North-east, where in the 1830s initial fixed-capital outlays could amount to £25,000 or £35,000, and even greater in a few cases,[2] the average figure suggests that mining enterprise may have been similar in the scale of its demands on individual investors to those in the other major growth industries of iron and cotton,[3] certainly the variability of firm size, with relatively small- to medium-sized enterprises predominating numerically throughout the nineteenth century, was a feature these industries shared in common.

Evidence from particular regions and collieries are broadly consistent with our capital–output data. An annual production of 40,000 tons in Yorkshire and the East Midlands was regarded as relatively large in the 1840s, while in South Wales a figure of 30,000 tons was taken to signify an output associated with operations on a substantial scale, for which a maximum of £10,000 is reckoned to have sufficed for sinking and working capital. In Staffordshire pits were being opened for sums rarely exceeding £3,000 or £4,000.[4] The Aberdare Coal Company, one of the

[1] See *List of Mines* and below, 386–91.   [2] Flinn 1984, 193–4.
[3] Crouzet (ed.), *Capital Formation in the Industrial Revolution* (London 1972), 37–8.
[4] A. J. Taylor 1967, 98.

earliest coalowning partnerships formed in South Wales, commenced trading in 1837 with a capital of less than £5,000, while £6,000 was the partnership capital of the Alloa Coal Company in Scotland, formed in 1836 to take over an existing colliery then raising about 60,000 tons a year.[1] When Alfred Barnes and his father took over the Grassmoor collieries in Derbyshire on lease in 1846 their starting capital was £6,000. In the North-east, where the largest colliery enterprises were located, the average fixed-capital requirements implied by our calculations of average mine size and our capital–output estimates amounted to slightly less than £19,000.[2] Fordyce observed in 1860 that the most numerous class of colliery concerns selling coal other than for landsale possessed capital of between £8,000 and £25,000.[3]

Initial sums of several thousands of pounds which were necessary for the establishment of a colliery trading on more than a local landsale basis were beyond the resources of most individuals. By 1830 most wealthy landowners were retreating from colliery enterprise, as the size of enterprises and the risks associated with mining grew, preferring the role of royalty recipients to that of entrepreneurs. In the North-east the scale of capital requirements consequent upon deeper mining and the intensification of competition is illustrated by the expenditure of between £80,000 and £100,000 in a single winning to the Bensham or Maudlin seam at Monkwearmouth, completed in 1834 after eight years' sinking, when coal was drawn at a depth of 474 metres. At the Murton winning, commenced in 1838, coal was found in the Hutton seam at a slightly higher level and took five years to reach, but water problems necessitated a total expenditure exceeding £250,000, and even in 1860 the project was described as 'unproductive'.[4] Such enormous unforseen costs, coupled with lengthy delays between investment and returns and the risk of incurring major losses, led some of those wealthy landowning proprietors who continued to produce coal to enter into partnerships.

Perhaps less than 15 per cent of coal production came from landed proprietors in 1830, falling to half that level by the 1870s and becoming negligible by 1913.[5] Buddle noted that in the North-east even by 1830 only eight out of fifty-nine landed proprietors were still actually producing coal, though among the largest of these the collieries of Lord Londonderry and the Earl of Durham continued to figure among the

---

[1] Morris and Williams 1958, 139; John L. Carvell, *One Hundred Years in Coal: The History of the Alloa Coal Co.* (Edinburgh, 1944), 28–32.
[2] Stephens thesis, 151.   [3] Fordyce 1860, 44.
[4] Ibid.   [5] See footnote 2 on p. 12.

nation's biggest coal producers until the 1890s, when these private proprietorships were converted into limited companies.[1] The Marquis of Bute did not sell his last colliery (to the Consett Iron Co.) in the North-east until the 1890s.[2] However, while in certain areas a few very large landowners continued to be important as coal producers and provided finance for investment, even before the joint stock legislation of the 1850s, the rapid growth of new enterprises had diminished the relative contribution of landed colliery owners to coal production—even in the North-east.

Similar patterns may be identified elsewhere. In Cumberland coal production was dominated by landed estates until 1840, after which three of the major families, the Seahouses in 1842, the Curwens in the 1850s, and the Lonsdales in 1888, leased their mines to others.[3] From their inception, the smaller and newer mines were developed under lease. In the West Midlands much production from Warwickshire pits came from collieries under landed-owner occupation in the 1840s, by Sir Roger Newdigate, F. Parrott and Partners, and the Bedworth Charity. In South Staffordshire, Lord Dudley's important collieries were partly leased and partly worked directly throughout the century; in North Staffordshire most large landowners had adopted leasing by the 1840s, although Lord Granville kept his Shelton Collieries until their exhaustion in the late 1880s.[4] In the west of Scotland most mines were worked on lease by 1830, though the collieries belonging to the Duke of Portland and Lord Eglinton both produced coal until the last quarter of the century.[5]

The Lothians and Fife, however, continued to be an aristocratic stronghold: the Dukes of Buccleuch and Hamilton, Marquis of Lothian, Sir John Hope, Sir George Clerk, Sir Philip Durham, Joshua Wilson, the Earl of Elgin, and Captain Wemyss together employed nearly half the work-force in this district in 1842, and several of these men or their heirs were active still thirty years later. The Durhams, Balfours, the Earl of Stair, and the Wemyss families continued to be active coal producers in 1913.[6] Lancashire and Cheshire also depended in part upon landed coal-owners for capital and enterprise in the early nineteenth century; the Bridgewater collieries near Manchester remained a private concern until 1913, though they were operated by trustees for much of the nineteenth century. The Earl of Balcarres was only the most distinguished of

---

[1] See below 465.
[2] J. Davies thesis, 495–6.
[3] Ward 1971, 74, 93–6.
[4] Sturgess 1971, 173–204.
[5] Ward 1971, 78–80.
[6] Hassan thesis, 78–80.

Lancashire landowners to exchange proprietorship for partnership when the Wigan Coal and Iron Company was formed in 1864, and ten years later the Duke of Bridgewater and the Earl of Bradford were exceptional in their continued involvement in mining coal. In Cheshire the Lords Vernon kept the Poynton and Worth collieries throughout the period. In Yorkshire, too, the Fitzwilliams retained their Elsecar Collieries until 1913, though by 1900 six times as much revenue accrued from royalties as from colliery profits. The Lister-Kayes also continued to operate pits near Wakefield until World War I.[1] The position in the East Midlands was probably the same; The Moira Collieries of the Marquis of Hastings remained independent until the 1880s, Lord Middleton's Nottinghamshire mines until the 1870s, and those belonging to W. P. Moorewood down to 1913, but several more smaller landed coal-owners were active until the 1880s.[2]

Of the major coal-mining regions, South Wales and the South-west were, throughout the period, the least dependent upon landed capital, although exceptionally in 1848 the Radstock collieries were reclaimed after a court case by the Marquess of Waldegrave and worked independently up to 1913. The Marquis of Bute was responsible for sinking his first colliery in South Wales to prove the steam-coal seams at Cwmsaerbren in the Rhondda in the 1850s, but the aim was to raise royalties. Collieries were taken over in the 1880s and 1890s when lessees failed, but Bute was not essentially a coal producer.

Despite the gradual withdrawal of landowners from large-scale colliery enterprise, independent ownership by no means vanished completely. Throughout the nineteenth century the mining of coal from drifts, levels, or shallow pits intended for local landsale was the province of the independent proprietor.[3] In the 1840s small shallow landsale pits working the Thick Coal in South Staffordshire and Worcestershire could commence production with an investment of a few hundred pounds, within the reach of the butties operating on a sub-contract basis. Mining on this scale needed relatively little capital for a given output of a few thousand tons a year, for the average life of the 'mine' was short; less than ten years in most cases. The prospect of short-term gains from a relatively low investment of this kind explains why local capitalists, merchants, brewers, and corn dealers, for example, were active as sole proprietors during the first half of the century, assisted in the East

[1] Ward 1971, 70, 75; A. H. Dodd, *Industrial Revolution in North Wales* (Cardiff, 1933), 189–97.
[2] A. R. Griffin 1971, 28, 110–111.
[3] Morris and Williams 1958, 116–8; J. Davies thesis, 494–502.

and West Midlands by production under the butty system which allowed working capital to be minimized.[1] In South Wales a similar diversity of trading activities provided the financial basis for individual enterprise, among the most successful independent adventurers being those of David Davis (Blaengwawr) and Samuel Thomas whose pits were financed from the profits of shopkeeping, and Thomas Powell, whose mercantile wealth provided the basis for the development of steam-coal production at Aberdare in the 1840s and 1850s, the profits of his Monmouthshire house-coal pits providing a supplementary source of finance.[2] The steep slopes of the Pennines provided another favourable environment for the capitalist of modest means, and north-east Lancashire was the location for numerous drift workings and shallow shafts under sole proprietorship throughout the century. When H. W. Hobart, owner of the Facit Colliery, who began his working life down a pit at the age of seven, was asked how he became a coalowner he replied: 'I were careful and saved't brass and bought it'.[3]

As the private funding of colliery enterprise, either by landowner or petty capitalist, became subject to increasing limitations in the context of technological and commercial developments, both landowners and other individuals sought to share financial burdens and risks with others through some form of partnership. Because of its long history, intensive working, and high capitalization, coalmining in the North-east was generally organized on a partnership basis before 1830, and several landowners. Lord Ravensworth and R. W. Brandling, for example, operated collieries both on their own account and in partnership with others.[4] The role played by the wealth of local families was a pattern common to all of the major coalmining regions; and is exemplified by contributions of the Blundells and the Knowles in Lancashire, the McKillops and Wilsons in Scotland, the Parrotts and Newdigates in the West Midlands, the Charlesworths and Clarkes of Yorkshire, and in the East Midlands the Wright and Barber families, though for several of these and many similar families the social ascent which wealth from colliery or other types of enterprise had made possible by 1830 had, through the purchase of land, already propelled them into the ranks of the new gentry.[5] In the North-east, wealth accumulated by trading as merchants in corn, timber, wine, linen, and other goods, or as a result of enterprise in shipping, brewing, banking, or from profits arising out of

[1] C. P. Griffin thesis, 230 passim.
[2] Walters 1980, 71.   [3] Challinor 1972, 207.
[4] Flinn 1984, 209.   [5] Ward 1971, 100–1.

the production of glass, chemicals, and lead, together formed tributaries which fed the numerous colliery partnerships established in the early nineteenth century.[1] Moreover, many of the coalowners in the North-east in 1830 were second generation coalowning families, notably the Lambs, Strakers, Cooksons, Potters, Cochranes, Mowbrays, and Richardsons, all of whom helped to finance the expansion that occurred in the North-east in the 1830s and 1840s.[2]

Local capital from trading was supplemented by investment attracted by railway development, for following the building of the Stockton and Darlington Railway and its rivals from 1825 Workington financiers purchased tracts of coal-bearing land and proceeded to sink substantial collieries.[3] Such was the mode of entry into the industry of the Pease family, whose collieries around Bishop Auckland, beginning with the Adelaide near Shildon which was opened in 1830, became one of the largest coal producers in the North-east during the mid-nineteenth century, and one of Britains largest producers of coke. The original partnership, which included Edward and Joseph Pease and four others, began with a share capital of £40,000 distributed equally; but when Joseph Pease and Partners, as it became later, was turned into a public limited company in 1898 the Pease family held the major share.[4]

Joseph Smith invested his capital and experience as a railway contractor in the coal industry through the partnership which he entered upon with James Joicey in 1837, the year which also saw the formation of the £100,000 Clay Cross 'Company' in Derbyshire, again dominated by leading railway contractors and their financial backers, who included George Stephenson, George Carr Glyn, George Hudson, and Morton Peto.[5] The origins of another firm, later to become a major coal producer in Yorkshire, included two railway contractors, George Pearson and John Woodhouse, who together with John Buckingham Pope, a London coal factor and partner in Crigglestone Cliffe Colliery since 1843, formed a partnership to sink a new pit at Altofts in 1851, which became known as the West Riding Colliery. By 1854 the firm had become Pope and Pearson. Richard Pearson, by this time senior partner in the Darfield Colliery near Barnsley, subsequently became the major partner in the Denaby Main Colliery Company, formed to work a new

[1] Benwell Community Project, Final Report 6, *The Making of a Ruling Class*, 10–15, 30–1.
[2] Ibid.   [3] Sturgess 1971, 13.
[4] NuRO Johnson ZWI/4, report books, 188–281.
[5] *The Times* 9 Feb. 1872, 12, 31 May 1881, 5; *CG* 6 Mar. 1861, 165; Clay Cross Company Ltd, Clay Cross, uncatalogued accounts and papers, including articles of agreement.

lease acquired from the Fullerton family in 1863, the other partners comprising J. B. Pope, by then partner, too, in the New Sharlston Colliery, Edward Baines junior, another New Sharlston partner and grandson of the Leeds Mercury owners, and Joseph Moxon Kirk, a dyer from Halifax. After the replacement of Kirk by Joseph Crossley, the carpet manufacturer who bought the former's quarter share in 1867, and the supercession of Edward Baines junior by his father, Sir Edward Baines, the foundations were laid for the conversion to limited liability in 1868 of the forerunner of Denaby and Cadeby Main Colliery Co.[1]

Professional mining engineers were another source of new partnership capital. Perhaps the most distinguished partnership of this kind was that which brought together John Buddle, 'King of the Coal Trade', Addison Potter, fitter and cashier, and T. Y. Hall, the salaried viewer, each holding an equal share in the Stella Coal Company formed with a capital of £26,000 in 1835. Within four years the leading north-country viewer, Mathias Dunn, had purchased a share in the partnership; he was replaced on his death in 1859 by the resident viewer, Robert Simpson.[2]

Iron masters were another identifiable group which contributed to the finance of coalmining, for well before 1830 most large iron masters owned collieries, and outside the North-east many of the large producers of coal were also iron manufacturers, a reflection of the importance of the iron trade as the second most concentrated market for coal. During the second quarter of the century an increasing number of iron masters began to exploit their mineral leases by developing a sale-coal trade. Within four decades virtually all the iron firms in South Wales, several of the larger integrated producers in the West of Scotland, and others in the West Midlands, south Lancashire, south Yorkshire, and south Derbyshire were also raising coal for sale as well as for internal consumption.[3] The ironmaking firms, typically with a fixed capital of at least £20,000, were the major financial successors to the landowners, inasmuch that many of the largest coal-producing enterprises during the first three-quarters of the nineteenth century were iron–coal partnerships.

---

[1] John Goodchild, 'Some notes on the early history of Denaby Main', *South Yorkshire Journal*, 4 (1972), 1–5; John Goodchild MS, 'Pope and Pearson and Silkstone Buildings', 11–15; John Goodchild, 'Great Northern Railway . . .', 1–5.

[2] DuRO Stella NCB I/TH/19(i); NCB I SC 466 (10), 607 (31, 36).

[3] Morris and Williams 1958, 60; Youngson Brown thesis, 47; A. J. Taylor 1967, 99; Birch, *Iron Industry, The Economic History of the British Iron and Steel Industry 1784–1879*, (1967), 197–9; Hopkinson thesis, 322–7, 355; Williams 1962, 38–41, 197–211.

As a mode of business organization the partnership existed in several different legal forms, but whether under common-law partnership, the Cost Book variation, or as an unlimited liability joint-stock company, the implications for business finance were essentially the same. Allotted proportions of share capital and an obligation to meet all calls upon that capital provided an initial basis for operations, coupled with a presumption that expansion would be financed from subscriptions proportional to the original shareholding, unless an individual's stake in the firm was to diminish. The Cost Book type of partnership offered a solution to this particular problem as shares were transferable; moreover, without expensive legal costs, the Cost Book company could expand capital without limit and could include up to twenty partners. Against this, however, was the possibility that at the monthly or bi-monthly meetings of shareholders which characterized this form of undertaking frequent divisions of profits might occur should such a policy be decided, an eventuality with might hamper capital accumulation and inhibit long-term marketing strategies.[1] Few examples of this partnership type survived outside non-ferrous metal-mining partnerships, the firm of Nixon, Taylor, and Cory, formed in 1855 to sink the Navigation Colliery, representing an exceptional—and successful—example.[2]

The common law partnership continued to be the form of undertaking most frequently adopted within the industry, though enlarging capital by increasing the number of partners could alter radically the original form. In the 1840s the Wingerworth Coal Company in south Derbyshire, which originally consisted of two local coalowning families, was transformed by the injection of finance from additional partners with interests in Liverpool shipping and trade, and from a local lead merchant and paint manufacturer.[3] The rise of the Ashington Coal Company originated in 1849 when a £2,500 partnership was formed by William Dickinson, founding head of a Newcastle steamship company in 1847, Francis Turner, viewer or colliery engineer, and Joseph Wright, who may have been a close associate of Lord Londonderry. Two other partners were invited to join them, partly to pay off the debts of their Black Close Colliery and partly to provide additional funds for the new venture. One was John Henderson, a Durham businessman whose wealth was founded on his father's carpet factory. Between 1850 and 1869 several changes occurred in the composition of the Ashington

---

[1] Walters 1977, 98; Cottrell 1980, 9–10.
[2] *MJ* 10 July 1852, 326, 20 June 1858, 303, 28 Aug. 1852, 422, 12 Mar. 1853, 151; Walters 1980, 72–3.
[3] Hopkinson thesis, 387–8.

partnership, beginning in 1851 when the principals of a firm known as Harrison Carr and Co. were appointed as managers and fitters, of whom John Harrison and Carl Lange introduced some of their capital into the coalmining enterprise. After the entry into the company of two leading families, the coal-owning Priestmans in 1869 and the Milburns, prominent shipowners, in 1879, the partnership emerged as one of the major coal producers in the region.[1]

Not only did the composition of particular partnerships alter; partners often belonged to more than a single enterprise. The Stella Coal Company illustrates this effectively; each of the partners, at one time or another, held shares which interlocked the Stella Coal Company with Benwell, Elswick, Wallsend and Hepburn, Walbottle, Heaton, Shent Hill, Backworth, and Throckley collieries.[2] When the Lamb family, through Joseph Chatto Lamb, also became shareholders in Stella, it meant that the South Hetton and Ryhope Colliery companies also became interconnected, as did Cramlington and Seaton Delavel.[3] Occasionally partners fell out over policy, particularly on the issue of an increase of capital, which in a partnership was normally on a proportional basis related to each partner's share. In 1858 partners in the Woolley Coal Company near Wakefield (who included a clerk in Holy Orders and a future governor of Wakefield Gaol) commenced litigation against Sir John Lister Kaye, who had refused to subscribe his share towards the enlarged capital stock.[4] One method of avoiding sudden calls on partners in this way, which also avoided the need for a new co-partnership deed, was an agreement among the partners that 5 per cent interest on each partner's capital should remain in the business as part of the capital stock, available for distribution later should circumstances allow. The 5 per cent retention arrangement had long been practised in the Newton Chambers partnership, and under reorganization in 1862 capital attributed to Thomas and John Chambers, £24,431 and £10,018 respectively, should remain in the business at 5 per cent interest until the respective shares reached £40,000 and £24,000. Until that time the partners were to draw salaries only, of £750 and £700. Thomas Newton, the third and senior partner, already owned a £40,000 'ordinary share' with an additional £24,621, defined as a loan, which likewise earned a

[1] NuRO Ashington NCB 15/5; NCL, local biography no. 3, 165.
[2] Benwell Community Project Final Report 6, *The Making of a Ruling Class* (Benwell, 1979), 10–13, 91–112.
[3] Ibid.
[4] John Goodchild MS, The Woolley Coal Company.

return of 5 per cent, but in principle was available for withdrawal at any time.[1]

This not uncommon practice, or some variation upon it, is in sharp contrast to the uncontrolled demands associated with high living which drove the associates of Lord Londonderry and John Bowes to distraction, though even by the 1830s the economic tides were running against them and their kind of undisciplined business management. When in 1833 Londonderry's finances were in a desperate state (not for the first time) John Buddle was contacted to consider the implications for the collieries and to advise. Sir Henry Browne, Londonderry's solicitor, wrote to tell him that Lord Londonderry has 'seriously resolved to make the sacrifices that are absolutely necessary . . . The ship is on the shore, and a gale of wind blowing right on, but by heaving useless ballast overboard, such as pictures and villas, I trust a way will be found to bring him up at last . . . Would Lord Londonderry live more economically, think you, abroad or at home for 3 or 4 years to come?'[2]

Partnerships did sometimes extend beyond families and localities. John Nixon, a mining engineer from the North-east, allied himself with two Bristol merchants and a Welsh farmer to work steam coal in South Wales, and in further developments his partner was William Cory, the leading London coal merchant, and Hugh Taylor, a substantial coalowner in the North-east. Archibald Hood, a Scottish mining engineer, later persuaded two Liverpool capitalists to back him in working coal in the Rhondda. But even in South Wales—the coal industry's most spectacular new frontier in the mid-nineteenth century and for that reason almost certainly the region most heavily penetrated by capital from elsewhere—by Bristol merchants, London coal merchants, mining engineers from Scotland and the North-east, and Liverpool manufacturers and merchants[3]—before 1870, at least, external entrepreneurial capital never dominated coal as it had earlier dominated iron production.

Durham had begun to attract capital from London even before 1830, notably in the formation of the Hetton Coal Company in 1820, soon to become one of the three largest colliery enterprises in the North-east. Arthur Mowbray, formerly manager of Londonderry's collieries adjacent to the Hetton royalty but possessing experience in banking

---

[1] T. S. Ashton and Sykes, *The Coal Industry of the Eighteenth Century* (Manchester 1929), 159–161. SCL, Newton Chambers TR 450/3/26; SCL Newton Chambers NCB/1/SC/466(10). For a similar arrangement see SCL Wharncliffe Silkstone NCB 1429/1.

[2] DuRO, first deposit NCB 1/JB/187.

[3] Morris and Williams 1958, 141–2.

too, according to Londonderry, 'by dint of prowling round the Royal
Exchange and Stock Market ... completely got Hetton under weigh in
London'.[1] Access to metropolitan finance for coal mining in the North-
east, however, seems to have depended upon the coincidence of either
family or local connections, for almost all of the eleven founding
partners in the Hetton enterprise possessed such links, including some
with mining. This seems to have been true of those partners either substituted for, or added to, the partnership, which by 1831 had increased
to twenty. These included John Gully, surely the most flamboyant
partner: a former prize fighter, tavern-keeper, and subsequently a
punter, he became a successful race-horse owner, diversified his assets
through financial interests in Hetton and invested his winnings in collieries at Thornley, Wingate Grange, and Trimdon.[2]

Disturbed by Hetton's rapid success based on external capital, in 1833
Buddle remarked upon the ruination of a 'splendid trade', which he
predicted would 'not be worth any gentleman's while pursuing in future
as a gentlemanlike business, as heretofore. It will fall into the hands of
grasping speculators and neck or nothing adventurers in joint stock
companies. I have been apprehensive of this ever since the Hetton Company got fairly afloat and other adventurers came into the field.'[3]
Buddle's predictions proved only partly accurate, for while landed
gentlemen did indeed continue to play a diminishing role as entrepreneurs, many decades were to pass before joint-stock companies became
the predominant form of business organization. In 1836 the Hetton
partners, erstwhile challengers of the status quo, combined with Lambton and Londonderry to purchase the North Hetton Colliery to prevent
its acquisition by precisely the type of joint-stock companies Buddle
had feared as a consequence of the repeal of the Bubble Act in 1825. It
had seemed likely during the second quarter of the century that both by
occupation and geographical location the composition of investors
would alter and that the joint-stock company would herald a new era of
capital mobility. Hence the excitement in the North-east when, following the repeal of the Bubble Act in 1825 which extended to the Crown
power to grant charters of incorporation with personal liability of its
members, the boom in the iron trade in the 1830s brought London
capital to the region on an unprecedented scale. The Durham Coal
Company was formed in 1836, followed in 1837 by the Northern Coal

[1] DuRO Londonderry D/LO/C150 Buddle to Iveson 22 Dec. 1820.
[2] I. Ayris, '*Elemore Colliery and the Hetton Coal Company*' (NPL, n.d.), 8–12.
[3] DuRO Londonderry D/LO/C142, 27 Aug. 1833.

Company, each with a nominal capital in transferable shares of £0.5m.[1] Pits were sunk, collieries opened out, but within a few years—which were marked by shareholders' investigating committees, a sacked investigator (whose personal recriminations were published as a front page advertisement in the *Mining Journal*), and the alteration of the venue for shareholders' meetings from London to Darlington to *Norwich* (when all directors were removed)—the companies collapsed. Both were wound up with huge financial losses, which in the case of the Northern Mining Company exceeded the original capital subscribed.[2] John Bowes, whose position as an established landowner with coal interests in the North-east probably led to his appointment as honorary director of the Durham Company, revealed his private views on the venture following his short-lived appointment: 'Our friends of the Coal Company are both knaves and fools ... I will not stand any more nonsense on the part of these fellows'.[3] In South Wales the £0.5m. Blaenavon Iron and Coal Company attracted similar criticism in the trade press, where London directors were accused by the ironmaster, David Mushet, of being 'money market sharpers'.[4] Joint-stock companies with unlimited liabilities, however, were few in number, and the unfavourable publicity accorded to these early examples and others (including that of the Northampton Union Coal and Mining Company which in 1837 sank a pit three hundred yards deep in the midst of Northamptonshire before raising coal which 'miners' employed by the company had first put in) afforded a cautionary lesson to other speculators and would-be investors.[5]

While it has not been possible to quantify the relative importance of proprietorial capital compared with other sources before the 1860s, the unmistakeable conclusion is that of an overwhelming preponderance of private wealth in the formation of capital in the industry; that arisocratic landed capital was of small and diminishing importance, while the transfer of capital from iron to coal was increasing; that financing was local and personal, reflecting the industrial and commercial composition of élites and of lesser groups within the regions; and that inasmuch that much of the capital investment outside South Wales was undertaken by a generation of colliery owners preceded by others, coalmining profits provided much of the finance for growth before 1855.

[1] Fordyce 1860, 105–6.

[2] The details are recorded in the *Mining Journal*, 6 Mar. 1841 to 9 Apr. 1843, 292; W. Green, 'Chronicles and Records of the Northern Coal Trade in Durham and Northumberland', *TNEIME*, XV (1865–6), 237.   [3] Mountford thesis, xxii.

[4] *MJ* 7 July 1855, letter.   [5] Galloway 1904, 19.

iv. Firms and finance after 1855: patterns of ownership

By the passage of the Limited Liability Act of 1855 and the Joint Stock Companies Act of 1856 such legal advantages as the right to sue, transferability of shares, and the option of limited liability became generally accessible; but while during the depression of the 1860s company promoters became active, principally in achieving the conversion of large, well-established partnerships into limited companies, the rate at which joint-stock incorporation occurred was slow and for many years scarcely affected the formation of *new* coalmining enterprises. Coalproducing iron companies, however, did figure in the conversion activity, between 1863 and 1867 and again during the boom of the early 1870s when they led the movement towards incorporation.[1] Most were conversions in which the vendors took a relatively large proportion of the issued capital, which is why the growth in the number of companies did not necessarily imply a proportionate expansion of real investment expenditure before 1913; though the composition of shareownership could change, usually slowly, broadening the sources of capital at a later stage in the company's history.[2] None the less, irrespective of the real effects of limited liability the data generated in the legal process of incorporation are particularly important, because of the information contained in these sources concerning the occupations or business interests of the founders of companies and of shareholders, and their geographical location.

A considerable improvement in the quantity and quality of financial data from companies themselves also enables us to proceed beyond an analysis of share capital and the finance of winning collieries to examine the different ways in which assets were built up, whether from retained profits, debentures, mortgages, or loans, and to the finance of working collieries. Most of our detailed information upon initial finance is taken from the data for limited companies found in the Dissolved Companies files, which although informative are not without ambiguity. The description of the occupation or business interest of founders and shareholders is bound to be imprecise; equally, the description 'coalowner' or 'colliery proprietor' need not signify a person whose entire investment was in that firm or even in other colliery firms. This description may indicate little concerning the true source of his wealth even in terms of

---

[1] Cottrell 1980, 190, 128–30.
[2] F. Lavington, *The English Capital Market* (London, 1921), 202; Peter L. Payne, *The Early Scottish Limited Companies 1856-1895* (Edinburgh, 1980), 19.

its accumulation during his lifetime; moreover, the 'founders' of companies as listed under the Articles of Association were not always the prime movers in company formation, though the latter were almost certain to be among those listed.

For these reasons more weight should be attached to the names and occupations of shareholders, an approach which although in theory raises questions of feasibility, in practice, because the majority of firms did possess a shareholding structure in which it is possible to identify the names and occupations of the principal owners, proves to be a fruitful exercise. Although in a statistical sense the 112 firms which have been analysed in this way cannot be regarded as a sample, they do represent each of the seven major regions. The *number* of firms in each region as a proportion of those included in the *List of Mines* for 1913 is small, ranging from around 3 per cent for Scotland and South Wales to 7 per cent in the case of Yorkshire and the East Midlands, and any conclusions drawn upon the basis of our data is vulnerable to the charge of being unrepresentative. However, because the sample is weighted towards the larger companies the firms do represent a total of at least 40 per cent of national employment in 1910, slightly less for Lancashire and Cheshire and the East Midlands. Thus, in terms of output and employment the data are more representative of the industry as a whole than the number of firms might suggest, and therefore, so far as the sources of capital for the industry as a whole, the results of our survey would seem to be a valid basis for generalization.

Further reservations should be made, however, since the capital accounts of individual firms vary in the degree to which they represent reality, depending upon accounting practices adopted within each company. Capital expenditure was frequently debited to revenue, effectively resulting in under-capitalization. The firm of Henry Briggs and Son and Co., for example, in which a fixed asset to output ratio fell from 9s. per ton in 1876 to 5s. 6d. per ton in 1908–13 (simultaneous with growth in output by two and a half times) underwent a process whereby extensions and new work could not have been fully capitalized.[1] Offsetting this tendency towards under-capitalization, which was present in nine of the companies for which relevant data were available, was the inflation of capital value caused by an inadequate depreciation allowance. Carlton Main and (prior to 1908) the Main Colliery Company providing examples of this very widespread practice, but evidence of which,

---

[1] Bro LU Special Coll MS 160, Briggs MB, 1865–1913.

by the nature of omission, is difficult to produce except on a random basis.[1] Another common feature of nineteenth-century company formation was that of marked under-capitalization at the time of initial purchase when the price was decided. A spectacular example of this occurred in 1864, when the collieries belonging to the Consett Iron Company were purchased for £10,193; the colliery asset figure given for the first full year of production was £15,175 to yield a fixed asset to output ratio of merely 10*d*. per ton.[2]

Often the under-valuation of assets prior to conversion to company organization was the result of expert valuation, which might produce estimates on the basis of the sum collieries might be expected to command were they to be sold at current market prices, which depended heavily upon the state of the coal trade; or the basis for valuation might be a predicted income as judged by an expert witness, as in the case of the Cannock Chase Colliery Company in 1857. In 1870–1 John Bowes and Co. was valued at £1m. to £1.2m. when the managing partner considered an outright purchase. At the height of the boom two years later, the viewer T. E. Forster valued the company at three times the figure, whereupon the prospective buyer lost interest.[3] It seems more likely, however, that when companies in difficulties were valued prior to changing hands the bias in capitalization would have been downwards and the overall trend a reinforcement of the tendency towards under-capitalization.[4]

Our evidence is necessarily confined to one or two dates in the history of each company, almost all of them after 1870 and most after 1890; consequently some of this material may fail to reflect changes in company structure and sources of finance over time. The company data are weighted heavily towards structure and capitalization at the time of foundation, and tend to under-record changes in shareholdings to an unverifiable but probably considerable extent. While potentially invalidating our analysis, this under-recording in share transfers must be placed in the context of the actuality of company formation in the nineteenth century, when the flotation of such companies did not necessarily herald the disappearance of the partnership type of organization, dominated either by family or close-knit kinship or trading interests,

---

[1] SCL, Carlton Main MD 4080–9, DM 1872–1913; GlaRO Main D/DMC, uncatalogued directors' annual reports, 1900–7.

[2] A. S. Wilson thesis, Table II.2; BSNRRC Consett Iron Company Statement of Fixed Assets 13251.

[3] Mountford thesis, 137.   [4] A. S. Wilson thesis, 36.

but was often merely a formal registration as a joint-stock company. Neither did the coming of limited liability legislation bring about a marked increase in net investment, since before 1900 almost all of the early joint-stock companies formed took the form of an exchange of claims upon assets to a greater or a lesser extent.[1]

When the Manchester company promoters, David Chadwick and Henry Davis Pochin, floated Staveley Coal and Iron as a limited company in 1864, the original purchasers also included five other businessmen from the Manchester area who together took less than half the paid up capital, amounting to £600,000; the assets taken over from Richard Barrow's original firm were valued at £449,324.[2] The motivation which led the Manchester capital to the north Midlands was the prospect, in a context of a growth of domestic iron and coal demand from 1859 and foreign demand from 1862, of exploiting the opportunities made available by the new company legislation.[3] Several factors help to explain Richard Barrow's decision to sell the firm. He was indebted to his retired brother, John, who had loaned £260,000 for investment in the business. Much of his own fortune, accumulated in trading in an earlier career, had been absorbed by the extensive development of iron and coal production since 1840, for net profits of the firm during the twenty-two years ending in 1863 fell short of gross investment by at least £45,000.[4] Besides, at the age of 76 he was a bachelor without an heir. Such circumstances were ideal for conversion, and it has been suggested that the Manchester men's connection with Staveley also led to the subsequent conversions of Sheepbridge Coal and Iron, and John Brown.[5]

Our sample reflects the common practice whereby many of the 'new' companies adopting limited liability were merely reconstructions or conversions of established companies or partnerships. Under such circumstances the pattern of shareholding revealed by the Dissolved Companies data depict a state of affairs which both pre- and post-dated the year of Association, and therefore extend the period for which the resulting generalizations are valid (see Table 2.9).

The pattern of ownership revealed by Table 2.9 underlines the financial dominance of 'coalowners' or 'colliery proprietors', although both

---

[1] For a discussion of the possibilities and limitations of the files of dissolved companies see Peter L. Payne, *The Early Scottish Limited Companies 1856-1895* (Edinburgh, 1980), 4–18, 45–8, 84–95.

[2] BSCEMRRC Stanton and Staveley 2034/2/1, Annual Report 30 June 1864, and Memorandum and Articles of Association.

[3] See the detailed account of the role of this group of financiers in Cottrell 1980, 124.

[4] BSCEMRRC Stanton and Staveley, 2034/2/50 Account Book, John Barrow; 2034/1/1 detailed balance sheets 1841–63.   [5] Chapman 1981, 71.

descriptions are inexact inasmuch as they are terms used by persons to describe themselves and consequently do not conform to a strict definition. Neither term necessarily denotes coalmining as the primary business concern, and in the course of the nineteenth century the relative importance of iron and coal production in many of the major iron and coal companies (which present the greatest problem of strict definition in the absence of adequate employment data) altered over time. It is not possible, therefore, to identify satisfactorily all of those coalowners whose interests also lay primarily or substantially in iron production; and in any case from the mid-nineteenth century iron masters who raised coal to supply their own furnaces became increasingly aware of the need for a professional approach towards the exploitation of mineral resources, even if their interests fell short of raising coal for sale as well as for consumption.

No less than 46 per cent of those with a stake in colliery companies in the North-east were described either as coalowners or colliery proprietors, compared with 14 per cent in the West Midlands. The reasons for these differences are to be found in the differing numbers and sizes of companies. In the West Midlands and to a lesser extent South Wales companies were numerous and small companies were relatively heavily represented, whereas in the North-east, Lancashire, and Yorkshire companies were fewer and likely to be larger. Consequently, coalowners, whom one may regard with some justification as substantial 'capitalists', were more likely to own a larger share of the industry in those regions where capital was more intensively invested. The second largest group consisted of those 'not gainfully employed'; a nice description which in fact might conceal business interests but which generally refers to people possessing inherited wealth—wives, widows, and spinsters—the origin of which is obscure but which must have included business. Nationally those 'not gainfully employed' accounted for 14 per cent, but again regional variations are of interest. This category was relatively important in the West Midlands, but not so in Scotland and the North-east. Again, it seems likely that a larger number of smaller companies in the West Midlands was the factor which explains the difference, ownership fragmentation allowing smaller investors with private means to play a more important role. The contribution of the professions amounted to 11 per cent (14 per cent if 'engineers' are included), a proportion which exceeds that for which iron masters, or businessmen taken together, were responsible. These figures imply that a substantial portion of partnership capital was met in small units

Table 2.9. *Occupations and business interests of shareholders in coalmining companies*
(per cent of ownership in each region)

	Scotland	North-east	Lancs.	Yorks.	East Midlands	West Midlands	South Wales	Average
1. *Industrial*								
Coalowners	28	46	38	34	20	20	26	32
Iron masters	17	—	1	—	17	4	14	5
Other industrial	3	7	7	7	6	6	—	8
2. *Professional and private*								
Professional	5	10	16	14	14	16	9	11
Engineers:								
Mining	1	—	2	3	3	3	3	2
Other	—	—	1	2	—	3	2	1
Shopkeepers/Tradesmen	—	—	—	—	—	—	3	$\frac{1}{2}$

Others in coal trade	—	—	—	—	2	—	½
Not gainfully employed	6	12	16	17	14	24	17	14
3. *Others*								
Landowners	—	3	5	—	1	1	7	3
Merchants	8	1	3	6	11	1	3	4
Banks and financial companies	9	8	7	12	10	12	2	8
Fragmented ownership	20	10	3	5	4	9	14	10

Weighted mean (1896–1905 employment).

The table refers to the structure of ownership within 112 firms considered separately, consequently each firm within the regional sample carries an equal weighting in the summary which results. No account, therefore, is taken of the differing size of companies or of differences in the abslute amount of capital which shareholders possessed in them.

Sources: Based on information contained in the files of the Registrars of Joint Stock Companies in England and Wales, and Scotland. Those of dissolved companies are located in the PRO, document classification BT 31/ (in Scotland at SRO, West Register House, BT 2/). Files of active companies are to be found at the Companies Registration Offices and Edinburgh. The data for 112 companies were obtained after searching files (empty or missing) for more than twice that number.

realizable by private but non-capitalist wealth. A broader categorization, which comprises all private and professional persons (the professions, engineers, shopkeepers, tradesmen, and 'others in the coal trade'), land-owners, and those 'not gainfully employed'—so as to represent all individuals receiving income either from professional or private sources—yields a share in national ownership of 34 per cent. This compares with 44 per cent for all business interests, which includes coal-owners, iron masters, and other businessmen.

While Table 2.9 provides some indication of the sources of investment, it throws no light on the capital structure and financial organization of the industry. From 1895, however, when reliable data on employment by firm become available, and by making certain assumptions in the absence of complete information on capitalization, it becomes possible to offer tentative generalizations. Thus, Table 2.10 presents employment figures by type of firm, used as a proxy for the relative distribution of investment interests. In 1895 less than 10 per cent of the mining work-force was employed in public companies, rising to 17 per cent by 1913. Private companies, which in comparison with public companies were in theory less accessible to personal investors, increased their share of employment from 45 to 57 per cent, the corollary being the declining importance of unlimited companies and individual partnerships and proprietorships from 30 to 10 per cent. Regional variations were important, the major regions most affected by the spread of public limited company formation being Scotland and South Wales, where the last twenty years of our period brought about the enormous development of coal production for export.

Employment figures suggest that though sizeable as a proportion of national employment and of appreciable dimensions in Scotland, the East and West Midlands, and increasingly in the North-east, the part played by South Wales iron masters in the development of coal resources had diminished considerably by the end of the century. The shareholding analysis presented in Table 2.9 confirms the late nineteenth- and early twentieth-century picture, though a corrective is supplied to the apparent importance to be attached to the role of iron interests in the West Midlands, a region in which the major centres of iron and coal production were in decline. Thus, whereas the proportion of iron masters' shareholdings in Scotland and the East Midlands in our sample are 19 and 21 per cent, the figure for the West Midlands is 5 per cent. When we exclude businessmen in coal and iron, sundry business interests emerge as a group of some importance in most regions but

Table 2.10. *Distribution of employment by type of firm, 1895 and 1913* (percentages)

Region	Coal and iron companies		Limited coal companies				Unlimited companies, partnerships, and proprietorships	
			Public		Private			
	1895	1913	1895	1913	1895	1913	1895	1913
Scotland	25.8	22.8	16.8	29.8	21.8	38.0	35.6	9.5
North-east	12.1	18.0	3.9	6.9	49.0	68.7	35.0	6.4
Cumberland	17.2	7.5	—	—	39.4	58.2	43.4	34.2
Lancs./Cheshire	8.4	7.1	11.8	13.7	50.1	66.4	29.7	12.8
North Wales	1.4	—	11.0	1.3	66.5	84.9	21.1	13.8
Yorkshire	11.6	9.8	5.1	15.4	52.5	63.0	30.8	11.8
East Midlands	25.9	26.1	5.0	2.4	36.7	55.3	32.5	16.2
West Midlands	25.7	21.2	6.2	4.5	36.9	62.9	31.1	11.4
South Wales	14.7	12.6	15.6	36.9	52.8	43.9	16.9	6.6
South-West	—	—	4.2	3.1	49.5	73.4	46.3	23.5
UK average	16.0	15.6	9.3	17.2	44.7	56.9	30.0	10.2

Sources: List of Mines, 1895 *and* 1913; *Stock Exchange Yearbook,* 1896 *and* 1914; *Mineral Statistics,* 1890–1913.

especially in South Wales, where (apart from the shipowning interests which owned the United National Collieries) all business interests in our sample were external to the region. The industrial development of Yorkshire, Lancashire, and the West Midlands was not accompanied by similar local business investment in coal mining to any great extent, though other sources indicate that some individuals who describe themselves as 'coalowners' in fact possessed wider business interests in engineering and textiles.

The regional spread of ownership was somewhat more marked among the professions. Individuals within the legal and other professions owned between 9 and 17 per cent of shares in all regions, apart from Scotland. Mining engineers, none of them necessarily local, formed a recurring, if small, element in capital funding (between 2 and 4 per cent of total capital) in all regions; except in Scotland and the North-east, a discovery which is compatible with the impression that successful mining engineers from the north migrated to the newer inland coalfields to exploit their expertise and invest their savings. Individuals or interests describing themselves as 'merchants' accounted for only 3 per cent of ownership nationally, as did landowners who accounted for 5 per cent in Lancashire (largely because of the Wigan Coal and Iron Company whose main shareholder might equally well be described as a 'coalowner') and 7 per cent in South Wales. In 1913 Lancashire was the region where concentration of landed capital was probably the greatest. South Wales appears to have been less prominent, but our figures are derived mainly from the Main Colliery Company and the Glamorgan Coal Company, and all the landowner-coalowners in question were external to the region.

Outside the industrial, private and professional, and landowning and merchant groups (which, including 'those not gainfully employed', acounted together for 80 per cent of total ownership) came the institutional owners. Banks and financial companies accounted for 8 per cent of ownership nationally, compared with 10 per cent in the form of fragmented holdings, raised largely by the public flotation of shares on the Stock Exchange. Altogether, non-industrial sources accounted for about one-half of the total capital employed. We have, however, indicated that those 'not gainfully employed' must have included wealth derived from business, while a few landowners and some merchants also combined industrial activity with mercantile or estate enterprise; perhaps, therefore, 60 per cent or more of the shareholders included in Table 2.9 derived their wealth from industry.

Table 2.9 suggests that institutional investors were important only in certain regions: in Yorkshire where 15 per cent of ownership is attributable to this group, and in the West Midlands where the figure is 14 per cent. A different picture emerges, however, when these figures are seen in conjunction with those for fragmented, or 'public', ownership, i.e. those shares widely dispersed in small units to numerous small investors whose occupations or business interests are impossible to trace. In Scotland, the West Midlands, and the North-east ownership arising from either public flotations or from institutional investment represented between 29 and 21 per cent and was substantially less in only in Lancashire and Cheshire. Public participation in the form of fragmented ownership was greatest among Scottish firms, which at 20 per cent was twice the average figure. At the other extreme, companies in Lancashire and Cheshire, the East Midlands, and Yorkshire recorded respectively 3, 4 and 5 per cent in this category, though in each case the ownership share attributed to banks and financial companies was above average.

South Wales is the only region where coalmining finance has been the subject of detailed research, from which Walters concluded that public participation was very low. During the coal famine it is true that capital did begin to flow in from outside the region and that this was closely related to the creation in 1872–4 of new public companies. But over the longer trend Walters's research showed that even in the 1890s, the next occasion when a large number of private partnerships were converted into public limited-liability companies, little *new* public capital was raised. Furthermore, the inactivity of the equity market did not coincide with increased activity in the market for fixed-interest sums to finance new investment, either in South Wales or elsewhere.[1] Of the £7.5m. of share capital of publicly quoted South Wales colliery companies in 1910 barely 14 per cent took the form of public subscription for new investment, and these publicly quoted companies themselves only accounted for 40 per cent of the region's coal output. Walters concluded that the South Wales coal industry was primarily financed by partners' subscriptions, calls on shares, and retention of profit, and that the stock market was unimportant as a source of finance.[2]

Even at Powell Duffryn, the largest British coal producer in 1913 with a paid up capital of £1.8m., the dispersion of originally private holdings was a recent development; growth depended minimally upon finance

---

[1] Walters 1980, 87; Youngson Brown thesis, 106.
[2] Walters 1980, 71–9, 87.

raised from the public. In this respect Powell Duffryn is more representative of industrial finance than the Fife Coal Company, the second-largest coal producer with a paid up capital of £1.2m., which beginning in the 1890s did turn to the public to help finance large-scale expansion.[1] The third-largest producer, Lambton Collieries Ltd. formed in 1913 with a paid up capital of £0.9m., had already been acquired from Lord Durham by Sir James Joicey in 1896.[2] The financial history of these two concerns, Lambton Collieries and James Joicey and Co., which eventually merged under the Joiceys, represent the opposite end of the spectrum to that which the Scottish company symbolized, and exemplified in extreme form the private accumulation of capital which typified most colliery enterprise before 1914.

The relative unimportance of publicly subscribed capital is not explicable in institutional terms, for in South Wales (where stockbroking and the dissemination of intelligence flourished from 1870) public flotation of shares was certainly possible from early in the history of joint-stock company formation.[3] However, the public evinced little interest in colliery shares even when they were offered, which explains why the few public issues which were made were concentrated in the years of bouyant trade. Even in the 1890s, when net investment coincided with the growing acceptance among colliery owners of the advantages afforded by limited liability—trends which were conducive to greater public involvement in the raising of new capital—the actual contribution of additional finance from this source was small. The issuance of preference shares indicates an attempt by coalowners to offset the unpopularity of colliery shares, though often the preference shares were issued to replace ordinary shares as part of financial reconstruction. Under such conditions the public was seldom invited to subscribe, and when coal shares eventually did find favour conversion issues were those on offer, involving little or no contribution by the public towards net investment.[4] Analysis of shareholders' regional origins offers further evidence that in other regions too, though with the exception of Scotland, public participation was low relative to other sources of finance.

Our company shareholdings sample reveals that over the seven major regions fully 38 per cent of total paid up capital originated from outside the region and points to marked regional variations (see Table 2.11). Intra-regional capital accounted for 93 per cent in Scotland and 76 per

---

[1] Hann 1922, 5, 8, 15, 18, 21, 26–9.
[2] Companies House BT 31/3358/20012; Lambton Collieries SRO Fife Coal Co. BT 2/449.
[3] Walters 1980, 87–8, 118.   [4] Ibid.

Table 2.11. *Shareholders in coalmining companies,*
by geographic origins
(percentages)

	External	Local
Scotland	7	93
North-east	40	60
Lancashire	24	76
Yorkshire	38	62
East Midlands	37	63
West Midlands	52	48
South Wales	57	43
Weighted Mean	38	62

All firms have been given equal weighting irrespective of size. The mean figure is weighted by regional
employment.

Sources: As for Table 2.9.

cent in Lancashire, compared with only 43 per cent in South Wales and
48 per cent in the West Midlands, the two major capital-importing
regions. In the West Midlands, where the main centres of iron and coal
production were in decline from the mid-century, the local iron masters,
typically regarded as 'large capitalists' and potentially important as
shareholders, were not major investors in colliery companies after about
1880. In that region the existence of relatively large numbers of small-
and medium-sized companies offered accessible forms of participant
investment and may help to explain its record of capital imports. In
South Wales the shift towards the coal-export trade seems to have
exercized a greater attraction for capitalists, the professions, and mercantile sections of the wider investing community compared with the
major local industrial groups.

Table 2.10 showed that public limited coal companies were relatively
unimportant in 1895, employing fewer than 10 per cent of all colliery
workers, though it is possible that public limited coal and iron
companies may have doubled that proportion. In 1913 barely 17 per cent
of mining employment was provided by the coal companies, while even
after a generous allowance for the number of miners employed by
public coal and iron companies has been made certainly fewer than

one-third of all miners worked in public companies even in 1913. This ownership structure is evidence of a lingering suspicion among contemporaries of the consequences of abandoning control of a firm's resources. When large amounts of cash were required, either for major new capital projects or the acquisition of another colliery, calls were made on partners' or shareholders' private wealth, which explains the limited contribution made by financial institutions and public shareholders already noted. In South Wales, for which the detailed evidence is best, public and institutional subscription seems to have grown even more slowly than in England and Scotland. The history of Powell Duffryn provides an extreme example of the ability of the private wealth of shareholders to supply share capital adequate to purchase and to sustain expansion. The purchase price of Thomas Powell's collieries in 1864 was £365,000, of which £100,000 was paid in cash by the new company's ten shareholders, drawn from the London railway and engineering contracting fraternity led by George Elliot. The remainder was paid by instalments completed in 1871; meanwhile, further acquisitions meant that between 1864 and 1886 the company's handful of shareholders found £755,000 from their own reserves without contributions from dividends.[1]

v. Sources and application of funds

Reviewing colliery accounting practices in the nineteenth century, the distinguished statistician and economist, Josiah Stamp, remarked that, 'It seems as if every year has to cover its own expenses, so to speak, out of revenue without touching the original investment'.[2] In our examination of thirty companies for which accounts exist for varying periods between 1854 and 1913 it is rarely possible to be certain that net profits (defined as gross profits minus deductions for depreciation, rates, and taxes) do not already incorporate deductions for capital items. To the extent that the working-cost account does include some items of capital funding over and above that of mere depreciation,[3] retained profit

---

[1] Walters 1980, 74.

[2] *The Accountant* 2 Jan. 1937, 16. I am indebted to Prof. Leslie Hannah for this reference.

[3] Perhaps the most significant evidence of this practice in relatively large firms comes from Staveley, where Charles Markham's maxim was to charge to revenue account when in doubt. BSCEMRRC Stanton and Staveley 2034/2/2–3 MB 25 Aug. 1866, 30 Aug. 1867. There are many other examples, including SCL Wharncliffe Silkstone NCB 1429–1; WaRO Griff CR 1169/22, 49, 150, 167; StRO Walsall Wood D876/39; BUL, BR 14/ii–iii/Cannock Chase Colliery MB, 20 May 1889.

figures must be regarded as minimum values and underestimate the actual amount of profit ploughed back into capital development. Of the thirty-one companies, Clifton and Kearsley, the Fife Coal Company, and Walsall Wood Colliery retained at least 50 per cent of total net profit; five, including Powell Duffryn, Butterley, Blaenavon, Main, and Newstead Collieries, retained between 30 and 41 per cent; nine recorded ratios of between 20 and 29 per cent, and only five companies retained less than 10 per cent of net profit, including the Hamstead Colliery Company which recorded a marginally negative rate.

Of those companies for which more detailed information survives, the Fife Colliery provides an example of a leading exponent of profit retention; at least half the net profits during the period 1873 and 1913 were ploughed back into capital expansion. This company experienced the fastest rate of growth of all the companies investigated, increasing its output from 70,000 tons in 1872–3 to more than 4.3m. tons in 1913. This expansion was achieved both by the sinking of new collieries and by taking over existing ones, the company's policy of amalgamation meaning that much of the retained profit was effectively capitalized in the form of already-productive capacity.[1] Morris and Williams instance the Ocean Coal Company which between 1865 and 1875 distributed only £204,000 out of total profits of £493,300, using £182,000 (37 per cent of total profit) to pay calls on new shares issued to open up additional pits.[2] A. R. Griffin noted that Bentinck Colliery in Nottinghamshire was sunk in the 1890s largely out of the profits of the New Hucknall Company and that Sherwood Colliery was begun with profits made at Hucknall Colliery, both ventures presumably requiring substantial retained profit.[3]

Our evidence, and that of Walters, Morris and Williams, and Griffin, offers no support for the view that a considerable number of collieries customarily distributed all profits.[4] Even some of the large profit retainers found it necessary to raise capital from other sources (Powell Duffryn is one example) while others, which Butterley exemplifies,[5] appear to have relied almost entirely upon profits (except, in this case, for debentures of an unknown value) to finance capital growth. Among our company sample only Carlton Main affords a clear example of an

[1] A. S. Cunningham, *The Fife Coal Company Ltd. The Jubilee Year, 1872-1922* (Leven, 1954), 12, 22; Augustus Muir, *The Fife Coal Company: A Short History* (Leven, 1954), 1–2, 4–6, 8–10, 13–16, 19–22; SRO BT 2/449.   [2] Morris and Williams 1958, 147.
[3] A. R. Griffin 1971, 106.   [4] Mitchell thesis, 276–9.
[5] DeRO Butterley 503/B Butterley Co. Certified Accounts 1881–1914 (2 vols.); 503/B directors' annual reports in Company Minute Books 1888–1919 (2 vols.).

internal capital shortage, which was due to considerable pressure from shareholders who from 1884 (following eleven barren years of no return) demanded that a high proportion of company profits should be distributed in dividends. This explains why the capital expansion that occurred in 1896–1913 led to the raising of further share capital.[1] There are, however, reasons to believe that the importance of profit retention is understated in our company sample, if not for the entire second half of the nineteenth century, and perhaps for the early years of the twentieth century. Walters's figures for twelve South Wales companies between 1899 and 1914 show non-divided profit amounting to 38.5 per cent of total profit, a third of which was allocated to reserves with most of the remainder allocated to capital projects, depreciation, and the servicing of debts.[2] Comparing reserved profit with other sources of finance for capital expenditure, profit ranks second after share or partnership capital, but Walters's figures refer to capital expenditure rather than to total (stated) company assets. Even so, especially after 1894, a greater relative importance of profit reinvestment in South Wales is plausible on the basis of the profitability of steam-coal at that time, though Walters's figures also reflect extreme variability in the proportion of profits retained by coal companies.

From the mid-century it is possible to identify the constituents in the supply of finance for seventeen colliery companies across the regions, and from the dissolved companies files at the PRO it is possible to analyse balance sheets for thirty more companies for the period between 1908 and 1913. On the basis of a single balance sheet for each company (in 1910) the primacy of share capital is confirmed, as is the variability between companies, but when reserves and current profits are combined the figure for the average percentage of total company capital is 18 per cent,[3] indicating a greater relative importance of profits in the

---

[1] SCL Carlton Main DM, 1872–1913, MD 4080–9, vols. II–IX, Minutes of AGMs and annual balance sheets.

[2] Walters 1977, 295–7, Table 44.

[3] These were the Edinburgh Collieries, John Watson Ltd., Summerlee and Mossend, United Collieries Ltd., Wilsons and Clyde, South Hetton, Bell Brothers, A. Knowles and Son, Cross Tetley and Co., Garwood Coal and Iron, Collins Green Co., Sutton Heath and Lee, Astley and Tyldesley, Rothervale Collieries, Wheldale Coal Co., Denaby and Cadeby, Wollaton Colliery Co., Bolsover Colliery Co., Shirebrook Colliery Co., Cannock and Rugeley, Shelton Iron and Steel, Littleton Collieries, Fenton Collieries, Sandwell Park Colliery, D. Davies and Sons, Lewis Merthyr Consolidated, Nixon's Navigation, Partridge Jones and Co., Powell's Tillery, and Glyncorrwg Colliery Co. The data came from the dissolved companies files PRO, SRO and from the Companies Registration Offices in London and Edinburgh.

finance of colliery companies generally at that time than do the figures from our main company sample between 1860 and 1913—and almost certainly reflecting the favourable condition of the coal market in the pre-war period. While the proportions of profit ploughed back into the industry by these firms were considerable, the relative importance of profit in aggregate may be judged only by comparing this source of finance with others: share capital, debentures and mortgages, bank loans, and trade credit. Though annual 'average share capital' is a notional entity devised to provide a broad indication of the relative size of share capital, our company sample of seventeen suggests some interesting comparisons (Table 2.12). Only in six companies did ordinary and preference share capital comprise less than 79 per cent of subscribed capital (the mean figure) and only in one below 60 per cent. All firms relied to some extent upon retained profits. The exceptionally high figure of 13 per cent for the Fife Coal Company appears to have been the result of a relatively low capitalization which could only support operations on the level associated with Fife from supplementary funding. Butterley was another company which was markedly under-capitalized in terms of share value and relied a good deal on profit retained for development.

In both cases, and in that of Powell Duffryn, debentures and mortgage loans assumed increasing importance towards the end of the century and the years after. Fife had none in 1873–88, but debentures represented 9 per cent of total capital in 1889–1907, rising to between 10 and 20 per cent in 1908–13. Powell Duffryn's financial history reveals a similar chronology, as do those of Main and, later, Lochgelly; at Carlton Main the 10 per cent figure for 1880–99 grew to more than 20 per cent by 1900–13, marking the development of Grimethorpe Colliery purchased in 1896. Only Henry Briggs and Son contradicts the trend: debentures averaging 5 per cent or less in 1867–92 were raised to finance continuing expansion during the low prices and profits of the late 1870s and 1880s. There is little evidence, however, to suggest that levels of under-capitalization can be related, even in a crude fashion, to the role and extent of profit retention in the growth of firms. Staveley's growth depended upon ploughed back profit but exhibited a fairly high capitalization; for a company of its size, Consett's level of capitalization was not especially high—retained profits were evidently an important source of expansion. This absence of any clear pattern merely underlines the fact that the relationship between capitalization levels, profit, and company finance were influenced by a variety of factors: the differences

Table 2.12. *Composition of company capital, 1860–1913*
(percentages)

	Share capital	Debentures and mortgages	Bank loans	Trading credit	Retained profit	Total as percentage of company
Fife Coal Co., 1873–1913	78½	6½	2	—	13	N.K.
Walsall Wood Colliery Co., 1877–1913	58	29	10		3	86
Powell Duffryn Steam Coal Co., 1888–1913	78	13½	3½	—	5	66
Main Colliery Co., 1890–1914	98	2½	—	—	4½	69
Briggs, Son and Co, 1866–1913	81	6	—	10	3	73
East Cannock Colliery Co., 1872–1913	63½	7½	10	16½	2½	75
Mitchell Main Colliery Co., 1883–1913	64½	7½	—	23	5	68
Cannock Chase Colliery Co. 1860–1911	85½	1½	5	5½	2½	86
Lochgelly Iron and Coal Co., 1873–1913	80½	9½	1	8	1	N.K.
Bolckow Vaughan and Co., 1866–1914	85½	11	2½	—	1	82
Staveley Coal and Iron Co., 1864–1913	91	7	—	—	2	79

Hamstead Colliery Co., 1875–1908	77	$19\frac{1}{2}$	—	$3\frac{1}{2}$	—	88
Newstead Colliery Co., 1879–1913	$92\frac{1}{2}$	—	$\frac{1}{2}$	5	2	89
New Hucknall Colliery Co., 1878–1913	$81\frac{1}{2}$	$2\frac{1}{2}$	2	$9\frac{1}{2}$	$4\frac{1}{2}$	86
Wigan Coal and Iron Co., 1864–1913	90	$5\frac{1}{2}$	—	$4\frac{1}{2}$	—	96
Clifton and Kearsley Co., 1885–1913	$82\frac{1}{2}$	$9\frac{1}{2}$	$1\frac{1}{2}$	7	4	77
Mean	79	10	2	6	3	80

Sources:

Fife coal Co.: ScRO, CB3/131/7 balance sheets and annual reports.

Main Colliery Go.: GlaRO D/DMC balance sheets.

East Cannock Colliery Co.: StRO D/429/m/B

Mitchell Main Colliery Co.: SCL, NCB 601 and 608A balance sheets.

Cannock Chase Colliery Co.: balance sheets in Directors' Minute Books, uncatalogued.

Bolckow Vaughan and Co.: BSNRRC 14603 (1866–61 and 1873–99) and 04902 (1881–1913). Annual Reports and Accounts.

Staveley Coal and Iron Co.: BSCEMRRC 2034/2/32–3 balance sheets.

Newstead Colliery: BSCEMRRC 2034/3/13, balance sheets.

Wigan Coal and Iron: LaRO, DDX/127/40–74 and WiRO, D/D Hai Box 14, Directors' Reports 1864–1914.

Clifton and kearsley Colliery Co.: LaRO, NCCK 5/1, balance sheets.

Henry Briggs & Son and Co.: Bro Special Collections MS 160, MB balance sheets.

Lochgelly: ScRO, CB 2/131–2; 155–9.

Carlton Main: SCL, MD 4080–9, MB balance sheets.

New Hucknall: NoRO NCB 1/41, balance sheets.

Hamstead: StaRO D 876/10–17, MB balance sheets.

Walsall Wood: StaRO D 876/39, MB balance sheets.

between the true and stated asset value, the rate of growth of output, the chronology of expansion, and the capital–output ratios and their determinants defined by the condition of each company's operations.

The mean share attributable to retained profit for our seventeen companies was 3 per cent, but at 10 per cent was exceeded more than three-fold by debentures and mortgages; a category within which, however, the inter-company differences were very much greater than was the case with profits and in any case were used, for the most part, by partners or business associates. Walsall Wood, Carlton Main, and Hamstead each recorded debentures and mortgages amounting to between one-fifth and one-third of their financial input, while four companies, Newstead, New Hucknall, Cannock Chase, and Main, recorded less than 3 per cent. Until the later nineteenth century the use of mortgage was wide-spread, freehold and colliery property providing the security, whether from insurance or building societies, banks, or individuals; the same was true of mortgage debentures, which gained in popularity in the late nine-teenth century. When Staveley was first formed as a limited company the vendor, John Barrow, agreed to leave £100,000 of his capital on a 6 per cent mortgage on an annual basis, an arrangement which the Staveley directors preferred rather than borrowing from the bank.[1] In 1869 the company directors issued debentures in order to disengage from Barrow, at the same time securing commitments for between three and seven years from the largest fifty shareholders who immediately took up debentures to the value of £90,000.[2] Two years later a further debenture was issued to shareholders for £30,000 for five or seven years to meet wagon purchase.[3] Later, debentures were issued to meet the costs of developing new collieries, the largest of which was £0.25m. in 1911—for the development of Hickleton Main and the Yorkshire Main Collieries.[4]

In general, and particularly among coal companies, borrowing on debentures became more popular during the deflation of the 1880s and early 1890s, for they offered greater security at lower interest rates than could be obtained from the banks; debentures also carried the option of liquidation or possible renewal on improved terms. Unlike mortgages, debentures could be secured on a floating charge, though especially after the 1890s colliery securities became more popular, particularly in South

---

[1] BSCEMRRC Stanton and Staveley 2034/2/31–2 balance sheets, 2034/2/2 MB 1 Sept. 1866.
[2] BSCEMRRC Stanton and Staveley 2034/2/3 MB 21 Dec. 1868.
[3] Ibid., 23 Oct. 1871.
[4] Ibid., 2034/2/10 MB 23 Jan., 26 Sept. 1911.

Wales.[1] Among these companies relying most heavily upon debenture and mortgages, Walsall Wood recorded the highest with 30 per cent and Hamstead 19.5 per cent; both were small- to medium-sized firms measured by subscribed capital and asset values. Hamstead was barely profitable and Walsall Wood's record was also poor, yet Walsall Wood retained the greatest proportion of profit of all companies in our sample, excepting Fife. Whereas the latter, however, was able to do this and to pay handsome dividends from highly profitable trading, the Walsall Wood directors appear to have found it necessary to forego dividend ditribution to ordinary shareholders because of a capital shortage, hence the need for high gearing. It is possible that the histories of these two firms are symptomatic of a capital shortage in the region; due to the absence of larger coalowner investors common in other regions, mortgage and debenture capital became especially important for raising funds.

Whereas the relative importance of retained profits and loans may have been different in South Wales compared with other regions, such is not the case when comparing mortgage loans and debentures with other forms of borrowing. Cottrell's research into the archives of the Midland Bank suggests that banks, especially in the Barnsley district, played an important role in Yorkshire financing colliery enterprise.[2] Such notable examples as Clay Cross, in which George Carr Glynn, the banker, was a founding partner, and the John Bowes partnership, whose further development at the Marley Hill Colliery beginning in 1841 was underpinned by considerable loan capital from the Northumberland and District Bank, offer further support for this view.[3] For many years the John Bowes partnership managed to remain solvent despite heavy indebtedness by a string of mortgage, personal, and bank loans which were in an almost perpetual state of renewal. Capital expenditure was only one of the reasons for increasing debt, for John Bowes indulged in spectacular extravagance: addiction to travel and gambling led to the acquisition of the Théâtre des Variétés in Paris, of which he became the director[4] in order to promote the ambitions of an actress and thereby advance his marriage prospects. In a confidential report to the partnership's main lessor, the Earl of Strathmore's solicitor analysed the reasons for this extraordinary financial history, which continued until the death of John Bowes in 1885. He noted that for a very long time the partnership had

---

[1] Walters 1977, 128. [2] Cottrell 1980, 198, 215–16.
[3] Mountford thesis, 10–17. [4] Ibid., 98.

been sustained throughout mainly on credit maintained 'primarily by the popular belief that Mr Bowes was an exceedingly rich man and by the known fact that Mr Palmer was undoubtdly an able man of business'.[1] Continued heavy indebtedness and further deterioration of finances in the difficult year of 1844, marked by strikes, the end of the Vend, and banking failures, had prompted Bowes to find an additional partner, Charles Mark Palmer, whose injection of capital proved to be critical in the short run and his expert management an asset in the longer term.[2]

Other firms in the North-east were less fortunate, many of which, according to Matthias Dunn, were in debt to three local banks which failed, forcing collieries into bankruptcy or sale at nominal values.[3] Burnopfield and Tanfield Moor Collieries both passed into the hands of John Bowes by arrangement with the North Durham and District Bank (their creditors) shortly after they became bankrupt in 1849, as did the bankrupt Crookbank Colliery.[4] In 1857 the sequence was repeated, John Bowes and Partners facing difficulty in meeting wage payments and fearing imminent bankruptcy,[5] yet only a few years elapsed before bank manager (and colliery owner) Johnathan Richardson was extending loans, as he had done in the past, for the acquisition of another colliery.[6]

Once a creditor was committed to a large extent, the logic of avoiding bankruptcy and of continuing to extend credit often seemed to be compelling. For such a reason Earl Strathmore, the principal lessor, was advised by his solicitor against allowing the Partnership to become bankrupt, for Bowes was 'the owner of an enormous enterprise . . . and liable for vast sums which however great the value of the assets they represent, could not be met from the resources of the firm itself . . .';[7] limited liability was seen to offer a solution to secure greater control over the partners, the price of which would be substantial shareholdings to be undertaken by the Strathmore family. Not only the aristocracy or wayward individuals, however, presented difficulties for lenders. The East Cannock Colliery Company was formed in 1870 and almost immediately encountered financial difficulties due to the faulty nature of the seams, unanticipated difficulties in sinking, an explosion, and a strike. The directors used the threat of liquidation against debenture

---

[1] Quoted in Mountford thesis, 162–3.
[2] Ibid., 31–3.   [3] Dunn 1852, 360.
[4] Mountford thesis, 58–9, 96–109.
[5] Ibid., 107–109.   [6] Ibid.
[7] Ibid., 162–3.

holders and bankers to secure greater funding, and in order to avoid the risk of receiving perhaps either half or nothing, debenture and shareholders agreed to suspend repayment, the bank allowing a further overdraft increase at an enhanced rate and in return for first charge on the company's entire debt.[1] Just as James Joicey, under not dissimilar conditions, had made an offer for John Bowes's royalty in the 1840s, so the company promoter, Henry Davis Pochin, made an ungenerous bid for East Cannock. This was rejected: but Pochin acquired the company soon after at well below the real asset value, when liquidation became inevitable.[2]

The histories of John Bowes and East Cannock might be regarded as exceptional in some respects, but they illustrate the risks that lenders ran. They also suggest reasons why research shows that from the mid-nineteenth century banks played a limited role in the long-term financing of colliery enterprise. The sample of thirty companies' balance sheets for 1908–13 shows a figure of one per cent as the share of loans to stated company assets, and our longer period sample of seventeen gives a figure of 3 per cent. None of the Yorkshire firms in our sample relied at all on bank loans, which overall accounted for only 2 per cent of colliery companies' cash flow. The Consett Iron Company, an important coal producer, was exceptional in that when it was founded in 1864 a number of leading creditors of the defunct Northumberland and Durham District Bank (which itself had loaned large sums to the firm's predecessors, the Derwent Iron Company) became shareholders in the company.[3] Largely as a consequence of the acute capital shortage experienced in the 1880s and 1890s, the Yorkshire company, Carlton Main, ran up a substantial overdraft with the Sheffield and Rotherham District Bank, which as a result influenced several important financial decisions made within the firm. The bank was not, however, in any sense a source of long-term funding.[4] For the other companies in the survey there is little evidence that bank or other financial institutions acted as long-term investors. In a few, however, for example the Ashington Coal Company, Pease and Partners, and Butterley, several of the directors were also partners in, or directors of, local banks, holding positions of potential influence by which loans might be obtained without appearing in the company balance sheets.

[1] StaRO East Cannock D/429/m/B, MB, General Meetings, 7 June 1878, 3 Oct. 1879, 21 June 1880.
[2] Ibid., MB, Directors' Meetings, 19 Aug. 1880; MB General Meetings, 18 Aug. 1880, 15 Sept. 1880. [3] A. S. Wilson thesis, 30–7.
[4] SCL Carlton Main MD 4080–9, Directors' Minutes, 6 Dec. 1878.

While we may conclude that banks did not play a vital role in the provision of long-term finance it is clear that the overdraft, often substantial in size, might prove critical in the short term. When Charles Markham tried to raise £100,000 for more than a year in 1869 the bankers refused and it was left to Staveley's shareholders to provide a loan on debentures.[1] In the case of Staveley and those companies which shared interlocking directorates (especially the Tredegar Iron and Coal Company, Bolckow Vaughan, Sheepbridge Coal and Iron, and John Brown) inter-company loans were the preferred alternative to bank loans, despite the opposition of the Staveley chairman, John Barrow, who must have regarded the temporary loan to competitors as a perverse use of the firm's resources; he, however, was not also a director of the other companies.[2] Never a recipient of such loans, Staveley frequently loaned funds until such time as they were repatriated for colliery development, for once the years of heavy indebtedness were left behind with the boom of 1872–3, calls on shareholders were sufficient to finance Staveley's long-term expansion, which included the formation of subsidiary companies. The recipients of Staveley loans (chiefly Bolckow Vaughan and John Brown), repayable at three months' notice, seem to have been regarded as relatively long-term commitments. A similar pattern of inter-company loans existed between parent and subsidiary companies: the Newstead Colliery Company, a joint venture between Staveley and Sheepbridge in 1872, Firbeck, formed in 1913, Brodsworth Colliery, formed in 1907 jointly with Hickleton Main Colliery Company, and the wholly-owned subsidiary, Yorkshire Main, provide examples.

This incestuous movement of funds between coal and iron-coal companies of course minimized interest payments flowing out of the industry, but it may also have reflected the low esteem attaching to colliery property as loan security for much of the nineteenth century.[3] John Bowes, perhaps not the most dispassionate witness, made this point in 1843, when neither a colliery lease nor an insurance policy proved acceptable to London capitalists when they were approached to supply some of the initial capital outlay for the Marley Hill colliery development. Writing to another partner, Bowes wrote, 'We require £10,000 of which I can advance £4,000 (if I am successful at Doncaster Races,

<hr />

[1] Chapman 1981, 80.

[2] BSCEMRRC, Stanton and Staveley 2034/2/4, MB 4 Aug. 1872, 24 Feb., 23 June, 27 Oct. 1873, 24 July 1874; 2034/2/5 MB 16 Dec., 28 Oct. 1876, 2034/2/6 MB 29 Mar. 1886, 2034/2/8 MB 23 Apr. 1901, 2034/2/9 MB 28 Nov. 1904.   [3] Walters 1977, 131–2.

more)',[1] a characteristic example of his boundless optimism which not surprisingly potential lenders, as yet uncommitted to his business ventures and personal extravagance, chose not to share. Colliery proprietor and manager Emerson Bainbridge's serious approach to mining enterprise some sixty years later was in complete contrast, but he, too, stressed the difficulties in securing external finance, which as a result of the need to sink deeper mines had greatly increased fixed-capital needs, and which by 1900 might require £300,000. In general, he regarded the credit standing of colliery proprietors as 'very bad', though conceded that in 1897, a year of particular financial difficulty, the banks had acted as their 'chief friends'.[2]

Bainbridge's general assessment of the banks' attitude to coalmining companies was echoed in 1900 by a manager on the Midland Bank's main board, whose diary recorded: 'Our board is very prejudiced against collieries'.[3] This did not mean that financial assistance, even over several years, was never forthcoming from the banks; at times of financial reconstruction, bridging finance was made available; on adequate security, when debentures and reliable personal guarantees were forthcoming, secured loans were made to coalmining companies. However, the uncertainties involved in mining and the physical waste of assets presented difficulties additional to those involved in manufacturing enterprise.

Justification for banking caution is demonstrated by the Midland's experience with the Flimby and Broughton Moor Coal and Fire Brick Company between 1897 (the year when the banks in general had been praised for their support to colliery companies) and 1905. Between 1897 and 1902 an initial loan of £10,000 had increased to £35,500, but the predictions of the colliery owners had been confounded by a faulted seam and led to revised expectations of imminent profitability. At this point dissention among the proprietors drew the bank into discussions of amalgamation with an adjacent colliery in the possession of a successful mining engineer, whose price for agreement involved long-term support from the bank.[4] The risks involved in long-term support are illustrated in the banking account of the Moss Hall Coal Company Ltd., which in 1903 had paid no dividend for nearly twenty years yet had accumulated debts exceeding £0.3m.[5]

---

[1] Quoted in Mountford thesis, 131–2.
[2] *RC Coal Supplies* 1904, XXIII, QQ 10971, 10976–83.
[3] Midland Bank Archives, Acc 26/2–183 Diary of S. B. Murray, 25 Jan. 1900.
[4] Ibid., Acc 26/10 431–3, 204, 241, 264, 371, 446.
[5] Ibid., 431–136.

Even companies possessing relatively secure financial foundations could expect mostly limited short-term support. Thus, in 1886 the Sheepbridge Coal and Iron Company found the Shefield Banking Company calling in a loan of £20,000 which had been issued on debenture in 1884 renewable every six months. The Sheepbridge directors were informed that the bank saw no particular risk attaching to the £35,000 debentures in its possession (security for the loan plus overdraft) but the bank 'did not desire that the heavy indebtedness should continue'; the bank also objected when the Sheepbridge directors proposed a call on shares to reduce indebtedness at the bank but not to pay off the debentures.[1]

Financing certain elements of fixed capital took somewhat different forms, varying between companies and over time, though evidence is insufficient to generalize with confidence. In the North-east before 1850 the early railway companies offered to provide wagon stocks and means of transport,[2] thereby relieving intending colliery investors of considerable capital costs estimated to account for some 30 per cent of deep-sinking costs, including engines, track and rolling stock.[3] Some existing colliery companies sold their main railways and sidings to the railway companies, as did Staveley, for example, in 1864, though continuing to purchase wagons.[4] Wagon purchase was also the policy of the Wingerworth Coal Company, at Newton Chambers, Cannock Chase, and Wharncliffe Silkstone.[5] The turning-point probably occurred round about 1850, when following fierce criticism on this count railway companies proposed that coalowners should provide wagons and that allowances in respect of charges be made for their use, a policy which became widespread.[6]

Methods of financing the acquisition of wagons, however, differed from company to company. In order to transfer some of the capital burden partners or shareholders were encouraged to purchase rolling stock as private individuals, for which they received rent from the company. By the 1860s wagon companies offered arrangements by which payments could be switched out of capital account and extended over a period of years, usually seven, when ownership passed to the colliery company.[7] Under the redemption-hire arrangement wagons

---

[1] BSCEMRRC Stanton and Staveley 2034/7/5 MB 27 Nov. 1884, 10 July, 28 Aug. 1886.

[2] Dunn 1852, 337–40.   [3] Vamplew thesis, 372–9.

[4] BSCEMRRC Stanton and Staveley 2034/2/1 MB 24 Oct. 1864.

[5] SCL Newton Chambers TR 462/4/17; Hopkinson thesis, 388; SCL Wharncliffe Silkstone NCB 1429/1 MB 18 Mar. 1865; BUL Directors' Minutes 26 Feb. 1870.

[6] Vamplew thesis, 374–5.   [7] WaRO Griff CR 1169/22 Annual Reports 16 Sept. 1894.

were regarded as a realizable asset which companies could pledge to the wagon companies for cash, a form of short-term loan. Powell Duffryn raised £46,000 in this way in 1886 in agreements over several years, which Walters interpreted as a sign of strained capital resources;[1] a similar expedient was adopted by the Main Coal Company on a smaller scale in 1890, when a temporary capital shortage was solved by transferring the burden to revenue, wagon hire becoming a part of current costs.[2] Few instances have survived however, where, as in the case of Staveley and of the Main Colliery Company, wagon companies actually loaned money—in one instance on the security of wagons, and in another on consols.[3]

Housing finance was another component of capital separable from the basic sinking and opening-out costs of a colliery, but alternative methods of providing finance for workmen's houses enabled many companies to minimize the capital burden; or to the extent that much of the company-owned colliery housing was on a self-financing basis capital costs were substituted for working costs. Where housing or wagons were operated at a profit they augmented cash flow. Whereas most colliery housing was built by the companies (and at Griff, at least, was charged to revenue account), a common method of reducing capital expenditure was to invite partners, shareholders, landlords, and other wealthy individuals to build houses on company land which colliery companies proceeded to hold on lease, or for which they offered a guaranteed minimum rent. Debenture issues were the preferred method of finance adopted by Powell Duffryn and Newton Chambers, and the New Hucknall Colliery Co. took up a mortgage loan to finance cottages needed to ensure that new or expanding collieries were amply supplied with labour.[4] An expanding mining population in remote districts offered incentives to speculators to build, thereby relieving the coal companies, but the return was not always a sufficient inducement. In 1904 William Armstrong was urging the Peases to build cottages despite the activities of private builders in the Eldon district, not only because the rents charged by the Peases he regarded as excessive but also because Bolckow Vaughan was erecting 600 cottages for leasing to company

[1] Walters 1977, 133–4.
[2] RC Coal Supplies 1904, XXIII, QQ 11987–11989.
[3] Walters 1977, 133; BSCEMRRC 2034/2/6, MB 10 Nov. 1883.
[4] WaRO, Griff CR 1169/22 Annual Reports 26 Sept. 1894, 6 Sept. 1895; C. P. Griffin thesis, 508; SCL, Wharncliffe Silkstone, 1429/1 25 Jan., 25 Apr. 1859, 22 Oct. 1866, 5 Jan. 1867; DuRO Stella, NCB/I/SC/108 (355); Walters, 1980, 83; NoRO, New Hucknall, NCB NHCC 1/15. SCL, Newton Chambers, TR 450/6/2; BSCEMRRC Stanton and Staveley 2034/7/5 MB 24 Mar. 1887.

workers.[1] In 1883 directors of the Hamstead Colliery Company established the Hamstead Building Company to lease freehold land on leases of ninety-nine years, offering to guarantee the initial expense of house-building up to £100. The directors justified such a venture to share-holders by explaining that they regarded it to be important to appropriate the company's capital for workers' housing—but the directors could hardly have expected the higher rate of return earned by the Building Company compared with that earned by the colliery.[2]

Building clubs enabled a relatively small number of workmen to obtain their own houses. In the 1840s James Baird loaned £40 to colliers with which to form a building club, each contributing 2s. 6d per week towards the cost of a cottage for £38.[3] Forty years later, Charles Markham encouraged the establishment of the Staveley Works Building Society to achieve this aim, and granted £600 to add impetus to the promotion of housing in the Brimington new mining area in 1882. The provision of large numbers of houses in the Warsop and Polbrook districts in the 1890s was arranged through a Shirebrook building firm, from whom Staveley leased several hundred cottages over twenty-one years, including a break clause in the tenth year in the event of the collieries ceasing production. At the large new winning at Yorkshire Main over one thousand houses were planned in 1910, Staveley undertaking to find tenants for the builders at a given rental.[4] Building clubs, similar in principle to those encouraged by Baird and Markham though organized in various forms, grew in popularity towards the end of our period. In the North-east co-operative societies controlled by committees dominated by miners promoted home ownership in a region where tied housing was very common. By building houses for tenants, with an option to buy over a number of years, or by making advances to members wishing to build their own houses, the co-operative building societies attracted many thousands of members between 1890 and 1913, as did the Welsh miners' building clubs.[5] Similar to the Co-operative Societies of the North of England, they differed in that the bank, instead of the co-operative society, loaned money on receiving security based on subscribed funds and the guarantee of trustees.[6] Finally, following

---

[1] NuRO 725/B14/564 Armstrong's Report.

[2] StaRO Hamstead, D 876/10 MB 24 May 1881, D 896–11, 1 Feb. 1883, D 896–12 6 Feb. 1888.

[3] McEwan thesis, 169.

[4] BSCEMRRC Stanton and Staveley 2034/2/6 MB 11 Aug. 1882, 2034/2/7 MB 4 Feb. 1891, 2034/2/7 MB 26 Nov. 1895, 28 Jan. 1898, 22 Nov. 1898, 2034/2/10 MB 25 Oct. 1910.

[5] Bulman 1920, 265–6, 301–3; H. S. Jevons 1915, 646–8.

[6] Ibid.

the Industrial and Provident Societies Act in 1903, organizations were established to take advantage of loans available from the Public Works Loan Board. One such body was Messrs. Welsh Garden Cities Ltd., formed in 1910, which inaugurated several co-partnership schemes offering a 5 per cent return on money invested by shareholder tenants. E. M. Hann, General Manager of Powell Duffryn, was the chairman of one such co-partnership society, which in Pengam Garden Village developed an entire community in the centre of the Rhymney Valley, close to Powell Duffryn's Britannia Colliery.[1]

In those instances where infrastructural investment was undertaken in addition to houses, by building hospitals, schools, churches and chapels, libraries, meeting halls, and institutes, normally either the company or partners or wealthy individuals acted in a private capacity providing at least the initial capital sum required.

Rental agreements were also not unusual—for example at the Derbyshire company, Sheepbridge Coal and Iron, where after requesting that an institute be built the works committee agreed to pay rent equivalent to 6 per cent of the capital expenditure of £1,300. A Primitive Methodist Chapel was financed in the same manner.[2] In several instances, however, virtually an entire town was built by a colliery company. At Ashington in Northumberland the Ashington Coal Company provided housing, schools, water and gas supplies, drains, roads, and social facilities; by 1913 this company had built 2,500 colliery houses which had cost at least an estimated £0.25m.;[3] Consett owned more.[4] In total, however, national non-housing social investment was small compared with capital embodied in workmen's housing.

Because of its importance in new enterprise formation and the expansion of existing firms, our discussion has concentrated mainly upon the process of fixed-capital formation. The need to acquire substantial amounts of capital within a relatively short period posed a problem. However, when capital investment is converted into capital costs, which is how the problem of capital formation presented itself to colliery owners once the initial capital had been raised, the difference between the mining and manufacturing industries is not substantial. The industry's cost structures are examined in detail in Chapter 6, but while an analysis of working costs presents no problems, unfortunately,

[1] Bulman 1920, 292–4.
[2] BSCEMRRC Stanton and Staveley 2034/7/5 MB 28 July 1889; 2034/7/6 MB 29 May 1899.
[3] NuRO Ashington NCB AS/2, AS/23.
[4] A. S. Wilson thesis, 173.

thanks to contemporary accounting practices, total costs are difficult to identify. If, however, we define capital costs as expenditure on mining operations (including land), then estimates imply capital costs not exceeding 14 per cent of total costs throughout our period; after the 1880s a downward trend to roughly 8 per cent is discernible.[1] This trend is explicable only in terms of the rise in relative importance of the other two major components: labour costs and other working costs, of which the largest by far were the former. There is a discernible trend in labour costs which rose from slightly more than 50 per cent of total working costs at the beginning of our period to roughly 70 per cent at the end. Other working costs, which included mainly timber, iron, and ropes, accounted for over one-third in 1830, falling to below a quarter by 1913.

Colliery owners, and contemporaries who wrote about the industry, tended to assume that working capital would take care of itself under normal circumstances—when coal and sales accounts were in balance. An analysis of the sources of working capital is complicated by the differences between the cost structures and the character of manufacturing industry compared with mining; for the risks associated with the uncertainties of mining, due to geological and physical factors, present difficulties for those seeking to separate sources of finance contributing to fixed-capital formation from those providing working capital. Our company sample shows that fixed assets as a proportion of total assets averaged 67 per cent, though barely a quarter of our company sample revealed a ratio below that. Furthermore, the structure of working costs was such that wages comprised between 55 and 70 per cent of the total. The cost of materials, chiefly pitwood, iron castings, and ropes, represented between 10 and 16 per cent. Suppliers were clearly responsible for most of the trade credit, which among our company sample accounted for 6 per cent of their financial resources, 8 per cent for our 1908–13 sample. The cost of maintaining stocks, which were small, was insignificant.

The main gap in the flow of revenue and current expenditure was that occasioned by the three-month settlement of payments for coal associated with the bill of exchange. But while many colliery companies did take advantage of this source of credit, discounting bills at the bank before maturity, it seems probable that at least the important constellation of iron and coal companies in which H. D. Pochin was a key figure

[1] Costs are analysed in Chapter 6.

from the 1860s—Staveley, Sheepbridge, Tredegar, Bolckow Vaughan, and John Brown—adopted another policy, which he explained to Staveley's shareholders in 1872: 'The policy of this company is carried on rather differently than at most places. We pay cash for all we receive and accept no bills.'[1] The same was true of David Davies, of the Ocean Coal Company.[2] However, many steam-coal companies in South Wales concentrated upon the trading connection to secure economies in working capital, which explains why some of them sold through export merchants at the ports, though for financial and organizational reasons most colliery sales agents sold through middlemen.[3]

Working capital in the form of picks, drilling gear, candles, and explosives were typically for much of the nineteenth century purchased by the miners themselves, either from an employer or through co-operative arrangements between the men and local storekeepers. Only safety lamps were supplied at the company's expense in most collieries, even in the twentieth century.[4] In those areas, particularly in the West and East Midlands, where sub-contracting was common, a butty might supply tools, carts, and horses, and pay wages, thereby removing all responsibility for the major items of capital expenditure from the coalowner. From the mid-century, however, sub-contracting on this model was in decline.[5]

Much more important, at least before 1870, was the minimization of a firm's cash outflow by the long pay. Fortnightly payment of wages was the norm in most regions, and at collieries in South Wales and Scotland monthly intervals between payment were not uncommon, allowing for fortnightly drawings in advance. The practice at the Llynvi Coal and Iron Company in South Wales was to pay workers only six times a year, a proportion of the payment taking the form of notes accepted by local shops and by the company's bankers: 'the company are evidently benefited by being released from the necessity of finding cash advances . . .' commented the Truck Commission Report in 1870.[6] Payment in kind had diminished with the decline of the butty system and truck legislation since 1830. In 1870 a few strongholds where company stores existed and payment in goods or notes instead of cash persisted were to be found in some parts of South Wales and Scotland, but their

---

[1] BSCEMRRC Stanton and Staveley 2034/2/13 MB 31 Aug. 1872.
[2] Walters 1980, 84.   [3] Ibid.
[4] *Truck Committee Report* 1908, LIX, paras 11–12.
[5] A. J. Taylor 1967, 98.
[6] *RC Truck* 1871, XXXVI, 58.

disappearance was hastened, though not entirely eliminated, by the Truck Act of 1872.[1]

Colliery finance was distinctive, in that whereas liquidity was necessary in manufacturing industry to levels which could meet unforseen contingencies arising from trading and from calculable (and insurable) commercial risks, coalowners faced uncertainties associated with natural phenomena, of fire or flooding, against which, at least before 1875,[2] no insurance could be secured. While such risks were greater during the initial sinking phase, the effect of flooding or fire resulting from a new sinking upon adjacent collieries could be damaging; furthermore, just as the emergence of geological faults could unexpectedly raise working costs by effects on the wages bill, similarly water could cause working (and capital) costs to increase through pumping costs. These were uncertainties completely unpredictable and to the single-pit colliery enterprise especially could prove to be disastrous, as the history of the Hamstead Colliery Company demonstrates. Formed by a group of prominent West Midlands businessmen in 1875, including Richard Chamberlain and William Kenrick, sinking and opening out continued until 1883 and profitable working was achieved in 1888; but in 1898 a fire caused the closure of most of the colliery for five years, destroying all hopes of attaining profitability.[3]

Such characteristics implied the need for conservative financial policies if a colliery was to survive. They also help towards an understanding of why it is difficult to separate the provision of fixed and working capital, for the degree of liquidity which was prudent to cover the risks affecting random damage to colliery property could also cushion a colliery during periods of trading difficulty. When in 1864 colliery owner Horace Walker attempted to reform Wharncliffe Silkstone's accounting procedure, the viewer, Parkin Jeffcock, protested against any distinction being drawn between capital and working expenses. Working capital required liquidity which depended upon profits, and profitability was particularly important for providing working capital and liquidity, because managers commonly perceived the deduction of depreciation as an appropriation of profits, rather than as a cost of conducting business; therefore, the option not to charge depreciation may be seen as one method of maintaining liquidity.[1]

---

[1] *Truck Committee Report* 1908, LIX, paras 11–12.
[2] *SC Lords Coal Trade* 1830, VIII, 2; Galloway 1904, 8–10, 111–135, 143–5.
[3] StaRO Hamstead D 876/10 MB 4 May 1875, D 876/11 10 Oct. 1883, D 876/17 12 Oct. 1909.

Advising Staveley's directors in 1868, viewer William Armstrong recommended that regular amounts allocated for depreciation should be invested,[2] advice which was also offered by H. S. Hoskold at a meeting of the Federated Institute of Mining Engineers more than twenty years later, when he criticized the lack of such redemption funds which should, he thought, ideally be held in the form of consols or similar securities.[3]

The reaction of J. B. Simpson, mining engineer and colliery owner associated with several collieries in the North-east, is revealing, for he denied having heard of collieries practising such a policy: 'Depreciation was generally a sum that was floating about, which was at the beck and call of the company when they wanted the money'.[4] Redemption funds did, however, exist, and were often held in the form of consols. A policy which linked depreciation to levels of profitability was widespread in the industry (even at Staveley as late as 1890 Pochin was suggesting that it was time that 'the question of depreciation . . . should be dealt with in a systematic and definite principle'),[5] but it should be seen in the context of another common practice, of writing off capital expenditure against revenue, the effect of which was to depress the level of profit. A frequent corollary of such policies was unsystematic depreciation linked to profit levels and debt avoidance by holding a reserve. In 1866 Charles Markham stated that it would be possible to withdraw up to £30,000 from Staveley before having to discount bills, 'which I trust will never be resorted to by the Staveley Company'.[6] Six years later, Pochin explained to shareholders who were pressing for higher dividends that it was as well to keep a little cash in hand. This sentiment was repeated by Emerson Bainbridge in 1895, when he stressed the importance of keeping a 'sufficient reserve fund for emergencies'.[7] It seems that the more prosperous, well-established colliery companies maintained cash balances more than adequate to meet anticipated needs for working capital. An extreme example of this, perhaps, is provided by the Rhymney Iron Company, which from the time its capital account was closed in 1849 until 1875 met *all* expenditure from revenue.[1] Similarly, the expan-

---

[1] SCL Wharncliffe Silkstone NCB 1429/1, 14 Nov. 1864, 1 Aug. 1868.

[2] BSCEMRRC Stanton and Staveley 2034/2/13, MB 17 Aug. 1868.

[3] H. D. Hoskold, 'Notes upon Redemption of Capital Invested in Collieries', *TFIME*, III (1891-2), 744. [4] Ibid.

[5] BSCEMRRC Stanton and Staveley 2034/2/7 MB 28 Jan. 1890.

[6] Ibid., 2034/2/2 MB 27 Aug. 1866.

[7] *RC Coal Supplies* 1904, xxiii, QQ 11011.

sion of the Ashington Coal Company's operations between 1880 and 1913, when output rose tenfold to reach 2.2m. tons, was financed from partners' and family wealth and profits, conservative financial policies also being evident in the high level of reserves and cash balances.[2]

As a proportion of the total assets of the thirty companies for which information is available in 1908–13, reserves averaged 9 per cent, though this level probably exaggerates the norm for the nineteenth century as a whole. An analysis of the reserves held by eighteen companies between 1865 and 1913 reveals an average of around 10 per cent of total assets held in the form of reserves, depreciation funds, or liquid assets, the range among the fourteen companies where reserves could be identified extending from less than 2 per cent to 25 per cent. Those percentages exclude the external investment of reserved funds by loans to other, mainly coal and iron, companies, or in the form of securities or shares in industry and trade, or consols. Differences in the levels of reserves between firms depend heavily upon the time period for which the data are available. The level of reserves was inevitably higher in booms than in slumps and was higher between 1890 and 1913 (and especially between 1900 and 1913) than in preceding periods. A number of the firms in our sample, however, Mitchell Main, Cannock Chase, East Cannock, and Butterley, established large capital reserves over the long term, and the same was true of David Davis and Co. and Cardiff Steam Collieries.[3] Reserves were the norm in the industry.

Under certain circumstances, particularly company formation or reorganization, and in small-scale enterprise, capital shortage might result from under-capitalization, not an uncommon condition in coal-mining. The Nottinghamshire partnership of Wakefield, North, and Co. mining coal at a dozen smallish pits, and which depended upon Thomas Wakefield, partner also in several diverse enterprises, for capital, reveals a precarious financial history which ended in Wakefield's bankruptcy in 1847. A. R. Griffin has described the firm's cash-flow difficulties which Thomas North, the managing partner, tackled by seeking revision of leases on less onerous terms, by postponing small payments to creditors, by squeezing wages, and by neglecting safety; he was also driven to

[1] Walters 1980, 58.
[2] NuRO Ashington NCB AS/5, ZMD/54/4–5.
[3] Walters 1977, 139. The figures are not exactly comparable.

exaggerate mining difficulties and to trespass on coal to which the firm had no right.[1]

Small-scale enterprises were often under-capitalized from the beginning, and as a result of fires or flooding an inability to raise capital to give time to solve these problems forced closure. Such a common sequence in the nineteenth century underlines the dubious analytical distinction between fixed and working colliery capital. When in 1858 the Woolley Coal Company in West Yorkshire completed a colliery extension (shaft and pump paid out of revenue) the partners searched for another to raise additional finance, and after failing to do so resolved that the remaining partners should contribute to working expenses on a proportionate basis. This precipitated the withdrawal of one of the partners, which even litigation could not prevent. Four years later, the principal partner, John Marsden, also a local solicitor with much experience in colliery affairs and presumably aware of financial sources, declared that in order to pay workmen's wages he had given the company's assurance policies to the landlord, already the largest creditor, as security for further support. Inundation in 1862–3 seemed to destroy hopes of survival, when Marsden wrote to the solicitors of another partner, Captain William Armytage, RN, in desperation 'Surely 1,400 acres of coal on 53 years lease at £120 per acre, when it is worth from £250 and £280 per annum according to the average of the district ought to be worth something ... I am borne down with anxiety attendant on this business and must beg for relief and for such suggestions as Captain William Armytage or you, as his advisers, have to make ...'[2] The conversion of this partnership into a limited liability company in 1867, following an optimistic assessment of the productive potential and profitability by the viewer, Thomas Woodhouse, proved to be a satisfactory way for Marsden to reduce his relative commitments to the firm, eventually selling his shares after the boom in 1874.[3] The Woolley Coal Company lacked the financial resources to cope with the risks which in mining were always close at hand, but none the less managed bare survival. Yet to possess such resources implied an ability also to avoid the problems

---

[1] A. R. Griffin, 'Thomas North: Mining Entrepreneur Extraordinary', *Transactions of the Thornton Society*, LXXVI (1972), 58–9.

[2] One example is provided in the origins of the New Hucknall Colliery Company, which was formed in 1879 to take over the Hucknall Huthwaite Colliery, then two years in arrears on royalty payments to the Duke of Portland. A. R. Griffin 1971, 103. For other examples see C. P. Griffin thesis, 229–30.

[3] John Goodchild MS, Woolley Coal Company.

of shortages of working capital, which though cyclical manifested themselves, as did the incidence of natural disasters and the eventuality of
geological setbacks, as sudden unforeseen difficulties.

Those which lacked resources to cope with periods of depressed
prices often also suffered from unfavourable cost structures and from a
shortage of working capital.[1] Relaxation of mine rents and royalties
might offer temporary relief, but survival depended upon changes in
colliery management rather than finance—or the rapid return of high
coal prices, which especially after 1874 were long delayed. Under such
circumstances smaller firms found themselves in difficulties, Hoyland
Silkstone and Wharncliffe Silkstone for example, which in 1883 were
offered for sale by the partners to Newton Chambers.[2] The capital
shortage experienced by the Yorkshire and Derbyshire Coal and Iron
Company in the late 1870s and early 1880s should not be taken merely
as an indication of general capital shortage (though this was a period of
low price and profits for coalowners) but as a symptom of under-
capitalization; for whereas when the company was formed in 1872 with
a nominal capital of £100,000 finance was easily obtained, by 1878, when
production at the Carlton Main Colliery actually began, trading conditions and the terms for borrowing had deteriorated.[3] The Sheepbridge
Coal and Iron Company experienced similar problems of capital
shortage from its formation in 1864 until the boom of 1871–3 generated
sufficient profits to solve them. Although the company was capitalized
at £500,000 the valuation announced in 1865 amounted to £265,744, substantially larger than the purchasers had expected. In 1869 the chairman,
managing director, and former owner of Sheepbridge, William Fowler,
described the company as being 'destitute of working capital'. Personal
loans from directors and from one external lender, in 1867 and 1868,
redeemable in 1869, plus an overdraft of up to £25,000 taken almost to
the limit in that year, led Fowler to urge 'constant watchfulness and
care'.[4]

In the short term and in extreme circumstances, such as during the
trading depressions of the late 1870s and early 1880s and in the difficult
year of 1897, banks were not unsympathetic to credit-worthy firms.

---

[1] For example, Whitwick Colliery, CG 30 May 1884, 856–74; see also C. P. Griffin thesis, 263–
70; CG 19 Aug. 1881, 308.
[2] SCL Newton Chambers TR 450/8/6; Wharncliffe Silkstone NCB 1429/1.
[3] SCL Carlton Main MD 4080–9 annual balance sheets, MB 27 Nov. 1872, 6 July 1873, 27 Feb.
1873, 2 May 1873, 9 Dec. 1873, 6 Apr. 1874, 12 June 1874, 26 Aug. 1874, 6 Jan. 1875, 5 May 1875, 5
Sept. 1877, 2 Jan. 1878.
[4] BSCEMRRC Stanton and Staveley 2034/7/2 MB 15 Nov. 1865.

From the beginning of its operations in 1864 the Powell Duffryn colliery relied on overdraft facilities at Glyn Mills Currie and Co. (though these disappeared in the 1880s). From the 1890s both the Cardiff Steam Coal and the Main Colliery companies used overdraft facilities.[1]

In the West Midlands, Cocks and Biddulph agreed to loan Cannock Chase Colliery Company £15,000 in 1877 on the security of preference shares, though after a year that loan became repayable at one month's notice.[2] During the same trading recession the Yorkshire and Derbyshire Coal and Iron Company (later to become Carlton Main) secured an overdraft with the Sheffield and Rotherham Bank, though the managers insisted on the condition that the remaining hundred shares of the company should be issued and called up, and that any future overdraft should not exceed £20,000, unless underwritten by the personal guarantees of one or more of the directors or shareholders. The response of the directors was to renegotiate loans on the personal liability of shareholders, offering to pay 5 per cent on mortgages and less than 7 per cent on ordinary loans. With considerable reluctance, the directors also agreed to guarantee an excess overdraft of £6,000 with their personal liability.[3]

Ultimately the bank's support depend upon the resources of individuals. In several cases family connections with banks or directorships may have facilitated the maintenance of liquidity at times when it was threatened; for example, for the Priestmans of the Ashington Coal Company, the Briggs of Henry Briggs and Son, the Knowles of Andrew Knowles and Son, the Peases of Pease and Partners, Charles Carlow of the Fife Coal Company, and Thomas Newton and Arthur Chambers, of the firm of Newton Chambers. Only in the latter case is there evidence of exceptional utilization of the bank's resources. An overdraft limit of £14,000 in 1870 allowed to increase to £20,000 when there is a reference by the partners to a shortage of capital. By 1880 the overdraft had reached £87,647, when the firm was on the verge of a joint-stock flotation capitalized at £0.65m.[4] With the exception of the Wrights' long-standing commitment to Butterley, and the relatively short-lived involvement of J. Carr Glyn and Glyn and Co. with the Clay Cross Company, however, banking connections tended to occur after coal-owners had become successfully established businessmen. That the

[1] Walters 1980, 84.
[2] BUL, BR 14/ii–iii/Cannock Chase Colliery, MB 19 Dec. 1877.
[3] SCL Carlton Main, MD 4080, 6 Dec. 1878, 6 Jan. 1879, 7 July 1879, 3 June 1879.
[4] SCL Newton Chambers TR 450/8/4, 7, 8, 16.

banks were, or could be, important to coalmasters in periods of general commercial difficulty is suggested by the formation of the J. and J. W. Pease bank after the commercial crisis of 1857. The crisis precipitated the eventual failure of the Northumberland and Durham District Bank, which then held colliery and other industrial securities valued at £350,000, excluding those underpinning a debt of £750,000 to Consett, to which Johnathan Richardson, the bank manager, had leased mineral rights.[1] John Bowes and partners grew large during the mid-nineteenth century by taking over collieries either in decline or pressed into liquidation, the bank to which the partnership was indebted figuring more than once in the sale of bankrupt collieries to which the bank had also been creditors.[2]

In summing up the evidence on financing the coal industry between 1830 and 1913, it is important to underline the differences between the longer gestation period in mining compared with other industries, particularly for medium-sized firms and larger, and the high risk level associated with mining arising from natural as distinct from commercial factors, though the coal industry was not, of course, insulated from these either. The coincidence of demand both for fixed and working capital during the period of gestation meant that during the initial phase of colliery enterprise, revenue, and therefore profits, were simply not available for ploughing back. This explains why private wealth was a principal source for initial capital investment. After a lag, profits retained in the business provided supplementary resources for expansion through additional calls on partners or shareholders, typically small in number even in 1913. Public subscription played a very limited role, and even when new capital was introduced to firms undergoing conversion from proprietorships, partnerships, or private companies to public companies, such flotations did not necessarily involve additional net investment. Much of the capital invested originated from within the coal industry, augmented by contributions from iron masters and other major business sources, but capital from professional groups and owners of private wealth also played an important role, both inside and outside public companies. The same is true for the provision of long-term loans in the form of mortgages or debentures to supplement other sources. Short-term loans and bank overdrafts provided temporary finance, overdraft and trade credit supplying working capital and emergency resourcing to enable collieries to cope with commercial

[1] *SC Bank Acts and Commercial Distress* 1857–8, V, 324–5.
[2] Mountford thesis, 59.

crises or to meet other contingencies. Relatively high levels of reserves, held either in suspense or depreciation funds or in the form of liquid assets, are indicative of cautious financial policies associated with the maintenance of ownership and control, offering limited scope for the role of external finance before 1914.

Appendix 2.1. Constant price index for capital (sinking) costs, 1830–1913

Current price series for the major items used in sinking and opening out a new colliery are not difficult to assemble, but deciding upon the weights to be attached to the multiple inputs poses serious problems; in particular, that of identifying the labour component in the sinking and equipping of a new mine before disaggregating the various capital components. Itemized cost accounts for sinking can be found in textbooks and in the periodical literature, but only exceptionally are labour costs separated from material costs in each of the different processes involved in winning and completing a new colliery. Yet such separation, while unnecessary in an analysis of alterations in asset structures, is critical in analysing the changing costs of a process. The earliest usable valuations apply to two pits in the North-east in 1839 and 1841, which give a cost breakdown of 45 per cent for labour, 35 per cent for engines and plant, 20 per cent for other materials.[1] At another unnamed colliery in Durham the cost of shafts was reported to have been 48 per cent of total capital costs.[2] Two more observations, both from Staveley collieries in the East Midlands sunk in the 1850s, reveal figures of 45 per cent and 38 per cent for labour, 34 per cent and 26 per cent for engines and pumps, and 21 per cent and 36 per cent for materials.[3] Four of these observations, however, referred to pits of above average size and technical endowment; consequently for our purpose these proportions need to be adjusted to reflect a national average, taking into account the considerable amount of drift mining and small shafts to be found in most regions. A distribution for the mid-nineteenth century of 52 per cent labour, 28 per cent engines and plant, and 20 per cent other materials was considered to satisfy these requirements.

For the later period archival information is even scarcer. The Merthyr

---

[1] NuRO Armstrong 725/B20, report books 95–101; NEI Johnson Shelf 4, vol. 9 reports 5 Jan. 1841. [2] Fordyce 1860, 47.

[3] BSCEMRRC Stanton and Staveley 2034/3/12 Hollingwood and Seymour Colliery new sinkings capital accounts, 1857–63.

Vale deep sinking in South Wales in the 1870s indicated shaft/plant ratios of 32.5 per cent for labour costs, and 21.5 per cent for tubbing and castings, timber, bricks, and nails.[1]

Assuming that one-third of labour costs were expended on surface work and the erection of machinery, and that one-third of material costs (excluding tubbing and castings) were similarly consumed, this leaves roughly 40 per cent of total costs (as defined in this case) attributable to expenditure on shafts. As this includes outlay on non-mining elements (houses for example), a figure of 46 per cent would be a more accurate estimate relating to the shaft component of mining as distinct from colliery capital.[2] In the 1880s a comparable proportion for shaft sinking at Staveley's Markham colliery was 42 per cent.[3] In 1909 Redmayne used as an example a colliery in which the sinking costs alone represented 55 per cent of total costs, though as the 'total' excluded such major capital items as railways, railway stock, and cokeworks an adjusted figure of 48 per cent seems to be justified. In another example, when railways and cokeworks were included in 'total capital costs', sinking costs can be put at roughly 40 per cent.[4] In a third example, quoted by T. F. Brown and G. F. Adams, shaft sinking and opening out underground were reckoned to be 43 per cent of total costs.[5]

Unfortunately, accounts in the later period were designed to identify the costs of successive *stages of the processes* of sinking and surface construction, stages in which labour and material costs are combined. As surface arrangements and technical endowment became more advanced it seems inevitable that the labour component would diminish as a proportion of total cost. However, a corollary of deep sinking accompanied by greater technical endowment is the augmentation of the capital element in costs. This follows from the fact that, in effect, large pits substitute capital for working costs, resulting in overall initial endowments with a capital bias. On balance, the effect of two conflicting trends upon the labour–capital ratio in newly-sunk collieries seems likely to have been to increase capital intensity over time, but at a

[1] Walters 1977, Table 30, recalculated.

[2] For the difference in definitions in mining and colliery capital see p. xxx.

[3] BSCEMRRC Stanton and Staveley 2034/3/2, Markham Colliery Sinking, capital accounts.

[4] Redmayne 1914, II, 189–90.

[5] Brown and Adams 1881, 95–6. Three other figures, referring to 1881, 1887, and 1892, put labour costs of shaft sinking as percentages of total costs at 43.5 per cent, 50 per cent, and 46.5 per cent. John Daglish, 'The Sinking of Two Shafts at Marsden for the Whitburn Coal Company', *PICE*, LXXI (1883), 195; J. H. Merivale, 'Notes and Formulae for Mining Students', (1887), 176; and Galloway, quoted in H. S. Jevons 1915, 193–4.

modest rate of substitution. Accordingly, we have adopted weights by which the labour–capital component falls from 52 per cent in 1840, to 45 per cent in 1880, and to 40 per cent in 1910.

A problem of disaggregation still remains, the solution for which we must rely on other sources. Expert contemporary estimates, taken together with evidence from our analysis of the fixed asset structure of collieries, suggest that a reasonable average figure for the shaft-sinking component only (that is, excluding the costs of equipping a new colliery) is 45 per cent. There seems to be no compelling reason why this should have altered between 1880 and 1910, since as pits became deeper and more technically sophisticated a rough balance between shaft-sinking costs and 'construction' and plant costs was probably maintained. The contribution of labour to shaft sinking was necessarily high. In *A Text Book of Coal Mining*, published in 1892, H. W. Hughes quoted Brown and Adam's figure of 75 per cent (in 1881) and materials at 25 per cent.[1]. An American example for 1903 attributed 79 per cent of the costs of a sinking to labour (when hand power and explosives only were used).[2]

Adopting 75 per cent as the labour costs in shaft sinking implies that when expressed as percentages of the overall cost of shaft sinking and equipping the colliery in around 1880, 33.75 per cent (i.e. 75 per cent of 45 per cent) comprises labour costs in shaft sinking, and 11.25 per cent (i.e. 25 per cent of 45 per cent) was attributable to materials used in shaft sinking. Therefore, where the overall labour component is 45 per cent in 1880 (50 per cent in 1850 and 40 per cent in 1910), the proportion of labour in equipping alone (excluding shaft sinking) must be 11.25 per cent (that is, 45 per cent less 33.75 per cent), leaving a residual 43.75 per cent for materials in construction and furnishing (mainly plant).

Assuming, for the reasons advanced earlier, that changes were uniform over time, it is possible to apply these values in estimating the proportions for the entire period. In this process of maintaining a balance between labour and non-labour costs (50:45:40 at benchmark dates 1850, 1880, and 1910), the ratio between shaft sinking and other work, is altered over time, the ratio falling from 47.6 per cent in 1850 to 42.7 per cent in 1910. These figures compare closely with Redmayne's figure of 45 per cent in 1910.

The disaggregation of the materials component depends upon our

---

[1] Brown and Adams 1881, 95–6.
[2] T. A. Rickard (ed.), *The Economics of Mining* (New York, 1907), 14.

estimates (derived from company data)[1] of the values of different categories of fixed capital, defined for this purpose as excluding all buildings except those directly related to mining operations. Amending these to exclude the shafts or 'mines' category, which consists mainly of labour costs in sinking, capital costs in this restricted definition may be allocated as follows: plant and coke works 66 per cent, railways and wagons 22 per cent, and brick works and buildings 12 per cent. These weights, which need to be deflated to levels representing their weighting in the overall (that is, capital plus labour) cost of new mines are derived from company data for the second half of the period; but in the absence of relevant information we are compelled to assume that the relative proportions also apply to 1830–70 (and to assume stability within the two periods). These categories may be regarded as equivalent to those referred to by Feinstein, who has constructed price series for 'plant and machinery', 'rolling stock', and 'other construction work'.[2]

While Feinstein's price indexes serve our purpose for most of our period, only decadal averages are available before 1855. We have found it necessary, therefore, to reconstitute the relevant annual price series for 1830–54. In the absence of a price series for rolling stock in this period we have merged railways and wagons with the plant and machinery index for those years. The weights Feinstein attributes in the 1830–54 series are, when adjusted for our requirements: plant, railways, and wagons—engineering wages and iron; building and brickworks—building wages, timber, bricks and iron. And to these we have added weights for materials used in shaft sinking—bricks, timber, and iron. The final constant price index for capital costs has been calculated and expressed in 1900 prices. In order to distinguish between, on the one hand, bricks, timber, and iron used in shaft sinking, and on the other, items of plant themselves, it was necessary to subdivide the plant and coke works category accordingly. Following our estimate that in 1880 some 11.25 per cent of the materials were consumed in shaft sinking (i.e. bricks, iron, and timber), and taking into account trends in colliery construction over time, we have devised a set of distributions between these three material inputs. Assuming regular and uniform changes over time, in which the labour component falls by 0.2 per cent per annum from 1840, the final weights, including labour, were derived as shown in Table 2.13.

Feinstein's 'plant and machinery' index was devised as a general

---

[1] See Appendix 2.3, especially Tables 2.15 and 2.16.
[2] Feinstein 1972, Table 63.

Table 2.13 *Input weights for shaft sinking, 1830–1910*

	Labour	Colliery plant	Railways and wagons	Surface buildings	Materials used in shaft		
					bricks	timber	iron
1830	54		31	5	3	5	2
1840	52		33	5	3	5	2
1855	49	25	11	5	3	4	3
1880	44	28	12	6	4	3	3
1910	38	33	13	6	4	2	4

industrial category and, *faute de mieux*, the use of this index requires the assumption that the price of colliery plant and equipment moved in step. His figures for rolling stock, based on Mitchell's analysis of railway company accounts, appear to exclude the cost of rails, an omission which, however, is unlikely to distort the series sufficiently to disqualify its adoption for our railways and wagons category. Finally, Feinstein's 'other construction work' index, based on Maiwald, which refers to brick costs and basic materials, is readily applicable to our buildings category. The index is presented in Table 2.14.

Appendix 2.2. Estimates of capital formation

All figures are either of peak years or, where appropriate, of cycles post-peak to peak, the justification being that peak years may be regarded as having produced conditions closest to full capacity. Moreover, since the course of each cycle shows a tendency to rise rapidly followed by a more gradual fall, a procedure which adopted peak years with trough-to-trough cycles gave erroneous cycle lengths, especially in the period 1907–13 when 1913 was the peak of an incomplete cycle. The output data used in column 2 of Table 2.1 are of detrended production from an eleven-year moving-average, though the figure for 1913 was interpolated from the shorter trend in order to avoid distortion of the total. An added advantage of this procedure was that where the peak year for certain indicators was not generally chosen, the relationship is not unduly affected, since our calculations in effect show estimates of capital *around* the peak.

The capital–output ratios presented in Table 2.2 (column 3) are based on estimates made by experts and appeared in contemporary mining literature. The key figure is 10s. per ton, which was quoted in 1894 in an article on 'The Profit of Coal Pits' by G. P. Bidder, chairman and managing director of the Cannock Chase Colliery Company and director of the Main Colliery Company in South Wales.[1] A similar figure was implied by capital estimates for the industry made a few years later by J. B. Simpson and by James Joicey, both prominent colliery

---

[1] Bidder 1894, 808. Bidder's figure referred to capital employed in 'the original and subsequent development [sinking and opening out], sidings, plant of all kinds and working capital'. However, working capital, which of course is excluded from our capital–output ratio, probably counted for 6 to 10 per cent of mining assets (see pp. xxx–x). Taking this into account, Bidder's figure of 10s. has been adopted for the benchmark year 1900 since his estimate referred to a year when price and output were substantially below the peak of 1900.

Table 2.14. *Constant price index of capital sinking cost estimates, 1830-1913*
(1900 = 100)

1830	69.1	1851	63.6	1872	96.1	1893	81.5
1831	70.5	1852	64.7	1873	109.4	1894	81.5
1832	68.3	1853	70.1	1874	101.4	1895	79.2
1833	69.3	1854	78.3	1875	90.9	1896	79.2
1834	71.0	1855	80.3	1876	87.0	1897	80.4
1835	69.7	1856	80.7	1877	81.8	1898	82.7
1836	77.9	1857	75.5	1878	77.6	1899	90.0
1837	78.7	1858	71.6	1879	74.1	1900	100
1838	75.9	1859	71.1	1880	76.0	1901	98.6
1839	77.7	1860	71.7	1881	75.0	1902	93.0
1840	77.8	1861	71.3	1882	77.4	1903	91.1
1841	74.7	1862	72.0	1883	76.7	1904	89.6
1842	69.9	1863	74.0	1884	75.8	1905	87.5
1843	64.9	1864	77.3	1885	73.4	1906	90.1
1844	65.4	1865	79.6	1886	70.7	1907	95.5
1845	72.4	1866	81.9	1887	70.4	1908	96.7
1846	74.0	1867	77.1	1888	71.2	1909	93.4
1847	74.3	1868	74.0	1889	76.8	1910	93.9
1848	67.5	1869	74.0	1890	88.1	1911	95.5
1849	65.8	1870	77.0	1891	87.6	1912	98.6
1850	64.4	1871	82.5	1892	85.2	1913	104.6

Sources:
1. Hewers' wages, UK mean (see below).
2. Plant: 1830–54, engineers' wages from A. L. Bowley and G. H. Wood, 'The Statistics of Wages during the Nineteenth Century (Part XIV), Engineering and Shipbuilding', *JRSS* LXIX (1906), 190, and iron prices from W. S. Jevons, 'On the Variation of Prices and the Value of Currency since 1782', *JRSS* XXVIII (1865), 317. For 1855–1913 see C. H. Feinstein's 'Plant and Machinery Index' in *National Income*, Table 63.
3. Railways and wagons: 1830–54, as 2 above; 1855–1913, C. H. Feinstein's index of 'Railway Rolling Stock' in *National Income*, Table 63.
4. Buildings: 1830–54, Building wages from A. L. Bowley, 'The Statistics of Wages in the United Kingdom during the last Hundred Years (Part VIII) Wages in the Building Trades' *JRSS* LXIX (1901), 112.
5. Bricks: 1845–1913, follows Maiwald's sources. Laxton's *Builders' Price Books* provide data for 1845 onwards only and contains no retrospective data. The 1830–1844 extrapolations based on the Gayer, Rostow, Schwartz index of domestic commodities are the least satisfactory of all our indices. Only the minimal proportion of total capital costs, bricks, justifies proceeding further with the construction of the overall index.
6. Wood: 1845–1913 follows Maiwald (1845–1913) and Feinstein (1830–44), except that in the latter case the series for Quebec yellow pine, employed by Feinstein, has been omitted as unsuitable, leaving our price series referring only to memel fir. Unfortunately we have no data on either the type of wood used by collieries in this period or on the prices of timber originating from out-

Sources to Table 2.14 (cont.)

side the Baltic. A lack of information on duties further complicate this exercise. As in the case of bricks, however, our timber weighting is small and errors in this series, while regrettable, need not invalidate the overall index.

7. Iron: 1830–1913, W. S. Jevons, 'On the Variation of Prices', 317. 1846–1913, Prices of common bars given in Mitchell and Deane 1962, 493.

owners in the North-east.[1] In an article published in the *Colliery Managers' Pocket Book* in 1903, edited by R. A. S. Redmayne, John Merivale adopted J. B. Simpson's estimate (of 9s. per ton), the explanation for which was that the scale of operations in Northumberland, the specific subject of his discussion of profitability, justified this figure,[2] but for the industry nationally this implied a higher figure. These various estimates—or implied estimates—of 10s. per ton later became the subject of discussion in the Samuel Commission, when Sir Josiah Stamp confirmed that this figure would have been correct for the 1890s, but that a higher figure would have been more accurate for the years between 1900 and 1913, though not by a large percentage.[3] But both his own aggregate figures for capitalization in 1913 and those cited by S. O. Davies produce a figure much closer to 10s. than to the 15s. which Stamp thought might have been reached just before the War; Jeans's 1907 estimate implied 11s. per ton.[4] In the context of increasing depths, widths, and difficulties in mining, the figure adopted is 10s. per ton at current prices in 1900 rising to 10s. 10d. for the cycle round the 1907 peak, to reach 11s. 2d. for the years between 1907 and 1913. From 1900 we have extrapolated backwards. The figure of 8s. per ton for 1890 derives in part from a statement made by G. Lewis that a modern colliery (say roughly 250,000 tons a year) would require approximately £100,000 to equip and open out.[5] When adjusted for price changes this figure is suitably below the 1900 estimate, thereby allowing for a certain growth of capital–output ratios in the 1890s as deeper collieries were won. A further growth in average levels of capital–output (at constant prices) between 1883 and 1890 seems likely in view of the closure of many of the smaller collieries on the outcrop, which had enjoyed a brief existence during and after the coal famine. This explains why a figure of 7s. at current prices has been

[1] Simpson 1900, 10, 25; *The Times* 22 May 1901.
[2] John H. Merivale, 'The Profits of Coalmining', in Redmayne (ed.), 1903, 45–6.
[3] *Samuel Commission* II, Part A, QQ 5270, 5286–8.
[4] Ibid., para. 119 and III, 272; *Eight Hours Committee*, 1907, XV, QQ 14893–911.
[5] G. Lewis, 'Presidential Address', *TFIME*, X (1892–3), 3–4.

adopted, based on mining engineer Arthur Sopwith's hypothetical example.[1] For the same reason, average levels of capital–output would have risen, though less steeply, between 1873 and 1883, and if steady rates of growth at constant prices had been maintained during those years than the current price figure for the peak in 1873 is likely to have been around 9s. 7d., the figure adopted here. For 1866, four years after the sinking of two shafts instead of one became a statutory requirement for safety reasons, we have relied upon the mining engineer G. C. Greenwell's estimate that a £10,000 outlay would be needed to produce an annual output of 30,000 tons,[2] though an allowance for the disproportionate effect of smaller than average and therefore less efficient collieries which flourished during the pre-boom years of the 1870s warrants a slight upward revision to 7s. In the absence of estimates from reliable sources the figures for 1826–54 are problematical and may be described as guesses based on the probable movement of capital–output ratios, at constant prices, during these years. While considerable data exist for the North-east for the 1830s and 1840s, the highly capitalized character of the industry in this region, which supplied almost a quarter of national coal production, provides an unrepresentative basis for simple extrapolation to the rest of the country. Buddle's often-quoted estimate of capital stock for the Tyne and Wear industry in 1829 of between £2.1m. and £2.2m. implies a capital–output ratio of 6s. 3d. to 6s. 6d. per ton.[3] Because of deeper working in this region, however, the North-eastern ratios are likely to have been relatively high in the 1830s and 1840s, after which they will have fallen relative to national levels, as drift and outcrop mining in other regions gradually gave way to the larger scale operations justified by market developments. It is suggested, therefore, that a growth in capital–output ratios of a shilling at constant prices between 1826 and 1854 is a plausible, perhaps even a conservative, assumption. The figures in column 3 of Table 2.2 also assume, on the basis of impressionistic evidence, that changes in mining practice and coalfield growth occurred mainly from about 1840 (see Chapter 4).

After deciding upon estimates of capital–output ratios, at current costs, these were converted to constant prices by applying the sinking-cost index devised in Appendix 2.1. The productive capital totals (Table 2.1, column 4) are calculated by multiplying these ratios by detrended output. Annual capital formation (column 5) is an average

[1] A. Sopwith, 'Depreciation of Colliery Plant', *TSSEWIME*, IX (1883), 143.
[2] G. C. Greenwell, 'The Rating of Mines', *TNEIME*, XIV (1865), 95.
[3] *SC Lords of Coal* 1830, VIII, 52.

about the peak year, being the average rate of growth in output
between one peak and the next multiplied by the middle peak capital-
output ratio, and is an approximation of the rate of investment at that
peak. The investment lags (column 6) are those previously estimated
on the basis of sinking times which vary according to the depth of
mines—the unproductive capital estimates which follow from these
(column 7) are the product of annual investment rates and these lags,
which were of crucial importance in influencing capital–output rates.

The evidence on mine depths derives from the Children's Employment Commission of 1842–3, Matthias Dunn's enumeration of the
depth and thickness of coal seams in 1852 in *Winning and Working*,
Leifchild's data for the North-east from The Midland Mining Commission of 1843, several Royal Commissions on accidents in the 1840s and
1850s, and the very valuable Samuel Commission.[1] The latter is particularly useful in containing a comprehensive analysis of output from
different depths on the basis of data covering 85 per cent of the industry, broken down by regions (though it refers only to 1913).
Almost all of the early data refer to average depth of shafts, rather
than to the average depth from which coal was wound; but since we are
attempting to assess capital employed the difference is of little significance, as the discrepancy would affect working costs rather than
capital. Interpolations for the intervening cycles are based on our
knowledge of the progress of the industry and sundry contemporary
observations.

Investment lags estimated by combining sinking times with mine
depths enable us to estimate unproductive capital, which are the
product of annual investment rates and these lags (column 7 of Table
2.1). The total replacement capital (column 8) is the sum of productive
and unproductive elements (columns 4 and 7) and the gross capital-
output ratio (this figure divided by output).

The historic capital estimates are derived in a similar manner. Beginning with our estimate of £6m. in 1826, the cumulative historic capital
(column 11) is constructed by adding for each cycle the net additions to
capital made during that cycle (column 10). The latter are calculated by

[1] Estimated average depths of UK mines, derived from regional depth estimates, which were
weighted by regional output estimates were interpolated between 1840 and 1913 (and extended
to 1827–38) as follows (metres):

1872–38	100	1874–83	170
1839–47	110	1884–90	190
1848–54	120	1891–1900	230
1855–66	130	1901–07	270
1867–73	150	1908–13	310

adding the increase in productive capital to the net change in unproductive capital. The formula is as follows: new productive capital = increase in output peak to peak × average capital–output ratio; change in unproductive capital = the difference between one cycle and the preceding cycle.

Thus, for the 1854 peak (cycle 1848–54) the increase in historic capital is estimated as follows:

$$(72.8 - 55.2\text{m. tons} = 17.6\text{m. tons}) \times \frac{(\pounds 0.40 + \pounds 0.39)}{2}$$

$$+ (\pounds 2.38\text{m.} - \pounds 2.0\text{m.}) = \pounds(17.6 \times 0.295)\text{m.} + \pounds 0.83\text{m.} = \pounds 7.78\text{m.}$$

The historic capital–output ratio at each peak (column 12) is calculated by dividing historic capital by output. Depreciation was assumed at 4 per cent before 1873, and 5 per cent thereafter, calculated in column 13 from the (unrounded) capital–output ratio: that is, capital (column 12) divided by output (column 2). Total depreciation throughout the course of any post-peak to peak cycle may be approximated as the average output over that cycle (the mean of peaks), multiplied by the number of years in that cycle, times the average of depreciation rates for that peak and the preceding peak. The amount of depreciation which should have taken place over any cycle, on our assumptions based on best practice, of 5 per cent post 1873 and 4 per cent before 1873 are reasonable rates to assume as normal, (column 14) and may be compared with our estimates of net investment over that cycle in column 10.

Each of the calculations, which are based on estimates of varying reliability, are subject to margins of error. The capital–output estimates are the key to reproducible capital figures, while historic capital is also critically dependent upon the estimate for 1826. Any error at that stage will have been magnified in subsequent cycles because of the cumulative character of the exercise, but the marginal error expressed as a percentage will have decreased over time. Mining capital in constant prices has been converted to current prices and shown in Table 2.2.

Appendix 2.3. Estimates of mining and colliery asset structures

The shaft component excepted, balance sheets and colliery accounts do offer a method by which to estimate the relative values of different items in the fixed-asset structure, though there are difficulties which need to be considered. Not surprisingly, the method of accounting and the subdivision of assets recorded is different from company to company, which presents problems of comparison. Differences in definition are more problematical, since it is clear that many commonly named assets, 'pits' for example, lack a common definition. Depreciation allowances differ, too. Faced with the need to try to present a more detailed picture of asset structure, however, it is possible to make calculations which achieve a degree of reconciliation between the various accounts and which we regard as sufficient to justify adopting the results as crude averages indicative of asset structure as a whole and on the basis of which limited generalizations can be made. A further problem arises from the fact that the company data including detailed material on tangible assets is not only limited in volume, deriving from less than a dozen major colliery companies, but is also confined, at least for more than a single company, to the period after 1870. A small amount of surviving evidence on the asset structure prior to 1870 was discussed in Appendix 2.2.

It is clearly hazardous to generalize concerning asset structure, partly because of the paucity of data, partly because the industry was so diverse. After 1870, however, data from company accounts become relatively more abundant and contain greater detail, which renders possible a disaggregated analysis of fixed mining and colliery assets. The estimates contained in Table 2.15 should be regarded only as indicative of the probable composition of the mining assets of sizeable colliery companies. The problems of interpreting correctly nineteenth-century colliery accounts include the need to reconcile unorthodox accounting and genuinely eccentric asset structure with what seems likely, on the basis of other company accounts, to have been more conventional practice, in conformity with an asset structure that was typical of mining and colliery operations. For example, the accounts of some companies—Briggs, Carlton Main, Walsall Wood, and New Hucknall—excluded specific values for railways, yet we know that they existed; we must conclude, therefore, that this item was included in 'colliery plant'. The same is true for wagons, the possession of which has been established but which were entered as part of either colliery plant or railways; for it seems fairly clear that colliery plant, railways, and wagons were assets common to all colliery companies. In these instances we have recast the accounts on the basis of crude average values (and proportions) which relate to the mining capital of these companies where these items are specified, hypothesizing a capital structure for those companies where the accounts lacked detailed definition, but at the same time attempting

Table 2.15. *Composition of mining assets, 1870–1913*
(percentages)

	1 Colliery plant	2 Railways ways	3 Wagons	4 Coke works	5 Brick works	6 Horses	7 Gate roads
Lochgelly, 1873–1903	$52\frac{1}{2}$	$12\frac{1}{2}$	34			1	
Lochgelly 1906–13	72[a]	28					
Carlton Main 1880–1909	$84\frac{1}{2}$		$10\frac{1}{2}$	5			
Henry Briggs 1879–1900	$97\frac{1}{2}$[a]				$2\frac{1}{2}$		
Consett 1864–1914	83[a]	17					
Ashington 1884	$75\frac{1}{2}$	$20\frac{1}{2}$			4		
Hamstead 1875–1908	$86\frac{1}{2}$		$\frac{1}{2}$		3		10
Walsall Wood 1877–1913	$78\frac{1}{2}$		$9\frac{1}{2}$		12		
New Hucknall 1879–1913	87		5	$7\frac{1}{2}$		$\frac{1}{2}$	
Powell Duffryn 1888–1913	87	$6\frac{1}{2}$	$6\frac{1}{2}$				
Crude average	$80\frac{1}{2}$	$8\frac{1}{2}$	$6\frac{1}{2}$	$1\frac{1}{2}$	2	—	1
Crude average ex-Lochgelly 1873–1903	$83\frac{1}{2}$	8	$3\frac{1}{2}$	$1\frac{1}{2}$	$2\frac{1}{2}$	—	1

[a] Includes some valuation for pits.

Source: Lochgelly: ScRO, CB2/131–2; 155–9. Carlton Main: SCL, annual balance sheets in Directors Minutes, II–IX. Henry Briggs: LCA, balance sheets and annual reports in Directors' Minutes. Consett: BSNRRC, 13251, statement of fixed assets. Ashington: NuRO, NCB/AS/12, valuation of assets 1884, 2MD 54/26, valuation of assets 1868, NCB/AS/6, valuation of assets 1880, AS/18/1, valuation of assets, 1898. Hamstead: StRO, D876/10–17, balance sheets and annual reports in Directors' Minutes. Walsall Wood: StRO, D876/39 balance sheets. New Hucknall: NoRO, NCB1/13–15 balance sheets and annual reports. Powell Duffryn: balance sheets, Powell Duffryn Ltd., Stanhope Gate.

to preserve the individuality and basic variety of the evidence from sampled firms. Furthermore, the possibility still exists that in some companies items assessed as parts of 'colliery plant' ought to be separately valued as coke works, brick works, horses, or the like, though it is at least certain that any errors in this direction would risk only minor distortion of the figures. However, with regard to brick works, coke works, and horses, for which there are numerous gaps, it seems preferable to refer to averages not for collieries as a whole but of averages *for collieries where such assets existed* (or were valued separately). The figures which result (Table 2.16) indicate three-quarters of mining assets to have comprised colliery plant, 11 per cent railways, 5.5 per cent wagons, 4 per cent coke works, 3.5 per cent brick works, and horses roughly one per cent.

Table 2.16. *Revised mining-asset structure, 1870-1913*
(percentages)

	Colliery plant	Railways	Wagons	Coke works	Brick works	Horses
Lochgelly	61½[a]	20	8	6[b]	3½[b]	1
Carlton Main	75½	8	10½	5		1[b]
Briggs	79½[a]	8	3	6[b]	2½	1[b]
Consett	76[a]	14	3	6[b]		1[b]
Ashington	74½	17½	3		4	1[b]
Hamstead	86	9	½		3½	1[b]
Walsall Wood	69½	8	9½		12	1[b]
New Hucknall	75½	8	5	7½	3½[b]	½
Powell Duffryn	76½	6½	6½	6[b]	3½[b]	1[b]
Mean	75	11	5½	4	3½	1

[a] Includes some valuation for pits; see below.
[b] Estimated.

By far the largest item, colliery plant, was itself a composite category in which some companies (not only those in our sample) included such items as 'pits' or 'sinking pits', or that of land, houses, and farm buildings, so that even when we have adjusted the figures for plant to take into account railways, wagons, coke works, and horses, 'colliery plant' may still incorporate at least part of the value of the mine or the shafts themselves. Among the companies in our sample, Briggs, Consett, and Lochgelly adopted this practice. But any distortion which might be expected to result from this definition is likely to have been extremely limited; only the Briggs and Consett figures show colliery plant with above-average values, and even then the deviation from the norm is very small. Briggs and Consett are the only companies in our group for which it is possible to identify pits and plant separately, but the valuation of plant is so low (at only a quarter of mining assets) as to suggest that much of the value of plant has been incorporated into the 'pits' category. Only Briggs presents a plausible example of the distinction between the value of 'pits', accounting for 29 per cent of stated assets, engines and machinery 54 per cent, and moveable plant 17 per cent. Our discussion of sinking costs revealed the importance of shaft building and the difficulty of estimating their magnitude.

However, determining what proportion of capital was necessary for shaft sinking and opening out underground presents less difficulty than deciding *the proportion of this cost which was effectively capitalized in company accounts*. Any search for a solution of this problem is bedevilled by the disparate methods and principles of accounting practiced by colliery companies, though it is possible to assess the level of under-capitalization to be found among our company sample. The historic ratios at current prices calculated independently (largely from technical rather than company data) for the industry as a whole may be regarded as the capital–output ratios which firms *should have possessed had they been fully capitalized*. A comparison of the companies' stated capital–output ratios in peak years with industry-average ratios will reveal the extent of under-capitalization which our evidence from company accounts had suggested was widespread. Indeed, the results confirm this supposition. For nine companies the estimated level of company capitalization before 1900 was roughly 90 per cent of the true level and nearer 80 per cent thereafter to 1913. It also seems probable that the costing of shafts and colliery plant were those elements which were almost entirely responsible for under-capitalization, compounded by a degree of confusion between the two categories. Clearly, if shafts comprised some 40 per cent of capital costs then a proportion of this value must have been incorporated in the company assets. Moreover, the greater likelihood is that shafts were under-capitalized by an amount accounting for the entire under-capitalization of assets, rather than under-capitalization of each element in mining assets by appropriate amounts.

The implication of such a judgement is the need to amend our earlier estimates of the distribution of mining assets. If we fix the proportions for railways, wagons, coke works, brick works, and horses at the level of 25 per cent of mining assets, the remaining 75 per cent in 'colliery plant' should then be reallocated in such a way that 40 per cent of the total is attributed to shafts, as suggested by the literature.[1] The result is to reduce colliery plant to 35 per cent of total mining assets. Such a re-adjustment may imply a less than perfect balance between shaft and colliery plant, but arguably any doubt about the figures can be proportionate only to the conceptual problems involved in deciding exactly what constitutes 'shafts' as distinct from 'plant'. The revised formula requires a revision of the distributions of mining capital in 1870–1913 as follows: value of shafts 40 per cent; colliery plant 35 per cent; railways 11 per cent; wagons 5 per cent; coke works 4 per cent; brick works 4 per cent; horses 1 per cent. We must stress the tentative character of this exercise, and that the variety of the estimates found in the company and technical data indicate clearly that at any single point in time differences between collieries tend to swamp changes over time in 'average' ratios.

We are left with important omissions, the first being the asset value of main-gate roadways, for among all the data we have examined, only two firms, Hampstead and Briggs, appear to have attributed underground roadways to fixed assets.[2] The explanation probably lies in both companies' practice of working coal by the longwall retreating method, which involved initial capital expenditure on main-gate roads and stall headings prior to mining. Coal which was won in the process of driving these roads and headings was sold, and its value deducted from the costs. Between 1884 and 1908 approximately 10 per cent of fixed colliery plant was attributed to this item at Hampstead, and 5 per cent at Briggs between 1879 and 1908. None of our other companies worked longwall retreating, and we have no information from other sources except a statement from an accountancy textbook in 1909, which regarded the attribution of costs incurred in underground roadways to working costs as having been normal colliery practice.[3] Between 5 and 10 per cent of mining assets as defined by the company, and 3 to 6 per cent as in our revised definition which includes the shaft, sinking/labour element and underground roadways, could, on the basis of our average percentage estimates of mining capital, equal or exceed the asset value of coke works and brick works. Clearly, two observations cannot form an adequate basis on which to recast our figures on mining and colliery

---

[1] See Appendix 2.1.

[2] StaRO Hamstead, D 876/11 Directors' Reports 1881, 1884; LCA 1708/15 Anon 'Down Amongst the Coals: Descriptions of the Collieries and Works of Messrs H. Briggs, Sons and Co Ltd, near Normanton', 7–29.

[3] J. Mann and H. Judd, *Colliery Accounts* (London 1909), 68.

capital, but the conclusion to be drawn from the Hampstead accounts should not be disregarded completely as a guide to the relative magnitude of this item in the industry's capital structure. Each colliery must have possessed several miles of underground main roads which, there is little doubt, had they been capitalized would have reached that scale of importance.[1] Neither the exclusion of this component from fixed assets as we have defined them, nor the probability that our figures underestimate mining and colliery capital, should be overlooked.

[1] In 1861 twenty miles of underground road and railway were in operation at the collieries of Staveley Coal and Iron Company: CG 13 Apr. 1861, 231.

CHAPTER 3

Labour Supply and the Labour Market

i. Size and structure of the labour force

By 1913 roughly one in every five males employed in mining, manufacturing, and building was a colliery worker. As the sixth-largest industrial employer of males in 1841, coalmining rose to third place among the largest industries in the transport, building, manufacturing, and mining sectors, and by 1911 was second only to the conglomerate census category of metal manufactures, machines, implements, vehicles, and precious metals. The number of colliery workers had risen from an estimated 109,000 in 1830 to 1,095,000 in 1913 (Table 3.1),[1] which represented a rise from 5 per cent to nearly 12 per cent of all employment in the mining, manufacturing, and building sectors. While manufacturing employment more than doubled and building employment grew threefold, the size of the coalmining work-force increased ten times during the same period, 1841–1913. This reflected not only the immense growth in coal production,[2] also approximately tenfold, but also the labour intensity which was characteristic of this major growth industry.

With the exceptions of the 1860s and 1890s, estimated decadal growth rates in employment exceeded 30 per cent; in the 1840s the rate is estimated to have reached 50 per cent. After 1871 the upward trend was interrupted only during the slump following the 1870s boom, when employment fell in three consecutive years in 1876–8, in 1893, and in 1896.

A marked disparity in the growth of regional employment existed; Scotland grew at 8.7 per cent a year compared with 4 per cent in South Wales (Table 3.2). In the 1850s and again in the 1870s Yorkshire and the East Midlands were the regions of greatest acceleration in coalmining

---

[1] The figures for coal mining employment are revised estimates, presented in Tables 3.1 and 3.2; the methods by which they were arrived at are explained in Appendix 3.1. Employment figures for purposes of comparison with other groups are those in Phyllis Deane and W. A. Cole, *British Economic Growth, 1688-1959* (Cambridge, 1969), 143, Table 31.

[2] See Chapter 1.

Table 3.1. *National and regional estimates of coalmining employment, census years 1831–1913*

	1831	1841	1851	1861	1871	1881	1891	1901	1913
Scotland	14,500	21,110	31,750	37,920	47,650	53,800	75,600	99,000	137,900
North-east	21,400	31,000	38,850	50,050	74,300	94,500	121,500	152,800	224,500
Cumberland	1,900	2,500	3,680	4,620	5,000	6,000	7,600	8,700	10,800
Lancs. and Ches.	14,700	20,450	32,450	46,300	54,500	63,200	80,500	91,900	107,100
North Wales	2,600	3,600	4,850	6,540	9,000	9,900	12,500	13,000	15,800
Yorkshire	9,100	13,110	21,500	32,810	44,050	59,200	80,500	103,400	159,600
East Midlands	5,100	6,840	10,750	20,270	29,500	45,500	65,100	84,800	110,900
West Midlands	18,100	23,380	34,750	45,720	54,000	43,400	49,600	62,000	80,800
South Wales	16,600	24,750	32,300	42,980	57,000	71,600	115,600	149,800	232,400
South-west	5,300	6,600	7,400	8,600	11,500	11,500	13,200	13,200	15,400
Totals	109,300	154,040	218,230	295,810	386,500	458,600	621,600	778,700	1,095,200

Sources: See Appendix 3.1.

Table 3.2. *Annual percentage rates of growth in male coalmining employment, by region, 1830–1913*

	1830s	1840s	1850s	1860s	1870s	1880s	1890s	1900s
Scotland	4.6	8.7	1.3	3.2	0.84	3.4	3.4	3.5
North-east	3.9	6.0	2.9	1.9	5.6	3.0	2.4	4.0
Cumberland	4.3	8.0	2.2	0.7	2.1	2.6	1.5	2.3
Lancs. and Ches	3.7	6.8	4.3	1.2	2.3	2.2	1.4	1.9
North Wales	4.2	−0.2	4.1	1.7	3.0	1.3	1.0	2.2
Yorkshire	4.3	6.9	5.5	1.7	5.5	3.1	2.7	4.7
East Midlands	3.0	6.6	8.8	2.8	7.3	3.7	3.0	3.0
West Midlands	3.1	5.0	3.2	0.4	−1.2	2.0	1.8	2.4
South Wales	5.5	4.0	3.3	2.0	3.4	6.2	3.4	4.4
South-west	1.2	1.4	1.5	0.5	2.4	1.9	−0.8	1.4

Sources: As for Table 3.1. the figure for 1830 was based on extrapolation from output.

employment, though thereafter, with the exception of the rapid growth in the South Wales coalfield in the 1880s and the remarkably slow growth in Scotland during the late 1890s, regional rates converged. Among the major regions only in the West Midlands was a net loss of employment recorded, which occurred in the 1870s. If cyclical reductions in the work-force occurred, which was to be expected in those regions where coal production was dependent on the iron trade or later upon the comparably volatile export market, the intra-decadal trends were sufficiently strong to conceal them. Even in South Wales, where only once from the 1880s did employment grow less rapidly than in any other region, net losses occurred during the years of greatest adversity from 1874 to 1878, during 1885 and 1886, and in 1895 and 1896.

The colliery work-force was almost entirely male, for at each census between 1841 and 1911 the number of working women in, or at, coal mines was between 4,000 and 6,000; as a proportion of the total labour force this represented perhaps 3.5 per cent in 1841, the year before underground employment became illegal, and 2.5 per cent in 1851; it fell to below half that figure after 1861. Before the 1842 Act, female employment underground was found mainly in East Scotland (where every fourth underground employee was female), West Lancashire, West Yorkshire, Monmouthshire, and East Glamorgan. In Eastern Scotland coal bearers carrying bags of coal from surface to face and back were almost always women or girls, as miners regarded the jobs too degrading for men.[1] One-third of the women and girls interviewed by the 1842 Commission reported having dead or disabled fathers, and a significant number of other girls came from large families.[2] Although, typically, women so employed were wives and daughters (or widows) of colliers, the attitude of miners as expressed in the *Northern Star* reflected a mixture of humanitarian, economic, and sexist motives: 'Remove the females, keep them at home to look after their families; decrease the pressure on the labour market . . .'[3]

Lord Ashley's bill proposed to prohibit the employment of women and very young children underground, and although a general opposition on principle was very limited, the short-term effects of such a ban generated considerable concern. Collusion between employer and workers led to considerable evasion of the Act, precisely because of the

[1] *SC Children's Employment Commission* 1842, XVI, Appendix I, 91.
[2] Hair thesis, 233.
[3] Quoted by John thesis, 230. The following paragraph draws heavily on the same source, 180–6, 254–6, 264, 410–20, 477–8, 533–4, 549.

coincidence of incentives to do so; but within ten years the pressure from Mines Inspectors upon employers had virtually ended the underground employment of women. Even above ground the small numbers employed thereafter were concentrated in South Staffordshire and West Lancashire, where 'pit brow lasses' worked at the pithead, picking coal refuse, sorting, riddling, and washing coal, pushing and pulling trams at the surface. Females under the age of ten were prohibited from undertaking such work in 1872, and the prohibition extended to girls under twelve in 1887. Sporadic attempts by philanthropists, trade unionists, and miners from districts where women were not employed met opposition from female surface workers, who successfully defended their right to work in 1866, 1887, and again in 1911, by which time the barely 6,000 women workers accounted for less than one per cent of the total mining population, compared with 4 per cent in 1841 (7 per cent including females below the age of twenty-one).

In so far as women's employment was affected, the legislation of 1842 was of limited economic importance (except, perhaps in Lancashire), but the clauses affecting children's work were central to the economics of colliery working, for restrictions on the supply of child labour was a sensitive issue in an industry experiencing very rapid expansion. The Coal Mines Act of 1842 resulted from two major influences: the contemporary movement for social reform, in which legislative restriction on the work of children and women followed logically from the 1833 Factory Act; and the conviction shared by many nineteenth-century public figures, including Lord Ashley who introduced the Coal Mines Bill, that preventing infants from working released them for moral and religious education, perceived as the critical influences which might civilize the labouring population and counter tendencies towards social disintegration.[1]

Clearly, because women accounted for such a small proportion of underground workers the wider aims held by some of the reformers could only be promoted were children's employment to be regulated; but although the conditions of child labour in the mines were deplorable, conventional morality was far more outraged by the sensational revelations of the condition of women workers underground—despite the latters' opposition to restrictive legislation. Verbatim accounts of their working lives in the 1842 *Report*, illustrated in woodcuts, engaged public sympathy and provoked an outcry. Ashley referred to the evils

[1] A. Heesom, 'The Coal Mines Act of 1842. Social Reform and Social Control', *HJ*, 24 (1981), 469–88. The following paragraph draws heavily on this source.

revealed by the Commissioners as 'both disgusting and intolerable', while the *Quarterly Review*'s commentator described the 'modes of existence as strange and as new as the wildest dreams of fiction. The earth seems now for the first time to have heaved from its entrails another race to astonish and move us to reflection and sympathy.' This view was echoed in the *Morning Chronicle*, where the report was calimed to resemble 'a volume of travels in a remote and barbarous country' and referred to 'the dead beneath the surface of the earth'.

Reports of women who drank, swore, and worked naked in the pits, who were believed to be sexually immoral and unfit to be wives and mothers, produced the sensational reaction in public opinion at large anticipated by Lord Ashley, but conditions of child labour, too, brought sufficient sympathetic response, at least outside the mining regions, to enable him to overcome the opposition of landed coalowner MPs—who could dispense with female labour, where it existed, with little difficulty, but who found limitation on child labour a more disruptive prospect and ensured evasion of the Act for many years. Furthermore, not until the Coal Mines Regulation Act of 1860 was restriction placed on the underground employment of boys up to the age of twelve, or ten if they could provide a certificate of education.

Child workers under 15 years probably comprised 13 per cent at the mid-century, and including those below 20 years (referred to in the industry as *juveniles*), for 30 per cent.

Between 1851 and 1871, Scotland, Lancashire and Cheshire, Yorkshire, and the East Midlands demonstrate relatively high levels of dependence upon juvenile labour. Hair's figures derived from the 1842 Commission show that child labour below the age of sixteen was greater than average in Pembroke, the Lothians, West Lancashire, Fife, and Yorkshire; below average children's employment was to be found in East Lancashire, Monmouth, Glamorgan, and the Tyne.[1] It is doubtful whether it is possible to link the differences in the proportion of juveniles employed to differences in the division of labour. The crucial factor in determining the relatively minor regional variations in the proportions of juveniles employed appears to have been the demand for labour in mining compared with alternative locally-available employment.

The mean age of entry of nearly two thousand children interviewed by the 1842 Commission, each of whom entered the industry between

[1] Hair thesis, 168.

1835 and 1841, was 8.8 years. This ranged from an average of 9.9 in Scotland and 9.2 in the North-east to 8.7 in Yorkshire, 8.6 in South Wales, 8.4 in Derbyshire, and 8.1 in Lancashire.[1] A total of some five thousand children aged between five and ten were working underground in 1841. Hair argued that lack of technical sophistication was a key reason explaining the proportion of children to adults employed, intensive child labour being a corollary of technical backwardness. Support for this view derived from evidence in 1841 of the smallest proportions of children in coalfields where rails and engines were employed most extensively.[2] There are, however, exceptions, as Hair points out, for in the North-east, a technically advanced mining region in the 1840s, the introduction of the relatively sophisticated system of air coursing actually increased the number of boys required as 'trappers', the children who tended the trap doors required to guide the ventilating current, which they opened to allow loaded and empty tubs or wagons to pass in and out;[3] these doors were later made self-acting.

Such was the introduction by which, in 1847, ten-year-old Thomas Burt began his career from trapper boy to national mining leader and Member of Parliament. Later in life he described 'the clatter, bustle, confusion, darkness, flickering lamps, shadowy figures' which remained vividly in his memory. He recalled that the putters, or hauliers, who were employed in propelling the loads of coal from the collier's working place to the horse roads or to the shaft, relieved the monotony each time they pushed their tubs through his trapdoor; 'otherwise dullness and loneliness were then oppressive', which on occasion induced sleep and caused danger.[4] The substitution of pony haulage for hand putting underground also generated a demand for boys as pony putters, an occupation which was both dangerous and arduous, for it involved driving the ponies along narrow, uneven roads, attempting to prevent them from galloping out of control at crossings and turnings. The tubs pulled by the ponies were clumsy and ponderous, and when on gradients were liable to fall off the rails, requiring considerable strength and technique to replace them.[5] He remembered his experience as a pony driver working fourteen and fifteen hours a day: '. . . so tired, listless and utterly used up was I when I reached home at nights that after dinner I not infrequently threw myself, unwashed upon the bare floor and fell fast asleep'.[6] The memory of another feature of underground employ-

---

[1] Ibid., 164–5.   [2] Ibid., 169–72.
[3] Ibid., 173.   [4] Burt 1924, 50, 54–5.
[5] Ibid., 52, 76–8, 82; Galloway 1898, 150.   [6] Burt 1924, 82.

ment which left a similarly strong impression, reminded him that on entry underground he had never seen 'so many crutches, so many empty jacket sleeves, so many wooden legs. The risk, the toilsomeness, the disagreeableness of the work made me wish to be elsewhere.'[1] Anticipating, perhaps, similar reactions from potential young recruits should they be given the choice, John Chambers opposed the legislation to reduce the minimum age of employment below thirteen, which would have enabled children to experience work at local engineering workshops, where no such restriction existed or was proposed. He feared that once children had experienced employment outside the mines they would be unlikely to remain willing, potential recruits for the collieries.[2]

Before promotion to pony putting at the age of sixteen Burt had a spell as a water loader, when except for a pony he worked entirely alone, saturated throughout the night as he baled water into tubs which he then removed in preparation of a working place for the hewer the following day.[3] At the age of seventeen he became a hand putter, which involved manhandling tubs of coal to the flat or station before they were placed upon rolleys and removed to the shaft by horse or engine. This task required exceptional strength and stamina, and was reserved for 'active powerful young men' who could sustain excessively hard work over long hours, shifting tubs of coal weighing up to a quarter of a ton.[4] Burt's experience, vividly described in his *Autobiography*, accords roughly with the viewer George Johnson's description of the gradation of labour in the pits of the North-east in the 1830s: from trap-door keepers (aged 12–14 years), rolley drivers (stronger boys aged 12–14, who used wheeled sledges to haul coal), putters (aged 15 to 22/3, coal hauliers by any means), and hewers, and his account makes it clear that age was a major criterion of job function in that region.[5] Several contributors to the 1842 Commission made it plain that the employment of very young children was indispensable to the working of some mines. Children aged between six and ten (one case cited a four-year old) were widely employed in the thin seams of the Coalbrookdale district of Staffordshire for this reason. In Warwickshire, on the other hand, the large size of coals was said to militate against the employment of young boys.[6] In some of the thinnest seams in Yorkshire, however, some

[1] Ibid., 84.   [2] SCL, Newton Chambers, TR 453/5.

[3] Burt 1924, 92.   [4] Ibid., 52.

[5] *SC Accidents in Coal Mines* 1835, V, Q 1322; Galloway 1898, 148–152; Hair thesis, 164, 212, 384.

[6] *SC Children's Employment* 1842, XVI, 9–10.

children were even employed as hewers, though most were putters;[1] 'When the main roads are four feet and a half high the mine may still be rendered sufficiently convenient for the work people, and the coals may be conveyed along the roads to the foot of the shaft by ponies or asses. But when the main roads are under four feet, the coals can no longer be conveyed along these roads by ponies or asses, or even by adults or young men; they can only be conveyed by children.'[2] Hence the opposition to the 1842 Act which rendered underground working by children below the age of ten illegal—and hence evasion of the Act.[3] Despite the progressive legislation on ages in subsequent years, and the elimination of many of the completely unskilled jobs (such as trapping and rolley driving), the picture of the division of labour conveyed by the *Report of the Eight Hour Day Committee* in 1907 is substantially the same in the North-east as hitherto described, where the division of labour was still the most advanced. Boys were introduced to the pit at the earliest age legal and received gradual promotion to the face after roughly seven years of apprenticeship following oncost work, though this division of labour according to age was not universal in other regions.

While unsupervised hewers were invariably adults, in Scotland and South Wales adults also worked as putters and drawers, and generational promotion which was typical of the North-east was exceptional in South Wales. There, boys entered the pits not as drivers working their way up to putting and hewing, but as trainee hewers or hauliers.[4] Children were employed because the early pits required a large number of jobs which either adults, because of their size, could not perform, or which children, even infants, could perform as well as men, notably trapping and keeping roads clear. Cost, however, was the main criterion. Nicholas Wood reported to the Select Committee on Accidents that if men were to be employed as trappers many collieries could not be worked at a profit.[5] On the other hand, Tremenheere found that a dozen years after the 1842 Act the majority of reported violations occurred only in the thin-seam districts.[6] There is also, of course, an overwhelming body of evidence to show that juvenile labour was accepted as the norm in colliery districts and that the vast majority of adult miners

[1] Ibid., 70.
[2] Ibid., 45.
[3] *SC Accidents in Coal Mines* 1854, IX, QQ 1232–4.
[4] *Eight Hours Committee* 1907, XV, QQ 483–7.
[5] *SC Accidents in Coal Mines* 1835, V, 1123.
[6] *SC Accidents in Coal Mines* 1854, IX, QQ 1232–4.

wished their sons to enter the mine at as early an age as possible.[1] This was largely for financial reasons, or course, but partly (so the argument ran) to ensure that boys could get accustomed to the mine at the earliest possible age (and hence improve the prospects of becoming a face worker). This fact may not in itself contradict the existence of a movement for the increase in the minimum age which the Miners' National Association claimed to be leading in the 1860s, but there was considerable disagreement amongst observers on how universal this desire to raise the minimum age was amongst miners themselves.[2] Certainly one year before a ten-year age limit was adopted in the Mines Act of 1842 the miners at Dixon Green Colliery belonging to the Bridgewater Trustees forced the manager to rescind a ban imposed on underground labour by children below the age of twelve, because they objected to the degradation of otherwise having to carry out boys' work—a matter of status and probably of earnings too.[3]

The 1842 Commission contains a mass of evidence on the evils of underground employment for children. Witness after witness testified to the difficulty and arduous nature of the work, the psychological effect of the mine in inducing terror in small children (especially among trappers left in the dark for hours on end), the very long hours, and the system of bullying (particularly by older boys) which was used to enforce discipline. Hair adds a corrective to this by pointing out that many children looked foward to commencing work, since it marked their entry into the adult world and at first had the atmosphere of an adventure.[4] Numerous interviews with the commissioners could, however, demonstrate how ephemeral the excitement of such an initiation was, for they stress the sheer drudgery of work underground. Most of the younger children described it as such. It is also clear that the abuse of juvenile labour did not disappear with the 1842 Act, even if one exempts the violations of the Act that occurred in the 1840s and early 1850s. In 1865 Thomas Burt, whose own experience had not been marred by gratuitous persecution, none the less drew a gloomy picture of the great mass of colliery boys beginning to work at the age of ten to twelve permanently foregoing education and confined to the pit for ten hours a day.[5] While many witnesses described juvenile labour at this time as

---

[1] *SC Children's Employment* 1842, XVI, QQ 606, 611, 213; Burt 1924, 108; *SC Dearness and Scarcity* 1873, X, Q 3238.

[2] See Thomas Burt's evidence to *SC Regulation and Inspection of Mines* 1865, XII, and the subsequent criticisms, 161–5.   [3] Mather 1970, 323.

[4] Hair thesis, 181–2.

[5] *SC Regulation and Inspection of Mines* 1865, XII, Q 1–161.

distinctly laborious and injurious to health[1] others argued that the work was light; but few disagreed that danger was present.[2]

In Scotland and in South Wales many children, in the former the vast majority, worked at the face on entering the pit, and no formal apprenticeship arrangements existed as they did in the North-east. There, as in Lancashire and Cheshire, Yorkshire, and the East Midlands virtually all boys commenced employment as haulage workers. The apparent contrast between such practices in the English and other coalfields, however, is expalined by the fact that outside England haulage was not specifically an adolescent occupation, while 'hewers' in South Wales and Scotland performed ancilliary work as well as cutting and loading the coal.[3]

In 1841, when it first becomes possible to estimate fairly accurately the age structure of the mining labour force, 31 per cent of all male miners were, by contemporaries' definition, juveniles, and 30 per cent in 1851 and 1861 (Table 3.3). Within the juvenile labour force the effects of the 1842 Act reduced the number of children aged five to ten working underground from about 5,000 (or more than 3 per cent in 1841), to 1,209 children below the age of nine in 1851, 835 in 1861, and 219 in 1871. Since all of this employment was illegal these census figures are almost certainly underestimates. Meanwhile, a compensating increase in employment of ten to nineteen year olds occurred which had the effect of maintaining the proportion of colliery workers below the age of twenty, at least until 1871. The effect of the 1842 Act upon the proportion of juvenile labour was negligible, although it is possible that the 27 per cent figure for 1841 might be an underestimate by the census. Throughout the period to 1871, therefore, the labour force was very young, with at least 48 per cent of the total employees aged between twenty and thirty-nine, and a further 30 per cent under the age of twenty. A marked decline in the employment of younger children, from about 12 per cent at the mid-century to below 4 per cent by 1911, can be associated with a declining rate of juvenile recruitment following the 1872 Mines Regulation Act, which prohibited the full-time employment of boys under twelve, and anyone from working more than ten hours a day or fifty hours a week. The same Act stipulated half-day schooling for boys aged ten to thirteen and as a consequence severely reduced the attraction of employing them. The Forster Education Act of 1870

---

[1] Ibid., QQ 4391–4402; 4669–77, 5687–92, 5754–60, 6791–6802.
[2] Ibid., QQ 10638–73, 10742–45, 10761–74, 7385–89, 7394–97.
[3] These generalizations are based on *Eight Hours Committee* 1907, XV, Pt II, 26–139.

Table 3.3. *Age structure of the male labour force, showing percentage employment in different age groups, 1841-1911*

Age Group	1841[a]	1851	1861[b]	1871	1881	1891	1901	1911
5–9		$\frac{1}{2}$	$\frac{1}{2}$					
10–14	(31)	$12\frac{1}{2}$	$12\frac{1}{2}$	$10\frac{1}{2}$	6	6	5	4
15–19		17	17	$17\frac{1}{2}$	17	18	16	16
20–44		54	54	56	$58\frac{1}{2}$	58	$60\frac{1}{2}$	$60\frac{1}{2}$
45–64	(69)	$13\frac{1}{2}$	14	$16\frac{1}{2}$	16	17	18	
65+		$2\frac{1}{2}$	2	2	2	2	$1\frac{1}{2}$	$1\frac{1}{2}$

[a] The figures for 1841 are estimates. It is possible to estimate male and female employment in 1841 as 34 per cent of the male work-force, comprising 18.5 per cent below the age of fifteen and 15.5 per cent aged between fifteen and twenty. These calculations are based on the assumption that the 1842 *Childrens' Commission Report* was correct in concluding that the average starting age was nine years.

[b] The data for 1861 refer to England and Wales only since the census data for Scotland in this year have a different (and incompatible) age breakdown. The 1851 data, available for England, Wales, and Scotland on the same basis, indicate the age strcture in Scotland to have been closely comparable with that of the rest of the country. Scotland's adult mining population was slightly larger than in the rest of the UK, with (in 1851) 50.5 per cent of employees in the age group 20–39 compared to 48 per cent in England and Wales.

Sources: Based on census and calculations from the census.

(which obliged local authorities to provide schooling though not as yet to compel attendance) for children of the same age group also reinforced the trend away from the employment of young boys. Not until 1887 was a legal minimum age of twelve introduced throughout the industry.

Meanwhile, technical advance, particularly in ventilation and underground transport, was a major factor reinforcing the trend away from the employment of young boys. Those aged twelve to thirteen years fell from 11,000 to barely 3,300 between 1873 and 1884; at the same time, nearly 6,000 youths aged thirteen to sixteen (probably hurriers and drivers) were replaced by steam traction.[1] The recruitment of older boys continued until the 1890s, when the fifteen to nineteen age group fell as a proportion of the total labour force, a reduction which may have been related to the increasing discrimination which the sons of miners were said to have exercised in this period when choosing future employment, especially in the urban coalfields, favouring instead either staying longer

[1] R. Nelson Boyd, 'Collieries and Colliery Engineering', *CJ* 10 Nov. 1893, 820.

in school or entering one of the growing range of alternative occupations.[1]

Among the adult male mining population a significant shift in age structure occurred between 1861 and 1881. As the population generally was living longer and fatality rates fell, the falling proportion of young juveniles recruited to the industry was accompanied by a marked ageing in the mining population, to which the rapid influx of young adult recruits in the early 1870s contributed.[2] The progressive growth in importance of adult labour which began in the 1850s continued, apart from a slight interruption in the 1880s and early 1890s. However, by comparison with the age structure among males in occupations other than mining the adult labour force was relatively young.[3] Two factors may be cited to account for this. Firstly, adult recruits attracted by the industry were more likely to be below forty or forty-five than above. In this sense, therefore, adult recruitment acted as a rejuvenating mechanism which arrested somewhat the natural process of ageing. Secondly, the tendency for the labour force to age over time at the same rate as the male population generally was impeded, to some extent, by the heavy fatal-accident rate and the high rate of wastage due to permanently incapacitating injuries.[4] Because of this high wastage rate, which affected all ages, juvenile recruitment alone was insufficient to restore entirely the age balance in the industry; therefore, an enlarged recruitment of young males may be regarded as an important contributing factor in maintaining the age structure. Before attempting to quantify this influx into the industry and to chart its chronology, however, it is necessary to consider the scope for occupational mobility by examining further the labour processes involved in mining coal, the division of labour practised, and the elements of skill.

[1] *Eight Hours Committee* 1907, XV, QQ 12338–44.

[2] Since changes in the period 1861–71 are obscured by differences in age classification, the figures for 1851 and 1861 for the age group 40–9 have been divided and distributed equally between the younger and older age groups, transforming these classifications into groups (20–44 and 45–64) comparable with 1871–1911. Thus, in percentages:

Age group	1851	1861	1871	1881	1891	1901	1911
20–44	54	54	56	$58\frac{1}{2}$	—	$60\frac{1}{2}$	$60\frac{1}{2}$
45–64	$13\frac{1}{2}$	14	14	$16\frac{1}{2}$	16	17	18

[3] Compare the national figures in Mitchell and Deane 1962, 12.

[4] See below 582–4.

ii. The work process

Commissioner Thomas Tancred's report on mining in the west of Scotland in 1842 combined technical detail with exact observation:

In whichever way the coal is worked the labour of the collier is the hardest with which I am acquainted. The thickness of the seam affords him more space to work in than is the case in the general yet he seldom stands to his work. The ordinary posture is leg doubled beneath him, and the other foot resting against, reclining his body to one side so as often nearly to touch the shoulder; he digs his pick with both hands into the lower part of the coal, or into a stratum of fire-clay, or some other softer material beneath the coal. In this way he picks out an excavation often for a considerable distance under a mass of coal, beneath which he half lies to work. When he has after two or three hours' labour undermined as much as he judges it prudent to attempt; he inserts iron wedges by means of a heavy hammer between the coal and the roof above it, by which, and by the weight of the ground above, the mass of the coal is detached and falls. The cramped posture, the closeness of the subterranean atmosphere loaded with coal dust, and the smoke of his lamp, and at times with sulphurous exhalations, together with the bodily exertion, cannot fail to be very exhausting.[1]

More then seventy years later, H. S. Jevons described the work of the South Wales colliers:

Usually the first thing he does is to 'hole' or cut away the shale from underneath the coal which is to be brought down. This is done by means of a pick, and in order to more effectually discharge this task, the collier is compelled, if the seam is not very thick, to adopt a very cramped and uncomfortable position—in many cases, indeed, he has to lie sideways at full length on the ground in order to be able to swing his pick in such a way as to win the coal satisfactorily. When it is neccessary to support the weight of the coal during the holing process, short wooden sprags, or props, are placed under the edge of the coal at frequent intervals, and when the holing work has been completed the sprags are withdrawn and the huge pressure of the overlying strata causes the mass of coal to fall forwards and downwards and be crushed. The collier and his assistant now set to work to fill the coal into the tubs or trams brought to their working place by hauliers with the aid of ponies ... When the tram is loaded the collier chalks on it the number of his stall so that the weigher and check-weigher at the surface will know to which man they must credit the weight of coal brought up in each train ... When the working space has been cleared, the collier sets props to support the roof, the roadways with their tram lines are

---

[1] *Children's Employment Commission* 1842, XVI, 334-5, para. 59.

brought forward nearer to the new coal face, and the preceding operations are repeated.[1]

This description, written in 1915, reveals how little the actual extraction of coal had altered.

Underground production workers were responsible for cutting, loading, and moving the coal from face to surface; they were also responsible for attaching whatever coal container was used onto the winding rope—and sometimes for the screening of coal before it was wound to the surface. The maintenance staff were responsible for deadwork, preparing, and ensuring that workings remained in a suitable condition to allow continuous production, advancing the face, and driving roads. Above ground the tasks were more varied, involving movement and preparation of coal as well as the maintenance and repair of colliery equipment and horse care. These functions were common to the industry in all regions, but the allocation of these tasks varied. In this sense there was no common division of labour; individuals with apparently identical job descriptions in practice performed quite different tasks, depending upon geological factors, technology, methods of working, and labour custom.

Regional and intra-regional differences existed in method and in the division of labour, but the sequence of manual hewing and filling the coal into containers, whether sledges, barrows, corves, or tubs, was essentially unchanged in most collieries throughout the century. The movement of coal from coal-face to primary roads, described as 'putting' in the North-east, 'hurrying' in Yorkshire, was affected by technical improvements, though limited until the third quarter of the century in their significance. On secondary haulage routes, for much of the period and for most mines, a mixture of human and animal power continued to dominate. Variations in geological conditions were important influences upon regional, even local, differences in the degrees of physical exertion required to carry out particular tasks. In the North-east, for example, it was necessary to rip the coal, which called for considerable strength and expertise, and where explosives, first introduced in 1810 but slow to spread, were not used to bring down the coal, called for almost continuous use of the pick. In South Wales, by contrast, the coal almost fell away.[2] Over time, however, marked reduc-

---

[1] H. S. Jevons 1915, 610–11.
[2] *Eight Hours Committee* 1907, XV, Q 8314–5.

tions in the severity of work occurred in all regions. For hewers the use of explosives, in those districts where it was safe to do so, was a major labour-saving device.[1] In underground haulage the replacement of sledges by wheeled trams and rails, and the increasing use of animal and later mechanical haulage eased the work considerably. Surface labour may also have been less onerous in its physical demands as a result of transport improvements. None the less there can be little doubt that the 1830s and early 1840s stand out as a time of extreme exploitation, whether in the form of female and child coal bearers, largely confined to Scotland, or the utilization of unassisted child labour for putting, or in the form of infant labour for trapping. For adult workers the principal benefits in terms of reduced physical exertion came from the reductions in hours during the century, which were extensive.[2] To be set against this, however, was the rising temperature of the deeper mines which produced an increasing proportion of coal from the late nineteenth century. Especially in the concealed coalfields of Lancashire, Yorkshire, the Midlands, and South Wales the problem of heat was particularly serious, with temperatures of more than 90 degrees fahrenheit frequently encountered in pits of depths around 300 metres or more.[3]

We have stressed the physical demands of mining coal particularly in the hewing and putting processes, for this reflects the focus of contemporary accounts of mining labour. Miners insisted, however, that in addition to sheer strength a substantial degree of skill was necessary to extract the coal with safety and with maximum economy of effort. The importance of muscle power is underlined by the tendency for men working as hewers, who were regarded as performing the most onerous of the physically demanding jobs, to take on other colliery work round about the age of fifty-five, eventually retiring altogether between the ages of sixty-five and seventy, should they survive.[4] That the skill of the hewer was to be equated with age, experience and mental attitude is implicit in Buddle's opinion, that unless boys were initiated into pitwork below the ages of ten or eleven they would never become colliers.[5] He drew a distinction between pitmen—middling-good pitmen and pitmen—who differed from colliers (described merely as 'underground workers') in their lack of long experience of work underground, which he thought to be an effective preparation only if commenced in

---

[1] Hair thesis, 128–9, and see below 249–55.
[2] See below.   [3] Benson 1980, 34–5.
[4] RC Trade Unions 1867, XXXIX, Q 11893; Burt 1924, 108.
[5] DuRO NCB 1/JB/1786 Buddle to Lambton.

childhood: 'our peculiar race of pitmen . . . can only be kept up by breeding',[1] declared Buddle in 1842.

Some forty years later, the Inspector of Mines for Staffordshire remarked on the decline in the custom whereby a contractor took on a half dozen apprentices, who were 'regularly brought up as miners and consequently made better colliers than we now meet with. They now come from the ploughtail and other kinds of work when the wages in the mines are good, and some of them stay; consequently they are not good colliers, and are not fit to be in a mine; they cannot take care of themselves and they do mischief.'[2]

Lindsay Wood reckoned that, on an average, twelve months were needed to convert a surface worker into a hewer, and a further six months to transform men fresh to underground work into effective colliers.[3] Normansell, for the Yorkshire miners, thought between two and two-and-a-half years were necessary for the complete transformation from unskilled labour to competent hewer.[4] This seems to be excessive to judge from the experience of Robert Smillie, later to become the leader of the Lanarkshire miners, who entered the industry as an unskilled labourer from Belfast. After working underground as a pumper and drawer, practising hewing in his spare time, he was promoted to the face, where at the end of six months he was reckoned to have been a 'more or less competent collier'.[5] He was one of many Irishmen recruited initially as bearers or other kinds of oncost workers, with time progressing to the face.[6] Alexander Gillmour, however, managing partner of an Ayrshire colliery, declared it to be impossible to convert 'an intelligent labourer' into a 'collier proper', and even though they might make tolerable oncost men assisting the collier, the latter, he implied, suffered from the former's inexperience, not only because of their threat to safety.[7]

Evidence that such circumstances did occur is provided by the complaints of Yorkshire miners in the 1880s and 1890s against the influx of unskilled workers entering the mines, 'so that the men can get very few tubs'.[8] As a result, coalowners were faced by attempts to restrict the entry of green labour into the industry for reasons relating to their threat to mine safety and to wage rates and colliers' earnings—but also

---

[1] Quoted in Flinn 1984, 339.
[2] Jonathan Presto, *Five Years of Colliery Life* (London, 1884), 5.
[3] *SC Dearness and Scarcity* 1873, X, Q 3357.   [4] Neville thesis, 159.
[5] Campbell 1979, 44.   [6] Hassan thesis, 240; Corrins thesis, 322.
[7] *SC Dearness and Scarcity* 1873, X, Q 6858.
[8] Neville thesis, 159.

because of the possible effects of an enlarged labour supply upon the informal system of 'patrimony', whereby sons were trained by fathers. Restrictive clauses are to be found in many union rule books in Scotland,[1] in some instances entry to the trade becoming negotiable at a price or on demonstration of achievement after a short trial period.[2] The nature of the demand for labour, however, which occurred in spurts, meant that some recourse to green adult labour was inevitable; hence the failure of the Scottish miners' policy of entry restriction and the espousal in the 1860s of emigration as a solution to a short-term labour surplus.[3]

Anxious to control the labour supply, in 1874 the Yorkshire miners proposed the imposition of an upper age limit of eighteen for new entrants to the industry, but they were clearly too late; for the huge influx attracted during the preceding boom already rendered such a policy superfluous in the succeeding depression. Frank Machin later stressed that this proposal was symptomatic of an unshakeable belief, 'widely held by miners, that coal face work was a highly skilled job'.[4] In 1861 the Special Rules for the Midland Inspection District came to include a regulation which ensured that inexperienced hewers would work under supervision at all times, after it was discerned that stallmen had been leaving them to work alone at the end of a shift.[5] Nearly thirty years later the Yorkshire Miners' Association advanced a proposal to the Miners Federation of Great Britain that men aspiring to become face workers should spend a compulsory period of pre-coal-face employment lasting for two years,[6] a provision apparently incorporated in the 1887 Mines Act,[7] but evidently honoured as much in the breach as in observance at pit level. In 1910 the Yorkshire miners reiterated their objection to the introduction of unskilled workers, whom they described as 'absolutely unnecessary' and a danger to the whole of the men at work in the mines.[8]

In the North-east, where most coal was hard and difficult to work, a characteristically rigid hierarchical structure avoided many of the difficulties experienced in other regions, for putting had been a necessary prerequisite for graduation to hewer status throughout the nineteenth century. This explains why in that region a novice who began as a door

[1] Campbell 1979, 44. [2] Ibid., 268.
[3] Ibid. [4] Machin 1958, 403.
[5] C. P. Griffin thesis, 393, 401.
[6] Neville thesis, 324.
[7] *Coal Mines Regulation Act* (16 Sept. 1887) 50 and 51, Vict Cap lviii.
[8] Neville thesis, 324.

keeper or boy trapper with nothing more than strength and experience could proceed to become in due course a putter and eventually a hewer, usually at the age of twenty-one and rarely below eighteen.[1] The miners' skill, therefore, was in effect a product of experience in the mine, the ability to interpret the sounds and smells of danger, to adopt safe working procedures as a matter of habit. These could vary from district to district, from colliery to colliery, so that in one pit a new recruit could hasten to perform tasks which in another might risk danger or impede efficient production.

The extremely lengthy system of apprenticeship in the thick coal seams of south Staffordshire was exceptional; for example, there a man would not be given charge of a stall until he had worked as a miner for twenty years because of the difficult and dangerous nature of the work, though reinforced, no doubt, by restrictive practices.[2] After hearing evidence from miners and from employers on the subject, the middle-class observer J. M. Ludlow concluded that while he accepted the employers' view that the physical labour required of a collier 'may be performed by any man with sufficient thews and sinews to carry it on', the requirement of 'a familiarity with the peculiar dangers of the occupation, and a caution in guarding against them' were equally necessary, 'which nothing but long experience can supply'.[3] A collier from South Wales described precisely the nature of his skill: 'It takes a man years to pick up all the indications of danger a pit gives forth; the ignorant . . . man . . . does not know when his Davy lamp is out of order; he does not know what the indications of gas are; he does not know anything of the strata, the setting coal may rumble its warning, but to his ear it has no meaning'.[4]

A Scottish collier who first entered the pit in 1913 recalled his father's skills as a 'picksman' at the face:

He used light holding picks, some long in the grain, others shorter. He had heavier picks for cutting the coal and breaking it up, heavier picks still to deal with stone work. For coal that was easy to bore he had a fast borer, for difficult or hard coal a slower borer. He also had a cleaver for cleaving borings out of a hole, a stemmer for stemming the shothole, a heavy hammer, or mash, a mash-axe, wedges, splinters, and so on. He had almost a hutchful of tools. In con-

---

[1] Burt 1924, 52; *SC Children's Employment* 1842, XVI, 206–8.

[2] *Eight Hours Committee* 1907, XV, Q 11439–54.

[3] J. M. Ludlow, 'Account of the West Yorkshire Coal Strike and Lock Out of 1858', *Trade Societies and Strikes* (London, 1860), 1314.

[4] Quoted in Campbell 1979, 44.

trast, all that a stripper—a miner working on a machine-cut face—needed was a shovel, a pick, sometimes a pick with a mash end, and a mash.[1]

A song in the dialect of the North-east, known among miners as 'pit-matic', describes how an experienced pitman warns a novice at the face how to test the coal, to ensure that it was secure, by 'jowling' with his pick haft before beginning to hew:[2]

> Jowl, jowl and listen, lad,
> Ye'll hear the coalface workin,
> There's mony a marra missin', lad,
> Because he wadn't listen lad.
>
> Me father aalwes used to say,
> Pit-wark's mair than hewin',
> Ye've got to coax the coal along,
> An' not be rivin' an tewin'.

These accounts indicate the possibilities of transforming mining from the crude pick and shovel got by 'green' labour to the relatively skilled process required to maximize the output and condition of coal while minimizing danger. The implication is that the term 'hewer' encompassed face workers of widely varying skills (through application and experience) and performance. The possibility of achieving high performance, however, explains the presumption of craftsmen status on the part of those hewers, (certainly fewer than 50 per cent of all miners) who aspired to excel in getting coal—regardless of how others outside the industry might regard coalmining, and the reality of the ease with which, when trading conditions warranted, other colliery workers could expand the hewing force, while other workers inexperienced in pitwork took their places.[3]

So far we have concentrated on the hewers, who were productive in a way that other underground workers were not. Whereas, however, in some regions hewers constituted an easily identifiable group performing specialized tasks, such a marked division of labour was not characteristic of colliery workers in all coalmining regions. In the North-east the division of labour was far in advance of that in other regions throughout the period; here hewers merely cut and broke up the coal, perhaps spending an entire day at the same part of the face, moving very little,

---

[1] Ian MacDougall, *Militant Miners* (Edinburgh, 1981), 6.

[2] 'Jowl and Listen' in Frank Atkinson, *Life and Tradition in Northumberland and Durham* (London, 1977), 7146.   [3] See above 204–5.

while the deputies were responsible for setting the timber and stone-work. Distinct grades of labour performed putting, haulage work on the primary roads, maintenance, and so on.[1] In South Wales, on the other hand, hewers had to 'rip the roads and timber the roads and cut bottom and stand timber, and keep the whole of their working place in safe working order, and their working place would extend back for 50 years'.[2] In South Wales, Scotland, and Lancashire, the hewer was responsible, at least in part, for putting the coal as well, though even less specialization of function was characteristic of the Cumberland coal mines.[3] In the South Wales and Midland coalfields hewers did all the face work, including timbering and stonework,[4] whereas the Yorkshire practice was closer to that of the North-east, with a relatively high degree of specialization though falling short of the North-east.[5]

It needs to be stressed that these are generalizations, for labour prac-tices outside the North-east did not show a degree of widespread uniformity peculiar to that region. Elsewhere, different collieries were said often to adopt systems of working according to the needs perceived by individual colliery managers. But increasing job division was a trend which during the century was intensified, partly as a consequence of the changeover from pillar and stall to longwall, for the lengthening faces which longwall facilitated encouraged such a development.[6]

In addition to the trappers, the pony drivers, the putters and their assistants, who might include fillers, comprising the main categories of non-hewing underground labour in the coal mines of the North-east in the mid-nineteenth century were others, variously described in different regions yet whose combined functions were similar. These included: the bottomers, or onsetters, who supervised traffic entering into, and departing from, the pit bottom; timbermen, who constructed and main-tained underground roads and passages in good order and carried out repairs to roofs and partitions; and, in the North-east, wastemen, who also ensured that door stoppings were sound, that ventilation in the waste was satisfactory, and who stowed waste; brushers, or redesmen, who finished off the formation of working roads and kept them in order. 'Crush' and 'creep', which became more common with the pro-gress of longwall mining, intensified the problems caused by sudden

[1] Dunn 1852, 89; H. S. Jevons 1915, 611–12.
[2] H. S. Jevons 1915, 611–12; *Eight Hours Committee* 1907, XV, Q 9769.
[3] *Eight Hours Committee* 1907, XV, QQ 8315, 10932, 16954; Rowe 1923, 57–68.
[4] Rowe 1923, 57–8.
[5] *Eight Hours Committee* 1907, XV, QQ 10916–9.
[6] See below 339.

dips in roof or floor, uneven roofs occasioning danger and uneven gradients in roads increasing the haulage effort required; hence the important role of roadsmen. The final category of underground workers was the firemen, whose responsibility was to monitor noxious fumes and ignite gases.

Above ground were the joiners and carpenters, enginewrights, smiths, masons, and bricklayers, though from the mid-century an increasing proportion of these skilled tradesmen went below ground as longwall mining methods spread across the country. As fixed engines came to be applied to underground transport, fitters and later electricians also found themselves working underground together with the less-skilled miscellaneous group which performed other services down the pit: the horsekeepers, lampmen, pumpmen, storemen, and furnacemen, the timekeeper, overman, and underviewer or under-manager. Remaining on the surface together with some of the skilled tradesmen were the pick sharpeners, cartmen, horsemen, saddlers, wagonwrights, wagon riders, banksmen, wagon fillers, storekeepers, and heapkeepers, as well as those engaged in weighing, screening, and in some cases washing, the coal. Whether above or below ground, all categories except hewers were referred to in the trade as oncost workers, in conformity with the accounting division between hewing, or getting, costs and oncosts.[1]

The proportion of surface workers in the total labour force in the UK was around 20 per cent in 1873, when annual returns are first available, remaining at that level until 1913. Between coalfields the range was between 25 and 27 per cent in South Staffordshire and 14 to 16 per cent in South Wales. A constant ratio overall might seem surprising in a period when the amount of surface work was regarded as on the increase, and led to the introduction of new categories of surface workers in the statistical returns beginning in 1893.[2] Two alternative explanations suggest themselves. One is that weighing, screening, washing, and tippling, as Walters points out, were not labour-intensive and were partly automated; the other is that the greater productivity of labour underground, especially of haulage workers, helped to offset

[1] Compare the discussion in Flinn 1984, 329–334, relating mainly to the early nineteenth century, with the organization of labour presented in 'Return showing the average number of hours daily and weekly worked . . .' 1890, LXVIII, 215, and evidence presented in the *Eight Hours Committee* 1907, XV, 26–139.

[2] Mines Inspectors' Reports, annually from 1873. The change was due to the 1887 Coal Mines Regultion Act, which included surface transport workers and those employed in the preparation and coking of coal.

whatever increase occurred in the surface labour force.[1] Before 1873 no national figures exist. T. J. Taylor gave figures for the North-east in 1844 and 1853 when underground workers accounted for 77 per cent of total employment;[2] in the only other early figures which have come to light, those of Mines Inspector Joseph Dickinson for Lancashire, Cheshire, and North Wales in 1853, show a comparable figure of 82 per cent.[3] Taken together, this evidence suggests that both before and after 1873 the ratio of surface to underground labour probably remained stable.

Annual official statistics do not differentiate between hewers and oncost underground workers, which makes it very difficult to compare these two elements and their relationship to the total labour force. The only documentation for the early period refers to the North-east, included in a parliamentary report produced in 1847. The figures contained therein refer to more than one hundred collieries in Northumberland and Durham and enumerate hewers separately from all other workers.[4] The variations between collieries were large, ranging from 23 per cent at Springwell to 56 per cent at Trimdon and Sheild Row; the overall average ratio was 38 per cent. Classification by districts reveals that collieries in the newly opened Tees district operated with higher hewer ratios than those in the Tyne and Wear, which suggests that the age of collieries may have been an important determinant. It is, of course, not difficult to explain why this should have been the case, for younger pits typically possessed shorter haulage routes and therefore a higher proportion of hewer to haulage workers. Size of output does not seem to have been a crucial factor. In 1846 the proportion of hewers to all other colliery workers employed by Lord Londonderry was 50 per cent; at the Earl of Durham's collieries, 44 per cent.[5]

Evidence for thirty-seven Northumberland collieries in 1873 (covering 76 per cent of output) indicates hewers accounted for 48 per cent of all workers.[6]

Clearly, random examples such as these provide too flimsy a basis for generalization, except that proportions varied between collieries and

[1] Walters 1977, 283–5; SC Dearness and Scarcity 1873, X, Q 1978.
[2] SC Accidents in Mines 1854, IX, Q 1044, ev. of T. J. Taylor, viewer.
[3] Mines Inspectors' Reports 1854 (XIX), 712.
[4] Report on Mining Districts 1847, XVI, Appendix B, 423.
[5] Report on Mining Districts 1846, XXIV, 397, 399. In 1856 Liefchild gave figures for South Hetton Colliery, in which hewers as a proportion of underground workers was 46 per cent, 1854, 182–3.
[6] SC Dearness and Scarcity 1873, X, QQ 3019–3023, ev. of G. B. Forster, coalowner and mining engineer.

that no dramatic changes can be detected. However, even though it seems unlikely that substantial alterations occurred in the ratio of hewers to other workers in the North-east, we need to remember that the organization of work in that region, where the division of labour was highly advanced, was the exception, especially before the 1860s. At the other extreme was South Wales where hewers were required to perform 'dead work' tasks other than getting coal, and implies the existence of a higher proportion of men hewing in those regions compared with the North-east.[1] Precise estimation is ruled out, however, by the complication due to the proportional increase in oncost work that must have occurred, particularly after 1840, when pit work began to predominate over level working in South Wales.[2] It is not worth attempting to produce national averages before the 1880s, for it is impossible to judge the combined effects of the increasing age of pits against the rising productivity of haulage labour needed to offset the lengthening haulage routes; improved face productivity, stemming possibly from the greater use of explosives and the spread of longwall mining outside the North-east, will also have affected the hewer–oncost labour ratio. Not until the late nineteenth century is there to be found the first reliable breakdown of labour in coalmining on a national basis.

Table 3.4 compares the division of labour in the industry in 1889 and 1905, and although the two returns define labour categories differently, it is possible to compare the proportion of face workers to underground workers. Taking the period 1889 to 1905 as a whole, the proportion of face workers varied from less than 50 per cent in the North-east to 67 or 68 per cent in Scotland. The only significant changes occurring between these two dates were the falls in the proportion of hewers to oncost workers in South Wales and in Lancashire and Cheshire, possibly associated with the rapidly ageing pits in those districts. Overall, the hewer ratio fell slightly. A comparison of these regions at either date, moreover, illustrates graphically how completely the allocation of labour to different categories depended upon custom within the region.

Only in the North-east is it possible to interpret these figures as an accurate reflection of the actual division of *labour time*, as distinct from the division of workers as individuals. In this region the quite precise demarcation of labour justifies the conclusion that roughly 47 per cent

[1] A less advanced division between dead work and other tasks was commonly practised in Yorkshire, but dead work was present to a greater or lesser extent in all regions, since whoever set the timber the responsibility for maintaining it was the hewer as he worked. *Eight Hour Day* 1907 XIV QQ 10916–21, 506; Daunton 1981, 584–5.
[2] Walters 1977, 201; Morris and Williams 1958, 50–3.

Table 3.4. *The division of labour, 1889 and 1905*
(as percentages of underground labour force)

1889	Face workers	Haulage workers	Others underground	Surface labour as percentage of total employment
Scotland	6.9	19.4	12.6	15.2
North-east	49.9	25.3	24.8	19.9
Cumberland	67.1	21.9	11.0	21.4
Lancs. and Ches.	61.5	19.5	19.0	16.5
North Wales	60.3	22.8	16.9	16.2
Yorkshire	61.6	23.8	14.5	18.0
East Midlands	68.1	19.6	12.3	20.6
West Midlands	61.1	25.2	13.7	21.9
South Wales	60.5	15.4	24.1	14.5
South-west	53.9	25.2	20.8	15.7
UK	60.5	21.3	18.3	17.9

1905	Officials	Hewers	Fillers	Face workers	Drawers	Road makers and repairers	Others underground	Surface labour as percentage of total employment
Scotland	4.0	59.4	7.3	66.7	13.6	13.2	2.4	17.2
North-east and Cumberland	4.9	47.5	1.2	48.7	22.6	20.3	3.4	20.2
Lancs. and Ches.	3.2	46.1	10.3	56.4	19.0	19.4	1.9	18.4
North Wales	2.9	49.8	11.2	61.0	18.5	14.2	3.4	0.7
Yorkshire	2.6	48.4	12.0	60.4	20.7	13.6	2.6	20.2
East and West Midlands	3.0	44.4	17.9	62.3	21.1	11.0	2.5	20.2
South Wales	2.3	55.6	1.8	57.4	14.9	22.0	3.3	13.5
South-west	2.7	45.0	20.3	65.3	15.5	13.3	3.1	15.9
UK	3.4	50.1	7.7	57.8	18.9	17.1	2.8	15.6

Sources: 1889, 'Return showing the Average Number of Hours Daily and Weekly Worked . . .' 1890, LXVIII, 215; 1905, *Eight Hours Committee* 1907, XIV, 26–139.

of underground labour time was devoted to hewing, about 1 or $1\frac{1}{2}$ per cent to filling coal at the face, 22 to 23 per cent to hauling coal (both on secondary and primary routes), 20 per cent to road making and repairing, and 5 per cent to supervisory work. For the other regions the figures are less revealing. The high proportion of hewers in Scotland and the Midlands reinforces what is known concerning the imperfect division of labour prevailing in these regions, and the fact that hewers were engaged in tasks other than simply getting coal. The levels of face labour in Lancashire and Cheshire and Yorkshire indicate a division of labour intermediate between the North-east on the one hand and Scotland on the other. South Wales does not fit neatly into this categorization according to labour division, even though colliery working there was not characterized by precise demarcation. The major explanation for the low proportion of hewers in South Wales was the high proportion of labour employed in roadmaking necessitated by typically highly vulnerable roofs, which also doubtless absorbed some of the labour time of face workers too. Since the coal was generally so easy to hew this was not inconsistent with efficient working. The adoption in different regions of differing definitions of the labour process (or rather, of the duties assigned to individual men) renders it impossible to relate precisely statistics on the division of labour to the impact of geological or technical factors.

Influences upon the division of labour were gradual, with the exception of the sudden and profound effect of the 1908 Eight Hours Act. The critical innovation was the imposition of an eight-hour limit on winding coal rather than on time spent working from bank to bank, the immediate result of which was a sharp reduction in the hewer oncost ratio in South Wales, Lancashire, and Scotland and a lesser reduction occurring in the North-east.[1] Again, age might be regarded as an important factor in explaining the differential effects of the legislation, but only because in those districts hewers continued to work long hours. In the North-east the shift system was such that although hewers worked shorter spells, haulage workers were on duty for very long hours, which explains why the Eight Hours Committee predicted that South Wales and Lancashire would be affected far more than other coal-producing areas. In the North-east the compulsory reduction of hours of haulage workers, which were almost invariably longer than those of face workers, caused an imbalance in the allocation of respective labour times,

---

[1] See McCormick and Williams 1959, 222–38; Rowe 1923, 115–16; Walters 1977, 213.

necessitating either, or both, a rearrangement of the shift system and an increase in the proportion of oncost workers to face workers. In some cases it became necessary to arrange the demotion of hewers back into haulage workers.[1] Such re-arrangements could not fail to affect the productivity of colliery enterprise, which is considered in Chapter 6.

iii. Labour recruitment and migration

Our discussion of the division of labour, the elements of skill, and the effects of legislation indicate the existence of an enormous potential for the employment of males ranging from the skilled tradesmen to the unskilled labourer, and that even the hewer's task was within the capability of those possessing sufficient strength once the necessary experience (one or two months) or the customary longer period of 'apprenticeship' (one or two years) had been completed. It would have been surprising, therefore, had regional migration not been a consequence of demand and an important source of labour supply.

Data relating to growth in the labour supply in the regions indicate that while expansion was rapid throughout the period it was not uniform, which prompts the question: why have the origins of this hugely increased labour force been sought generally in recruitment within the colliery communities rather than in migration? Employing a definition of 'colliery districts' first used by T. A. Welton in his book *England's Recent Progress* in 1911, Caircross presented figures which depicted the balance of natural increase and migration for these districts for all decades between 1841 and 1911 in England and Wales. While underlining the varying regional totals which comprised the averages for different decades, his main conclusion was that although population growth in the colliery districts was more marked than in any other designated groups of registration districts (urban or rural), only one-sixth of the expansion in colliery population over the period as a whole derived from net migration, the remainder arising from natural increase.[2] By reconstituting these figures with the aid of the census, however, it appears that in the 1840s and 1850s the importance of migration into the 'colliery districts' was much greater than this, accounting for almost one-third of the population gain (Table 3.5).

[1] NuRO Ashington NCB/AS/88.
[2] Caircross 1953, 70–2. The categories of districts identified by Caircross were 'large towns', 'northern towns', 'southern towns', 'residential towns', 'military towns', 'rural towns', and 'colliery districts'.

Table 3.5. *Migration between colliery districts in*
England and Wales, 1841-1910

	Population growth	Gain by migration	Percentage growth by migration
1841–50	308,101	82,287	27
1851–60	312,642	103,467	33
1861–70	486,684	90,860	19
1871–80	745,397	84,474	11
1881–90	471,055	90,303	19
1891–1900	652,137	85,158	13
1901–1910	837,590	113,999	14

Sources: T. A. Welton, *England's Recent Progress* (London, 1911), 70–1;
Cairncross 1953, 78–80; Censuses of England and Wales.

The rapid rate of natural increase in these areas was attributed mainly to a high birth rate which, while not remarkably high in colliery districts in 1841–51, exceeded the national average by 42 per cent in the 1870s and even in the 1900s was 33 per cent above it.[1] This kind of analysis, however, contains serious shortcomings because of the data base employed, and may be regarded as no more than a very approximate guide to recruitment into the mining industry. In the 'colliery districts', as defined by Welton and Caircross, the figures are distorted by the existence of urban growth occurring within the registration districts but only indirectly linked to the coalfield; thus, in the registration colliery districts (which included total populations of five million inhabitants) the ratio of miners to other male occupations rarely exceeded 50 per cent and usually fell below one-quarter of the total.[2] A more detailed analysis of the South Wales data by Brinley Thomas[3] suggested that short-distance migration was important in that region, the Glamorgan coalfield depending to a considerable extent upon labour recruited from the neighbouring counties of Carmarthen, Brecknock, Monmouth, Somerset, and Devon. In 1861–70 about 70 per cent of migrants were recruited from neighbouring areas, though long distance migrants assumed greater importance in the 1870s and 1880s and continued to

[1] Ibid., 77–83.   [2] Ibid., 72.
[3] Brinley Thomas, 'The Migration of Labour into the Glamorganshire Coalfield 1861–1911', *Economica*, X (1930), 275–294.

expand in periods of bouyancy in the coal trade of South Wales. From other sources, it seems likely that Durham may have experienced substantial immigration in the 1840s and the 1860s, when major disputes prompted colliery owners to replace local miners with men from Cornwall, Dorset, Lancashire, Staffordshire and Shropshire.[1]

As South Wales may be regarded as a relatively remote mining region by comparison with others experiencing rapid growth, it seems likely that short-distance migration may have been important in other regions, too. But neither the analysis conducted by Brinley Thomas nor that by Caircross can take account of colliers who moved in and out of the registration districts between two censuses, thereby escaping enumeration altogether. Probably of greater importance is the failure of either study to measure migration within individual registration areas, with the result that movement from a surrounding rural area to a nearby colliery, albeit several miles distant, may have been interpreted as part of internal recruitment, consequently underestimating what otherwise might reasonably be regarded as migration, at least from the standpoint of those who moved.

The only research to have tackled this problem, albeit on a limited scale, is that of Alan Campbell, whose study *Lanarkshire Miners* included an analysis of the persistence rates of miners in two districts and for several villages within those districts between 1841–51 and 1861–71.[2] In the larger of the two, Coatbridge, where the number of miners employed averaged more than 1,500 between 1841 and 1861, persistence rates were 14.2 per cent and 16.7 per cent in 1841–51 and 1851–61, rising to 23.3 per cent in the following decade; whereas at Larkhall, averaging fewer than 400 in the same period, more than 40 per cent of all colliers and miners remained within the district, though that figure fell to 32 per cent in 1861–71. At the village level persistence rates were lower, in most instances, than for the district as a whole, which suggests that many miners who remained within a district none the less altered their place of residence. Inasmuch that the rates for the two districts tended to converge over the period analysed they reflect the different chronological phases of mining development experienced by the two districts. Thus, mobility was highest in Coatbridge during the 1840s and 1850s, a period which coincided with rapid mineral exploitation and high population growth, a combination characteristic of Larkhall only in the 1860s.[3]

---

[1] Mountford thesis, 25; *MJ* 10 Apr. 1844, 17 Aug. 1844; *CG* 16 Dec. 1865, 471, 20 Dec. 1865, 510, 13 June 1867, 527, 10 Aug. 1867, 127.　　　　　　　　　　[2] Campbell 1979, 165–8.
[3] Ibid., 66.

There is evidence to suggest, therefore, that the migration of miners from one colliery to another, either within or between regions, was considerably more prevalent than figures relating to 'colliery districts' imply. Descriptive evidence abounds on this kind of inter-colliery movement, though apart from Campbell's research there is little quantification. It is apparent, however, that it was common for a miner to move home voluntarily in search of higher wages and better working conditions, affording superior opportunities for higher earnings, more stable employment, or greater comfort and convenience provided by housing accommodation close to a pithead—though negative influences also played a part. Throughout the 1830s and 1840s a considerable number of miners from north of the Tyne travelled to the new collieries in south Durham.[1] In 1842 about one-third of the 'boys' at Tyne collieries who discussed migration with an observer said that they had already changed collieries three or more times; that is, before the age of sixteen.[2] The system of annual hiring may have encouraged these migrations once a year, for coalowners often paid travelling expenses and in the North-east provided free housing. Recalling 'a wandering gypsy life', Thomas Burt described how by the time he was fifteen his father had worked at seven or eight different collieries in Northumberland and Durham, and lived in at least eighteen houses. Burt's own life as a miner, which began in 1847, was similarly migratory within the North-east region, though eight years were spent at Seaton Delaval.[3] Robert Smillie worked at four different collieries during his first five years as a hewer in Lanarkshire. Each of his employers were located in different villages but all were in the Larkhall district,[4] which lends support to Hair's suggestion that migration was far greater within coalfields than between them, estimating an annual migration of between 10 and 35 per cent of colliers in the North-east, where movement was most intense, during the first half of the nineteenth century.[5] The next most migratory region was probably Scotland, both between the nearly contiguous coalfields and within them. In 1842 the clerk of Dundyvan Ironworks referred to Scottish colliers as 'a wandering race'.[6] At the Baird's collieries in Coatbridge the persistence rate of colliers was never more than 25 per cent between 1851 and 1871, and even at Larkhall, regarded as a relatively stable colliery community in comparison with Coatbridge,

---

[1] Hair thesis, 37.   [2] Ibid., 38.
[3] Burt 1924, 24, 50, 136.   [4] Campbell 1979, 167–8.
[5] Hair thesis, 144; this conclusion was based on Hair's analysis of parish registers.
[6] Quoted in Campbell 1979, 164.

the figure was between 32 and 47 per cent. Many years later, Keir Hardie recalled the intermittent character of coalmining in many districts where working for a short time alternated with movements to other districts.[1] Outside the North-east and Scotland it seems likely that probably not less than 10 per cent of the colliers moved their homes each year before 1850, a level of migration which contemporary descriptions of this movement imply was peculiar to coalmining and untypical of other industries.[2]

After 1850 circumstances altered, with the decline of annual hiring and changing trends in the provision of accommodation by coalowners; while the disappearance of the small, rapidly exhausted mines which compelled frequent movements of labour also had the effect of reducing the incentives for perpetual motion. Yet it is possible, even in the North-east where such changes were most marked, to trace evidence of internal migration for the later period, too. At the Consett Iron Company's Garesfield Colliery between 1855 and 1914 approximately 15 per cent of the hewers moved away from the colliery each year, of whom between 30 and 50 per cent had spent only brief working spells there. The annual turnover at Chopwell Colliery, where the average age of migrants was thirty,[3] was as high as 40 per cent a year. Young men, unmarried or with growing families, were the most typical of the short-distance migrants who responded readily to the prospects of material gain. In evidence to the Committee on Dearness and Scarcity in 1873, Joseph Pease remarked that between one-third and one-quarter of a mining population was constantly on the move; among the settled majority inter-colliery movement was common, but migration out of the district was rare.[4]

Evidence from other regions is less plentiful, though doubtless short-distance migration within the industry was more likely to occur wherever houses were provided. The opening of new pits in any area, of course, would stimulate such a movement, though especially in South Wales workmen's trains also played a role, fetching miners to collieries opening up further down the valleys and returning them, at the colliery company's expense, to their homes.[5] When new collieries were being opened up in the East Midlands during the 1860s and 1870s, Staveley's Newstead Colliery was adversely affected in the competition for labour

[1] Ibid., 165, 171.
[2] Hair thesis, 44–5.
[3] Marshall thesis, 304–5.
[4] SC Dearness and Scarcity 1873, X, QQ 4312, 1322.
[5] RC Mining Royalties 1890–1, XLI, QQ 5518–9.

by Hucknall Colliery, for it meant that miners hitherto walking seven miles to Newstead from Hucknall now faced a choice of pitwork closer to home. Workmen's trains run by the Midland Railway Company eased this difficulty, but Charles Markham expressed dissatisfaction with the commuters they brought to the pits, whom he described as 'the waifs and strays of labour'.[1] Competition for labour from Chesterfield resulting from new collieries opening up at Sheepbridge and Dronfield led Markham to embark upon more housebuilding by the Staveley Coal and Iron Company. How far a 'constant migration of miners' remarked upon by contemporaries in the Midland district in 1859, in South Wales, and in other expanding coalfields was also to be found in other established fields, however, as it did in the North-east after the 1870s, we do not know.[2]

The lack of evidence on the long-distance migration of established colliers suggests that wage differentials alone were rarely sufficiently marked to encourage movement of this kind. Furthermore, while there seems to have been relatively little opposition to new men entering mining by changing their occupation within mining districts, there is evidence of opposition from miners towards geographical mobility,[3] especially in view of the often considerable cultural and social isolation of the more remote mining districts, which at least before the 1870s provided fertile ground for resentment and hostility towards newcomers. Before 1870, however, certain types of long-distance migration qualify the picture. Long before 1830 the unrivalled reputation of miners of the North-east for their skilled 'pitmanship' had stimulated requests to leading viewers like Buddle, to recommend or supply pitmen to serve in the collieries of Cumberland, Scotland, and Wales, where local labour was often described as ignorant and inexperienced.[4] This trickle of experienced hewers to the rapidly developing coalfields was entirely different in its contribution from that provided by the influx of unskilled Irish beginning in the 1830s, many of whom entered the Scottish coalfield to take the place of striking miners. According to one official of the Dundyvan Colliery in 1843, since 1837 at least 4,000 such migrants had stuck to the trade.[5] Similar evidence was forthcoming from Durham, where it was estimated that about one-third of the strike

[1] BSCEMRRC Stanton and Staveley 2034/3/9C Markham's reports 16 Dec. 1863, 29 Oct. 1872.
[2] C. P. Griffin thesis, 401; Morris and Williams 1958, 236–7, A. R. Griffin thesis, 68.
[3] SC Dearness and Scarcity 1873, X, Q 4609.
[4] Hiskey thesis, 292.
[5] Report on Mining Districts 1844, XVI, 38.

breakers brought to Durham during the 1844 strike, again mostly Irish, though some from South Wales, had continued to work in the industry and were gradually assimilated into the community.[1] In the same year the Marquis of Londonderry wrote in reply to a query from the West Yorkshire Coalmasters' Association that Irishmen 'thought at first rather inefficient hands are now tolerable workmen', sufficient encouragement for the subsequent importation of Irishmen to Wakefield, under the observance of extra police.[2] Staveley was another company which recruited long-distance migrants, and where in the 1860s between 20 and 25 per cent of Staveley's work-force were Irish. They resided at Chesterfield, several miles distant travelling to the collieries by train, whereas two-thirds of the miners lived in company dwellings on the spot. Of the migrants entering the collieries only 10 per cent were born within ten miles of Staveley village; nearly 40 per cent moved distances of between ten and thirty miles. One-half the household heads in the model community built at Barrow Hill to accommodate them were under the age of thirty.[3]

According to Morris and Williams, the Irish who found their way to South Wales assumed the role of labourers in the coal-producing iron firms, whereas the Cornish miners, possessing basic mining skills (though mystified by the Welsh language) could take their places at the coal face after a month or two.[4] Irish penetration into Scottish collieries was more effective; by 1871 the proportion of Irish-born men aged twenty and over in selected Scottish towns on the coalfield was extremely high: 1 in $3\frac{1}{2}$ in Airdrie, 1 in 4 in Glasgow, 1 in 6 in Hamilton, and 1 in 7 in Kilmarnock, though not all were employed in coalmines.[5] Movements of miners from Lancashire, Cheshire, and South Wales to the North-east occurred in the 1840s, when Cornishmen were also on the move as blacklegs, though some were 'persuaded' to return by local miners.[6] Even so, the sheer rate of migration in the 1840s and 1850s, approaching one-third of the growth of population in the colliery districts, implies an inability of the industry to rely solely upon mining labour to meet the demand. From the 1830s agriculture and the depressed outwork trades provided a less spectacular, but probably more permanent, addition to the coalmining population.[7] In South

[1] *Report on Mining Districts* 1846, XXVI, 397; *MJ* 13 July 1844, 237; 3 Aug. 1844, 261; 17 Aug. 1844, 277.   [2] Machin 1958, 61.
[3] Chapman 1981, 48–9.   [4] Morris and Williams 1958, 236–7.
[5] G. M. Wilson thesis, 84.   [6] Welbourne 1923, 74.
[7] Hair thesis, 58–62.

Wales preference was given to 'local peasants' and only in the eastern districts were English migrants easily absorbed,[1] reflecting a prejudice against long-distance migrants which Alexander MacDonald noted as a general phenomenon in the colliery districts.[2] It seems likely that agriculture and other domestic trades contributed the major flow of migrants from outside the colliery districts after 1850, too, though the rash of strikes in 1858 and in the mid-1860s found coalowners again seeking replacements from the regions of declining mining activity of one kind or another. Lancashire and Yorkshire coalowners favoured Staffordshire as their main source, both in 1858 and in the 1860s, though some came from Derbyshire and Warwickshire.[3] Other coalowners sought Cornishmen. In 1865 the owners of Cramlington Colliery recruited several hundred miners from Cornwall and labourers from Dorset, though some returned home paid from miners' funds;[4] the Staveley Coal and Iron Company's agent was in Cornwall for the same reason in 1866, and the Shotts Iron Company among other Scottish collieries was fishing in the same waters—not for the first time.[5] In 1867 the Earl of Durham's representative was in Cornwall offering free transport to his collieries in return for a year's contract.[6] Small wonder that the *Colliery Guardian* should have reported an 'exodus of Cornishmen to the mining districts' at that time.[7]

For the first time, sizeable emigration of miners, according to Alexander MacDonald, from 1864 began to transform a labour surplus into a scarcity.[8] For five years, beginning in 1865, miners and quarrymen emigrating to the US (many of them Cornish miners suffering from the collapse of the copper industry in 1866) averaged more than 7,000, falling back to slighly more than 5,000 in 1870–3 as the great boom in coal-mining reached its peak.[9] The surge of migration which accompanied it involved the transfer into the industry of railway servants, policemen, framework knitters, tailors, shoemakers, agricultural labourers, and others mentioned in evidence to the Dearness and Scarcity Committee in 1873.[10] Regional differences may be discerned. Alexander MacDonald

[1] Morris and Williams 1958, 237.
[2] *SC Dearness and Scarcity* 1873, X, Q 4609.
[3] Machin 1958, 85, 107, 119–20, 334, 337, 361, 367, 378; Challinor 1972, 73.
[4] *CG* 16 Dec. 1865, 471–2, 30 Dec. 1865, 510.
[5] Chapman 1981, 48–9, 149; *CG* 15 Dec. 1866, 467, 5 Jan. 1867, 8; Brown 1953, 38.
[6] *CG* 13 June 1867, 527.
[7] *CG* 10 Aug. 1867, 117–27.
[8] *SC Dearness and Scarcity* 1873, X, 4715–18.
[9] 'Return of the Number of Miners and Quarrymen . . . 1861–1872', 1873, LXI, 37.
[10] *SC Dearness and Scarcity* 1873, X, QQ 961, 2018, 290.

argued that in Scotland agricultural labourers and other rural workers were no longer attracted to the mining industry as they used to be[1] (though as he made this point in the context of a polemical argument about high death rates and low wages it may have been an exaggeration); similarly, in the North-east the coal famine did not, apparently, lead to a dramatic increase in labour recruitment.[2] Yet there is evidence from Yorkshire and South Staffordshire that high wages during the boom attract external labour into the mines.[3] There was also a shortage of juvenile labour in Lancashire.[4]

The changeover to a decade of net outward movement from the industry must have been dramatic, but of course decennial averages tend to exaggerate the abruptness of the transformation. The net inflows associated with the decade 1871–80 were certainly almost all limited to the early 1870s boom, and many newly-recruited miners must have left the industry once the short-lived boom was over, especially, of course, after 1874. The percentage gain by migration in the colliery districts averaged only 14 per cent between 1871 and 1910. What seems likely, however, is that the migrants of the late nineteenth and early twentieth century were at least as diverse in origin as those of the earlier decades. Reviewing the period shortly before World War I, H. S. Jevons remarked upon the migration into the high-wage South Wales coalfield of large numbers of agricultural labourers from South and mid-Wales, Somerset, and Devon, and of similarly large numbers of 'men of the most miscellaneous previous employments, mostly from Bristol, Gloucester and the Midland towns'.[5] The tendency was for workmen to go from the older coalfields to the new and rapidly developing fields, which is why Jevons also compared the migration to south Yorkshire and Fife with that taking place in South Wales. Echoing William Armstrong and Joseph Pease in the 1870s,[6] his view of migrants originating outside the rapid growth areas was that they were 'the least desirable and responsible class. They have been weeded out from the mines of the older coalfields, perhaps during the period of depression, and they do not compare well with the indigenous population of the districts to which they come.'[7]

---

[1] Ibid., QQ 4594–8.
[2] Ibid., QQ 1318, 3687.
[3] Ibid., QQ 2686; Johnathan Presto, *Five Years of Colliery Life* (London, 1844), 5.
[4] *SC Dearness and Scarcity* 1873, X, QQ 3994–99, 4045–54.
[5] H. S. Jevons 1915, 286–7.
[6] Ibid., 287, 264; NuRO Armstrong 725/B11/81; *SC Dearness and Scarcity* 1873, X, QQ 4330, 4420.
[7] H. S. Jevons 1915, 624.

Attempts to introduce foreign labour were rare and confined principally to Scotland, where colonies of Irishmen, and later Germans and
Poles, worked in pits largely separate from Scottish miners, whose·
union resented the cheap immigrant labour. In South Wales two or
three localities existed where the populations contained concentrations
of Irishmen, Spaniards, and Italians, but the presence of non-Irish
foreign migrants in the coalmining regions was a phenomenon dating
only from the late nineteenth century.[1]

The other type of long-distance immigration was that associated with
the transfer of supervisory and coal-face skills, which did, however,
involve movement from one coalfield to another. It is exemplified by the
entry of many Staffordshire miners into Monmouth in the 1860s.[2] Even
so, contrasted with the volume of short-distance intra-coalfield migration the scale of the movement must have been small, as the relatively
low net migration into the colliery districts after 1871 indicates. What
these figures conceal, however, is the extent to which either before and
after 1871 there might have been a net movement of non-mining labour
into the industry.

iv. The supply of mining labour and occupational mobility

It is pertinent to note that juxtaposed with H. S. Jevons's discussion of
migration is a reaffirmation of the truth in the epigram 'once a collier
always a collier' which, taken in conjunction with the remark that 'the
sons of miners for the most part adopt their fathers' vocations' suggests
a further dimension of labour mobility which hitherto we have considered only indirectly and in non-quantitative fashion. For unanswered
questions remain as to the balance between 'internal' recruitment,
defined as juveniles, themselves the sons of miners, and 'external'
recruitment, comprising the movement of adults from other occupations, or their sons, to mining. Neither the research of Cairncross nor
Thomas addressed itself to this problem, the perspective which
informed their exposition of migration owing more to geography than
to demography, and which therefore failed to reflect the extent to which
the mining industry recruited from within the mining population. Until
the mid-century, at least, coalmining was sometimes combined with
other forms of employment, such as fishing, navvying, and seasonal agricultural work, a practice which, though how widespread we do not

[1] Ibid., 623; Benson 1980, 190–1.
[2] Morris and Williams 1958, 235–7.

know, complicates any discussion of occupational redistribution.[1] Yet such problems have meant that except for casual observation of the kind quoted above very little information is available either on generational recruitment or occupational mobility.

Campbell's study of the Lanarkshire miners is an exception. Using marriage registers as a basis, Campbell surveyed the occupations of the fathers of colliers married in Coatbridge and Larkhall between 1855 and 1875, which revealed that 46 per cent of the fathers of miners in the Coatbridge sample were miners, compared with almost 60 per cent in Larkhall. Qualitative evidence from other regions would suggest that these proportions were below average and that the character of the Coatbridge labour force especially, containing just over 41 per cent born outside the county and a 45 per cent ratio of Irish men to others, was exceptional and unrepresentative of the colliery population as a whole. Larkhall's Irishmen accounted for 17 per cent of the labour force, and more than 67 per cent were born in the county.[2] Both were, in a sense, frontier settlements, though phased at different times. The relatively high levels of occupational mobility exhibited there might have existed also in similar regions which were geographically remote and experienced rapid rates of growth from a relatively small base. However, Campbell's study, though interesting in illuminating the demographic aspects of labour mobility in a small part of Lanarkshire and suggestive at a more general level, cannot provide a workable model for a wider enquiry into national trends and characteristics between 1830 and 1913, for the census data are not available after 1881. It is possible, however, to utilize the contemporary and local evidence adduced so far and to pursue the problem of inter-occupational migration in the industry indirectly.[3]

[1] Samuel 1977, 66.
[2] Campbell 1979, 171–3.
[3] An alternative method, which was rejected, involved the construction of estimates of family size in the colliery districts, and from these the likely number of male children that miners and their wives generated in different decades. Such an exercise would require the reconstruction of key demographic characteristics based on registration district data from censuses and Registrar General's Reports. It might have been possible to adopt the Cairncross/Welton definition of 'colliery districts', to which birth and death rates could have been applied in order to proceed to regional analysis. This, however, would have implied an assumption that each of the colliery districts, which differed in the extent of miner concentration, showed common demographic characteristics, and to deduce these on the basis of those calculated for a limited number of colliery districts, containing, in several instances, high proportions of non-mining populations, seemed to be a serious methodological weakness. The redefinition of colliery districts, on the other hand, raised the fundamental, but problematical, question as to the number of miners who should reside in a registration district in order to justify the designation accorded to any particular area

To calculate the size of the labour force internally generated we have estimated juvenile recruitment, by taking the proportion of juveniles in the industry at census years as the basis for juvenile recruitment during the previous decade (Table 3.6). Line 10 of Table 3.6 estimates the number of adult entrants to the industry required in each decade to compensate for the shortfall in recruitment from juveniles—except in the 1870s and 1890s when juveniles appear to have satisfied the industry's entire need for new labour. This line, therefore, is a guide to the extent of external adult recruitment from other occupations, and by extension is indicative of labour demand. Three problems arise, however, in the interpretation of Table 3.6. Firstly, is it correct to assume that all adult recruits were non-miners, in the sense that they had never previously been employed within the industry, or might some of them have left employment in mining and then returned? Secondly, what proportion of juvenile recruitment came from the sons of men already employed in it? What was the level of recruitment of boys from families where the household head was not a miner and might, therefore, constitute a significant trend in 'external' juvenile recruitment? Finally, what was the level of emigration of miners from the United Kingdom and was it large enough to influence significantly the estimates in Table 3.6?

We have already referred to H. S. Jevon's supposition that once a miner always a miner to have been close to the truth. Evidence given by a Derbyshire miner to the 1842 Commission affords corroboration of a commitment to the industry which fell short of this extreme, but which nevertheless strengthens the presumption that even for those miners who did leave the industry the departure was likely to be temporary and possibly involuntary. He had begun life as a miner but experienced spells of employment in the stocking and iron trades before resuming pitwork. He explained that although it was 'sad, slavish work', he 'was brought up to it, and always like it best'.[1] As this preference was reinforced by favourable wage differentials in comparison with most kinds of employment for which miners were equipped, it may have held good for most times, but probably broke down during periods of

---

as a 'colliery district'. These difficulties together with the enormously labour-intensive recalculations such an approach would involve, prompted the choice of the alternative method, for the doubts aroused by the latter seemed to be much more easily resolved, though not all are entirely satisfied.

[1] Quoted in Hair thesis, 68.

Table 3.6. *Estimates of juvenile and adult recruitment to coalmining, 1831–1911*
('ooos except where stated)

	1831–40	1841–50	1851–60	1861–70	1871–80	1881–90	1891–1900	1901–10
1. Employment	129.4	177.7	248.9	332.1	413.0	519.5	682.0	893.1
2. Juvenile recruitment	50.2	64.2	87.4	106.9	104.4	148.1	162.5	205.9
3. Growth of employment	44.7	66.5	77.3	90.5	72.1	163.2	156.8	255.3
4. Mortality rate (per 1,000)	16.0	15.5	15.5	15.4	15.0	12.5	12.5	11.5
5. Deaths	20.7	27.5	38.6	51.1	62.0	64.9	85.2	102.7
6. Wastage through injury	7.1	10.4	14.0	14.8	19.0	17.4	18.0	22.0
7. Gross increase in labour supply	72.5	104.4	129.9	156.4	153.1	245.5	260.0	380.0
8. Average age of recruitment	9.01	11.23	11.23	12.0	13.24	13.33	13.42	13.75
9. Adjusted juvenile recruitment	45.7	73.2	99.7	133.7	154.5	222.1	247.0	329.4
10. Adult recruitment	26.8	31.2	30.2	22.7	−1.4	23.4	13.0	50.6
11. Juvenile recruitment as percentage of total supply	63	70	77	85	101	90	95	87

^a Figures for 1831–40 refer to male and female employment, those for 1841–1911 to males only.

Sources: Appendix 3.2.

depression, particularly that which followed the boom ending in 1873.[1] Consequently the figures presented in Table 3.6 must be seen for what they are: decadal averages of net juvenile and adult recruitment. Thus, the bald statement that in the 1870s juvenile recruitment equalled the total labour needs of the industry conceals the influx of thousands of adult recruits from non-mining occupations whose departure occurred as suddenly with the onset of the depression in 1874.

This phenomenon poses less of a problem for our decadal averages when (as in the 1870s) the entire process was confined within a decade, but in 1888–91 and 1899–1901 it is conceivable that adult recruits entered the industry towards the end of one decade before leaving it at the beginning of the next. To set this problem in perspective, however, the period 1873 to 1878 is unique throughout the century for the severity and protracted nature of the depression: even after the booms of 1888–91 and 1899–1901 total employment and output continued to rise. Consequently, apart from the mid-1870s there was no necessity for significant numbers of recent recruits to leave the industry. It is possible that the marked fall in earnings that coincided with the slump might have encouraged newly recruited miners to return to their former employment, but for the period before 1850 Hair assembled evidence which suggests that once men had been introduced to work in the pits they were reluctant to move away.[2] Demand for labour between 1830 and 1873 was so bouyant that there are good a priori reasons for supposing that relatively few recruits to mining would have left thereafter, though one cannot discount the possibility that some surface labourers or tradesmen may have returned to employment outside mining. Even the labourer William Brown, while reluctant to send his sons to work in the pit, had himself remained in the industry for twenty-five years, which to judge from the autbiographical evidence presented in 1873 could only be explained in terms of relative earnings and material wellbeing:

I have shorn corn with a sickle for my living in harvest time for years in succession, when there has been short trade; I have mowed grass and corn with a scythe; I have worked in a forge; I have broken down stones on the high road, and I have done everything that I could do for an honest living; but cutting coal is the hardest work I ever did.[3]

---

[1] In 1875 the Mines Inspector for Scotland remarked on the coincidence of an exodus of men attracted to the mines during the boom, with a favourable demand for workers in railway construction and a higher rate of wages. Campbell 1979, 166.

[2] Hair thesis, 66–8.

[3] *SC Dearness and Scarcity* 1873, X, Q 5888.

The Eight Hours Inquiry contains evidence which reveals a considerable regional diversity in the demand for labour from external sources,[1] and is entirely compatible with what we know of the employment needs of different areas and collieries. Since levels of employment did not fall (except in the mid 1870s), there was scant incentive for newly recruited miners to leave the industry. At the same time, regional and intra-regional disparities in rates of growth must have resulted in an exodus from the industry in a few relatively isolated cases, though this problem is dealt with more satisfactorily in the context of the regional recruitment estimates. The second difficulty concerns the possible number of external juvenile recruits and potentially is more serious. Many sources noted the extent to which juvenile recruitment in the mining districts was limited to the sons of miners. Our evidence for the last two decades of our period suggests that the children of miners were less inclined than formerly to follow their fathers in the pit and more likely to seek jobs elsewhere.[2] However, the very absence of job opportunities for juveniles in colliery districts prior to about 1890 might have also acted as an incentive for juveniles from non-mining families to seek work in the pits. Although the popular and contemporary view of mining was that of a hereditary closed shop, the fact that large numbers of external adult recruits entered the industry in 1830–73 reveals this to have been untrue, and raises the question of the possible importance of external juvenile recruitment.

The principal factor operating against it was the fact that traditionally a boy followed his father into the pit and received much of his training from him; 'Men ... brought up in the pits themselves generally wish their boys to work in the pit', was a view repeated more than once in the evidence offered to the Children's Employment Commission in 1842.[3] The hereditary nature of coalmining in the North-east, where free colliery housing and limited alternative employment opportunities were the prevailing characteristics, is hardly surprising, but a similar phenomenon has been found in Leicestershire, where in the mid-nineteenth century circumstances were completely different. Colin Griffin found a very high proportion of colliers to have sent their children into the pits: at Lord Moira's three collieries, for example, 83 per cent of colliers' children had entered the mines.[4] In 1833 Benjamin

[1] *Eight Hour Committee* 1907, XIV, Pt III, QQ 5504, 5602, 3918–20, 3921 and Appendix 6.
[2] Ibid., Pt II, Q 12338–44.
[3] *SC Children's Employment Commission* 1842, XVI, Appendix I, 611, ev. of John Menham, underviewer Garforth Colliery; ibid., 605, evidence of Nicholas Wood, viewer of Killingworth, Hetton, etc. Also XV, 267.   [4] C. P. Griffin thesis, 453.

Biram, the agent in charge of the Yorkshire collieries of the Earl Fitzwilliam, expressed concern at the consequences of the increasing recruitment, mainly of 'little boys ... who as they grow older are appointed to more important posts—and all have the notion that if they behave properly at your lordship's collieries their employment is for life. The collieries by this means become over-stocked with men'.[1] At the mines belonging to the Bridgewater Trust in Lancashire a similar policy of free access to employment for colliers' boys led to a serious over-supply of labour in the pits and prompted measures to remedy the situation. Hitherto, collier's sons could expect to enter the mines and progress to become full getters of coal. The restrictions imposed to limit recruitment, by cutting intake and rendering promotion more difficult, nevertheless proved temporary when trade recovered and boomed in the early 1850s.[2] A contemporary writing in 1860 described the custom among Scottish colliers to regard their 'profession as a sort of hereditary right, which has descended from generation to generation and for which they had to undergo a regular apprenticeship'.[3] Greatly to the surprise of one commissioner who interviewed many boys in North Stafford-shire in 1842, he discovered that they themselves experienced a prefer-ence for mining: '... nineteen out of twenty will say I'd rather be a collier than farmer or potter'.[4]

Yet temporary spurts of demand for labour are much more likely to have been met by adult workers than by juveniles, who by physical capacity as well as legislation were limited as to the work they could do. The 1842 Commissioners concluded, '... the great body of the Children and Young Persons employed in these mines are of the families of the adult workpeople engaged in the pits, or belong to the poorest popula-tion in the neighbourhood'.[5] The *Report* contained no specific reference to the proportion of children brought to the mine by their fathers, though the discussion of ages implies that parents were in favour of putting their own children to work at the earliest possible age, and justi-fied the practice on the grounds that they themselves began work at that age. In the west of Scotland it was noted that, 'Drawers to colliers are generally their own children, or younger brothers or sisters ...' and similar supporting evidence for miners' children to follow fathers into

---

[1] Quoted in John Addy, *A Coal Iron Community in the Industrial Revolution* (London 1969), 34.
[2] Mather 1970, 67.
[3] A. Miller, *Coatbridge, Its Rise and Progress* (Glasgow, 1864), 187.
[4] Quoted in Hair thesis, 67.
[5] *SC Children's Employment Commission* 1842, XV, 267.

the pit came from other major regions too.[1] The only reference to parents refusing to set their children to work in the pits came from the West Midlands, and refers to the butties and wealthier miners who preferred to engage pauper apprentices rather than their own children.[2] In 1865 Thomas Burt noted that in the North-east even the workmen with good wages put their children to work in the pit from the age of ten.[3] Customs, therefore, as well as poverty explain this pattern, and it was reckoned good for a boy to become used to work underground at the earliest possible age in those regions where an experienced hewer commanded status as well as higher wages, though evidence from the same source implies that the pattern was less pronounced in some of the urban industrial mining areas.[4]

Evidence for the later nineteenth century is less abundant but nonetheless testifies to a continuing tradition of internal hereditary recruitment. V. G. Hall's study of Northumberland during the period 1890 to 1914 revealed that 'In all districts it was still common for the boy to receive a training in the skills of hewing from his father or another family member; and to enter hewing as the "marra" (mate) of that family member'. The suggestion that family members other than fathers could supervise boys widens the possible scope for recruitment to nephews and brothers as well as sons, though nevertheless the ability of 'non-mining juveniles' to enter the industry would seem to have been extremely low except when demand was very high.[5] In the Fife coalfield, Abe Moffat, one of fourteen children who first worked in the pit in 1910 when aged fourteen, wrote of his wife, father, mother, grandfather, and grandmother, who also worked as miners or at the pithead.[6]

Conclusions regarding juvenile recruitment are problematical. The level of external juvenile recruitment should have peaked in the 1830s and 1840s when overall recruitment was at its height, intensified, perhaps, by the 1842 Act which reduced, albeit slightly, the potential supply from within the mining community. In all probability, however, this was a temporary phenomenon. By the mid-century the growth of the mining community enabled it to supply the bulk of the industry's demand for juveniles. Simultaneously, the exploitative use of pauper apprentices was curtailed by the 1842 Act and by other legislation. In the

---

[1] Ibid., XVI, Appendix Pt. I, 344, XVII, Appendix Pt. II, 9–22, 827.
[2] Ibid., XVI, Appendix Pt. I, 167.
[3] *SC Regulation and Inspection of Mines* 1865, XII, Q 95–6.
[4] Ibid., Q 99.   [5] Hall thesis, 23.
[6] Abe Moffat, *My Life with the Miners* (London, 1965), 9–10.

second half of the century, however, the figures in Table 3.6 undoubtedly conceal a trade-off between, on the one hand, a small but
growing number of miners' sons who failed to become miners, and, on
the other, the entry into the mines of a small number of children
originating from non-mining families but most of whom were probably
nephews and other distant kin. Such evidence as there is points to the
very limited degree of external juvenile recruitment, both in the early
period before 1870 and at the beginning of the twentieth century.
Evidence that in the period 1890 to 1914 juveniles in coal mines were
often dismissed if their father or brother left the pit[1] suggests that it
must have been extremely difficult for juveniles without mining kin to
gain access to the industry, especially in the rural coalfields.

The calculations above take no account of the numbers of emigrant
miners, mainly to the United States, but there is no reason to suppose
that the trends presented are seriously misleading as a result. Alexander
MacDonald argued that the low prices of the 1860s had driven
thousands of Scottish miners to America, an observation, however,
made in the context of a polemical point about low wages and poverty.[2]
A parliamentary return of 1873 records that 60,000 miners emigrated in
1862–72,[3] though the vast majority of those were undoubtedly metal
miners. However, even supposing a relatively small number of these to
have been coalminers (perhaps between 5,000 and 10,000) and all settled
permanently (a large number are known to have returned), it is possible
that Table 3.6 considerably understates the gross increase in labour supply and the scale of recruitment that would have been needed to compensate for these emigrants. There would appear to be no possibility of
estimating the number of coal miners who emigrated. Statistics on emigration compiled by Brinley Thomas in *Migration and Economic Growth*
are insufficiently disaggregated to be of use in an occupational analysis.[4]
It is safe to argue that continental emigration can hardly have featured
much before 1860, so our estimates for the first three decades are
unlikely to require attention. From MacDonald's evidence on the 1860s,
coal miners are unlikely to have figured prominently among the ranks of
the permanent migrants. Official statistics begin in 1875 and suggest that
assuming coalminers to have emigrated to the same extent as other
workers in Britain, considerable numbers (in the region of 20,000 a

---

[1] Hall thesis, 23.
[2] *SC Dearness and Scarcity* 1873, X, Q 4634.
[3] *Return of Miners and Quarrymen* 1861–1872, 1873, LXI, 37, return no. 142.
[4] Brinley Thomas, *Migration and Economic Growth* (Cambridge, 1954), 268–72.

decade) might have left the UK industry in the 1880s and 1900s (but not in the 1890s when emigration fell off markedly). It is, however, highly unlikely that coalminers emigrated as regularly as other workers, since two of the main spurs to emigration, structural and chronic cyclical unemployment, affected them much less than other groups of workers in the nineteenth century.[1]

Consequently the most that can be said here is that the figures in Table 3.6 for the 1860s, 1880s, and 1900s may contain errors in which gross labour requirements are understated because of the failure to include an allowance for permanent emigration. A conservative estimate (at least for the 1880s and 1900s) would place this under-counting at several thousand miners, which would push up the adult recruitment figures (because of the need to displace the emigrants) by the same amount. Juvenile recruitment as a percentage of total supply in the 1860s, 1880s, and 1900s is likely to have been several percentage points lower than is indicated in the figures in line 11 of Table 3.6. Supposing miners to have emigrated at levels of 50 per cent below the frequency of other occupations, the percentage in line 11 would need to be lowered by between 5 and 7 points for those decades. The overall trend, as indicated in the decadal estimates, would be unlikely to be affected.

With these provisos in mind, Table 3.6 may be regarded as showing broadly the level of juvenile recruitment, with the balance made up by adult or 'external' recruitment from other occupations. The years between 1831 and 1860 (and especially between 1831 and 1850) emerge as a period of substantial external recruitment. As a whole, in these three decades approximately 30 per cent of the industry's newly recruited labour force originated from the movement of adults engaged in occupations other than mining, especially in the 1830s and 1840s. The 1870s also stand out as a period of unprecedented levels of adult recruitment, which between 1871 and 1875 averaged 18,300, compared with annual figures for previous decades which fell well below 20 per cent of that level. After 1875 the decade saw an equally massive exodus from the industry, when more than three-quarters of the number of adults recruited in 1871–5 returned to, or sought other, employment. Remarkably, it was also during this decade that juvenile recruitment exceeded supply, coinciding with the unprecedented movement into, and then away from, the industry. In the 1890s juvenile recruitment accounted for 95 per cent of the industry's net demand for labour, higher than in any other decade save the 1870s.

[1] SC *Dearness and Scarcity* 1873, X, Q 4637.

Except for hewers, and in the short-term for colliery labour in general, the generalization that 'on the coalfield shortage of labour rather than excess prevailed'[1] appears to be an exaggeration. The spreading of work which was very common in the industry reflected coal-owners' concern to retain selected workers whose qualities were specific and included more than skill.[2] The fact that under-employment was the characteristic condition in the industry testifies to the long-term overall excess supply, though periods of shortage did occur in certain mining regions. This is indicated by the inter-regional variations in the estimates of external adult recruitment (Table 3.7), which may be interpreted as a symptom of the strength of demand for labour. Among the large, older coal mining regions only the North-east recorded net recruitment of adult males from outside the industry in as many as three decades; during the 1830s and again in the 1860s and 1870s. The other regions recruiting non-mining adults were South Wales (in the 1830s, 1860s, 1880s, and 1900), the East Midlands (from the 1850s to the 1880s), and Yorkshire (from the 1860s to the 1890s). In the 1870s an outflow occurred in the West Midlands, Lancashire and Cheshire, and even Scotland, marginal losses continuing in the West Midlands and Lancashire and Cheshire in the 1880s, but also after 1900 joined by the North-east and Scotland. The explanation for the regional patterns in external recruitment raises the question of the relationship between differential wage levels and comparative inducements, a problem which can be examined only after regional wage patterns have been established.[3]

v. Labour intensity: days and hours

Neither skill requirements nor wage levels presented coalowners with an overall difficulty in filling their collieries with labour, except in the very short run and in certain districts.[4] The number of miners employed is, however, inadequate as a measurement of the supply of the labour inputs to the industry; for just as the actual supply of colliery workers was affected by legislation, custom, and the employment policies pursued by coalowners and trade unions, likewise such influences had an effect upon the days and hours of working, as did the nature of colliery enterprise in the nineteenth century. The seasonal character of the domestic coal trade and the cyclical nature of the demand for furnace coal,

[1] Samuel 1977, 48.
[2] See below 747–57.
[3] See below 278–9.
[4] See above 204–7.

Table 3.7. *Estimates of labour recruitment in the regions, 1831-1910 (males)*

	1831-40	1841-50	1851-60	1861-70	1871-80	1881-90	1891-1900	1901-10
A. Adult recruitment ('000s)								
Scotland	4.5	4.3	−0.1	0.3	−4.4	4.3	1.0	4.1
North-east	6.3	2.9	4.5	10.9	6.2	−1.9	2.2	4.5
Lancs./Ches.	3.4	5.4	5.7	−0.9	−3.9	−0.6	−2.7	−4.3
Yorkshire	1.2	3.9	4.4	3.7	5.8	3.0	3.8	12.9
East Midlands	0.7	1.6	5.2	2.8	6.6	4.5	2.4	−2.8
West Midlands	3.1	7.2	5.9	0.2	−13.2	−5.0	1.2	−0.2
South Wales	5.4	3.5	4.2	3.6	3.2	16.7	5.2	26.7
B. Juvenile recruitment as a percentage of gross supply								
Scotland	56	73	101	98	127	86	97	91
North-east	59	81	78	70	83	104	96	95
Lancs./Ches.	64	69	74	105	119	102	111	117
Yorkshire	77	67	74	80	77	91	90	78
East Midlands	75	72	58	80	71	84	92	108
West Midlands	68	59	69	99	194	137	94	101
South Wales	57	74	77	85	88	71	90	72

The above presents the results only of the calculations for the regions. The methods are identical to those used in Table 3.6. Juvenile recruitment percentages above 100 correspond with negative adult recruitment shown in A, which are explained by an indigenous shortfall of the latter due to death, injury, or retirement.

and later for exports, meant that a policy of engaging sufficient labour to meet the needs of a colliery at times of maximum demand necessitated short-time working, from year to year—and even within the year for collieries supplying the landsale domestic house coal market.[1] Conditions of the supply of labour also contributed to the origins of a persistent, long-term labour surplus, resulting in part from the customary progression of colliers' sons in traditional coal-mining districts to become pit lads, possessing the aspiration ultimately to become hewers. This was a phenomenon which in the 1830s and 1840s presented an increasingly serious problem for the managers of the Yorkshire mines owned by the Earl Fitzwilliam and of the Lancashire mines owned by Lord Egerton, later by the Bridgewater Trustees. When trade was poor work was spread among miners at the Worsley mines, mainly as a humanitarian approach to the problem of surplus labour;[2] whereas on the estates of the Lords Bradford and Crawford the accumulation of a labour reserve was an integral part of employment policy designed to render the work-force more amenable.[3] Both policies, however, also ensured that labour would be available to accommodate an upturn in trade.

The butties of south Staffordshire pursued similar policies to those of Lords Bradford and Crawford, and the notoriety earned by the district as a source of blackleg labour owed much to the continuance of a labour surplus.[4] Similar circumstances in the East Midlands before the 1890s explains the existence of a substantial number of 'marketmen', who lacked regular work and depended upon the daily decision of a pit official for day-to-day employment. Tending to depress wages and to reinforce the disciplinary powers of the butties, the 'marketmen' enabled the coalowners to extend short-time working so as to retain the potential services of men who were not even on their pay lists.[5] Even in the North-east, where until the 1840s at least the annual bond had included guaranteed minimum earnings and employment for most face workers, the increasing vulnerability of colliery enterprises to the discontinuities in demand arising from commercial, rather than purely seasonal, factors had led to the exclusion of these guarantees by the coalowners in 1831—henceforth the subject of recurrent disputes.[6] When in 1844 the coalowners of the North-east decided to replace the annual

---

[1] Walters 1977, 193; A. R. Griffin 1971, 115.
[2] Mee 1975, 155–8; Mather 1970, 224–5.
[3] Mather 1970, 325.
[4] Taylor thesis, 124–5, 148–9, 136, 160.
[5] A. R. Griffin 1971, 115.   [6] See above 217.

bond by a monthly contract, T.J. Taylor explained the change in policy as the result of a chronic labour surplus, the consequence of 'high wages' and 'the habit of pitmen to bring up their families in their own occupation'.[1] The reference to high wages was doubtless designed to counter the miners' bid to improve rates, but the short-time working which involved the loss of between two and four or even more days per fortnight was presented as evidence to support his claim.[2] When the coal-owners had first removed the minimum-wage employment guarantee they had made it clear that they wished to reserve the right to lay a pit idle on a regular basis should commercial conditions require it, a principle which became general in the rest of the industry where annual bonds did not exist and where the general policy was to adopt short-time working to reduce output until an improvement in prices justified full-time working.[3]

Long-term unemployment was not a feature of the nineteenth-century mining industry. Owing to the almost uninterrupted growth of the industry, a growth not accompanied by rises in productivity large enough to displace labour, structural unemployment was virtually non-existent. Nor did seasonal unemployment feature very much in the period after 1830, at least in the larger collieries in the major regions, while cyclical unemployment was felt in the form of short-time working rather than long-period lay-offs. The lack of official statistics on unemployment is, in this case, indicative of its absence, though a few isolated data appear to strengthen this assertion. A study of the unemployment relief figures from the Miners' Permanent Relief Fund in Durham indicates that unemployment (defined here as five consecutive days without work) affected less than 0.25 per cent of the work-force on average between 1883 and 1913, and that even in the worst year (1908) the proportion rose to only 0.66 per cent.[4] A return from the West Cumberland Miners' Association to the 1866 Royal Commission on the Depression of Trade and Industry reported that less than one per cent of the work-force could be considered unemployed in the long term.[5] Writing in 1903, W. J. Ashley described coalmining as a trade 'in which there is usually little complete unemployment; where slack times means

[1] *Report on Mining Districts* 1846, XXIV, 392–3.

[2] Ibid., 394.

[3] Brown thesis, 190–1; Walters 1977, 237–8.

[4] Marshall thesis, 231.

[5] 'In the coal mines the workmen are not discharged, but in depression the workmen are employed less days per week, so that men always have some work'. *RC Depression on Trade and Industry* 1886, XXII, Appendix Pt. II, 93, West Cumberland Miners' Association.

fewer days for all rather than complete loss of work for many',[1] and there is abundant evidence in from the Children's Employment Commission, the Midland Mining Commission, and Reports on the State of the Population in Mining Districts[2] to indicate that short-term working was common before the 1870s boom, though it is difficult to judge whether it was less pervasive than in the depression of the late 1870s and 1880s.

Variations in the length of the working week and short-time working were important features of the industry. In addition to the climatic, geological, accidental, and seasonal factors which sometimes occasioned such discontinuities in employment, variations in the length of the working week and short-time working comprised two main types: firstly, those imposed by employers, taking the form of the closing of the entire pits for a number of days each week, and secondly, those voluntarily entered into by the men who restricted their own labour by working fewer days than possible. The former was the typical reaction of management to depressed trade and lowered prices; the latter the familiar response by labour to high prices and prosperity.

In the case of voluntary restriction the motivation was two-fold; firstly it coincided with high wages and amounted to a conscious leisure preference; secondly, the withholding of labour under such conditions was felt to be beneficial in maintaining high prices and wages, thereby prolonging the boom. In 1845 Tremenheere reserved particular vehemence for an attack on this practice which he described as widespread in Lanarkshire, Fifeshire, Staffordshire, and the North-east, and not unknown to occur in other regions, for short periods, as well.[3] However, the limited effectiveness of such restrictions on output, even in Scotland where the 'darg' was the most persistent form of stinting output and sometimes secured gains during an upswing,[4] suggests that employers' labour policies were the more important explanation for perpetuating part-time employment over the long term. For the investment cycle was such that the booms stimulated additions to capacity which materialized only after the peaks had passed, yet which the economics of colliery working dictated should become, and remain, operational, because new faces promised either lower costs or higher revenue product.[5] The additional employment created tended to offset

---

[1] Ashley 1903, 55.
[2] See also Brown thesis, 190–1; Evison, 'Central Region', 51; Benson 1980, 61; Burt 1924, 90, 111.
[3] See the *Reports on Mining Population*, esp. 1844, XVI, 30–53.
[4] G. M. Wilson thesis, 277–8.   [5] See chap. 6.

losses of manpower occasioned by the closure of exhausted pits or the temporary, or permanent, shutdown of mines dictated by commercial considerations.

The existence of highly competitive conditions in the industry from the 1840s and the weakness of organized labour during the slumps enabled coalowners to find workers at lower wages,[1] conditions which satisfied the employers' preference for continued production in order to minimize working costs. Taking the restraint on productivity in the booms together with the adjustment of workers to lower wages in the slump, the combined effect upon output was to slow down contraction following each expansion. It cannot be overemphasized that the widespread existence of under-employment in the coalmining industry in the form of three- or four-day working or less[2] has the effect of falsely inflating the level of 'employment' as indicated by nineteenth-century statistics, and largely explains the apparent paradox implied by the coincidence between fluctuating annual production per man-year and the uninterrupted growth in employment.

In attempting to measure labour input—and indeed labour productivity—it is necessary to identify and measure variations in the length of the working week and the extent of short-time working, both of which were prevalent but for which the data are limited in the period they cover, partial in regional coverage, and largely descriptive.[3] The evidence does indicate a considerable disparity in the number of days worked by hewers in the different regions. This originates partly in differences in the state of trade within the country at any one time, partly in different custom (for example, the tendency in the early period for some regions to operate a six-day week and others a five- or five-and-a-half day week, or six in one week and five the next), and partly in differences in the response of labour to common problems (such as the decision to strike or to restrict work during booms). At best, therefore, the resulting series on days worked can purport to reflect the average hypothetical situation,

---

[1] Even in 1829 Buddle remarked on this in evidence quoted in William Green, *The Chronicles and Records of the Northern Coal Trade* (Newcastle, c.1866), 229; and see below 556–61, 752.

[2] See below 240–8.

[3] For the period 1860–90 numerous references in the parliamentary papers make it possible to construct a UK average of days worked, and for the North-east a regional series exists. To extend the UK series before 1860 presents serious difficulties since most of the evidence is limited to 1842–6, taken from the 1842 *Children's Employment Commission*, the *Midland Mining Commission*, and *Reports on the Mining Population*. For other years guesswork has been based on the movement of coal prices and a detrended series of coal output, together with a few isolated references from other sources.

and it seems sensible to concentrate on changes over time rather than attempting to embrace the full range of regional variations.

There is, however, a problem arising from the sources, for much of the parliamentary evidence prior to 1870 contains an element of confusion between figures reflecting the number of days on which pits were open and those indicating the number of days on which hewers actually worked on average, a difference which is explained by the prevalence of voluntary absence from work, or 'absenteeism', as coalowners and commentators preferred to describe a phenomenon whereby miners might work fewer days than those when the pits were open, and which observers and employers condemned. An element of uncertainty, therefore, complicates any attempt to measure attendance at work, which except for certain holidays often differed from region to region and district to district, the result of individual choice. In this sense, miners have always been prone to absent themselves from work.

In 1860 Robert Slaney MP, an otherwise well-informed observer but knowing nothing of the coalmining industry, tried to explain why a three-day working week was common among miners when economic circumstances allowed. A visit underground had convinced him of the rationality and justification for such a practice:

It may be, in consequence of getting high wages he works a shorter time, but if the Hon. Member has not been, as I have been, down to the bottom of a coal pit he will hardly conceive the hardships the miners undergo. You go down to a working in which you cannot walk upright; you walk on and find a number of men without a single rag on above their waists, picking at the coal in every painful attitude, you can conceive; then there come draughts of air, to shield themselves against which they must put on their woollen jackets, after being in profuse perspiration; they will then take you to a spot where they will ask you if you ever heard of such a thing as bad air, and they will put in a light, which will immediately burn blue, and you have such a horrid smell that you desire to leave the place as quickly as possible; therefore they have a good deal of painful work, and they do as much in 12 hours that way as many men do in 24, when you look at the real hardships which they have to go, putting aside the chances of accident to which they are subject.[1]

Whether pushing and dragging coal-laden tubs weighing half a ton or more from the face, which was the putter's task, or getting the coal, several tons a day, often from awkward positions, which was the hewer's role, face work was exhausting, made worse by conditions of

[1] *SC Masters and Operatives* 1860, XXII, Q 510.

heat, as in the Shropshire pit visited by Slaney, and by water. Yet even in 1913 only a tiny proportion of miners were at work in collieries where hewing was mechanized. H. S. Jevons described the hewers' work in 1915 as requiring 'seven or eight hours of almost incessant strenuous physical exertion' with pick and shovel: 'working continuously, as some must do, in a dripping wet place generally leads to diminished vitality and disease. Whilst some seams are very wet, others are too dry, so that there is constantly coal dust in the air which is somewhat unwholesome to breathe and highly dangerous.' Moreover at the end of a shift the miner could face a walk often up to three miles to the shaft, which in wet mines meant a 'trudge through pools of black slush, water percolating from the roof'.[1]

It would be plausible to envisage high absentee rates falling after the mid-nineteenth century when hours of such unrelenting toil became shorter. Yet in South Wales the habit of losing several days a month in the 1840s survived the changing character of the trade from one based on coal for iron production to steam coal for export, so that in 1871 it was found that following pay day each month, 'Monday is not a working day; sometimes Tuesday they do not go in. Saturday is always a contracted day in the number of hours' work.'[2] At Earl Fitzwilliam's collieries, in South Yorkshire, 'reckoning Monday' was generally regarded as a holiday, and Tuesdays too, in good times. In Lancashire 'reckinin Saturday' occurring at fortnightly intervals was still customarily followed in the 1860s by 'three day bacchanals, beer drinking and eating'.[3] In Staffordshire about half the miners were paid by the stint (an agreed quantity of coal which could be worked in any number of hours that they chose) rather than by the day, and two and occasionally three days work could be accomplished within twelve hours, depending upon agreement with the butty on what constituted a day's work. Day workers present in the pit for twelve hours were renowned for their absenteeism. 'St Monday is honoured with punctilious observance and Tuesday is known locally as "shackling day"'. Easter, Whitsuntide and Christmas are observed by a whole week's feasting and recreation and Autumn months bring village wakes.'[4] Remarking upon a recurrence of regular holiday-making on fortnightly 'pay Mondays' in Derbyshire, in 1861 the *Colliery Guardian* expressed approval of the

---

[1] H. S. Jevons 1915, 610–15.
[2] Quoted in Walters 1977, 224.
[3] Mee 1975, 161; Challinor 1972, 69.
[4] *CG* 5 Jan. 1872, 14.

magistrates' apparent determination to check this recurrence of a former traditional practice.[1]

Ironically, the weekly pay (increasingly regarded by workers to be preferable to fortnightly or monthly pays, because it offered better prospects of avoiding indebtedness to employers) could in some instances provide the worst arrangements for employers from the standpoint of regular working. Such an instance was that of the weekly-paid Staffordshire pitworkers whose post-pay behaviour drew criticism from the editor of the *Colliery Guardian*, and the suggestion that employers there should adopt fortnightly pays.[2] Weekly pays were conceded by many employers during the boom of the 1870s, the subsequent trend continuing in that direction, particularly in those collieries where managers could exercize a degree of effective control over attendance. No doubt Normansell, leader of the Yorkshire miners, was trying to portray the advantages for employers of the adoption of shorter hours when in 1860 his report to the National Association for the Promotion of Social Science he described the effects of the introduction of the eight-hour day in south Yorkshire since 1858; he made no mention of the improved physical productivity of hewers but stressed their greater regularity when working shorter hours. Long hours of work he associated with irregular working: 'The young thoughtless and improvident as a general rule have two or three days spreeing and drinking ... because they know that they will have the opportunity of working all the hours God sends in the latter part to fetch up their lost time'. He remarked on the men's 'steadier habits' since the 1858 reform, which meant that pits had not lain idle for one or two days in each pay.[3]

Widespread observance of 'St Monday', however, symbolic of voluntary absenteeism, survived, for it was not only custom but the system of working and economic conditions which explains its persistence; the relatively high earnings of face workers, the main practitioners, and payment by piece-rates enabled them to make up losses at other times. Not surprisingly, therefore, absenteeism was cyclical, increasing when piece-rates and the demand for labour was high. A *Colliery Guardian* report in 1872 referred to such a phenomenon in the Forest of Dean, where repeated wage rises 'far from promoting the industry and comfort of the miners, appears to have had an opposite effect, for whereas they used to

---

[1] *CG* 26 Oct. 1861, 266.

[2] Henry Johnson 'South Staffordshire Coalfield', in Samuel Timmins (ed.), *Birmingham and the Midland Hardware District* (London, 1866), 21–34; *CG* 3 Aug. 1861, 22.

[3] Quoted in Machin 1958, 343.

be satisifed with "Saint Mondays", Tuesday and Wednesday are now habitually cannonised'.[1] This cyclical aspect of absenteeism Normansell also acknowledged.[2] During the boom of the 1870s Alfred Hewlett reported to shareholders of the Wigan Coal and Iron Company that 'the men resolved to restrict output of coal by working shorter hours on each day, and only on certain days in each week. This restriction has been acted upon, and has told most seriously against the advantageous working of the mines'.[3] Buoyant trading conditions were often accompanied by a similar pattern of restriction in the west of Scotland and in South Wales.[4] At the Bedlington Colliery, in Northumberland, in 1900 colliery manager John Weeks reflected on the reasons for a diminished output produced by a greater number of hewers on the pay sheets compared with the previous year. An influenza epidemic was one factor, but 'idleness following on higher wages' he reckoned was the other. The number of men off work continued to rise 'still further stimulated by the increase of wages accompanied by constant work'.[5]

Cyclical gains sometimes endured over longer periods. For example, after the boom of the 1870s Northumberland coalowners agreed to observe 'baff' Saturday as a general holiday following each pay day, but in 1885 officials of the miners' union conceded that the necessity for their members to work the Baff Saturday to sustain incomes had led the owners to alter their attitude, henceforward regarding it as a working day.[6] At Griff Colliery, in Warwickshire, where earnings were high, manager Melly reported in 1895 that summer working had dropped to three days a week at the company's three pits, and that Easter had brought an even greater loss of work than the employers had desired: 'in consequence I came to blows with the stallmen on two occasions and fined all the absentees 5s. which I hope will have the effect of getting them back to work with more reasonable time after each holiday'. Since at least 1893 Melly had made a determined effort to reduce the number of holidays taken at Griff, which then amounted to one month in all, five days at Easter, five at Whitsun, three in August, four or five at Christmas and the same at Bedworth Wake, and two at Chivers Coton Wake.[7] In comparison with examples from other regions these are generous

[1] Quoted in Benson 1980, 58.
[2] *SC Dearness and Scarcity* 1873, X, Q 660.
[3] LaRO Wigan Coal and Iron DXX/127/40-7.
[4] G. M. Wilson thesis, 275; Walters 1977, 224-5.
[5] NEI Weeks MS9/1 Weeks's Report 25 April 1900.
[6] *CG* 10 July 1885, 67.
[7] WaRO Griff CR/1169/22-3 Annual Reports.

holiday periods, but while the precise occasion for the celebration of occasions, other than the main religious festivals, differed from region to region, observance continued into the twentieth century.

Extended holidays were one manifestation of absenteeism, but in 1915 an official committee found that custom was also a continuing influence on the pattern of miners' week-to-week working patterns.[1] Contrary to a supposition that arduous labour would require days off to recover from sustained spells of hard work, it was found that those days on which most absenteeism occurred were influenced more by custom than physical need, though as it happened maximum exertion customarily immediately preceded pay day—which was the signal to rest. In Scotland, an idle-pay Saturday was almost invariably followed by Monday off, while the best attendance occurred towards pay day. In the North-east most took Monday off work, attendance thereafter gradually improving until the end of the pay. In Lancashire, Friday was pay day and consequently on Saturdays the pits were poorly attended and only slightly better on Mondays, a pattern unaltered for more than fifty years, except that the precise days which colliers chose to take off altered as the pay day changed; the survival of a similar pattern is to be found in South Wales and in the Midlands, too.[2] Beyond custom or collusion, the option to be absent from work remained the choice of the individual. The leading Scottish coalowner, J. S. Dixon, explained to the Eight Hour Day Committee in 1907: 'There is no hard and fast rule that the miner must work so many days a week. A miner takes an idle day whenever he wishes, but, of course, if he persistently does that, the manager may dismiss him';[3] though he might have added that such an action would have depended on the state of the labour market.

With so much depending upon short-term considerations and upon individuals' inclinations, absenteeism is extremely difficult to measure. An attempt to quantify trends in absenteeism among miners by the West Yorkshire Coalowners' Association for the period between 1875 and 1913 was less than successful, but the unanimous view of colliery owners and managers in this region was that absenteeism had invariably increased when wages rose and the pits worked full time; the converse was also affirmed, as was the view that underground workers were those principally responsible for absenteeism. A few returns recorded average annual absenteeism, above and below ground, to have been 9.2 per cent

---

[1] Report of a Departmental Committee on Conditions Prevailing in the Coal Mining Industry due to the War 1914–16 col. 7939 xxviii. 1, 11–16.

[2] Ibid., Benson 1980, 58–60.   [3] *Eight Hours Committee* 1907, XV, Q 641.

in 1905, 10.7 per cent in 1910, and 9.2 per cent in 1913, but these were regarded as neither representative nor reliable. None the less, the coal-owners evinced no doubt that absenteeism was due to the 'attractions of sports, racing etc. to men who consider he [sic] can earn a week's wage if he takes at least one day off per week'.[1]

The aims of collective action are clear; to help sustain high prices, and to allow miners to do less work for the same, or more, money, for on some occasions in Scotland wages in the short term were forced up, at least temporarily.[2] For the individual miner exercizing independent choice, his motive was usually leisure of various kinds: race meetings, elections, displays, as well as fairs and festivals, religious or otherwise—and fair weather absenteeism was also common. In South Wales the *eisteddfodau* afforded particular occasions when holidays were taken, as was Hogmanay in Scotland.[3] For some miners the purpose of a day's freedom from work was to drink alcohol, or to recover from it; the pattern of drinking in the Fife coalfield was described by an observer who noted that the miners confined excessive drinking to pay night, the day, or perhaps the two, following, and holidays, especially at Hogmanay.[4]

It seems likely that the justification for blaming drink as causing laziness and absenteeism, a common complaint among coalowners at the beginning of our period, had diminished considerably by 1900, partly as a result of truck legislation and the prohibition of the payment of wages in public houses, which had been an especially common practice in South Wales, South Staffordshire, and Scotland in the first half of the century.[5] This legislation was anticipated by the policies of many coalowners who, like Richard Barrow of Staveley, refused to pay his men through butties for fear they might pay out at the pub.[6] George Stephenson at Clay Cross and the Peases in Durham sacked habitual drunkards and opposed the licensing of new premises.[7] Morality may have been an important consideration in adopting such policies, but inasmuch that in the minds of contemporaries drink and irregular work habits were inter-related, the attempts to contain the consumption of alcohol was congruent with the economics of colliery working. By World War I, however, the national trend away from intemperance had

---

[1] LCA 1708/12 WYCOA, 31–2.

[2] G. M. Wilson thesis, 275–7.

[3] Walters 1977, 234–5; Benson 1981, 58–9.

[4] Quoted in Benson 1981, 151; see also W. R. Lambert, 'Drink and Work Discipline in Industrial South Wales 1800–1870', *Welsh History Review*, VII (1975), 289–306.

[5] *RC Truck 1871* XXXVI, 5.   [6] Chapman 1981, 150.

[7] Ibid.; Benson 1980, 151.

carried the miners with it, and an official investigation into absenteeism concluded, rather coyly, that drink was 'less the cause of absenteeism than may have been supposed'.[1] None the less, while mortality from alcohol was lower than the national average, one survey concluded that mining towns were second only to the major ports in the incidence of drunkenness.[2]

As mining became more capital-intensive, managers found themselves under pressure to reduce voluntary absenteeism in order to maximize continuous production, which might explain why Newton Chambers experimented with weekly instead of fortnightly pays in the early 1860s. But when attendance by the workmen did not improve, the scheme was abandoned: 'We should not object to weekly pays', remarked John Chambers, 'on condition they would bind themselves to work every day in busy seasons, having their holidays in the slack seasons'.[3] Richard Barrow's tactics in 1863 included conceding a wage increase to Staveley's hewers conditional on regular working, instead of missing Mondays and occasionally Tuesdays. The problem surfaced again in 1889 and 1896 and had yet to be completely solved some thirty years later, when C. P. Markham grumbled before the Samuel Commission about excessive absenteeism and the frequentcy of local wakes and race meetings to which he thought it was connected.[4]

Actually estimating absenteeism accurately is extremely difficult, even for the twentieth century, for not until 1913 are there national and comprehensive regional figures (though for six months only). Two separate regional series—for hewers in Durham and in Northumberland[5]—provide the basis for constructing a voluntary absenteeism series for the North-east between 1873 and 1913, which is presented in Appendix 3.3. This evidence suggests variation between 5 and 13 per cent, resembling rates recorded in some South Wales collieries from the 1890s.[6] It also provides support for the interpretation of absenteeism as a cyclical trade-related phenomenon, revealing no marked secular trend upwards other than might have been expected during the boom conditions from around 1900. Cyclical changes were superimposed upon patterns of attendance which were largely customary and which, while altering in detail, appear to have remained at roughly the same

---

[1] *Report of a Departmental Committee on Conditions Prevailing in the Coal Mining Industry due to the War* 1914–16, cd. 7939 xxviii. 1, 16.

[2] Dingle, 'Drink and Working Class Living Standards 1870–1914', *EHR*, XXV (1972), 610.

[3] SCL, Newton Chambers, TR 453/5.   [4] Chapman 1981, 149.

[5] See Appendix III.   [6] Walters 1977, 224.

frequency and for the same reasons. In 1915 a Select Committee examined national figures of absenteeism as it affected all colliery workers and concluded that in 1913 avoidable absenteeism (after adjusting the figures for absence due to accident and sickness) amounted to less than 5 per cent.[1] The regional data available from 1899 (Appendix 3.3) suggest that the North-east, South Wales, and Scotland were areas of lower than average rates, whereas in the predominantly urban coalmining regions of Lancashire, Yorkshire, and the West Midlands higher than average levels were recorded. This pattern suggested that alternative employment opportunities for miners' wives might have had the effect of reducing the pressure upon miners to work the maximum shifts possible.[2]

The inter-regional differences revealed in the national 'snapshot' figures of no more than a few percentage points justify adopting the evidence on the North-east as an indicator of general trends in absenteeism. From 1873, therefore, data assembled relating to the number of days on which pits were opened have been deflated by the series on rates of absenteeism among hewers in the North-east. Before 1873 evidence has been gathered on the number of days actually worked. The various series used to produce Table 3.8 are presented in Appendix 3.3 where the sources and methods are explained, and the results compared with Barnsby's series for the Black Country and Slaven's for Govan.

It must be emphasized that prior to 1894 the series is experimental, and the results need to be tested against both contemporary and secondary data. The former make it abundantly clear that weekly variations in the number of days worked were the norm. The parliamentary literature covering the period 1830–50 makes it clear that restriction, both voluntary and imposed, was a common feature of the industry. Restriction of labour during the massive boom of 1872–3 is well attested.[3] The extent of voluntary restriction, however, evidently varied markedly between individuals, which explains why when Ralph Moore, Mines Inspector for the east of Scotland, recorded wages and earnings of individual colliers he drew a distinction between 'good' and 'average' collieries mainly by the criterion of regularity of attendance rather than skill.[4]

The degree of regional variation in employment opportunities may be tested, to a certain extent, by comparing the national series for the

---

[1] *Report of a Departmental Committee on Conditions Prevailing in the Coal Mining Industry due to the War 1914–16* cd. 7939 xxxiii, 1, 11–16.

[2] *Eight Hours Committee* 1907, XV, Q 6047.

[3] See above 242–3.

[4] *Reports of the Inspector of Mines for East Scotland* 1868–87.

Table 3.8. *Estimated days per week worked by hewers, 1830-1913*

1830	5	1851	$4\frac{1}{2}$	1872	4	1893	4.6
1831	$4\frac{1}{2}$	1852	$4\frac{1}{2}$	1873	4.3	1894	4.7
1832	4	1853	4	1874	4.0	1895	4.4
1833	$3\frac{1}{2}$	1854	4	1875	3.9	1896	4.5
1834	4	1855	$4\frac{1}{2}$	1876	3.9	1897	4.7
1835	$4\frac{1}{2}$	1856	$4\frac{1}{2}$	1877	3.5	1898	4.7
1836	$4\frac{1}{2}$	1857	$4\frac{1}{2}$	1878	3.3	1899	4.9
1837	5	1858	4	1879	4.4	1900	4.8
1838	5	1859	$4\frac{1}{2}$	1880	4.6	1901	4.5
1839	$4\frac{1}{2}$	1860	$4\frac{1}{2}$	1881	4.6	1902	4.7
1840	$4\frac{1}{2}$	1861	$4\frac{1}{2}$	1882	4.8	1903	4.6
1841	4	1862	$4\frac{1}{2}$	1883	4.8	1904	4.6
1842	3	1863	$4\frac{1}{2}$	1884	4.5	1905	4.6
1843	$3\frac{1}{2}$	1864	$4\frac{1}{2}$	1885	4.4	1906	4.8
1844	4	1865	$4\frac{1}{2}$	1886	4.6	1907	4.9
1845	$4\frac{1}{2}$	1866	$4\frac{1}{2}$	1887	4.7	1908	4.5
1846	$4\frac{1}{2}$	1867	$4\frac{1}{2}$	1888	4.8	1909	4.5
1847	$4\frac{1}{2}$	1868	4	1889	4.9	1910	4.6
1848	$4\frac{1}{2}$	1869	$4\frac{1}{2}$	1890	4.7	1911	4.6
1849	$4\frac{1}{2}$	1870	$4\frac{1}{2}$	1891	4.7	1912	4.9
1850	$4\frac{1}{2}$	1871	$4\frac{1}{2}$	1892	4.7	1913	4.8

Sources: Appendix 3.3.

period 1830–94 with the regional series which are available after 1894.[1] The national series fluctuates appreciably in the first two decades of our period, but achieves a greater degree of stability (within the context of cyclical movement) in the 1850s and 1860s. On average, 4.2 days a week were worked in 1830–42, thereafter $4\frac{1}{2}$ becoming the norm over the cycle. Regional differences clearly did occur: for example, the *Labour Gazette* data show days lost in any one year were often twice as great in the midland regions than in the North-east; however, the chronology of pit opening reveals the trade cycle to have been the fundamental determinant in all regions.

Whereas the number of days worked was dependent on a combination of custom, individual choice, and trading conditions, hours were the subject of legislation. Before 1842 boys' hours frequently exceeded the twelve-hour maximum introduced by law in that year, and through-

[1] *Labour Gazette* 1894–1914.

out the nineteenth century were at least as long (and before 1872 generally longer) than those worked by adults. The Act of 1842 did little to reduce the average length of hours for boys, though almost certainly it helped to eliminate the very long hours of thirteen and more in the worst regions. The Mines Regulation Act of 1872 led to an effective reduction in the hours of young persons under sixteen to no more than ten a day. Thereafter, the hours of juvenile workers appear to have kept in line with those of their adult unskilled fellow workers underground, whose hours also came within the ambit of legislation for the first time.[1]

Any discussion of working hours in the mining industry is bedevilled by the very concept of a working hour. Legislation in 1872 and 1908 had the effect of reducing hours during which coal was wound, which as it included both travelling time to the face and meal breaks exceeded the hours of labour actually worked at the face; descending into the pit or ascending from it also involved 'waiting time'—the amount of time spent in a work environment from pithead to pithead, or bank to bank as it was known—and was greater than the winding time. Because of these complications not even the Eight Hour Day Committee in 1908 succeeded in reaching a common definition of the working day.[2] Furthermore, at least before 1860 a fixed or common working day for hewers and for piece-rate haulage workers did not exist. Until then the length of the hewers' working day often determined the hours of other workers, since haulage and maintenance workers were generally needed throughout the coal-getting shift and often for a period after the shift had ended. A greater regularity in working hours after 1860 may have originated in the North-east. There the wider introduction of multiple-shift systems on a large scale in the 1850s encouraged the regularization of work patterns, which became the norm in other regions, too, though South Wales and to a less extent Lancashire were exceptions.[3] Consequently, voluntary shortening of the length of the working day was much less common after 1860 (when hours began to be reduced) than in the earlier period, when a twelve-hour nominal shift was the norm. Then it was common for miners to work shorter days in addition to, or instead of, fewer days, wherever and whenever the level of piece-rate wages allowed. Especially before 1860 input from labour was, as we have seen, also affected by voluntary restriction, which reflected leisure

[1] *Children's Employment Commission* 1842, XV, 118–34, 268; Flight thesis, 144–9, 178–9, 264–7.
[2] McCormick and Williams 1959, 226–7.
[3] *Eight Hours Committee* 1907, XV, 26–126; LSE Webb Coll. E Section A, Vol. XXVI, 135–151.

preference, perhaps limited consumption opportunities in pit villages and a desire to maintain high prices and wages, though a similar mechanism can be identified continuing into the twentieth century; measuring this phenomenon, however, offers considerable scope for disagreement.

The most comprehensive study of hours in British industry, by M. A. Bienfield, contains a dubious analysis of miners' hours of work. On a slender empirical basis Bienfield maintains that in the late eighteenth century hewers worked only six or seven hours a day, but that by 1842, according to the Report of the 1842 *Children's Employment Commission*, twelve hours had become the norm. He maintains that a dramatic extension of hours occurred in the 1830s as a result of the rise of inter-regional competition, the appearance of subcontracting, and the disappearance of the stint.[1] However, none of the regional studies of the industry have identified such a change and the existence of considerable stinting after 1842 throws doubt on its alleged absence in the immediately preceding decade;[2] in Scotland, where the 'darg' was more effectively implemented than in any other region, restriction was intermittently used from the 1820s.[3] Bienfield goes on to interpret the reduction in hours of the 1850s and 1860s as a result of 'share-the-work' arrangements rather than of 'actual reductions in hours';[4] but this is a dubious distinction, since reduced hours in this period were regarded as one method by which miners could attempt to raise wages collectively, and by so doing establish a basis for shorter hours without unacceptable cuts in living standards. The stint was employed in the twin roles of maintaining wages and coal prices and of achieving the practical limitation of the working day. For this reason it is difficult, without precise information in the nature of industrial bargaining in this period, to distinguish wage rises from hours reductions, but both may be generally associated with the increasing strength of labour in this period (particularly in its cyclical upswings), with the rise of the county unions after 1858 and of the Miners' National Association after 1863.[5]

As for the important reductions in the 1870s, Bienfield incorporates his analysis into a general interpretation which he advances to explain

---

[1] Bienfield 1972, 26–7, 55–8, 79–80.

[2] Yet Bienfield also notes that 'The falling wages and irregular employment of the early 1840s made the men willing to work very long hours on those days on which they could obtain work, as the idle days meant they had ample leisure but little income', ibid. 79. See above.

[3] G. M. Wilson thesis, 274.

[4] Bienfield 1972, 93–4, 101.

[5] Machin 1958, 52, 290, 343; A. S. Wilson thesis, 273–81.

the history of working hours during the last two centuries. The thesis relates falling hours of work to rapid real-wage inflation, when the employee's preference system shifted decisively away from (further) increases in wages in favour of shorter hours, a model which, he maintain, fits the national picture in 1871–4, 1919, 1948, and 1960–6. It is not clear, however, that the mining industry validates this mechanism. The main changes in hewers' hours occurred in the 1860s in Scotland, the North-east, and Yorkshire, and in the 1870s and 1880s in the East and West Midlands and in South Wales. Real earnings did rise fairly sharply in the early 1860s and in the 1870s boom, but fell back markedly in the latter part of both decades. The rise in real earnings in the mining industry, indeed, was as great in 1878–91 (and of course more sustained) than in the early 1870s,[1] while average changes in hours were much more marked in the 1860s and 1870s.

A further mistaken presumption is that hours assume prominence in industrial bargaining only when real wages rise sufficiently to induce a shift in workers' preferences away from income and toward leisure. In the mining industry, however, hours had been at the centre of industrial relations since at least 1831, when pitmen in the North-east requested a twelve-hour working day for boys on arrival at pit shaft, superceding the fourteen hours at the face required by the bond;[2] in the 1840s, under the impetus of a campaign co-ordinated by the National Association of Great Britain and Ireland formed in 1842, miners in the North-east, Scotland, Lancashire, and Yorkshire, adopted a strategy of limiting earnings and hours of work, as a means of maintaining coal prices—and wages.[3]

Since the 1850s the miners had petitioned Parliament for an eight-hour day for boys, a movement initiated in the west of Scotland and carried south of the border by Alexander MacDonald in 1856.[4] When a few years later hours restriction for boys was under discussion by colliery workers and coalowners, John Chambers, of Newton Chambers, expressed the opinion that miners were 'craftily driving at limitation of their own hours through child legislation . . .'.[5] Thereafter, the Miners' National Union maintained the pressure in the 1860s and early 1870s, as did the Miners' Federation of Great Britain after 1888.

---

[1] See below 568.

[2] NEI Watson 5/9/76, memo respecting pitmen's grievances, 1831; Hylton Scott thesis, 58–9.

[3] A. J. Taylor, 'The Miners' Association of Great Britain and Ireland, 1842–8', *Economica* 22 (1955), 53.

[4] A. S. Wilson thesis, 274. Machin 1958.

[5] SCL Newton Chambers TR 453/5.

The research of McCormick and Williams offer a firmer foundation for further analysis. Building upon their estimates of hours of work in 1850 to 1880 and in 1905,[1] parliamentary papers have been employed to refine and to supplement their figures by estimating hours for each region in 1842, 1890, and 1913. This involved a lengthy process of evaluation in the light of often conflicting data. Averages of weekly hours necessarily conceal substantial intra-regional variation, especially in the early period, and must be regarded as averages over the trade cycle; for it is certain that hours varied cyclically even in the late nineteenth century. Despite reservations, in the absence of an alternative source, the 1842 *Childrens Commission* is the starting point for the pre-1860 analysis of hours. In using this evidence it has been assumed that a five- rather than a six-day week was worked in all regions, since although pits were opened for six days the widespread practice of making Saturday a half-day holiday and pay-week holidays meant that, particularly in the case of hewers, rarely were more than ten days worked in each fortnight.[2] Meal times are also included in our estimates, following the practice adopted by the commissioners and by succeeding inquiries into hours.[3] The broad margins of error in these 1842 figures must be borne firmly in mind, for the evidence upon which they are based sometimes contains discrepancies of up to three or four hours between the reckoning of employers and workers. Much of this is attributable to inconsistent definitions, for employers often applied a strict definition of work as time spent at the coal face, whereas employees sometimes (but evidently not always) included time taken to travel from their homes to the pithead as part of the working day.[4] Resolving differences has been a matter of judgement.

In 1842, when the first reliable figures become available, the length of the average working week for hewers was sixty hours, which compared with up to eighty-four hours a week for some unskilled or oncost underground workers. There are few indications which might suggest more than slight reductions in hewers' weekly hours before 1860, the fall in hours of hewers in the North-east in the 1850s probably resulting from

---

[1] McCormick and Williams 1959, 237–8.

[2] And because of this assumption it is possible that hours worked by oncost workers in 1842 may have been underestimated. *Children's Employment Commission* 1842, XV, 122–5 provides the justification for this important basis of the exercise.

[3] Approximately three hours a week (to allow for meals) could be subtracted from the 1842 figures for weekly hours since the Commission gave 30 to 40 minutes as the daily average time so spent. *Children's Employment Commission* 1842, XV, 122–5.

[4] Ibid., 109.

the introduction of the $7\frac{1}{2}$-hour shift in Northumberland in 1852–6.[1] Appreciable falls took place in the 1860s, except in the West Midlands and South Wales, and marked reductions accompanied the intense boom conditions of 1872–3 which coincided with the Coal Mines Regulation Act of 1872. By reducing boys' hours to no more than ten a day the Act caused a general contraction in the length of the working day for other workers, particularly for oncost men.[2] Legislation in the form of the 1908 Eight Hours Act also lowered working hours, affecting non-hewers in the North-east most of all.

The intervening period, according to Rowe, was not one of significant hours reduction,[3] but there is evidence that between these two major pieces of legislation further falls did take place, a consequence of economic conditions combined with growing trade-union strength and pressure, when the Miners' Federation of Great Britain adopted the eight-hour day as a major policy objective.[4] In South Wales, where the 1887 Mines Regulation Act had led to some reduction in hours following the restriction on boy's hours, in 1888 the miners persuaded the coalowners to concede the first Monday in each month as a holiday, later defending 'Mabon's Day', as it came to be called in honour of the miners' leader, when attempts were made to withdraw it.[5] Evidence given to the Eight Hours Committee and before the Royal Commission on Labour also referred to a fall in hours throughout Yorkshire and Cumberland in 1890, in parts of the North-east and Lancashire in 1891, and to a gradual and continuing long-term reduction in most coalfields, as those regions which lagged behind the average were able to narrow the difference.[6] Table 3.9 presents the estimated hours at benchmark years between 1842 and 1913.

Differentials in hours between grades of workers lessened over time, resulting mainly from legislation on juvenile hours. Differences in hours persisted none the less; though whereas in the 1830s and 1840s a differential of three or even four hours separated the daily working hours of hewers from others, by 1905 an hour's difference was more likely. One small group of workers lagged behind in these improvements, for the Eight Hour Day Committee reported that those in positions of special responsibility, colliery officials, overmen, deputies, examiners,

---

[1] LSE Webb Coll. E, Section A, Vol. XXXI.
[2] Flight thesis, 264–7.   [3] Rowe 1923, 59.
[4] Bienfield 1972, 93–4, 101.   [5] Evans 1961, 320.
[6] RC Labour 1892, XXXIV, 26, 15, 20; Eight Hours Committee 1907, XV, Q 5119–20, 7389, 10487–91, 10498–52; Appendix 15; Eight Hours Committee 1907, XIV, Q 275, XV 5516, 5140.

Table 3.9. *Estimated hours of adult miners by region, 1842-1913*

	1842	1850	1860	1870	1880	1890	1905	1913
Hewers								
Scotland	60	60	60	44	44	44	44	42
North-east	60	60	54	$35\frac{1}{2}$	$35\frac{1}{2}$	37	35	35
Cumberland	60					$41\frac{1}{2}$	37	37
Yorkshire	54	60	60	54	48	$44\frac{1}{2}$	$42\frac{1}{2}$	42
Lancs. and Ches.	54	53	52	50	$47\frac{1}{2}$	47	46	42
North Wales	60						$45\frac{1}{2}$	
East Midlands	66	66	66	64	$51\frac{1}{2}$	49	$46\frac{1}{2}$	42
West Midlands	66	59	54	54	48	48	$45\frac{1}{2}$	42
South Wales	60	58–72	58–72	58–72	56	51	$47\frac{1}{2}$	44
South West	54						$42\frac{1}{2}$	
Weighted average	60	60	58	50	46	45	43	41

Unskilled underground workers

Scotland	60–72	60	60	44	44		47½	44
North-east	60–72	54	54	54	54		52	44
Cumberland	60–72							
Yorkshire	60	60		54	48	45		44
Lancs. and Ches.	60		54	54	50	49		44
North Wales	60–72							
East Midlands	70–84	66	66	64	51½	49		42
West Midlands	60–72	59		54	48	43		42
South Wales	60–72	58–72	58–72	58–72	56	49		44
South West	54–60							
Weighted average	65	59	58	55	51	48	47	43

Sources:

1842: *Children's Employment Commission*, 1842, XV, 106–13.

1850–1880c: B. M. McCormick and J. H. Williams, 'The Miners and the Eight Hour Day' (based on Board of Trade, *Accounts and Papers* (1890), LXVIII, 591–666).

1890: Ibid., 238 (compromise figures based on evidence from the Miners' Federation of Great Britain and Home Office Return) and *Royal Commission on Labour*, 1892, Group A, Vol. I, Vol. XXXIV, Precis of evidence 8–37.

1905: McCormick and Williams, 'The Miners and the Eight Hour Day', 238 (Eight Hour Day data).

1913: Estimate

and firemen tended to work longer hours than other workers, with the single exception of those who attended the pumps whose hours were usually the longest of all. Deputies and firemen were required to descend underground before (or at least with) the first men to go down and to remain until the last man had reached the surface.[1] Not until 1890 does evidence become available on the proportion of miners working different hours in the regions. This reveals that Lancashire, Scotland, and South Wales were those where workers employed for maximum hours were more numerous proportionately than elsewhere.[2]

The major feature of the period between 1890 and 1905 was the campaign for the eight-hour day waged on principles similar to those which informed policies of output restriction before 1870. Rowe maintained that hours of work remained largely unaltered between 1888 and 1908, though conceding the possibility of a small decrease gained by hewers in certain districts in the Midlands and by transit workers in Somerset and the Forest of Dean.[3] Yet the evidence suggests that he may have underestimated the actual reduction in hewers' hours. Ascertaining hours in this period was complicated in the minds of contemporary observers by the question of winding and travelling time from, and back to, the pithead. Winding time could vary considerably from one pit to another and was usually longer at older pits, but between fifteen and thirty minutes each way was an average in this period.[4] The effect of the Eight Hours Act which came into operation in July 1909 is less easily identified than might have been supposed, since the Eight Hours Day Committee failed to collect evidence on hours according to a common definition and no official investigation followed the Act's implementation before 1914. We are forced, therefore, to rely upon the 1905 data; the 1913 figures are estimates predicated on the predicted effects of the Act and upon those few observations actually made. In those regions already working an eight-hour day—Scotland, the South-west, and the East and West Midlands—the effect of the Act was negligible. In the North-east, too, where the Act became operational only in 1910, hours remained about the same for hewers (though a three-shift system was introduced) but did increase for oncost workers, to about nine hours or

---

[1] Ibid., XV, Q 413-5, 456-8.

[2] Bienfield 1972, 123-6.

[3] Rowe 1923, 115.

[4] *Eight Hours Committee* 1907, XV, Q 739, 8641, 11110-1, 10574, 12688. The Eight Hours Committee found the average length of the working day in 1905 to be 8¼ for hewers and 9¼ for workers, Pt. 1, 11.

so. Those regions most affected were Yorkshire, Lancashire and Cheshire, and South Wales, where the average reduction was probably about one hour,[1] representing falls in the hours of hewers by about 7 per cent in South Wales and 9 per cent in Lancashire and Cheshire. South Wales, however, was exceptional in remaining significantly above the overall average of 41 hours in 1913. Over the country as a whole the hours of non-hewers were reduced by about fifty minutes a day.[2]

Piece-rate wage increases might be regarded as having been a contributory factor to the shorter working day by enabling earnings to rise without necessitating more work (there is no evidence that miners ever contemplated a wage reduction in return for shorter hours); essentially, however, hours reductions were achieved in two ways. Trade union pressure was important and was instrumental in securing the Acts of 1872 and 1908, which had the support of wider, political opinion. Apart from the reductions which followed this legislation, however, the main reduction in hours resulted from a process of negotiation, in which it is scarcely possible to disentangle the wages and hours issues. It seems probable that miners themselves preferred to keep open options between shorter hours and higher wages when entering into negotiations. As one contemporary observer put it: 'It is not that the men want to get very large wages. I do not believe that they do; but they want short hours and more leisure and a higher price for their piecework.'[3] It has been argued that because of the decline of sub-contracting and the increase of trade-union power in a period of buoyant trade coalowners found it impossible to drive men harder in order to compensate for the curtailment of hours. Their response was limited to attempts to increase the number of days worked and to maximize the number of shifts; for employers saw good reasons for trying to reach agreements on fixed-shift working in order to rationalize management and guarantee output.[4] Without detailed knowledge of the particular bargaining processes, however, the exact nature of the trade-off between wages and hours must remain speculative, though the growing concern expressed by some coalowners over 'absenteeism' is indicative of an anxiety over the need to compensate for the effects of the Eight Hours Act.

---

[1] McCormick and Williams 1959, 232–4; *Sankey Commission* 1919, XI. For Yorkshire: QQ 6403, 6406–13, 6487–94, 6663–6; for North-east: QQ 5119–23, 5134–7, 5345–55, 5851–5, 5494–6, 6180–201.

[2] Rowe 1923, 116.

[3] Martin, in evidence to *Dearness and Scarcity Commission*, quoted in Walters 1977, 231.

[4] Mitchell thesis, 167–183.

Table 3.10. *Estimates of nominal and actual hours worked in the British coalmining industry, 1842-1913*

Average of	Nominal hours	Days worked on average per week	Actual weekly hours
1841–9	63	4.12	51.9
1850–9	59½	4.35	51.8
1860–9	58	4.45	51.6
1870–9	53	4.03	42.7
1880–9	49	4.67	45.8
1890–9	47	4.66	43.8
1900–8	45½	4.67	42.5
1909–13	42	4.68	39.3

Sources: Derived from Tables 3.8 and 3.9; for the method see Appendix 3.3.

It is clear from the considerable changes and variations in the length of the shift and the number of days worked that employment figures alone are misleading as a measure of the input to the industry of labour as a factor of production. Yet there are serious problems in progressing from an estimate of nominal hours worked, presented in Table 3.9, to estimates of actual hours worked. Only the central importance of this consideration encourages an attempt to do so; the assumptions underlying this exercise and the methods by which nominal hours are transformed into actual hours worked are presented in Appendix 3.3. The accuracy of the resulting estimates shown in Table 3.10 is subject to limitations, but there can surely be no doubt that the comparisons between nominal and actual hours offer a superior guide to the input of labour into the industry. The estimates suggests that hours actually worked by miners remained constant between 1842 and 1870, despite a fall in the nominal length of shifts. As a consequence firstly, of the voluntary short-week working which accompanied the early seventies boom, and secondly, the enforced idleness which followed the ensuing slump, the 1870s saw a dramatic fall in the number of hours actually worked. In the 1880s more hours were actually worked compared with the previous decade, but thereafter actual hours worked underwent a progressive decline, as days worked per week remained stable (over successive cycles) and the nominal length of shifts fell. By 1913 the *average* number of hours actually worked had fallen below 40 hours, lower for hewers.

As a more reliable guide to the input of labour as a factor of production and as one element in the pattern of miners' employment these figures are of intrinsic interest, but they will assume even greater significance in subsequent discussions of labour productivity and of miners' standard of living.[1] The perceived reasons for avoidable absenteeism, as well as the phenomonen itself, are also important for an understanding of coalowners' attitudes to labour and to labour policies. It is clear that coalowners commonly drew a distinction between workers possessing habits of regularity from those who did not, a division which was reflected in policies aimed at attracting and retaining a reliable core of hewers. To achieve this, many coalowenrs sought to modify customs and contracts and to impose greater control and regulation of workers. In this process law and government, as well as the labour policies of colliery managers, played their part.

vi. Contracts, labour regulation and work discipline

The recruitment of miners in the early nineteenth century depended partly upon bringing children into the mines, a process which the methods used to retain workers reflected. Mining fathers were anxious to secure colliery work for their sons, but in the periods of rapid growth not all movement into the mines was voluntary. The 1842 Children's Employment Commission found the hiring of parish apprentices to have been common in Yorkshire, Lancashire, and not unknown in the west of Scotland; in south Staffordshire the practice was most widespread of all.[2] From the Union Workhouses of Walsall, Wolverhampton, Dudley, and Stourbridge boys were sent into the mines on trial at the age of eight or nine, bound as apprentices for twelve years. Throughout that period the wretched boy received no pay, except that allowed to him by the 'master' to whom he was apprenticed; typically a collier, or in south Staffordshire a butty who took the earnings credited to his apprentice as compensation for board and lodging and 'instruction in the art and mystery of hurrying and thrusting'.[3] Most children, who were not parish apprentices, were hired by the colliers as assistants to hewers and putters, whereas the proprietors hired those children or

---

[1] See Chapters 6 and 7.
[2] *Children's Employment Commission* 1842, XV, 51–6.
[3] Ibid., 55.

young people who performed tasks contributing indirectly to the running of the mine rather than getting coal direct: as horse drivers, engine boys, air-door tenders, hookers-on, and carters and the like. Contracts were not normally for a long period, though in South Wales the usual mode of hiring was by the month. There, it was said, 'the collier's boy is, to all intents and purposes, the property of his father (as to wages) until he attains the age of seventeen years, or marries; his father receives his wages, whether he be an air-door boy of five years of age or a haulier of fifteen.'[1]

In the North-east, where there were no parish apprentices, children were hired directly by the colliery proprietor, not infrequently at the behest of parents; but unlike adult hewers and putters children were not required to sign the bond,[2] the key to recruitment throughout the North-east for most hewers at the beginning of the period. Specifying in detail the duties, rates of payment, penalties imposed for certain transgressions or neglect, either relating to the quality of coal got, absence from work, or other forms of unacceptable behaviour, the bond was renewed annually (when inducements in the form of cash and beer were not uncommon) and was enforceable by law.[3] In 1842 Dr Mitchell noted that unbound men were not well spoken of, consisting 'chiefly of newcomers or of men with whom their former employers had declined to enter a new engagement'.[4] Binding, therefore, was a method of retaining the best workmen for a year at a time, initial recruitment to collieries depending upon family or personal recommendation from existing employees.[5]

By 1831 certain aspects of the bond had become irksome: work and wage guarantees, notice to quit colliery housing, fines, and forfeitures for short measure[6]—though the length of contract was not among the miners' complaints. Compromises were reached on each of these issues, except for the coalowners' refusal to renew the undertaking to pay a guaranteed wage, and their insistence that they would continue to lay pits idle when to work them would be uneconomic. The 1832 bond excluded the guaranteed minimum wage, and although it was reintroduced in 1838 re-emerged as a central issue in the dispute of 1844. On that occasion the coalowners substituted a monthly contract for the

[1] Ibid.
[2] Ibid., XVI, 149, Appendix Pt. I.
[3] Scott thesis, 58.
[4] *Children's Employment Commission* 1842, XVI, Appendix I, 150.
[5] Ibid., 158–9 ev. of Thomas Cockin, colliery manager for Pease.
[6] NEI Watson 5/9/76c.

annual bond, to which the miners reacted by proposing a bond of six-months' duration. This was only one of several issues involved during the seventeen-week strike in 1844, which ended when miners returned to work on employers' terms; these included a monthly bond, without minimum guarantees either on employment or wages, and enforceable, as before, under the law.[1] George Elliot, who at the time was the under-viewer at Monwearmouth colliery, later referred to the restoration of annual binding in Durham—at the miners' request—during the boom of 1854, when coalowners also conceded a guarantee of minimum employment under the bond.[2] The reintroduction was neither widespread nor effective, however, and when in 1862 coalowners attempted to extend annual contracts throughout the North-east the bond became a rallying point for the newly formed miners' union of Northumberland and Durham.[3] Reflecting different bargaining strengths, the Northumberland miners resisted, and in the process split from the Durham miners whose organization disintegrated completely in 1865. When miners found themselves strongly placed to negotiate in the boom of 1872 the revived Durham Miners' Union succeeded in forcing coalowners to agree to fortnightly contracts,[4] so ending a system of hiring which had been productive of disputes and litigation and had prompted condemnation from a lawyer acting on a coalowners' behalf.[5] In other regions long contracts had virtually disappeared by 1840, the monthly or fortnightly agreement having replaced them. In Lancashire debtor miners sometimes bound children to their employers as surety, and in south Staffordshire 'bondsmen' continued to be employed hauling coal, for which at certain times they were entitled only to ale as payment; but these were vestiges of an earlier age.[6]

The decline of the bond and long-term employment contracts did not end resort to litigation to enforce discipline. Prosecution over a broken bond in the North-east had its more widely applicable counterpart in the Master and Servant Act of 1823, which made it a criminal offence for a worker to break his contract (by verbal or written agreement) and was punishable by fine, or a maximum period of three-months' imprisonment with hard labour. The use of this law, or the threat to prosecute, was not uncommon in the mining industry, especially in south Staffordshire where prosecutions were twice as high as in any other county

---

[1] NEI Watson 5/9/76a; Scott thesis, 60–5; *RC Trade Union* 1867–8, XXXIX, Q 13612.
[2] *SC Dearness and Scarcity* 1873, X, Q 7607.
[3] Welbourne 1923, 115.
[4] Ibid., 123–4, 138, 146.
[5] Ibid., 144.
[6] Galloway 1898, 167–8.

during the mid-nineteenth century.[1] The involvement of coalowners as magistrates adjudicating in other coalowners' cases was not unusual in this region, and the same was true in Lanarkshire, according to the miners' leader, Alexander MacDonald. Describing the contempt with which Lanarkshire miners regarded local justices, he declared: 'They are not only well-to-do grocers, retired publicans or colliery owners: of 100 men or so . . . the jurors are the managers, the publicans, the grocers and the doctors to the works'.[2]

From South Wales, William Menelaus, manager of the Dowlais Collieries since 1856, told the Royal Commission on the Labour Laws in 1874 that in his experience the law had seldom been employed to discipline workers leaving without due notice. His own policy had been to impose fines with the threat of imprisonment in the event of non-payment. He had invoked the law only where the working of the pits or plant seemed to be seriously at risk as a result of an employee's action.[3] A detailed analysis of prosecutions under the Master and Servant Acts in south Staffordshire indicates a cyclical pattern occurring in the boom when the incentive to find more remunerative or less dangerous work, or shorter hours, was greatest because the possibilities of finding such opportunities were best.[4] In the spring of 1858 colliers in the West Riding, where the fortnightly contract was in operation, declared their objection to the legally required two-weeks' notice, which the miners attorney, W. P. Roberts, agreed to test in the courts. A number of miners who took action in expectation of the outcome were imprisoned under the Master and Servant Act for leaving work without due notice, a judgement to which the *Colliery Guardian* attached considerable importance,[5] presumably as a warning to colliers and an encouragement to employers. While local conditions varied, it seems that the number of convictions as a proportion of prosecutions indicates that employers used the courts as a warning and as a means of getting men back to work, the employer often offering to drop charges should the men return to work out contractual agreements.

Another cruder method of retaining labour was by the long pay, which is the explanation offered by Morris and Williams for the persis-

[1] Woods 1982, 93–115; D. Philips, 'The Black Country Magistracy 1835–60', *Midland History*, III (1975–6), 161–190.

[2] Quoted in Campbell 1979, 219; MacEwan thesis, 171. For examples outside Staffordshire and Scotland see *CG* 25 June 1869, 16 Jan. 1868, 20 Feb. 1858, 89.

[3] *RC Labour Laws* 1874, XXVI, QQ 575, 510–13, 516, 519, 557.

[4] Woods 1982, 93–115.

[5] *CG* 20 Feb. 1858, 89.

tence of company stores and truck shops in South Wales long after the elimination of isolated locations which may have justified this widespread practise.[1] During the ten years following the Truck Act of 1831, which outlawed the payment of wages in kind, monthly contracts and monthly pay days with fortnightly and sometimes weekly 'drawers' in the form of credit from shopkeepers or employer, had been superceded in many districts by fortnightly contracts and fortnightly pays. The transition was slower, however, in parts of South Wales, south Staffordshire, and the west of Scotland, particularly among coal-producing iron firms, where miners' wages tended to be relatively low and more volatile than in the house-coal districts.[2] Although the colliery owners of Lanarkshire and Ayrshire had already substituted fortnightly for monthly contracts before 1831 and by 1860 had dispensed with the formal notice as part of colliers' contracts, the Scottish coal-producing iron masters, notably the Bairds, Merry and Cunningham, the Summerlee Iron Company, the Dundyvan Iron Company, the Govan and Calder Iron Companies, and the Monkland Iron and Steel Company, afforded notorious examples of company stores which required miners to trade as a condition of credit from their employers.[3] The Truck Committee of 1870 concluded: 'The real pressure lies not in the cash advance clerk or the shop managers' conduct, but in the system of lengthened pays and draws, which is so adjusted as to render it far more convenient for the needy workman to betake himself to the company's shop and accept all its terms'.[4]

The Scottish evidence, however, suggests that even the fortnightly pay was insufficient to keep miners out of debt in a region where the demand for coal was dominated by the highly fluctuating demands of the iron and steel industry. Truck was rare in the North-east, though debt was not. Thomas Burt referred to the regular, though not high, wages which enabled his family to settle debts before moving on to another colliery—a customary constraint upon mobility and necessary to avoid threat of prosecution. Yet the strike of 1844 thrust even the 'small thrifty family' into debt,[5] an indication of the precarious balance between miners' earnings and expenditure. Some coalowners regarded the truck shop as an opportunity to charge excessive prices to a captive work-force. The bookkeeper who ran the store at the Darley Main Colliery in Barnsley in 1842 explained his master's approach to the

[1] Morris and Williams 1958, 226.
[2] Hair thesis, 364.
[3] Campbell 1979, 34, 105, 205.
[4] *RC Truck* 1871, XXXVI, 64.
[5] Burt 1924, 89–90, 39.

workers: 'we cannot force you to deal at our shop, but you cannot force us to employ you'.[1] Not all employers who owned truck shops exercised compulsion on dealing, though in Scotland, where in the 1840s an estimated 20 per cent of miners' monthly wages were described as 'mortgaged in advance', the practice was common.[2] A list of truck stores in Scotland compiled twenty years later by Alexander MacDonald implied their use by more than twenty thousand workers in the pits and ironworks; perhaps 40 per cent of Scottish colliers were thus affected.[3] Retail profit, however, was almost certainly diminishing in importance as an explanation for the continuance of truck practices after the mid-nineteenth century.

The rationale for truck payments to the employees of Lord Dudley, the largest colliery proprietor in south Staffordshire, was explained by the manager of the Round Oak Ironworks in evidence to the Commissioners: 'With working men it is always desirable to have something in hand because then we have a line upon them which prevents them from occasionally moving away without giving notice . . .'[4] Such inescapable logic probably explains why in the coal and iron-making districts of south Staffordshire, South Wales, and Scotland truck was so difficult to eliminate completely, even after the prohibiting legislation of 1831, 1842, 1860, and 1871.[5] For many miners, therefore, the lower paid, the less provident, and those with large, young families, the struggle to remain free from debt was inevitable and rendered more difficult by the perpetuation of long pays and truck. In 1852 Tremenheere condemned truck payment and the indebtedness associated with it, not merely on social grounds but because in good times men were prevented from moving to the efficient pits, while in bad times the inefficient pits could survive on the basis of labour which, in effect, was tied to them.[6] The payment of wages at public houses become illegal in 1842 but the practice persisted, especially in those districts where truck was in evidence, but also in Yorkshire, Durham, and Derbyshire.[7]

In 1842 J. M. Fellowes, Sub Commissioner for Derbyshire, explained how the butties, who in most coalfields were paid every other Saturday night, others at monthly or six-week intervals, were allowed weekly drawers of 'subsistence money'. 'On the butty receiving the money he

---

[1] SC Payment of Wages 1842, IX, Q 3313.
[2] Inspectors' Reports 1844, 20.   [3] Campbell 1979, 237.
[4] Quoted in Woods 1982, 93–115.
[5] G. M. Wilson thesis, 62–3, 71.
[6] Report on Mining Districts 1852, XXI, 439.
[7] Hair thesis, 236; Morris and Williams 1948, 230–1; G. M. Wilson thesis, 64.

appoints the colliers and children to meet him, either at his own home or some beer shop he has an interest in, and generally keeps them waiting until he considers it has answered his purpose well enough, when the landlord produces the change and his bill.'[1] The payout of wages at public houses seems to have been the most pervasive for longest, however, in Scotland, where in 1866 the drink trade was said to be almost entirely in the hands of employers, some having defended truck shops as a means of controlling, and therefore reducing, alcohol consumption on the spot—thereby checking absenteeism.[2] Such arguments received little sympathy from the Inspectors, among whom Tremenheere in 1852 expressed particularly strong views on a practice which he regarded as actually discouraging sobriety and thrift.[3]

Tremenheere was largely instrumental in reducing truck and payments from public houses, following a campaign in which he succeeded in enlisting the support of a number of colliery proprietors who were persuaded that reductions in absenteeism would result. As public-house wage payments were usually associated with sub-contractors or butties, who often had an interest in the store, coalowners threatened them with dismissal or withdrawal of further credit facilities unless they discontinued truck and beer-related wage policies.[4] Such an approach, reinforced by a growing public opposition to truck, achieved considerable success, as was demonstrated by the discontinuance in 1857 of the extensive truck system of William Baird, one of Scotland's two largest employers of mining labour. Including the compulsory use of the company stores by Baird's employees in receipt of advances on wages, the Baird's truck system was described by a lawyer investigating truck prevailing in Scotland in 1854 as 'an organisation for applying coercion'.[5] James Baird had defended the system in cross examination, but three years later Alexander MacDonald ensured that truck became an issue in an election contested by James's brother, George, who to avoid unpopularity removed compulsion from shopping at the company's stores. Other employers chose to observe the letter of the law but to retain illegal practices in effect. One such strategy was to pay wages from an office adjacent to the company's public house and store, which in some cases made more than a marginal contribution to trading revenues (references were made to returns of between 5 and 10 per cent) provided a continuing

---

[1] Quoted in Williams 1962, 62.
[2] *Mines Inspectors' Report*, XIV, 215–18.
[3] Cassell thesis, 96–8.
[4] Ibid., 99; Morris and Williams 1958, 230–1.
[5] Campbell 1979, 216, 221.

incentive for associating payment with immediate expenditure.[1] Thus, while the historian of truck is impressed by its rarity in colliery districts by 1871,[2] the practices continuing in some iron and coal companies, in South Wales and in Scotland especially, necessitated further legislation in 1887 and 1896 before truck finally disappeared.[3]

Another custom which affected labour discipline, yet which despite employers' efforts to end it survived into the twentieth century, was the allowance of 'free' beer. In south Staffordshire and Derbyshire beer was supplied to miners at the pit bank without charge, a custom which in the 1840s John Thomas Woodhouse, viewer and principal agent at Church Gresley Colliery in Derbyshire, decided to discontinue because of many instances of 'persons never going to their homes at all, but stopping fuddling all day and night in public houses and coming to work at the colliery next morning'.[4] His attempt, made in 1842, provoked a strike; sixty years later the practice had almost disappeared, though 5,000 Staffordshire miners were still receiving beer free of charge, their daily allocation having been reduced from two quarts to one quart, adjusted for shorter shifts.[5]

Weekly pays, which became one of the aims of miners' unions, were gradually adopted after 1870, when trading conditions from time to time enabled workers to negotiate this reform at colliery or district level. In some districts, however, these were still a matter for negotiation shortly before World War I.[6] In the period before 1870, when long pays were most common in the indebtedness they encouraged which not even fortnightly pays could always avoid, left the worker vulnerable to discrimination when seeking other employment, thereby affecting labour mobility. For in some districts movement between pits required a quitting certificate, or discharge note, from the last employers, whose disinclination to provide one hampered, even though it did not always prevent, movement, depending upon the state of trade.[7] A report, however, that a certain miner's services 'are no longer required at this colliery', was a transparent code intended to discourage other employers from offering him work. Except in South Wales and in some parts of

[1] RC Truck 1871, XXXVI, 5.
[2] G. Hilton.
[3] G. M. Wilson thesis, 64-5, 71.
[4] RC Trade Unions 1867-8, XXXIX, QQ 11903-6.
[5] Truck Acts Committee 1908, LIX, Q 162.
[6] But in Scotland not until 1910 did the Joint Conciliation Board finally conclude an agreement on weekly pays, GLA Scottish Coalowners UGD 161/3/48.
[7] Hassan thesis, 229.

Scotland,[1] the discharge note seems to have been systematically employed almost entirely in relation to strike activity as a method of blocking alternative employment opportunities for the industry's trou-·blemakers.

In South Wales, however, the intention which lay behind it was to 'check the mobility of labour without notice, and to curb the intransigence of those who did not comply with the discipline of the mine'.[2] The note could also indicate experience, or lack of it, which it would be to the employer's interest (especially in the fiery mines) to know. The quitting certificate, or 'free lines' as it was called in the Scottish Lothians, resembled the discharge note, a guarantee that the recipient was free from debt or engagement to his former employer, though free lines presented by some of the large coalowners operating the system during the turbulent 1840s, began to include information on a collier's character.[3]

Even in South Wales, however, the state of trade and the relative strength of labour demand were important influences upon the timing and extent of the use and effectiveness of the note, for neither workers nor coalowners were united across the coalfield before 1873. In that year the newly formed Monmouth and South Wales Collieries Association formally adopted a resolution not to employ workmen previously in the employment of other members of the Association unless they could present discharge notes.[4] The masters were not unanimous in their attitude to such a policy. Sir George Elliot, representing the Powell Duffryn Company, and Mark Curtis, of the Ebbw Vale Iron and Coal Company, objected to a clause implying that discharge notes would be withheld even though formal notice had been worked satisfactorily. The Association agreed to exclude such an eventuality, the two major Welsh producers thus effectively destroying the disciplinary advantages of the system which had attracted other members, especially those concerned to squeeze out agitators, curb strikers and crush the unions altogether. The note could be used, however, in connection with a particular strike at an associated colliery. Two factors prevented the effectiveness of such a policy. One was the expansion in the demand for labour and the competition from collieries which remained outside the Association; the other was the growth of miners' opposition to the discharge note. That became a bargaining counter during the negotiations between

[1] Morris and Williams 1957, 286–193; Machin 1958, 108.
[2] Morris and Williams 1957, 286.   [3] Hassan thesis, 229.
[4] This paragraph draws heavily on Morris and Williams 1957 and L. J. Williams's thesis.

employers and workers' leaders over the introduction of a sliding scale, which culminated in the Caeru strike of 1894–6 when employers abandoned the discharge note. In no other region was the attempt to extend the practice of discharge notes carried so far, and its failure in South' Wales, except in the short term in connection with specific strikes, is a pointer to its limited use in other regions.

Workers' contracts often embodied formal regulations even outside the North-east, and in Scotland often resembled a shortened version of the bond,[1] which usually contained clauses relating to more than wages and employment. A pitman's bond, dated 1851, at the Stella and Townley Collieries in Durham specified the terms of hiring, enumerated which tools were to be supplied by the workmen and which by the owner, contained a detailed list of rates according to size and quality of coal got, taking into consideration mining conditions in the seams, indicated the precise methods of working, the days and hours of work, and warned that a fine of 2s. 6d. deducted from wages would be imposed for disobeying any of the owner's terms and conditions.[2] A similar set of 'Rules, Regulations and Suggestions' for miners employed at the Washington Colliery in Durham also specified fines for lack of punctuality, irregular working, swearing, ill-treatment of other workers or pit ponies, and for taking matches or intoxicants into the pit. The similarity of rules enforced at other collieries in the 1840s and 1850s suggests a widespread uniformity between, as well as within, regions,[3] though the Clay Cross colliery in Derbyshire specifically prohibited workmen from keeping dogs or fighting cocks in the cottages belonging to the owners, and from introducing them into the works.[4]

The range of offences usually comprised within the general category of 'improper conduct' or 'neglecting work' is indicated by a listing of the reason for which fines were deducted from colliers' wages at the Wingate Grange Colliery and at Haswell Colliery during an eight-month period in 1844. In addition to those imposed for major breaches of contract—by sending up tubs of coal either mixed with slate and stones or deficient in weight, by refusing to work, by leaving work early, and hewing improperly—they included 'disobeying orders, damaging safety lamps . . . throwing coals at the putters, removing safety lamps

---

[1] Hassan thesis, 228.

[2] NEI ZB/5 Pitman's Bond, 1 July 1851.

[3] Specimen colliery rules for miners in the North-east, East Midlands, Lancashire, and Yorkshire are reproduced in *Mines Inspectors' Reports* 1854, XIX, 757–9.

[4] *Children's Employment Commission* 1842, XVII Appendix Pt. II, 347 'Regulations for Workmen Employed'.

placed as a guide to the workmen, hewing coal off the wall sides, using gunpowder for blasting the coal contrary to orders'.[1] The special features of the rules in force at the Shotts and Coltness Iron Works in the 1840s included the entitlement of each collier to exceed the customary darg, and to make it possible for the employer to set aside the traditional strict rotation which hitherto governed the winding of each 'hutch' to the surface. Coltness contracts required men to move between pits in the event of an accident, which conflicted both with the tradition of stopping work on such occasions and the customary notion of a working place in the pit as a matter for mutual agreement. In order to counteract the colliers' restrictions on apprenticeship, the Shotts Iron Company rules required each collier to take charge of, and instruct, any labourer whom the company chose to employ, for which a 'reasonable renumeration' was to be allowed.[2] Similar rules relating to the removal from working places without notice, and the acceptance of labourers as assistants without consultation (whom in this instance the stallman working by contract would have to pay), were introduced at the Staveley Company in 1866 and precipitated a major strike.[3] More common were clauses which penalized absence from work, dirty coal, and short measures, and although the latter became the subject of legislation in 1860 the scope for grievance arising from such policies persisted.

Representative of pre-compulsory colliery rules were those introduced by James Darlington, manager of Ince Hall Coal and Cannel Company's colliery at Wigan, which included twenty-nine rules applying to workmen and seventeen instructions for underlookers. Most were concerned with safety and fines for neglecting the recommended measures, but a few dealt with discipline relating to production.[4] On the whole, the early Mines Inspectors approved of printed rules which related to safety, endeavouring (unsuccessfully) to persuade most collieries to adopt this practice. But the Mines Inspector, Henry Mackworth, noted and sympathized with the miners' hostility to printed rules, 'for the rules for safety where they do exist are generally mixed up with rules for work and payment'.[5] The barrister, J. M. Ludlow, was also critical of the rigorous tone of some colliery rules, and instanced those he had seen in West Yorkshire which, he told a meeting of the National Association for the Promotion of Social Science in 1860, '. . . bristle so

[1] *MJ* 6 Jan. 1844, 461.
[2] Campbell 1979, 106–9.
[3] Williams 1962, 110.
[4] Cassell thesis, 202–3.
[5] Quoted in Cassell thesis, 203.

with fines and penalties that they suggest rather a prison than a trading concern'.[1]

As a result of the Inspector's pressure, those common elements in printed colliery rules relating specifically to safety were codified to form a set of Special Rules under the Mines Inspection Act of 1855. Mackworth's fears that these, too, would be received by the men with suspicion proved to be justified, for adoption of these rules came to be regarded initially as the occasion for an intensification of labour discipline. The Act required all collieries to adopt by-laws in accordance with a general safety code as formulated under the Mines Regulation Act of 1850, together with a set of Special Rules designed to meet local conditions. The General Rules, drawn up on the basis of a code formulated by a committee including the Mines Inspectors, but which was dominated by coalowners, were uncontroversial; they were limited in scope and detail, largely incorporating the principles of best standard practice as existing in the North-east. Special Rules were intended merely to allow modifications to, or exceptions in detail from, the General Rules to take account of their applicability to particular coalfields, localities, and even some individual collieries where geological conditions or organizational factors justified such amendments. They were drawn up by coalowners, mainly through trade associations or *ad hoc* meetings, before submission for approval by the Home Secretary, to whom the Mine Inspectors were responsible.[2]

The reasons why these Special Rules proved unpopular with workers was that some employers saw the framing of such regulations as an opportunity, to quote one critical Inspector, 'to impose upon the workmen stringent regulations respecting the hours of work, wages, and quality and quantity of work, which would be immediately resisted if attempted in a more open manner'; thus such items prejudicial to the men, hitherto figuring in bonds and contracts relating to conduct, appearance, or attendance at Divine Service on Sundays,[3] were among those excised from Special Rules proposed by some of the coalowners.[4] Mackworth's comment quoted above reveals an awareness of the risks associated with regulation and a recognition that the Special Rules (between thirty and seventy for each colliery) required careful scrutiny before approval. But the size and complexity of the task which faced the

---

[1] J. M. Ludlow, 'Account of the West Yorkshire Coal Strike and Lockout of 1858', *Trade Societies and Strikes*, Report of the National Association for the *Promotion of Social Science* 1860, 32.

[2] Cassell thesis, 209, 216, 222–3.   [3] Quoted in Cassell thesis, 225.

[4] Ibid., 239.

small number of Inspectors, not all of whom may have been as concerned over the scope of the Special Rules as Mackworth, was immense, with the result that some of the Special Rules approved for some districts sanctioned penalties for behaviour unrelated to safety. Furthermore, even though the Inspectors may have exercised particular care in their deliberations in the process of inspecting the special draft rules, many managers recognized that by printing the colliery rules relating to workers' behaviour affecting commercial performance (normally contained in contracts) on the same notice as the legally enforceable Special Rules, the distinction between the two would become blurred to the labour force.[1] The significant difference between the contract and Special Rules was that violation of the latter might be punished by a fine of £2 or three-months' imprisonment.

The by-laws continued to be a matter for concern among miners, and in 1863 the South Yorkshire Miners' Association, the most forceful of all miners' unions at that time, complained in particular of those which gave employers the power to confiscate corves below weight—which had nothing to do with safety. In west Yorkshire several employers continued to insist on 'detaining money' from miners, from which fines for the breach of colliery rules were deducted.[2] The Special Rules drawn up by the Scottish coalowners included clauses which enjoined all colliers to 'work at their appointed coal faces continuously industriously and without necessary interruption while the shift continues', prohibiting all underground meetings of workmen.[3] Undoubtedly the intention of the Inspectors was to promote safety in the mines, but the scope to reinforce the disciplinary powers of employers long after the modifications of 1860 is clear from evidence to the Royal Commission on Labour in 1892; then it was explained that the Master and Servant Act empowered the coalowner to prosecute individual colliers for transgressing not only the innumerable provisions of the Mines Act, but also the contract of employment.[4] South Wales coalowners had taken steps to 'avoid the inconvenience and publicity associated with magistrates' courts' by arranging for miners to be given the option of paying fines at the local library. Some coalowners were also not averse to mobilizing community pressure to discipline workmen by posting an offender's name in some conspicuous place in the colliery; such a method was alleged to have had 'a far more deterrent effect upon him than any punishment he may receive at the hands of the magistrate, while it prevents a great deal of

---

[1] Ibid., 225.
[2] Machin 1958, 304, 211.
[3] Campbell 1979, 107.
[4] RC Labour 1892, XXXVI, 156.

friction between the management and men'.[1] By the early years of the twentieth century fines for disciplinary purposes had almost disappeared, the fear of dismissal, according to the agent of the Lancashire and Cheshire Miners' Federation discouraging miners from reporting what remained of this illegal practice to the Inspectors.[2]

Though abuses were still to be found, methods of labour discipline had altered much since the 1830s and 1840s, when the substantial child labour force had offered greater scope for harsher regimes, including corporal punishment. Nardinelli's analysis of corporal punishment in factories at this time led him to conclude that the evidence was consistent with the hypothesis 'that corporal punishment increased the productivity of child labour', a conclusion based on the presumed association of greater discipline and higher productivity with the observed coincidence of corporal punishment and higher wages.[3] Children in coal mines were excluded from his investigation, and the concentration of corporal punishment in the East and West Midlands (at least, as reflected in evidence to the *Children's Employment Commission*), where wage levels and productivity were low but where the butty system predominated, suggests alternatively that in the coal industry the mode of organization and hiring arrangements were major influences upon the incidence of corporal punishment. The prevalence of child employment in the context of an extended working family unit before 1842 in any case complicates an analysis of the relationships posed by Nardinelli.[4]

From the 1840s two influences tended to reduce the amount of crude physical discipline in mines. One was the decline of the big butty system which, because reward was directly related to intensive driving of those in the sub-contractor's employment, offered the greatest scope for abuse. A Nottinghamshire miner recalled his own experience in the 1830s and 1840s at the Pinxton pits, where 'A few of the butties . . . were humane and kind, but others were most cruel and brutish'; some of their supervisory employees he described as 'slave drivers, [who] would arm themselves with a stick or thong, fix themselves in some convenient spot, and as a lad (about naked) came by with his wagon, which he had

---

[1] Ibid.

[2] *Truck Acts Committee* 1908, LIX, QQ 7853, 7860, 7877, 7881, 7885, 7894.

[3] Clark Nardinelli, 'Corporal Punishment and Children's Wages in Nineteenth Century Britain', *EEH* 19 (1982), 283–95.

[4] The most unambiguous statement to this effect referred to South Wales and the west of Scotland, but this is also a possible interpretation of the situation in most other regions excepting the North-east; *Children's Employment Commission* 1842, XV, 51–2; A. R. Griffin 1971, 42–3.

to push, would strike him on the back . . .'.[1] in south Staffordshire the butties were the principal offenders in abusing parish apprentices.[2] Typically under-capitalized on the margins of profitability, the mines which operated under the big butty system faced competition with the new pits sunk in the East Midlands from the 1840s and later from those in north Staffordshire and in neighbouring districts.[3] Improved equipment and mining methods conducted under the supervision of salaried officials heralded a more systematic, more humane, approach to labour discipline.[4] Reinforcing these changes were the Mines Act which, beginning in 1842, gradually removed children from underground, though even after the Act of 1872 children between the ages of twelve and sixteen were still permitted to work fifty-four hours a week underground, and not until 1900 was the age limit underground raised to thirteen.

Outside the big butty system sub-contracting was also associated with particularly hard driving of juvenile and adult workers too. One Scottish coalowner told the Commission in 1844, 'The contractors do the work for us cheaper than the masters can get it done', a remark which is consistent with the comment embodied in the Commissioner's Report that the contractors 'take more out of the men'[5]—the result of hard driving. It seems likely, too, that one of the influences of the Inspectors was to encourage the appointment of more intelligent supervisory labour. The Inspector for the Midland District repeatedly drew attention to the importance of this factor in explaining differential colliery performance.[6] In 1852 the Inspector referred to the existence of 'a great deal of ignorance' among colliery officials and underground stewards, who often couldn't write and many of whom 'lacked sufficient knowledge to perform their duties adequately', neglecting discipline and safety.[7] Ten years later the Inspector's Reports noted improvements in the quality of mine management in the Midlands, a trend which was to continue.[8]

Between 1830 and 1870 the character of labour discipline in most regions had altered, therefore, as the result of legislative and other changes. Legislation against truck payments and the disassociation of

[1] Quoted in A. R. Griffin 1972, 43.
[2] Ibid., 53–4.
[3] A. R. Griffin 1971, 43; A. J. Taylor 1967, 101.
[4] C. P. Griffin thesis 298.
[5] Quoted in Campbell 1979, 212–213; see also Hair thesis, 169.
[6] C. P. Griffin thesis, 311.
[7] Ibid., 311–12; A. J. Taylor 1967, 200.
[8] C. P. Griffin thesis, 311.

wage payments from public houses, the introduction of regulation, and the inspection of coal mines which transformed the age structure of the labour force, helped to diminish, though they did not entirely eliminate, the scope for cynical coercion based on indebtedness, intimidation, and hard driving in those regions where such practices had flourished most. Trends away from these were reinforced by legislation, by the growth of trade unions and by a gradual improvement in the quality of management and supervisory staff. None the less, historians have drawn attention to two developments which, in contrasting ways, were intended to strengthen the miners' work orientation and to threaten the mining tradition of self-imposed work pace and the hewers' artisan status. Both the extent and effectiveness of these policies are matters for dispute.

vii. Labour supervision and welfare policies

A considerable body of literature exists[1] which stresses the changes in management–labour relations consequent upon alterations in work organization described in Chapter 4. The distinctive element which has been seen as critical in longwall working, compared with the bord and pillar method which it superceded, was the greater scope for managerial supervision underground, one effect of which, it is argued, was a deterioration in labour relations. This occurred, the argument runs, because the adoption of longwall mining allowed increasing specialization of function among larger teams of miners working longer faces, facilitated a higher degree of supervision by managers, and by requiring a more disciplined performance from the individual miner thereby led to a decline in his independence as an artisan. This general hypothesis, supported in several twentieth-century studies of mining, has been challenged recently by Daunton, who concluded that in the era of non-mechanized cutting before 1913 the difference in working method was not sufficiently great in its effect upon group or individual behaviour to justify attaching significance of the kind often attributed to it. He shows, for example, that when attempts were made to change the technique of extraction in South Wales in the 1860s the difficulties encountered by managers were temporary problems of adjustment; the changes did not introduce a long-term divergence between the two systems.[2] On

---

[1] For example, S. Wellisz, 'Strikes in Coal Mining', *British Journal of Sociology*, 1953, IV, 357; C. Goodrich, *The Miners' Freedom* (Boston, 1925), 26–35; E. L. Trist and K. W. Bamforth, 'Technicism: Some Effects of Material Technology on Managerial Methods and on Work Situation Relationships' in T. Burns (ed.) *Industrial Man* (London, 1969), 335–6.

[2] Daunton 1981, 583.

balance, the evidence appears to support Daunton's argument that the crucial difference in work organization came only with longwall *machine* mining, when the processes of undercutting, ripping, and filling were entirely separated and performed by different groups (and different shifts) of workers.[1]

Pillar and stall working remained the dominant practice in Lanarkshire throughout the second half of the nineteenth century, and consequently no change in working practice was to be observed.[2] Elsewhere in Scotland a fundamental shift to longwall working occurred in the period after 1850, but in their study of the 'Independent Collier' Campbell and Reid argue that although this facilitated the greater division of the non-face labour force it changed the work of the hewer relatively little.[3] G. M. Wilson's study of miners in the west of Scotland puts a greater emphasis on the introduction of longwall working (and there would appear to be a difference of opinion between Campbell and Wilson on the true extent of longwall working in the region). Quoting a Scottish mining engineer named Bailes, who argued that one of the greatest advantages of longwall mining was the supervision it made possible, Wilson points out that at the time Bailes was writing, in 1874, longwall teams rarely exceeded four people, though the evolution of large-scale team longwall mining occurred later.[4] Even this argument, however, is not fundamentally at odds with Daunton's analysis. Not only did longwall working facilitate a higher degree of specialization within larger teams, it also encouraged a greater degree of managerial supervision because the face had to move forward uniformly, which required greater co-ordination of effort (between worker and worker and worker and management). Nevertheless, work pace was largely group-determined. Allocation of working places, however, was decided by the overman, except in the North-east where 'cavilling' enabled hewers to share good and inferior, or 'abnormal', places by drawing lots.[5]

Daunton stressed the fundamental difference that accompanied the introduction of multiple-shift working, in which different shifts performed three distinct processes (moving the face forward every twenty-four hours); and that this was the product of machine cutting only. Because the crucial advance in the division of labour came with machine cutting and not with longwall itself, the effects prior to 1913 were confined largely to Scotland—and even there to a limited extent. None of

[1] Ibid., 583–4.
[2] Campbell 1979, 109.   [3] Campbell and Reid 1978, 58.
[4] G. M. Wilson thesis, 36.   [5] Daunton 1981, 584.

this is to deny that the introduction of longwall working had some effect on labour relations and working arrangements, but simply emphasizes the fundamental role of machine cutting while minimizing the degree to which managerial control actually accompanied the spread of longwall mining in the pre-face mechanization period.

Longwall mining probably accounted for 75 per cent of UK output by 1900, and dominated except in south Staffordshire, the North-east and North Wales.[1] Studies by Campbell, Campbell and Reid, and G. M. Wilson point to an increasing trend in the second half of the nineteenth century whereby owners and management made deliberate attempts to itensify managerial control and destroy the degree of independence so valued by the hewer as craftsman.[2] That status was illustrated in the report of an agent in Lanarkshire, reporting that in one pillar-and-stall working the overman never saw the men at work, who refused to be observed; whenever he approached the hewers they stopped and waited until he passed.[3] After 1900 the change-over to mechanized longwall mining played a small part in the erosion of the degree of independence retained by hewers, for machine cutting did necessitate greater regimentation. However, longwall teams remained small, for the most part, and consequently the overall process of managerial supervision was also limited in scope. The managerial drive to draw up shorter-term contracts for hewers, to increase the number of supervisory staff, to increase the pace of work, and intensify a complex process of 'social coercion and ideological pressure' met with mixed success.[4] There were considerable regional and intra-regional variations. Thus, for example, Alexander MacDonald claimed that apprenticeship regulations were observed in Clackmannan, Fife, Midlothian, and East Lothian, but could not generally be enforced in Lanarkshire, Renfrewshire, Linlithgowshire, and the bulk of Ayrshire.[5] At a more fundamental level, miners resented managerial control, and the existence or non-existence of longwall mining was far from being the fundamental determinant of their ability to resist it. Describing the system in twentieth-century County Durham, Douglass argues that even where longwall working had been introduced and when as a result the deputy was 'always in or near the face', in practice his powers of supervision were no greater than they had been under pillar-and-stall working.[6] Longwall teams still worked under their elected leaders, and men habitually refused to accept super-

---

[1] See below 338.
[2] Especially Campbell 1979, 105–9.
[3] Douglass 1977, 218.
[4] Campbell 1979, 105–9.
[5] Ibid., 109.
[6] Douglass 1977, 218.

vision and advice from deputies, refusing to be 'spied upon'.[1] Such evidence as this helps to explain the co-existence in the North-east of England of a high degree of labour division in pillar-and-stall working on the one hand with a high degree of independent craft status for the hewer on the other. This independent status was so well established that it could survive the transition to longwall working, although it would have been weakened, presumably, by the adoption of machine methods. Thus, while the decision to employ pillar and stall or longwall in British mines depended in part, upon the search for improvements in labour productivity through better organization, the question of artisan status, self-imposed work pace, and managerial supervision depended on a much wider group of factors than on this transition alone.

One major consideration of the extent to which control could be exercised over workers was the sheer demand for labour, which eventually led to the removal of long-term contracts, long pays, and other policies intended to secure and retain labour. In 1867 one of Staveley's managers explained that the company's policy was to compete in the labour market by wage adjustments and reductions in hours in order to keep, or attract, colliers.[2] The manager of the Brancepeth Colliery, belonging to Straker and Love in Northumberland, reported in similar terms: 'As soon as the price of coal increases we raise the wages, because we find that if we do not pay men as well or better than our neighbours we lose them'. William Armstrong repeatedly advocated a similar policy to the managers of collieries for whom he was viewer, though he attached considerable importance, too, to housing policy.[3]

Within the North-east (and Scotland, to a lesser extent) colliery housing formed part of the miners' contract, but elsewhere miners were free to move, subject to monthly, but increasingly from the mid-century, fortnightly notice. One effect must have been to increase the importance attached to the provision of colliery housing, not only as a method of attracting the best hewers, but to retain them either by offering the advantage of proximity to the pit or superior and more comfortable accommodation.

Colliery housing was widely regarded as forming an important element in the managerial strategy for labour recruitment and retention. For although 'free' housing was virtually unknown outside the North-east, tied housing was associated in other districts, too, with the

[1] Ibid., 219–20.
[2] RC Trade Unions 1867–8, XXXIX, Q 13587–8.
[3] Ibid., Q 119897.

possibility of eviction in the event of unsatisfactory performance or insubordination, more especially in connection with trade-union activity and strikes.

In the 1870s William Armstrong wrote to Bolckow Vaughan's directors, telling them that 'cottages are now the chief item to assure [sic] large production. Every colliery proprietor is increasing his housing accommodation and vying with his neighbours in the scale of comfort they afford to entice and retain men, and it is of no use to hope for regular work or large quantity unless the workmen are well housed and in a position near their work'. Time and time again, especially in relation to the opening of new pits, Armstrong recommended house building to retain a 'good staff of men'[1]—by which he meant reliable hewers. Elliot described the process by which newly developed pits generally attracted 'a loose stray class of working people until you get more of them and select them'; the reservation of colliery housing for supervisory workers and for the most valued hewers was a method of securing and keeping a supply of the latter.[2] This view was echoed by William Armstrong in a letter advising the directors of Tredegar Colliery in South Wales. He referred to 'a lot of waifs and strays running about who failing to find a place where money is easily acquired have frequently left without notice and not one worth looking after—and until some improvement takes place in wages I fear men will still leave the county at times ... and unless you can offer accommodation to strangers, you cannot maintain your working complement'.[3] The company secretary of Carlton Main Colliery in Yorkshire enunciated a principle, widely held among coal-owners and managers, that 'where houses are provided, it is the means of ensuring a steady class of workmen and regularity of work'.[4]

In 1873 the Quaker coalowner, J. Whitewell Pease, reckoned that the only way to get more men was to give them houses, which was his own method of recruiting and keeping the 'respectable resident men',[5] a class of colliers very different from those described by Leifchild as 'always shifting about the same as navvies: ... if the shop doesn't suit they are off'.[6] Charles Markham reckoned that workmen's trains introduced by

---

[1] NuRO Armstrong 725/B8/117; 725/B11/81-6; 725/B14/564.
[2] *RC Trade Unions* 1867, XXXIX, Q 11391.
[3] NuRO Armstrong 725/B11/81 Report.
[4] SCL Carlton Main MD 4080-89 Directors' Minutes 1878.
[5] *SC Dearness and Scarcity* 1873, X, Q 4399.
[6] *Children's Employment Commission* 1842, XVI, para 192.

Staveley in 1860 offered one solution to difficulties of recruitment to rural collieries, but that they tended to attract only 'the waifs and strays of labour' from Chesterfield, whence some of the colliery workers at the Newstead Colliery were drawn.[1] The Clay Cross managers' desperate measures to obtain labour at the height of the early 1870s boom included the offer of drink; 'the only remedy for this state of things', Markham informed his co-directors 'appears to be the erection of additional houses'.[2]

The manager of the Dowlais Iron Company was explicit in his expectations of the beneficial effects of housing provision in developing a sober and responsible work-force: '. . . if a workman has a comfortable house over his head, he will by degrees regard air, water, and drainage as necessaries of life. He will have no inducement to go to the Public House. He will save money. He will insist upon having some time at his disposal for reading, gardening, and the society of his wife'.[3] Some twenty years later, in 1877, William Armstrong spelled out to the Staveley and Sheepbridge joint managing committee his solution for improving the quality and regularity of labour at Newstead colliery in rural Nottinghamshire. After describing the current labour force as 'an inferior lot, brought from every handicraft and trade and hence unfitted for work of this kind', he advised that with everyone competing for men:

you must run with the stream . . .. If you cannot persuade building societies or builders to invest in erecting cottages I see no alternative but your erecting them. Goose fairs and country hoppings are easy pretexts for keeping the men at home, and in wet and winter weather the long walk is frequently given up to the prejudice of the colliery . . . I suggest you . . . recover your capital within the terms of your lease and you will then have the men under your control and you can rely upon a better and more regular class of workmen . . .[4]

Considerations of labour supply thus provided the major justification for house building in coalfields undergoing rapid development in locations remote from towns.

While the *economics* of colliery housing were less than compelling, many coalowners were persuaded that considerations of regularity and

[1] BSCEMRRC Stanton and Staveley 2034/3/9c 29 Oct. 1877, Markham's Reports; Chapman 1981, 49.   [2] Ibid., 26 July 1872.
[3] G. P. Smith thesis, 116.
[4] BSCEMRRC Stanton and Staveley 2034/3/9a, Armstrong's Report on Newstead Colliery, 10 Oct. 1877.

quality of the labour force justified such investment. Rent-free housing was the single most powerful lever on labour, though limited almost entirely to the North-east, conferring income in kind and relative comfort but which during a dispute might be threatened by eviction. Mass evictions occurred during the pitmen's strikes in the North-east in 1831–2 and 1844, at Wingate Grange in 1849, at the Brancepath Collieries of Straker and Love in 1863, at West Cramlington Colliery in 1865. G. M. Wilson counted eighteen instances when evictions occurred in Lanarkshire between 1842 and 1874, and in Yorkshire and the East Midlands they have been identified in 1844, 1858, and 1861, at Henry Brigg's Collieries in 1862–3, Newton Chambers's Thorncliffe Colliery and at Denaby Main in 1869, and at Lord Crawford's Lancashire collieries in 1853. Later, evictions at Ushaw Moor Colliery in 1883 and at Silksworth Colliery in 1890 were exceptions in a period when transparent coercion ran the risk of major trade-union reaction and public outrage.[1]

The scope for mass evictions among the work-force became increasingly limited, for when coalfields expanded, alternative forms of housing provision developed, becoming available in all but the most distant and isolated locations. However, the decline in tied housing did not substantially improve miners' security, for while the typical tenure available allowed the customary right to remain in housing through short periods of unemployment, none the less as tenants at will they were vulnerable to eviction. When company housing was at its peak, certainly before 1870, perhaps one-third of miners were company tenants, more in the North-east and in Scotland than elsewhere, which indicates the extent to which coalowners were in a position to employ housing as an instrument of policy. A similar proportional concentration in these two regions persisted until 1913.[2]

The substitution of tenancies at will for rent-free housing, which Daunton has charted during the last quarter of the century, has been explained largely in terms of market forces.[3] The lengthy periods of

[1] Richard Fynes, *The Miners of Northumberland and Durham* (Sunderland, 1873), 28–31, 119–20; Welbourne 1923, 38, 54, 75–6, 115, 127; G. M. Wilson thesis, 257; Machin 1958, 119, 287, 362–3; Challinor 1972, 46–7.

[2] The only reliable (though incomplete) figures available for 1913 are those presented in the *Samuel Commission* III 247–9 Table 37 which refer to houses rather than workers. Taken in conjunction with the size of the work-force and the average number of workers who lived in each colliery house, the proportion of miners living in colliery housing may be estimated at roughly 50 per cent in the North-east, just over a third in Scotland, less than 10 per cent in South Wales, and between 15 and 20 per cent in Yorkshire and the East Midlands. Elsewhere the proportions were probably similar to, or less than those for South Wales.

[3] Daunton 1980.

under employment encountered after 1874, a time of doubtful profit-ability for most collieries, prompted the coalowners to try to eliminate the opportunity costs incurred when miners were not at work yet enjoying rent-free accommodation in company housing. The financial return on coalowners' housing investment during this period appears to have been low and falling. Yet it is clear that while financial return was one consideration influencing coalowners' decisions on house building and housing policy, much more important were the labour management strategies of individual firms, affected powerfully by the geographical location of collieries in relation to accessible supplies of labour and the retention of experienced and steady working miners.[1] The change in attitude towards housing policy from the 1880s may be interpreted as the effect of a combination of factors, therefore, for coinciding with diminishing profitability and the growth of coalmining in urban dis-tricts, the rise of trade-union strength helped to impose constraints upon the effectiveness of a policy of housing provision as one form of labour regulation.[2] This trend away from company housing towards the close of the century did not see the end of it, however, for in the newly developing coalfields of Yorkshire and the Midlands entire model col-liery villages sprang into existence. While they exhibited some of the fea-tures of the old pit villages, because of the entirely rural location of the new collieries they were conceived on a new scale and built to much higher standards of social amenity and architecture.[3]

Whereas housing combined both a potentially coercive as well as an attractive aspect, the development of a row or two of colliery houses into a village marked the transition to more subtle possibilities of wel-fare provision, whereby employers might adopt paternalist policies in pursuit of a measure of 'social control' over the work-force, or designed to achieve 'communal sociability' possibly unrelated to ulterior motives concerned with workers' performance.[4] Precise definitions of social control are difficult to formulate, but the writings of historians who have examined this phenomenon suggest that the key feature is the separation of the unintended effects of economic, political, and legal systems upon workers' attitudes and behaviour from the conscious efforts of a class, or group of employers, which attempts to impose notions of what are regarded as suitable habits and conduct for another

---

[1] See above 279–80.

[2] J. Melling, 'Employers' Industrial Housing and the Evolution of Company Welfare Policies in Britain's heavy Industries: West Scotland 1870–1920', *IRSH*, XXVI (1981), 257–9.

[3] See below 288–9.   [4] Joyce 1980, 93.

class, or group of workers, upon the latter. The agencies through which social control has been seen to operate include principally religion, education, and the sanction of public opinion. An alternative stress upon the context and process of people's working lives has placed 'community', whether nurtured by employers or emerging as a spontaneous manifestation of living and working in close proximity, at the centre of the process of social control, in which work is regarded as having been the supreme influence. Under conditions in which the presence of a coalowner as major property owner or as dominant employer loomed large, the influence of employers penetrated entire institutional structures extending into housing, schools, church and chapel, institute, and club; local government, the administration of law and of poor relief were further, though more direct, manifestations of patriarchal dominance which Joyce has identified in the cotton towns and industrial villages of Lancashire during the second and third quarters of the nineteenth century.

In a different geographical and industrial context, Hassan has described the evolution of a 'new community of deference' in Midlothian coalmining during the second quarter of the century, when the feudalistic values of the aristocratic landed entrepreneurs were adapted to the perceived requirements of the management and control of a rapidly growing mining population.[1] In this process coercion is seen as being gradually superceded by more subtle forms of influence, at the centre of which was the provision of company housing and local amenities. But such practices were also widespread where mining was not under aristocratic control.[2] Moreover, landowning mining entrepreneurs were not immune to industrial unrest, and at times the owners and managers of such collieries employed similar measures to force strikers back to work as the major industrial capitalists did—including evictions from colliery housing, the use of blacklegs, and victimization. Housing and associated policies affecting the everyday lives of miners and their families stemmed less from the feudal imperatives of aristocratic paternalism than from an industrial logic, in which housing and amenity provision on the one hand, and on the other anti-unionism coupled with the cultivation of deference, might be complementary; which is why the influence of aristocratic presumptions and principles

---

[1] Hassan, 'The Landed Estate, Paternalism and the Coal Industry in Midlothian, 1880–18', *Scottish Historical Review*, LIX (1980).

[2] See below 283–4.

upon social relations in the coalfields should not be regarded as crucial in determining labour or welfare policies in the nineteenth century.[1]

Contemporary practitioners of the methods by which various forms of indirect influence on workers' attitudes and behaviour were sought referred merely to 'paternalism', though the implied philanthropic, or enlightened, benevolence normally associated with that term, especially when applied to the administration of aristocratic estates, rarely seems to have been uppermost in the minds of contemporary practitioners. George Elliot, Powell Duffryn's manager, observed that 'a little of the paternal system is very useful because you can keep your men in times of difficulty'.[2] In 1873 the Quaker coalowner, J. W. Pease, told the Royal Commission of the economic justification for what he called 'philanthropy', which he stressed 'in the form of free housing, pig styes, gardens, etc. is a sound investment for colliery owners, even if there was no higher motive than keeping your men comfortable. I believe it pays.'[3] For many years the Peases had provided schools, reading rooms, mechanics institutes, and a cottage hospital. The company employed two 'missionaries' to perform partly secular and partly religious duties, including house-to-house visiting, when parents were urged to send children to school; all adults were encouraged to use other facilities, to save with building societies, and to accept advice 'on sanitary and other matters'. One key provision missing from these amenities was the public house, no fewer than twenty-six having been closed by the Peases in the 1860s, all of which had been run formerly by foremen and 'gaffers' at the collieries.

Such paternalist policies aimed at fostering a sense of community— whatever other ultimate motives may have existed (and even among Quakers evidently they were not always based on altruism)—were not new. An Edinburgh accountant's report on the Alloa Coal Company prepared for prospective purchasers in 1833 included an explanation of expenditure on such items as the support of the colliery band, the provision of a bible to each collier on marriage, the establishment of soup

---

[1] Roy Hay and Joseph Melling, 'Public Service and Private Progress: Business Welfare in British and Australian Mining: mid-19th to mid-20th Centuries', presented to the Eighth International Congress of Economic History, Budapest, August 1982, 8–13. These authors present Scottish evidence. For examples of the policies of English aristocratic colliery owners see Mee 1975, 182–3; A. J. Taylor, 'The Third Marquis of Londonderry and the North-east Coal Trade', *DUJ*, new series, xvii (1955–6), 21–7; Mather, 1970, 320–33. A. J. Heesom, 'Entrepreneurial Paternalism: The Third Lord Londonderry (1755–1854) and the Coal Trade', *DUJ*, NS, XXXV (1974), 253–5.   [2] *RC Trade Unions* 1867–8, XXXIX, Q 11411.

[3] *SC Dearness and Scarcity* 1873, X, Q 4399.

kitchens in time of hardship, the building and running of a colliery school, and the opening of a hospital during the recent cholera outbreak; expenditure which the accountant suggested external assessors might regard as charges to load on colliery assets. He noted, however, that expenditures of this kind were 'sanctioned by long continued usage, and are considered not only necessary and proper, but highly beneficial in the management of the colliery in securing the fidelity and attachment of the men, who it is believed are the most orderly and well disposed class of men collected with any colliery in Scotland'; he added, 'their wages, moreover, are lower than what is generally paid at other collieries'.[1] Henry Briggs saw a somewhat different relationship between wages and social provision. He told the 1842 Commissioners: 'I am of opinion that high wages do men harm where they are not sufficiently educated'. He described the facilities available to his miners, which consisted of Sunday and evening schools, recreational evenings, and a very successful horticultural society. This amounted to 'a system already beginning to show evidence of manifesting a beneficial tendency in creating a friendly feeling between the employers and the men and in keeping the latter from the public house'.[2]

Barrow's conviction that his miners were 'too fond of drink' was fundamental to his welfare policies at Staveley in the mid-nineteenth century, for he admitted that although one objective in providing schools was 'to enable the rising generation to receive the benefits of Education', he added: '. . . At all events, I hope the schools will restrain them from attending the public houses . . .',[3] reflecting a concern widespread among Victorian employers. Another measure designed to discourage workmen from frequenting public houses was the provision of dining institutes, a practice common in Scotland, where a midday meal at low cost was the inducement.[4] At Wharncliffe Silkstone avoidance of public houses was a condition dictated by the directors in return for a contribution towards the purchase of instruments for the colliery brass band.[5] At Gateshead Colliery, in Kilmarnock, the Duke of Portland furnished a miners' library including only books which were 'fitted to promote intellectual, moral, and religious improvement of readers', one rule requiring exclusion of any book 'containing unsound opinion or having a dangerous tendency'.[6]

[1] SRO Alloa 17/592/3.
[2] *Children's Employment Commission* 1842, XVI, Q, 171.
[3] Chapman 1981, 153.   [4] Ibid., 155.
[5] SCL Wharncliffe Silkstone NCB 1429/1, 7 July 1867.
[6] G. M. Wilson thesis, 102.

To amenities some employers added occasions for communal celebration and entertainment. At the Emmaville Colliery of the Stella Coal Company in 1861 J. B. Simpson declared a day's holiday for the five hundred employees to enable them to attend a public 'soirée'. The Emmaville Cricket Club played their opponents, and to the accompaniment of the colliery band the assembled miners and their families took tea in a marquee, where Simpson made a speech. After referring to the existence of chapel, school, and reading room, he dwelt on the success of the Grand Lease Royalty, and drew contrasts between 'the alehouse gatherings of former times' and the decorous occasion then being enjoyed.[1] Barrow adopted a similarly paternalistic posture at Staveley, presiding at open-air gatherings and temperance meetings; and under the Markhams, too, from the mid-century the Staveley Works Mechanics Institute became a centre for the company's annual soirées, which were popular occasions held in wakes week. By the end of the century a local newspaper correspondent claimed to have detected 'a better moral tone and more cordial relations between masters and workmen' in those Derbyshire colliery districts 'where the owners had interested themselves in workers' recreational facilities'. By that time Staveley's policy, under C. P. Markham, continued to include the provision of amenities, but the Memorial Hall, built in 1893, and the Club, opened in 1904, contained not only dining and reading rooms but billiard tables and a bar,[2] features which suggest a retreat from the sterner morality characteristic of early and mid-Victorian employers' welfare. Not far distant from Staveley, however, Emerson Bainbridge's Bolsover Colliery saw community development established from the 1890s on the basis of a strict code of behaviour.[3]

By the very nature of coalmining, the face-to-face meeting of owner and worker, save in the smallest pits, was exceptional, especially underground, but on the surface too, where there were no factory walls to contain owners and workers. While the agent or colliery manager visited underground, with increasing regularity after the Mines Act, pit conditions offered limited scope for the furtherance of paternal relations between those in command and those mining coal. As landed colliery enterprises were typically survivors from an earlier period and therefore more likely to retain a style of quasi-feudal character, the paternalism associated with them tended to perpetuate a stability resulting from a traditional form of deference[4] which was at times the

---

[1] *CG* 12 July 1862, 34.   [2] Chapman 1981, 148–168.
[3] See below 288.   [4] Hair thesis, 9.

despair of trade-union leaders. In a carefully prepared report on miners' dwellings in Yorkshire and submitted to the National Conference of Miners in 1863 the author praised the quality of cottages provided, but noted that 'those who lived in them are nailed as fast to his lordship's pits and the customs of his lordship's colliery stewards as the trees are to his lordship's park. They have their cottages, gardens, pigstyes, etc. . . . yet the men have no resisting power . . . These men are as thoroughly feudalised as were the Britons in the day of "William, the Norman" . . . for these reasons we object to living in a coalowners' house.'[1] The remedies urged were savings, self-help, and home-ownership—exactly the same elements contained in the policy pursued by G. T. Clark, managing trustee of Dowlais from the 1850s, the purpose of which was clear to him: 'Whenever I hear of a good worker my first impulse is to induce him to save a little money, to build himself a house, and to give me some security that he will not leave his work'.[2] Clark also associated home ownership with tranquil labour relations, for he categorized the typical strike-prone collier as young, lacking savings, and who 'at worst' could migrate, whereas older and steadier house-holders were more prepared 'to wait on market forces'. Long-standing employment for a colliery owner was regarded by others too as conducive of respect for, and attachment to, employers, particularly by the landed coalowners.[3]

Landed coalowners, industrial capitalists, viewers, and workers all acknowledged the importance of assisting in the process of settlement, especially in the non-urban coalfields. When Thomas Burt moved to Choppington Colliery, Northumberland, shortly after it opened in 1860 he was critical of the lack of 'cohesion' and the absence of 'public spirit' in the village. 'As yet', he recalled, 'there were no schools, no reading rooms, no lecture hall, no cooperative store': none of the facilities which he associated with a stable and settled community, but which later also included a workmen's hall, provided by the company, but managed by a workmen's committee and used for trade-union meetings.[4] This community-development policy Burt described as producing a laudable 'enhancement of social life'. That the policy of constructive paternalism was not the monopoly of landed coalowners is even more evident in the policy of the Clay Cross Company, which from the beginning in the 1840s provided a range of educational and social amenities for their

---

[1] *Transactions and Proceedings of the National Conference of Miners* 1863, 51.
[2] Smith thesis, 30.
[3] Ibid., 14; Hassan thesis, 285–7.
[4] Burt 1924, 137–141.

Derbyshire miners: a workmen's institute containing a library, a 'free' medical service, including pay during sickness and disablement by accident, a brass band, cricket club, fornightly dancing, and various societies designed to meet the interests of enthusiasts. Costing each employee a small, but compulsory, deduction from wages, the resulting community drew special praise from Samuel Smiles, who in 1864 described it as a model for large employers of labour.[1]

Another example of a constructive recruitment policy was that pursued by the Throckley Coal Company in Northumberland, which since its formation in 1867 had adopted a similar approach to that described at Clay Cross. Respectable family men, particularly those with Methodist convictions, were favoured by the proprietors, whose policy was the subject for comment by a reporter for the *Newcastle Daily Chronicle* in 1897:

... for a pit village it is claimed that in orderliness and prosperity of its people it is second to no other in Northumberland and Durham. More than half of the miners are total abstainers, for the prohibition of drink, dogs and pigeons keeps away those that are inclined thereto, and the result of the repulsion of these free-livers is a sort of artificial selection of steady workmen, who have in the course of years formed themselves into an industrious, peaceable and thriving community ...[2]

Noting that attendance at both chapels in the village was high, he observed that the miners also attended work on Monday mornings 'in an efficient condition—guiltless of "after damp" from any Saturday and Sunday potations', another respect in which Throckley's reputation was deemed to have been exceptional.[3]

That circumstances, rather than business structure and organization, were the critical influences on community policies is suggested by the attempts of large joint-stock companies to create communities in the late nineteenth and early twentieth centuries. When in the 1890s the Griff Colliery Company opened new pits in Warwickshire the cottages built to accommodate miners were followed by the opening of a 'Mission Room' used for mothers, Sunday schools, and for services by Wesleyan lay preachers. A reading room was opened for colliery workers, as was a skittles ground; allotments were laid out and sports and gardening clubs formed to compete for company prizes. Not all of these ventures succeeded, but a few years later a lending library, founded by

[1] Samuel Smiles, *Life of George Stephenson Railway Engineer* (London, 1864), 328–30.
[2] Williamson 1982, 80.   [3] Ibid.

the manager's wife, was in operation, and various recreational and mining classes took placed in the Mission. Griff's manager, E. F. Melly, remarked, 'I think on the whole it is a comfortable colliery village and most of the rough ones, who got in at first, when we wanted tenants, have been turned out'.[1] Even at the end of our period a new colliery town, for example, Bolsover and Cresswell in Derbyshire, Woodlands and Denaby Main in South Yorkshire, might have most of its public institutions—schools, parish church, co-op, local hotel, and sports ground and clubs—built and largely controlled by the company that sank the pit and built the houses.[2]

The continuity of pit-village formation to be found in the newly expanding regions in the East and West Midlands and south Yorkshire may be regarded as evidence of the persistence of long-established assumptions concerning the character of labour in isolation, the methods of promoting good relations, and of recruiting reliable workers. This also suggests that the tendency of studies of paternalism in the early nineteenth century to limit its significance to that period have overlooked the extent to which, certainly in mining, the need to socialize a migrant or inexperienced work-force continued to present a problem throughout the nineteenth century. Thus, when the first of the several colliery villages established by Emerson Bainbridge's Bolsover Colliery was begun in Derbyshire in 1892, the *Colliery Guardian* reporter noted that 'the village will be governed, as far as possible, by a council of men themselves; and drunkenness and swearing and gambling will render offenders liable to instant dismissal'.[3] Combined with this stern moral imperative was the provision of schools, incorporating a large hall for public meetings and entertainment, and a miners' institute, including reading room, sports, games, and committee rooms, and a large library. Resembling arrangements in most such institutes, members' subscriptions paid the rental to the company, any surplus proceeds being applied to village needs. A bowling green, skittle and quoit grounds, a cricket ground with pavilion, and a miniature rifle range completed the recreational amenities. At nearby Old Bolsover was Bolsover Castle, long since vacated by the Duke of Portland, who allowed public use of the extensive grounds for flower shows and other activities. Cresswell Colliery, a few miles distant, was the site of a similar model village, though larger in scale than Bolsover. In south Yorkshire,

[1] WaRO Griff, CR 1169/22–75.
[2] H. S. Jevons 1915, 655–6; Bulman 1920, 274–8, 288–9; Chapman 1981, Chapt. 6.
[3] *CG* 30 Sept. 1892, 611.

the Woodlands Model Village, built by the Brodsworth Main Colliery Co. under the guidance of chairman Sir Arthur Markham, brought to colliery village building unprecedented distinction, when in 1905 the architect who designed the cottages won a prize in a competition sponsored by the *Country Gentleman* in connection with the Letchworth Garden City. The social buildings were similar in range to those at Bainbridge's villages. Having counted the cost, Bulman commented on the valuable seams and the long life expected of the colliery as factors justifying an expenditure of over £200,000, and added: 'The health and happiness and efficiency of workpeople cannot be expressed in £.*s*.*d*. but apart from higher considerations they are a valuable asset in any industrial enterprise.'[1]

Many joint-stock companies and landed enterprises shared another policy in common before the 1870s: the proscription of trade unions. The Earl Fitzwilliam, otherwise praised for his social provisions, was criticized in 1863 by the union in south Yorkshire for his refusal to allow his colliers to unionize,[2] a policy similar in its combination with community development to that pursued by the great anti-union companies of Clay Cross, Staveley and Butterley, in the East Midlands, and of Newton Chambers and Denaby Main in south Yorkshire.[3] The policies of these companies illustrate the 'subjugatory deference' which has been seen in another context as a characteristic of the communal basis of deference during the mid-nineteenth century.[4] In 1867 Staveley's chairman praised Charles Markham for his determined resistance to trade unionism among the men, and informed the shareholders, 'your directors will continue to contribute by every means in their power to the comfort of the workpeople, by giving the best wages to all industrious workmen by providing them, as far as practicable, with convenient cottages, gardens, etc., and by supporting schools for education of children and other facilities for their intellectual and moral instruction.' Having spent £1,000 in the previous year on 'religious and educational purposes for the improvement and wellbeing of employees' children' the directors agreed to contribute a further £2,000, and thereafter to supplement workmen's subscriptions towards the provision of similar social expenditure by adding 25 per cent.[5] A similar policy, which combined

[1] Bulman 1920, 278.
[2] *Transactions and Proceedings of the National Conference of Miners* 1863, 51.
[3] J. E. Williams 1962. The anti-union record of Newton Chambers is contained in the accounts of labour disputes reported in the *Colliery Guardian*.
[4] Joyce 1980, 95.
[5] BSCEMRRC Stanton and Staveley 2034/20/1, AGM 1866, 1867.

expenditure on welfare and proscribed trade unions, was adopted by
Richard Pope, managing director of Denaby Main at the new Denaby
Colliery when it opened in 1867. Nevertheless, strikes and lockouts
punctuated the company's history.[1] One of Pope's contemporaries,
Charles Binns, manager of Clay Cross, acknowledged the conditional
nature of his company's paternalism: in 1872 he informed a deputation
of miners intending to form a union that if they proceeded he would
withdraw all the company's assistance to schools, chapels, and other
social institutions.[2] This notion of a mutual contract—welfare in return
for union-free labour relations—was also shared by J. T. Woodhouse,
mining engineer and agent to the Marquis of Hasting's collieries; the formation of a union, he argued, 'breaks entirely the old lines of good faith
as between master and men, and they depend upon this union for coun-
sel and advice, and assistance, and they lose all kindly feeling, and all the
old lines are completely destroyed as between master and men, and it
then comes down to a hard line, and from that moment all good feeling
is lost. The master is soured, loses his temper, and will do nothing for his
men.'[3]

By its nature, evidence that workers opposed community policies is
difficult to find, though in the 1850s miners at Wharncliffe Silkstone
resisted, and successfully defeated, attempts at social intervention.[4] On
the other hand, initiatives for social provision sometimes originated in
workers' requests. Miners at Shotts Iron Company in 1835 had petitioned their employers for an infants' school, 'to improve the moral
habits and industry of their workmen', for which the men had already
saved a sizeable sum, which the company agreed to increase threefold.[5]
At other collieries, however, colliery schools were frequently poorly
attended; those, for example, provided by Frances Ann, Marchioness of
Londonderry, who in 1867 announced a future policy for her Durham
pits of employing only boys possessing a certified ability to read and
write.[6] Miners' initiative lay behind the building by Hamstead Colliery
Company in 1884 of a reading room and library, where directors agreed
to provide the capital expenditure to meet the miners' offer of rental
payments. The directors' minutes noted that the pub was the only place
available in which the men could either read, discuss, or hold meetings,

[1] J. Macfarlane 'Denaby Main: A Yorkshire Mining Village', B.S.S.L.H. 25, 1972, 109–113.

[2] Chapman 1981, 160.

[3] RC Trade Unions 1867–8, XXXIX, QQ 11978.

[4] Pat Spaven 'Main Gates of Protest', in Royden Harrison (ed.), Independent Collier (London,
1978), 206.   [5] McEwan thesis, 168.

[6] DuRO Londonderry D/LO/B455.

and agreed readily to a venture 'to benefit them morally and intellectually and for their mutual improvement'.[1] Such a policy was entirely congruent with that advocated by leading mining engineers H. F. Bulman and R. A. S. Redmayne in their 1896 textbook on mining, in which they advised on the relationship between managers and miners: 'An unfortunate task of the viewer is to carry through unpopular decisions. It is well, therefore, that he should cultivate relationships with them. This he may do by taking a personal interest in their reading rooms and institutes, their athletic clubs, their musical band, or in some of the various institutions which usually exist in colliery villages'.[2]

Historians have interpreted the significance of what might be termed constructive paternalism in various ways. Some have seen it as an attempt to secure 'social control' or 'ideological hegemony': to secure a more compliant workforce by imposing, by more or less subtle methods, the ethics of middle-class morality, sobriety, and regular habits upon the labouring population. L. J. Williams, though, has questioned whether the involvement of coalowners in community affairs was intended to achieve social control. He argues that in those rural company towns and villages where a colliery dominated employment the power structure was so unambiguous that the financial assistance provided by coalowners to community activities may be interpreted as an attempt to *disguise* the degree of control in their possession.[3] Joyce's research on work and locality suggests that while economic or financial provision was sometimes important in the case of large employers, the 'constraints of laissez faire ideology on paternalist practice meant that cultural . . . provision always bulked largest'.[4] Thus, sick clubs, insurance and provident funds, and educational provision of various kinds were pump primed by the coalowners who introduced them—but workers' contributions were compulsory, at least during the first half of our period. Such pit clubs were condemned by trade unions; 'if the miner claims the benefit of the fund created out of his own wages, the payment to him is called a "gift" by the masters'.[5] Joyce stresses

the wholesale penetration of everyday manner and feelings, the necessity of comprehending the complex social effect of the working-class people made for

---

[1] StaRO Hamstead, D 896/11 Directors' Minutes 30 Sept. 1884.

[2] Bulman and Redmayne 1896, 65.

[3] L. J. Williams 1980, 108.   [4] Joyce 1980, 152–3.

[5] *Transactions and Proceedings of the National Conference of Miners* 1865, 49. For an example of the unequal benefits obtainable from a company sick benefit fund see the evidence of Charles Markham, *RC Trade Unions* 1867, XXXIX, QQ 11519–97.

themselves: the *milieu* of ordinary life were impregnated with the authority and influence of an elite, so that the habit of neighbourhood community, expressed in the terminology of sociology as 'communal sociability' was the source of subordination as well as class selfhood.[1]

Thus, whether as a result of conscious efforts to mould attitudes and behaviouir or not (and Bulman and Redmayne certainly felt that constructive paternalism was managerially effective), Joyce sees as the principal source of social 'cohesion' (to use Thomas Burt's term) the institutions so frequently provided by employers, whose dominating influence over people's lives, both at work and elsewhere, was almost inevitable; the mere fact of the employer's permeation of a locality reinforced the feelings of 'community', in which deference was always a potential, though conditional, feature.

Two institutions have been regarded as critical, both by those who favour the interpretation of paternalism as a means towards 'social control', and by those who stress communal sociability and deference. Colls has argued that schools were intended to promote harmonious relations through indoctrination by careful supervision of the curriculum by coalowners and managers; whereas Duffy has stressed the philanthropic approach designed to elicit gratitude and loyalty from workers. Joyce's research on Lancashire, however, stressed the role of elementary school provision in particular, which schooled the worker from his or her earliest days into the 'reputation of a paternal elite and very often into an environment dominated by a particular employer ...'.[2] This was precisely the process which in 1843 mining trade unionists in the North-east had hoped to avoid, by establishing schools as well as providing relief during periods of sickness, and death benefits. At that time Thomas Hepburn, the miners' leader, urged them to seek greater control over the schools.[3] In many cases colliery schools were managed jointly by owners and miners' representatives, the latter sometimes dominating a colliery's Educational Society Committee, to which compulsory contributions were made by all miners.[4] At Gartsherrie, however, the Bairds allowed little scope for colliers to influence the curriculum, which was determined by the master and included such texts as *Ready Work for Willing Hands, Truth Always Best*, and *Self-taught Men*, revealing a preoccupation with a morality stressing industry and self-help.[5] The growth of colliery schools, either built entirely or partly

[1] Joyce 1980, 116.   [2] Joyce 1980, 172.
[3] CG 31 May 1862, 425.   [4] Pallister 1968, 32–8.
[5] Campbell 1979; G. M. Wilson thesis.

financed by coalowners, is best documented for the North-east where company housing was most extensive and the opportunities for community policy greatest.

Historians are faced with the problem, however, that few coalowners have left their attitudes towards education on record. The Revd W. Hick, from County Durham, told the Newcastle Commission in 1858 that in his view pit-owners did not regard the educated pitman more highly than he who lacked education, while another contemporary drew a contrast between the socially stable communities of lead miners of the Wear and Tees Valley (where educational provision had been made available by the mining companies) and coalmining communites in the same district where the miners were described as 'a recent heterogeneous, fluctuating and rapidly increasing population, earning high wages, which they know no way of spending but in the gratification of animal appetites'.[1]

Though historians disagree over the precise effect upon coalowners' policy towards colliery schooling of the miners' strike of 1844, there is some agreement that, while philanthropic inclinations may have influenced some coalowners in making school provision in the 1830s and 1840s, two other considerations were of major importance: the need to secure educated responses from labour, which it was anticipated would lead to improved relations and reduce, if not remove altogether, the threat of future strike action, and the achievement of a greater labour discipline necessary in pits which were becoming deeper and more dangerous to mine.[2] Unambiguous statements of intention were made by Robert Brown, agent for the Duke of Hamilton's Lanarkshire estates, who argued that more education, especially of females, would help to reform the mining population, diminish their inclination to strike or restrict output, and increase their willingness to work hard.[3] With the exception of Lord Londonderry, by 1842 all of the leading coalowners in the North-east had provided educational facilities for their workers.[4]

The 1840s were also years of school building in South Wales, where, as part of a comprehensive set of community provision which included cottages, churches, reading room, library, savings and insurance schemes and a medical fund (to which workers were required to

---

[1] Quoted in Pallister 1968, 33.

[2] Colls 1976, 156; Heeson, 'Entrepreneurial Paternalism: The Third Lord Londonderry (1775–1854) and the Coal Trade', *DUJ*, NS, XXXV (1974), 165; Brendan Duffy, 'Coal, Class and Education in the North-east', *Past and Present* 90 (1981), 146–7, 150–1.

[3] G. M. Wilson thesis, 103.

[4] Brendan Duffy, 'Coal, Class and Education in the North-east', *Past and Present* 90 (1981), 148.

contribute), Dowlais developed perhaps the most comprehensive schooling system, for infants, adolescents and adults.[1] G. T. Clark regarded education as a means of disciplining the minds of his workers, of inculcating a capacity for 'painstaking industry combined with good moral conduct'. This policy was also seen as training a supply of literate, dutiful, and well-behaved clerks and agents: '. . . moral training . . . teaches the workforce to deny himself present pleasure in order that he may provide for the evil day'[2] when no work would be available; thus the philosophy offered was one of acceptance as well as that of self-help, and Clark appointed only those certificated teachers whose philosophical approach he approved of, and preferably, when possible, those hitherto educated in the company's schools. The principle whereby priority in employment favoured men schooled at Dowlais meant that in 1881 W. T. Clark could claim that 'almost all the workforce had been through his schools, and certainly all the clerks'. Such an employment policy, coupled with compulsory deductions from workers' wages to support the school, amounted to a strong incentive for children to be enrolled, though very high enrolment concealed high absenteeism and early withdrawal.[3]

In districts not dominated by a single company the situation was very different, although even in company schools the amount of time spent in these institutions was very small. The limited amount of education available to children in the mining villages may be deduced from the requirements introduced in the 1860 Mines Inspection Act, which obliged children to attend night school twice weekly for a total of six hours. Evasion of the law, however, was simplified by the clause which waived these requirements for child mineworkers between the ages of ten and twelve years if they could present a certificate to indicate a basic reading and writing ability. The difficulties of enforcement were compounded by the unreasonable expectations of children—and parents— implied by the legislation. Even under the 1872 Coal Mines Regulation Act children aged between twelve and sixteen were permitted to work a fifty-four hour week, and before that time often worked far more.[4] All of this suggests that schooling cannot have been a major influence on the lives of most miners and their children, whatever may have been the coalmasters' motives in making such provision.

Whether the result of devious or altruistic motives, many owners of

[1] Smith thesis, 27.
[2] Ibid., 16, 71–6.   [3] Ibid., 77–81.
[4] *Children's Employment Commission* 1842, XV, 268; *RC Labourer* 1894, XXV, 318.

large collieries regarded the building of churches and chapels, or at least providing financial support, as forming part of their responsibility to local mining populations. However, coalowners' policies in this respect are even less researched than those relating to education. Chapman's examination of the policies of Derbyshire colliery owners suggests that they were more concerned to meet workers' denominational preferences than to promote a particular dogma. Richard Barrow, for example, was an Anglican, but presided at the first meeting of the Primitive Methodists for whom he had provided a meeting house. Two of Staveley's managers, who were Wesleyans, told Charles Markham, Barrow's successor, that 'the better class of workman' was averse to the Church of England and persuaded the directors to build a Wesleyan Chapel, but financial support was also extended to other denominations—and the Roman Catholic Church—according to workmen's preferences.[1] At Dowlais, too, W. T. Clark acquiesced in the wishes of his workers to offer non-sectarian education.[2] Moore's study of mining communities in Durham concluded that religion, particularly Methodism, was a powerful influence in some colliery villages,[3] though no one has ever explained convincingly why it took root in one village but not in another. Wherever Methodism flourished, however, its influence seems to have been to reinforce the sense of community. The language used by Methodists was highly suggestive of their common orientation; prayers were directed towards the community's spiritual and moral needs.

An examination of social relations in the North-east led Moore to conclude that industrial harmony was promoted by the consonance of religious affiliation of employers and workers, specifically the membership of nonconformist chapels and the espousing of principles for which they stood. The case he makes for the North-east is persuasive, though important exceptions can be made.[4] The community orientation of Methodism, however, particularly in its strongholds of the North-east and South Wales, but also in parts of Lancashire, Yorkshire, and the East and West Midlands, proved to exercise a powerful social as well as religious influence. To the extent that in many instances employers were identified with the church or chapel they patronized, the links between work-place and place of worship were strengthened, the loyalties and sense of obligation merged, and the hierarchical authority underpinned.

---

[1] Chapman 1981, 155. [2] Smith thesis, 86.
[3] Moore 1974, 126–30; 226–7. [4] Ibid.; Chapman 1981, 162.

Describing the west of Scotland, however, G. M. Wilson argues that religion was not a powerful influence on the social life of the mining community, which depended far more upon the pub or friendly society than either church or school.[1] Certainly G. T. Clark seems to have seen these institutions as competitors. When he promoted his campaign against the beer houses and spirit shops operating in Dowlais in the 1850s he blamed them for '. . . doing those harm that the schools and chapels are doing good'.[2] Despite his opposition to licences for public houses in the district, however, magistrates felt unable to comply with his wishes. Likewise, independent friendly societies competed with the Dowlais company schemes for sick funds and savings, which Clark regarded as a means of enabling workers to become financially independent. For this reason he had no objection to his own employees belonging to self-help schemes outside the company; in 1870 fewer than 5 per cent of the workers held accounts in the company's savings bank scheme, which had been in existence since 1852.[3]

What actual effects employers' welfare policies had upon labour relations in general is difficult to judge. There are instances where relations were harmonious where such provisions were made, notably at Fitzwilliam's collieries, at the Worsley Mines of Lord Francis Egerton, and at the Ashington and Butterley Coal companies. In the mid-nineteenth century harmonious labour relations may well have been related to the Butterley Company's substantial expenditure on schools and churches—though the practice of offering tied houses to miners[4] and their families probably assisted God's Work. In evidence to the Commissioners, one employee claimed that the company's educational facilities offered one means of social advancement, and the little butty system introduced round about 1850 was another means of securing promotion, removing frustration among the ambitious.[5] During the later nineteenth century the Ashington Coal Company, where rent-free housing in this remote company town was a privilege and where the Ashington police constable was virtually an employee, labour relations were rarely disturbed by even the threat of strikes, until 1897 when a four-day strike was called over the employment of non-union labour.[6]

Adopting similar welfare strategies from the 1840s, though without the addition of rent-free housing, the firm of Henry Briggs experienced

[1] G. M. Wilson thesis, 105–9.
[2] Smith thesis, 25.   [3] Ibid., 29–31.
[4] Mather 1970, 331–2; Mee 1975, 142; *Report on Mining Districts* 1853, XL, 782–97.
[5] *Report of Mining Districts* 1851, XXIII, 472.
[6] NuRO Ashington ZMD 54/3–5.

appalling labour relations in the 1850s and 1860s, as did Clay Cross and Staveley in the 1860s, and Denaby Main from shortly after the new colliery was opened at Denaby in 1867.[1] G. M. Wilson concluded that throughout much of the west of Scotland 'Although schools and churches were being built in increasing numbers, often by employers, they seem to have had little effect on industrial relations in spite of the fact that some employers saw them as a means of making their work force more peaceful and more submissive'.[2] Such objectives, especially when they were sought in relation to the larger collieries which were usually those able or willing to invest in constructive philanthrophy, were likely to require for their successs the simultaneous pursuit of firm policies towards labour relations in the narrower sense. Those of William Baird in the west of Scotland exemplify this policy of constructive philanthrophy and labour repression, differing only in scale and degree from many other sizeable colliery enterprises.

The Bairds' policies at Gartsherrie, which involved the provision of workers' institutes, including private baths, swimming baths, reading and sports rooms, a Total Abstinence Society set up to arrange lectures and concerts, and from 1852 a colliery band, schools, and churches, together represented a degree of comprehensive social intervention which appears to have achieved the subordination of a collier community to an extent undocumented elsewhere. Between 1830 and the 1860s, according to Campbell, the 'irregular and dissolute characters' who had flooded into the Coatbridge district were 'hammered into a docile and disciplined work-force ... transforming a turbulent locality into a peaceful industrial town'.[3] In 1851 a Commissioner declared that in his opinion the Bairds had been rewarded for their paternalistic philanthropy by 'a general steadiness and good conduct of their people at Gartsherrie who rarely gave them any trouble by joining strikes or in any subordination'.[4] The Bairds, of course, also banned trade unions as part of their social contract, the quid pro quo for amenity provision, and it may be that employers' welfare policies at the anti-union companies of the East Midlands—and of others—in this way helped to retard trade-union development.

A comparable battery of institutional and environmental control and influence established at Dowlais appears to have been less effective in subduing the work-force than the suppression of labour organization

---

[1] See below 655, 661–4.
[2] G. M. Wilson thesis, 105–9.
[3] Campbell 1979, 22.
[4] Quoted ibid., 225.

achieved by occasional trials of strength. Thus, despite at least two generations of workers exposed to the company's sustained and compulsory moral education, the stoppage at the company's collieries in 1875, which lasted nearly four months, caused G. T. Clark to reflect upon recent deteroriation in the work habits of his colliers: 'Of late years the great mass of men employed in the ironworks and collieries have been content to do as little work as possible and . . . often done in a slovenly manner. All this, if curable at all, can only be cured by years of financial distress, and by such personal privation, out of which and out of which alone, a more healthy state of things can be expected to rise.'[1] In his capacity as chairman of the Board of Guardians he was responsible for instituting a policy denying out-relief to strikers (though not to the widows and elderly whose support from their children on strike was affected) on the grounds that the thrifty could manage without parish assistance.[2] Even after three months in dispute Clark remarked: 'They have ample wages . . . they are pretty well-to-do and can hold out, I dare say for 3 months'.[3] The policy towards the able-bodied strikers he described approvingly as 'severe as possible'. Those locked out were offered relief conditional upon a labour test, but even this was withdrawn in the third month, a tactic to force the miners back to work at one of the reopened Dowlais collieries; by the fourth month not one able-bodied collier or underground haulier was receiving relief in any form.[4]

Difficulties of interpretation arise when assessing the importance of social control, even when policies aimed at achieving it were unaccompanied by otherwise reactionary labour policies. The existence of an apparatus aimed at socialization, for whatever motive, is not itself a proof of its effective functioning. Thus, in the west of Scotland, 'Although schools and churches were being built in increasing numbers often by employers, they seem to have had little effect on industrial relations in spite of the fact that some employers saw them as means of making their workforce more peaceful and more submissive.'[5] Not only is there evidence that facilities provided by employers were either managed by the workers or neglected or rejected by them, there is also uncertainty concerning the extent and frequency of single-employer control within a region, area, district, or locality. Benson has suggested that dominance by a single employer was less typical than many his-

---

[1] Smith thesis, 176.   [2] Ibid., 175.
[3] Ibid., 176.   [4] Ibid., 177-9.
[5] G. M. Wilson thesis, 105-6.

torians have assumed; that wherever they lived almost all miners had access to one or more pits run by a number of different coalowners, and that this became more common in the second half of the nineteenth century as the urban coalfields, outside the already heavily populated districts of west Scotland, west Yorkshire, Lancashire, and south Staffordshire, developed.[1] Nor were the number of villages and towns in which mining was the only, or even the predominant, form of employment as large as some have suggested. The histories of Bairds and Dowlais probably illustrate conditions where the potential for effective labour control was greater than elsewhere. Even in the isolated colliery village dominated by a single employer it seems probable that the extent of his influence was at all times subject to challenge.[2] Macfarlane has argued that single-employer domination might result in powerful influence, but was likely to have been divisive and to lead to a clear demarcation between 'company men' and 'union men'; such a polarization led to conflict, at Denaby Main and at Staveley, rather than to control.[3] Except for a few very large companies operating in newly developing districts in rural areas, constructive philanthropy diminished in importance as managerial effort concentrated upon attempts to maximize labour effort through more systematic job control, improved methods of remuneration, and, increasingly from the 1880s, combined action through coalowner's associations to limit the growing strength of trade unions.

Appendix 3.1. Estimates of coal mining employment

Before the 1872 Coal Mines Regulation Act no attempt was made to collect detailed national employment statistics, either by the Mines Inspectors or by Robert Hunt. Some figures and contemporary estimates for employment do exist, however, and may be used to check the accuracy of the early population census figures, which beginning in 1841 provide details of the number returned as coalminers.[4]

Comparison of the census figures with the Inspectors' returns under

---

[1] Benson 1981, 81–5; Hair thesis, 20–1.
[2] Ibid.   [3] Macfarlane 1972, 100.
[4] For many regions the *Children's Employment Commission* provides figures, which have been supplemented as follows. The North-east: NuRO, Coalowners' Survey 1828, *SC Lords Committee* 1830, VIII, 54, ev. of Puddle; *Midland Mining Commission* cvii–cviii, ev. of Leifchild; *Report on Mining Districts* 1847, XVI, 401; 1844 list published in *Newcastle Journal* (quoted in *SC Accidents* 1854, IX, 93–4, IX, 93–4). For Lancashire and Cheshire: J. Dickinson, 'Statistics of the Collieries of Lancashire, Cheshire and North Wales', *Lit. Phil. Soc. Manchester*, XII (1853–4), 71–107.

the 1872 Act, and subsequent acts, shows that the former are consistently lower than the numbers given by the Inspectors—by about 8 per cent in 1881 and by 5 per cent in 1901. In the early years, too, a sizeable category of 'unspecified miners' were probably almost all colliery workers, and consequently the actual total was almost certainly substantially greater than the figure returned in 1841. Similar remarks apply to the 1851 and 1861 censuses, though the margin of error is likely to have been less. In estimating the figures for the early census years to 1871 the following assumptions have been made: first, that miners over the age of sixty-five did not necessarily retire[1] but continued to work at less onerous jobs on the surface, though the numbers were insignificant; second, that the 'unspecified miners' category in the census should be divided according to the ratio of recorded coalminers to recorded metal and other miners in each county, though no such problem arises in 1851 and after 1871; and third, that owners, agents, etc. are excluded.

In 1841 the figure for female miners refers to coal only and assumes that unspecified females, most of whom were in non-coalmining counties, were not coal miners in other counties either. In 1861 no female coalminers were recorded, which may mean that we have underestimated their number, perhaps concealed within the female 'labourers' category. From 1864 the Inspectors made estimates of employment in their areas by extrapolating from the 1861 census on the basis of their knowledge of developments in the district, and these figures were published as a preface to the annual *Reports* 1864–72. Since the census understated the position, the estimates were too low, but there can be little doubt that the pattern of steady growth which they show, followed by rapid acceleration after 1870, is broadly accurate. The employment position between 1871 and 1876 is very unclear largely as a result of the coincidence of a considerable boom in the coal trade with the introduction of compulsory returns of under-and-above ground employment under the 1872 Act. In 1872 Joseph Dickinson, Inspector for North-east Lancashire, compiled a retrospective table of employment from 1851,[2] but as it turns out to be virtually a straight-line interpolation between census figures it is of dubious value. Inspectors' regional estimates in the late 1860s include unexplained jumps of considerable magnitude from one year to the next and presumably indicate drastic upward revision of previous estimates.

---

[1] *RC Trade Unions* 1867–8, XXXIX, 178.

[2] A return showing the number of male coalminers employed in and about the coalmines of Great Britain, annually 1864–1872.

Registration under the 1872 Act improved reliability enormously.[1] A very large increase in numbers occurred in almost every district between 1872 and 1873 (though by about 25 per cent which is the magnitude unless non-coalminers are eliminated). There are, however, identifiable inaccuracies; for example, the north Staffordshire district figures for 1864–72 must also have included ironstone miners, and require deflating—by perhaps 8,000 in 1872 and by 3,000 before; whereas the Scottish figures appear to have excluded iron and shale miners. After allowing for these imperfections and adjusting accordingly (using the output figures as a check), the Inspectors' estimates do seem to provide a reliable basis. They should not, however, be used as published, since until 1893 they refer to *all* mines under the Act, which means that the figures include employment in stratified ironstone, shale, and fireclay mines. For most counties this is not a serious problem as the output of minerals other than coal was trifling, only a per cent or so; in some cases, however, the amounts involved were more considerable. From 1894 onwards the figures are of coal mines only, though since many of these also produced iron and clay over-counting persisted.

The output of minerals other than from collieries declined both relatively and absolutely over time; therefore, the *degree* of over-counting (and consequently the size of the adjustments necessary to obtain the 'true' total) was reduced. In the years immediately after 1873, however, non-coal miners made up a sizeable proportion of those recorded under the Regulation Act. Taking 1875, the first year in which the Act can be said to have been operating smoothly, roughly 8.2 million tons of other minerals were recorded (not counting the Cleveland and Lincoln ironstone districts which produced no coal). Coal production at that date was 133.3 million tons, which suggests that iron, fireclay, and shale represented 5.8 per cent of the total output. In 1893 the figure had fallen to below 4 per cent and was barely 1 per cent in 1913. The production of these minerals involved employment of some magnitude, consequently the numbers so employed need to be deducted from the totals published under the 1872 Act if we are to reach an accurate figure for coalmining employment. This is possible for some areas, notably Scotland, Cleveland, and Lincolnshire, where the figures have been subtracted; for other areas the procedure has been to divide the remaining employment figures proportionately to regional tonnages.

Such an exercise requires the assumption that productivity in

[1] Inspectors' Report 1872, LIV, 41.

ironstone, fireclay, and shale workings was the same as in coalmines. At first sight this might appear to be a very dubious proposition; and, indeed, for the individual minerals there is no such identity. Productivity in ironstone workings was generally lower than in collieries, as the seams were thin and the material hard, while output per man was slightly above average in easily-won clay and shale seams. Overall, however, these influences may be assumed to balance; thus, while the county figures may err very slightly (too low where clay but no iron was mined and too high where the reverse applied) the numbers involved are not likely to be large.

For the early part of the period up to about 1890, when the contribution of other minerals to the total was largest, the deductions made are likely, if anything, to be too low, since the Scottish shale and fireclay miners can be eliminated. Apart from Cleveland the main other concentration of non-coal miners was north Staffordshire. Fireclay in England and Wales was never more than 2 per cent of any county's total output and generally much less.

After 1890, when the Scottish figures are no longer given separately, and especially after 1894, when mines not producing coal are eliminated from the *Mineral Statistics* Tables, the position is slightly different, as the output of iron ore from coal mines in 1900, for instance, had fallen to 1,722, 391 tons out of a total non-coal yield of 4,554,620 tons (39 per cent). By then, however, other minerals represented only 2 per cent of total production from coal mines, therefore the upward bias to our adjustment will be very slight—probably fewer than a thousand out of 750,000, though it is not possible to obtain a reliable control for this.

Accepting that the figures obtained by this exercise are subject to a small margin of error, which is likely to make the final adjusted totals slightly too high up to about 1890 and slightly too low after that date (and the differences from the totals under the Regulation Act understated in the early period, overstated after 1890), the results reveal differences between the 'true' total number of coal miners and the Regulation Act totals of about 40,000 in the mid-1870s, 30,000 by 1885, and 25,000 by 1894; thereafter the figure rose to 30,000 by 1910. In percentage terms these represent reductions of 8 per cent in 1875, 6 per cent in 1885, 3.5 per cent in 1895, and 2.9 per cent in 1910. The estimates of annual employment between 1830 and 1913 are presented in Table 3.11.

Appendix 3.2. Juvenile and adult recruitment estimates

Notes to Table 3.6

Line 1   Mean of beginning and end years for 1831–80. Mean of annual data for 1881–1910.

Line 2   Census figures for the number of male workers in industry under twenty years of age (male and female for 1831–40) in following census year.

Line 3   Growth in male labour force over decade.

Line 4   Occupational death rate based on Registrar's General's Decennial Supplements; for 1830–60: Hair thesis, Table 5, and Cairncross 82.

Line 5   Based on line 4 and line 1.

Line 6   There are no figures on the number of miners permanently incapacitated by injury. The best treatment of non-fatal accidents appears to be that by Benson,[1] who argued that there is sufficient evidence to indicate that the ratio of non-fatal accidents to fatal ones claiming less than five lives remained constant at roughly 100:1. The number of non-fatal accidents in different decades was estimated by taking the number of deaths from all accidents, save explosions, and multiplying them by 100. How many of these were permanently incapacitating, however, is still a matter for conjecture. Although injuries may have occurred to underground workers which prevented them ever returning to face or roadways, many did not leave the industry permanently but were found surface jobs. At a guess, not more than one in fifty non-fatal accidents led to retirement, and even this is likely to be an upper estimate. The estimates used in this line were derived as shown in Table 3.12.

Line 7   The sum of lines 3, 5, and 6.

Line 8   These are rough estimates of the average age of juvenile entry to the industry in different decades. Assuming the age structure of the juvenile population to be uniform, the number of juveniles in the industry under 15 as a proportion of those aged 15–19 expresses the proportion of a five-year period (in each decade) occupied by the under-15 age group, and this figure deducted from 15 represents the average age at which

[1] Benson 1980, 39–44.

Table 3.11. *Estimates of annual coalmining employment: revised Inspectors' returns (eliminating non-coal miners) 1871–1913*

	Scotland	North-east	Cumber-land	Lancs./Ches.	North Wales	York-shire	East Midlands	West Midlands	South Wales	South-west	GB Total	UK Total
1871	47.7	74.3	5.0	54.5	9.0	44.0	29.5	54.0	57.0	11.5	386.5	388.5
1872	51.3	80.1	4.5	57.5	9.5	51.0	37.3	55.0	62.0	11.5	419.7	421.7
1873	58.5	93.1	4.8	63.7	12.6	56.1	42.3	54.6	65.0	12.5	463.2	465.2
1874	60.2	96.5	5.5	65.2	13.6	59.9	46.8	56.3	70.5	13.0	487.5	489.2
1875	56.4	99.9	6.3	66.9	13.3	60.6	47.3	56.1	69.6	12.7	488.1	490.6
1876	54.5	98.7	5.8	62.7	11.6	59.4	47.8	52.5	65.2	12.1	469.8	471.1
1877	52.1	96.8	5.6	60.6	10.5	59.0	46.3	47.1	63.8	11.4	452.7	453.9
1878	51.9	91.1	5.6	60.9	9.4	58.3	44.8	43.9	62.5	11.1	439.5	440.7
1879	52.8	88.4	5.7	62.1	9.8	58.7	46.4	43.0	65.3	11.5	443.7	444.8
1880	53.1	93.1	5.7	62.3	9.9	59.1	45.0	41.6	67.9	11.0	448.7	449.7
1881	53.8	94.5	6.0	63.2	9.9	59.2	45.5	43.4	71.6	11.5	458.6	459.6
1882	53.2	97.0	5.9	64.2	9.9	60.1	45.7	46.2	73.6	11.3	467.1	468.1
1883	54.3	98.7	6.2	66.0	10.0	61.8	47.6	44.2	79.2	11.5	479.5	480.5
1884	55.4	100.8	6.3	66.0	10.0	62.6	48.7	42.6	82.7	11.8	486.9	487.8
1885	56.5	100.5	6.6	65.9	9.1	62.3	50.5	41.0	84.3	12.0	488.7	489.6
1886	58.8	99.5	6.6	66.7	9.1	64.6	50.6	41.3	84.2	11.9	493.2	494.1
1887	61.1	100.4	6.7	67.3	9.6	65.7	51.1	39.5	85.9	12.0	499.3	500.1
1888	59.1	102.6	6.4	67.8	10.0	65.9	52.8	41.7	90.4	11.9	508.4	509.2
1889	62.1	107.4	6.3	70.2	10.6	68.7	55.8	44.7	98.1	12.1	535.9	536.6
1890	71.0	115.0	6.9	76.3	11.2	75.4	61.8	49.8	108.7	13.2	589.2	590.0

1891	75.6	121.5	7.6	80.5	12.5	80.5	65.1	49.6	115.6	13.2	621.6	622.4
1892	80.1	122.5	7.4	83.5	12.4	85.1	68.3	50.1	116.6	12.8	638.4	639.2
1893	80.2	129.9	7.7	86.0	12.2	86.7	70.8	52.6	116.9	12.4	655.4	656.2
1894	85.4	134.7	8.1	87.6	12.4	89.5	72.8	53.8	123.6	12.1	680.0	680.9
1895	85.0	134.0	7.6	86.7	12.0	87.2	72.1	52.0	125.1	12.3	674.0	675.0
1896	79.2	135.6	7.6	83.1	11.2	87.8	71.4	52.5	124.3	13.0	665.8	666.8
1897	80.1	136.1	7.6	83.6	11.3	87.9	71.9	51.7	125.9	11.6	667.6	668.6
1898	83.7	138.1	7.7	82.8	11.2	89.4	73.3	52.7	128.0	12.6	679.3	680.3
1899	87.3	143.3	7.7	82.8	11.7	93.1	75.5	55.2	132.0	12.2	700.7	701.7
1900	95.1	150.3	8.3	87.1	12.3	99.0	80.5	58.6	146.9	13.0	751.2	752.2
1901	99.0	152.8	8.7	91.9	13.0	103.4	84.8	62.0	149.8	13.2	778.7	779.6
1902	100.0	156.6	8.8	92.5	13.0	105.8	87.7	64.6	153.9	13.4	796.3	797.1
1903	102.7	161.0	9.1	94.4	12.9	107.8	89.9	64.6	158.4	13.0	813.8	814.6
1904	103.8	163.2	8.8	93.1	12.6	110.1	90.3	61.8	162.3	12.9	818.8	819.6
1905	104.9	168.1	8.8	93.1	12.4	110.8	90.7	62.5	164.9	13.1	829.2	829.9
1906	106.3	175.1	8.9	91.7	12.7	113.8	93.1	63.6	173.8	13.3	852.2	852.9
1907	115.4	184.3	9.2	94.7	13.7	122.3	99.5	67.3	189.4	14.1	909.9	910.7
1908	123.1	192.0	9.3	99.6	14.9	133.5	101.3	68.8	200.9	14.4	957.7	958.5
1909	124.4	198.3	9.7	102.9	14.7	139.3	103.7	71.2	204.1	14.9	983.1	983.9
1910	128.7	210.4	10.2	103.8	15.0	145.4	105.0	72.7	212.3	14.8	1,018.2	1,018.9
1911	128.9	214.7	10.3	103.2	15.2	146.3	107.0	74.4	220.3	15.3	1,035.5	1,036.3
1912	133.6	216.8	10.5	104.9	15.5	151.2	107.9	77.5	224.7	15.0	1,057.8	1,058.6
1913	137.9	224.5	10.8	107.1	15.8	159.6	110.9	80.8	232.4	15.4	1,095.2	1,096.0

Sources: See Appendix 3.1.

Table 3.12. *Fatalities and injuries caused by accidents, 1831-1910*

	Number of fatal accidents, excluding deaths from explosions	Estimated non-fatal accidents	Estimated number permanently incapacitated
1831–40[a]	3,546	354,600	7,092
1841–50[a]	5,197	519,700	10,394
1851–60[a]	6,999	699,900	13,998
1861–70	7,422	742,200	14,844
1871–80	9,514	951,400	19,028
1881–90	8,725	872,500	17,450
1891–1900	9,017	901,700	18,034
1901–10	10,977	1,097,700	21,954

[a] Based on Hair's guesstimate of a fatal accident rate of 5:1000 and counting explosions at 2:1000.[1]

juveniles must have commenced work in order to have occupied the under-15 category for this length of time. Thus, for example, in 1911 20 per cent of the under-20 category were under 15 and 80 per cent were aged 15–19 than under 15, juveniles must have occupied the under-15 category for an average period of 1.25 years (i.e. a quarter of five years). If juveniles occupied this category for 1.25 years, then the average age of entry must have been 13.75 years. A serious problem arises, however, with the figure for the 1830s, since it is evident that the 1841 Census considerably understated the number of children in the under-15 age group. The 1841 Census figure works out at a starting age of 11.23 years (the same as for 1851 and 1861), but Hair notes that the average starting age of juveniles interviewed by the 1842 Commissioners was under nine years.[2] Consequently, the 1841 figure has been revised here to take account of the fact that there were probably more children in the under-15 category than in the 15–19 age group in 1841. The proportion aged 15–19 has also been revised. The above method of estimating ages can be expressed arithmetically as shown in Table 3.13.

[1] Hair, 'Mortality from Violence in British Coal Mines 1800–50', *EHR* 2nd ser. XXI (1968), 560.
[2] Hair thesis, 164.

Table 3.13. *Age of juvenile entry to the industry*

Census year	Proportion of juveniles		under-15 as % of 15–19	Number of years occupied by under-15 (previous column × 5)	Average age of entry (previous column minus 15)
	under-15	15–19			
1841	$54\frac{1}{2}$	$45\frac{1}{2}$	119.78	5.99	9.01
1851	43	57	75.44	3.77	11.23
1861	43	57	75.44	3.77	11.23
1871	$37\frac{1}{2}$	$62\frac{1}{2}$	60.0	3.0	12.0
1881	26	74	35.14	1.76	13.24
1891	25	75	33.33	1.67	13.33
1901	24	76	31.58	1.58	13.42
1911	20	80	25.0	1.25	13.75

Line 9   The number of male juvenile recruits in line 2 has been adjusted here to take account of changes in the average age of entry to the industry. The figures in line 8 were subtracted from 20 to obtain the figure for the number of years during which juveniles counted in the subsequent census as under 20 could have entered the industry. Thus, for example, in 1851 when the average age of entry was 11.23 years, the juveniles recorded in that year as under 20 could only have joined within a period of 8.77 years. The total number of juveniles in the census year was then divided by 8.77 to obtain an annual flow figure. This figure multiplied by ten represents the adjusted decadal juvenile entry.

Line 10   Line 7 minus line 9.

Line 11   Line 9 as a percentage of line 7.

Appendix 3.3. **Estimates of coalminers' working days and hours**

The first key assumption is that hewers constituted 40 per cent of the labour force throughout the entire period. The reason for having to make this assumption is the absence of an accurate breakdown of the time spent in hewing as distinct from other work, yet it is necessary to adopt a weighting in order to combine the estimated nominal hours of hewers with those of surface workers—which were longer. Only in the North-east was the mining process so subdivided as to reflect the actual division of labour time spent on hewing, and the data describing employment categories (in 1844 and 1905) show the proportion of hewers in the labour force at about 40 per cent. This figure has been proxy for hewing time. Though objections can be conceived, none the less such an assumption seems defensible. It is true that the age of collieries tended to increase the ratio of hewers to oncost workers, but there is no evidence of this having occurred in the industry as a whole between 1889 and 1905—when data are available (Table 3.4), a period when the potential disadvantages of ageing were likely to have grown as pits became much deeper and larger. As collieries aged, more haulage labour was needed, yet haulage was a major source of productivity increase to offset the lengthening haulage routes; while face productivity (possibly stemming from the use of explosives, and later mechanization) were influences tending to reduce the hewer/oncost ratio.

The second assumption is that the hours of surface workers were equivalent to those of unskilled underground men, which is justified merely on comparability of job types. Surface employment as a percentage of total employment was 18 per cent in 1889 and 16 per cent in 1905 (Table 3.4).

The figures for nominal hours of work resulting from these calculations were then multiplied by the estimated number of days worked—though for the period before 1873 evidence on actual days worked has been used. Thereafter estimates of the number of days worked are based on the number of days pits were open, and to achieve comparability with the pre-1873 data have been deflated by a series of rates of absenteeism among hewers in the North-east (Table 3.12). The average UK series for days worked, 1830–1913, is presented in Table 3.8, for which the sources were as follows: 1894–1913—*Labour Gazette*, 1895–6, and *Colliery Year Book and Coal Trades Directory* (1927), 707; 1873–1894—North-east Average based on *PP*, 1886, XXIII, Q 11, 688 and *SC Dearness and Scarcity*, 1873, X, QQ 3034 and 3401-6. Before 1873 the principal sources used were the 1842 *Children's Employment Commission*, the *Midland Mining Commission*, and *Reports on the State of the Population in Mining Districts*. Guided by impressions gained from these, the movement of coal prices and a detrended coal-output series provided the main basis for the resulting estimates. See also the detailed sources for Table 7.15.

The most valuable secondary source against which we may test the plausibility of our own national UK series (Table 3.8) is that devised for Scotland by Slaven.[1] Using various parliamentary and newspaper sources, he constructed a series representing the number of days

Table 3.14. *Hewers' absenteeism in Northumberland and Durham, 1873-1913*
(weighted average, percentages[a])

1873	9.9	1887	7.2	1901	12.0
1874	9.4	1888	7.5	1902	10.4
1875	9.6	1889	8.9	1903	9.9
1876	6.5	1890	11.5	1904	9.0
1877	5.7	1891	11.4	1905	8.7
1878	5.2	1892	8.7	1906	9.7
1879	5.8	1893	7.6	1907	10.7
1880	6.5	1894	7.8	1908	12.7
1881	8.2	1895	7.8	1909	11.5
1882	8.4	1896	7.4	1910	11.3
1883	8.3	1897	7.9	1911	11.9
1884	8.3	1898	9.0	1912	10.5
1885	7.3	1899	10.1	1913	13.6
1886	6.8	1900	12.0		

[a] Voluntary absenteeism only—excludes men off sick; the Northumberland data for 1873–78 have been deflated to allow for sickness.

Sources: 1871–78 BPP, 1886, XXIV; 1879–1913 *Sankey Commission*, appendix 23; NRO/NCB/ C/254 and 368.

worked by hewers in Scotland between 1856 and 1913. The movement of this series corresponds reasonably closely to that of the UK estimates, though on average the Scottish series reflects lower levels of employment. The most notable feature of Slaven's series is that despite the use of fairly round figures (the half-day is the discrete interval as with our UK series prior to 1873) the trend over time is quite smooth. Both the UK and Scottish series stand in strong contrast to the index of days worked devised by Barnsby for the industry in the Black Country.[2] Formulated in terms of the number of days worked each week on average through the year, Barnsby adopted the rather broad interval of the day (which in itself would tend to emphasize fluctuations) and the resulting series moves quite violently at times. Years of depression are particularly emphasized (for example, 1842 and 1843 when 1–2 days only were worked each week throughout the year, and the late 1870s when only 2–3 days were worked), as are the peaks (through the assumption that a six-day week operated throughout the century). The fundamental criticism of Barnsby's index is that it involves the translation of descriptive statements of the state of trade into an arithmetic index, a process which is

[1] Slaven thesis, Table 20.   [2] Barnsby 1971, 234–5.

Table 3.15. *Estimates of absenteeism in the coal industry, 1899-1913*

| | Percentage of all workers June–Dec. 1913 | Index (UK = 100) | | | |
| | | Hewers | | All under-ground | |
		1899	1905	1899	1905
United Kingdom[a]	10.7	100	100	100	100
Scotland	6.5	80	85	75	82
North-east[b]	10.6	77	63	72	56
Lancs. and Ches.	10.6	139	179	137	177
Yorkshire	13.8	123	126	128	130
East Midlands[c]	10.3	99	98	103	103
West Midlands[d]	12.2	150	123	143	125
South Wales	10.9	70	66	82	75

Notes: [a] Weighted average of the regions for 1913.
[b] Includes Cumberland throughout.
[c] Includes Warwickshire in 1899 and 1905.
[d] Excludes Warwickshire in 1899 and 1905.

Sources and methods: Data for 1899 and 1905 was taken from *Eight Hours Day Committee.* 1907 XIV, Appendix C, Table III. Data for 1913 was taken from *Sankey Commission*, III, Appendix 22, F, 35. The figures for 1913 are based upon the numbers absent as a percentage of all men in all the colliery books. The figures for 1899 and 1905, however, are based on the average level of attendance during the week deducted from the highest number of persons employed in any one day of that week. This approach underestimates absenteeism considerably, and because of this the actual figures for 1899 and 1905 have been rejected in favour of an index which expresses absenteeism in each region as a proportion of absenteeism nationally. Figures for all dates refer to involuntary (e.g. sickness and accidents) as well as voluntary absenteeism.

notoriously speculative and in its particular execution is misleading. It is conceivable, of course, that employment in the Black Country did fluctuate more acutely than elsewhere, and that Barnsby's index captures this. At the same time, some of his extremely low figures (for example, one day a week for the whole of 1842) are palpably incorrect and can be contradicted from parliamentary sources. Moreover, his higher estimates (for example, six days working a week in 1870–4) are also flatly contradicted by well-known evidence. His estimates of the effects of the Great Depression on employment are certainly exaggerated.

CHAPTER 4

Technology and Working Methods

i. Access technology: boring, sinking, drainage, ventilation, and lighting

The continuing primacy of manual labour and physical exertion in actually getting coal at the face was a corollary of the minimal employment of coal-cutting machinery before 1913. This raised the question in the minds of some contemporaries, since echoed by many historians, that this reflected badly upon British colliery owners and managers. Such a view warrants careful consideration, but needs to be put in the context of the advances in other forms of technical innovation critical to an industry in which it became necessary to dig deeper, to search more widely for new sources of coal supply, and to mine thinner seams. The virtually continuous growth of production from pits which increased in number until the 1880s, and in size, required improved techniques for removing coal, raising it to surface, and maintaining and operating miles of underground passages. In the nineteenth century the two major areas of technical advances lay in *access* technology, which enabled the coal to be reached and worked in increasingly safe conditions, and in *operational* methods, which involved the laying out of workings, getting the coal (though this was least affected), and transportation to the surface; the preparation of coal for sale was the final and increasingly important stage of production affected by technical improvement. The examination of developments in each of these various processes which follows proceeds in a broadly logical sequence, following operations from virgin land to coal sale.

In the early nineteenth century the work of prospecting new coalmines, boring to find the coal, laying out surface plant to sink, and supervising the actual sinking operations, was largely in the hands of the consulting viewers, most of whom were trained, and many based, in the North-east.[1] A landowner wishing to establish the presence of coal on his property. its depths and thickness, would engage one such specialist

---

[1] Flinn 1984, 69–80.

to view the property, make borings, and report on the feasibility of mining. The landowner's choice then lay between financing a colliery himself or, more likely, offering a lease at a royalty, hoping to attract risk capital on the strength of the viewer's report. Despite mistakes, which sometimes involved substantial expenditure without return, this system was adequate so long as mining operations were concentrated in exposed coalfields, or where concealed strata were newly exploited, such as those in the pioneering development of the South Wales valleys in the 1840s and 1850s.

As the depth to which it was necessary to sink to find new coal increased, and as it became vital to pursue the seams further under the concealing strata, the need for boring before sinking became more important; new techniques of exploration were devised or adapted to coalmining, and more local expertise developed. Thus, from the 1860s, when coal was being sought in Fife, and especially in the concealed part of the coalfield extending from Yorkshire across the East Midlands, a new class of specialized surveying and boring contractors began to emerge. By 1913 several such firms were in operation, obtaining leases or options from landowners and boring and proving the coal before attempting to persuade a colliery company to take over the actual winning of the colliery. The pioneer company's income generally came from reimbursement of its costs by the colliery company, to which was added a tonnage payment on coal raised, calculated on the difference between the royalty paid and that which would have been asked had the coal already been proved; sometimes shares were substituted for cash payments.[1] Sinking boreholes was not a cheap process. During the twenty years before 1913 eighteen bores, mostly between 600 and 900 metres, made in Yorkshire cost an estimated £167,100 and a similar average cost of £10,000 was estimated for bores in Nottinghamshire during the same period.[2] Already by the second quarter of the nineteenth century boreholes of up to 275 metres were common, at least in the North-east where Dunn described as normal the practice whereby several bores were made as part of a single exploration in order to establish seam inclination, faulting, and other characteristics which might present difficulties in mining. The method widely in use to prove coal seams was that of percussive boring, which involved the use of iron rods and a chisel, or in soft ground a wimble, or scoop. Not only sinking the bore and retrieving samples but also interpreting the results required the

---

[1] *Sankey Commission*, III Appendix 63.
[2] Ibid., Appendix 83, also II, QQ 17235–332.

skill of specialists,[1] hence the development of independent contractors, and later companies, to meet these needs.

Boring technology improved slowly. The amount of manhandling and manipulation of perhaps 200 metres of heavy iron rods was reduced by the application of steam power, while the introduction, also in the 1840s, of hollow rods through which water was injected to lubricate the chisel and to flush out waste was an innovation which speeded up the process. By 1862 portable steam engines and boring frames were widespread in seams of some depth, and the use of ropes enabled much lighter apparatus to be employed. These developments culminated in 1865 in the introduction by Mather and Platt of a steam engine to lift the rope using a pulley, an improved version of boring machinery which marked the end of a phase of innovation.[2]

The 1860s saw the beginnings of hydraulic lubrication techniques and core recovery, which were accompanied by the most important innovation of diamond core drilling, a method which made it possible to increase the rate of sinking and to recover the whole strata. The new technology consisted of industrial diamonds set into an annular crown, which when rotated rapidly cut a circular hole enclosing the strata and facilitated the retrieval of a solid core for detailed sectional analysis. This advantage, added to its speedier progress and lower cost for deep bores, led to the rapid adoption of diamond drilling in the 1870s and 1880s, though even after 1900 improved percussive methods were still more suitable for boring through soft strata.[3] For most mining expansion, however, the diamond-drilled core-recovery technique signalled the transformation of mine sinking into a much more predictable process, which revealed clearly the kinds of strata to be penetrated and the precise location of water and coal—the two most important geological considerations affecting the development of new coalfields. The risks accompanying sinking were thus diminished, though the fundamentals remained largely unaltered.

Advances in boring, particularly by improving the quality of information concerning the underlying strata, could not fail to affect sinking, though the skill requirements increased as the complexities of deep mining also grew. As in boring, sinking operations were conducted in the early nineteenth century by a subcontractor working under contract price, and while involving company, rather than independent, enterprise

[1] Dunn 1852, 37–9; Kerr 1904, 12–23; Pamely 1904, 11–16; Greenwell 1855, 106–14.
[2] Kerr 1904, 21–3; Hughes 1904, 24–6; CG 3 May 1862, 349–50.
[3] Kerr 1904, 23–6; Hughes 1904, 27–31; Pamely 1904, 17–23; CG 20 May 1898, 881.

by the end of the period, this basic relationship between sinker and landowner—though usually between sinker and colliery owner—remained unchanged. Sinkers advised colliery owners, as well as supplying experienced men to carry out the various jobs involved in sinking which might include walling, putting in timber, wedging cribs, installing and changing pumps. The contract price typically excluded the cost of rods, pumps for sinking, standing sets, and other materials, but contractors often provided their own sinking gear, kibbles, trams, running platforms, and similar appliances. Not surprisingly, in the early nineteenth century men from the North-east virtually monopolized the skills required in carrying out such operations, which increased in difficulty as mining depths grew. When Stephenson's Snibston Colliery was in the process of sinking in the 1830s local sinkers had to be replaced by Durham men, whom he sent for when the Leicester men failed to cope with the large volume of water gushing out of the Keuper marl. By substituting tubbing for brick lining and introducing more efficient pumps the Durham sinkers succeeded in stemming the flow and reached the main coal after nine months sinking.[1]

As the scale and sophistication of sinking methods increased, the type of skills developed in the North-east and in Lancashire, another deep-mining area by the 1850s, were transmitted to other regions, a process in which professional mining engineers together with subcontracting sinkers working under supervision played an important role.[2] Some engineers, acting as consultants, began to specialize in sinking operations; notably, for example, Walker and Foulstone, who in the 1880s used their experience of sinking deep mines in South Wales, Yorkshire, and Derbyshire to establish specialist services in those regions. John Higson, the Lancashire mining engineer, was consulting engineer in charge of the Ashton Main sinking to the Saltpetre and Black Mine Seams in 1874–82, and the contractor who actually carried out the operation, reaching depths exceeding 850 metres, was James Stanfield of Ashton.[3] The deepest sinking in South Wales at that time, the Harris Navigation that reached 640 metres, was the responsibility of T. Forster Brown, formerly a Durham mining engineer who had become a partner in a firm which specialized as consultants on deep mining especially in

---

[1] C. P. Griffin thesis, 698–9.
[2] *CG* 3 July 1858, 67; 'Aldwarke Main Colliery, Sinking of the No. 1 Deep Mine', *JBSMS* I (1876), 225–7.
[3] *CG* 25 June 1886, 1017, 11 Mar. 1881, 387.

South Wales.[1] In some of the very large colliery companies, however, resident engineer-managers took charge of sinkings.[2]

The precise technology to be employed depended upon the sinking depth and geological conditions, particularly whether water-bearing strata presented boring difficulties. In general the principle was to sink quickly, commensurate with safety and economy, which the employment of specialist contract labour could help to ensure. Before the Hartley disaster of 1862 deep pits commonly possessed only a single large divided shaft, though by the 1840s the incorporation of two shafts was gaining favour, an upcast shaft used for winding and close to this a downcast shaft used for pumping. Mostly circular in England and Wales, though mainly rectangular in Scotland, the diameter of shafts depended on the daily volume of coal raised, ventilation requirements, and the purpose for which they were to be designed. In the small, shallow mines the dimension might be no more than 1.5 metres, and four times that for large, single divided shafts. By 1913 high-output mines typically contained paired shafts of 2.5 to 3 metres or single shafts of 3.5 to 4.5 metres.[3] Typicality, however, is a concept of dubious relevance to mining operations. In 1830 shaft-sinking conditions ranged from simple drifts into hillsides and shallow shafts struck into dry strata, to very deep mines exceeding 400 metres; in the North-east often in the extreme watery conditions encountered in the concealed coalfield under the magnesian limestone, first won in the 1820s.[4]

Under dry conditions sinking techniques were simple, though difficulties increased with depth. Once the topsoil had been penetrated and lined, either with wood or brick to prevent loose material running into the shaft, sinking proper commenced. Using plumb lines to ensure verticality, work proceeded from wooden staging, with space to allow kibbles, containing debris, to pass through. Picks, shovels, and hand rock-drills were the tools employed during the early nineteenth century, as was gunpowder, except in watery strata where rocks tended to crack and aid percolation; later, steam, compressed air, and electric drills were introduced. By 1900 percussive drills similar to modern road-mending equipment were in use. Pickwork, drilling, and blasting produced rubble, which was raised in kibbles, or bowks (self-tipping

---

[1] CG 22 May 1891, 887; Wilkins 1888, 725.

[2] For example, W. H. Chambers at Denaby and Cadeby Main, and C. E. Rhodes at Rotherham Main. CG 14 Apr. 1893, 675, 19 June 1891, 1055.

[3] Dunn 1852, 42–3; Forster Brown 1924, 26–41; Kerr 1904, 30–2.

[4] Galloway 1904, 12–19; Flinn 1984, 20.

kibbles), at first simply attached to a rope. Economy and safety were improved from the mid-century by the introduction of guide ropes, which not only allowed two kibbles to be used, speeding operations, but also reduced the danger of damage to the shaft and injury to the men. In 1875 William Galloway patented twin guides, and he also devised improved counter-balanced doors to cover the shaft top. During the early years ventilation was extremely poor, and both firedamp (methane) and chokedamp (carbon dioxide) posed serious problems. Later, a short drift to a furnace and wooden bratticing to just above the working level provided a draught, while after fan ventilation became normal an iron pipe conveyed fresh air from a small surface fan to pit bottom.[1]

Even more of a threat to sinking was the presence of water, its removal, and/or prevention from entering into the workings, which proved to be the most difficult aspect of shaft sinking. In shallow and relatively dry sinkings the water accumulation could be removed in water tubs, or in kibbles using a horse-gin, but where the flow was considerable the problem was solved either by installing a small steam pumping-engine or by coupling pumps to a winding engine. For workings on any scale and at depths exceeding 30 metres, even in 1830 steam pumping was the rule. However, where water-bearing limestone or sandstone—or even worse, quicksand—was penetrated, enormous feeders of water amounting to several thousands of gallons per minute might be encountered, as at Murton (sinking 1838–43), Marsden (1877–84), and Blackhall (1909–13), all in County Durham. Since this water usually contained sand or grit, the wear on the pumps was considerable. Thus in the Murton winning, where steam engines generating 1,500 horsepower were employed in pumping, no fewer than three tanneries were required to supply leather for the pump buckets. Murton's water problem was exceptionally large, however, and from the 1870s the introduction of the Pulsometer steam pump (a modified Savery engine with no rubbing parts) could cope with flows up to about 2,500 gallons per minute (the flows at Murton, Marsden, and Blackhall each exceeded 9,000 gallons). About 1900 electric centrifugal pumps solved this problem.[2]

Pumping costs could be considerable, and consequently for operational reasons continuous pumping was to be avoided if possible.

[1] Kerr 1904, 32–4; 62–6; Hughes 1904, 99–103; Forster Brown 1924, 37–8.
[2] Forster Brown 1924, 32–5, 39–40; Hughes 1904, 110–11; Pamely 1904, 541–5, 537; Galloway 1904, 14–15; Kerr 1904, 307–11.

Methods of preventing water entering the shaft were already in use in 1830. Under conditions where water pressure was heavy, cast iron had been substituted for wooden planking, or 'tubbing', and masonry. Cast-iron segments were widely favoured for greater strength, durability, and because they were relatively water tight. Iron tubbing was built up by segments to a ring, or 'curb', offset like brickwork, with lead seals filling the gaps. By this method pumping was temporary until the tubbing was complete, which, when made of the requisite strength, permitted sinking to proceed in dry conditions below the water-bearing strata.[1]

Again, greater depths and difficulties occasioning greater risks and higher costs brought about increasing interest in the improvement and speeding up of the sinking process during the last quarter of the nineteenth century; this followed the sinking through Permian rocks beginning in parts of Yorkshire and the East and West Midlands in the 1860s. The Kind Chaudron method, a French invention, was first employed in Britain in 1877. It involved boring a narrow advance shaft, enlarged by a rotary heading which was made watertight with a box stuffed with moss; rings of iron tubbing were placed on this as the sinking progressed, effectively blocking off the watery strata as a result of the hydrostatic pressure which helped support the weight of the tubbing until it was secured permanently. The Kind Chaudron marked an advance upon existing methods, though the process was slow, costly, and proved to be unsuitable for sinking large shafts, or in quicksand.[2] This last problem was solved by Poetsch's freezing technique, first employed in Britain at the Washington Colliery in Durham in 1902. By this method a set of boreholes were driven through the quicksand, or watery strata, the smaller pipes contained with the main bore pipes providing a channel through which was pumped calcium chloride, returning by the longer pipe until the ground was frozen solid. To avoid cracks, sinking was effected without explosives and segmented tubbing was installed in the usual manner.

A variant, Gobert's system, used ammonia vapour; it could be used at greater depths and for successive strata. These various advances in sinking methods meant that by 1913 shafts of 6 metres could be sunk absolutely vertical with little technical difficulty, and as mines were driven deeper mine shafts assumed a more permanent character.[3] At first tubbing or lining were employed only to seal off water from workings,

---

[1] Hughes 1904, 111–18; Kerr 1904, 35–40; Flinn 1984, 75–7.
[2] Hughes 1904, 118–21; Kerr 1904, 54–9; Forster Brown 1924, 33–4.
[3] Hughes 1904, 121–2; Pamely 1904, 83–8.

but increasingly the practice was to line top and bottom sections with brickwork, and later to line the entire shaft.[1]

Very few mines could be worked without pumping machinery of some sort, for even deep tubbed-off mines were not entirely impervious, while the grooved iron-ring gutters were often insufficient to maintain dry conditions. A proportion of small adit mines requiring pumping only for workings below bottom drainage level still existed during the mid-century, for which hand or horse power sufficed, but the number of such mines and their share of total output was very small and in decline. A few mines still relied on water wheels for pumping but this was increasingly rare. The well-known example at Beamish, in Durham, was replaced by steam power in the 1830s. By far the greatest part of the pumping load was carried by steam engines, ranging from small portable units of a few horsepower to huge Cornish and horizontal compound engines of 5,000 horsepower or more. In many small mines engines were used for both winding and pumping, the latter taking place at night and at weekends. Until quite late into the nineteenth century the technology of steam pumping was often very simple, sometimes relying upon Watt, or even the primitive Newcomen-type, engines, for they were relatively cheap to install, reliable, durable, and easy to maintain—features which also meant that movement to new sites was not difficult. These engines used low steam pressures, but most collieries had little incentive to economize on fuel, since dust or small coal was generally of little value before the 1870s;[2] indeed, burning slack lessened the problem of waste disposal.

Where the amount of power required was considerable (perhaps exceeding 200 hp), either for sinking operations, or in deep, wet mines, or where the ready saleability of small coal as coke or for local manufactures encouraged economizing on colliery consumption, the Cornish beam engine offered considerable advantages. The capital cost of this type of plant was high, due mainly to the massive construction, but fuel consumption and running costs were minimized; as the stresses were relatively low reliability was superior to other types. For these reasons Cornish engines represented the best-practice technology until the last quarter of the century, when they began to be superseded by horizontal compounds of various types.[3] Horizontal engines found favour for

---

[1] Hughes 1904, 104–7; Forster Brown 1924, 37.

[2] Hughes 1904, 307–9; Galloway 1904, 478–9; Kenneth H. Rogers, *The Newcomen Engine in the West of England* (Bradford-on-Avon, 1976), 45–6.

[3] Hughes 1904, 295–6; Pamely 1904, 388–96; Forster Brown 1924, 183–94.

several reasons, for whereas the fuel consumption of Cornish engines was superior, and the end-of-stroke shocks eliminated by applying the Davy differential valve gear, horizontal compounds were more compact, offered greater flexibility in the speed of operation which was extremely smooth when used with the Davy gear, and were cheaper to install. They were also manufactured by a wide variety of makers who offered service agreements, and in addition to their use in pumping they were applied to electricity generation and to winding, and sometimes to both simultaneously.

Until the late nineteenth century pumping operations tended to be conducted from the surface, but the trend thereafter was to transfer the engine to pit bottom, applying it directly to the pumps. Such an alteration economized on pump rods (which were expensive, required considerable maintenance, and bulked large in the shaft) and enabled the engine to work continuously on a light load at low cost.[1] Such rearrangements became possible once the danger and losses involved in bringing steam down to the engine had been solved, while the advent of electricity, first applied to pumping at Trafalgar Colliery in the Forest of Dean in 1881, the difficulties of transferring operations from the surface diminished even further. However, not until after 1900 when centrifugal pumps were introduced did electrification become widespread; they could pump dirty water, they were efficient, flexible, and relatively trouble-free and could be coupled directly to fast-running electric motors.[2] Stimulated, in part, by the increasing relative value of small coal and facilitated by improvements in the efficiency both of engines and pumps, the fuel economy with which an ever-increasing load was pumped improved continually between 1830 and 1913.

Such improvements in the technology of mine drainage were vital to enable the continued expansion of mining in the concealed coalfields and the working of deeper and deeper seams in existing fields. However, in certain areas technology failed to overcome the particular geological difficulties so successfully neutralized in deep mines. Under wet conditions continuous pumping could only be economic where effective tubbing minimized the water flow. In shallower mines in sandstone and limestone strata, where water entered workings through cracks and faults in strata above the tubbing, working became extremely difficult. Abandoned workings soon became submerged and these affected adjacent working mines. The risks of breaking through effectively

---

[1] Forster Brown 1924, 189–91; Pamely 1904, 416–537, describes the variants in detail.
[2] Pamely 1904, 556–64; Forster Brown 1924, 191–2.

sterilized large tracts of coal because of the need to leave barriers to prevent breakthroughs, and because pumping was too costly on such a
scale. These were the conditions affecting south Staffordshire, which
deteriorated sufficiently during the mid-century to stimulate legislative
action in order to promote drainage. In 1873 a local voluntary scheme
was replaced by a general compulsory arrangement under the direction
of a Drainage Commission.[1] Progress was slow, however, a report issued
in 1920 remarking on the resemblance of a large part of the coalfield to 'a
waterlogged rabbit warren'.[2] Under local conditions less intractable
than those in the Black Country, colliery proprietors and landowners
were capable of combining together, sharing the costs of driving soughs
to drain coal seams common to their royalties but mined separately. An
important example of this was the arrangement between Newton
Chambers and Co. and the Earl Fitzwilliam, who together financed a
2,770-metre sough driven for the purpose of draining the Park Gate and
Silkstone Seams of coal in south Yorkshire. The cost amounted to
£10,000 and the project took six years, beginning in 1838.[3]

Once sinking was completed and drainage assured it was then necessary to lay out underground roadways to develop the coal seams and to
act as haulage and ventilation routes. Pillars of coal, varying in size
depending on depth, seam inclination, and rock hardness, were left to
support the shafts and surface installations, and main roads were driven
through them, each designed to service a large part of the mines area
and, where possible, to slope gently down to the shaft to facilitate
drainage and to minimize the effort of coal haulage. Subsidiary haulage
routes branched from the main roads and working levels, or gate roads,
which were abandoned once the coal which they developed was
extracted, were driven off these. Main and secondary roads were driven
in pairs for ventilation purposes and were connected at intervals by
crosscuts which were normally closed off, one serving as the intake and
the other carrying the return air. There was obviously a trade-off
between maximizing the height and width of the main roads for convenience of operation and minimizing costs; the point of intersection
was determined by the hardness of the strata and the consequent
expense of driving, the method of haulage employed, the volume of air
flow, and the quality of roof and floor. Sometimes changes in these conditions necessitated an enlargement of the roads, as for instance when

---

[1] A. J. Taylor 1967, 91.
[2] See *Report of the Committee on the Drainage of Mines in the South Staffordshire Coalfield* 1920,
XXI, 881.   [3] Hopkinson thesis, 353.

horses were substituted for human labour in Scotland in 1842, or when twin-track rope haulage was introduced.[1]

These permanent roads, which in larger collieries extended for many miles, were intended to last throughout the lifetime of the mine and with minimum maintenance, though cost considerations imposed limitations on such a policy. In most cases baulks of larch, fir, or pine, 0.2 to 0.3 metres thick, were employed in roadways depending on roof pressure; these were often set with square 'caps' to spread the load and combined with cross-timbers spaced as closely as seemed necessary to support the roof. Occasionally the roof was especially sound, requiring timber only in certain places; at junctions, for example. More frequently conditions were poor and extensive timbering was essential, especially in South Wales. The lifetime of pit props varied from months to years, depending on the crush.[2]

A more permanent solution was to use a brick lining, but this was much more expensive in initial cost due to the greater excavation needed, the price of bricks, and the labour-intensiveness of brick-working. Nevertheless, brick lining with an eliptical section and packing with soft sand was generally regarded as requiring minimal maintenance and in the long term was relatively cheap as well as safe. Colliery owners tended to limit this type of construction to the immediate area around the shaft bottom and to particularly bad places. Iron and steel girders, followed by light steel props, began to replace timber in some mines towards the end of the century. The tensile strength, lesser bulk, lightness, and non-inflammability of metal supports were widely recognized, and although they cost two or three times as much as timber they lasted four to six times as long and needed less attention. High initial cost, however, was a disincentive, except in districts where geological conditions led to rapid deterioration of timber and in some newer, larger colliery companies where long-term planning was more in evidence.[3]

Unless roads were well constructed and adequately maintained the dangers presented by crush and collapse might be costly in economic and human terms. Spontaneous combustion posed a similar threat, and as mines became deeper and as workings moved further from the shaft, improved ventilation to introduce or increase fresh air underground

---

[1] Redmayne 1914, 3, 27–39; Bulman and Redmayne 1906, 135–6; Kerr 1904, Chapter 7; SRO Newbattle GD 40/90–111, Gibson's Reports for 1842 and 1843.

[2] Kerr 1904, 152–62; Hughes 1904, 132–7; Pamely 1904, 224–32.

[3] Pamely 1904, 232–7; Kerr 1904, 161–72; Redmayne 1914, 3, 73–8. For a detailed account of the logic of substitution see the reports of Griff's colliery manager WaRO Griff CR 1169/22–4, and 1169/22–9.

assumed increasing importance. By the early nineteenth century some collieries in the North-east were traversed by as many as thirty miles of underground passages, which presented considerable possibility for the accumulation of explosive gas. Already well established by 1830 was the system of coursing air through the workings by means of wooden partitions, or brattices, as was the splitting of currents to reduce the distance travelled. Even in the North-east, however, these methods were not widespread, and the use of furnaces at the pit bottom to draw air through the upcast shaft was standard practice in large collieries. In Scotland, the West Midlands, and South Wales even more primitive methods of ventilation prevailed, for typically mines in these regions were small and often employed no ventilating aids at all.[1]

Furnace ventilation was widely adopted after 1830, especially in deep mines, for the increasing volume of air being drawn through the workings improved its effectiveness, which was further enhanced in some of the largest mines where several furnaces were installed. None the less, the problems associated with furnace ventilation were still considerable—the risk of explosion, the difficulties of relighting, the dangerous and unpleasant conditions for the men being wound in furnace shafts, and the difficulty of carrying out repairs. The search for alternatives brought a brief popularity for steam jets placed in the upcast shaft, and following their adoption in the 1840s received endorsement by the 1852 Select Committee on Accidents in Coal Mines; but it was soon demonstrated that they were less powerful than furnaces and more expensive to run.[2]

The future lay with the fan. Mechanical ventilators had been devised before 1830 (Buddle had installed a mechanical ventilation fan at Hebburn Colliery in 1807), but the capacity of these early devices was small and in any case was unnecessary for the deep mines of the North-east, where furnaces were most efficient. The installation of a steam-driven fan at the top of a shaft in a colliery near Paisley in 1827 marked a forward step in the history of mechanical fan ventilation,[3] but more decisive developments followed in South Wales, where in the peculiarly predominant shallow workings inadequate draught rendered the furnace unsatisfactory as a mode of ventilation, both on economic and safety grounds. The need for improved ventilation, however, increased

---

[1] Galloway 1898, 518–22 and 1904, 256–68; Moss, K. 'Ventilation of Coal Mines' in Mining Association of Great Britain (London, c.1924), 126–49.
[2] Galloway 1904, 269–86; SC Coal Mines 1852, V, 4–5.
[3] Flinn 1984, 135–6.

in the 1840s with the development of the gassy steam-coal seams. These had occasioned several explosions in the single-stall workings characteristic of Welsh mines and which were particularly conducive to the accumulation of gas. Of the variety of experiments with air pumps, rotary pumps, and fans one of the most successful was the W. P. Struve ventilator, an air pump developed in Wales and first installed at Eaglebush Colliery in 1849; this coincided with the installation of the first Brunton fan, again in South Wales.[1] These were followed by the Waddle and Schiele fans introduced in the 1860s, but the most successful of all, because of its higher efficiency, was the Guibal fan, developed by a Professor of Mineral Engineering at Mons University in Belgium, and patented in England in 1862. The diffusion of this new technology was stimulated by a series of articles which from 1850 appeared in the proceedings and transactions of the professional engineering bodies. The articles demonstrated, on empirical and theoretical grounds, the relative inefficiency of furnaces (measured by coal consumed) compared with fan ventilation, and justified the substitution of fan for furnace.[2] A comparison with other forms of ventilation in 1874 revealed that, with a single exception, all ventilators and fans were at least twice as economic because of low coal consumption (the Guibal fan nearly four times as cost efficient), quite apart from their other safety advantages.[3]

South Staffordshire, in most respects backward in working practices, lagged in the adoption of fans, for fire damp in the thick coal had long been dispersed by driving air headings in the upper seams, a method introduced first in Lord Dudley's mines before 1810 and for which its exponent, 'Hell-fire Jack', had received a gold medal. This innovation coupled with the prevalence of small pits earned for the region a reputation for relatively few explosions, with the result that not even furnaces were introduced until the 1860s, when they were found necessary to ventilate the deeper mines.[4] Elsewhere, perceived unreliability or reservations concerning the power of centrifugal fans delayed widespread transfer to the new ventilation systems; even in South Wales the furnace continued to dominate until the mid-1860s.[5] By that time the increasing

---

[1] Morris and Williams 1958, 64.

[2] For a complete list of the thirty-eight articles appearing in the various regional *Transactions* between 1850, beginning with W. P. Struven, 'The Ventilation of Collieries, Theoretically and Practically considered', *TNIEME*, X (1850–1), 22–57, see U. E. Nicholson, *A Glossary of Terms used in the Coal Trade of Northumberland and Durham* (Newcastle upon Tyne, 1888), 142–5; Moss 1924, 141; Kerr 1904, 333–44.

[3] E. Bainbridge, 'On the Prevention of Colliery Explosions', *CG* 20 Mar. 1874, 377.

[4] A. J. Taylor 1967, 93.   [5] Morris and Williams 1958, 66.

power, economy, and reliability of fans had overcome prejudice, besides which the relative value of furnace fuel small coal began to rise.

By 1876 two hundred Guibal fans had been installed in the country as a whole.[1] Among the first to adopt this important innovation were the owners of Elswick Colliery, near Newcastle, in 1864, followed by the Stella Coal Company, at the Addison Pit, in 1866.[2] Two years later the Londonderry viewer, Daglish, installed a fan at Framwellgate Colliery 'in deference to the Inspector of Mines as to the inefficiency of ventilation'.[3] In 1868 Staveley's viewer, William Armstrong, advised in favour of installing Guibal fans into two of the company's pits, on economic as well as upon safety grounds; in one instance the fan superseded a furnace located at the foot of a wooden partition down which a constant stream of running water was the only form of fire prevention.[4]

Fuel economy, improved safety, constant running, and uniform operation were factors which justified the switch from furnace to fan, but in some instances the most important reason was probably the need for sufficient air to ventilate workings nearing exhaustion or requiring extension, and which otherwise would suffer physical limitations of mining operations at worst, or at best necessitate additional shaft sinking. Such was the case at Unsworth in Lancashire in 1871, when George Elliot, who had installed several fans in South Wales, was asked to advise the proprietors on the prospects for expanding production from a pit worked for more than twenty years.[5] The *Colliery Guardian* was clearly impressed with the outcome and quoted Elliot: 'He thought no injustice would be done to coalowners if it were stipulated that henceforth there should be neither furnaces nor steam boilers used in pits; he advocated getting rid of fires in the pits, and blasting powder, but urged the adoption of ventilating fans'.[6] By 1890 very deep mines, especially those in the North-east, provided the only exception where furnaces rather than fans were at work, the most successful being the Guibal, Schiele, improved Waddle and Walker, and Cappel fans. The trend in designing these was towards the smaller, faster-running fans of the Schiele and Cappel types to replace the large, slow-running fans of the second and third quarters of the century, with the result that by 1900 the

[1] Galloway 1882, 253–6; Moss 1924, 141–7.

[2] W. Cochrane, 'Description of Guibal's fan at the Elswick Colliery', *TNEIMME*, 1864, XIV, 73–81; CG 2 Feb. 1894, 207.

[3] DuRO, Londonderry, D/LO/B320(6) vii.

[4] BSCEMRRC Stanton and Staveley 2034/3/9c Markham's Report 20 Jan. 1877; CG 15 June 1894, 112.   [5] CG 18 May 1894, 937.

[6] CG 21 Apr. 1871, 424.

centrifugal fan could be designed to generate a sufficient flow for efficient ventilation of the deepest mines.[1] Only a very few furnaces remained in use by 1913. Electric motors also soon proved their suitability for driving fans directly and were favoured for their greater efficiency and reliability. By the end of 1913 over 50,000 horsepower of electric motors were applied to ventilation.[2]

Allied with these developments in the means of generating currents of air through the workings, leaks were reduced at connecting points by substituting cloth for wood in brattices; the development of self-closing doors for haulage roads both dispensed with fallible juvenile labour and facilitated leak-free operation.[3]

Improved ventilation did not depend entirely upon the replacement of furnaces by mechanically operated fans, for the circulation of air within the mines was powerfully affected by the methods used to extract coal, the hewing of coal from a long face facilitating air flows effectively dispersing gas in otherwise potentially dangerous seams. Where coal was worked in confined spaces and blind recesses the accumulation of gas afforded a constant threat of explosion, which is one of the main reasons explaining why, from the mid-nineteenth century, men of high standing among mining engineers began to advocate the substitution of longwall for pillar-and-stall or bord-and-pillar methods of extraction.[4]

Face workers, especially hewers, depended on lighting for both earning capacity and safety, for as the level of illumination rose their ability to work effectively and to spot danger in the roof or floor improved. Lighting improvements, however, were the consequence of concern aroused by a growing number of catastrophic explosions for which naked lights were blamed. The history of the development of the safety lamp, which relied on a wire gauze and later a glass cover to shield the flame from inflammable mine gases, is well known. First introduced in 1815, twenty years later a House of Commons Committee criticized the Davy Lamp as dangerous to use. In 1843 the South Shields Committee also underlined the dangers of the various other lamps invented since the Davy—those of Stephenson, Clanny, Upton and Roberts, William Martin, Richard Ayre, and of Mueseler and Lemielle from Belgium; no

[1] J. B. Simpson, Presidential Address, *TFIME*, III (1891–2), 557; R. Nelson Boyd, 'Collieries and Colliery Engineering', *CG* 10 Nov. 1893, 819; Hinsley, 'The Development of Coal Mine Ventilation in Great Britain up to the end of the Nineteenth Century', *TNS*, 1969–70, XLII, 28–9, 31–4.　　　　　　　　　　　　　　　　　[2] *Mineral Statistics* 1913 and 1914.

[3] Kerr 1904, 347–52; Hughes 1904, 341–4.

[4] Galloway 1904, 250.

lamp was safe unless used in well-ventilated conditions. Most highly regarded was the Mueseler, which represented an improvement over the Clanny by adding to its cylindrical glass protection and gauze above the glass a device to separate burnt gases from the incoming air. Particularly because of the superior illumination, the Mueseler was preferred by the experts to either the Clanny or the Davy lamp, but even the Mueseler barely generated half as much light as a single candle. The Biram lamp, invented by Earl Fitzwilliam's agent in 1849, contained a reflector behind the wick and gave high illumination, but from one side only.

Between the review of safety lamps in 1835 and the legislation of 1911, the official attitude, that they improved safety under appropriate conditions and when properly used, did not alter; but the dangers associated with them under different circumstances were none the less still sufficiently apparent that neither the Coal Mines Act of 1872 nor of 1887 rendered use compulsory. This came in 1911, when the Mines Act divided mines into those which were, and those which were not, required to use safety lamps, depending upon the proportion of firedamp present.[1] Contemporaries criticized the safety lamp for having increased danger, in some instances, especially in the North-east, for it was instrumental in making pillar extraction possible on a large scale and at greater depths. Even the partial removal of pillars produced hazardous conditions owing to the increased breakage of coal and the consequent release of firedamp.[2] Unfortunately, the prospect of safer working with the aid of lamps tended to induce complacency and encourage misuse by the men. The defects of the lamp were, none the less, real, and the inadequacy of the light they radiated continued to check the speed of work without removing danger.

An article which appeared in the *Colliery Guardian* in 1881 following the Penygraig explosion quoted the views of Mines Inspectors from several districts, each of whom referred to the dangers of the Davy, Clanny, and Stephenson lamps, which were the most commonly used. Dickinson, Wales, and Cadman recommended the adoption of self-extinguishing lamps, such as the Mueseler, which on contact with an explosive current went out.[3] However, in very fiery mines not even the Mueseler lamp was absolutely safe. In a paper delivered to the Manchester Geological Society in 1882 the author described the safe lighting of

[1] Galloway 1904, Chap. XXIII; A. R. Griffin 1977, 118–20.
[2] F. Hinsley, 'The Development of Coal Mine Ventilation in Great Britain up to the end of the Nineteenth Century', *TNS*, 1969–70, XLII, 28–9, 31–4.
[3] *CG* 1 July 1881, 11.

coal mines as 'eminently unsatisfactory', reflecting on twenty years during which less progress had been made than in ventilation, winding, or winning.[1] Thus, although the introduction of the safety lamp had made some improvement in the safe removal of pillars, especially in the North-east between roughly 1820 and 1850, its role should not be exaggerated, either then or later.[2] It should also be stressed that the use of safety lamps was essentially a defensive practice. For wherever the workings were (or were thought to be) free of gas, or where gunpowder was used, despite their higher running costs the superior illumination offered by naked lights (candles, later oil lamps, and from the beginning of the twentieth century, carbide lamps) meant that naked lights were preferred. A paraffin lamp gave eight times as much light as a Davy and three times as much as an improved glassed lamp, such as the Marsault or Mueseler. Naked lights remained the norm in Scotland and large parts of the North-east as late as 1913 (when there were only 0.3 safety lamps per underground worker in Scotland and 0.7 per man in the North-east).[3]

Electric lamps were slow to be introduced, for the early models were heavy, expensive, lasted less than a full shift, and were unsuitable for rough treatment because they used wet acid. After 1900, however, their popularity increased, especially in Yorkshire and the East Midlands where they represented 11 per cent of the total in use in 1913—when the national figure for electric lamps was slightly less than 5 per cent. The safety lamps most popular by that time were the Clanny and Marsault designs, which were similar in type though the latter incorporated double gauze for extra safety. Together these lamps accounted for 82 per cent of the total in 1913.[4] The pit bottom and main gate roads were illuminated by open torch lamps during the early nineteenth century, but the second half saw the spread of gas lighting. The Emma Pit, owned by the Stella Coal Company, pioneered the use of natural gas for this purpose in the 1850s[5] while in Lancashire at about the same time the Kirkless Hall and Ince Hall Companies attracted comment for having introduced gas lighting into their mines (at depths exceeding 810 metres) where lamp posts were erected along the principal tram roads for considerable distances at the intake levels.[6] Such an expedient in deep fiery

---

[1] CG 10 Mar. 1882, 385, 16 June 1882, 943.

[2] Hair 1968, 550–4; Dron 1928, 150–69; Galloway 1898, 506–8, 513–16, and II 304–24.

[3] The national average was 0.85 safety lamps per underground worker. *Mineral Statistics* 1913; Galloway 1898, 509–15; Kerr 1904, 384–5.

[4] *Mineral Statistics* 1913.   [5] CG 6 July 1891, 9.

[6] CG 30 Jan. 1858, 74.

mines enabled the managers to ban naked lights altogether and to insist upon miners using safety lamps. On William Armstrong's recommendation, a similar policy was adopted at Blundell's Lancashire Collieries a few years later.[1]

Beginning in the 1880s, electric light began to supersede gas-light installations underground at pit bottom and in main gate roads, though diffusion was relatively slow until after 1900. Staveley's underground workings, gas-lit at least from 1861, were converted to electric light in 1891, though one of the first electric light systems installed underground was that of the Cannock Chase Colliery in 1883.[2] Communications underground began to improve from 1880, when Lord Elphinstone invited the General Telephone Agency Company Ltd. to experiment at Carberry Colliery near Inveresk before the installation of the first telephone system in a British mine. The report of this development, which appeared in the *Colliery Guardian*, underlined the importance of continuous information on the functioning of pumping and other gear below and above ground, both from an economic and safety standpoint, but we do not know how rapidly this innovation was adopted.[3]

ii. Working methods

The underground layout of mines and the methods of coal extraction may be divided into 'longwall', and 'pillar and stall' or 'bord and pillar'. Within these categories many variants existed, while techniques peculiar to some localities combined elements of both; consequently classification is difficult. Indeed, it is scarcely an exaggeration that there were as many variations as there were different seam characteristics. Standardization of technique proceeded slowly, as the merits of the simple types of longwall and pillar and stall were recognized and as the technological capacity to get coal by them were developed. It is important, however, to emphasize from the outset that longwall as it was understood in the century before 1913 differed from the method described as longwall in the mid-twentieth century—whereby coal was got in straight strips a hundred metres or more wide. Nineteenth-century longwall mining generally involved the coal-face advancing in a stepped line, or fanning out from the bottom, to form a series of well-defined working places which were the province of one or two hewers and the putters who

---

[1] D. Anderson, 'Blundell's Collieries, Technical Developments', 168–9.

[2] *CG* 13 Apr. 1861, 231; J. Roger Francis *History of the Cannock Chase Colliery Company* (Rugeley, 1981), 18, 28.   [3] *CG* 16 Apr. 1880, 623.

removed the coal from the face. None the less, team working and labour specialization did become more common. In the East Midlands and parts of the West Midlands working places were much longer, perhaps 30–50 metres, in the hands of a 'little butty' where up to ten men worked a face advancing continuously.[1] The width of the working places also varied with seam thickness and hardness and problems were often encountered in ensuring that the face advanced uniformly. Even the introduction of coal cutters did not necessarily bring about a transition to 'true' longwall: sometimes the machines were man-handled from stall to stall.[2] None the less, the fundamental difference between longwall and pillar and stall existed from the beginning, for by longwall extraction a given length of face was worked in a single line along which coal was removed in one operation.

In 1830 most coal was got by one of several variants of pillar-and-stall working, while longwall mining was mainly confined to Shropshire, the South-west, and to certain thin seams elsewhere.[3] By pillar and stall, bord and pillar, or other variations, work was divided into two separate extractive operations, the feature which distinguished such techniques of extraction from longwall. 'Whole' work under pillar-and-stall working consisted of driving a number of bords, or passages, parallel to each other, between pillars, or stoops, from which the coal was taken, leaving the pillars of coal to support the roof. These bords were connected at suitable intervals by cuts which intersected the coalfield to form a honeycomb.

The discontinuance of this wasteful method of extracting coal occurred first in the North-east, where the bord-and-pillar method, often known as the Newcastle system, involved a second working to

---

[1] *CG* 4 Mar. 1881, 334, from Manchester Geological Society 1881.

[2] A. R. Griffin, *Coalmining* (London, 1971), 50–2; Galloway 1904, 246; Hughes 1904, 159–60.

[3] Galloway 1904, 245–7. The following descriptions of various working methods are drawn from a wide range of sources, but chiefly Galloway 1904, 227–55; Dunn 1852, 74–121; Kerr 1904, Chap. 7; Hughes 1904, Chap. 7; Granville Pool 'Historical Survey of Methods of Working' in Mining Association of Great Britain, *Historical Review of Coal Mining* (London, *c.* 1924), 42–63; Bulman and Redmayne 1906, Chap. 9–13; John Hedley, 'On Mines and Mining in the North Staffordshire Coalfield', *TNEIME*, II (1853), 235–48; James Morgan, 'The Mining and Working of Coal Mines in North Staffordshire, *NSIMME*, VII (1884–5), 58–68, 85–96; Henry Johnson, 'South Staffordshire Coalfield: Method of Working, Ventilation, Extent and Duration of Coalfield', in Samuel Timmins (ed.), *Birmingham and the Midland Hardware District* (London, 1866), 21–6; J. T. Woodhouse, 'The Progress of Coal Mining in the Counties of Derby and Nottingham', *TNEIME*, X (1861–2), 117–31, 137–47; H. B. Coke, 'Longwall in Derbyshire', *JBSMS*, I and II (1876–8), 70–6; A. R. Griffin 1971, 4–5; Jonathan Unsworth, 'Half a Century of Lancashire Coal Mining', National Association of Colliery Managers' Proceedings, II (1906), 292–316; R. A. S. Redmayne, 'The "Double Stall" Method of Working Coal', *JBSMS*, X (1887–8), 29–43.

remove more of the coal hitherto remaining as pillars; by 1830 Buddle had modified the Newcastle system to secure some of the advantages of longwall working. Coal in areas or 'panels' of between eight and twelve acres were divided by thick coal barriers, in which separate ventilation systems were maintained. Access was by the working roads and ventilation courses which penetrated the solid walls of coal (up to fifty metres thick) surrounding the panels. Resembling bankwork in layout and longwall in method, the roofs of the panels were left to settle and collapse by the natural process known as 'creep', so avoiding disturbance of workings in other panels. 'Broken' work consisted of pillar removal, which by the traditional methods of the North-east occurred after the bords had been driven to the extremities, whereas in pillar-and-stall working, the two operations almost merged into one.

Bord and pillar and pillar and stall were the principal types of a general method of extraction which at one extreme resembled longwall. Figures 4.1 to 4.10 show these variants. The basic system, prevalent in the 1830s in Scotland, Cumberland, and parts of Lancashire, Yorkshire, the North-east, and South Wales, is illustrated in Figure 4.1. Here a large proportion of the coal—up to half, or more in exceptional cases—was lost, being left behind to prop up the roof; even when the pillars were recovered the coal was much crushed. This very inefficient system gradually died out as better methods were developed but was still in use in places in the 1850s and later. A modification of the system called 'single stall' (Figure 4.3) was practised in South Wales; this also involved much waste and encountered ventilation problems due to gas accumulating in the stalls, though the method persisted until the last quarter of the century. The predominant system prevailing in South Wales until after the 1870s consisted of pillar and stall in which the 'whole' working, when the bords were driven to the limits of the extraction area, was

Key to Figs 4.1–10

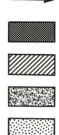

Working place

Coal left permanently for support

Coal to be worked

Goaf-usually packed with waste

Boundary of area being worked

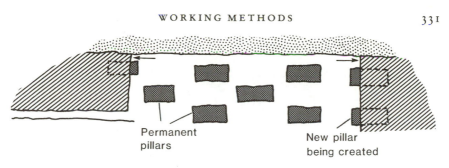

Permanent pillars

New pillar being created

Fig. 4.1. Pillar and stall

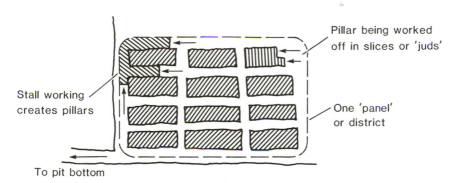

Pillar being worked off in slices or 'juds'

Stall working creates pillars

One 'panel' or district

To pit bottom

Fig. 4.2. Modified pillar and stall or bord and pillar

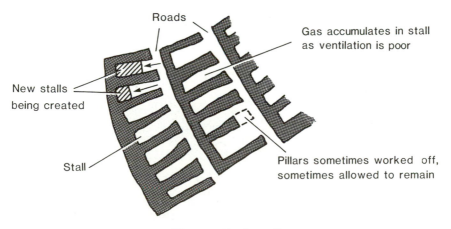

Roads

Gas accumulates in stall as ventilation is poor

New stalls being created

Stall

Pillars sometimes worked off, sometimes allowed to remain

Fig. 4.3. Single stall

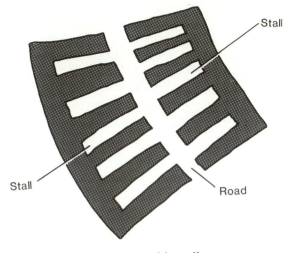

Stall

Stall

Road

Fig. 4.4. Double stall

Permanent pillars

Each 'side of work'
kept separate and
sealed off after coal
was extracted

Fig. 4.5. Square work

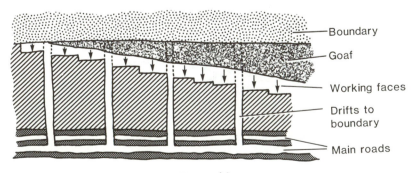

Boundary

Goaf

Working faces

Drifts to
boundary

Main roads

Fig. 4.6. Lancashire system

immediately followed by 'broken' work, which saw the removal of each contiguous pillar formed by the stall driven off the heading (Figure 4.4).

In south Staffordshire the whole of the Thick Coal, up to 10 metres, was got by 'square work' (Figure 4.5). This involved blocking out 'sides of work' about 50 by 100 metres surrounded by barriers of coal. These were worked with a number of permanent pillars, which when all the coal removable safely had been got were sealed off to prevent the spread of gob fires in the gassy workings. Despite attempts to work the Thick Coal longwall in stages, this remained the normal practice and clearly involved much unavoidable waste; working coal overhead also considerably increased the danger of roof falls which caused many deaths.

The much improved version of pillar and stall working which was becoming general in the North-east by the 1830s is illustrated in Figure 4.2. The result of improved lighting and ventilation underground, the system of blocking out large sections and driving narrow bords with large pillars of from 20 to 60 metres (square or oblong), depending on depth, was known as 'panel' working. As soon as the panel was blocked out the pillars were worked off back to the gate road and almost all the coal got with the minimum of small; ventilation was also made much easier and the floor and roof could be allowed to squeeze together thus eliminating the problems otherwise caused by 'creep'. This system gradually replaced that which left small, permanent pillars, though panel working was especially suited to seams of 1 to 2.5 metres thickness.

Two other main systems of working fall somewhere between pillar and stall and longwall: the 'Lancashire System', and the 'bankwork' layout found in Yorkshire and the East Midlands. The former involved driving roads some 20–40 metres apart from the gate roads to the boundary then working back either longwall or by blocking out pillars (Figure 4.6); this was common practice in Lancashire, Cheshire, North Wales, and north Staffordshire. Bankwork consisted in driving wide bords and working the banks they blocked out back to the main roads, leaving thin permanent pillars between banks (Figure 4.7). For a long time in Yorkshire this method persisted in improved form, whereby bankwork in sets sometimes proceeded along stepped longwall faces (Figure 4.8); whereas in the East Midlands longwall proper rapidly superseded bankwork in the 1840s.

The survival of pillar-and-stall methods in some districts depended partly upon its suitability for particular coal seams and partly upon the ability of mining engineers to adapt the traditional pillar and stall so as to compete with longwall working under similar geological conditions.

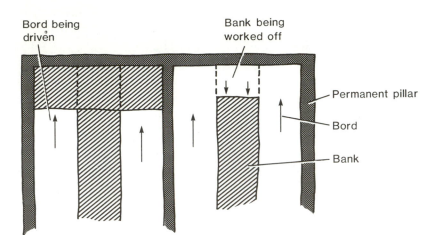

Fig. 4.7. Bankwork or bord and bank

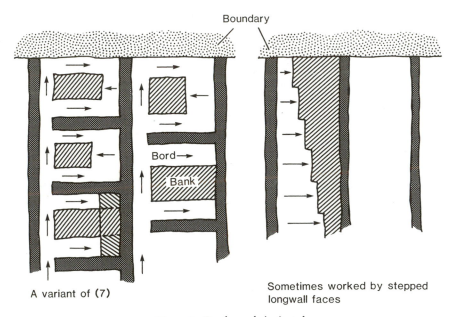

A variant of (7)

Sometimes worked by stepped longwall faces

Fig. 4.8. Bankwork in 'sets'

The thickness of seams in Durham, parts of Scotland, and in the Swansea district of South Wales, where roofs were typically poor and wet conditions were widespread, proved especially favourable to the persistence of pillar and stall. Reinforcing its survival in these areas was the narrowing price differential between large and small coal, thereby reducing one of the major advantages of longwall over pillar-and-stall working.[1] Indeed, in those districts where there was no clear advantage in utilizing one or other method there is abundant evidence that some form of pillar and stall or longwall existed in different seams side by side in the same mines.[2] At Briggs's Whitwood Colliery in the 1860s a combination of stoop-and-room and longwall systems were employed in working the Stanley six-foot seam.[3] And even in the North-east by the 1890s[4] the longwall system was used to work away the larger pillars between 20 and 40 metres square.[5]

In 1852 Matthias Dunn set out the conditions under which longwall methods were most suitable, and offered the greatest advantages.[6] Those conditions included thin, hard coal seams capable of bearing pressure, an abundant supply of land, rubbish or ironstone mixed with coals or debris for filling the hollows, water-free roofs, and the workings free from buildings or rivers. Among the principal advantages which he emphasized, one was cheaper working cost, but greater importance was attached to the higher proportion of large coal yielded in longwall working; simple and effective ventilation was also an advantage stressed by Dunn.[7] Although longwall was initially more expensive, principally because of the packing which it necessitated and the continual maintenance and control of roofs, working costs were lowered by the smaller amount of timbering needed and because the tram roads were short, minimizing the cost of upkeep for maintaining rails and sleepers. The short, more direct roads in longwall working also facilitated the adoption of simpler haulage and ventilation techniques, while by assisting the collier to undermine the coal the weight of the roof at the face helped to reduce labour and drilling operations to a minimum. Moreover, where gunpowder had been used it could be dispensed with altogether in many cases, except perhaps in stonework or ripping operations. Where the cost of longwall working exceeded that of alternative methods, the yield of large coal, and hence the enlarged revenue product, could more than offset the incremental cost.[8]

[1] See below.

[2] E. Mammett, 'Various Methods of Working Coal in Yorkshire', *TMIME*, 1869, I, 25–31.

[3] *CG* 31 May 1862, 431.   [4] *CG* 10 Nov. 1895, 820.

[5] George Elliott, viewer at the Londonderry collieries advocated the adoption of longwall there in the 1850s. DuRO Londonderry D/LO/B/62.

[6] Dunn 1852, 76.   [7] Ibid., 87–8.

[8] James Turrington, 'General Underground Layout and Working Arrangements for a New Colliery', *Mining Engineer* 1912, XVI, 235; *CG* 4 Mar. 1881, 334, 1 Dec. 1871, 553, 24 Nov. 1871, 529; W. O. Wood, 'The Long Wall Workings at East Hetton Colliery', *NEIME* 1875–6, XXV, 21–69.

Warrington Smyth's review of mining methods, reported to the Government School of Science in a lecture delivered in 1858, underlined the leadership of the East Midlands in the extent and practice of longwall working, though Shropshire, too, was included among the counties where the system was managed best.[1] Longwall had also been introduced in Somerset and a few districts in north Staffordshire, and by the late 1860s had advanced considerably in Lancashire, in the steam-coal seams of South Wales, and in Scotland, though as yet, especially in the last three regions, the instances were few before the mid-century.[2] Among the leading viewers the advantages of longwall were beginning to be acknowledged in other regions, too. Thus, George Elliot, viewer and engineer at Lord Londonderry's collieries from 1851, introduced longwall working which he then described as 'the greatest improvement in this century for producing the coals large and cheap and also the saving of timber'. 'I have had the honour', he told His Lordship, 'in defiance of all the colliery viewers in the Trade, of being the first man to carry out this system in the County of Durham . . .'.[3] But even such an enthusiast for longwall as George Elliot, praised by Matthias Dunn for his practical achievements in its introduction, acknowledged the need for a necessary minimum set of geological conditions to justify altering a working system in order to maximize the marketability of output and to achieve the real economies and safety advantages which longwall could offer;[4] for this reason longwall made little further progress in Durham before 1870, except to work off the gigantic pillars of some of the deepest collieries.[5]

Longwall working spread steadily after 1830, but especially between 1860 and 1880. This was in part a recognition of its superior safety and efficiency, but owed something, too, to the greater proportion of large coal that could be got by longwall, increasing incentives to raise the whole seam and, especially after 1880, to the greater proportion of output from the thin seams for which longwall was particularly suited.[6] Once goaf-packing techniques had been perfected, longwall working

[1] *CG* 23 Jan. 1858, 52–3.

[2] Ibid.; *Coal Supply* 1870, XVIII, 546, 564.

[3] DuRO D/LO/B/62.

[4] Dunn 1852, 88.

[5] *CG* 25 July 1868, 73, 17 Nov. 1871, 511.

[6] The advantages of longwall were stressed repeatedly in the *Colliery Guardian* for more than fifty years after Dunn. They were contained in reports, articles, and correspondence. For example: 23 Jan. 1858, 52; 6 Feb. 1858, 88, 17 Nov. 1871, 511, 4 Mar. 1881, 334, 5 Apr. 1881, 547, 29 Apr. 1881, 656, 25 Nov. 1881, 863, 13 Nov. 1885, 773, 13 Jan. 1882, 56, 27 May 1898, 945. For quantitative estimates of the effect of changing from pillar and stall to longwall see p. 337 fn. 2.

also gave better ventilation, more control over roof and floor, and the considerable economic advantages of greater productivity and lower working costs. For these reasons, by 1870 longwall working had advanced to account for over half Scottish output, all East Midlands production, nearly half in South Wales, and for smaller proportions elsewhere. By 1900 only the North-east, Cumberland, North Wales, south Staffordshire, and certain thick seams elsewhere still employed the improved pillar-and-stall layout to any degree; about three-quarters of UK output was got from longwall faces advancing from the shaft (Figure 4.9).[1]

Longwall retreating, by which roads were driven through to the boundary before working back (Figure 4.10), saw limited employment in the period before 1913, and was applied principally in the steep, thick seams of north Staffordshire and Warwickshire, and in parts of the North-west on the Lancashire system described above. The chief technical advantage of longwall retreating was that it left the roof to collapse behind the workings and eliminated the problems of gas accumulation in the goaf. Where the roof was soft, however, there were problems in keeping the roads open and the percentage of small coal was higher than from longwall. Capital costs were higher and opening out times much longer, consequently despite the lower working costs of retreat mining most collieries worked ordinary longwall.[2]

The full potential for working economies from longwall depended upon the response of labour as well as the careful management of the conditions of operation. When in 1859 William Armstrong advised the owners of West Staveley Colliery to alter the traditional pillar-and-stall working to a form of longwall system, he acknowledged that 'some little difficulty may at first arise in getting all parties to accommodate themselves to it, but I have purposely so contrived it as to involve as little departure as possible and the difference is very trivial from your present system of working so far as regards the men'.[3] Initial opposition from miners was not unusual, and appears to have been particularly marked when attempts were made to introduce longwall methods in South Wales in the 1860s. But opposition could be bought off, and depended upon the negotiation of new cutting-rates for hewers. John Nixon, who prosecuted some of his colliers for refusing to work long-

[1] Estimated from 1900 output and data on working methods in the sources quoted above and *Coal Supply Commission* 1903, XVI. The references are too numerous to record and may be found in the index to the Report under the headings 'Coalfields' and 'Systems of Working'.

[2] Ibid.; *Samuel Commission* III, 254–9; Hughes 1904, 161.

[3] NuRO Armstrong 725/B5 22 Oct. 1859, Reports.

wall, eventually succeeded in persuading most of the work-force to accept the change by gradually reducing the thickness of the pillars until holing the stalls into one another became both evidently sensible and remunerative.[1] Enhanced earnings one way or another usually proved to be the solvent of hostility, so that miners' resistance was only a short-term problem occasioning little delay in the spread of longwall where coalowners chose to adopt it.

For example, the introduction of longwall at Briggs's Whitwood Colliery in 1863 met no objection from the miners, other than that which stemmed from an insistence on securing extra payment. Local miners reacted differently one year later when the owners of another West Yorkshire colliery, Hudson's Victoria, imported eight experienced Derbyshire miners to demonstrate the new system, for they struck, refusing to accept a new and, it was argued, more intensive working without increased pay. The owners countered by replacing the Derbyshire miners by their striking miners, who agreed to work the new system 'in order to fix a fair and remunerative price for the work'. Within a fortnight a mutually agreed list of piece-rates signalled the introduction of coal getting by longwall.[2]

Employers in South Wales, however, proved to be less successful in altering other working practices designed to maximize the advantages of large outputs.[3] Under favourable conditions deep mining, and longwall in particular, allowed pressure from the roof to cause the undercut coal to fall without further assistance. The practice in many collieries in other regions, and in the North-east under pillar-and-stall conditions too, was for the mine to work double shifts, the second shift loading the coal from the previous one to raise the rate of daily output; hauliers and other oncost workers worked a long single shift. When John Nixon, the principal advocate of double-shift working, tried to introduce such a system in his South Wales collieries in the 1860s he encountered resistance. This was despite Nixon having tried to allay the apprehensions of his colliers by arranging for some of them to visit collieries in the North-east where shift work was common.[4] Aware of colliers' objections to it because of the disruptive effects on their social lives, he tried to persuade them to agree to an increase in the number of men working to a stall from one to three, but without success,[5] an illustration of the

[1] Morris and Williams 1958, 61.
[2] Machin 1958, 130–2.
[3] Morris and Williams 1958, 260.
[4] Ibid.   [5] Ibid., 260–1.

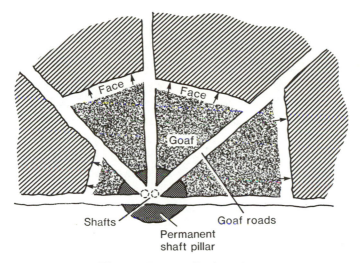

Fig. 4.9. Longwall advancing

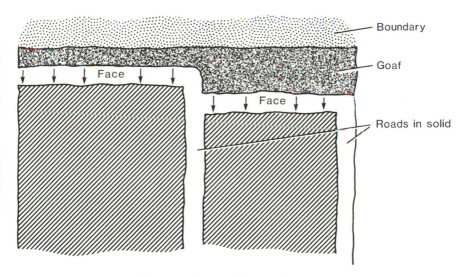

Fig. 4.10. Longwall retreating

continuing importance of working practices in affecting the cost of producing coal.

iii. Innovation at the face

The use of gunpowder to bring down coal and for blasting rock was well established before 1830, for wherever the coal was hard to hew, in conditions where ventilation was good and the risk of firedamp explosions sufficiently low, its effect was to raise productivity, to increase output, and reduce working costs—though at the expense of producing more small coal.[1] The invention of the first safety fuse by William Bickford in 1831 reduced the risks of ignition by the shot firer, but serious explosions caused by shots igniting firedamp continued to occur.[2] There was, however, no official attempt to prohibit the use of gunpowder. The difference in face productivity with and without gunpowder obviously varied greatly. In 1854 T. J. Taylor reckoned that gunpowder increased the output of hard coal by between 20 and 30 per cent, though under different circumstances the gain may have been minimal.[3] Supposing a gain of between 15 and 20 per cent to have been about average and that between 35 and 40 per cent of the underground work-force were hewers, the implication is an overall improvement in output by between 5 and 8 per cent. This is not, however, equivalent to a simple cost reduction, for the value of coal got by gunpowder was usually less because of the lower yield of round coal, which invalidates direct comparison. Further, despite Galloway's statement that 'gunpowder had come into use in all parts of the kingdom',[4] it should not be assumed that gunpowder was adopted widely in all regions, nor was its introduction necessarily permanent; the extent to which gunpowder was actually used before 1870 is highly problematical, for reasons other than the mere absence of relevant quantitative data. One is the effect of explosions, which, whether the direct consequence of shot-firing or not, induced caution among some managers and some miners. Viewers and Mines Inspectors advised against its use in fiery seams.[5] After the Oaks Colliery disaster in 1847, when seventy-three people died, the proprietors of Lundhill Colliery, also located in the Barnsley district,

---

[1] Galloway 1898, 485–6.
[2] Galloway 1904, 372.
[3] RC Accidents 1854, IX, Q 1094, T. J. Taylor's estimate.
[4] Galloway 1904, 372. Galloway's statement is based on Dunn, but from a passage in which he referred specifically to the North-east, where during the second quarter of the century blasting 'was fast being introduced'. Dunn 1844, 49.   [5] Ibid., 63.

reintroduced wedging instead of gunpowder. When in 1867 a new manager tried to revert to the use of gunpowder, the men struck—successfully—on grounds of safety and loss of earnings.[1] In 1863 Thomas Embleton, viewer for Wharncliffe Silkstone, advised the abandonment of shot-firing which he considered unsuitable in that area, drawing attention to the loss of life and capital resulting from a series of explosions in the Barnsley district.[2] At Seaton Delaval, economic reasons explain the rejection of gunpowder, for while there was no safety threat it had been prohibited because of the tendency to increase the proportion of small to large coal.[3]

How widespread were such limitations on the use of gunpowder, either in fiery mines for fear of explosion or in others in order to maximize large-coal production, we do not know. When legislation was introduced to improve the safety of shot-firing in 1884, only parts of South Wales and to a less extent Lancashire were expected to be seriously affected, as only in these areas were shots still used in the coal.[4] Even in Lancashire, the advocates of substituting longwall for alternative working methods and simultaneously dispensing with gunpowder, notably the Mines Inspector (and former colliery manager) Peter Higson, and John Warburton, manager at Dukinfield, began to secure movements in this direction from the 1860s.[5] Widespread agreement existed among mining engineers that among the reasons why, under suitable geological conditions, longwall was preferable to other forms of working was the higher yield of large coals and, related to this, the possibility of employing gravity to bring the coal down; the superincumbent weight of the strata squeezing the coal forward, which, following the removal of sprags or wedges, came away in good condition.[6] From an economic standpoint, therefore, the claim that longwall 'coupled with the adoption of explosives lifted productivity quite substantially at the coal face'[7] is misleading. Not only did this depend upon the ease or difficulty of holing or undermining the coal,[8] but even where the geological conditions were favourable the volume of output might have risen as a consequence of the use of gunpowder while the *value* of production fell.

[1] CG 27 July 1867, 76. [2] SCL NCB 1429/1/1113 24 Feb. 1863.
[3] NuRO 725/B20/273 Armstrong's Report.
[4] Galloway gives examples from Durham in 1850 and Derbyshire in 1857, Galloway 1904, 372.
[5] CG 19 May 1882, 739; Anderson, 'Blundell's Collieries; Technical Developments', 92.
[6] TMIME, II (1870–1), 29, XII (1882), 29, XIII, 29; CG 17 Nov. 1871, 511, 5 Apr. 1881, 547, 29 Apr. 1888, 656, 25 Nov. 1881, 863.
[7] A. R. Griffin 1977, 108. [8] Hyslop 1870, 292–305.

The progress of longwall mining, which accelerated from the mid-century, may be taken as a rough indirect indication of the decline in the use of gunpowder, which according to Emerson Bainbridge, writing in 1874, was by that time employed chiefly in the driving of headings and stone drifts and in removing the roof and floor of a seam.[1] Reinforcing this trend from the 1860s was the introduction of hydraulic wedging machines to break the coal, the expansion of the wedge by hydraulic pressure forcing the coal out and producing a lower proportion of small and waste. In the years before 1873 George Elliot had introduced several such machines into pits where blasting was dangerous. The extent to which the machines could be applied, however, depended on the difficulty of holing; in particularly hard coal holing still required gunpowder to loosen the coal.[2] The merit of the Haswell Mechanical Coal Getter, the success of which was reported to the Midland Institute of Mining Engineers in 1884, was that in addition to dispensing with gunpowder, these coals got by the mechanical wedge, though costing more labour per ton, were harder, more enduring, and greater by 17 per cent than could be got by pick and wedge, or by blasting.[3] Even in pits where shot-firing was not practised at all at the coal-face, however, gunpowder might continue to be used in stone drifting and in making roadways.

In 1879/80 two sources examined the state of blasting practice in some detail: a paper by W. Y. Craig,[4] and a set of reports made by the Mines Inspectors.[5] Both emphasized the enormous range of conditions, from those where gunpowder was unnecessary to those where its use was essential for profitable working, the principal determinant of which was the hardness of coal. Details were given of the extent of the use of gunpowder in the North-east (especially in the hard coal seams of Northumberland) where 43 per cent of production was got with explosives.[6] In that region, men often favoured using gunpowder to minimize physical effort, but the most important argument was the increase

[1] CG 20 Mar. 1874, 376.

[2] A. Lupton, 'The Use of Hydraulic Machines for Breaking Down Coal', TMIMCME 1869–70, 14–24; Coal Supply Commission 1871, XII, Committee C, QQ 1980–99; SC Dearness and Scarcity 1873, X, Q 7583–7; H. S. Walker, 'Elliott's Multiple Wedge', TNEIMME, 1885–6, X, 233–40.

[3] Robert Miller, 'The Haswell Mechanical Coal Getter', TMIME, IX (1884), 273–86.

[4] W. Y. Craig, 'Prohibition of Blasting in Coal Mines: its Effect on the Cost of Production', TNSIME 1879–80, IV, 53–9, 93–101, 179–91.

[5] Hobart House Library, 'Reports by Her Majesty's Inspectors of Mines on the Use of Gunpowder in Blasting in Mining' (unpublished, bound with 1880 Mineral Statistics).

[6] Ibid.; Reports of J. Willis and T. Bell.

in costs, from 6*d*. to 2*s*. per ton, which would result should it be banned.[1]

Between 1880 and 1913 a variety of new explosives were introduced; notably Bobbinite, an improved 'safety' gunpowder, and the gelignite/dynamite family of explosives designed by Nobel and others. Gelignite had five times the blasting power of gunpowder, dynamite three times, but all the patent explosives were more expensive, costing 3*d*. a ton (50 per cent) more for getting coal, though less for stonework.[2] The share of coal got by gunpowder compared with safety explosives was probably down to a quarter by 1913, though regional differences continued to be important; pits in the North-east and Scotland were the largest users.[3] The advent of safety explosives reduced the risk of explosion considerably after 1880, and the general reliance on shot-firing by the end of our period is plain; at less than 1*d*. per ton explosives were highly cost-effective and there could be no thought of banning their use; efforts were made to devise safer compounds. Only towards the very end of our period did the gradual adoption of mechanized coal cutting presage the decline in the use of explosives.[4]

For most of the century coal getting remained unaffected by mechanization, the hewer typically removing coal from the face with the aid of picks and wedges of various sorts, hammers, and shovels or forks to lift the coal into tubs. Tools, the shape of which varied regionally and with seam hardness, were made of wrought iron until that was gradually replaced by steel in the fifty years before 1913. By 1890 interchangeable steel picks were widely used, but even steel picks required sharpening—within a single shift if the coal was hard—hence the need for every colliery to employ a skilled pick-sharpener. The basic technique of hewing also changed little; the coal was undercut or 'kirved' at the bottom for a depth of up to a metre and brought down with picks, wedges, or explosives. Hand drills of various sorts were also devised over the century, particularly for shot-firing but also for applying wedges.[5] Similar tools and techniques were used in driving headings and roadways through rock, though after Stanley's heading machine was invented and first introduced at the inventor's Nuneaton Colliery in the 1880s, these, too, became widely used. However, effective use of these

---

[1] W. Y. Craig, 'Prohibition of Blasting in Coal Mines: its Effect on the Cost of Production', *TNSIME* 1879–80, IV, 53–101. [2] Kerr 1904, 69, 76.

[3] *Mineral Statistics* 1905 and 1913.

[4] *CG* 23 Sept. 1898, 561; *Coal Supplies Commission* 1903, XVI, Q 2710, W. E. Garforth.

[5] *CG* 19 Aug. 1890, 258; Hughes 1904, 38–48; Bulman and Redmayne 1906, 108–13.

machines was limited to very thick seams, where they doubled the speed of hand ripping.[1]

The obvious way to reduce the hewer's labour, improve productivity, and lower costs was to substitute some mechanical means of under-cutting the coal, which was by far the most arduous part of coal getting. The practicability of achieving this, however, awaited the introduction of compressed-air motors from 1849 (when the first-known instance of such an installation occurred at the Govan Colliery), though the wider application of compressed air followed the patent taken out by James Atkinson Longridge in 1856. Compressed air offered an effective supply of power underground, for it allowed transmission into a mine in any direction and for almost any distance; unlike in steam-power systems, heat, moisture, and condensation were non-existent. The absence of faulty joints eliminated much of the need for repair, which in any case was relatively simple in compressed-air systems, as was part replace-ment.[2] However, the relatively high cost of compressed air in com-parison with steam and the tendency to lose power over long distances ensured only a gradual transition from one to the other.

By the time compressed air was well established in the 1880s, compact and portable electric cutters of increasing reliability and efficiency began to offer competition, the first instance of electricity applied as motive power occurring in 1887.[3] Until shortly after 1900 the lack of an adequate power supply to carry long distances underground was partly overcome by the development of compressed-air technology, though the loss of power when negotiating bends continued to be a distinct drawback especially in working thin seams, for which compressed-air plant was too bulky and cumbersome for effective operation.[4] The increasing proportion of coal which came from thin seams and the con-tinued safety uncertainties associated with electrical power under-ground until 1904, when official clearance was given following a Home Office investigation,[5] explains why even in 1905 compressed air still powered one-half of the undercutting machines in operation.[6]

---

[1] G. Blake Walker, 'Coal Getting by Machinery', TFIME, 1889–90, I, 123–6; CG 15 Aug. 1890, 258; Kerr 1904, 12.

[2] Nicholas Wood, 'On the Conveyance of Coals Underground in Coal Mines', TNEIME, 1854–5, III, 239–318; John Warburton, 'Compressed Air as a Power for Underground Purposes', TMIME, 1871, III, 233, 328.

[3] Paull thesis, 57.

[4] R. Nelson Boyd, 'Collieries and Colliery Engineering', CG 10 Nov. 1893, 820.

[5] Coal Supplies Commission 1904, xxiv, Q 10921; Byatt 1979, 92.

[6] Mineral Statistics 1905.

The relatively slow advances made by compressed air during the third quarter of the century should not be allowed to conceal the importance of this invention in the history of mechanization, for the flexibility, in particular the underground portability, afforded by compressed air rendered possible the initial development of commercial coal cutters. This occurred with concentration upon the basic cutting principles; the percussive type, which consisted of picks and later chisels to imitate the action of a miner's hand; and the rotary, which actually undercut the coal, consisting of a motor and haulage unit in addition to a cutting tool.[1] Among the various types on offer the two which dominated undercutting technology were the disc cutters, consisting of a rigid circular plate with rotating cutters on the circumference; the chain machine operating as a coal saw; and the bar cutter, whose toothed, tapered rods rotated at right angles to the face. From the 1890s the new generation of chain cutters offered a strength and reliability comparable with disc machines, and the versatility of bar cutters. Even in 1913, however, 60 per cent of the total cutting machinery consisted of disc cutters.[2] Both bar and disc cutters worked on the principle of using moving teeth to cut away the bottom of the seam, or the rock below, to a depth of between 1 and 1.5 metres, preparatory to wedging, or blasting; the deeper the cut the better, which is why towards the end of the period the more robust endless chain cutter began to be favoured.[3]

There is a suggestion that the first commercial use of cutters occurred before 1850, but as a permanent phenomenon coal-cutting machinery emerged as commercially successful (though in only a handful of pits) from the 1860s.[4] The pioneer was probably the West Ardsley Coal Company at Bingley in west Yorkshire, the owner of which, W. S. Firth, installed a mechanical pick at the Balaclava Colliery in 1860. Other Yorkshire firms followed this example in the 1860s and 1870s, notably those managed by George Blake Walker—the Lidgett and Wharncliffe Silkstone collieries—where in 1863 rotary-cutting machines patented by Firth and Hurd were installed for experimentation.[5] In 1892 Wharncliffe

---

[1] See Pamely 1904, 966–96; D. Burns and G. L. Kerr 1904, 546–87. *The Modern Practice of Coal Mining* (London, 1908), especially Chapters VI and VII.

[2] *Mineral Statistics* 1913, 147–8.

[3] See Crankshaw, H. M. 'The History of Machine Mining', in Mining Association of Great Britain, *Historical Review of Coal Mining* (London, *c.* 1924), 64–81; Hughes 1904, 68–72.

[4] *CG* 16 Jan. 1874, 85; W. T. Embleton, 'On a Patent Self Acting Hydraulic Coal Cutting Machine', *TNEIME* 1864–5, XIV, 83–92.

[5] *CG* 10 May 1862, 361–70, 25 Oct. 1862, 335, 7 June 1862, 451, 22 Nov. 1862, 417, 6 Dec. 1862, 445, 6 Aug. 1869, 127; G. Blake Walker, 'Coal Getting by Machinery', *TFIME* 1898–90, I, 126.

Silkstone was described as the largest user of coal-cutting machines in England.[1]

The other major innovator was Baird, the large Scottish iron and coal producer, whose experiments with a mechanical pick in 1864 led to the development of the Gartsherrie machine (a medal winner at the Philadelphia Exhibition in 1876).[2] Of the endless chain cutter variety, this was the first machine to have incorporated cutters proper (rather than modified pick-teeth) with a self-hauling action and a movable jib.[3]

The reasons why the advance of mechanical cutting was slow during this early phase of innovation seem to be neither a lack of interest by the various professional associations, nor inadequate communication of technical developments through the trade journals. Beginning in 1865, competitions were arranged and prizes were offered for machines which could cut coal successfully, but such efforts were virtually ignored by coalowners, and attracted the interest of very few engineers or inventors.[4] After the 1870s boom the interest in machine cutters appears to have declined, exemplified by the Baird's eventual abandonment of chain-cutting machines in the course of a labour dispute beginning in 1894. Nearly twenty years were to pass before similar machinery was reintroduced at Gartsherrie.[5]

The first reliable statistics of coal-cutting machinery refer to 1902, and are presented in Table 4.1. Only 426 of these were undercutting machines, the remainder consisting of portable drills and heading drivers: more than 90 per cent of the former were disc type. About one-third of the true coal cutters were electrically powered. In total 4.16 million tons of coal were mechanically cut, rising to 24.6 million tons by 1913. A total of 2,897 machines were recorded then, but if again we discount hand drills the number falls to 2,035 undercutting machines. Of these, 64 per cent were electrically driven, and 740 were powered by compressed air; 61 per cent were disc machines. The output of longwall undercut coal, therefore, was probably about 22.5 million tons, or 7.8 per cent of total output. The limited application of coal-cutting machinery is revealed in Table 4.1, and equally striking is the regional disparity in the distribution of machine-cut coal in 1913; the overall UK figure was 8.6 per cent, whereas in Scotland 22 per cent of the region's output was cut by machines, exceeding the pro-

[1] SCL Wharncliffe Silkstone NCB 1429/1 DM 16 Jan. 1863.
[2] CG 11 Mar. 1892, 463.
[3] Corrins thesis, 235–8, 242.
[4] CG 22 Mar. 1872, 303–17, 8 Nov. 1872, 513–26, 16 Jan. 1874, 85.
[5] Corrins thesis, 242.

Table 4.1. *Coal-face mechanization, by region, 1913*

	Number of mines with coal cutters	Number of undercutting machines	Power sources (percentages)		No. of percussive machines	Total no. of machines	Output per machine ('000 tons)	Percentage of region's output	No. of face conveyors	Percentage output from seams less than 3 ft wide
			electricity	compressed air						
Scotland	288	832	83	17	44	876	10.7	22.0	125	38.3
Northern	89	223	59	41	442	665	5.3	6.0	58	28.0
Lancs./N. Wales	106	186	19	81	207	393	5.4	7.7	27	18.9
Yorks./E. Midlands	164	602	55	45	71	673	11.3	10.4	86	12.5[a]
W. Midlands/South	48	96	73	27	79	175	7.5	4.6	2	3.4
South Wales	41	96	38	62	19	115	5.6	1.1	61	13.3
GB total	736	2,035	64	36	862	2,897	8.5	8.6	359	18.1

[a] West Yorkshire alone, 27.7 per cent.

Sources: 1913 *Mineral Statistics*, p. 148; *Samuel Commission*, III, 184–7.

portion in any other region. Why, even by 1913, had the diffusion of cutting technology proceeded so slowly, and how are the disparate regional patterns to be explained?

Both the Eight Hours Committee and a report drawn up by the North of England Institute of Mining Engineers contained instances of increases in output per man shift resulting from face mechanization by as much as 65 per cent—but only obtained under certain optimal conditions.[1] An important pre-condition for effective coal cutting included a fairly strong roof and a level floor which left a parting about 8 centimetres below the coal (identical circumstances required for the introduction of longwall working—which was another necessary condition for cutting machinery), and a space of about 1.2 metres between the props and the face to allow machine manœuvrability.[2] Long faces were important because they reduced the need to shift the machine to a new starting position after traversing a face, and maximized continuous cutting. Under favourable conditions, by 1900 machines were able to cut perhaps two or three times faster compared with hand hewing. Needing fewer openings and roadways, such a system of mechanized longwall working reduced deadwork and maintenance requirements and some of the haulage labour and stonemen associated with these tasks, though the manhandling and maintenance of machinery also required labour. In mines characterized by weak roofs, close timbering, steeply inclined seams, heavily faulted and uncrushed coal, getting machinery of any kind had little to offer in competition with hand hewing, for example in South Wales. Similarly in south Yorkshire, where the cleat, or breakage line, in the coal was so well defined that it broke away easily under roof pressure and came down with little effort, coal cutters were completely unsuitable. Neither pillar and stall nor stepped longwall offered suitable conditions for undercutting by machine for, apart from the need for space to manœuvre the machinery, considerable extra weight and faster cutting speed required long faces for efficient operation. Difficulties over mechanization thus arose out of both practical and economic considerations.[3]

Short faces and pillar and stall systems favoured the use of portable,

[1] *Eight Hours Committee*, QQ 874–921, 1142, 2750, 654, 1031, 1075, 5620, 6257; 'Report of Committee upon Mechanical Coal Cutting', *TFIME* 1903, XXVI; Paull thesis, 151.

[2] See the detailed discussion by a pioneer in the use of cutting machinery, G. Blake Walker, 'Coal Getting by Machinery', *TFIME* 1889–90, I, 74–5; *CG* 25 Jan. 1901, 182.

[3] *RC Coal Supplies* 1903, XVI, QQ 874–921; *Samuel Commission* III, 184–7; Burns and Kerr 1904, 508–11; Paull thesis, 166–7.

wheeled or hand-held, percussive drills worked by compressed air, which were used mainly for pillar working in the North-east, and in north Staffordshire and Warwickshire where steeply sloping seams rendered cutting difficult otherwise. Where the coal was soft, however, cutting costs were unlikely to be less compared with hand hewing, for machinery tended to become clogged and in South Wales actually became buried.[1] Under certain conditions, therefore, percussive machines might be economic, but their significance in the context of technical development in the industry as a whole is considerably less than the progress of other types of machine. Possessing an annual output capacity of 2,500 tons, compared with the 11,000 tons of a disc machine,[2] it is important to draw a distinction, rarely made in recent commentaries on mechanization, between the two types of 'machine' so different in scale and commercial implications.

Inventor Frank Hurd, of Firth & Hurd, claimed that coal-cutting machinery had become reliable even by the 1870s;[3] but without questioning his objectivity, this opinion needs to be seen in the context of a characteristic of coal-cutting machinery throughout the nineteenth century—the critical importance of adapting machines to suit local colliery conditions. It is significant that several of the pioneering innovators, coalowners or managers, were partly involved in the invention or modification process, and that in those instances which have come to light where the machinery was not in part adapted by colliery engineers, visiting engineers were necessary to set up the machines and to advise during the experimental stage, even where conditions for machinery were favourable. This was the case at the collieries of Baird and of Wharncliffe Silkstone, where the experimental period was about ten years, and much later at Radford Colliery in Nottinghamshire, where from the manager's initial inquiry made in 1878 cutting machinery of one make or another was in experimental use for nearly twenty years—perhaps an extreme example of cautious experimentation.[4]

Machine makers were sometimes criticized by mining engineers for a

[1] *Samuel Commission* I, 331–69; Kerr 1904, 96; Pamely 1904, 946–9; Burns and Kerr 1904, 509–14.

[2] *RC Coal Supplies* 1903, XVI, especially QQ 874–921 and 1031, 1075, 5620 and 6253; Paull thesis, 62–5.

[3] Frank Hurd, 'Electrical Coal Cutting Machines', *TFIME* 1902–3, XXV, 108–10.

[4] Corrins thesis, 235–6; SCL NCB 1429/1 MB numerous entries 1863–72; NoRO NCB, MB 1878, 29 Oct. 1907. Lancashire collieries were supplied with patent coal-cutting machinery by J. S. Walker, a Wigan engineer. *CG* 30 Dec. 1870, 722. The Nottinghamshire specialist was Manlove and Alliott.

lack of preparation and research into which kind of machine suited the particular requirements of collieries and mines,[1] though practical experimentation did yield technical improvements, notably affecting gearing and cutter design; after 1900 the substitution of skids and enclosed motors for rails promoted both efficiency and safety, as did the introduction of wheeled transport for machinery at the face.[2]

The uncertainty surrounding the technical operation of coal-cutting machinery was accompanied by considerable economic risk, for when the cost of supporting equipment, air-compressing machinery, air pipes, and engines were added to the cost of cutters and to maintenance costs, several thousand pounds were required for initial outlay on a small plant with seven machines in operation. George Blake Walker, Wharncliffe Silkstone's manager, calculated that in order to cover capital costs, from which he excluded such investment as might be necessary to alter the faces, roadways, supports, and so on to accommodate the machines for optimal performance (which another expert reckoned could add ten times the cost of cutting machines), he would need a figure of between 11 and 15 per cent saving on getting costs; in a similar calculation he carried out in 1900 the figure had become 23 per cent.[3] Walker's reports on his practical, but also experimental and systematic, experience of machinery are invaluable in elucidating those factors which rendered savings of those orders of magnitude difficult to obtain (or widely considered to have been unattainable). These were human as well as geotechnical, though on the latter he was most unequivocal: 'as the seam decreases in thickness the cost of production necessarily increases, as will the relative advantage of mechanization'.[4]

Apart from the limits geology imposed on the technical capabilities of machines, until 1900, at least, their efficient operation required optimal labour organization and supervision. Walker explained that machine work tended to regularize output because

the machines must be kept going and it will not be permitted that they shall be hindered by coals not being filled out. Thus, men who are in the habit of losing time will be got rid of. The system will be modified to some extent. Probably one leading man will have three or four times the usual length of face, and

---

[1] M. Millington, *TFIME* 1902, XXV, 3; *Coal Supplies Commission* 1903, XVI, 35, 45.

[2] Paull thesis, 295; 'Report of Committee upon Mechanical Coal Cutting', *TFIME* 1903, XXVI, 23.

[3] G. Blake Walker, 'Coal Getting by Machinery', *TMIME* 1885, X, 73–80.

[4] Ibid., 80.

employ a number of fillers who can be concentrated in force at any desired point so as to get the coal filled out rapidly. The faces will move forward at a great rate, and the breakage of timber will be less. The tendency of the roof will be to break more regularly and there will be less tendency of [sic] the places to fill in.[1]

Nearly thirty years later, Frank Hurd also stressed the importance of close supervision when cutting machinery was introduced, as well as emphasizing the need for coalowners to motivate managers in ensuring effective organization.[2]

Working miners, too, faced novel face technology with apprehension, but contemporaries remarked that normally this could be overcome by adjusting payment.[3] Archival evidence seems to support this view, and suggests that the occasional condemnation of miners' hostility by the editor of the Colliery Guardian seems to have been a misjudgement.[4] It was certainly not consistent with the observation made in the report of the Coal Conservation Committee of 1918: 'Reference is sometimes made to the hostility of labour to changes in methods of mining and more particularly to the use of mechanical appliances underground. We do not regard this impression as well founded.'[5]

The introduction of machinery usually involved negotiations over wage rates and did produce friction and resistance in some instances, but Mammett's wide experience of these matters in his capacity as a viewer in Yorkshire and the Midlands during the later nineteenth century led him to advise Staveley's managers, then experiencing difficulty, that 'This is commonly the case when machine work is introduced but no doubt in time the difficulties will disappear with perseverance'; and they did.[6] Elsewhere, W. E. Garforth noted that he had detected opposition from some mining officials who found themselves with additional workloads as a result of machine breakdowns, while managers often objected to the extra supervision which machine mining required. He thought that prejudices against machinery were beginning to disappear by 1900,[7] but in evidence to the Coal Supply Commission in 1903–5

[1] Ibid.

[2] Frank Hurd, 'Electrical Coal Cutting Machines', TFIME 1902–3, XXV, 110.

[3] G. B. Walker, 'Coal Getting by Machinery', MIME 1885, X, 74; RC Coal Supplies 1903, XVI, 125; Paull thesis, 155.

[4] CG 10 Sept. 1897, 480;. NoRO Wollaton Colliery, DM 15 Sept. 1903; WaRO Griff Colliery Co., Sept. 1897, Sept. 1907; BSCEMRRC 2034/3/9d 16 Dec. 1895 Mammett's Report.

[5] Coal Conservation Committee 1918, VII, 62.

[6] BSCEMRRC Stanton and Staveley 2034/3/9d 16 Dec. 1895 Mammett's Report.

[7] CG 10 Sept. 1897, 480.

coalowners and managers were criticized for their conservative approach to mechanization, even by the Mines Inspector for east Scotland where cutting machinery found the most receptive response: 'there is a sort of *vis inertiae* that you have to overcome at a great many collieries before you can get any new system introduced'.[1]

There is evidence to suggest that beneath the prejudice there were often sound reasons for conservatism—even disregarding the uncertainty of the technology—unless the correct geological conditions existed and unless suitable mining methods were in operation so as to maximize the advantages and justify investment. In 1896, J. Morrison, manager of Cramlington Colliery in Northumberland, warned those of his fellow mining engineers then contemplating the introduction of coal-cutting machinery that, while there was no difficulty in working the machinery, too often 'the subsequent labour of following the machine, getting out the coal and attending to the workplace and keeping the face in a fit condition had generally been found a source of greater difficulty and cost than was expected when the machines were introduced'.[2] R. F. Spence, of Backworth Colliery, declared that in his experience the profitability of machine cutting depended upon how much the way on which the machine ran required laying, for the thrust of the machines was often so great that each sleeper had to be 'stayed' and the way very carefully prepared and laid.[3]

Given all these reservations and the limited progress of mechanization, why did the substitution of cutting machines for hand labour commend itself at all to the innovators? And why did diffusion begin to accelerate after 1900? Wharncliffe Silkstone's first experiment began in 1863 shortly after a labour dispute, which, however, was unrelated to wages and working practices.[4] More pertinent is the difficulty this new colliery was facing in the thin seams, for the proportion of small coal and 'smudge' increased as output expanded. One result was a decision to close one of the thin seams, though an imminent rise in rent which threatened the firm's profitability underlined the vulnerability of colliery enterprise unless coal of sufficient size and quality could be offered on the market. These were the circumstances in which in 1863 mechanized picks were introduced. While that decision was taken at the begin-

---

[1] *RC Coal Supplies* 1903, XXIII, QQ 670, 1077; S. F. Walker 1902, 138.

[2] *TNEIMME* 1896–7, XLVI, 74–5.

[3] Discussion of G. Blake Walker, 'Coal Getting by Machinery', *TMIME* 1885–6, XI, 179.

[4] SCL Wharncliffe Silkstone NCB 1429/1 MB 15 Apr. 1858, 28 Jan. 1859, 25 Apr. 1859, 23 Apr. 1863.

ning of a boom there is no evidence that labour shortage was an important consideration.[1] The adoption of coal-cutting machinery at High Royds Colliery in south Yorkshire coincided with a strike in 1864, as did that at the Oaks Colliery, but the success of mechanization here is not known.[2] The same is true of the machine, described in the *Colliery Guardian*'s report in 1865, at Kippax Colliery, near Leeds, where a 'self acting hydraulic coal cutter' had been in successful operation for several months, saving $2\frac{1}{2}d$. per ton over hand labour.[3] The beginning of permanent coal-cutting operations at Wharncliffe Silkstone also dated from 1872, as a result of a decision to raise the output of the Park Gate thin seam by at least 20 per cent, and while at that time the scarcity of labour was acute, as in all coalmining regions, it is significant that the Directors' Minutes contain references not only to the improved speed of the machine enabling a rapid expansion of supply to an over-heated market, but also to the greater size of the coals, which meant effectively more large coal for sale at higher prices.[4] The Baird's initial experiments with machinery beginning in 1864, according to his machinery suppliers, were the consequence of 'endless strikes and complications with labour',[5] though this is the only evidence to this effect.

Labour shortage seems to be an obvious reason to explain the heightened interest in cutting machinery in 1872; then the demand for coal was so great that so long as the coal could be cut and supplied quality was a secondary consideration. Furthermore, wage rates increased so enormously that, even though prices rose faster the illusion of high wages may have stimulated interest in cost-cutting machinery, in spite of the magnitude of the savings at that time being either unknown or uncertain.[6] The 1870s boom also marked the introduction of cutting machinery at the Wigan Coal and Iron Company's pits.[7] Twenty years later, again in periods of high demand and scarce labour, and in particular when hewers were unwilling to work in difficult thin seams except at what seemed to managers to be excessive rates, machine cutters were adopted by Garforth at the pits of Pope and Pearson, and at those collieries with whom Emerson Bainbridge was connected.[8]

As labour cost accounted for the major proportion of total costs, it is

[1] Ibid., 27 Nov. 1862, 16 June 1863, 17 Dec. 1863.
[2] Machin 1958, 338; *CG* 14 Jan. 1865, 27.
[3] *CG* 15 May 1865, 341.
[4] SCL Wharncliffe Silkstone, NCB 1429/1 DM 30 Mar. 1872, 3 Oct. 1873, 11 Apr. 1874.
[5] *CG* 28 Feb. 1873, 243.   [6] Corrins thesis, 235–8.
[7] *SC Dearness and Scarcity* 1873, X, Q 1173.
[8] *CG* 10 Sept. 1897, 480, 23 Sept. 1898, 561.

hardly surprising that labour saving was a major consideration, though geological factors were critical. Caleb Pameley, author of the *Colliery Manager's Handbook*, regarded the threshold above which machine cutting could yield economic results to have been 2 shillings per ton for hand cutting, noting, however, that figures above that were exceptional. For collieries whose survival depended upon working thinner seams— which almost inevitably meant higher hand-labour costs—mechanization offered some hope so long as other conditions were suitable.[1] This explains the interest shown in coal cutters by Consett, Ashington, Pease and Partners, and Staveley around 1900, and at Briggs in west Yorkshire, and Pope and Pearson,[2] where the Stanley Main Seam was approaching exhaustion after forty-five years of continuous working.[3] W. E. Garforth, colliery manager of Pope and Pearson, explained the logic of introducing cutting machines at the new hard, thin seam discovered in 1890: 'Without higher productivity in thin seams we cannot compete with the thick seams of South Yorkshire',[4] though failure to agree new tonnage prices with the miners for hand cutting had also been a consideration. Perhaps the most remarkable illustration of how a heterogeneous mixture of working methods and machinery reflected differing geological conditions in seams worked by a single enterprise is provided in a report on Ashington Colliery in 1912.[5] Of seven seams differing in depth from 44 to 163 metres and varying in seam thickness from an average of 0.75 metres to between 1.2 and 2 metres, four were worked by the bord-and-pillar method, two mainly by longwall, and the remainder by a mixture of both. Machines were in operation in both of the Yard and Bensham thin-seam longwall workings, and also, curiously, in the High Main thicker seam worked by pillar and stall. As the directors had resolved several years earlier that a switch from hand to machine cutting should take place wherever possible, the factors which explain the heterogeneity relate to physical or geological constraints that rendered hand working relatively uneconomic.

The history of Ashington's eclectic conversion to mechanization is particularly instructive, because when in 1895 the Yard seam, the only

[1] Pamely 1904, 946.

[2] A. S. Wilson thesis, 150–8; NCB/AS/18/1; ZMD/54/2–5; NCB/AS/23; BSCEMRRC 2034/27 MB 26 May 1893, 21 July 1893, 27 Dec. 1894, 16 Dec. 1895, 26 June 1897.

[3] LCA 1708/15, 'Down Among the Coals'; Bro SC ME 160, MB 7 July, 1 Aug. 1889, Directors' Report 1904; CG 10 Sept. 1897, 480, 23 Sept. 1898, 561.

[4] CG 10 Sept. 1897, 480.

[5] NuRO NCB AS/18/1.

seam to produce house coal, became the first to be so affected, the Directors' Minutes recorded that the object was 'chiefly of improving and increasing the produce of large coals',[1] a response to complaints received from customers concerning the quality (by which was meant size) of export coals. Subsequently, similar complaints met with the same response, and by 1912 some 50 per cent of Ashington's coal output of 2 million tons was cut by machines.[2] The Fife Coal Company was another major exporter which by 1913 relied heavily on electrically operated coal cutters.[3]

The cost savings from machine cutting were reckoned to be less important than the increased yield of large coal and the extraction of more coal from a given area. Walker's experiments in 1885 had resulted in savings on hand labour of between 2s. 8d. and 4s. 6d. in hard, thin seams of up to a metre, whereas saving in the yield of coal was between 8s. 8d. and 10s. 5d.[4] Similar results were obtained at Wharncliffe Silkstone in 1892, though in the 0.5 metre seam the increase in coal yield was 8s. 5d., compared with 9s. 8d. saving on hand labour.[5] These point to the greater importance of a reduction in slack which cutters could offer in all but the thinnest of the thin seams where cutters were at all economic—below 1.2 metres. Taken together, the savings implied in Walker's experiments (under optimal conditions) represent between 15 and 20 per cent of total working costs in very thin, hard seams, though less as a proportion of total costs and less in thicker and softer seams. This was also the conclusion of a survey carried out by the NEIME in 1903.[6]

The importance of market considerations as a principal motive for mechanizing cutting, though within geological constraints, was not new. In 1873, George Elliot explained that his own experiments since the 1850s had been carried out with an eye to profitability and prices: 'The great principle of the coal cutting machine was not so much to economize or cheapen the get of the coal as it was to get a large yield of what we call large merchantable coal'.[7] Even though the price ratio of small to large 'merchantable coal' altered after the boom, diminishing the relative difference, the motive to secure large coal remained the most

---

[1] Ibid.
[2] NuRO Ashington ZMD/54/2–5; NCB/AS/23.
[3] Muir 1952, 14–17.
[4] G. Blake Walker, 'Coal Getting by Machinery', *TMIME* 1885–6, X, 80.
[5] *CG* 11 Mar. 1892, 463.
[6] 'Report of the Committee upon Mechanical Coal Cutting', *TFIME* 1903–4, XXVI, 141–6.
[7] *SC Dearness and Scarcity* 1873, X, Q 7582.

frequently quoted even after 1873. For actual operating conditions could eliminate the cost savings otherwise possible only under optimal experimental arrangements. This was the view, based on practical experience, of leading mining engineers and viewers, Lindsay Wood in the North-east, and Emerson Bainbridge, who was knowledgeable of conditions in Yorkshire and the East Midlands.[1] In 1903, W. E. Garforth, Pope and Pearson's colliery manager and inventor of the diamond-disc coal cutter, who possessed nearly thirty years' experience of mechanization, illustrated the commercial significance of coal cutting for market considerations. He described the getting of two lots of one thousand tons in the same colliery, from the same face and under identical conditions—except that one batch was cut by machine and the other by hand; in the market the difference was 7d. per ton in favour of machine-cut coal.[2]

The reasons why the pace of mechanization at the face accelerated during the early years of the twentieth century are sufficiently important to deserve separate treatment,[3] but before doing so it is interesting to consider the extent to which the relatively slow progress of coal-cutting machinery before 1913 has been exaggerated, and at the same time accorded undue attention. First, in 1913 only 3 per cent of coal exceeding 1.2 metres was machine cut,[4] which tends to corroborate the opinions of contemporary observers concerning the economics of machine mining, and suggests that we may deduce that probably 40 per cent of all coal being produced at that time was unsuitable for machine cutting. Second, irrespective of seam thickness almost all coal produced in South Wales was too soft to be won by the technology available in 1913.[1] After allowing for one-third of this originating from seams under 1.2 metres, we may add a further 6 per cent of national output as unable to sustain machine cutting. Soft seams elsewhere added perhaps a further one per cent to raise the share of the national total below the critical thickness too soft for mechanized cutters to 10 per cent. The existence of steep seams, frequent flaws, poor roofs, and uneven floors in seams not already included in our schematic survey might justify defining an extra 5 to 10 per cent of coal production as completely unsuitable for mechanized cutting under prevailing technology. Another unquantifiable proportion of production came from collieries with a short life which rendered it

---

[1] *TNEIMME* 1876, XXV, 197; *CG* 15 May 1890, 258.
[2] *RC Coal Supplies* 1903, XVI, A 2711 W. E. Garforth.
[3] See below.
[4] *Mineral Statistics* 1913; *Samuel Commission* III, Appendix 18:10.
[5] *RC Coal Supplies* 1903, XVI, QQ 4170, 4401, 8260.

uneconomic to introduce cutters, either because their capital cost would not be amortized in time or because it would be too expensive or difficult to rearrange existing workings. The latter applied particularly to mines not working longwall, although most of these were to be found in thicker seams. In total, perhaps a further 5 to 10 per cent of coal production was, or was perceived to be, too difficult to adapt, or came from mines lacking sufficient reserves to justify capital expenditure, notably in Staffordshire and the South-west.

Because of the high capital costs involved, virtually no mines raising fewer than 20,000 tons a year, and most with double that output, could make coal cutters pay. The smallest mine where coal cutters were in use was in Scotland and employed only sixty-four men (fifty-two underground), consistent with an output of about 20,000 tons and two machines. The mean of all collieries was 905 men, while for mechanized getting the figure was 465.[1] Amounting to perhaps 5 per cent, mines below this size were responsible for a tiny percentage of the output and most will have been included among the thick-seam mines, but another couple of percentage points may be deducted for small mines. Within the total of between 62 and 72 per cent of coal which essentially for geotechnical reasons may be described as unsuitable for mechanized cutting, was that proportion of coal, 14 per cent, consumed in carbonization (for which quality considerations were unimportant), principally in Durham and south Yorkshire.[2] Our schematic analysis suggests that only between one-quarter and one-third of coal mined in 1913 was geologically suitable for mechanized cutting, which places the 8.6 per cent mined in this way in 1913 into a different perspective from that which assumes that 100 per cent of coal could have been cut by machinery. None the less, the diffusion of machine cutting still appears to have been a protracted process. Within the 25 to 33 per cent of coal which theoretically could have been cut economically by machinery but which was not, why did entrepreneurs delay? A. J. Taylor has interpreted this as evidence of entrepreneurial failure, implying elements of irrationality or ineptitude in the decisions of business leaders from the late nineteenth century.[3] Our research supports the findings of Greasley's recent examination of the problem in the period 1902 to 1938, which stressed the essential rationality of technical choice.[4]

[1] *Samuel Commission* III, Appendix 18:10; *List of Mines* 1913.

[2] Calculated from *Mineral Statistics* and *Coal Conservation Committee* 1918, VII, 693.

[3] Taylor 1961, 86; Taylor 1968, 69; Neil Buxton, 'Entrepreneurial Efficiency in the British Coal Industry Between the Wars', *EHR*, 2nd Series, XXIII (1907). Buxton qualified this view in 1978, 112–15.   [4] Greasley 1982, 247–68.

By ignoring the progress of electrification, however, the reasons for it, and the induced innovation associated with it before 1913, Greasley's otherwise convincing analysis of the diffusion of machine cutting in the twentieth century disregards a key factor in this process, which is of particular importance for an analysis of the earliest stages of diffusion. Although compressed air had rendered mechanical coal cutting possible, transmission below ground was difficult and not always satisfactory. Perceptions of fire risk made electricity unpopular with colliery managers and Mines Inspectors before 1904, for cable faults were common during the early years of electricity.[1] Nevertheless, by 1913, 62 per cent of electrical horsepower in mines was underground.[2]

Electricity was first used successfully for lighting purposes in collieries in 1878, and on a small scale for pumping in 1881; two years later, the first electric haulage gear was installed at Mostell Colliery in west Yorkshire.[3] The firm of Henry Briggs and Sons introduced a powerful electrically operated pump at the St John's Colliery, Normanton, in 1887, at the same time that a small Parsons turbine was installed to drive a lighting generator.[4] Except for lighting and pumping, however, electrification in general was slow. The explanation for the continuing lead in power transmission established by compressed air was the use of the inferior direct current (DC) system, which had high transmission losses and was inflexible, added to which was the real danger of explosions caused by sparks. After about 1895, however, the large firms began to switch to alternating current (AC), which with the aid of transformers made it possible to use varying voltages to suit different tasks and involved very low transmission losses because of the high voltages possible. Well-shielded AC motors and light armoured cables produced no sparks, removing the danger from electric motors regardless of their location within the colliery.[5]

In this period, too, the advantage of centralizing power production increased, especially for collieries which installed by-product or gas-recovery coke ovens and/or exhaust-steam turbines fed from high-pressure steam-winding engines, arrangements which ensured a supply of cheap fuel for dynamos. The price of small coal relative to large

---

[1] Byatt 1979, 92.
[2] Ibid.
[3] LCA 1708/12 'West Yorkshire Coalfield', 24.
[4] *CG* 5 Sept. 1890, 370.
[5] Lupton, Parr, and Perkins, *Electricity as Applied to Mining*, iii, 157–8; Kerr 1904, 105–11.

increased significantly from 1900 onwards, further stimulating the construction of centralized plant with high fuel economy, to maximize saleable output and increase profitability. A centralized power plant might use 12–20 pounds of (cheaper) steam per hour, as against 80 pounds for direct-steam plant. Even if total losses in transmission and electric motor reached 50 per cent, fuel cost was still reduced by half to two-thirds.[1] The introduction of such a system also permitted, indeed encouraged, the reorganization of other aspects of colliery plant, such as pumping, winding, haulage, and the employment of coal cutters.

The progress of electrification was unspectacular at first. Although most large collieries, and almost all new ones, used electricity for surface and pit-bottom lighting in the early 1900s, few used it for power generation. The 1907 Census of Production records 11,809 kW of steam-driven dynamos in all mines, which at 90 per cent conversion gives 166,500 horsepower, or less than 7 per cent of total mining power plant.[2] By January 1913, electric horsepower at collieries had risen to over 628,000 in 1,471 mines; nearly 50 per cent of all mines were using electricity, which accounted for about one-quarter of the total power of all kinds employed in coal mines (Table 4.2).

The regional distribution was uneven, South Wales using nearly 3,200 hp per million tons (and recording the greatest average power per mine), Scotland over 2,800 hp, but Lancashire a mere 110 hp per million tons; the national average was 2,185 hp per million tons, or 427 hp per mine; relatively few mines used large amounts of power in the North-east. Sectoral distribution was also uneven, with most electric power applied to haulage (25 per cent of electric horsepower) and pumping (45 per cent) underground, notably in South Wales and Scotland. Surface uses were also unevenly spread, South Wales using many electric winders, Yorkshire a good deal for coal preparation.[3] Electricity clearly made dramatic progress in coal mining in the period immediately before the war, and was undoubtedly a major new development; much more significant at that time than mechanization of cutting, the progress of which was to be influenced very much by electrification between 1909 and 1914. In 1913 two-thirds of all machine cutters were powered by electricity (Table 4.1).

The coal industry has been criticized for the tardy application of electricity. The fear of danger expressed by colliery managers when

---

[1] Arnold Lupton, G. D. A. Parr, and H. Perkins, *Electricity as Applied to Mining* (London, 1906), 153–71; George M. Harvey, *Colliery Electrical Engineering* (London, 1928), 8–24.
[2] *First Census*, 16.   [3] *Inspectors' Reports* 1913; Byatt 1979, 92.

Table 4.2. *Electricity in coalmines, 1913*[a]

	Number of mines using electricity	Horsepower			Mines	Millions to output
		Surface	Underground	Total		
Scotland	319	26,279	93,361	19,640	375	2,818
North-east	272	64,837	79,422	144,259	530	2,459
Lancashire and Cheshire and North Wales	320	55,955	51,245	107,200	335	1,469
West Midlands and South-west	132	9,141	35,294	44,435	337	1,571
South Wales	294	90,581	91,237	181,818	618	3,199
Total	1,471	256,676	371,422	628,098	427	2,185

[a] All mines under Regulation Act.
Source: 1913 *Inspectors' Reports.*

opposing electrification has been regarded by a historian of the electrical industry as evidence to support the contemporary view that colliery managers possessed only sufficient technical expertise to enable them to resist innovation. Coalowners, too, have been condemned for a lack of interest in electric power.[1] Several factors suggest that although, no doubt, conservatism and lack of understanding or expertise existed among decision-makers at the collieries caution was fully justified, at least before 1904 which marked the turning point in colliery electrification.

Byatt estimated the capital costs of electric transmission systems per unit of prime moving capacity to have fallen below alternative sources only after 1905; that until then fuel-saving was insignificant in comparison with best mechanical practice. He also described the passive attitude of electrical engineers towards the special needs of the coal industry. They neglected the development of motors for coal cutters; not until 1903 was a three-phase motor available, bringing about an important improvement in safety.[2] In 1904 a report of a Home Office Departmental Committee's investigation into the safety of electricity provided official approval, so removing safety reservations as a deterrent to electrification.[3] From 145 electric coal cutters in use in 1902 the number rose to perhaps 2,000 by 1912.[4] Thus, only after 1904, when the economic upswing began and coal demand and wage costs rose, could colliery owners turn to a novel, superior, and safe source of power; relative backwardness in the electrical industry retarded progress in the coal industry. None the less, the Committee had revealed a considerable amount of ignorance within the latter concerning the skills and knowledge necessary to take charge of electric coal cutters; some thought an electrician was required, others a pitman.[5] For example, Matthew Habershon, manager of the Newton Chambers collieries, attached little importance to the need for electrical knowledge: 'all he has to do is to switch on and off and stop if he finds anything wrong'.[6] T. Y. Greener, however, general manager of Pease and Partners, expressed his preference for a combination of fitting and electrical skills. Not until 1909 was an Electrical Inspector of Mines appointed to monitor colliery practice.[7]

For many years the comparative cost advantage of electricity over steam did not seem to be so great as to compel coalowners to discard

[1] Byatt thesis, 301, 298.
[2] Byatt 1979, 92, fn. 59.　　　　[3] Ibid., 93.　　　　　　　　[4] Ibid.
[5] Calvert thesis, 102.　　　　　[6] Ibid., 102.　　　　　　[7] Ibid., 107, 139.

one for the other. Consulting engineer Henry Armstrong gave different advice on this, depending upon the particular plant and working conditions.[1] Even at the sinking of Ellington Colliery in 1910 a comparison of electric and steam power for winding (though not for haulage, pumping, and ventilation, for which electricity was already used) led to the conclusion that electricity would be more expensive to install and to run.[2] In the case of isolated collieries the capital needed to build an independent power supply could deter. The directors of Cannock Chase Colliery in north Staffordshire, for example, distant from the industrial Midlands, spent £21,259 on a station and transmission lines which were expected to be self-financing within six years. Sopwith reckoned that his colliery's electricity unit costs were actually lower than a commercial quotation for the erection of a power station to supply Cannock Chase, an offer conditional upon a guaranteed level of demand from every colliery in the district.[3] In this instance the resources and future prospects of a successful company were sufficient to encourage and enable independent initiative to be taken, but what we know of the median colliery size and the variability of operating conditions between collieries suggests that both the structure and organization of the industry probably reinforced the retarding influence of the electrical industry. Conservatism seemed to be justified before 1904 when electrification presented a safety hazard, while even after 1904 savings from innovation seemed to be at best uncertain and less than dramatic.

Evidence from archival sources suggests that the age and layout of a colliery were important influences on face mechanization, and that when a programme of new pit-sinking or reorganization was either in progress or under consideration—especially if it included electrification—experiments with machine cutting were encouraged, which as a consequence could be conducted at moderate marginal cost.[4] There are several examples of such a sequence after 1900: at the collieries of the Lochgelly Iron and Coal Company, Barber, Walker and Co., the Fife Coal Company, Powell Duffryn, Wollaton Colliery Company, the Ashington Coal Company, and the Cannock Chase Colliery Company.[5]

---

[1] NuRO Armstrong, 725/B14/492–503 Reports on Lambton Collieries.

[2] NuRO NCB/AS/23; ZND 54/4–5.

[3] Francis 1980, 28–9; Sopwith, 'Electrification of Cannock Chase Colliery', *TFIME* 1912–13, 45, 350.

[4] *Digest of Evidence* I, 366–9, 446; Pamely 1904, 948; Buxton, *British Coal Industry*, 114–15.

[5] SRO CB 2/131 Directors' Report 1909; G. C. H. Whitelock, *250 years in Coal* (Derby and London, 1957), 44; *List of Mines* 1905 and 1913; Muir 1952, 22; Hann 1922, 21–2, 39; NoRO Wollaton NCB Directors' Minutes 28 Feb. 1902, 19 Mar. 1902, 29 Aug. 1902, 23 Oct. 1902; NuRO Ash-

1. Pithead, St Hilda's Colliery, South Shields, c. 1840

3. Women and Children Hauling Coal, *c.* 1840

4. Face Workers, c. 1900

5. Early Coal Cutters—Disc and Bar types, c. 1913

PRICE LIST.

TERMS.—Nett Cash on the 14th of the month following delivery.   These prices are subject to alteration without notice.

	Per ton of 2,240 lbs. at pit.		Per ton of 2,240 lbs. at pit.
Best Main—The best Coal produced in Derbyshire		**Large House Nuts**—Through 3-inch and over 2-inch screen	
Best Main Cubes—Through 5-inch and over 2½-inch screen		**Hand-Picked Deep**—An ideal coal for Farmers	
Large Main Nuts—Through 2½-inch and over 1½-inch screen		**Hand-Picked Cobbles**—A first-class kitchen coal	
Hasland Brights—Through 8-inch and over 4½-inch screen		**Treble-Screened Cobbles**— Through 5½-inch and over 3-inch screen. A splendid all-round coal.	
Best Derbys—Through 10-inch and over 5-inch screen		**Cobbles**—A very useful coal	
Derby Cubes—Through 5-inch and over 3-inch screen		**Deep Hard Nuts**—Through 3-inch and over 1½-inch screen. A first-rate hard nut.	
Derby Large Nuts—Through 4½-inch and over 2-inch screen		**Hand-Picked Hards**—A first-rate steam coal ..	
Best House—Over 2½-inch screen .. .. A superior coal suitable for all household purposes.		**Best Loco**	

6. Clay Cross Company Price List, 1910

Coal Exchange.

7. Interior of the Coal Exchange, *c*.1900

8. Mr Briers' Hearses at Whitwick Colliery after the Disaster of 1908

The complete replacement of all power plant by a central steam-electric installation was an increasing trend among the larger colliery companies after 1900.

There is evidence, too, to suggest that the cost-raising effects, anticipated or consequential, of the Eight Hours Act from 1909 also seems to have stimulated investment in plant and machinery, including electrification, as a counter measure;[1] though how important the fillip was is impossible to guess. The specific conditions favouring mechanization and electrification are obscure, for except for the Scottish region the *List of Mines* records the use of coal cutters and electrical power only on a regional, rather than colliery-by-colliery, basis. We have delineated a pattern of technical innovation which was much influenced by differing regional endowments and reflecting the various combinations of techniques and locally modified technology designed to minimize costs under contrasting conditions. Coal-cutting machinery was introduced where seam width and quality dictated their use as the only option for profitable mining; hence the Scottish lead.[2] Electrification, however, was applicable to all mines for haulage and pumping, as well as for coal preparation. It seems probable that the geological factors which sharpened the incentive to Scottish owners to install coal cutters also stimulated electrification to expedite the entire production process. In South Wales, however, where geological conditions were in marked contrast, electric horsepower per million tons of output in 1913 exceeded that of Scotland (Table 4.2). The North-east, which contained both thin and thick seams, was third in order of electric-power use. It may be significant that each of these three regions contained major exporting companies and that South Wales and the North-east were the locations of the very large mines; Lancashire and the West Midlands exhibited very limited export-orientation, contained the lowest proportions of large mines, and recorded the slowest rate of electrification. Yorkshire possessed roughly the same number of very large mines, as did Scotland, and as an exporting region Yorkshire grew rapidly shortly before 1913. This suggests that if size was an important influence upon the pace of electrification, then geological conditions, which necessitated greater

ington ZMD/54/2–5; NCB/AS/23; Francis 1980, 18, 28, 34; Sopwith, 'Electrification of the Cannock Chase Colliery Company', *TIME*, 45 (1912–13), 350.

[1] Bro Briggs SC/MS 160, Directors' Report 1910; BSCEMRRC Stanton and Staveley 2034/2/10 MB 19 Feb. 1909; Hann 1922, 41.
[2] See the discussion in Greasley 1982, 246–54.

emphasis on machine cutting in Scotland, is the factor which most likely explains the contrast with Yorkshire. Certainly, the regional disparities in machine use and in the application of electric power are not susceptible of an interpretation which stresses entrepreneurial failure to assess the advantages of new technology; but in as much that the availability of electricity was an important influence upon mechanization, the size distribution of mines and collieries also seems to be relevant to any explanation of the pattern of diffusion of machine cutting before 1913.

In considering the dynamics of technical progress in the pig iron industry in the North-east, Allen has argued that evidence which is consistent with rationality, manifest in innovations introduced to minimize costs and maximize profit, does not disprove the entrepreneurial hypothesis: that theoretically profit-seeking entrepreneurs may nevertheless approach new technology with a lack of vigour.[1] This is an argument which draws a distinction betweeen entrepreneurial behaviour which ensures profit and that which adopts new technology and introduces best practice *before* profitability is threatened. The beneficial consequences for industrial productivity in an industry where entrepreneurs exhibit vigour rather than mere rationality is to strengthen its competitive position. In the Cleveland iron industry Allen identified both rational decision making and the absence of sufficient entrepreneurial vigour; scrapping and rebuilding of plant took place, but the pace of innovation was too slow.[2]

Adopting a similar approach in assessing technical progress in the coal industry, our evidence supported the view that, particularly in the mechanization of coal cutting and electrification for which statistics are available (though only after 1900) the pattern of diffusion appears to have been rational on the whole; the factors which explained the speed of diffusion also suggest that entrepreneurial vigour existed, but that it was in a geological context very different, much more varied, and difficult compared with that which faced American colliery owners, with whom they have been compared unfavourably. However, technology—and especially the mechanization of coal cutting which has tended to preoccupy historians of the industry—is only one dimension of entrepreneurial behaviour, which for a fuller assessment must await our examination of the industry's productivity record, the institutional framework, and the character of the business élite.

---

[1] Robert C. Allen, 'Entrepreneurship and Technical Progress in the North-east Coast Pig Iron Industry: 1850–1913', *Research in Economic History*, 6 (1981), 59–61.
[2] Ibid.

iv. Haulage and winding

The efficient and economical transport of coal from the working place to the surface was one of the most important aspects of mining technology and proceeded in most cases in three consecutive stages: face to haulage road, haulage road to pit bottom, and pit bottom to surface.

Face transport consisted mainly of short-distance movements to concentration points, although in small or new mines coal might go direct to pit bottom. In the early years of our period human labour was almost universally employed for such operations: boys and youths, but also girls and women in some areas, notably Scotland, Lancashire, and Yorkshire. By the 1830s most collieries used wheeled trams, or wagons with iron rings, running on light rails or wooden boards, although in some areas, north Staffordshire, Shropshire, west Yorkshire, and parts of Lancashire, sledges were still employed. In Scotland, however, women still carried coal from the face on their backs. At this time, too, the coal was often transhipped into larger trucks or trams at the haulage road, occasioning considerable labour cost and breakage, though by the 1840s trams were approaching the face to avoid the disadvantage of transhipment.[1]

Other improvements followed, as a consequence of the 1842 Mines Act forbidding women and young children underground, and because increasing output was demanding better techniques. Ponies, generally not much higher than a metre, which had previously been confined to main roads were introduced into Durham in the mid-1840s and their use spread steadily thereafter; a greater throughput, reduced costs, and less arduous labour for the putter or haulage hand were the results. By 1913 most face haulage was still pony work, while mechanization spread slowly. There were then 73,000 horses and ponies in mines under the Regulation Act, and were especially common in the Northeast, where pillar-and-stall working was still widespread. There the horsepower-per-million-ton ratio was 429, followed by South Wales at 295; some were at work in main haulage, but most were employed for face-to-road duties.[2]

Low levels of horse use reflected either the use of hand power, in Lancashire especially, or in some cases mechanization. The extension of rope haulage to faces from the 1880s was slow, and was often

[1] *Children's Employment Commission* XVI, para. 207; Dunn 1852, 14–15; Galloway 1904, 344, and 1882, 115–17.
[2] Nicholas Wood 1855, 260–1; Galloway 1904, 344; Dunn 1852, 15; *Mineral Statistics* 1913, 69.

concomitant with the introduction of electric haulage and mechanized cutting. Horse putting, especially over short distances, was economical, flexible, and required little capital, whereas adoption of rope haulage at the face entailed enlargement of gate roads and frequent changes as the face advanced.[1] The use of conveyor belts at the face was beginning to gain favour by 1913, in Scotland and South Wales especially, but as yet they were uncommon elsewhere.[2] Employed in conjunction with machine cutters, under optimal conditions the conveyors (mostly American at this time) offered large returns. Consisting of a trough which ran along the length of the face through which ran an endless scraper chain, the coal was cast into the trough by the fillers before the scraper chain drew it to the main gate for loading into trams.[3] At Consett's Langley Park Colliery, which in 1904 faced closure because the seam was extra hard, cutters converted what was previously an uneconomic seam on account of the high cost into a profitable one. By hand labour the amount of steam coal produced at Langley Park Colliery had been 1.8 tons per man-shift; this was raised to 3.75 tons with the Diamond Coal Cutter, but in conjunction with the conveyor the figure increased to 8 tons per man-shift. The produce of round coal by hand labour and blasting was 32 per cent, which the coal cutter had increased to 48 per cent, rising to 72 per cent when a conveyor was used. Equally significant to these striking gains in productivity were the reductions in working costs which arose from reduced deadwork and from economies in roadway maintenance.[4]

Even under ideal physical conditions, however, large improvements in throughput and cost reductions were available only to collieries of comparable size to those of Consett or Ashington, for capital investment in heavy-duty rails, haulage units, and ancillary plant rendered the use of conveyors economic only along extended longwall faces; none of those described in operation in 1904–5 were less than 60 metres in length. Such characteristics limited their use to thin-seam working, though these conditions also offered savings on the height of gate roads. Maximization of conveyor's potential throughput also implied the

---

[1] Ponies were more suited to shorter distances. Hughes 1904, 191.

[2] *Mineral Statistics* 1913.

[3] A. R. Griffin *Coalmining* (London, 1971), 122.

[4] W. C. Blackett and R. G. Ware, 'The Conveyor System for Filling at the Coal Face, as practised in Great Britain and America', *TFIME* 1904–5, XXIX, 477–9, 492. At Ashington Colliery a conveyor employed in the Yard Seam raised tonnage per man shift from 0.75 to 3, and the percentage of round coal from 70 per cent (using screens) to 75 per cent. Ibid., 467.

employment of large teams of miners along a face, supervised and monitored to maintain a pace of working to match conveyor speeds.[1]

As colliery sizes rose, increased haulage distances along lengthening main roads posed a much greater threat to supply than did the absence of mechanization at the face. Until the third quarter of the century horse or human agency was preferred for the horizontal roads. These used either trucks on rails or broad-wheeled 'rolleys' on a wooden floor, since difficulties arose when ropes were operated horizontally over long distances and because horses were economical and versatile. The substitution of horse for human power was a process accelerated by the 1842 Act, though horses were less economic for short runs and were useless where the roof was low.[2]

Steam power had become standard for winding on dip slopes by the 1840s, often in conjunction with inclined self-acting planes, though horse whims were sometimes employed to pull small loads. From this time, however, steam power also began to be applied to main-road haulage, a substitution made possible by the perfection of wire ropes and by better arrangements for underground engines supplied by steam from the surface.[3] Wire ropes were introduced from the Harz mines in Germany in 1834, but lengths of only 90 metres proved to be insufficient to enable colliery engineers to switch from horse, or hand, putting to rope haulage, which offered most savings at greater depths. The manufacture of wire ropes of any length by R. S. Newall in 1840 solved this problem and heralded the diffusion of mechanical haulage. By the late 1850s stationary steam engines underground, combined with wire rope, had almost entirely supplanted horses at the face in some of the large collieries of the North-east; the Tail Rope Committee's report, published in 1868, described the system as having been perfected so as to be applicable under any condition of wagonway, whether crooked, steeply graded, or with several branches.[4]

The first system of mechanized haulage to come into wide use was the main and tail rope, whereby the engine wound two ropes: one hauled the loaded trams to the pit bottom, the other pulled the empties in

[1] Ibid., 487.

[2] Nicholas Wood 1855, 270–6; Granville Poole, 'History and Development of Underground Haulage', Mining Association of Great Britain, *Historical Review of Coalmining* (London, c. 1924), 89–104; Dunn 1852, 14–15; Galloway 1904, 340–3.

[3] Dunn 1852, 214–16; Poole 1924, 96–7; Galloway 1882, 261, and 1904, 343–7. Compressed air was also employed occasionally.

[4] *CG* 23 Jan. 1858, 59–60; 'Report of the Tail Rope Committee', *TNEIME* 1867–8, XVII, Appendix.

round a pulley at the far end, drawing the main rope behind. This system was easy to operate, requiring only a single set of rails; it could work branches well and reach speeds of 15 miles per hour. Against this, power consumption was high, wear was considerable, and delivery irregular, and its continued popularity in the North-east until the end of the century suggests that by 1900 coalowners in that region were becoming conservative, almost backward.[1] The main alternative was the use of endless chains, which had been recommended as cheapest by the Tail Rope Committee in 1868. Widely used in Lancashire and taken up in the late 1860s by firms in the North-east, one disadvantage of endless chain was that as the number of branches worked increased its economic value declined, for the extra branches required the erection of additional pulleys and the employment of men or boys to attend to them; and in the endless-chain system the application of driving power to the chain, typically heavier than the wire rope, was more difficult. Endless-chain systems were soon superseded by improved rope haulage and later were mainly used on surface. In most respects the system was similar to endless rope haulage.[2]

The endless rope system, which eventually superseded endless chains, was slow to be applied at first. It consisted of a double line of rails with a continuous wire or steel rope driven either directly by an underground engine or via another rope from the surface. Trams could be attached at any point to the rope which moved at about walking pace. Not surprisingly, the transfer from chain to endless rope occurred first in the Wigan district of Lancashire, where the two systems were so similar. Reviewing the state of haulage technology, the Tail Rope Committee remarked on the novelty of the endless-rope system which was still in its experimental stage in 1868. Already by 1870, however, the viewer William Armstrong had become convinced of the superiority of endless rope over all other haulage systems and was advising his client companies accordingly, at the same time impressing upon them the importance of high and continuous levels of output to reduce working costs.[3] Once clips had been devised to connect tubs securely to ropes, and automatic detachers introduced, the use of pulleys and ropes increased this system's superiority. By 1892 Hughes could write: 'nine out of every ten

---

[1] Poole 1924, 97–8; Kerr 1904, 243–8; Hughes 1904, 200–2, 226; 'Report of the Tail Rope Committee', *TNEIME*, 1867–8, XVII, Appendix, 1–177.

[2] 'Report of the Tail Rope Committee', *TNEIME*, 1867–8, XVII, 70–7; CG 8 Aug. 1890, 216; Kerr 1904, 249–52; Hughes 1904, 202–5.

[3] NuRO Armstrong 725/B7 Report.

systems which have been put to work during the last ten years are endless rope, with the probable exception of the North of England, and
even there the system is rapidly gaining ground'.[1] The explanation for
the adoption of this innovation was the greater regularity of tubs which
facilitated handling; the light weight and durability of ropes, which
saved power and maintenance; slower speed, which enhanced safety; an
even distribution of load; and relatively low labour requirements.
Against this, twin rails meant more capital in the roadway, but even this
could be reduced by working with passing places and sets of tubs.[2]

The pace of diffusion of mechanized haulage of all kinds appears to
have been steady. After about 1840, when the first installations are
recorded in the deepest mines of the North, to the 1900s the technology
was continuously refined. Nicholas Wood's review of underground
haulage technology which appeared between 1854 and 1857 had stimulated interest in improving systems.[3] A major stimulus was afforded ten
years later by the detailed analytical review conducted by the Tail Rope
Committee set up by the North of England Institute of Mining
Engineers and published in 1868. Galloway referred to this report as one
of the most valuable contributions ever made to mining literature,
'showing marvellously low costs per mile ton';[4] likewise, R. Nelson
Boyd regarded this to have marked the beginning of general adoption of
iron and steel wire-rope haulage.[5] From the mid-1870s most new
installations used endless ropes, but the working and cost advantages of
one system over another do not appear to have been great enough to
induce wholesale changeover at any stage, which helps to explain why a
mix of technologies was employed. The larger collieries became the
greater was the advantage in cost and operating convenience that
mechanized haulage had over horses, but the wide mine size distribution which existed ensured the continuous survival of horse haulage,[6]
the cost of which compared favourably with mechanical methods. Even
electric motors made slow progress, despite their advantages; only
151,000 horsepower had been installed by January 1913, when the two
major user-regions were South Wales and Scotland.[7]

[1] Hughes 1904, 226.   [2] Dunn 1852, 214–16.
[3] Nicholas Wood, 'On the Conveyance of Coals Underground in Coal Mines', *TNEIME* 1854–
5, III, 239–318.
[4] Galloway, 'Secondary Haulage', *TFIME* 1896–7, XII, 257.
[5] R. Nelson Boyd, 'Collieries and Colliery Engineering', *CG* 10 Nov. 1893, 819.
[6] *CG* 15 Apr. 1898, 673; W. P. Laws, 'Costs of Haulage Underground', *Mining Engineering*
1896–7, I, 177.
[7] Kerr 1904, 252–67; Hughes 1904, 205–26; Poole 1924, 98–100.

Winding the coal from pit bottom to surface saw improvements of similar importance. In the early nineteenth century most mines were relatively shallow and small, and consequently horse gins, or even windlasses, sufficed; adit mines, of course, needed no winding plant, although workings below level were becoming common. None the less, even in the 1830s some collieries had outputs of 100,000 tons a year, particularly in the North-east, and these required large winding plant. Between these two extremes most needed some sort of steam winder, usually a beam engine and often of simple Newcomen or Watt type. Many raised the coal in two or three stages, as engine power was low and long ropes difficult to manufacture and maintain; in smaller collieries one engine both wound and pumped. In many cases in South Wales, and occasionally elsewhere, water-balance engines, using the weight of water in the descending cage to raise the loaded one, remained sufficient until the 1860s. These were frequently only a means of power transmission—the water being pumped back up again—but were economical for small outputs. In south Staffordshire, the East Midlands, and Shropshire a single engine frequently raised coal from two or more pits.[1]

In the 1840s larger winding engines of up to 200 horsepower began to be introduced, mainly in the North-east and Lancashire at first, and these continued to be the norm until the 1870s; many collieries in Durham dispensed with the beam driving flywheels, and many Derbyshire collieries employed a hanging rope with pulley for counter-balancing to achieve swifter winding. Horizontal twin-cylinder engines soon became the standard practice thereafter; compounds were introduced in the 1880s and improved versions of this basic configuration, generally driving the winding drum directly, were characteristic of winding plant up to 1913, some of which might generate 750 horsepower or more.[2]

Electric winders also began to be introduced in the 1880s but these spread very slowly before 1913, except in South Wales where two-thirds of the 34,000 horsepower in electric winding was to be found. The reasons for this slow take-up are to be found in the development of exhaust-steam turbines, worked in conjunction with high-pressure winding engines at very high efficiency, to generate electricity for other purposes.[3]

[1] Galloway 1904, 325–8 and 336–7; Dunn 1852, 16–18; Morris and Williams 1958, 70–1; T. Smith 1836, 27; Flinn 1984, 102–4.
[2] Galloway 1904, 327–8; Kerr 1904, 185–8; Forster Brown 1924, 170–6; CG 1 Aug. 1890, 175; George Watkins, 'Vertical Winding Engines of Durham', TNS 1955–6, XXIX, 205–19.
[3] Forster Brown 1924, 180; Buxton 1978, 107, 109.

Developments in the means of transmitting power were even more important for winding technology. In the 1830s flat hemp ropes were most commonly employed, although especially in Lancashire endless chains were preferred. The latter were found to be too heavy for depths above about 92 metres, and by 1865 fewer than a dozen were still in use. Wire ropes were first introduced in the early 1840s; they were flat, but although the men were at first distrustful of their safety, occasionally causing strike action in the early years, they soon became accepted.[1] During the second half of the century flat ropes were superseded by round ropes, which offered advantages of greater strength and durability and were cheaper than flat ropes, few of which remained in use by 1900. As the depths from which coal was wound increased, various methods of counter-balancing the load were devised: tailropes, spiral winding drums, continuous ropes, and chains, of which the two former were most used.[2]

Improved methods of bringing coal to bank on the surface were for the most part simple in principle and operation before mechanization. Although Curr had introduced wooden corves with guides in the late eighteenth century these had not been widely adopted. At the beginning of our period, baskets or tubs, swinging freely in the shaft, were the normal means of raising both coal and men. In the 1830s, however, T. Y. Hall introduced cages with rails laid on the bottom on to which the tubs could be wheeled and raised to the surface thereby eliminating transhipment, while wooden or iron rail-guides in the shaft ensured that the winding was straight. Such cages were eventually adopted everywhere and were made double- and in some instances triple-decked to increase capacity.[3]

Thus, the main technical and economic aspects of winding, motive power, ropes, and cages, were developed to a high level by 1900; loads and speed were able to match output at relatively low cost. Since the men were also raised and lowered by the winding engine much attention was also paid to safety. Wire guides prevented the cages hitting the shaft walls and the cages were roofed to protect against falls of stone. Automatic brakes on the guides in case of rope failure were devised by Fourdrinier and others between 1847 and 1864, but these were inconvenient to operate and attention was thereafter concentrated on making

---

[1] R. S. Williamson, Presidential Address, *TFIME* 1896–7, XII, 84.
[2] Galloway 1904, 332–3, 337; Forster Brown 1924, 173–5, 197–8; Kerr 1904, 190–2, 197–200.
[3] Galloway 1904, 328–9 and 1882, 211–18; Forster Brown 1924, 172–3; Kerr 1904, 201–9.

the wire ropes, guides, fastenings, brakes, and signalling systems as fool-proof as possible.[1] The enormous power required to empty two or three decks at once and to replace the full for empty tubs led to the adoption, from the 1880s, of hydraulic rams, first introduced at Clifton Colliery in Nottinghamshire, and at Emerson Bainbridge's Nunnery Colliery in 1890. Until after 1890 tubs were removed by the use of movable plat-forms tilted by steam-powered machinery so as to set the tubs in motion. Another method of ensuring tub dispatch was to use suspended platforms attached by ropes to separate drums, with counter-balancing weights to adjust the platform level. By the use of a powerful brake on the drum the cage was lowered deck by deck; 'keps' to hold the cage at top and bottom, were also introduced. All of these innovations helped to eliminate accidents involving winding failures and at the same time helped to reduce the cost of bringing coal to bank.[2]

v. Preparation and by-product technology

Most coal could not be sold without some processing in order to remove impurities, and graded according to size. The degree of cleaning and grading needed varied considerably over time, depending on the type of coal and its market: some consumers required very precise characteristics while others were less particular, showing more sen-sitivity to price than to quality. Thus, at one extreme the household market was principally for large coal exceeding about 2 centimetres in diameter and which was free from impurities, such as shale; the boilers of steam engines, however, especially those at collieries, tended to be fed with the cheapest slack.[3] Considerations concerning the suitability of small coal for making good coke, and the proportion of small in total output, also influenced decisions on treatment, for finding markets for non-caking small coal was a persistent problem which much of the research into coal preparation was designed to solve.

In 1830 both the market and the preparation technology were rela-tively unsophisticated; large quantities of small coal were wasted, either by throwing back into the goaf or by burning at the surface.[4] At this time production was concentrated, for the most part, in reasonably thick seams at moderate depth and free from dirt partings. For this reason coal could be brought to the surface in good condition; only the size of

---

[1] Galloway 1882, 259–61; Kerr 1904, 212–20.
[2] CG 8 Aug. 1890, 216.   [3] Flinn 1984, 106–8, 247–8.
[4] Ibid., 30–1.

the lumps obtained imposed a constraint on saleability in the context of an otherwise largely undifferentiated demand. In many areas coal-owners could afford to throw away much of the small coal, because its value was less than the cost of production and prices of large coal were sufficient to ensure profitability.[1]

These conditions obtained until roughly the 1870s, by which time annual output had quadrupled to 120 million tons. Between 1830 and 1870 perhaps 2,750 million tons of coal were raised and another 750 million tons sterilized underground in barriers, pillars, and waste.[2] At this period it was becoming increasingly difficult to find good, clean seams to replace areas worked out, and increasingly coalowners were compelled to turn to thinner seams with more dirt partings and which yielded a smaller percentage of large coal. Customers were also more particular after the 1873 boom which had led to increased consumption of small coal, but this had been followed by a period of lower prices and over-capacity, producing a buyers' market until the mid-eighties. The euphoria surrounding the boom of 1872–3 also brought about reworking of old seams and much new sinking to inferior coal, the effect of which was to intensify the move towards discrimination by consumers.[3]

Meanwhile, the composition of demand had been changing away from household markets towards industrial uses and exports. Pressure on mineowners to process their coal, therefore, began to increase, especially in certain areas such as South Wales where the disposal of small coal was problematical. As the growth in production of steam coals from deeper seams grew during the third quarter of the century, the increasingly large pillars required drew attention to the waste of small coal for which there was no alternative economic use; hence the shift to longwall working in South Wales in the 1860s.[4] A further trend reinforcing the need for more thorough preparation was the increasing size of collieries, which both brought larger and larger amounts of coal to the surface and made it economically feasible to build specialized large plant to clean coal. This pressure was alleviated, partly by the recovery in demand and also by the willingness of some consumers to continue to purchase small coal even after the sharp price differential between small and large coal had diminished somewhat. For their part,

---

[1] Flinn 1984, 106–8.

[2] Calculated from output figures and *Coal Supply* 1871, XVIII, Committee E.

[3] *SC Dearness and Scarcity* 1873, X, QQ 992–7, 1929–31, 2682, 2768, 2889, 3110–15, 3166–7, 3266–7, 3372–3, 3589–90; W. R. Chapman and R. A. Mott, *The Cleaning of Coal* (London, 1928), 117–18.

[4] Morris and Williams 1958, 50–1.

colliery owners began to recognize that it was less efficient to pay men to sort the coal underground in cramped conditions by the indifferent light of the safety lamp, than to bring it all to the surface for processing, although even in 1913 some house-coal collieries still insisted that the coal was filled using a fork-shaped 'riddle'.[1] The results of all these pressures were twofold: increasing care in grading the coal according to size, and much greater attention to the removal of dirt from small coal—which in practice meant washing it. These trends intensified.

In 1830 coal preparation meant screening out large from small coal. This was most obviously a feature of, and a problem in, the North-east coalfield's London market, but applied to a greater or lesser extent to any area which produced coal for coastwise shipment, for urban markets, or for the iron industry—in practice, most coalfields. Many collieries avoided the problem by riddling or otherwise sorting the coal at the face, attempting to raise only large coal and selling it without any treatment. In industrial areas, such as Lancashire and Yorkshire where there was a ready market for small coal in mill boilers, colliery owners tended to raise and screen; in coalfields serving mainly household and general markets, such as the East Midlands, Warwickshire, Yorkshire, and South Wales, the favoured practice was to riddle underground; often the coal was both riddled and screened.[2]

The process of separating large from small coals began with the hewer, who in the steam-coal seams was usually paid only for large coal. Heavy fines and the confiscation of tubs were introduced to reinforce this system in Northumberland in 1859 when it was the subject of dispute, but not until the boom conditions of 1872 did the miners successfully negotiate an ending to the separation of coals underground.[3] In South Wales and in Derbyshire owners introduced 'Billy Fairplay' into the collieries, a machine installed at the surface to separate large from small, the latter passing through a screen and deducted from a hewer's get to establish pay entitlement.[4] Hitherto, a colliery official had arbitrarily estimated the amount of small and reduced payment accordingly, but the new device met with opposition from the men, suspicious of the accuracy of the scales and critical of the width between the screen bars. In riddling districts, notably Yorkshire, riddles were

---

[1] Chapman and Mott 1928, 117; *Digest of Evidence* I, 151–70, 281–9, II, 38–9.
[2] Galloway 1904, 361–2; *Coal Supply* 1871, XVIII, Committee E, 535–634.
[3] Burt 1924, 128.
[4] *SC Dearness and Scarcity* 1873, X, Q 7599; *CG* 12 Dec. 1884, 934; Morris and Williams 1958, 259.

withdrawn when trade was good, for consumers were competing to purchase coals; but when conditions deteriorated and consumers' demands became more precise, the need to ensure that large coal only was supplied occasioned the reintroduction of riddles underground. Wage rates were often adjusted upwards in such circumstances to compensate for the extra time involved in riddling, but miners were rarely satisfied.[1] Again, as in the North-east, Yorkshire miners negotiated to discontinue coal separation during 1872, at a time when few collieries required it. With the onset of depression, however, riddles were reintroduced, especially in the thin-seam district of west Yorkshire, and despite strikes on a considerable scale the Coalmasters' Association forced reintroduction of the riddling requirement in 1879. In collieries where, when markets for small coal improved, differential rates were paid for large and small coal, the extent of the differences became a repeated focus for disputes.[2]

It was, however, pre-eminently the North-east that pioneered and employed screening techniques. The London market, which from the beginning dominated the coalfield, demanded only large coal, and consequently even in 1830 before dispatch from the pits all seasale collieries sorted their output by tipping it on to grids of bars set roughly 2 cm. apart. Boys and old men then picked out the extraneous matter, and only the coal remaining on the screens, about two-thirds of the total, was sent to London. The rest was either sold without further treatment to local markets or screened again over $\frac{3}{8}$ of an inch bars, the 'nut' coal thus produced going to export, household, and manufacturing markets. Often much of the coal less than a centimetre across was unsaleable, and after colliery consumption, miners' coal, and that which was saleable had been extracted, the remainder was burnt, returned underground, or used for road mending; sometimes a third screening yielded even smaller coal, leaving only coal dust as completely unsaleable.[3] Similar practices continued to be normal until the 1880s and spread to other coalfields, screening tending to supersede hand riddling in some of the worst-affected districts. The deep and badly faulted pits of Lancashire suffered particularly from the production of dirty coal. In the 1840s some success was achieved with Walker's patent cylindrical coal riddle, a steam-powered revolving screen for separating slack from

---

[1] Machin 1958, 204, 245.

[2] Ibid., 246–7.

[3] Galloway 1904, 361–2; Flinn 1984, 107–8; *Children's Employment Commission* 1842, XVI, Appendix, 154–7, Dr Mitchell's Report; *Coal Supply* 1871, XVII, Committee C, 'Waste in Working'.

round coal. By 1849 eight collieries, including Ince Hall, Haigh Colliery, and the Ladyshore and Agecroft Collieries (respectively belonging to J. Pearson and Andrew Knowles and Sons) were employing this device, which dispensed altogether with riddling underground. In 1858, on William Armstrong's advice, screening was also introduced at Blundell's Collieries.[1] Owners of south Yorkshire collieries at that time seeking to establish a foothold in the London market found it necessary for the first time to screen the coal in order to compete with Wallsend coal, 'upon which', a *Colliery Guardian* correspondent observed, 'every care is bestowed'.[2] This new departure also coincided with the agreement between the Great Northern Railway Company and south Yorkshire coalmasters, whereby whereas hitherto all coal from the Silkstone seam, irrespective of the colliery of origin, had borne the label 'Silkstone', henceforward the name of the colliery supplying the coal would also identify Silkstone coal.[3] Such an important development, a victory for repeated pressure by the Newton Chambers directors, had the immediate effect of providing an incentive, hitherto absent, for the careful preparation of coal at all pits, and to stimulate independent advertising by the proprietors. Sensitivity to complaints was a necessary condition for survival under certain conditions, and when Wharncliffe Silkstone's directors received complaints concerning quality (i.e. size) in 1862 they set in motion the monitoring of corves, introduced hand-picking if necessary, purchased cisterns for washing, and built reservoirs to ensure an adequate water supply.[4]

In many collieries, however, especially those outside the sophisticated London market, screening continued to be crude in the extreme. Tubs were emptied by turning them upside down, spilling the coal on to a fixed screen from which the large lumps were picked out and thrown into a wagon. The banksmen proceeded to separate cobbles with the aid of pronged forks, leaving the remainder as slack.[5] In the 1880s, when the relative market values of large and small coal differed by about 40 per cent, the incentive to maximize production of the former grew, intensified by the increase in deep mining which tended to enlarge small-coal production. As one colliery manager from Wigan explained: 'The good old times, when almost anything that looked black would sell, had passed away and complaints of dirty coal are now one of the ills

[1] Anderson 1967, 171.
[2] *CG* 14 Mar. 1858, 103.　　　　　　　　[3] *CG* 6 Mar. 1858, 153.
[4] SCL Wharncliffe Silkstone NCB 1429/1, DM 27 Feb. 1862, 27 Oct. 1864.
[5] LCA 1708/12 'West Yorkshire Coalfield', 27; *CG* 4 Feb. 1898, 219.

which every colliery manager had, more or less, to bear'.[1] He described the changes induced by trade depression in Brinsop Hall Collieries in 1882, where belts made of steel wire carried the coal on to a moving screen, replacing two hand rakers, while the slack (in very small quantities) fell on to a shute and into a wagon. By maximizing round coals, avoiding breakage in screening, and keeping the coal free from dirt the prospects for profitability increased.[2] Hence the trend towards greater selection, more washing, and the rescreening of coal into multiple sizes applicable to diverse purposes.

Coal-crushing and washing plant was introduced into William Baird's collieries from the late 1870s, followed by mechanized sorting plant; in 1886 Bairds became the first Scottish company to commence briquette manufacture.[3] Emerson Bainbridge expressed his opinion that probably more progress had been made in screening and washing coal in the 1880s 'than in any department of management'.[4]

While most energy was directed into reducing the proportion of small coal produced, particularly by the steamcoal collieries from the late 1850s, the insistence of purchasers in periods of slack trade that screens of a larger mesh should be used at the collieries and at the docks[5] intensified the search for alternative methods of small-coal utilization. Symptoms of this trend were the experiments carried out by T. Y. Hall, and later the formation in 1861 of the Compressed Coal Company Ltd., followed by the London Patent Coal Co. in 1866, each for the purpose of manufacturing small coal compressed into bricks.[6] Coalowners in the North-east, Scotland, Yorkshire, and Derbyshire subsequently expressed interest in such a possibility in later years, but not until the late 1880s did the conversion of slack to combustible fuel begin to become sufficiently economic to induce even the steam-coal owners of South Wales to raise more than a tiny amount of small coal to bank, though these were the leaders in the manufacture of briquettes, or patent fuel. This process was much more important in Continental Europe, especially as a means of improving German brown coals, though it was a Leeds engineering company, Yeaton and Co., which designed the most successful brick-making machinery, which was

---

[1] A. H. Leach, 'Improvements in Screening Arrangements', *Proceedings Manchester Geological Society* 1885, 15 (1886), 95.

[2] Ibid.

[3] Corrins thesis, 244–5.

[4] *CG* 15 Aug. 1890, 258.

[5] Morris and Williams 1958, 59.

[6] *CG* 20 July 1861, 36, 18 Aug. 1886, 104.

exported to European producers in considerable numbers in the 1880s.[1] The process consisted of forming into bricks under heavy pressure a mixture of small coal with 6–10 per cent of pitch, in order to make otherwise useless duff steam coals saleable. The plant was mainly located at the ports and produced hard bricks, ranging from egg shaped and sized nuts for domestic use to large blocks weighing several pounds. By the late 1850s about 80,000 tons per annum were being exported, three-quarters from Swansea and smaller amounts from Liverpool and London. The markets were principally for marine consumption in the Mediterranean and a scattering over many Asian and American countries. Output grew steadily: by 1900 it had reached a million tons and more than doubled by 1913, when 93 per cent was exported.[2] At first, unwashed coal was used, as the South Wales small was fairly clean; much was double-screened export refuse. Later, however, washed and dried small was substituted. Patent fuel was more or less equal in calorific value and more easily handled than coal; much was used for railway locomotives. Manufacturing costs were high, but prices correspondingly so, and depending on the price of small coal the trade seems to have been generally profitable.[3]

Much more important than patent fuel manufacture was the coking of small coal, for which market conditions differed. In 1830 coke was made principally from large coal, and coking plant was chiefly concentrated in the main iron-producing areas of South Wales, Shropshire, and Staffordshire. The technology was fairly crude, coking occurring in open heaps or open-topped brick boxes, usually with a central brick chimney to improve the draught. However, small coals could not be used with this method since they choked the draught.[4] Coking technology improved substantially, the impetus coming from both the supply and the demand side. The latter stemmed particularly from the development of the iron industry on Teesside, and to a lesser extent from the railways which until about 1870 used mainly coke. The coking of west Durham small coals, which were particularly suitable, grew rapidly in the 1840s. There were over 2,000 ovens in Durham by 1847, perhaps 7,500 in 1860, and 14,000 in 1877, at which time coking capacity was 4.1

---

[1] A series of articles 'Notes on the Preparation of Coal for Coking', are contained in *CG* 22 Apr., 29 July, 28 Oct., 9 Dec. 1887; Morris and Williams 1958, 59.

[2] G. Franke, *A Handbook of Briquetting* Vol. I (London, 1916), 1–22, 260–3; *Digest of Evidence*, I, 274–8, II, 28–92; *Annual Statements of Trade* 1855–1913.

[3] *Digest of Evidence*, I, 274–8; 78–92.

[4] *Children's Employment Commission* 1842, XVI, Appendix II, 44; Mott 1936, 25–9, 54; Galloway 1904, 364.

million tons a year.[1] The largest coke producer in Britain in the 1840s was John Bowes and Partners, whose Marley Hill Colliery possessed 424 beehive ovens in 1849, and more than 600 a few years later; about two-thirds of Marley Hill's output of nearly 200,000 tons a year was coked.[2] From the late 1850s the declining consumption of coke by the railways was more than offset by the rapid growth of the iron industry which stimulated the expansion of coal and coke production; in some cases in response to the demand for coke generated within the iron-works, in others (as at Consett and Dowlais from the 1860s, and Bairds) as a conscious policy of diversification into salecoal and coke produc-tion. By the late 1860s more than half Consett's coke production was sold to other iron producers, and beginning in the 1860s Bairds became the leading Scottish coke producer.[3] At the Staveley Iron and Coal Company large-scale investment in coke production was a response to the unsaleability of slack from the collieries in the late 1860s. In 1873 the directors agreed that 'as a means of using the surplus small coal the company should build ovens'.[4]

Collieries unconnected with iron production also looked to coke ovens as an outlet for unsaleable slack; almost from its foundation coke production was regarded by Wharncliffe Silkstone's directors as a valuable counterweight to the highly seasonal household trade on which the colliery was chiefly dependent.[5] The neighbouring Newton Chambers collieries had supplied coked coal for its furnaces since 1825, but it was not until the firm's natural iron-ore resources were exhausted in the 1860s that the emphasis from iron to coal production altered, with the result that coke was manufactured for supply to the Sheffield steel and blast furnaces, as well as for internal consumption.[6]

Giving evidence before the Coal Supply Commission in 1903, C. E. Rhodes, manager of the extensive collieries belonging to John Brown, the Sheffield steel manufacturer, remarked on the importance of coking small coal in enabling many companies to survive depressed periods of trade, partly because of improvements on the supply side affecting costs, but also because improved methods of handling small coal had

[1] A. L. Steavenson, 'The Manufacture of Coke in the Newcastle and Durham Districts', *TNEIME*, VIII, 1859–60, 109–35; Mott 1936, 44–5.

[2] Mountford thesis, 61.

[3] A. S. Wilson thesis, 101; Morris and Williams 1958, 88–9; Corrins thesis, 348–50.

[4] BSCEMRRC Stanton and Staveley 2034/2/4 MB 23 May 1873.

[5] SCL NCB 1429/1 DM 2 Feb. 1858, 21 Aug. 1863, 17 Apr. 1869, 17 Nov. 1873.

[6] *Thorncliffe News*, 4 June 1954.

rendered it more marketable, resulting in a trend towards higher prices relative to large coal.[1]

The rapid growth in the demand for coke brought about the perfection of beehive coking technology between 1845 and 1873, which also led to the recognition that strongly caking small coal made better coke than large coal, and saw large coal being deliberately crushed for coking.[2] Oven design was standardized as a circular brick oven with a sloping floor, and before long, crude trough washers were installed to reduce ash (dirt) content before coking.[3] Improved types of oven, at first recovering only the waste gases for boiler heating, later utilizing all the decomposition products (the chief of which were ammonia, tar, and benzole), were slow to be taken up in Britain. Most improved ovens were designed in Germany and Belgium, but because the coal was unsuitable for beehive ovens there was a strong incentive for the development of long, tall, narrow ovens with side flues.[4] The foremost gas-recovery design was that of Coppee, which became favoured in Britain from 1870, especially in South Wales where the coal was most similar in quality to Continental types. Elsewhere, the economic justification for preferring Coppee to beehive was less clear, for resource endowments were rarely comparable with those of South Wales and the coke produced was generally regarded to have been inferior to beehive coke—except when the coal, as in South Wales, was free from impurities.[5]

Full by-product recovery ovens were used in gasworks early in the nineteenth century, but it was not until the 1860s that they appeared in collieries in the French Simon-Carves design, and nearly another twenty years elapsed before they were tried in Britain. Improvements on the principle were made in France, Belgium, and Germany, whence originated the popularization of by-product ovens in Britain in the late 1890s. In the new types of ovens volatile substances were condensed and utilized, and in the process of gas manufacture it became possible to produce various preparations of ammonia, including sulphate of ammonia for use in making artificial manures, tar, which formed the basis for benzole, carbolic acid, naphthalene, creosote, anthracine, and gas pitch used in asphalting. The value of the gas, extra coke, and the by-products could reach 5s. per ton of coke at a time when coke fetched 14–

[1] *RC Coal Supplies* 1903, XVI, QQ 4932–3.

[2] Dunn 1852, 327; Galloway 1904, 364; Meade 1882, 15.

[3] A. L. Steavenson, 'The Manufacture of Coke in the Newcastle and Durham Districts', *TNEIME*, 1859–60, VIII, 109–35.   [4] Mott 1936, 55–6.

[5] Ibid., 61–3; Meade 1882, 198–201; *CG* 14 Sept. 1888, 383.

15s. a ton. Coke yield alone could be 10 per cent or more higher, depending on oven design and the type of coal.

In view of these manifest advantages, very rapid substitution of by-product for beehive ovens might have been expected. In fact, 80 per cent of British coke output came from beehive ovens in 1900, 13 per cent from retort ovens, and only 7 per cent was by-product coke. Only in about 1910 did beehive output fall below half, and in 1913 the proportions were about 40 per cent beehive, 50 per cent by-product, 10 per cent retort; in Durham beehive coking was even more resilient.[1]

There are many reasons for this apparent slowness to innovate. Early by-product ovens, which were small, were not very efficient in comparison with later ones; capital costs were relatively high, as were maintenance, repair, and operating costs; they produced fewer by-products than those of later design, and a coke yield barely greater than the beehives yet which was of inferior quality by comparison. Beehive coke was harder and until 1900, at least, could support a larger charge in the blast furnace; consequently customers preferred beehive coke and would pay a price premium. The effect, however, was to reinforce prejudice and encourage technical conservatism among British coke-producers. Two other factors unfavourable to more rapid innovation were the slow growth of coke output, which the simple and reliable beehive oven could sustain without difficulty, and the limited contact between the coal industry and professional scientists. Under such circumstances the initial lack of enthusiasm for by-product technology is understandable.[2] Yet the turning-point occurred in 1900, when profit possibilities altered as coal prices rose. The history of coking technology at Consett provides an illustration. Faced with rising coke costs from the late 1880s, due principally to coal costs higher than those of their competitors, the directors erected by-product ovens after hearing the experience of one of the directors, David Dale, also managing director of Pease, the second largest coke producer—where the first installation of Simon Carves ovens ten years before had not proved commercially successful. For this reason beehives were installed at Consett in 1892.[3] Twelve years later, however, fifty Otto Hilgenstock by-product ovens were erected, probably in response to the innovations introduced at Bolckow Vaughn and Bell Brothers in 1901.[4] Similar

[1] Mott 1936, 64–70, 85; Mountford thesis, Appendix F; Digest of Evidence I, 37–78; Samuel Commission II, 341; Mineral Statistics 1905–13.
[2] Mott 1936, 68–83; Digest of Evidence II, 39–78.
[3] A. S. Wilson thesis, 159–62.
[4] Ibid., 112–14.

developments were occurring elsewhere, at John Bowes Ltd., Blundell's Collieries, and notably at Staveley,[1] where C. P. Markham's remarkable engineering development involved the construction of three blast furnaces, one hundred simplex ovens by 1908, and by 1912 a further fifty Huessener ovens. The beginning of Staveley's major investment in heavy chemical manufacture marked the origin of Staveley Chemicals Ltd.[2]

The burgeoning of by-product investment around the turn of the century does not demonstrate a late awakening to the commercial possibilities but rather a change in economic conditions, which rendered by-product investment profitable. Research chemists engaged by Newton Chambers (exceptional in this respect) to experiment with coal distillation in the early 1880s had achieved technical success—but the Rockingham Colliery plant built to develop its commercial potential was a failure. Not until 1900 did either the Rockingham Gas Works or a patent oil works make a profit; however, the company's by-product investment achieved a major success with the patent IZAL germicide, soon to be followed by a range of disinfectants, insecticides, antiseptic soaps, and liquid detergents, for public health and industrial uses.[3]

By-product recovery ovens increased rapidly from 1900, the proportion of coke output produced in these ovens rising from 7 to 15 per cent by 1905, reaching 50 per cent in 1913; retort ovens did not exceed 13 per cent before 1913, while beehives fell from 80 per cent of coke production in 1900 to 40 per cent in 1913.[4]

Both coking and briquetting technology were clearly of crucial importance to profitability for some collieries, and were inextricably linked with the progress of preparation technology. The first moves towards wet cleaning came from the coking market, since screening and picking was sufficient for large coal. Small coal could not be picked by hand, of course, and often contained too much dirt to make good coke. Moreover, the effect of washing coke was not only to clean it, but to produce coke which was tougher and of larger than average bulk.[5] The first coal-washing plant in Britain was of French design: a Bérard jig

---

[1] Mountford thesis, 163; Anderson 1967, 176; Chapman 1981, 97.

[2] Chapman 1981, 97.

[3] SCL TR 450/8–25, Directors' Minutes 25 June 1883, 24 Mar., 29 Sept. 1884, 29 June, 26 Oct. 1885, 25 Jan. 1887, 2 Apr. 1892, 28 Jan. 1889, 27 Apr. 1896, 26 Apr. 1897, 10 Apr. 1899; *Thorncliffe News* Supplements, 2 Apr., 4 June, 9 July 1951.

[4] *Mineral Statistics* 1905–13; Mott 1936, 55; Mountford thesis, Appendix F.

[5] *CG* 29 Apr. 1887, 604.

built in 1849 in Newcastle by James Morrison, who bought up otherwise worthless dirty slack from the Lambton Collieries, washed and coked it and sold it for a profit. He did the same later in Wigan.[1] Green and Bell's Coal Cleansing Machine was first installed at Framwellgate Colliery in 1856, and Robinson's patent washers were introduced at Blundell's Colliery in the late 1850s,[2] but not until George Gilroy's open-transfer method, in operation at the Ince Hall Coal and Cannel Co. Colliery in Wigan from 1864, did some of the large coal and iron firms, such as the Wigan Coal and Iron, Ebbw Vale, and the Sheepbridge and Clay Cross companies build washers to clean the small coal. These early machines were quite small, handling up to 10 or 12 tons per hour, and were built in groups of two or four; they cost about $1\frac{1}{2}d.-2d.$ per ton to operate.[3]

Several types of jig washer existed, mostly of European design and based on metal-mining technology. All used the principle that the coal was lighter than the refuse, which when agitated in water allowed separation. Some plants in Wigan and Durham were simple trough washers, in which a mixture of coal and water flowed over wooden troughs; most were fully-enclosed boxes. They were not particularly efficient, for though the coal came out clean 10–15 per cent remained in the dirt; none the less, they more than justified their expense.[4]

An improved British design, the Sheppard washer, became popular, especially in South Wales where twenty-four had been built by 1880, and sixty by 1890 with a capacity of about four million tons.[5] The technology was refined further with the development of the Lührig washer; this used a bed of feldspar particles, parallelepiped in shape, which allowed the dirt to fall through when the water moved upwards but formed a solid bed when they fell back, retaining the coal. Large numbers of increasingly large Lührig plant were built after about 1895, and by the end of the century the Baum washer, which graded the coal as well as washing it, also gained in popularity. Staveley, Rothervale, Mitchell's Main, and Denaby and Cadeby Main were among those introducing Lührig dressing appliances before 1904. Powell Duffryn installed a Humboldt type, whereas the complex of screening and washing plant at Blundell's collieries consisted of mechanically operated tipplers,

[1] *CG* 20 May 1889, 700; Chapman and Mott 1928, 101–2, 105; Galloway 1904, 366.

[2] *CG* 29 Apr. 1887, 604; Anderson 1967, 172.

[3] G. Gilroy, 'Coal Washing in Use at the Ince Hall Coal and Connell Company's Collieries', *TNEIMME* 1866, XV, 127–9; Chapman and Mott 1928, 105–6.

[4] Chapman and Mott 1928, 103–9, 112–17.

[5] Ibid., 109–12.

shaker screens, and wire picking belts fitted with loading booms.[1] It is
significant that it was these large colliery companies which were the
innovators in Britain of advanced screening and washing techniques,
often building central plant installations to serve a group of collieries,
for these required heavy capital investment and large outputs to ensure
economic operation; examples include the major complexes at Barlborough (Staveley Iron and Coal Company) in 1893, at Aberaman
(Powell Duffryn) in 1903, and at Bothwell Castle (Baird and Co.) in 1900,
where collieries were connected to electrical power stations.[2]

The factors which explain these developments is the trend towards
the mining, in non-coking areas, of thinner and dirtier seams, and the
growing differentiation of coal consumption, especially in export
markets, which demanded close control of coal size, all of which
necessitated investment in coal preparation. Emerson Bainbridge told
the Commissioners in 1904: 'I have been driven to wash against my will',
and explained that washing at his collieries had 'not been done so much
for the purpose of making a profit, as to make unsaleable coal saleable',[3]
an expedient dictated by competition. He, as did James T. Forgie, a
leading figure in the Scottish coal industry, and T. E. Forster, the
prominent North-eastern mining engineer, independently expressed the
view that since 1880 improvements in screening and washing were more
important than any other developments in the industry before 1900.[4]
The Coal Supply Commission in 1903–5 reported that in many coalfields about half the large firms had modern screening and washing plant
and were taking trade from the rest, while it was reported that 40 per
cent of Monmouth collieries had washeries and were grading into more
and more sizes.[5]

Even so, in 1904 George Blake Walker reckoned that Britain still
lagged behind Continental collieries in such techniques, particularly
those of Germany. His judgement may not be disregarded, for since
1873 he had made repeated visits to Westphalia to observe techniques,
noting the efficiency of German methods where more precise mixtures
were available for use in mechanical stokers. Whereas in Britain coalowners usually offered four sizes—large coal, large nuts, pea nuts, and

[1] Ibid., 115–17, 119–21.

[2] Ibid., 178; CG 31 Oct. 1890, 705; BSCEMRRC Stanton and Staveley 2034/2/7 MB 23 Feb.
1892; Hann 1922, 15; Anderson 1967, 174.

[3] Coal Supplies Commission 1904, XXIII, QQ 14713, 11056, 11058.

[4] CG 15 Aug. 1890, 258, 21 Feb. 1896, 365, 17 June 1898, 1089; T. E. Forster and H. Ayton,
'Improved Coal Screening and Cleaning', TNEIME, XXIX (1889/90), 51.

[5] Digest of Evidence I, 26–38.

slack—their counterparts in Germany offered many more. The explanation he offered for the lead was historical and geological; that Westphalian coal producers had encountered particular difficulties due to a 'contorted coalfield', containing folding strata and crushed seams, which from the beginning had forced them to make greater use of washing.[1] By 1913 an estimated 14.4 per cent of UK output, or 42.3 million tons, was washed. Washing plant was not evenly spread over the country, however: in 1925 over 40 per cent of Yorkshire and South Wales output was washed but only 13 per cent in the North-east and 18 per cent in Scotland; the UK average was then 28.3 per cent.[2] Another return for 1913 shows that in collieries comprising 94 per cent of output an average of 2.9 per cent of gross output became refuse after screening and washing, ranging from 4.5 per cent in Scotland to 1.6 per cent in South Wales, though some of the coal contained in this dirt was recovered. An estimated 3.25 million tons was left underground.[3]

By the late nineteenth century the declining quality of coal mined from deeper and thinner seams, more dirt and an increasing percentage of small coal resulting therefrom, an increasingly sophisticated market, and the massive strides occurring in washing technology meant that by 1913 nearly 15 per cent of coal and probably half the small coal was being washed, either to turn it into a marketable product or to increase revenue product and profitability; over 4 per cent was being coked for metallurgical purposes, and about $3\frac{1}{2}$ per cent of South Wales output was going to manufacture patent fuel. It seems likely that while overall profits in the industry were sustained by a buoyant demand for coal, between 1895 and 1913 the widespread adoption of modern washing, coking, and briquetting plant were important influences on inter-firm differences in profitability—for the real costs of mining coal were rising.[4]

[1] *RC Coal Supplies* 1904, XXIII, Q 10698.
[2] Chapman and Mott 1928, 125–8.
[3] *Coal Conservation Committee*, 1918, VII, 669–70.
[4] See below 510–11.

CHAPTER 5

Business Organization and Management

i. Colliery size and productivity

The speed and extent to which technology advanced and was applied to mining coal—and to coal preparation—depended much upon the effective administration and control of firms, the relations between them in market transactions, and the structure of enterprise. Already by 1830 some colliery enterprises had reached considerable size, exceeding a thousand workers, especially in the North-east where the country's deepest pits were to be found. Perhaps not surprisingly, therefore, in 1833 John Buddle, agent to the Marquis of Londonderry, advised his employer to regard the coal trade 'as a sheer matter of business in every respect, which in plain truth it really is, and nothing else'.[1] Throughout the period the trend towards an increase in the size of collieries and of coalmining firms continued, though with marked regional differences. Difficulties arise, however, in charting this process of increasing size, partly because even from 1854, when Robert Hunt's *Mineral Statistics* and the *Reports* of the Inspectors of Mines provide information on county and regional production, inconsistency and incomplete recording render these figures unreliable. Furthermore, even from 1894, when colliery-by-colliery employment figures are available in the *List of Mines*, variability in the definition of a 'colliery' results in less than perfect data. The mining unit might consist of a pit or a drift or a combination of both. The characteristic of the pit was the vertical access to a series of roads leading to the coal faces, whereas a drift, or level, led horizontally or by slope from a hillside face into the workings. Pit layout depended upon geological factors. In the North-east, where seams workable in the 1830s ran deep, several seams might be tapped from a single shaft, whereas shallow seam locations, in Lancashire for example, favoured the sinking of several shafts, each often referred to as a pit, from which distinctive seams would be mined.[2] The seams were

---

[1] DuRO Londonderry, D/LO/C142, Buddle to Londonderry, 19 Nov. 1833.
[2] Flinn 1984, 49–51.

critical in determining the duration of a pit's working life, the shallower ones surviving often for less than five years. Pits usually operated as sub-units within the mine or colliery for the purposes of getting coal and employment, though they might be linked underground by common drainage or ventilation systems.

A 'mine' is defined here as consisting of one or more pits which from an organizational and operational standpoint collectively form a mine, or colliery, as a single *productive* unit. We have attempted to rectify anomalies in the *Mineral Statistics* and *List of Mines* and to correct for omissions the resulting figures for 1913, 1895, 1880, and 1860. When applied to the revised output estimates they show average mine size at these benchmark years (Table 5.1). The sources and methods of doing so are explained in Appendix 5.1.

The overall trend in the annual average output of mines is of un-ambiguous acceleration: a 41 per cent increase in the twenty years between 1860 and 1880, 45 per cent during the fifteen years which followed, and a rise by 64 per cent over the next eighteen years. Between 1860 and 1895 the mines of the North-east and of South Wales were above average size, the former by a factor of around two, and only the East Midlands had joined these two major regions above the average by 1880. Until after 1880, however, the North-east continued to be the dominant large-scale producer by a wide margin, no region having achieved an average mine size comparable with the figure for the North-east of 62,800 tons in 1860. Walters's detailed figures using parish returns for Aberdare suggest that in the 1860s and early 1870s the average size of steam-coal collieries in South Wales were twice the level of the overall regional average in 1860, and about half as much again of the 1880 figure. The North-east too, however, Durham in particular, contained mines very much larger than average, which the sizeable numbers of relatively small mines in Northumberland depressed, as did those of Pembroke-shire, Breconshire, and Carmarthenshire in the case of South Wales.[1] In Yorkshire, Lancashire, and the East Midlands marked deviations about the mean from one district to another cautions against simple generali-zations concerning the significance and causes of trends in 'size' measured by averages, especially before the 1890s. From that time, how-ever, when the data are more reliable, generalizations are possible with fewer qualifications. The most rapid increases in average mine size between 1895 and 1913 occurred in Yorkshire and the East Midlands;

---

[1] Walters 1977, 268.

Table 5.1. *Number and average size of mines, by employment and region, 1860–1913*

	1860		1880		1895		1913	
	Number	Av. output ('ooo tons)	Number	Av. output ('ooo tons)	Number	Av. output ('ooo tons)	Number	Av. output ('ooo tons)
Scotland	427	26.0	500	36.5	491	58.6	463	91.7
North-east	283	62.8	380	91.9	347	114.8	395	142.7
Cumberland	28	42.9	35	48.0	39	48.3	37	59.5
Lancs./Ches.	406	30.3	480	41.3	399	57.1	335	73.5
North Wales	70	25.7	85	28.6	59	48.3	45	77.9
yorkshire	387	23.8	460	38.0	364	62.7	297	147.0
East Midlands	200	28.5	280	47.8	247	78.2	189	178.3
West Midlands	500	23.0	520	30.1	400	40.3	307	67.9
South Wales	400	35.5	457	46.3	490	67.4	569	99.9
South-west	90	16.6	110	17.7	99	21.3	68	43.6
Average	2,791	31.5	3,307	44.3	2,935	64.6	2,705	106.2

Sources: Recalculated from *List of Mines* and regional output figures (Appendix 1.1). See Appendix 5.1.

the slowest were recorded in the North-east and Lancashire. These variations, which are a continuation of earlier trends, clearly reflect rapid expansion into new areas with few large mines, the stagnation of output in Lancashire, and the long-standing higher-than-average size of mines in the North-east. The mines of Fife, the area of rapid growth within Scotland, also experienced a rise in average size.

However, the mean colliery size conceals a wide range of sizes throughout the period, which it becomes possible to analyse in terms of underground colliery employment from 1895 (Table 5.2). They reveal a *median* colliery size of 125, compared with a mean employment per mine of 235. One-third of all working collieries employed fewer than 50 people, only 13 per cent above 500, and 3 per cent (76 mines) over one thousand. Large numbers of small collieries continued to exist, but in addition to the many tiny pits of south Staffordshire and the levels in the Forest of Dean even South Wales possessed an above-average percentage, for numerous levels and drifts continued to exist, especially outside the steam-coal districts. Small mines were fewest in the North-east and the East Midlands, followed by Scotland where most were of medium size. The percentage of mines employing more than 500 people was highest in the North-east (27 per cent), whereas in South Wales the distribution was skewed, with many large pits and few in the 200 to 600 range.

Between 1895 and 1913 the average size of collieries rose considerably, as the number of working mines fell from 2,935 to 2,705. As output was increasing, the mean colliery size rose from 235 to 410 workers, compared with an increase in the median from 125 to 210. The proportion of those employing fewer than 50 had fallen, those employing more than 500 had risen, and in 1913 12 per cent of all mines employed more than one thousand men underground. Between 1895 and 1913 Scotland still contained relatively few large mines and a lower percentage of small mines than any other region. Yorkshire contained a higher proportion of mines employing more than one thousand underground workers, followed by the East Midlands and the North-east, but South Wales ranked second only to Yorkshire in mines employing more than two thousand.

Technology and the depth of pits were closely related to mine size in the nineteenth century. As pits became deeper, in some regions it was seldom practicable for a company to sink more than a couple of pits at a colliery site. One effect was to encourage the sinking of larger pits in order to concentrate capital expenditure. While in such instances the

Table 5.2. *Size distribution of mines by employment and region, 1895 and 1913*
(percentages)

	below 50	50–199	200–399	400–599	600–799	800–999	1,000–1,499	1,500–1,999	over 2,000	Number of collieries
1895										
Scotland	26	41	21	8	2	1		1		491
North-east	22	12	27	17	11	4		6		347
Cumberland	33	15	36	10	5	—		—		39
Lancs./Ches.	28	27	30	11	4	0		—		399
North Wales	37	28	16	13	5	2		—		59
Yorkshire	33	28	15	8	5	4		4		364
East Midlands	23	19	32	13	6	3		4		247
West Midlands	52	26	11	7	3	1		1		400
South Wales	37	27	14	6	6	4		5		490
South-west	55	17	20	7	1	—		—		99
Total number of collieries	973	781	609	280	146	70		76		2,935

1913										
Scotland	18	31	23	14	9	3	2	0	—	463
North-east	23	11	13	14	11	9	11	5	3	395
Cumberland	32	16	22	14	8	3	2	—	—	37
Lancs./Ches.	23	18	26	16	9	3	3	—	—	335
North Wales	27	21	13	17	6	11	4	5	—	45
Yorkshire	38	17	11	4	3	4	8	5	8	297
East Midlands	22	9	15	17	13	6	11	5	4	189
West Midlands	46	19	10	6	6	4	5	1	1	307
South Wales	34	23	15	7	6	1	4	4	5	569
South-west	43	16	18	13	5	4	—	—	—	68
Total number of collieries	794	538	451	300	209	116	153	71	73	2,705

Source: List of Mines.

motive for establishing a large mine might have been unrelated to considerations of productivity or operational economics, the possibility none the less exists that benefits of this kind resulted from size. In the literature of industrial economics the economies of large-scale production have figured prominently. The scope for technology to improve labour productivity, either by changes in the working methods or by introducing new technology, have already been identified, albeit necessarily in non-quantitative terms except in certain instances. Did the trend towards larger mines reflect a greater efficiency associated with size?

Since coal is not a homogeneous product, different levels of labour productivity can coexist at similar profit margins, depending upon different conditions in the various markets for diverse coal types. Moreover, labour productivity in Walters's detailed study of comparisons between average costs per ton of coal at Powell Duffryn's pits, similar in age, led him to conclude: 'It appears that, among like pits in like conditions, greater scale of operations brought advantages in factor prices'; within certain bounds of comparability, it seemed that the larger the colliery the lower the costs, though because mining conditions varied so widely evidence of scale economies could not be discerned in every case.[1] Evidence provided by the collieries of the Staveley Coal and Iron Company between 1894 and 1913 lend support to this general observation, the larger than average collieries of Markham I, Ireland, and Barlboro registering lower-than-average working costs, compared with the Bonds Main, Hartington, and from 1905 Seymour, pits.[2] But detailed comparisons between productivity and costs in the various collieries belonging to Consett showed no such positive correlation with mine size; indeed, the costs at Hunter Pit were consistently lower than those at Chopwell, even though the former was of more recent origin and actually produced diminishing outputs; Langley Park increased output, but costs increased simultaneously as productivity fell. A. S. Wilson concluded that the actual size of pit was of small significance to cost functions.[3]

Labour productivity, fundamental to cost levels in the coal industry, depends upon two fundamental factors: geological constraints on production, and capital endowment. Output per man varied according

---

[1] Ibid., 276–8.
[2] BSCEMRRC Stanton and Staveley 2034/2/32–3 cost and profits data; *List of Mines*.
[3] A. S. Wilson thesis, 149–51.

to seam thickness, condition of floor and roof, and the length of haulage routes, as well, of course, as the proportion of face workers to others. Furthermore, the massive variation in capital–output ratios between one colliery and another must have affected labour productivity considerably, though under conditions of disparate geological constraints on production higher levels of capital investment, while raising productivity, might not yield differing levels of output per man in comparison with other pits. There are, therefore, serious methodological problems in establishing the relationship between labour productivity and mine size. It is difficult to envisage how it could be possible to hold such factors as geology and capital endowment constant in order to meet the necessary precondition for assessing a degree of correlation between productivity and colliery size; data do exist, however, which enable us to observe relationships between the two, even though it may not be possible actually to prove those relationships.

By using four sets of data, relating to collieries on the Tyne and Wear in 1843,[1] to a sample of Durham collieries for 1893–5 and for 1908–10,[2] and to another sample of Northumberland collieries averaged over the period 1893–1913,[3] it is possible to deduce relationships between productivity—defined here as output per man-shift (except in the first case where output per man-year has had to be used) plotted against colliery output and mine size. While there are reservations concerning the validity of the 1843 data, the results of a similar exercise based on the firmer empirical foundation of the later material are not at variance.

[1] Liefchild's list, *Report on Mining Districts* 1847, XVI, 437–9. The data refer to fifty-eight collieries which represented well above one-half of the saleable output from the North-east region (compare returns located NEI ZC 14–15 and also Dunn's list in *On the Coal Trade*, 214–6). Reservations arise concerning the minor distortions consequent upon the (unavoidable) use of output per man-year rather than output per man-shift as the measure of productivity, which might conceal variations due to the number of days worked in each year. There is a possibility, too, that the rapid expansion of the industry in these districts at that time meant that some— perhaps several—collieries were either at an early stage of operational life, or undergoing new sinking. More serious, however, is that the output data probably refer only to seasale coal and excludes a substantial proportion of production, resulting in underestimates of actual productivity; NEI ZC 14, 15.

[2] DuRO/NCB I/Co/86/358, 358a, 402–6, 441, 482, 501, 526, 540, 555, 577, 586, 595, 612, 627, 651, 673: a series of coalowners' returns. On a colliery-by-colliery analysis for 1893–9 and 1908–10 (where the means of output and productivity over the three-year period were calculated) there were forty and forty-eight observations respectively, representing in 1893–5 22.5 per cent of total Durham output and 27.2 per cent in 1908–10.

[3] NuRO/NCB/C/160, 169–171, 180, 188, 193, 195, 197, 204, 212, 217, 224, 246, 254, 259, 267, 286, 291, 292, 300, 313, 368: a series of coalowners' returns. Data for Northumberland relate to thirteen collieries (for which the mean of output and productivity over the entire period 1893–1913 was calculated) representing about 52 per cent of the county's output.

None reveal an observable correlation between productivity and size of productive unit. The Durham data, based on Durham Coalowners' Association Returns, which are thorough and reliable, show low and high productivities both at collieries with low production levels as well as in highly productive collieries. The implication that low-output collieries might be associated with either a positive or a negative correlation between size and output per man is consistent with the critical relationship between geological conditions and capital endowment, which largely explained differing capital–output ratios and patterns of technical innovation.[1]

Given the deficiencies of our data, it remains to consider whether the outcome of a hypothetical exercise, in which it might have been possible to hold capital investment and geological factors constant, would have produced similar conclusions rejecting the hypothesis that colliery size influenced productivity. It is plausible to conceive of a hypothetical example of two collieries in which we suppose that operating at full, or nearly full, capacity, A produces 100,000 tons from one seam and B produces 200,000 tons from two seams of identical depth and structure; and in which B has precisely twice the amount of capital invested as A. First, there is no reason why, by employing identical systems of face technology, hewers' productivity in A should differ from that in B. Second, only if the average length of roadways (per ton of output) varied would colliery B reap economies of scale; whether this were the case would depend on mine layout. If in the case of colliery B the main roadways served both seams, then some labour saving would be possible; but it would be minimal under conditions of fully mechanized haulage. Where main haulage roads served two or more seams, labour savings from road construction and maintenance might be appreciable. Finally, greater savings might result, and economies of scale secured, in surface preparation, washing, and coking of coal, though this, of course, implies increased capital investment, especially from the 1880s. Since the bulk of labour in the industry was engaged in hewing or putting (activities only marginally affected by scale), our conclusion that variations in capital

---

[1] Our conclusions may be tested by the correlation coefficients, the results of which are as follows: Tyne and Wear (1843) −0.05; Durham (1893–5) −0.14; Durham (1908–10) −0.05; Northumberland (1893–1913) +0.25. Thus is demonstrated the complete absence of any correlation between colliery size and labour productivity. It was also possible to conduct a similar exercise using the Durham sample for 1893–5 together with supplementary information on coal types produced by each colliery, available in the *Mineral Statistics*. Again, no obvious correlation between labour productivity and the type of coal produced emerged, though the number of observations it was possible to use was insufficient to establish this conclusion beyond doubt.

endowment and geology swamped any relationship between size and productivity is hardly surprising. The most likely response to low productivity by managers was thus less likely to have been an expansion in the size of operations (as distinct from increasing output within a given size of colliery) to secure operating economies, than in greater efforts to increase capital efficiency, or 'improve' geology by the working of more productive seams, or the adoption of a policy of product enhancement—by attention to coal preparation.

It has been established that in Scotland the average size of mines using cutting machinery was considerably greater than that of the all-mine average. The smallest mine using coal cutters in 1913 employed only sixty-four workers, consistent with an output of about 20,000 tons—roughly the annual output from a single coal cutter. The mean size of mechanized mines in Scotland was 465, compared with 305 in all collieries. The median figure was 400 for mechanized mines compared with 210 for all collieries.[1] This suggests that while size was largely irrelevant in contributing directly to labour productivity, its indirect importance lay in justifying investment in new technology—though the Scottish figures suggest a relatively modest size threshold before coal-cutting machinery became economic. The general concentration of coal cutters in thin seams is also consistent with our conclusions which place geological, technological, and human factors as the major determinants of productivity.[2]

Where conditions were unsuited to mechanization at the face, the alternative strategy in the face of increasing costs was to close some pits and to sink others with the aim of extracting coal from the most accessible and/or from those offering relatively high marginal revenues. The possession of more than a single mine, and certainly access to more than a single seam, was necessary for the implementation of such a policy, especially in the short to medium term; and yet the size of mines carried implications for the economics of colliery working which differed, depending upon whether the pits or levels belonging to an enterprise were relatively small and shallow, whether they were easily maintained during closure, or whether the mines were deep and large—of the type characteristic of the South Wales steam collieries.[3] Here, heavier fixed costs and prevailing geological conditions rendered closure

[1] *List of Mines* and *Samuel Commission* III Appendix 18:10.
[2] See above 352–64. See also *Samuel Commission* III 58, 44; J. Johnston, *Statistical Cost Analysis* (New York, 1960), 97–102.
[3] Walters 1977, 263–6.

more problematical, especially for the single mine-owning enterprise or for those dependent on only a few collieries.

Where conditions were suitable, however, the concentration of production at a single pit, or in a small number of pits in close proximity, did offer once-and-for-all economies by ensuring the more economic use of fixed capital. When William Armstrong was asked to report on the Blundell's collieries in 1853 he criticized the 'extraordinary number of pits and the small produce from each, with the necessity, from the distance over which the coal is taken by the drawers, of an excessive number being employed', expressing amazement at the operation of no fewer than seventeen separate engines to draw coal and pump water from the three collieries, Pemberton, Ince, and Chorley. His remedy was the immediate introduction of the 'North country practice . . . concentration of work both above, and underground . . . wherever practicable the self acting plane should displace labour—working plans closely kept up to the face—the number of pits reduced and the aggregate tonnage if possible largely increased'.[1] Over the next twenty years a thoroughgoing transformation followed along these lines, involving the closure of several pits, the leasing of others and the opening of more, the provision of central workshops, and the rationalization of modernized machinery for pumping, ventilation, and haulage.[2] Armstrong was to proffer similar advice to other colliery owners, and even fifty years later criticized 'the scattered condition of . . . working faces in several seams', and 'high upstanding charges chiefly caused by heavy and extensive pumping operations . . .'. He advised closure of the worst workings, but maintaining others in order to maintain output at sufficient levels to avoid increasing overhead costs.[3]

J. G. Weeks, manager of Bedlington Colliery in Northumberland, quantified the costs and benefits of temporary or permanent closure in a review of working costs conducted prior to a decision whether to close one of three pits then working only five days each fortnight, from which the rough annual tonnages were 230,000, 180,000, and 150,000. By adjusting the output of the three pits for quality differences (as indicated by the relative prices of coals raised from each) Weeks showed that the smallest pit, the 'Doctor', which produced the smallest proportion of 'best' coals, had getting costs 12 per cent higher than the other two. Weeks calculated savings to be gained by closing the small pit and

[1] NuRO Armstrong 725/B5/185–8, Report.
[2] Anderson 1967, 131–61.
[3] NuRO Armstrong 725/B14/547–64, 671–7, Reports.

concentrating production, of the same level, in one or other of the two remaining pits. Taking account of differences in pit and screeners' wages, increased percentage of large coal from the largest pit, reduced cost of horse feeding, fewer mechanics' and labourers' charges, reduced house rent and coal allowances, the total was $5\frac{1}{4}d$. per ton on an output of 570,000 tons: equivalent to roughly 10 per cent savings from the costs of the two relatively efficient pits hitherto working short time, together with the third. These calculations took into account the extra costs necessarily incurred in maintaining in good order (timbering in the roads and air courses which in the pit earmarked for closure were extensive), 'so that when required to be restored little delay or expense be occasioned'.[1] The flexibility of the multi-pit colliery illustrated by Bedlington's history was denied to the single-pit colliery. The principle underlying Weeks's policy was to maintain levels of output produced more efficiently by concentration and full-time working at two pits, in order to bring to an end the relatively inefficient short-time working at three pits. By so doing Bedlington's costs could be reduced, a goal which for the less flexible enterprises implied actually increasing output despite difficulties in selling more coal.

Temporary closure was unusual among the steam coalowners of South Wales, save in exceptionally adverse circumstances; multi-mine ownership was not typical, the depth and size of mines imposed heavy fixed charges, and bad roof conditions in any case rendered such a policy extremely risky.[2] Indeed, even where a company owned several mines—Newton Chambers, for example—joint risks and the fixed costs to insure against flooding or general deterioration which might affect pits remaining at work meant that temporary closure was, in some instances, not a feasible option even for a multi-pit colliery enterprise.[3] In theory, it was possible to minimize costs none the less, by limiting production within a mine to a seam or a section of a mine, which because of prevailing prices justified partial production short of pit closure. This was the principle on which Weeks recommended the closure of the Doctor Pit at Bedlington in 1878, when low prices, especially for coals other than of the large, 'best' type, rendered continued working uneconomic.[4]

In 1894, Mammatt advised the Staveley managers on costs at three districts of Markham No. 1 colliery, recently expanded but where

[1] NEI Weeks 9/1 Report to Directors 1 Nov. 1878.
[2] Walters 1977, 265.
[3] SCL Newton Chambers TR/101 DM 27 Nov. 1905.
[4] NEI Weeks 9/1 Report to Directors 1 Nov. 1878.

production had temporarily ceased due to poor trade: '. . . it is not advisable to work any of this inferior and more costly coal as long as the full output can be maintained from the other and more cheaply worked coal'.[1] The determinants of a seam's profitability were current prices and demand and, despite problems connected with discontinuous working, managers opened and closed faces on the basis of prevailing prices.

The maintenance of full output in sections of a colliery or mine was in accordance with best practice; rather than spreading work over numerous under-exploited faces, the work-force, or at least the hewers, were usually redirected to other working seams or pits. The need to honour customers' contracts, to maintain a skilled or regular work-force, and to meet some of the unavoidable fixed charges if a mine was to remain workable when demand recovered, together provided the economic justification to avoid complete closure:[2] '. . . working places always suffer by stoppage, and in some cases to a very serious and expensive extent',[3] wrote J. Hyslop in *Colliery Management* published in 1870, hence the incentive to maintain continuous and regular working, which, pit by pit or even seam by seam, the larger collieries and the larger firms were best placed to achieve.

ii. Industrial concentration and the growth of firms

The scope for variation in order to minimize costs, both in the short and long term, depended much upon the size of firms, the extent and character of ownership and control, and the systems and quality of decision making. Mine size alone appears to have been unimportant as a direct determinant of productivity;[4] however, the absence of technical economies of scale do not rule out the possibility that the size of enterprises (which might contain numerous mines and collieries) offered cost advantages[5]—through a greater command of capital for investment in modern technology and by possessing greater flexibility of working operations, including the option of moving machinery from one pit to another. Furthermore, as marketing became increasingly important size could offer economies of scale in coal preparation, for only on the basis

[1] BSCEMRRC Stanton and Staveley 2034/3/9d Mammett's Reports 7 Dec. 1894, 18 Jan. 1892.
[2] H. S. Jevons 1915, 260–1; Walters 197, 266–8.
[3] J. Hyslop 1870, 289.
[4] See above 391–98.
[5] A. J. Taylor 1961, 64; A. S. Wilson thesis, 150.

of volume production could the specialized marketing operations of the major exporters be economic.

Except on a random basis for certain firms, output data on mine, colliery, or colliery enterprise are not available before 1913. As a proxy for output, therefore, figures for colliery employment recorded in the *List of Mines* (beginning in 1894) have been used, supplemented by various sources to provide information on the preceding period.[1]

We can do little more than guess the degree of concentration before 1894, for few actual figures are available either of output or employment. Evidence has been assembled from various sources, but the information refers to different years and sometimes includes figures for employment which are only indirectly related to coal production. Our best guess is that during the early 1870s, when our observations are more plentiful than at any other time before 1894, the ten largest coal producers probably accounted for about 10 per cent of total output (Table 5.3). In order of size, Bolckow Vaughan, the Lambton Collieries, Pease and Partners, John Bowes and Partners, J. Joicey, and Straker and Love were the largest North-eastern colliery firms.[2] Wigan Coal and Iron[3] was of similar size to Bolckow Vaughan; Powell Duffryn ranked fifth, or thereabouts, and the Dudley enterprises in south Staffordshire and Ebbw Vale shared ninth and tenth places with the Londonderry collieries;[4] Butterley and Blaenavon collieries were perhaps marginally smaller.[5] Thus it seems that even though the trend in mine size was upwards and the number of multi-colliery firms increased, the industry was not characterized by a high level of concentration. Even in 1913 the ten largest coal producers accounted for only 10 per cent of colliery employment (9 per cent in 1894), and probably roughly the same expressed in terms of output. The largest fifty companies in 1894 employed 28 per cent of all colliery workers, rising to 31 per cent by 1913.

At the regional level important differences can be identified, though only from 1894 is it possible to be confident of generalizations. Beginning with the North-east, where both the large mine and business enterprise was more prevalent throughout the period than in other regions, it seems likely that between 1840 and 1873 concentration altered little,

---

[1] For a justification of this method and a discussion of estimates of firm size see Appendix 5.1.

[2] The figures for Bolckow Vaughan, Lambton Collieries, Pease and Partners, John Bowes and Partners, James Joicey and Straker and Love and Londonderry Collieries refer to 1872, Mountford thesis.

[3] LaRO Wigan Coal and Iron NCW i 1/1–2, Get Books; C. G. 21 Sept. 1867.

[4] Walters 1977, Table 32; A. J. Taylor 1967, 99; C. G. 24 Aug. 1867, 161.

[5] DeRO Butterley 503/B Statement of coal raised . . .; NuRO 725/B8/82 Armstrong's report.

Table 5.3. *The ten largest employers of colliery workers, 1894 and 1913*

1894		1913	
Ocean Coal (SW)	7,917	Powell Duffryn (SW)	14,779
Lambton (NE)	7,500	Lambton (NE)	13,905
William Baird (Scotland)	7,405	Fife (Scotland)	13,853
John Bowes (NE)	6,535	William Baird (Scotland)	11,408
Wigan Coal and Iron (Lancs.)	6,303	Harton (NE)	10,196
David Davies and Son (SW)	5,743	GKN (Dowlais) (SW)	9,929
Bolckow Vaughan (NE)	5,743	Bolckow Vaughan (NE)	9,463
Nixon's Navigation (SW)	5,351	Ashington (NE)	8,985
Powell Duffryn (SW)	5,113	Wigan Coal and Iron (Lancs.)	8,928
Dowlais (SW)	4,652	Nixon's Navigation (SW)	8,887

perhaps at around 25 per cent of production coming from the largest ten firms, rising to 36 and 38 per cent in 1894 and 1913 (Table 5.4).

In comparison with the North-east, South Wales, with the second largest average mine size by 1860 and remaining above average until after 1895, contained fewer very large firms before 1873, but even then (within the industry context) experienced relatively high levels of concentration. It is estimated that whereas in the North-east in 1873 the ten largest firms employed 26 per cent of colliery workers, in South Wales the figure was 41 per cent, falling to 35 per cent by 1913.

Scotland was the only other region possessing coal companies of a size comparable with South Wales and the North-east, the ten largest Scottish firms in eastern Scotland having an estimated 29 per cent of the regional work-force in 1873, and a similar figure measured by employment in the whole of Scotland in 1894. By 1913, however, this proportion had risen to 45 per cent, which signified a higher industrial concentration in Scotland than in any other region. The ownership pattern in Scotland also differed from that in England and Wales, with many more Scottish firms owning numerous collieries scattered across several counties. The figures for Lancashire were 37 per cent and 37 per cent in 1894 and 1913, compared with 39 per cent rising to 43 per cent in the East Midlands.

By 1913 the variation in the degree of industrial concentration in the regions was relatively small, with only Scotland (45 per cent) and the East Midlands (43 per cent) exceeding the 40 per cent level for the ten largest firms, and not even the West Midlands figure fell below 30 per

Table 5.4. *Estimated share of regional employment of the ten largest coal producers, 1873-1913*

	c. 1873[a]	1894	1913
Scotland	29[b]	29	45
North-east	26	36	38
Lancs./Ches.		37	37
Yorkshire		30	36
East Midlands		39	43
West Midlands		31	31
South Wales	41	36	35

[a] Estimates.

[b] East Scotland only, 1875.

Sources:

1873 *List of Mines*; Mountford thesis; NLW 1274, South Wales Coal-owners' Papers; Inspectors' Reports, 1875.

1894 *List of Mines*; NCB I/LO/86(1)–1322, Durham Coalowners' Annual Returns; SCL MD 2699, South Yorkshire Coalowners' Annual Returns; Bro LU, West Yorkshire Coalowners' Annual Returns; Raybould thesis.

1913 *List of Mines*; NCB I/LO/86(1)–1322, Durham Coalowners' Annual Returns; NLW 1274, South Wales Coalowners' Annual Returns; SCL MD 2699, South Yorkshire Coalowners' Annual Returns; Bro LU, West Yorkshire Coalowners' Annual Returns.

cent. When the shares of the three largest firms in each region are calculated Scotland again emerges with the highest level, 24 per cent, followed by the East Midlands at 20 per cent. Scotland was also the region where the level of concentration increased most rapidly between 1894 and 1913, when the ten largest firms almost doubled their share of the region's output. Elsewhere the rise was less dramatic, but only in South Wales did the proportion fall.

Considerable concentration existed at the local level: in Fifeshire, where the Fife Coal Company accounted for half the output, in south Staffordshire, where a half-dozen iron firms produced half the coal in that area, and in the steam-coal districts of South Wales where fourteen firms produced two-thirds of the output. At the national level the growth of industrial concentration between 1894 and 1913 shown by the employment figures is a one per cent increase in the share attributed to the largest ten producers; taking the biggest fifty firms, the figure of 28 per cent in 1894 had risen to 31 by 1913. However, the overall average size of collieries almost doubled, from 3,742 employees in 1894 to 6,785 by 1913. Averaging the top ten companies in each region in 1913 shows regional differences: the North-east and South Wales possessed the largest average colliery employment figures, 8,510 and 8,157 respectively, followed by Scotland, 6,206, Yorkshire, 4,915, the East Midlands, 4,821, Lancashire, 4,290, and the West Midlands, 2,664. Among the ten largest companies in 1894, five were in South Wales, three in the North-east. In 1913 four were in the North-east and three in South Wales. When the largest fifty firms are analysed the dominance of the North-east and South Wales among the big colliery employers is diminished somewhat, though both in 1894 and 1913 the North-east headed the list, with sixteen and seventeen, followed by South Wales, with fourteen and thirteen. Yorkshire, with seven, was third in both years, followed by Scotland and the East Midlands, both with four among the largest in 1894 and five in 1913. Five of Lancashire's producers were included in 1894 and three in 1913. Both in 1894 and 1913 three of the nation's largest ten coal producers were primarily iron and steel manufacturers: Baird, Bolckow Vaughan, and Dowlais (GKN in 1913). Pease and Partners ranked twelfth in both years; by 1913 Staveley and Consett had replaced James Joicey and the Londonderry collieries as thirteenth- and fourteenth-largest colliery employers.

The effects upon size by the emergence of combinations of companies, which while retaining separate identities shared common proprietorship, are not captured in our analysis of concentration, but although spectacular individually such instances do not modify the general conclusions. The most remarkable instances was the complicated structure built up by D. A. Thomas who, beginning with Cambrian Collieries which became a limited company in 1895, proceeded to acquire the Glamorgan Coal Company in 1906, the resulting merger forming the basis of the Cambrian Trust, a holding company formed in 1908. After taking over the Naval Colliery in 1908, the Albion Steam Coal Company in 1909, and in the following year the Fernhill Collieries Ltd., comprising the Fernhill and Dunraven Collieries and Britannic Merthyr, this amalgamation became the Consolidated Cambrian Ltd. in 1913.[1] The combined employment in 1913 exceeded the size of Powell Duffryn's labour force by some 12 per cent.

Also concealed within the *List of Mines* figures are the alliances of ownership resulting from the creation of subsidiary companies which, having a separate identity, are recorded for official purposes as in-

---

[1] H. S. Jevons 1915, 320–3; Walters 1977, 65–6, 273.

dependent colliery enterprises. As for example in the case of the formation of the Newstead Colliery Company in 1872, a joint venture
between Staveley and Sheepbridge, the purpose of which was to sink a
new colliery in a fresh royalty, a device repeatedly employed when these
two companies began to develop the south Yorkshire mineral deposits
after 1900.[1] Staveley's other subsidiaries were Brodsworth Main Colliery
Co. Ltd., formed jointly with Hickleton Main Colliery in 1907, followed
by the wholly-owned subsidiary, Yorkshire Main, a few years later.
Another joint venture with Sheepbridge brought about the formation of
Firbeck Main Colliery Co. Ltd. in 1913. Meanwhile, in 1901, jointly with
the Sheffield Coal Company, Sheepbridge had promoted the Dinnington
Main Colliery Co. Ltd., followed by the wholly-owned subsidiaries of
Maltby Main Colliery Co. Ltd. in 1907 and Rossington Main Colliery
Company Ltd. in 1911.[2] The Tredegar Iron Company possessed two off-
shoots shortly before 1913, Oakdale Navigation and Markham Steam
Coal Colliery Companies.[3] It is difficult to establish the extent of such
concealed concentration, especially when partnerships or private
limited companies were involved. Among large public companies, however, the amount of unidentified hidden concentration is likely to have
been insignificant in its effect upon an analysis of concentration
patterns.

Even more difficult to assess are the effects of interlocking directorates which were extensive, upon the conduct of business. Before
considering this aspect of ownership and control, however, the extent
and form of concentration in the industry requires explanation in terms
of the economic advantages of size. Evidence presented above suggested
that the significance for labour productivity of mine size was negligible.
Cost economies could be achieved by the concentration of output into a
single or into a few mines, which could be supplied with pumping and
ventilation from a single power source; but while offering considerable
economies in fuel such measures saved very little labour, the major
element in costs.[4] Such considerations, however, depended upon
geological conditions, except under circumstances where management
was lax, as in the remarkable, though by no means unique, case of
Blundell's collieries in the 1850s.[5] Furthermore, this was an argument for
the concentration of production into the minimum number of pits

---

[1] BSCEMRRC Stanton and Staveley 2034/3/10. Memorandum and Articles of Association,
Newstead Colliery Company, 1878.
[2] Chapman 1981, 132.   [3] Walters 1977, 274.
[4] See below 496–511.   [5] See above 396.

possible, rather than a justification for a particular size of colliery enterprise. The other source of saving associated with production was that
arising from the provision of power of lower unit costs from a central
electric station, though electricity was not a major influence before 1903,
the exceptions even then occurring in firms which were already large.[1]
Especially during the first half of the century, however, there were other
cost advantages associated with size arising from the possession and
utilization of ancillary colliery plant, such as railroads and rolling stock,
coking facilities, and ships. In the 1830s, with few exceptions, those
colliery enterprises which attained the largest size depended upon seaborne trade—especially the highly organized marketing arrangements
involved in supplying the London market, which necessitated extensive
investment to transport and distribute the coals.

By the early 1870s probably five of the top ten coal-producing firms
were also iron producers: Bolckow Vaughan, Wigan Coal and Iron,
Pease and Partners, the Dudley Trustees, and Ebbw Vale; though
Dowlais, Blaenavon, Butterley, Staveley, and Consett were other large
iron and coal companies. The entry of John Brown into coal production
in 1872–3 exemplifies the motives which may have lain behind the
adoption of a similar strategy by other steel producers. Quite simply, in
recent years the company had experienced difficulty in securing coal on
long contract, which for any large iron or steel producer was of critical
importance. H. D. Pochin explained to shareholders that the directors
had intended to obtain more and more control over the raw materials,
and to reduce the cost of coal at the furnace mouth. By acquiring
Aldwarke Main and Carr House Collieries, however, the company
found itself with one-third more than the furnaces could consume—
which led to the construction of more blast furnaces.[2] Before the 1880s
every one of the large-scale coal producers in Scotland were also iron
producers,[3] and the same was true, with the exception of Powell
Duffryn, of the South Wales industry;[4] and, though none appeared
among the largest ten firms at national level, likewise the major coal
producers in the East and West Midlands.[5] Many of the iron firms, such
as the Bairds, William Dixon, and Clay Cross, had initially been coalmasters but had embarked upon iron production either as a profitable

[1] See above 361–3.
[2] *Sheffield Daily Telegraph* 26 June 1873.
[3] Youngson Brown thesis, 97.
[4] Morris and Williams 1958, 83–8.
[5] J. E. Williams 1962, 36–43, 197–204; Hopkinson thesis, 374–89; A. J. Taylor 1967, 99.

investment *per se*, or, as in the case of Clay Cross in the 1840s and 1850s, as a method of consuming small coal and slack in the form of coke for blast furnaces.[1] One of the strongest incentives to control the supply of raw materials, however, was the fluctuating character of the iron trade, accompanied by potential fuel shortages from an industry in which supply was inelastic at the peaks.[2] Moreover, as the economics of iron production required large-scale operations and a continuous output, the implication for the size of iron/coal enterprises ensured the dominance of the coal-producing iron firms as the largest outside the North-east before the 1880s. The role of internal coal supplies to the iron producer is also evident in the Staveley Colliery manager's report to the directors in 1901, when under circumstances of a depressed market for the company's pig iron: 'According to costs as shown in the trade report we cannot produce iron at a remunerative figure, taking the present market value as a basis, but if the raw material be reckoned at prime cost without intermediate profit there is still a margin on the right side'.[3] The alternative of closing furnaces was rejected on the grounds that disposal of the company's furnaces coal would become even more difficult. The implication was that by adopting favourable transfer costs for coal used in the furnaces iron production should be subsidized. In companies accustomed to much less orthodox accounting procedures compared with the norm at Staveley, such an arrangement was probably widespread.

Diversification was another important influence on industrial structure and the growth of firms, the impulse intensifying, not surprisingly, in periods when the iron industry was in difficulties—in the 1860s and again after the early 1870s boom into the 1880s. During the depression in the iron trade in 1865–7, for example, the sinking of a new large colliery by the Sheepbridge Iron Company and the acquisition of another were part of a policy motivated by the search for partial insurance against the periodic collapse of the iron market, which house and steam coal might mitigate.[4] The high quality of Welsh steam coal meant that from the third quarter of the century the coal trade exercised a special attraction in that region, irrespective of the state of the iron trade. After the Dowlais Iron Company acquired the Penydarren lease in 1859, the

[1] *The Times* 1 Dec. 1913, 26.

[2] George Elliott explained the position vividly: 'If there is a scarcity of coal you know not what to do; you must have it at any price', *SC Dearness and Scarcity* 1873, X, Q 7533.

[3] BSCEMRRC Stanton and Staveley 031428/75, MB 26 Feb. 1901.

[4] BSCEMRRC Stanton and Staveley 031428/71, MB 14 Sept. 1863, 31 Aug. 1866, 9 Sept. 1867, 14 Sept. 1868.

manager, Menelaus, emphasized the advantages of working the coal at about 1,000 tons a day more than was justified by output from the furnaces, which he considered was then at a level above which the risks of continued production were too great. He argued that such a policy would require no new pits after the initial sinkings and very little capital outlay for disposal of the coal, other than relatively small amounts of circulating capital. He claimed: 'It is well known that the iron master under the same circumstances can always work his coal cheaper than the coal owner',[1] though to his reasons (the provision of more regular employment and the use of small coal as furnace fuel) should be added the lower wages paid to colliery workers employed in mines belonging to iron-masters. Whereas the latter consideration was important for iron/coal producers elsewhere, however, the revenue productivity of the steam-coal collieries from the 1860s was so favourable that Dowlais began not only to sell coal but to purchase furnace coke to replace it.[2] Even by the early 1870s over one-third of the total, and one-half of large, coal at Dowlais was sold. Especially from the 1860s, iron-making companies in the North-east, Scotland, the East Midlands, and Yorkshire also began to raise coal for sale as well as for consumption, which explains how, by 1900, such companies as William Baird, Dowlais (later GKN), the Peases, Staveley, Consett, and Butterley figured among the largest twenty coal producers in the U.K.

With the exception of the Wigan Coal and Iron Company, all of the remaining firms among the top twenty in 1913 conducted substantial exporting trade. Powell Duffryn, the Lambton Collieries, the Fife Coal Company, Ashington, Nixon's Navigation, the Ocean Colliery Co., and the Londonderry Collieries each possessed overseas depots, and either owned subsidiary shipping companies or hired steamers for trade with large customers ordering on a scale comparable with the Admiralty.[3] The Wigan Coal and Iron Company, probably one of the three largest coal employers in the early 1870s, and ninth in 1913, may be classified as the name implies, but in fact coal came to dominate the firm's activities soon after its formation in 1865, the first limited-liability company involving the amalgamation of separate interests. Whereas, in explaining size, other firms we have alluded to fit broadly into one or other category (iron-producing or exporting enterprise, including the London trade), the extent of the Lancashire company's operations resulted almost entirely from the fact of merger between the Haigh and Up-

[1] Morris and Williams 1958, 88.   [2] Walters 1977, 11.
[3] The Times 1 Dec. 1913, 26; Walters 1977, 301-5.

holland Collieries, the Kirkless Hall Coal and Iron Works (each valued at more than £0.6m.), the Standish and Shevington Cannel Company (£0.3m.), and the tiny Broomfield Colliery.[1] Coalmining assets represented the major part of the company's assets, and coal and coke sales accounted for approximately three-quarters of the total sale values in the 1860s and 1870s. This amalgamation created one of the largest, at that time possibly the largest, of all coal-producing enterprises, and raises the question of how important mergers were in influencing size.

Partnerships and business alliances of various kinds were frequently changing their composition and character during the nineteenth century, long before the limited-liability legislation of the 1850s and 1860s facilitated the formal and more permanent combinations of business organizations. Because of the restrictions under partnership law, even relatively large colliery enterprises were in the hands of a few partners, and almost invariably some of these held major shares in other firms. The links which maintained continuity between them over time usually centred on family connections. Shifting patterns of colliery ownership contributed to industrial concentration, which the growth in colliery size due to geo-technical considerations had already intensified. By the 1840s the huge landed enterprises in the North-east were being challenged in size by the newly formed Haswell, Hetton, and South Hetton coal companies.[2] As the demand for coal grew, colliery expansion in the North-east took the form of mining at increasing depths as well as in an increase in the number of producers, and depth in particular reinforced the trend towards larger size. However, colliery proliferation also stimulated attempts to increase industrial concentration, as restriction became a motivating force among large established enterprises. The joint acquisition in 1836 of the operating North Hetton Colliery by the Earl of Durham, Lord Londonderry, and the Hetton Colliery Co. was designed to steal a march on the Durham Colliery Co., the new joint-stock company which appeared to threaten the oligopolistic power of the three major producers.[3] Defensive expansion also explains some of the acquisition made by the owners of Barber Walker in the East Midlands, who between 1838 and 1857 were reputed to have purchased collieries in order to restrict their output and stifle competition.[4] Similarly, the process by which John Bowes and partners grew to

---

[1] LaRO DDX/127/44, Wigan Coal and Iron Company Ltd., Memorandum and Articles of Association, 5–14.   [2] Hiskey 1983, 2–7.
[3] D. Spring, 'The Earls of Durham and the Great Northern Coalfield 1830–1880', *Canadian Historical Review*, 33 (1952), 242–3.   [4] A. R. Griffin 1971, 67.

become one of the ten largest coal producers from the 1840s was the out-right purchase of existing pits from competitors who were either bank-rupt or in decline.[1] Charles Palmer's shrewd assessment of the desirabil-ity of the Bowes Partnership acquiring Springwell Colliery and railway from the Grand Allies was based on his anticipation of the interest in obtaining it from Joicey, who had become a rival as a consequence of his recent expansion of coal production around Tanfield and Beamish: 'I think it would be a dangerous thing to let him have it, for should he join with Southern and get his coals down by a cheaper and shorter route than us it would be a very serious matter. Already he is underselling us by 6d. or 9d. per ton, although he pays higher than we do ... It will be more satisfactory for us to have the concern ...'.[2] For the most part, however, this pattern of expansion through acquisition, for one reason or another, is untypical of the other large North-eastern producers at that time.

The formation of the Wigan Coal and Iron Company in 1865 was an example of a merger in what was to become a classic manner, whereby private groups of owner-managers sought to realize benefits of merging their enterprises in a consolidated limited-liability company by issuing shares to the public. With a paid up capital of £1.5m. and a coal output of 1.4m. tons in 1866, the company immediately became one of the lead-ing enterprises on a national level, posing problems of policy formula-tion and managerial structure and practice which soon precipitated a boardroom crisis and occasioned public interest.[3] The origins of the merger, however, are to be found in the impending retirement from active involvement by Lord Crawford from his Haigh and Upholland Collieries, which provided an opportunity for John Lancaster and his partners of Kirkless Hall Coal and Ironworks to diversify from iron to coal.[4]

Mergers were not important in the industry before the 1890s, and even then by comparison with developments in manufacturing indus-try, which experienced three peaks in merger activity, 1888–90, 1898–1900, and 1909–11,[5] were limited in number and extent. With a few spectacular exceptions, most of the large firms which developed in the

---

[1] Mountford thesis, 58–77, 153, 200.

[2] Ibid., 65.

[3] LaRO Wigan Coal and Iron DXX/127/38 Extraordinary General Meeting 13 Jan. 1870, 1–35.

[4] J. A. Peden, 'The History of Kirkless Iron Works', unpublished B.Ed. dissertation; C. F. Mott Training College 1965, 32–5.

[5] Leslie Hannah, 'Mergers in British Manufacturing Industry 1880–1918', *Oxford Economic Papers*, 26 (1974), 5–7.

course of the nineteenth and early twentieth century grew by a process of internal expansion; by sinking pits on existing and newly acquired royalties, and in some instances establishing subsidiary companies in the process. Expanding coal production by iron companies resulted either from a desire to control raw materials or to diversify from, to complement, or offset fluctuations in iron production, and increasingly from the 1880s to compensate for the relative decline in the profitability of iron and steel production.[1]

Ironworks tended to expand coal production by sinking their own pits. Sale-coal companies grew large in response to an 'export' trade, to London from the North-east during the first three-quarters of the century, but increasingly from the 1860s for shipment overseas. Strategic and commercial considerations, rather than the expectation of substantial technical and cost advantages in production, appear to have been the major influences in the growth of large-scale enterprise. Even by 1913, when the degree of concentration was probably not very different, taking the largest ten or twenty coal producers, from that which existed in the 1840s, Macrosty concluded that 'singularly little' had been achieved in the way of amalgamation in this industry.[2]

iii. The structure of mining management

Discussion of management structures is bedevilled by terminology, which differed from regions and over time. In the managerial hierarchy of the North-east the term 'viewer' normally referred to a mining engineer, who in his capacity as head viewer, resident or otherwise, was retained by several coalowners; a viewer also accepted commissions to write specific reports for other coalowners in addition to the regular progress reports on those collieries within his continuing and prime responsibility.[3] Contemporaries drew a distinction between a mining engineer and a viewer, the latter possessing the ability to undertake the general direction of a large colliery 'as to the scale and disposition of its workings and also with regard to whatever requires a profound theoretical as well as complete practical knowledge of obtaining the coal economically and safely. ... The viewer not only being a person of education, but who is presumed to have the best information and the largest experience as to all matters connected with mining.'[4] Viewers

[1] See below 534-5.
[2] H. W. Macrosty, *Trusts in British Industry* (London, 1907), 95.
[3] Flinn 1984, 52-63.   [4] Quoted in C. P. Griffin thesis, 305.

constituted an élite, and together with agents or resident viewers employed in most cases on a full-time basis and through whom the viewers' instructions were carried out, they formed a professional managerial cadre which existed in its most highly developed form in the North-east and in Scotland well before 1830.[1] Matthias Dunn described the system in 1849 and compared it with that existing in other regions:

the collieries of the north of England are all managed directly by viewers and agents employed by the owners, who have no personal interest to militate against their duty of maintaining good machinery, and of providing ample materials and attendance for the workman—the said viewers being more practical and scientific than many managers of collieries elsewhere, as, from the comparative smallness of the works, there does not appear that necessity to employ scientific men—hence many persons are entrusted with the management of collieries who do not at all understand the subject ... in many of the southern coal-fields, the working of the pits, the supplying of materials, and the dealings with the workmen, are let to contractors, or butty colliers, who raise the coal by the ton; and as these persons have only a temporary interest in the work, they naturally save at all points—hence may be attributed the numerous deaths produced by deficient timbering, neglect of lamps, bad ropes and chains, deficient machinery....[2]

He also regarded the economics of colliery working under this system, without salaried managers, as inferior to that associated with practices in the North-east. Dunn, of course, himself a viewer from that region, was hardly impartial in these judgements, but the general comparison was echoed by others.[3]

The transition towards full-time resident head-viewers, the forerunners of the general colliery managers, was a natural progression, for in many cases resident viewers, in the North-east especially, were former pupils or apprentices of general viewers, whose patronage was important in securing the most desirable appointments at the largest collieries. For example, after reporting upon Blundell's collieries in Lancashire in 1853 following the death of Richard Blundell, William

---

[1] Flinn 1984, 57–64.

[2] *MJ* 10 Mar. 1849; Dunn 1852, 74–82.

[3] 'You will not find the majority of our coal mine managers are men possessed of a knowledge of the principles of what they are doing, and of the practice of other districts, except what they have seen. ...' W. Smyth, mining engineer and lecturer at the School of Mines in London, regarded as the exception to this generalization perhaps two or three dozen men in the country—undoubtedly the northern viewers. *SC Mining Accidents* 1854, IX, Q 1878–80. See also Mackworth's assessment of managerial standards in South Wales, *Inspectors' Reports* 1854, XIX, 822.

Armstrong's unqualified condemnation of their state was followed by the substitution, on his advice, of William Greener, a Durham viewer, for the resident agent, Thomas Sheratt—and his two sons who assisted him; William Armstrong became consultant viewer to Blundells.[1] Experience and expertise in deep mining was thus transferred to Lancashire where the shallower seams were rapidly being worked out and deep sinking about to begin. The first of a series of Greeners to manage the Blundells', Pemberton, and Ince Collieries, William Greener, was killed by a roof fall in 1865 while carrying out his duties as a consultant viewer at Rainford Colliery. His successor, again on Armstrong's recommendation, was another Durham viewer, William John Laverick Watkin, under whose management Armstrong's overall plan for the modernization and expansion of Blundell's collieries continued. Armstrong's role in the transformation of Blundell's collieries exemplifies the process of the diffusion of mining practices and working methods, which had long occurred through the medium of the viewers, especially those in the North-east where experience in deep mining gave them unrivalled knowledge of mining problems and their solution.[2] Mining engineers from the North-east were favourite managerial appointments in the collieries of other regions, especially in the rapidly developing coalfield of South Wales; for example, Joshua Richardson, Samuel Dobson, William Gray, George Wilkinson, John Nixon, and George Elliot. Archibald Hood, too, from Scotland, became associated with one of the large South Wales collieries.[3] Even by the 1830s, however, some regions were beginning to produce their own mining engineers, familiar with the distinctive geology of the region and prepared to advise on the most suitable methods of extraction.[4]

Although some of these North-eastern 'experts' acted as head viewers, it was increasingly as consultant viewers acting in a purely advisory role that such figures made their contribution to the industry. Indicative of this trend from the mid-century is the relationship between William Armstrong and H. D. Pochin and his associates. Prior to, and consequent upon, the incorporation of Staveley, Sheepbridge, Bolckow Vaughan, and the Tredegar companies (for which Armstrong's

---

[1] Anderson 1965, 83, 86, 89.

[2] Ibid., 89–91.

[3] Morris and Williams 1958, 54–5.

[4] Notably J. T. Woodhouse, who acted as viewer for collieries in Yorkshire and in the East Midlands: C. P. Griffin thesis, 304–5, 311. John Edward Mammett, from Yorkshire, succeeded William Armstrong as consultant viewer for Staveley.

advice was sought on valuation, prospects, and future policy) his subsequent annual or biennial reports on the collieries (and later those of J.
E. Mammatt) provided an invaluable basis for the decisions taken by
directors and colliery managers.[1] Armstrong also acted as viewer in a
similar advisory capacity to numerous other collieries, including those
of Pease and Partners, Seaton Delaval, Blundell's collieries in Lancashire, Bolckow Vaughan, and Denaby Main in Yorkshire.[2] In this way,
by disseminating and securing the implementation of best-practice
mining methods and technology, viewers continued to play an important role in the joint-stock era, though this affected principally the largest collieries. Such outstanding nineteenth-century viewers as Buddle,
until his death in 1843, and later, William Armstrong, J. T. Woodhouse,
John Daglish, J. R. Landale, the Woods, the Forsters, the Simpsons, the
Forster Browns, the Embletons, 'general viewers' as they were sometimes called, formed informal 'schools' of apprentices, whose graduates
subsequently became part of the viewing network.[3] Outside the North-
east viewers of Armstrong's calibre, often referred to as 'the father of the
coal trade' in the nineteenth century,[4] were in short supply. In the 1860s,
J. T. Woodhouse, consulting viewer for large collieries in Yorkshire and
the East Midlands, was described by the Mines Inspector for the Midland District as 'an oasis in the desert', though lesser mining engineers
offered similar advisory services.[5] In South Wales only two viewers were
practising through resident viewers in the 1850s, which explains why the
tripartite system of management was unusual in that region. Thomas
Powell, proprietor and manager of a handful of house-coal collieries,
found that, because of the growing number of pits under his control by
the 1850s, it became necessary to appoint underground managers to
work under mining engineer Samuel Dobson who was appointed as
viewer.[6]

The transition from traditional management structures to full-time
professional salaried managers is exemplified by the changes at Staveley,
where before incorporation in 1865 eminent mining engineers, Woodhouse and Jeffcock, had been responsible for the colliery management as
viewers.[7] A report in the *Colliery Guardian* explained that 'the growing
importance of the work and the extension of the undertaking suggested

[1] BSCEMRRC Stanton and Staveley 2034/3/9a and 9d, Reports of Armstrong and Mammett.
[2] NuRO Armstrong 725/B1–23 Report Books.
[3] Walters 1977, 58–9, 186–9; C. P. Griffin thesis, 305; Hassan thesis, 212–14; Flinn 1984, 59.
[4] *TNEIME*, XIV (1897–8), 170–2.   [5] C. P. Griffin thesis, 305.
[6] Walters 1977, 153.   [7] *CG* 13 Apr. 1861, 231.

the propriety of engagement of a resident viewer', which resulted in the appointment of Martin Seymour, who in 1861 was described by the same observer as contriving 'to exercise professional energies'.[1] The mode of organization underground was to employ two or three men to a stall perhaps 40 metres long, though in some places as long as 80 metres even in 1867. The stallmen, hewers who were paid by contract prices per ton, let out the stall to other men for whose work, efficiency, and safety they were responsible, though these workers received payment (by the yard, and loaders by the ton) from the company. The resident colliery manager, first Martin Seymour, and later James Campbell and his progeny, had overall responsibility for the pits, though he was guided by the annual advice of consultant viewer William Armstrong, and after his death by Edward Mammett. Ultimately decisions were made by the managing director, Charles Markham, subject to agreement by his co-directors, but Charles, and later his son, C. P. Markham, effectively assumed critical decision-making powers.[2]

While many viewers' reports contained commercial and financial advice in addition to that on mining practices, the viewers were essentially experts in mining rather than in management in general. There were, of course, important exceptions, notably that of George Elliot who, as one of three leading viewers working in the North-east, was appointed to report on the South Wales collieries of Thomas Powell in 1864. On the basis of the report he decided to raise the capital with which to form his own company and to develop the vast mineral potential which he found. This marked the transition for George Elliot from a role which was primarily advisory, as an expert in mining management, to that of chairman and managing director of a major company, concerned with the problems of how much to produce as well as how to produce it; with the sources of finance as well as with colliery accounts; and with access to markets, marketing methods, the acquisition of leases, and of general administration; it also marked the formation of Powell Duffryn.[3]

These were areas of management with which some viewers, notably those in the employment of landowners, were already familiar. Benjamin Biram, third in the line of a dynasty of viewers on the Yorkshire estates of the Earl Fitzwilliam, performed the roles of general manager, accountant, sales and marketing manager, labour manager, and mining engineer

[1] Ibid.
[2] Chapman 1981, 84–5.
[3] Hann 1922, 3–5, 8.

from the 1830s,[1] and the same was true of George Samuel Fereday Smith, a mining engineer appointed in 1837 by the Bridgewater Trust to manage the Trust's coal and canal enterprises.[2] Price and wage determination resulted from managerial decisions at the Duke of Buccleuch's collieries between 1834 and 1875, the outcome being a matter for subsequent report to the Duke.[3] Indeed, the extent to which authority sometimes passed from proprietor to manager is illustrated by the failure of the Marquis of Lothian to win a legal action in the Court of Sessions, where in 1836–7 John Williamson, manager of Newbattle Colliery, was accused of having exceeded his authority in his manner of conducting marketing policy during the preceding three years.[4]

The subject of managerial specialization and its relation to coal-owning proprietors is considered below, though outside the estates, in large partnerships and in the new joint-stock companies, the division between responsibilities for mining management and business management was inevitable, as the size of collieries and companies grew and as mining operations and business activities became more complex. These trends explain why even by 1840 the employment of salaried agents and under-managers was common in the large coal-producing ironworks, where the mines agent was usually one of several departmental managers responsible to the general manager or to the proprietor. Sale-coal collieries owned by non-resident proprietors also tended to employ salaried professional agents and managers;[5] even where proprietors were resident, however, the shortage of adequately trained practising viewers comparable with those in the North-east, at least until the mid-century, meant that a single viewer rarely divided managerial responsibility between several collieries.[6]

The role of resident viewer or general colliery manager is illustrated by the experience of George Greenwell, who on completion of a four-year apprenticeship under T. E. Forster at Haswell Colliery in 1842 became resident viewer at the Blackboy Colliery, Bishop Auckland, where Forster was head viewer (and simultaneously viewer for several other colliery owners). In 1848 Greenwell became resident viewer for John Bowes at Marley Hill Colliery, though he was still subject to the control of Nicholas Wood, partner, chief engineer, and consulting viewer to the partnership. Both the overman and the master engineman

---

[1] Mee 1975, 99.   [2] Mather 1970, 98–9, 267–9, 346–7.
[3] Hassan thesis, 209–10.   [4] Ibid., 210.
[5] Hopkinson thesis, 355; Chapman 1981, 88–9; Walters 1977, 161.
[6] Ibid.

from Blackboy Colliery followed Greenwell to Marley Hill.[1] He records a daily round which began at 5 a.m. when he entered the pits located within a radius of five miles to examine the workings, usually accompanied by the overman. Charles Palmer, the managing partner with special responsibility for sales, generally rode to the collieries once or twice weekly, and because of the responsibilities of Wood and Palmer outside the partnership Greenwell found himself immersed in all aspects of colliery management. After a late breakfast, time was spent in the office attending to colliery accounts and checking efficiency, or visiting the coke ovens, brickworks, railway, or inspecting machinery.[2] Labour management was also his responsibility, and he recorded his supervision of the eviction of striking miners in 1844.[3] In 1854 he became sole manager (viewer and manager) of Radstock Collieries in Somerset, where he took charge of a dozen pits, large and small and 'antiquated in character', where the main problems were water and inadequate shafts. By close attention to, and alterations in, production, pricing, and marketing, Greenwell solved the outstanding problems, with the result that 'productivity rose, costs fell, and profits rose on larger contracts', whereupon he became sole manager of Lord Vernon's collieries at Poynton in Cheshire in 1863. Owing to the ill health of his predecessor, again he found collieries in a poor state, where there was 'nothing for it but to tighten up the reins', which he did until 1876 when he became visiting consultant engineer. Thereafter he was consultant to several collieries in the North, in Lancashire and Yorkshire.[4] When John Chambers was appointed manager in charge of the collieries of Newton Chambers in 1859, a schedule of duties required him to 'confer and work amicably with the principal viewer [in this case an underviewer answerable to Chambers as manager] and so arrange the operations as to produce best possible results'. John Chambers was also to inspect the whole of the underground works once in three months: 'and make faithful report of some point and every savings of expense that can be brought about in and out of pits ... keep detailed records of costs and price per ton; monthly accounts: wages and sales ready for inspection to instruction of General Manager'.[5] His other major responsibility was to direct labour, enforce discipline, and exercise continuing control of the quantity and quality of production.

[1] G. C. Greenwell 1899, 58–62, 83–5, 100, 110–15.
[2] Ibid., 123.   [3] Ibid., 117–19.
[4] Ibid., 131, 138, 163, 207–8, 212, 225.
[5] SCL, Newton Chambers, TR 470 MB 22 Dec. 1859.

In 1860 underviewers, or colliery managers, became responsible for the supervision and control of a colliery in terms defined by the Mines Act of 1860, itself a codification of best practices which had long been adopted in the North-east to ensure safe and efficient working of the mine, and normally effected through overmen or underlookers who belonged to a supervisory body of under-managers.

By this time the appointment of mines inspectors and the codification of their responsibilities brought legal sanctions affecting safety a step closer. As yet, however, the law provided very little incentive towards effective management. The Inspection of Coal Mines Act of 1855 laid down seven General Rules to be implemented by the Inspectors. These Rules were intended to ensure 'adequate' ventilation, the fending of air pits or shafts when not in use, signalling to allow communication between the surface and pit bottom, adequate braking on all winding gear, and safety valves and gauges fitted to steam boilers.[1] Special Rules aimed at improving safety by introducing detailed regulations concerning mine working were the responsibility of colliery owners, though the regulations had to be acceptable to the Home Secretary.[2] Beyond establishing clearer responsibilities of managers and the accountability of owners for keeping their pits in a safe condition, before 1872 the law was not a major force for the improvement in managerial methods. To the extent, however, that the General and Special Rules represented more or less a codification of best practices already long practised in the North-east,[3] underviewers, or colliery managers in other regions, who under the Mines Regulation and Inspection Act of 1860 became responsible for the supervision and control of working mines, began to assume similar functional relationships to overmen and underlookers as did the supervisory under-managers in North-eastern collieries.

Before the 1860s it was still possible for an owner to manage his own colliery assisted by an underground agent, but in the large collieries a professional salaried colliery manager with overall responsibility for mining management became the rule, a trend which the formation of joint-stock companies intensified. Within such management systems, however, it was still possible for subcontract to survive in some form, though unknown in the sale-coal collieries of the North-east and severely criticized in general by Dunn in 1849.[4] In the major iron-making districts subcontract was a very common mode of organization

---

[1] 18–19 Vict. C 108 Clause 4.   [2] Cassell thesis, 215–16.
[3] Ibid., 220–40; see below.   [4] *MJ* 10 Mar. 1849.

during the first half of the century, especially in the Midlands, York-shire, and North Wales. Typically, the owner or lessor's agent would take responsibility for accounts, administration, and sales, while the subcontractor—the charter masters of Shropshire and Derbyshire, the chalter of North Wales, or the butties of south Yorkshire and Stafford-shire—agreed to raise a certain volume of coal at a given price, a contract normally of short duration. The actual getting of coal and management of labour underground was often under the supervision of deputies or 'doggies', employed by the charter masters for this purpose, though the latter bore responsibility for cutting, hauling, and winding coal, prop-ping roofs, filling goafs, providing timber, tools, tubs, and ·horses.[1] Owners undertook to sink the shaft and to supply drainage, ventilation, and winding equipment, the fixed capital of mining enterprise, though in the West Midlands shaft sinking and driving levels were often left to the charter master. In this region, too, contracting was on a larger scale and survived longer, the big-butty system dominating coal production in the West Midlands at least until 1870.[2] Under this system contractors, often working in partnership, reached agreement with the mine owner. Formal contracts often regulated the precise division of responsibilities concerning the extraction of coal, the recruitment as well as manage-ment of labour, and either the right to sell the coal after payment of rent or royalty, or remuneration at agreed piece-rates on delivery of the coal to the owner or lessee. Under such an arrangement in the 1840s, at Oak Farm Colliery in south Staffordshire, two butties employed 130 men and 18 horses in three pits; the control over routine working was left to a 'doggy' or under-manager. In place of the professional salaried manager, therefore, the management of such mines was in the hands of men, mostly ex-miners, whose livelihood depended upon the margin of profit between their costs and the prices received from the coalowner.[3]

Fifteen butties were under contract to work mines on Lord Dudley's estate in the 1840s. The justification for this system was explained before the Midland Mining Commission in 1843 by Richard Smith, resident viewer on his lordship's estate. He argued that butties got results, though they needed watching closely.[4] The major advantages he saw as the simplicity of dealing with one man rather than with a labour force, and described the butties as 'shock absorbers between management and men, taking in slack times much of the odium of [sic] unpopular

---

[1] Flinn 1984, 55–7.
[2] A. J. Taylor 1967, 99.
[3] Ibid., 99–100.   [4] Fereday thesis, 128.

decisions'.[1] More vulnerable than permanent agents, they were also more expendable. There were other reasons, too, why the butty system should have been so common in the West Midlands, where the lack of potential professional managers is revealed in a report on that district in 1850. Typically, mines in south Staffordshire were small and shallow, the geology of that area ensuring that most could sustain continuous working for not more than a few years.[2] Besides the butties, about sixty mine agents, described as a 'superior class of persons', were also to be found charged with the supervision of coal pits, and of whom it was said: 'about 15 cannot write or read ... there may be 25 who are educated men: the rest, say about 20, are in a sort of intermediate state as regards intelligence.[3] In their hands the butty system was regarded as the principal explanation for the unskilful mining of coal in south Staffordshire in particular, and was related to 'neglect of discipline and measures of safety'.[4]

Subcontract was not limited to the Black Country. In South Wales ironmasters began by subcontracting their collieries, so far as it was possible, under the general supervision of a mineral agent. In 1846, when as part of a reorganization of the administration of the Dowlais Iron Company Sir John Guest decided to begin to pay employees direct, no fewer than forty contractors had agreements with the company. Not all contracts were discontinued, but subcontracting became limited to the levels and patches (that is to say, the smaller, more temporary and less capital-intensive work).[5] Thereafter, the Dowlais collieries were managed by a series of agents and managers, under whom worked numerous underground overmen and managers.[6] The switch to direct salaried management seems to have been related to the sinking of deeper pits. The simultaneous existence of subcontract and direct supervision which henceforward persisted at Dowlais was also to be found at the Cyfarthfa Works, though the relative importance of subcontract diminished in significance during the second half of the nineteenth century.[7] The same is true of Bairds, where during the early nineteenth century the overall management of the pits was the responsibility of George Baird, while the more technical aspects of colliery supervision were taken care of by William Cameron, a former collier. The extent of their managerial control, however, was mostly limited to the sinking and opening out of a pit, the working of which became the responsi-

[1] Quoted in ibid., 130.   [2] A. J. Taylor 1967, 85–7.
[3] Quoted in Raybould thesis, 134.   [4] Quoted in A. J. Taylor 1967, 100.
[5] Walters 1977, 158.   [6] Ibid., 162.   [7] Ibid., 158.

bility of a subcontractor for an agreed price per ton of coal, though some contracts committed the company to pay oncost men directly. Coincident with the growth in coal production for sale in the late 1860s, a policy of greater centralization and managerial control by salaried managers seems to have been introduced, a development in part explained by an improvement in communications between collieries and by the requirements of safety regulations, notably the 1872 Coal Mines Regulation Act which compelled the appointment of certificated managers. As a result, whereas in 1872 four managers were responsible for forty-four pits in the Gartsherrie district, by 1888 seven had charge of thirty-four, and certificated under-managers were to be found in most pits.[1]

In the East Midlands the big butty system survived in some collieries until the 1870s, though some large coal producers, Butterley for example, by the 1850s had modified the system by reducing the scale of subcontracting and exercising continuous control over colliery and shafts, for which the company's manager was responsible. Under this little butty system (which was still in operation in 1913) the butties' responsibility was the recruitment and payment of hewers and haulage workers, rarely more than ten in number, though occasionally as many as twenty.[2] In Nottinghamshire at the mid-century, typically three contractors or stallmen, who were usually experienced miners, rented a gate-road or stall and supplied two loaders, two stovemen, a dayman, two holers, and a boy. The contractors paid tonnage 'prices', carried out all the setting and drawing of timber, removed all coal after holing, and blasted where necessary,[3] but the difference between this system and the big-butty system was that sinking and opening out was carried out by sinkers on contract, and that on entering the pit the subcontracters were obliged to work coal in a single stall as directed by the colliery manager. After 1860, but especially after the Mines Act of 1872, the subcontractors were also subject to a degree of supervision consistent with the observance of safety requirements. For some time, however, the butty continued to negotiate an overall contract price per ton of coal delivered at the pithead, and to hire and pay men according to an agreement in which the proprietor had no part. The provision of tools, horses, and equipment was in some instances the responsibility of the subcontractor, but the trend was away from such arrangements.[4]

[1] Corrins thesis, 264–6.
[2] A. R. Griffin 1971, 29, 32; J. E. Williams 1962, 410–11, 586, 639–41.
[3] CG 16 Jan. 1858, 41.
[4] C. P. Griffin thesis, 297–8; Neville thesis, 286–7; BRO Lu WYCOA, MB 16 Nov. 1909.

A corollary of the decline in the managerial role of the butty was the need to alter managerial structures. When Sir Robert Clifton commissioned John Daglish to report on his colliery in 1871, the result was a recommendation to abolish the inefficient butty system altogether;[1] but that report was criticized by a Midland viewer as indicating a misunderstanding on the part of a man from the North-east who knew nothing of Midland mining practice.[2] In 1876 another local mining engineer produced a similar report, outlining what he regarded as an ideal system of management, offering the advantage of retaining those elements of the stall or little butty system which ensured the closest supervision under self-interested workers but which would also provide greater control over labour recruitment and organization. He recommended the appointment of a consulting engineer, who would occasionally attend the colliery and report, a certificated colliery manager, and three deputies as assistants, though hiring and firing was to be the prerogative of the colliery manager.[3] Under various forms and degrees of managerial control, the little butty system survived throughout much of the East and West Midlands during the mid-nineteenth century, whence it spread into Yorkshire, extending as production increased.

From the beginning the Mines Inspectors were critical of the defects of subcontract systems, and the increasing danger of deeper mining intensified their concern over the safety implications of the separation of responsibility underground from colliery management.[4] From the coalowners' standpoint the working of larger, deeper mines involving greater capital outlay provided an incentive to ensure that safety and profitability should not be jeopardized by the irresponsible mining practice underground of subcontractors working to maximize short-term advantage yet endangering lives and risking financial losses.

By the 1870s boom many of the larger firms had, to a large extent, already adopted the new practice embodied in the 1872 Mines Act. Under this legislation it became a statutory obligation for every colliery employing more than thirty men to engage a duly trained and certificated manager capable of drafting and enforcing safety regulations, thereby providing a powerful impetus towards a centralization of managerial control.[5] Only in the smallest pits could butties continue to

[1] NoRO, Clifton misc: Valuation, 1871.
[2] Ibid.
[3] NoRO, Clifton misc: Report 17 June 1876.
[4] A. J. Taylor 1967, 100–1; C. P. Griffin thesis, 298–302.
[5] A. J. Taylor 1967, 101; C. P. Griffin thesis, 301.

operate without supervision. In all other pits the butty, or stallman as he came to be called, could purchase and erect timber, but to avoid the risk that he might economize beyond the limits of safety the legislation placed the responsibility for safety squarely upon the shoulders of colliery managers to whom, henceforward, the stallmen were responsible. The same was true of the purchase and use of candles, safety lamps, and gunpowder, until legislation between 1872 and 1887 removed their supply to centralized control. Further regulation of the stallman's supervisory role resulted from the 1887 Act, which required the appointment of deputies whose function was to assist certificated managers in their duties.[1] Indeed, the erosion of the stallman's role led to an attempt by Leicestershire employers to dispense altogether with a subcontract system, and to pay day wages to all colliery workers irrespective of task, the intention being to eliminate the incentive for stallmen to skimp on safety. However, not until the 1890s was the stallman's control over wages subject to regulation, the outcome of pressure from the miners' union.[2] Under certain circumstances coalowners sought to perpetuate the little butty system well into the twentieth century; as at the collieries of Henry Briggs, for example, where the closest possible supervision of miners was required to ensure that hewers holed, or undercut, the coal in the dirt below the coal to increase the yield of large coal.[3] The practice was one similar to that in many other collieries in the district, and made for greater headroom, less ripping, and reduced oncosts. Not until 1910 was a compromise, similar to that in Derbyshire, agreed with the miners' union, the effect of which was to remove the word 'butty' from the price lists and to place two men in charge of a stall; each was to contain four workers whose entire wages were to be drawn by the two 'chargemen'.[4]

The extent of managerial supervision below ground depended in part upon the methods of working. The mining engineer, George Bailes, maintained that, in theory, longwall working afforded greater scope for supervisory control, not only because a face of up to 50 metres (rarely longer before 1900) provided more space and vision, but because if the advantage of longwall mining was to be fully exploited safely the face (and the miners) must move forward in steps at a steady pace. For this reason miners should work in larger teams, instead of in couples as in the pillar-and-stall or stoop-and-room systems, and this facilitated division of labour between digging and

---

[1] C. P. Griffin thesis, 302.
[2] Ibid., 302–3.
[3] BRO, Briggs SC MS 160, MB 22 Nov. 1909.
[4] Neville thesis, 289.

filling simultaneously with cutting and hewing.[1] From an efficiency standpoint the small-butty system, in which groups of around half a dozen men worked together under participant supervision, might be an effective arrangement.[2] It contrasted with conditions under the pillar-and-stall system where limited working space reduced the potential for effective supervision by overmen, whose appearance in some Lancashire mines was the customary signal for miners to down tools.[3] Even in long-wall mining, however, implementation of managerial control depended on miners' compliance.[4]

Whereas the large-butty system was usually associated with participant supervision at the pit level, the small-butty system, with which the longwall mines of the East Midlands and Yorkshire especially were associated, maximized group incentive within stalls only. Under such an arrangement the oncosts arising from the overall colliery operations were met by the enterprise, and minimized the harmful long-term consequences of the large butty's drive for maximum exploitation within his contract price. In 1870 Thomas Cottingham, owner of collieries at Neston, North Wales, referred to the concomitant effects of the introduction of longwall in the Wrexham and Ruabon district, attributing the greater amount of coal saved in comparison with mining under pillar and stall to better supervision and management: 'The charter system has been suspended and men are not left to themselves. In many cases the viewers never went down the pits more than once every six months and the over-men once a month perhaps. . . . Now there is more supervision on the part of owners and managers.'[5]

iv. Influences on managerial practice

Apart from the search for efficiency and greater control over the quality of coal raised, safety was another consideration which eventually compelled coalowners to ensure at least minimally qualified managerial supervision underground, as required by law. In the context of nineteenth-century scientific knowledge, efficient mining was not always compatible with safety, though viewers in the North-east regarded their

---

[1] George M. Bailes, *Modern Mining Practice IV* (Sheffield, 1907), 18–22.

[2] G. M. Wilson thesis, 32–3.

[3] Carter L. Goodrich, cited in J. Goldthorpe, 'Technical Organisation as a Factor in Supervising Works Conflict', *British Journal of Sociology*, X (1959), 215. See also above 226–7.

[4] See above 226–7. On the subject of job control in the nineteenth century, see Joseph Melling, 'Non-commissioned Officers': British employers and their supervisory workers, 1880–1920', *Social History* 5 (1981), 187–94.   [5] *Coal Supply* 1870, XVII, QQ 1854–6.

own record in this respect as beyond criticism. In 1849 Matthias Dunn contrasted the long-term commitment to the management of collieries by viewers and agents (in the North-east) with the temporary character of contractors and butties, whose motivation to ensure adequate timbering, ropes, chains, lamps, and machinery was limited.[1] In private, Buddle made it clear that he regarded his prime obligation was to obey his employer—rather than to advise in that disinterested manner implied by Dunn's public statement, which emphasized the lack of personal (financial) interest in the collieries they managed, and their practical and scientific approach to mining and working.[2]

Yet, so convinced was Dunn of the close connection between mining efficiency, safety, and the role of viewers, that in the 1840s he was a leading advocate, among other enlightened viewers from the North, for the introduction of government inspection—though he was virtually alone in his support for compulsory powers to be vested in inspecting officers.[3] The origins of legislation embodied in the first Mine Act in 1850 were to be found in a series of serious explosions, beginning at Haswell in 1844 and Jarrow in 1845, the combined effect of which was to galvanize public opinion and government. Seymour Tremenheere, the architect of the 1850 Act, interpreted the explosion at Risca Colliery in 1846 as the prelude to many more: 'The collieries of South Wales are every year extending more down the vallies, and becoming deeper and more liable to accumulations of explosive gas. Their number is also increasing, with the probable continuance of the great demand for iron, likely still further very considerably to increase. . . .'[4]

The details of the history of coal mines regulation do not belong here.[5] Tremenheere's proposals resembled those of Dunn and Playfair, inasmuch that each envisaged the establishment of an inspectorate comprised of an élite possessing high technical and scientific qualifications. Political opposition to intervention in the industry, however, came from the coal interests in the Commons, the Cabinet, and above all in the Lords, while in the North-east a permanent secretariat monitored developments for the coalowners. Practical difficulties of inspection in an industry consisting of nearly two thousand collieries was self evident; scientific understanding of the causes of explosions was very limited,

---

[1] *MJ* 10 Mar. 1849.   [2] Hiskey thesis, 127.
[3] Cassell thesis, 115.   [4] Quoted in ibid., 113.
[5] The following paragraphs draw heavily upon O. MacDonagh, 'Coal Mines Regulation: The First Decade, 1842–1852', in Robert Robson (ed.), *Ideas and Institutions of Victorian Britain* (London, 1967), 71.

and concern was expressed lest the introduction of inspectors should encourage viewers and managers to accept diminished responsibility, yet leaving inspectors with responsibility without power.

Rearguard political opposition was eroded by publicity given to a series of colliery disasters and by the reaction to the reports, initiated by the government, of 'eminent scientific men' on their causes. These inquiries also offered general observations on safety, adding the force of scientific authority to the pressures hitherto exerted by Tremenheere from within the administration, by the South Shields Committee, including reformist viewers, and by the mining unions. The result was the setting-up of the Lords Committee, appointed in 1849, to inquire into 'The Best Means of Preventing the Occurrence of Dangerous Accidents in Coal Mines . . .'.

The four inspectors appointed under the Mines Act of 1850, the outcome of the Lords' Select Committee's recommendations, were offered access only to those mines where a fatal accident had occurred, or by invitation from the colliery owner. After recording and reporting an accident the inspector's role was advisory, indeed at the personal level the ratio of inspectors to mines meant that nothing more could be expected; more than fifty years later, by which time their number had risen to thirty-eight, the local Commission regarded the ratio to be inadequate still, though random visiting had replaced inspection by invitation. By 1911 the industry was served by eighty-three inspectors.[1]

Had frequency of colliery visits determined the inspectors' limits of influence, the effects upon standards of safety—and managerial practice—would have been very small indeed, especially during the nineteenth century. Certainly, the influence of the early mines inspectors in the 1850s and 1860s was slow to spread in regions outside the Northeast, and according to one inspector, none of them 'had occasion to make any suggestions for the prevention of accidents which had not previously been carried into effect at various mines'.[2] Before 1872 they acted without legal sanctions to prevent dangerous mining practice— even though the inspectors had to be practical engineers possessing a minimum of seven years as colliery managers, and to have passed an examination in mining science. Colliery managers, meanwhile, were not required to possess certificates of competency.[3] This was a state of affairs which, following the Oaks explosion in 1866 and that at Ferndale

---

[1] Buxton 1978, 139.
[2] Mackworth, quoted in *MJ* 7 July 1855, 149.
[3] Cassell thesis, 71.

in 1867, led the *Colliery Guardian* to quote, approvingly, W. W. Smyth's observation: 'as long as we find collieries managed by a shopkeeper or joiner, or half-educated young "gentlemen", a nephew of the owner, we must expect that accidents will occur, which would be preventable under better auspices'[1]—a preface to his plea for professionalization of colliery management by certification dependent upon training and experience.

Despite the absence of legal powers and their limited scope for personal contact with colliery managers, and within the constraints of resources at their disposal, the handful of inspectors did make some impact upon the regions for which they were responsible. Influence was exercised by writing annual reports on their regions, analysing and commenting upon the particular geological conditions and working methods[2]—in a manner hitherto almost entirely limited to literature dealing with the North-east. From the beginning, the Mines Inspectors appointed under the 1850 Act were expert mining engineers: Matthias Dunn for the North-east, Joseph Dickinson for Staffordshire and Lancashire, Charles Morton for Yorkshire, and Kenyon Blackwell, replaced by Herbert Francis Mackworth, for South Wales. Dunn's experience was mostly as check viewer to large collieries in the North-east, and as a writer of treatises on mining practices; Dickinson also originated from the North-east, but practised as a manager in South Wales and in Scotland; Mackworth, too, possessed practical experience in South Wales. In 1855 the Inspectorate was increased from four to twelve, those added to the list being selected after examination by Nicholas Wood, the prestigious North-eastern mining engineer, viewer, and colliery owner, and Warington Smyth, later to become President of the Geological Society. They chose Atkinson, Alexander, Hedley, Higson, Brough, and Evans.[3] In the absence of a detailed mining code of rules for pit working and management, their responsibility was to advocate the safest, and therefore in most cases the most advanced, methods of mining and working coal,[4] but the scope for extensive influence in this way was severely limited by the number of collieries it was physically possible for Inspectors to visit; before 1855, once in four or five years was the limit, according to the two Inspectors responsible for Staffordshire and Lancashire and South Wales, should every colliery

---

[1] *CG* 14 Dec. 1867.

[2] O. MacDonagh, 'Coal Mines Regulation: The First Decade, 1842–1852', in Robert Robson (ed.), *Ideas and Institutions of Victorian Britain* (London, 1967), 84.

[3] Cassell thesis, 118–22.

[4] Ibid., 142, 219.

in their respective districts receive a call,[1] and not much more frequently until 1872, for the number of mines increased as the Inspectorate was enlarged. Lacking coercive powers before 1855, attention paid to those where serious accidents occurred would not necessarily result in improvements, and even after the 1855 Act, which marked the introduction of a code of safety, Inspectors could only report danger to the Home Secretary, and could not force mine closure should owners or managers refuse to act to remove the cause of danger. The Home Office could, however, decide to prosecute.[2] There is some evidence, though, from Mines Inspectors themselves, that their advice was frequently accepted. In 1854 Wynn began to think that 'the dullest mine agent is now aware than an ill-ventilated mine cannot be a profitable one'.[3] The relation between profit, safety, and effective management control was also the theme pursued by Mackworth when advocating the 'Newcastle system' of management, whereby the appointment of superintending viewer or mining engineer could, he thought, remedy the 'ignorance of the overmen' which he encountered in South Wales and Monmouthshire. In 1853 he reported that several, though not a majority, of proprietors in that region had adopted such an arrangement after persuasion, and that it had been proved to have been both the safest and most economical managerial system.[4]

The Safety Code adopted in 1855, though compulsory only from 1860, embodied standards accepted and enforced by managers in the best-managed collieries, the General Rules setting these out in detail representing merely a general application of existing practice in the North-east. The Special Rules, which allowed flexibility to suit local conditions, but often including between 30 and 70 specific regulations regarding sound colliery practice, related more to mining methods and management than to technology.[5] None the less, the Inspectors' *Reports*, which were often reproduced, in full or in abstract, by the *Colliery Guardian*, which commenced publication in 1858, offered a wealth of detailed information concerning winning and working and the techniques of mining coal at many collieries in various parts of the country. Inspectors' evidence was also prominent in the various reports of committees and commissions, instituted and paid for by the government, which dealt with the technical problems of mining, beginning

---

[1] Ibid., 143.

[2] Ibid., 215, 219, 240–4.   [3] *Inspectors' Reports* 1854–5, XV, 47, 105.

[4] *Inspectors' Reports* 1854, XIX, 803. Progress was reported, too, in the East Midlands. C. P. Griffin thesis, 311.   [5] Cassell thesis, 222–5.

with the various reports on accidents in the 1850s and 1860s. Of wider implication were the reports of the Coal Commission in 1870 and of the Royal Commission on the Dearness and Scarcity of Coal in 1873, which systematically related the economics of colliery working to management and working methods. A. J. Youngson Brown concluded that the Dearness and Scarcity report did more to advance mining knowledge than any other investigating body in the nineteenth century,[1] though in fact the 1870 *Report* of the Coal Commission was more comprehensive. In the short term, the supply of suitably qualified certificated colliery managers was insufficient, and marked improvement in the quality of management awaited the emergence of a new generation of managers. Because of this, the Mines Act of 1872 did not immediately eliminate entirely the continued existence of the non-resident mining engineer who was sometimes registered as certificated colliery manager for several collieries simultaneously—a division of specific responsibility for the implementation of General and Special Rules affecting safety which the Act implied should form part of the duties of a full-time resident colliery manager. Furthermore, the Act permitted managers already responsible for mine management on a day-to-day basis to receive managers' certificates without the need for formal qualifications.[2]

As mining explosions continued to occur, discussions of accident prevention focused increasingly upon the need for the education and training of colliery managers in the elements of science and practical mining, culminating in the provisions contained in the 1887 Mines Regulation Act;[3] first and second class management certificates were introduced under this Act, the former requiring a minimum of five years practical experience, and two for the lesser qualification. The Act also empowered the Secretary of State to set up special courts of inquiry into accidents, though not until the Act of 1911 did he acquire the power to revoke certificates of competence. The year 1911 also marked the effective implementation of a provision, first introduced in the Act of 1872, which involved working miners, or their nominees, in regular mines inspection.[4]

The growing concern for safety and the introduction of inspection had other indirect effects upon mining practices and management, for the necessity for coalowners and viewers to react to government, in the

---

[1] Youngson Brown thesis, 91.
[2] *CG* 28 Aug. 1885, 335; C. P. Griffin thesis, 311.
[3] Cassell thesis, 99; Calvert thesis, 80–2, 92–9.
[4] Walters thesis, 22.

first instance to the proposal to establish an inspectorate and subsequently to provide legislative support, led to the growth of professional organizations embracing many of the leading viewers and mining engineers. Possessing a history of incipient professionalization even before 1830, it is not surprising that the first of the regional associations established on a permanent basis was the North of England Institute of Mining and Mechanical Engineers, formed in 1852,[1] a body not without influence on management and mining methods across the coalfields. The origins began in a discussion among mining engineers in the aftermath of the explosion at Seaham Colliery. Among them were Matthias Dunn and George Elliot, who proposed that the advantages derived from professional argument and discussion should be extended 'and that what had then the character of a friendly coterie should become a recognizable body working under fixed rules and with aims that should be clearly defined'.[2] When the Society was formed, those specific aims comprised regular meetings to discuss ventilation, the prevention of accidents, and 'for general purposes to do with winning and working of collieries'.[3]

The geographical scatter of subscribers to the *Transactions* of the North East Institute is unknown, but their deliberations were often reported, and sometimes reproduced, in the *Colliery Guardian*. The South Yorkshire Viewers' Association was formed in 1857, though the latter's history was intermittent until it became the Midland Institute of Mining Engineers in 1869, when its rules were revised to bring them more closely into line with those of the northern institute: to meet monthly, to discuss means for ventilation, the prevention of accidents, winning and working, and the advancement of the science of mining and engineering.[4] The South Wales Institute of Engineers, which was formed in 1864, from the beginning included mining matters in their publications,[5] and in 1867 the South Staffordshire and East Worcestershire Institute of Engineers formed a mining branch. The Chesterfield and Midland Counties Institution of Engineers followed in 1871, and the mining engineers of north Staffordshire a year later. The Manchester Geological and Mining Society, established in 1838, originated from different considerations from those of the 1850s and 1860s, but the wider

---

[1] Flinn 1984, 68.   [2] J. E. McCutcheon 1955, 45–7.
[3] *MJ* 10 July 1852, 11 Sept. 1852, 444.   [4] *TMIME*, I (1870), 1–3.
[5] The following paragraph draws heavily upon Calvert thesis, 117–21, and R. Buchanan, 'Institutional Proliferation in the Engineering Profession, 1847–1914', *EHR* 2nd series, XXXVIII (1985), 41–52.

functions of accumulating and communicating scientific knowledge and practical experience of coal mining was part of the essential justification of the Manchester Society from its inception. None the less, this body was the last to join the central Federation of the Institutes, formed on the initiative of the North of England Institute in 1889 when total membership was 1,239, rising to 3,277 by 1914. The volume and variety of articles published in the proceedings of the regional, and from 1889 incorporated in the nationally distributed *Proceedings*, together with discussion, reflect at least a potentially valuable influence on mining technology and colliery practice during the second half of the nineteenth century. Moreover, the combined result of the rise in the number of professional mining engineers and the diminution in the numer of mines meant that whereas in 1890 the ratio of professional engineers to mines was below 1 to 2, by 1914 the ratio had altered to 1.2 to 1; in 1890 there were two professional mining engineers for every thousand colliery workers, compared with three from 1900.[1]

To be set against this evidence of increasing professionalization of the mining engineering and management profession is the lack of specialist education facilities, either at senior managerial or underground supervisory level. Before the establishment of the Inspectorate, only the Royal School of Mines, originating in the Museum of Economic Geology in 1837, offered any form of instruction in Mining Science.[2] Described by Hedley and by Lothian Bell as too remote in its London location to be of any general use, the renamed School of Mines and Science in 1851 employed Warrington Smyth to lecture on mining and mineralogy, Robert Hunt, lecturer in applied mechanics, Dr Lyon Playfair, lecturer in natural history, and Andrew Ramsay, lecturer in geology. Between 1855 and 1875 the School produced fewer than one hundred associates, though this figure increased fourfold in the following twenty years. However, only 10 per cent entered mining as managers or mining engineers.[3]

Critical of the School's failure to link theory with mining practice, Nicholas Wood had attempted to establish an institution in the Northeast in the 1850s, but failed for lack of financial support. Intermittent pressure from the North-east Institute of Mining Engineers for the formation of a specialist college of mining also failed for lack of business support. In 1880 leading coalowners endowed a chair of mining at the

[1] Calculated from ibid. and *List of Mines*.
[2] Roderick and Stephens 1972, 107.
[3] Ibid., 105–8, 110.

Armstrong College of Physical Science in Newcastle,[1] an institution which within a few years had overtaken the Government School of Mines as the main source of qualified Mines Inspectors, and counted Sir Richard Redmayne and Lord Cadman, successive Professors of Mining at the University of Birmingham, among their graduates.[2] Other developments in higher mining education were those taking place in Sheffield, beginning with evening lectures at Firth College in 1882 and the appointment of a Professor in 1892, though not until 1910 was a Department of Mining and Metallurgy established, and no students enrolled for the degree before 1919. From 1896 a diploma course proved more successful.[3] Birmingham was also the centre of initiative in the 1880s, but the department of coalmining and colliery management, under the Professor of Mining appointed in 1883, lapsed for lack of support until it was revived nineteen years later. With R. A. S. Redmayne as Professor, the Mining Department offered a curriculum designed to train practising and consulting mining engineers, colliery managers, teachers of mining, and mines surveyors, and included a spell of practical mining and experience in research laboratories in addition to a grounding in relevant scientific theory.[4] By that time Professors of Mining had been appointed, too, in Glasgow, Cardiff, Manchester, and Leeds; Durham University also offered degrees in mining.[5]

Sanderson concluded that 'scarcely any industry had more university attention lavished on it than mining',[6] but the attraction for British graduates of opportunities in the colonies, especially India, was one factor restricting the flow of mining graduates into the industry at home. The statistical information is patchy. Between 1871 and 1885 eighty-nine students who left Armstrong College had become qualified mining engineers,[7] four of whom were coalowners and three assistant government inspectors. In Cardiff, forty-four collieries employed mining engineers educated at the College.[8] Between 1905 and 1914 one-third of the thirty-three students after leaving the Mining Department at

---

[1] Ibid., 110–11; Sanderson 1972, 86.

[2] Roderick and Stephens 1972, 112–13; Sanderson 1972, 87–8.

[3] Roderick and Stephens 1972, 114.

[4] J. Wertheimer, 'The Training of Industrial Leaders', *TFIME*, XXIII (1901–2), 494–500; R. A. S. Redmayne, 'The Mining Department of the University of Birmingham', *TFIME*, XXVIII (1904–5), 465.

[5] Ibid.; Roderick and Stephens 1972, 113.

[6] Sanderson 1972, 87.

[7] NUL Special Collection, Principal's Report 1895–1919.

[8] Sanderson 1972, 141.

Birmingham University were in a managerial capacity at British collieries.[1]

Unfavourable comparisons were drawn between the size of the flow of highly qualified recruits to the mining industries in Britain and Germany. Since 1776 the state-run Freiberg Mining Academy, located geographically in the middle of mining activity, was at the centre of a network of major mining schools in each of the mining districts in Germany, which recruited students from preparatory secondary schools.[2] In Germany recruitment to the Mines Inspectorate was limited to students possessing diplomas or degree qualifications based on training at a mining school or university, their duties were more widely defined, and the number of inspectors was larger. The incentive to undertake the undergraduate-level training, therefore, was greater. A further disincentive for British students to read for a degree or diploma was that until 1903 five years of experience was required in order to qualify to sit the examination to become a certificated colliery manager, which for a graduate amounted to a total of eight years of apprenticeship status.[3] The colliery manager's certificate was aimed at a much lower level of technical and scientific knowledge than was expected of a graduate, or the holder of a diploma. Under the Coal Mines Regulation Act of 1903, the degree offered by Newcastle College became the first to receive official sanction by the Home Office in connection with the Colliery Managers' examination, exempting graduates from two of the five years practical experience required of other candidates.[4] By this time the certificates had been divided into two classes, a step taken in 1884 to accommodate the lesser requirements of under-managers and subordinate colliery officials normally recruited from among working miners. In 1911 certification of colliery deputies became law, filling a critical gap at the supervisory level.[5] There is evidence, however, which indicates that the 'scope and character of the examinations set by the Home Office lagged behind the advance of mining technology',[6] and standards differed between districts. Mechanization increased danger, and electrification in particular posed serious problems underground, sufficiently serious in their effects to justify the formation of a Departmental Committee in 1902 to investigate

---

[1] This figure is an overestimate, as some of the graduates specialized in metal mining. I am grateful to the Mining Department of the University of Birmingham for permission to consult the Register of Old Students (1938).

[2] Roderick and Stephens 1972, 105–6.

[3] Calvert thesis, 110.

[4] NUL Special Collection, Principal's Report 1895–1918, Durham College of Science.

[5] Calvert thesis, 93–9.　　　　　　　　　　　　　　　　　　　　[6] Ibid., 126.

the use of electricity in mines, and to inquire into the level and type of skills and expertise deemed necessary.[1]

The origins of this tardy development of mining education were to be found in the growing concern for safety, but in addition to an improved scientific understanding of mining operations, colliery managers needed to ensure discipline in promoting safety, which also implied greater orderliness and systematization in working;[2] to the extent that safety was improved, the stoppages which otherwise often resulted from accidents diminished and continuity of production increased. In 1890 the President of the National Association of Colliery managers reminded his members that 'a colliery manager's first duty is to provide for safety of men under his employment . . . next to see that he gets his coal at the cheapest possible cost consistent with the safety of the men under his supervision and the efficient opening-out of the mine';[3] minimization of the proportion of small to round coal, and the mining of clean coal in good condition were next among the priorities. The introduction of compulsory certification of colliery managers increased the likelihood of the managers' ability to achieve all of these aims, for the knowledge required and the discipline needed to promote safe mining also contributed to economy of working. The majority of colliery managers, therefore, remained underground agents of the companies which employed them, and inexperienced in company affairs in the wider sense. A. J. Taylor has remarked upon their preference for practical experience rather than theory, and for proficiency in mining engineering rather than in mines organization and the principles of management.[4] In this respect, the published proceedings of the Managers' Association differed little from those of the Institutes of Mining Engineers, which were almost exclusively concerned with geology or technology, with only occasional discussions of methods of working and costs.

It is possible to identify a few distinctive preoccupations held by colliery managers which were not reflected in the publications of the engineering institutions. From its inception in 1887, in response to the new responsibilities for the safety of workers imposed by the Coal Mines Regulation Act of that year, the National Association became a focus for opposition to that legislation, and orchestrated attempts to influence future legislation. Thereafter, the *Proceedings* illustrate managers' concern with their professional status and with their reaction to simul-

---

[1] Ibid., 102–6.
[2] *Inspectors' Reports* 1854–5, XV, 115–16, Mackworth; H. S. Jevons 1915, 369.
[3] *CG* 12 Sept. 1890, 400.   [4] A. J. Taylor 1968, 61–2.

taneous conflicting pressures from owners and workers. From 1900, however, the issues which absorbed increasing space were the proposed reduction in miners' hours, falling work pace, and increasing absenteeism; rarely did the contributors raise broad policy issues, preferring to concentrate upon labour discipline, productivity in the pit, and the quality of output.[1] A. J. Taylor has referred to their 'toughness and pragmatism', sometimes combined with a reluctance, or inability, to show vision.[2] In 1891 William Jenkins, Consett's general colliery manager, wrote to David Dale, managing director, claiming to have detected 'a good deal of conservative feeling on the part of colliery managers in the way of unwillingness to attempt anything new'.[3] But this was hardly true of all colliery managers; of John Turner, for example, who from certificated colliery manager rose to become general manager of the reinvigorated Moira Collieries in Leicestershire in the 1890s.[4] Jenkins's observation should perhaps be seen in the context of Consett's practice of internal recruitment of managers,[5] but a similar policy also prevailed at Staveley, both at senior level and at the level of individual colliery management, where heredity afforded a route to succession for three generations of the Humble family.[6] The Harrisons at Barber Walker and Co., the Meachams at Hamstead, the Sopwiths at Cannock Chase, the Coopers at the Earl Fitzwilliam's Parkgate Colliery, provide other examples of hereditary managerial succession.[7]

Overall colliery performance depended at least as much upon the framework provided by those above them in the managerial hierarchy, and the lead given by company managers and managing directors. These men were, in effect, successors to the estate managers and chief viewers of the early and mid-century, for they were expected to possess commercial as well as theoretical knowledge, practical expertise and organizing ability, and an understanding of the principles underlying colliery organization. It seems probable that a shortage of such well-qualified professional general managers continued throughout the century,[8] and that they found their way into the largest, and perhaps the

---

[1] *Proceedings of the National Association of Colliery Managers*, from 1887.

[2] A. J. Taylor 1968, 62–3.

[3] A. S. Wilson thesis, 187.   [4] C. P. Griffin thesis, 310.

[5] A. S. Wilson thesis, 186.   [6] Chapman 1981, 87–9.

[7] C. P. Griffin, 'Robert Harrison and the Barber Walker Company: A Study in Colliery Management 1850–90', *TTS* LXXXII (1979). StRO Hamstead, D 876/15 MB 15 Oct. 1894; BUL BR 14/ii–iii/Cannock Chase Colliery, MB 26 June 1912; *CG* 6 Jan. 1871, 15.

[8] On Britain's relative shortage of professionally qualified colliery managers see J. Wertheimer, 'The Training of Industrial Leaders', *TFIME*, XXIII (1901–2), 494–500.

most profitable, companies. The implication, should such a supposition
be correct, is that at least in the medium and small firms, and probably
in many of the larger enterprises, owner control and management was
the norm, and that in most firms the colliery manager was little more
than an underground agent working directly to proprietors who took all
major managerial decisions.

v. Ownership, control, and management

Just as the increasing difficulties of mining coal safely and more
efficiently led to the rise of professional mining engineers and certificated colliery managers, similarly the growing complexity of policy formulation and business administration in large organizations required
increasing professionalization, either in the conduct of proprietors or
their salaried managing executives. The interesting question then arises
whether this division of managerial responsibilities was accompanied by
a change in the location of control in those corporate enterprises which
in terms of size, technology, and complexity of organization represented the most progressive section of the industry.

An analysis of ownership and control in the nineteenth century is
simplified to some extent by the relatively small amount of institutional
(and therefore concealed) shareholding; for the most part shares were
owned either by individuals whom we can identify, or they were dispersed in public holdings by owners who may be assumed to have
played no part in management. Banks and finance companies played a
role in capital provision, but not a dominant one. Complicating our
analysis, however, are the limitations of the data. Our Dissolved
Companies 'sample' of 112 firms at best account for some 40 per cent of
regional output, and little more than one-tenth of the number of firms in
the regions in 1913.[1] The firms are, on the whole, large, and for that
reason untypical; and they almost certainly contain a bias towards
publicly-owned (and therefore professionally managed) companies.
A few company histories provide supplementary information, but
they are least satisfactory in revealing decision-making processes in any
detail. While it is possible, therefore, to attempt an assessment of the

---

[1] Initially the sample was intended to include the largest companies in proportion to regional
shares in total production. Missing BT 31 files and those containing no useful data before 1913
meant that the 112 company sample is in a literal sense the random residual after searching for
data from more than twice that number of companies.

role played by major shareholders as directors (that is, the extent to which the boards of companies included major shareholders), it is not possible to gauge fully the impact of owner-directors in the decision-making process.[1]

Some recent investigations by economists into ownership and management control have begun with a structural rather than a behavioural approach, in an attempt to identify potential rather than observed control. The extent of potential ownership-control can be measured in two ways by the use of the Dissolved Companies sample. First, evidence on the extent to which the directors of companies were major shareholders in that company may be taken as an indirect indication of the extent to which firms were run (or potentially run) by owners. In practice, the criteria of what constitutes a 'major' shareholder presents few problems. Almost all the companies in the sample displayed either an unmistakable dominance of shareholdings and directorships by a few individuals, or conversely indicate that directors were 'professional' appointees, possibly holding a handful of shares which in all probability represent part remuneration, but never possessing a proportion sufficient to command a major influence on policy.

In the following analysis, therefore, shareholder control is deemed to exist in all private and public companies wherever no more than eight identifiable individuals owned at least 50 per cent of the shares. In the case of 'mixed' companies (defined below) a figure of 33 per cent is deemed sufficient to indicate potential owner-control. It is necessary to make the assumption here that directors with few or no shares in the company were more likely to be appointed as a result of recognized skills or knowledge of the industry, although the possibility of a degree of patronage cannot be entirely discounted. Nor is it possible in practice to distinguish ordinary directorships from more 'prestigious' and influential posts, such as chairman and managing director, partly because of lack of evidence in many cases and partly out of ignorance of the true power and influence which it was possible for holders of these more prestigious positions to exercise.

The second measure of ownership or management-control concerns the extent to which shares were widely dispersed (as in truly 'public' companies), or concentrated in the hands of a few individuals (as in

---

[1] This is a problem which has been acknowledged by investigators of modern business structure, and which, because of the paucity of case studies, led Nyman and Silberston to adopt 'a structural rather than a behavioural analysis ... emphasizing potential rather than observed control'; S. Nyman and A. Silberston, 'The Ownership and Control of Industry', OEP, NS 3 (1978), 81.

private companies or those effectively private). Although this does not prove ownership or management control, it remains more likely that truly public companies with dispersed shareholdings would be professionally managed and controlled, whereas those in which shareholdings were concentrated in limited hands might come under the control of the owners. There are obvious difficulties. While it has been possible to identify certain companies as 'public' or 'private' (a judgement made on the basis of the observed distribution of shares and made irrespective of the nominal status of the company), it was also essential to create a third category of 'mixed' companies, in order to describe those firms in which although a large proportion of the shares were in the hands of 'public' (and therefore largely anonymous) share-holders, a significant (indeed, a potentially controlling) proportion nevertheless were in the hands of a few identifiable individuals. Even so, concentrated shareholding does not constitute proof of owner-control, since these 'private' or 'mixed' companies might still be controlled by non-shareholders, or might be companies in which ownership had become diluted due to bequests, wills, and other non-market share transfers over time, passing from the hands of deceased controllers to trusts or female relatives who took no role in the running of the company. The analysis of 'public', 'private', and 'mixed' ownership is none the less revealing when placed alongside the analysis of director-ships and major shareholdings; in this comparison more light is shed on the relationship between potential ownership-control (as measured by the preponderance of major shareholder-directors) and the structure of ownership itself. The two measures are set out in Table 5.5.

The percentage figures given in the Table should not be interpreted too precisely, since in the case of each region only some ten to twenty companies are involved—though they tend to be among the largest. The trend they point to is an accurate reflection of the sample data. Almost two-thirds of the companies in the sample were controlled by a limited number of major shareholdings. There were, however, important regional variations. Potential ownership-control was especially marked in the North-east, Lancashire, and Yorkshire; it was below average in other regions, and was particularly low in South Wales. Thus, although it was the 'common' practice over the country as a whole, for directors to be major shareholders in the companies they ran, in no less than three of the major regions—namely Scotland, the West Midlands, and South Wales—only about half of the firms in our sample were identifiably owner-controlled.

Table 5.5. *Ownership and management control of colliery companies*
(sample)

	Percentage of companies in which:		Designation of company (%)		
	(a) major shareholders controlled the board	(b) directors were not major shareholders	Quasi-public[a]	Private[a]	Mixed[a]
Scotland	50	50	40	50	10
North-east	86	14	8	78	14
Lancashire	80	20	13	73	14
Yorkshire	86	14	7	57	36
East Midlands	60	40	30	50	20
West Midlands	54	46	31	46	23
South Wales	42	58	50	33	17
Unweighted Av.	65	35	26	55	19
Weighted Av.	66	34	26	56	18

[a] These terms refer not to the nominal status of the company but to its ownership characteristics.

Sources: PRO BT 31/files of dissolved companies, and files at Companies' House; SRO BT 2/files.

Over half of the companies in the sample were private, or effectively 'private', companies in which ownership was confined to a limited number of identifiable individuals. This proportion agrees quite closely with that of the percentage of firms in which major shareholders controlled the board of directors, and while the two phenomena are not directly equivalent (that is, a few private companies were controlled by non-shareholders and a few of the companies in which major shareholders dominated the board were what we have termed 'mixed' companies), there is none the less a close relationship between 'private' status (as defined here) and potential owner-control, with the core of ownership-control occurring in private of effectively 'private' companies. The spread of 'private' companies was considerable—it was high in the North-east and Lancashire, but low in South Wales where shareholdings were unusually well-dispersed. The concentration of 'private' ownership in the North-east and Lancashire accords closely with the high degree of ownership-control in those regions.

The distribution of truly public companies was also diverse. Forty to fifty per cent of companies in South Wales and Scotland had highly-fragmented ownership, in which it was impossible for shareholders to dominate the board. In Yorkshire and the North-east there were few firms of this kind in our sample, though in the case of the former there was a large number of 'mixed' companies—firms in which shareholding was quite fragmented but in which a few individuals held enough shares to control the board; the data for Yorkshire, in fact, indicate that two-thirds of these 'mixed' companies were dominated by a few major share-holders. The number of truly public companies was also very small in Lancashire, a factor obviously connected with the dominance of major shareholders in this region.

A region-by-region analysis reveals that in the North-east, Lanca-shire, and Yorkshire the bulk of the companies in our sample were controlled, or at least potentially controlled, by a handful of major shareholders, and the vast majority of these were 'private' companies in the sense of having a very limited dispersal of shareholdings; the only qualification refers to Yorkshire, where a considerable proportion of potential ownership-control can be traced in the 'mixed' companies overall share fragmentation—much greater but in which a limited number of shareholders nevertheless dominated the board. In Scotland, the East and West Midlands, and South Wales potential ownership-control was less marked, though it still applied to roughly 50 per cent of the companies in the sample; share fragmentation was relatively advanced, particularly in South Wales.

Potential ownership control can be related, in large measure at least, to the conclusions reached in the earlier discussion of partnership capital and its sources (see Table 2.2). The concentration of potential ownership-control in the North-east, Lancashire, and Yorkshire must be related to the importance of coalowners as shareholders in these regions; 'coalowners' or 'colliery proprietors' held between a third and a half of all company shares in Yorkshire, Lancashire, and the North-east, and it is precisely this group of individuals one would expect to see most active in owner-management. The East Midlands, West Midlands, and South Wales, on the other hand, possessed few coalowner-shareholders, though an appreciable number could be identified in Scotland. There was, moreover, a larger-than-average representation of the private ('not gainfully employed') shareholders in the West Midlands and South

Wales, and it seems reasonable to argue that on the whole these share-holders were less likely to assume, or to wish to assume, control of the companies in which they invested. Further than this it is probably unwise to generalize. There were complicating factors in three of the regions, for although in the West Midlands, the East Midlands, and South Wales the proportion of coalowner-shareholders was below average, a fair proportion of iron masters was to be found among share-holders in the East Midlands, and the same is true of 'other business-men' in South Wales. When examined in the context of our evidence on sources of capital, the data assembled here on ownership-control implies that these non-coalowning business groups were less interested and less active in direct ownership-control, when compared with indi-viduals who saw mining as their chief business activity. Even so, the pos-sibility that these other business groups did exercise a degree of ownership-control in the mining industry cannot be entirely dis-counted.

The limitations of the data have already been rehearsed in connection with the use of this sample to identify sources of capital.[1] Part of the difficulty in interpreting and assessing the significance of the results stems from the chronological limits of the material—firstly in being con-fined to the period 1870–1914 with a bias towards 1890–1914; and secondly in its snapshot quality, in that it attempts to describe a con-stantly changing pattern of ownership or management control by means of data on shareholders and directors at one or two points in a com-pany's history. There are, however, firm a priori grounds to argue that the picture presented here is part of a long-term transition from ownership-control (and concentrated shareholdings) to professional control (and more dispersed shareholdings). Thus, while the data pre-sented here indicate that potential ownership-control was still dominant in the industry in the last two decades of our period (that is, about two-thirds of companies in the sample were potentially con-trolled by major shareholders and bearing in mind that owner-control was less likely in large companies), it was none the less more infrequent than hitherto. Unfortunately, the lack of data on ownership at mid-century makes it rather difficult to prove this proposition conclusively. Furthermore, the recent appearance of studies which call into question the generally accepted picture of greater management control in the twentieth century raises doubts concerning the historical inevitability of

[1] See above 136–40.

the growth of the corporate economy and the replacement of ownership by management control.[1]

There is clearly a different theoretical problem relating to ownership and management control which has yet to be examined. The evolution of the professional company manager was an important nineteenth-century trend, and was the basis for any management control which did exist in our period. The archetypal management-controlled company may be depicted as consisting of a board of non-owner directors chosen because of their knowledge of the industry or their skill in management, working in close collaboration with a professional manager or managing director. On the other hand, the evolution of professional management was not a trend which need *necessarily* have interfered with the mainten-ance of ownership control. Boards could still comprise owner-directors who might dictate the pace of investment and development and control the evolution of policy, while working with a professional manager. But it is also possible that owner-directors possessed power only in theory; in practice delegating it to professional managers or managing directors.

When David Dale became the chief executive of Consett through his family's shareholding on the company's formation he played a central role in resurrecting the company by restoring financial control and guiding policy. He retained a directorship when he left the company to join Pease and Partners as managing director, where Sir Alfred Pease was so impressed by the delight Dale took 'in the drudgery of figures' that before long he became a partner in the Pease colliery enterprise, and later vice-chairman. He also became chairman of Consett serving on coal and finance committees.[2] Elevation from his position as pro-fessional manager to director and partner represented a formalization of an arrangement by which effective power was acknowledged by a partial transfer of ownership, which was not uncommon. A similar history describes the development of the major Lancashire firm of Pear-son and Knowles. In 1848 the colliery-owner Thomas Pearson appointed Thomas Knowles, a former pit boy, sinker, collier, and at that time overlooker at the company's Ince Hall collieries, as colliery manager. When Thomas died in 1855 his son offered Knowles a partner-ship, of which he soon became chairman and managing director. Although it is true that the presence of shareholder-directors made ownership-control possible, it does not constitute proof of the existence of owner control, nor does it indicate the location of managerial authority.

[1] S. Nyman and A. Silberston, 'The Ownership and Control of Industry', OEP, NS 3 (1978), 97–9.   [2] A. S. Wilson thesis, 313–14; *Wigan Observer* 5 Dec. 1883, 5.

Although the two phenomena are in part connected there is an important distinction to be made between the evolution of the professional colliery manager and the appearance of powerful, non-shareowning managing directors. The transition which occurred, for example, in William Baird and Company after the late 1870s is typical of this trend. Before 1878 the Baird partners, who were all family members, held active administrative posts in the firm. After 1878 six new professional bureaucrats came to power, only one of whom was related to the Bairds.[1] It does seem important to make a distinction between this kind of change—the evolution of professional *company* management—and the development of the skills and numbers of good *colliery* managers. The former was a threat to owner control (and might affect company policy); the latter was not. Walters notes that in South Wales by the 1870s it was rare to find a colliery without a professional manager; but although some owners did leave responsibility for active company management to an underground agent, it was more common for owners and partners, with the assistance of salaried agents, to manage their own affairs.[2] When the Staveley Coal and Iron Company was formed in 1864 the Manchester investors who secured the conversion held one thousand of the six thousand £100 shares then issued, the Barrows' holding 1,250, and the remainder dispersed among more than one hundred investors, principally from the Manchester area.[3] Under our definition of ownership types Staveley was 'mixed', the control of management policy resting with the board of directors, consisting of the major shareholders. The power of the Barrow family, the former proprietors, waned after the death in 1865 of Richard Barrow, the first chairman, Pochin succeeded him, but it was Charles Markham, Richard Barrow's appointee as managing director and chief engineer in 1863, who soon established a personal dominance on the board by sheer experience, expertise, and personality.[4] On Markham's death in 1888, H. D. Pochin recalled that he 'had so ably conducted the affairs of this Company for some 25 years that it was with something like fear and trembling that we lost his controlling hand',[5] an explicit indication of how professional managerial power had dominated decision-making at Staveley. His successor was an administrator within Staveley, but from 1894 C. P. Markham, Charles's eldest son, was chairing annual general

---

[1] Corrins thesis, 287.
[2] Walters 1977, 159–68.
[3] Chapman 1981, 71.
[4] Ibid., 74–5.
[5] Ibid., 85.

meetings. His appointment as chairman in 1903 coincided with a period of rapid business development which, so far as Staveley was concerned, owed much to the new chairman's exercise of engineering and administrative skills, as well as the entrepreneurial flair inherited from his father.[1]

The details of Staveley's history underline the impossibility of deducing the location of power from positions held in the managerial structure, and highlights one of the chief difficulties in assessing the relationship between the board of directors and the company manager. Was the latter the mere servant of the former, or did he directly influence policy and investment, perhaps presenting the board with choices which he, because of his specialized knowledge and professional full-time application, could regard as effectively already made? Even where the minutes of the boards of directors are available they contain few clues to the decision-making process; it is unclear whether decisions made at managerial level were merely passed on to the board for more or less automatic confirmation, or whether the non-executive directors took an active part in managerial and investment decisions.

Valuable evidence on the role of boards of directors comes from the archives of a handful of major companies. First, at Carlton Main the crucial role of the board is revealed in five main areas which, according to the surviving minutes, accounted for the bulk of directors' time: negotiation for new leases, search for new sources of capital, negotiation of sales contracts, issues concerned with transport costs, and investment programmes.[2] In all these areas, particularly the last, however, it remains uncertain whether, in general, managers or directors set the pace. In Carlton Main's case it is clear that a crucial role was occupied by the consulting engineer, T. W. Jeffcock, who was himself a director and shareholder, though by no means the most important. Evidently day-to-day management resided with Jeffcock but it would also appear that he exercised a disproportionate influence over long-term strategy as well.[3] Similarly, evidence relating to Henry Briggs and Son points to a controlling influence residing with the chairman and managing director, rather than with the board as a whole. Thus, for example, in 1870 the power to negotiate leases, which rested originally in the board of directors as a whole, was transferred to chairman and managing director, two posts

[1] Ibid., 85–7.
[2] SCL Carlton Main MD 4080–9, 19 Jan. 1874, 4 Nov. 1879, 30 Mar. 1887, AGM June 1901 and May 1907, 2 July 1880, AGM May 1881, June 1883, and May 1884, 27 Mar. 1906, 30 Oct. 1906.
[3] Ibid., 4 Oct. 1876 and AGM May 1878, 15 Sept. 1896.

which the Briggs family effectively controlled. The board appears to have had a liaison function (that is, between the chairman and managing director on the one hand and the shareholders on the other) rather than an executive one. Shareholders might exert a considerable influence at rare moments, for example the decision to abandon profit-sharing in 1875, but this is almost a case of the exception proving the rule.[1] Both these Yorkshire companies were what we have designated 'mixed' in their ownership structure—companies with a high degree of ownership fragmentation in which, nevertheless, a few identifiable individuals can be seen as directors and potential controllers. However, the detailed company data suggests that in the case of both firms effective power was rather more limited, perhaps involving one or two professional managers in each. The board of directors was evidently not impotent, but in practice agreed to a delegation of authority in which the potential ownership-control of final policy was combined with, and to some extent replaced by, management control of much of the decision-making process, at least most routine decision-making.

The ultimate example in management control must be considered to be the Fife Coal Company. As managing director, Charles Carlow (and later his son Charles Augustus Carlow) assumed complete dominance of long-term strategy. In 1897 Charles Carlow set up what appears to have been a highly advanced system of policy committees, each of which was concerned with a different aspect of company policy but each embracing all twenty-three of the company's collieries on such matters as costs, prices, capital investment, and so on; since Carlow sat on every committee his control of all aspects of policy must have been considerable.[2] Similarly, at the Wigan Coal and Iron Company one man, in this case the manager Alfred Hewlett, wielded disproportionate power. Only five years after incorporation, in 1870 a major dispute broke out at the company, when a section of the board accused Hewlett of assuming the functions of directors; not only taking decisions on such matters as the ordering of equipment, managerial appointments, contracts for sales, and capital allocations, but actually carrying out these decisions without the prior approval of the board. The course of the dispute makes it clear that Hewlett was exceeding his powers, since whoever made the decision in practice such matters were always to be laid before

[1] BroLU Special Coll. MS 160, Henry Briggs, MB, Reports of Directors, 16 Feb. 1882. Worker-directors, one being chosen by the worker-shareholders each year, sat on the board between 1869 and 1886; 29 Apr. 1870, 23 Nov. 1888, 23 May 1890.

[2] Muir 1952, 19–22, 3–11, 120; SRO BT 2/2826/2–5.

the board for confirmation. Even so, Hewlett survived the crisis, largely through a good deal of shareholder support, and continued to run the company for forty years or more,[1] during which time Wigan presents a portrait of a classic professionally-managed company; although here, as elsewhere, the precise role of the board is unclear, it is certain that Hewlett was no mere servant. Comparisons between Staveley, Fife, and Wigan would suggest that management control was not confined to any particular pattern of ownership structure. Fife was a public company with a widely dispersed shareholding, one in which major shareholders do not seem to have been present as directors; both Staveley and Wigan, on the other hand, could perhaps best be described as 'mixed' in structure, though Wigan was a company in which one or two individuals (landed aristocrats) progressively increased their controlling interest. In Wigan's case, therefore, there seems to have been a conscious decision to delegate control to a non-owning professional manager. Under somewhat different circumstances a similar delegation occurred at Staveley.

Two major Welsh companies, Powell Duffryn and Main, appear to have travelled far along the road to professional management control. As the principal financier and moving spirit in forming Powell Duffryn in 1864, George Elliot, distinguished mining engineer, multi-colliery owner, and entrepreneur, dominated company policy from its inception, though a disastrous diversification into iron production at the peak of the early 1870s boom hampered colliery development during a period of indifferent company performance after 1874. After becoming a baronet, in 1877 Sir George Elliot was squeezed out of active management participation, but as further problems accumulated he was recalled as managing director in 1880. However, dissension among the directors, partly concerning Sir George's wire-making business, eventually led to his resignation in 1888. Thereafter, company policy was formed by a joint management committee consisting of four directors, one of whom, A. G. Ogilvie, also became chairman. As part of this reorganization the post of general manager in charge of all colliery development was created; E. M. Hann, an experienced colliery manager within Powell Duffryn, was appointed and worked directly under Ogilvie to whom he was responsible, though Hann claimed that his own influence domi-

---

[1] LaRO Wigan Coal and Iron, DDX/127/38 Proceedings of EGM 13 Jan. 1870, 1–35, 68; DDX/127/39, Reply by Mr Hewlett to Charges Made Against Him by Mr John Lancaster and Mr Thomas Part, Jan. 1870; Wigan Coal and Iron, DDX/127/40–74, Directors' Report Dec. 1885 and 1895; DDX/127/73; Newspaper cuttings from *Wigan Examiner* 8 Feb. 1896; *Wigan Observer* 17 Sept. 1918.

nated investment and technical strategy. The effect of these changes appears to have involved a reassertion of management control during the decade following Elliot's departure.[1] This was a development which may have been assisted by share fragmentation and increasing levels of external ownership. The developing authority of professional management at the Main Colliery Company, too, may have owed something to the dispersion of ownership, though the precise role of Main's directors remains difficult to assess. Since outside technical expertise was sought on several occasions this might imply an unwillingness or inability to delegate to management within the company. Despite a good deal of share fragmentation, numerous major shareholders or their representatives held board membership and this, too,[2] might be taken as a sign of some continuing owner-control. Since in the case of both firms shareholdings became more and more fragmented over time, the probability is that the powers of the owners and the board of directors in entirety diminished as those of professional managers increased. At Powell Duffryn, where from 1888 the management committee was in control of policy, the directors also acted as executive managers.

The last four companies on which we have information, Butterley, Ashington, Cannock Chase, and Andrew Knowles and Sons, appear to fall into the category of privately owned, owner-controlled firms. The management structure at Butterley is obscure, and the precise powers of William Bean, the company's chief agent, unknown, but it would seem that the Wright family (effectively the sole owners) continued throughout the period to control company policy.[3] Much the same was true of the similarly long-established firm of Andrew Knowles and Son Ltd., the Knowles family continuing to own more than 50 per cent of capital after incorporation in 1874 and providing both chairman and managing director.[4] The Ashington Coal Company was owned and managed by coalowners who were (or at least regarded themselves as) competent policy makers. Directors were present at all policy meetings, held monthly with the manager and head viewer, whose responsibility was to issue reports on proposed developments and to make recommendations on company matters. The company operated with a firm distinction

---

[1] Hann 1922, 4–5, 8–9, 13, 16–17; PRO BT 31 30728/1487c.

[2] This view is based on the impression of anonymity gained from the Directors' Reports contained among the uncatalogued collection of records of Main Colliery Co. Ltd., GlaRO, Main D/DMC; PRO BT 31 1984/8488; PRO BT 31 31167/29139.

[3] Mottram and Coote 1950, 24; DeRO Butterley 503/B MB 1888–1919; 503/B/39 Notes for a History of Butterley Company; 503/B Share and Debenture Ledger Book.

[4] *Wigan Observer* 27 Jan. 1894.

between management and financial affairs; and control of the latter was left entirely in the hands of owner-directors.[1] Ashington's structure would appear to present a clear example of a private owner-controlled company.

The Cannock Chase Colliery Company's history provides another example of this, and illustrates how the essential character of a firm under ownership control could survive family differences and the introduction of outsiders into management at senior level. On its formation in 1860 the Company was owned predominantly by a handful of families residing in London, including the major shareholder and managing director. He was John Robinson McClean, who until his death in 1875 ran the company together with a local colliery manager and occasional advice from an incomparable combination of George Elliot and William Armstrong. A few years after McClean's death the leading director became the mining engineer George Parker Bidder, whose shareholding in the company became large only after his appointment as a director in 1878, since when until his death in 1896, by which time he was chief executive, he was described by the chairman, Colonel Lewin, as having been 'emphatically the prop and stay of the Company'.[2] The McCleans and the Lewins, however, continued to own more than half the ordinary shares, the Bidders ranking second in order of importance. In the reconstructed company in 1902 these three families owned all the shares, a Bidder and a McClean were joint managing directors, with Arthur Sopwith, the company's mining engineer since 1875, appointed as colliery manager in 1878, and general manager and non-shareholding director following George Parker Bidder's death in 1896.[3]

When the Bidders and McCleans relinquished their executive roles in 1908 Arthur Sopwith became general manager, colliery management becoming the responsibility of S. F. Sopwith as certificated colliery manager, a change heralding the first major step in managerial control separate from ownership.[4]

On the basis of company histories it has been possible to argue that successful company managers and managing directors should be regarded as the successors to estate managers and viewers of the early

[1] NuRO Ashington NCB/AS/5; ZMD/54/1–5; *Newcastle Daily Chronicle* 13 Nov. 1903; *Newcastle Daily Journal* 12 Aug. 1907; J. Jamieson, *Northumberland at the Opening of the Twentieth Century* (Brighton, 1906), 21.

[2] BUL BR 14/ii–iii, Cannock Chase Colliery, MB 4 Mar. 1896.

[3] Ibid., 30 Sept. 1862, 19 Feb. 1873, 4 Nov. 1877, 27 Mar. 1878, 4 Mar. 1896, 31 July 1901, 26 June 1912.

[4] Ibid., 27 May 1908, 26 June 1912.

nineteenth century, that the supply of such men was limited, and that one implication of this is the continuing dominance of owner-control, at least in the medium and smaller firms. Even among our few examples from larger firms there are marked variations in the structure of ownership, management, and control, and no single pattern emerges. The dissolved companies data on potential ownership-control indicated that such control was the norm, embracing almost two-thirds of the companies in the sample. But if a detailed case study of each were possible, an unknown proportion of this two-thirds might be seen to be effectively management controlled, whereby directors possessed limited or circumscribed powers. Probably in almost all of these firms the board of directors would have constituted the final policy-making and executive authority, but it has not proved possible to discover how often this authority was actually invoked. In those companies in which owners were not directors (just over one-third of the whole), ownership-control of the firm was still possible through shareholders' meetings, but is unlikely to have been common.

Limitations of the data in the dissolved companies sample and of archival sources render generalization about the industry as a whole problematical. Both our samples are heavily biased in favour of large companies—which might be thought to have contained above-average levels of 'public' and fragmented capital and a higher degree of management control than was normal for firms as a whole. There are grounds for believing, though, unfortunately, inadequate evidence to prove, that smaller firms would have been private, limited-shareholding companies in which owner-directors would have a considerable impact on policy and management. Professional managers (an expensive commodity) might be entirely eschewed in favour of advice on contract from viewers and consultant engineers. Where they were employed managers would be less able, less knowledgeable, less well paid, and probably less powerful. Owner-directors in these smaller to medium-sized companies, possessing a close knowledge of the firm and possibly of the industry as well, might be expected to have wielded more power than their equivalents in the larger public or semi-public companies.[1] Since most directors were part time, it would seem likely that their ability to control policy would have been greater in the smaller, more accessible undertakings, where a rapidly acquired working knowledge of the

---

[1] The big butty system would form an exception, since under this arrangement contracted management held effective power at colliery level. But it is doubtful whether this system was at all widespread after about 1850.

collieries was possible. An undertaking the size of the Fife Coal Company, however, with its twenty-three collieries in Fife alone (thirty-two if one includes associated concerns),. required a man of undivided interests and uncompromising energy, and also needed a fairly large management team.[1] Consequently, if our detailed company surveys suggest that the dissolved company material may have overestimated the degree of true ownership-control in the industry, this needs to be set against the likelihood that by its concentration on the larger companies the dissolved companies material itself probably understates the true level of ownership-control. That this was the case seems all the more likely when considering the financial constraints under which the smaller and medium-sized firms were compelled to operate. Where capital programmes and development required a limited number of partners or shareholders to subscribe increased capital from their own pockets, their ultimate control over investment and development decisions must have been very great indeed.

C. P. Griffin's detailed account of colliery development in Leicestershire and south Derbyshire, an area of small-scale enterprise where corporate transformation was very slow to take place, reveals that in those limited liability companies which were formed characteristically ownership and control remained in the same hands: 'the modern limited liability company, with its divorce of ownership and control and the employment of a paid manager subject to an anonymous and largely absentee board of directors, was not typical (if, indeed, it existed at all) of the Leicestershire and South Derbyshire coalfield in the late nineteenth century'.[2] If such were the conditions among incorporated firms there can be little doubt that among the rest the identity between ownership, control, and management was complete. Where public flotation of capital was involved, or where partners in large companies were very wealthy men, the power of professional managers to raise the necessary funds was likely to have been so much greater; hence even at the end of our period, the power and effectiveness of these men with whom their company became identified was considerably enhanced, and following suitable preparation not infrequently perpetuated through nepotistic managerial succession.

---

[1] Mineral Statistics 1910; Muir 1952, 1–2, 4–6, 8–9, 10, 13–14, 16, 19–20, 22; Charles Carlow, the manager in question, is the subject of a biography in the forthcoming *Dictionary of Scottish Business Biography*. I am grateful to Dr Maurice Kirby and to the editors for allowing me to refer to this entry.

[2] C. P. Griffin thesis, 265.

vi. Business leaders

Several problems arise in any attempt to present a profile of coalowners, not least the paucity of data. The sources which offer the most extensive information referring to a large number of the founders of firms are the dissolved companies files, which provide evidence on the occupations of founders. However, nothing more than their place of residence and their occupation or business interests are included in the files, and imprecision is abundant. There is no indication of the extent to which, for example, a person's colliery interests were primary or supplementary to other business interests he might possess; neither is there any clue to the source from which a lifetime's accumulation of wealth has originated, for there are no details of family or parental background.

The founders of the companies, as listed in Articles of Association, were not always the prime movers in company formation, who might consist of perhaps one or two individuals among a long list of signatures, or might not even appear at all, if local solicitors acted on their behalf. Furthermore, because the dissolved companies files are more abundant for the later nineteenth and early twentieth century, this data will reveal neither changes that may have occurred during the course of the nineteenth century nor major shifts in the composition of coalowners as a group.

For an impression of the picture over a longer period we have been compelled to rely upon various contemporary and secondary sources, parliamentary inquiries, directories, technical and trade journals, newspapers, and regional and local histories, with the result that our survey cannot offer a systematic basis for generalization—except in the sense that the trawl for information has been systematic. The size of the industry was so large, ownership was so diffuse, and the structure and organization of colliery enterprise was so varied, that in many instances it has been impossible to distinguish participant-owners from effective policy makers, or to identify the extent of decision-making involvement by individuals, variously described as agent, viewer, general manager, managing director, or chairman; the identification of the chief executive is sometimes difficult even within those firms which are reasonably well documented, and as most of our observations depend upon a few lines from an obituary the fragility of the foundations of this exercise will be apparent. However, this approach does make it possible not only to refer to actively participating coalowners and business leaders during the first and second half of our period, but broadens the kind of information available on social background, education, training and experience and interests both inside and outside the industry.

Our sample of founders extracted from the dissolved companies files is similar to that employed in analysing share ownership, and exhibits the same strengths and defects. It refers principally to the period after about 1880. Because of the procedures involved in forming companies it seems likely that the sample is biased by the inclusion of the professions and 'capitalists', and is weighted towards larger companies; fessions and 'capitalists' and is weighted towards larger companies, whereas other sources subsequently employed in our analysis of business leaders probably includes some professional managers who were not at the same time proprietors. Table 5.6 measures the proportion of company founders falling into different occupational and business groupings; each individual is counted once and the Table takes no account of the differing amounts of capital possessed by founders or of the varying size of companies which they founded.

The most frequent form of description given by signatories to articles of association was that of 'coalowner' or 'colliery proprietor' (28 per cent), almost certainly reflecting the typical circumstances surrounding the formation of a company by the owners of a firm already doing business. The proportion of founders so described, however, varied between regions, from 44 per cent in the North-east to 7 per cent in the West Midlands. Next to coalowners or colliery proprietors the largest single group consisted of those 'not gainfully employed', numbering 13 per cent nationally. Here, too, regional variations are striking, varying from 6 per cent in Scotland and 7 per cent in Lancashire, to 20 per cent in the North-east and the West Midlands. These differences may conceal the diversity of interests among wealthy, well-established business, banking, and landed families in the North-east, whereas the high figure for the West Midlands might be the result of the highly fragmented ownership pattern in the coal industry of the region, which allowed small investors with private means to play an important part in company formation.

Eleven per cent of all founders were 'businessmen' and a further 8 per cent were iron masters. When coalowners, iron masters, and other businessmen are combined, they represent in total 47 per cent of company founders, slightly more than the proportion for ownership itself. Thirteen per cent were from the professions and another 9 per cent were professional engineers, a category which included contractors; merchants also accounted for 9 per cent, which revealed both groups as having played a larger role in company formation than in

Table 5.6. *Occupations and business interests of company founders*
(percentages)

	Scotland	North-east	Lancs.	Yorks.	East Midlands	West Midlands	South Wales	Average[a]
1. Business								
Coalowners	36	44	35	23	26	7	13	28
Iron masters	25	3	6	2	9	8	5	8
Other business	1	5	11	10	4	8	29	11
2. Professional and Private								
Professional: legal	4	2	7	14	6	9	6	6
others	5	—	6	12	4	13	12	7
Engineers: mining	5	5	6	2	9	3	5	5
others	3	—	2	7	9	11	4	4
Shopkeepers/tradesmen	—	—	—	—	2	3	4	1
Others in coal trade	6	6	6	2	4	7	3	5
3. Others								
Landowners	—	3	—	—	—	—	3	1
Merchants	6	12	11	14	8	8	6	9
Bankers and financiers	1	—	3	2	2	2	—	1

[a] weighted mean (employment)
Source: as for Table 2.9, where the basis for the sample is explained.

capital provision. 'Others in the coal trade' (including managers, agents, and secretaries), engineers, and shopkeepers and tradesmen were also of slightly greater numerical significance as founders than as shareholders.

By combining coal masters, professional mining engineers, and 'others in the coal trade', we arrive at a figure of 38 per cent as a very conservative measure of the involvement as proprietors of those already connected with the industry. However, as many iron masters possessed collieries as a subsidiary activity, the relative importance of which grew from the 1880s, it is reasonable to include their contribution to the founding of colliery enterprise with that of other groups identified entirely with coal; which raises the proportion of founders whose business activities were already partly or wholly dependent upon coal production to 46 per cent. These groups held 40.5 per cent of shares; more than three-quarters of these, however, were in the hands of coalowners.

If we make allowance for the connections between coal production and the coal trade, and for the probable inclusion among those 'not gain-fully employed' of wealthy businessmen to whose success colliery enter-prise had contributed yet for whom public dissociation from industry was a symptom of social aspiration, then we might conclude that at least 50 per cent of those in our sample involved in company formation were very familiar with, even though they may not have depended for their success entirely upon, the coal industry. It seems likely that this under-estimates the extent to which the industry recruited entrepreneurs and capital from within the industry, especially before 1880, for the dissolved companies data, which consists of a few remains of limited companies only, necessarily provides a partial picture of firms best placed to involve those lacking first-hand knowledge of the industry. The widely publicized disasters which attended London capitalists' ventures into limited-liability coal companies in the North-east in the 1840s sounded a warning of the consequences of uninformed specula-tion in the coal trade.[1] Even extended partnerships, therefore, remained predominantly local, and tended to be based on kinship and connec-tions with coal. For another group whose trading activities were also separate from coal production yet whose success depended upon coal, movement into the industry occurred later and took a different and more successful course. The availability of output figures for steam-coal collieries in South Wales enabled Walters to identify with considerable accuracy the entry into the industry of coal exporters and shipowners beginning in the 1870s. The data also revealed that whereas the

[1] See above 131-2.

engineers, iron masters, and retail shopkeepers tended to sink pits them-selves the mercantile element acquired their pits as going concerns.[1]

Our examination of the sources of capital and the occupational com-position of the founders of coal companies provides some indication of the sorts of people attracted to, and willing to commit risk capital in, the industry, but our discussion of managerial structures and organization revealed the difficulties of deducing from an objective structure the loca-tion of the power to make strategic policy decisions. The tentative nature of conclusions arising from an analysis of dissolved companies data and company archives underlines the necessity, in order to illu-minate managerial behaviour, of attempting to identify the decision-making élite in the industry. This we have done by an essentially eclectic process, the necessary consequence of the paucity of secondary or pri-mary sources from which to reconstruct even the most basic informa-tion on the social origins, education, training, and careers of more than a few of the business leaders in this industry. We have attempted to reveal chronological changes in the characteristics of business leaders by focusing upon two cohorts: those born before 1831 but who were active in the industry at least until 1850, and those whose birth occurred between 1830 and 1870. The logic of this division is our assumption that effective managerial contributions occurred after the age of twenty, and that a twenty-year period of active leadership should be a necessary qualification for inclusion in the élite. The divide also separates, broadly, those business leaders whose formative years pre-dated the railways and were active in the period when iron was the dominant determinant of market conditions, from the later cohort which experienced the forma-tive influences of intense competition as the inland coalfields were developed, and when exports emerged as central to the industry; the latter period also saw the emergence of the company form of organiza-tion and the rise of the professional company manager. We have excluded from the élite those colliery managers who did not also exercise executive power—or at least did not powerfully influence decision-making at the company, partnership, or proprietor level—for we are concerned with that body of men who undertook the *strategic* decisions which determined the mobilization and deployment of resources. In total, we have assembled biographical details of 172 business leaders, eighty-one of whom are included in the pre-1831 cohort, though basic information is far from complete for all of these or for their successors after 1830.

[1] Walters 1977, 87.

Table 5.7 shows that the social origins of the first cohort, indicated by father's occupation, were predominantly related to the coal industry. Of those for whom the information is available, 26 per cent of fathers were coalowners, 15 per cent viewers or colliery managers, and 5 per cent were mining engineers. This excludes iron masters, accounting for a further 8 per cent, some of whom were certainly involved in the production of coal though not for sale. Another 5 or 7 per cent represented working miners and 7 per cent were merchants of one kind or another. Depending upon definition, therefore, 44 per cent, and possibly more of the business leaders included in our sample were the sons of fathers involved in the industry. Landowners, farmers, and estate agents accounted for 20 per cent, and probably included some possessing experience in surveying and mineral estate development.

It is impossible to be other than arbitrary when trying to classify fathers by social status; none the less, tentative conclusions may be made. Few business leaders emerged from a working-class background (only four out of sixty-one known cases). George Elliot exemplifies the exceptional rags to riches success which was so rare in the coalmining industry. The son of a working miner, Elliot was born at Gateshead in 1815, beginning as a pit lad at the Marquis of Londonderry's Pensher Pit nine years later. His mathematical abilities commended him to the colliery viewer who agreed to his apprenticeship with Thomas Sopwith, land and mining surveyor, after which, at the age of twenty-one, he returned to Pensher Colliery as overman, succeeding shortly to the position of under-viewer at Monkwearmouth, then the deepest pit known. Three years later he became head viewer, undertook consulting work for others, and together with bankers Backhouse and Maunsey became managing partner of Washington Colliery. In 1843 he took out a lease of extensive mines at Usworth and commenced sinking on his own account. By 1851 he had also become chief viewer for the collieries of the Marquis of Londonderry. In the 1860s he purchased Pensher Colliery, where he had begun as a pit lad, and after making a valuation of Thomas Powell's steam-coal collieries led the formation of the Powell Duffryn Steam Coal Company Ltd. in 1864 to purchase Powell's and other collieries in the Aberdare and Rhymney valleys. For the next thirteen years he remained principal proprietor, general manager, and moving spirit: he resigned in 1877, was re-called in 1880 as part of a managerial reform, and finally removed from office in 1888.[1] Joseph Love, a miner's son who began as a pit lad in Northumberland,

---

[1] Hann 1922, 3–13.

Table 5.7. *Occupations of fathers of business leaders*
(percentages)

	Pre-1831	Post-1830		Pre-1831	Post-1830
Coalowners	26	39	Other business	7	1
Viewers, colliery managers	15	13	Not gainfully employed	3	—
Others in the coal trade	—	—	Merchants	7	—
Working miners	7	3	Shopkeepers/tradesmen	3	1
Mining engineers	5	7	Banks, finance	—	—
Other engineers	2	10	Landowners and estate agents	7	—
Iron masters	8	13	Farmers	10	3
			Other	—	10

The sample consists of 81 before 1831, 19 of whose origins were not known, compared with the unknown origins of 23 out of a sample of 85 after 1830. The percentages refer to the totals excluding those not known.

Key: Sample occupations:
Social Class I: landowner, merchant, clergymen, those not gainfully employed.
Social Class II: coalowners, viewers, senior colliery managers, mining and other engineers, iron masters, farmers, school-teachers.
Sources: As for Table 2.9, where the sample is explained.

developed his entrepreneurial skills as a travelling salesman in dry goods and as a building contractor, before joining his father-in-law, a timber merchant, in a new venture; this began in 1840, when the firm of Straker and Love opened out Brancepath Colliery.[1] This enterprise, though size-able, could not compare either with those of Sir George Elliot or with North's Navigation Colliery, formed in 1889, or with those of Pearson and Knowles, a partnership in which Thomas Knowles, who began as a pit boy and whom we may assume was the son of a manual worker, rose within the firm to become managing partner and later company chair-man.[2] It seems likely, too, that John Lancaster, whose origins are similarly obscure, but who was described as a self-taught mechanic, worked his way up by experience and application to become mineral agent to Lord Mostyn and later the manager of Earl Granville's collieries and ironworks; Lancaster also became a colliery proprietor, and was appointed the first chairman of the Wigan Coal and Iron Company.[3] Of similarly modest origins was Joseph Hargreaves, who rose from trapper boy at one of Charlesworth's pits at the age of eight to become general manager in charge of all of the west Yorkshire pits belonging to Charles-worth, one of the major coal producers in the region.[4] Even more important, however, were the achievements of David Davies, the son of a farmer who began as a sawyer with his father, branching out into building construction before becoming a partner in a railway contract-ing firm. He was nearly fifty years of age when in 1868 he leased coal in the Rhondda, and together with other partners formed David Davies and Co. The Ocean Coal Company, a merger of two firms, was formed in 1887, and in 1893 Deep Navigation Colliery was taken over, by which time William Jenkins, a professional mining engineer trained by W. T. Lewis, had become general manager.[5]

One of the most successful entrepreneurs who entered the industry from outside was Charles Mark Palmer, the son of a timber merchant who left school and travelled to France where he was to learn the language and search for orders on behalf of his father's new venture, Palmer, Beckwith and Co., coal fitters. At the age of twenty-two, Palmer returned to the North-east and joined with John Bowes to form the Marley Hill Coking Company in 1844, simultaneously taking on the sole responsibility for selling the company's coke and accepting a full share as managing partner of Marley Hill in 1847. Although his impor-

[1] University of Durham, Dept. of Paleography, 'Local Necrologies', 21 Feb. 1875.
[2] *Wigan Observer* 5 Dec. 1883, 5.   [3] *Wigan Observer* 23 Apr. 1884, 7.
[4] Goodchild 1978, 123.   [5] Walters 1977, 52, 61-2.

tant iron shipbuilding ventures absorbed considerable time, energy, and capital, none the less Palmer continued as managing partner of Marley Hill, becoming chairman and managing director, and until 1860 undertaking detailed managerial responsibilities. When John Bowes and Partners became a limited company in 1886 Palmer was one of the two largest shareholders. The demands upon time by his parliamentary commitments, and by the financial difficulties of the ill-fated Tyne Plate Glass Co., however, proved to be a serious drain upon Palmer's entrepreneurial commitment to the John Bowes Company, and he retired in 1895. His successor as managing director was his eldest son, Alfred, whose full-time commitment allowed the termination of the post of head viewer, held continuously by Cuthbert Berkley since 1863. From 1901 Berkley's son took over general superintendence of the coking collieries, and two others, one of whom was Claud Bowes Palmer, Charles's third son, managed the others, the ultimate management control resting with Alfred Palmer.[1]

The attribution of social class to business leaders' origins within a five-category schema inevitably involves arbitrary decisions, especially in trying to decide between classes II (major businessmen and senior managers) and III (small businessmen and middle managers); but probably no more than 28 per cent of business leaders in the first cohort originated from classes other than I and (predominantly) II; skilled manual workers and below were insignificant numerically as a source of upwardly mobile recruits. In the second cohort the proportion originating from classes I and II was even higher, at 84 per cent. Unfortunately, the difficulty in identifying the educational backgrounds of this cohort provides inadequate evidence—only in twenty cases is information available—and, as might have been expected, records either grammar or some kind of nonconformist-academy schooling for almost all. In eight instances business leaders had also spent time at a university, though few stayed long enough to graduate. William Dixon, son of the founder of Dixon's coal company, attended Glasgow University,[2] as did James Merry, of Merry and Cunninghame.[3] Colliery and landowner John Dodgson Charlesworth was an MA of St John's College, Cambridge,[4] while the manager he appointed in 1866, T. W. Embleton, son of a viewer from Newcastle, was a graduate of the University of Edinburgh, who also completed an apprenticeship under his uncle (another

---

[1] Mountford thesis, 29–32, 138, 155, 138, 149, 152–3, 175, 183.
[2] Byres thesis, 810.   [3] SDBB (forthcoming).
[4] John Goodchild, 'John Dodgson Charlesworth', DBB.

mining engineer). After more than twenty years as Charlesworth's general colliery manager, at the same time consulting for Lord Mexborough and for Wharncliffe Silkstone, Embleton became a proprietor involved in managing Monk Bretton.[1]

University education supplemented by mining engineering apprenticeship was also the pattern for some of the leading viewers and managers, notably John Daglish who was associated for a critical period in the management of the Londonderry collieries,[2] and George Greenwell, whose major responsibilities during the course of his career as viewer and later resident manager included undertakings at the John Bowes collieries, followed by those at the Earl Waldegrave's Radstock collieries in Somerset, and the Poynton collieries belonging to Lord Vernon, in Cheshire.[3] In the West Midlands, J. R. McClean, founding proprietor of Cannock Chase Colliery Co., pursued a combination of science and mathematics at university, followed by an engineering apprenticeship,[4] an education which resembled that of Charles Markham, Staveley's key figure from 1863, inasmuch that after reading chemistry at Edinburgh University Markham was also trained as a civil engineer; both began their careers in railway construction.[5] Thus, education at a grammar-type school or academy, followed by sciences at a university and subsequent apprenticeship under a practising engineer, either civil or mineral, was the pattern of experience for an élite corps of business leaders in the industry. For the 'father of the coal trade' in the nineteenth century, William Armstrong,[6] consultant to the greatest colliery enterprises, but proprietor of, or partner in, none, secondary education at Dr Bruce's academy followed by science at Edinburgh University, articles to Nicholas Wood at Killingworth and practical experience at other collieries, formed the classic basis for the career of the most distinguished and almost certainly one of the most influential figures in the industry until his death in 1897.[7] It is interesting to note that while his expertise was obtained in this orthodox fashion, the means by which it became so widely diffused was the influence of the group of Manchester financiers led by H. D. Pochin, the former druggist's apprentice, whose constellation of coal-producing iron companies were committed to Armstrong's care as consultant viewer.[8]

[1] *TFIME* VII (1893–4), 222–7.
[2] *TFIME* XXXIII (1907–8), 201–4.   [3] Greenwell 1899, 11–28, 110, 131, 163.
[4] *The Times* 16 July 1873, 5.   [5] Chapman 1981, 72–3.
[6] *TNEIME*, XIV (1897–8), 1702.   [7] Ibid.
[8] NuRO Armstrong 725/B5–13 Reports on Staveley, Sheepbridge, Bolckow Vaughn, Tredegar; Chapman 1981, 70–2.

During the first half of our period consultants continued to provide instant access to breadth of experience, a vital ingredient in the apprenticeship of the business élite, though which could serve as a substitute for proprietary inheritors. Proprietors, partners, or directors, who began as viewers or professional managers typically were mobile until the formation of a firm to which they became financially committed; for professional managers, other than those in service on the landed estates, multi-colliery management for more than one proprietor was an alternative method of enhancing income and extending experience. Simultaneously, in the 1840s Nicholas Wood was managing partner in the Hetton Coal Company, partner in the North Hetton Coal Co., Marley Hill, and three others, in addition to which he was sole owner of the Blackboy Colliery and two others.[1] T. Y. Hall, another leading mining engineer in the North-east, was viewer at North Hetton, Blackboy, and the Stella Coal Company, of which he was also a founding partner.[2] Reinforcing this diffusion of experience among the business élite, particularly of professional mining engineers, was the movement out of the North-east to other regions where the problems posed by mining at greater depths provided incentives to encourage geographical mobility.

Sir George Elliot's progress to South Wales, where he founded Powell Duffryn, is a spectacular example of professional mobility, as is that of Archibald Hood, whose apprenticeship in the Scottish pit where his father was colliery manager began a long career, during which he was mineral agent and engineer at the Dundyvan Works of Dunlop and Wilson, the colliery manager for a mineral owner from whom Hood subsequently took a lease and formed a partnership with others in Scotland and finally in 1863, having moved to South Wales, established the Glamorgan Coal Company.[3] George Greenwell and James MacMurtrie were two other mining engineers from the North-east whose technical expertise and managerial experience were secured by collieries in Somerset, Cheshire, and South Wales,[4] as was that of T. E. Forster, who in taking over the management of the Machen collieries in 1858 took on as apprentice Thomas Forster-Brown. After several years as a professional consultant in partnership with Samual Dobson, Forster-Brown

[1] *Newcastle Daily Chronicle* 20 Dec. 1865.

[2] NCL William Fordyce 'Memoir of T. Y. Hall Esq. Mining Engineer'.

[3] *CG* 21 Nov. 1868, 449, 29 Dec. 1893; Hassan thesis, 158–60; Phillips 1925, 208; Walters 1977, 55–6.

[4] See above 414–5, also C. J. Down and A. J. Warrington, *The History of the Somerset Coalfield* (Newton Abbott, 1971), 162–3.

became part-owner and director of the Great Western Colliery Company Ltd., in the development of which he played a key role.[1]

A similar pattern is revealed by the career of W. T. Lewis (later Lord Merthyr), who upon leaving a local school joined his father as engineer at the Plymouth Iron Works to serve an apprenticeship for five years. Thereafter, Lewis became assistant engineer and clerk to W. S. Clark for the Marquis of Bute, who was then only seventeen, though soon Clark's poor health led to Lewis entering into partnership with Clark as mineral agent for the Bute estate, whom he succeeded on his death in 1864. As a result Lewis became responsible for the management of the Bute Merthyr Pit, the first deep sinking in the Upper Rhondda Valley. By the 1870s Lewis had purchased his own collieries, culminating in the formation of the Lewis Merthyr Consolidated Collieries in 1900, though outside the Rhondda Lewis acquired other pits, too.[2]

Business leaders born after 1830 were similar in social background to their predecessors. Of those whose father's occupation is known, 39 per cent were coalowners, 13 per cent viewers and managers, 7 per cent mining engineers and 3 per cent were otherwise engaged in the coal trade; a futher 12 per cent were iron masters. Excluding iron masters, 61 per cent of our representative sample of business leaders sprang from a coalmining parentage; a further 3 per cent of fathers were ordinary working men. These figures suggest a trend towards the recruitment of business leaders from within the industry in which inherited authority, consequent upon ownership or managerial influence, were important contributory factors. The social composition of the business élite also seems to have narrowed during the late nineteenth century, for among the second cohort 28 per cent may be regarded as having originated from outside classes I and II; if the four vicars were to be identified as class III (alongside middle management) instead of class I, that figure would rise to 33 per cent. Among those of humble origins in our sample, Joseph Hewitt rose from junior clerk to solicitor and became a managing director, though in the relatively small firm of Fountain and Burnley.[3] The greatest success was that achieved by Alexander Roxburgh, the son of a forester and coal salesman; he began as a pit pony driver, became bookkeeper and accountant before being appointed as general manager of the Alloa Coal Company in 1873, and was admitted as a managing partner with a minimal shareholding in 1884.[4] The career

[1] Walters 1977, 58.   [2] Ibid., 52.
[3] John Goodchild, 'Joseph Hewitt', DBB.
[4] SDBB (forthcoming).

of John Turner, who began as a pit lad in Derbyshire, became a trainee under a local consultant viewer for four years and achieved a colliery managers' certificate in 1886, provides another unusual example of upward mobility. But Turner was an exceptional figure, for a succession of managerial appointments in the East Midlands, beginning as commercial manager of the South Leicester Colliery Co. in 1880, culminated in his becoming general manager of Moira Collieries, Leicestershire's largest colliery enterprise, in 1893.[1]

Such a career pattern, however, was unusual and the careful preparation of a handful of vicars' sons, as well as the son of a master of Eton, may be regarded as an indication of the status accorded to successful mining engineers.[2] In our second cohort, public-school education was the preparation for nine of the forty-nine known histories; fifteen were educated at grammar schools, and seventeen at nonconformist academies. Eight took advantage of the provision of technical-school evening instruction. An increasing importance attached to formal education is reflected, too, in the rise in the proportion of those attending university: 24 per cent compared with 10 per cent in the pre-1831 cohort. J. H. Merivale's father, a rector, sent his son to a private school, proceeding to Armstrong College of Science in Newcastle, followed by articles for four years as a mining engineer at South Hetton and Murton Collieries. Although he became check viewer to several collieries in the North-east, his marriage into a distinguished viewing family, the Liddells, must have consolidated his position as manager at the Netherton Colliery of the Broomhill Company, in which Merivale became managing agent as Liddell's successor.[3] Charles Chetwynd Ellison was sent by his father, who was also a vicar, to Clifton College, followed by King's College School of Mines; subsequently he served time in the RNVR, before becoming articled to Emerson Bainbridge at Nunnery Colliery.[4]

As one of the leading mining engineers, and from the late nineteenth century entrepreneur and manager in several important colliery companies, Bainbridge typified the leaders of this élite in the later period. The son of a retail and wholesale draper who also owned interests in collieries in the North-east, Emerson Bainbridge of Sheffield, as he was sometimes known to distinguish him from his father, Emerson Muschamp Bainbridge, was educated at Edenfield House in Doncaster,

---

[1] C. P. Griffin thesis, 239, 310.

[2] Outstanding among this group was the vicar's son, Alfred Hewlett, chairman and managing director of the Wigan Coal and Iron Company: *Wigan Observer* 17 Sept. 1918.

[3] *TFIME* LIV (1916), 364. [4] *TFIME* LXV (1922), 44–5.

before proceeding to the University of Durham where he studied mathematics and mine engineering. After completing articles as a mining engineer on the Londonderry estates in 1870, at the age of twenty-five he was appointed manager of the Duke of Norfolk's collieries near Sheffield, became managing director of Nunnery Colliery, in which he possessed a controlling interest, four years later, and went on to participate in the formation of New Hucknall Colliery Company, Bolsover Colliery Company, and the Griff Colliery Company, the first together with his father and other capitalists from the North-east; Griff was a joint venture with the Knowles family, hitherto important coalowners in Lancashire. He became a director of Blackwell Colliery, the Hatfield Main Colliery, the Newbiggin Colliery Company, and several railway companies. Like Sir George Elliot, he was also called upon to offer expert evidence before several government inquiries. His role in founding colliery communities on progressive lines brought him to the forefront of coalmining entrepreneurs identified with the social as well as economic advance of the industry before 1914.[1]

Comparable in stature in his professional achievements was Charles Carlow, born in 1849 and educated at Dunfermline High School, who by the age of nineteen had become assistant manager of a Midlothian colliery. Four years later, having obtained a first-class certificate in colliery management and already possessing a reputation as an outstanding mining engineer, he was appointed as first manager of the Fife Coal Company, formed in 1872 to acquire the Beath and Blairadam Colliery Company. His policy of the closure of redundant capacity and the concentration of production from the most productive seams and investment in new pits was accompanied by experimentation with coal cutters, coal-working machinery, the introduction of electricity below and above ground, the utilization of by-products and improvement of the company's coal-shipping facilities, and expansion into new markets. He was appointed to the board in 1893, and in 1895 became managing director, to which appointment in 1907 was added that of company chairman. His biographer concluded that the dominance of the Fife Coal Company in the Scottish coalfield was attributable to Charles Carlow's personal achievements.[2] Andrew McCosh, who for much of the late nineteenth century was the key figure at William Baird and Co., was the son of a lawyer and banker; he was educated at the Scottish

---

[1] *The Times* 13 May 1911; NCL Local Obituaries, I, 145–7, 178–9; J. H. Stainton, *The Making of Sheffield 1865-1914* (Sheffield, 1924), 348–9.

[2] See SDDB, forthcoming.

universities, though he also completed articles as a civil and mining engineer before his managerial career began.[1]

It is difficult to generalize about managerial remuneration. The validity of the suggestion that colliery managers' salaries were insufficient to attract high-quality entrants to the industry is at least open to question, for the significance of average salaries for 'colliery managers' of £400 in 1913[2] is not self evident without defining a 'colliery manager'. Clearly, the duties, degree of expertise, range of responsibilities, and scope for initiative varied considerably, depending upon the size and number of pits under his command. Certificated colliery managers were usually located at middle-management level, though in large companies they were likely to have been subordinate both to a general colliery manager possessing responsibility for several pits or collieries, as well as to a managing director or general manager. The certificated colliery managers who were likely to have received remuneration averaging £400 were essentially technical or under-managers, and while mining operations depended on them for day-to-day efficiency, the major policy decisions affecting investment, finance markets, innovation, and industrial relations were the concern of managers with access to partners or to a board of directors, or who were represented on it.

In the 1850s Dunn implied that a viewer in charge of a single colliery might expect remuneration of £400 or slightly less.[3] When George Greenwell was appointed to the Radstock Collieries (producing round about 100,000 tons) in 1853 his salary was £500, plus a horse and gig, rent-free house, free coal, and grass for a cow. After 1858 he became entitled to 4 per cent of the profits of the collieries when they exceeded £1,000.[4] At that time it was reported that viewers maintaining checkviewing contracts with several colliery owners earned considerably more than £400, and that the leading viewers, such as Wood, Woodhouse, and Forster, could earn at least £2,000.[5] The scattered evidence in company archives suggests that the salaries of general managers were sometimes twice or three times the level of pit or colliery managers, exceeded by those of managing directors perhaps by a similar multiple, especially in some of the large companies in which it was common practice to link remuneration of top managers to profits or dividends.[6] If we

---

[1] SDBB (Forthcoming).
[2] A. J. Taylor 1968.   [3] Cassell thesis, 126.
[4] Down and Warrington 1971, 163.   [5] Cassell thesis, 126.
[6] In 1893 John Turner's salary, when appointed as general manager of the Moira Collieries (output c. 0.25m. tons), was £1,000 plus a percentage on sales (though he regarded this as merely a

assume that science graduates were sensitive to career opportunities, including remuneration, in the twenty years before 1900, then at least graduates of Glasgow University favoured mining engineering (the most common route to senior management) as much as railway engineering. Both appear to have been slightly less attractive compared with marine engineering and much less so than civil engineering, but except for the powerful attraction of general engineering, these were the most favoured careers of all.[1]

Among the leading colliery proprietors was also to be found a recognition of the increasing importance for their successors within the family to substitute professional training for learning by doing within the company. Approximating to perfection as a preparation for his role as chairman and managing director of the nation's largest colliery combine was that undertaken by D. A. Thomas (later Lord Rhondda), the son of a wealthy coalowner. Clifton College, followed by Cambridge University, where he proved to be a brilliant mathematician, was the prelude to a spell in the sales office of his father's Cambrian Collieries, followed by two years' experience in a stockbroker's office intervening between that and subsequent experience underground. Following his father's death in 1879, D. A. Thomas became managing partner in Cambrian Collieries at the age of twenty-three. As chairman and managing director of the company formed in 1895 he also laid the foundations for the spectacular series of amalgamations culminating in the Cambrian Combine. The motivation which explains his achievements is clear from his remark that 'Business is a modern equivalent of war. . . . Business attracts the man who loves conquest, who loves to pit himself against vast odds, who could not live without strain of effort.'[2]

Even among the largest colliery companies in 1913, however, graduate decision-makers were exceptional. Professionally qualified engineers, through apprenticeship and later by examination, were more common, and yet even in some of the largest companies key decisions

'clerk's salary'); Arthur Sopwith's salary as General Manager of Cannock Chase (output c. 0.5m. tons), was £1,000 in 1898. William Allott, General Manager of the collieries of Newton Chambers, received £900 annual salary in 1899. In 1912 P. Mushamp, agent and works manager of New Hucknall Colliery (output c. 1m. tons), received £700. These figures illustrate the difficulty of generalization without conducting an extensive survey taking account of colliery size and comparable responsibilities. C. P. Griffin thesis, 239; BUL BR 14/ii-iii, Cannock Chase Colliery, MB 30 Nov. 1898. NoRO New Hucknall NCB 1/15/312; SCL Newton Chambers, TR 450/450/ 8-52.

[1] Sanderson 1972, Table 14.
[2] Quoted in Phillips 1925, 213-14; *The Times* 1 Dec. 1913.

lay in the hands of owner-managers lacking in formal training. Jonathan Priestman, for example, was the son of a tanner with whom, after leaving the Society of Friends' School in York, he experienced managerial responsibility; but through his father's shareholding and influence the younger Priestman became managing director of Consett between 1860 and 1869, in that year becoming managing partner in the Ashington Coal Company. Together with his two sons he subsequently carried on, simultaneously, a separate business to become known as Priestman Collieries, establishing the Priestman family as major coal producers in the North-east.[1] James Joicey, founder of the partnership of James Joicey and Co. in 1839, received a mercantile education followed by an apprenticeship as mining engineer at South Hetton; by the time of his death in 1863 he and his brothers had developed an enterprise consisting of ten flourishing collieries.[2] James Joicey's eventual successor as head of the firm was nephew James, son of the founder of J. and G. Joicey, the Newcastle engineering firm. The young James's first business experience was as an office clerk, succeeding his uncle in 1881 at the age of thirty-five. His subsequent success lay in extending the activities of this private limited company, incorporated in 1888, and culminated in the formation of another company to acquire the Lambton Collieries in 1896.

Together with the original Joicey firm, by 1913 the Hetton Coal Company controlled the largest coal output in the UK, the result of a positive managerial reorganization, mechanization, and capital investment in the collieries acquired by the Joiceys. The chairman of the new company was Lord Joicey, then aged sixty-five; his sons, J. Arthur and Sydney Joicey, who were managing directors of Joicey and Co. Ltd., were also managing directors of the Lambton and Hetton Collieries Ltd.[3] This provides an illustration of the ability of owner-controlled firms either by retaining managerial authority within a family, or by entrusting it into the hands of a succession of professional managers, to succeed in staying abreast of those organizations which were symptomatic of the expansion of corporate capitalism. Among the largest twelve companies in 1913, control and the exercise of managerial authority was maintained by the Joiceys, the Bairds, the Woods, the

[1] NCL, 'Local Biography', 3, 43–7.

[2] R. Welford, Men of Mark Twixt Tyne and Tweed (Newcastle, 1895), 645–9.

[3] NCL Local Newspaper Cuttings, 70, 72–3; J. Jamieson, Northumberland at the Opening of the Twentieth Century (Brighton, 1905), 99; Newcastle Weekly Chronicle, 28 Nov. 1936, and 30 Jan. 1937; R. W. Stenton, Northern Worthies, 2 (Newcastle upon Tyne, 1932), 166; The Times 1 Dec. 1913.

Priestmans, the Thomas's, the Peases, the Dales, and the Davies, though with differing degrees of participation in their business organizations.[1]

The line between professional and proprietorial interests and influences were blurred even in some of the largest companies. George Elliot had been general manager of Powell Duffryn, of which he was also a principal proprietor, between its formation in 1864 and 1888, except for an interruption in 1877 until 1880. Under his second period as chief executive, the collieries' manager, F. M. Hann, was appointed to assist him, together with the commercial manager. Originally trained at Hetton Colliery in Durham, Hann has been described as 'the inspiration of all future development' at Powell Duffryn; for after Elliot left the company Hann became a member of the managing committee formed to provide the effective management which by that time was regarded as beyond the capability of a general manager alone. The committee included representatives of three proprietorial families, while Hann was the senior professional manager appointed to it. However, by 1910 Hann had become the tenth largest shareholder in Powell Duffryn and proceeded to secure managerial positions for his sons.[2] Charles Markham, initially the professional managing director of Staveley Coal and Iron, became a major shareholder in the subsidiary Newstead Colliery Company when that was formed, and of which he was a member of the managing committee.[3]

Just as recruitment appears to have narrowed to favour those from social classes I and II, and from coalowning or coal-managerial families, the frequency of experience outside the industry was probably diminishing too. Of the pre-1831 cohort, 21 per cent spent their entire career within the same firm, compared with 27 per cent for the second cohort; 42 per cent, compared with 61 per cent, spent a period with at least one other colliery enterprise. Of the pre-1831 cohort, 37 per cent worked for some time outside the industry, compared with only 11 per cent of the later cohort. When those who possessed experience both in other firms within and outside the industry are combined, the extent of experience in more than one colliery enterprise is 57 per cent for the first cohort and 66 per cent for the second.

An analysis of directorships held by coal-company directors in 1890 and 1910 reveals a concentration in industries either directly or in-

[1] The companies with which they were associated were the Lambton Collieries, William Baird, Harton Coal, Ashington, Pease and Partners, Nixon's Navigation, and Ocean Coal.

[2] Walters 1977, 175–6.

[3] BSCEMRRC Stanton and Staveley 2304/3/10 Memorandum of Association, Newstead Colliery Co.

Table 5.8. *Directorships held by business leaders*
(percentages)

	1890	1910		1890	1910
coal only	11	17	wagon	4	6
iron and steel	11	15	insurance	7	2
utilities	11	12	estate and building	9	—
domestic railways	9	16	shippig and shipbuilding	11	3
electric power	—	3	overseas minerals	4	4
banking and finance	9	3	other	14	19

Source: Directory of Directors. Includes those directors listed who are known to have a major share in coal production as proprietors or directors, and who held a minimum of two directorships in coal (or coal–iron) companies. 'Other' includes a diverse collection, none of which exceeds two directorships: ore, oil and chemicals, fireclay brick and tile, tinplate, engineering, wire rope, brewery, etc. The sample size in 1890 was 45, and in 1910 121.

directly related. In 1890 directorships were fairly evenly distributed, mainly between iron and steel, shipping and shipbuilding, public utilities, domestic railways, estate and building, banking and finance (Table 5.8). Eleven per cent of the sample held directorships in coal companies only, a figure not exceeded by any other single category. Between 1890 and 1910 the number of directors holding a minimum of two directorships in addition to that of the company with which each was identified (the criterion which defined the sample) had increased nearly threefold. Seventeen per cent held directorships in coal-only companies, 16 per cent in domestic railways, and 15 per cent in iron and steel. After public utilities, all other categories fell below 6 per cent. Evidence of recruitment, career patterns, and directorships conveys an impression of an industry in which, while experience with more than a single firm became more common within coal and related industries, experience outside the industry probably diminished and business leadership became increasingly inbred. Before considering the performance of this business élite, however, it will be necessary to examine the dynamics of colliery enterprise and the industry's record of productivity and profitability.

Appendix 5.1. Mine and firm-size estimates before 1913

While contemporary average regional and county production may be calculated from Hunt's *Mineral Statistics*, the *List of Mines*, and the *Reports* of the Inspectors of Mines, the figures are of doubtful reliability, due to incomplete recording, and in some cases (especially before 1880) a failure to keep up-to-date. Even after 1894, when colliery-by-colliery employment figures are available, we cannot be absolutely confident of the accuracy or significance of the averages implied in the *List of Mines*, not least because of the continued lack of a consistent definition of what constituted a 'colliery'.

The most serious complications arise from three principal defects. First, the *List of Mines* included many mines which were either closed, or where mining had been suspended, or which were in the process of sinking. Sometimes employment figures are included even so, presumably referring to the men employed in sinking and driving. Secondly, under the Mines Regulation Act fireclay mines were included in the *List of Mines*, even though their production of coal was either very small or nonexistent; but it is not always possible in the earlier years to separate and exclude fireclay mines. The third problem arises from inconsistencies in the description of collieries. These were especially prevalent in the data relating to Yorkshire and the East Midlands; less so, but nevertheless present, in Lancashire, the North-east, and the West Midlands. In Yorkshire, for example, different seams were often given in the *List of Mines* as separate collieries—thus, South Kirkby, Barnsley; South Kirkby, Haigh Moor; South Kirkby, Beamshaw. In the East Midlands a difficulty arises from references to mines called no. 1, no. 2, etc. The *List of Mines* commonly treats the group as a single colliery, even when two separate seam names are attached associated with it. In most cases the practice adopted in the *List of Mines* has been accepted, though when it is clear that, for example, mine 1 and mine 2 represent two distinct operations they have been regarded as separate entities. An examination of data other than the number of mines included in the contemporary lists reveals the difficulty which officials experienced in compiling mineral statistics. For Nottinghamshire in 1913, for example, the *List of Mines* recorded 55 mines, 53 sets of figures for underground employment, 50 for surface employment, mentioned 42 separate mine names, and 48 separate under managers. The West Midlands mines were often divided into 'parts' under butties, but these have generally been regarded as a single mine, and the same is true of the Lancashire number 1 and 2 mines. In the North-east pits belonging to a single colliery, for example, Bedlington 'A' and Bedlington 'Doctor', or Ashington 'Carl', 'Bothal', and 'Duke', have, too, been lumped together.

Before 1894 the problems are greater. Hunt's *Mineral Statistics* often counted companies (particularly ironworks) collectively, thereby omitting many pits and levels, and often collieries remained in the list long after closure. Since the data are so poor, and in any case conceal important differences (for example, the relative size of intra-regional differences due to contrasting types of coal mined within a single region), we have calculated average and median mine sizes for four dates: 1860, 1880, 1895, and 1913. The first two dates were chosen to avoid the particularly defective data of 1854 to 1858, and the effects of legal and definitional changes that occurred during the 1860s to mid-1870s, when the boom and slump presented problems of recording which further undermined the credibility of the statistics (Table 5.1).

Measuring the output of firms involves difficulties through lack of data except for certain regions. The use of coalowners' association records in South Wales enabled Walters to establish the mean size of steam-coal collieries for members between 1860 and 1913.[1] It would be

[1] Walters 1977, 268–9.

possible to conduct a similar, though less satisfactory, exercise from similar sources for the North-east and Yorkshire (though only after 1890), which is inadequate as a basis for generalizations on the industry as a whole. As a proxy for output, therefore, we have used figures for colliery employment, recorded in the *List of Mines* beginning in 1894, supplemented by various parliamentary, trade journal and archival sources to provide information on the preceding period. Because of differences in productivity and (especially in the case of coal-producing iron firms) the uncertainty which surrounds the definition of 'colliery workers', notably those on the surface, it is not surprising that a comparison of coal-production figures for the largest seven companies in South Wales in 1910 yield a different rank order from that based on the *List of Mines* employment data. Six of the seven companies were identical in ranking and one-half were in correct sequence, though ordering by both criteria produced the same ranking in only three cases. On the basis of considerably less complete data for firms belonging to the associations of the Durham, south Yorkshire, and west Yorkshire coalowners (which prevent any presentation of an adequate set of output hierarchies), and in the complete absence of adequate production series for other regions, the use of employment figures as a proxy for size seems to be amply justified.

CHAPTER 6

The Economics of Colliery Enterprise

i. Productivity: measures, hypotheses, and evidence

The conventional view of nineteenth-century trends in productivity in coalmining is based on Taylor's 1961 estimates of output per man-year (OMY). These showed that from 1851 until the 1880s the industry enjoyed increasing returns; thereafter, 'the tide of productivity ebbed and flowed, but each recovery was less pronounced than its predecessor'.[1] Estimates of output per man-shift (OMS) for Durham miners between 1879 and 1913 seemed to confirm the downward trend.[2] Since that time historians have largely accepted Taylor's analysis—even critics of his diagnosis of the reasons for declining productivity having also accepted, in its statistical dimensions, the essential outline of the course of development of the industry.[3] Our recalculation of production and employment in Chapters 1 and 2 indicate somewhat different trends, for they imply higher levels of OMY before 1880 and a lower rate of increase during the third quarter of the century (Table 6.1). Whereas Taylor's decennial figures implied an increase in productivity by about 36 per cent between 1851 and 1871, revised figures suggest a rise of some 5 per cent, which is roughly the same as the recalculated growth in OMY for the twenty years preceding 1851. Far from confirming the 'firmly upward' trend in OMY Taylor identified during the third quarter of the century,[4] the revised estimates suggest barely a perceptible improvement from the 1850s, which even in the 1860s was still below 5 per cent over the decade.

There is, however, broad agreement in the movement of OMY from the 1870s. A sharp decline between 1871 and 1874 coincided with the

---

[1] A. J. Taylor 1961, 49.

[2] Ibid., 56, and Appendix 6.2.

[3] Walters 1975, 280–303; McCloskey (ed.) 1971, 289–95, and discussion 296–309; Lars Sandberg, 'The Entrepreneur and Technological Change' in Floud and McCloskey (eds.), *The Economic History of Britain since 1700* (1981), 2, 116–18; Greasley 1982, 246; Hirsch and Hausman 1983, 145–57.

[4] A. J. Taylor 1961, 49.

limitation of hours legislation in 1872. This had the effect of reducing the hours of transit workers and inevitably affected hewers' hours, a potential setback for productivity reinforced by the leisure-inducing boom that occurred in the same year.[1] The collapse of the boom and the adoption of measures to counteract the effects of hours limitation were the factors which explain the rise in OMY after 1874; an OMY of 341 tons, achieved in 1883, representing an increase by almost one-third. Thereafter, the trend was firmly downwards, though at the regional level important differences may be identified, both in absolute levels and in the degree of change (Table 6.1).

Table 6.1. *Estimated labour productivity in the regions, 1831-1881*
(tons per man-year)

	1831	1841	1851	1861	1871	1881
Scotland	214	213	246	306	324	392
North-east	327	323	376	382	397	382
Cumberland	316	320	243	283	280	300
Lancs./Ches.	279	279	281	281	272	305
North Wales	231	194	271	292	278	273
Yorkshire	319	321	298	287	291	309
East Midlands	333	338	308	291	288	316
West Midlands	315	321	300	249[a]	326	389
South Wales	277	283	310	326	291	311
South West	151	152	176	174	183	183
Average	285	284	298	301	314	335
(A. J. Taylor)			220	272	300	326

[a] Affected by trade slump.
Sources: Tables 1.1 and 3.1.

Historians who have addressed the problem of measuring productivity are agreed that figures for output per man-shift (OMS) are preferable to OMY,[2] because OMS takes account of days worked and is therefore a more accurate measure of labour productivity. In the absence of such a national series before 1897 we have used the estimates of days worked, presented in Table 3.8, as a basis for calculating the number of shifts actually worked in a year. Estimated output per man-

[1] Ibid. The change in the sources for employment estimates from 1871 detracts from the validity of a strict comparison in the years to 1874.
[2] Beginning with A. J. Taylor 1961, 51-4.

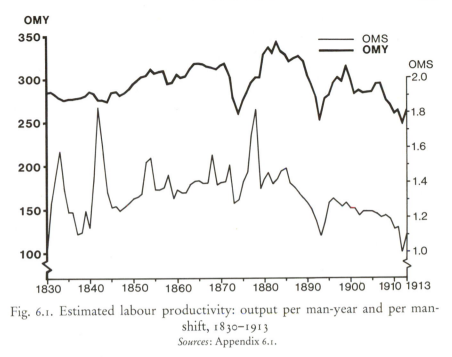

Fig. 6.1. Estimated labour productivity: output per man-year and per man-shift, 1830–1913

Sources: Appendix 6.1.

shift plotted in Figure 6.1 alongside OMY extends the existing series, beginning in 1897, backward to 1830. Even output per shift, however, is less than satisfactory as the most accurate measure of labour productivity, for it disregards variations in the duration of shifts, which altered considerably between 1830 and 1913. Contemporaries were quick to draw attention to the effects of the 1908 Eight Hours Act upon productivity, and historians, too, have referred to the depressing effect of legislation which necessitated an increase in the number of men at the face. Taylor incorporated this in his analysis of an alleged general decline in underground productivity (measured in man-years) which he identified beginning in the 1880s.[1] Phelps Brown noted the importance of hours reduction in calculating productivity,[2] while recent econometric analysis, based on Walters's Welsh data, by Hirsch and Hausmann presents generally accepted trends in OMY, but also offers conclusions which imply that the number of hours worked should be an important consideration in any attempt to interpret productivity trends, especially after the Eight Hours Act.[3] A consideration of hours, however, raises a

[1] Ibid.
[2] E. H. Phelps Brown and M. H. Browne, *A Century of Pay* (London, 1968), 175–82.
[3] Hirsch and Hausman 1983, 145–57.

more fundamental question concerning the measurement of productivity; for even supposing, as seems likely (at least after 1909), that hours reductions explain the decline in OMY, there is a danger of forgetting that OMY (and to a less extent OMS) has remained at the centre of dicussions of industrial productivity merely because the data are available to measure it. The superior measure, output per man hour (OMH), if it can be estimated, may reveal important differences in trend hitherto concealed by OMY and OMS, and invite reassessment of the industry's record of physical productivity.

Estimates of OMH, therefore, are prerequisites for the next stage in analysis of the industry's productivity performance. Beginning in 1894, the availability of annual data on the number of shifts worked, recorded in the *Labour Gazette*, facilitates this exercise, though before then our OMH estimates, beginning in 1840, will not allow precision in the timing of changes. The sources used and the assumptions on which the figures in Table 6.2 are based are explained in Appendix 6.1. They represent actual, rather than nominal, hours worked each week, for the former offer a more accurate guide to historical reality and a more precise assessment of labour inputs. Estimated hours actually worked by miners remained constant between 1842 and 1870, despite a fall in the nominal length of shifts. The number of hours actually worked in the 1870s fell sharply, the combined result of voluntary short-week working

Table 6.2. *Estimated hours of work and hourly productivity, 1842-1913*
(OMH)

	Output per man-year (tons OMY)	Output per man-shift (tons OMS)	Hours worked during year (50 weeks)	Output per man-hour (tons OMH)
1842–9	280.6	1.36	2,595	0.108
1850–9	302.1	1.39	2,590	0.117
1860–9	310.8	1.40	2,580	0.120
1870–9	292.2	1.45	2,135	0.137
1880–9	329.5	1.41	2,290	0.144
1890–9	290.4	1.25	2,190	0.133
1900–8	286.4	1.27	2,125	0.135
1909–13	259.6	1.11	1,965	0.132

Sources: Appendix 6.1.

which accompanied the 1870s boom, followed by the enforced idleness in the ensuing slump.[1] More hours were spent working in the 1880s than in the 1870s, but after the 1880s working hours declined progressively, as days worked per week remained stable (over successive cycles), and the nominal shift fell. Had hours of work affected productivity directly, the expectation would have been a marked fall in OMH in the 1870s, followed by a more general decline beginning from the 1880s, in line with OMY and OMS. A comparison of the three measures reveals significant differences. OMY and OMS are not incompatible, though the former does imply a more sustained rise in productivity from the mid-1840s to the late 1870s (and early 1880s) than the data on shift productivity, an increase of about 11 per cent before 1872. While corroborating the upward trend in productivity, the OMH figures are a few percentage points higher than OMY or OMS, at around 15 per cent perhaps, before the 1870s boom. OMH moved upward very sharply in 1860/9–1870/9, greatly assisted by the shorter working week. Improvements in OMH continued into the 1880s, followed by a fall before the decade ended (since the figures for 1890–9 are based essentially on hewers' data for 1890); but it fell only as far as the level of the 1890s, on which relatively stable plateau OMH remained until 1909.

Beginning in 1894, shift data from the *Labour Gazette* make it possible to construct estimates of hourly productivity in the regions. The sources and methods used in preparing Table 6.3 and Figure 6.2 are explained in Appendix 6.1, but the crucial assumption is that hours fell by equal amounts between benchmark years. The graphs, which compare the course of OMY, OMS, and hourly productivity in six major regions, reveal similar relative performances, because differences in hours between the regions by this time were small; shorter hours worked in the North-east tended to raise productivity relative to others, but this reordering was the exception. However, a comparison of OMH in the regions indicates divergencies of considerable importance. Whereas the OMS data showed a gradual but perceptible decline from 1894 to 1909, followed by a sharp downward acceleration to 1913, the OMH figures suggest a more or less stable trend; the exceptions were South Wales and the North-east, where a fall in hourly productivity appears to have occurred between the mid-1890s and 1909. The national series falls marginally in 1896–1909, though we have noted above that average OMH for the 1890s as a whole was, if anything, lower than that for 1900–9; from which we may infer that neither the 1890s as a whole

[1] Taylor 1961, 49; Walters 1975, 293–4.

Table 6.3. *Estimated output per man-hour, by region, 1894–1913*

	UK	Scotland	North-east	Yorks.	Lancs./Ches.	East Midlands	South Wales	West Midlands
1894	0.126		0.148	0.125	0.121			0.151
1895	0.137	0.153	0.144	0.139	0.126	0.141	0.108	0.150
1896	0.141	0.157	0.147	0.135	0.129	0.147	0.110	0.158
1897	0.139	0.158	0.148	0.128	0.128	0.147	0.112	0.166
1898	0.137	0.160	0.152	0.132	0.134	0.149		0.169
1899	0.140	0.163	0.149	0.130	0.132	0.146	0.119	0.167
1900	0.136	0.160	0.147	0.129	0.127	0.145	0.110	0.165
1901	0.137	0.160	0.147	0.132	0.130	0.144	0.115	0.147
1902	0.133	0.158	0.145	0.132	0.128	0.141	0.110	0.143
1903	0.136	0.156	0.146	0.135	0.131	0.148	0.109	0.141
1904	0.137	0.158	0.146	0.132	0.129	0.155	0.110	0.141
1905	0.137	0.159	0.147	0.134	0.128	0.160	0.111	0.144
1906	0.137	0.163	0.146	0.136	0.133	0.165	0.111	0.150
1907	0.136	0.152	0.144	0.131	0.127	0.153	0.109	0.159
1908	0.138	0.165	0.147	0.129	0.130	0.161	0.110	0.152
1909	0.137	0.168	0.143	0.131	0.122	0.160	0.110	0.144
1910	0.131	0.163	0.131	0.129	0.118	0.156	0.099	0.145
1911	0.133	0.164	0.139	0.129	0.118	0.162	0.103	0.145
1912	0.118	0.147	0.122	0.114	0.104	0.139	0.096	0.133
1913	0.130	0.160	0.132	0.128	0.114	0.154	0.109	0.140

Sources: Appendix 6.1

nor the following decade should be regarded as periods of noticeably falling productivity.

After relative stability between 1894 and 1909 the marked fall may be explained, at least in part, by the introduction of the Eight Hours Act, which especially in the North-east (where only oncost workers were affected), Lancashire, and Cheshire, and more temporarily South Wales (where the reduction in hours was greatest), was reflected not only in annual or shift productivity but also in output per man-hour, for more workers needed to be employed to compensate for hours limitation. Scotland, the East Midlands, and Yorkshire suffered relatively little from the effects of the Act.[1] Even in South Wales, however, the impact of the Act may have been exaggerated by historians. The claim that labour productivity fell between 1909 and 1910 because of legislation disregards the timing of implementation,[2] which in South Wales was postponed until July 1909. While productivity by all measures fell furthest in South Wales relative to other regions (OMY, OMS, and OMH), from 1910 that relative decline was checked and began to move into reverse. At a national level, the decline in productivity of 1909-13 remains the only clear instance of a downward trend in the period beginning in 1894, but was mainly the result of trends peculiar to two of the largest coalmining regions—South Wales and the North-east—and was clearly the consequence of legislation.

Thus, two strikingly novel conclusions emerged from these exercises incorporating OMH estimates at national and regional level. First, contrary to the widely accepted decline in productivity from the early 1880s, implied by OMY and OMS, hourly productivity, after rising steadily with a temporary set-back in the late 1880s, remained roughly stable in the period between the 1890s and 1909. Second, estimated hourly productivity levels were much higher at the end of our period than at the beginning, a contrasting picture compared with that implied by OMY and OMS, which indicated levels appreciably higher in the 1830s and 1840s than on the eve of World War I.

The common view is that a secular decline in labour productivity, identifiable from the early 1880s, was the consequence of a combination of factors; these included a deteriorating resource base and the ageing of pits which resulted in a fall in the ratio of hewers to oncost workers, managerial weaknesses, and the effects of 'recalcitrant labour', or of the reaction of miners to an improvement in wages from the 1880s onwards.

---

[1] McCormick and Williams 1959, 225. H. F. Bulman, 'The Multiple Shift System of Working', CG XCIX, 1910, 467-8.   [2] Walters 1975, 280-2, 299.

A

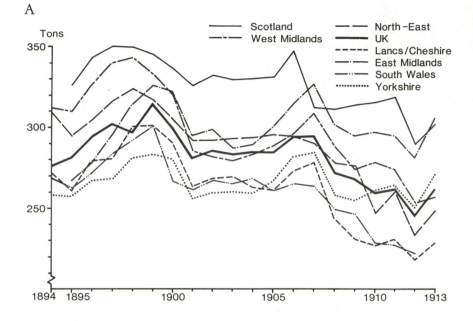

Tons

B

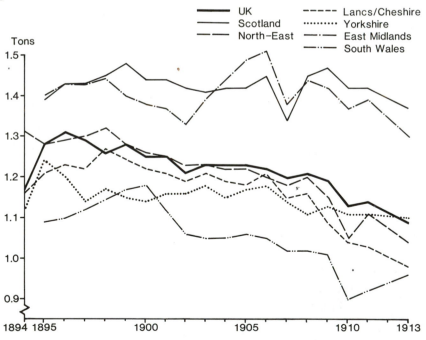

Tons

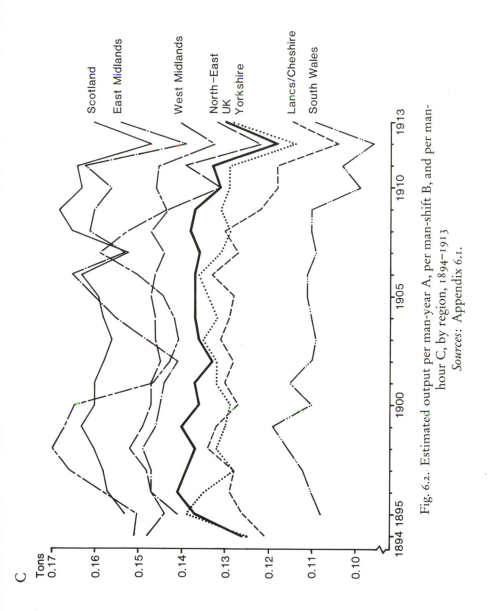

Fig. 6.2. Estimated output per man-year A, per man-shift B, and per man-hour C, by region, 1894–1913

Sources: Appendix 6.1.

The OMH figures suggest that the conventional view, which stresses the irreversible process of diminishing returns setting in during the 1880s, might need revision. However, before trying to provide answers to the question why the trend in hourly labour productivity was *not* one of decline in the second half of the century, a brief consideration of trends in total factor productivity (TFP) is warranted, at least for comparative purposes.

Measuring the contribution to productivity of factors other than capital and labour is fraught with difficulties. This is not only for the reason that TFP (variously calculated) has attracted damaging criticism on methodological grounds,[1] but is due also to the peculiarities of the mining industry, in which changes in the quality of the resource base are impossible to isolate from technological and organizational influences. Our attempts at calculating TFP, therefore, should be regarded with considerable scepticism, and merit serious attention only when compared with the course of labour productivity over the long term, the estimates for which will bear more weight than TFP before and after 1890. Table 6.4 (the sources and methods for which are described in Appendix 6.2) presents inter-cyclical comparisons of average percentage changes in output, capital, and wages, with TFP set alongside similar changes in OMY (which we noted understated OMH). The data will not

Table 6.4. *Intercyclical rates of growth in output, capital, wages, total factor productivity, and output per man-year, 1832-1913*

	Output	Capital	Wages	TFP	OMY
1832/7–1838/47	0.1786	0.6975	0.0965	−0.1825	0.0084
1838/47–1848/54	0.6014	0.4373	0.0254	0.1571	0.0352
1848/54–1855/66	0.1145	0.5443	0.1351	−0.1956	0.0172
1855/66–1866/73	0.5959	0.2532	0.5849	0.2069	0.0060
1866/73–1874/80	0.2137	0.3008	0.0284	0.0641	0.0030
1874/80–1881/90	0.1803	0.2064	0.1827	0.0021	0.0640
1881/90–1891/1900	0.1707	0.3024	0.4213	−0.1637	−0.1073
1891/1900–1901/7	0.4063	0.1944	0.5893	0.0419	0.0100
1900/7–1908/13	0.0240	0.0993	0.0627	−0.0984	−0.0865

Sources: Appendix 6.2.

[1] Stephen Nicholas, 'Total Factor Productivity Growth and the Revision of Post 1870 British Economic History', *EHR*, 2nd ser. XXXV (1982), 83–95.

support short-run analysis, but if they may be accorded any importance it should be in affording a long-term chronological perspective on the industry; they help to clarify the character of the industry's productivity dilemma by endorsing (or at least being consistent with) conclusions suggested by archival research. Table 6.4 reveals a check to OMY beginning in the 1890s; total factor productivity fluctuated between the cycles, a decline in the 1890s coinciding with the pause in labour productivity, as did the further drop in the cycle after 1908. Two alternative methods of estimating TFP yielded not dissimilar results, though indicating an inferior record of factor productivity throughout the entire period (Appendix 6.2). Calculated on different bases and for a period beginning only in 1856, the trends in TFP presented by Matthews, Feinstein, and Odling Smee[1] are not inconsistent with those in Table 6.4. There is a distinct difference, however, between movements in the two labour-productivity series, the annual percentage growth rates falling from the 1860s according to MFOS, with a temporary upward shift around 1900. Beginning in 1856 their series does not reveal the large fluctuations, including absolute reductions, in TFP before the 1860s.

Sufficient confidence may be attached to the OMY estimates presented in Table 6.4 to justify disregarding the MFOS labour-productivity figures before 1873; furthermore, although it proved possible to estimate OMH only on a decadal basis, the unambiguous upward trend, until the set-backs of the late 1880s and after 1908, suggests that the OMY series understates the difference between total factor productivity and output per man-hour. There is sufficient similarity in the downward trend in TFP revealed in both series, even though calculated from different sources, to confirm the probability of a declining rate of productivity growth. However, our estimates for the early nineteenth century suggest that TFP was even then subject to reversal. These may be explained to a large extent by the increasing geological constraints on production, which even before the last quarter of the century restrained productivity. A comparison of the rate of growth of output, capital, and wages (on which the calculation of TFP depended) in Table 6.4 suggests that by the late nineteenth century the scope for substituting capital for labour was limited. The same conclusion is prompted by comparing estimates of the flow of resources into the industry measured by wages, resource costs, and net investment per ton averaged over cycles between 1830 and 1913. This reveals net investment to have represented a share of

---

[1] R. C. O. Matthews, C. H. Feinstein, and J. C. Odling Smee, *British Economic Growth 1856-1973* (Oxford, 1982), 229, 232–3, 462–7.

less than 12 per cent averaged over all cycles, and in some fell below 8 per cent; the proportion represented by wages remained relatively steady at around 70 per cent. Almost certainly, the explanation for a falling rate of growth in productivity lies in deep coalmining. Technical change was aimed largely at gaining access to coal from areas previously unworked (both geographically and geologically), and at developing surface and underground transport facilities; only indirectly might productivity be enhanced by reducing bottlenecks and by improving the flow of output. Before the 1880s at least, this permitted coal to be won and worked at increasing levels of output per man-hour (labour productivity was aided somewhat by improvements in the age, and therefore, in some sense in the quality, of workers), but improvements in technology led to growth in output only, and not directly to higher productivity. The course of labour productivity (OMH) over the long term may be interpreted as signifying the success of the industry in raising, and—with only temporary set-backs—holding steady output per man, despite the increasing difficulty of technology in countering diminishing returns caused by geological factors.

Before the 1870s, the analysis of which on the basis of decadal figures is bedevilled by the colossal boom and slump, all three measures of labour productivity point to a steady but modest rise in contrast with A. J. Taylor's designation of the period as one of sharply rising productivity. In the light of our examination of the nature and extent of technical innovation and changes in working methods before 1870 this lower figure seems to be more plausible, such limited advances that occurred before 1871 being little more than sufficient to make it possible to mine at lower depths, at greater distances from the shaft, and in gassier, less accessible seams. Taylor regards shot-firing to have been the 'general practice in all coalfields' by 1850,[1] and implied gains in productivity, but Galloway merely referred to blasting with gunpowder as having 'come into use in all parts of the Kingdom',[2] and which, we have argued, was limited in its use to certain locations and conditions, and declined with the progress of longwall mining. Productivity was almost certainly more affected by important improvements in the conveyance of coal to the shaft,[3] but the contribution to productivity levels outside the deeper mining regions of the North-east and parts of Lancashire before the 1860s is unlikely to have been large, and the same is true of improvements in ventilation. As increasing attention was paid to the quality of

[1] Taylor 1961, 57.
[2] Galloway 1904, 372.   [3] Taylor 1961, 56.

coal, partly in response to growing inter-regional competition and partly to developments in the market for coal, the effect was to increase oncost working, whether due to riddling underground or because additional labour was needed for screening and coking at the surface.

Finally, gains in productivity from improved haulage methods were offset to some extent by a decline in workers' hours, by perhaps 15 per cent between 1842 and 1870. In the absence of alternative sources of appreciable productivity gains, it seems likely that the transition to longwall helped to raise output per man,[1] though by an increment difficult to quantify. *Ceteris paribus*, regardless of the method of working, the output per man-year, shift, or hour was higher from a thick seam of six to eight feet than from a thin one of three feet or less, the reason being that in a thin seam the hewer had to spend much of his time cutting away dead rock in order to get at the coal, which reduced the time spent on extraction; alternatively the hewer worked in cramped conditions not conducive to a high rate of production.[2] Differences in productivity resulting from such circumstances were much greater than the relatively small gains to be made by working longwall rather than by an efficient pillar and stall in any given seam. Indeed, changing to longwall from pillar and stall, though undoubtedly increasing hewers' OMH might mean a reduction in total OMH should the new system increase oncost ratios. None the less, as the techniques of goaf packing improved, the trend was for thicker seams to be worked longwall, rendering longwall more applicable to more and more areas, notably the Midlands, Scotland, and South Wales. The cost advantage of longwall, however, still lay emphatically in working thin, hard seams. The optimal economic conditions for longwall are shown schematically in Figure 6.3.

Accompanying the improvements in technology was a growth in the

---

[1] For a different view see ibid., 57.

[2] In 1896 Bulman and Redmayne referred to an actual case from the North-east, and concluded that OMS by longwall was 4.18 tons, compared with 3.16 tons by pillar and stall—a difference of more than 32 per cent. Fowler's experience of longwall in Derbyshire before 1870 led him to conclude that the output per hewer was between 1½ and 2½ times higher in 'long work' than in 'narrow work'—though, of course, only a portion of the coal from pillar-and-stall working was 'narrow work'; Bulman and Redmayne 1896, 243-7; George Fowler, 'Further remarks on the different methods of working coal', *TMIME* II (1870), 67. The latter was part of a series of articles on this subject which appeared in the first two issues of the Transactions of the Midland Institute of Mining Engineers: Edward Mammatt, 'Various Methods of Working Coal in Yorkshire', *TMIME*, I (1869), 25-32; Philip Cooper, 'Different Methods of Working Coal', *TMIME*, I (1869), 44-51; George Fowler, 'Further Remarks on the Different Methods of Working Coal', *TMIME*, II (1870), 64-74; Philip Cooper, 'Further Observations on Different Methods of Working Coal', *TMIME*, II (1870), 12-18.

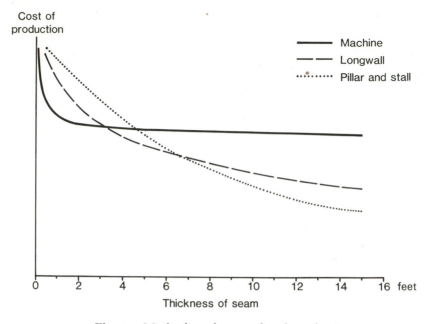

Fig. 6.3. Methods and costs of coal production

number of large firms, which the Sankey Commission concluded was associated with higher output per man-shift. This logic, however, was at fault, since the results of the statistical exercise were biased by the influence of the new large collieries opened up in recent years in the East Midlands and Yorkshire.[1] There is further justification for discounting technical economies of large-scale production as a source of productivity gains: at least in the North-east there was no correlation between mine size and labour productivity.[2] It is possible, of course, that economies of scale derived from financial and managerial advantages, though given the low degree of industrial concentration and the small number of large firms in the industry, especially before the 1890s, scale economies as an influence on output per man are unlikely to have been appreciable (though they will have affected costs). An analysis of OMS in the North-east reveals the collieries of some large firms, Consett, Bowes, Joicey, Wearmouth, and South Hetton, to have possessed high levels in the 1890s, whereas in 1913 this was true only of Consett, Joicey, and Wearmouth. Throughout the period, however, outputs per man-shift at the collieries of Bolckow Vaughan were low.[3]

At the national level, the rise in OMH in 1860/9–1870/9, relative to

[1] Dron 1928, 111–12.   [2] See above 393–4.   [3] Ibid.

OMY and OMS, might be explicable by an improvement in the quality of labour inputs or by variations in the work pace, but the evidence is against either as an adequate explanation. One possibility is that managers increased work intensity by raising the work pace, but the problems of identifying such an influence are severe. Work pace varied between individuals and cyclically (with higher intensity of work in slumps to compensate for lower price-rate wages), and also altered over the long term, as wages moved upwards and labour custom evolved.[1] Certainly sound a priori reasons exist for doubting that a reduction in the length of the working day of x per cent would lead necessarily to a commensurate fall in output, since shorter hours allow a higher intensity of effort. Intensity of work resembled hours and absenteeism inasmuch that it was geared to the wages that miners could earn on any particular day, and might vary, either over the cycle or with the facility or disposition of the hewer. Thus, Redmayne maintained that 'when the miner really works hardest is when the mine is on short time . . . and if the pit only works three days, seeing he is paid on piece work, he will work harder per day on those days than on five days if the pit works five days'.[2] And Hugh Bell: 'If trade were bad, the tendency was for men to work better and more regularly; if trade were good, the opposite took place. Men lost more time in good times than in bad, and that applied not only, as might be expected, to the piece worker, but also to a very large extent to the dayman, whether he is underground or on the surface.'[3]

Changes in work pace in practice, moreover, are virtually inseparable from technical change. The reduction in the length of the working day in the North-east in the 1850s and 1860s, for example, was dependent, at least partly, on inter-related changes in technology and productivity: 'The short hours of the hewers are dependent on the "double shift" system. This system was brought about not by owners but by a different method of working. The "wedge system" required two men working together; the "blasting system" requires only one man to be at the "coal face" at a time.'[4] Referring to a later period, it was noted that, 'Mechanical drills save about 20 minutes a day, and the work is not so severe as it

[1] See Chapter 3. For a recent discussion of changing effort bargains generally see C. Littler, *The Development of the Labour Process in Capitalist Societies* (London, 1982), 65–73.

[2] From discussion of a paper by E. C. Rhodes, 'Labour and Output in the Coal Mining Industry in Great Britain', *JRSS*, XCIV (1931), 530.

[3] Ibid., 533; also 'Experience tells us that increased wages do not as a whole impel miners in the direction of more strenuous production', *CG* 3 May 1907, 823.

[4] *RC Labour* 1892, XXXIV, Group A 16; LSE Webb Collection, Sect. A, Vol. XXVI, 135–51.

used to be, but the men will exert more energy per minute or per hour, than they did before over the longer period'.[1]

Consideration of the human contribution to productivity necessitates a distinction between the efficiency of the worker and the work pace itself. Abundant circumstantial evidence exists to justify the assumption that efficiency improved as the combined result of amelioration in health and housing, diet, and physical well-being, which may have been enhanced by shortening of hours. Such improvements may be regarded as involuntary and unintentional forces working for increased productivity. By contrast, work pace is either voluntary or dictated. A defensible hypothesis might interpret the growth of trade-union, and later of a more overtly political, consciousness among workers as having encouraged the viewpoint which regarded work pace as of critical importance, comparable with wages and hours and therefore an important point of focus in industrial relations[2]—although inevitably in bargaining with employers work pace remained as a sub-text, concealed in negotiations over cutting rates. Yet while organized labour in the mining industry evidently came to value leisure more and more, the concept of leisure had more to do with time spent away from the pit than with a lower work pace when at work. Because of this, the effort expended per hour (should that be measurable) is unlikely to have been affected by any conscious reduction over the century. A Mines Inspector noted in 1873 that 'men do not work worse underground, there is an *esprit de corps* with men, a sort of rivalry, and they will do their work well. I cannot believe in statements that the men are doing badly, but they are doing it in less degree.'[3] The Yorkshire owner, Robert Tennant, believed that men had 'worked better during the time that they have worked, but they have worked less hours'.[4] Theoretically consistent with one implication of Tennant's evidence, increasing absenteeism may have lowered OMY, whereas OMS might have been raised to compensate. Evidence for Durham, for which absenteeism figures are available from 1880, reveals a pattern of slow, secular growth, punctuated by isolated peaks in boom years, though with consistently high levels between 1907 and 1913.[5] Yet this trend before 1907 coincides with a slow fall, too, in the OMS of hewers,[6] suggesting a relationship which is not consistent with the thesis that men sought to compensate their

[1] Ibid.

[2] See E. J. Hobsbawm, 'Custom Wages and Work Load', in E. J. Hobsbawm, *Labouring Men* (London, 1960).

[3] *Dearness and Scarcity* 1873, X, Q 434.

[4] Ibid., Q 2718.

[5] *Sankey Commission* III, 42.

[6] See above 473–4.

preference for more leisure time with a renewed work intensity; and there is no obvious reason to suppose that the relationship between hours and effort and work were different in the decades immediately preceding 1880.

Although there are numerous references by owners to slack working amongst the men, most of these can be identified as complaints about absenteeism rather than work pace.[1] It is more likely, therefore, that the increasing efficiency of labour (here measured purely in terms of health and fitness) led to an increase in output per man than that the work pace was actually reduced. If we can assume that this was indeed the case, then the rise in OMH in 1860/9–1870/9 relative to OMY and OMS is explicable neither by an improvement in the 'quality' of labour inputs (for this period encompassed the boom when the collieries absorbed, temporarily, large numbers of workers from outside the industry), nor by changes in effort. Improved access technology and a higher volume of capital investment were key factors, annual average investment rising to levels higher by 50 per cent in real terms during the cycles 1866/73 and 1873/83 compared with the two previous cycles.[2] The effect was to offset rising capital–output ratios and contribute to the rise in labour productivity. This in turn offset the decline, hitherto identified measured by OMY and OMS, until sometime towards the end of the 1880s. At this point our interpretation differs from all other historians of the industry, for whereas they have accepted the onset of a decline in productivity in the early 1880s which continued almost unabated, though to a different extent from region to region, our OMH estimates focus upon a temporary drop, probably in the late 1880s, followed by a recovery and a period of stability until 1909. Average working hours in 1880 (assuming, as we have, that hewers constituted 40 per cent of the work-force)[3] were 49 falling to 47 in 1890, a drop of 4 per cent. The weekly averages of days worked, according to our estimates, were identical in the 1880s and 1890s, and cannot, therefore, have caused any variation in productivity. The greatest difference between the 1880s and the 1890s occurred in the area of productivity, as ordinarily measured by OMY or OMS; the former fell from 329 to 290 tons a year, the latter from 1.41 to 1.25 tons per shift. Within a context of constant working days and a mere 4 per cent drop in hours, this reduction in labour productivity by some 11 to 12 per cent is the phenomenon requiring further analysis.

The fall in productivity between the 1880s and 1890s was the largest

[1] See above 241–6.   [2] See above Table 2.1.   [3] See Appendix 6.1.

fall, indeed the only marked fall, before 1909, and resulted from more than a single cause. Exceptionally high strike activity was one important contributory factor, for major strikes in the North-east in 1892, in the inland coalfields in 1893, and in Scotland and in South Wales in 1898,[1] depressed OMY by reducing output. Their effect was also to lower OMS, because our initial calculations of the number of shifts worked each year ignored the effects of strikes; they were designed to measure the effects of variations in the state of trade, and are based on the number of days worked each week during periods of trade uninterrupted by strikes (but allowing for absenteeism) multiplied by fifty working weeks. The implication is that during the strike periods the employment denominator remains the same while the output numerator falls, thereby deflating productivity estimates. When regional productivity data for the 1890s is recalculated on a non-strike basis (by substituting productivity estimates for preceding and succeeding years), the revised national productivity estimates raise the level of output per man-hour in the 1890s, leaving a fall in hourly productivity of 5.5 per cent, rather than the 7.7 per cent implied by the uncorrected data. The difference between the fall in OMY and OMS on the one hand (now barely 10 per cent) and the fall in OMH (5.5 per cent) becomes explicable largely in terms of the 4 per cent fall in hours.

We are left with the need to explain why OMH should have actually fallen by about 5 per cent, sometime around 1890, when for the rest of the century the trend was either upward, prior to 1880, or static beginning in the 1890s. One further complicating factor is the cyclical movement in trade, for the relatively depressed 1880s tended to inflate productivity figures. The relationship between falling trade and rising productivity lies essentially in the contraction of the labour force, a probable consequence of which was to increase the proportion of relatively skilled labour, while falling wages led to a greater work intensity and the mining of less marginal seams. Certainly, a comparison of productivity in the depressed 1880s with that of the buoyant 1890s needs to take account of such factors, and justifies the argument that the productivity for the 1880s is artificially high: that it exaggerates the true rise in output per man from the 1870s to the 1880s, and overstates the decline from the 1880s to the 1890s. None the less, productivity did fall temporarily, and requires explanation.

Two views, not entirely incompatible, have been advanced by historians to account for the check to labour productivity, though per-

[1] See below 725, 736–9.

ceived by them as a secular, rather than as a short-term, phenomenon. Both explanations contain in common the opinion, succinctly stated by Walters (though relating specifically to South Wales) 'that diminishing marginal returns did contribute to the long-term decline of overall labour productivity of coalmining after the 1880s, and possibly provide the only long-term causal factor of which we can be certain.'[1] The deteriorating resource base apart, however, A. J. Taylor emphasized managerial weaknesses in the industry, in failing to adopt technology and exploit potential economies of large-scale enterprise sufficiently to counter diminishing returns; he has also referred to 'a relapse in effort' by those in the industry.[2] More recently, and specifically in the context of South Wales, Walters placed his emphasis firstly, upon the disproportionate increase in underground oncost workers due to the long-term effect of diminishing marginal returns, and secondly, upon 'the stagnation and slight fall in hewers' productivity after 1888, which was a reaction to the improvement in wage rates down to 1913.[3] In an econometric reworking of data used by Taylor and by Walters, Hirsch and Hausman endorsed Walters's interpretation of the negative role of labour, but denied the importance of diminishing returns.[4]

The longer a mine had been worked, the more distant were the faces from the shaft, the further the men had to travel, and the greater the oncost work. The time a hewer could spend at the face was an important influence on the amount of coal that could be produced in a shift, and thus affected productivity, while, unless the mine was working retreating, the length of roads needed constant upkeep.[5] It is possible that the significant increase in travelling time underground which occurred between roughly 1890 and 1905 may have originated in the 1880s, though its effect was probably only marginal in its overall contribution to the fall at that time. None the less, for South Wales Walters calculated that while only 54 per cent of output came from collieries more than twenty years old in 1890, by 1913 the proportion had risen to 72 per cent.[6] Increasing oncost ratios were, therefore, inevitable, especially after the 1908 Act. In 1925 nearly 60 per cent of all UK miners were employed in mines sunk before 1885 and 73 per cent in those sunk before 1896.[7] Clearly, the influence of diminishing marginal returns varied depending on the age of the coalfield, and may, perhaps, be

[1] Walters 1975, 296. [2] Taylor 1961, 69.
[3] Walters 1975, 296, 299. [4] Hirsch and Hausman 1983, 145–57.
[5] Walters 1975, 295; *Eight Hours Committee* 1907, XIV, QQ 8641, 10574, 11110–1, 11645, 12688; III, Q 739. [6] Walters 1975, 295.
[7] *Samuel Commission, III*, 175.

advanced as the most important factor also in the relative decline of Durham—which until about 1890 was one of the highest productivity areas but which by 1907 recorded levels of no more than average productivity. Both Taylor and Walters have argued that variations in work intensity were characteristic of miners and were related directly to earnings. Buoyant trading conditions from the late nineteenth century, especially from 1900, they argue, elicited a diminution of effort from miners whose 'basic efficiency' deteriorated as a result, a view receiving some endorsement from Hirsch and Hausman.[1]

That such a relationship existed was widely believed by contemporaries. A report from Lancashire noted a falling off in the output of some mines, the daily 'get' in 1873 falling short of the 1869 figure by 10 or 12 per cent on average, though this was attributed as much to a scarcity of underground oncost labourers and a limited supply of lads due to legislation, as to lower work intensity.[2] Nearly ten years later, the Inspector of Mines for Durham reported on a similar relationship between wages and productivity, prompting a comment in the *Colliery Guardian* that this was characteristic of coalmining everywhere, though to a less extent than in Durham.[3] It is clear, however, that these observations refer to short-term responses, for which there is much supporting evidence. But movements in hourly productivity do not lend support to the existence of a clearly identifiable cyclical relationship between earnings potential and work intensity, the levels of which seem to have been at least as much affected by custom and special factors. Another possible explanation for any change in productivity trend, albeit temporary, round about 1890 might be found in hours reductions at that time, for while in most regions these occurred gradually (at least between 1872 and 1908) in certain regions where quite substantial falls were recorded between 1887 and 1893 the fall in OMY was very marked.[4] However, appreciable reductions in OMY also occurred in Scotland, where no comparable diminution in hours was recorded.

We have already underlined the significance for (declining) productivity not only of the age of pits but also the width of seams.[5] From 1900, when statistical information is available, the output from seams of less

---

[1] The phrase used by Taylor 1968, 54; Walters 1975, 296, 299; Hirsch and Hausmann 1983, 141–55, though their analysis is invalidated by their use of percentage additions to hewers' standard wage rates as a measure of wage trends, and they have applied this dubious proxy for wages to all colliery workers. See below, Appendix 7.1.

[2] *CG* 25 Apr. 1873, 429–30.   [3] *CG* 29 Sept. 1882, 509.

[4] South Wales, the North-east, and Lancashire. See Chapter 3 and Fig. 6.6.

[5] See above 352–5, 489.

than a metre was 17 per cent, yet in the three areas producing the highest proportion of coal from thin seams (Scotland, Northumberland, and west Yorkshire)[1] the percentage of coal cut by machinery was greatest, too.[2] Seam thickness, therefore, while an important influence, should not be regarded as the single major determinant of falling labour productivity; for by 1900 a growing acceptability of electrification and mechanization offered a solution—and OMH figures show a recovery.

A possible solution to this puzzle of a lapse in productivity is provided by our historic capital estimates which, after the relatively high levels of gross investment during the 1860s and 1870s, show a sharp fall over the 1883/90 cycle to barely two-thirds of the earlier levels, followed by recovery in the two succeeding cycles 1890/1900 and 1900/1907 at levels more than double those of the 1880s; they fell again in 1907/1913.[3] This sequence is consistent with a falling off in hourly productivity during the late 1880s to 1890s as a result of the drop in investment in the preceding cycle. Only very high levels of investment in the rest of that decade could, with the usual lag, check the fall in labour productivity. Thus, whereas capital per worker in 1873 is estimated at £123, rising to £156 by 1883, a marginal fall followed, leaving the 1890 figures lower than that in 1883. Between 1890 and 1900 capital per worker increased again to £160.

At a national level, the decline in productivity of 1908–13 remains the only clear instance of a downward trend in the period beginning 1894, the result of trends peculiar to the two largest coalmining regions and clearly the consequence of legislation. Otherwise, this picture of stability in rates of hourly productivity from the 1890s is evidently at odds with the conventional view of a secular decline in productivity, as a consequence, in part, of a deteriorating resource base, the ageing of pits, and a fall in the ratio of hewers to oncost workers. All of these factors (together with an increase in travelling and winding time) have been shown to have operated during the late nineteenth and early twentieth century; yet except for two brief checks, one of which is explained by hours legislation, without a significant reduction in hourly productivity.

The question then needs to be asked, how diminishing returns came to be successfully countered after the setback round about 1890, as evidenced by the conflicting movements of OMH and TFP? In the absence of other influences peculiar to the late 1880s and early 1890s it is tempting to regard increased mechanization and underground

[1] *Samuel Commission*, III, Appendix 10, 18, 184–7.
[2] See above Table 4.1.　　[3] See above Table 2.1.

electrification as having been important elements contributing to the maintenance of a stable OMH thereafter. It partly explains the substantial increase in real gross capital investment that occurred during the ten-year cycle ending in 1900 compared with the previous cycle, and which was sustained at relatively high levels until 1913. However, capital investment was lower relative to labour inputs after 1900, and much of it took the form of new resource development, either by deepening existing pits or sinking new ones; face mechanization, while increasing, was still relatively limited.

The experience of the Ashington Coal Company exemplifies the chronological sequence of increasing geological difficulties followed by face mechanization. From 1893 it is possible to calculate seam thickness and the changes occurring in the proportion of coal got from the six different seams mined at the company's four collieries. Before the mid-1860s the High Main seam was the sole source of output; with the addition of the Main and Low Main seams after 1868 these became the main sources of coal. Thereafter, the decline of the Low Main seam as a major resource coincided with the rise of the Yard seam. It seems clear that the thickest seams were worked first, the progressive working out of the Main, Low Main, and High Main (which was the first to be worked, abandoned in the 1880s and reopened in 1898 with the sinking of Linton Colliery) necessitating the opening up of new seams; hence the rise to prominence of the Yard coal in the late 1890s and early 1900s, which was both thinner (the company's thinnest) and less productive than the Main coals, but which yielded high-quality house coal. The development of this seam, however, involved the introduction of mechanical cutters in 1895, which transformed a hitherto uneconomic seam into a central source of the company's coal supply.[1]

Though putters' shift productivity fell sharply as a result of the Eight Hours Act, introduced in Northumberland in 1909, and provides adequate explanation for the overall check to labour productivity at Ashington's collieries, the 1890s were a period when diminishing marginal returns at the face were clearly manifest in the decline in hewers' productivity. This implied either the effects of lengthening haulage routes and/or the failure of Ashington's managers to improve haulage techniques sufficiently. There is evidence from other companies, too, that successful colliery enterprise depended upon the tapping of new, richer seams to offset declining productivity in those becoming exhausted. The original Carlton Main Colliery, sunk to work

[1] NuRO Ashington ZMD/54/2-5; NCB/AS/23.

the highly productive Barnsley seam in the 1870s, was eventually closed in 1910; by which time the acquisition and development of the large new Grimethorpe Colliery in 1900, followed by the sinking of the even larger Frickley Colliery which came into production in 1908, offset the tendency towards declining productivity and rising costs which prompted this policy.[1] At Staveley's collieries, too, differences between the levels of productivity point to the critical influence of the resource base and the changing proportions supplied by individual collieries. Here dramatic changes occurred in the relative importance of the new, large collieries, beginning in the 1890s when the high-productivity pits of Markham 1 and Barborough overtook the ageing Seymour and Hollingwood Collieries. By 1901, however, Warsop Main, where production, which began in 1895, exceeded Markham's output; though together these two large collieries produced 47 per cent of the total, rising to 62 per cent by 1913.[2] A new sinking, Markham 2, proved unsuccessful owing to the deep, hard seam which was thin and difficult to hole, and despite the use of coal cutters it was abandoned—because the price of coal and the amount of small produced required much higher physical productivity than was possible.[3]

The more productive seams attracted investment not only within regions but from areas where inferior resources posed a much greater problem. Thus, the Knowles family, leading Lancashire coalowners, joined with Emerson Bainbridge in taking over Warwickshire collieries, forming the Griff Coal Company in 1888.[4] Shortly after, Merry and Cunninghame and the Coltness Iron Company from Scotland were sinking pits in the same district.[5] The Wigan Coal and Iron Company was sinking pits in Nottinghamshire at about the same time.[6]

There is evidence, therefore, which suggests that variations in geological constraints, or in types of coal produced by different collieries, was a vital factor at the colliery and regional level; and were more important than, though not of course unrelated to, technological progress (and advances in knowledge) which gave access to resources and enhanced production possibilities in the industry. The variety of levels

[1] SCL Carlton Main MD 4080, May 1878, AGM, May 1906 AGM, May 1908 AGM; working costs and OMY calculated from AGMs 1882–1909 and SCL SYCOA, MD 2699–1–25, *Mineral Statistics* and *List of Mines*.

[2] J. E. Williams 1962, 175–9; *List of Mines*; BSCEMRRC Stanton and Staveley 2034/2/32–3 detailed balance sheets.

[3] BSCEMRRC Stanton and Staveley 2034/3/9d Mammatt's Report 6 May 1893, 17 Dec. 1894, 24 June 1895, 16 Dec. 1895.   [4] PRO BT 31/17294/1.

[5] WaRO Griff CR 1169/22/299, 326.   [6] CG 18 Feb. 1898, 303.

of, and trends in, productivity, therefore, have considerable implications for any interpretation of the industry's performance at national as well as at the regional level. Although regions may be ranked in order of average labour productivities—Scotland, the East Midlands, and the North-east above the UK average, with South Wales well below all others—the corollary that those exhibiting high productivities were 'superior' to those below them does not necessary follow. This is not only because of the geological differences so critical to explanations of inter- and intra-regional disparities, but because the more appropriate indicator of a colliery's performance as a commercial entity—revenue productivity—yields a different ranking from the physical productivity measures.

The record of shift productivity nationally was inferior by comparison with that of revenues per man-shift after 1888, a fairly steady decline in OMS contrasting with a sharply fluctuating, but none the less unmistakable, rise in £ms (Figure 6.4).[1] These national estimates conceal important regional differences, however, which are identifiable reasonably accurately only from 1894, when annual data on shifts makes it possible to estimate OMH and revenue product per man-hour (d/MH), by applying the regional price series to the OMH figures (Figure 6.5). The results reveal that while the East and West Midlands and Scotland both record OMH and d/MH values above the UK average, South Wales—which consistently recorded the lowest physical productivity at levels well below all other regions—fell below only the East Midlands and Scotland in revenue productivity. A high commercial value of output enabled the South Wales coal industry to sustain high-cost production, and while in South Wales high-revenue productivity reflected the buoyancy of international trade for the high-quality steam coal of this major exporting region, 'quality' was the result of working methods and investment in preparation, as well as of natural resource endowment.[2] Revenue productivity in Scottish mines was also sustained by favourable export prices, but face mechanization was another important contributory factor[3] which enabled Scotland to record the highest average OMH between 1894 and 1913. The export factor was minimal in the commercial success of the East Midlands, as was face mechanization; here the high quality of the natural resource in newly developing parts

---

[1] It has not been possible to estimate OMH annually until 1894; hence the use of OMS to calculate revenue productivity from 1882, an inferior measure but one which nevertheless indicates a difference in physical and revenue productivity over the longer period.

[2] See above 384.   [3] See above Table 4.2.

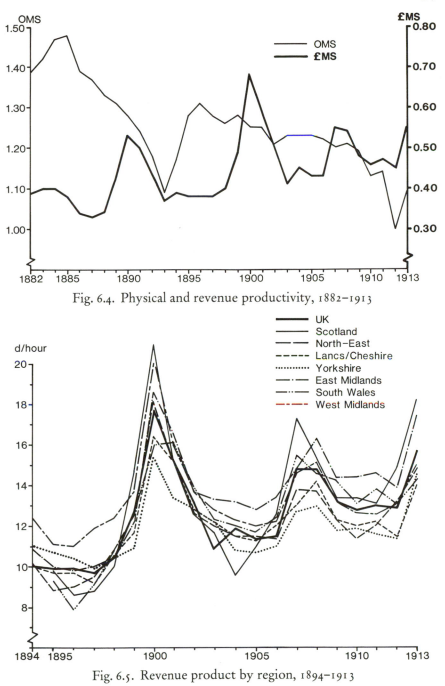

Fig. 6.4. Physical and revenue productivity, 1882–1913

Fig. 6.5. Revenue product by region, 1894–1913

Sources: Appendix 6.1 and *Mineral Statistics*.

of the region provide the key; and there, too, advanced working methods and coal preparation contributed to the combination of high physical and revenue productivity.[1]

The level and trends in revenue product, fundamental to any discussion of the economics of coal production, cannot be explained without reference to the important developments that occurred from the 1880s in the preparation and marketing of small coal, for the rise in small-coal prices relative to other coal prices was only indirectly the consequence of an expanding demand for fuel. In order to transform potential demand for small coal into effective consumption, innovations were required to render inferior, and often unusable, slack into a commercially acceptable state.[2] Developments in this direction were particularly marked in South Wales, and are reflected in the contrast between physical and revenue productivity. Where coal sales were less dependent upon quality and less constrained by competition (for example, the coal-producing iron companies before the 1890s) control over working costs assumed a relatively greater importance. But in the production of coal for sale it was revenue, rather than physical, productivity which in the economics of colliery enterprise was the critical factor influencing commercial policy and colliery practice.

ii. Working costs

The concept of marginal productivity was not part of the language of nineteenth-century coalowners, but even in collieries lacking proper cost accounts (the vast majority) its implicit application preceded many decisions pertaining to colliery strategy; whether to discontinue production either temporarily or for all time, whether to seek coal elsewhere, possibly in another coalfield. High or low, rising or falling, labour productivity might lead to different decisions in different regions, depending upon the trends and future expectations of coal prices. For example, Consett's Langley Park Colliery experienced rapidly declining labour productivity after 1903, but because of the rising trend in the price of non-coking coals, mechanization and an expansion of production from marginal deposits was the policy adopted.[3] At Staveley's new Markham No. 2 colliery a decision to discontinue working in 1898, after only four years during which cutting

---

[1] See above Table 6.3.   [2] See above chap. 4, v.
[3] A. S. Wilson thesis, 157.

machines were introduced to improve physical productivity, was the consequence of low prices and the need to reduce the relatively high proportion of slack. Only when prices reached high levels ten years later was Markham No. 2 colliery reopened, though at first operating slightly lower productivity levels than before.[1] While trends and levels of productivity were important in affecting costs, costs in relation to prices were the key determinants in the economics of colliery enterprise.

In order to analyse colliery costs data have been assembled and presented in Figures 6.6 and 6.7. In an industry containing such marked regional variations and diversities within regions, localities, and even within colliery companies, the validity of generalizations are subject to reservation, and the various caveats and qualifications expressed in our discussion of costs should be borne in mind throughout the following analysis. Before 1870 average working-cost series have been assembled for a mere handful of collieries, some referring to large coal or only to coal shipped, the effect of which is to inflate the figures. Figure 6.6 shows the various cost series, together with labour cost only for Elphinstone and Govan. The superimposition of a series of estimates for hewers' wages per shift provides a useful guide to the movement of working costs in this period, in which the number of observations is small, the collieries for which data were found for the years before 1860 are different from those for which we have cost figures after 1860, and for which a gap in our information exists during the 1850s. The justification for using the wage rate as a proxy for working costs is to be found in the discussion of cost structures[2] and in the close conformity between the movements of the wage-rate index and of the average working-cost index shown in Table 6.5. The basis of this index, derived almost entirely from colliery archives, is variable in coverage and comparability. Between 1830 and 1868 we must rely upon fewer than ten separate series in any single year, but they are discontinuous, of uncertain definition, and in some cases are of doubtful accuracy; for this reason we have not attempted to calculate an average for the early period.

No pretence will be made that the resulting average for 1868–1913 is an accurate statistic, but when slight differences in definition are allowed for the series is none the less strongly indicative of the levels and movements in colliery costs. Several of these series are continuous, or virtually so, throughout the entire period; none extends over a period shorter than sixteen years and most exceed twenty-five years. This

---

[1] BSCEMRRC Stanton and Staveley 2034/3/9d 16 Dec. 1892, Mammatt's Report.
[2] See below 501–3.

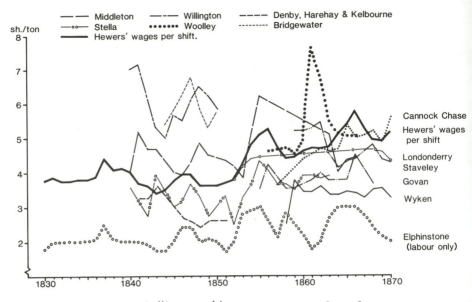

Fig. 6.6. Colliery working costs per ton, 1830–1870

Sources for Figures 6.6 and 6.7

Ashington, NuRO/1352/37/1–3; 538/8.
Astley and Tyldesley, LaRO, NCA t3/2.
Bedlington, NEMI, Weeks MS, 9/5.
Bell Bros., B.S.N.R.R.C. 04793, Comparative Balances, Profit and Loss Accounts 1873–1913.
Briggs Son and Co., L.C.A., 1708/13.
Butterley, DeRO, 503/B Certified Accounts vol. II and Managing Director's annual reports.
Cannock Chase, BUL, Balance sheets, 273/4.
Carlton Main, SCA, Director's Minutes 1879–1910, MD 4081–4088; South Yorkshire Coalowners'
    Association, Annual Reports, 1910–1913, M.D. 2699.
Clay Cross, Ledgers at Clay Cross Company, Clay Cross (uncatalogued).
Consett, Wilson thesis, Appendix B.1(i).
Darfield Main, SCA, NCB 601 and 608A.
Denby, Harehay and Kelbourne, NoUL archives, Dr. E 123/1–8.
East Cannock, StRO, D/429/m/B.
Elphinstone, SC *Dearness and Scarcity*, 1873, x, 328.
Govan, Slaven thesis, Table 34 and University of Glasgow Archives UGD/1/28/1–6.
Griff, WaRO, Annual Reports CR 1169/22.
Heaton, NuRO, 2WI/3.
Lochgelly, ScRO, CB2/218.
Londonderry, DuRO, LO/B/104(4) and Additional Ledger 'A'.
Main, GlaRO Trade and private ledgers, D/DMC (uncatalogued).
Middleton, LCA, MC 36–8.
Mitchell Main, SCA, NCB/601 and 608A.

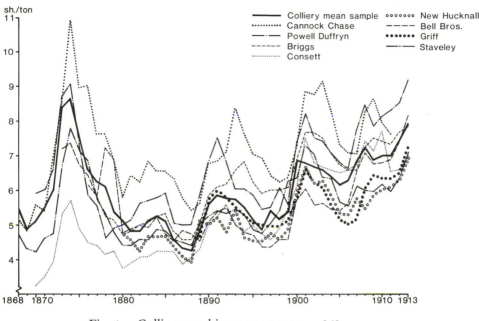

Fig. 6.7. Colliery working costs per ton, 1868–1913

Newbattle, ScRO, GD 40/94–111.
New Hucknall, NoRO, Balance Sheets NCB 1/40.
Newton Chambers, SCA, NCB/705 and 737.
Pelton, NuRO, 725/B6–B19.
Powell Duffryn, Walters 1977, Table 32.
Radstock, SoRO, DD/WG/49.
Staveley, BSCEMRRC, Stanton and Staveley 2034/2/32–3 and 303, detailed balance sheets.
Stella, DuRO, NCB I/SC/106.
Walbottle, NuRO 599.
Wharncliffe Silkstone, SCA, NCB 1280/1429/1.
Wigan, Coal Supply Commission (1903) I, p. 120.
Willington, NuRO 2WI/3.
Woolley, John Goodchild MS, Woolley Coal Co. Box 2.
Wyken, CoRO, 285/24/1–3.

Notes on the data

Ashington figures refer to labour costs and are excluded from the composite average index. Other series referring only to labour costs are Denby, Harehay and Kelbourne, Elphinstone, Govan, and almost certainly Wyken. The Bedlington figures refer to large coal only before 1869, as do those for Powell Duffryn for the entire series. The figures for Newbattle and Radstock refer to coal sold, and those for Heaton and Willington to coal shipments.

Table 6.5. *Index of average colliery working costs, 1868-1913,*
and of hewers' wage rates
(1900 = 100)

	Wage rate	Working costs		Wage rate	Working costs		Wage rate	Working costs
1830	46.4		1858	55.1		1886	58.3	67.1
1831	48.3		1859	55.3		1887	61.1	64.0
1832	46.4		1860	57.2		1888	62.8	63.4
1833	46.4		1861	58.3		1889	70.2	70.7
1834	47.3		1862	58.6		1890	84.7	80.5
1835	46.9		1863	59.1		1891	88.4	85.9
1836	48.2		1864	63.5		1892	85.3	85.4
1837	54.9		1865	67.1		1893	81.6	84.1
1838	50.5		1866	71.4		1894	83.0	80.5
1839	51.1		1867	65.6		1895	78.8	94.4
1840	49.7		1868	61.4	80.5	1896	77.6	72.6
1841	46.0		1869	61.0	71.9	1897	79.0	79.9
1842	44.8		1870	64.0	75.6	1898	82.7	75.0
1843	42.5		1871	66.3	76.8	1899	87.7	79.3
1844	43.5		1872	81.4	110.8	1900	100.0	100.0
1845	46.9		1873	96.9	121.3	1901	106.0	99.4
1846	49.2		1874	92.4	125.6	1902	99.0	98.2
1847	49.3		1875	76.6	109.8	1903	95.8	96.3
1848	45.0		1876	72.5	99.4	1904	92.7	94.5
1849	44.8		1877	66.0	92.7	1905	90.5	90.2
1850	44.8		1878	61.9	89.6	1906	92.1	88.4
1851	46.0		1879	56.8	79.3	1907	101.0	101.2
1852	46.9		1880	59.5	75.6	1908	106.8	106.1
1853	52.2		1881	60.1	71.3	1909	102.1	101.2
1854	59.6		1882	60.8	71.3	1910	101.4	103.1
1855	62.9		1883	63.1	74.4	1911	101.9	103.0
1856	65.4		1884	65.4	76.8	1912	103.5	108.5
1857	59.0		1885	60.8	73.8	1913	112.3	127.4

Sources: Working-cost index is calculated from the sources for Figure 6.7. The wage-rate index is calculated from Table 7.3.

larger number of series also includes many large multi-colliery companies, and makes it possible to include fairly continuous data from all
of the major regions. None the less, the definition of working cost is far
from uniform, a spectacular example of this being Ashington's virtual
disregard of non-labour costs in its working-cost accounting[1]—and

[1] NuRO Ashington NCB/AS 5; ZMD/54/1-7.

which has been excluded from the later series for that reason. From time to time many collieries included elements which we would regard as capital expenditure, one result of which is to produce sharp annual variation in some series, but which our average cost figures from 1868 tends to smooth. Nevertheless, the diversity in movements of individual series occurs within upper and lower limits not so markedly divergent as to undermine the exercise of averaging a series for 1868–1913. Ignoring the extraordinary coal-famine period, the turning-point in cost trend occurred in 1888–9 when from the lowest recorded average of 1887–8 a rise in costs began which, though temporarily reversed between 1893 and 1899, carried prices well above 6s. per ton. The peaks in 1901 and 1908 were followed by the highest figure of the entire period in 1913. Costs also followed short-run movements in prices during the booms, demonstrating the obverse of labour productivity (which, as we have seen, tended to fall at those times) when the dependent relationship between the two is apparent. The rise in costs at current prices by some 50 per cent between the 1860s and the early 1900s is only slightly less pronounced when expressed in constant prices, and the substantial rise which coincided with the successful impact of organized labour beginning in 1888–9 is unmistakable.

Examination of the various series individually and by regions reveals a greater degree of conformity after 1870 than before, and is explicable mainly in terms of the reservations already expressed concerning the early data. Before 1870 annual fluctuations in output and sales tended to be greater, which caused costs to fluctuate more widely, too, and on the whole colliery firms were much smaller. Some regional differences emerge after 1870: lower than average costs in the North-east, roughly average in Yorkshire and the East Midlands, and relatively high in South Wales, though the picture is complicated there by the cost series applying to large coal only and the proportion which that represented of all coal. Elsewhere, insufficient observations have been made to justify any conclusions, but although incomplete the picture is broadly consistent with relative regional productivity levels until the early years of the twentieth century, when the North-east and the East Midlands changed positions.

Wages were the major component in working costs. A detailed survey of the structure and composition of a sample of colliery costs, published in the *Colliery Guardian* in 1871,[1] implies that if we may assume that depth is acceptable as a crude proxy for size, then with a

---

[1] *CG* 2 June 1871, 586–8.

single exception wage costs in smaller collieries bore a higher proportion to total working costs than in others; in three of the four smaller
collieries this figure exceeded 70 per cent, whereas only one of the
medium to large collieries had wage costs exceeding 62 per cent; the
range was between 58 and 77 per cent. Our own colliery sample confirms an average figure in the low to middle 60s for the 1860s, and frag-
mentary data for the 1840s and 1850s point to a figure around the 60 per
cent level for that period.

Both before and after the *Colliery Guardian* survey the overall proportion of wage costs was similar, within the range of 50 to 75 per cent,
but marked differences occurred between those figures which in some
collieries appear to have fluctuated sharply in any year. Our much more
reliable data, which beginning in the 1860s increases in volume and
detail, indicate a general rise in the ratio of wage to total working costs
beginning in the 1880s, after which figures above 70 per cent are normal,
with the upper limit exceeding 80 per cent in some collieries. Similar
levels were revealed in evidence to the Mining Royalties Commission in
1889–90.[1] Given the long-term relative stability, or gradual increase, in
the ratio of wage costs to total working costs, it is possible that the
weakness of our cost data before 1870, and especially before 1860, concealed an increase in this ratio in the early to mid-1850s, when our wage-
rate series suggests that a sharp upward movement became
permanent—unlike the rise in wages levels in the early 1860s which
almost immediately returned to former levels when the boom collapsed.
The coincidence, however, of the upward shift of the ratio in the late
1880s with a rise in the wage-rate series together provides confirmation
of the reality of this alteration in the structure of colliery costs.

This was a development which contemporaries had long associated
with efficiency: 'when the percentage of wages is the highest', explained
the author of the 1871 article, 'the actual cost of working is usually the
least'.[2] But this depended in part upon the relative proportions of
certain categories of labour. Underground wage costs were, of course,
the main component, accounting for round about 80 per cent of all wage
costs at Briggs's collieries in 1860 and again in 1885, rising to 85 per cent
by 1910[3]; at Staveley the comparable figure was about 85 per cent in 1860
and remained at around that level in 1876.[4] At Ashington the 1885 figure

[1] *RC Mining Royalties* 1890–1, XLI, Q 14167.
[2] *CG* 2 June 1871, 588.
[3] LCA 1708/13, Schedule of Sales and Costs.
[4] BSCEMRRC Stanton and Staveley 2034/2/32–3, detailed balance sheets.

was 75 per cent.[1] A different categorization, that of 'getting' and oncost wages, offers no better basis for generalization, because of the difficulty of definition and regional variations in the degree of job specialization. In South Wales such a division reveals getting costs to have been only a fraction of total labour costs: about one-third from 1870 when Walters's continuous cost series begins,[2] and a similar proportion at Ashington and at Staveley's three main pits in the same year. But the comparable figure at Staveley was nearer 42 per cent in 1880, rising to 50 per cent until the early 1900s. This remarkable difference is partly explicable by the different systems of work organization in the regions, where the roles of face workers were not the same.

As we have found so often, therefore, accurate generalization is scarcely possible. The analysis by Isaac Hodges of the course of under-ground wages at two seams of the Whitwood collieries of Henry Briggs and Son concluded that they contributeds two-thirds of the rise in total working costs at the collieries, which between 1860 and 1910 had nearly doubled. Hodges stressed the percentage addition to wages since 1885 as the main underlying cause for rising wage costs.[3] It should be noted, however, that taking all of Briggs's collieries over the longer period between 1876 and 1914 labour costs per ton rose by 47 per cent, at the same time that percentage additions to wages in west Yorkshire, the outcome of agreements between the West Yorkshire Coal Owners' Association and the trade unions, were of the order of 40 per cent.[4] West Yorkshire wage rates were certainly under pressure from the higher earnings possible in the south Yorkshire pits, where a similar upward pressure on cutting rates at various collieries arose from alterations in the thickness of seams and differences in the thickness of dirt.[5] At Carlton Main Colliery, for example, where costs were rising from the 1880s, wage costs accounted for 63 per cent of total working costs, com-pared with between 68 and 72 per cent at Briggs. The difference, how-ever, was attributable less to the level of piece-rates than to average earnings, dependent upon contrasting geological conditions. The Barns-ley seam worked at Carlton Main was simply more productive than the seams worked by Briggs, and by the time (because of approaching exhaustion) Carlton Main's costs had begun to rise to intolerable levels,

[1] NuRO Ashington, NCB/AS 5; ZMD/54/1–7.

[2] Walters 1977, 255–6, Table 31.

[3] Isaac Hodges 1910–11, 175–9.

[4] Board of Trade, *Rates of Wages and Hours of Labour in various Industries in the UK*, Library of the Department of Employment, 71–2; Board of Trade, *Seventeenth Abstract of Labour Statistics* (1915), 7.   [5] SCL MD 2699–13, SYCOA Report, 25 Apr. 1904.

the directors had acquired Grimethorpe Colliery which shortly after 1900 had been developed sufficiently to produce coal more cheaply than the original Carlton Main, the closure of which soon followed.[1]

In 1906 J. G. Weeks explained the additional 6*d*. per ton (9 per cent) by which Bedlington Colliery's working costs, carefully recorded and analysed regularly, had risen since 1894. Wage increases were part of the answer, and more accurate costing may have explained part of the rise, but he considered the major reason to have been the working of the Bensham and Plessey seams, which were thinner and less cheaply worked than the Low Main which had hitherto provided the company's main coal supply.[2] Wage costs were regarded as fundamental to an explanation of the higher working costs of Consett's collieries, which rose by 100 per cent between 1868 and 1913, for labour costs increased by one-and-a-half times and accounted for three-quarters of the cost inflation. The striking disparity in the level of labour costs at each colliery, however, underlines the significance of differences in resource productivity underlying labour-cost differentials.[3] In 1895 Mammett reported on the Hartington Colliery workings to Staveley's directors, and remarked on the disadvantage of working the Hartington Silkstone seam where high getting prices were necessary due to the thickness of parting in the seam. Because of the extra amount of work required of the hewer to remove the thick clod to get at the thin bottom coal, high rates had to be offered to attract men to work the seam at all.[4]

These various case studies, therefore, suggest that in some collieries the rise in wage costs may be regarded in part as a result of an upward adjustment of cutting prices in order to exploit a deteriorating resource base, though from 1889 the existence of strong trade unions was also a factor which influenced overall wage costs.[5] While productivity levels at the Briggs collieries were relatively low in comparison with other west Yorkshire collieries, none the less levels were reasonably stable in the 1890s and early 1900s,[6] though the directors were protecting their company's financial position by investing heavily outside the industry.[7] The rise in non-hewing costs, which reached twice the 1885 level in 1910, Hodges attributed entirely to the strictures contained in the various

[1] SCL Carlton Main MD 4080–9, AGM 1880; LCA 1708/13, Schedules of Sales and Costs.
[2] NEI Weeks MS, 9/1 Directors' Reports, 11 Jan. 1906.
[3] A. S. Wilson thesis, Appendix B1(i).
[4] BSCEMRRC, Stanton and Staveley 2034/3/9d, 16 Dec. 1895, 6 July 1891 Mammatt's Reports.
[5] See below 747–57.
[6] Measured by OMY. Bro LU Special Collections MS, WYCOA, statements of output 1890–1913; *List of Mines*.   [7] LCA Briggs 1708/13, MB 1866–1914.

Mines Regulations Acts relating to hours and safety. One consequence of this was the doubling in the number of deputies in 1910 compared with 1885. After 1910 additional costs imposed on collieries included the national minimum-wage agreement in 1912, the new Mines Act, and the Insurance Act.[1] Nevertheless, there are plausible grounds for believing that diminishing returns were also a factor, and that haulage routes in the thin Silkstone and Warren seams involved higher oncosts.[2]

Diminishing returns might have been expected to account for the rise in Ashington's oncosts, both surface and underground, at a faster rate than hewing costs after 1900, for by 1912–13 underground oncost labour actually exceeded the costs of winning coal.[3] On a return which showed working costs at Bolckow Vaughan's collieries a manager had scrawled: 'best seams in many of our pits are practically exhausted, thinner and more expensive seams are being worked. Workings are much further away from shafts causing increased cost.'[4] Both in the collieries belonging to Briggs and those of Ashington surface costs declined as a proportion of labour costs, the potential increase in labour costs involved in more screening and greater product differentiation being offset by the mechanization of these processes, and also by a reduction in the amount of labour per ton needed in winding, bank work, and general labour. Wages and labour costs, therefore, were critical to the colliery cost structure, and because the economizing of labour, especially of hewers, was economic for only a small proportion of coal producers before 1913, the burden of offsetting diminishing marginal returns, higher wages, and legislative enactments lay in other directions.

After labour, the next largest component of working costs was materials and stores, which in the *Colliery Guardian* survey in 1871 varied between 5 and 18 per cent, but averaged 12 per cent.[5] Materials and stores consisted of pit timber, rails, castings, ropes, candles, oil rails, and grease, but might also include pit wagons. These are similar proportions to those revealed in our company data, though the *Colliery*

[1] Isaac Hodges 1910–11, 175–9.

[2] LCA 1708/15 Anon., 'Down Among the Coals', Bro Special Collections MS, 160, MB, 1904 Directors' Report.

[3] NuRO Ashington Colliery Weekly Pit Bills, 1352/37/1–3, Pit Bills with Abstracts 1879–1912, 538/8 Colliery Group Statistics.

[4] A. S. Wilson thesis, 162. Evidence of the increasing difficulties presented by deteriorating geological condition is to be found at the Wigan Coal and Iron Company, and of Bell Brothers. *Report to the Board of Trade on the Relation of Wages in certain Industries to the Cost of Production*, 1891, LXXVIII, 13; BSNRRC Bell 04793, Comparative Balances, 1873–1913.

[5] *CG* 2 June 1871, 568–8.

Guardian survey suggests that larger collieries tended to register higher material and store costs as a proportion of total working costs compared with the smaller collieries. At Briggs the figures were 14 per cent in 1860 in one seam and 13 in another, remaining at roughly the same level in 1885 when the figure for all the company's collieries was 9 per cent; the same level was recorded for 1910, by which time in the Stanley Main and the Haigh Moor seams the figure had fallen to 10 per cent. According to Hodge's analysis the burden of stores had been limited by the fall in prices of timber and ropes, and from the 1890s the substituting of long-lasting steel for timber.[1]

Horse feed varied between 1 and 7 per cent in the *Colliery Guardian*'s review, averaging 4 per cent,[2] though a higher figure probably obtained before the mechanization of main-road haulage. At Briggs the cost of horse feed relative to other costs remained static, and the increasing efficiency of horses 'under modern conditions' was offset, according to Hodges, by reducing working hours.[3] In 1871 the *Colliery Guardian* survey put expenditure on fuel, mainly in pumping and ventilation, as varying between 2 and 7 per cent of total working cost.[4] At Briggs's collieries boiler fuel costs were contained by boiler economy,[5] a dramatic illustration of this in progress at another colliery being the reduction in the real cost of fuel for Consett's boiler by nearly 50 per cent between the 1860s and the 1890s.[6] At the three collieries of Bell brothers the combined cost of material, stores, and horses, but excluding coal for colliery consumption, averaged 10 per cent of working costs in the 1870s, 11 per cent in the late 1890s and in 1909–13, and another 4 per cent for fuel consumption in the 1870s, varying between 3 and 4 per cent until 1913.[7] Taken together, materials, stores, horse-keep, and fuel for colliery consumption add up to the proportions which 'stores costs' represented in the steam-coal collieries of South Wales, between 20 and 25 per cent between the 1860s and 1913.[8] Finally, rents and royalties in the *Colliery Guardian* report varied as a proportion of working costs between 5 and 14 per cent.[9]

The contribution of rents and royalties to the costs of coalmining became the subject for political debate in the 1880s, when the TUC passed a resolution proposing the abolition of royalties, as 'a tax upon

[1] Isaac Hodges 1910–11, 175–9.   [2] *CG* 2 June 1871, 568–8.
[3] Isaac Hodges 1910–11, 175–9.   [4] *CG* 2 June 1871, 567.
[5] Isaac Hodges 1910–11, 170–9.   [6] A. S. Wilson thesis, 168.
[7] BSNRRC Bell, 04793, Comparative Balances, 1873–1913.
[8] Walters 1977, 252.   [9] *CG* 2 June 1871, 567–8.

our staple industries . . .'[1] and which placed limitations on wages and profits. Abolition of royalties also became part of the Liberal Party's programme.[2] Inter-regional differences in royalty levels, and variations from seam to seam, complicate the identification of trends, but archival data from a dozen collieries offer a clearer picture from the 1880s, by which time the relatively high levels set during the 1870s boom had begun to fall. An index of average royalties presented in Table 6.6 shows royalty levels returning to those of the early 1870s in 1889–91, and again in 1900–1; thereafter, royalties were at similar levels to those of the 1880s. A different picture is presented by comparing average working costs with average royalty levels (though the two series contain only some colliery series in common). These suggest that as a percentage of working costs royalties declined from the relatively high levels of the early to mid-1870s, when they reached 9 per cent, until the early and mid-1890s—reflecting post-boom lag before royalties were adjusted downwards. After another rise in the late 1890s, the 1900s saw royalty levels at their lowest levels throughout the period since 1873. Unambiguously, therefore, over the long term archival evidence suggests that the burden of rents and royalties was downwards.

Rates and taxes, principally poor rates, did not exceed 5 per cent and averaged 3 per cent in the *Colliery Guardian* survey;[3] Hodges attributed to this a figure of 4 per cent as the proportion of Briggs's working costs in 1860, rising to 5 per cent by 1885 and 6 per cent by 1910. Management and establishment costs were the residual, at no more than 4 per cent, and remained steady round about that level at Briggs's collieries. These included 'general management', travelling agents, charges and damages, rates, and taxes; beginning in the early 1890s membership of the coalowners' association, and from 1897 Workmen's Compensation, were additional items. The only significant increase in relative importance, however, was the rise in rates and taxes from 2.4 per cent in 1885 to 4.3 per cent in 1910.[4] 'Establishment charges' at Staveley's collieries, which averaged 10 per cent in the 1860s, fell steadily from then on, to below 7 per cent in the 1880s, around 4 per cent in the 1890s, and below that level thereafter. Staveley's disaggregated working-cost series, the longest to have been discovered, is presented in Figure 6.8.

We have seen that the tendency towards increasing costs, which intensified towards the end of the century, could be counteracted by

[1] Quoted in *Sankey Commission* 1919, XII, Q 663.
[2] Sorley 1889, 74.   [3] *CG* 2 June 1871, 567–8.
[4] Isaac Hodges 1910–11, 170–9.

Table 6.6. *Index of average royalties*[a] *per ton and as a percentage of average working costs, 1873-1913*

(1900 = 100 = 7d.)

Year	Index	%	Year	Index	%	Year	Index	%
1873	96	7.8	1887	86	6.5	1901	107	5.3
1874	104	7.6	1888	82	6.8	1902	86	4.4
1875	104	8.6	1889	100	5.8	1903	89	4.8
1876	100	7.4	1890	93	6.9	1904	89	4.8
1877	107	9.3	1891	100	7.3	1905	89	4.9
1878	100	9.0	1892	93	5.0	1906	89	5.0
1879	79	6.0	1893	93	5.5	1907	96	4.6
1880	79	6.5	1894	93	6.9	1908	89	4.3
1881	89	6.5	1895	96	5.5	1909	93	5.5
1882	89	6.7	1896	93	7.1	1910	93	4.9
1883	82	6.5	1897	93	7.3	1911	86	5.7
1884	93	6.2	1898	93	7.4	1912	82	4.8
1885	79	6.0	1899	96	7.4	1913	86	4.8
1886	93	6.5	1900	100	10.0			

[a] Royalties include rent where applicable.

Sources: Average working costs are from Table 6.5. The royalty data are taken from fifteen colliery companies, but represent probably more than twice that number of collieries: Bell Brothers 1873-1913, BSNRRC, 04793 comparative balances and profit and loss accounts; Henry Briggs and Son 1876-1913, LCA 1708/13, MB and reports of directors; Cannock Chase, 1873-1913, BUL, directors' reports, accounts and papers; Consett (Home Collieries), Wilson thesis, Appendix B1(i); Dalton Main 1883-1913; Darfield Main 1880-1913, SCL, NCB 601 and 608A; Griff 1888-1913, WaRO, CR 1169/22, managers' annual reports; Main 1890-1913, GRO, D/DMC, balance sheets; Mitchell Main 1876-1913, SCL NCB 601 and 608A; New Hucknall 1879-1913, NoRO NCB 1/13-15, MB; Newton Chambers 1876-1913, SCL, NCB/704-737; Pelton 1873-1913, NuRO 725/B16-B19, Report Books of William Armstrong re Lord Dunsay 1867-1913; Powell Duffryn Directors' Reports and balance sheets, P.D. Ltd., Stanhope Gate, and South Wales Coal-owners' Association returns of output: royalty rates differ from those given by Walters 1977, Table 32, as the latter were based upon large coal sold only, rather than all coal; Staveley Coal and Iron, 1873-1913, BSCEMRRC/2034/2/32-3 and 303, detailed balance sheets.

achieving higher productivity, or at least checking its fall, either through technological change and alterations in working methods, or by organizing large-scale colliery enterprise in order to exploit cost economies arising from fixed-cost elements. Depending upon how fixed costs were defined they could be considerable. The *Colliery Guardian* article suggested a figure of between 25 and 30 per cent in 1870,[1] which was slightly less than that advanced by Bidder, of the Cannock Chase Colliery Co., in 1894, when his hypothetical example implied a figure

[1] *CG* 2 June 1871, 567-8.

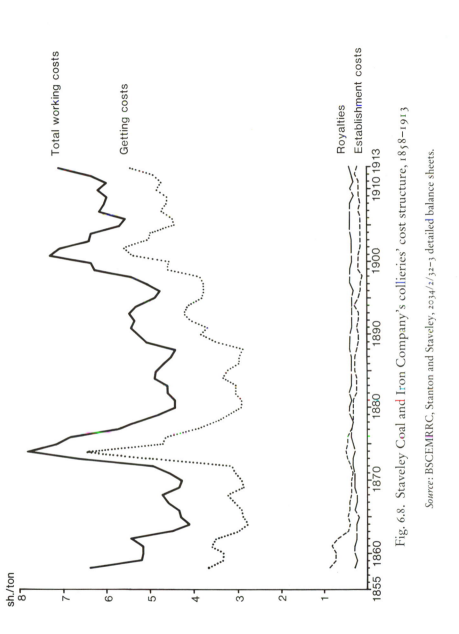

Fig. 6.8. Staveley Coal and Iron Company's collieries' cost structure, 1858–1913

Source: BSCEMRRC, Stanton and Staveley, 2034/2/32–3 detailed balance sheets.

closer to 40 per cent. Apart from the small fixed-rental element, management or establishment charges, and rates and taxes, oncosts were incurred irrespective of production, and Bidder stressed the continuing payments necessitated by safety imperatives, by the need to keep the pits clear of water, the roads clear, the roofs well supported, and the horses fed; continuous ventilation was also an unavoidable cost, whether or not a colliery was actually raising coal.[1] Actual costs assembled by William Armstrong in the course of considering pit-closure policies at Pease's Eldon Colliery implied oncost figures, irrespective of whether coal was being raised, of between 36 and 38 per cent.[2] The *Colliery Guardian* article also drew attention to the often substantial body of joiners, smiths, and labourers customarily employed at a colliery but who were necessary in such numbers only because of the otherwise unavoidable work caused by accidents and renewals due to carelessness in the pit and inadequate supervision, a cost which the author estimated at between 8 and 12 per cent of the working cost.[3] In the minds of some coalowners, however, depreciation and sometimes interest payments were included as working costs, which although irregular as cost-accounting practice must have underlined the advantages of continuous full-time working. At Pelton Colliery, for example, capital costs added an average of 5 per cent to working costs between 1868 and 1913, though the annual burden varied between 42 per cent and zero.[4]

Our working-cost series reflects imperfectly the changes in the real costs of mining coal. It is possible, however, by deflating working costs by a composite input price index, to eliminate the effect of changing input costs, the resulting series comprising a measure of the remaining influences (that is, other than wages and material costs) upon working costs per ton.[5] Such a series may therefore be regarded as an alternative measure equivalent to, but different from, total factor productivity, incorporating the impact of the changing quality of the resource base, of technology, and of all capital inputs—not just those related to working technology specifically, since capital expended on access technology alone would none the less reduce the costs per ton of working coal; for example, by allowing a constant or expanding scale of production. Real working costs, by these calculations, rose by perhaps 50 per cent during

[1] Bidder 1894, 808.

[2] NuRO Armstrong, 725/B14/675-7, Report.   [3] CG 2 June 1871, 588.

[4] NuRO Armstrong 725/B6-10, 11, 12, 14, 15, 19, Reports to Directors.

[5] This calculation adopted a weighting of the wage index of 5, and of 1 for a composite material-costs index (equal brick, timber, and iron prices from the sinking cost index).

the twenty-five years before World War I, and again implies that the deterioration in the resource base (in so far as it affected working costs) occurred more rapidly than did technological improvements. It suggests that while the countervailing influences of improved working methods and technology, and the consequent exploitation and greater relative importance of superior coal deposits, proved sufficient to check the fall in labour *productivity* (OMH), they were insufficient to stem the tendency for *costs* to rise. In the context of rising real working costs and (as indicated by our sinking-cost index) of capital costs, favourable revenue productivity was the key to sustained productive investment and to profitability.

iii. Profitability

The outcome of the unavoidable struggle to counter diminishing returns and the tendency for capital and working costs to rise, to a great extent determined the profitability of the industry. For while in the very short term price fluctuations were the major determinants of profit, tonnage was regarded as the primary factor influencing potential profitability in the longer term. Preparation and marketing, of course, contributed to the ability to actually sell the coal, maintain high levels of production, and to boost revenue product.[1]

Profits may be regarded either as rewards to investors and colliery-owning entrepreneurs, or when expressed as a return on assets as an indication of the efficiency of capital. Unfortunately the difficulties surrounding the estimation of rates of return on capital were almost as great at the end of our period as at the beginning. In 1920 H. F. Bulman pointed out that,

Any general statement about the return received on the capital which is invested in collieries is apt to be misleading. The truth is that at some collieries it receives a very large return; at some, much capital is altogether lost or remains unremunerative for years; and there are many collieries which pay well occasionally when the selling price of coal is high, but in normal years do little more than pay their way....[2]

He quoted a special report, commissioned in 1915 at the request of the Monmouthshire and South Wales Coal Owners' Association, which showed 1914 profits for almost all the working collieries producing

---

[1] Bidder 1894, 810–11; WaRO Griff, CR 1169/22–258, Melly's report.
[2] Bulman 1920, 206.

steam coal. Of these seventy-nine firms, twenty-nine were working at a loss or at zero profit on ordinary capital; 37 per cent were earning a profit of less than 1s. a ton, and 32 per cent were earning more than 1s. per ton. About one-fifth of all steam coal in the region was produced at a loss or at zero profit—even in a year of buoyant trade.[1]

Contemporaries seem to have agreed on the level at which, 'taking one year with another', a fair and reasonable return was being made on capital invested in coal mining. Bidder described the problem in an article entitled 'The Profits of Coal Pits' which was published in *The Nineteenth Century* in 1894:

The business is one of a very fluctuating character. There are occasionally periods of inflation, when the profits are excessive; they are invariably followed by periods of depression, usually of much longer duration in which little or no profit is realisable. Moreover, in any individual colliery profits are liable to disappear entirely, apart from rise and fall of markets, in consequence of accidents, failure of seams, faulty ground, or other contingencies impossible to be foreseen. . . . It is also to be noticed that some time must always elapse before a colliery can be developed sufficiently to earn profits, and during this period the capital is necessarily unproductive. Now there are many opportunities for investing money far less risky and fluctuating than the coal trade by which a return of 5 per cent or upwards can be obtained. It seems, therefore, not unreasonable to expect a return somewhat higher than 5 per cent on colliery capital. Further, it must be remembered that the life of a colliery is limited by the extent of workable coal that can profitably be won from it, and therefore in addition to interest an annual sum must be provided for the redemption of the capital sunk. Taking all these circumstances into account, an annual return of 10 per cent on the capital, to include both interest and depreciation or redemption of capital, is surely a very reasonable remuneration. To put the same thing in other words, no man would embark his money in colliery property unless he had a fair prospect of obtaining at least this return for it.[2]

In 1919 Sir Josiah Stamp explained that (for much the same reason as outlined by Bidder many years before) excess profits duty had been imposed at above 9 per cent for collieries, compared with 6 per cent which had been deemed 'the proper figure for a "natural industry"',[3] though he stressed that in determining the allowances under the Excess Profits Duty Act these figures bore no relationship to actual profit levels. He did, however, express his personal opinion that 'the market rate to attract capital in the coal mining industry . . . must necessarily be higher than the other rate'.[4]

[1] Ibid., 207–8.   [2] Ibid., 808.
[3] *Sankey Commission*, I, Q 789.   [4] Ibid., Q 794.

A similar view was common among coalowners in the nineteenth century. In 1847 Joseph Pease declared: 'I never consider that I have made a profit till I have realized something over and above the interest which the money would have fetched in the market'.[1] Indeed, the deduction of an 'appropriate' rate of interest before declaring net profit, or adding 5 per cent to partners' capital, was not an unusual practice at that time,[2] though the advent of corporate enterprise probably began the trend towards the discontinuance of such a convention. Henry Curer Briggs told the Trade Union Commission in 1867–8 that his expectation of profitability was 'something less than 10 per cent return on capital on average'.[3] In the course of discussions over sliding scales in 1875 the coalowners of South Wales differed among themselves as to the precise percentage which might be regarded as essential as an assured return on investment, 5 per cent on capital, 4 per cent for redemption, and an unspecified figure for risk, or up to 20 per cent including 10 per cent on capital.[4] The latter figure, however, may well have reflected the inflationary influence of the coalowners' experience of the early 1870s, which even as they deliberated moved sharply into reverse.[5] As the insistence upon a notional element of interest as a component of gross profits weakened, so the claims upon them became increasingly specific and the subject of informed professional debate. In the absence of legal requirements some accountants and managers favoured the payment of dividends from capital, as it enabled a company to pay dividends during its early years of existence, usually a critical period of nil return for colliery enterprises. First in the *Accountant* in 1876 and later in *The Engineer* in 1883, proposals were made to adopt a formal accounting procedure which equated depreciation with a cost equal to the value of an asset consumed during a year. However, colliery managers resisted this innovation on the grounds that depreciation could only be afforded if profits were made, thereby reflecting the prevailing practice within industry.[6]

Actual practices varied between companies; depreciation was allowed irregularly, depending upon the availability of gross profits sufficient to cover accumulated depreciation, and sometimes, in accordance with the method recommended by Arthur Sopwith in 1883,

[1] *SC Commercial Distress* 1847, VIII, Q 4835.
[2] SCL TR 450/5126 Newton Chambers partnership deed 1863; Walters 1977, 283.
[3] *RC Trade Unions* 1867–8, XXXIX, Q 12673.
[4] Walters 1977, 284.   [5] See below.
[6] R. P. Brief, 'Depreciation Theory in Historical Perspective', *The Accountant*, 163 (1970), 737–9.

colliery manager at Cannock Chase, was accompanied by a reserve fund maintained to meet emergencies.[1] The practice of depreciating to nil, or to the break-up value of the plant over a thirty- or forty-year period, was a common one, but by no means universal. Emerson Bainbridge told the Commissioners in 1904: 'I think the best plan in managing a colliery . . . is to hand to your shareholders the money that is made, keeping back a sufficient reserve fund for emergencies. In the concerns I have to do with we never put aside any redemption sum.'[2] Even towards the end of our period, R. A. S. Redmayne also regarded the regular and systematic amortization of capital, either by means of a sinking fund or by taking out an insurance policy to mature at the end of a lease, as exceptional, preference being accorded to declaring higher dividends.[3]

The allowance for wear and tear as a charge against revenue for tax purposes, introduced in 1878, was an indication that this aspect of depreciation was receiving greater attention, though the precise formulae (a fixed amount per ton, a percentage of fixed or of specific assets) varied among those companies which did adopt systematic annual depreciation. Throughout the period, however, large numbers of firms, especially in the North-east where because of the relatively few large public companies the influences towards advanced accounting practice were weaker than in other regions, pursued outdated procedures. This was the conclusion of Sir Josiah Stamp, when during the early years of the twentieth century he examined the colliery accounts submitted to the Inland Revenue. The entire mine assets, below and above ground, were stated in a single sum unaltered for many years: 'Some of the pits being 120 to 140 years old it did appear as though some kind of statement of total worth was used in those days, but there was no conception that there ought to be some clear relation between the charges in that and the annual . . . profit and loss account. It seems as if every year has to cover its own expenses, so to speak, out of revenue without touching the original investment.'[4] Stamp implied a 'system' of accounting similar to that in practice at the Dowlais Iron Company during the second and third quarters of the nineteenth century, whereby items of capital expenditure normally appeared in the profit and loss account as a cost

[1] Arthur Sopwith, 'Depreciation of Colliery Plant', *TSSEWIME*, 9 (1883), 133–46; J. R. Edwards, 'British Capital Accounting Practices and Business Finance 1852–1919: An Exemplification', *Accounting and Business Research*, 10 (1980), 245, for practices at Shelton Bar Iron Company.

[2] *Coal Supply Commission* 1904, XXIII, Q 11011.

[3] Walters 1977, 285.

[4] Josiah Stamp, 'The Accounting Research Association', *The Accountant* XCVI (1937), 16. I am grateful to Professor Leslie Hannah for this reference.

for the year of expenditure, with income bearing all capital as well as revenue outlays immediately they were incurred.[1]

After reviewing accounting procedures in the 1840s and 1850s, William Jenkins reported to the trustees that even expenditure amounting to nearly £35,000 on the Dowlais Branch Railway would have been treated as an Estate 'or as a set of Pits and cleared off out of profits'.[2] During the early nineteenth century such common practice reflected the widespread lack of understanding of the significant difference between capital and revenue expenditure when measuring profit, but even after such issues became the subject of discussion among accountants and managers systematic depreciation accounting (incorporating the distinction between capital and revenue) did not achieve widespread acceptance, even among the large companies, before 1900.[3] It is true that during the late nineteenth century a consensus was emerging (at least, in theory) in favour of a more rational accounting practice, both amongst managers and auditors, and that a sentiment began to be expressed that formal annual depreciation was advantageous to managers and directors since it allowed them to undertake new work or repairs without consulting shareholders.[4] But such considerations were more important to the professionally managed and publicly owned companies, since it was the non-shareholding (or at least the non-controlling) managers of these companies who had most to gain by the adoption of such a practice. We have seen, however, that in the coal industry large publicly owned companies and professional non-controlling managers were not at all characteristic of most colliery enterprises even in 1913.

If directors could charge items to revenue rather than to capital account when cash flow permitted, this was one method of concealing the size of real profits from customers—and from the trade unions—though other shareholders might not wholeheartedly approve of such a policy. Thus, in reply to Staveley shareholders' queries in 1866 Markham had stated that when in doubt an item was charged to revenue rather than to capital account, while Pochin sought to allay the suspicion of one shareholder bold enough to query the company's accounting procedures, with the reply: 'Like every other trading

[1] Edwards and Baber 1979, 142, 148.
[2] Ibid., 145.
[3] Ibid.; J. R. Edwards, 'British Capital Accounting Practices and Business Finance 1852–1919: An Exemplification', *Accounting and Business Research*, 10 (1980), 241–3; A. C. Littlejohn, *Essays in Accounting* (Illinois, 1966), 83.
[4] R. P. Brief, 'Depreciation Theory in Historical Perspective', *The Accountant*, 163 (1970), 737–9.

community, in some cases they were making a decent profit, but it was not advisable to let their customers know this'.[1] He also explained that any report issued which referred to the company's purchase of a railway property for £60,000 and its subsequent sale for nearly five times that figure would be injurious to the company, as well as being incorrect. None the less, the proceeds of the sale referred to were placed in a 'suspense account'.[2] Indeed, the general approach of the Staveley directors was typified by the statement made by Benjamin Whitworth in 1866 when he admitted that 'it was quite true that the directors had not put the best face upon matters. They had been very liberal in their allowance for the depreciation fund and the insurance fund and they had rather tried to make the balance sheet look unfavourable rather than the contrary'[3] in order to avoid adverse local publicity. Even at Staveley a systematic depreciation policy was still not in force in 1890, though revenues were set aside in a depreciation fund from time to time.[4] Furthermore, with the object of concealing the true position in 1874, £70,000 'disappeared' from profits.[5] At the same time, Pochin argued in favour of increasing capitalization in order to enable the company to appear to be paying lower returns on capital, a reaction prompted by the presumed effect of the company's highly prosperous circumstances upon the miners then in negotiation over wages with Charles Markham.[6]

The directors of Carlton Main were so secretive in their financial dealings that they refused permission for the royalty owner Lord Wharncliffe's auditors to review the company's books.[7] In 1887 the directors urged upon those attending the annual general meeting the importance of maintaining secrecy regarding dividend payments, for fear that public knowledge might adversely affect dealings with customers, negotiations over leases, and wage bargaining.[8] Throughout the pre-war period the company's annual reports remained confidential, and in 1910 even shareholders, then numbering about sixty, were denied information on output, costs, or assets.

Many of the companies whose accounts have survived reveal the current expenditure on capital items, or the transference to a reserve of resources for the future purchase of engines, wagons, or machinery.

---

[1] BSCEMRRC Stanton and Staveley 2034/2/13, 30 Aug. 1867.
[2] Ibid., 30 Aug. 1867.   [3] Ibid., AGM 31 Aug. 1866.
[4] Ibid., 28 Jan. 1890.   [5] Ibid., 28 Aug. 1874.
[6] Ibid., 28 Apr. 1873.   [7] SCL MD 4080–9, 30 Dec. 1890.
[8] Ibid., AGM 1887.

From its formation as a limited company in 1883, when Emerson Bain-bridge and the Knowles family acquired Griff Colliery, for several years the profits of the old colliery were applied to pay interest on the capital raised to develop a new pit.[1] Undisclosed charges against revenue made before striking the profit balance actually increased at the coal-producing Shelton Bar Iron Company after 1900, a period of financial stringency when improvements, extensions, and new work occurred. This was despite the report of an external special audit carried out in 1892, when the company's balance sheet was criticized as an inaccurate presentation of its 'pecuniary position'. Such practices, differing in detail but similar in principle, indicate the limitations of profit measure-ment before 1914, and the need to regard any figures, especially of net but even of gross profit, as less than completely reliable.[2]

Profit measures which failed to incorporate a proper distinction between capital and revenue expenditure rendered them of especially doubtful validity as an indicator of a company's performance, for capital expenditure and reported profit were represented as alternatives.[3] Colliery accounts, however, make it clear that the profit figures revealed annually were viewed primarily as a measure of resources available for distribution, while separate costing data formed the basis for managerial decisions directly affecting the mines. Best practice in the larger collieries was the maintenance of up-to-date itemized input-costs per ton—pit by pit, and often seam by seam. Thus, while output costing was regarded as the key to profitability, for the most part leaving prices to be determined by market forces, the method of profit measurement had the effect of ensuring a conservative policy of expansion with existing resources, freedom from reliance on external finance, and the perpetua-tion of ownership and control.[4]

The risks of coalmining investment throughout the nineteenth century are abundantly illustrated in the history of colliery enterprise. In 1829 Buddle had remarked that no stronger proof of great risk could be adduced than that insurance companies would not insure colliery enterprise (which continued to be the case nearly fifty years later).[5] When Liddell and Smith reported on the mineral enterprise on the

---

[1] WaRO Griff CR 1169/10 Oct. 1893.

[2] J. R. Edwards, 'British Capital Accounting Practices and Business Finance 1852–1919: An Exemplification', *Accounting and Business Research*, 10 (1980), 245, 252–3.

[3] Edwards and Baber 1979, 142.

[4] Ibid., 142–8.

[5] Quoted in J. B. Simpson 1900; LCA 1708/12 'West Yorkshire Coalfield', 23.

Dudley Estate in the 1840s the remark was made that 'it is generally accepted that money in trade will pay at least 10 per cent',[1] implying that this was a reasonable yardstick with which to compare the profitability of coalmining investment. In 1857 T. John Taylor, the Northumberland mining engineer, remarked upon the increasing financial risk attaching to coalmining as a consequence of the deeper and larger sinkings. Seaton Delaval Colliery, which cost £200,000 to sink, produced no dividend at all for the first eighteen years, and it was twenty years before the Monkwearmouth winning was completed.[2] Reviewing the record of losses in the industry, in 1881 another observer remarked upon the great prizes to be gained in the trade: 'Such prizes are necessarily rare and fall to the lot of a few but . . . men are sanguine enough to suppose that they will be the favourites of fortune . . . until they find that mortality and misfortune are a heritage common to all'.[3]

Bankruptcy rates among mining firms are unknown because the data necessary for calculation do not exist, except in Scotland. Analysis of the Scottish data for the period 1850 to 1879, however, indicates coalmining to have suffered a high failure rate in comparison with all manufacturing industries. The figures also suggest that not until the late 1870s did depressions significantly affect the frequency of bankruptcies.[4] High risk and high rewards for the successful continued to be the conventional description of the history of investment in the industry, and was echoed by H. F. Bulman in 1910 in a special article printed in the *Colliery Guardian*: 'It is only the chance of making large profits that attracts investors and if large profits are not forthcoming there will be increasing difficulty in getting the capital needed for colliery undertakings'.[5] In *The Economics of Coal Mining*, published in 1928, Robert Dron remarked that past history showed that capital would only be attracted to coalmining ventures when there was a prospect of at least double the rate of interest on government securities.[6] Sir Josiah Stamp, referring to the pre-war industry, considered a return below 9 per cent was 'extraordinarily low in relation to the risks involved',[7] an opinion disputed by some contemporary observers, and later by others.[8]

[1] Quoted in Raybould thesis, 442.

[2] M. Littlewood, 'The Risks and Losses of Coalmining', *British Society of Mining Students*, V (1881), 176.   [3] Ibid.

[4] M. S. Moss and J. R. Hume, 'Business Failure in Scotland, 1839–1913: A Research Note', *Business History*, XXV (1983), 7–9.   [5] CG 19 May 1910, 961.

[6] Dron 1928, 29.

[7] *Sankey Commission*, I, QQ 780–0.

[8] Richardson and Wallbank 1911; A. J. Taylor 1961, 65; Gregory 1968, 180–1.

Differences between the levels of profitability at the peaks, in 1872–3, 1890–2, and 1900–1, and those during the intervening years was very marked, and colliery enterprises formed during, or immediately following, one of these booms faced either unprofitable existence or a lengthy struggle for survival. The Skegby Colliery Company in Nottinghamshire is an example of the first, for after the conversion from a partnership in 1873 to sink the Sutton Colliery there followed twenty years of financial failure and largely unsuccessful, though ruthless, economies, which earned for Sutton the nickname of the 'bread and herring pit'.[1] The origins of the eventually successful Carlton Main Company near Barnsley stemmed initially from its foundation in 1872, coming into production only during the slump of the late 1870s. The costs of raising capital on 10 per cent preference shares, loans, and overdraft to complete the development represented a huge financial burden, and not until sustained profitability beginning in the mid-1880s was the company's survival assured.[2] The strength of the boom in the early 1870s took even George Elliot by surprise, so large were the profits at that time. He told a Select Committee in 1873 that although he possessed widespread experience of other businesses 'the coal trade was certainly the least lucrative', describing current profit levels as 'unnatural'.[3]

Inadequate data, differing contemporary definitions, and ambiguity in evidence, notably in the references to interest and depreciation, render the reconstruction of the levels of profit and rates of return extremely difficult, especially before the 1880s. Before attempting to construct a company profit series, however, we must consider the existing series and estimates available to historians.

Estimates of the actual rates of returns on capital in the North-east before 1857 made by Buddle and T. J. Taylor suggested that, after making allowances for interest and the redemption of capital, mining profits amounted to less than 4 or 5 per cent, or somewhere between 4 and 5 per cent, on the capital embarked in enterprise. J. Whitworth Pease regarded 5 per cent as the maximum average 'interest' in the North-east during the twenty years preceding 1867 or 1868.[4] That was the period, of course, which saw the sequel to the collapse of the vend and the growing effects upon coalowners in the North-east of

---

[1] A. R. Griffin 1971, 162, 178 fn. 3.
[2] SCL Carlton Main MD 4080–9 MB, 27 Feb. 1873, 2 May 1873, 9 Dec. 1873, 6 Apr. 1874, 12 June 1894, 26 Aug. 1874, 6 Jan. 1875, 5 May 1875, 5 Sept. 1877, 2 Jan. 1878, 6 Dec. 1878, 6 Sept. 1878, 23 Dec. 1878.
[3] *Dearness and Scarcity* 1873, X, QQ 7536–9.
[4] Simpson 1900, 23.

investment in inland coalfields in the Midlands and Yorkshire, which accompanied the spread of railways. William Armstrong drew attention to the process of competition which, especially after the short-lived boom ending in 1854, had damaging effects on profitability in the North-east, followed by a period of deterioration in the early 1860s exacerbated by depression in the iron trade, war in America, and the disturbed state of continental markets.[1] Between the boom of the early 1870s and that of the early 1890s figures of not more than 3 or 4 per cent were quoted as the average yield on capital invested.[2]

Two series of annual profits may be obtained for the late nineteenth century. The first is based on Stamp's attempt to produce annual esti-mates of aggregate profits derived by grossing up from a sample of actual colliery profits. This was reported in the *Economist* beginning in 1890,[3] though as there is no indication of the number of observations on which his calculations were based his series remains suspect. The other series is that presented by Thomas Richardson, MP and John A. Walbank, the latter an accountant, who together produced a pamphlet designed to advance the argument in favour of a minimum wage, and to consider the 'adequacy' of colliery profits to sustain such a wage at reasonable levels. Their sample included the profit and loss accounts of sixty-five public companies for all, or part, of the period between 1898 and 1910. Stressing that both successful and unsuccessful firms which together produced approximately one-third of total coal output formed the sample, and that the profit figures themselves were probably under-estimates, the authors concluded that the average 'Total Profit' as a per-centage of 'Total Capital' (Ordinary, Preference, and Debenture) was 11.8 per cent per annum. They did acknowledge, however, the question-able reliability of capital defined in this manner, for it differed in many cases from current valuation and in some instances may have been dis-torted by over-valued assets, the result of 'watering'. The authors defended their exclusion of depreciation from their calculations of rates of return by pointing to the absence of depreciation allowed for the wear, tear, and replacement of miners.[4] Setting aside the moral impli-cations of the normal use of depreciation as an accounting concept, Wallbank and Richardson's approach is clearly unhelpful for the pur-pose of comparisons with alternative investments. The relatively high

[1] NuRO Armstrong 725/B15/567 Report to Directors of Hartlepool Railway and Harbour Company.   [2] *CG* 17 Feb. 1891, 275.
[3] J. C. Stamp, 'The Effect of Trade Fluctuations upon Profits', *JRSS*, LXXXI (1918), 574–8.
[4] Richardson and Wallbank 1911, 14–15, 30–2.

levels of profitability implied in their publications echoed remarks
uttered by the Chancellor of the Exchequer in 1901, provoking a sharp
rejoinder in *The Times* from James Joicey, who, in defence, referred to
the Board of Trade estimates based on wage costs and revenues between
1886 and 1900; these implied a return of barely 6 per cent before
depreciation.[1]

We have attempted to compensate for the weaknesses of the figures
employed in contemporary polemics by presenting three different
measures of profitability obtained from other contemporary sources.
The first is the profit per ton of coal raised; the second is a sample of
company profits; the third is a series of estimated average aggregate
profits from coalmining, based on income tax returns. As the data inputs
for each of the three series utilize different sources, a comparison is of
interest in our search for valid generalizations on the level and movement of profitability.

The profit per ton measure was widely employed by colliery owners
and managers as an indicator of performance over time. Indeed, in those
coal and iron companies whose accounts did not distinguish between
coal and iron assets, profit per ton normally calculated on the basis of
differences between pithead prices and working costs was the only yardstick available. As a measure of profit margins at the colliery level the
regular recording of gross profit per ton has produced series which for
some collieries have survived over relatively long periods and are presented in Figure 6.9.

There are several reasons, however, why profit-per-ton figures may
be employed as little more than a rough guide to the level and
chronology of profitability, precluding confident generalizations relating to inter-colliery profitability. Because the sample is so small before
1870 (and changes radically in composition) a mean would be unjustified
as an indication of trends. The overall impression presented by Figure
6.9 is that margins of gross profit per ton varied between 6*d*. and 2*s*. for
much of the 1840s, falling in the late 1840s and early 1850s to around 1*s*.,
and rising in the mid-1850s to return to previous levels by the end of the
decade. The mean gross profit per ton hovered around 1*s*. 6*d*., until the
spectacular jump that occurred in 1872–4 revealed in Figure 6.10. Beginning in 1876, the level remained close to 6*d*. until 1889, rising to a peak of
2*s*. 7*d*. in 1890. After six years between 1892 and 1898, when margins fell
back below 1*s*., higher levels obtained, the peak in 1900 carrying profit

[1] *The Times* 22 May 1901; Board of Trade, *Wages, other Costs, and Profits*, 1903, LXIV, 783.

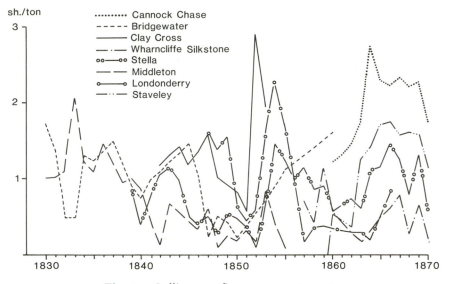

Fig. 6.9. Colliery profits per ton, 1830–1870

per ton to 3s. 7d. Thereafter, except for very low levels of 7d. and 8d. per ton in 1909–11, the post-1900 average figure remained appreciably above 1s. per ton. Losses among our sample were few throughout the period, and from the 1870s only Clay Cross, Cannock Chase, and Wigan Coal and Iron recorded profit-per-ton levels noticeably below those of others in our company sample. Among the remainder, no single company consistently out-performed others in this respect. In the 1870s and 1880s Staveley, Bell Brothers, and Ashington secured high profit per ton, and these were joined by Briggs and the Fife Coal Company in the 1890s; by 1900 the Londonderry Collieries and Fife had taken the lead, though Powell Duffryn's figures were superior to those of Fife during the years immediately preceding World War I. The pattern suggests a connection between the quality of coal produced for sale, particularly steam coal for export, yielding relatively high levels of profit per ton, though there were important exceptions. The ironmaking firms of Bell Brothers and Staveley continued to rank high in this respect throughout the period; on the other hand, except during the boom of 1900–1, the steam-coal producing Main Colliery Company did not figure among the best performers. Taking the sample as a whole, there does appear to have been a relatively close convergence in the direction and levels of profit per ton in the period following the boom of the 1870s.

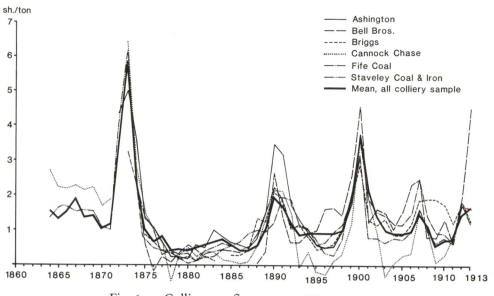

sh./ton

——— Ashington
—— Bell Bros.
----- Briggs
·········· Cannock Chase
—·— Fife Coal
—··— Staveley Coal & Iron
——— Mean, all colliery sample

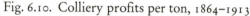

Fig. 6.10. Colliery profits per ton, 1864–1913

Sources for Figures 6.9 and 6.10

Ashington Coal Co, NuRO/NCB/As5, and ZMD/4/1–7.
Bell Brothers, BSNRRC 04793, Comparative Balances, Profit and Loss Accounts 1873–1913.
Bridgewater Collieries, F. C. Mather, *After the Canal Duke* (Oxford, 1970) appendix A and C.
Briggs Son and Co, LCA 1708/13 Minute Books and Reports of Directors 1866–1914.
Butterley Iron and Coal Co, DeRO 503/B/85, Detailed Schedule; 503/B Profit and Loss.
Cannock Chase Colliery Co, BUL, Annual Balance Sheets, 1860–1913.
Carlton Main Coal Co SCL, MD 4080–9, Annual Balance Sheets, Directors' Minutes I and II.
Clay Cross Coal and Iron Co, Company archives, Balance sheets.
Darfield Main (see Mitchell Main).
Dowlais, Walters 1977, Table 42.
East Cannock Colliery Co, StRO D/429/m/B Minute Book of General Meetings 1871–1914.
Fife Coal Co, ScRO CB3/131/7; Dissolved Companies Files; BT/2826/3–5.
Griff Colliery Co, WaRO CR 1169/22 Managers' Annual Reports 1893–1913.
Lochgelly, ScRO CB2/115–123; 202, 214–16, 218, 249, 318; NLS M 12306.
Londonderry Collieries, DuRO LO/B/318 Daglish's Report; D/LO/B 320 (231); B 452 (1); D/LO/104(4); D/LO/B Additional Ledger 'A', Revenue and Private.
Main Colliery Co, GlaRO printed balance sheets 1890–1914.
Middleton Colliery, LCA, MC 36–8, ledgers 1830–56.
Mitchell Main Colliery Co, SCL NCB 601 and 608A.
Newbattle Colliery, ScRO GD 40/94–11, Lothian Ms.
New Hucknall Colliery Co, NoRO NCB 1/40–1, Balance Sheets.
Nixon Taylor and Cory, Walters 1977, Table 42.
Oakthorpe Colliery, C. P. Griffin, thesis, p. 277.
Powell Duffryn Coal Co, Company archives, Papers and Accounts, Minute Books 1864–1913 and estimated output.
Radstock Colliery, SoRO DD/WG/BOX 49.
Staveley Coal and Iron Co, BSCEMRRC 2034/2/32–3 and 303, detailed balance sheets.
Stella Coal Co, DuRO NCBI/SC/466(12), NCBI/SC/527(3).
Walbottle Colliery, NuRO/599 Colliery accounts.
Wharncliffe Silkstone Coal Co, SCL NCB 1280/1429–1.
Wigan Coal and Iron Co, LaRO DDX/127/40–74 and WiRO D/D Hai Box 14 Directors' Reports.
Woolley Collieries, John Goodchild MS, Box 2.

Whereas many managers regarded profit per ton as an indicator of performance, for proprietors the rate of return on capital invested was the ultimate test. The data required to calculate a rate of return on assets are available for only a few of those firms for which profit-per-ton data have been assembled, though information has been found for some other companies. While we are able to make only a very imperfect comparison of these two measures for a mere handful of companies, therefore, nevertheless an examination of financial returns for nineteen firms does provide a useful indicator of profitability related to assets in large to medium-sized companies (see Table 6.9 below). As in the calculating of profits per ton, attempts have been made to ensure that profits and assets data are on a comparable basis, but the peculiar nature of nineteenth-century accounting has meant that difficulties remain.

With two minor exceptions (Wharncliffe Silkstone and Clay Cross), all profit data are net, after deduction from gross profits of rates, taxes, and appropriations to meet depreciation for sinking and for other capital funds, though the precise categories differed from company to company and in any case are rarely fully traceable from the accounts themselves. To this extent our company data may be considered to be as comparable as the state of contemporary accounting practices will allow. In addition to the problem of definition is that which is presented by the variety in the type of collieries for which data have survived over lengthy periods. Of the nineteen firms, seven are iron and coal companies, though two of them (Lochgelly and Wigan) had a relatively small proportion of their assets committed to non-coal production (none at Lochgelly by the 1890s); while the data for Clay Cross refer exclusively to gross coal profits as a percentage of assets in coal. However, four of the companies, Bolckow Vaughan, Butterley, Sheepbridge, and Staveley, had substantial assets in, and therefore profits from, iron and steel production. There is some evidence, from Bolckow Vaughan, Butterley, and Sheepbridge, that these integrated firms may have been less profitable, especially towards the end of our period when profits from coalmines were advancing over the long term, though the companies with the worst record were the Hamstead and Walsall Wood Colliery Companies. The inclusion of profit data from iron and coal firms may be regarded as both beneficial and advantageous: beneficial in the sense that since integrated firms played an important part in the mining industry it is advisable to incorporate data on their profitability; disadvantageous only in the narrower sense that profits from items other than coal are necessarily included in the sample.

Yet this apparent problem presented by profits accruing from items other than coal (and which also complicates our treatment of assets) applies, in varying measures, to most other firms in our sample. Some earned profits from processing coal, especially as coke manufacturers, or from transporting coal, or from such commonly associated colliery activities as brickmaking, farming, and house-building for rent, each featuring among colliery assets and, according to our limited evidence, in most cases earning low rates of return. As late as the 1890s Griff's colliery manager risked prosecution by vastly over-charging for the stores sold to the miners, which the Mines Inspector described as having produced 'an unholy profit' to the company, and compelled a change in policy (which none the less the manager envisaged as enabling the company to make a moderate profit from this source).[1] Among those firms in our sample which earned income from non-coalmining investments, Briggs became the outstanding example, for 40 per cent of that company's assets were in that form—mostly in securities. Typically, other companies held a few per cent of assets related to brickmaking, wagons, houses, farm stock, or land. Such items earned varying profit rates, a more detailed breakdown of New Hucknall's accounts revealing a consistently lower return on colliery assets compared with coal-only profits as a percentage of mining assets.

Whether the inclusion of profits from these activities is to be considered a drawback depends upon the object of our exercise. The sample affords an imperfect guide to profits from coalmining, but a better guide to the profitability of *companies* producing coal. The existence of external investment does, however, colour any comparison of inter-firm profitability. Those possessing higher levels of external investment unrelated to colliery enterprise (but excluding iron and steel) were better placed to sustain prolonged periods of poor trade, while those with lower levels appear to have secured maximum returns during upswings, especially in 1889–91, 1899–1901, and 1912–13.

Average returns on assets are presented in Table 6.7. The methods by which these have been calculated are explained in Appendix 6.2, where it is concluded that as the direction of error in contemporary accounting was one of under- rather than over-valuation, the figures should be regarded as overestimates of the true rate.

The average net rate of return on the assets of all companies in the sample over the period 1865 to 1913 was 8.2 per cent. Of the five

[1] WaRO Griff CR 1169/22, 10 Oct. 1893.

Table 6.7. *Average return on companies' coalmining assets, 1860-1913*

	1860–4	1865–9	1870–4	1875–9	1880–4	1885–9	1890–4	1895–9	1900–4	1905–9	1910–13
Clifton and Kearsley					2.4	3.8	10.5	6.7	18.7	8.1	2.0
Cannock Chase	14.4	17.9	23.1	4.3		3.0	9.1	3.5	11.3	4.2	
Bolckow Vaughan		6.6	9.9[a]	4.0	3.6	2.8	2.3	5.5	5.5	7.5	6.8
Briggs and Co.		13.7	14.9	3.6	1.1	5.4	11.3	9.6	12.0	9.1	11.0
Wigan Coal and Iron			8.8	1.9	1.7	2.2[b]	5.4	8.8		5.2[c]	5.4
Main							6.5			6.4	3.3
Staveley		11.2	15.7	5.3	5.0	6.3	9.0	10.7	19.8	11.5	12.1
Powell Duffryn							5.0	2.7	12.7	10.9	10.5
Wharncliffe Silkstone	3.3	9.3	22.0[d]				3.0	1.9	10.4		5.3
Carlton Main					2.3	10.0	23.6	13.6	10.5	4.3	5.9
Fife									11.6	5.3	11.3
Lochgelly					−1.4	0.7	8.9			6.9[e]	10.2
Newstead					7.2	3.7	13.1	6.0	19.2	10.4	9.8
Average		11.0	15.1	3.9	2.9	4.4	8.9	6.8	13.4	7.5	7.7

[a] 1870, 1872–4. [b] 1885–9, excluding 1886. [c] 1907–9. [d] 1870–2. [e] 1906–9.

Sources: As for Figure 6.9.

companies for which more than 10 per cent is recorded under-capitalization is partly responsible, in the case of both Mitchell Main (15.3 per cent) and East Cannock (10.3 per cent, 1882–1913), while Fife's figure of 11.1 per cent refers only to 1908–1913. Carlton Main's 10.5 per cent return refers to 1880–1913 and excludes the period of zero return on assets since the formation of the company in 1873, the effect of which would be to reduce the figure to 8.5 per cent. Only in the case of New Hucknall does there appear to have been a relatively unambiguous 'high' rate of return of 10.5 per cent between 1879 and 1913. Of the remaining companies, in only two were rates of return below 5 per cent recorded, 1.9 per cent for Hamstead and 4.6 per cent for Walsall Wood; Bolckow Vaughan's figure was 4.8 per cent for the period 1879–1913 compared with 5.3 per cent between 1865 and 1913. In the case of Cannock Chase, Briggs, Staveley, Wigan Coal and Iron, and Sheepbridge the inclusion of figures before 1879 has the effect of raising the rates of return; subtantially for Cannock Chase, from 5.7 per cent for 1879–1911 to 9.3 per cent in 1860–1911; from 8.4 per cent at Staveley in 1879–1913 to 9.1 per cent in 1863–1913; and for others by very small amounts.

Within the limitations of the data a general conclusion seems possible that net rates of return on the assets of large and medium-sized firms fell below 10 per cent over the long term, even when the boom of the early 1870s is included in the series; that in the short term spectacular levels were achieved, usually for fewer than three years, and that beginning in 1900 levels were higher than in preceding decades. Moreover, it appears that where comparisons are possible the differential profitability of firms was not related to *margins* of gross profit on coal, which seem to have been remarkably similar from one colliery to another over the long term.

Whereas our company data provides an indication of the profitability of coal-producing companies, it is possible to construct estimates of all coalmining profits in the UK by utilizing the tax assessments published annually by the Commissioners of Inland Revenue beginning in 1855. There are difficulties in the form these data take: presentation was in the form of five-year moving-averages; the figures refer to *all* mines, rather than to collieries only;[1] until 1908/9 to 1910/11 the figures are of national aggregates; the tax assessments are based on royalties as well as profits; and all losses are counted as zero profits, which particularly in years of bad trade tends to overstate colliery profits in total. While the

[1] And therefore excludes profits from iron production in iron and coal producing firms.

latter defect has not proved possible to remedy, by methods described in Appendix 6.3 estimates for coalmining profits (necessarily omitting depreciation and excluding losses) are presented in Table 6.8. The early figures are especially suspect, a detailed explanation for which is given in Appendix 6.3, and even though an attempt has been made to improve on previous profit estimates, direct comparisons with the figures from our company sample is not possible for two reasons; the exclusion of losses in the tax data and the omission of depreciation.

The assessment-based estimates provide a breakdown by counties for five-year periods centred on 1908/9, 1909/10, and 1910/11, and for Scotland data referring to preceding periods are available. The latter show rates of profits to have been significantly below those realized in England and Wales, and that Scottish royalties were slightly higher than those south of the border. The figures suggest that few Scottish companies can have made profits from coalmining in the late 1870s and early 1880s. The detailed data for 1908–11 reveal very high profit rates in South Wales, in Fife, Lanarkshire, Yorkshire, and Warwickshire, and low rates in Nottinghamshire, Derbyshire, and Monmouthshire. These refer to counties between which rates of expansion differed, and where the age of coalfields varied. Conclusions based on these data, therefore, are problematical.

If we accept the validity, with some reservations, of the assessment-based estimates of coalmining profits, it becomes possible to calculate a rate of return on historic capital; first, converting the weighted sinking-cost index into a five-year moving average; second, by dividing the total income-tax profits by the cost index to produce profits at constant prices; third, by calculating annual historic capital figures by interpolation from the peak-year figures; and finally expressing profits as a percentage of capital. The result is a gross annual rate of return on capital investment in the form of a five-year moving average. There are several reasons why the resulting percentages may be regarded as no more than a crude indicator of mining profitability before depreciation over the long term, for the income-tax profit figures are unreliable in the early years and overstate profits in the slumps; they do not give peak values because they are five-year averages. The weighted index introduces another fairly crude element in our formulae, and historic-cost capital can be interpolated only on a straight-line basis.

Juxtaposition of both the company-based and the assessment-based series in graph form in Figure 6.11 reveals a marked similarity from the 1870s boom until 1913, though it is important to bear in mind the

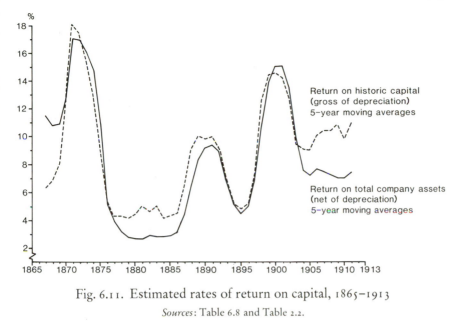

Fig. 6.11. Estimated rates of return on capital, 1865–1913

Sources: Table 6.8 and Table 2.2.

important differences in the components of each measurement, and in particular that the assessment-based figures are before depreciation. If we regard the tax assessment-based estimates in this way and our company data are indicative of the experience of the large and medium-sized firms, only in the 1860s does there appear to be a difference in the movement of profits per ton. For whereas the assessment figures show a very modest rise during the early 1860s the profit-per-ton data indicate a sharp increase which, beginning in the early 1860s, continued until 1867–8, faltered, and rose to unprecedented heights in 1872 and 1873. Thereafter, levels of profit per ton moved together.

Moreover, setting aside those series which we know to be gross-profit figures, there is striking similarity, peaks excepted, between inter-colliery profit-per-ton levels and movements from the 1870s boom, when sufficient series can be assembled to justify limited generalization. The assessment-based profit data (which excluded losses and therefore overstated even gross profits during the slumps) reveal maximum estimates of coalmining profitability below 6 per cent between 1854 and 1867, rising to almost 20 per cent at the peak of the coal famine, returning to 4 or 5 per cent between 1876 and 1886. During the boom of the 1890s the figure was 10 per cent, 5 per cent in the trough of the mid-1890s, from which it rose to more than 14 per cent in the early 1900s.

Table 6.8. *Estimated aggregate coalmining profits, 1848-1913*

5 years centred on	'Profits' all mines (£ m.)	'Profits' coal only (£ m.)	Net royalty (d.)	Detrended output (m. tons)	Total royalties (£ m.)	Net coal profits (£ m.)	Coal profit (d.)	If 20% under-recording	
								£ m.	d.
1848/9	2.37	1.66	5.14	57.6	1.23	0.43	1.80	0.76	3.17
1949/50	2.34	1.64	5.14	60.3	1.29	0.35	1.39	0.68	2.69
1850/1	2.81	2.02	5.16	62.9	1.35	0.67	2.57	1.07	4.10
1851/2	2.89	2.08	5.16	65.4	1.41	0.67	2.45	1.09	3.98
1852/3	2.97	2.15	5.18	68.0	1.47	0.68	2.40	1.11	3.91
1853/4	3.01	2.16	5.18	70.4	1.52	0.64	2.18	1.07	3.65
1854/5	3.82	2.87	5.21	72.8	1.58	1.29	4.25		
1855/6	3.89	2.92	5.21	75.4	1.64	1.28	4.08		
1856/7	4.02	3.02	5.23	77.8	1.70	1.32	4.08		
1857/8	4.20	3.15	5.23	80.2	1.75	1.40	4.20		
1858/9	4.44	3.33	5.26	82.7	1.81	1.52	4.42		
1859/60	4.52	3.39	5.26	85.2	1.87	1.52	4.27		
1860/1	4.57	3.45	5.28	87.7	1.93	1.52	4.15		
1861/2	4.83	3.68	5.28	90.3	1.99	1.69	4.49		
1862/3	5.08	3.89	5.30	92.8	2.05	1.84	4.75		
1863/4	5.61	4.38	5.30	95.2	2.10	2.28	5.74		
1864/5	5.74	4.53	5.33	97.9	2.17	2.36	5.78		
1865/6	5.48	4.37	5.33	100.9	2.24	2.13	5.06		
1866/7	5.54	4.46	5.35	104.0	2.32	2.14	4.94		
1867/8	5.89	4.76	5.38	107.2	2.40	2.36	5.28		

Year							
1868/9	6.34	5.08	5.38	110.5	2.48	2.50	5.54
1869/70	7.28	5.69	5.40	113.4	2.55	3.14	6.65
1870/1	10.55	8.31	5.40	116.6	2.62	5.69	11.71
1871/2	14.11	11.53	5.52	119.5	2.75	8.78	17.64
1872/3	14.61	12.08	5.76	122.1	2.93	9.15	17.98
1873/4	14.09	11.72	6.0	124.5	3.11	8.61	16.61
1874/5	12.90	10.85	6.0	126.8	3.17	7.68	14.54
1875/6	10.09	8.50	6.0	130.1	3.25	5.25	9.70
1876/7	7.50	6.21	5.98	133.7	3.33	2.88	5.16
1877/8	6.67	5.50	5.95	136.9	3.40	2.10	3.67
1878/9	6.73	5.52	5.93	140.4	3.47	2.05	3.50
1879/80	6.73	5.51	5.90	143.4	3.53	1.98	3.31
1880/1	7.06	5.79	5.88	146.3	3.58	2.21	3.62
1881/2	7.60	6.27	5.86	148.5	3.62	2.65	4.27
1882/3	7.52	6.23	5.83	151.1	3.67	2.56	4.06
1883/4	7.49	6.51	5.81	154.3	3.73	2.78	4.32
1884/5	7.15	6.13	5.76	158.3	3.80	2.33	3.53
1885/6	7.29	6.25	5.76	162.7	3.90	2.35	3.46
1886/7	7.45	6.41	5.74	166.2	3.97	2.44	3.53
1887/8	8.81	7.66	5.74	169.1	4.04	3.62	5.14
1888/9	10.87	9.63	5.71	171.9	4.09	5.54	7.73
1889/90	12.05	10.80	5.71	174.1	4.14	6.66	9.19
1890/1	12.32	11.12	5.69	176.7	4.19	6.93	9.41
1891/2	12.68	11.50	5.69	180.0	4.27	7.23	9.65
1892/3	12.28	11.16	5.66	184.0	4.43	6.82	8.90
1893/4	10.51	9.56	5.66	188.5	4.45	5.11	6.50
1894/5	9.08	8.26	5.64	193.0	4.54	3.72	4.61

Table 6.8. (cont.)

5 years centred on	'Profits' all mines (£ m.)	'Profits' coal only (£ m.)	Net royalty (d.)	Detrended output (m. tons)	Total royalties (£ m.)	Net coal profits (£ m.)	Coal profit (d.)	If 20% under-recording (£ m.) (d.)
1895/6	8.90	8.09	5.64	197.4	4.63	3.46	4.20	
1896/7	9.49	8.65	5.62	200.8	4.70	3.95	4.73	
1897/8	12.03	10.98	5.62	204.5	4.79	6.19	7.27	
1898/9	17.64	16.19	5.59	208.6	4.86	11.33	13.03	
1899/1900	20.26	18.70	5.59	212.7	4.96	13.74	15.50	
1900/1	21.19	19.62	5.57	217.0	5.03	14.59	16.13	
1901/2	21.24	19.70	5.57	222.6	5.16	14.54	15.67	
1902/3	20.00	18.60	5.54	229.2	5.29	13.31	13.94	
1903/4	16.37	15.17	5.54	234.6	5.42	9.75	9.98	
1904/5	16.40	15.15	5.52	239.5	5.51	9.64	9.67	
1905/6	16.64	15.38	5.52	243.5	5.60	9.78	0.65	
1906/7	18.46	17.07	5.52	247.8	5.70	11.37	11.02	
1907/8	19.34	17.90	5.52	253.1	5.82	12.08	11.45	
1908/9	19.68	18.35	5.52	258.6	5.95	12.40	11.52	
1909/10	20.03	19.07	5.52	264.7	6.09	12.98	11.76	
1910/11	19.61	18.23	5.52	270.1	6.21	12.02	10.68	
1911/12	21.52	19.96	5.52	273.1	6.28	13.68	12.02	

Sources: As for Table 1.1; Sir Josiah Stamp 1916, 220–1; 'The Effects of Fluctuations of Trade on Profits', *JRSS* LXXXI (1918), 563–600; *RC Mining Royalties* 1893, XLI,360–1; *Sankey Commission* 1919, XIII, Appendix 5; *Colliery Yearbook* 1927, 665. See also Appendix 6.3(c).

Between 1903 and 1911 average profitability was stable at 9 or 10 per cent. Over the period 1865 to 1911 the average rate of return on historic capital was 8.6 per cent per annum.

Similarly, the 1865 to 1913 annual average estimate of 8.2 per cent as the rate of return on company assets contains elements of exaggeration because of the tendency for assets to be under-valued. The two measures are not comparable as they stand, because while the company data contains some element of depreciation the tax data excludes any such allowance, which is why the rate of profit requires adjusting to produce a figure gross of depreciation. A full 4 or 5 per cent per annum depreciation, as suggested by our estimate of the true rate of depreciation,[1] is likely to be too large an increment, because many companies did allow for depreciataion at some level, though unsystematically and irregularly. A plausible, if rough, estimate of 11 or 12 per cent gross return on company assets would be an upper estimate because of the under-valued asset data on which it is based, but a more reasonable figure might be 10 or 11 per cent per annum. From the 1870s the company data reveal similar trends and orders of magnitude identifiable in the tax-based figures, except for the peak in that decade, which reached 17 per cent; the trough from the late 1870s to the mid-1880s, when returns fell to only 2 per cent, was followed by a period after 1903 when the rate stabilized at 7 per cent.

Our two measures of returns, therefore, produce estimates over the long term, beginning in 1865, of 8.6 per cent (or less) for profits on historical capital, and 10 or 11 per cent for profits as a percentage of company assets, both gross (or estimated gross) of depreciation. It is quite possible, of course, for the first measure to be disregarded on the grounds that our data on historic capital are quite notional and theoretical. None the less, the results do seem to be plausible when compared with the company data, which, though limited in range and susceptible to distortion by exceptionally high or low values in individual companies' profit data, are related to actual company assets and may claim to be representative of the experience of some larger firms. That these

[1] This estimate is based on the depreciation practices of Powell Duffryn, Lochgelly, Clifton and Kearsley, Walsall Wood, the Staveley and Sheepbridge and other companies with whom H. D. Pochin was connected, New Hucknall, Shelton Bar Ironworks (also producing coal). The source for Shelton Bar Ironworks is J. R. Edwards, 'British Capital Accounting Practices and Business Finance 1852–1919: An Exemplification', *Accounting and Business Research*, 10 (1980), 241–5. For the remainder the sources are those listed in Table 0.0. Irregularity in the provision for depreciation was the normal practice at Staveley, Sheepbridge, and other related companies, Carlton Main and the Main Colliery Company.

data should show a higher rate than that on historic capital as a whole was predictable, for greater than average size conferred some profit advantage, perhaps by attracting high calibre managers, while the sheer survival of the companies over a long period implies above-average profitability; it seems likely too, that the more successful companies were those who tended to preserve data. Over the long term, therefore, the average annual gross return on capital in coalmining was probably around 8 or 9 per cent, though probably two or three percentage points higher for larger companies. Net of depreciation the figures are roughly 8.7 per cent—or less if redemption is allowed for—in the case of larger companies, and on a similar basis 2 or 3 per cent below this for all coalmines. A long-term average, however, conceals the characteristic pattern of very high returns in a series of price and profit explosions lasting for no longer than two or three years, with low returns during the intervening periods. When the series are adjusted for price changes to show the real value of profits the measures conform closely, the greater amplitude of fluctuation revealed in the company series and the break in trend levels around 1900 remaining as the two major features.

Both sets of figures demonstrate that except for the few boom years, and even after 1900, the average returns were substantially less than the 10 per cent rate which contemporaries regarded as a reasonable minimum. The boom centred upon 1900 marked a break in trend, after which the rate of profit continued at levels markedly above those which obtained during all preceding decades; higher indeed than relative price levels which were also at their highest historic secular level. This might seem to be surprising in view of the industry's rising costs in this period, and underlines the strength of demand which underpinned profits.

This secular increase in the relative profitability of coal proved especially beneficial to coal-producing iron and steel companies, some of which (even from as early as the 1860s) had developed and expanded not just to achieve vertical integration to control resources and minimize costs, but also to diversify production. The assessment-based profit series enables us to establish the context for the intensification of this trend from the mid-1880s, for it is possible to compare the movement of profits per ton of coal with a similar series simply calculated for iron production. Without comparable estimates of capital–output ratios the absolute differences in profit levels are meaningless, but a comparison of the relative levels are instructive. Whereas before the mid-1880s iron profits per ton exceeded those for coal, thereafter, except at the peaks, the opposite relationship was maintained. Consequently, from the 1880s the relatively low profitability of iron and steel production stimulated further backward vertical integration and the expansion of coal production. Such a sequence of events explains why Bairds, Scotland's major iron-making firm producing perhaps a quarter of Scottish pig iron output in 1882, for a time became the largest Scottish producer of coal; by 1900 most of the profits came from coal. Reviewing Baird's experience between 1899 and 1904, Andrew K. McCosh, managing director, expressed the opinion that other Scottish iron masters had also relied for at least half their profit from coal sales.[1] There is further evidence of the relative increase in the importance of coal profits for iron producers, from companies in England and South Wales as well as Scotland: the Shotts Iron Company, Merry and Cunninghame, Coltness, the Summerlee and Mossend Company, Guest Keen and Co. and Rhymney, Wigan Coal and Iron, Staveley, Butterley, Consett, and Bolckow Vaughan.[2] To varying degrees coal became the key to improving profitability in these major coal and iron companies, and evidence from the movement of relative profitability suggested by the assessment-based series points to the late 1880s as the probable starting point for this trend.

Just as our profit data defined the general financial context in which such business decisions were made, similarly the history of the major coal and iron companies lends further support to the suggestion, prompted by our survey of company profits, that the coal-producing iron firms fared worse than the colliery companies. Even so, the redirection of effort and resources into coal production for sale was a trend which, stimulated by changing relative profitabilities in the markets for coal and iron, from the mid-1880s offered an opportunity for British iron masters to reduce the financial consequences of competition from increasingly fierce foreign competitors in markets for iron and steel.

iv. The distribution of profits and rewards to coalowners

With the caveat made above concerning the deficiencies of the income tax data, it seems that in total royalties exceeded coalowners' (gross)

---

[1] P. L. Payne, *Colvilles and the Scottish Steel Industry* (Oxford, 1979), 51.

[2] Ibid., 53–4; Chapman 1981, 75; Walters 1977, 10–11, 16–17, and generally, 49–50; A. S. Wilson thesis, Table II; and BSNRRC Consett 02250, Profit Statement; BSNRRC Bolckow Vaughan 04794, Comparative Statement; WRO D/D Hai Box 149 and LaRO Wigan Coal and Iron DDX/127/44 Expenditure and Income Accounts; *CG* 4 Jan. 1895, 17.

profits in the 1850s and 1860s, during the second half of the 1870s and 1880s, and again in the mid-1890s. The opposite occurred from the end of the 1860s until 1876, between 1888 and 1894, and again after 1896. These estimates suggest that for much of our period landed proprietors found little incentive to work, rather than to lease minerals to others, and helps to explain the continuing decline of direct involvement by landowners in the production of coal.

The disposal of profit by colliery companies differed considerably in the proportions distributed to shareholders, reflecting the diverse treatment accorded to depreciation, redemption, and expenditure for development. Some companies were committed to paying interest on debt resulting from loans or debentures, either contracted in the course of initial flotation when the original proprietors sought to realize all or part of their assets in liquid form, or resulting from the need to finance substantial capital development, though our examination of the composition of company capital suggests that this was not normally a major drain on cash flow. In attempting to discover the proportion of profits retained in the business for development we face the problem of definition, and encounter the difficulty of precisely what has been included in 'net' profit figures. For example, in 1876 Sheepbridge's shareholders were informed of 'a clear profit of £18,883 0s. 4d. after maintaining the Works in efficient repair, taking the stocks at the reduced market prices of the day, providing for all bad and doubtful debts and placing adequate sums to the Redemption and Depreciation Funds'.[1] It is rarely possible to be certain that net profits, so defined as gross profits less depreciation rates and taxes, do not already incorporate deductions for capital items made before even trading profits were calculated (but often not recorded in a company's balance sheets). We must regard the retained profit figures extracted from them as minimum values. The case of Wigan Coal and Iron illustrates the need for caution, for while superficially the balance sheets yield an average figure for retained profits of 2.5 per cent between 1864 and 1913, they also record substantial additions to capital stock in many years, which, since these were accompanied by stagnant share capital values and no capital funding occurred, must have been funded from profits. The resulting extraordinarily low figure, therefore, is entirely artificial, but the absence of adequate data from the balance sheets prevents the calculation of a more accurate one.[2]

[1] BSCEMRRC Stanton and Staveley 2034/2/14 1 July 1876.
[2] LaRO Wigan Coal and Iron, DDX/127/40–74 and WRO D/D Hai Box 147, Directors' Reports 1865–1914.

Excluding Wigan Coal and Iron, a hierarchy of thirty-one firms has been assembled for which a sustained analysis of balance sheets is possible for most of the period from the early 1870s, though several begin in the 1850s and 1860s. They include firms from all regions and range in size from Powell Duffryn, employing nearly 15,000 colliery workers in 1913, to East Cannock with fewer than 900. Those companies retaining the highest proportion of net profits were Clifton and Kearsley (57 per cent), the Fife Coal Company (50 per cent), Walsall Wood (50 per cent), New Hucknell Colliery Co. (41 per cent), Powell Duffryn (40 per cent), and the Butterley Company (38 per cent). Of these six companies, three may be categorized as large and three of medium size, the smallest of which (Walsall Wood) employed barely one thousand colliery workers. A detailed breakdown of the balance sheets of twelve coal companies in South Wales which refer to the period 1899 to 1914 similarly reveals no correlation between size and the relative proportion of gross profits retained. In all, these companies, varying in size, distributed dividends which averaged 61.5 per cent of profit, and none paid out less than 49 per cent.

We conclude that, on the basis of our admittedly limited evidence, the factors which determined the distribution of profits depended less upon size than upon the policy of directors in any company. It seems likely that public companies were under greater pressure to distribute than others. An examination of the proportion of retained profits year by year reveals a definite, if imperfect, cyclical trend, with peaks in the years when profits peaked, notably 1871-3, 1890-2, 1900-2, and 1906-7, and troughs in the worst years. This finding does not contradict an earlier observation that actual capital expenditure was undertaken in roughly equal amounts irrespective of the phase of the cycle, though it does suggest that timing in the planning of capital projects was influenced by capital accumulation in the booms.

Details of the volume of capital allocated to reserves and external, or non-colliery, investment are available for eighteen companies, although there are differences in definition and in the time-span covered. The nature of the accounts and balance sheets renders it essential to distinguish between reserves, the allocation of which is unclear but which in most cases may be treated as 'cash in the bank', and external capital investment, in which it is possible to trace the movement of reserved funds to non-colliery interests. The average of our company sample which extends for some back to the 1860s, but mostly from the 1880s, is 16 per cent allocated to reserve, depreciation funds or liquid assets, and to outside investments, though this is almost certainly an overestimate. In several companies, however, substantial sums were accumulated over the long term: Briggs and Co., Cannock Chase, and East Cannock all possessed between one-quarter and one-half of their total assets in the form of reserve and/or outside investments. A number of others, Butterley, Clifton and Kearsley, New Hucknall, Main, and Walsall Wood, possessed between 10 and 20 per cent of their assets in this form. Furthermore, the possession of assets in the form of reserves and external investment was the norm rather than the exception; of all the firms in the company sample, only Powell Duffryn and Consett have yielded no evidence, though this is scarcely proof that reserves did not exist. The investment of reserves outside the company, either in physical assets or in claims on other companies, was less common than the possession of reserves. Of the eighteen companies we have examined, fourteen held reserves of one kind or another, but only eleven invested externally, of which four—Mitchell Main, Briggs and Son, Fife Coal Company (after 1900), and the Ashington Coal Co. (again probably only in the later period)—invested sums in excess of 10 per cent of total assets outside the company.

Our discussion of the distribution of profits, particularly as this affected reserves and investments revealed among our company sample, implied a relatively high proportion of profits distributed in the form of dividends, though highest mainly after 1900, as reserves accumulated. Wallbank and Richardson analysed the profits and dividends of sixty-five firms between 1898 and 1910, a sample which included profit- and loss-making companies. Total ascertainable profits, which included transfers to reserves and debenture interest and was gross of depreciation, averaged 11.8 per cent between 1898 and 1910, while dividends on total paid-up capital was 7.8 per cent, implying two-thirds of profits distributed to shareholders.[1] Based on comparable data Walters analysed the record of a dozen companies in the South Wales Steam Coal industry between 1899 and 1914, to produce a figure of 61.5 per cent for distributed profits. The range was limited, between 73.9 per cent for United National Collieries (1903–14) and 49.3 per cent for Burnyeat (1904–14); both collieries were of similar size, and there was no correlation between the size of companies and the proportion of profits distributed.[2]

With the aid of company archives and the annual *Stock Exchange*

[1] Richardson and Wallbank 1911, 14–15, 30–2.
[2] Walters 1977, 294–5, Table 44.

Yearbooks, it is possible to assemble figures for ordinary dividends as a percentage of paid-up capital for about a dozen firms in the 1880s, nearly double that number for the 1890s, and over thirty after 1900. Except for average dividends of 10.3 per cent and 12.9 per cent in 1890 and 1891, levels between 1883 and 1899 fluctuated between 2.4 per cent and 6.7 per cent; the overall average was 5.3 per cent. In 1900 the figure was 19.7 per cent, and reached 13.4 and 13.5 per cent in 1907, 1908, and in 1913; otherwise the norm fell well below this. The overall average between 1900 and 1913 was 10.5 per cent. Year-to-year dividends tended to lag behind profits as post-peak dividends were sustained by reserves accumulated at the peak; the corollary was an amplitude in dividend fluctuation which was less than that in total profits. We have calculated average dividends from 1883 and plotted these alongside the Wallbank and Richardson series from 1898 and 1910 (Figure 6.12).

Walters has drawn attention to the failure by many proprietors in the steam-coal industry of South Wales to realize their aspirations, even including those associated with some of the most successful companies. Others produced even less impressive records; the Cardiff and Swansea Smokeless Steam Coal Company paid only one dividend in nineteen years of existence before it was sold back to the Corys as chief creditors, though this was regarded as a failure which was exceptional in character, even for colliery companies 'which must be looked upon more or less as speculations'.[1] Hoyland Silkstone Colliery, sunk early in 1874 and won in 1876 after an investment of £200,000 was never profitable and went into liquidation in 1888.[2] The Glamorgan Colliery, similarly profitless between 1892 and 1890, paid its first dividend in 1908. Even Powell Duffryn's shareholders received no dividends from its formation in 1864 until 1889, though the early 1870s boom was highly profitable. One of the most disastrous histories was that of the collieries formerly belonging to the Aberdare and Plymouth Company, which failed in 1882. The collieries were subsequently taken on by the Hankey family, who were the mortgagees and inexperienced in colliery management. After twenty-two years working, during which they became part of Hill's Plymouth Company, the continuing losses had accumulated a debit on profit and loss account amounting to almost £300,000 in 1904.[3] The record for the longest surviving unprofitable colliery was probably held by the Hamstead Colliery Company, whose chairman, Richard Chamberlain (Joseph's son) was an expert mathematician, who when he

[1] Quoted in Walters 1977, 287.
[2] CG 29 June 1888, 921.   [3] Walters 1977, 287–8.

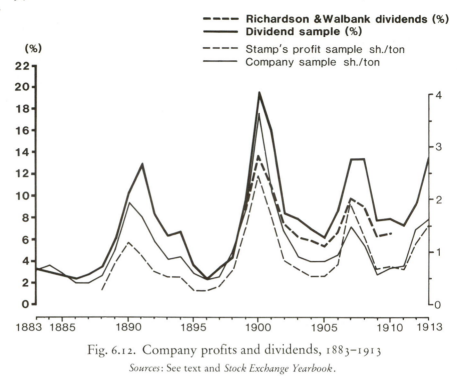

Fig. 6.12. Company profits and dividends, 1883–1913

Sources: See text and *Stock Exchange Yearbook*.

was Mayor astonished councillors with his slide-rule computations. This was a skill evidently employed to little effect in the boardroom, for between 1875 and 1908 the colliery company paid dividends barely averaging 2 per cent—actually exceeding net profit.[1]

The speculative character of the industry was generally recognized, yet Payne's analysis of the longevity of Scottish joint stock companies in the nineteenth century revealed that the average life of dissolved companies in Scottish coalmining was 20.9 years, compared with an average of 16.4; within the industrial classification only textiles, clothing, and footwear showed a comparable longevity (21.1 years).[2] The average for iron and steel companies was 14.8 years, slightly below the average for the categories mining and manufacturing. This result is in sharp contrast to the picture presented by Slaven for Western Scotland, where perhaps between 1854 and 1870 no fewer than 91 out of a total of 145 firms went out of existence, though simultaneously 122

---

[1] StaRO Hamstead D876/10–17, Balance Sheets; D. H. Elletson, *The Chamberlains* (London, 1966), 8.

[2] Peter C. Payne, *The Early Scottish Limited Companies 1856-1895* (Edinburgh, 1980), Table 25.

new entrants were identified, an overall picture suggesting a high rate of turnover.[1] It seems likely, however, that the differences reflect two different populations of coal-producing firms, with the trend towards deeper sinkings and larger companies towards the end of the century imparting a greater degree of stability among major coal companies. It is also true, however, that a common convention among colliery viewers was to assess the future profitability of a colliery over twenty-five or thirty years, a popular length of period for redemption schemes, which also suggests that within the industry, even early in the nineteenth century, the time horizon for investment and entrepreneurial decision-making extended to a relatively long term.

Our examination of rewards in the industry began with the observation of contemporaries as to the level prospective investors might regard as offering a reasonable return on capital. We conclude that on the basis of our estimates not even the large colliery companies could expect to achieve levels of 10 per cent, net, over the long term. None the less, investors and entrepreneurs were forthcoming even during the virtually profitless period between the boom of the 1870s and the mid-1880s, to establish and expand colliery enterprise, though we saw that increasingly both capital and entrepreneurship tended to originate from within the industry from the late nineteenth century.

Probate records have been used by Rubenstein to present an inter-industry comparison of wealth left by businessmen on decease. As an accurate assessment of business wealth or success, this source contains weaknesses, for not only does it take no account of the transfer of wealth during a lifetime but land was excluded from probate valuation. While many of the leading coalmining entrepreneurs are known to have acquired land on a large scale, we do not know whether as a group they possessed a greater hunger for land than entrepreneurs and managers outside coalmining. There are limitations, therefore, to the kind of comparison undertaken by Rubenstein.[2] None the less it seems worthwhile drawing attention to the conclusions that emerged from his analysis, pending new estimates of wealth based on death-duty registers.

In view of the relatively low overall profitability of coalmining it is not surprising to discover that by comparison with other major industries, cotton, engineering, brewing, chemicals, and iron and steel,

[1] Anthony Slaven, *The Development of Western Scotland 1750-1960* (London, 1975), 123.

[2] Values of estates were obtained from the Probate Registry and biographical detail supplemented from sources referred to above. A particularly useful analysis of a business élite in Northumberland is contained in Benwell Community Project Final Report Series 6, *The Making of a Ruling Class*, especially 10–14.

non-landed coalowners did not figure prominently among the millionaire population before World War I, and the same is true, excluding chemicals, of half-millionaires.[1]

Six millionaire coalowners were among those who died between 1840 and 1919, and twenty-eight half-millionaires, which compared with eight iron and steel millionaires and thirty-eight half-millionaires during the same period, totals which placed both industries well below cotton manufacturing in personal wealth creation. A comparison of non-landed lesser wealthy businessmen who died between 1850 and 1869 produces a slightly different picture, for while those in cotton manufacturing and engineering outnumbered those in the coal industry, the six coalowners exceeded brewers and chemical manufacturers, and iron and steel producers, among whom only two left wealth amounting to between £160,000 and £500,000. Thomas Powell, founder of the forerunner of Powell Duffryn before the enterprise was sold to George Elliot and his consortium of contractors, left £250,000 in 1863, and Joseph Straker, the Northumberland timber merchant who established the successful Straker and Love partnership based initially upon the Brancepath Colliery in 1840, left £300,000 in 1867. His partner, the son of a miner and a former pit lad, was Joseph Love, who after a spell as a travelling salesman of dry goods, as a shopkeeper, and as a building contractor, married into the Straker family, and with investment support from the Strakers proceeded to develop one of the most successful Durham colliery enterprises. At his death in 1875 he was a millionaire, by which time Joseph's son, John Straker, was the other principal partner, with interests, too, in Cowpen and North Seaton Coal Co., and the Eastern Railway Company. John Straker also owned more than twelve thousand acres of land in Northumberland, and at his death in 1885 left slightly less than £1m.

Just as the Strakers founded their coalowning dynasty, which brought immense wealth before the end of the century, so did the Joiceys, though the origins lay in James Joicey's 'mercantile education' followed by an apprenticeship as a colliery viewer and mining engineer at South Hetton. In partnership with a railway engineer he leased coal, and together with his brothers John and Edward in 1837 formed the

---

[1] See Tables 3.3 and 3.4 in W. D. Rubinstein, *Men of Property: The Very Wealthy in Britain since the Industrial Revolution* (London, 1981). These tables omit businessmen who were also active colliery owners, whose coalmining activities constituted their primary interest: notably George Elliott and John Knowles. Lindsay Wood, who died in 1920, left £0.85m. I am grateful to Dr Rubinstein for revealing to me the identites of those whose fortunes formed the basis for his tabulations.

partnership of James Joicey and Co. Soon the partnership owned ten flourishing collieries, and, together with brother George, James established the Newcastle engineering firm of J. and G. Joicey, though George died in 1856. In 1863 the first James Joicey left a personal estate valued at less than £100,000, but his brother Edward, who died in 1879, left more than £500,000 and two years later his brother John left £710,495. He was succeeded by his nephew James in 1881, who henceforward controlled the family's large and rapidly growing colliery empire, to which his contribution was both consolidation and extension, including the takeover of Hetton Collieries and Lambton Collieries. When he died in 1936, as Lord Joicey, he left an estate valued at £1.5m., with personal holdings in coal companies amounting to shares to the value of £200,000 each in James Joicey and Co. and in Lambton Collieries Ltd. He was also a major shareholder in the Shirebrook Colliery Co. in the East Midlands, a director of numerous railway, shipping, and goldmining companies, and the proprietor of three North-eastern newspapers. The Joiceys, the Strakers, and especially Joseph Love, were exceptional inasmuch that their wealth stemmed from colliery owning, whereas the wealth of most other major coal-producing millionaires and demi-millionaires before 1880 resulted from the combination of other activities, especially iron production.

Many of the largest producers of coal who died as millionaires during the first three-quarters of the century, William and James Baird, Richard and William Crawshay, and Francis Wright, held their primary investments in iron, as did demi-millionaires from the Baird and Crawshay families, Sir Josiah Guest, Alexander Cunninghame, and James Merry. All are recorded as iron masters. So too is Richard Barrow, although his initial wealth originated in overseas trade, which was subsequently invested in his brother's iron-making firm at Staveley. On his death Richard Barrow left £500,000. Compared with nineteen millionaires and demi-millionaires for the entire period to 1914, whose primary economic interest was coal production, thirty-three other individuals in the same wealth category possessed subsidiary interests in coal. As these figures include coal-producing iron masters the changing relative importance of coal and iron production and profitability from the 1880s prevents a precise comparison, but the undoubted long-term weakness of coal as a sole basis for very substantial accumulation of wealth, certainly before the 1880s, seems a reasonable conclusion to draw.

The wealthiest figures within the industry were colliery proprietors, though rarely was considerable wealth generated in a single generation. One striking feature, however, is the ability of a few leading mining engineers to achieve wealth on the basis of a professional career followed by coalownership. When Lindsay Wood died in 1920 he left £853,834, and six years later John Bell Simpson left £812,171. Both came from leading families in the North-east, possessing a tradition of professional mining engineering, the status of viewers, and proprietory interests in collieries. Lindsay Wood was the youngest of four sons of the prominent viewer Nicholas Wood, manager of the Hetton Coal Company and one of the John Bowes partnership, who at his death in 1865 had left £400,000. Lindsay succeeded his father as manager at Hetton, but the foundation of his fortune lay in his large shareholding in the Harton Coal Company, and he was also a director and eventually vice-chairman of John Bowes and Partners; he held directorships, too, in insurance, railway, and electric power companies. He was created a baronet in 1897. The career of John Bell Simpson resembled that of Lindsay Wood, for he was also the son of a prominent mining engineer, Robert Simpson, adopted his father's profession, inherited some of his father's managerial appointments, and became a managing partner, following his father, in the Stella Coal Company. His directorships concentrated upon electric power companies.

The process of enhanced accumulation evident in the history of North-eastern coalowners and mining engineers is to be found, too, in the newer regions of coalmining development. Charles Markham, Staveley's first managing director, left £233,893 in 1888, but his son Charles Paxton Markham left £611,305 nearly forty years later. Emerson Muschamp Bainbridge left £407,715 in 1892, while his son, Emerson, left £461,769 in 1911. Resembling in his career pattern both the first generation Markham and Bainbridge, though from considerably humbler circumstances, George Elliot progressed from professional engineer to become a wealthy coalowner and the industry's first leader to receive a baronetcy, who on his death in 1893 left £561,044. Some of this fortune, however, flowed from his highly successful wire and rope manufacturing enterprise. Samuel Thomas, the Welsh colliery owner, left £200,000 in 1879, but his son David A. Thomas, First Baron Rhondda, left £1,169,000 when he died in 1918, after achieving growth and extension of his father's colliery interests in a similar fashion to James Joicey. Thomas, however, who served as MP for Merthyr Tydfil in 1888 and 1906, quit political life in disillusion, and from 1907 rejoined his brother to establish the Cambrian Combine. Unlike Thomas, John Nixon, the son of a tenant farmer, was a mining engineer yet shared with Thomas a commercial flair and enormous business drive, which by developing the coalfield in the Aberdare district enabled him to leave £1,155,069 on his death in 1899. William Thomas Lewis, the son of an engineeer at the Plymouth works, was of a similar mould, combining a knowledge of mining engineering with business ability, who after becoming the mineral agent for the Bute estate in 1864 subsequently acquired control of pits of his own in the Lower Rhondda. The founder of Lewis Merthyr Consolidated Collieries in 1900, when he died in 1914 as the first Baron Merthyr he was a half-millionaire. John Thomas North, founder of North's Navigation Collieries in 1889, was also a half-millionaire when he died in 1896, but his fortune was based upon wealth accumulated from speculations in the guano trade in South America, which subsequently he invested in coal on the advice and under the active supervision of T. Forster Browne, the successful Welsh mining engineer.

In Scotland the iron and coal magnates dominate the scene. James Baird, second generation, left £1,190,868 on his death in 1876; Andrew McKosh, son of a lawyer and banker and a professional civil and mining engineer who was managing director and subsequent partner at Bairds, left £818,546 in 1916. William Weir, son of a small farmer but also a nephew of William Baird and who became principal partner of the company, left no less than £2,220,000 when he died in 1913. Wealthy Scottish coalmasters left lesser sums: Sir John Wilson, of Wilsons Clyde and Co., left £603,892 in 1918, Archibald Russell in 1904 left £506,170, and in 1933 Sir James Wood left £506,598.

In comparison with other industries, and especially, of course, compared with commerce and finance, excluding the aristocratic coalowners coalmining was not the basis for many very large fortunes, and among the few exceptions a wealthy, even moderately wealthy, parentage, and training in mining engineering seems to have been the most common combination likely to achieve it. Few received honours, the exceptions consisting of the creation of a single peer, Lord Joicey, and a handful of baronetcies and knighthoods. Few took an active part in national politics in an arena where they were over-shadowed by the coalowning aristocrats, especially during the early period of factory and mining legislation. Thereafter, their proprietorial role as coalowners declined, as they became rentiers, relying on royalties, rather than profits, to augment their land-based wealth.

Of the coalmasters, portrayed in the polemics of class dialectic during the early twentieth century as the bogeymen, Rubinstein concluded that the wealthiest coalowners were relatively homogeneous in background and in career patterns, politics (Conservatism) and religion (Anglicanism), and that few of them achieved national renown.[1] The implication may be that 'larger-than-life entrepreneurs' were especially scarce in coal compared with other industries, but the rewards in mining depended much upon mining engineers, who figured either as proprietors or professional managers among the top wealth-holders. Their continued application was necessary to successful enterprise under conditions of intense competition and of diminishing returns, and the pattern of directorships and external investment underline the narrowness of their business interests, which in most instances were related in some way to coal. Similarly, the political arenas they chose to inhabit were mainly professional and local. Often residing in locations remote from the major cities and most far distant from London, the paternalist role was commonly adopted, seemingly more appropriate in pit villages which in many cases were built by the coalowners who might expect to benefit indirectly by concerning themselves with the development of the communities they helped to create.

Appendix 6.1. Coalminers' productivity

Output per man-year has been recalculated on the basis of revised output and employment estimates presented in Tables 1.1 and 3.1, and differ, therefore, from previous estimates for the period before 1881. Inter-censal employment estimates before 1871 are straight-line extrapolations between the revised figures for census years. Estimates for output per man-shift are the result of applying absenteeism rates (Table 3.14) to the OMY series to produce OMS. Hourly productivity was obtained by transforming the estimates for nominal hours worked in each region at benchmark years (Table 3.14) into a national series of actual weekly hours worked by miners (Table 3.15). Estimates of nominal hours worked by miners were presented in Table 3.1, but need to be translated into the number of hours actually worked by miners in order to obtain a more accurate estimate of labour inputs in OMH. The difficulty in doing so arises from the considerable degree of individual choice open to miners, especially until the 1860s, for neither hewers nor piece-rate haulage workers adhered to a fixed working day. For most

---

[1] Ibid., 76–8.

other workers the time spent at work depended upon hewers' hours, and usually extended over a long period. It is possible that the Commissioners failed to acknowledge this characteristic of miners' working patterns which enabled them to work considerably shorter shifts than those nominally available. Even so, it seems inconceivable that an overestimate of hours in the 1840s, which would have resulted from such a misunderstanding, could have been so large as to produce OMH levels commensurate with, or even remotely approaching, those of 1890–1913. That would require an error of between 13 and 17 hours a week. Greater regularity in working hours was introduced when multiple-shift systems began to be widely adopted (in the North-east in the 1850s), and spread to other regions where multiple-shift working was absent.[1] Consequently voluntary shortening of the working day became less common after 1860 (when hours began to be reduced) than in the preceding period, when a twelve-hour nominal shift was the norm. In the later period, miners took their rest less in the form of shorter days than in daily absenteeism. Nominal weekly hours before 1860 must be seen as averages over the trade cycle, for cyclical variations in hours formed a major feature of the industry. A report from the Cumberland Miners' Association in 1886 observed that, 'In prosperity the hours are not so long, the workmen working by piece earn better wages and they do not work as long. In depression the hours of labour increase. The men stop longer hours to try and earn more wages.'[2] For this reason all evidence should be judged with particular caution for, at least before 1860, variability, from year to year and between regions, was characteristic of the pattern of working hours.

The starting point was the 1842 Children's Employment Commission, the only comprehensive survey for the pre-1860 period. It was assumed, in using this source, that miners worked a five-day (rather than a six-day) week in all regions, since although pits were opened on six days the widespread practice of half-day holidays and pay-week holidays meant that rarely, particularly in the case of hewers, were more than ten days worked each fortnight;[3] because of this assumption, however, the hours of workers in 1842 may be understated. The estimates after 1842 are based on McCormick and Williams's figures[4] supplemented by Parliamentary Papers, except those for 1913 which are essentially

[1] See above 249.
[2] *RC Depression of Trade and Industry* 1886, XXII, Appendix D, 92–4.
[3] *Children's Employment Commission* 1842, XVI, 122–5.
[4] McCormick and Williams 1959, 232–4.

estimates based on the predicted effect of the Eight Hours Act[1] and on those few observations that were actually made. This involved several broad assumptions. First, it was necessary to use hours as a guide to the volume of labour inputs, which immediately posed the problem of how to deal with the time taken within the shift for travelling underground and for meals. The second problem was raised by the possibility of variations in work intensity. It was decided to include meal times in the hours estimates, since this was the practice adopted by the Commissioners and by succeeding inquiries into hours. Approximately three hours a week could be subtracted from the 1842 figure on hours to allow for meals, since the Commission gave thirty to forty minutes as the daily average time taken.[2] All estimates of hours of work include travelling times underground and winding in the length of the working shift, but trends in mining practice during the century indicate a lengthening in the amount of time necessarily spent in this 'unproductive' activity, as pits grew deeper and larger and required longer haulage routes. The Eight Hours inquiry recorded haulage routes varying in length from a few yards in some of the new pits to one-and-a-half miles in some of the older ones, which involved daily travelling time underground of up to forty-five minutes;[3] and we may assume that technical improvements hardly affected this situation, at least before 1900, the length of time being related closely to the size and age of pits and to the infrequency of shafts. After 1880 the construction of improved roads may have allowed a quicker walking pace, but is unlikely to have reduced travelling time significantly.

Even after 1900 haulage machinery was rarely employed to convey men to the face. Man-riding was practised in South Wales to some extent, but elsewhere the dangers deterred miners and managers, and at Clifton and Kearsley collieries near Manchester, for example, experimental man-riding was abandoned as too dangerous.[4] A return relating to 91,155 Durham miners in 1907 showed that more than 91 per cent walked to their place of work, travelling distances in the North-east varying between one and three-and-a-half miles.[5] Man-riding was described as impractical in south Staffordshire mines because the workings were so scattered.[6] Apart from the Eight Hours Inquiry the other

---

[1] As reported in the *Eight Hours Committee* 1907, XIV and XV.
[2] *Children's Employment Commission* 1842, XV, 118–22.
[3] *Eight Hours Committee* 1907, XV, Q 739.
[4] Ibid., QQ 8641, 11110–1.
[5] Ibid., QQ 10574, 12688.
[6] Ibid., Q 11645.

source offering evidence on travelling time is the Royal Commission on Labour, a comparison of the two indicating a marked increase between 1890 and 1905. Since travelling time was mainly a function of the increasing age of pits, not before the late 1870s or 1880s is the effect on productivity likely to have been appreciable. However, before 1880, and since the early 1840s when meal breaks of between half an hour and one-and-a-half hours were recorded by the Children's Employment Commission, their length probably fell as the length of shifts lessened, which may have acted as a corrective to any increase in travelling time before 1880. It does not seem implausible, therefore, to conclude that increases in non-productive labour time of this kind were not important influences on productivity.

The possibility that variations in the intensity of work influenced productivity has been dealt with in the text in the discussion of wages, hours, and absenteeism. The next stage was to transform actual hours worked by hewers and unskilled underground workers in different regions at bench-mark years into a composite national average hours series for all UK miners, for each decade, beginning in 1842. This was possible in a general way only by making the assumption that hewers constituted 40 per cent of the labour force (or rather that hewing time constituted 40 per cent of labour time) throughout the entire period;[1] and that the hours of surface workers were equivalent to those of unskilled underground men (even though we know that *some* surface workers worked much longer hours). The figures of average hours of work were then multiplied by the estimated number of days worked (Table 3.8) in order to arrive at actual weekly hours in different periods (Table 3.10). By dividing output by actual hours it was possible to produce a series of OMH by decade. It cannot be repeated too often that the resulting series are, themselves, the outcome of an accumulation of estimation exercises, which, while explained and justified step by step, none the less mean that at most the trends revealed command more confidence than the actual estimates.

Appendix 6.2. Total factor productivity

The figures in the second column of Table 6.4 show inter-cyclical average changes in total factor productivity; limitations imposed by the

[1] This percentage is based on T. J. Taylor's figures for the North-east in 1844 *Reporting on Mining Districts* 1847, Appendix B; a 'Return showing the Average Number of Hours Daily and Weekly Worked . . .', 1890, LXVIII, 215; and *Eight Hours Committee* 1907, XIV, 26–139.

capital estimates used in this exercise, which were for cycles only, dictated the calculation of total factor productivity in this form.[1]

In addition to the series presented in Table 6.4 which we shall call TFP^1, two other series were calculated, TFP^2 and TFP^3, in which the formulae were essentially the same but with some variations. The differences were as follows:

TFP^1 was obtained from the formulae: proportional change in output — share of labour × proportional change in wages — share of capital × proportional change in capital; the shares were derived from the data by regressing output of coal on wages and capital stock. The resulting coefficients were used as weights for each of the inputs.

TFP^2: the same formula was adopted, but the estimated depreciation data were used as a proxy for the capital input.

TFP^3: the same formula was adopted, but estimated coal profits were computed as a proportion of the value of output to arrive at the weight to be assigned to capital, a method justified by the industry's highly competitive structure, at least after 1840, and near constant returns to scale.

The data used in this exercise were as follows: Labour input was measured as total wages, obtained by multiplying coal output by wage costs per ton. Calculation of wage costs per ton were based on wages per shift per hewers (Table 7.15); the particular weights attached to hewers, skilled day men, and other colliery workers were broadly in

	TFP^2	TFP^3
1832–7/38–47	−0.1995	+0.2240
1838–47/48–54	+0.2056	+0.9955
1848–54/55–66	−0.2877	+0.0490
1855–66/67–73	+0.2113	−0.9230
1867–73/74–83	−0.0127	−0.5140
1874–83/84–90	+0.0548	−1.1310
1884–90/91–1900	−0.2878	−0.2850
1891–1900/01–07	+0.0054	−1.0880
1901–07/08–13	−0.0653	−0.9708

[1] In conducting this exercise I am most grateful for the advice and assistance of my colleague Professor Ashok Parikh.

line with the breakdown published in the Board of Trade Return on 'Wages, Other Costs and Profits 1886–1902' (LXIV, 783). The capital input in TFP[1] was estimated historic capital stock, beginning with the base estimate for 1826, to which gross investment figures were added to obtain changes in historic capital stock (Table 2.1). All data were in constant prices.

Appendix 6.3. Profits and profitability

(a) Profit per ton

The size of the sample is small—fewer than a dozen before 1850, and rarely as many as twenty even after 1880. Many of the series are discontinuous, and there is uncertainty in many cases regarding the precise composition of 'profits' recorded in the colliery accounts. Even figures which appear to have been regarded as gross profits per ton, which account for more than half the series, may have been reduced by the common practice of charging capital expenditure to revenue account, which of course inflated working costs.

Another problem arises from the combination of non-mining coal activities, which though in most cases were insignificant none the less may invalidate some inter-colliery comparisons. This is less likely, however, to affect the gross profit per ton series (which refers to coal production only) than the net profits series, which relate to business enterprise as a whole. Our profit-per-ton series includes both gross and net figures, though even some of the gross profit figures might be underestimates, and the net profit figures are not entirely consistent with each other, as it is not clear in many cases precisely which elements have been incorporated in costs or deducted from revenues. For example, from the accounts of the Lochgelly Coal and Iron Company it is possible to calculate a series for gross and net profits per ton, the former usually many times as large as the latter; but yet another series was recorded at intermediate levels between the two and labelled 'profit per ton', though it is impossible to discover why it differed from the other two. Of nineteen series, most of which extend between the 1870s and 1913, the average gross profit per ton for ten of them for which continuous figures were available was between 1s. and 1s. 2d. per ton, against a working cost which averaged 6s. The Staveley figure was 1s. 1¼d. for the period 1879 to 1913, but rose to 1s. 4d. when extended back to 1863. The figure for Cannock Chase was 8d. between 1879 and 1913, rising to 1s. 1½d. for the period 1860 to 1911, in each case the inclusion of the boom of the early 1870s imparting a sizeable inflationary effect upon average profitability, though levels in the 1860s were also relatively high for both companies.

Unfortunately, the series for three South Wales collieries, Dowlais, Nixon Taylor and Cory, and David Davies, end in the mid-1880s and offer no basis for comparison with most of the other series since they refer to profits from the sale of large coal only (which in the case of David Davies, for example, formed only 80 per cent of total production in the early 1880s).[1] The profit-per-ton figures of the Welsh firms, therefore, are inflated, though inter-colliery comparisons within the region are not invalidated completely. Walters regarded the very high profitability of Nixon Taylor and Cory, the figures for which are based on large coal sold, to have been less representative of the South Wales steam-coal trade than the profit records of large coal produced by David Davies and Co., or by Powell Duffryn.[2] Neither the margins at Powell Duffryn's collieries nor of the Main Colliery differed from the overall average among our company sample from the 1880s onwards.

(b) Company profitability

A widely employed method of measuring the return to investors in an industry is that which expresses dividends as a return on market share values, but we have rejected this on practical grounds. Publicly quoted coalmining companies were few before 1900; even in 1890 the *Investors' Monthly Manual* included barely a dozen colliery companies, of which six were in South Wales, although many coal and iron firms were, of course, listed. As our archival data applied to nineteen firms, which in several cases covered considerably longer periods and including enterprises which, certainly before 1900, were more representative of coal producers than were genuinely public limited companies, our research effort concentrated on this alternative approach. An added advantage was that the supporting archival evidence allowed some evaluation of the significance of figures appearing in the balance sheets, especially in the case of iron and coal companies, or other colliery concerns not involved exclusively in mining coal. A further justification for not using the p/e ratio is the widespread existence of concentrated family ownership even among large colliery companies. High gearing of shareholding capital towards owners who may be assumed to have been less sensitive

---

[1] I am indebted to Dr Rhodri Walters for confirming this difference, by letter, 12 Apr. 1983.
[2] Walters 1977, Table 42.

to movements in share prices renders the *p/e* ratio of dubious value as a measurement of rates of return. Unfortunately, the data required to calculate a rate of return of this kind is not available for all firms for which profit-per-ton data have been assembled, though the information has been found for some other companies.

Inter-firm comparisons of profit performance inevitably depend upon the comparability of asset valuation. In all cases, except that of Clay Cross, the data refer to total assets and thus refer to coal companies rather than to coal production only. There were, however, no inflexible rules covering the valuation of companies upon which their assets figures were to be based. Data from Consett and Bell Brothers have been discarded completely because of absurdly low initial valuations duly incorporated in all subsequent statements of asset value; for Ashington no asset data have survived. By comparing the output of each of the remaining companies with the fixed asset figures to ascertain whether the capital–output ratio was at all credible, it has been possible to judge the accuracy of asset valuations. The balance sheets of Bolckow Vaughan, Carlton Main, Powell Duffryn, Staveley, Wharncliffe Silkstone, and Wigan revealed plausible asset valuations, and those of Cannock Chase and Main possessed realistic asset values on the whole despite minor inconsistencies—a low initial capitalization in the case of Cannock Chase, and irregular depreciation rates at Main. Each of the remaining companies, Briggs, Butterley, Fife, and Lochgelly, Mitchell Main, and East Cannock, do, however, raise problems, for all reveal assets which are obviously under-valued and result in exaggerated rates of return. It seems likely that this might be a general characteristic of other companies in our sample too, however, since the direction of error in contemporary accounting was one of under- rather than over-valuation.

(c) *Profits based on tax assessments*

Published annually in *Reports of the Commissioners of Inland Revenue* beginning in 1855, the assessments related to the tax year April to April, and are based on the average gross value added of all mines for the preceding five years; for this reason they appear as a five-year moving average centred three years prior to the year of assessment; the figure for 1900–1, for example, referred to the period 1899/1900, in which April 1897 to April 1898 is the key year.[1] Stamp drew attention to the

---

[1] See *British Incomes and Property: The Application of Official Statistics to Economic Problems* (London, 1916), 184; J. C. Stamp, 'The Effect of Trade Fluctuations upon Profits', *JRSS*, LXXXI (1918).

tendency for prices to lag behind profits, a perverse and unexpected relationship which he explained as the result of a technicality embodied in the procedures required by Section 133 of the 1842 Income Tax Act.[1] There are other defects in the series, too, only some of which can be remedied. Until 1911 the figures refer to *all* mines rather than to collieries only; assessments for coalmines separately beginning in 1911/12 to 1914/15, referring to the five-year periods centred upon 1908/9 to 1911/12; until 1908/9 to 1910/11 the figures refer to national aggregates; the tax assessments are based on royalties as well as profits; and all losses are counted as zero profits, which particularly in years of bad trade tends to overstate colliery profits in total, a defect which it has not been possible to remedy.

It is possible, however, to construct estimates for colliery profits net of royalties. By taking the proportionate values of the output of tin, copper, lead, and iron ore, which are known,[2] and allowing a further notional 3 per cent of total receipts from the sale of zinc, fireclay, silver, and barytes, it is estimated that the ratios of coal to total mining profits increased from 75 per cent in the 1850s to 93 per cent by the end of our period. The elimination of royalties from the figures depends upon our previous discussion of changing royalty levels, which suggested averages of $5\frac{1}{4}d$. for the 1850s and 1860s, rising to $6d$. for the five-years' average around the peak of 1873–4, falling back to $5\frac{1}{4}d$. by the mid-1890s, and remaining at that level.[3] As royalties were generally levied on sales (sometimes on sales of large coal only), output was reduced to saleable percentages according to our consumption estimates for 1840 and 1855, when colliery consumption and waste were estimated to have been 13 and 11 per cent respectively, declining until the 1870s boom. The result was a series of adjusted royalty rates which were then multiplied by detrended output to produce total estimated royalty payments; when subtracted from total 'profits' the figures showed coalowners' profits; these were then reduced to tonnage rates. All profit figures derived from the assessments are distorted, however, due to the unavoidable exaggeration during trough years, when losses were understated. The early estimates are especially suspect. A sudden sharp rise in profits in 1853/4 is difficult to explain, for the very nature of a five-year moving average precludes such a discontinuity. Since there is no evidence of any large addition to the scope of the returns, each mineral being specified in the

---

[1] J. C. Stamp, 'The Effects upon Profits', *JRSS*, LXXXI (1918), 573.
[2] Mitchell and Deane 1962, 129–30, 155, 159–60.
[3] See above 506–8.

1842 Act when assessments began, the unavoidable conclusion is that prior to the 1858 assessment, which referred to the previous five years, considerable under-recording (or evasion) by up to a fifth of the total must have occurred, though the Inland Revenue reports include no reference to it. In calculating coalowners' profits before 1854 we have assumed under-recording on this scale in both coal and other mines.

Generalizations on profitability before the tax-based figures became reliable are even more problematical, because of the lack of data. The close correspondence between price and profit levels (indicated both by the assessment-based estimates and our company-sample averages, of profit per ton) suggests that price movements before 1860, for which our data are better than for costs and profits, may be regarded as an acceptable proxy for the purpose of indicating levels and movements in profitability in the short term. Pithead prices rose above 5s. per ton in the mid-1830s and in the late 1840s, and although they fell to around the 4s. per ton mark of the early 1830s and early 1840s, the mid-1850s saw prices continue at levels around 5s. per ton, below which, except for isolated years, they were never to fall again. In subsequent periods, when the price of coal moved to higher trend levels, working costs also adjusted upwards, which, if we can assume a similar mechanism at work in the 1850s and 1860s, could explain why the assessment-based profit series reveal no appreciable change in the level of profitability in the 1850s as compared with the 1860s, or, supposing the estimates inflated to compensate for under-recording are valid, by comparison with the 1840s either. Because they are five-year moving averages the assessment-based estimates conceal the extent to which profits fluctuated, a phenomenon which is very marked in our company-sample data.

CHAPTER 7

Standards and Experiences: The Miners

i. Wages, earnings, and the cost of living

'What is the price of champagne in Wigan? . . . Is there much champagne drunk in your district?'[1] These questions posed to miners' leaders giving evidence to the Dearness and Scarcity Committee in 1873 were doubtless intended to reveal the heights of luxurious consumption sustained by the considerably inflated earnings of miners at the peak of the boom—then about to collapse. The Yorkshire miners replied that 'champagne was unheard of until coal consumers began to talk about it', since when miners had been known to subscribe to buy a bottle for tasting.[2] Such experiences, however, were rare, and even at the peak were well beyond the reach of the majority of colliery workers. For fundamental to their living standards was the structure of wages and earnings, affected by geography, function, and grade within the industry, by age and sex, and the trade cycle.

Hewers' wages were largely determined by two factors: the geological structure of coal seams, and the hewers' own, often self-imposed and self-regulated, pace of work. Differences in work pace allowed two workers operating in identical conditions to receive unequal wages; similarly, identical work pace might also produce contrasting earnings under different geological conditions. The wages of those putters paid by the piece would also vary according to work rate, and were affected, too, by problems encountered in haulage. Such variability in the influence on wages meant that the earnings structure for the majority of workers in the industry depended upon separately negotiated price lists, one for each seam and several for each colliery; and it is not—nor has it ever been—practicable to identify the impact of each on miners' wages. Furthermore, because the majority of coalminers were not time-paid workers, the notion of an average wage earned in a 'normal' week is inapplicable. For this reason the historian is faced with intractable diffi-

---

[1] *Dearness and Scarcity* 1873, X, QQ 3969–70, 7386–7.
[2] Ibid.

culties, rendering the measurement of those elements in the miners' standard of living which allow quantification more difficult methodologically than those for other workers. A large volume of information on wages is available (relating mainly to the post-1870 period); taking the form of money earnings per shift, the data conceal large-scale, though infrequent, deviations of as much as 25 per cent either side of the stated average. None the less, while accepting the impossibility of precision, there are grounds for regarding these averages as typical, with sizeable deviations possible but infrequent.

As early as the 1830s, and possibly earlier, the notion of an average day's work (in Scotland known as the 'darg' and in Staffordshire as the 'stint') was widespread in the industry, and consequently individual price lists tended to be structured so as to coincide with this norm. The 'darg' or 'stint' represented the amount of coal produced by a hewer in one day, and it was evidently raised or lowered many times during the first half of the nineteenth century; reduced as wages and prices rose and increased as they fell.[1] In Northumberland and Durham this practice was eventually institutionalized in the form of the 'county average', an average level of daily wages to which all pits had to correspond. In other regions, too, this concept of a base rate was employed, though the sum might vary more from pit to pit than it did in the North-east. Variations in the level of daily wages, whether between individual men or between pits, were likely to be greater during periods of boom or depression than they were in 'normal' times.

The evidence on daily wage rates is abundant but imperfect. For the period prior to 1870 it is necessary to rely on data drawn largely from parliamentary reports, supplemented by archival evidence which generally relates to particular firms or collieries. The parliamentary material is relatively rich for the 1840s and late 1860s, but contains gaps for the 1830s, 1850s, and early 1860s. It is impossible, therefore, to construct a table of year-to-year changes without considerable interpolation, this being based mainly on the available coal-price series with which movements in wages tended to synchronize, with a lag. The data are not always in agreement, and difficult choices of accepting one piece of information in favour of another have often been unavoidable. For the years after 1870 abundant evidence is available on wage trends, and the problem resolves itself into adopting the most accurate and appropriate method of summarizing it.

---

[1] *Midlands Mining Commission* 1843, XIII, 91.

The deficiencies of the material must be borne firmly in mind. Wage data refer mainly to hewers, who probably comprised less than one-half of all colliery workers.[1] The wages of other coalminers are extremely difficult to determine before the introduction of district-wide collective bargaining in the second half of the period, and it is not possible to construct an index of year-to-year changes for these grades of workers before the 1880s. The paucity of information on the wages of juvenile labour is particularly frustrating, since it obscures the examination of family earnings and makes it difficult to examine changes over time in the demand for, and remuneration of, oncost labour. Furthermore, although the evidence lends itself to the analysis of wage trends in each of the major regions, a series for the minor coalfields—Cumberland, North Wales, and the South-west—is not available before the 1870s; it is possible, therefore, only to point to the probable course of wages on the basis of the other indexes. Finally, although attempts have been made to produce daily wage-rate figures which reflect net earnings, after deductions for such items as candles, pick sharpening, powder, and so on, the evidence from which the data are derived is frequently itself ambiguous. The amount of money deducted in this way was in any case small—perhaps $2d.$ or $3d.$ a shift—and was likely to be of greater importance relative to total wages in the first half of the period.[2] The core of the evidence on wage rates, which is the product of a large number of separate, often lengthy, calculations, is presented in Appendix 7.1.

Figure 7.1, which shows the movements of hewers' shift wages in the seven largest regions, indicates clearly the pronounced short-term variations in wage rates in the industry, though the degree of annual fluctuation is seen to be far greater in the case of Scotland, the North-east, and South Wales than in the other regions, a result, no doubt, of their considerable dependence on export markets. The trend in the case of the inland English coalfields is slightly less irregular, though the booms of 1856, 1866, 1873, 1890, and 1900 are clearly emphasized. Wage rates in these coalfields moved closely together (long before the adoption of common federation scales in the late 1880s),[3] though for most of the period wages in the East Midlands and in Yorkshire were appreciably higher than those in Lancashire and Cheshire and the West Midlands. Rates in the North-east and South Wales ran closely together (apart from

---

[1] See above 210–11.
[2] Rather larger in South Wales, perhaps $3d.–6d.$ a shift. See Morris and Williams 1958, 222.
[3] See above 265–6.

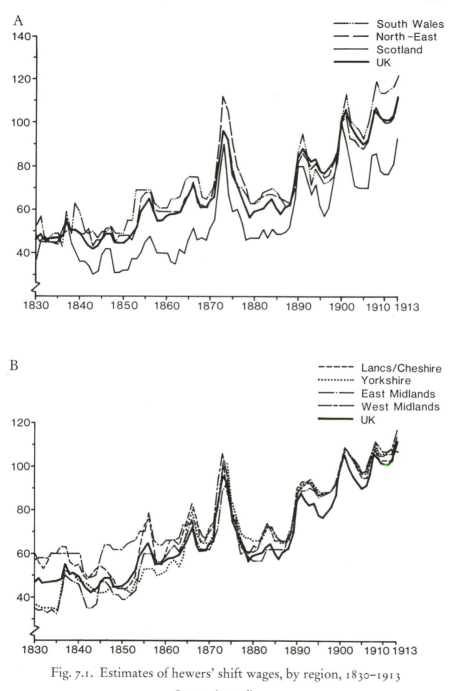

Fig. 7.1. Estimates of hewers' shift wages, by region, 1830–1913

Sources: Appendix 7.1

the early 1870s boom which was more marked in its repercussion on wages in the North-east); in Scotland, apart from a brief period in the 1830s and a slightly longer one in 1888–1900, wages were considerably lower than average. Apart from the period 1830–50 when wages in most regions stagnated and in some actually declined, the movement of wages was clearly upward. The degree of fluctuation in annual wage rates before 1850 was less marked than that in the rest of the period, and this can be explained either in terms of imperfect competition or of the initial failure of labour to respond fully to the price mechanism (or indeed of employers' resistance to their response). We must be aware, however, of the extremely sparse evidence on wage rates for the early period, which may have imparted an exaggerated stability to the series.

The evidence assembled so far has been confined to wages per shift and to the movement of these nominal rates of pay over time. The take-home pay of miners, however, was dependent not only upon how much could be earned each day, but on the regularity of employment; on the number of days worked each week and each year. Our earlier discussion of employment, both in connection with labour supply and productivity, was based on an empirically defensible assumption that neither long-term nor seasonal unemployment was at any time significant in the industry between 1830 and 1913, and that even cyclical unemployment took the form, typically, of short-time working. The tendency for employers to close pits for a number of days each week in times of bad trade, combined with the proneness of miners to restrict their working in good times, were important influences on earnings, tending to dampen the effect of recession on wage levels and to smooth wage movements at the peak.

In the 1830s and 1840s employment fluctuated markedly, but achieved a great degree of stability, within the context of cyclical movement, in the 1850s and 1860s. On average, 4.2 days a week were worked in 1830–42, after which 4.5 was the norm over the cycle. Regional differences clearly did occur. For example, in the Midland regions the number of days lost in any one year was often twice the loss in the North-east (though differences in voluntary absenteeism may have reduced the overall impact of this on earnings). On the other hand, changes over time in the number of days on which pits were open were synchronized, the cycle being the fundamental determinant. Voluntary rates of absenteeism also varied from one region to another (from 6–14 per cent according to figures for 1899 and 1905), and here differences in employment opportunities, together with the extent of female and

Table 7.1. *Index of estimated wages and earnings per shift of hewers, 1830-1913*
(1900 = 100)

	Wage rate	Earnings		Wage rate	Earnings		Wage rate	Earnings
1830	46.4	48.3	1858	55.1	45.9	1886	58.3	55.9
1831	48.3	45.3	1859	55.3	51.8	1887	61.1	59.8
1832	46.4	38.7	1860	57.2	53.6	1888	62.8	62.8
1833	46.4	33.8	1861	58.3	54.7	1889	70.2	84.4
1834	47.3	39.4	1862	58.6	54.9	1890	84.7	82.9
1835	46.9	44.0	1863	59.1	55.4	1891	88.4	86.5
1836	48.2	45.2	1864	63.5	59.5	1892	85.3	83.5
1837	54.9	57.2	1865	67.1	62.9	1893	81.6	78.2
1838	50.5	52.6	1866	71.4	66.9	1894	83.0	81.3
1839	51.1	47.9	1867	65.6	61.5	1895	78.8	72.3
1840	49.7	46.6	1868	61.4	51.2	1896	77.6	72.7
1841	46.0	38.3	1869	61.0	57.2	1897	79.0	77.4
1842	44.8	28.0	1870	64.0	60.0	1898	82.7	81.0
1843	42.5	31.0	1871	66.3	62.2	1899	87.7	89.5
1844	43.5	36.2	1872	81.4	67.8	1900	100.0	100.0
1845	46.9	44.0	1873	96.9	86.8	1901	106.0	99.4
1846	49.2	46.1	1874	92.4	77.0	1902	99.0	96.9
1847	49.3	46.2	1875	76.6	62.2	1903	95.8	91.8
1848	45.0	42.2	1876	72.5	58.9	1904	92.7	88.8
1849	44.8	42.0	1877	66.0	48.1	1905	90.5	86.7
1850	44.8	42.0	1878	61.9	42.6	1906	92.1	92.1
1851	46.0	43.1	1879	56.8	52.1	1907	101.0	103.1
1852	46.9	44.0	1880	59.5	57.0	1908	106.8	100.2
1853	52.2	43.5	1881	60.1	57.6	1909	102.1	95.7
1854	59.6	49.7	1882	60.8	60.8	1910	101.4	97.2
1855	62.9	59.0	1883	63.1	63.1	1911	101.9	97.7
1856	65.4	61.3	1884	65.4	61.3	1912	103.5	105.7
1857	59.0	55.3	1885	60.8	55.7	1913	112.3	112.3

Wage rate: Average (weighted by employment) of the regional series. 100 = 8 s. ½ d.
Earnings: Wage rate × days worked per week (Table 3.8). 100 = 7 s. 9 d.
Sources: See Appendix 7.1.

juvenile employment outside the industry, seem to have been the major
influences.[1]

It is possible to estimate earnings, first by calculating a national wage
series, which is achieved by weighting the regional wage series (see
Appendix 7.1) by regional employment, and by weighting the results by

[1] See above.

Table 7.2. *Index of estimated potential earnings of hewers by region, 1873–1913*
(1900 = 100)

North-east 1873–1893

Year	North-east
1873	99
1874	84
1875	70
1876	61
1877	50
1878	45
1879	54
1880	57

1894–1913

Year	North-east	Scotland	Yorks.	Lancs. and Cheshire	East Midlands	West Midlands	South Wales
1894	75		81	87			
1895	71	60	70	76	68	69	70
1896	69	56	75	80	69	76	68
1897	74	62	80	82	74	82	71
1898	80	74	87	86	80	84	
1899	86	83	92	93	92	94	83
1900	100	100	100	100	100	100	100
1901	99	88	97	99	101	99	107

Year							
1881	59						
1882	63						
1883	64						
1884	61						
1885	57						
1886	59						
1887	60						
1888	60						
1889	69						
1890	80						
1891	83						
1892	77						
1893	72						
1902	89	78	95	98	101	101	101
1903	88	70	90	91	91	92	99
1904	86	67	87	88	84	88	97
1905	84	68	86	84	81	84	88
1906	88	70	92	88	85	88	99
1907	99	84	105	102	98	107	112
1908	102	79	105	95	99	104	118
1909	100	70	97	91	93	97	111
1910	96	73	100	93	97	101	115
1911	96	74	103	98	96	99	114
1912	101	79	109	103	106	108	121
1913	112	90	119	113	117	119	129

Sources: See Appendix 7.1; *Labour Gazette* 1894–1913; North-east, 1873–94 based on *BPP*, 1886, XXIII, Q 11, 688, *Dearness and Scarcity* 1873, X, Q 3034, and 3401–6 and *Sankey Commission*, appendix 23.

estimates of the number of days worked. The composite national wages
and earnings series thus produced are presented in Table 7.1. Table 7.2
compares the course of earnings in the main regions between 1894 and
1913 (from 1873 for the North-east), the only period for which a regional
breakdown is possible. The earnings series represent wage rates
weighted by the number of days on which coal was wound, and ignore
the effect of absenteeism; they reflect, in effect, the course of maximum
potential earnings. The comparative course of these regional indices is
sufficiently similar to justify the notion of a common experience for
hewers in which the trade cycle was the dominant factor, though
accompanied, too, by a regionally disparate chronology of movements
in earnings—which were marked. Thus, for example, the peak of earnings was 1900 in all regions except South Wales (where it was 1901),
though in the succeeding cycle two regions (Lancashire and Cheshire,
and Scotland) peaked in 1907, and the other three in 1908. The amplitude of fluctuation (visible from the degree to which the various indices
depart from one another after the common base in 1900) was quite
different in the case of each, with South Wales gaining the most and
Scotland actually losing ground in 1900–13. These differences were due
much more to differences in employment opportunities than to
variations in wage rates.

One symptom of the complexity of labour organization in the mining
industry was the existence of numerous different grades, ranging from
pit deputy to surface labourer, which also implied a complex wages
structure. Fortunately, for practical purposes it is possible to identify
five or six key grades which illustrate the differentials that resulted.
Again, while the period between 1886 and 1914 is relatively well documented and has been treated by Rowe for the period before 1886,[1] no
published treatment of wage differentials in mining exists. Table 7.3
combines the data given by Rowe for 1888 and 1914 with the Wage
Census data for 1886 (which in any case is the substantive source for the
1888 figures),[2] and on the basis of scattered evidence in parliamentary
and secondary literature continues the analysis back to 1830.

Differentials within the industry remained fairly uniform over 1886–
1914. On the whole, hewers gained rather more than skilled day-wage
men, except in the minor regions at least; putters gained rather less than
hewers, while unskilled labourers gained roughly as much. The relativi-

---

[1] Rowe 1923.

[2] A summary of the *Wage Census* data is given in *Rates of Wages in Mines and Quarries in the UK* 1890–1, LXXVIII, xi.

Table 7.3. *Wage differentials at various dates, 1830-1914*
(Hewers' wage at each date = 100)

	Skilled day-wage men	Underground labourers	Juveniles	Older putters	Women
1830	96		48		
1842					
1846		51			
1849	100		45		
1856		57			
1859	96		48		
1860	100		52		
1862	90	46	60		23
1866		46	46		
1869		61			
1870		55			
1873		50			
1877	92		50		
1878		77			
1880	100				
1883	85	75	43		30
1886	90	72	40	78	37
1888	95	65		76	
1914	87	66		73	

Sources: Returns of Wages Published between 1830 and 1886, 1887 LXXXIX, 134-45; *Children's Employment Commission*, 1842 XV, 154-8; Leifchild 1854, 185-6; Bulman and Redmayne 1896, 46-50; *Reports on the State of the Population in Mining Districts*, 1844-1846; A Dalziel, *The Colliers' Strike in South Wales* (Cardiff, 1872), 9; Benson 1980, 67-71.

ties indicated in Table 7.3 tend to conceal regional differentials, but these were not great (to the extent that regional differentials in the division of labour necessitated different grades of worker); and in any case, not enough evidence exists for the years before 1886 to extend the analysis very far. It suggests that differentials before 1886 were not greatly different from those hitherto. Annual data point clearly to the influence of the trade cycle, with hewers' earnings increasing relative to time-paid workers during upswings but falling during downswings.

Table 7.3 indicates that the ratio of juvenile to adult workers' wages remained fairly constant over the period, particularly after 1842 when the lowest grades of juvenile workers were eliminated. Between 1842 and 1886 juvenile workers between the ages of fourteen and eighteen received between 45 and 60 per cent of the adult hewer's wage. By 1886 'putters' were earning considerably more (probably three-quarters of the hewer's wage); but by this time the majority of young men so employed were aged eighteen to twenty-one, and this in fact, more than anything else, was the reason for their increasing wage relativities. Juveniles below the age of eighteen continued to earn no more than half the adult wage. Underground labourers received only between 50 and 60 per cent of the adult hewer's wage between 1846 and 1872 (when admittedly because of the unprecedented earnings of hewers the ratio was at its lowest). Consequently, differentials for labourers must have improved somewhat over 1872–86 in order to reach the level of 65–66 per cent pertaining in 1888 and 1914.[1] The differentials of the skilled day-men contain the greatest variation, largely because of considerable differences in skill and experience. Excluding deputies and other supervisory staff, the wages of skilled day-men fluctuated at levels around 86–96 per cent of the hewer's wage, and this was a fairly constant ratio throughout the period. Meanwhile, adult surface workers (excepting craftsmen) would earn rather less than unskilled workers underground. Women surface workers (the majority employed in Lancashire) earned wages which were less than one-third of the hewer's wage before 1886, and barely more thereafter. On the basis of this evidence, therefore, it seems reasonable to regard the movement of hewers' wages as an adequate (if not completely accurate) guide to the wages of other grades of colliery workers, especially after 1886 when many rates were dictated by the same sliding scales or agreements that governed hewers' wages.

The central problem in converting the earnings series into an index of real earnings arises in constructing a cost of living index covering the entire period. Various measures of the cost of living utilized by historians attain a considerable degree of agreement in the period after 1890, and there can be little doubt that, at least on theoretical grounds, the Ministry of Labour's Retail Price Index for 1892–1913 (the only national retail price series for the whole of this period) should be superior to any other. The greatest difficulties of selection occur in relation to the period between 1850 and 1892, for before 1850 there is virtually no choice at all other than the Gayer, Rostow and Schwartz index. Thereafter, for reasons explained in Appendix 7.1, we have chosen G. H. Wood's index, based on the Board of Trade 1903 *Report on Wholesale and Retail Prices*, on many printed works, and on numerous 'personal inqui-

---

[1] The values for 1878, 1883, and 1886 appear to be inflated by the slack trade of these years relative to the early 1870s and 1888–1914, and were probably untypical.

ries' in major centres of population.[1] The unweighted means of a number of commodities of ordinary consumption were checked 'by estimating independently at various periods the cost of a given quantity of various articles commonly used in artisan households'.[2] Wood also made an estimate for rent, an element excluded from the index reproduced by Mitchell and Deane.[3] When recalculated so as to include rent, Wood's index coincides closely with that of the Ministry of Labour after 1982—perhaps because common sources were used. This conformity of the series in 1892 strengthens the credibility of Wood's estimates for the preceding period, and simplifies the splicing together of the series in 1892.

None of the few regional indexes which have appeared since Wood's have substantially modified his picture, except that presented by Barnsby;[4] but since Barnsby's index fluctuates more acutely than the available wholesale price series serious doubts arise as to its accuracy. For the period 1830–50 the Gayer, Rostow, and Schwartz price index has been used despite its various shortcomings;[5] partly because in comparison with Sauerbeck (wholesale) and Black Country (retail) indexes in the late 1840s the distortion likely to result from splicing the GRS with the Wood index would be less than were either of the alternatives employed. Thus, whereas for the 1830–50 period our cost of living index remains suspect, but inevitably so, Wood's series, as presented by Mitchell and Deane, has been recalculated in order to accommodate an allowance for rent. Similarly, the Ministry of Labour's Index of Retail Prices for 1892–1914 has also been amended so as to comprise a weighted index of food, clothing, and rent.

The resulting cost of living index, shown in Table 7.4, reveals the overall deflationary trend which will be familiar to historians, but showing that the cost of living fell before 1850 only by swinging dramatically from peak to trough, each peak lower than the last, but still pronounced when compared with the years immediately before or after. A mild inflation in living costs occurred between the late 1850s and the early 1870s, amounting to roughly 10 per cent over the whole period, whereas the succeeding twenty-five years saw prices fall by almost 30 per cent. In addition to these chronological trends in movements in the cost of living

[1] G. H. Wood, 'The Investigation of Retail Prices', *JRSS*, LXV (1902), 685–90.

[2] G. H. Wood, 'Real Wages and the Standard of Comfort since 1850', *JRSS*, LXXII (1909), 95.

[3] Mitchell and Deane 1962, 343–4.

[4] Barnsby 1971, 221–2.

[5] See A. J. Taylor (ed.), *The Standard of Living in Britain in the Industrial Revolution* (London, 1971), xxiv–xxv.

Table 7.4. *Index of estimated living costs and of real earnings, 1830-1913*
(1900 = 100)

	Cost of living	Real earnings		Cost of living	Real earnings		Cost of living	Real earnings
1830	134	36.1	1858	112	40.8	1886	102	54.7
1831	135	33.6	1859	111	46.7	1887	100	59.8
1832	130	30.0	1860	115	46.4	1888	100	62.7
1833	126	26.9	1861	117	46.9	1889	102	70.2
1834	122	32.2	1862	115	47.7	1890	102	81.3
1835	119	36.9	1863	112	49.4	1891	103	84.0
1836	135	33.6	1864	111	53.6	1892	102	81.9
1837	134	42.7	1865	112	46.1	1893	999	78.9
1838	139	37.8	1866	118	46.5	1894	96	84.7
1839	148	32.4	1867	124	49.4	1895	94	77.0
1840	145	32.2	1868	122	41.8	1896	94	77.4
1841	139	27.6	1869	117	48.7	1897	97	79.8
1842	126	22.2	1870	117	51.2	1898	99	81.8
1843	113	27.4	1871	118	52.4	1899	97	92.5
1844	114	31.7	1872	123	55.0	1900	100	100.0
1845	118	37.2	1873	125	69.2	1901	101	98.4
1846	121	37.9	1874	121	63.5	1902	101	95.9
1847	137	33.8	1875	118	52.6	1903	103	89.1
1848	115	36.8	1876	116	50.7	1904	103	86.0
1849	104	40.4	1877	118	40.6	1905	103	84.1
1850	103	40.8	1878	116	36.5	1906	103	89.3
1851	102	42.3	1879	111	46.9	1907	105	98.1
1852	102	43.1	1880	114	50.0	1908	107	93.6
1853	109	39.9	1881	112	51.2	1909	107	89.3
1854	123	40.2	1882	113	53.7	1910	109	88.9
1855	127	46.6	1883	111	56.7	1911	109	89.5
1856	127	48.4	1884	109	56.0	1912	113	93.3
1857	121	45.5	1885	105	53.1	1913	113	99.2

Real earnings = Earnings ÷ cost of living index
Sources: See Appendix 7.1.

there appears to have been a decrease in the amplitude of fluctuation in living costs after about 1860, a phenomenon possibly explained by inadequacies in the GRS index but a transition also to be detected in Wood's retail index for the 1850s and 1860s. This suggests that the trend towards less severe short-run fluctuations in living costs beginning in mid-Victorian Britain was not a statistical aberration and marks the origins of a genuinely new phase in the history of the cost of living.

One of the main problems in employing a single cost of living index is its inability to make allowance for regional variations in prices, yet Hunt's analysis of regional variations in the cost of living in the period 1850–1914 suggests that the degree of variation encountered was fairly minimal.[1] Food prices were generally lower in the large towns and cities than in rural areas. In the early part of our period (particularly 1830–50) this disparity was probably exacerbated by the presence of truck, which raised food prices in the remoter mining villages. Hunt regarded the trade-off between lower urban food prices and the value of (predominantly rural) cottage gardens as roughly equal, consequently the cost of food in urban areas may have varied relatively little from that in rural ones.[2] There is evidence of the existence of large allotments and gardens in many mining areas, most of them predominantly rural, while in the urban coalfields there was less opportunity for the growing of food.[3] Variations in the cost of miners' coal were not significant.

The main factor distinguishing the urban and rural cost of living was rent, urban rents being significantly higher than rural ones. There can be no doubt that workers in the urban coalfields were at a disadvantage. Free and subsidized housing were generally features of the remoter rural areas; workers elsewhere (for example, parts of west and south Yorkshire, the East and West Midlands, and Lancashire) competed in a more pressurized house market.[4] However, although it is possible to discuss these differences the magnitude of this variation in terms of our regional breakdown is not measurable, since few of our regions are entirely rural or urban measured by residence patterns of mining families before 1870, and none after that time. On decline since the 1840s, by 1870 truck was exceptional outside certain districts in Ayrshire and Lanarkshire, South Wales and Monmouthshire, and south Staffordshire;[5] though David Dale of the Consett Iron Company claimed that truck made a 10 per cent difference to those coalmasters who practised it,[6] an ambiguous expression which leaves open the extent to which miners' real earnings were diminished. As the extent and form taken by truck before 1870 varied widely, it is impossible to build its effects into any calculations of incomes, but to note merely the prevalence of truck in

[1] Hunt 1973, Chapt. 2.

[2] Ibid., 100.

[3] Barnsby 1971, 231, argues that in the Black Country 'allotments were not widespread, nor were gardens usually large'.

[4] See below.

[5] See above.

[6] RC Truck 1871, XXXVI, 5.

[6] G. H. Wood, 'Real Wages and the Standard of Comfort since 1850', JRSS, LXXII (1909), 95.

certain districts until the 1870s, when legislation hastened further the disappearance of trucking practices.

Efforts have already been made in the calculation of the wage data to deduct the costs of all items (such as candles, powder, pick sharpening, etc.) essential to the miner's job, though some of these deductions began to be phased out towards the end of our period. Other deductions, for children's education, sickness benefit, and union fees, for example, are not included as there seems to have been no identifiable standard national pattern. The portion of the budget ascribed to clothing in the cost of living index may well be an underestimate for workers in an industry such as mining. But even were such costs calculable, none of these additional considerations would materially affect the value of the index in its ability to describe the broad movement of price changes as they affected miners and their families. It is possible that further distortion in the course of real wages resulted from the effects of involuntary absenteeism from sickness and lay-offs caused by accidents, or of strikes and lockouts. Walters estimated that approximately 5 per cent of shifts were lost each week due to sickness and accidents,[1] the effect of which would have been to reduce money wages by the same percentage annually. However, since the number of shifts lost in this way varied little year by year, the indexes of wages, earnings, and real earnings would have remained unaltered. From 1891, when accurate data on the number of working days lost through disputes are available,[2] it can be estimated that 3 per cent of possible shifts were lost in this way, which suggests that a 3 per cent deduction from annual money wages and earnings should be applied.

Having calculated miners' wages and earnings and the cost of living, it is possible to produce an index of hewers' real earnings, as shown in Table 7.4. This shows that after 1842 real earnings rose strongly, though erratically. The impact of the cost of living on the earnings index has generally been to further emphasize year-on-year and secular change, since the two indexes often move in opposite directions (most notably during the 'Great Depression'). Real earnings fluctuated greatly in 1830–42, but on average the trend was stationary or slightly downwards (the mean index for these years as a whole is 53, slightly below that of 1830 itself). From 1842 to the mid-1860s, however, real earnings rose fairly steadily and even peak-to-peak (1846–66) real earnings increased by at

[1] Walters 1975, 293, quoting *Eight Hours Committee* 1907, XV, 359, 393.
[2] Board of Trade, *Reports on Strikes and Lockouts*, annually 1891– .

least 50 per cent, marking a critical period of improvement in material standards of life. Thereafter, the exaggerated troughs of 1868 and 1878, and the even more marked peak of the early 1870s, resulted in a decade when miners experienced severe fluctuations in the material conditions of life. From the trough of 1878 real earnings rose dramatically during the next twenty years, as wages rose and prices fell. The increase in real earnings from trough to peak (1878–1900) can be measured at two-and-a-half times, though this exaggerates the average rise, which when measured from 1883 to 1900 was 70 per cent. Mean real earnings over the period 1900–13 remained roughly stationary. Thus, although real earnings in the mining industry rose throughout most of the period 1830–1914, truly decisive improvements were confined to two periods, each of twenty years, from the mid-1840s to the mid-1860s and during the last two decades of the century.

The use of this kind of evidence on earnings and real earnings to assess the extent of poverty and deprivation presents considerable problems but may be attempted. To his 'Index of Rent and Commodities' Wood attached money values for the cost of living. The level in 1850 was £1, and although based on budgetary data from 1903 was extended back to 1850 by checking actual expenditure at different times. Our difficulty lies in assessing the accuracy of his figures in estimating average household expenditure in the period before 1900. The figures Wood gave for the end of the period closely approximate Rowntree's estimate of the expenditure necessary to maintain a family of two adults and two children.[1] Thus, Rowntree's figure for 1899 is 18s. 10d. and Wood's 19s. This provides a basis, therefore, upon which it is possible to compare the money value of hewers' earnings with the money value of the cost of living, in order to assess the adequacy of the former in meeting the cost of the latter. It seems unlikely that Wood was justified in extending his cost of living series back to 1850, and to push it back to 1830 would be even more indefensible, for this would show a cost of living of at least £1 in the 1850s and up to 25s. for the preceding period. These levels of 'average expenditure' are extremely high, exceeding by a considerable margin our estimates of hewers' earnings for most years between 1830 and 1860. Comparisons with the budgets collected by William Nield for Manchester and Dukinfield in 1836 and 1841 suggest that they are so high as to be misleading. Among the budgets for nineteen families, three of them for families of two adults and two children,

---

[1] B. S. Rowntree, *Poverty: A Study of Town Life* (London, 1908), 103.

these were respectively 16s. 9d., 18s. 4d., and 12s. 9d. a week in 1836, and 19s. 1d., 21s. 3d., and 14s. 6d. a week in 1841. The figures calculable from Wood's series are 24s. 7d. for 1836 and 25s. 3d. for 1841.[1]

Calculations of this sort are, of course, bedevilled by changes in the composition of a budget over time, and in average levels of expenditure. The limited diets of the first half of the nineteenth century (based primarily on bread, potatoes, and a little meat) contrast quite strongly with the enriched diets of the later-nineteenth century, when typically they incorporated dairy produce, vegetables, and imported meat, representing a much higher protein content. Thus, in the early period both the 'mean' and 'subsistence' diet were relatively cheap. Yet despite its shortcomings we are reluctant to ignore completely the opportunity which Wood's data afford for describing the course of living standards in the nineteenth century. For the period 1870–1914, at least, the money series of the cost of living is reasonably accurate. Figure 7.2 compares the course of his cost of living series with that of hewers' earnings.

A third series is added to represent the course of subsistence expenditure. This is based on Rowntree's allowance for food and rent, which constitutes 78 per cent of the normal expenditure of a family of two adults and two children.[2] Consequently, the course of the subsistence series follows that of Wood's cost of living index, but at a lower level. Income below this third line was likely to result in what Rowntree termed 'primary poverty': physical need despite perfectly rational expenditure. These three series (cost of living, cost of subsistence diet, and earnings) are all extended back to 1830, though it must be emphasized again that the 1830–70 data should be interpreted in the light of the above comments and accepted as a set of little more than best guesses. The slender margins of comfort experienced during the volatile years between the late 1860s and the late 1870s is suggested strongly by Figure 7.2. Earnings were close to subsistence in 1868 and actually reached that level in 1878; meanwhile, during the peak of 1871–5 the margin of prosperity was extremely wide. The decade 1868–78, however, stands in total contrast to the period which followed. After 1878 until 1896 earnings rose sharply as the cost of living fell, and rose only gradually thereafter. The gap between the cost of living and take-home pay widened consistently in the last three decades of our period.

The evidence for the 1850s and 1860s suggests an uneasy proximity

[1] William Nield, 'Comparative Statement of the Increase of Expenditure of Certain Families of the Working Classes in Manchester and Dukinfield in the Years 1836 and 1841', JRSS, IV (1841), 320–4.   [2] B. S. Rowntree, Poverty: A Study of Town Life (London, 1908), 105, 110.

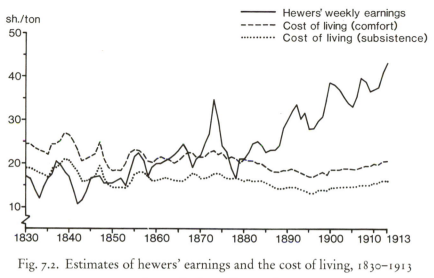

Fig. 7.2. Estimates of hewers' earnings and the cost of living, 1830–1913

Sources: See Appendix 7.1 and 7.2.

between levels of earnings and levels of subsistence expenditure, though even with our generous (that is, late-Victorian) definition of the cost of living, hewers' earnings are seen to have moved steadily above, and away from, subsistence levels in the years beginning in about 1850. It is difficult to comment on the early years of our period. It was certainly the low-point in terms of real earnings and material standards of life. The level of earnings in the troughs of 1833 and 1842 was so far below that of subsistence (even allowing for our generous and anachronistic definition) that these years must have been accompanied by acute hardship; the level of earnings in these years is well below the expenditure indicated in Nield's budgets. Immediately adjacent to these troughs low earnings were characteristic, and consequently it is reasonable to speak of a period of at least six years (1832–4 and 1841–4) in which poverty among miners was widespread. It is evident that, at least until 1860, the earnings of women and children (which are not included in the earnings series) must have been especially important in raising family incomes above the poverty line. Unfortunately, while the importance of family earnings seems to be self-evident, serious theoretical problems present themselves which hinder a simple calculation of the extent and contribution of the earnings of wives and children to the miner's family economy. It may be assumed that the majority of families whose livelihood depended on the industry were headed by a male worker, who received the levels of take-home pay indicated in the previous discussion.

It is, however, extremely difficult to estimate the potential contribution made to earnings by wives and children. Adolescents, who were widely employed, cause difficulties because their earning capacity within the family was short-lived. The phenomenon of life-cycle variations in the standard of life, first pointed to by Rowntree, is now well-attested: families are most vulnerable when they contain young children, but relatively better off when juveniles attain working age. Wives, too, although only exceptionally employed within the coal industry after the mid-1840s, were employed elsewhere where opportunities existed, but here also for only some part of their lives.

The proportion of juveniles (aged under twenty) in the mining industry fell from slightly above 30 per cent at the beginning of our period to 20 per cent in 1911;[1] thus, even at the end of the period one in every five wage packets belonged to a juvenile and must be considered to have been adding to family earnings. Female activity rates in mining counties varied from 47 per cent in Lancashire in 1851 to 21 per cent in Durham, though these rates had fallen appreciably by the end of the period.[2] In the discussion of wage rates earlier it was possible only to make very general statements about juvenile wages. The wages of boys varied between roughly one-third and one-half of the hewer's wage, depending on age. Without more detailed information on the structure of miners' families we are reluctant to generalize on the potential contribution of juveniles to the family economy, though statistics of employment, indications of female activity rates, and our data on wages structure suggest that the earnings of children and adolescents, and wives to a less extent, might have added as much as 40 or 50 per cent to the weekly income of a large number of families at some temporary stage in their life cycle. How this compared with families either outside the mining counties or identified with other industries we do not know.

Limited comparison with other occupations may be conducted both in terms of changes over time and in absolute levels of income. Williamson's comparative estimates of average annual male earnings in 1827, 1851, 1881, and 1901 suggested that, except in 1881 when they were exceptionally low, 'miners' earnings exceeded those of the vast majority of all manual workers—whether agricultural labourers, 'manual workers in commodity production',[3] building trade workers, railway employees, or non-agricultural labourers. These estimates, however, are vitiated by

---

[1] See above.   [2] Hunt 1973, 127–8.
[3] Jeffrey G. Williamson, 'Earnings Inequality in Nineteenth-century Britain', *JEH*, XI (1980), 720 and Appendix, Table I.

the underlying assumption that unemployment among unionized workers was higher than that among workers who lacked union organization. The comparison presented in Table 7.5 is necessarily selective, reflecting the coverage of the data available on actual wage rates, and compares money wages of hewers with those of other specific categories of skilled and unskilled manual workers. The figures reveal hewers to have earned considerably more than unskilled workers. In the period before 1890, however, their wages compared unfavourably with those of skilled (apprentice-served) urban workers, such as fitters and shipwrights or compositors. (These remarks do not apply to 1873, however, when the unprecedented level of wages in the mining industry put these at, or very near to, the top of the wage league). The wage increases in the mining industry of 1888–90 were sufficient to raise hewers' wages to levels comparable with those of engineers and shipwrights. Further increases after 1890 in long-term rates of pay meant that by 1900 hewers received substantially more than almost all skilled workers in the UK.

Two other considerations must be borne in mind. The dates selected here for comparison are all boom years, and since miners' wages were subject to greater cyclical fluctuation than others their average wages between these peaks will have been lower than the levels indicated here. On the other hand, the hewer's wages given here represent shift wages multiplied by days worked—and therefore reflect, reasonably accurately, weekly levels of pay. In the case of the other occupations,

Table 7.5. *Wage comparisons, 1854-1900; national averages*
(shillings and pence)

	1854	1866	1873	1883	1890	1900
Hewers	19/2	25/10	32/9	24/5	32/2	38/7
Engineering (fitters, piece-rate)	28/-	27/3	30/3	31/6	32/2	34/8
Shipwrights (piece-rate)			32/3	31/6	33/10	34/3	36/8
Textiles (dyers)	18/-	20/-	21/6	24/-	24/-	24/-
Clothing (boot and shoe operatives)						26/-
Printing (compositors)	24/-	25/-	27/9	30/-	29/-	32/-
Seamen (highest UK rates)			22/6	18/9	22/9	22/6
Agricultural labourers: Board of Trade	10/8	11/6	13/4	13/3	13/0½	14/5½
Hunt		14/3½				17/2½

Sources: Unpublished Board of Trade return Library of the Department of Employment, London, 'Rates of Wages and Hours of Labour in Various Industries in the United Kingdom' (1900).

however, the figures represent standard time rates (or piece-rates converted into average standard rates) only, and are likely to be higher than
actual take-home pay. Taken together, these two factors will tend to
counteract each other and justify confidence in Table 7.5 as presenting a
reasonably accurate comparison of wage levels in those occupations.
Further comparisons may be made over a longer period by comparing
index numbers for the income of different occupations. By taking series
of money wage rates for five groups of workers and for all UK workers
calculated, or recalculated, to base 1900, it was possible to compare relative changes in wages, though not in their absolute levels.

The series for hewers displayed both a strong cyclical, but also a
strong upward, trend over the period 1830–1913: a gradual upward
movement (setting aside cyclical factors) from 1843–73, and a much
sharper upward trend from 1886 to 1913. Money wage rates for hewers
were twice as high in 1913 than in 1838. The series for cotton workers'
wages was equally inflationary, though in this case the upward trend
was far smoother and less subject to cyclical variation. The improvement in building workers' wages over the same period was slightly less.
In contrast, the wages of agricultural labourers in England and Wales
(like those of shipbuilders) increased by less than 50 per cent over the
same period; here a marked upward movement was confined to 1852–
74, and even after 1886 agricultural wages increased very slowly. Among
the occupations described here, therefore, workers in coalmining and
cotton gained more, measured by the movement of wage rates, than
those in agriculture and shipbuilding. Comparison with the Wood
average UK series indicates that a strong upward trend in wage rates was
the norm rather than the exception for industrial workers, wages overall
roughly doubling between 1830 and 1913. Yet wages in mining were distinguished by their profound cyclical character, which appears in
neither the UK average nor in the series for cotton workers. This feature
of wages in the mining industry has been remarked on elsewhere,[1] and
its origin lies essentially in the wage–selling-price mechanism which
characterized coalmining and a few other industries, notably iron and
steel manufacture.[2]

---

[1] The source for these calculations was Mitchell and Deane 1962, 343–51. The UK index was
that of G. H. Wood (as continued by Bowley to 1910). The strong cyclical element in miners'
wages has been underlined by A. Slaven, 'Earnings and Productivity in the Scottish Coalmining
Industry during the Nineteenth Century: The Dixon Enterprises', in P. L. Payne (ed.), *Studies in
Scottish Business History* (London, 1967), 217–49.

[2] A. A. Hall, 'Wages, Earnings and Real Earnings in Teesside: A Reassessment of the Ameliorist
Interpretation of Living Standards in Britain, 1870–1914', *IRSH*, 1981, 204–6, 209–10.

Instructive though these varied comparisons of monetary remuneration are, when we focus upon both real wages and real earnings important differences emerge. The inclusion of weights for unemployment and under-employment inevitably exacerbates the cyclical element already present in the wage pattern, but inter-industry differences in the incidence of cyclical influences also affected the relative earning of workers in different industries, shown in Table 7.6. Specifically, levels and movements of wage rates understate the miners' earnings experience. Except for the deep troughs of 1842–3 and 1875–8 the coalmining industry managed to preserve a working week of four to five days. By comparison with unskilled workers and casual labourers at the extreme, but even compared with certain skilled and semi-skilled workers particularly in heavy engineering, shipbuilding, and iron and steel manufacture, chronic cyclical fluctuation in employment opportunities posed considerably less of a threat to the earnings of colliery workers.[1] For this reason they occupied a unique position in the nineteenth-century industrial wage and earning structure. Much uncertainty surrounded weekly levels of take-home pay: this is perfectly clear if one attempts to examine weekly or monthly income in preference to annual averages (though of course the same applies, to a differing extent, to all occupations). The scale of this uncertainty was probably not as great as that in metallurgical and in other capital-sector industries;[2] even so, by comparison with those employees working in industries in most of which wage rates were fixed (subject only to periodic arbitration), and levels of employment relatively steady, most coalminers experienced unpredictable weekly incomes as well as chronic uncertainty from cyclical fluctuations.

There is some evidence that the diets of miners and their families possessed certain distinctive features by comparison with the pattern of food consumption typical of artisan and semi-skilled families. The higher earnings of miners in the later-nineteenth century enabled them to eat more and better food than many working-class groups, and even in the years before the wage surge which began in 1888 some mining families, especially those with multiple incomes, enjoyed a relatively high standard of life. John Burnett, for example, quotes the example of a budget in the 1870s of a miner, his wife, and three working sons, with a weekly income in excess of £2 10s. The family ate 14 lbs of meat per week, and spent 3s. 3d. per week on coffee, tea, and sugar, and 2s. on

---

[1] Ibid., 204–9.
[2] Ibid.

Table 7.6. *Comparisons of real earnings estimates, 1830–1913*
(1900 = 100)

	Hewers UK[a]	Sheffield trades[b]	Black Country miners[c] (1899 = 100)	Teeside iron and steel[d]	London artisans[e]
1830	36				56
1831	34				51
1832	30				52
1833	27				55
1834	32				57
1835	37				57
1836	34				53
1837	43				50
1838	38				50
1839	32		37		47
1840	32		29		49
1841	28		22		48
1842	22		6		55
1843	27		16		55
1844	32		46		56
1845	37		62		53
1846	38		65		49
1847	34		58		47
1848	37		48		52
1849	40		59		55
1850	41		53		58
1851	42	77	59		59
1852	43	78	62		61
1853	40	75	47		57
1854	40	65	43		54
1855	47	63	36		54
1856	48	66	47		53
1857	45	72	42		54
1858	41	70	51		59
1859	47	71	45		57
1860	47	71	33		56
1861	47	64	28		55
1862	48	65	39		56
1863	49	69	40		56
1864	54	73	76		56
1865	56	79	52		58

Table 7.6 (*cont.*)

	Hewers UK[a]	Sheffield trades[b]	Black Country miners[c] (1899 = 100)	Teeside iron and steel[d]	London artisans[e]
1866	56	80	37		58
1867	49	71	38		58
1868	42	66	40		59
1869	49	70	59		62
1870	51	74	70	81	65
1871	52	83	75	80	65
1872	55	84	70	106	65
1873	69	82	75	110	67
1874	63	77	69	103	72
1875	53	74	44	82	74
1876	51	74	35	71	75
1877	41	71	22	66	75
1878	36	70	15	55	75
1879	47	71	14	55	78
1880	50	73	22	67	77
1881	51	78	35	70	80
1882	54	84	31	66	81
1883	57	84	39	79	82
1884	56	76	33	60	85
1885	53	74	34	58	87
1886	55	73	34	54	88
1887	60	78	44	58	90
1888	63	81	62	65	91
1889	70	89	81	68	91
1890	81	91	79	90	93
1891	84	90	70	71	95
1892	82	81	78	51	94
1893	79	79	81	64	95
1894	85	83	68	71	99
1895	77	89	66	70	102
1896	77	98	65	74	102
1897	80	101	62	73	104
1898	82	98	72	77	100
1899	92	104	100	80	102
1900	100	100		100	100
1901	98	94		82	100
1902	96	88		74	98

Table 7.6 (cont.)

	Hewers UK[a]	Sheffield trades[b]	Black Country miners[c] (1899 = 100)	Teeside iron and steel[d]	London artisans[e]
1903	89	89		75	97
1904	86	85		71	97
1905	84	85		78	96
1906	89	92		88	98
1907	98	92		92	99
1908	94	83		80	97
1909	89	84		76	96
1910	89	92		79	95
1911	89	97		81	95
1912	93	99		77	94
1913	99	101		83	96

Sources:
[a] Table 7.4.
[b] S. Pollard, 'Real Earnings in Sheffield, 1851–1914' *YBESR*, 9 (1957), 56–7.
[c] Barnsby, 'The Standard of Living in the Black Country', 238.
[d] A. A. Hall thesis, Appendix 6A (Puddlers).
[e] R. S. Tucker, 'Real Wages of Artisans in London, 1729–1935', reprinted in A. J. Taylor (ed.), *The Standard of Living in Britain in the Industrial Revolution* (London, 1975), 27–31. Real wages only.

tobacco and beer.[1] Naturally, this was a family at the height of its earning power and miners were rarely so well off. C. P. Griffin quotes the 1842 example of a family in Leicestershire receiving an income of 18s. per week; out of a weekly expenditure of 13s. 11½d. this family consumed 5 lbs of meat (costing 2s. 8½d.), tea, sugar, coffee, salt, soap, etc., at 1s. 6d. per week, and 3 gallons of beer at 9d. per week. Flour accounted for one-quarter of total expenditure,[2] as against 22 per cent in the example quoted by Burnett.

In 1891–4 a society calling itself the Economic Club undertook a survey of the consumption and expenditure of thirty-six families (within twenty-eight occupations); two were miners from Leicestershire. Evidence on expenditure as a whole showed that for those two families food and drink made up 61 and 65 per cent of all weekly outgoings—quite a high figure (though by no means the highest) for families in the

[1] J. Burnett, *Plenty and Want* (London, 1966), 191–2.
[2] C. P. Griffin thesis, 331.

survey as a whole. The amount of expenditure on rent was 10 per cent and 15 per cent of all expenditure, roughly average for other families in the sample. The most striking evidence in the survey concerned diet. Only 16 to 17 per cent of expenditure on food and drink was spent on flour and bread, but 46 and 53 per cent was spent on meat, representing the highest proportion of any occupation in the sample (even though several of those drew higher weekly incomes). Conversely, expenditure on other items of food, vegetables for example, was low. Expenditure on tea represented 5 and $5\frac{1}{2}$ per cent of outgoings on food and drink, while for alcoholic drink the proportions were 6 and 7 per cent; only two other families in the survey had (or would admit to) a higher level of expenditure on alcohol.[1] The Economic Club survey tends, therefore, to reinforce the impression that miners ate more meat than other working-class families and drank more beer than was usual in most other occupations; both facts are probably a reflection of current perceptions of occupational requirements and the physical demands of the job; certainly both received support from prevailing cultural traditions.

It is also conceivable that within mining families more attention was given to the cooking and preparation of food than was the case with many other working-class families of the period. In a general observation on working-class diet, Elizabeth Roberts remarked that,

... historians who believed that traditional English peasant cooking disappeared with the Industrial Revolution might well be right about textile areas and large conurbations, but would be wrong about smaller urban areas where 90 per cent or more of married women did not go out to full-time work, where it was possible for traditional skills to be continually handed down from mother to daughter, and where the women had the time to devote to dishes which required both long hours of cooking and of preparation.[2]

Miners' wives and daughters living at home, particularly outside the urban coalfields, would have fulfilled this role, for activity rates among miners' wives especially was relatively low in those major coalmining regions where alternative occupations were less abundant. These regional variations in consumption and expenditure and in the non-monetary remuneration of miners are of interest, if difficult to measure, because they provide substance to an otherwise abstract notion of the standard of living, or degree of comfort, which depended also upon the

[1] *The Economic Club*, 'Being the Expenditure of Twenty-eight British Households 1891–94' (1896).
[2] E. Roberts, 'Working Class Standards of Living in Barrow and Lancaster, 1890–1914', *EHR*, XXX (1977), 315.

effects of occupation, housing, and social environment, and upon health and mortality.

ii. Occupational mortality and health

'The most painful feature of the coalmining industry is the heavy toll it takes on human life by accidents causing death or injury'; this statement made by H. F. Bulman in 1919[1] merely echoed similar remarks made by generations of observers, within and outside the industry. Such remarks punctuated mining history each time disasters killing large numbers of miners in a single pit underlined the peculiar risks involved for the underground worker: the Lundhill disaster in Yorkshire in 1857, the New Hartley in Northumberland in 1862, the Oaks in Yorkshire in 1866, Blantyre in Lanarkshire in 1877, and Abercarn the following year in Monmouthshire, Albion Cilfyndd in Glamorgan in 1894, and the biggest disasters of all—at Hulton in Lancashire in 1910 when 344 men died, and the Universal, Senghenydd, Glamorgan, in 1913, when 439 lives were lost.[2]

While disasters of this magnitude were characteristic of the industry in this period, and distinguish miners from other occupations, the periodicity of major accidents tends to distort the long term picture of occupational mortality; for data on death rates were not collected on an annual basis before 1851, when records began as a consequence of the Inspection of Coal Mines Act of 1850. Beginning in 1860–2 (also in 1871, 1880–2, 1890–2, and 1900–2) the Registrar General published data for mining and for other occupational groups. Freed from the daunting process of statistical reconciliation necessitated by this discontinuity in data after 1850, Hair's analysis of mortality during the pre-statistical era was based on figures of fatal colliery accidents. He concluded that there was a dramatic fall in the rate of mortality caused by explosions between the 1810s and the 1840s, principally explained by the introduction of the safety lamp and better ventilation, but that there were considerable regional variations in accident rates.[3] The most accident-prone districts were the Black Country, where the thick coal led to numerous falls of roof, South Wales, where single-stall working and poor ventilation led to high mortality, Lancashire, where there was a high proportion of gassy seams, and Cumberland, where similar problems applied. There is

---

[1] Bulman 1920, 61.

[2] Baron F. and Helen Duckham, *Great Pit Disasters: Great Britain 1700 to the Present Day* (Newton Abbott, 1973), 302–7.   [3] Hair 1968, 545–61.

little evidence on rates of decline in mortality before 1850 except for the North-east, which had plainly fallen from above to below average in danger between about 1820 and 1840, a result of better ventilation and possibly the employment of the safety lamp. Accidents from causes other than explosions do not seem to have declined to any measurable extent.[1]

Certainly as far as the North-east is concerned, but perhaps under-estimating the improvement there may have been in other areas, Hair's broad conclusions may be accepted, though the actual figures are suspect since they depend on his estimates of the work-force in different coalfields at various dates. It would be possible to compile alternative series based on new regional employment estimates, but the general picture is unlikely to be very different and consequently quantification has been attempted only from 1851 when Hair's study ended. Concentrating on deaths from explosions, many contemporary observers and later historians held the view that the effect of the introduction of the safety lamp may have been negative because it caused the working of previously unsafe pillars, but Hair's quantitative re-examination of this question led him to conclude that such a conclusion was incorrect. He was silent, however, on the increase in deaths from falls which might have resulted from inferior lamp illumination.[2]

Representativeness is far from being the most intractable problem in the use of the official data available from 1851, for there are immense differences of approach, classification, and comprehensibility located in each of the beginning-of-decade surveys. The evidence is a statistical minefield, and it seems unlikely that enough data exist to put each of the different sets of figures for each of the periods on to a common, or fully comparable, basis. Unlike the Census itself, the Registrar General's data on occupational mortality did not go into detail where classifications overlap or are confused, and consequently it is impossible to adjust the figures accurately. The major difficulty in comparing different dates comes firstly from a degree of confusion prior to 1880–2 over whether the 'occupied' or the 'occupied and retired' categories are being recorded (death rates are naturally higher amongst the latter), and secondly over significant changes in the age classification and age groups chosen for study, which apparently affected the comparability of the figures for different decades. Because of these and other difficulties the data on occupational mortality given below must be treated with caution. Only a limited amount of information can be obtained from

[1] Ibid. [2] Ibid., 550–1, 554.

Table 7.7. *Mortality rates in various occupations in England and Wales, 1851-1902*
(per thousand)

	1851[a]	1860–2[b]	1871[b]	1880–2	1890–2	1900–2
Occupied males	20.0	13.5	15.0	16.0	16.0	14.0
General labourers		23.5	25.5	27.0[c]	21.0	32.5
Agricultural labourers		17.5	19.0	16.5	17.5	15.0
Building trades	18.0	17.5	19.0	14.5	16.5	13.0
Iron and steel workers	16.5	14.0	16.5	13.0	16.0	13.0
Iron miners		16.0	16.0	11.0	12.0	12.0
Coalminers	16.0[d]	15.5[e]	15.0	12.5	12.5[f]	11.5[g]

[a] With the exception of the figure for coalminers, workers over the age of twenty only are included here. The figures for 1860–2 onwards are from the *Registrar General's Annual Reports on Births, Deaths and Marriages.*

[b] England only; Wales excluded.

[c] Figure refers to London only.

[d] An estimate based on the movement of the death rate in the 'colliery districts' derived from Cairncross 1953, 82.

[e] Two different figures are calculable for this date, one for 1860–1 taken from all deaths amongst coalminers, and one for 1860–2 referring to death rates in three regions only. Both are affected somewhat by the higher-than-average fatal accident rate (when compared to the 1860s as a whole) of 1860–1. The figure given here is a compromise estimate.

[f] The figure for Scotland (for miners aged fifteen and over) was 11.9; *Supplement to the 38th Annual Report of the Registrar General of Births, Deaths and Marriages in Scotland*, C. 7583, 1895.

[g] The figure for Scotland, as defined above, was 11.8; *Supplement to the 48th Annual Report of the Registrar General of Births, Deaths and Marriages in Scotland*, cd 2790, 1906.

them, and much of this is subject to qualification in the light of the descriptive evidence.

Benson has remarked on the frequency with which coalminers were killed at work: 'between 1868 and 1919 a miner was killed every six hours, seriously injured every two hours and injured badly ... every two or three minutes'.[1] That coalmining was very dangerous there is no doubt—and killed managers as well as men[2]—but by placing the statistical record of miners' overall mortality in the context of the experience of other groups of workers in the nineteenth century a different perspective throws into relief the miners' relative position (from the 1870s at least) and suggests the need for a closer scrutiny of the statistics and of their interpretation than has been attempted hitherto.

[1] Benson 1980, 43.

[2] At Blundell's collieries in Lancashire between 1854 and 1896 each of a succession of general managers was killed underground: Anderson 1967, 138.

Table 7.7 shows mortality per thousand in six different occupations, including coalmining, and also for occupied males as a whole. The highest rate of mortality was encountered by general labourers, though the course of this group's mortality over time is distorted by changes in classification introduced into successive censuses. The general effect of these changes was to decrease the numbers classed as such and confine the group to a lower and lower section of the community, typically more and more impoverished (hence the very high death rate in 1900–2 amongst what is effectively the casually employed). Although an unskilled group, agricultural labourers experienced a level of mortality only slightly higher than the average for occupied workers as a whole. Building workers and workers in the iron and steel industry (both mixed groups socially, though with a preponderance of skilled men) encountered mortality rates in excess of those for occupied males in 1860–1 and 1871 (though all figures for these dates are questionable) and levels equivalent to, or slightly below, the average in 1880–2, 1890–2, and 1900–2. The same is true of coalminers; by the time the more reliable statistics are available in 1880–2 mortality in these occupations is significantly below the average for occupied males. Furthermore, throughout the period 1880–1900 mining appears to have been a healthier occupation than most. Two tentative conclusions may be made at this stage, therefore. Firstly, mining appears to have been a relatively 'healthy' occupation—or at least possessed a labour force with a relatively low level of occupational mortality. Secondly, the difference between levels of mortality in mining and in other occupations appears to have increased after the 1870s, when a quite dramatic amelioration in mortality rates occurred in the industry. The uncertain nature of the statistics prior to 1880–2 must qualify, but probably not entirely invalidate, this conclusion.

By using our employment figures it has been possible to calculate death rates for the period between 1850 and 1873; after that date official statistics are available on death by accidents in mines under the Coal Mines Act of 1872 (Table 7.8). The death rates per thousand employees can be split into mortality by explosions, from falls of roof and side, from shaft accidents and other miscellaneous underground mishaps (mainly on haulage), and surface mortality. The latter was fairly stable, declining only very gradually from about one per thousand in the 1850s and 1860s to 0.96 per thousand in the 1880s and 0.78 per thousand in the 1900s.

Four phases may be identified in mortality as a whole: a rapid decline

Table 7.8. *Miners' mortality from accidents, 1851–1913*

Years	Total deaths	Deaths per thousand					Deaths per million tons
		below ground			above ground	total, above and below ground	
		explosions	falls etc.	in shafts			
1851–5	985	1.2	1.9	1.2	1.0	4.1	13.9
1856–60	1,018	1.2	1.8	0.9	1.0	3.7	12.4
1861–5	967	0.6	1.6	0.6	1.0	3.0	10.2
1866–70	1,158	1.0	1.4	0.5	1.2	3.1	10.7
1871–5	1,101	0.5	1.2	0.4	1.1	2.3	8.2
1876–80	1,169	0.9	1.1	0.3	0.9	2.4	7.8
1881–5	1,045	0.4	1.1	0.2	0.8	2.0	6.0
1886–90	1,032	0.3	0.9	0.2	1.0	1.8	5.6
1891–5	1,050	0.3	0.8	0.2	0.9	1.5	5.4
1896–1900	958	0.1	0.6	0.1	0.8	1.3	4.3
1901–5	1,082	0.1	0.8	0.1	0.8	1.3	4.5
1906–13	1,402	0.4	0.7	0.2	0.8	1.4	5.0

Source: Annual Reports of the Inspectors of Mines, 1850–1913.

from about 4 per thousand in the early 1850s to 2 per thousand by about 1875, little improvement between 1875 and 1885, another considerable fall to 1.3 per thousand by the late 1890s, and stagnation thereafter. Throughout the entire period it is immediately apparent that in all but the most exceptional years of major disasters the largest category of fatalities was falls of ground or roof, usually in small incidents affecting fewer than half a dozen miners. These accounted for just under 40 per cent of the total in 1850–70, rising to 45 per cent by the 1880s, at which level they remained. Deaths from explosions were the next largest category until about 1880, but were declining rapidly from roughly one per thousand in a 'normal' year (one with no major disaster) in 1850, to 0.1 per thousand from the late 1890s onwards. Miscellaneous accidents, which include haulage and other machinery accidents, remained remarkably constant over the period at roughly 0.5 per thousand, rising almost imperceptibly up to the mid-1860s to 0.7, then sinking back to 0.5 within ten years. After 1880 this was the second largest category. Finally, shaft deaths, including persons falling from the surface, declined very rapidly between 1850 and 1870 from more than 1 to 0.4 per thousand, and thereafter more gradually to 0.1 by the late 1890s.

It is impossible to assess the relative importance of those factors responsible for this improvement. Legislative intervention was obviously critical, but the effectiveness of a colliery's safety policy depended much upon managerial practice, which is why successive Acts following that of 1872—in 1887, 1896, and 1911—saw a tightening up and more effective implementation of measures already adopted in the best-conducted mines.[1] However, despite enlarged responsibilities under the Act of 1887 (following a rash of serious explosions in 1879) the number of Mines Inspectors did not increase until 1911, and not until that year did the certification of colliery deputies become law, a critical gap at supervisory level. Following the *Report of the Royal Commission on Mine Accidents (Rescue and Aid)* in 1907, an Act was passed in 1910 which empowered the Secretary of State to require all mines to provide rescue apparatus manned by trained brigades, and ambulances and appliances also suitably manned. Many contemporaries, however, regarded the principal problem of deaths and injuries in the mines to be the lack of training of young people, especially school leavers, whose deaths continued to be a cause for serious concern.

Regional differences in rates of mortality from accidents may be analysed from the annual *Reports of the Inspectors of Mines* beginning in

[1] This paragraph draws heavily upon Calvert thesis, 85–139.

1860 (Table 7.9). South Wales recorded the highest levels, followed by the West Midlands and Lancashire. The East Midlands possessed the best record, fatal accidents averaging about one-half of the rate in South Wales. Contemporaries attempted to explain differences in terms of colliery size, capital investment, and managerial attitudes towards safety measures, particularly during the mid-nineteenth century,[1] factors which would help to explain the lower accident rates in the North-east, Yorkshire, and the East Midlands—though South Wales also possessed collieries of above average size. Again, the butty system was generally regarded as inimical to conscientious management and safety—notably in south Staffordshire[2]—yet forms of subcontract also prevailed in the East Midlands and Yorkshire, without apparent adverse effects.[3] Moreover, as the amount and quality of inspection increased the importance of these factors must have declined, but variations in regional mortality remained marked. This puts the onus firmly on geological factors, and particularly on the incidence of roof falls (which were normally responsible for the majority of deaths among underground workers), in accounting for the regional variations which occurred.

Commenting upon regional variations generally in 1882, the Registrar General expressed the opinion that differentials in occupational mortality were largely explained by differences in death from accidents; for while the death rates of coalminers were described as 'surprisingly low . . . considerably below that of all males', the Registrar General also drew attention to coalminers' high fatal-accident rates, which was exceeded only in other forms of mining, in stone and slate quarrying, and in fishing. Levels of mortality, however, varied greatly from region to region, as revealed in figures which compared the average mortality for occupied males in England and Wales in 1880–2 (one thousand) with five areas. For Derbyshire and Nottinghamshire the figure was 734; the West Riding 772, Durham and Northumberland 873, Lancashire and Staffordshire each 929, and for South Wales the figure was 1,081.[4] While differences in fatal accident rates exaggerated regional variations in mortality they do not conceal sizeable inter-regional disparities in non-accidental occupational mortality. In fact, however, those regions recording a higher than average proportion of deaths due to accidents—South

[1] SC Coal Mines 1852, V, QQ 539–41, 564, 889, 1036.

[2] SC Regulation and Inspection of Coal Mines 1865, XII, QQ 7021–6; Midland Mining Commission 1843, XIII, 70–86; RC Accidents in Coal Mines 1852–3, XX, QQ 4207, 3831–47, 3113–31.

[3] See above.

[4] Registrar General's Annual Reports on Births, Deaths and Marriages, 1882 Supplement, xlix–lii.

Table 7.9. *Mortality from mining accidents in the regions, 1860-1913*
(per thousand)

	Scotland	North-east	Lancs.	Yorks.	East Midlands	West Midlands	South Wales
1860/4	2.08	4.1	3.2	2.0	2.1	4.1	3.9
1865/9	2.1	2.6	4.5	4.0	2.3	3.4	5.2
1870/4	1.8	1.9	3.3	2.1	1.8	3.1	3.2
1875/9	2.9	1.5	3.4	2.1	1.2	2.6	3.8
1880/4	1.9	1.9	2.5	1.6	1.5	2.6	3.4
1885/9	2.0	1.4	2.6	1.6	1.1	2.5	2.5
1890/4	1.5	1.1	1.6	1.4	0.9	1.6	3.1
1895/9	1.8	1.2	1.5	1.2	0.9	1.8	1.8
1900/4	1.7	1.1	1.3	1.1	0.8	1.7	1.8
1905/9	1.6	1.3	1.3	1.2	0.9	1.6	1.8
1910/14	1.5	1.1	1.5	1.1		1.2	1.9

Sources: *Annual Reports of the Inspectors of Mines*, 1860–1913. The figures for South Wales (1874–1913) are from Finlay Gibson 1928.

Wales, south Staffordshire, and Lancashire—also displayed relatively high levels of occupational mortality. In the case of Lancashire, where the death rate from natural causes is extraordinarily high from the 1890s, exceeding all other regions by far, a part of the explanation is probably related to age structure, though the favourable level of natural mortality in the East Midlands cannot be ascribed to age structure. Other factors, especially wages, working conditions, and housing must have played an important part, for these were important influences upon health, some of which were peculiar to miners.

Table 7.10 presents a comparison of the relative important of miners' deaths caused by accident in the major coalmining regions. These figures show the sharp fall which occurred nationally in fatal accidents between 1880–2 and 1890–2, and the relative stability between 1890–2 and 1900–2. In 1880–2 each of the regions had a comparable proportion of deaths due to accidents, though in 1890–2 and 1900–2 it is evident that Lancashire and Staffordshire had a rate slightly above average; in South Wales the proportion of deaths due to accidents was very high indeed even after 1890–2. Unfortunately, when tabulating regional differences in occupational mortality the Registrar General employed a refined version of the crude data, in which deaths amongst different occupations

Table 7.10. *Percentages of miners' deaths caused by accidents, 1880-1902*[a]

	1880–2	1890–2	1900–2
North-east	22	13	15
Lancs.	21	16	14
West Riding	21	14	14
East Midlands	22	14	13
Staffs.	19	16	15
South Wales	21	24	20

[a] Refers to males aged 25–65 years of age.

Source: Registar General's data revised and represented by Dr Thatham for the *Eight Hour Day Committee*, 1907 XV, Appendix 27.

were expressed in terms of their relationship with the number of deaths among occupied males generally. This is less than ideal for our purpose, though the data can still be used. Expressed in this way, the comparative regional rates of mortality are shown in Table 7.11. It is evident that Lancashire, Staffordshire, and South Wales had relatively high levels of occupational mortality—the three regions, in fact, which displayed a higher-than-average proportion of deaths due to accidents.

Clearly, differences in fatal accident rates do underlie regional variations in mortality, but even when deaths due to accidents are deducted, considerable regional contrasts in mortality patterns remain. In 1890–2, for example, the figures for all deaths show the East Midlands to have possessed a mortality of only 68 per cent of the level in South Wales, while the figure for deaths from natural causes was 71 per cent (Table 7.12). A similar comparison for 1900–2 reveals 70 per cent as against 76 per cent. Perhaps the most startling result of the exercise is the indication of a very high death rate from natural causes in Lancashire in 1890–2 and 1900–2, which exceeds that of all the other regions. This is probably (in part at least) related to age structure, and the preponderance (relative to national levels) in Lancashire of adults aged 45–64. It is doubtful, however, whether all differences in natural mortality can be related to age structure; the favourable level in the East Midlands, for example, cannot be thus ascribed. Other factors, especially wages and standards of living, but also housing and conditions of work, must have played an important part. Thus, while differences in fatal accident rates did exaggerate regional variations in mortality, there is evidence that

Table 7.11. *Deaths of coalminers in relation to deaths of all males, 1880-1902*[a]
(1,000 = England and Wales mean in each triennium)

	1880–2	1890–2	1900–2	1800–2	1890–2	1900–2
North-east	949	870	742	81	68	82
Lancs.	1,009	1,171	939	86	92	104
West Riding	839	980	732	72	77	81
East Midlands	797	800	633	68	63	70
Staffs.	1,009	1,073	807	86	84	89
South Wales	1,173	1,272	903	100	100	100

[a] Refers to males aged 25–65 years of age.
Sources: As for Table 7.10.

sizeable differences in natural mortality alone remain. Differences on average amount to some 20 per cent between low and high death-rate regions. Can these be explained by the varying incidence of miners' diseases? Table 7.13 presents a comparison of causes of death in those mining areas for which data is available.

The most dramatic contrasts occur in the 'respiratory' diseases category and, to a certain extent, in phthisis. The unavoidable problem with these kind of data lie in different diagnoses by different doctors, who often confused phthisis with respiratory diseases. Nevertheless, there are grounds here for seeing certain regions, Lancashire, the West

Table 7.12. *Non-accidental deaths of coalminers in relation to similar deaths of all males, 1880-1902*[a]
(1,000 = England and Wales mean in each triennium)

	1880–2	1890–2	1900–2	1800–2	1890–2	1900–2
North-east	736	755	634	80	78	88
Lancs.	794	979	803	86	101	111
West Riding	664	838	629	72	87	81
East Midlands	620	690	550	67	71	76
Staffs.	822	906	684	89	94	95
South Wales	924	965	721	100	100	100

[a] Refers to males aged 25–65 years of age.
Sources: As for Table 7.10.

Table 7.13. *Percentages of miners' deaths due to major identified causes,*
1880-1902[a]
(data from triennia 1880-2, 1890-2, and 1900-2 combined)

	Phthisis	Diseases of the nervous system	Diseases of the circulatory system	Diseases of the respiratory system	Accidents	Rest
North-east	14	9	15	17	17	29
Lancs.	11	8	11	29	17	24
West Riding	14	7	12	24	16	27
East Midlands	13	8	13	19	17	30
Staffs.	10	8	13	28	16	25
South Wales	12	6	11	26	22	23

[a] Refers to male miners between the ages of 25 and 65.
Sources: as for Table 7.10.

Riding, Staffordshire, and South Wales, as having experienced relatively high mortality from these causes. Respiratory disease is, of course, closely associated with lung congestion to which miners were particularly prone. It is unclear, however, why the North-east and East Midlands should have been relatively shielded from the effects of lung complaints, but there is no treatment of this problem in the Registrar Generals' reports. Lung diseases are obviously associated with depth of working, adequacy of ventilation, type of coal and coal dust, and the presence of stone dust (identified by contemporaries as a key factor), but it is unclear whether the North-east or East Midlands were favourably placed in any of these respects. Our regional analysis thus remains inconclusive. At the national level, apart from deaths due to accidents, which were 2.3 times the national average, death from respiratory diseases was the single cause of death affecting miners more than the national average—higher by one-fifth.[1] In his 1882 Report the Registrar General underlined the apparent immunity of miners from tubercular diseases, so commonly associated in the nineteenth century with over-work and poor living conditions. The 1892 Supplement revealed that miners suffered less severely than other occupations from constitutional diseases, that their mortality from pthisis was 41 per cent

[1] Ibid., 1892 Supplement, lxxxix–lxxx.

below average, 16 per cent below average in the case of cancer, and 29 per cent in that of diabetes. Mortality from alcoholism was one-third of the national average.[1]

Two factors caution against translating these better-than-average levels of occupational mortality into conclusions concerning the industry's health record. The first of these is differential age structure. The industry contained a marked preponderance of workers in age categories 20–39 or 20–44.[2] This imbalance was especially favourable to overall levels of mortality, for miners' mortality at ages 25–55 was below the average for occupied males, whereas at other ages it was equal to, or in excess of, that average. Since men aged 20–44 constituted some 60 per cent of total employment in mining, the effects of this 'excess', especially in the pre-1870 period, were important. The second, related, consideration is the extent to which miners were a 'picked body of men', in which the constitutionally weak and physically less powerful men were excluded, either in the selection of recruits or by an inability to do the job and gain promotion to hewers.[3] The Registrar General argued to this effect in 1882, and the theme was developed in subsequent reports.

In the course of the Sankey Commission, Sidney Webb took up the idea to argue against the apparently benign mortality record of the industry, but Dr J. S. Haldane, an authority on occupational health and mortality in mining, denied that any process of selection took place. He agreed, however, that the proportion of young men in the industry was much larger than in most occupations. Webb cited evidence that the proportion of men between 20 and 45 was 58 per cent for all trades, 42 per cent for agriculture, and 69 per cent for coal-face workers, and argued that this was proof that weaker and older men were forced to drift out of the industry. He went on to argue that because men dropped out of the industry at a relatively early age their 'sickness rate' (which would be a more reliable indicator of their true state of health) would be much higher than the death rate might suggest. According to him, the miners' friendly societies had a very much higher level of sick benefit per year than ordinary friendly societies. However, Haldane rejected the idea that the data on death rates after age 55 was proof that miners became prematurely exhausted, and was quoted as describing these figures as 'totally unreliable'. Another witness did agree, however, that mining was a 'selective' industry, in the sense that only the stronger boys went into it and because men retired

[1] Ibid. [2] See above.
[3] Ibid., 1882 Supplement, xlix–l.

from it relatively early (though no proof of either assertion was offered).[1] Probably the most that can be said on the basis of the evidence is that the industry's predominantly young age structure was a factor favourable to health and occupational mortality, but that this is not in itself proof of premature exhaustion or retirement amongst older miners.

The uncertainty over the true nature of occupational health in the industry at the time of the Sankey Commission warns against attempting to probe further into the state of miners' health before the 1880s, though the controversy has a long history.[2] On balance, the literature undoubtedly points to quite substantial improvements in health over the first thirty or forty years of our period, improvements in which it is rather difficult to distinguish purely occupational advances from wider amelioration in the general standard of life. The idea that miners were 'knocked up' between the ages of 45 and 55, with only a small proportion continuing work thereafter, was prevalent in the early part of our period. Many a miner was said to be 'a disabled man, with marks of old age upon him, when other men have scarcely passed their prime'.[3] There must have been in this period, as the 1842 Children's Commission implied, considerable regional and even intra-regional variations in standards of health brought about by differences in working conditions—the height of seams and roadways, the degree of ventilation, the amount of water, the method of lighting, the depth of the mine, the hardness of the coal, and the length of the working day all having an influence on miners' health. Possibly the chief factor in improving standards of health after the 1840s was the reduction in hours worked. Although there are no reliable figures on occupational mortality for the period 1830–60 which reflect this improvement,[4] most observers seem to indicate that it did take place. J. S. Haldane argued (admittedly on the basis of imperfect statistical evidence) that the death rate amongst miners was one-third higher than the average for occupied males in the mid-nineteenth century, but that since 1850 it had fallen more rapidly than in most other occupations. It is tempting to attribute this post-1850

---

[1] *Sankey Commission* 1919, XI, QQ 18, 230–7, 7091–8, 6821–4, 18534–5.

[2] *SC Accidents in Mines* 1835, V, QQ 396–1420, 1859–61; *SC Accidents in Coal Mines* 1852–3, XX, QQ 1552–4. For pessimistic interpretations by miners' leaders, see *SC Regulation and Inspection of Mines* 1865, XII, QQ 2302–4, 11079; *Dearness and Scarcity* 1873, X, Q 4655.

[3] *Children's Employment Commission* 1842, XVI, quoted in C. P. Griffin thesis, 371.

[4] Our own data for this period are guesses, based on the movement of death rates in 'colliery districts'.

improvement to overall advances in wages and standards of life (particularly after 1888) than to specifically occupational improvements.[1]

Contemporaries were agreed, however, that miners suffered unduly from several occupational diseases which were peculiar to, or consequent upon, their work. Bronchitis resulted from poor ventilation, and rheumatism from working in wet places, but peculiar to coalminers was a condition popularly known as 'black spit' which in the 1830s was identified as pneumoconiosis, a chronic form of asthma caused by inhaling coal dust.[2] Stone dust caused silicosis, the most deadly of the lung diseases. The other major occupational disease was nystagmus, an eye condition which was the result of working in poor light and was associated particularly with the use of safety lamps instead of naked lights.[3] Minor, though doubtless potentially incapacitating, complaints included 'beat elbow' (caused by constant use of the pick) and 'pit knee' (caused by kneeling at the coal face).[4] Benson concluded that as the nature of work changed relatively little over the century the prevalence of these minor incapacities could not have diminished over time,[5] but this overlooks improvements in protective clothing and the introduction of sharper steel picks, which may have reduced the prevalence of knee and elbow complaints.

The descriptive evidence of miners' health and occupational diseases may appear to conflict with the statistics of occupational mortality, but on closer consideration of the latter the discrepancy does not seem to be significant. Occupational mortality rates in the mining industry for the period 1830–60 have been estimated at roughly 16 per thousand, a figure which appears less benign when one recalls the favourable age structure of the industry in this early period, and the relative paucity (compared with 1881–1911) of miners aged 45–64. The growth over time in the relative size of the group (from $13\frac{1}{2}$ per cent of total male employment in 1851 to 18 per cent in 1911)[6] makes the decline in rates of occupational mortality over the century as a whole all the more notable. This favourable age structure in the early period may go some way towards explaining the contradiction between relatively low rates of occupational mortality (for example, our estimate of 16 per thousand for 1830–60 compares with 20 per thousand as the mean for occupied males in 1851) on the one hand, and the descriptions of unhealthy working conditions and premature exhaustion on the other. The distinct possibility that

[1] *Sankey Commission* 1919, XI, Q 6823, and Appendix 43.
[2] Flinn 1984.   [3] *Sankey Commission* 1919, XI, Q 18392.
[4] Ibid., Q 9061–75.   [5] Benson 1981, 63.   [6] See above Table 3.3.

prior to 1880–2 the number of deaths among older workers may have been under-recorded and those among retired miners ignored altogether leads one to suspect the earlier data of understating the true level of deaths in the industry. Improvements in occupational health undoubtedly took place after the 1860s and 1870s, and the figures for miners for 1880–2, 1890–2, and 1900–2 undoubtedly reflect a sharp fall in mortality—the early data must understate the true rate. The fall over time, therefore, may well have been greater than that suggested in Table 7.5, which also shows that by 1900–2 coalminers enjoyed a level of occupational mortality lower than all the other occupations included. This reflects higher-than-average wages and earnings, more than specifically occupational conditions, although a favourable age structure will have contributed something to the difference. There does seem to be a demonstrable connection between the untypically sharp fall in mortality of miners after the 1870s on the one hand, with the untypically sharp rise in wages which they encountered over the period from the 1880s to 1913, on the other.

Financial provision for miners and their families in the event of ill health, incapacity through accident or old age, or mortality resulting from accident, depended largely upon their own ability to save. For most the alternatives were those offered under the Poor Law or by charity, and in this respect miners' well-being in periods of adversity was subject to the same limitations which faced other occupational groups in similar circumstances. One exception was the success of colliery disaster funds, which each time elicited from the charitable public tens of thousands of pounds, though Benson has calculated the proportion of miners' families to have benefited from such subscriptions during the century at no more than one-eighth of all miners killed in the industry.[1] The forms taken by charitable provision varied between regions. Mid-way between charity and employers' self-interest, the payment of 'smart' money to colliery accident victims was very common in the North-east. Injured miners or children were entitled to receive medical care and payment in compensation, perhaps followed by transfer to a lighter job. Similar practices were followed by substantial colliery employers in other regions, and were sometimes accompanied, as in the North-east, by systematic provision for bereaved widows, who occasionally received permanent pensions.[2]

[1] Benson 1981, 177.
[2] Ibid., 177–8; Roy Earwicker, 'Miners' Medical Services before the First World War: The South Wales Coalfield', Llafur, 2, 1981, 39–50.

Large firms often provided medical facilities and retained the services of a doctor for the treatment of miners and their dependants, an arrangement financed by various (often compulsory) contributory schemes, which combined workmen's wages, deducted at source, and owner's contributions. In some instances a more extensive system of medical insurance developed, for coalowners recognized that it was in their own—as well as in the miners'—interests to secure the latter's insurance against death, disablement, and sickness. Consequently colliery insurance funds, initiated by coalowners, grew in number during the first three-quarters of the century, and membership of the colliery insurance fund became a condition of employment. Based on the compulsory subscriptions of workers, the benefits they offered were modest, and declined after relatively brief periods of illness or incapacity. Inexpertly managed and rarely open to inspection by the contributors, colliery funds caused suspicion of malpractice by employers; besides which the funds were actually unsound, and too often administered (and sometimes abused) according to an employer's inclination.[1]

These various limitations, set in the context of a highly cyclical industry, stimulated the incentive to save, once the margin of disposable income rendered savings possible. Various types of clubs assisted the temporary postponement of consumption from month to month, but increasingly from the mid-century co-operative stores, savings banks, and building societies became the repository of miners' longer-term savings, though the establishment of some of these, too, had been encouraged at colliery level by employers.[2] Miners' permanent relief funds, which grew in number during the second half of the century, though eventually designed to insure miners and their dependants against the financial loss occasioned by colliery accidents also sometimes provided pensions and medical relief, and operated along friendly society lines.[3]

Between 1862, when the Hartley disaster was the catalyst leading to the formation of the first permanent relief fund in Northumberland and Durham, and 1881, seven such organizations covered each major coalfield in England and Wales.[4] Permanence, separate and efficient administration, deductions from wages at source by employers, and attractive benefit levels are the features which explain the movement's success among miners, despite initial hostility shown by the trade unions.[5] By 1890 membership exceeded 40 per cent of all coalminers, the major

[1] Benson 1981, 179–81. [2] Ibid., 183. [3] Ibid., 187.
[4] CG 5 Apr. 1862, 267. [5] Benson 1981, 187–8.

strongholds being the North-east, Lancashire and Cheshire, and South Wales and Monmouthshire, each of which recorded at least 50 per cent membership.[1] By that time, however, their importance had reached a peak for two reasons: the taking-on of friendly society functions by miners' unions, which from the 1880s increased in strength; and the Employers Liability Act of 1880, which offered workers the opportunity of contracting out of the relief funds in preference for the national scheme, though this option was bitterly opposed by employers in Lancashire, who locked out the miners when they sought to exercise this prerogative.[2]

The history of miners' savings and insurance researched by Benson testifies to the inaccuracy of the conventional view that miners were feckless, short-sighted, and completely lacking in resources to be called upon in times of domestic crises. These arose from the physical risks miners faced as well as from the financial insecurity associated with a fluctuating industry.[3] We have stressed that by comparison with workers in other capital-goods industries miners' earning enjoyed a degree of protection resulting from the prevalence, during depressions, of short-time working rather than unemployment. However, trade-union policies took account of this well-established practice by excluding the payment of unemployment benefit,[4] in which respect, as the only principal group of industrial workers to do so, again the miners were exceptional.

The incentive still remained, therefore, to save and to insure against unforeseen contingencies, and this became increasingly possible after the mid-century, as miners' earnings and their standards of living rose. Of course, there were regional differences, and in one respect miners in the North-east revealed a degree of prudent provision which was unique, not only within the industry but by comparison with all occupational groups. This was in their arrangements for superannuation. Since 1862 the Durham Miners' Relief Society had introduced a contributary superannuation scheme, which became the model also for miners in Northumberland and Cumberland. Financed entirely by miners' subscriptions, amounting to 6d. weekly before 1915, those eligible to benefit were those miners who were either unfit for further employment, or aged sixty or more. In addition to a weekly pension of 8s., benefits were available for temporary incapacity. By the end of our

[1] Ibid.
[2] Challinor 1972, Chapt. X passim.   [3] Ibid., 172–89.
[4] W. R. Garside, The Measurement of Unemployment (Oxford, 1982), 14–15.

period almost 90 per cent of all miners in the North-east and Cumberland, representing nearly 20 per cent of all miners in the UK, belonged to the scheme, and were the largest occupational group insured for superannuation.[1] John Errington, treasurer of the Durham society, claimed in 1919 that the £2.3m. paid out to miners since its formation had saved many miners from the Poor Law,[2] and may be regarded, therefore, as having helped sustain at least one large section of the mining population at the stage when, typically, living standards were most vulnerable.

iii. Housing and environment

Housing provision was an important determinant of the standard of living, and depended on the terms of housing contracts, the level of rents, and the quality of housing. As is the case with many other aspects of the industry these elements are not difficult to measure or assess in 1913, but become increasingly obscure the further back the analysis is taken. The Samuel Commission published comparative tables for 1924 and 1913,[3] the latter referring to about 75 per cent of total output but probably covering a greater share of housing, since we may assume that the larger firms would have been the most likely to have returned details and to have owned substantial numbers of houses. In addition to these data is a certain amount of descriptive material, especially for the North-east and Scotland, which when combined with our employment and output series may form the basis of very rough estimates of the numbers of company-owned colliery houses at earlier dates. If we assume that the omissions from the Samuel Commission survey contained the same distribution between the number of houses leased, rather than directly owned, it is possible to make estimates of the different types on the basis of our estimates for colliery housing in total. These placed the stock of company housing at 139,000 in 1913, probably 140,000 or thereabouts in 1890, and (even more speculatively) perhaps 46,000 in the mid-1860s and 20,000 in 1830. At all times, slightly less than half of these houses were to be found in the North-east, and a further 17 to 19 per cent in Scotland.

By 1913 the proportion of miners living in company housing had declined, though the calculation of the precise extent is not possible

---

[1] *Report of Departmental Committee on Old Age Pensions* 1919, XXVII, QQ 5148–57.
[2] Ibid., QQ 5206–39.
[3] *Samuel Commission* III, Appendix 18, Table 37, 247–9; *Mineral Statistics* 1913.

from the Samuel Commission data. It seems likely, however, that about 12 per cent of the work-force lived in company houses in 1913, compared with perhaps 33 per cent in 1830,[1] most of which were rented by miners and their families; a few were held on lease, and in the North-east some were free.

One of the most striking features of the nineteenth-century housing market in colliery districts was the variety of provision. In the North-east the companies provided approximately half the supply, with the remainder provided by speculative builders. In South Wales, where land was expensive and rarely granted freehold, the variety of housing type and agency of provision was greatest. Housebuilding in South Wales was largely a speculative, profit-making activity, essentially a form of income for a rentier class. Coalowners were involved only to a limited extent, though before the 1870s, especially in the newer and remoter parts of the coalfield, some company houses were built. A more important phenomenon, however, was the rise of the building clubs; in the period after 1878 about a quarter of new houses built in the central part of the coalfield were provided by these agencies. Though limited, owner-occupation, therefore, was more extensive in South Wales than elsewhere. Whereas in 1913 the national proportion of miners living in their own houses was perhaps some 7 per cent, the proportion in South Wales at this time was in the region of 19–20 per cent. A further 23 per cent of houses were owned or leased by colliery companies, and the remaining 57 per cent owned by landlords.[2]

How is the variety and geographical spread of the different kinds of housing provision for miners to be explained? The incentives for providing company housing certainly changed over time, and were stronger for various reasons at the beginning of our period than at the end. The need to attract labour to remote parts of any coalfield was a major consideration, especially before 1870, but was present, too, in some of the inland coalfields even after 1900. The belief that housing could attract and retain a more stable and reliable work-force was another justification for company housing, forming a part of some employers' competitive strategy.[3] The importance of company provision in the remoter parts of the coalfield is admirably illustrated in Martin Daunton's map

[1] Ibid.; Benson 1981, 105. The 1830 figure is a guess based upon impressions given in *Reports on State of the Population in Mining Districts* 1844, XV, 1845, xxvii, 1846, xxiv, 1848, xxvi; *Dearness and Scarcity*, 1873, X; *RC Labour* 1892, XXIV and XXXVI; *Eight Hours Committee* 1907, XIV, XV.

[2] P. N. Jones, 'Colliery Settlements in the South Wales Coalfield, 1850–1926', University of Hull, *Occasional Papers in Geography*, 14 (1969), 8–12, 41–5; Benson 1981, 109; Daunton 1980, 146.

[3] See above 277–80.

of colliery housing in County Durham, in which he grades the geography of the coalfield according to the extent of company provision.[1] Here, lack of alternative sources of housing, together with remoteness, were the key factors in motivating a company to provide houses; the absence of company houses was most noticeable in the larger industrial settlements along the Tyne, where colliers tended to live among an industrial proletariat and share its housing.[2]

Even in the inter-war period colliery houses continued to be built, as they had been before the War, as close as possible to the pithead—a deliberate policy on the part of employers which combined convenience for pitwork with deterrence from seeking alternative sources of employment. By the end of our period this policy was aimed especially at recruiting juveniles, in order to make it difficult for recent school leavers, living at home, to work anywhere except at the pit.[3] An illustration of this principle in operation in the North-east was the allocation of colliery housing according to a points system based upon whether a man was married and the number of children he had; houses were given as a priority to a stable work-force of married men with children, with the latter, in their turn, going down the pit.[4] Almost paradoxically, however, the effect of housing provision by competing companies in adjacent areas (such as in the North-east and parts of Scotland, south Yorkshire, and the East Midlands) actually encouraged labour mobility and migratory habits, as companies attempted to vie with one another, especially in the remoter areas, for a supply of labour.[5] At the same time, company housing offered flexibility, and in the event of colliery expansion might be used to attract a supply of younger unmarried miners from outside the immediate area by insistence that families already living in colliery housing should take in lodgers; despite complaints, this practice continued down to the First World War, and was a valuable company weapon in obtaining a supply of short-term, mobile labour.[6]

Daunton has argued that it would be misleading to look only at the 'manipulative' colliery company in the study of housing provision. Particularly later in the century workers, rather than owners, became

[1] Daunton 1980, 155.   [2] Ibid.

[3] P. H. White, 'Some Aspects of Urban Development in Colliery Companies 1919–39', *Manchester School of Economic and Social Studies*, XXIII (1955), 278.

[4] Daunton 1980, 173.

[5] See above; also Campbell 1979, 165–8.

[6] See *Samuel Commission* II, QQ 7989–95; H. S. Jevons 1915, 657–8. As a condition of tenancy the workers at Pease and Partners were required to accept their unmarried male colliery employees as lodgers. Moore 1974, 67.

increasingly committed to the free-house system. As the costs of house-building increased, employers came to have a different perception of the relationship between fixed and variable costs. Despite the large number of company houses in the North-east, one-third of all men received no housing assistance at all. In the 1890s in Durham three-quarters of married men were in receipt of a free house, but by 1913 this had fallen to just over one-half. Meanwhile, in place of the free house in the North-east increasingly employers chose to provide financial assistance towards the rent, an allowance added to the wages to compensate for the lack of a free house.[1]

This did not prevent certain employers (for example, the Ashington Coal Company) building a large number of houses where expansion in a remote section of the coalfield dictated it.[2] Similarly, in the expanding coalfields company housebuilding continued.[3]

For miners who were not housed by coalowners and companies the three alternatives were to rent from a private landlord, to become an owner-occupier, or to share lodgings with another miner. The latter was common at those times, and in those districts where production and the labour force grew rapidly; even in 1911 nearly 10 per cent of all houses in the North-east and in South Wales were sub-let, though these regions possessed the worst overcrowding of all, which in South Wales was getting worse. Elsewhere, the percentage of dwellings sub-let was low and declining.[4] The growth of private tenancy depended partly upon the willingness of builders and landowners to invest in house provision and partly upon the rising incomes of miners, but was stimulated, too, by the rise of organizations which promoted and facilitated owner-occupancy.[5] There is evidence, from Yorkshire, the East and West Midlands, Scotland, and especially from South Wales, that from the mid-nineteenth century house purchase was not unusual among miners.[6] In the most rapidly-growing regions where speculative building contractors failed to keep pace with demand, miners joined together to form building clubs which, with the advice of a secretary (who was usually an accountant), arranged a single contract for multiple house-building. The system began in Yorkshire, and during the second half of

---

[1] Daunton 1980, 151–65.

[2] The Ashington Coal Company built 837 houses in 1898–1904, and in 1914 2,500 houses. NuRO/NCB/AS23.

[3] Bulman 1920, 252, 274–8, 282, 284, 289; Daunton 1980, 166–7; *Samuel Commission* III, Q 10018–2.

[4] H. S. Jevons 1915, 642–3; Benson 1981, 106.

[5] Benson 1981, 109–10.   [6] H. S. Jevons 1915, 646.

the century became common in South Wales. Respected men of substance in a district would act as trustees of the fund, and the bank as guarantor. When each member's contributions reached perhaps a quarter of the cost of a dwelling it was purchased on a mortgage, from which time it became the responsibility of the member.[1] Such an enterprise involved sustained saving by miners for as many as twenty-five years, at a monthly rate of between fifteen and twenty-four shillings. In the late nineteenth century some 25 per cent of all new houses erected in the coalmining districts of South Wales were those contracted by miners' colliery clubs. As a result, the rate of owner-occupation in the South Wales coalfield was nearly three times that in the Principality as a whole.[2]

The other form of organization which attracted increasing support from miners in the late nineteenth and early twentieth centuries was the co-operative society. The basis of housebuilding was an extension of retailing, and the policy of paying dividends and interest thereon encouraged the accumulation of funds for a down payment on a house. The co-operative societies began to build houses themselves, offering occupying tenants the option of becoming owners by paying higher rents for a period to meet repayment; but some societies also advanced members loans for house purchase. Beginning in 1884, the Co-operative Society in Newcastle-upon-Tyne, most of whose several thousand members were colliery workers, spending tens of thousands of building houses during the following thirty-five years, and more than twice that sum was advanced for house loans.[3]

The popularity of building clubs and co-operative societies in the North-east, however, while it indicated the aspirations of miners to become owner-occupiers, was not a consequence of low average rents. For though these were characteristic of the region, building clubs and co-ops thrived, too, in South Wales, where rents were higher than in all other coalmining regions.

There is a dearth of adequate, regionally-based data on rental levels for all but the very end of our period. At the same time, in all periods the rents paid varied markedly with the quality of the house. The most expensive in 1913 were the newly-built, and particularly the model housing developments, especially those in areas where competition from the private sector was weak. Bulman's statement, that a newly-built house of average size would cost 6s. 6d. a week to rent, is broadly

[1] Ibid., 646–7.
[2] Benson 1981, 108.   [3] Bulman 1920, 265–6.

accurate but conceals considerable regional variation.[1] Some of the rents indicated, even for a miner earning 30s. a week, must have been prohibitive, and it is not difficult to explain why many miners lived in the smaller, older, and cheaper houses which observers often condemned.

The fullest information on regional variations in *average* rental levels comes from the *Samuel Commission*; this produced data for 1913, from a sample of rented houses in each of the regions, and is summarized in Table 7.14.

Table 7.14 indicates wide variations between the regions in rents actually paid, variations which must have had a significant impact on differential standards of living. Undoubtedly the cheapest accommodation on a mass scale was found in Scotland. Table 7.14 shows cheap rents to have predominated in all the more rural coalfields: in the North-east, Cumberland, North Wales, the South-west, and of course Scotland (altogether representing roughly 37 per cent of national output in 1913) where houses (admittedly of contrasting quality) could be rented at half the cost possible in other areas.

What evidence there is points to the fact that a differential between urban and rural rents was typical of the nineteenth century as a whole, though was rather less marked in 1850 than in 1914. By the 1840s urban cottages in Staffordshire, Derbyshire, Cheshire, and Lancashire cost 1s. 3d. to 3s. 6d. a week, only a little more than the run of rural rents. An investigation carried out by the *Morning Chronicle* in 1849–50 suggested that the rents paid by unskilled labourers in towns were about 1s. to 2s. a week higher than the equivalent rural levels. This gap widened over time, as rural rents remained at low levels while those in towns climbed steadily. Rents in the larger provincial towns in 1897 were approximately double those of rural rents. The Samuel Commission figures suggest a similar relationship for colliery districts in 1913. It is not possible, of course, to adopt a mechanistic urban–rural distinction; at least during the first half of the period rents in many of the urban portions of relatively rural coalfields (such as in the North-east and Scotland) were lower because expectations were lower; furthermore, an area with abundant free housing would possess lower rental levels, reflecting lower expectations and lack of competition. However, rents were more or less uniformly high in South Wales where much colliery housing was in rural locations. With these exceptions, from the 1840s onwards a widening gap existed between the cost of renting

[1] Ibid., 318, actual rents for various regions are given: 277, 280–1, 283, 286, 291, 299, 303, 306, 310, 320.

Table 7.14. *The distribution of house rent levels in 1913*

Rent level in shillings	Percentage of houses in each region								Number of houses in sample	Stock of houses owned by colliery companies
	0–2s.	2s.–3s.	3s.–4s.	4s.–5s.	5s.–6s.	6s.–7s.	7s.–8s.	8s.+		
Scotland	16	35	31	14	2	1	—	—	26,145	26,000
North-east	11	22	37	4	21	4	1	—	393	62,000
Cumberland	—	27	44	21	8	—	—	—	1,503	1,500
Lancs./Ches.	1	12	33	34	15	4	1	—	4,672	5,000
North Wales	1	6	61	28	3	—	1	1	345	500
Yorks.	—	4	15	19	25	34	4	—	14,212	15,000
East Midlands	1	6	18	34	19	19	2	1	9,026	70,000
West Midlands	1	19	22	32	17	7	1	1	3,888	5,000
South Wales	1	5	15	25	35	14	4	1	11,897	13,000
South-west	8	32	39	10	10	—	—	—	478	1,000
UK	6	18	24	22	16	12	2	—	72,559	139,000

Source: Samuel Commission III Appendix 18, Table 37.

houses in rural coalfields and the costs of renting them in the larger towns or cities.[1]

Whereas information on rents is sparse before 1913 accounts of the quality of colliery housing are abundant throughout our period, though discrimination is required in distinguishing inter-regional differences from changing standards of colliery housing over time. Particularly in the new and remoter parts of British coalfields, colliery housing in the 1830s and 1840s appears to have shared much in common, both in design and quality, with the housing of agricultural labourers. In descriptions of colliery areas the two often appear indistinguishable, and even for the standards of the time colliery housing was probably poor in quality, possessing all the features which made rural housing of this period notorious. Thus, for example, houses built in the North-east in the early nineteenth century were usually cottages with low windows, and lacking provision for sanitation and drainage. However large his family, no miner had more than two rooms.[2] Writing of miners' housing in east Cumberland, Allan Harris notes that even by the standards of the time they were 'wretched hovels' (in the words of a contemporary observer); they were built of stone and of local slate or thatch. Many consisted of a single ground floor only, and were designed in a similar fashion to local agricultural cottages.[3] The best quality miners' housing of this very early period was undoubtedly provided by the paternalistic landowner–coalowners, such houses existing in sufficient numbers in the 1830s and 1840s to present a contribution to rural miners' housing. Both the quality of the houses themselves and the appearance of the surrounding colliery community was likely to be superior, as Tremenhere noted of the Fitzwilliam collieries in Yorkshire.[4]

Certain improvements seem to have occurred by the mid-century. By 1845 nearly all British miners lived in houses of stone or brick, which must have represented a considerable improvement since 1830 when some miners must have lived in the infamous mud or daub cottage pioneered by the impoverished agricultural labourer. Even though in 1845 probably about one-third of colliers lived in one-roomed houses, the majority had begun to aspire to more spacious accommodation. William Cobbet, an expert on rural housing, declared the colliery houses of the North-east to be 'very solid and very good', though one rather

[1] Hunt 1973, 79–80, 88–92; Liefchild 1854, 189–90; *Dearness and Scarcity* 1873, X, Q 6623.
[2] Bulman 1920, 250.
[3] A. Harris, 'Colliery Settlements in East Cumberland', *TC and WAAS* 1974, 136–7.
[4] Mee 1975, 142; Benson 1981, 93.

than two storeys was still characteristic, as were two rooms, possibly with an attic.[1]

Colliery housing in Scotland was almost universally inferior, and there can be little doubt that throughout the period conditions were worse than any other region. In 1844 Tremenheere noted that the typical colliery house in the Lothians was '... rather a hovel than a cottage, having nothing but the ground floor. Some consist of only one, others of two rooms, from 10 to 14 feet square each. Many of the older ones have no ceiling; vacancies in the roof let in the wind and rain, and the floor is damp, being often little more than the natural ground.'[2] He remarked on the tendency for accommodation to fall well short of the standard usually found in England. Miller's description of colliers' housing in Coatbridge, twenty years later, recorded that it consisted generally of one apartment, scantily furnished, with two bed places; the only solution for large families was to convert two such one-roomed apartments into one dwelling. All the houses were of one storey, and thatched or tiled. R. H. Campbell succinctly summed up Scottish miners' housing between 1830 and 1880: '... the miners' row was squalid and remained so'.[3]

Scottish housing standards continued to fall below those in other regions, as the *Report of the Royal Commission in Housing in Scotland* in 1917–18 showed, but elsewhere progress can be detected from the mid-century at least, when in evidence to a Select Committee in 1854 George Elliot remarked on recent improvements in the quality of colliery housing. He referred to the development of two kinds of houses in the North-east—one designed for a grown-up family of several adults, and another for a young couple with children. The latter comprised a downstairs room sixteen feet by seventeen, with fireplace and oven, and an upper room of the same dimensions; the houses would possess a pantry and back door, but only very rarely a privy. For grown-up families there was an additional room at the back of the house.[4] Leifchild, writing of the same district at around the same time, noted that most of the houses were two- or three-roomed cottages. In observing that the quality of housing was much superior at the newer, more recently developed, collieries, he gives direct evidence that housing was improving rapidly as the coalfield expanded, and that the more recently

---

[1] Hair thesis, 265–7.
[2] *Report on Mining Districts* 1844, XVI, 10–11.
[3] A. Miller 1864, 178; R. H. Campbell, *Scotland Since 1707* (1969), 191.
[4] *SC Accidents* 1854, IX, QQ 996–9.

built houses were superior. He also noted that each row of houses generally possessed a large oven common for all the inhabitants, but that there were no conveniences, communal or otherwise.[1] Further improvements in colliers' housing in the North-east can be traced in the 1860s and 1870s, when, Scotland aside, the literature of the period is generally favourable towards housing development.

A more critical outlook re-emerges from about 1880. Both the abundance of comments on housing in this period, and its generally critical content, are reflections of an increased awareness of the importance of housing in living standards generally.[2] Miners themselves were often critical of their homes. John Robertson, Chairman of the Scottish Union of Mineworkers, probably had most grounds for complaint. He argued that the houses were usually too small and often badly constructed. The collection of official statistics on overcrowding (first incorporated in the 1891 Census) advanced this argument too; while the number of persons living more than two to a room in England and Wales as a whole was only 9.1 per cent, in selected mining districts it was anything between 17 and 44 per cent.[3] The notion that poor quality miners' housing was due essentially to its antiquity was also challenged; it was argued increasingly that even the new houses built in the North-east were inferior, since they conformed to the standards of the existing provision.[4] But it was also suggested that the key factor in the quality of miners' housing was environmental and social rather than purely occupational; thus it was maintained that miners' housing in Scotland was no worse than that provided for other workers in the region.[5]

There is little evidence that the quality of miners' housing deteriorated in the period 1880–1914, or that overcrowding became more acute. The census data for 1901 and 1911 reveal that in all coalmining areas, excepting Fife, Warwick, and South Wales, house provision had at least kept pace with population growth. Only in the North-east, Glamorgan, and Monmouth did the figures exceed five persons per dwelling. However, the acute overcrowding problem in the North-east was not a new phenomenon. The only region to experience a new housing crisis in this period was the rapidly-expanding South Wales field; only here was overcrowding on the increase. It is reasonable to conclude, therefore, that the increased attention received by miners' housing and its short-

[1] Liefchild 1854, 189–90.   [2] Benson 1981, 95–8.

[3] Sankey Commission 1919, XI, Q 8837.

[4] Ibid., QQ 8585–6; 'Report on the Local Government Board by Dr Darra Mair on Wickham Urban District', Annual Report of the Medical Officer of the Local Government Board, 1906–7, 39.

[5] Sankey Commission 1919, XI, Q 24106–7.

comings after 1880 were the result of changing perceptions, rather than of any new crisis. This does not imply, however, that housing pressure was absent in particular districts within the regions. The experience in South Wales, where rapid growth in coalmining development had led to intense housing demand in certain areas, was not unique, though appeared in more acute form there than in any other region.[1] When the 'central' region of the south Yorkshire coalfield was opened up in 1875–1900, an increase in congestion of houses in the area, overcrowding, and a rise in average household size followed. The quality of housing was superior to the existing stock in the region largely because of the provision of the 1875 Public Health Act, but in the newly developing parts of the coalfield drainage, sanitation, and water supply problems presented difficulties.[2]

In this respect, pit villages suffered the deficiencies common to rural housing generally, but since, even in the remoter parts of the coalfield, miners tended to live in greater densities than agricultural workers these problems were all the more serious in their impact on health and well-being. J. Y. E. Seeley provides a detailed study of sanitary facilities in over a hundred villages in the North-east of England in the 1870s, where very few villages possessed underground drains and few were supplied with their water from a water company. Fresh water supply was a major problem in colliery villages to the end of the nineteenth century and, of course, prior to 1914 the ash closet and ash pit were the most sophisticated forms of excrement disposal available. Only miners who lived in large towns, admittedly a growing number, could reasonably expect anything better. Even in some colliery settlements developed after about 1870 adequate systems of drainage and water supply were not laid down until the early twentieth century.[3]

Folklore insists that the miners' cottage presented a more congenial impression from inside than outside, and that miners and their wives kept well-maintained rooms and possessed abundant furnishings. There is sufficient evidence to indicate this to have been the case, though the homes of hewers were those most likely to have borne out the truth of this generalization. Leifchild was not the only observer to point out the contrast between the external and internal appearance of colliery houses; in the 1840s he described the interiors as typically 'comparatively showy and costly', many included 'an eight-day clock, a good

[1] Jevons 1915, 638–43.
[2] Macfarlane, 'Denaby Main: A South Yorkshire Mining Village', *BSSLH*, 1972, 86; Evison thesis, 291–358.   [3] Seeley thesis, 286–315.

chest of drawers, a fine four post bedstead—the last two often of mahogany, and sometimes of a very superior kind'.[1] He also noted that as free coals were provided for most households in the North-east large home fires burned day and night.[2] Miners appeared to have shown a taste for contemporary creature comforts and, on the whole, their incomes from the 1870s onwards were sufficient to enable them to indulge at least some of these tastes. John Normansell, the Yorkshire miners' leader, giving evidence to the 1873 *Select Committee on Dearness and Scarcity*, reported that he was '. . . glad to be able to say to the Committee that we have got more harmoniums, and more pianos and more perambulators than we ever had before'.[3] The favourable internal aspect of miners' housing was only possible, of course, where a great deal of female labour was devoted to its upkeep, and it may have been more pronounced in the rural than in the urban coalfields for this reason, though in the latter the earnings potential was greater.

This contrast between the external and internal appearance of miners' housing points perhaps to a more fundamental contradiction in their standard of living and style of life. At least in the second half of our period, miners were, for the most part, relatively well-paid, though still subject to serious cyclical fluctuations in the wages they received. Often it seems, however, that the houses in which they lived reflected little of their comparative affluence. The choice they possessed in housing was indeed very limited; almost all were forced to live close to the pithead and many (as in the North-east) were 'compelled' (either by employers or by local tradition) to live in company-provided houses. The rural environment in which the many miners found themselves further constrained the housing opportunities available to them, and at the same time usually entailed a lower standard of sanitary and social facilities. In the early period, before 1850 certainly and to a lesser extent in 1850–70 as well, miners probably endured a lower standard of housing than that enjoyed by skilled and semi-skilled workers in the towns. Improvements in many regions (and certainly in the North-east) can be traced in the 1850s and 1860s, as miners, even in rural areas, began to distinguish themselves, both in terms of income and life-style, from other rural workers. By the 1890s their incomes were sufficient to allow the purchase of relatively good-quality housing accommodation, but there were evident problems in rural areas in translating money incomes into improved standards of housing. Particularly in the North-east and

[1] Liefchild 1854, 191.   [2] Ibid., 28.
[3] *Dearness and Scarcity* 1873, X, Q 7384.

Scotland, good quality and sufficiently proportioned housing was rarely available, and miners tended to accept a relatively low standard, in the remoter parts of the coalfield.

When assessing living standards of coalminers, therefore, with the exception of South Wales, where rents tended to be considerably higher than in all other regions, and of the North-east and Scotland where rents tended to be substantially lower than elsewhere, the main influence of rent levels varied within regions depending upon the character of pit location, whether urban or rural. However, whereas this might imply that in real terms miners' earnings in the North and Scotland were enhanced by cheap housing, the typically inferior quality of accommodation in those regions, as in other rural areas, cautions against such a generalization.

iv. Mining communities

Close to the pit, often separated geographically and by the nature of their occupation from workers in other industries, large numbers of pitmen and their families experienced an unusual degree of rural isolation and occupational homogeneity in the mining villages where they lived. Reinforcing and perpetuating these features was the phenomenon of the 'family pit', defined by working miners as a well-organized pit which was the centre of a stable social group; where sons followed fathers to the coal face, and social relationships between men working underground was that of family. Communities possessing these features existed in the early nineteenth century, but became more common after 1870 as mining moved eastwards and away from long-established centres of population. Even in those districts where the mining population was diluted by workers in other occupations, the miners' unusual hours and patterns of employment, the unmistakable appearance of the underground colliery worker as he travelled home (unwashed until the advent of pithead baths after 1900) from the pit in daylight, and the ritual which accompanied pit deaths, and especially major disasters, contributed to a sense of mutuality among miners and a status apart from society at large.[1] This was the image conveyed vividly by the parliamentary and official investigations into the social conditions of the mining population in the 1840s.

[1] C. Storm Clark, 'The Miners, 1870–1970: A Test Case for Oral History', *Victorian Studies*, XV (1971), 67–8. A personal retrospective view is presented in Williamson 1982, 87–8.

The extent of isolation and the degree of introversion is difficult to assess, as is the validity of contemporaries' generalizations concerning the behavioural characteristics of the mining population. None the less, during the first half of the century the objective differences between the patterns and hazards of miners' working lives and their modes of living compared with other occupational groups were sufficient to have produced an environment, varying in the degree of uniqueness, which virtually imposed shared experiences of a kind which produced the phenomenon sometimes described as 'community'.[1] The aggregation of people in groups relatively homogeneous in their occupation, distinctive in kind, presented problems which necessitated various forms of local organization and association, whether initiated by employers or workers. Though differing according to geographical, local, and historical influences, and varying in the degree of socio-political cohesion or social stability, continuity, or change which they exhibited over time, such mining communities were a reality at one end of the spectrum of the mining environment. Neither uniform throughout the mining regions, nor static in time even where the archetypal mining communities existed, the rural pit village none the less continued to represent the popular image of the mining community long after the growth of mixed and 'cosmopolitan' urban mining districts became the norm.[2]

Despite critics of 'community' as a sociological entity, mining communities—with all their local differentiation, both spatially and chronologically—contain sufficient similarities through the experiences of the miners and their families who lived in them to justify further examination of their essential characteristics and their history. A problem presents itself in the absence of a general study of the mining community as a whole in the nineteenth century, either in its structural or subjective manifestations. None the less, a fairly extensive literature points either to particular examples of individual communities or to particular themes in their development, which may be merged to yield at least a limited and provisional account of mining communities before 1913.

The mining population dwelt in diverse environmental conditions, ranging from small, isolated nucleated settlements and industrial villages

[1] See the discussion on the concept of community in A. MacFarlane, 'History, Anthropology and the History of Communities', *Social History* 5 (1977), and C. J. Calhoun, 'History, Anthropology and the History of Communities: Some Problems in MacFarlane's Proposal', 3 (1978), 363–72.

[2] The term used by Storm Clark to describe mining villages containing migrant populations. C. Storm Clark, 'The Miners, 1870–1970: A Test Case for Oral History', *Victorian Studies*, XV (1971), 51–69.

to industrial towns or even urban locations within city limits. Some of Britain's major new towns of the late nineteenth century included mining centres such as Ashington in Northumberland, Shirebrook in Derbyshire, and Conisbrough in the West Riding, as well as the coal-exporting ports of Cardiff, Hartlepool, and Goole. Each of these towns grew much faster than the national rate of urban population increase, which between 1801 and 1921 was roughly ninefold. Each of the coal-producing towns contained a population of at least 2,500, of which at least 50 per cent of the male workforce were employed in mining, the definition adopted by C. M. Law of a 'mining centre'.[1] Law's calculations from the Census of 1911 produced an estimate of more than one hundred mining centres, most of which were new settlements, recorded very high rates of growth, and contained populations none of which exceeded 20,000—many containing fewer than 10,000 inhabitants. The total population of these mining centres was 1.5 million, compared with 0.1 million in 1851. On Law's definition of a mining centre, there-fore, the proportion of miners who might have lived in the stereotype mining community which formed a separate urban entity may have been, at most, 57 per cent in 1911 and no more than 14 per cent in 1851.

Among these mining centres were to be found stereotyped mining communities of folklore, which consisted of a remote village or small town containing numerous rows of terraced houses, a few shops, numerous pubs, a chapel, and perhaps a school. Many examples could be listed in South Wales, Northumberland, Durham, south Yorkshire, and parts of the East Midlands, and especially by 1913 within the con-cealed coalfield extending from east of Nottingham to the Leeds–Selby area.[2] In the expanding and relatively prosperous high-wage districts within the major coalmining regions rural influences may have pre-dominated, but many miners—possibly a majority—lived not in isolated pit villages but in large industrial towns or on the edge of cities, which possessed diverse occupational structures and in which urban influences were dominant: for example, Bradford, Barnsley, Leeds, Wakefield, Castleford, Manchester, Burnley, Bolton, Blackburn, Wigan, St Helens, Dudley, Wolverhampton, West Bromwich, Glasgow, Hamilton, and Kilmarnock, and these tended to be the points of focus for labour organization and activity from which radiated influence in the surrounding areas. Even of those miners in 'isolated' pit villages, many

---

[1] C. M. Law, 'The Growth of Urban Population in England and Wales, 1801–1911', *Transactions of the Institute of British Geographers*, 41 (1967), 125–43.

[2] Benson 1981, 81.

lived within reasonable proximity of a small town, and at the mid-century even those communities most dependent on coalmining rarely recorded one miner for every three occupied males, though this was to alter in the late nineteenth century as deep mining led to increasing concentrations of mineworkers, some in large mining settlements such as Ashington, Bedlington, Earsdon, Tanfield, Ryton, and the Rhondda. At the extreme, the Census of 1911 reveals the urban district of Darfield in south Yorkshire to have possessed a mining-occupation ratio of 80 per cent; Ashington, Earsdon, and Bedlingtonshire in Northumberland, Tanfield and Annfield Plain in Durham, Featherstone, Boulton upon Dearne, and Wombwell in Yorkshire, Bolsover in Derbyshire, and the Rhondda, each recorded at least 70 per cent of their male populations as miners. Apart from the population of the Rhondda (55,784 total occupied males, 41,145 mine workers), none of these urban districts contained a total population exceeding 9,000, and half were below 5,000. There was therefore, at the very least, a greater diversity of settlement than has been popularly assumed.[1]

In our discussion of the 'typical' colliery community it must be remembered that a large proportion of miners, namely the substantial numbers who lived in large towns or on the edge of cities, are effectively excluded. The communities which they inhabited will have possessed more in common with the urban and industrial patterns of experience and behaviour shared by the majority of the British people after 1851, and will have been equally open to the wider social and political influences affecting the urban industrial population as a whole. Even among the rest, those who lived in small towns and villages, the notion of a common experience must be a qualified concept. In the period before 1850 three main types of colliery settlement may be distinguished—firstly, the sub-village or hamlet comprising a few houses or single row close to the pithead; secondly, a pit village of between 400 and 4,000 people, a large proportion of whom would be employed in a local pit; thirdly, a group of villages or quasi-villages strung along a road or railway. Even before 1850, however, there were large industrial settlements in the Black Country and parts of Lanarkshire, Yorkshire, Lancashire, and South Wales in which miners were merged more completely with and South Wales, in which miners were merged more completely with munities often found themselves closer to, and more dependent upon, existing towns or cities. In the well-established coalfields exhibiting a

---

[1] R. Gregory, *Politics and the Miners* (Oxford, 1968), 2, Table I; Benson 1981, 82–5.
[2] Hair thesis, 20–1.

particular pattern of settlement (for example, the North-east), the opening up of a new mine led to the creation often of a compact mining settlement with a stereotyped (usually grid-iron) plan of housing layout. In the West Midlands or the Carmarthenshire anthracite coalfield where expansion was less pervasive newer development more frequently took the shape of a linear expansion of existing nuclei along the major or minor thoroughfares. In less developed areas still, or in areas where a small, perhaps short-lived, colliery was opened, the isolated hamlet continued to appear.

The kind of settlement which developed depended ultimately on local topography. Thus, South Wales, dominated by the valley, underwent a sequential development different from that in many other regions: firstly, the driving of the railway to the head of the valley and the growth of colliery communities along its course; secondly, the development of communities along the tributaries of the main valley; and finally, with improved transport facilities and greater mobility of labour, workers became less dependent on living close to their place of work, and larger, more diffuse communities were created, often involving a rejuvenation of the head-of-valley settlement.[1]

As with the archetypal colliery community, which is part myth and part reality, there is a set of archetypal demographic characteristics to which the mining community corresponds, at least in theory. Evison's study of the opening up of a new part of the south Yorkshire coalfield after 1875 illustrates these characteristics. Three-quarters of employed males worked in the collieries, and 90 per cent of women of working age had no employment. Influx of migrants to work at the new collieries of the region led to a male imbalance in the population, and eventually to a higher household and family size. As the new community developed, the female age of marriage became lower and the population growth rate increased due to higher birth rates. Both the infantile and general death rates increased at first, but when the community was fully established both began to decline, though those males aged 25–44 remained at greater risk than the equivalent age group in other communities. Evison's study is only one of a limited number of such demographic studies of colliery communities, but it tends to reinforce the overall picture gradually being pieced together by research on national and local occupational statistics.[2]

[1] P. N. Jones, 'Colliery Settlements in the South Wales Coalfield, 1850–1926', University of Hull *Occasional Papers in Geography*, 14 (1969), 4–6, 33–91.
[2] Evison thesis, 345–406.

The conventional view of miners was expressed by Redford long ago, that they were 'a notoriously prolific section of the population'.[1] Since then, Hair's analysis of the colliery districts before 1850 revealed them to have been composed of families possessing an unusually large proportion of children, of younger adults (predominantly male), and where older women represented a smaller proportion than young females. Such demographic imbalances were associated with the periods of rapid migration into the colliery districts between 1830 and 1860.[2] A comparison between colliery districts, one each in Durham and South Wales, where the proportion of miners to all occupied males was 30–40 per cent, demonstrated relatively high birth and fertility rates accompanied by lower illegitimacy rates, the high natality and fertility conforming to characteristics normally associated with imbalances in age and sex structure consequent upon heavy immigration.[3] However, a special study carried out by the Registrar General in 1884–5 revealed that miners and their wives had the lowest age of first marriage of nine occupational groups (24.06 for men and 22.46 for women),[4] which suggests that imbalances in age and sex structure provide only part of the explanation for the demographic characteristics normally associated with mining communities. The independent researches by Friedlander and by Haines have pursued the possible connections and interactions between migration, natality, marriage, employment, and family structure, the result of which, despite different emphases in interpretation, is a considerable measure of agreement.

Using Welton's registration district data for the pre-war period since 1881, Friedlander identified a relatively high rate of population growth resulting from imbalance caused by migration in the earlier period, and leading to a high rate of natural increase after 1881. He concluded that coalmining areas could be characterized as high in migration, nuptiality, fertility, and mortality, and that the transition to the small family was slow by comparison with the population of England and Wales as a whole or with rural areas only.[5] Using data from the 1911 *Census of Fertility*, Friedlander also showed that even where age of marriage was 'controlled', on average, compared with all families, the families of coalminers produced an additional child. His explanation was not primarily demographic, depending entirely on age and sex structure, but rested on

---

[1] A. Redford, *Labour Migration in England, 1800-1850* (Manchester, 1964), 56.
[2] Hair thesis, 75–6.   [3] Ibid., 90–1.
[4] *49th Annual Report of the Registrar General*, 1886. See Haines 1977, 259.
[5] Friedlander 1973, 50.

partners' priorities and decisions regarding family size. Friedlander hypothesized that large families were the result of conscious decisions by spouses who had taken into account the limited opportunities for women's employment in colliery districts, and the certainty that the husband's earnings were likely to fall as age diminished his physical capacity for high-earning work at the colliery. An early age at marriage together with high marital fertility offered compensating effects on incomes perceived to be advantageous. While a large family could provide extra income at a relatively early stage of the life cycle (perhaps after about a dozen years' marriage), from the first-born, the youngest unmarried son could prolong the benefit of additional earnings relatively late in the life cycle, probably at that point when the householder's income was beginning to fall.[1] Thus, Friedlander argues, '... relatively early marriage and high marital fertility ... provided a kind of life insurance or a pension scheme particularly suited to their special occupational characteristics'.[2] In support of this conclusion, calculations from the 1891 *Census* showed that in Glamorgan, Monmouthshire, and Durham the average number of children above the age of ten for each family head was between 10 and 30 per cent higher in England and Wales as a whole. Female employment was also shown to have been relatively low in coalmining counties. The data could not be used to reveal earlier retirement among miners compared with other workers, though impressionistic evidence showed earnings to have fallen more rapidly with advancing age.[3]

These various conclusions relating demographic characteristics to socio-economic factors received confirmation from a similar study conducted by Haines. On the basis of the censuses of 1851, 1861, and 1871 he identified sixty-one registration districts where male employment in mining accounted for 10 per cent or more of the total, which he defined as mining areas. When compared with others the results demonstrated mining areas (so defined) to have exhibited significantly higher overall fertility, marital fertility, and marriage rate, low rates of female employment, and less out-migration.[4] As Haines's definition of mining areas permitted a relatively low percentage of miners, the support for Friedlander's study is far from robust, though his hypothesis is certainly not weakened inasmuch that miners were found to have experienced the trends hitherto identified. None the less, Friedlander's interpretation, particularly of the relationship between early marriages and high

[1] Ibid., 40–5.   [2] Ibid., 51.
[3] Ibid., 46–9.   [4] Haines 1977, 267–79.

fertility, is open to doubt, for although early marriage was a cause of larger families this does not necessarily imply that conscious choice of the family size contributed to this trend. Obviously it would be a crude over-simplification to claim that miners had no control at all over fertility; but there is no evidence to justify assuming that the degree of control was considerable. To the extent that choice was relatively limited, family size may be seen much more as the result of the early age of marriage, which is explained by the ability of young men, aged eighteen to twenty-one years, to enter upon the high-earnings stage in the miner's life cycle.

Local evidence suggests that perhaps both Friedlander and Haines have exaggerated the importance of occupational factors as causes of high fertility and large families. A study of coalmining community in 1890–1914 underlines the crucial importance of the rural and urban dichotomy for an analysis of features regarded as peculiar to mining areas; the sex- and age-structure imbalances which characterized the 'mining districts', in the coalfields of the North-east and South Wales, were found to have been absent in many cases from the urban—and even from the mixed-economy—coalfields that developed more fully after the mid-century.[1] Unfortunately, the effect of this on the marriage rate cannot be measured, because the extent to which women from mining families married non-miners is unknown. It seems plausible to suppose, however, that where female employment opportunities were greater, and where marriage outside the mining community was possible, then women's age at marriage may have been higher and fertility lower. Even so, the motivation for marrying early and to conceive quickly and often was undeniably strengthened by purely *occupational* considerations, and was the subject for comment by a Poor Law Commissioner at the time. He stressed employment opportunities for children as the explanation for the tendency of mining families to have large families.[2] Contemporary references to miners' preference for their wives to be fertile—and in many instances for them to prove it before marriage[3]— may be compared with oral evidence which suggests that large families were preferred in order to secure 'a period of affluence in middle age'.[4] To be set against this, however, is the fall in average family size during the last two decades of the period, which the Medical Officer of Health for Bedlington attributed to conscious family limitation.[5] Evidence from

[1] Hall thesis, 183–4.   [2] Quoted in ibid., 181.
[3] Ibid., 181–2.   [4] Chaplin 1977, 9–29.
[5] Hall thesis, 253–4.

these various sources thus points to the need to register changes over time and to distinguish between rural or semi-rural, and urban coalfields when describing demographic and socio-economic characteristics of mining communities, implying a further qualification to the concept of mining community at least in the late nineteenth century.

Hair offered some evidence to show a relatively low age of marriage before 1850. Lists of colliery disaster victims suggest that normally colliers married in their mid-twenties, though few before age twenty. Evidence from the east of Scotland points to a lower age (because of their need for a female coal-bearer) and teenage marriages were not unusual for Welsh males either; according to witnesses before the 1842 Employment Commission wives were usually younger than husbands.[1] The period of very high migration between 1830 and 1860 produced the age and sex imbalance which favoured early marriage, and can be expected to have influenced the succeeding generation even though secular migration on that scale ended. How influential purely occupational considerations were upon marriage and fertility relative to the demographic imbalance is difficult to assess; but there is reason for supposing that after the 1870s, when colliery districts were no longer characterized quite so markedly by predominantly male and youthful populations, the purely occupational factors probably assumed increasing significance. Another reasonable hypothesis is that the widespread rise of living standards experienced by the working population in general after 1850, and particularly during the 'Great Depression' beginning in the 1870s, also influenced miners' families in their attitudes to family size, but that because of the peculiar problems encountered by the coal industry were affected less than other groups of workers who did limit families; consequently the size of mining families fell more slowly by comparison.[2]

Likewise, as coalfield development in the regions became increasingly located within, or in close proximity to, urban districts, colliery populations in those regions most affected by this trend were less likely to have been influenced by the occupational considerations outlined by Friedlander and Haines. Women might marry outside the industry and take a greater part in employment, while miners' sons, less subject to parental influence, were faced with more alternative opportunities for work compared with the sons of miners in the rural areas. In such

[1] Hair thesis, 253–4.

[2] The widening differential in the rate of decline in average family size between different occupations is noted in Haines 1977, 253.

situations, because of a later age of marriage for women and the greater chance of female employment, large families may have become less common. Consequently the occupational factors which influenced early marriage and contributed to larger families might still have operated in urban coalfields but with diminished intensity. The declining importance of these influences, moreover, will have been weakened further by the quite dramatic shift to an over-abundant supply of internal recruits to the industry, particularly in the 1890s;[1] especially in the urban coalfields this development must have been accompanied by an exodus, at least of potential miners, from the industry, thereby contributing to a further erosion of the mining community stereotype.

One further point is relevant in relation to the model. For although Friedlander, Haines, and other writers have isolated certain demographic characteristics which miners tended to possess and which therefore coloured the culture of their communities, not only did these apply to a minority of miners before 1914 but—as Haines's double-edged methodology betrayed—other occupational groups (including agricultural labourers, workers in shipyards, and iron and steel workers) might share the same or similar characteristics. Mining did not, therefore, correspond with a unique set of demographic features, but did emphasize certain elements which, at least in part, other occupations might share.

The physical appearance of the archetypal colliery community is a familiar one, and is captured in Redmayne's description of Hetton-Le-Hole in County Durham:

... the discomfort and inconvenience of the dwellings ... a lack of adequate water supply, an outside tap shared between several householders, communal ash bins close to the cottage doors, bad roads with a dreary outlook—for pit heaps dotted here and there, with their monotonous regularity of outline and colour, cannot be said to have other than a depressing effect on the landscape. There was also an entire absence of buildings of any comeliness—the church of drab yellow brick, or an edifice of wood and corrugated iron, the Methodist Chapel, perhaps a little more impressive, though also frequently of the same drab colour.[2]

Similar descriptions of mining communities, both in the North-east and elsewhere in Britain, abound. They took many diverse forms in the nineteenth century, from the descriptions in Tremenheere's *Report on the State of the Population in Mining Districts* of the 1840s, through the parlia-

---

[1] See above.

[2] A. S. Redmayne, *Men, Mining and Memories* (London, 1942), 8, quoted in Colls 1977, 16.

mentary inquiries of the Victorian and Edwardian period, to the indictment contained in the social realist novel looking back from, or set in, the 1930s.[1]

These descriptions represent our view of the 'objective' colliery community—the community seen dispassionately from the outside; but, of course, in reality these descriptions are far from being objective portraits. Almost all come from 'outsiders', the bulk of them (as with the official and parliamentary literature) the product of middle-class observers probing an unfamiliar phenomenon. The sense of remoteness and alienation is revealed in the reports of the early and mid-nineteenth century but is present, too, in contemporary commentary in the twentieth century. Where the 'detached eye' was not motivated by the values of middle-class culture, he was, as in the example of the social-realist novel, prompted by an exaggerated sense of spiritual alienation (vaguely Marxist in derivation), a desire to present a sombre perspective. These descriptions are essentially false, but being externally imposed are therefore misleading; they tell us less than we might suppose about how miners saw themselves and their homes.

The dichotomy between observable 'reality' and self-image is conveyed most effectively in Mark Benney's *Charity Main: A Coalfield Chronicle*, and although this relates to the period at the end of the Second World War its relevance is scarcely diminished. The civil servant Johnson, the classic detached eye, describes the room he rents in the colliery village, a room furnished in the 'modern style',

... with infinite care and sacrifice and the most appalling bad taste, at the great Co-operative Society store in the city. . . . Never surely was so genteel a vision imposed so incongruously on its surroundings. The cottage, the village, the slagheap behind the village, all insisted on a black, raw, elemental scheme of life, where the cardinal virtues might flourish but the refinements and comforts were never intended to have place ... [The room was furnished by a young couple] who from newspaper and radio had gathered ill-defined images and desires at variance with the slagheap, and had symbolised their experience with the aid of a hire-purchase account.[2]

There is some indication here that the inhabitants of the 'dreary' colliery community saw their lives in a distinctly different perspective from that of the observers who visited them. In part, this may have been the result of a process of habituation—an acceptance of the drab,

[1] For a discussion of the latter see Colls 1977, 184–91.
[2] Benney 1946, 18.

exterior appearance of their environment. But both nineteenth- and twentieth-century mining families placed a high value on physical comforts and modern (mass) tastes; many nineteenth-century observers drew a contrast between the cheerless external aspect of miners' dwellings, and the physical comforts, expensive trappings, and relative luxury of the interiors.[1] In 1850 a visit to Abercarn and Gwyther collieries was reported in the *Morning Chronicle*, where the reporter drew attention to the cleanliness of the interiors 'crammed with furniture [described as 'showy and good'] and walls bedecked with a profusion of coloured prints and lithographs'.[2] If one felt compelled to discover the community's self-image it is surely to be found in the interior condition of homes, rather than in housing exteriors, and insiders might view the community in a different light altogether. Thus, George Parkinson, writing in 1912 of his own village upbringing, perceived the simplicity of the Wesleyan chapel but not its ugliness—for him the chapel was associated with warmth, light, emotion, and drama.[3] Much the same might be said of the modest architecture characteristic of church halls, colliery schools, mechanics institutes, and co-operative stores which might form the amenity infrastructure of the typical mining community, as in the Northumberland village of Throckley shortly after the Throckley Coal Company began mining coal in 1867. For whatever their external appearance pit villages were the centres of a wide range of social activities, which included concert performances by local choirs and brass bands, whist drives, dances, flower and vegetable shows, billiards, and exhibitions; outdoor recreation consisting of competitive cricket and football (for this was the home of Throckley Villa), pigeon fancying, whippet racing, and an annual sports day and picnic.[4]

By whatever process, the author of the manuscript poem of the late 1830s, 'The Pitman's Pay', certainly felt that the spread of Methodist Sunday Schools, the opening of savings banks, and the dissemination of 'useful knowledge' through cheap publications had already resulted in a noticeable improvement in the quality and temper of the home life of miners in the North-east.[5] Indeed, 'The Pitman's Pay' is one of the key documents used by Colls in his attempt to analyse the colliers' percep-

---

[1] See above.

[2] Reported in *Morning Chronicle*, 19 June 1850, 302.

[3] George Parkinson, *True Stories of Durham Pit Life* (London, 1912), 9, 13.

[4] Williamson 1982, 51–6, 62–3.

[5] NuRo Society of Antiquaries, ZAN M18 18/Preface, 8.

tions of themselves through their songs. In this he drew attention to what he interpreted as a collective egotism, reinforced by a genuine sense of social and geographical isolation, which developed at the latest from the 1830s and 1840s. Colls identifies a cultural revolution which split the North-eastern mining communities into two—one consciously respectable and the other 'degraded', almost in a celebratory sense, and identified the Methodists as the pioneers of this cultural revolution—though also conceivably the group whose moral conduct and activities attracted people already inclined towards such values and behaviour. One of the principal weapons of methodist influence in the north, the Sunday School Union, was described by its local historian as 'an opposing phalanx to the surging masses of the discontented, disloyal and sceptical'.[1]

The validity of this notion of polarization accompanied by what might be regarded as pacification of a turbulent mining labour force is difficult to assess, for the influence of Methodism was certainly not in only one direction. Ralph Elliott, underviewer at the Marquis of Londonderry's collieries offered evidence that in 1844 many miners were encouraged to strike by the 'Ranter preachers, who made a religious question out of it, to induce the men to stick to their pledge and stand out. Some few also of the local Wesleyan preachers, who are working men principally, lectured on behalf of the union.' Once the strike had begun, 'lower and less educated classes of local preachers, belonging chiefly to the sect of Primitive Methodists, frequently had recourse to appeals to religious feelings of their hearers to keep up excitement ...' and to sustain the strike. T. J. Taylor, a northern coalowner, referred to the tendency for Methodists and ranters to be the spokesmen and the most difficult to deal with because they were usually of superior intelligence and generally showed 'skill, cunning and circumvention'. Tremenheere's 1846 report also alluded to the role of the Primitive Methodists, who 'by a certain command of language and by an energetic tone and manner had acquired an influence over their fellow workmen and were invariably the chief promoters and abettors of the strike'. They were consequently among the first to be dismissed by the masters as soon as the strike was over.[2] A working miner from Durham later recalled an instance when a colliery manager dismissed a lay preacher because of his 'Methodist innovation and irregularity'.[3]

---

[1] This is developed in Colls 1977, Chapts. 2 and 3.
[2] *Report on Mining Districts* 1846, XXIV, 390, 397.
[3] George Parkinson, *True Stories of Durham Pit Life* (London, 1912), 38.

Methodism could instil self-confidence and independence, producing trade-union leaders whose methods may appear to have been moderate by the standards of socialist historians but whose effectiveness in promoting miners' material well-being was possibly greater than might have been achieved by alternative means under the prevailing balance of power between coalowners and trade unionists.

There is a difficulty, however, in judging how far the ranting style of Methodist preachers was merely adopted by union activists to promote their secular aims. In the 1860s William Brown, an agent for the West Yorkshire Miners' Association, who was a regular singer at a Wesleyan chapel, became one of the most active agents in that district and in the Midlands. J. T. Woodhouse, viewer in that region, described how Brown tried to organize miners in Derbyshire. At Church Gresley he hired the People's Hall from the Primitive Methodists and lectured 'in a quasi-religious form ... giving out a text and shouting from it'.[1] Later he became the agent for the North Staffordshire Miners' Association.

At the broader level, of culture and community, it is possible that religious influences were particularly strong in affecting the pattern of life and leisure, especially but not exclusively in the rural pit villages,[2] and the processes of working-class improvement in all its guises— teetotalism, Owenism, Chartism, trade unionism, friendly societies, and clubs—in their various ways contributed to the destruction of the popular culture which had existed before 1830 (though Colls emphasized that much of this survived even so). Colls argues that the songs of the 1830s and 1840s mark the appearance of class pride and local chauvinism, and current with this was a popular appreciation of the importance of coal in the life of the nation, a belief in the dignity of labour and in the rights of organized labour. By the second half of the nineteenth century, however, a transformation had occurred in which the two strands of the original cultural revolution had merged. Bob Cranky, the self-opinionated, hard-drinking, dialect-speaking, labour militant hero of the early nineteenth-century popular song, 'The Pitman's Pay', is transformed into Jack Spring (the hero of Patterson's *Colliery Village Life*)—teetotal, liberal, wise, Methodist—a transformation which, according to Colls, mirrored a real one in society.[3] Certainly this seems to be consistent with the changing leisure patterns, hitherto dominated by the coarser sports until the early nineteenth century, to

---

[1] *RC Trade Unions* 1867–8, XXXIX, QQ 11906–15, 16371–443; *Dearness and Scarcity* 1873, X, Q 5682.   [2] C. P. Griffin thesis, 480–4.

[3] Colls 1977, Chapts. 2 and 3.

the more 'rational recreation' from the mid-century: from cock fighting, dog-, bull-, badger-, and bear-baiting and prize fighting to football and cricket, floral and horticultural competitions, pigeon fancying, band concerts, and railway excursions.[1] Colls's extrapolations from song and novel to social life are bound to remain contentious and, in practice, fallible; but in presenting the collier's self-image, which is absent in contemporary middle-class descriptions of the community, he substitutes for the appearance of the community the attitudes of the people who lived there.

There seems little doubt that religion, particularly Methodism, was a powerful influence in some colliery villages, though no one has ever explained convincingly why it took root in one village but not in another. Methodist influence reinforced the sense of community. The language used by Methodists was highly suggestive of their communal orientation. Prayers were directed toward the communty's spiritual and moral needs. 'The chapels were cultural centres in the village; at least, they were non-drinking, non-gambling, social centres and almost the only legitimate source of entertainment for the women.'[2] At the same time, Methodist society was a community within a community, one in which ties of friendship and kinship were as significant as the nominal demands of membership of a religious group. It is difficult to gauge the impact of religion at the national level. The community-orientation of Methodism and Nonconformity generally must have been an especially powerful influence in its strongholds of the North-east and South Wales, but also in parts of Yorkshire, Lancashire, and the East Midlands. Elsewhere the picture is unclear. Neither the Church of England nor Catholicism emphasized community to the same extent, and neither, it appears, held such a close grip as Methodism over community life. Describing the west of Scotland, G. M. Wilson argued that religion was not a powerful force in the social life of the mining community. Community feeling was generated more commonly around the pub or the friendly society than the school or the church.[3]

It is possible, however, that Colls's characterization of the 'degraded' miner—echoing Liefchild's account of the 'lamentably degraded' character of miners in the North-east in the 1840s—is over-drawn as a generalized description of miners living in established mining centres. For Liefchild's precise reference was to miners in the new pit villages, which depended heavily upon migrant labour, 'a peculiar mischievous and

[1] C. P. Griffin thesis, 479–80.
[2] Moore 1974, 126–30, 226–7.　　　　　[3] G. M. Wilson thesis, 105–9.

unlettered race', in the unsympathetic portrayal by Liefchild, though he also remarked on the 'gregarious habits, clannishness and moral insulation' of miners in general. He noted that pitmen's wages were relatively high but criticized their patterns of expenditure and the forms of leisure which they favoured.[1] Colls's imaginative explanation for the rise of the 'respectable' miner may have underestimated the social and cultural transition which, almost inevitably, tended to accompany the development of turbulent, isolated frontier villages into settled, more stable communities.[2] None the less, the general view of miners as possessing low status may be regarded as the accepted view of their social condition.

Status is a concept which for the nineteenth century is neither easily measured nor defined. In the 1830s the more highly paid grades of mining labour were at least as well paid as comparable grades of skilled workers;[3] contemporary assessment in 1842 drew a favourable comparison between the earnings of the mining population as a whole and those, not only of agricultural labourers, but of urban textile workers. As for their 'moral condition'—that was reported to have been 'better than the lower orders in towns'.[4] None the less, the view (among middle-class observers) of miners at that time as clannish, improvident, prone to 'luxurious' rather than essential expenditure (deemed to be the cause of their 'degraded' character), was widespread. Describing Scottish miners in 1869, Bremner identified a 'want of sympathy' between collier and mason, tailor, shoemaker, carpenter, and other tradesmen: 'Were his said position to be regulated by the amount of his earnings, the miner would stand above a large proportion of the working classes; but he appears to be indifferent to rank, provided he is allowed to enjoy life according to his own notions'. Bremner remarked on miners' lowly position on the social scale, evidenced by their existing amusements, their notoriety for poaching, and their drinking: the miner was 'a rough sort of fellow' in his view—though yielding to the civilizing influence of education by the 1860s.[5]

There is, however, a remarkable contrast between such characterizations of the 'degraded miner' and miners' perceptions of their own status. Campbell and Reid have portrayed hewers in the traditional mining communities of Lanarkshire in the second and third quarter of the century as having been 'proud men', who regarded themselves as

---

[1] *Children's Employment Commission* 1842, XVI, paras. 112, 31–2, 145, 147; David Bremner, *The Industries of Scotland* (Glasgow, 1869), 20–1.

[2] Pollard 1978, 139.   [3] Flinn 1984, 393.

[4] *Children's Employment Commission* 1842, XVI, paras. 228–31.

[5] David Bremner, *The Industries of Scotland* (Glasgow, 1969), 20.

skilled tradesmen and compared themselves to craftsmen in other industries:[1] 'Pride in his skill and resentment of interlopers', according to Campbell and Reid, 'were ... as much important parts of the value system of the independent collier as of the independent artisan'.[2] This was manifested in a habit, at least among Scottish hewers, of refusing to work in front of visitors, whether workers from a neighbouring section or supervisors; this also helps to explain the restrictions imposed upon entry to miners' trade unions, protecting status and relative earnings potential. Earnings differentials also provided a basis for self-improvement.[3] The practice of piece-rate payment and lack of close supervision encouraged the face worker to regard himself as an independent contractor, rather than as a wage hand.[4] This method of organization—containing a clearly defined élite within the work-force—was similar in the North-east, though less marked elsewhere.

The major cause of the erosion of this sense of independence by the 1870s has been identified as the growth in the power of the large coal-producing iron masters, though the persistence of a self-image of independence in the smaller collieries, which employed most miners, helped to contribute to the survival of the respectable and self-improving miner,[5] the spearhead of mining trade unionism for most of the nineteenth century.[6] Campbell's comparison between the failure of trade unions in urban Coatbridge with their resilience in rural Larkhall, between the miners as 'degraded slaves' in the former and the 'honourable men' in Larkhall, underlines the cultural differences which might distinguish urban mining districts from rural communities, though by the 1870s the illusion and aspirations to independence had begun to disappear.[7]

Nevertheless, despite the erosion of a sense of occupational status, feelings of insularity and village pride could create a tremendous sense of community in the rural coalfields. Speaking of his own upbringing in a Durham colliery village, Sid Chaplin claims that 'One was hardly aware of the villages next door'. Thus, if boys from another village had the temerity to enter one's own, says Chaplin, they would be stoned until they fled. 'Marrying out', between members of different villages, was rare. Above all, one's own village was meant to be 'sufficient', both in terms of social facilities and spiritual horizons.[8] The sense of

[1] Campbell and Reid 1978, 57. [2] Ibid., 62–3.
[3] Ibid., 61. [4] Ibid., 62.
[5] Ibid., 65–70. [6] See chapter 8.
[7] Campbell 1978, 102. [8] Chaplin 1977, 5–6.

belonging to a community was overpowering: '. . . the one thing about being born into a mining community is that "ye knaa whe ye are". You know who you spring from, you know who you belong to, your roots are firmly embedded. In fact at times you feel almost imprisoned in a past that isn't entirely yours, a past that belongs to the community.'[1] This sense of being imprisoned by a communal past and a communal history, a feature, perhaps, of most tightly-knit and insular communities, inevitably offered both advantages and disadvantages.

The other feature of colliery village life which accompanied insularity was a fierce sense of independence. There were, of course, exceptions to this, but their importance may have been exaggerated by historians intent on examining agencies of 'social control'. The paternalistic employer—both aristocratic and capitalist—did exist, in the early part of the period, particularly in the remoter rural areas.[2]

One of the owners of Throckley Colliery built both school and chapel and subsidized the village brass band; and involvement in the affairs of the pit village they owned and dominated saw Major Stephenson occasionally playing for the football team and shooting with miners, while his wife was accustomed to visit the sick and advise on child rearing. According to one personal account, this capitalist paternalism does not seem to have been regarded as unduly oppressive by the local population who regarded the coalowner neither with hostility nor deference.[3] The operation and ethos of local communities depended much upon the existence of social amenities and religious institutions, but also the involvement of coalowning proprietors, and—from the late nineteenth century—of their professional and managerial staff—in local administration: by serving on Boards of Health or as Poor Law Guardians, and by becoming nominated functionaries, notably as JPs.[4] Presumably because of the classifications adopted by those who compiled the official returns of the names and occupations of JPs, except for well-known coalowners it is not possible to identify this occupational group, which is obscured by the description 'esquire'.[5] In Monmouthshire, Glamorgan, and Derbyshire it is clear that colliery proprietors and some colliery managers had been appointed to the county benches at least since the 1870s—though in the older regions, notably Durham, somewhat earlier. Similar information for the boroughs and cities reveals a similar picture,

---

[1] Ibid., 3.   [2] See above 281-99.
[3] Williamson 1982, 60-2.   [4] L. J. Williams 1980, 106-8.
[5] 'Return giving names . . . of all J.P.s for the counties of England and Wales 1888', LXXXII, 193; 'Return giving names . . . of all J.P.s for the Boroughs and Cities of England and Wales', 1886, LIII, 237.

though systematic analysis is bedevilled by variable descriptions and overlapping definitions.

The assumption that such public service contributed towards the greater cohesion of community, more widely defined, is dubious, however. On the one hand the activities of a local participating élite might reinforce a sense of community, but equally it might intensify the sense of *class* oppression, particularly through the activities of coal and iron masters as JPs and Guardians. In the colliery villages of Sid Chaplin's youth, in Durham shortly after the First World War, he found a powerful spirit of independence developed though the union lodge— the lodge was the village, and the latter gained its sense of identity and independence from its links with organized labour.[1] There was almost certainly a strong correlation between village independence and union strength, and since in all regions (except in South Wales) the pit lodge was the basis of union organization, this growing spirit of independence is one that must be traced from the emergence of the first county unions in the late 1850s.[2]

The sense of community among miners was also reinforced by village activities, many of which were free from employer intervention and control. Robert Moore's use of newspaper reports indicated that throughout at least the last third of the nineteenth century the colliery villages were the sites of almost continuous and enthusiastic activity. These included bands, orchestras, gardening, dog racing, knur and spell, pitch and toss, popular lectures, the Mechanics Institute, football, rowing, running and other competitive sports, picnics, and outings of various kinds.[3] This portrait of frenzied social activity is a much-needed counterweight to the frequent, largely middle-class, descriptions of the village as drab and insanitary settlements. Life in mining villages should not be confused with the conditions of living.

Two of the most abiding pastimes for men in colliery communities were drinking and gambling. Gambling was not only common, but, more remarkably, almost any activity (and certainly all sports and pastimes) became an excuse to gamble; all gambling was organized by and for the men themselves, with no outside intervention or organization. At least amongst a section of the male population, often 'all hell was let loose' on Friday and Saturday nights, even in a community of only some 900 or 1,000 people, the consequence of heavy drinking. Probably a perennial feature of colliery life, this none the less was muted

[1] Chaplin 1977, 12–14.
[2] See below chapter 8, ii.   [3] Moore 1974, 77.

wherever Methodism had gained influence, which in certain areas, such as the North-east, must have been widespread. Heavy drinking can be associated particularly with the 'degraded' condition of the early nineteenth-century miner—though how much of this was sensationalism on the part of middle-class observers and how much a dispassionate account of truly general conditions is difficult to say. Describing the newly-created community around Coatbridge in the 1830s, Miller spoke of the drunken brawls and general lawlessness which kept all peaceable folks in their homes at night;[1] improvements in these conditions occurred, however, in the later 1840s. One estimate of crime rates published in the *Journal of the Statistical Society* in 1839 ranked the mining counties as a whole well below London, the manufacturing districts, and the rural counties,[2] and while these levels also reflected the effectiveness of policing, there is no obvious reason to suppose that policing in mining counties was either very much worse or very much better than in both rural and manufacturing districts; mining populations were to be found in both kinds of locations.

The social life of the two sexes was almost completely segregated—all 'serious' drinking, gambling, and sport was indulged in by men, alone.[3] Common family traditions which continued through the generations, and in particular a common youth culture, were also a force for community solidarity. Family relationships were inevitably close in these relatively isolated communities, though of course this might produce friction as well as cohesion. Children and adolescents were tied more closely to their parents and other kin by the practice of colliery recruitment—children entered the mine on leaving school, recruited by employers who actively used kinship ties to effect a supply of new labour, and would, either immediately or on entry to the face, work an 'apprenticeship' of some kind with their father, brother, or other relative.[4] The pattern of one's future life was laid down and was difficult to escape. Promotion to the face and to the status of hewer brought financial independence and made marriage possible. A system of 'betrothal' seems to have operated in some sense, at least in the North-east, with marriage usually following on from (rather than preceding) pregnancy. Multi-generational ties were surprisingly strong. Sid Chaplin, for

[1] Miller 1864, 17.

[2] R. W. Rawson, 'An Inquiry into the Statistics of Crime in England and Wales', *JSS* (1839), 337–8; J. Fletcher, 'Progress of Crime in the United Kingdom', *JSS* (1843), 224.

[3] Benney 1946, 24.

[4] See above 205–6.

example, records that it was common for the eldest son to be adopted by his grandparents—and he felt more affection for his grandmother than his mother.[1] As many writers have noted, families were also united by fear, since mining was a dangerous occupation which all male family members faced, the threat of death or serious injury must have acted as a familial and communal bond.[2]

There is no need to idealize or sentimentalize the effects of living in a small, relatively isolated community. The classic problem of such communities, lack of secrecy, was fully in evidence in mining villages and towns. This applied to income as well as to the details of family life. According to Benney, the income of every family was known to all the people of the village—largely because of the fact that the weekly pay, worked out by the checkweighman, was public knowledge. Benney comments, 'The pretensions of urban living were impossible here. No family could assume higher standards than its income warranted without incurring ridicule. Here, perhaps, [was] part of the reason why miners made their demands on life as a community, not as individuals.'[3] Lack of privacy was also a powerful incentive toward convention and conventional living.

Similarly, social rank and status within the community were well-defined and more-or-less immutable. The position of a man in society was noted and acknowledged—'gaffer', craftsman, collier, surface worker, youth, and so on—and he was expected to behave in accordance with his position. Reinforcement of these rigidities of social structure resulted from family influence at the colliery as well as in the home. In most regions boys commenced work as drivers and putters prior to promotion to the face, whereupon they were likely to work with their father, brother, or some other relative, and family ties remained integral to the process of apprenticeship.[4] Daunton's observation that 'in the North-east entry to work was always outside the orbit of the family . . .'[5] is thus misleading. It might be possible to argue that juveniles in the North-east were less dependent on their seniors than in South Wales because they were paid directly by the management (whereas elsewhere subcontracting of juveniles was still the norm at the end of our period); but this may be regarded as an accounting, rather than a socially significant, distinction.

[1] Chaplin 1977, 16–17, 30.
[2] Williamson 1982, 135–6; J. Lawson, *A Man's Life* (1932), 49.
[3] Benney 1946, 24.
[4] Colls 1977, 95; Chaplin 1977, 27–8.
[5] Daunton 1980, 590.

Communal life was also reinforced by the well-defined and distinct life styles which men and women would separately adopt; naturally, this applies generally to most societies, but the division of work and leisure amongst the sexes in the archetypal colliery community was arguably stronger than that operating in most other nineteenth-century occupations and communities. Colls draws attention to the egotistical, regional, and sexual chauvinism of the North-eastern miner, in which the perception of one's work conferred superiority.[1] Many miners in the North-east composed songs about work and about people at work (though as Colls points out this might be contrasted to the choir traditions of South Wales), and geographical and social isolation enforced this act of self-celebration. Concepts of virility and manliness enter these songs most clearly in the post-1830 period; manhood was synonymous with mining—a fact accepted, of course, by the entire community.[2] Chaplin declared that 'The very nature of pit work made most women slaves, wives and daughters all'.[3]

In the rural coalfields, and indeed in perhaps most mining districts before the 1850s, the pattern of family life revolved around the males, especially because of the absence of alternative employment for women and young girls, other than seasonal agricultural work and a small amount of domestic service. The domestic roles of wives and unmarried daughters, however, were onerous, their function being to provide the domestic base, often for several males working different shifts, to make their work possible.[4] Such duties were often sufficient to keep a daughter at home irrespective of employment opportunities. The miner's wife was virtually confined to the domestic arena; only in the urban or mixed coalfields could women penetrate the otherwise male-dominated area of work and leisure.

Even in those regions where women could find employment in the collieries, underground before 1842 or, for a few, on the surface thereafter, starting a family usually heralded retirement. The growth of domestic service, dressmaking, and the professions such as teaching, hardly affected the tradition in mining families for girls to stay at home until marriage, and even fewer wives found employment outside the home. Mining districts in the North-east rarely recorded the employment of more than 14 per cent of their female population, compared with between 20 and 30 per cent in non-mining districts in the same region.[5]

[1] Colls 1977, 52–4, 121–2.   [2] Ibid.
[4] Benney 1978, 20.   [3] Chaplin 1977, 29.
[5] Haines 1977, 242–7; Freidlander 1973, 46–9.

However, unwaged women were not necessarily economically inactive, for miners' wives commonly took in lodgers,[1] who especially among the poorer families provided an important source of additional income. None the less, a rigid sexual division of labour was a prominent feature of the industry, formed a major element in social experience, and contributed to the self-image of communities. Traditional patterns of behaviour survived; in 1946 an observer remarked on the women he encountered at 'Charity Main', that 'the thought of a man doing housework of any sort was considered . . . as being too ludicrous to be entertained'.[2]

Colliery communities in rural parts of the coalfields were sufficiently small and closed for deprivation—and the perception of what constituted deprivation—to be reasonably similar in the experience of all families; for despite variations in families' incomes and differing standards of living, the environmental constraints of living in a colliery community, its alleged 'drabness' and poor social facilities, were experienced by everybody.[3] The 'degradation' found in so many of the mining villages observed by people like Tremenheere and Liefchild in the early nineteenth century affected all the inhabitants, though in various degrees. Referring to miners in Coatbridge, Miller argued that *as a class* they were improvident, spending their money freely and leaving the future to chance, the majority living in poverty and debt.[4] Whereas Colls explained the gradual supercession of the older tradition of degradation and excess by the new ethic of respectability under Methodist influence,[5] it is possible to doubt whether it was as influential in the long term as a general improvement in the miner's standard of living, which can be dated with certainty from the 1850s. The growth of communications was another influence, but especially important in dissolving the cohesion of pit villages was urbanization, though this influence was felt more in some coalfields than others. A glass manufacturer from St Helens described this process as he witnessed it in south Lancashire: 'Colliers have a bad name; they used to live as it were isolated from everyone, and were rough and ignorant; to some extent they are so still but towns have grown up around coalpits of late years. . . . The Colliers have now been forced to mix with their fellows and have improved accordingly.'[6]

[1] In Moira, a Leicestershire colliery village, in 1871 one-third of the houses contained lodgers. C. P. Griffin, 'Three Generations of Miners' Housing at Moira, Leicestershire, 1811–1934', *Industrial Archeology Review*, 1 (1976–7), 280–2.   [2] Benney 1978, 20.

[3] Miller 1864, 182.   [4] See Evison thesis, 421–6, for an example.

[5] Colls 1977, 77–83.   [6] Quoted in Challinor 1972, 251.

The conscious efforts of trade-union leaders reinforced this 'civilizing' process; drunkenness, profligacy, aggression, and unruly behaviour were counter to the image of responsible, respectable trade unionism, on which depended the prospect of something approaching negotiation between equals—as had certainly been established by the Yorkshire miners by the 1860s, and later in the same decade by the miners of Northumberland and Durham.[1] A report of a union dinner, which appeared in the *Miners' Advocate* in 1845, captures the mood even then among those seeking to advance the miners' interests. The report referred to 'the prognostications of some that miners could not meet at a convivial feast without a fight', but the occasion had passed off peacefully, for it was explained that 'the union has knitted them together, made them better neighbours, better husbands'.[2]

For whatever reason, changes did occur, transforming what were sometimes virtually lawless and primitive communities, hastily erected, attracting a restless population, into something more representative of, and acceptable to, mid-Victorian standards. A definition of the nature of these 'improved' communities, in which transport, rising living standards, unionization, and industrialization gradually eroded a peculiar community cohesion, is difficult to find. Chaplin has focused upon their negative aspects, in particular the elusive phenomenon of spiritual deprivation. He found himself 'so shaped and moulded by the village that in many ways I remained inextricably its prisoner . . . willingly and for life'.[3] Yet in Chaplin's experience this process of socialization occurred in a context of emotional constriction, in which family affection was never displayed, mothers were never kissed, and people remained silent upon their innermost feelings.[4]

We have no way of judging the validity of this verdict, for personal responses to similar circumstances might differ widely. In searching for influences which may be regarded as peculiar to life in nineteenth-century mining communities, however, and the effects which are not inconsistent with Chaplin's account of personal relationships, the high risks of injury and death stand out. These have been adduced as the reasons explaining the custom, 'based on grim, sad experience', whereby mothers and wives invariably saw their menfolk out to work, whatever the shift, and stayed up for their return.[5] It has been suggested, too, that

[1] See below 681, 697.
[2] Quoted in Challinor 1972, 252.
[3] Chaplin 1977, 34.
[4] Ibid., 16–19.
[5] J. Lawson, *A Man's Life* (London, 1932), 49.

the constant threat of danger, which may help to account for the inhibited emotional display alluded to by Chaplin, simultaneously underwrote a degree of marital equilibrium.[1] The fundamental basis for enduring alliances, however, was the socio-economic element of the contractual obligation implied in marriage, so crucial in mining communities which allowed very limited scope for women's employment.[2]

Chaplin felt unable to counter the oppressiveness generated by the constricting relationships produced by limited social networks, and the inhibiting influence upon personality which he thought they exercised. The experiences of George Parkinson and James Brown, however, suggest that Chaplin's responses should not be interpreted as representative of a sentiment widely held. Parkinson's experience and attitudes were powerfully informed by his religious beliefs and his role as lay preacher, which almost guaranteed a sense of self-fulfilment.[3] The life of James Brown and his family, however, offers perhaps a more reliable— though by no means infallible—guide to the ordinary working miners' perception of life down the pit and in the village.[4] Beginning in 1883, from the age of eleven he spent 52 years in three pits, mostly as a hewer for the Throckley Coal Company, in the community constructed by the local owners after 1867. This formed the basis for Brown, and for others who moved to the village, to build a life for themselves as far as they could, 'free from the constraints of the company and its rules and the vicissitudes of winning coal'.[5] The development among the mining population of necessary habits of mutuality, supplemented by neighbourliness often rooted in kinship, and the interaction between the various institutions, organizations, and associations—the co-operative store, the union lodge, the numerous recreational societies—some established by the company, others by the miners and their families, were neither consciously defensive nor static.[6] Williamson has described how these local groups contributed both to a reinforcement of a 'prevailing sense of belonging to a particular place and a particular class', but which simultaneously introduced and sustained considerable diversity, offering outlets for self-expression and opportunities for fulfilment at various levels; 'To come from Throckley meant precisely this—to be recognized as someone who shared in the associational life of the village'.[7]

[1] Williamson 1982, 135–6.

[2] D. H. Slaughter, *Coal is Our Life: An Analysis of a Yorkshire Mining Community* (London, 1956), 228.

[3] George Parkinson, *True Stories of Durham Pit Life* (London, 1912), 153–5.

[4] Williamson 1982, 1.   [5] Ibid., 230.

[6] Ibid., 136, 230–1.   [7] Ibid., 63.

It is difficult to determine how widespread and how typical was the archetypal mining village of the kind represented by Throckley, which even in 1913 contained well below 3,000 inhabitants and retained its truly rural character.[1] This contrasted with the environment of colliery workers in the Black Country, to which well before 1830 iron production and metal manufacture had been drawn to exploit the area's coal. By the mid-century collieries were scattered in districts within a four-mile radius from Tipton, wherein blast furnaces, mills and forges, rolling mills, and engineering shops were almost ubiquitous; but in close proximity, too, were to be found a variety of unrelated trades, including leather, glass, and paper.[2] Such a diverse industrial structure within an extensively urbanized region produced a social environment in which the lives of colliers and their families could be freer from paternalist influence, more open to external forces, and less introverted as a group, for they lived and worked in towns and sizeable industrial villages, such as West Bromwich, Dudley, Wolverhampton, Walsall, and Tipton, each possessing populations which even in 1861 exceeded 30,000, with only slightly fewer in Bilston, Willenhall, Wednesbury, and Rowley Regis.[3] Lancashire was similar in this respect.

Elsewhere, too, it is evident that an increasingly large number of miners lived in towns and cities, as some villages expanded to become urban districts and as others were drawn into the ambit of cities and absorbed into an even more extensive and heterogeneous socio-economic network. Certainly no region was homogeneous in this rural–urban classification. While even in 1913 the majority of miners in Scotland, the North-east, and South Wales dwelt in rural locations—though what proportion resembled Throckley we do not know—large minorities in these regions lived in cities or industrial conurbations. In Yorkshire and the Midlands there was perhaps a finer balance between rural and urban workers in the industry. In any case, the distinction between 'rural' and 'urban' is not an easy one to define, and an estimate of the number of miners living in different-sized communities may not be adequate. It seems probable, for example, that miners living in the larger colliery settlements (such as Ashington in Northumberland, or the Rhondda in South Wales) exhibited a mixture of 'rural' and 'urban' characteristics. Similarly, miners who lived in the large towns and cities of Yorkshire or

---

[1] Ibid., 56.
[2] G. C. Allen, *The Industrial Development of Birmingham and the Black Country* (London, 1929), 87, 457, Table II, 458 Table IV, 459 Table V.
[3] Ibid., 98.

Lancashire would still have possessed many of the traits associated with mining as an occupation (that is, the traits identified here in the discussion of the colliery community), but would at the same time have exhibited many of the wider trans-occupational characteristics of urban dwellers in the later nineteenth century.

Essentially, we are concerned here with occupational characteristics which achieved their fullest expression in the closed, isolated, single-industry villages of the rural coalfields, but which might also be identified, to a lesser degree perhaps, even among miners who lived in large towns and cities. Similarly, the qualities which writers have identified as characteristic of mining communities—their patriarchal aspects their communal independence, their emphasis upon community, religion, and family relationships, their cohesion, their lack of emotional expression, even their social life and pastimes—were all features that might be identified in other occupations and communities, but were simply more visible, more clearly defined, in the mining villages. The distinction is perhaps one of degree rather than substance. Even so, the combination of these characteristics, in a particular manner and to a certain extent, did help to create an identifiable community. Despite the misconceptions that stem from external observation and from community chauvinism from within, the archetypal colliery village did represent a pattern of life, the elements of which genuinely encompassed a large, though probably declining, proportion of colliery workers. As a model, a figment based on reality, the notion of the mining community affords limited illumination; but in the absence of empirical evidence which would enable us to proceed further than purely local generalization, its value remains for the light it sheds on the lives of miners and their families.

Appendix 7.1. Sources and methods for wage estimates

Any attempt to construct a series of wage rates in the industry must begin with J. W. F. Rowe's *Wages in the Coal Industry* (London, 1923), the main aim of which was to trace the changes in daily wage rates in the regions between 1888 (or 1879 in the case of Durham and Northumberland) and 1914, and relate these differences to the published district scales. Rowe observed that the actual rise in shift wages in this period was generally in advance of the rise indicated by the printed scales which stated the position of wages above the respective base year (1879 or 1888). This difference, which was roughly 25 per cent of the 1879 or 1888 rate on average, was due to changes in base rates (the going rate for a 'normal' day's work) which were renegotiated at pit level throughout the period. Because Rowe was only interested in wage levels at two points in time, it remains necessary to calculate the annual movement of wage rates, firstly from the percentage fluctuations in the scales, and secondly from an estimation (necessarily speculative) of the likely timing of changes in base rates considered at the coalfield level.

The calculations involved contain several difficulties. The approach adopted by Rowe was to take the *Wage Census* data of October 1886,[1] which is in the form of weekly earnings, and divide by the number of days worked in each of the regions according to a parliamentary return dated 1890.[2] The difficulty lies in deciding to which year the 1890 return refers. The output data given in conjunction with the report refer unambiguously to 1889, though this cannot be taken as a certain indication that the employment data do too. At any rate, it is most unlikely that the 1886 *Wage Census* data are divided in these calculations by exactly the right figure (namely the number of days worked in October 1886). If the data do refer to 1889 the magnitude of the error may be as great as 10 per cent (that is, half a day a week); if it refers to 1887 or 1888 the error will be much less than this. In addition to this problem, the *Wage Census* covered only about 16 per cent of underground workers in the industry, and in some regions the figure was less than 10 per cent.

This raises questions about the representativeness of the census and the validity of the selection involved. The days-worked data in the 1890 report appear to refer to hewers working a full week (that is, one with no absenteeism) and the Rowe analysis depends upon the implicit assumption that the *Wage Census* also selected workers who worked for the full number of shifts. Despite these reservations, there are too many uncertainties to allow a convincing revision based on different assumptions; neither the date of the days-worked data in the 1890 Report is certain, nor is the basis on which the 1886 wage figures were calculated. If a significant error does occur, the bias will almost certainly be in the direction of overestimating the number of days actually worked by miners in 1886, thereby underestimating the size of shift wages received.

---

[1] A summary of the *Wage Census* data is given in *Rates of Wages in Mines and Quarries in the UK*, 1890-1, LXVIII, xi.

[2] 'Return Showing the Average Number of Hours and Days Daily and Weekly Worked by Men and Boys . . . in and about Mines in the UK', 1890, LXVIII, 215.

This will tend to exaggerate the extent to which wage rates appeared to rise over the period 1886–1914.[1] Consequently, the base-rate daily earnings as calculated by Rowe have been retained.

The problem of constructing base rates for 1886 does not directly affect the relative movements of wage rates in the period 1870–1913, since these are based on percentage additions (and subtractions) to district scales. Mitchell's analysis of the timing of movements in the base rates after 1886 is accepted here with only minor revisions, but the problem of transforming scales into annual indexes remains.[2] The most comprehensive source for the study of wage rates in the industry in this later period consists of the material collected, or inherited, by the Board of Trade's Department of Labour. Each year after 1893 the Board of Trade issued a detailed account of monthly fluctuations in this and other industries, but also published separately data relating to the period before 1893.[3] Not all of this material can be accepted uncritically, though in practice it was found that the series were accurate, except for the 1860s when errors were evident in many of the scales.[4] The approach adopted here has been to take the Board of Trade series which depict wage-rate fluctuations and convert them into a seasonally adjusted figure for each year (that is, the sum of monthly levels of wages above or below standard divided by twelve). In this way the resulting indexes for 1871–1914 reflect the full impact of seasonal changes which were often considerable, and the result is thereby distinguished from indexes which record end-of-year figures only, or those based on the average of maximum or minimum levels during the year.[5]

The evidence for Scotland and South Wales before 1870 is abundant but requires judgement in reconciling conflicting data.[6] In making such

[1] There is no uncertainty surrounding the 1914 shift wage-rate figures, which are based on Finlay Gibson's evidence to the *Sankey Commission* 1919, XIII.

[2] Mitchell thesis, 203–7. The revisions affect figures for south Yorkshire and north Wales.

[3] This is contained in a unique and unpublished document located in the Library of the Department of Employment, St James's Square, London. It contains wage data going back to the 1860s. See 'Rates of Wages and Hours of Labour in Various industries in the UK 1850–1905', 64–88.

[4] Except for Scotland, where the west of Scotland series given for 1871–80 appeared to be unreliable, or at least unrepresentative, and is not used here.

[5] The end-of-year format is used in the series contained in Department of Labour, *Seventeenth Abstract of Labour Statistics* (1915), 70–1.

[6] This is because in Scotland, in the first half of the period, wage rates varied considerably between east and west, and in South Wales and Monmouthshire wages varied appreciably between the workers in sale-coal collieries and those in the pits of ironworks, while wages in Pembrokeshire were appreciably lower than in the rest of the region. Differences also existed in other regions, notably in the West Midlands, where in Staffordshire before the 1880s wages were considerably higher in the thick-coal districts than in the thin-seam areas, and higher in the south

judgements, both for these regions and for the remainder of the evidence, which is very sparse indeed, we have relied upon our price data, which seems wholly justified in the light of the relations between wages and prices analysed in Chapter 8. Wage movements in adjacent coalfields have also been taken into account, especially where it is known that coalowners colluded and miners participated in common activities to influence wages. For example, for the North-east, prices have provided the basis for wage-rate movements in the 1850s and 1860s, a sharp rise in the early 1850s, common to other regions, followed by stagnation between 1858 and 1863, and another upward shift to 1866. The main problem for Yorkshire occurs in the 1830s; again price movements have informed our judgement. Both Middleton pithead, and Hull export, prices began to fall after 1837 and we assume that wages followed; there was a sharp rise in the early 1850s to a peak in 1855–7. For Lancashire and Cheshire the Manchester price series is particularly crucial for the 1830s, though again there are many gaps in subsequent decades. The only continuous series for the West Midlands comes from Botham's thesis on north Staffordshire and refers to 1850–67, but the figures are considerably below those found in contemporary data for south Staffordshire, the major district in the region at that period, and the chronology differs slightly. The Barnsby series for south Staffordshire follows a significantly different course over time, which might also be attributed to the region's heterogeneity. However, the remarkable absence of any inflation in his series in 1852–6 must be unrepresentative at least, while sufficient evidence is available from elsewhere in the region to indicate that the Barnsby index for these years is unreliable. Eric Taylor's series, which begins in 1865, is taken from Board of Trade data, but appears to be exceptionally high, in common with much of the data from this source prior to 1871, probably due to a misleading assessment of changes in the standard rate.

The greatest difficulty is posed by the East Midlands. As south Yorkshire and north Derbyshire coalowners colluded, or attempted to collude, on prices and wages, we have adopted Yorkshire wage movements as a proxy for the East Midlands when no observations can be found for the latter.

than in the north. Durham wages levels were lower than those in Northumberland, though moving in step. Morris and Williams 1958, 220–1; Hunt 1973, 52 fn. 1; *Dearness and Scarcity* 1873, X, Q 4479. The sources forming the basis for wage estimates are listed below. The price series used in bridging the gaps and reconciling conflicting evidence are those presented in Table 1.9.

Table 7.15. *Estimated hewers' shift wages, 1830–1913*
(1900 = 100)

	Scotland	North-east	Cumberland	Lancs./Ches.	North Wales	Yorks.	East Midlands	West Midlands	South Wales	South-west
100 =	8s. 10d.	8s. 5d.	6s. 9½d.	7s. 7d.	6s. 11½d.	8s. 4d.	8s. 7d.	6s. 8½d.	7s. 7d.	5s. 1d.
1830	48	37		(60)		(37)	(35)	57	52	
1831	45	(46)		(56)		36	(34)	(58)	57	
1832	45	48		(53)		(35)	(34)	(58)	45	
1833	45	(45)		(56)		(35)	(33)	(58)	47	
1834	45	(45)		(60)		(35)	(34)	(58)	49	
1835	45	44		60		(34)	(32)	60	49	
1836	51	(48)		(63)		(42)	(40)	(60)	43	
1837	56	(50)		(63)		(52)	(50)	(60)	59	
1838	45	(51)		(56)		(51)	(48)	(60)	49	
1839	40	(50)		(54)		(50)	(47)	(60)	63	
1840	36	(49)		(55)		(48)	(46)	60	59	
1841	36	49		50		47	41	52	50	
1842	34	51		48		(46)	35	49	49	
1843	30	43		(50)		(44)	(35)	49	50	
1844	31	46		53		42	(37)	(50)	47	
1845	39	(46)		(54)		42	47	(58)	50	
1846	42	51		53		42	47	64	50	
1847	42	52		(50)		44	(45)	64	52	
1848	31	45		(48)		45	(41)	(62)	49	
1849	31	48		44		44	41	(62)	49	

Table 7.15. (cont.)

100 =	Scotland 8s. 10d.	North-east 8s. 5d.	Cumber-land 6s. 9½d.	Lancs./Ches. 7s. 7d.	North Wales 6s. 11½d.	Yorks. 8s. 4d.	East Midlands 8s. 7d.	West Midlands 6s. 8½d.	South Wales 7s. 7d.	South-west 5s. 1d.
1850	32	48		44		44	39	(62)	49	
1851	32	48		(44)		43	39	(64)	55	
1852	37	(46)		46		42	(41)	(65)	55	
1853	37	51		(50)		48	(43)	(66)	69	
1854	40	(65)		63		(57)	53	70	69	
1855	45	(68)		(73)		(63)	(60)	70	69	
1856	48	(68)		76		(63)	(60)	79	69	
1857	43	60		(66)		63	(60)	66	63	
1858	40	(59)		(55)		60	(56)	64	61	
1859	40	(59)		55		61	(56)	64	61	
1860	40	(59)		(60)		62	(59)	66	61	
1861	36	(59)		(66)		65	(62)	66	65	
1862	35	(59)		66		67	(64)	66	65	
1863	42	59		(64)		64	(61)	(67)	66	
1864	40	65		(70)		68	(65)	73	73	
1865	46	67		(76)		73	(70)	73	75	
1866	51	72		(83)		80	(76)	74	75	
1867	46	63		76		69	(66)	74	75	
1868	47	62		66		65	(62)	68	66	
1869	48	(61)		66		65	(62)	67	65	

Year										
1872	92	84	95	71	83	70	83	90	92	76
1873	113	96	106	89	102	84	102	92	112	90
1874	104	91	95	93	101	80	89	84	105	67
1875	94	79	78	80	85	68	79	74	90	59
1876	86	70	73	71	78	56	77	66	80	60
1877	79	70	67	66	70	53	64	63	74	54
1878	77	67	61	61	67	53	61	63	70	46
1879	78	63	60	58	67	53	61	63	63	47
1880	77	63	64	57	66	53	61	65	63	47
1881	77	64	62	57	66	51	62	66	65	47
1882	77	68	68	57	67	56	69	70	66	51
1883	77	69	72	62	72	61	74	70	67	47
1884	79	70	72	62	72	61	70	68	67	51
1885	77	68	68	62	69	61	66	66	66	49
1886	77	65	66	62	65	61	66	65	65	49
1887	76	62	65	62	65	61	66	66	64	50
1888	75	62	66	70	67	62	68	66	63	52
1889	77	72	74	70	75	70	75	72	69	65
1890	83	87	89	85	89	84	90	86	82	80
1891	89	95	91	89	92	87	93	88	86	80
1892	98	84	92	89	93	88	93	83	83	74
1893	95	72	93	90	93	89	94	81	79	67
1894	98	79	90	89	91	88	91	83	81	72
1895	94	75	87	86	88	85	87	79	78	62
1896	86	72	87	87	88	86	88	81	75	57
1897	86	73	88	88	88	87	88	81	76	61

Table 7.15. (cont.)

100 =	Scotland 8s.10d.	North-east 8s.5d.	Cumberland 6s.9½d.	Lancs./ Ches. 7s.7d.	North Wales 6s.11½d.	Yorks. 8s.4d.	East Midlands 8s.7d.	West Midlands 6s.8½d.	South Wales 7s.7d.	South-west 5s.1d.
1898	74	81	83	89	88	89	89	89	74	86
1899	84	86	88	93	93	93	94	93	82	91
1900	100	100	100	100	100	100	100	100	100	100
1901	91	103	105	109	109	109	109	109	113	112
1902	80	93	101	106	107	107	107	107	101	107
1903	71	92	97	103	105	103	105	103	99	105
1904	70	89	94	99	102	99	101	99	97	104
1905	70	88	94	95	99	97	98	98	93	102
1906	70	91	94	95	100	97	98	99	100	104
1907	85	100	104	102	107	105	104	105	109	115
1908	86	107	108	107	112	110	109	111	119	118
1909	78	102	105	103	108	106	105	107	114	119
1910	77	100	105	103	107	106	105	107	114	120
1911	77	100	106	103	107	107	106	107	115	123
1912	81	102	108	103	107	108	106	108	117	123
1913	93	111	118	113	115	117	114	117	122	122

Figures in brackets indicate estimates based on the movement of coal prices or on the movement of wages in neighbouring regions.

Sources and Methods:

1830–1870: the main sources are as follows: *Children's Employment Commission*, 1842; *Midland Mining Commission*, 1843; *State of the Population in Mining Districts*, 1844–59; *SC Accidents in Coal Mines*, 1873; *Reports of the Inspector of Mines for East Scotland*, 1868–87; DuRO D/X/411/93 *Selected Tables of Northern Collieries*, 1843; William Green, *The Chronicles and Records of the Northern Coal Trade* (Newcastle, 1866); *Returns of Wages Published between 1830 and 1886*, 1887 LXXXIX, 134–5; John Knowles, 'On the Coal Trade' *Transactions of the Manchester Geological Society*, Part II, Vol. XX, 1888; Eric Taylor thesis, 555; Bowley, *Wages in the UK in the Nineteenth Century* (Cambridge, 1900), 101–7; Hair thesis; E. W. Hunt, *Regional Wage Variations* (Oxford, 1973), 46; Morris and Williams 1958, 217–22; Evans 1961, 244–5; F. W. Botham, 'Workers' Living Standards in North Staffordshire, 1750–1914 (unpublished Ph.D. thesis, LSE 1982), 211, 309.

1871–1913: The central sources are: Board of Trade, 'Rates of Wages and Hours of Labour in Various Industries in the United Kingdom, 1850–1905' (unpublished returns kept at the Library of the Department of Employment in London) and Board of Trade, *Annual Returns of Rates of Wages and Hours of Labour*, 1893–1913. These Board of Trade data were weighted as follows:

North-east: Northumberland 25; Durham 75

Lancashire: Based on figures for SW Lancs.

Yorkshire: South Yorks 50 in 1870 rising to 60 in 1890; west Yorkshire 50 in 1870 falling to 40 in 1890.

East Midlands: Based on figures for Nottinghamshire.

West Midlands: North Staffs 40; south Staffs 60.

South-west: Forest of Dean 50; Somerset 50.

Other sources used for 1871–1913 are *Dearness and Scarcity*, 1873; *Report of Inspector of Mines for East Scotland*, 1868–87; *Royal Commission on Labour*, 1893; *Royal Commission on the Depression of Trade and industry*, 1886; *Rates of Wages in Mines and Quarries in the UK*, 1890–1; Hunt 1973; Bulman 1920; Rowe 1923. Annual percentages are added to the figures given the Board of Trade data in order to allow for changes in base rates in 1886–1914. These percentages are based, in the case of the inland coalfields, on Mitchell thesis, 203–11. In the case of Scotland, the North-east, Cumberland, South Wales, and the South-west they are based on equal annual percentage additions. The total addition required, based on the comparison of wages in 1886 and 1914, is taken from Rowe 1923, 41–57.

For Scotland we have relied on the Elphinstone price series in order to check Bowley's data, and for this reason rejected Youngson Brown's 1855–75 series, which appeared too static. For South Wales the earnings data provided by E. W. Evans has been adopted as a basis for the period between 1830 and 1849, though the wage data he gives for 1849–1912 are largely invalidated because of the apparent disregard of changes in the standard, and particularly for 1852–60 presented unbelievably high figures. Finally, data for the minor regions were deemed insufficient to attempt the construction of a series before 1871, when the Board of Trade data became available.

Secondary and printed contemporary sources for the period after 1870 are adequate to plot regional wage rates, by employing the Board of Trade data, incorporating seasonal variations, and inflating in order to take account of additions to basic rates.

For the purpose of analysis, Table 7.15 may be divided into two sections, the first running from 1830 to 1870, the second to 1913. The sources for the first half are mainly parliamentary and secondary, and for the most part are familiar to historians. The source material for 1871–1913 is much more abundant, particularly after the establishment of district collective bargaining in the 1870s.

Appendix 7.2. Prices and the cost of living

The price series available for 1850–92 include the Sauerbeck index of wholesale prices, G. H. Wood's index, designed to reflect changes in national retail prices, and Barnsby's retail price index for the Black Country. The Sauerbeck index suffers from the typical weakness shared with other wholesale price series, the food components displaying extreme volatility and tending to exaggerate retail price movements. Barnsby's index is highly erratic (exceeding the movements of Sauerbeck's wholesale series in the 1850s) and even if accurately reflecting price movements within the region seems unlikely to be applicable to the rest of the country. G. H. Wood's index of the cost of living (excluding rent) exhibits annual fluctuations and relative magnitudes similar chronologically to the Sauerbeck index (unlike Barnsby's) though at lower levels, and compares closely with Hall's Teeside index for 1870–1914. While resembling the Wood and Barnsby indexes in trend, the Sauerbeck index appears to overstate movements in retail prices, particularly the fall associated with the 'Great Depression' from the mid-1870s.[1]

The defects of other existing indexes warrant closer attention to Wood's index, which hitherto has been largely discounted by historians. Mitchell and Deane criticized it because Wood described it as 'experimental', and they warned others not to use it 'for purposes other than for which it was computed'.[2] Closer examination suggests that they were too cautious, and that Wood's index is the most reliable available indicator of living costs in the nineteenth century. It was based on the Board of Trade's 1903 *Report on Wholesale and Retail Prices* and many printed sources (thirty-three are cited for the period 1850–1901), and upon 'personal inquiries' in Manchester, Bristol, Huddersfield, and elsewhere. The unweighted means of a number of commodities of ordinary consumption were checked 'by estimating independently at various periods the cost of a given quantity of various articles commonly used in artisan households'.[3] An estimate of rent was also included, though this is not given in the index as quoted by Mitchell and Deane, an important omission.

His painstaking approach to statistical problems, together with the use of a wide array of sources, suggest that Wood's series was probably as thorough as the contemporary evidence would allow, and was the result of careful preparation. The regional spread of evidence was wide, and though biased somewhat towards large towns may be accepted as a sufficiently valid basis for a national average. The food component is unweighted, but it is known that food prices tended to move in step during this period; besides, Wood made efforts to check his results against actual consumption and expenditure. Furthermore, there is close agreement between the Wood and the Ministry of Labour's index after 1892, though this is probably explained by the use of identical sources and may not be regarded as an entirely independent check. Nevertheless, the coincidence of the two series in 1892 justifies confidence in the reliability of Wood's pre-1892 estimates, and enables us to splice the two series

[1] For an assessment of the relative merits of various price indexes, including those of Sauerbeek, G. H. Wood, and Gayer, Rostow, and Schwartz, see A. J. Taylor, *The Standard of Living in Britain in the Industrial Revolution* (London, 1971), xxxix–xxv, and Flinn, 'Trends in Real Wages, 1750–1850', *EHR* Second Series, XXVII (1974), 395–411. See also Barnsby 1971, and C. P. Griffin, 'A Critical Comment', *EHR* Second Series, XXIV (1971), 220–39. A. A. Hall's Teesside index is to be found in his article on 'Wages, Earnings and Real Earnings in Teesside, A Re-assessment of the Ameliorist Interpretation of Living Standards in Britain, 1870–1914', *IRSH* XXVI (1981), 205.

[2] Mitchell and Deane 1962, 343.

[3] G. H. Wood, 'The Investigation of Retail Prices', *JRSS*, LXV (1902), 685–90.

together without difficulty. There seemed to be no convincing justification for using the Phelps-Brown and Browne index, which leans heavily
on Bowley and Wood.[1] None of the regional indexes to appear since
Wood's have modified the picture implied by his series, Barnsby's being
the single exception, but which is vulnerable to criticism because of fluctuations which exceed those even of the wholesale price series.

Before 1850 Wood's retail price figures refer to isolated years only,
and are open to criticism on other counts, too. The Gayer, Rostow, and
Schwartz series is sophisticated, but contains the obvious disadvantage
of describing wholesale price fluctuations, and includes a large number
of commodities not generally entering into working-class consumption
(or, at least, were not consumed in proportion to the weights accorded
to them in the index). Distortion in the final index may arise, moreover,
from the necessity of splicing the Gayer, Rostow, and Schwartz index
with Wood's retail series in 1850, the effect of which could be to exaggerate the fall in prices which began in the late 1840s (assuming that
wholesale prices stand at higher levels than retail prices in the 1840s, and
that they tend to fall faster and further during a recession). On the other
hand, the Gayer, Rostow, and Schwartz series stands at a relative level
below that of the Sauerbeck (wholesale) and Black Country (retail)
indexes in the late 1840s, which suggests that any distortion which
might result from the splicing of the Gayer, Rostow, and Schwartz
series with the post-1850 Wood index will produce less distortion in
trend than were alternative available indexes for 1830–50 to be
employed.

While the Gayer, Rostow, and Schwartz index must be accepted unaltered, it is possible to recalculate Wood's 1850–92 series in order to
incorporate an allowance for rent, the result of which is to modify the
downward movement in the cost of living as rents underwent inflation.
For the period 1892–1913, to the partial Board of Trade indexes given by
Mitchell and Deane, we have also added rent, the result being a weighted
index of food, clothing, and rent.

Appendix 7.3. Earnings

Inevitably, the course of earnings over time displays a much greater
degree of year-to-year variation than that of wages. Years of low wages

---

[1] Phelps-Browne and Browne 1968, 220–39.

were most likely to be ones of reduced employment, and those of high wages of full employment, and consequently the amplitude of cyclical fluctuations is intensified. Average levels of hewers' earnings in the UK fell in 1830–3, and then rose slowly to reach a peak in 1837, which was not reached again until the mid-1850s. From the peak of 1837, earnings fell to 1842 and then rose (a little more gradually) to the peak in 1856. The troughs of 1858 and 1868 were separated by a period of upward movement in earnings. The peak that occurred in 1873 was naturally unprecedented in its scale, but the trough of 1878 brought earnings temporarily back to their level in the 1840s. Cyclical activity was as pronounced in the years between 1880 and 1913 as it had been in the rest of the century, but despite these fluctuations a marked secular increase in earnings took place in this period.

The severity of year-to-year fluctuations and the chronic uncertainty and irregularity which accompanied the take-home pay of piece-rate miners was the central feature of their standard of living. Although hewers suffered most in this respect (because both their wage rates and their employment opportunities varied with the state of trade) non-hewers also experienced considerable short-run fluctuations in their earnings, owing to movements in the number of days on which pits were opened. It is no exaggeration to say that the overriding problem in discussing the earnings of nineteenth-century coalminers comes in assessing the extent of this irregularity. A comparison of two alternative earnings series devised for hewers at Govan Colliery by Slaven, and for Black Country miners by Barnsby[1] (both of which are indexes and consequently do not allow comparisons of relative levels) is, nevertheless, instructive. In monetary terms, Barnsby's index is by far the lowest. Slaven's series for Govan hewers is the only long-run example of actual earnings available. The Govan index has a higher level of variation than our UK average figures, but then the experience of an individual colliery is likely to exhibit greater variability than an average. However, Slaven also assembled a series purporting to represent the average course of Scottish miners' earnings, the major characteristic of which was extreme fluctuation. The Barnsby index showing the earnings of Black Country miners also revealed marked year-to-year fluctuations, though of somewhat lesser amplitude compared with the Scottish series. The annual fluctuations in Barnsby's index, however, are essentially the result of his method of

[1] Barnsby 1971, 220–39; A. Slaven, 'Earnings and Productivity in the Scottish Coal Mining Industry during the Nineteenth Century: The Dixon Enterprises', in P. L. Payne (ed.), *Studies in Scottish Business History* (London, 1967), 217–49.

estimating employment, upon which doubt has already been cast.[1] The variations in the Scottish series showing miners' earnings are caused not so much by the employment data as by violent fluctuations in the stated day-wage rates, variations which do not receive support from the wider parliamentary literature. For these reasons the series of national averages presented above may be regarded as reflecting the general, somewhat hypothetical, experience; while more excessive variations could always be found at the level of the individual colliery (and more so at the level of the indivdual miner), it is unlikely that the average regional experience (itself a highly refined and artificial concept) could have differed significantly from the trend revealed in Tables 7.2 and 7.4.

[1] See above, Chapter 3.

CHAPTER 8

Industrial Relations and Wage Determination

i. The coalowners' associations

The determination of wages cannot be examined as a wholly disembodied process separate from changes in political climate. Such important developments as the extension of the franchise, the growth of socialist ideas, and the appearance of political parties appealing directly to the working classes were long-term influences which had as one of their effects the strengthening of a radical element within mining trade unionism, and which indirectly affected the unions' tactics and strategy over wages and conditions; similarly, a general philosophy which approximated to economic liberalism provided the underpinnings of employers' attitudes and actions, manifested either independently or as members of coalowners' associations.

Coalowners' attempts to establish formal and informal associations have a long history, but of the two major aims which typically stimulated efforts to combine, the regulation of prices proved to be a weaker foundation for the formation of permanent associations than the wish to present a united front in their relations with workers. The exception was the United Coal Trade Association, which long before 1830 had controlled prices, wages, and conditions of employment throughout the North-east, until the disintegration of the vend. Aspirations to continue to exercise comprehensive regulation even after 1850 were frustrated, for competition had destroyed the possibility of agreement between owners of a sufficient proportion of coal output from the region to achieve effective control even in the short term.[1] For this reason those coalowners of the North-east who continued to believe in the desirability of combined action concentrated upon two areas where mutual support might temper the effects of competition. One was to limit costs by maintaining control over labour; the other was to promote the interests of the trade by acting as a pressure group, specifically to influ-

---

[1] See above 68–9.

ence, and sometimes to modify, government intervention through legislation. The latter policy led to the formation of the Mining Association in 1854, a permanent body which included representation from most regions. The Association undertook to encourage inventions and improvements affecting safety, to promote mining education, and to discuss the 'commercial interests of the trade': by which was meant tariffs and taxation, relations with canal and railway companies, harbour boards, and similar bodies. In these activities, coalowning Members of Parliament (never a large group) who figured largely among the Mining Association's membership, played an important role, as they did in influencing legislation relating to safety in mines and working hours.[1]

Price and wage determination were specifically excluded from the Association's terms of reference. Such matters remained the primary concern in the North-east of the United Coal Trades Association—the body which for many years provided the leadership and sustained the impetus of the Mining Association.[2] Until the mid-nineteenth century, industrial relations in the North-east hinged upon the annual contract which laid down wages and conditions of employment, and was the subject of collective agreement between the Coal Trades Committee, representing employers, and the miners' sporadic combination—which after its collapse in 1844 heralded a period of nearly twenty years when trade-union organization (though not strike action) was non-existent.[3]

While the North-eastern coalowners' control over labour was long-established, formalized, and extensive before the 1860s, the power of coalowners in other regions was intermittent, exercised differently, and varied in degrees of effectiveness. Evidence is sparse and the picture it gives of coalowners in Yorkshire, especially west Yorkshire (the most active in collusion before 1860), might be misleading as a measure of effectiveness.[4] Nowhere, however, were the iron and coal producers more formidable than in the west of Scotland, where coal masters exchanged information on workmen, fixed wages, and acted in concert to implement their decisions, which included the provision of legal aid to enforce evictions upon striking miners.[5]

The two key factors which explain the aggressive approach to

---

[1] SCL Newton Chambers TR/453/5 Reports of Proceedings 1860–1862, 1866.

[2] NuRO North of England United Coal Trade Association, Minute Book, Annual Report 1872: CG 23 Feb. 1867, 176.

[3] Welbourne 1923, 28–43, 64–115.

[4] Machin 1958, 39–40, 45, 47; J. E. Williams 1962, 90; A. R. and C. P. Griffin 1972, 98–9, 101–3, 106; Neville thesis, 184–223; Challinor 1972, Chaps. 4 and 10.

[5] Campbell 1979, 81, 210.

the coal-producing iron masters were, first, their sensitivity to price changes determined by extreme fluctuations in the price of iron, and second, the tendency for the largest producers of coal also to be iron manufacturers. Thus, the onset of depression in the iron industry almost invariably provided the cue for the companies to impose wage cuts, which their power as large employers enabled them to enforce; whereas in the booms they were able to restrain, though not prevent altogether, the upward pressure on wages. The exercise of power by these producers closely resembled the sequence of events in major disputes in the North-east.[1] A limited strike would be organized against perhaps three major firms, while those not on strike financed those hitherto employed at the target firms; other owners would provide similar financial support, based on tonnage, to compensate those owners against whom action had been taken. Such action would lead to a lock-out throughout much of the district. The recruitment of blacklegs, sometimes through a professional strike-breaker, in those regions where colliery housing was important, especially in the North-east and Scotland, was the signal for evictions. This provoked agitation and threats which led to the appointment of special constables, sometimes police intervention, and occasionally culminated in the mobilization of troops to quell riotous assembly, public disorder, destruction of property, or physical violence. The sequel to disputes of such a character often included the offer of rewards, prosecution, victimization, the circulation of blacklists among employers, and even attempts to arrange for the denial of relief from the Board of Guardians, a sequence which could only leave a legacy of hostility towards employers—and to those who acted as magistrates and Guardians.[2]

The features here described were those of the worst disputes, and while they were characteristic of almost all of the major strikes that occurred before the 1860s, and several after that time, it should be remembered that not all disputes turned into strikes or lockouts, and that miners achieved successes as well as suffering defeats. The reasons for this are two-fold. One is simply the relation between the supply of, and demand for, labour, that influenced the relative strength of one side or the other—irrespective of the degree of organization. The other is the lack of permanence of the coalowners' associations and the difficulty they encountered in presenting a united front to miners. Even the associations formed in Scotland before the 1860s (indeed, until the

---

[1] Welbourne 1923, 28–123.
[2] Machin 1958, 81–100, 143–57; Barnsby 1980, 39–41; A. R. Griffin 1971, 80–4.

1880s) could be described as formal organizations for relatively brief periods only, re-emerging at times when changes in trading conditions or demands from workers required concerted action. By the 1860s, however, the emergence of a sale-coal trade, especially when it began to develop within iron-making districts, reduced the ability of coal producers to agree to common wage policies and, except under critical circumstances, to act in concert. Thus, a contemporary observer analysed the inhibiting effects of the multi-product structure of the iron and coal firms upon union and employer organization in the west of Scotland: in the 1860s sale-coal producers raised wage rates, whereupon iron masters' colliers who were denied a similar rise went on strike. The iron masters could not agree upon concerted action. Some extinguished the furnaces and kept the pits in operation, thereby undermining the coal-owners' position: 'Unfortunately this antagonistic position rather tends to induce discontent among the workmen, it is a state of things gradually becoming more marked, and was unknown throughout the mining districts when the interests of the employers were less complicated and better identified'.[1] Meanwhile, sale-coal producers in the Lothians had acted in concert over wages in 1837, 1842, 1856, and 1860, securing implementation by mutual support and sanctions.[2] In South Wales, too, employers in the Rhondda and Aberdare Valleys had acted together on wages in 1848 and 1858, and in 1866 brought about the formation of the South Wales Bituminous Collieries Association.[3] Despite the appearance of sale-coal owners' associations, however, Welsh coal producers experienced difficulties similar to those facing their Scottish counterparts. They failed to impose wage reductions in attempts made in 1861, 1865, and again in 1866, the latter occasion prompting G. T. Clark, of the Dowlais Iron Company, to remark to other representations of association members that, 'having failed so signally in acting together we had better now and in the future act separately'.[4]

When the sale-coal proprietors were fighting a strike in 1871, iron masters promoted coal sales from their pits; two years later, the iron masters fought to resist wage increases while sale-coal proprietors refrained from action, keeping their pits open.[5] Similar divisions of interest were to be found in south Staffordshire;[6] and to a lesser extent

[1] Quoted in Youngson Brown thesis, 130.
[2] Hassan thesis, 170.
[3] Evans 1961, 83.
[4] L. J. Williams thesis, 18–19; Morris and Williams 1958, 275.
[5] Morris and Williams 1958, 280–1.
[6] Barnsby 1980, 45–9; Taylor thesis, 125–7.

in north Derbyshire and south Yorkshire the coal-iron price and wage connection was a factor affecting industrial relations.[1] As sale-coal production in the East Midlands and Yorkshire increasingly dominated mining activity in these regions the owners of sale-coal collieries began to assume greater prominence in promoting collective action, though not until 1890 did formal organization become permanent.

For example, in the 1830s Henry Briggs was chairman of a coal and ironmasters' association which covered the entire West Riding; but it disappeared in the 1840s. According to his son, H. C. Briggs, it re-emerged briefly in 1853 as an association of sale-coal producers in the course of a dispute with a newly-formed miners' union which was pressing for a wage increase.[2] After five months of 'a stand-up battle' the miners won the advance, which became more or less general throughout the district. None the less, the west Yorkshire coalmasters refused to recognize the union.[3] Five years later, coalowners again acted in concert, this time in support of three firms which sought to impose wage reductions tacitly agreed by coalowners throughout west Yorkshire. The 'special collision', to use Henry Briggs's description, that resulted[4]—a euphemism for what a report in the *Colliery Guardian* referred to as 'a struggle for entire mastery',[5] not merely in fixing wages but in deciding whether colliery owners should be free to employ non-unionists, lasted nearly nine months, ending in victory for the employers after a general lock-out of virtually all west Yorkshire miners for eight weeks. In 1860 the idea of 'a sort of assurance society against strikes' was mooted, and in 1863 a change in working practices was imposed by west Yorkshire coalowners acting in collusion.[6]

West Yorkshire coalowners continued to associate informally and intermittently until 1890, and from 1873 took part in a joint committee, together with trade union representatives, to settle disputes on the model already introduced in south Yorkshire, Northumberland, and Durham.[7]

In South Yorkshire that development had first occurred in 1866, and was the culmination of a remarkably successful exploitation of the divisions among employers referred to in a report appearing in a Sheffield newspaper.[8] Intermittent organization against miners had

[1] Hopkins thesis, 401–3.
[2] John Goochild MS 'Some Early Yorkshire Coalmasters' Associations', *South Yorkshire Journal*, 6 (1970), 6. [3] *RC Trade Unions* 1867–8, XXXIX, Q 12489.
[4] Ibid., QQ 12495, 12501, 12507. [5] *CG* 16 Oct. 1858, 249.
[6] Machin 1958, 119. [7] Ibid., 175–7.
[8] Ibid., 280.

failed to lead to the degree of cohesion achieved by colliery owners in west Yorkshire, and this is probably explained by the intense competition between Yorkshire coalowners on the Derbyshire border with coal-producing iron masters in Derbyshire, who themselves were divided in their inclinations towards combination. However, when the South Yorkshire Miners' Association was formed in 1858 (during a campaign the success of which contrasted with the failure of west Yorkshire miners) and showed signs of becoming more than a temporary phenomenon, coalowners responded by forming a new association.

Giving evidence to the Royal Commission in 1867–8, John Chambers, partner in Newton Chambers and the colliery manager, explained that the masters' combination was a direct response to the policy of the union, whose officials 'took notice of the state of the district, took notice of those they considered weakest collieries, either in firmness of nerve or in moneyed resources, and then commenced strike at those collieries.'.[1] Glossing, one suspects, the coalowners' intentions, a *Sheffield Independent* report declared that destruction of the union was not their aim, though they could not allow themselves to be subdued by one.[2] This referred to the colliery owners' insistence that they reserve the right to employ non-union labour.[3] The strike of 1860, ostensibly over a rise in wages, then became a battle for recognition and the extent of managerial power. A succession of strikes involving collective action by the coalowners to resist the union followed, but not until 1865 did they agree to meet and negotiate with SYMA officials, a process the outcome of which was the adoption of John Normansell's 'reference system' for solving disputes, involving representatives from both sides.[4] This provided a *raison d'être* for a formally organized and continuous owners' association which lasted until 1876, by which time wage reductions and heavy membership losses had seriously weakened the balance of power[5]—and removed the necessity for employers to combine.

A similar, and simultaneous, story of the parallel growth of employers' and workers' organizations is to be found in the North-east, where in 1852 a Steam Collieries Association, consisting mainly of Northumberland firms, was formed, underlining the divergence in interest between the soft- and hard-coal producers. Unable to achieve price control, wage restraint promised the next most important key to

[1] *RC Trade Unions* 1867–8, XXXIX, Q 14436.
[2] Machin 1958, 296–9.
[3] *RC Trade Unions* 1867–8, XXXIX, QQ 14438–55.
[4] Machin 1958, 349–50.
[5] Ibid., 454–7.

profitability in an increasingly competitive trade, and consequently 1864 brought the formation of a Steam Collieries Defence Association.[1] This followed a similar development among Durham coalowners immediately following an 'equalization' of wage rates carried out by a sub-committee of the main association in 1853. The agreement envisaged an initial fund of £50,000, based on contributions according to colliery output, to support those collieries affected by strike action and to assist in obtaining labour from other districts in pursuance of defeating strikes. Colliery owners were required to undertake not to employ any striker, irrespective of his possession of a clearance certificate.[2]

The agreement was to come into effect after three-quarters of the trade (calculated on the vend) had signed it. Whether it did become effective is not clear, but Durham coalowners acted in concert in 1862, when they achieved more success than did their counterparts in Northumberland in reimposing the bond and in crushing a newly formed trade union.[3] The development away from the United Coal Trades Association by the Northumberland Steam Coalowners owed something to secession from the joint miners' union by the Northumberland miners in 1864 to form the Northumberland Miners' Mutual Confident Association, led by Thomas Burt. The rapid growth of the steam-coal trade provided a more favourable climate for workers' opposition, in contrast with the relatively depressed soft coking-coal sector during the early 1860s, and must have helped to explain the different outcome of the 1862 dispute. Successful resistance by the Northumberland miners was followed by the formation of the Steam Collieries Defence Association. By agreement, Northumberland owners pledged to refrain from making any concessions 'however trifling . . . unless in pursuance and in accordance with a resolution of a meeting of the Association regularly convened'.[4] Collieries were rated according to output to provide a 'protection' fund to compensate collieries affected by strikes, and legal assistance was offered to members carrying out the association policy of evicting strikers. In the case of a dispute, the colliery in question received a visit from a representative appointed by, and from among, the members of the Defence Association, who would accompany the colliery owner's representative to examine the problem and to recommend action. Thereafter, the

---

[1] NuRO Steam Collieries Association: General Meetings Minute Book.
[2] NEI Misc Deposit ZA66 Memorandum and Agreement 1855.
[3] Welbourne 1923, 48, 123-4.
[4] NuRO Steam Collieries Association, MB 2, 122, 159-60, 195.

Association conducted all negotiations—mostly with colliery workers' representatives, occasionally with the trade union.[1]

General wage levels were agreed by a wages committee (consisting of viewers) which from time to time reported to the general meeting the results of periodic comparative surveys of wages being paid in the county; these provided a standard for judging claims from individual collieries.[2] By 1872 buoyant trade had enabled the miners' union to consolidate its position, the leaders so impressing the colliery owners as negotiators that they refused to entertain applications from individual collieries, insisting that claims should be presented by the union executive only. The employers probably regarded the executive as more amenable to persuasion and argument than the rank and file,[4] though the sheer volume of independent demands being presented to the Association increased the burden of administration and tended to threaten the existence of orderly wage agreements across the coalfield. None-the-less, the executive of the union objected to its added responsibility of filtering wage applications before they reached the owners. This presaged the formation of the Joint Committee in 1873.[5]

A regularization of industrial relations also occurred in Durham after the union recovered from its collapse in 1865, re-forming on a permanent basis in 1869. The long-established strength of Durham coalowners had (despite divisions) enabled them to crush the union over the issue of the bond in 1865, though in fact the bond was not widely reintroduced thereafter.[6] The boom of the early 1870s enabled the Durham Miners' Association to bring coalowners' representatives to a meeting with union officials in 1872, the first formal gesture of recognition, which was followed by the termination of the bond and the formation, at the miners' request, of a joint committee.[7] When the boom turned into slump in 1874 employers in Northumberland and Durham joined together to form a very different kind of subcommittee, with a brief to plan and enforce general wage reductions—which were subsequently implemented initially without consultation with the unions.[8]

[1] Ibid. Steam Collieries Association, MB 2, 122, 159–60, 195.

[2] Ibid., MB 3, 338.

[3] Ibid.

[4] Ibid. In 1872, after a union deputation had agreed to accept a 10 per cent rise instead of the 15 per cent requested for boys and hewers, the deputation withdrew '. . . promising to use its influence with the Boys to keep them steady in their work'.

[5] Ibid.

[6] Welbourne 1923, 138–146.

[7] NuRO Steam Collieries Association, MB 3, 198, 204, 215, 310, 324.

[8] Ibid.

It soon became clear that a wages policy applied throughout the North-east would not be workable, because of the different circumstances and interests involved in the soft- and hard-coal districts.[1] The soft-coal owners, whose collieries produced about one-sixth of the total output of Northumberland, felt under pressure from their Durham competitors who paid lower wages than those agreed by the Steam Collieries Association, and different reductions were subsequently sanctioned by steam-coal owners.[2] Sliding scales, which were rejected by the owners in 1872 when Northumberland miners had proposed their introduction, were adopted there in 1879, two years following their introduction on a separate basis in Durham.[3] Henceforward, sliding scales and, following their discontinuance ten years later, conciliation processes dominated industrial relations in the North-east. Both owners and workers maintained a very high rate of participation in their respective organizations, particularly in Durham where throughout the 1870s and 1880s members of the Coalowners' Association accounted for at least three-quarters of coal output in the region.[4]

The evidence on combination in other regions before 1870 is obscure. Coalowners in the Wigan district met regularly to discuss wages, and in 1855 the South Lancashire and Cheshire Coalowners Association was formed in response to the initiative of the Mining Association.[5] However, Challinor has explained the survival of the Miners Association of Great Britain and Ireland for a longer period than in any other region, in terms of the employers' weakness at that time; no formal organization of coalowners has been recorded again until a revival in 1885, which was also short-lived.[6] Coalowners in the East Midlands probably colluded on wages as an adjunct to their attempts to regulate prices, the prime object of the Erewash Valley Coalowners' Association in the 1830s and early 1840s. In 1844 coalowners of Derbyshire, Nottinghamshire, and Leicestershire combined to destroy incipient trade unionism stimulated by the MAGBI. A lock-out, followed by the issuance and implementation of the 'document' effectively removed trade-unionist activity for twenty years and hence the need for employers to combine, until the formation of the South Derbyshire Miners' Union in 1867—when Leicestershire and south Derbyshire

[1] Ibid., 356–67, 380–1.
[2] Ibid., 466; ibid. MB 1, 167, 456.
[3] Webster thesis, 154–6.
[4] DuRO NCB I/Co/86 (1)–(1322), Coalowners' Returns.
[5] Challinor 1972, 50.
[6] Ibid., 46–7.

owners reintroduced the black-listing policy which had succeeded in 1844.[1] Colliery owners in north Derbyshire found themselves in direct competition with those in south Yorkshire, but remained aloof from the South Yorkshire Coalowners' Association until an amalgamated association, including coalowners from both districts, was formed in 1874.[2]

Hitherto the SYCOA had financed its activities, which included compensation to member firms who lost production through strikes or lock-outs sanctioned by the Association, by levies according to size of output, but the new joint organization was formed with an initial capital of £200,000 issued in £10 shares, minimum membership consisting of two for each 1,000 tons of coal raised.[3]

In fact the Association was short-lived, for the unity which seemed possible in the 1870s boom belied the realities of historical experience in the years of unexceptional trading conditions, and which, as coal prices fell during the slump, brought the renewal of intense competition between the two districts. The attempt to bring the north Derbyshire owners into a system of joint committees and orderly bargaining failed, with the result that in 1876 the Yorkshire system itself collapsed.[4] The incentive for organized resistance to trade unions had thus vanished with the boom, as it did in other regions. The continuity and strength of owners' associations before the boom should not be judged by the achievements in the North-east and Yorkshire, where the balance of power was not so uneven as to remove the need for the existence of a negotiating body. Even in Yorkshire, shortly before the boom several leading employers had continued to translate their hostility to trade unions by refusing to employ trade unionists. In Lancashire, the collieries belonging to the Knowles family were involved in a lock-out of all union labour for nearly eighteen months, and received the support of other major north Lancashire firms, including those of Hargreaves and Richard Evans.[5] Trade unions also encountered particular difficulty in achieving recognition in the iron-making districts, but the campaigns of the 1860s and the formation of the Miners' National Association in 1863 stimulated trade-union activity in the rapidly expanding inland coalfields on a scale unprecedented since the 1840s. In the intervening

[1] A. R. and C. P. Griffin 1972, 98–108.

[2] J. E. Williams 1962, 90.

[3] *CG* 17 July 1874, 93; *CG* 4 Dec. 1874, 829.

[4] J. F. Goochild, 'Some Early Yorkshire Coalmasters' Associations', *South Yorkshire Journal*, 6 (1970), 6.

[5] See *RC Trade Unions* 1867–8, XXXIX, QQ 16209–10, 16260; Challinor 1972, 204–6.

period of relative quiescence anti-union sentiments had only occasionally surfaced during specific disputes, but the reactions of coalowners in
the 1860s reflected little change in attitudes, for the most part, since
those which had destroyed the trade unions in the 1840s.

Attitudes towards trade unions held by many business leaders, such
as Sir William Alleyn of Butterley, William Jackson of Clay Cross,
Charles Markham of Staveley, John Knowles, J. B. Pope of Pope and
Pearson (later Denaby Main), Joseph Love, of Straker and Love, and
G. T. Clark, of Dowlais, were not dissimilar to those of the landed coalowners of the North-east. During the strike of 1844 Lord Londonderry
received an invitation from the committee of the miners' union requesting a meeting between 'bona fide coalowners and their late workmen'—
instead of the viewers who normally conducted labour relations. Lord
Londonderry's reply was that his Lordship 'has nothing to do with such
committees . . . but will treat with his own colliers and pitmen and none
others . . . he states his men all acknowledge they had nothing to
complain of but were compelled by the force of the union to fight the
battles of others; he will not wait much longer before peopling his
collieries with others'.[1] and he didn't. Greenwell's evidence, based on
experience as viewer at several collieries in the North-east, in Somerset,
and in Lancashire, is consistent with this approach to labour relations,
even in the 1860s, as a family problem;[2] as are those of the reactionary
coalowners of north Derbyshire and south Yorkshire.[3] Any differences
in attitude to trade unions of the long-established paternalist landed
enterprise and those of the major joint-stock companies of the 1860s is
difficult to discern.

One of the most vehement critics of trade unions in the 1860s was
Charles Markham, managing director of Staveley, which until 1874
remained outside coalowners' associations. In 1867 he was quoted in the
Colliery Guardian, when he emphasized the company's determination
'to either crush the union or keep their works closed'. This uncompromising posture meant the dismissal of half the company's workers, but
received support from a large group of non-unionsts already employed
at Staveley's pits and who formed a non-union society; miners were also
recruited from Staffordshire and Yorkshire to fill the places of the
expelled trade unionsts.[4] Markham was the most coherent exponent of

[1] *MJ* 27 July 1844, 255.
[2] *RC Trade Unions* 1867–8, XXXIX, Q 13620.
[3] *RC Trade Unions* 1867, XXXIX, QQ 11916–42.
[4] *CG* 13 Jan. 1867, 74.

anti-trade-union policy at this time, and he reported how Staveley had successfully resisted the attempt of the Derbyshire Miners' Union to recruit members in 1866.[1] Markham appeared to see the butty system as the main weapon against them: 'I believe in everything being done by contract and piece work. I think that it will become universal, and that the only mode of getting rid of trade unions will be by adopting an universal system of piece work.'[2] He considered trade unions to be unacceptable because they destroyed the paternalistic relationship between men and employers. He argued that the establishment of permanent unions would lead to the end of all social ties between capital and labour. In these circumstances the firm would no longer contribute to the social welfare of the mining community at Staveley: '... we should break up our schools and let the men do what they like ... [because] we never could have any reliance upon our men'. All social relationships would be severed as the directors would feel no moral obligation to do anything for the benefit of the men and their families.[3]

The directors agreed that in addition to the £1,000 expenditure in 1866 on religious and educational purposes for 'improvement and well being of employees' children' (a decision taken before the lock-out), four annual instalments of £2,000 would be spent on welfare of this kind, thereafter providing the equivalent of 25 per cent of sums spent by the workmen.[4] A similar strategy, of support for dissidents and welfare expenditure, was adopted at Clay Cross, where an 'Insurance and Free Labour Society' was formed, the president of which was Charles Binns, the company's managing director.[5]

After several months of the campaign to resist the trade unionists' attempts to secure recognition, the coalowners issued a statement declaring that unless the men destroyed the books and rules of the association not one of the former trade unionists would be employed. Unqualified victory went to the coalowners, and Markham accepted a silver claret jug and salver, paid for and presented by working miners on their own initiative, the fund receiving subscriptions from 2,556 workmen each of only 6d. or less.[6] A dogmatic proponent of *laissez faire*, his opposition to combined action among the masters complemented his

---

[1] BSCEMRRC Stanton and Staveley 2034/1/2 June 1866.
[2] *RC Trade Unions* 1867–8, XXXIX, Q 11723.
[3] Ibid., QQ 11654–56.
[4] BSCEMRRC Stanton and Staveley 2034/1/2 MB June 1866.
[5] *CG* 30 Mar. 1867, 293.
[6] *CG* 13 Jan. 1867, 74, 7 Sept. 1867, 212–13; *RC Trade Unions* 1867–8, XXXIX, QQ 11627–8.

hostility to trade unions, against whom he waged an independent battle. The successful outcome of the trial of strength in 1866–9 embittered labour relations in these collieries for many years. Not until Markham was dead was his successor able to enter into negotiations with officials of the Derbyshire Miners' Union.[1]

In south Yorkshire resolution of the dispute was less clear cut, but after a strike–lock-out lasting for eighteen months at the collieries of the major 'free labour' companies, Denaby Main and Newton Chambers, it was agreed (in part as the result of arbitration involving the Mayor of Sheffield and A. J. Mundella), that trade unionists and non-union labour would be employed. In these collieries, too, a period of uneasy relations followed after a period in the 1860s which marked a nadir in industrial relations comparable with that in the mid-1840s.[2]

The approach to industrial relations in general, and to trade unions in particular, typified by Charles Markham, Charles Binns, Sir John Alleyn, John Chambers, Lord Londonderry, J. B. Pope, W. H. Chambers, G. T. Clark, John Knowles, Joseph Love, and Fisher Smith represented the extreme end of the spectrum, but their attitudes and actions were influential, for they controlled relatively large firms whose success in resisting the advance of trade-union recognition provided powerful precedent and reinforcement for the many smaller firms who had less room for manœuvre to cut costs when trade was depressed, though who were more vulnerable to loss of workers in the booms. None the less, some employers and managers acknowledged that a price was paid by those who adopted a high profile in anti-unionism. In 1866–7 George Greenwell, whose experience included the bitter disputes at the John Bowes collieries in 1849 where he was viewer, expressed what was probably a more widespread, less extreme, and more representative view. When asked to define a strike he replied: 'Generally speaking, . . . a combination of workmen which may take place at an individual colliery cannot be called a union, because that is a mere family matter. But I think that immediately it extends beyond the precincts of one colliery, and a combination is made, i.e. between one colliery and another, then it becomes a union . . .' Asked for his attitudes to trade unions, he answered: 'I have not opposed myself point blank to the union; but to a certain extent so long as they conducted themselves properly, I have admitted a certain right that they have to have a union. I have not gone

---

[1] Chapman 1981, 83–4.
[2] MacFarlane 1972, 215–16; Pat Spaven 'Main Gates of Protest' in Royden Harrison, 1978, 201–7; MacFarlane 1978, 194–5.

dead against it, and perhaps that is a reason why it may not have affected me so seriously as others.[1]

Evidence from several regions thus lends suport to C. P. Griffin's conclusion, based on the events in south Derbyshire, that the claim by Hamish Fraser that by the 1850s and 1860s employers had 'learned to live with unionism' and were coming to appreciate its value, is not generally applicable in the coalmining industry.[2] Only in Northumberland and Yorkshire was it even partly true; in 1868 John Chambers, hostile in principle to trade-union interference with managerial decisions over whom to employ, none the less expressed grudging acknowledgement of the good sense and reason shown by Normansell and other union leaders in south Yorkshire.[3] The decision of the Northumberland Steam Collieries Defence Committee to funnel all disputes through the miners' union implied a similar acceptance that it was a responsible body. But the speed with which wage cuts were planned and implemented without consultation with the unions in Northumberland and Durham in 1874 suggests that the apparent acceptance of trade unions as a constructive institution during the 1870s boom had more to do with the balance of power rooted in economic conditions.

Elsewhere, too, economic expansion in this period created the conditions in which newly formed trade unions succeeding in winning recognition from employers, who at last agreed to meet union officials and discuss the creation of negotiating machinery. However, when the boom ended, coalowners in South Wales, Scotland, south Staffordshire, Cumberland, Leicestershire and Warwickshire, Derbyshire, and Nottinghamshire forced wage reductions so substantial that they provoked strikes and caused lock-outs.[4] Those unions not destroyed entirely were severely crippled for at least a dozen years, for the counter-attack, even in the relatively well-organized Yorkshire region, took the form not only of reducing wages but saw the reintroduction of several measures which eroded earnings and/or increased work intensity; in South Wales these included non-payment

---

[1] RC Trade Unions 1867–8, XXXIX, QQ 13620, 13623.

[2] W. H. Fraser, *Trade Unions and Society* (London, 1974), 73–6, 97–100; C. P. Griffin, 'Colliery Owners and Trade Unionism: The Case of South Derbyshire in the Mid Nineteenth Century', *Midland History* VI (1981), 120.

[3] RC Trade Unions 1867–8, XXXIX, QQ 14526–8.

[4] NuRO Steam Collieries Association, MB I 356–8, 367; Machin 1958, 354; C. P. Griffin thesis, 665; Welbourne 1923, 190–1; L. J. Williams 1976, 83–4, 92; Evans 1961, 115–129; Challinor 1972, 148–9; C. P. Griffin, *The Leicestershire and South Derbyshire Miners 1840-1914* I (Coalville, 1982), 120–2.

for trams containing more than a percentage of small coal and extending hours; in Yorkshire, reversion to riddling underground, the reintroduction of the 21 cwt. ton and tickets of leave, and the confiscation and abolition of coal allowances.[1] The mid-1870s also saw attempts to terminate or undermine the checkweighman's position.[2]

After Northumberland and Durham the longest surviving colliery owners' association in 1913 was in South Wales, which originated in the formation of the Aberdare Steam Collieries Association in 1864. At first controlling no more than 15 per cent of the entire coalfield, it was absorbed in the enlarged and reconstituted Monmouthshire and South Wales Collieries Association in December 1873. This broader organization, whose members controlled about 70 per cent of the total production in the coalfield, included sale coal and coal-producing iron masters, who merged their different interests in the cause of unity following two major defeats by the miners in 1871 and 1873. The greater priority was to destroy the Lancashire-based Amalgamated Association of Miners, which had encouraged the sudden growth in trade-union membership in South Wales, and provided assistance with strike strategy.[3] In 1875 the coalowners effectively eradicated organized trade unionism in the region after a lengthy strike and lock-out. The owners' victory was accompanied by the introduction of a sliding scale, but the inclusion of minimum rates proved a serious limitation upon the ability of owners to press for the most favourable wage agreements possible when coal prices entered their dramatic decline from 1876. The result was that within five years 45 per cent of the membership had withdrawn from the association, which came to represent less than one-half of total coal production[4]—though shortly before the 1893 strike membership accounted for about two-thirds of the tonnage. Even among those who remained, some members sought to negotiate covert agreements outside the sliding scale, as several non-members had already done.[5]

Although a fluctuating membership weakened the association, the financial policy of levying members on an annual, rather than on an *ad hoc*, basis was a source of potential strength.[6] Williams's detailed

---

[1] Evans 1961, 123; Machin 1958, 458–62.
[2] Machin 1958, 489.   [3] L. J. Williams 1976, 83.
[4] *RC Labour* 1892, XXXVI, 18.   [5] L. J. Williams 1976, 89.
[6] Ibid., 82. The model was that long established by coalowners in the North-east in connection with the vend. Such was the method for financing members involved in strikes adopted by the Steam Collieries Defence Association in 1864, by the West Yorkshire Coalowners' Association from 1890, and by the South Yorkshire Coalowners' Association from 1901. NuRO Steam Collieries Association MB Defence I, Rules . . .; BRO West Yorkshire Coal Owners Association,

account of the Association's early history illustrates problems common in kind to other regions (where iron producers were also important producers of coal), though perhaps less extreme than those which demonstrated the fragility of owners' unity in South Wales. The persistence, too, of firms which either refused to deal with trade unions or declined to be members of an owners' association also imposed limits on the effectiveness of owners' collective policies.

Other more permanent associations date from the 1880s, and mark the revival of trade-union membership. Lanarkshire coalowners formed an association in 1886 in anticipation of a dispute over wages and output restriction announced by the miners' leaders, and resolved to extend financial support against strikes at any colliery belonging to members. The immediate target fund for this purpose was set at £10,000. Led by John Cunninghame and Robert Baird, the association introduced a sliding scale, in agreement with the miners, in 1887. A few years later, only about one-quarter of Lanarkshire miners were employed by coal masters belonging to the association, though the newly formed Fife and Clackmannon Coalowners' joint-conciliation machinery set up in 1902, applying also to Fifeshire and Ayrshire, was reckoned to embrace a high proportion of miners in the Fife and Clackmannon district.[1]

South Yorkshire coalowners took similar steps, reviving an association which in 1874 had been described by the *Colliery Guardian* as 'the most powerful combination of colliery owners in the kingdom', and had included coalowners from north Derbyshire.[2] That had long since disintegrated, and the new body formed in 1886 was exclusive to coal masters from south Yorkshire, under the chairmanship of J. D. Ellis, manager of John Brown and Co.[3] The secretary, Parker Rhodes, reflected on the general need for combination among coalowners: 'If he stands alone he no longer deals with his own men and he can neither commend or obtain fair treatment except by effective combination.'[4] Parker Rhodes was a persistent advocate of federation with coalowners in other areas, and in 1890 was present, along with other leaders of associations from Lancashire, south Staffordshire, Cannock Chase, Derbyshire, and south Yorkshire, as the 'Federated Mineowners', to

---

Minute Book 29 July 1890; SCL MD 2699–11, South Yorkshire Coal Owners Association, MB Feb. 8 1900, 2699–13, 25 Apr. 1902.

[1] SRO (W) Lanarkshire Coalowners' Association CB 8/1–2; *RC Labour* 1892, XXXVI, 30.
[2] *CG* 4 Dec, 1874, 829.   [3] *CG* 16 Jan. 1885, 103.
[4] SCL SYCOA MD 2699–6, MB 15 Jan. 1895.
[5] *CG* 7 March 1890, 363.

negotiate with the Miners' Federation.[1] As a result of this meeting, which impressed upon coalowners the relative weakness of their organization, the west Yorkshire owners established a new coalowners' association, modelled on south Yorkshire, of which Henry Curer Briggs was elected chairman.[2] Federation, however, proved to be a tenuous collectivity, and even at the regional level Parker Rhodes's desire to integrate south and west Yorkshire owners remained unfulfilled. Even more damaging to coalowners in both areas, but especially those in south Yorkshire, was the complete lack of discipline among Derbyshire owners, whose independence frequently proved to be the Achilles heel of the south Yorkshire employers.

The occasion for the establishment of the SYCOA in 1886, according to Parker Rhodes, had been 'the aggressive attitude of the leaders of the men, the rising power of their union and the ceaseless agitation as to wages . . . In consequence the Miners' Union lost prestige and rapidly decreased in number and power. . . . As the danger from this quarter grew less, the cohesion among the owners themselves grew less also, and today [1889] the Society is weaker than at its formation by reasons of some defections'. Those defections had occurred over the 1888 dispute resulting from the SYMA pressing for wage increases. The owners' position had been undermined by owners in north Derbyshire who conceded the rise; West Yorkshire employers had also exhibited weakness. As some members chose temporary profit-taking, opposition by the association became untenable, and was withdrawn.[3] A joint committee was in operation, though unresolved disputes were sent to arbitration; after the 1893 strike a conciliation board was formed, but proved to be temporary. Its revival in 1898 was for the purpose of dealing with a wages claim and for regulating the agreement for a two-year period. During the boom of 1900–1 the South Yorkshire Coalowners' Association was reorganized, and for the first time, following the practice of South Wales coalowners, established a reserve fund to be invested until required.[4]

In 1906 Parker Rhodes remarked on the change in attitudes and policy of the men's leaders compared with a few years before, noting: 'They express their claims with vigour, and they sometimes support, very likely against their own better judgement, claims which are not reasonable in themselves, but no one can help observing that they rely

---

[1] SCL SYCOA MD 2699–11, MB 8 Feb. 1900; BRO, WYCOA Minute Book 25 Mar. 2 Sept. 1890.   [2] SCL SYCOA MD 2699–3, MB 13 Jan. 1890.

[3] Ibid.

[4] SCL SYCOA MD 2699–11, MB 8 Feb. 1900.

much more on the strength of their case and on their reasoning powers with reference to it rather than on a policy of threats and bluster as used to be the case'.[1] The explanation for the joint committee having met not once during that year, however, was in part, on Parker Rhodes's own admission, due to the 'exercise of a good deal of tact on more than one occasion to postpone and ultimately avoid meetings which in my judgement would not have been to the benefit of those sitting on our side of the table'.[2] The record of the joint committee, for whatever reason, appears to have been successful in resolving those differences brought to it, and the membership of the association increased, until by 1913 Barber Walker and even the troubled Denaby and Cadeby Company, which had left in 1904, had become members.[3] Still, however, the managers and directors of a handful of important member firms, Carlton Main in particular, opposed the Yorkshire Miners' Union outright, and encouraged an alternative union dominated by butties.[4]

An increasing inability, especially after the introduction of the railways, to control prices, meant that coalowners' associations became overwhelmingly concerned with aims shared in common: of minimizing labour costs, whether resulting from wage rates, the effect of safety legislation, or reduction in hours. In so far as trade unions assisted in the promotion of miners' aspirations, and from the 1860s were invited to offer evidence in official inquiries, the masters' associations flourished when defence was needed to resist a campaign. The fiercest attacks upon trade unions came from several of the large firms, the owners of which, at least during the 1860s, were in most cases opposed to collective membership of organizations, whether of coalowners or of working miners. Even those employers who later joined owners' associations enjoyed an uneasy relationship with other members, as a result of a greater frequency of disputes and the costs necessarily borne by them on others' behalf. Thus, as alliances the associations resembled the trade unions.

Common interests shared within a district or part of a coalfield, rather than throughout even a region, were cut across by divergent interests arising from geological and market differences; and because of this, coalowners' associations faced persistent difficulties in securing sufficient support to implement policy. The catalyst which gave to the coalowners outside the exporting regions a greater, though still limited, degree of

[1] SCL SYCOA MD 2699–13, MB 25 Apr. 1902.
[2] SCL SYCOA MD 2699–18, MB 25 Mar. 1907.
[3] SCL SYCOA MD 2699–16, MB 8 Feb. 1905, 2699–25 6 Feb. 1914.
[4] Neville thesis, 304.

unity, at least within regions, was the formation by the county unions of the inland coalfields of the Miners' Federation in 1889. While enabling coalowners to retain their administrative and financial independence the need to respond to, and deal with, a single major body representing miners' interests brought about the centralization of industrial and parliamentary policy. The Federation's policy of rejecting sliding scales and the employment of Federation-wide strike action in support of resistance in any district clearly amounted to a challenge to employers which required a comparable organizational response, the outcome being a change in the pattern of disputes and a growth in collective bargaining.[1]

In regions unaffected directly by the formation of the MFGB, coalowners struggled to achieve unity. In Lanarkshire, for example, sliding-scale arrangements proved difficult to settle because the refusal of so many employers to belong to the association made members reluctant to divulge information on profit per ton, which the leaders of the coalowners had hoped to adopt as the linkage point for wages. At the same time, certain actions were ruled out 'to keep right with the Public', hence the coalowners' reluctant decision to agree to the appointment of a neutral chairman of the conciliation board in 1902 irrespective of his views on whether a limit should be imposed on the size of any wage reduction.[2] There is thus ample evidence that certainly before 1889 the weakness of trade-union organization had provided insufficient incentive for coalowners to relegate differences in economic interests in order to sustain an effective combination.

Quantification of the strength of coalowners' associations is frustrated by lack of data. Figures for a single year offer an unsatisfactory measure of long-term membership, but the evidence presented to the Labour Commission relating to 1892 does provide a snapshot of comparative strengths in the coalfields, when considered in terms of the share of a region's output 'controlled' by an association. Furthermore, membership data which have survived, for Durham, south and west Yorkshire, and South Wales, suggest that 1892 was not an exceptional year (whereas the year of the 1893 strike would have been). In all regions membership fell considerably below 100 per cent, Durham claiming to control more than any other coalfield and accounting for in excess of 80 per cent.[3] Associations of colliery owners in South Wales,[4] south

---

[1] Arnot 1949, 92–119.
[2] GLA UGD Coalowners' Joint Committee 161–65–8, 161–82.
[3] DuRO NCB I/CO/86 (1)–(1322)–(45) Coalowners' Returns.
[4] Dalziel 1895.

Staffordshire and east Worcestershire,[1] and Fife and Clackmannan[2] each commanded about two-thirds of the output from those districts, as did the south Yorkshire coalowners.[3] In west Yorkshire the proportion under control of the association formed in 1890 was about one-half.[4] The situation in Lancashire is less clear; in 1892 the existence of such an association to deal with industrial relations was denied, the Lancashire witness reporting the non-existence of joint committees and the complete independence of each coalowner who 'dealt with his own men in his own way'. Three years later, however, the secretary of the South Yorkshire Coalowners' Association had referred to the existence of a fighting fund established by Lancashire owners three or four years before,[5] which suggests that in 1892 an association was about to be formed in Lancashire. Certainly Lancashire owners had combined in the past.

The Lancashire Coal Trade Association, formed in 1877 recruited throughout Lancashire and Cheshire, but it seems to have been preoccupied with transport matters as 'the infirmity of the colliers' unions' caused the masters little concern'.[6] The Association assumed a major role, however, in reaction against the Employers' Liability Act of 1880.

The contracting-out clause of this legislation introduced to extend freedom of contract to employees was interpreted as an attack on employers' freedom to conduct their own labour relations; consequently the Lancashire coalowners had insisted that a condition of employment in the region was membership of the Lancashire and Cheshire Permanent Relief Society. This organization had been formed in 1872 to assist miners and families in the event of death or injury through accident. Most of the financial contribution came from miners but the coalowners managed the fund, so it is not surprising that the miners, who were critical of the high costs and partiality exercised by management, should object strongly to the coalowners' reactionary policy. Thus began the greatest dispute in the history of the region, and the violence and vindictiveness which accompanied it soured industrial relations for many years.[7] Reviewing industrial relations in the region since the 1880s, an outside observer referred to a succession of 'miserable strikes following strikes in weary and often futile repetitions, of lock-

---

[1] *RC Labour* XXXVI, Pt. I, QQ 10832, 11646–7, 13421, 133736–8.
[2] Ibid., 35.
[3] SCL SYCOA MD 2700, Membership Sheets 1884–1916; *RC Labour* 1892, XXXIV, 41.
[4] Bro LU, WYCOA 1708/12 'West Yorkshire Coal Industry'.
[5] *RC Labour* 1892, XXXIV, 34; SCL SYCOA MD–6, Annual Report, 15 Jan. 1895.
[6] Quoted in Challinor 1972, 149.
[7] Ibid., 162–3.

outs and actions at law. The cumulative effect is an estrangement between masters and men . . .'.[1] No evidence of an association similar to that in other regions has survived, but in 1898 coalowners in south and west Lancashire formed an association which concerned itself entirely with matters arising from workmen's compensation.

In the East Midlands and in Cannock Chase associations existed but their strength is unknown. In the latter district twenty-four of the thirty collieries belonged, which suggests that a high proportion of output probably came under its control from its formation in 1888.[2] The Griffins have identified the revival of the Erewash Valley Coalowners' Association in 1892, and of the Leen Valley Coalowners' Association in 1893, though both were merged to combine coalowners in the three East Midland counties and Warwickshire in 1899 to form the Midland Counties Colliery Owners' Association. No measurement of membership, however, has been possible.[3]

Numerical strength was not the only novel element in trade-union development in the late nineteenth century, for the MFBG's policy of securing minimum-wage legislation was interpreted by coalowners, particularly those in South Wales (and to a lesser extent south Yorkshire) where 'abnormal places' intensified miners' demands for an alteration in the system of payment, as the inevitable precursor of higher costs and lower productivity. The profound discontent among the miners of South Wales over this issue eventually erupted, first in the conflict of 1898 and subsequently at Tonypandy, both events evoking widespread sympathy across the mining regions, and which have been interpreted as symptomatic of an atmosphere of suspicion between colliery owners and miners.[4] However, the politicization of industrial relations in South Wales where the Liberal consensus based upon an assumption of inherent mutuality of interests began to give ground to a philosophy predicated on the affirmation of mutual antagonism, is barely perceptible in other regions, and made little political impact even in South Wales before 1913.[5]

Despite relatively high levels of solidarity, from the 1890s at least, fundamental economic differences continued to hinder a transition to unity among coalowners at the national level. Colliery owners were divided in 1893, and again in 1912 colliery owners in the high-cost

[1] Quoted in Gregory 1968, 57.
[2] RC Labour 1892, XXXIV, 101.
[3] A. R. and C. P. Griffin 1972, 107–8.
[4] L. J. Williams 1980, 99.
[5] Gregory 1968, 184–9.

districts of South Wales and Scotland evinced unqualified hostility to minimum-wage legislation (indeed, arousing the suspicion among Liberal leaders that no negotiated settlement would satisfy them)[1] whereas in the Federated districts reservations were expressed mainly concerning feasibility rather than principle; their assumption being that the level at which the minimum would be fixed would fall below existing wages in these areas. Furthermore, the effect of the compromise imposed by government through legislation, requiring statutory determination of wages, paradoxically strengthened existing centrifugal tendencies in industrial relations. For just as in the 1890s local officials had been given the responsibility of ensuring that awards made at district level were correctly applied to each price list, so the 1912 Act required the establishment of joint district boards which, under an independent chairman, were to fix a minimum wage for each district. Thus, trends which since the 1880s might have been expected to have led to the consolidation and centralization of coalowners' associations were counteracted by others which reinforced long-established differences between, and within, the mining regions.

Employers' policies towards labour were mainly determined by the extent to which miners accepted the frequent wage adjustments deemed necessary by employers to compensate for price changes, either upwards or downwards. Such a relationship formed part of the model of competitive market capitalism accepted as one of the broad economic orthodoxies of the age, and was of particular applicability to the coal industry in which labour costs were the major part of working costs. Hence the fierce resistance to wage claims, the hostility to safety and hours legislation, and the continued opposition, in many districts until the 1880s and 1890s, to trade unions.[2] Most strikes, and resistance to them, were local and shortlived, and even where a union extended support to the strikers at one firm as a test, down to the 1860s employers tended to regard mutual support of the stricken firm as an appropriate and reasonable response, meanwhile maintaining production. Sometimes that which began as a dispute over wages became an issue over union recognition, the proselytizing activities of the country unions, the MNA, the AAM, and later the MFGB, leading to more disputes of this kind. Investment in community facilities and welfare in an attempt to win the loyalty of colliery workers, and the formation of company unions, were alternative strategies, which appear to have been of limited effective-

---

[1] Peter Rowland, *The Last Liberal Government's Unfinished Business 1911-1914* (London, 1972) 148.   [2] L. J. Williams 1980, 99.

ness;[1] though one notable pioneering experiment—in profit sharing—did survive until 1875.[2]

The experiment began at the firm of Henry Briggs and Son in 1865, where after a dozen years of deteriorating and turbulent labour relations culminating in the strike of 1862, which turned into a lock-out of trade unionists, followed by evictions, blackleg recruiting, riot, and police action, a solution was sought in a profit-sharing scheme. Having failed to destroy the union, this unique experiment was aimed at weaning men away by undermining its influence. Improved profitability was one expected result, but H. C. Briggs made it clear that if co-partnership, as he called employee share-ownership, was to be deemed a success, the trade unions must wither away. Rewards to employees through dividends moved with the trade cycle, but likewise union membership boomed from 1868, whereupon Briggs rejoined the masters' association. When the tide of prosperity turned and in 1874 the company announced the reintroduction of riddling (the issue which had sparked off the 1862 dispute) and imposed wage reductions, the miners struck. The discontinuance of bonuses on wages in 1875 marked the termination of profit sharing, and a return to traditional forms of labour relations, though from the 1870s concentrating, as were employers in other regions, upon the introduction of sliding scales as the favoured method of removing conflict from the process of wage adjustment; from the mid 1870s and in the early 1880s this meant wage reductions.

After a period of regress in the 1870s and early 1880s, trade unionism in all the major regions began to pose renewed threats to coalowners' authority, as membership increased and, at least for the inland coalfields, federation achieved unprecedented co-ordination of policy. Coalowners again responded by the formation of associations, which this time achieved the status of a national coalition embracing employers in the inland regions, and which secured a degree of permanence similar to that of the trade unions. In this later phase of association, coalowners showed less inclination to recruit non-union labour *en masse* to replace strikers, preference being shown towards the lockout combined with the payment of substantial financial indemnity to employers involved, and the use of the discharge note.[3] None the less, divisions which resulted from

[1] Wilson Thesis, 258; Neville Thesis, 308; and see below.

[2] This section draws heavily on R. A. Church, 'Profit Sharing and Labour Relations in England in the Nineteenth Century', *IRSH* 16 (1971), 2–8.

[3] Williams, 1976, 218–63. The impression given by the minutes of the Coalowners' Associations of South and West Yorkshire and of Scotland to this effect is borne out by the data contained on a national basis in the Board of Trade, *Report on Strikes and Lockouts, 1888–1899*.

production for different markets and from the variable incidence of prosperity or depression in the markets for differing coal types were persistent influences tending to perpetuate coalowners' divergent interests. This explains why the initiative which most frequently determined events came from the trade unions, to which coalowners, with rare exception, merely reacted, and sometimes over-reacted.

ii. The growth of trade unions

There is demonstrably a close association between the level of wages in the industry and the level of trade-union membership, but it is difficult to establish the causation, partly because of the lack of data on union membership. There is some truth in Buxton's assertion that a wealth of published material now exists on the activities and development of organized labour in the coal industry, and that most of the geographical and chronological gaps in knowledge have been filled.[1] However, the actual dimensions of labour organization in any period before the years immediately preceding World War I are still difficult to ascertain. Difficulties arise not only in counting the number of men who belonged to formal unions, but equally important is the problem of equating the numbers so organized with the effective level of collective association within the industry. Since the basic unit of labour organization was the pit, it would be unreasonable to expect a comprehensive documentation of labour organization in all periods. Collective association has only become measurable where miners have looked beyond their own place of work to the possibility of district, coalfield, or national organization. Judged in this way, the extent of formal representation was extremely limited, at least prior to the 1890s, the reasons for which are well known.

Small-scale production in scattered locations was typical of the industry outside the North-east until the 1870s, and discouraged the formation of permanent organizations. Wide and recurrent fluctuations in coal prices further weakened any potential basis for sustained unionization, even though in some regions hewers' earnings in most years might compare with those of skilled workers in other industries where trade unionism had succeeded in establishing permanent roots. The result was that in most regions before the 1860s conditions allowed only a rudimentary organization among miners, the strength of the ephemeral

[1] Buxton 1978, 147.

unions which were characteristic of the period being located at the district, rather than at national or even regional, level. The activities of employers' associations were also instrumental in weakening some miners' unions, which, while claiming a continuous existence from the third quarter of the century, none the less almost disappeared after the 1870s boom, achieving permanence only after the late 1880s.[1] Evidence for the existence and membership of unions prior to 1870 is extremely sparse, and presents the inevitable difficulty of deciding whether this is a problem of evidence only or is indicative of minimal trade-union organization.

Local unions were reported to exist in most regions during the 1830s, though sporadically and limited to a duration of one or two years. An organization formed in 1831 to embrace colliers throughout the North-east collapsed in 1832, when coalowners reacted strongly against un-official action to enlarge the gains achieved in 1831.[2] Indeed, survival of trade unions depended much, throughout the nineteenth century, upon the attitudes and policies of employers; action taken by Lancashire coal-owners in 1830 aborted the newly-formed Friendly Society of Coal Mining, an organization in whose brief history links had been estab-lished with miners in Staffordshire and Yorkshire.[3] Affiliation by some groups of miners to the National Association for the Protection of Labour, which in 1834 had also stimulated union organization in South Wales, was an indication of the aspiration towards an arrangement which would provide mutual support between unions in different districts; on which basis the Miners' Association of Great Britain and Ireland was formed in 1841.

Originating at Wakefield, where a brief period of unionization had occurred in 1833, the 'Colliers' Philanthropic Society' was established under the leadership of David Swallow, victimized for previous trade-union activities. The Society's initial aim was to petition Parliament to redress miners' grievances, and towards this end support was received from miners in the North-east.[4] Before long, associations existed in Staffordshire, Monmouthshire, Scotland, Lancashire, Leicestershire, and the North-east. Reporting a meeting of colliery delegates to form a permanent commitee representing, all paying members, in January 1844 the *Mining Journal* recorded a national membership figure of 32,148. About two-thirds of the members were in the North-east,

[1] Clegg, Fox, and Thompson 1964, 15; Benson 1980, 177, 189, 208.
[2] Welbourne 1923, 38–43.
[3] Evans 1961, 40–1, 43 ff.
[4] Machin 1958, 44–7; Challinor 1972, 36–8.

while the remainder came almost entirely from Yorkshire and Lanca-shire.[1] Shortly before the major strike in support of a 20 per cent rise in wages in the North-east in March 1844, the union's secretary, John Hall, claimed the support of 60,000, a figure accepted a few years later by Tremenheere, but who in 1847 put the figure for current membership at between 20,000 and 30,000.[2] Without doubt, claims in later sources that the Association's membership reached 70,000 or 100,000 are highly dubious.[3] Even so, by contemporary standards the possible range of between 30,000 and 60,000 membership at the peak represent an out-standing measure of support for a trade union, even though the geo-graphical concentration was narow. Unprecedented, too, was the MAGBI's full-time independent executive appointed in 1844, and a national delegate conference which met at least twice a year.[4] One-half of the subscriptions were retained by the district unions, who main-tained also a quasi-independent existence which, while conducive to independent action, soon proved to be the undoing of the MAGBI; complete centralization, however, was quite beyond the limitations of the state of trade-union organization at that time.[5] Coinciding with the imprisonment of the Lancashire union's leaders for their involvement in Chartist activity, the down-turn in trade in 1848 effectively destroyed the Miners Association as a national organization: thereafter, even the county unions struggled for survival.[6] The union of miners in Northumberland and Durham survived the 1844 defeat but finally collapsed in the slump of 1847–8.[7]

In catalysing discontent, focusing attention upon grievances, and pro-viding confidence, albeit short-lived, to organize, campaign, and in some localities to take more forceful measures to secure improvements, the MAGBI was a formative influence in providing experience of collective organization and, for a few, of leadership.[8] At the same time, the failure of collaboration between local unions meant that on the next occasion when large-scale unionization occurred, in the early 1870s, no similar national organization was attempted. Meanwhile, only the Miners' National Association, formed in 1863 under the leadership of the

---

[1] *MJ* 6 Jan. 1844, 1. Miners in Denbighshire were reported to be too poor to become paying members.

[2] *State of the Population in Mining Districts* 1847 XVI 14.

[3] Arnot 1949, 41.

[4] A. J. Taylor 1955, 47.   [5] Ibid.

[6] Challinor and Ripley, *The Miners' Association: A Trade Union in the Age of the Chartists* (London, 1968), 40.

[7] A. J. Taylor 1955, 35.   [8] Ibid., 45–60.

Scottish miners' leader, Alexander MacDonald, was successfully established on a national basis, though unlike the discredited MAGBI the activities of the MNA (renamed the Miners' National Union in 1875) were limited to those of a pressure group in support of legislative reform. Given the central importance of safety to miners' well-being, and the feasibility of achieving progress on a national basis, the role adopted by the MNA appears to have exhibited both a sense of priorities and a realistic appraisal of the limited possibilities at that time of introducing an effective, co-ordinated wages policy within the framework of prevailing industrial relations.

The period between 1830 and 1850 has been identified as having marked a transition—at least in the major coalfields of the North-east—from a system of industrial relations based upon the master–servant relationship (determined by custom in which wage manipulation was minimal and involving magistrates at Petty Sessions in the event of infraction of a signed agreement) to a stage where wage bargaining was central and persistent.[1] The bond traditionally offered miners a guarantee of job stability, recognition, and reward for artisan status, but wage rates and working practices were negotiated annually, when employers might revise the terms and conditions for the following year. In fact, although the only method of striking legally was to refuse to be bound at binding time, miners did take action in combination, frequently, but on a local basis.[2] The repeal of the Combination Acts in 1824, and the modification in 1825, removed the stigma and hindrance of illegality, but the burst of trade-union activity that followed was short-lived, for poor communications, slack trade, and the hostility shown by employers, continued to render formal trade-union organization, instead of temporary inchoate combination, extremely difficult. Lack of experienced leadership was another handicap, which among miners was briefly overcome with the emergence of Tommy Hepburn, whose union, when it was formed in 1830, embraced miners in Northumberland and Durham, staged two strikes, in 1831 and again a year later; on each occasion marking a co-ordinated attempt to improve the terms contained in the bond. The first collapsed after two weeks, but the second continued for several months, during which time work stopped at pits where the majority belonged to the union, and where the strikers received financial support from those remaining at work.[3] The aim of

[1] Welbourne 1923, 26–7; Rimlinger thesis, 48.
[2] Flinn 1984, 399.
[3] Welbourne 1923, 28, 36–7, 38–43.

this strike, and of the major strike of 1844 mounted by the MAGBI, was to renegotiate such factors as wages, conditions, hours, systems of weight and measurement of output, and fines and forfeitures, the occasion each time being the annual binding.

The traditional view of the annual contract, recently described as 'the slavery of the yearly bond' which in 1844 miners sought to abolish, has also been endorsed by Pollard, who interpreted the bond as an arrangement which rendered miners 'only a degree less unfree' than the typical Scottish miner serfs in the eighteenth century.[1] The contrary interpretation of the bond as a contractual agreement, renegotiable at annual intervals, is suggested by the attempt of miners in the North-east to perpetuate rather than to abolish the annual bond, opposing the coalowners who wished to shorten the duration of contracts and eventually to terminate binding. On each occasion when miners were in general dispute—in 1831, 1832, and 1844—what was at stake, in part, was the possible loss of guaranteed regular employment, and compensation for periods of enforced idleness; commitments which coalowners showed increasing reluctance to concede should they apply to an entire year.[2] This change in attitude may be seen as the erosion of custom as a basis for industrial relations, a development induced by the weakening and ultimately the collapse of the vend, which coincided with the intensification of competition in the marketing of coal and increasing uncertainty in trading activity.[3] It is significant that the temporary reintroduction of annual binding in Durham in 1854, though probably on a much less rigorous basis than before, occurred during a major boom when miners were in a position of strength.[4] However, when in 1863 owners gave notice of their intention to reintroduce yearly agreements in Northumberland, the new generation of miners in this district refused to accept them. The *Newcastle Chronicle* commented: '. . . that which their fathers had considered security, they called slavery'. In the North-east the so-called Third Union (after those of 1830–1 and 1842–4) was born with this campaign; yet in parts of Durham annual binding was not finally abolished until 1872, by which time the employers appear to have lost all interest in it.[5]

[1] Webourne 1923, 144–5; Dave Douglass, 'The Durham Pitman', in Samuel 1977, 272; Pollard, 'Labour in Great Britain' in Peter Mathias and M. M. Postan (eds.), *The Cambridge Economic History of Europe* vol. vii, 1 (Cambridge 1978), 136.

[2] *Dearness and Scarcity*, X, Q 7607; Scott thesis, 59–176.

[3] NuRO Steam Collieries' Association, General Meetings, 459, Report.

[4] Scott thesis, 59–176.

[5] Quoted in ibid.

The tardy emergence of miners' permanent trade unions has been explained by a historian of industrial relations as, in part, almost an inevitable consequence of their socio-economic position:

The brutalised condition of the miner was reflected in the dirt, neglect and habitual drunkenness prevailing in many mining villages . . . violence was never far from the miner's life either at work or at leisure. His basic needs remained simple and his tastes were largely customary, hence the increase in absenteeism during booms . . . Habitual drunkenness led to 'irregular habits' and drained the miner's meagre income, impairing his ability to create and sustain trade unionism.[1]

The validity of this stereotype of the dissipated miner, capricious and irresponsible, has been seriously questioned above, and when a perspective is adopted focusing on a local, rather than a district or national, level of organization before the 1880s, the picture which emerges suggests that much of the literature on miners' trade unionism which begins from the standpoint of the late nineteenth and early twentieth centuries is misleading. A survey of colliery strikes during the period between 1800 and 1850 left Hair with the impression that '. . . the majority of colliers were eager to combine locally and to strike on local issues, but that they distrusted wider combinations and some of the regular trade union leaders'.[2] Conversely, one should not take the absence of formal coalfield labour organization as proof of no organization at all. The bulk of any organization on the coalfields of England and Wales in this early period was at the level of the individual pit, and involved a direct confrontation with the management over the crucial questions of wages, price lists, weights and measures, fines and forfeitures, hours, and conditions. The majority of strikes in this early period appear to have been unsuccessful, probably because they were conducted in the downswing.[3] But one would expect to find greater success in claiming higher wages and more favourable conditions during periods of rising prices. Temporary combinations of pit lodges might occur to settle individual issues, but these collapsed, either with the settlement of the dispute or with the coming of the downswing.[4] In Scotland, the 1830s witnessed the emergence of short-lived trade unions at district level, which after 1842 were loosely knitted together for the first time, though the individual pit lodges retained effective autonomy.[5]

---

[1] Burgess 1975, 169–171.
[2] Hair thesis, 425.
[3] Ibid.   [4] Evans 1961, 86.
[5] G. M. Wilson thesis, 90–1, 118–29.

Despite the tenuous character of the early unions it is possible to identify elements of continuity in the major centres of intermittent activity. Beginning in the boom of the 1850s, several attempts were made to establish permanent trade unions. The Lancashire and Cheshire Miners' Association, formed in 1850, was particularly active in strikes in the 1850s,[1] and some six or seven thousand pitmen were said to be members of a union in the North-east in 1850. Yet ten years later when, frustrated by collective action, especially by miners at steam collieries, all coalowners (including house- and gas-coal producers) decided to reintroduce annual hiring contracts, the union had to be revived.[2]

The first permanent county district union was formed in 1858 during a strike of Yorkshire miners against a wage reduction. West Yorkshire miners already possessed a history of intermittent organization, and in resisting employers in 1858 chose three of the major collieries as the object of their industrial action, enabling other miners to work and to support those on strike. The employers' reaction was to lock out miners at other collieries and to evict workers' families, at the same time imposing conditions before the pits could reopen. These included strict observance of colliery rules, the abandonment of restricted eight hours working, and an end to the support of miners already on strike. By the fourth month of the strike, more than three thousand miners were either on strike or locked out. In the course of the struggle the miners formed a union, following a visit by Alexander MacDonald, the Scottish miners' leader, and received assistance from local miners who had been involved in previous abortive associations; prominent roles were undertaken by a local Alderman, G. W. Harrison, a Wakefield corn merchant, 'Wesleyan reformer, temperance advocate and Liberal', Richard Bayldon, a road surveyor who became treasurer of the Wakefield and Methley branch of the union, and John Helmer, a Leeds draper, who was also president of the local co-operative and provision society.[3] The most important figure, however, was James Pyrah, who for nearly thirty years had been a pitman for Henry Briggs. Miners in the Barnsley district extended their support, and before the end of 1858 both the South Yorkshire Miners' Association and the West Yorkshire Miners' Association were in existence.[4] Defeat over recognition and exclusive trade-union employment when west Yorkshire coalowners locked out all members

[1] Challinor 1972, 45.

[2] *State of the Population in Mining Districts*, 1850 XXIII, 43; NuRO Steam Collieries Association, General Meetings MB 2, 141–3, MB 3, 39–46; Welbourne 1923, 115.

[3] *CG* Apr. 1858, 247, 24 June 1858, Oct. 1858, 216, Aug. 1858, 135; Machin 1958, 84–5.

[4] *RC Trade Unions* 1867–8, XXXIX, QQ 12782–4, 12927.

for nearly nine months destroyed the union, until it was re-established on a permanent basis in 1863, stimulated by the upsurge of widespread enthusiasm for organization resulting from Alexander MacDonald's campaign to amend mining legislation.[1]

Meanwhile, South Yorkshire miners, who, in the absence of a masters' combination of comparable strength and cohesion as shown by West Yorkshire coalowners succeeded in winning a relatively short strike against a wage reduction in 1858 and persisted with their association, soon became the model for centrally organized, financially sound, moderate, effective mining trade unionism.[2] Such policies achieved for the SYMA a reputation outside the district of dominating industrial relations; 'the union are the masters there' was the comment of Henry Briggs from the perspective of West Yorkshire;[3] but John Chambers, managing director of the Newton Chambers collieries in South Yorkshire, and initially hostile to trade-union interference, remarked on how well-informed on trade and economic matters the miners' officials were, and how, during the period since he had dealt with the SYMA, those officials had replaced violence with reason in labour relations.[4]

They also represented the spearhead of miners' trade-union organization. In 1860 the secretary of the SYMA reported to a Select Committee that there existed 'a partial sort of organization in Lancashire, a little in Cheshire; trifling in Derbyshire; none at all in Staffordshire and Warwickshire'.[5] When the Royal Commission on Trade Unions reported a few years later, the permanence of trade unions established in the interim was still uncertain. From a North-eastern perspective, in 1867–8 George Elliot noted how permanent unions did not exist in Durham (though Northumberland miners were organized) and related this in part to the system of annual binding. When asked whether this practice removed the power of trade unions, he replied:

It does so to a great extent, excepting at the time when the contract has to be made; the union operates then, and it operates very strongly. The men combine amongst themselves, but I am bound to say that the union is not a universal thing with us, though it crops up occasionally about the binding time. I do not think a regular system of unionism prevails at any of my collieries, excepting societies for self support in sickness and so on.[6]

---

[1] CG Oct. 1858, 249, 281; Machin 1958, 341–50.
[2] Machin 1958, 341–50.   [3] Ibid., 350.
[4] RC Trade Unions 1867–8, XXXIX, QQ 14526, 14534. For a similar appreciation of the constructive role of trade unions see the evidence of P. Cooper, Yorkshire Coalmaster, Q 14209.
[5] SC Masters and Operatives 1860, XXII, Q 575.
[6] RC Trade Unions 1862–8 XXXIX, Q 11351.

At Elliot's collieries in South Wales no union existed 'excepting the spontaneous combination which arises if there is the least interference with them [the men]',[1] a situation which despite the absence of formally constituted trade unions enabled miners to mount effective collective action over particular issues. It was reported that neither in Derbyshire, Leicestershire, Nottinghamshire, nor Warwickshire did miners' unions exist at the time of the Royal Commission,[2] though in fact in 1864 confidence generated by the activities of MacDonald's Miners' National Union in other larger coalfields had prompted the reformation of a union of Leicestershire miners which, after a successful strike in 1864, adopted such a low profile as to become invisible outside the county.[3] In other East Midland counties the coalowners had checked any advance threatened, and at no colliery more effectively than at Staveley, whose viewer recalled that 'a spasmodic effort' at unionization '... was blown out'.[4]

Just as the short-lived Derbyshire and Nottinghamshire Miners' Association had collapsed in 1863, the district unions which came into existence in South Wales in 1864 were quickly snuffed out by the coalowners, whose reaction against the Welsh miners' initiative marked the origins of a permanent masters' association.[5] In south Staffordshire before 1863, which saw the formation of the short-lived South Staffordshire and East Worcestershire Amalgamated Miners' Association, there is no record at all of local unions existing on more than an *ad hoc* basis,[6] and in Durham, where in 1865 only two years after the Northumberland leaders had assisted in organization, the Durham Coalowners' Association once more destroyed the union with the greatest potential membership.[7] Witnesses before the Royal Commission in 1867–8 compared the lack of permanence of trade unionism in most regions with the strength of organizations in Northumberland,[8] West Yorkshire, and South Yorkshire[9] where between 1858 and 1868 membership had grown from about two or three thousand to seven thousand. In west Yorkshire, where the permanent associated dated from 1863, membership stood at about one-half that level.[10] Yorkshire (not, as it has been claimed, the North-east[11]) stands out as the region where the most suc-

---

[1] Ibid., Q 11363.   [2] Ibid., QQ 11510, 16536.
[3] C. P. Griffin, *The Leicestershire and South Derbyshire Miners 1840– 1914*, Vol. I (Coalville, Leicester, 1981), 118.   [4] *RC Trade Unions* 1867–8, XXXIX, Q 13, 550.
[5] L. J. Williams 1976, 82–3.
[6] Taylor thesis, 117, 128.   [7] Welbourne 1923, 138.
[8] *RC Trade Unions* 1867–8, XXXIX, QQ 11766, 14280.   [9] Ibid., Q 11383.
[10] Ibid., QQ 16, 097–16, 102, 13027; Machin 1958, 148–50.   [11] Burgess 1975 180–2.

cessful attempts were made to establish permanent district unions and to inaugurate a new phase in the development of collective bargaining in the industry.

Studies of the Lanarkshire miners reveal a state of affairs somewhere between the intermittent, spontaneous unionism characteristic of most other regions before 1858, and the permanent type of labour organization which emerged for the first time in Yorkshire in that year. These unions tended to collapse in times of recession and await the return of bouyant trade for recovery.[1] Although they do not merit the description permanently constituted, these unions none the less enjoyed a strength and secured a degree of intra-regional co-operation unique to Scotland in this period, warning against equating parochiality with powerlessness before the emergence of the county district unions from the late 1850s.

The Royal Commission is hardly the most reliable source from which to gain an impression of the impact of trade unions. For the most part the witnesses were either employers or employers' men who argued that unions served no useful function. All sources agreed that trade unions came to prominence and strikes occurred at times when trade was brisk, but that invariably the men's organizations were weakened and destroyed during recessions.[2] Most witnesses, however, particularly those from Yorkshire and the East Midlands, argued that unions had no effect on wages, that all general wage advances would have taken place without the help of trade unions, and that strikes against reductions in downswings were almost invariably failures.[3] Possibly a more objective viewpoint, however, was expressed by G. C. Greenwell, who with disarming understatement argued that trade unions might prove beneficial to workers because,

... when times are good people rather than submit to a strike would give an advanced wage because they do not like the threat of a strike to be carried out ... I think that the increase of prosperity in the business with the increase in demand for coal increased the demand for labour, and that therefore the price of labour rose because its value increased. I do not think that the owners are such angels that they would give a rise quite of their own accord but I should say that the owners gave it because they were obliged to do it in order to get labour.[4]

---

[1] Campbell 1979, 247–63; G. M. Wilson thesis, 118–41.
[2] See, for example, *RC Trade Unions* 1867–8, XXXIX, QQ 11480, 12330, 13638.
[3] See, for example, Ibid., QQ 14296, 14015.
[4] Ibid., QQ 13656–8.

On the trade-union side, too, the preference for avoiding costly strikes was accompanied by a desire to establish some form of conciliation and arbitration. In 1860 Richard Mitchell of the SYMA had told the Select Committee on Masters and Operatives, 'it is seldom that we have an opportunity of reasoning with our employers',[1] and noted that the representatives of fifty Yorkshire collieries supported a bill to establish councils of conciliation—so long as JPs were not given the responsibility of appointing chairmen.[2] A few years later, joint committees of employers and union representatives met regularly to solve disagreements.

Two other factors may be regarded as having encouraged trade-union development in the 1860s. Alexander Macdonald's Miners' National Association is widely considered to have been an organization which encouraged accommodation with coalowners other than in the political arena, whose leaders failed to provide a lead in industrial policy, and who, in general, refused to support local strikes involving the district association. Such a policy, culminating in the 1868 decision to deny support to miners who found themselves locked out, firmly advocated conciliation and arbitration which miners were advised to urge upon employers.[3] Irrespective of the merits or disadvantages of such a policy, the MNA did encourage the formation of trade unions; and by its own success, albeit limited in scope and short of financial strength, the size of membership affiliated to it inspired a degree of confidence in some kind of mutual support across the coalfields, even though many of the district associations formed under the stimulus of the MNA in 1863 and 1864 disappeared shortly thereafter. Moreover, the structure established by the MNA, of a hierarchy beginning with the miners' lodge, a district and county association, and a federated national assembly, became the basis for subsequent labour organization in the industry when the economic climate for trade-union growth became more favourable.

The other factor which has been regarded as having assisted the growth of trade unions is the Checkweighman's Act of 1860, though as this legislation depended entirely upon the power of the miners to insist on the appointment of a checkweighman, modifications embodied in subsequent Mines Acts to strengthen his independence from employers were also important, culminating in clauses included in the Mines

---

[1] SC Masters and Operatives 1860, XXII, Q 721.
[2] Ibid., Q 583.
[3] Burgess 1975, 185.

Regulation Act of 1887.[1] The Webbs stressed the checkweighmen's positive role, reflected in the numbers who became full-time trade-union officials, in defending miners both against sharp practice and victimization, though frequently becoming the object of victimization themselves.[2] Burgess, however, has disputed this interpretation, emphasizing the likelihood of a checkweighman becoming compromised by receiving regular wages irrespective of trading conditions.[3]

Setting aside, for a moment, the role of checkweighmen, the intention behind the Act of 1860 was to protect workers against the bullying and fraud perpetrated by employers. This was symptomatic of a policy endorsed by the MNA aimed at progress through legislative reform rather than by direct action, through conciliation rather than militancy, and not all trade unionists welcomed it. Thus, in 1863–4 opposition to the MNA emanated from Lancashire and south Staffordshire, whence the short-lived Practical Miners' Association drew most support, and where organization was particularly difficult because of the fragmentation of the coalfields and divisions between miners' interests. When in 1868, encouraged by the MNA, local leaders met to discuss the organization of an effective county union, the assembled delegates formed the Amalgamated Association of Miners, which as it was designed to become a national centralized body inevitably ran into competition with the MNA. Under the leadership of Thomas Halliday, a policy of centrally administered financial suport for strikers was the key factor which won support of miners in south Staffordshire and Worcestershire, who had been abandoned by the MNA in their strike of 1864; South Wales miners, among whom trade unionism was a relative novelty, also responded to this promised opportunity to tap the financial resources from other regions, where trade unionism amongst miners was better established.[4]

By 1873 the AAM, limited still to these three regions, claimed a

[1] G. D. H. Cole, 'Some Notes on British Trade Unionism in the Third Quarter of the Nineteenth Century', *IRSH* 11 (1937), 1–23; Challinor 1972, Chapts. 5–8; Arnot 1949, 54–6; A. R. Griffin 1971, 76.

[2] S. and B. Webb *History of Trade Unionism* (1920) 289–91, 453.

[3] Burgess 1975, 167. But giving evidence in 1867–8 the miners' agent, William Brown, explained the checkweighmen's inability to exercise independence from employers unless a strong union existed to support him; 'otherwise he can be dismissed immediately and has no power.' In this respect the checkweighman was 'partly under the masters'—meaning under their thumbs rather than in their pockets.

[4] Arnot, 1949, 46–61; Chris Fisher and John Smethurst 'War on Supply and Demand: The Amalgamated Association of Miners and the Forest of Dean Colliers, 1869–75', in Royden Harrison 1978, 144–8; Challinor 1972, Chapt. 5.

membership of 99,000 compared with a published figure of 123,000 for the MNA, though the actual figure was closer to 104,000.[1] Even though the number of miners each organization claimed to represent may have been similar, the AAM could not claim for its constituent unions the degree of permanence already achieved by some of those belonging to the MNA. Among the membership of the MNA in 1875 35,000 were in Durham, 17,000 in south Yorkshire, 16,000 in Northumberland, 10,000 in west Yorkshire, and 17,000 in the six separate Scottish unions (of which the only semi-permanent body was that of the Fife and Clackmannan miners, whose union was formed in that year.[2] The respective financial balances of the Durham and south Yorkshire miners were each one-half as large as the combined resources of the AAM unions. Through the highest weekly contributions levied by the SYMA of 1s., a fund of £34,000 had been estbalished to provide death, sickness, and trade benefits. Members of the Durham Miners' Association had accumulated a fund of £37,000 from contributions of 9d. for all three benefits, or less for one or two; the west Yorkshire and Derbyshire and Leicestershire unions required contributions of 8d. and 7½d. for all benefits. For other unions the maximum subscription was 6d. and, except for the Northumberland miners who could obtain sickness and death benefits only, the priority was trade benefit.[3] Since 1862, however, many miners in Durham, Northumberland, and Cumberland had contributed also to the Permanent Relief Society, pioneered by the Durham miners who for a weekly subscription of 6d. could claim benefit, either as a result of accident, or when they became permanently unfit for work.[4]

The failure of miners in Lancashire and Cheshire, South Wales, and south Staffordshire to establish county unions demonstrated the unsuitability of the MNA's loose federal structure for their needs, for under the MNA's general policy, they were denied the support promised within the centralized structure of the AAM. However, the difficulty of reconciling local with wider interests proved too much, and despite the AAM's initial successes, notably in expanding trade unionism in South Wales, the disappearance of the early 1870s boom revealed the contradictions built into the structure of the AAM. The tradition of local

[1] *Dearness and Scarcity* 1873, X, QQ 4488–90.

[2] LSE Library Webb Collection (E) XXVII, 73. The Leeds Conference of 1873 recorded higher financial balances for several unions, but the relative financial strengths were similar to those implied by the Fynes figures in the Webb Collection.

[3] Ibid.

[4] See above 598–9.

separatism and the proliferation of district organizations undermined centralized control and defeated any prospect of withstanding the employers' counter-attack in the depression. As membership declined rapidly, the leaders accepted an overture from the MNA to merge the two associations, and thus the Miners' National Union was established in 1875.[1] In a context of falling prices and limited funds, resistance to wage reductions was not sustainable. At county level such unionism that did continue remained firmly attached to the principles of conciliation and sliding scales in accordance with the policies of the MNU, which continued to seek legislative reforms rather than narrowly economic aims, a policy for which an increasingly political orientation became necessary.[2]

The Miners' Federation of Great Britain was formed in 1889, in the midst of a wave of wage increases which accompanied the upswing of 1888–91. It has been seen by some historians as a revival of the AAM, in that its structure was slightly more centralized; it was centred on the inland coalfields and projected a more militant image than the MNU, though this simple dichotomy has been questioned and the similarities and continuities between the two bodies underlined. Eventually, in the later 1890s the MFGB rejected the policy of the sliding scale, which unions in the export coalfields, however, regarded as essential.[3] Two views have been advanced to explain the dramatic increase in mining trade unionism in the 1880s, following a period described either as instability or quiescence. H. A. Turner suggested that, hitherto, the élitism of miners' trade unions in the North-east had inhibited a more broadly based trade unionism among mineworkers.[4] Certainly, those who determined the objectives and methods of mining unions were the hewers who, at least until the very rapid expansion in trade unionism after 1889, comprised virtually the entire membership. In the North-east, where division of labour had progressed furthest, the hewers were an élite in the sense that the particular kind of skill they possessed, albeit accumulated by sheer experience, was greater than that of other colliery workers (excluding some craftsmen), that their earnings were higher, and their working hours shorter.

[1] Chris Fisher and John Smethurst 'War on the Law of Supply and Demand: The Amalgamated Association of Miners and the Forest of Dean Colliers, 1869–75', in Royden Harrison 1978, 144–8; Challinor 1972, Chapts. 5–8.
[2] G. D. H. Cole, 'Some Notes on British Trade Unionism in the Third Quarter of the Nineteenth Century', *IRSH* 11 (1937), 1–23.
[3] Fisher and Smethurst 1978, 114–48.
[4] H. A. Turner, *Trade Union Growth and Structure*, London, (1962) 191–2.

Hewers constituted some 40 per cent of all colliery workers in the North-east, but in most other regions, where specialization was less advanced, those proportions were higher, because hewers carried out less 'skilled' tasks and worked longer hours; they were in a weaker position, therefore, to establish an élitist posture in relation to trade-union organization and policy. The basic skills of hewing could be acquired without difficulty by colliery workers familiar with pit routine and discipline, and unskilled labour could be recruited to perform labourers' tasks on the surface or underground.[1] Furthermore, apart from the dubious assumption that in the nineteenth century the strength of miners' trade unions in one region depended upon the 'élitist' policies of those in another (distant) region, the membership policies of the unions in the North-east were not noticeably more restrictive than those adopted later in other regions where stable trade unions began to emerge.

In contrast to this structural explanation for the relatively tardy development of stable trade unionism among miners, Burgess advances a model which stresses a transformation in miners' attitudes, softened by the years of prosperity between 1850 and 1875 when the aspiration towards collective action on a national scale had been in abeyance.[2] The validity of this interpretation may be doubted, too, however, for setting aside the exceptional depression of the late 1870s, which succeeded the equally unprecedented prosperity of the preceding boom, secular trends in real wages and earnings were similar in the 1880s to those in the 1850s and 1860s, though in the 1880s at higher levels.[3] Certainly the newly emerging leaders, notably Keir Hardie and Robert Smillie, espoused different political ideas from the major figures whose formative experience was in the mid-nineteenth century; but the advance of socialism at the rank-and-file level was equally slow to affect their elected leaders in the 1880s, when attitudes are alleged to have been transformed.[4]

Much more important than changing ideologies were the economic changes which produced a sharp contrast in employment opportunities and aspirations from the mid-1880s by comparison with the prolonged and deep depression after 1874. The 1880s saw the resumption of adult recruitment into the industry on a scale similar to that of the 1860s, with overall recruitment 60 per cent higher than in the 1860s. The return of growth in coal production provided the climate of expansion in which miners' leaders, and the miners who flocked to join the unions, could

[1] See above 204–7, 229.   [2] Burgess 1975, 172–3.
[3] See above Table 7.4.   [4] Arnot 1949, 46–61.

envisage real prospects of greater prosperity, and afforded the opportunity to place upon the agenda of the employers and government
demands for the eight-hour day and a minimum wage. Not until the
twentieth century did these campaigns bear fruit, however; until the
more customary aims and methods had advanced miners' traditional
interests centred upon wages and working practices, which, from its
inception, were the preoccupations of the MFGB.

Beginning as a federation embracing the county unions in the inland
coalfields, membership expanded both there and geographically, and by
1907 the Federation comprised thirty separately constituted unions; yet
its structure remained firmly based on the familiar pattern of pit lodge,
district and county union, and federated national assembly, ensuring the
perpetuation of the centrifugal tendencies in industrial relations.[1]

National estimates of the number of miners belonging to trade unions
are probably less reliable than those for the regional totals on record,
but unfortunately the latter are very incomplete before the 1890s. It is
possible that at its short-lived peak in 1844 MAGBI membership
included 30 per cent of all coalminers, but it has been estimated that no
more than 10 per cent were members of trade unions in the early 1860s,[2]
when only in Yorkshire and the North-east had permanent organization taken root. The coal famine raised that proportion temporarily,
perhaps to above 50 per cent if measured by the combined affiliated
membership of the MNA and the AAM. However, it seems unlikely
that the percentage of mining trade-union membership exceeded 16 per
cent throughout the remainder of the 1870s and 1880s, until the remarkable acceleration after 1888. Table 8.1 presents membership data, the
accuracy of which is open to question before the 1890s.

They are minimum figures of trade-union membership, and for the
earlier part of the period inevitably contain omissions. The sources
occasionally contain two (or more) different estimates of membership
for the same year, and when this occurs the upper figure has been taken
(since membership figures were frequently revised upward in the light
of later and more accurate evidence). Omissions of entire regions, or
sub-regions, from the figures present a greater problem, and mean that it
has been found impossible to arrive at an accurate figure of total
membership prior to the 1890s. Those unionized in the UK industry
numbered some 250,000–300,000 in the 1890s, fluctuating thereafter to
peaks of around 650,000 in 1905–7, rising to 885,000 in 1910–13.

[1] Ibid., 67–8, 370–4.
[2] See above 676, and Benson 1980, 197–8.

Table 8.1. *Trade-union membership, 1874–1913*
(thousands)

	Scotland	North-east	Cumb.	Lancs./Ches.	North Wales and Monmouth	Yorks.	East Midlands	West Midlands	South Wales excl. Monmouth	GB total
1874		40.0				33.2	7.0	6.6		
1875		55.6		0.5		22.5	6.0			
1876		53.6	2.0			30.5	4.8			
1877		47.3	1.0			12.5				
1878			0.7		N.W. only	3.3				
1879			0.75			3.0				
1880		40.7	1.0		0.2	2.8		0.6		
1881		40.8	0.6		0.2	5.8		0.7		
1882		47.4	1.5	18.4	0.4	11.0		1.1		
1883		47.4	1.5	17.2	0.3	12.0	5.0	1.7		
1884		50.7	2.0	10.8	0.2	8.0	2.3	1.5		
1885		48.1	2.0	9.5	0.2	8.0		1.6		
1886		43.8	2.0	8.1	0.4	8.0		1.6		
1887	3.0	42.7	2.3	7.3	0.4	8.0		1.1		
1888	1.7	49.5	2.3	10.7	0.4	10.0		2.4		
1889	3.0	61.1	2.3	14.8	0.4	35.0	19.8	7.0	1.6	
1890	3.1	66.0	3.3	28.8	0.7	50.0	28.3	9.9	3.0	
1891	2.2	72.4	3.5	31.2	1.2	43.3	16.4	3.3		
1892	14.6	67.1	5.0	40.1	6.8	55.0	40.1	22.9	25.1	271.4
1893	20.9	67.4	3.7	39.6	5.1	55.0	42.4	20.2	23.8	273.5

Year											
1894	35.9	76.0	3.1	6.8	29.2	55.0	38.7			23.0	285.5
1895	20.9	78.9	2.4	3.8	27.8	50.4	36.8			16.7	258.0
1896	18.0	79.0	2.3	3.5	25.9	50.0	33.4			21.7	250.1
1897	15.7	81.6	2.7	2.7	26.5	50.0	33.4			19.0	250.2
1898	20.9	90.7	3.8		30.3	50.0	35.8			60.0	319.3
1899	47.9	102.2	3.8	7.9	30.3	51.0	41.5	31.8		104.2	416.1
1900	65.5	104.2	3.6	6.8	37.0	79.5	50.2	43.1		127.9	511.8
1901	64.5	100.0	5.2	8.8	39.8	89.2	51.2	40.6		124.1	552.3
1902	60.1	103.8	4.4	10.5	38.1	60.7	55.3	36.7		127.4	493.9
1903	59.8	110.1	4.0	13.8	36.6	60.5	54.0	35.0		125.6	493.7
1904	55.1	113.3	3.3	12.4	33.3	56.7	51.9	32.4		117.1	469.0
1905	56.7	114.7	3.2	12.0	34.2	55.2	50.7	31.8		111.0	465.4
1906	57.8	120.7	4.3	18.5	55.4	62.2	51.7	44.2		121.3	537.7
1907	79.5	137.9	5.1	23.1	75.4	79.1	58.9	64.4		135.8	664.8
1908	81.5	147.0	4.9	23.9	72.5	78.4	72.6	56.9		144.6	678.9
1909	85.2	152.9	6.8	24.6	67.6	83.8	79.9	52.3		141.2	685.1
1910	86.6	159.2	6.3	24.6	61.8	88.3	77.8	59.1		137.6	692.0
1911	93.3	189.3	7.5	22.6	74.1	92.9			129.1	120.0	728.9
1912	93.8	195.0	8.1	19.8	65.4	99.6			137.5	114.2	733.6
1913	110.8	203.4	9.9	25.0	89.6	126.3			166.6	154.1	885.8

Sources: Evidence is to be found for all regions in: Board of Trade, *Reports on Trade Unions*, 1889–1910; Thirteenth and Seventeenth *Abstract of Labour Statistics*, 1889–1913; the *Labour Gazette*; Webb Collection (E) XXVII. Supplementary evidence for the regions has been assembled as follows: Scotland: Arnot, 1949. Lancashire and Cheshire: Webb Collection (E) XXVII. Yorkshire: Machin, 1958; Neville thesis, 329; Webb Collection (E) XXVII. East Midlands: A. R. Griffin 1971; C. P. Griffin 1982; J. E. Williams, 1962. West Midlands: E. Hopkins, thesis. Figures are available for the 1873 district membership of the Miners' National Association in Fynes 1873, and the Webb Collection (E) XXVI, 73; but these are unreliable (see Challinor 1972, 94–6). Except for membership figures for the unions of the North-east and Yorkshire, no reliable series exist for the period before 1875, but for membership in occasional years see A. E. P. Duffy 'The Growth of Trade Unionism in England from 1867 to 1906 in its Political Aspects' (unpublished Ph.D. thesis, University of London, 1956) p. 251 where figures and estimates found in the Webb Collection have been reproduced.

The regional totals are of interest in the light of the evidence given to the 1868 Royal Commission on the relatively advanced state of trade unionism in the 1860s in Yorkshire, and evidence from other sources on the membership of the MNA and AAM during the coal famine. The figures show clearly that of all unions only those in Northumberland and Durham survived the depression after 1874 with a mass membership. Other regions failed to regain a mass membership until much later—in Yorkshire from 1889, in Scotland after the 1890s, and in Lancashire and Cheshire after 1892. Although the figures for the East and West Midlands are deficient, there are good grounds for timing the emergence of large-scale unionism there with that in Yorkshire, and with the founding of the MFGB in 1889. Formal union organization in South Wales was very limited prior to 1892, emerging in force only in 1898–9, when its rate of growth was unparalleled in any region. Table 8.2 reveals the proportion of miners unionized nationally, and in each of the regions in 1875 and thereafter at five-yearly intervals.

Throughout the period there was an intimate connection between the state of the industry, as reflected in prices and wages, and the level of membership. Trade-union membership rose sharply in booms and fell with equal rapidity in slumps, and no single figure should be taken as representative of an entire trade cycle. The only demonstrable association between membership and rising wages occurs in 1870–3, 1888–91, 1898–1900, and 1905–7. McCormick advances two resons why union membership should rise in booms: firstly, because price and wage rises allow workers to buy more goods (among which trade union members can be counted), and secondly, because the upswing of the cycle reduces the possible 'cost' of trade union membership in terms of the possibilities of victimization and job loss.[1] To these reasons can be added a third: that the benefits of union membership, particularly in the form of higher wages, were more immediately visible during booms, and that over an entire upswing a progressive widening of interest in the work of the union occurred as wages rose. Other benefits could also be achieved during this period, including shorter hours, reduced intensity of work, higher absenteeism, and increased restrictive practices. The secular boom in membership after 1888 must be associated, therefore, at least in part, with the trade buoyancy of the period 1888–1913, and particularly with that of 1888–1904, when coal prices rose relative to general price levels.

[1] B. J. McCormick 1979, 235–6.

Table 8.2. *Comparisons of trade-union density, 1875–1913*
(percentages)

	Scotland	North-east	Cumb.	Lancs./Ches.	North Wales	Yorks.	East Midlands	West Midlands	South Wales	UK
1875		56				(44)[a]				
1880		44	17		2	5		1		
1885		48	30	12		13		4		
1890	4	54	45	36.8	7	64	46	20	3	42 (1892)
1895	25	59	31	32	32	58	51		15	39
1900	69	69	43	42		80	62	73	87	68
1905	54	68	37	37		50	57	51	67	56
1910	67	76	62	59		61	74	81	65	68
1913	80	91		84		79	87		66	81

[a] Estimate arrived at by deduction from the SYMA figures the number of members located in Derbyshire (given by J. E. Williams 1962, 168).

Annual figures for the percentage unionized in the UK are as follows: 1892–4, 42 per cent; 1895, 39 per cent; 1896–7, 38 per cent; 1898, 47 per cent; 1899, 60 per cent; 1900, 68 per cent; 1901, 67 pe cent; 1902, 62 per cent; 1903, 61 per cent; 1904, 58 per cent; 1905, 56 per cent; 1906, 63 per cent; 1907, 73 per cent; 1908, 71 per cent; 1909, 70 per cent; 1910, 68 per cent; 1911, 71 per cent; 1912, 69 per cent; 1913, 81 per cent.

Sources: Board of Trade, *17th Abstract of Labour Statistics*. The original percentages are calculated from Table 8.1 together with regional employment data assembled in the preparation of Table 3.2.

iii. Trade-union policies: restrictions, strikes, and collective bargaining

Whether as members of formal or informal organizations, miners pursued a limited range of policies which displayed little variation throughout the entire period. The emergence of unions at different times does not appear to have fundamentally affected either objectives or methods, though different groups of workers at various times showed preferences for one strategy rather than another. The two major strategies were the strike and the restriction of output, though legislation was also regarded by leaders of the MAGBI, the MNU, and the MFGB as offering one way of promoting miners' material interests. There is every reason to believe that output restriction was considered as a tactic of equal importance with the strike, though evidently the former was much less successful in achieving the desired end.

Particularly during the years before about 1860, miners tended to regard the restriction of their daily output as potentially providing a solution to the problems of low wages, falling coal prices, over-production, and under-employment. Even until the 1880s, restriction was the fundamental policy option among miners in the west of Scotland for whom strike action was a second-best alternative to be employed only when restriction had failed.[1] Welbourne argued that the reason why the 1831 strike by miners in the North-east was accompanied by so much bitterness was that the restriction of output put into effect was interpreted by the employers as an infringement of managerial control.[2] Throughout the early nineteenth century restriction was practically synonymous with unionism. Welbourne maintained that restriction was undertaken mainly to prevent exhaustion and overwork, and to preserve the weak and the old from health-damaging competition,[3] though there is abundant evidence that the motives behind restriction were economic. In the North-east restriction was widely practised in 1825, 1831 and 1832,[4] and 1850, and in Yorkshire in 1843, 1844, 1858, 1863, 1865, 1867, and 1873.[5] As late as 1879 in Yorkshire and 1882 in Derbyshire miners' leaders gave serious consideration to such a policy, though decided against it.[6]

Tremenheere's reports between 1846 and 1858 contain numerous references to, and vehement criticism of, the policy of restriction.

[1] Campbell 1979, 265–6.   [2] Welbourne 1973, 39.
[3] Ibid., 25–6.   [4] Scott thesis, Appendix N.
[5] Machin 1958, 46, 52, 83, 118, 139, 176, 278, 315–6, 342–3, 385.
[6] Ibid. 468–90.

Referring to the MFGBI in 1847, he wrote: 'The combination enables the colliers to regulate the markets, and raise the price of coal. . .'[1] After reporting on restrictive practices in the North-east in 1850,[2] he observed later that, '. . . strikes . . . are harmless in comparison with the permanent combinations to reduce the amount of labour which are so general throughout the mining districts. . . .'[3] More than in any other region, however, the theme of restricting output lay at the root of the Scottish 'darg' which was employed widely in Scotland: 'Restricted working had been regularly adopted by West of Scotland miners since at least the eighteen-twenties and it remained a recommended policy of local unions until the eighties . . . Over the period 1842–74 it was implemented at district level and over large parts of the whole region during at least sixteen years'.[4] For miners' leaders in the west of Scotland restriction was essential, not only to raise wages but also to maintain effective collective organization; it was, indeed, the source of discipline on which that organization was based. Yet, like the strike weapon (or any union strategy) the darg proved more effective when prices were rising than when they were falling.[5]

Output restriction links the trade-union movement of the early years with the MFGB's campaign for the eight-hour day in 1889–1908. Page Arnot pointed out that it was the coexistence of falling prices and expanding output in the early 1880s which led the unions to regard over-production as the main problem.[6] Restriction of output was also some-times employed during the late nineteenth century by a militant rank and file in opposition to the sliding-scale policy espoused by mining leaders, though rarely with success.[7] The west of Scotland in the period 1842–74 may have been untypical in the extent to which restriction was commonly pursued and in the short term achieved some success, but elsewhere difficulty in securing sufficient support for collective action to be effective was the main reason for the failure of such a policy. In Durham, especially in the later period, many lodges refused to carry out a restriction order and the policy collapsed. 'Human nature is too strong for such arrangements', declared John Wilson, the Durham miners' leader—an oblique reference to the opposition from men whose earn-ings would suffer under restricted working.[8]

[1] *State of the Population in Mining Districts* 1847, XVI, 14.
[2] Ibid., 1850, 46.
[3] Ibid., 1854, 23–4.
[4] G. M. Wilson thesis, 44–7.
[5] Ibid., 274–83.
[6] Arnot 1949, 67–8.
[7] Evans 1961, 162.
[8] J. Wilson, *A History of the Durham Miners' Association, 1870-1904* (Durham, 1907), 176–9; Evans 1961, 163.

Underlying the choice between strikes and restriction were miners' views of the relationships between wages and coal prices. That they held a definite standpoint on this issue is certain. In the strikes of 1831 and 1844, employers and workers in the North-east used a barrage of information about the relationship between wages and prices to demonstrate the strengths of their respective positions. The belief that prices determined wages was widely accepted by both sides; the debate was primarily about whether miners in co-operation with employers as producers could do anything to maintain prices. In 1844 an address to the coalowners issued by the MAGBI pursued this theme of co-operative action in defence of the trade:

We have had to submit this year to a very great reduction in prices, and this we opine, if you as coalowners get once into the path of ruinous competition by underselling each other in the market and then endeavouring to reduce the wages to still keep a market, it is a process which is alike ruinous to both parties ... while the public, who are consumers, reap the benefit ...[1]

Such a theme was certainly not new to the North-east where, under the vend, prices and wages had been artificially maintained. Only when employers refused to consider price-fixing or declared such a policy impossible to achieve did miners seek to restrict output.[2] The failure to secure employers' collaboration in reducing output influenced Mac-Donald and the MNU in turning to parliamentary intervention, especially over hours, as the best long-term strategy. Viewed in this way, it is possible to argue that miners possessed a relatively sophisticated view of the economy; since the cycle dominated and since in the long run it was difficult to perceive real gains as wages rose and fell so rapidly, restriction of output was seen as the key to secular progress and as a method of moderating the vicissitudes of the cycle. The eight-hour movement and even the minimum-wage agitation may be interpreted as a continuation of this basic strategy into the twentieth century.

The alternative to output restriction was strike action, whether limited to a single colliery, pit, or lodge or extended to two or three separate enterprises as a contest, the outcome of which was sometimes tacitly regarded by employers and miners as a general settlement or standard; or in the form of a complete stoppage at district or county level. The strike (or strike threat) was flexible, but the difficulty of sustaining a strike on the basis of levies (for regular contributions adequate to meet such a contingency were rare even among the first permanent

---

[1] Quoted in Richard Fynes, *The Miners of Northumberland and Durham* (Sunderland, 1873), 50.
[2] See A. J. Taylor 1955, 52–4.

unions) prompted some union leaders to favour moderation in the use of the strike, and to persuade employers to negotiate on an agreed basis. The origins of continuous systematic collective bargaining in the coal industry have been identified in Durham in 1872, when the first Joint Committee was formed. Consisting of six representatives each from owners and the union, the committee possessed authority to settle all questions affecting individual collieries.[1] Northumberland's joint committee was established on the Durham model in 1873 (on a three to two majority vote of coalowners), in response to the union request.[2]

The distinctive feature of the Durham model was the authority of the Committee's decision, but for several years before it was established a similar system, operating on a voluntary basis and involving two representatives from each side, had, according to Normansell, secretary of the SYMA, settled hundreds of disputes in that district by the 'reference system', devised by him.[3] The system was agreed to by the coalowners after their defeats in 1864 and 1865, and ushered in a period of relative peace in the district, except for a number of major strikes and lock-outs at individual collieries over the closed-shop issue—a symptom of union strength.[4] Collective bargaining in west Yorkshire was resisted by a stronger, more cohesive group of coalowners than those in south Yorkshire, and west Yorkshire coalowners did not feel compelled to agree to the establishment of a joint committee until 1873 (as did Northumberland owners at the same time) under the pressure of an over-heated labour market.[5] These district committees were exceptional, and Burgess has argued that they were 'confined to districts where a class of miners' officials had emerged with sufficient power and prestige to control the malcontents. In these areas, the owners had little to lose and much to gain from recognizing the miners' representatives and agreeing to bargain with them'.[6]

Certainly collective bargaining was only accepted by employers where agreements could be adhered to—which required union discipline as well as adequate membership of coalowners' associations; but the latter acknowledged the advantages of orderly collective bargaining only in retrospect, and in each case was accepted on the unions' initiative and under pressure. Moreover, rank-and-file members supported the district unions when economic conditions favoured activity. An

[1] Burgess 1975, 182–3.
[2] NuRO Steam Collieries Association MB I, 198, 215.
[3] Machin 1958, 350.   [4] Ibid., 342–3.
[5] Ibid., 188.   [6] Burgess 1975, 188.

alternative organization advocating more militant policies was available to miners in 1864–5 in the form of the Practical Miners Association, yet this short-lived body won little support from Yorkshire miners.[1] Trade-union density in south Yorkshire was higher than in any other district during the 1860s, with the possible exception of Northumberland, at a time when the newly established 'cosmopolitan pits' might have been expected to have inhibited trade-union growth and collective action; yet Spaven found little evidence of dissatisfaction among rank and file with the union's policies until the depression of the late 1870s, and membership continued to grow until the 1876 down-turn. Meanwhile, the achievements of Normansell's strategy before that time, of moderation from a position of strength, included an eight-hour day, higher wages than in many coalfields, agreement on weekly pays, the 20 cwt. ton, and the appointment of a checkweighman.[2]

Gains in these areas were eroded after the boom of the 1870s, the sliding scale, which some trade-union leaders had been advocating during the boom but which coalowners had resisted, proving to be instrumental in this process. The introduction of formal sliding scales in the 1870s could do little to strengthen the already close proximity in the course of wages and prices. Porter has shown that the formation of the boards of conciliation and arbitration in the early 1870s occurred because the unions possessed insufficient strength to pursue a more militant policy but enough to convince the employers that conciliation was needed. This point was usually reached in the upswing when trade-union membership was increasing, notably in the early 1870s. But the introduction of permanent arrangements for conciliation and arbitration did not imply a diminished importance of the price–wage relationship. In 1874–6, for example, the Durham and Northumberland coalowners and union leaders declared prices to be the most important factor in the arbitrations of those years. The record of these arbitrations shows a close correspondence between wages and short-run price fluctuations, and the movement towards sliding scales owed something to the failure of some arbitrations and to a recognition that prices had governed wage movements in the past and in all recent arbitrations.[3] Another influence was the suspicion on the part of miners' leaders (especially those in Durham) that the wage reductions of 1873–7 were not justified by falls in prices;

[1] Chris Fisher and Pat Spaven 1978, 'Edward Rymer and "the Moral Workman"—The Dilemma of the Radical Miner under "Macdonaldism"', in Royden Harrison (ed.), Independent Collier (Hassocks, 1978) 237–9; Pat Spaven 'Main Gates of Protest', Ibid., 201.

[2] Machin 1958, 351.   [3] Porter 1970, 461–7.

which explains their wish to obtain independent evidence of price movements—which a sliding scale would formalize.[1]

In the event, arbitration alone can hardly be considered to have favoured the miners; of thirty-nine arbitrations made in 1865–1914 only eight did not lead to wage reductions, and only four produced increases.[2] In practice, the particular scale adopted simply reflected the balance of industrial forces operating at the time of the agreement, and contributed little towards the creation of industrial peace.[3] The sliding-scale wages system, did, however, tend to generate misunderstanding and disagreement arising from the complexity of the scales.[4] A regularly negotiated basis, or standard rate, was the fixed point in the system, though after 1888 a percentage addition to the standard rate was adopted as the basis for the piece-rates paid to most underground workers and the wages of surface workers, who were paid by time rates. In addition to piece-rates, paid according to the colliery price-list adjusted by the negotiated percentage, piece-workers also received supplementary wages, negotiated locally according to working conditions and designed to compensate miners working in 'abnormal' places, a term which was defined broadly, though with difficulty, by geological criteria.[5]

Labour's attitude to sliding scales varied a good deal. Miners' leaders in the North-east and in South Wales considered them the best way of fixing wages; in 1889 the Durham miners' executive affirmed its conviction that in practice, they offered the most equitable way of fixing and settling wages.[6] Labour representatives on the 1893 Royal Commission on Labour saw the sliding scale as the main buttress of industrial peace, though only Durham and South Wales representatives gave evidence to the Commission.[7] This position adopted by the leaders in the export coalfields appears to have had much to do with their belief that these regions depended more than others on long-term contracts, which could be permanently lost if disputes occurred.[8] The export coalfields were also most affected by extreme variations in prices, and consequently it was reasonable for trade-union leaders in these areas to attach importance to the need for sliding scales. Particularly in areas of weak unionism, such as South Wales, one attraction of sliding scales was

---

[1] Metcalfe thesis, 97–101.
[2] Porter 1970, 475.   [3] Porter 1971, 14.
[4] Benson 1982, 190.   [5] Ibid.
[6] Porter 1970, 467.   [7] Duggett thesis, 17–19.
[8] Clegg, Fox, and Thompson 1964, 19.

that they extended to the trade union an official and recognized role, and was therefore seen as an alternative to purely arbitrary, employer-dictated decisions.[1] Clearly, therefore, outside the North-east, sliding scales were often agreed to simply because the unions were weak and unable to resist them. Many trade-union leaders favoured sliding scales because they appeared to be effectively automatic, allowing deductions from wages without endangering discipline and membership.[2]

Partly for this reason, perhaps, eventually mining leaders in Yorkshire, who already enjoyed a regular joint-committee procedure for settling disputes, began to consider the system.[3] Yet the basic fact which most of the literature seems to have ignored in accounting for the introduction of sliding scales is that the system was merely an institutional variant of a long-established practice, based on the assumption that prices should govern wages. The sliding scales were disadvantageous to labour, however, to the extent that the maximum was far more important as a restrictive factor on trade unions in good times than was the minimum on employers in periods of depression.[4] At the same time, the scales were never truly automatic. In practice a scale rarely lasted longer than two years, for when it ceased to be appropriate in relation to the relative strength of the bargainers it was rejected, and when economic circumstances changed substantially a new scale was drawn up. When a scale continued for a lengthy period (as did the South Wales scale between 1892 and 1903), it should be seen in the context of the relatively stable bargaining positions of employers and workers.[5]

Sliding scales were eventually rejected by organized labour for a number of reasons, though it is difficult to establish their order of importance: partly from a growing recognition that the maxima and minima operated against the interests of miners, partly out of the growth of the concern with the minimum wage. Rejection was due also to the simultaneous development of the sustained boom of 1888–91, the formation of the MFGB, and the growth of its membership which encouraged a more aggressive policy. At the same time, many radical leaders and rank-and-file members, particularly those in the North-east and in South Wales, rejected the conciliatory policy of the established leadership. It has also been noted that the MFGB, and particularly the leadership in the inland coalfields, was more successful in rejecting slid-

---

[1] Morris and Williams, 'The South Wales Sliding Scale, 1876–9: An Experiment in Industrial Relations', in W. Minchinton (ed.), *Industrial South Wales, 1750-1914*, (London, 1969), 220.
[2] Garside 1977, 143–4.   [3] Porter 1970, 467.
[4] Ibid., 474.   [5] Porter 1971, 17–18.

ing scales because price fluctuations in these regions were less acute than in the export coalfields and because, for this reason, employers were more disposed to dispense with the system.[1] An additional factor, though difficult to measure, lay in the trend of productivity. Whereas in the iron and steel industry sliding scales tended to receive continuing labour support because of advances in productivity, which allowed piece-rate shift wages to increase over time, in the coal industry such rises in productivity that occurred did so against a background of diminishing returns, which placed restraints on the ability, or willingness, of employers to concede substantial rises in basic rates.[2] One of the aims of miners in rejecting sliding scales lay in the abolition of the maxima and minima;[3] thereafter, wages may still not have kept pace with prices during booms after their abolition,[4] but they almost certainly rose further than the earlier sliding scales would have permitted.

It would seem, therefore, that throughout the period a considerable degree of continuity may be identified in the response of organized labour to the problems and challenges presented. The twin weapons of the strike and of restriction of output were implemented recurrently throughout the period. Likewise, the close relationship between price and wage movements persisted as a dominant influence upon labour relations. At the same time, it would be absurd to argue that regional differences, whether in the extent and strength of unionism, in labour traditions and practices, or in the precise comparative course of wages and prices over time, did not entail certain differences in the policy adopted. Various examples can be cited of this disequilibrium, whether in the form of the struggle to establish a national union in the early period, in the conflict of the MNA and AAM in the 1870s, or in that of the MFGB and the North-eastern leadership in the 1890s and 1900s. Indeed, the establishment in the North-east of a powerful union before 1870, together with the achieving of a seven-hour working day for hewers, eventually came into conflict with the MFGB's attempt to establish a single national union, with its insistence on the eight-hour day as a central part of its programme. Differentials in wages and earnings between the regions also contributed to disunity, and there was no concerted attempt (even in the Minimum Wage Act) to establish a uniform national wage structure. Even in the post-1889 period the inability of the unions to challenge, or significantly erode, regional wage differentials

---

[1] Garside 1977, 143. [2] Ibid., 20–1.
[3] Clegg, Fox, and Thompson 1964, 462.
[4] See below 747 fn. 2.

does suggest that their power in relation to market forces was relatively limited. Regional differences in wage and other conditions led unions to attach to such issues as wages, conditions, hours, and employment (and in the early period such issues as truck, fines and forfeitures, arrestment of wages, and payment by weight) differences in priorities, and to pursue policies which varied—for example, in the degree of militancy. These differing preferences, however, were none the less expressed within the context of a common attitude to the basic strategy, which was concerned with the maintenance of the optimum level of wages within the limits dictated by prices.

Such was the aim which lay behind the legislative campaign to secure payment by true weight and the appointment of checkweighmen at the pithead, measures designed to obtain full payment for all coal got, by ending the widespread practice of confiscation and deductions from wages, which some employers maximized by requiring tubs to be 'rocked' before they could be accepted as full measure.[1] The Duke of Hamilton's mineral accounts in the 1840s reveal that 6 per cent of coal raised from his pits was not paid for,[2] and in 1860 a survey of weighing in some south Yorkshire pits showed similar losses in earnings by what was referred to by Scottish miners as 'a system of robbing . . . practised by the employers'. John Normansell (himself a checkweighman at Wharncliffe Silkstone from 1859 to 1863 and whose view therefore might have been biased) was convinced that the appointment of a checkweighman fully justified 10 per cent of any man's wages to support it; implying that earnings would be enhanced by at least as much when fair weighing practices were effectively implemented.[3]

Although the grievance was widespread, the local initiative in reforming the system was undertaken by the south Yorkshire miners, who had succeeded, before 1860, in securing the agreement of a few owners to pay by weight and to allow the miners to appoint a checkweighman at the pithead to monitor and record the coal got by each miner. The comparative strength of the Yorkshire miners had enabled them to insist upon an arrangement whereby the checkweighman was a man of their choice, a principle which occasioned an eighteen-week strike at the Oaks Colliery in 1858 and ended in a compromise agreement, conceding the employers' approval as also necessary.[4] With the precedents and pro-

---

[1] *Transactions National Association of Miners* 1863, 143.
[2] G. M. Wilson Thesis, 59–60.
[3] *Transactions National Association of Miners* 1863 53–68; Machin 1958, 13.
[4] *Transactions National Association of Miners* 1863, 186.

gress, albeit limited, obtained in south Yorkshire, Alexander Mac-
Donald took up these issues and campaigned for legislation under the
1860 Mines Inspection Act to require a similar system of measurement
by weight, and the appointment of miners' checkweighmen at all
collieries. This clause was fought by employers, who succeeded in insisting that checkweighmen's appointments should be voluntary, that all
such appointments must be made from among a colliery's employees,
and that a checkweighman's wages would be a matter for the miners
who paid him. Under such arrangements, a miner appointed by his
fellow colliery workers risked harrassment, or even dismissal.

At Henry Briggs's pits, for example, no difficulties were presented over
the implementation of the checkweighman's appointment under the 1860
Act, but other employers favoured dismissing all their men on some pre-
text and on rehiring to exclude the checkweighmen, forcing the men to
elect another from their number. Not surprisingly, four years after the
Act only eight checkweighmen were performing their duties in south
Yorkshire; Wharncliffe Silkstone dismissed Normansell for providing
information germane to an existing dispute; and there were other
instances of checkweighmens' dismissals, one in 1863–4 leading to a
seventeen-week strike at Straker and Love's collieries in Durham.[1]
Grievances concerned with weighing did not cease, either in Yorkshire
or in other regions. A number of successful court cases brought by
miners' unions during the 1860s reduced some of the worst abuses,
though until the 1870s complaints of faulty weighing machines were not
uncommon, and payment by weight continued to be an issue, especially
in Lancashire and Cheshire, after the 1870s boom.[2] Machin remarked
that in Yorkshire, at any rate, the position of the checkweighman was as
precarious in the mid-1870s as it had been in the 1860s—this in the
region where trade unionism was well established (though then small in
numbers);[3] in South Wales, checkweighmen 'became an accepted part of
colliery organization' in the 1870s, after the Dowlais company had
conceded the principle in order to avert a strike in 1869.[4]

The checkweighman's legal position was strengthened in 1872 and
again in 1887, when the Coal Mines Regulation Act gave power to any
checkweighman, appointed by a majority of the workmen paid by
weight, to recover his wages from all who were remunerated on this
basis; election was to be by ballot and the appointment was no longer

[1] Ibid., 58–9.
[2] G. M. Wilson thesis, 61; Challinor 1972, 81; A. R. Griffin 1971, 90.
[3] Machin 1958, 250 [4] Evans 1961, 92.

subejct to the employers' agreement. Thereafter, checkweighmen came to be appointed at virtually all collieries, and in most cases the miners' contributions towards his wages were deducted by arrangement with employers. None the less, weighing continued to provide a source of grievance and dispute, and some coal masters continued to resent the tendency of the miners to appoint union men to this potentially influential position. In 1904 the Lanarkshire Coalmasters Association heard one of its members insist that were checkweighmen to be sworn neutral, and union men debarred from that office, interference with colliery working by 'proclaiming idle days' would be much reduced and friction with the miners diminished.[1]

From the standpoint of trade-union development, the Webbs's conclusion is consistent with this Scottish view from the coal masters' perspective. The Webbs relate the legality of checkweighmen, and the mode of election under the 1887 legislation (by a committee—usually identical with the committee of the miners' lodge) to the rapid growth of miners' organizations from that date: 'The recognition of this legislative reform and promotion of collective action by the men has been a direct incitement to combination;[2] the compulsory levy in effect provided a branch secretary which the union did not need to finance; and those who filled the checkweighman's position possessed the qualities admirably suited to the post of trade-union secretaries.

Burgess has questioned the validity of this longstanding interpretation, asserting that it was not uncommon for the checkweighman to become an 'employer's man'.[3] No evidence is offered for this supposition, 'explained' by referring to the regularity of a checkweighman's wages which are assumed to have separated his interest from those of the rank and file; an implied charge of duplicity. There is, of course, a plausible alternative explanation for the conversion from action which precipitates conflict with employers to that which minimizes discord; in Normansell's case, moderation followed militancy as the most effective method of maximizing gains once the SYMA was firmly established. The fact that those trade-union officials during the period 1860 to 1887 who were former checkweighmen may have tended to favour moderate policies might be plausibly explained by the difficult legal position of checkweighmen before 1887, for not until then did the employers' veto disappear, giving the miners freedom to select by ballot whomsoever they chose.

[1] SRO(W) Lanarkshire Coalmasters' Association CB 8/1 Dec. 1904.
[2] Quoted in H. S. Jevons 1915, 465.   [3] Burgess 1975, 167.

A small minority of mining trade unionists, including Alexander Mac-Donald, favoured some form of co-operation as a means of controlling the organization of production and of avoiding the difficulties presented in relations with employers.[1] Proposals were advanced for the investment of union funds into co-operative production in Yorkshire in the 1840s and 1850s, but not until the immense profitability of the 1870s boom raised expectations of appreciable monetary rewards, as well as miners' collective independence though co-operation, was the experiment put into practice. Results were disastrous, for by the time the various ventures launched by miners' trade unions in Durham, south Yorkshire, west Yorkshire, and north Staffordshire reached the stage of company formation, share issue, and subscription, the boom had ended; miners faced wage reductions, and enthusiasm for the enterprise ebbed. Only the south Yorkshire company survived until 1876, but in that year the managing director resigned after failing to persuade the work-force of between 350 to 400 men (few of whom were trade-union members) to accept wage reductions. At the same time, miners showed a continuing reluctance to provide share capital, and the debenture holders who had entered the company through public subscription took possession in 1876. Durham miners lost £15,500, those in west Yorkshire £6,000, and in south Yorkshire £31,500. With trade-union membership falling sharply and coalowners pressing home further reductions, the vision of the co-operative alternative was shattered, if for no other reason, by the chronology of co-operative experiment.[2]

Burgess's interpretation of the role of checkweighmen and the significance of co-operation forms part of his general thesis that the period of 'great prosperity' between 1850 and 1875 influenced the outlook of a generation of trade-union leaders—for example Burt, Wilson, and Abraham, who also became respected figures in their local communities and in national trade-union politics. Under the influence of such leaders, and in a context of the proliferation of 'cosmopolitan pits' intensifying centrifugal tendencies within mining communities, 'class conflict gave way to class harmony'. Burgess cites the popularity of 'co-operative collieries' as evidence of this, though he chooses profit-sharing, rather than genuine co-operative societies owned by the unions, to illustrate his argument.[3] The union co-operatives, however, small in number, failures without exception, and experimented with only during the 1870s boom,

[1] Campbell 1979, 270–1.
[2] Machin 1958, 217–19, 228–9, 231, 414–25; H. S. Jevons 1915, 459–60.
[3] Burgess 1975, 172.

represented a modest alternative to capitalist ownership and control, whereas the profit-sharing scheme at Briggs and Son was almost unique. The basic premiss underlying the argument that moderate leaders were the consequence of the influence of prosperity between 1850 and 1875 is itself dubious, for although our estimates show wage rates to have risen sharply during the mid-1850s, the plateau that followed (at a level some 15 per cent above that of the 1840s) continued until the late 1880s, interrupted only by the sudden rise between 1872 and 1874.

Real earnings in the 1850s were about one-third higher than in the 1840s, and in the 1860s exceeded 1840s real earnings by about one-half. However, after the initial reaction set in during the slump which followed the exceptionally high earnings of the 1870s boom, the mid-century levels of 'prosperity'—to which Burgess attributes a catalytic effect upon trade-union leaders—were resumed and improved upon.[1] Yet according to Burgess it was the disappearance of prosperity which led to the transformation of miners' attitudes, culminating, at least in the inland coalfields, in the formation of the MFGB, rejecting class harmony in preference for class conflict. Manifestations of this are seen in the revival of collective activity on a broad front to obtain an eight-hour day by legislation, and a minimum wage. The period between the demise of the MAGBI and the formation of the MFGB is seen as a hiatus, which marked a deviation from the tradition of 'collective activity' (that is, aspirations towards inter-regional solidarity), at a time when the miner remained outside the mainstream of the labour movement.[2]

In its centralized structure the MAGBI had represented the views of those who wished to build a national organization in order to bolster weaker districts through a levy on membership; the alternative, which envisaged a national organization to act as a pressure group for legislative reform and propaganda, supported by a loose structure of autonomous district unions, was that which prevailed.[3] Between the collapse of the MAGBI until 1889 only two attempts were made to dopt a centralized structure; one was the virtually abortive Practical Miners' Association, formed by a dissident group within the MNA, and advocating mutual financial support of strikers in the other districts and a return to the more aggressive policies of the MAGBI. Most support came from south Staffordshire, where, under the MNA, miners had been denied

---

[1] See above Table 7.4.

[2] Burgess 1975, 172–3.

[3] Chris Fisher and Pat Spaven 'Edward Rymer and the "Moral Workman"', in Royden Harrison (ed.) *Independent Collier* Hassocks, 1978), 237–9, Chris Fisher and John Smethurst', 'War on the Law of Supply and Demand', 114–48.

such support, but whose precipitate action destroyed the PMA in 1865.[1]

The other experiment in centralized unionism occurred with the formation of the Amalgamated Association of Miners in 1869. Just as the PMA had been formed as a reaction to a lack of financial support from miners in other regions, Lancashire miners found themselves similarly isolated during the strikes and lock-outs of 1869. The AAM, therefore, represented another attempt by disaffected miners in a region where trade unionism was weak to tap the financial strength of other regions, where members were asked to contribute to a central fund designed to assist miners involved in local disputes.[2] Not surprisingly, the main support came from similarly poorly organized areas—south Stafford-shire, Wales, and the South-west. Described by Burgess as 'the militant rival of the Miners' National Union',[3] it lasted only six years, when aspiration eventually out-ran financial resources, marking another failure in centralized leadership. The contrast, drawn by both Challinor and by Burgess, between moderate MNU and militant AAM differs from the interpretation by Fisher and Spaven, who point out that the AAM was formed with the blessing and support of MacDonald, and emphasize that centralization was merely a method of strengthening trade unionism more appropriate to the largest and strongest areas; the leaders of the MNA shared with those of the AAM similar assumptions concerning objectives and tactics.[4] They accepted the need to secure reforms through legislation, to negotiate wages and conditions accord-ing to the state of trade, and, taking into account the same factors, to implement output restriction or strike action when necessary.

Where there is agreement between Burgess and Fisher and Spaven, however, is in their contention that real divisons among trade unions divided rank and file from the leaders, a phenomenon which Fisher and Spaven claim to have existed especially in the 'weaker' coalfields, but also in south Yorkshire and Durham,[5] while Burgess identified such divisions in Northumberland, too. Burgess also maintained that after 1875 the moderation of full-time trade-union officials stemmed from a shared priority to win recognition for their organizations and that they were prepared to collaborate with employers in order to avoid disputes and restrain the rank and file.[6] Fisher and Spaven claim to have detected

---

[1] Chris Fisher and John Smethurst', War on the Law of Supplyand Demand', 114–48.
[2] Ibid., Burgess 1975, 186.
[3] Burgess 1975, 192.
[4] Fisher and Spaven 1978, 233.
[5] Ibid., 237.
[6] Burgess 1975, 188–90.

'an acute awareness of the continuing injustices in the coalfields sharpened by a fighting spirit ... In particular this consciousness was expressed through demands for a minimum standard of reward'.[1]

We have found no evidence for such demands to justify the thesis of 'real division',[2] which claims that even before the 1880s the rank and file possessed a more acute awareness of injustices and a superior perception of priorities, objectives, and tactics than did most miners' leaders.[3] It is true, however, that divisions did occur in those districts where trade-union development was most advanced, if only because the requirement of discipline for effective organization was accompanied, inevitably, by the need to establish priorities in policy decisions affecting localities and individual collieries. Prior to the 1860s, it is doubtful whether the attempts to federate regional or county unions exercised any effect on the policies of these unions. Miners in the North-east had led the MAGBI, but failed to gain its active support for their strike in 1844; the avowed aim of preventing the importation of blacklegs between regions also failed. Throughout the union's existence the typical pattern was a firm base in the pit lodge, district meeting, and national conference, though the first was stronger than the other two.[4] After the demise of the MAGBI, unions were autonomous, a condition which not even the MNA altered, for it was in the localities that the funds primarily resided.

The first centralized unions—and even here the term covers a number of contrasting arrangements—appeared only after 1858, with the emergence of the first permanently constituted county federations. In south Yorkshire centralized control was relatively effective for nearly twenty years, beginning shortly after its formation in 1858, after an initial period of continuing recalcitrance by the local branches. Disaffiliation on a mass scale occurred in 1879–80, which led to a split of the SYMA into three virtually autonomous organizations.[5] Until then, under Normansell's energetic but moderate secretaryship, the lodges came under the control of the district committees, over whom the union leadership exercised firm control. Normansell affirmed that 'the recognition we

[1] Fisher and Spaven 1978, 233.

[2] Suggestions made by R. V. Clements that 'Many of the craftsmen's and miners' unions of this period did retain, if not the concept of a minimum standard of reward, at least the fighting attitude of earlier years that implied this objective': R. V. Clements, 'British Trade Unions and Popular Political Economy, 1850–1870', *EHR* XIV (1961), 101–3.

[3] Fisher and Spaven 1978, 215–17.

[4] A. J. Taylor 1955, 56–9.

[5] Spaven 1978, 213.

have got is through the power that we got by organization'—and rarely
was that power employed for the purpose of strikes.[1] For this reason
south Yorkshire, which in the 1850s was the location of bitter, local and
district-wide disputes, has been described as having been 'probably the
most consistently moderate of the major miners' unions' during the
second half of the century.[2] In structure, organization, and policies, the
SYMA was regarded by Alexander MacDonald as a model of an effective trade union, which he urged his own Scottish miners to emulate.[3]

It is difficult to gain a consistent impression of how other centralized
unions function. In areas such as west Yorkshire, the east Midlands, and
Lancashire, executive authority was evidently limited, with both general
membership levels and executive authority itself highly vulnerable to
movements in the trade cycle. After destruction in the 1840s, from the
1860s the classic example of powerful executive control was the Durham
Miners' Association (and, to a lesser extent, the Northumberland union
from the 1870s). Power was highly centralized; each lodge, irrespective
of size, was entitled to one vote on the executive council. The leadership
was opposed to strikes and favoured strong centralized funds. Since
there were approximately 200 lodges in Durham in the period 1881–
1913, centralized power was a considerable achievement, but even there
executive control was repeatedly (and increasingly) challenged by unofficial strike activity on the part of the more radical lodges.[4]

South Wales was always something of an exception to national
patterns of trade-union development and authority. Prior to 1898 there
was no regional union in South Wales, although growth can be traced at
the district-union level. Even in the period 1898–1913, the South Wales
Miners' Federation was an association of twenty fairly autonomous
district unions.[5] Whereas the English and Scottish unions were based
on the pit lodge, uinionism in South Wales was centred on the village
group: it is generally agreed that the former was a more powerful and
superior organizational structure.[6] However, Spavin has argued that the
tendency to join a union where one lived, rather than where one
worked (a tendency which evidently increased, in Yorkshire at least, as
pits became larger and travelling distances to them greater) led to a

[1] Machin 1958, 84, 341, 350–2.
[2] Spaven 1978, 201.
[3] Ibid., 203.
[4] Marshall thesis, 36–41, 44–5, 106–7.
[5] Evans 1961, 135; Arnot, *History of the South Wales Miners' Federation, 1914-26* (Cardiff, 1975),
75, 145–8, 321–7.
[6] Ibid., 14–15.

'discredited sense of pit-based identity and cohesion, but a heightened consciousness of the district union as an organic entity'.[1] This argument implies that miners who lived and worked in the same village were more likely to resent centralized authority, and that this may have led to the intensification of central executive authority from the 1890s. It does not, however, appear to be a particularly persuasive explanation of regional differences (for example, of why centralized authority was greater in the North-east than elsewhere).

Spavin also argues that geographical proximity to union district head-quarters (for example, Barnsley in the case of south Yorkshire) was a factor in the relative strength of executive authority; pits closer to Barnsley, and, in particular, pits located within an urban environment and an environment of urban politics, were more likely to acquiesce in the decisions by an executive leadership. More isolated mining communities with a distinct political tradition were more likely to be independent—militant or pacific depending upon other factors.[2] This detailed evidence tends to support the view, therefore, that before the 1880s, the fundamental divisions were local—rather than political, or hierarchical, as argued by Burgess and Fisher and Spavin. Local considerations, even at pit level, afforded the most potent sources of discontent, while the nature of grievances, preparedness, and ability of workers to organize, or, if organized, to mobilize, were also powerfully influenced by employers' attitudes and policies.

None the less, centralization did gain ground with the formation of the MFGB, whose leaders began to formulate an approximation to a national policy. From its base in the inland coalfields, the Federation grew in size and geographical extent. The Scottish miners affiliated in its early days, followed in 1899 by South Wales. In 1907 the remaining major exporting region, Northumberland and Durham, became permanent members. By that time the Federation comprised thirty separately constituted unions, yet its structure remained firmly based on the familiar pattern of pit lodge, district and county union, and federated national assembly, perpetuating centrifugal forces in industrial relations, even though common wage scales existed from 1889.[3]

Trends and characteristics of miners' trade unionism which can be identified before 1889 continued, and despite the higher national profile and more vigorous rhetoric the MFGB did not immediately herald a transformation of the movement. An increasingly radical rank and file

[1] Spavin thesis, 198.   [2] Ibid., 216, 627–30.
[3] Burgess 1975, 208–13; Spavin 1978, 215–17.

caused an increase in unofficial strikes in those counties where the executive authority was highly centralized and introduced this banned category of industrial action. In Durham only a single official strike occurred between 1869 and 1890 (that of 1879) but the level of unofficial activity rose steadily during the 1880s.[1] Nevertheless, all of Durham's moderate leaders were democratically elected, and it seems unnecessary to resort to a form of conspiracy theory, such as that employed by Burgess, to account for moderation, either in Durham in the 1870s or 1880s, or among the MFGB leaders after the 1893 strike.[2] It was not until the decisive wage rises of 1888–91 and the accompanying rise in mass membership that an aggressive policy became feasible under the conditions that obtained. Yet a growing gulf between this 'old' leadership on the one hand and the rank and file and its new leaders on the other did occur and is visible after the 1892 strike in Durham and the 1893 strike in the inland coalfields.[3] This gulf, which was to widen, was a feature of post-1888 unionism as well as of pre-MFGB days. Page Arnot maintained that it was only in the years after 1909 that the leadership of the South Wales Miners' Federation caught up with the more radical political consciousness of the rank and file.[4] Without exaggerating the extent of this gulf, it can be argued that an industrial militancy, influenced by a new socialist ideology, emerged and began to dominate the MFGB, but not until the immediate pre-war years.[5]

Throughout most of the period 1830–1913 the dominant ideology within which organized labour in the mining industry worked was firmly labourist, moderate, and reformist. The political traditions which endured in mining districts took root long before the emergence of socialism in the 1880s. The leadership was politically moderate and Liberal in complexion, and the counterpart to this in industrial policy was the almost universal acceptance that prices should determine wages, though underlying this doctrine were vague notions of a living wage, and, in the North-east during the early years, of the right to compensation for enforced idleness. Attitudes to social and political change in the early period were overwhelmingly moderate, even timid. Despite the assertion of Chartist and Owenite influence in the MFGBI,[6] A. J. Taylor has observed how '... a laudable concern about keeping within the

[1] Marshall thesis, 42–7. [2] Burgess 1975, 188–90.
[3] Garside 1977, 146; J. E. Williams, 'The Miners' Lockout of 1893', *BSSLH* 24 (1972), 15–16.
[4] Arnot, *History of the South Wales Miners* (1967), 375.
[5] Henry Pelling, *Popular Politics and Society in Late Victorian Britain* (London, 1968), 155–60.
[6] Challinor and Ripley, *The Miners' Association: A Miners' Union in the Age of the Chartists* (London 1968), passim.

framework of the law and avoiding political entanglements degenerated at times into an almost pathological fear of repression'.[1]

Nevertheless, for most of this period, within their localities miners enjoyed a highly developed sense of occupational solidarity, which contributed much to the growth of stable trade-union organizations from the 1880s. While Liberal and reformist for the most part, the leadership was heavily committed to the principles of democratic nonconformity, and contributed greatly to the democratization of political institutions in mining areas. Nonconformity strengthened the link with peaceful struggle and with Liberalism. The more established and long-standing this political tradition was (for example, in the North-east), the more difficult it was for socialism to dislodge. On the other hand, in those regions where the labourist tradition was weak and had proved ineffective—such as, for example, in South Wales—a new radical socialist (and later, syndicalist) ideology was gaining ground from the 1880s. The spread of a more radical approach to the problems facing miners occurred in all regions to some extent, and even in the most traditional mining areas can be seen as the source of the growing gulf between leadership and rank and file in the pre-war years. None the less, labourism and the labourist tradition retained a firm grip in all but the immediate pre-war years.[2]

While the industrial success of the MFGB was to gain influence over colliery price-lists, the emergence of the MFGB also marked the beginning of an attack on the non-socialist tradition. The rise in membership encouraged a more determined interest in the potential political strength of miners (particularly following the 1884 Reform Act) and renewed the concern with legislative reforms.[3] Yet this concern with a parliamentary approach owed more to the labourist and Liberal tradition than to socialism. In the North-east, the Durham Miners' Association played a major role in the attempt to pursuade miners to vote Liberal after 1884. Even in the first decade of the new century, when support moved away from the Liberal to the Labour party, the bulk of support for the Independent Labour Party and the Labour Representation Committee did not come from a socialist platform. The greatest rallying point for Labour was the demand for a legal minimum wage. The appeal of 'socialism', as far as it was represented in the Labour Party, was industrial rather than political.[4]

[1] A. J. Taylor 1955, 51.
[2] J. Saville, 'Some Notes on Ideology and the Miners before World War I', *BSSLH* 23 (1971), 25–7.
[3] Clegg, Fox, and Thompson 1964, 110–11, 240.
[4] Marshall thesis, 109–23, 170–2, 240.

The issues of structure and ideology raise the fundamental question of the nature of mining unions in this period, whether their status was as craft or sectional 'model' unions, comprising mainly hewers; and whether their ability to attract an undifferentiated 'mass' membership changed over time. This question is crucial to an understanding of unionism in this period, but unfortunately there is little evidence available. Clegg, Fox, and Thompson assert that the MFGB was the first union to recruit non-face labour and to concern itself with the rates of wages paid to haulage and surface workers.[1] Since there is very little evidence on the composition of unions before 1888 this is a difficult point to prove. In the North-east the county unions which emerged in the 1860s appear to have included, or attempted to include, all adult underground workers, though in view of the precise generational division of labour in this region the majority of these would have been hewers or other skilled workers. There is even less evidence on the other regions. The AAM is traditionally viewed as having been a radical alternative to the 'new model' approach of the MNU,[2] but whether this radicalism, which Fisher and Smethurst have argued has been exaggerated, originated in its ability to attract non-face labour into its ranks is difficult to judge. There is, however, abundant evidence that juveniles were given little or no support by the unions in the pre-war period. In the North-east the period after 1880 witnessed a wave of pit-lad strikes (an average of two a year between 1888 and 1907), almost all of them called without the support of the union, and generally contrary to instructions.[3] This may be seen as a conflict of generations and a manifestation of adolescent revolt, as much as an attack on sectional labour consciousness, but it may be more correct to see it as both.

The lack of data on the composition of mining unions prior to 1888 forces the interpretation back on to theoretical arguments. H. A. Turner regarded the pattern in mining as fairly typical of those industries in which permanent craft unions began to develop from the mid-nineteenth century. He argued that some groups of miners, notably hewers in the North-east, achieved 'a real degree of collective regulation by informal "natural" workers' associations'. The onset of industrialization and the emergence of intense competition between coalfields sub-

---

[1] Clegg, Fox, and Thompson 1964, 110–11.
[2] Buxton 1978, 150–1;Burgess 1975, 186.
[3] Welbourne 1923, 221; J. Woodhurst, 'Pit lad Strikes in England and Wales, 1888–1914', unpublished article, for which we are grateful to have seen; Marshall thesis, 84.

sequently plunged this group into uncertainty as to their status and power in the market. Then,

Partly in an attempt to maintain their own customary or traditional standards, they promote or support wider demands and mass organisation of workers not previously organised. Put among the original groups, the consolidation of an internal aristocracy in regular 'institutional' unions leads to their withdrawal from the general movement, the collapse of which then breed disillusionment and a retreat from organisation among others.

In these circumstances, the emergence of mass unionism at a later stage might actually provoke the active opposition of this original élite. While we have rejected Turner's explanation for the slow development of miners' trade unions before the 1880s, his supposition concerning the later development is consistent with the relations that prevailed between the MFGB and the North-eastern unions[1] (though in regions where the butty system prevailed this argument is irrelevant).

As the highest paid sector of the labour force with the greatest responsibility, the hewers' domination of miners' trade unions can scarcely be doubted. Moreover, Turner's argument that hewers needed to generate a wider movement in order to achieve their aims can be applied to many of the early labour struggles in the industry. The tendency of hewers to withdraw from the movement (retreating presumably to pit-level organization) is difficult to demonstrate, though it is probable that when organized unionism collapsed, pit-level solidarity, at least among a section of the work-force, remained. The dominance of these early unions by an élite of hewers and their inability to generate wider support, except temporarily during the upswing, was evidently a source of much weakness.

The MFGB marked a decisive transition to a mass union in which non-face and surface workers were included on a permanent basis, probably for the first time. To see the MFGB as an outright militant mass union would, of course, be a gross over-simplification. Despite gaining substantial wage advances, amounting to 40 per cent in 1888–90, MFGB leaders were forced to accept a 25 per cent reduction thereafter, and following the 1893 strike committed themselves to a policy of conciliation, which they were forced to defend against mounting rank-and-file criticism in the years ahead. Not even the MFGB succeeded in breaking away effectively from the tradition that prices governed wage rates.

[1] H. A. Turner, *Trade Union Growth, Structure and Policy: A Comparative Study of the Cotton Unions* (London, 1962), 191–2, and see above.

Thus, although sliding scales were rejected and reformist North-eastern leaders bitterly attacked the achievement of the union, at least with regard to some aspects of its policy, the MFGB was not so radically different from that of the earlier county unions as the language of its leaders might suggest. On the other hand, the success of the eight-hour movement and that for the minimum wage were significant advances on the achievements of the earlier unions.[1]

The transition from moderation to militancy, therefore, was gradual, progressing at different speeds in the regions. The reaction against the moderation of the county unions can be seen most clearly in Durham between 1893 and 1908. Not only did rank-and-file opposition to the leadership grow stronger, but on the DMA council itself a pro-MFGB group emerged, highly critical of Wilson's leadership; against the wishes of the leadership, rank-and-file demands forced the DMA to affiliate, eventually on a permanent basis, to the MFGB.[2] At the same time, it would be wrong to exaggerate the strength of this opposition, or to imply that leaders in the export coalfields could coerce members.

In South Wales, for example, where a moderate policy was pursued throughout the 1890s, an analysis of voting within the union shows that roughly one-quarter to a third of miners were devoted supporters of the sliding-scale system, and that in the face of much apathy and non-voting (turn-outs varied from 48 to 78 per cent) this was sufficient to ensure a democratic victory for Mabon's policies. On six occasions lodges in Durham were asked to vote on the DMA's recommendation to accept an offer made in accordance with sliding-scale principles, and only once rejected the recommendation put to them. Voting in favour was 55 per cent in 1876, 46 to 65, and 70 per cent in three votes conducted in 1882; 65 per cent in 1884; and 50 per cent in 1889.[3] There was, however, a distinct tendency for some lodges, generally the larger ones, to vote against moderation, and from these originated rank-and-file opposition to the DMA and support for the MFGB.[4]

---

[1] Contributors to the debate on the policy of the MFGB particularly after the 1893 strike are as follows: J. E. Williams, 'Militancy Amongst the British Coalminers, 1890-1914', BSSLH 13 (1966), 16; idem, 'The Miners' Lockout of 1893', BSSLH 25 (1972), 24; A. R. Griffin, 'The Miners' Lockout of 1893: A Rejoinder', BSSLH 25 (1972), 58-65; J. H. Porter, 'Coal Miners and Conciliation', BSSLH 26 (1973), 27-8. The limitations of both the Eight Hour Movement and that for the minimum wage are pointed out by Rowe 1923, 102-10; and McCormick and Williams 1959, 222-38.

[2] Marshall thesis, 71-81.

[3] Ibid., 103-4.

[4] Ibid.; Duggett thesis, 405-10.

We have already remarked on the essential continuity of trade-union policies, though hours restriction diminished in importance as a tactical weapon. The strike, however, continued to be the principal form of industrial action throughout the period. A detailed analysis of strikes at the county or pit level is quite beyond the scope of this study, but an examination of inter-regional differences provides the basis for instructive comparisons, as do similar exercises focusing upon the outcome of strikes and upon the methods of settlement. Neither minor nor major strikes are easy to enumerate for the pre-statistical period before 1888, when official Board of Trade returns begin; none the less, with the aid of regional studies, supplemented by contemporary printed sources, we have attempted an inevitably incomplete tabulation of the major strikes in most regions between 1830 and 1888, indicating their purpose and outcome (Table 8.3 presents the data and definitions).

Of ninety-six major strikes, 30 per cent aimed to raise wages, 60 per cent were undertaken to resist wage reductions, and of the remainder, one half (4 per cent) of these were aimed at obtaining improved terms and conditions of contract (including wages) under the bond. Of those for which information on the outcome is known (eighty-five from ninety-six), 26 per cent of major strikes were successful, 65 per cent failed, and the remainder ended in compromise. Marked regional differences are revealed, and while our figures might misrepresent the precise rank order, Lancashire and Cheshire, the west of Scotland, South Wales, and west Yorkshire appear to have been significantly more strike prone than other areas. Comparing major strikes in all regions, only south Yorkshire recorded more successes than failures, though the unions of Nottinghamshire, Derbyshire, and Leicestershire achieved three successes and two compromise results from ten major strikes. When compromise results are included in south Yorkshire's balance, the record shows only two failures from eight major strikes.

For the period before 1875 it is possible to present figures for the number of minor strikes for the west of Scotland, and for south Yorkshire; before 1870 for west Yorkshire; and between 1840 and 1853 only, for South Wales and Monmouthshire; lack of comparability prevents aggregative analysis, and because the ratio of major to minor strikes depends heavily upon how many of the latter were recorded it would be absurd to claim that the ratios are more than merely suggestive of a figure of about 5 to 1 in each of these areas, compared with perhaps one-third that level in south Yorkshire. It has not been possible to identify the outcome of minor strikes in three of these areas, but Wilson's

Table 8.3. *Analysis of major strikes, 1830–1888*[a]

	Number of major strikes	Reason			Outcome		
		for an advance	against a reduction	other	success	failure	compromise
Lancs. and Ches.	17	4	12	1	4	11	
West Scotland	15	7	8		5	9	1
South Wales	14	4	10		1	6	1
West Yorks.	12	5	7	1	3	9	1
South Staffs.	11 2	9		1	8		
South Yorks.	9	4	5		4	2	2
Notts./Derby/Leics.	9	3	4	2	3	5	2
Northd. and Dur.	7	3	3	4[b]	1	5	1
	96	29	58	8	22	55	8

[a] Major strikes are defined on the minimum criteria that miners from more than a single district took part, in which at least 750 workers were involved (the definition of a major strike late adopted by the Board of Trade), and which lasted for longer than one week. It has not been possible in every case, however, to identify all three of these criteria; consequently the figures will not bear the weight of anything more than very tentative conclusions.

[b] On three occasions the strikes occurred in connection with the terms and conditions of contract under the bond.

Sources: For Lancashire and Cheshire: Challinor 1972. West of Scotland: Arnot 1955; Youngson Brown 1953; G. M. Wilson thesis; Campbell 1979. South Wales: Evans 1961; Wilkins 1888; Collier thesis. West and South Yorkshire: Machin 1958; Neville thesis; Hopkinson thesis. South Staffordshire: A. J. Taylor 1967; Barnsby thesis; Eric Taylor thesis. The East Midlands: Williams 1962; A. R. Griffin thesis; C. P. Griffin thesis and 1982. Northumberland and Durham: Richard Fynes 1873; John Wilson, *A History of the Durham Miners' Association 1870-1914* (Durham, 1917); Metcalf thesis; Marshall thesis. These various sources have been supplemented by the *Colliery Guardian*.

detailed analysis of Lanarkshire shows a success rate before 1875 of 42 per cent for major strikes compared with 65 per cent for lesser ones. This suggests that the frequent minor strikes, often involving one or two collieries only, tended to result in a successful outcome for the miners, and usually secured wage increases. In south Yorkshire, by contrast, where union officials exercised tighter control over the lodges, minor strikes were exceptional from the 1860s, and grievances, including wage matters, were dealt with by the joint committee. Outside south Yorkshire, therefore, it seems that the lightning strike, limited in the numbers involved and in duration, was an almost perpetual feature of industrial relations. Wilson's Scottish evidence reveals the coincidence of strikes with fluctuation irrespective of actual wage levels, and that industrial action led to both wage advances and reductions occurring within a twelve-month period.[1] Almost all strikes were undertaken principally in order to improve, or to protect, wages, though occasionally additional grievances were aired and demands attached. Abolition of truck was a common complaint in some districts where the practice survived, though in Scotland truck was not a cause of strikes. Working practices peculiar to a locality, or to a single pit, could also prompt demands for changes in riddling coal, fairer weighing of coal, the appointment of a checkweighman, and the freedom to belong to a trade union.

Any attempt to explain the role of trade unions in differential regional strike pattern is hampered by lack of evidence concerning the minor strikes, but even the regional incidence of major strikes offers no clear basis for generalization. In those regions where the structure and organization of trade unions was under the firmest control of officials—in the North-east and from the late 1850s in south Yorkshire—the number of major strikes was at a minimum, while the East Midland counties unions, which experienced an extremely tenuous existence with limited membership, was also an area of relative peace. Here, the firmness of employers and union weakness would seem to have been the explanatory factors for the small number of major strikes before 1888. The high strike rate in Lancashire and Cheshire probably reflected the highly fragmented localized trade-union structure in the region, for membership was relatively high, albeit fluctuating, in the mid-nineteenth century. The figures also point to the discrepancy between the pacific public pronouncements of MacDonald and other Scottish mining leaders who emphasized the undesirability of strikes, and the actuality

[1] G. M. Wilson thesis, 236–8, 242, 244–6, 249.

of industrial relations in the Scottish coalfield. For by the standards of mid-Victorian Britain the Scottish industry was among the most strike prone of all regions, and comparable with the record of the Lancashire miners, commonly regarded as especially militant under the influence of the AAM. Clearly, the strike was not an exceptional weapon in Scotland, despite MacDonald's declared aim 'to have strikes blotted for ever from the body of the employers' and miners' experiences: Wilson cites several instances when MacDonald supported specific strikes but opposed them when he expected failure, and he defended strike action in evidence before the Royal Commission in 1867. Such evidence, both by action and by affirmation, is in direct contradiction to the portrayal of MacDonald and his contribution to the miners' interests by Challinor and other historians contemptuous of that which they refer to as 'Mac-Donaldism'.[1] Explanations for inter-regional differences in strikes and lock-outs before 1888 must await research into industrial relations patterns within the regions.

We are on surer empirical foundations after 1888, when it is possible to use the Board of Trade's annual reports on strikes and lock-outs. On the basis of these data historians have long been impressed by the relatively greater amount of industrial conflict in the coal industry by comparison with other industries, and the seemingly greater influence of the historical conditions of mining in explaining miners' exceptionally high strike propensity.[2] In the most recent attempt to analyse strike activity, Cronin challenged this view, denying that miners were more prone to strike than workers in other industries before 1920.[3]

However, when one adopts as the criterion working days lost through strikes in relation to numbers employed in the industry, a measure which takes account of the duration as well as the frequency of strikes, then coal miners emerge quite clearly as the group of industrial workers most involved in industrial conflict;[4] whether in the form of strikes *or* lock-outs, between which it is difficult to distinguish in the Board of Trade's data. Nonetheless, all historians have accepted the value, as well as the limitation of an analysis of industrial conflict which inevitably conflates strikes with lockouts. Cronin's study found mining

[1] Challinor 1972.
[2] K. G. J. C. Knowles, *Strikes: A Study in Industrial Conflict* (Oxford, 1952), 162–4, Gaston V. Rimlinger, 'International Differences in the Strike Propensity of Coal Miners: Experience in Four Countries', *Industrial and Labour Relations Review* 12 (1959), 389.
[3] James E. Cronin, *Industrial Conflict in Modern Britain* (London, 1979), 28.
[4] Compare the figures calculable from the two series on employment and on days lost in Mitchell and Deane, *Abstract*, Chapt. II.

strikes to have possessed a pattern of their own, determined by an 'internal logic of mining', and he suggested that miners were more important in influencing other workers to strike than *vice versa*.[1] This was the explanation for his relative lack of success in explaining the dynamics of industrial conflict in coal mining. An attempt to achieve this on the basis of our detailed research into the history of the industry before 1913 would be feasible, but within the limitations imposed by the present study can allow only of an examination of the chronology and broad causality at the national level, and the delineation of regional differences in the miners' propensity to strike.

The Board of Trade's annual reports on strikes and lockouts contain figures for the number of days lost through strikes nationally from 1891 and regionally from 1897; the disaggregated returns also provide figures on regional strike activity from 1894.[2] A careful check against the detailed returns (in which all strikes are listed prior to 1901 and all large strikes involving in excess of 750 workers, thereafter) and a comparison of the two figures reveals significant omissions from the summary data for the Edwardian period. The most important are the major regional stoppages of 1902 and 1909–10, but several minor adjustments to the final figures for the separate regions were also necessary, when it was clear that the Board of Trade's summary figures were understatements. The final revised estimates cannot claim to be accurate, and it has not been possible to rectify the omissions from both sets of data, other than major strikes between 1901 and 1913. Any error in this period, however, is most likely to be in the direction of understatement, and relative to days lost in major strikes is unlikely to have been large. There can be no doubt that the figures given in Table 8.4 are preferable both to those calculated by the Board of Trade and those in Mitchell and Deane.[3] A comparison shows the need for significant revisions, particularly in 1894, 1902, 1909, and 1910.

Table 8.4 gives details of the total number of working days lost through strikes between 1891 and 1913, nationally and by region. The revised data suggest that 55.5m. working days were lost between 1891 and 1900 (closely comparable with the Board of Trade's own summary reproduced in Mitchell and Deane) compared with 70 million days in 1901–13. Even allowing for small errors, there can be no doubt that the overall picture presented here is broadly accurate. Other historians who

[1] James E. Cronin, *Industrial Conflict in Modern Britain*, (London, 1979), 106–7.
[2] Board of Trade, *Reports on Strikes and Lockouts*, annually 1891–.
[3] Mitchell and Deane 1962, Chapt. II.

have used these data have been preoccupied with the industrial strife beginning in 1908 and continuing until World War I, in which miners' militancy, culminating in the peaks of 1910 and 1912, is accorded an especially important historic role.[1] Issues peculiar to miners—the Eight Hours Act and 'abnormal places'—are acknowledged to have led to the major strikes of 1910 and 1912, but there is a measure of disagreement whether miners' living standards and coalowners' profits were also important in precipitating strikes from motives of material discontent or increasing relative impoverishment. Phelps-Brown stressed the pressure on profit margins which predisposed coalowners to resist miners' demands,[2] whereas others have been more impressed by the provocative role of coalowners' profits after 1900, casting doubt on his interpretation of the causes of industrial unrest.[3] Among the material influences on miners, attention has been drawn to the fall in earnings after the Boer War, while more generally Pollard has emphasized the connection between industrial unrest and the failure of industrial workers' real wages to rise between 1902 and 1912.[4] Evidence on the course of profits and real wages in the coal industry suggest the validity of an analysis which offers a different emphasis.

Our estimates of profits and real earnings showed falls in both from the peak of 1901, the former modestly, the latter sharply from 1902. Profit rates levelled out at above pre-1900 levels. Miners' real earnings fell between 1902 and 1905, but only once marginally below the levels prevailing in the 1890s; recovered after 1905, and after a modest set-back resumed on a firmly upward trend from 1910 to 1913. It seems, there-fore, that both coalowners and miners experienced set-backs imme-diately after the boom of 1900, but by comparison with pre-boom trends and levels both also enjoyed improved rewards thereafter. The years when miners seem to have suffered the worst falls were those when disputes were few, before 1908; thereafter, a rising trend in earnings was in contrast to relatively stable profit rates. The juxtaposition of evidence on profitability with that on real earnings suggests that neither material discontent nor increasing relative impoverishment provide satisfactory

[1] Gaston Rimlinger, 'International Differences in the Strike Propensity of Coal Mines: Experience in Four Countries', *Industrial and Labour Relations Review* 12 (1959), 389–406; Gregory 1968, 178–91; Samuel 1977, 3; See also the quotation from H. G. Wells in K. G. J. C. Knowles, *A Study in Industrial Conflict with Special Reference to British Experience between 1911 and 1947* (Oxford, 1952), 4.

[2] Phelps-Brown 1959, 334.

[3] Gregory 1968, 180–1; Burgess 1975, 152–3, 215.

[4] Sidney Pollard, *The Development of the British Economy, 1914-1980* (London, 1983), 13.

Table 8.4. *Working days lost through strikes, 1891-1913*
(thousands)

	Scotland	North-east	Lancs. and Ches.	Yorks.	East Midlands	West[a] Midlands	South Wales	Minor regions	GB
1891									584
1892									5,376
1893									24,408
1894	6,766	37	47	129	33	47	212	37	7,308
1895	83	131	154	372	18	30	283	39	1,110
1896	35	316	17	383	11	21	186	41	1,010
1897	101	226	25	367	79	—	779	45	1,622
1898	134	94	61	657	139	5	11,885	4	12,979
1899	60	30	45	201	63	3	113	37	552
1900	47	32	42	149	43	24	248	16	601
1901	291	80	66	644	85		917	4	2,087
1902	1,327	88	1,177	1,863	1,445	742	2,470	100[b]	9,212
1903	145	35	20	515	22		651	10	1,398

Year									
1904	43	59	27	20	19	2	156	156	627
1905	97	48	320	93	41	47	633	22	1,301
1906	65	60	71	7		85	644	15	947
1907	128	115	5	41		50	220	8	567
1908	296	104	19	124	355	—	501	64	1,643
1909	90	295	111	1,153	298	283	799	27	3,056
1910	112	9,281	280	94	451	11	2,105	14	12,348
1911	137	150	386	344	22	27	2,923	130	4,119
1912	4,129	6,368	3,133	4,484	3,164	2,210	6,840	1,253	31,581
1913	54	151	322	52	22	35	658	3	1,297
Total 1894–1913	14,140	17,700	6,328	11,692		9,932	33,368	2,025	95,180
per cent	15	19	7	12		10	35	2	100
per cent employed[c]	13	20	11	14		18	209	4	100

[a] Figures for the West Midlands are minimum ones throughout.
[b] Estimate.
[c] Average of 1895, 1900, 1905, 1910 and 1913.

Source: Board of Trade, *Reports on Strikes and Lockouts.* For an analysis of the problems of definition and an appraisal of the weaknesses of the official statistics on strikes see K. G. J. C. Knowles, *A Study in Industrial Conflict with Special Reference to British Experience between 1911 and 1947* (Oxford 1952), pp. 299–305, and Michael Silver, 'Recent British Strike Trends: A Factual Analysis', *Journal of British Industrial Relations* XI (1973), pp. 66–9. See also Roger Davidson, 'Llewellyn Smith, the Labour Department and Government Growth', in Gillian Sutherland, ed, *Studies in the Growth of Nineteenth Century Government* (Cambridge, 1972), 227–62, which examines the institutional context influencing the scope and quality of the Labour Department's statistical data.

explanations of the influence of economic factors on industrial relations during the years of 'industrial strife' between 1908 and 1914; however, the movement of company dividends at high levels to compensate for the lean years between 1902–6 does sustain the credibility of this thesis.

Measured in a different way, by counting *days lost per employee per year*, rather than total working days lost in each year, the rate of strikes and lock-outs during the Edwardian period turns out to have been lower than in the late Victorian years. Even after our upward revision of the figures for 1901–13, as a result of which the figure for days lost per employee increases from four to five, the years between 1891 and 1900 appear to have witnessed greater disruption than did the later period, for eight days per employee per year were lost between 1891 and 1900.

When a similar formula is applied to regional data for 1891–1913, calculating the number of days lost in each region as a percentage of those lost nationally and comparing this figure with the proportion of miners employed in each region, the result is a measure of comparative strike intensity. The accepted view of South Wales as the most strike prone region by far is confirmed, accounting for 35 per cent of all working days lost in the UK, but only 20 per cent of total employment. Scotland was the only other region to possess a higher than average strike record (in the sense of days lost compared with employment levels), which accounted for 15 per cent of days lost through strikes but only 13 per cent of national employment. The North-east and Yorkshire recorded strike levels roughly commensurate with their size and importance as employers of labour, but Lancashire and Cheshire, the East and West Midlands, and the minor regions (taken as one unit) all had levels of strike intensity well below that which might have been predicted in accordance with their importance as employers of labour.

When the seven major strikes, accounting for 68.7 million working days, are excluded, there emerges a more accurate picture of what one might call incipient, or 'normal', strike intensity, which is presented in Table 8.5. The picture of 'normal' strike intensity has important differences from that presented in Table 8.4, though South Wales retains its position as pre-eminently militant; 41 per cent of all the days lost in the industry were lost in South Wales, a rate more than double that which the region's employment level might have predicted, and consistently high. By contrast, normal strike activity in Scotland, Lancashire and Cheshire, and the East and West Midlands was well below their expected norms, whilst the North-east had a level of stoppages less than half that of its place in national employment. Yorkshire was the only

Table 8.5. *Working days lost, excluding major strikes,*[a] *1891–1913*
(thousands)

	Scotland	North-east	Lancs. and Ches.	Yorks.	Midlands Midlands	South Wales	Minor regions	GB
Total	2,399	2,278	2,112	5,100	2,882	10,999	680	26,450
per cent	9	9	8	19	11	41	3	100
per cent employed	13	20	11	14	18	20	4	100

[a] The following strikes, included in Table 8.4, are excluded:

Scotland, 1894	6,500,000 working days
South Wales, 1898	10,900,000 working days
Federated districts, 1902	7,282,840 working days
Yorkshire, 1909	980,000 working days
North-east, 1910	9,200,000 working days
Rhondda, 1910–11	3,072,000 working days
Great Britain, 1912	30,800,000 working days

Source: Board of Trade, *Reports on Strikes and Lockouts*.

region to join South Wales with an above-average level of days lost, due mainly to high losses in 1894–1903.

No regional figures for working days lost exist for 1888–93, or for the numbers involved in each dispute, but data are available on the number of days on which strikes occurred, which offers supplementary evidence. Complications arise when information on the length of disputes alone is adopted as a proxy for either strike frequency or intensity. Table 8.6 suggests that in the critical period 1888–93, which saw the emergence of the MFGB, the highest strike activity was to be found in Yorkshire (where there were three times the level of strikes as one might expect to find from the region's employment level), followed by the East Midlands and the minor regions, where disputes were above average. Since, however, the minor regions contained a relatively high distribution of smaller collieries with smaller work-forces, these figures on the length of disputes necessarily overstate strike intensity as measured (were it possible) by an index of men involved and days lost. Yet the appearance of Yorkshire as a highly strike-prone region is probably genuine, marking a continuity with the years succeeding 1894 which were highly strike prone. By the criterion of strike duration, South Wales and Scotland appear to have been only moderately strike prone before 1894, and although the number of days lost in South Wales was

Table 8.6. *Duration of disputes in the regions, 1888-93*
(days)

	Total duration of disputes	Duration of of dispute as % of total	% employed in 1890
Scotland	1,485	10	12
North-east	569	4	20
Lancs. and Ches.	1,344	9	13
Yorkshire	5,475	37	13
East Midlands	1,880	13	10
West Midlands	264	2	8
South Wales	2,222	15	18
Minor regions	1,550	10	5

Source: Board of Trade, *Reports on Strikes and Lockouts.*

fairly high in 1894–7 it was not until 1897 that South Wales began to overtake Yorkshire as the leading region for strikes and lock-outs. However, it seems probable that both South Wales and Scotland may be under-represented by such figures, for if strikes were focused on the larger collieries in these regions (where they existed in considerable numbers) and thereby involved a greater loss of working days than figures on the length of disputes alone might suggest, the data in Table 8.6 will have understated the true strike intensity.

An analysis of the major strike issues between 1888 and 1913 reveals a pattern which also suggests an alteration taking place in the character of strikes in the industry, and links lower strike levels after 1900 to a diminishing importance of strikes intended to secure wages and wage-related improvements. Table 8.7 shows that between 1888 and 1899 23 per cent of all strikes were undertaken with the aim of raising wages, and 19 per cent for the same purpose in 1900–13. Resistance to wage cuts accounted for 23 per cent of strikes between 1888 and 1899 and 5 per cent in 1900–13. When strikes over price-lists are included, however, between 1888 and 1899 the percentage of strikes directly related to wages issues is 58 per cent, compared with 36 per cent for 1900–13.

Those percentages probably understate the importance of earnings-related issues, for although disputes over 'working arrangements' might be concerned entirely with how work was done, more commonly it represented a demand for higher wages in return for a change in working practices, and was often indistinguishable from piece-rates or price-list questions. Thus, including strikes concerning piece-rates and working arrangements, between 1888 and 1900 the figure was 71 per cent and 53 per cent between 1900 and 1913. This represents an appreciable drop in the importance of issues directly affecting wages in a period already identified as having exhibited a lower strike intensity than in the late Victorian years.

To some extent, the varying regional strengths of the unions may be compared by examining the rate of success or failure of the disputes undertaken: 'success', 'failure', and 'compromise' are all terms with considerable shades of meaning, for the statistical information available inevitably suffers from considerable imprecision. Reports on strikes and lock-outs provide valuable data, both on the results of disputes and on methods of settlement, which is at least suggestive. The UK aggregate data on days lost through strikes in mining and quarrying as a whole show the pronounced annual and cyclical fluctuations in the kind of result obtained from strikes by workers in the industry.

Table 8.7. *Major strike issues, 1888–1913*

Cause of dispute	As percentage of all strikes								
	Scotland	North-east	Lancs. and Ches.	Yorks.	East Midlands	West[a] Midlands	South Wales	Minor regions	UK
1888–99									
Increase in wages	17	13	34	26	44	26	21	21	23
Decrease in wages	40	2	19	21	22	38	7	36	23
Working arrangements	10	13	17	17	8	3	21	3	13
Price lists	4	10	16	11	13	3	25	7	12
Other	28	73	13	25	14	30	29	39	29
1900–1913									
Increase in wages	10	35	31	22	27	25	10	29	19
Decrease in wages	10	19	6	7	10	19	3	12	5
Working arrangements	16	19	16	18	20	12	15	24	17
Price lists	10	7	16	11	8	6	16	12	12
Other	56	41	31	41	35	35	56	24	46

Source: Board of Trade, *Report on Strikes and Lockouts.*

Predictably, the state of trade in the year in question was the main determinant of the outcome of strikes, reflecting the relative strengths of capital and labour. Consequently, more successful conclusions to disputes were achieved by unions in 1900, 1906, and 1912–13 than in other years. Failure was more common in 1901–4, and 1907–8. On average, measured in terms of working days lost between 1901 and 1913, a quarter of all disputes resulted in success, slightly more than a quarter in failure,

Table 8.8. *Analysis of results of strikes as percentages of working days lost, 1900–1913*

% resulting in:	Success	Failure	Compromise	Indefinite
1900	41	9	49	1
1901	11	36	43	
1902	7	41	51	1
1903	14	57	29	
1904	17	54	29	
1905	11	18	71	
1906	42	10	48	
1907	28	43	29	
1908	12	28	60	
1909	7	32	61	
1910	7	9	83	1
1911	6	14	75	5
1912	98	$\frac{1}{2}$	$1\frac{1}{2}$	
1913	54	24	21	1
average	$25\frac{1}{2}$	27	$46\frac{1}{2}$	1

These figures include days lost direct and indirect.
Source: Board of Trade, *Reports on Strikes and Lockouts.*

and almost half in compromise. A regional break-down, however, is available only on the basis of individual strikes (rather than days lost), though the analysis can be pushed back to 1888.

The UK figures for 1901–13 show certain differences from those analysed previously on working days lost, though the differences are not so great as to invalidate the analysis. Of all individual strikes in 1901–13, slightly more than a third resulted in success, slightly less than a third in failure, and the rest in compromise. It seems probable that evidence on days lost in aggregate (as opposed to evidence on individual strikes only) tends to give an impression of less successful strike activity, because of the tendency for longer disputes (which on average involved the loss of a large number of working days) to be less successful.

The main value of Table 8.9, however, is the regional variation which it reveals. Scotland's failure rate was relatively high, coupled with a relatively low rate of success; strikes in the North-east were reasonably successful prior to 1901, but thereafter fell to below one-third of the national success rate. The impression conveyed by other sources is that the high incidence of failure was largely attributable to pit lads, who struck frequently but, lacking bargaining power, to little effect. In both periods the failure rate in the North-east was in excess of the national average, but was especially so in 1901–13. The success rate in Lancashire and Cheshire, on the other hand, was above the national average, and the failure rate below in both periods. In Yorkshire the success rate was slightly above average before 1901, but markedly below average thereafter. The East Midlands had a highly successful record in both periods, and likewise the West Midlands (admittedly on the basis of a rather low overall strike activity) before 1901, but not later. The experience of South Wales ran directly counter to that in the West Midlands: strike activity there shows a marginally less-than-average success rate in 1888–1900, but in 1901–13 achieved more success than any other region. This remarkable post-1901 record derived largely from the ninety strikes conducted over the issue of non-union labour, nearly all of which were won by the union. The three minor regions were lamentably unsuccessful throughout 1888–1913.

The contrasts in the regions' success and failure rates is shown clearly in the proportion of disputes culminating in submission by the strikers; on average 27 per cent of all strikes in the UK ended thus, but the proportion was as high as 40 per cent in Scotland, 33 per cent in the North-east, and 34 per cent in the minor coalfields. The relatively low rate of submission by miners in the East Midlands cannot conceal the relative weakness in the position of organized labour in the region, evidence of which is the relatively large number of strikes which resulted in the importation of blackleg labour, or permanent colliery closure. Nine per cent of disputes ended thus, compared with a national average of 3 per cent. The importance of compromise in labour disputes was fairly uniform between the regions. If one excludes results in the West Midlands and minor coalfields, which had a rather untypical pattern, the number of strikes ending in a compromise settlement in 1888–1900 ranged between 32 per cent in the North-east and 44 per cent in the East Midlands and South Wales; between 1901 and 1913 the range was from 30 per cent in South Wales to 38 per cent in Yorkshire. While this continuity between the regions permits an analysis which concentrates essentially on success and failure, at the same time it must be remembered that the term 'compromise' inevitably conceals results of unequal benefit to workers and employers, and therefore may conceal a degree of regional differences in the achievements of the unions themselves.

It is evident from the foregoing analysis of the strike data and of the growth and policies of trade unions that one important reason for the excessive strike activity in the mining industry compared with others lay in the nature of wage regulation (or rather lack of it) in the industry. Even in the period of sliding scales that accompanied the 'Great Depression', no general agreement existed on exactly how coal prices should govern wages. Though obviously determined in the long run by price movements, wage rates were not so determined in the short run without either a process of collective bargaining or a trial of industrial strength. Before 1888 the trial of strength, in the form of a strike, most frequently on a very minor scale, was the dominant mode of 'resolving' disputes. From the 1860s there were exceptions, the most notable being the conciliation and pit-level negotiation fostered in Yorkshire by the SYMA, and this approach became formalized by the various joint committees which proliferated suddenly following the formation of the Durham committee in 1872.

Boards of conciliation and arbitration became widespread after 1888, a development of collective bargaining which, despite its deficiencies, has been described as perhaps the outstanding change to have taken place in the employer–worker relations of the industry between 1889 and 1914.[1] Contributing to this growth in orderly collective bargaining, by the agreement between the MFGB and the federated employers in 1889, was the mutual acceptance of the principle of the joint negotiation of wages over the entire federated area. By 1910 one-half of all coalminers were covered by collective agreements negotiated by the MFGB, whereas arrangements of this kind applied to only one-fifth of the entire British labour force.[2] Details of the method of settling disputes are available in detail from the Board of Trade sources only for 1888–1900, but they show that despite the industry's record of disputes leading to

[1] Benson 1982, 200.
[2] Ibid., 200.

Table 8.9. *Results of strikes and methods of settlement, 1888–1913*
(percentages)

	Scotland	North-east	Lancs. and Ches.	Yorks.	East Midlands	West[a] Midlands	South Wales	Minor regions	UK
Results									
Success:									
1888–1900	24	31	34	32	37	52	26	17	29
1901–1913	28	11	43	26	48	20	51	17	36
Compromise:									
1888–1900	36	32	43	40	44	29	44	37	39
1901–1913	32	35	33	38	35	47	30	56	34
Failure:									
1888–1900	40	37	23	28	19	19	30	46	32
1901–1913	40	54	23	36	17	33	19	28	30

Method of settlement									
Conciliation and negotiation:									
1888–1900	57	58	79	69	81	81	64	57	
1901–13									66
Official arbitration:									
1888–1900	2	7	1	3	2		13	4	4
1901–1913									5
Submission by labour:									
1888–1900	40	33	18	24	8	16	22	34	
1901–1913									27
Pit closure and use of outside labour:									
1888–1900	1	3	2	4	9	3	2	6	
1901–1913									3

Source: Board of Trade, *Reports on Strikes and Lockouts, 1888–1913*.

industrial action, the most common method of settlement was through conciliation and pit-level negotiation. Regional differences reveal 80 per cent of disputes to have been settled in this way in Lancashire and Cheshire, the East and West Midlands, and rather less than 60 per cent in Scotland, the North-east, and minor regions. Resort to an official arbitration was a relatively uncommon method of settling disputes, except in South Wales. The percentage of strikes settled by conciliation machinery (that is, official arbitration boards) or by the intervention of third parties, was only 4 per cent in 1888–1900, and 5 per cent in 1901–13.

Despite developments in collective bargaining, wages and earnings issues continued to cause disputes, especially in the period 1888–1900 when nearly half of all disputes were concerned with percentage additions to, or subtractions from, basic rates, and a further quarter over wage issues relating specifically to colliery piece-rates and working practices. Even in 1901–13, 24 per cent of strikes originated in additions to, or subtractions from, prevailing rates, and a further 29 per cent in colliery-based wage questions. Thus, though the development of collective bargaining was important in introducing a degree of orderliness and consistency in the handling of disputes, it did not end the high strike intensity. The explanation is to be found in two related factors, which were fundamental to the industry's record of strikes and lockouts: firstly the apparent impossibility of finding a way to reconcile movements in wage rates with the pronounced cyclical variations in coal prices; and secondly, the equally intractable difficulties which prevented the creation of a system of piece-rate earnings which could accommodate, and be adapted to, the short-run changes that occurred in working conditions at each colliery.

Clegg, Fox, and Thompson argued that wage pressures in the industry, particularly through price changes, were too powerful to be contained by conventional bargaining procedures.[1] From the end of the 1880s, therefore, the combination of collective bargaining across one or several regions, between representatives of rapidly growing trade unions and powerful coalowners' associations, introduced into the system of industrial relations a factor of scale. This meant that although minor issues were likely to be resolved without confrontation, whenever either of the two central problems affecting wages—coal prices and short-run changes in working conditions—became a major issue, regional or nationwide stoppages on an unprecedented scale were more likely to occur.[2]

---

[1] Clegg, Fox, and Thompson 1964, 461–2.
[2] Benson 1982, 200–1.

The first of a series of set-piece battles took place in Durham in 1892, when miners remained aloof from the MFGB; the strike involved a loss of 5.3 million days. The Scottish miners' strike in 1894 lost more than 7 million days. The strikes in South Wales in 1898 saw the loss of nearly 13 million days, and in the pit-lads' strike of 1902, which was unofficial and not concerted, more than 9 million days were lost. In 1910 strikes in the North-east and South Wales again brought the total days lost to more than 12 million. With the exception of the pit-lads' strike, which raised the issue of differentials, and those of 1910, which were a consequence of the Eight Hours Act, each of the other major strikes, or lock-outs, concerned wage issues of some kind. So, too, did the two epic battles between coalowners and miners: the 1893 lock-out, which was on a scale hitherto unknown in Britain, causing 24.4 million lost days; and in 1912 the first national stoppage, which caused 31.6 million days to be lost. Commonly known as the Minimum Wage Strike, the 1912 dispute was none the less concerned entirely with the two related issues of resolving the problem of the relation of wage rates to coal prices, and the creation of a piece-rate earnings system which could cope with local conditions of work.

The significance of the changes that had affected industrial relations in the industry between the 1880s and the end of the century were remarked upon in 1899 by John Chambers, chairman of the South Yorkshire Coalowners' Association, when he reminded members:

Experience has shown us that [the strike] cannot be used with effect today as it could have been fifteen or twenty years ago. Organization on both sides has relieved both the individual owner and the individual workman to a considerable extent from the pressure caused by a strike, and what would have been a question of weeks some years ago must now be measured by a much longer period of time.[1]

Just as the strikes of 1844 were unprecedented in scale and importance, similarly, though on an altogether larger scale, the strikes of 1893 and 1912, yet to come when Chambers made his observation, were of such magnitude that they deserve special attention, not least because their significance has been a matter of some dispute among historians.

[1] SCL MD 2699–10, SYCOA Reports, 14 Feb. 1899.

iv. Capital versus labour, 1893 and 1912

Following a 35 per cent fall in the selling price of coal, in June 1893 coal-owners in the Federated area demanded a 25 per cent reduction in wages. With the exception of Northumberland and Durham, all the English regional representatives at the special conference of the MFGB voted to oppose the reduction; neither Scotland nor South Wales were represented. The owners rebuffed the attempts at conciliation offered by the mayors of six major cities in the Midland colliery districts and in Yorkshire, and within a month 300,000 colliery workers in Yorkshire, Lancashire, and the Midlands were locked out. Apart from Northumberland and Durham, only in the West Midlands, the South-west, and Cumberland were men at work in English collieries.[1] The strike was accompanied by blacklegging, rioting, violence, and the intervention of troops. Neville has described the civil disorder that prevailed in the West Riding as unprecedented in degree since the Chartist campaigns of the 1840s, and it was in south Yorkshire that the climax was reached in the infamous 'Featherstone Massacre', which occurred after the Riot Act had been read at the Ackton Hall Colliery, where huge crowds, variously estimated at several hundred to three thousand (the official figure), had gathered to prevent the loading of coal. Troops sent to reinforce a local constabulary under strength opened fire to commence dispersal; two miners were killed and twelve were wounded.[2]

As the weeks passed and financial resources dwindled, support among the miners declined, and by October 1893 no fewer than 87,000 men were at work in the English coalfields, in addition to those in the North-east who had continued to work throughout the strike. The ageing Gladstone intervened during the fifteenth week of the dispute, and appointed the foreign secretary, Lord Rosebury, to initiate a conference involving the owners and leaders of the MFGB, to settle the dispute, pending which pre-strike wage levels continued for four months until a further arbitration was made. When that occurred, in August 1894, a 10 per cent reduction was awarded to continue until the end of 1895. Meanwhile a Conciliation Board, set up for 1894–5, was the body through which after 1895 the new rate of wages might be varied upwards, with an upper limit of 45 per cent on the 1888 standard, but

---

[1] Arnot 1953, 219–50.
[2] Neville thesis, 184, 198–210.

not downwards; the period over which adjusted rates might apply was a minimum of seven months.[1]

The origins of this dispute lay in the extreme price and wage fluctuations of 1888–91 which had coincided with the formation of the MFGB. The main preoccupation of the leaders of the MFGB between 1889 and 1893 however, was not wages but the massive legislative campaign for an eight-hour day. Falling coal prices in 1892–3 seemed to reinforce the logic of the eight-hour day, for it was congruent with the miners' time-honoured strategy of output restriction. But although the MFGB succeeded in implementing a week's holiday in 1892, the attempt at repetition in 1893 was defeated at the national conference. Page Arnot interpreted this important decision as a rejection of the notion that prices should determine wage rates (which was the economic rationale of restriction) and implied the miners' belief in 'the Living Wage Principle'.[2] At the Rosebury Conference in 1893 'the living wage' was a concept deployed in argument, coupled with an outright repudiation of the inevitability of a dependence of wages upon prices. It was argued that only provided a minimum wage was first secured should the wage–price mechanism be allowed to operate.[3]

This philosophy, forcefully presented in concert by leaders of trade unions possessing large and rapidly growing membership, was instrumental in strengthening the miners' resolve to resist the wage cut in 1893, and the coalowners' uncompromising insistence on the cut has been interpreted by Clegg, Fox, and Thompson as a pre-meditated attack on the MFGB itself.[4] By demanding wage reductions first in the smaller regions, employers tried to attack the Federation where it was most vulnerable, with the intention of dividing the miners before destroying the Federation by the lock-out. The non-participation of miners in the North-east in 1893 is explicable by their independence from the MFGB, but the possible charge that the Durham miners rejected solidarity with other English miners should be considered in the context of the lock-out of 75,000 miners of Durham for fifty-eight working days in 1892. It was a dispute which engendered immense bitterness, which Garside explains as the result of the miners' persistent refusal either to acknowledge the necessity for reducing wages when prices fell or to agree to

[1] Arnot 1953, 219–50.

[2] Ibid., 223–4.

[3] C. M. Percy, 'The Coal Dispute of 1893, Its History, Policy and Warnings', *Economic Journal* III (1893), 645; C. Edwards, 'The Lockout in the Coal Trade', *Economic Journal* III (1893), 655–6.

[4] Clegg, Fox, and Thompson 1965, 106–9.

settle through arbitration. Eventually the Bishop of Durham broke the deadlock, succeeding in assembling the miners' county Federation Board together with the Coalowners' Association at Auckland Castle, his official residence. Faced with mounting public criticism and a growth in resistance from union rank and file, the employers accepted the Bishop's appeal for humanity as a justification for tempering their immediate demands and backing down. The owners had, however, achieved their original terms set out when the dispute began. At no time did the Durham Miners' Association campaign for a minimum wage; they refused to participate in the 1893 lock-out, partly for this reason and partly as a result of financial exhaustion and the weariness induced by the struggle of 1892.[1]

The North-east, where a historically moderate leadership had steered a course independently of the other English regions, was characterized by strong unions and powerful coalowners' associations. In South Wales the relative strength of the owners contrasted with the weakness of trades unions, though as a result of the MFGB's campaign in the region unionism began to be transformed, culminating in 1898 in a six-month dispute in the cause of a minimum wage. As in South Wales, most Scottish miners remained outside permanent trades unions—only the five or six thousand Fife miners, according to Arnot, belonging to a fully established union before 1894.[2] The formation in that year of the first Scottish Miners' Federation, affiliated to the MFGB, saw 20,000 Scottish miners enroll and strike, staying out for fifteen weeks (seventeen in Fife) before they returned to work on the employers' terms.[3]

The varying responses from miners in the regions are explicable only by reference to several factors. One fundamental difference between the exporting regions and others was the greater acceptance in the former, because of the intense fluctuations historically characteristic of coal export prices, of the principle that wages must follow prices; as in parts of the North-east and South Wales employment depended upon exports and the willingness to concede the importance of wage flexibility, that was the cornerstone of policies espoused by an entire tradition of trade-union leadership. Another important variable which contributed to differences in policies and response from the 1880s was the numerical and financial strength of trade unions—and of coalowners' associations. Less susceptible to measurement, and internal to the

---

[1] Garside 1977, 142–6.
[2] Arnot 1955, 70–1, 76–88.
[3] Ibid.

unions, were the complex variations in the degree of cohesion between leaders and rank-and-file members, which could affect a union's stance over such major issues as hours output restriction, and minimum wage.

This is the theme pursued by Garside in his analysis of the 1892 Durham lock-out, and by J. E. Williams, addressing the subject of the more extensive 1893 strike. Both identify increased militancy among the rank and file, and a progressive divorce from the leadership. Garside maintains that the reason why union leaders accepted the sliding-scale principle in Durham was that it allowed deductions from wages without jeopardizing union discipline or cohesion, for the executives could avoid blame for wage adjustments determined automatically. Such sanguinity was not, however, entirely justified, for Durham sliding scales in operation between 1877 and 1889 antagonized the rank and file. The termination of the fourth and last scale in 1889 in favour of joint consultation was effected within a context of acute cleavage, according to Garside, between 'certain sections' of the rank and file and the leaders. This same disaffected, but increasingly influential, group also reacted against the conciliation machinery introduced at the end of the 1892 strike, when its operation in practice turned out to be essentially a sliding-scale mechanism.[1] Marshall has charted the cumulative political radicalization of the Durham miners from this time, accompanied by a widening rift between leaders and the rank and file.[2] A similar analysis has been applied to the 1893 strike by J. E. Williams, who argued that having committed themselves to conciliation when the dispute was settled, mining leaders felt compelled to defend policies of conciliation when they were attacked increasingly by the rank and file between 1893 and 1912.[3]

A. R. Griffin has disputed the assertion that all miners would have benefited had a more militant policy been pursued by miners' leaders between 1893 and 1912,[4] but Porter demonstrates convincingly that the restrictions imposed by the post-1893 conciliation boards and agreements effectively prevented miners from reaping full advantage of bouyant trade in the years down to 1912.[5] Indeed, the strike of 1912 (although precipitated by a push for a minimum wage) had its origins in the failure to achieve this objective in 1893, and the continuing prevarication of the miners leaders, especially in the North-east and South

[1] Garside 1977, 142–6.
[2] Marshall thesis 311–17.
[3] J. E. Williams, 'The Miners' Lockout of 1893', *BSSLH* 24 (1972), 15–16.
[4] A. R. Griffin, 'The Miners' Lockout of 1893: A Rejoinder', *BSSLH* 25 (1972), 58–65.
[5] J. H. Porter, 'Coalminers and Conciliation', *BSSLH* 26 (1972), 27.

Wales, in the face of mounting hostility of a growing rank and file wholly opposed to compromise over a guaranteed minimum.[1] That socialist ideology intensified this polarization after 1893 is generally agreed, though outside South Wales the spread of a form of syndicalism was limited and exercised influence at the earliest in Yorkshire from about 1910.[2]

Labour historians are divided on the outcome of the 1893 stoppage. A. R. Griffin, Page Arnot, and Challinor tend to regard the settlement, which led to the establishment of the Conciliation Board in 1894, as a victory for the miners, and Neville, too, is inclined to adopt an optimistic position. According to this view, the Conciliation Board's operation from 1894 reduced the intensity of wage fluctuations by comparison with the preceding period before 1888. Neville also rejects the alternative claim that the MFGB leaders were duped into agreeing terms at the Rosebury Conference, pointing out that the terms had been ratified immediately by a full conference of the MFGB.[3] Parker Rhodes, Secretary of the SYCOA, regarded the outcome as a compromise, and explained to the members that the coalowners agreed to negotiate only because 'united action couldn't have been maintained longer than it was' and that within 'a few days, or hours defections were inevitable, which would have brought about disaster'.[4] A few years later, he referred to the 1893 settlement as having 'rendered useless the sacrifices the coalowners had made'.[5]

It has been argued that greater stability of earnings followed the settlement, to which the owners' acceptance of a minimum level to base-rate wages (though not in itself a minimum wage) must have contributed, and that this led to more stable labour relations. But both Williams and Porter have described the new system of conciliation as essentially a variant of the sliding scale, which when trade was prosperous was heavily weighted in the employers' favour. For this reason the Minimum Wage Strike of 1912 is regarded almost as an inevitable consequence of the miners' failure to secure their objective in 1893–4. As for the effects on labour relations, the evidence is unclear, though the high level of strikes in the industry is not indicative of any marked improvement. Furthermore, a growing recognition by the unions of the

[1] Duffy thesis, 549–50; J. E. Williams, 'The Miners' Lockout of 1893', *BSSLH* 24 (1972), 16.

[2] Though this is a matter of dispute among historians: Neville thesis, 381–2; P. Davies thesis, 141–56.

[3] Neville thesis, 217–30.

[4] SCL SYCOA MD 2699–6, Reports Jan. 15, 1895.

[5] Ibid., 24 Jan. 1901.

asymmetry of conciliation, favouring employers in periods of expanding trade, tended to intensify divisions within the unions and to polarize colliery owners and workers, especially those sections of the rank and file whose commitment to a minimum living wage rendered a sequel to the 1893 strike unavoidable as their influence within the unions grew.

Symptoms of a growing polarisation between masters and men was the Miners' Federation support for nationalization of the mines, a proposal first introduced by Keir Hardie in the form of a Bill immediately after the announcement in the House of Commons that the strike of 1893 had ended.[1] The introduction, too, of a Bill to limit hours in 1892, heralding the first of many parliamentary debates on this subject until 1907, was another development tending to exacerbate relations between mine workers and certain colliery owners, whose continued opposition to hours reduction prompted Winston Churchill's memorable castigation:

Two more hours are demanded in the interest of economics. I do not wonder a bit at the miners' demand. I cannot find it in my heart to feel the slightest surprise, or indignation, or mental disturbance. My capacity for wonder is entirely absorbed not by the miners' demand, but by the gentleman in the silk hat and white waistcoat who has the coolness, the composure, and the complacency to deny that demand and dispute it with him.[2]

When eventually in 1908 the Eight Hours Act was passed the Federation switched its energies to achieving the minimum wage which had been denied in 1893.

The concept of, and aspiration to, a minimum living wage may be traced, intermittently at least, to the Miners' Association of the 1840s, and was related to the effects upon miners' living standards of violent fluctuations in wages to which they were accustomed but never reconciled. Various measures had been proposed over the years, which included combined action between workers and coalowners to sustain prices, or to reduce hours or limit output to attain the same effect. We have seen that intervention of these kinds was occasionally successful, but only in the short term. Erratic price and wage fluctuations continued to be a feature of the industry and provided the basis for the dispute of 1912. Kirby has emphasized that the nationwide significance which miners attached to what was known as the abnormal places

---

[1] *HC Debates* 4th Series, Vol. 18, 1235–6.
[2] *HC Debates* 4th Series, Vol. 191, 1332.

dispute is explicable by its provision of 'a substantive base for the miners' long-standing demand for a minimum wage'—a demand which had originally arisen in response to their experience of wage fluctuations after 1870.[1] Employers had always resisted such claims, and in particular saw the 1912 minimum wage agitation as a fundamental attack on the piece-rate system by the Miners' Federation.[2] Even so, the employers' determination to resist the claim differed in degree; those in the export coalfields, where wages fluctuated most, expressing the firmest opposition,[3] which is why the coalowners of Northumberland and South Wales rejected completely the proposals formulated by government.[4]

Largely originating in South Wales, the abnormal places dispute provided a spearhead for the larger issue of a minimum wage for all miners, one of the aims included in the manifesto of the South Wales Syndicalists', *The Miners' Next Step*, published in 1912, and in which industrial action was advocated to achieve it.[5] In September 1911 employers officially acknowledged the justice of the claim for some form of compensation to miners working in abnormal places whose best efforts were insufficient to enable them to earn a living wage, an admission to which the MFGB immediately reacted by resolving to proceed with the larger claim.[6] The bitterness which the ensuing dispute generated when an impasse was reached stemmed in part from this strategy, which irked the owners, but also from the effects of the Eight Hours Act, which they alleged had increased costs considerably in the region and justified resistance to measures which threatened to raise them further.[7]

For their part, Welsh miners had already demonstrated their disenchantment with conciliation in 1910, when a violent strike affecting a large section of the coalfield originated from a refusal to accept a wage adjudication—which was probably symptomatic of a longer history of opposition from rank and file to the boards set up in the wake of the strikes in the 1890s. The presence of an energetic group advocating syndicalist ideas also seems to have been important in radicalizing rank-and-file members.[8] The dispute in D. A. Thomas's Cambrian combine, itself over work in abnormal places, was greatly exacerbated by the employers' attempts to lock out all the workers, simply to put pressure

---

[1] Kirby 1977, 19. [2] Arnot 1953, 91–3.
[3] Kirby 1977, 19. [4] Arnot 1953, 99–101.
[5] D. Smith, 'Leaders and Led', in K. S. Hopkins (ed.) *Rhondda Past and Future* (Rhondda, 1975), 37–65.
[6] J. R. Raynes, *Coal and its Conflicts* (London, 1928), 125. [7] Rowe 1923, 102–3.
[8] R. V. Sires, 'Labour Unrest in England, 1910–14', *JEH* XV (1955), 257; R. P. Arnot, *A History of the South Wales Miners' Federation* (London, 1967), 375.

on those directly involved; for the effect of this extreme measure seems to have been to promote unity among the miners and to strengthen their determination to resolve the issue of the minimum wage.[1] According to Page Arnot, radicalization of the rank and file also affected ideas among the leaders of the South Wales miners, a transformation which appears to have had an increasing influence upon policies, though not until after 1909.[2] Before that time, according to Robert Smillie, South Wales miners had been over-awed by the beguiling, if unorthodox, approach of their moderate Labourist leader: 'If any friction arose and pandemonium—so easy to arouse, so difficult to quell—Mabon never tried to restore order in any way. He promptly struck up a Welsh hymn, or that magical melody "Land of My Fathers". Hardly had he reached the second line, when, with uplifted arms . . . he had the whole audience dropping into their various parts . . .'.[3]

Growing solidarity within the region, however, did not extend across the coalfields. A more moderate leadership in the North-east afforded one contrast with South Wales, but more fundamental in explaining the differences between the measure of resistance in Northumberland and South Wales was the presence in the former of cavilling, and the county average wages policy, both of which effectively removed the inequities and difficulties which arose in South Wales as a result of chronic geological faulting and poor working places. The obduracy of South Wales miners is explicable by the fact they had the least to lose, a situation which the events at Tonypandy during the Cambrian strike in 1910, when troops entered the town to quell a three-day riot, seemed to confirm.

The final campaign to secure the minimum wage was led by the MFGB, which formulated minimum wages for each of the regions. The basis adopted in January 1912 was 5s. a day for each man underground, and 2s. for boys. The Federated Colliery owners were more inclined than those outside the Federated districts to accept the minimum wage in principle, but sought safeguards against a reduction in miners' work effort, with a resulting decline in OMS[4] consequent upon its adoption. Prevarication frustrated the miners' leaders, and when acceptance was not forthcoming a conference was convened at which miners voted for a national strike, by 445,801 to 115,921. Counter-proposals by the government gained acceptance from neither side, divisions between union

---

[1] Arnot 1953, 60.
[2] R. P. Arnot, *A History of the South Wales Miners' Federation 1898-1914* (London, 1967), 378.
[3] Smillie 1924, 160.
[4] Neville thesis, 385-8.

members finding their counterpart among the employers, among whom those from Northumberland and South Wales insisted on outright rejection. Having failed to negotiate a compromise, the government introduced a Bill which embodied the principle of the minimum wage but included no figures. This was rejected as inadequate by the union, and by 244,011 votes to 201,103 voted to continue the strike, then in its fourth month. Many of the opposing votes came from South Wales, where the effects of the stoppage were the most extreme, and the Midlands, traditionally a moderate and high productivity region where the minimum wage was not of immediate relevance to local conditions. Their withdrawal of support meant the termination of the strike by the MFGB executive, which had failed to secure the two-thirds majority required to continue. The government's terms were accepted.[1]

From the miners' standpoint, the major defect of the resulting legislation was that while it protected workers against the inability, through no fault of their own, to obtain a living wage, the Act did not stipulate the actual wage level, which was to be decided by joint boards in each region. From the employers' standpoint, this afforded sufficient flexibility to enable them to resist and avoid the introduction of uniform minima.[2] According to Rowe, the minima granted fell well below miners' demands in the various regions, and except in Leicestershire, South Wales, and Somerset the Act barely affected average earnings. Scotland failed completely to secure an effective minimum wage.[3]

These conclusions may be tested by comparing the proposals advanced by the MFGB with the minima actually achieved under the joint boards in 1912; these may also be compared with the actual average rates of pay, calculated from the wages data (Table 8.10). Such a comparison reveals that the actual minima determined by the various district boards fell well short of miners' demands. The gap between average levels of shift wages for hewers in 1912 and the minima granted is sufficiently great in most cases to support Rowe's contention that the Act barely affected average earnings. This evidence alone, however, is insufficient to clinch the argument, for the number of abnormal places in each region will have affected the difference—though outside South Wales it seems likely that they were not sufficiently numerous to warrant a different conclusion. This does not, however, imply that the

---

[1] Arnot 1953, 91–103; D. H. Robertson, 'A Narrative of the Coal Strike', *Economic Journal*, XXII (1912), 383.

[2] Kirby 1977, 19; D. H. Robertson, 'A Narrative of the Coal Strike', *Economic Journal* XXII (1912), 305–6. [3] Rowe 1923, 107.

1912 minimum wage agitation was not historically important. Though unsuccessful in terms of the substantive short-term gains, none the less the campaign and the strike demonstrated the ability of the miners' organizations to mount and sustain a lengthy national strike, and to threaten the economy to such a degree that government felt impelled not only to intervene, as in 1893, but also to legislate on wages. Simultaneously, therefore, the coal strike which was 'indicative of the centripetal forces at work in mining trade unionism'[1] was also symptomatic of a growing involvement of the state in industrial relations in the coalfields. Phelps-Brown has suggested that the MFGB successfully manipulated the government by intimidation, obtaining, as it had over the eight-hours issue, a national settlement which unaided it could not have hoped to secure from employers; and he enlarged on the general significance of the 1912 strike, which he considered represented an important precedent, which was to enable the trade unions to compel

Table 8.10. *Hewers' rates of pay after 1912*
(per shift)

	Miners' proposed minima[a]	Actual minima determined by boards[b]	Average money wages[c]
Scotland	6 s.	5 s. 10 d.	7 s. 2 d.
North-east	6 s. 2 d.	5 s. 6 d.–5 s. 10 d.	8 s. 7 d.
Cumberland	6 s. 6 d.	6 s.	7 s. 4 d.
Lancs. and Ches.	7 s.	6 s. 6 d.	7 s. 10 d.
North Wales	6 s.		7 s. 5 d.
Yorkshire	7 s. 6 d.	6 s. 9 d.	9 s. 0 d.
East Midlands	7 s. 4½ d.	6 s. –7 s. 3 d.	9 s. 1 d.
West Midlands	6 s. 6 d.	6 s.	7 s. 3 d.
South Wales	7 s. 3 d.	6 s. 10½ d.	8 s. 10 d.
South-west	4 s. 11 d.	6 s. ½ d.	6 s. 3 d.
UK Average	6 s. 9½ d.	6 s. 3½ d.	8 s. 4 d.

[a] Arnot 1953, 92.
[b] H. S. Jevons 1915, 591, 602.
[c] Table 7.1.

[1] Kirby 1977, 20.

governments to offer concessions to demands which employers other-wise found completely unacceptable.

Undoubtedly a national strike posed a threat to the functioning of the economy, but the national settlement which was the outcome excluded a universal minimum wage (the objective for which the MFGB fought) and resembled closely the compromise proposals embodied in a Bill pre-pared by government during the course of the strike and which the miners had rejected. Among the coalowners, too, a substantial minority had continued to oppose the minimum concept included in government proposals for solving the dispute. It would seem that the final legislation introduced after the stoppage was ended constituted a genuine com-promise, with minorities on both sides continuing to remain dissatis-fied. Such an interpretation is at odds with Phelps-Brown's notion that the events in the coalfields and at Westminster in 1911 heralded a new era in industrial relations.[1] For even though the strike was indicative of tendencies within the industry which were conducive to corporatism, it concealed only temporarily an underlying preoccupation in the regions with local issues and local action; and even within regional branches rifts occurred in relations between leadership and some of the rank and file.

The persistence, albeit at a lower intensity compared with the late Victorian period, of numerous local, often unofficial, strikes, underlined the simultaneous centrifugal influences which were ever present in the industry before 1914, and which were important in contributing to the industry's reputation of being highly strike-prone. Our revised figures for days lost presented in Table 8.4 may not be strictly comparable with those readily available for other industries, which might also require revision. However, even on the basis of the Board of Trade figures pre-sented by Mitchell and Deane[2] the inter-industry differences in strike frequency is so great that revisions would be unlikely to alter the essen-tial picture. Measured by days lost per employee, mining and quarrying lost more than twice as many as textiles in 1891–1900, and slightly below double the figures for textiles in 1901–13. After textiles, the metal, engineering and shipbuilding industries recorded less than a quarter of days lost per employee in 1891–1900, and less than one fifth in 1901–1913: hence the reputation of the coalfields for militancy.

---

[1] Phelps-Brown 1959, 325–8; Kirby 1977, 21.
[2] Mitchell and Deane 1962, Chapt. II.

v. Wages and wage determination

Our discussion of the institutional developments and socio-political processes at work on the coalfields has stopped short of an explicit discussion of their relative importance in the determination of wages. That they played a part is beyond doubt; and yet for all the social and political significance of the trends which have been identified, an examination of wage–price relationships leads to an endorsement of Pollard's thesis, based on the period 1870–1914, that despite the relative strength of coalminers' unions the 'market' component of the determined wage must be accorded greater influence than organizational and institutional factors.[1] There was no evidence that the higher degree of formal union organization after the 1880s enabled wages to move more independently from the price mechanism. An analysis of the cyclical amplitude of movements in wages and prices reveal low rates of wage reduction in the downswings after 1883,[2] which therefore created an environment more favourable to trade-union growth than hitherto, strengthening the trades unions' ability to resist wage reductions commensurate with falling prices in subsequent recessions.

Three tests can be made to guage the role of trade unions in wage determination. Firstly, in an industry in which wages closely followed the course of prices it is possible to examine the impact of organized labour on this relationship. In the inland coalfields and Scotland, where wages increased measurably in excess of the price level, the more organized and formal unionism of the later period does seem to have modified the wage–price relationship existing before the late 1880s.

---

[1] Sydney Pollard, 'Trade Unions and the Labour Market, 1870–1914', *YBESR* 17 (1965), 111.

[2] This generalization is based on two exercises: (1) coal prices and wages were converted to indices and the rates of growth compared for each half cycle divided into upswings (1833/4–7 to 1909/10–13) and downswings (1837–42/3 to 1907/8–9/10), using the actual turning points for each series; (2) cycles were defined by measuring upswings as a percentage of previous peak (1835–7 to 1909/10–13), and downswings as a percentage of previous trough(1837–42/4 to 1908–10). The annual average rate of growth of wages revealed considerable variation in the amplitude of upswings, with a higher level of growth in wages in 1835–7, 1849/51–6, 1868/9–73, 1886/8–90/1— punctuated by relatively low increases in the intervening upswings. After the upturn of 1886/8–90/1 (the highest increase in wages over any upswing apart from that of the coal famine), however, the rate of increase in the remaining three upswings was relatively modest. The increases of 1886–90 were obviously an important incentive to the trade-union growth of those years, and moderate wage rises in succeeding upswings appear to have enabled this growth to be maintained. A more decisive role, however, seems to have been played by differing levels of wage reductions during downswings which, especially after 1883, were modest compared with the severe losses that occurred in previous downswings (and especially high in 1873–9/80).

The second test (suggested by Pollard) concerns the effectiveness of labour organization in reducing wage differentials within the industry (though of doubtful validity for miners' unions, which consisted overwhelmingly of hewers, for whom the maintenance of differentials was a continual aim). Here, too, evidence suggests that the impact of the more highly organized and formal unionism of the second half of the period was not particularly significant. Indeed, putters and unskilled underground workers gained rather less than did hewers in 1886–1914. Only the differentials of the skilled day-wage men fell during this period.[1]

The third test of the effectiveness of trade unions on wage determination concerns the relationship between the proportion that the total revenue generated by the industry bears to wages, on the one hand, with that of trade-union organization on the other. The mining industry was a particularly clear example of a system of labour relations in which the struggle between employers and employees was focused on the wage front. According to Burgess, wages were the focus for industrial relations in mining in the nineteenth century to a much greater extent, for example, than in either the building or engineering industries. Because wages and prices fluctuated so acutely, and because wage rates made up such a large proportion of total working costs, this encouraged a perception of the relationship between employers and employed as one that involved a struggle over the division of the industry's total product'.[2] There is considerable evidence to support this view. For most of the nineteenth century workers accepted that wages had to fluctuate with prices and revenue; the attempt to restrict output intermittently throughout the period was an acknowledgement that only by maintaining prices could wage levels be kept up. Similarly, all the negotiations with employers conducted under the apparatus of conciliation and sliding scales accepted the notion of a reasonable profit for coalowners and effectively condoned the transfer of the effects of market depression to wages. Only on very rare occasions did miners' representatives successfully challenge the proportion of revenue going to profit.[3] The annual figures can be broken down into cyclical averages, as in Table 8.11.

The problems of defining the wage–income ratio are of only technical significance, since whatever the method adopted the trend is the same. The proportion that the wage bill bore to the total revenue of the industry remained sstable in the long period between the 1830s and 1879, but rose significantly in 1880–96 and again after 1906. It is difficult

---

[1] See above Table 7.3.   [2] Burgess 1975, 215–6.
[3] Welbourne 1923, 174; see also Garside 1977, 143.

Table 8.11. *Ratio of total wages to total revenue 1833-1910*
(per cent)

	Definition A (Export prices– Hewers' wages)	Definition B (Pithead prices– Hewers' wages)	Definition C (Pithead prices– 'Wage Bill')
1833–43	36	42	
1844–52	35	45	
1853–60	33	46	
1861–70	35	46	
1871–79	32	41	
1880–87	40	69	
1888–96	50	77	69
1897–1905	51	77	67
1906–10	57	81	

Sources: By expressing wages as a proportion of the revenue (or 'income') of an industry, Phelps-Brown and Browne 1968, 69–70, have analysed the importance of labour compared with other productive factors, especially fixed capital. The application of this technique to coalmining presents problems, however, because of the difficulty of defining income and wages. Income has been calculated by multiplying output by pithead prices and by export prices, which may be regarded as alternative measures. As a proxy for the annual wage bill in the industry we have been compelled to multiply the number of shifts worked per year by hewers' wages, which inevitably yields an inflated total. Assuming, however, a constant proportion of hewers to other workers, and no marked shift in differentials, the concealed differentials between juvenile and adult and 'skilled' and unskilled workers will not distort the trend in the size of the wage bill relative to other constituents in income. In practice, the fall in the hewer–oncost ratio results in an exaggeration of the wage bill's relative importance during these later years, though the increasing average age of haulage workers and the rise in their average earnings over time will probably have offset this bias.

A parliamentary return (1903, LXIV, 783) is the source of the actual wage bill, presented together with the price of coal (defined as pithead prices times output) for the years 1886–1902. When the actual wage bill is compared with our wage–income ratio for the same period the latter appears to contain only slight exaggeration resulting from the use of the hewer's wage only in the equation, though as the parliamentary return itself tends to overestimate the wage bill, too, the difference between the two measures must be regarded as greater, and may have been between 10 and 20 per cent.

to attribute this change after 1879 to labour organization, since in the years between 1880 and 1887 unions were at their weakest; consequently, a 'market' explanation for this phenomenon seems more plausible. The increase in the wage–income ratio between 1880 and 1896 might be attributed in part to the depressed prices of many of these years (since the ratio is always higher in slump years), but since there is an unmistakable secular trend towards a higher ratio in 1880–1913, this can hardly be a sufficient or persuasive explanation. The dominant long-term factor was probably the effect of intensifying geological constraints, shorter hours, reduced work pace, and increased absenteeism, which together tended to depress labour productivity. This was accompanied by increasing labour costs per ton and higher shift wages, both of which led to a growth in the total wage bill.

Meanwhile, this growth in wages (both in the sense of wages per man-shift and wage costs per ton) was accompanied itself by a stagnant level of capital per man at constant prices. At the same time, the real productivity of capital could not increase, because most of the increments to fixed capital in this period (as calculated from our capital–output ratios) was expended in overcoming the problems stemming from increased depth of working. In this sense, therefore, the dramatic growth of output in the period 1880–1913 can be attributed to increasing labour inputs, and consequently the growing importance of labour (*vis-à-vis* capital) in this period was probably an important factor in the increasing ability of organized labour to gain a full share in the 'prosperity' of 1888–1913. The plausibility of this interpretation of the shift in the wage–income ratio is enhanced if the apparently abrupt change in the ratio in 1879–80 is regarded as largely artificial and caused by untypically low coal prices, and that this fall is merely coincidental with the beginning of a more fundamental secular decline in the proportion that wages bore to total costs and to total revenue. Even so, the timing of this change suggests that the ratio began to move prior to the emergence of the MFGB.

This organic change, therefore, appears to have been a causal factor in enlarging the unions' ability to compete with employers for a share of revenue, rather than the result of this increased competition. It is possible, however, to attribute to the MFGB an important role in the process of consolidating the advantages to be gained from the rise in the wage–income ratio, and translating it into concrete terms in the form of improved wages, reduced hours, and alterations in working conditions. The more formal unionism of the post–1889 period did not lead to an attack on wage differentials, largely because of the domination of the unions by relatively skilled face workers; nor could the shift in the wage–income ratio, which began in the cycle 1880–7, be attributed to the results of trade-union pressure, though its consolidation may have owned something to this influence. The impact of trade unions on wage rates appears to have had a measurable effect in Yorkshire, the East Midlands, and in

Scotland, but the history of differential productivity in the regions examined in Chapter 6 raises considerable doubts about whether the distinct performance of these three regions, as regards the respective course of wages and prices, can be attributed entirely to institutional pressure.

The effect of trade unions on productivity was the subject of research by Pencavel, who concluded that the growth of trade unionism between 1900 and 1913 explained the 'loss' of 2 or 3 per cent of production.[1] The completeness of the production function used in reaching this conclusion, however, is in doubt, particularly as it does not appear to take account of changes in the average lengths of shift worked between 1900 and 1913. What is perhaps more significant for our immediate purpose is Pencavel's conclusion (both on the basis of the wage–price correlation and on that of a more formal test) that there is no evidence from the export coalfields that the increased union power of the post-1900 period had any significant effect on wage rates when compared with the very limited power they possessed in 1878–92. He did not perform the same test for the inland coalfields, though our earlier analysis pointed to a circumstantial connection between the strength of the MFGB in Yorkshire, the East Midlands, and Scotland, and the fact that wage rates performed rather better than prices. When productivity trends are incorporated into the picture, however, it is more difficult to accept this evidence at face value. In those three regions, output per man from the 1880s fell less than it did in all other major regions. Consequently, the relatively improved performance of wages may have owed less to institutional factors than to favourable levels of output per man. Indeed, viewed in this way the comparative strength of the MFGB in these regions may have derived partly, or wholly, from their favourable record of productivity, which allowed wages to increase by more than the price-indicated level.

Rather than attempt to construct a complete model of the factors influencing wage levels in the mining industry, it is a more practical proposition to evolve from the foregoing review of industrial relations a descriptive framework which might help to account for the role of trade unions in wage determination. In the general sense, the likely effects of labour organization are fairly clear, involving a pressure for higher wages, lower productivity (through a variety of strategies including shorter hours, reduced intensity of work, increased use of restrictive

[1] John H. Pencavel, 'The Distributional Efficiency Effects of Trade Unions in Britain', *BJIR* 15 (1977), 137–56.

practices), leading to increased wage costs, and squeezed profit margins.

It is possible to consider the role of organized labour in influencing these factors in two senses—firstly, in terms of the gains achieved over the upswing (accompanied by losses in the downswing), and secondly, in terms of secular gains in which advances over the cycle as a whole must be recorded. In the period 1830–88 the prevalence of the first type of mechanism is clear: organized labour achieved wage (and other) advances over the upswing, but suffered defeats during the subsequent slump. Any secular advance in wage rates in this period appears to have been the result of price movements rather than union pressure. During the upswing, however, organized labour should be accorded an important role in gaining the full benefits of the price rises in that cycle. It can scarcely be doubted that had there been no labour organization at all, wages would not necessarily have followed prices, as employers would have been under no pressure to grant wage increases unless coincidentally a shortage of labour prevailed at current wage rates—the situation which arose only at the peaks. Conversely, in the period 1830–88 wages fell in the downswing because prices fell, but also because of the inability of weakened labour organizations (compared to those existing in the upswing) to resist wage cuts.

It could be argued that the post-1889 period marked a significant departure in the history of labour organization, in that for the first time membership remained relatively buoyant in the downswings. This made little difference to the comparative performance of wages and prices in the export coalfields, though it may have led to some increased resistance to wage cuts in the downswing in the inland coalfields. The ability of the MFGB to undertake this increased resistance lay primarily in the new conditions of trade created by the export-led boom, which provided the economic foundation for the establishment of permanently constituted unions even in counties not involved in exporting. The MFGB was the manifestation of this new phase in the industry's history, and without its effective operation miners' wages would have been more vulnerable to downward pressure during the downswings. The sheer size of the price increase of 1888–91 (which allowed a 40 per cent increase in additions to wage scales) meant that wage rates reached a level where a powerful and permanently organized union was possible. Secondly, the fact that prices did not return to pre-1888 levels (as they had after the early-1870s boom) provided the basis for wage rises over the cycle as a whole, a process repeated in the subsequent cycles down to 1913. Thirdly, the growing importance of labour inputs relative to those of capital after 1880 strengthened the potential power of organ-ized labour and led to an increase in the proportion that wages bore to the total costs of, and returns from, production. Finally, the favourable productivity record of some regions may have assisted miners in obtain-ing greater wage gains than their neighbours.

Any attempt to measure the comparative performance of the less formal unionism of the pre-1889 period with the national movement after that date is bedevilled by inadequate data before 1889. Suppose, therefore, that labour as a commodity in the market possessed no institutional defences whatsoever. Is it possible to trace a relationship between the movement of wage rates and that of demand for labour? Is it possible to identify periods when demand for labour does not satisfactorily account for its level of remuneration, and in which, therefore, institutional factors appear to have played a part?

The distinction between 'internal' recruitment (from within families where the household head was a miner) and movement from other occupations to mining is relevant to an attempt to answer these ques-tions.[1] While acknowledging the feasibility only of measuring these within broad margins of error, Chapter 3 contained a comparison of the demand for labour by decadal periods on this basis. The period of maxi-mum demand was 1840–60, when heavy recruitment from other occu-pations coincided with a relatively low level of 'internal' supply. Despite this, the level of wages in the industry rose significantly only in 1852–6. The main source of the attraction of labour to mining in 1840–52 (and also in the 1830s) was clearly the differential between wage levels there and those in other occupations. Bowley gives figures of average agricul-tural earnings in England and Wales for 1830 and 1840 of 11s. a week. In Ireland, wages of roughly 6s. a week in 1837, 7s. in 1838–46, and 8s. in 1847–54 are recorded.[2] In Scotland, agricultural wages of 9s. in 1834–5 and 14s. in 1860 can be calculated. In mining, on the other hand, average weekly earnings of hewers fell below 11s. a week only in the 1842 depression, and for most of the period 1830–52 ranged between 13s. and 17s. There can be little doubt, therefore, that wage rates in mining in the period 1830–52 were sufficiently high, relative to other occupational groups from which colliery workers were recruited, to attract labour.

It is difficult to know, however, whether there was a labour shortage in the period 1852–6 which might account for the signi-ficant wage and price rises of those years. Output rose by 16 per cent in

[1] See above 226–36.
[2] Bowley, *Wages in the UK in the Nineteenth Century* (Cambridge, 1900), 48–60.

this four-year period, but this was no faster than the average rate of growth for the 1850s as a whole. Since levels of productivity are unlikely to have altered much over this brief period, there seem to be no grounds for advocating a supply-side explanation for the growth of wage rates, unless there was a fall in labour supply for some unknown reason. Moreover, since the early 1850s witnessed a sharp rise in general commodity prices, the temptation is to ascribe the movement of prices and wages in mining to changes in demand rather than supply factors.

Demand for labour was relatively low in the 1860s, measured by a 1.5 per cent annual growth rate in the labour force and the net movement of the sons of miners to other occupations during the decade. Nevertheless, wages rose steadily from 1858 to 1866, followed by a fairly sharp fall to 1869. The weekly earnings of agricultural labourers in the mining counties in 1867–70 ranged from 14s. (or as low as 12s. in some of the Scottish coalfields) to 20s. (in Durham), while the earnings of hewers were in excess of 20s. a week throughout the entire decade.[1] This evidence suggests that a combination of reduced demand for labour in the industry, together with high wage relativities, prevented wages from falling; they continued to move upwards with prices until the cyclical fall of 1866–9. The reasons for this are difficult to identify. Possibly 'institutional' factors may have been important; the MNA and the county unions, which temporarily enjoyed considerable strength from 1858 to the mid-1860s, succeeding in maintaining artificially high prices, though the buoyancy of prices may have been equally instrumental; or possibly a combination of the two. But since demand for labour was fairly low and coincided with rising productivity levels in the 1860s, supply factors offer no reason to explain why the unions should have enjoyed a period of comparative strength. The alternative is to seek the primary forces in determining wage movements in prices, and factors related to the demand for labour.

The booms of 1870–3, 1888–91, 1898–1901, 1905–7, and 1912–13 saw marked increases in wage rates. The rate of growth in the labour force rose measurably during most of these upswings, as did output—though to a lesser extent. Could one postulate, therefore, conditions obtaining during these years in which a shortage of labour at current rates of pay could account for the wage rises that occurred? Employment increased by 43 per cent in 1871–5, by 22 per cent in 1888–91, by 15 per cent in 1898–1901, and by 10 per cent in 1905–7; with the exception of 1905–7

---

[1] E. E. Hunt, *Regional Wage Variation in Britain, 1850-1914* (Oxford, 1973), 64.

the rates of growth were well above average for the respective decades.

Levels of weekly earnings for hewers at the outset of booms were 24s.6d. in 1871, 24s. 4d. in 1888, 30s. 7d. in 1898, and 33s. in 1905. The earnings of new recruits to the industry is difficult to guess. Working on an upper limit of three-quarters, then their wages may have reached 18s. 4d. in 1871, 18s. 3d. in 1888, 22s. 11d. in 1898, and 24s. 9d. in 1905, which in every case would have been higher than those received by agricultural labourers, though lower, assuming full employment, than those received by building labourers in most of the coalfield regions.[1] It is possible, therefore, that a labour shortage might have existed, in the sense that potential recruits to the industry found alternative urban occupations more attractive than mining at these levels of pay, which meant that colliery owners were forced to increase mining wages in order to attract labour. It is true, of course, that juvenile entrants to the industry could rarely receive a higher initial wage than that offered by mining, but juveniles did not at any one time constitute a large reservoir of labour; moreover, during these boom periods there was evidently a need to attract adults as well, possibly through higher wages.

The forces attracting both adults and juveniles to (and away from) the industry were not, of course, entirely monetary. We have presented evidence to show that towards the end of the period the sons of miners became increasingly reluctant to enter the industry, which implies the necessity of a greater financial incentive to attract them.[2] Considerations of the basic unattractiveness of work in the industry make it impossible to base any argument purely on wage disparities. There are grounds, however, for regarding the wage rises of 1871–3, 1888–91, and 1898–1901, as having been motivated by a shortage of labour at the current rate, particularly in those coalfields (accounting for an increasingly larger proportion of output) where colliery employers faced competition from industrial occupations (though employers' ability to pay higher wages was also critical). It is possible, therefore, that supply-side factors made some contribution to the increase in wages. At the same time, contemporary comment on this subject, as well as an examination of the timing of changes, indicates that prices moved first, thus enabling hewers to press for, and to secure, higher wages. It seems unlikely that an increase in wage rates was needed to encourage transit workers to convert to hewers (essential to increase output during the boom, especially in the face of falling productivity), since presumably these

[1] Ibid., 64, 70.
[2] See above Table 3.6.

would have agreed to conversion at the old rates.

The most likely mechanism is that whereby prices moved first, encouraging hewers (supported by improving levels of labour organization) to claim higher wages. The effect of hewers' success in doing so, coupled with a degree of promotion for haulage workers who became hewers, was to leave a shortage of haulage workers, and led to a supply-side increase in the wages of unskilled and semi-skilled mine workers. The falling output per man which inevitably accompanied the upswing accentuated this labour shortage. There are also grounds for seeing a connection between the greater power of the MFGB in the inland coal-fields, and increasingly in South Wales and Scotland as well, with the high level of competition for labour which must have operated in these predominantly urban areas. Unionism in the North-east may have been less well placed because of the relative absence of other job opportunities except in certain districts. In this way, the rise of the MFGB is partly to be seen in the context of the growing importance of the urban coal-fields and the competitive pressures in the labour market generated by the mixed regional economies.[1]

The inevitable conclusion is that no single identifiable cause can be found to explain the movement of miners' wages during the period 1830–1913. Undoubtedly wages moved with prices, but the relationship was not necessarily automatic. Indeed, it was one which was exhibited against the background of a considerable amount of labour organization and trade-union activity, whether of the often informal and generally intermittent variety characteristic between 1830 and 1888, or of the more formal and sustained kind that occurred between 1888 and 1913. It would be erroneous merely to dismiss the MFGB as ineffective in its attack on the price–wage mechanism, for that would overlook its achievement in assisting the securing of wage rises commensurate with the unprecedented secular price rise of 1888–1913, and in three regions achieving a wage rise in excess of this. None the less, the fundamental mechanism was one in which price increases encouraged a push for higher wages, which needed and facilitated a growth in labour organization. The vital factor which distinguishes 1888–1913 from most of the period 1830–88 is that the price rise in the later period was secular and sustained, which for the first time (except perhaps from 1852–6) allowed a rise in wage rates and earnings which was not largely eroded in successive downswings. This was the real basis for permanent and powerful trade unionism.

[1] Though the North-east retained its position at the top of the wage hierarchy.

But if price inflation was the basis for the growth of wage rates and earnings, it was not the only factor. Any mechanistic correlation between wages and prices ignores both the changing relationship between the supply of, and demand for, labour (which is difficult to measure but which does not appear to have been identical in every upswing), and the struggle which it was necessary for organized labour to undertake to exploit the potential for wage increases and to resist, so far as it proved possible, reductions in pay levels. Considered within this context, the question of policy is a difficult one, for the crucial issue is not so much whether moderate or militant strategies were pursued—but whether the choice of policy was appropriate for the conditions prevailing. In the climate of low prices between 1875 and 1887 conciliation and arbitration offered some basis for negotiation in a period when unions, where they survived, were febrile and ineffectual. After 1888 the MFGB demonstrated the effectiveness of union pressure and militancy in rejecting sliding scales, and there is little doubt that the leaders of the unions in some coalfields (South Wales and the North-east in particular) were slow to recognize the opportunities for different policies. At the same time, all the evidence indicates that the *optimum* policy was dictated neither by union leaders nor by political ideology, but by prevailing economic conditions. In this sense, organized labour may be seen as having responded either more or less effectively to given conditions which were beyond its power to create.

CHAPTER 9

Coal, Economy, and Society, 1830–1913

It is difficult to exaggerate the importance of coal to the British economy between 1830 and 1913. When Britain's first Census of Production was taken in 1907 the coal industry was second to none in the value it added to the country's net output, representing approximately 14 per cent of the total. Nearly two-thirds of all coal entering world trade was mined in Britain, and after cotton goods, coal and iron and steel exports ranked roughly equal—each accounting for about 10 per cent of the total value in 1913. Except for the heterogeneous category of metal manufacture, machinery, vehicles and metal products, coalminers were the largest group of male industrial workers, exceeding a million by 1911.[1]

Their numbers, their unparalleled degree of trade union organization and their role in British political history further underline the critical importance of the coal industry for an understanding of British economic and social history, before and after 1913.

Describing the course of industrial change after the early railway age, Clapham remarked that 'behind and beneath the technical development of all the industries lay the coal and the technique of collier and mining engineer'.[2] Just as water power had helped to initiate industrialization, coal was the energy which not only gave Britain a unique advantage in establishing industrial leadership in the early nineteenth century, but proceeded to sustain and carry forward the process of industrialization in Britain. Simultaneously, coal fuelled industrial revolutions in other European countries which were either less favourably endowed with resources or lacked the expertise to exploit those in their possession.[3] At home, already in 1830 the volume of coal burnt in domestic hearths had been exceeded by that used in industry; by 1870 well over three times as much coal was providing

---

[1] Comparative figures from Mitchell and Deane 1962, 270, 305, 62; H. S. Jevons 1951, 675, 681.
[2] Clapham, *Economic History of Modern Britain II* (Cambridge, 1932), 99.
[3] Rondo Cameron, 'A New View of European Industrialization', *EHR* 2nd ser. XXXVIII (1985), 1–23.

energy for industry as for heating homes. Total UK consumption per capita rose roughly threefold between 1830 and 1913, when it slightly exceeded 4 tons. The proportion of UK coal output exported rose from less than about 2 per cent in 1830 to around 10 per cent in 1870; in 1913 the figure was 27 per cent. Throughout the entire period Britain continued to lead Europe both as a consumer and as a producer of coal per head of population, though from 1905 the US recorded a larger per capita consumption.[1]

The energy demands for the industrialization of Britain and of those parts of Europe which lacked adequate low-cost coal supplies generated a demand for British coal which resulted in an expansion of production by more than ninefold between 1830 and 1913, which compared with a tenfold increase between 1700 and 1830, a period half as long again. Flinn has shown how this expansion was achieved before 1830 with virtually no increase in the real costs of production;[2] in the nineteenth century, too, despite the tendency towards increasing costs, the price of coal relative to other commodities did not rise over the long term until the 1880s, the result of improved technology and methods of production. As in the period before 1830, in practical application advances in the technology of coal cutting were virtually non-existent before 1890. Even the use of gunpowder to bring down the coal was of relatively little significance when compared with innovations designed to enable deeper mining to take place, principally by improving the drainage, lighting, and ventilation of pits. Throughout the period—even in 1913—access technology was of far greater importance than the mechanization of coal cutting, yet the latter has dominated the debate among those historians who have sought to assess the industry's performance before 1913.

The great advances in mining, the gradual introduction of which yielded correspondingly gradual measurable effects on the industry were those which enabled coal to be reached and worked in safer conditions, and changes in operational methods for which a major inducement, in addition to maximizing the amount of coal removed from the face, was an improvement in the 'quality' or size of coal. From the 1830s improvements included methods of laying out workings, pumping by using more efficient engines, the substitution of cast iron for wooden tubbing, the adoption of mechanical fans for ventilation (especially from the 1860s), and safer and more efficient

[1] Ibid.   [2] Flinn 1984, 311.

transportation of coal to the surface. The contribution to productivity of all these improvements has been underestimated, as have the developments affecting the preparation of coal for sale, which effectively increased the proportion and value of saleable coal. The importance of the substitution of longwall for pillar-and-stall methods of extraction has also been underrated, largely because evaluations have been made in terms of increasing coal output per man rather than a higher per capita value of output. The contribution of the safety lamp to productivity, however, may have been exaggerated, though from the 1850s the illumination of the pit bottom and main gate roads by gas undoubtedly contributed to the more efficient conduct of mining operations.

The movement of coal from the face was a necessary condition for continuous working, and in achieving this the substitution of ponies for human labour beyond the main roads for face-to-main-road duties was significant from the mid-nineteenth century; steam power was also soon applied to main-road haulage. The key development in this direction, however, began in the 1860s, with the substitution of the endless wire rope for the chain system of haulage; this increased the regularity of tubs dispatched, facilitated handling, enhanced safety, and required minimal labour for efficient operation. Raising and lowering men in the shafts and winding coal to the surface from mines of increasing depth, at speed and with greater safety, was achieved not only by increasingly powerful winding engines but also, even from the 1830s, by the installation of guided cages, first using rails, then ropes, and later by the use of automatic tippers which were designed to avoid the transhipment of coal.

New safety devices permitted more rapid winding and helped to maintain productivity. The twentieth century saw the application of electricity, especially to lighting and to pumping and haulage, which effectively raised both the efficiency and safety of these operations. Such innovations ensured the continued expansion of coal production despite increasing geological difficulties, and while the application of steam power may be regarded as the most striking development in mining technology during the fifty years from 1830, the numerous minor innovations, but particularly the use of wire ropes, were crucial to achieving levels of productivity sufficient to restrain the real cost and price of coal. Throughout the nineteenth century, the raising of coal to the surface remained the critical bottleneck in an industry for which the supply of labour presented difficulty only at the peak of the booms, and in which the scope for substituting capital for labour was limited.

Almost as important as a limitation on production levels was the cost of, and capacity for, moving coal from the pithead to the consumer. While waterborne coal, shipped from greatly improved docks linked by feeder railways to the coalfields, continued to dominate the coastal and London trade originating in the inland coalfields, the mid-nineteenth century brought about a decisive shift in coal traffic from water to rail. At all except coastal markets, including London, by avoiding the need for trans-shipment the railways could offer lower rates compared with canals. During the 1840s and 1850s, therefore, partly because of the canals' limited physical capacity for carrying the volume of coal consumed by a rapidly industrializing economy. By 1870 railborne coal delivered in London exceeded that arriving by sea, although towards the end of our period the seaborne trade to London experienced a considerable revival. The railways were important not only in reducing transport costs for existing producers but also in bringing into the market mineral resources as yet undeveloped. The result was to expand the supply—and quality—of coal, and to introduce a degree of competition which finally destroyed the monopolistic elements in the regions: those exercised by canal companies and those resulting from the collusion of coalowners in certain regions—most remarkably, of course, in the form of the vend in the North-east.

The growth of competition coincided with an increasing differentiation in the demand for coal, as domestic consumption fell from 44 per cent of the volume sold in 1830 to barely half that figure by 1870. This period saw considerable progress in the application of steam power to manufacturing industry, and witnessed important developments in the use of coking coal for the furnaces, and the emergence of virtually new demands: for gas manufacture, the railways, and steam navigation. The iron and steel industry took a substantially larger share of coal production in 1869 than in 1830—25 per cent compared with 19 per cent—and by tonnage, consumption in 1869 was nearly five times as great. This spectacular growth was one consequence of the invention by Neilson of the hot-blast process in 1828, and later of the substitution of Bessemer steel for puddled iron from 1856. By reducing the cost and price of iron and steel, expansion in the demand for these items, so crucial to industrial growth at home and overseas, generated a derived demand for coal.

The combined effects of differentiation in the market, rapidly expanding demand, and intense price competition, strengthened the incentive not only to improve the marketability of coal but also to utilize the wasted coal which resulted from the crude methods of screening to separate large lumps suitable for household demand. The adoption of longwall working was another method of maximizing the proportion of large coals, though this step depended upon the suitability of geological conditions. The introduction of longwall working, increased attention to screening, and the branding and advertising of coal, by colliery as well as by seam of origin, were symptomatic of the intensification of competitive pressures during the third quarter of the century; so, too, were the changes in commercial organization which involved the gradual elimination of intermediaries, especially between coalowners and industrial consumers.

Accompanying these trends was the decline in the relative importance of the landed coalowners as producers, not only as a result of the retreat by some of them into the role of rentier, or royalty owner, as coal profits lost their attraction in comparison with royalty levels, but simply because the rapid growth in production attracted capital and enterprise from non-landed business interest. Even at the beginning of our period several of the largest landed colliery owners employed between one thousand and two thousand workers, falling into the category of 'gigantic' firms by the standards of early Victorian industry,[1] though by the 1840s they had been joined by a handful of large coal-producing iron manufacturers, a trend which was to continue. By the 1870s probably five of the ten largest coal producers were also iron and steel makers, each exceeding an output of a million tons. Among landed proprietors in 1907 only Lord Lambton's collieries, in second place, remained among the largest ten colliery enterprises with those of Lord Londonderry, included among the top twenty. Measured by employment, colliery enterprises still ranked among the largest firms in the early twentieth century. By comparison with levels of industrial concentration in other industries, however, the influence of these giant enterprises was potentially less.

The impetus to expansion derived from different sources. For the great landed entrepreneurs the exploration of mineral resources within their possession provided part of the logic for expansion, though the London trade offered economies of scale, as did the export orientation of the later generation of giant colliery enterprises. The advantages of vertical integration explained the large-scale coalmining activities of numerous major iron and steel companies, though in the late nineteenth century the further development of colliery enterprise offered financial advantages too. Giant firms were the exception in coalmining, as in most

---

[1] Crouzet, *Capital Formation in the Industrial Revolution* (London, 1972), 81.

other industries, and to that extent the problems associated with the raising of substantial capital, with employing a large labour force, and with organizing production and marketing, were encountered by a relatively small proportion of enterprises. None the less, they were sufficiently numerous and the problems associated with geology and mechanical engineering were sufficiently complex to give rise to a managerial class well before 1830. At first, professional managers originated almost exclusively from the North-east and Scotland, but subsequently others emerged in other developing coalfields to the south, where until the 1870s managerial expertise was in short supply. The later nineteenth century saw the full professionalization of mining engineers, on whose decisions, whether as proprietors or managers, the performance of the industry depended heavily. The ownership and management of colliery enterprise was dominated by families possessing connections with coal-owning or with some form of engineering, and it is suggested that the social basis of this élite narrowed over the period. Outside the industry their range of experience tended to be limited to activities related to some extent to coalmining, though vertically integrated iron and coal firms encouraged wider participation.

This relatively close-knit character of ownership and management, which in the older coalfields had already established self-perpetuating dynasties by the early years of the century, subsequently extended connections into the newer regions. The mobilization of capital, enterprise, and expertise was thus achieved despite the geographical extension of the industry. The limited comparative data available for other major capital-goods industries suggests that, at least on average, initial fixed-capital requirements were not dissimilar; the significance of such a tentative observation, however, is diminished considerably by the large inter- and intra-regional variations, which were more a matter of geological requirement than of choice. An important difference which did distinguish mining investment from that in manufacturing, at least until the late nineteenth century, was the inability of coalowners to insure against the very high risk associated with mining enterprise, a factor which must have strengthened the tendency towards internal financing from within the industry where the assessment of risks was more reliable, and from the heaviest coal-consuming industries. In regions where coalowner capitalists were less in evidence, however, particularly Scotland and South Wales, finance was forthcoming from private and professional sources even in the age of joint-stock companies.

Banks and finance companies comprised a relatively small group of shareholders, though this may understate somewhat their financial stake in the industry. None the less, the conclusion is that the industry's expansion was financed principally by private capital in both the corporate and the private sectors, that with few exceptions the geographical origin was intra-regional, and that reinvested profits were the major source of growth. Inasmuch as the ratio of fixed to total assets indicates the relative importance of the demand for working as compared with fixed capital, the problems associated with the provision of short-term finance may be regarded as less important. Moreover, unlike manufacturing industry, in which value was added to raw materials, the latter played no part in mining. Credit for the purchase of consumables and to meet wage bills was supplied by banks and by internal transfers within the industry. Interlocking partnerships and directors also played a role. The maintenance of relatively high levels of reserves was indicative of cautious financial policies associated with the retention of ownership and control—even in many of the large nominally public limited companies—and offered limited scope for the role of external finance before 1913.

Historians are generally in agreement that the supply of labour over the long term did not present coalowners with serious difficulty, despite the nature of an occupation generally regarded as dirty, dangerous, erratic, and of relatively low status.[1] To help account for the continuing flow of labour into the industry, supplementing internal recruitment from among miners' families, Pollard stressed the influx of agricultural labourers: 'it was not difficult to trump the lowly earnings on the land'. He also maintained that before 1850 a combination of social control by the magistracy, the yearly bond in the North-east, which made miners in that region 'only a degree less unfree' than serfs, and the widespread indebtedness among miners, together somehow helped to remove any threat of labour shortage.[2]

Pollard is correct to stress both internal recruitment and migration into the industry before 1850 as sources which perpetuated an abundant supply of mining labour, but the range of occupations from which migrants were drawn was much wider than agriculture, and reflected the miners' relatively high earnings, particularly those of hewers, in comparison with perhaps most manual workers. By contrast with others' findings, our calculations suggest that the years between 1831 and 1860 were a period of very substantial migration into the industry,

[1] Pollard 1978, 136.
[2] Ibid., 137.

when approximately 30 per cent of the net addition to the labour force originated from the movement of adults hitherto engaged in occupations other than mining. Thereafter, with the outstanding exception of the early 1870s, this form of migration was relatively limited, though South Wales was a major exception, as to a lesser extent was Yorkshire. Before 1860 the disparity between wages in coalmining and those in other manual occupations was the magnet which drew workers into the industry when the growth in output out-ran the ability of the mining population to fill the pits. Comparisons between hewers' wages and those of other selected categories of workers in other occupations during the later period suggests that the relatively greater financial rewards reinforced internal recruitment among miners' families.

Material attractions were sufficient to explain both the regeneration of mining labour and external recruitment without recourse to explanations relying, in part, upon various forms of 'social control' and the miners' bond. The latter offered miners in the North-east a degree of employment protection which they valued and fought to retain, and the high level of migration within the regions is ample evidence of a freedom to move to or, within, an industry experiencing secular expansion, in order to improve their terms and conditions of employment, despite restrictions imposed on the activities of trade unions. The latter were more effective as deterrents to mobility in the short term by ensuring fulfilment of contracts, but failed to restrain movement when slump turned into boom. The disciplining of an expanding labour force posed serious problems, and despite employers' attempts to introduce regularity into pit working the primitive face technology and limited face lengths, even under longwall, enabled the hewers to retain a degree of independence which, well into the later nineteenth century, helped to perpetuate work patterns which by comparison with manufacturing industry were irregular and difficult to control. In other respects, however, safety legislation assisted in the disciplinary process underground.

Because resource costs formed a relatively small part of total costs, the industry was less affected by the cost–price squeeze encountered by much of manufacturing industry during the mid-Victorian decades.[1] None the less, wages, by far the largest cost component, were carried upwards with the demand for labour in this period, and intense competition ensured that profitability probably remained below 6 per cent (gross of depreciation) before the 1870s boom. There is no evidence

[1] Roy Church, *The Dynamics of Victorian Business* (London, 1980), 43.

here, then, that coalowners reaped very large profits during the mid-Victorian boom, and certainly fell well below contemporaries' expectations. Thereafter, the figures were 13 per cent in 1870–6, 5 per cent in 1877–86, 8 per cent in 1887–96, and 11 per cent in 1897–1909; the company data suggested somewhat higher figures for all large companies. Edelstein's figures for these periods, which were calculated on a basis which did not permit any separation of coal from iron profits and used price–earnings share ratios, showed realized rates of return for publicly-quoted companies at lower levels than our estimates of rates of return on capital in the coal industry alone, but the movements show some similarity. Edelstein's comparison between the movement of profits from iron and coal with those of other industries revealed that during the periods containing the enormous coalmining booms of the early 1870s and the early 1900s (1870–6 and 1897–1909), realized rates of return were among the highest, and middling to high in 1887–96; whereas in 1877–86 and 1910–13 rates of return were among the lowest.[1] As coal prices were even more volatile than iron prices and were even more critical for coalowners' profitability, it seems probable that Edelstein's conclusions on the relative profitability of major iron and coal companies are also applicable to relative rates of return in the coal industry alone.

Just as profits, following prices, fluctuated sharply, so miners' wages were distinguished by profound cyclical fluctuations. In this respect they resembled the experience of workers in the iron and steel, shipbuilding, and other heavy engineering industries. However, because of the tendency of unemployment to be the exception among colliery workers—coalowners preferring to adopt short-time working in order to retain labour for future expansion—the contrast between the earnings of colliery workers and those of unskilled workers, casual labour, many semi-skilled, and even certain skilled workers in the capital goods industries, favoured mining labour. In 1830 the earnings of agricultural workers and unskilled labourers were below those of colliery workers as a whole, but the earnings of hewers compared favourably with those of the highest grades of Sheffield metal workers. Some twenty years later, a comparison between hewers' weekly wages and those of other various categories of workers revealed hewers' wages to be nearly twice those of agricultural labourers, slightly greater than dyers in the textile industry,

---

[1] Michael Edelstein, *Overseas Investment in the Age of High Imperialism: The United Kingdom 1850-1914* (New York, 1982), 153.

but only 80 per cent of the wages earned by compositors, and 68 per cent of fitters' wages. During the second half of the century a comparison of the real earnings of hewers with those of other groups of workers for which data exist—workers in the Sheffield trades, in the iron and steel industry on Teesside, and London artisans—indicate that miners experienced substantial absolute and relative improvements. By 1850 real earnings were higher than in 1830–4 by some 16 per cent, a level which had been achieved in the late 1830s, though the massive depression intervening in 1842–3 temporarily reversed this trend dramatically to produce real earnings below pre-1830 levels. Thereafter, a rising trend in the 1860s brought real earnings to average levels which were some 50 per cent higher than those of the 1830s. Between 1851 and 1913 hewers more than doubled their real earnings, whereas those received by workers in the Sheffield trades and by London artisans had increased by between 50 and 60 per cent, and Teesside iron and steel workers' real earnings remained much the same as in 1870.

In a recent assessment of the course of workers' real wages between 1850 and 1900, Hunt endorsed G. D. H. Cole's conclusion (based on calculations by Wood and Bowley) that they probably rose by between 70 and 80 per cent.[1] This may be compared with a rise in hewers' real earnings between 1850–5 and 1896–1900 of 110 per cent. After that, peak earnings held up well by comparison with those of other groups of workers. Yet even in 1913, the work of a miner—even a hewer—could be performed (if only barely adequately) by unskilled labour without great difficulty, a feat which makes the miners' earnings record particularly remarkable. It was explained by the interaction of economic conditions in the industry which set a ceiling upon earnings, and the strength and policies of organized labour. The unions became increasingly effective after 1888, when the export-led secular expansion was a key factor leading to a very substantial rise in miners' earnings. In the climate of low prices between 1875 and 1887 conciliation and arbitration afforded some basis for negotiation in a period when unions, where they survived, were febrile and ineffectual when confronted by employers in combination. Thereafter, under much more favourable economic conditions, the MFGB demonstrated the effectiveness of trade-union militancy.

Within a context of successful permanent trade-union development, the impetus for which derived much from the influence of labourism, one consequence proved to be a degree of solidarity among miners

[1] E. H. Hunt, *British Labour History 1815-1914* (London, 1981), 73.

sufficient to pose threats to the coalowners' authority. For, though far from complete, the unprecedented policy co-ordination, at least in the inland coalfields, was a symptom of the recognition of a measure of common interest, seen in terms either of occupation or class, which hitherto purely economic divisions had largely obscured and frustrated. For their part, the coalowners apparently lacked either a political commitment or an identification with class interests strong enough to override their economic interests, and to develop an effective national coalition. Consequently, even at the regional level, internal divisions which resulted from the various types of coal they produced for different markets, and unsynchronized prosperity or depression, tended to perpetuate coalowners' divergent interests. Their resulting weakness in association enabled miners' trade unions, especially those located in regions of relatively high labour productivity, to press home advantages corresponding to their market power.

The course of productivity has been a matter of considerable debate among historians and economists. Employing OMY as the measure, they have generally concluded that labour productivity declined from the mid-1880s, for which various explanations—entrepreneurship, the effect of wage rates upon miners' willingness to work, diminishing returns, and legislated reductions in hours—have been offered. Our revised output and employment figures suggest that the rise in output per man-year has been exaggerated before 1870, and that as a consequence the fall in OMY from the 1880s has been overdrawn. Even more important are the implications of the estimates for output per man-hour between 1840 and 1913 from which two strikingly novel conclusions emerged. First, contrary to the widely accepted picture of a decline in labour productivity from the early 1880s (as implied by OMY and OMS), hourly productivity estimates show only a temporary reversal of an upward trend occurring in the late 1880s, a recovery from which succeeded by relatively stable levels of productivity until 1909. Second, whereas OMY figures have hitherto indicated productivity levels in the 1830s and 1840s exceeding those after 1900, a comparison of hourly productivity estimates suggests that the secular deterioration in labour productivity, universally accepted in the literature, did not occur.

Estimated productivity levels appear to have been higher at the end of our period than at the beginning. A comparison of total factor productivity with labour productivity, however, reveals a tendency for TFP to decline from the 1880s and to fluctuate before that time. This contrast between the course of labour and total factor productivity has been interpreted as evidence of the effect of increasing geological constraints upon coal production under conditions which allowed limited scope for the substitution of capital for labour. The explanation for this was sought in the character of deep coalmining, for technical change was aimed largely at gaining access to coal to permit mining to take place in areas previously unworked (both geographically and geologically), and at developing surface and underground transport facilities, although some enhancement of productivity was obtainable away from the coal-face by reducing bottlenecks and by improving the flow of output. Before the 1880s, at least, these developments facilitated the winning and working of coal at increasing levels of output per man-hour during a period when labour productivity was aided somewhat by improvements in the age and quality of workers. However, this was achieved at the expense of resource and capital inputs which were themselves rewarded simply by growth in output rather than by higher total factor productivity.

The course of labour productivity over the long term may be interpreted as signifying the success of those in the industry, first in raising, then with only temporary set-backs holding steady output per man-hour, despite the increasing difficulty of countering diminishing returns caused by geological factors. The tendency, therefore, for historians to concentrate so much attention on the tardy adoption of coal-cutting machinery sometimes obscures the much more important developments in other forms of technology and in the spread of longwall mining; equally critical to the success of the industry was the continuance of a historic process by which the geological frontier was extended both spatially and in depth, a development made possible by new technology and advances in mining engineering. As a result, from the late nineteenth century an increasing proportion of Britain's coal was mined in 'newer' and deeper pits in the rapidly growing districts of south Yorkshire, Nottinghamshire, Warwickshire, and Fife.

The stimulus for this process, however, was only partly the inexorable drag on productivity exercised by geological difficulties; for while the movement of capital from older to newer areas helps to explain the expansion of the high productivity areas, in South Wales a very high revenue productivity led to the rapid growth of the region which possessed the worst record of labour productivity. That region, however, was in the vanguard of coal preparation and by-product technology, the importance of which has often been overlooked. Yet commercial success overseas was increasingly dependent upon sound product differentiation by the end of the century, when competition from other coal-producing countries began to emerge. Within the home market, too, competition required colliery owners to pay increasing attention to quality in a market which became increasingly differentiated according to the specific needs of industrial consumers and utilities. In one branch of this process of product diversification and improvement, that of coke production, British manufacturers maintained their lead throughout the century, but from the third quarter of the century continental European producers took the lead in oven design innovation for by-product recovery. Beehive ovens continued to dominate British coke production until after 1900, partly because of differential capital costs between the by-product recovery ovens and the beehives, and partly because the quality of British beehive coke was superior and found a ready demand at premium prices. However, when after a period of sluggish growth in coke demand coal prices rose dramatically from 1900 the economics of continental by-product ovens stimulated their rapid introduction into British industry. By 1913 such ovens dominated coke production.

Just as economic considerations were the key factors influencing the chronology of innovation in coking, likewise the adoption of coal cutters and conveyors at the coal-face were introduced when production costs were rising sharply, particularly in the geologically inferior areas within the Scottish region and in west Yorkshire. The quality of coal output, however, was at least as important an incentive to mechanize cutting as was cost, emphasizing the market orientation of an industry which, in this respect, makes it comparable to many manufacturing industries. Thinner seams yielded higher proportions of small and slack, which implied low-revenue product; under favourable conditions, longwall working, and later cutting machinery, could counter this trend.

The slowness with which cutting machinery was introduced before 1913 has often been criticized and may be presented as the conventional view of the technological performance of the industry. Mathias remarked on the fact that 'one quarter of American coal was being cut mechanically in 1910, but only a negligible fraction of British coal'. But equally relevant in assessing international performance is the superior progress of mechanical cutting in Britain compared with other European countries before 1914.[1] Furthermore, by analysing the geological conditions under which it was physically possible and economic to do so, and by considering carefully the size of colliery which could justify

[1] Peter Mathias, *The First Industrial Nation* (London, 1983), 378; Buxton 1978, 111, 179, Table 7.

or sustain investment in cutting and associated machinery, the conclusion was that by 1913 between 25 and 33 per cent of coal-faces located in conditions suitable for machinery were mechanized; this represents an effective rate of mechanization between three and four times higher than that implied by the widely quoted official statistics—and comparable with the rate of diffusion in the United States.

In the application of electricity to mining comparisons reveal American coalowners to have forged ahead; but they were largely free from the constraining factors of advanced age and established layout of mines which necessarily influenced British managers' technical choices and investment decisions. Until 1895 the electrification of British coalmines was hindered by the direct-current system then generally available, which was operationally unsatisfactory and unsafe underground. The greatly superior alternating current finally only received official approval for underground use from the Mines Inspectors in 1904. This coincided with a rise in both coal demand and wage costs, and marked the beginnings of an acceleration in electrification, particularly of pumping and haulage. The cost advantage of electricity over steam power was none the less insufficient, as yet, to encourage wholesale electrification in established pits.

In considering the dynamics of technical progress in the pig-iron industry in the North-east, Allen has argued that rationality, manifest in innovations introduced to minimize costs and maximize profit, does not disprove the entrepreneurial hypothesis which envisages profit-seeking entrepreneurs simultaneously approaching new technology with a lack of vigour. This argument draws a distinction between entrepreneurial behaviour which ensures profit, and entrepreneurial initiative which adopts new technology and introduces best practice *before* profitability is threatened. The beneficial consquences for industrial productivity in an industry in which entrepreneurs exhibit vigour rather than merely rationality (by implication attaching greater importance to short-run considerations) is to strengthen competitiveness.[1]

When a similar approach is adopted in assessing technical progress in the coal industry evidence supports the view that, particularly in the mechanization of coal cutting and electrification for which statistics are available after 1900, on the whole the pattern of diffusion appears to have been rational. The factors which explain the speed of diffusion also suggest that entrepreneurial vigour existed, but that the geological

[1] R. C. Allen, 'Entrepreneurship and Technical Progress in the North-east Coast Pig Iron Industry 1850–1913', *Research in Economic History* 6 (1981), 57–61.

context in which it was applied was much more varied, unpredictable, and difficult compared with that which faced American colliery owners with whom they have been compared unfavourably. The international coal market began to show signs of increasing competitiveness, which the Coal Supply Commission in 1871 signalled as heralding a decelera- tion in the growth of British coal exports. This prediction, based on the growth of coal production in Europe, America, Asia, and Australia, proved wrong only because of the unanticipated rate of expansion in the world demand for coal. For while British production continued to increase, the proportion it represented a world output dropped from 41 to 25 per cent between 1885–9 and 1909–13.[1] The United States and Germany were the major coal-producing countries where rapidly expanding iron and steel production generated massive demands for indigenous coal, which contributed to the erosion of British world dominance. The rise, also, of coal production in Russia, Japan, and (of special long-term significance to Britain) of India and Australia pointed to the probability that Britain's relative decline would continue. From 1900 the US became the world's major producer with almost twice the volume raised in the UK. Beginning in the late 1890s German coal out- put also rose more rapidly than that of the UK, from less than half the UK output in 1900 rising to 65 per cent by 1913. Lignite, or brown coal, which possesses a calorific value of about one-half that of coal, enlarged the German percentages but still left total German production behind the UK. French coal production was small, as was that of Russia and Austro-Hungary, the other main coal-producing countries (Table 9.1).

To some extent, therefore, British pre-eminence as a coal exporter may be seen as the consequence of several inter-related factors which the industry was peculiarly well placed to exploit: her emergence as the first industrial nation; the location and abundance of coal resources which had strongly influenced the development of a transport system and which, even before the secular expansion of coal exports, facilitated shipments overseas; the dramatic reduction in freight charges due not only to improved efficiency in shipping but to the structure and com- position of British overseas trade as a whole; and finally the critical role of mineral-fuel technology to the process of international industrializa- tion, which rendered an adequate coal supply a necessary precondition for industrial growth. For how long, however, could Britain expect to command 85 per cent of the world's trade in coal, as in 1900?

[1] Buxton 1978, 91.

Table 9.1. *Output of principal coal-producing countries, 1830–1913*
(million tons)

	UK	USA	France[a]	Germany		Belgium	Russia[a]	Austro-Hungary	
				coal	lignite			coal	lignite[b]
1830	30.5	0.8	1.8	1.8		2.3		0.2	c
1840	42.6	2.2	3.0	3.1	0.7	3.9		0.5	c
1850	62.5	7.5	4.4	5.0	1.8	5.7		0.9	c
1860	87.9	17.9	8.2	12.2	4.3	9.5	0.3	1.9	1.7
1870	115.5	36.1	13.1	26.0	7.5	13.5	0.7	4.2	4.0
1880	147.0	70.9	19.1	46.2	12.0	16.6	3.2	6.6	9.3
1890	181.6	140.9	25.7	69.1	18.7	20.0	5.9	9.8	17.3
1900	225.2	240.8	32.9	107.6	39.6	23.1	15.9	12.2	26.2
1913	287.4	508.9	40.2	187.1	85.9	24.0	35.5	17.5	35.8

[a] Including lignite.
[b] Lignite or brown coal which has approximately half the calorific value of coal.
[c] Included with coal.

Sources: UK: Table 1.12; USA: 1830–85; H. N. Eavenson, *The First One Hundred Years of American Coal Industry*, 432–4; 1885–1913; Finlay A. Gibson, *A Compilation of Statistics of the Coalmining Industry of the UK*, 214. France: Gillet thesis, App. Table 23. Others: B. R. Mitchell, *European Historical Statistics 1750–1970* (New York, 1976), 360–4.

Reinforcing these advantages, which may be regarded as uniquely favourable to Britain during a historic phase of world economic development, were factors internal to the economics of the British coal-mining industry. Their effect may be identified in international comparisons of productivity (OMY) which, despite their weakness as an accurate measure, differ so dramatically as to warrant attention (Table 9.2). They show that European producers experienced similar trends in labour productivity, tonnage per man-year either falling slowly or fluctuating around a relatively stable level from the mid-1890s. The trend in the US, however, rose in meteoric fashion. UK productivity remained above that of Germany, its closest European rival, until 1912 when German productivity reached that of the UK. American levels, however, which were about 50 per cent above British levels in the early 1890s, rose to more than two-and-a-half times as great by 1913, even though hours of work were probably shorter than those of British miners by that time.[1] In 1894 the hours of German mine workers, bank to bank, were reported to have exceeded those of their British counterparts by more than 5 per cent, though by 1907 working hours favoured German mine workers.[2] Because of these changes it is impossible to be precise in comparing trends in OMY, though the evidence suggests that the narrowing of the difference, culminating in the reversal of the rela-

Table 9.2. *International comparisons of labour productivity, 1885–1913*
(OMY)

	UK	USA	France	Germany[a]	Belgium	Russia	Austro-Hungary[a]
1885	325	—	190	263	166	134	177
1890	308	443	213	264	171	146	180
1890	281	450	202	256	169	173	175
1900	299	537	203	260	174	146	160
1905	285	560	202	242	159	153	187
1910	260	618	192	239	164	136	183
1913	262	681	200[b]	269	155[b]	—	207[b]

[a] Hard coal only.
[b] 1912.
Source: Finlay Gibson, 1922, 227.

[1] *RC Labour* 1894, XXXV, 325.
[2] *RC Labour* 1894, XXXV, 325; *Eight Hours Committee* 1907, XV, 321.

tive levels in British and German OMY after 1909, can be explained by the deleterious effects on mining operations of hours legislation in the UK. This conclusion is consistent with the prediction made in the report of the Eight Hours Committee that the hours worked in American and German mines after the Act would exceed those worked by British miners.[1]

The implications of productivity differentials for the comparative costs of producing coal were revealed in an article contained in an American Consular Report in 1897: 'Until lately no one would have thought of doubting the assertion that England produced the coal most cheaply. This, in fact, was the case until a comparatively recent period, but it is to be remarked that the United States long ago excelled England in the economic production of coal, and some districts in Germany even extract their coal under better conditions than England.'[2] Costs per ton were lower in the US than in Britain, but higher in Germany and Belgium, and the same was true for labour cost, the single most important component, though there is evidence to suggest that this was not explained by low wages in the British industry.[3]

Labour costs were dominant in all coal-producing industries, whereas the royalty element was non-existent in the US. Royalties, however, were relatively low in Britain compared with the rest of Europe.[4] None the less, Fine has argued that royalties adversely affected the British industry by deterring colliery owners from working the best seams that were available or in the best possible fashion.[5] This was the result, in his view, of the royalty system peculiar to Britain, whereby the separation of mine owner from landownership tended to prevent optimal resource development. He is unable to measure the deleterious effect this had upon productivity but he points to poor layout, haulage, and transportation consequent upon the division betwen land and mineral ownership. Fine's arguments are that the profitability of mine owners' investment depended in part upon economies of scale, that landowners' demands for a share in these profits, in the form of royalties, weakened the mine owners' incentive to undertake large-scale investment, and that such a system tended to discourage efficient organization and re-organization of the industry.[6] However, when royalty estimates are

[1] *Eight Hours Committee* 1907, XV, 321.

[2] *US Consular Report* Vol. 54, 200, May 1897, 55.

[3] Ibid., 55–7; Buxton 1978, 95.

[4] *RC Royalties* 1890.

[5] Ben Fine, 'Landed Property and the British Coal Industry Prior to World War I', *Birkbeck College Discussion Paper* No. 10 (1982), 7–11.   [6] Ibid.

compared with estimates of profits, they show that while royalties per ton actually exceeded profit per ton until the mid-1890s, thereafter until 1914 profit per ton ran at a level roughly twice the average of royalties; moreover, throughout this period royalties as a proportion of working cost averaged barely 5 per cent. Royalties, therefore, were less of a burden during the twenty years before 1914 than hitherto; moreover, the higher profit levels of this period suggest that there was no shortage of capital attributable to a drain into royalties.

To a foreign contemporary observer none of the cost elements seemed to be sufficient to explain international differences in production costs:

Granted that the rates of wages in the United States are nominally twice as high in Germany [larger by a smaller margin than those in the UK] it is evident that the question of cheapness in production does not depend entirely on the price of labour. . . . The fact is that the rate of wages, the skill of workmen, the number of hours of labour, and other factors of this kind do not alone influence the cost of production of coal: this remains subject to the natural advantages which certain countries possess over others. Thus, for example, the coal veins in the United Kingdom can be worked under more favourable conditions than those of other European countries, but are not as favourably situated as the American mines, of which a great number are worked in the open air or by means of inclined planes.[1]

The coal was found in seams which on the whole were thicker, closer to the surface, freer from faults, more level, and drier than those in British mines. The critical superiority of American over British resources lay in their ready accessibility; they did not require a comparable application of capital to land in the form of deep shafts, large mines, long roads, and machinery to service them merely in order to begin mining coal. Yet despite the mitigating factors adduced hitherto by McCloskey and Buxton,[2] authors of the most recent, and widely read, interpretations of British economic history in the nineteenth century, they share the conviction that in some way the coal industry fell short of what might have been expected, and that this failure contributed to Britain's relative economic decline. Such a view gained strength from the results of an important recent comprehensive, quantitative assessment of the performance of the British economy, which recorded an absolute decline in

---

[1] *US Consular Report* Vol. 54, 200, May 1897, 55.
[2] D. N. McCloskey, 'International Differences in Productivity?' in D. N. McCloskey (ed.), *Essays on a Mature Economy after 1840* (Princeton, 1971), 285–304; Neil K. Buxton 1980, 99–114.

total factor productivity in mining (representing the worst record in comparison with any other sector of British industry).[1] This evidence has been advanced to support the long-standing criticism of the industry's record, and attention has been drawn to the substantial rise in real costs between 1880 and 1914, more than in any other country.[2] Mathias registered serious reservations concerning the performance of the industry, while Crouzet concluded unequivocally:

One cannot exonerate the British coal industry from the charge of inefficiency. ... One noted a slackening of effort, a reluctance to accept innovation and to adapt to new situations, and a deterioration in industrial relations which although they were faults in common to other British industries, were to create a difficult future for this great industry; and in view of its role in the nation's economy, these faults certainly had a widespread negative influence.[3]

Further research suggests that unfavourable comparisons between British and American rates of innovation in cutting machinery have been exaggerated, that the professional associations of mining engineers were extremely active in exploring the possibilities of new technology, and that there is little evidence for a change in miners' willingness to work. In any case, our estimates of output per man-hour invalidates this allegation of a general inefficiency and the reasons for it. This does not mean that entrepreneurial deficiencies did not exist, even though the diffusion of cutting machinery does not seem to have been seriously hampered by irrationalities among mining entrepreneurs. In two particular areas of technology, however, coking and conveyors, coalowners and managers appear to have acted only in step with, rather than ahead of, immediately rational economic decisions. Thus, colliery owners and managers did not alter methods in advance of what seemed to be rational until the economics of coking rendered innovation clearly preferable. The same could be said of the lag in introducing conveyors at the face, though this was so closely dependent upon the age and layout of pits that, again, to justify investment the expected economic advantages had to be decisive in the particular circumstances—which contrasted

---

[1] Matthews, Feinstein, and Odling-Smee, *British Economic Growth* (Cambridge, 1983), 455.

[2] Peter Mathias, *The First Industrial Nation* (London, 1983), 378.

[3] Francis Crouzet, *The Victorian Economy* (London, 1982), 270. This view contrasts with that of Sandberg in whose general survey is endorsed the conclusion of D. N. McCloskey, 'International Differences in Productivity?' in D. N. McCloskey (ed.), *Essays on a Mature Economy: Britain after 1840* (Princeton, 1971), 285–304, in which it was argued that the coalowners were rational decision makers. Lars Sandberg, 'The Entrepreneur and Technological Change' in Roderick Floud and Donald McCloskey (eds), *The Economic History of Britain since 1700: 1860 to the 1970s* (Cambridge, 1981), 116–18.

especially with American collieries where face conveyors were introduced much more rapidly. Because the age and size of pits were
crucial influences on the economics of this kind of innovative investment, the industrial structure, characterized by large numbers of small
and ageing large pits, was inimical to rapid innovation in these particular
areas. So too, in comparison with the German industry, was the scale of
investment in new, large pits, which was also related to the relatively
recent development of a large and rapidly growing home demand.

During the period after 1900, when rapidly rising German productivity eventually overtook that in Britain, UK production rose by 62m.
tons, an increase of 28 per cent, compared with 80m. tons, a 74 per cent
rise in German hard-coal output. The scope for achieving a greater proportional technological transformation in Germany at that time is
obvious. Yet, on the whole, the commercial responses of British colliery
owners and managers in a context of a buoyant world demand for coal
proved sufficiently sensitive to market conditions that neither low
physical productivity nor small size could seriously alter an industrial
structure which exhibited one of the lowest levels of concentration
throughout British industry.

Detailed examination of the records of colliery enterprises reveals
that the variability and uncertainty which characterized the mining of
coal inevitably offered coalowners and managers a range of alternative
combinations of methods and technology most suited to geological and
demand conditions. None of the inventions affecting coal-getting which
became available in the nineteenth and (except in certain districts) in the
early twentieth century were sufficiently superior in cost advantage to
alone affect dramatically the ability of non-innovating collieries to
survive. This is partly because colliery owners could vary the quality of
coal according to the state of the market, which even late in the century
involved simply controlling the size of coal by the use of forks or
riddles, or by varying production between seams, and by washing.

Where eventually geological difficulties did combine with market
competition to press seriously upon the performance of collieries, in the
thin-seam districts in Scotland and west Yorkshire, cutting machinery
and conveyors could be incorporated within the existing industrial
structure. Another disincentive for colliery owners to withdraw from
the industry was the continuous growth in the demand for coal, and the
prospect, also on historical evidence, of the prospect of a sudden rise in
prices which might, albeit briefly, retrieve high profitability. A further
consideration was the knowledge that the scrap value of mining assets

was likely to be low in the event of closure;[1] hence the persistence into the twentieth century of large numbers of miners working in collieries sunk before 1876—and many before 1866. To be set against this, however, was the investment directed increasingly into the concealed coal measures of south Yorkshire, Nottingham, Warwickshire, and Fife, where the sinking of new, large pits in effect converted the fixed resource factor into a variable one, thereby offsetting the tendency in other coalfields of diminishing returns. Even so, features peculiar to the British coalmining industry in the nineteenth century had produced a structure and organization manifestly ill-suited to rapid adjustment or reorganization but which before 1914 had witnessed a largely successful record of labour productivity, adequate, though over the long term not excessive, profitability, increasing employment, and rising real earnings for colliery workers. The First World War and its effects heralded a transformation of the industry at its peak. For the first time in more than a century, the industry was to be faced with a contracting world demand, the emergence of serious international competition, and sources of energy competing with coal to an appreciable degree.

In two respects there is a sense in which the very success of the coal-mining industry before 1914 may have exercised serious negative effects, both on a major industry and indirectly on the economy as a whole. Its more pervasive effect resulted from the rapid rise in exports, at an annual average rate of 4.6 per cent between 1873 and 1913, and exceeding 10 per cent of the value of all British exports by 1913. By strengthening Britain's balance of payments and supporting the domestic price level, coal's success helped contribute towards the failure of British manufacturers who, partly as a consequence, experienced a rise in export prices relative to those of competitors.[2]

The second, less pervasive, effect of coal's success in diminishing Britain's economic position in other sectors arose from the close connection between coal and iron and steel production. For most of the nineteenth century relatively low-cost coal was an advantage of particular importance for iron and steel producers, and despite a rise in real costs fuel prices continued marginally to benefit the British iron industry in comparison with those of America or Germany during the early twentieth century.[3] However, by the 1890s access to lower cost raw materials

---

[1] Buxton 1978, 117.

[2] Matthews, Feinstein, and Odling-Smee, *British Economic Growth* (Cambridge, 1983), 455.

[3] Robert C. Allen, 'International Competition in Iron and Steel, 1870–1914', *JEH* XXXIV (1979), 929.

by iron and steel makers in these countries combined with superior productivity resulted in a sharp decline in British exports. A careful reconstruction of comparative-cost studies in the three countries showed that cheap raw materials were available and that a handful of steel-makers along the North-east coast did build modern integrated plants after 1900 with successful results, though the number was insufficient to transform the industry's flagging performance. Simple entrepreneurial failure, adduced by Allen, is one possible explanation.[1] Another possibility lies in the exploitation of readily available alternative opportunities, for many of the major iron- and steel-making firms possessed collieries which, from the 1890s and especially from 1900, offered an immediate defence against increasing competition from low-priced German iron and steel.

Expansion of relatively profitable coalmining proved an attractive option, which while cushioning iron and steel manufacturers from the full financial consequences of effective foreign competition, at the same time weakened the stimulus to adapt their relatively high-cost steelworks. In this sense, from the wider standpoint of Britain's manufacturing position, the success of coal exports during the Edwardian period proved to have been a mixed blessing. It has also been suggested that while coal was by far the largest freight carried by railways, well above three times the volume of general merchandise by 1913, the effect of 1.4 million wagons, mostly of small capacity, was to clutter up the tracks, to slow the pace, and increase the transport costs of merchandise destined for markets at home and overseas.[2]

A comparable mixture of the beneficial and the disadvantageous is to be found also in the social effects of coal. Negative aspects of the industry's commercial success arose from the continuing freedom of colliery owners to externalize the social costs of coalmining by disfiguring the landscape and indirectly by damaging the national health. In 1842 Leifchild described the transformation of rural areas brought about by the winning of new collieries: the 'dense volumes of rolling smoke—endless clatter of endless strings of coal waggons—the funereal colour imparted to the district—are surely sufficient to untenant the seats of the wealthy'.[3] During the first three-quarters of the century the substantial proportion of coal wasted was often burnt in vast heaps at the pithead, though some of the slack and dust was dumped to form huge unsightly heaps. Where mines were in the proximity of rivers and streams these

---

[1] Ibid.
[2] P. S. Bagwell, *The Transport Revolution* (London, 1980), 114.
[3] *Children's Employment Commission* 1842, XVI, 528–9.

often became 'turgid and unsightly' as a result of refuse-coal waste dispo-sal. When small coal experienced increased demand for coking, the elimi-nation of impurities by washing led some coalowners to utilize the local waterways for this purpose. The Royal Commission on the Pollution of Rivers noted that this practice increased from the 1860s, and that in the Chesterfield district in Derbyshire 'huge volumes of black water fed into brooks, streams and rivers'.[1] Lacking an outlet to the sea, the rivers and streams of south Yorkshire and the Midlands seem to have been the worst affected, for in periods of flooding meadows became covered with coal dust. Where coal was converted to coke, especially in south Durham and in South Wales, the local populations must have found the atmos-phere insufferable, for the despoliation resulting from the carbonic acid, sulphuric acid, and nitrogen produced in the process were clearly visible; they were described in a report in 1878: '. . . the growth of trees is checked or destroyed, fences are killed, crops of every description are injured, cat-tle suffer, and wool is made almost useless'.[2]

The extent of this was limited by comparison with the far more perva-sive pollution from domestic soot, which contained a considerably higher proportion of carbon and tar than soot from factory chimneys. Both, however, damaged the health of the population, not only during the periods of particularly dense smoke fogs, which at times completely enveloped industrial and populous areas, but by steadily exacerbating heart and lung conditions. An investigation in 1920 estimated that perhaps 20 per cent less sunlight was experienced in urban industrial districts, as a result of soot and smoke fogs, compared with rural areas.[3] Health deterioration involved costs, as did the damage to buildings, both public and private, the acid soot produced by coal burning, and the cost of repairs and maintenance. Living costs were also increased by air pollu-tion. An investigation conducted by the Manchester Pollution Advisory Board in 1918 concluded that average annual household expenditure on fuel and washing material used in the removal of urban industrial soot deposit exceeded £1 per year.[4] Some attempt had been made to reduce pollution by legislation passed in 1845, but only the emission of smoke from locomotives, manufacture, and trades had been defined as a nuisance under the law; meanwhile, domestic chimneys continued to be

---

[1] *Report of Commissioners on the Pollution of Rivers* 1874, XXXIII, 15-20, 65-7.
[2] Quoted in Anthony S. Wohl, *Endangered Lives: Public Health in Victorian Britain* (London, 1983), 214.
[3] *Report of Committee on Smoke and Noxious Vapour Abatement* 1920, XXV, 255-9.
[4] Ibid.

exempt from all control. In 1904 the Inter-Departmental Committee on Physical Deterioration condemned air pollution as one of the principal contributors to the poor health of the nation.[1]

The national economic importance of this labour-intensive industry found a parallel in the central role played by the miners in British industrial and political life. Yet the long-standing popular view of miners before 1914 survives: 'Long considered plain savages, they formed, together with their large families . . . a mass of several million people, mostly living in large isolated villages, self-contained and introverted'.[2] Crouzet's description presents an image of rural mining communities which were similar in their behavioural characteristics. The development of deep mining and the process of pit village formation in remoter sections of certain coalfields meant that the phenomenon of mining communities was perpetuated in a society which was overwhelmingly urban and industrial, though how many lived in such communities and how different they were from other settlements has yet to be established.

The entire mining community certainly displayed characteristics which set them apart from other groups of workers. Coalminers were peculiarly vulnerable to violent deaths—as were other workers in mines and quarries, and fishermen (whose accident fatality rate was even higher). Within a wider perspective, however, international comparisons of death rates from accidents towards the end of the century reveals the UK to have possessed the best record among the major coal-producing countries: compared with the United States, where the rate was more than double that of the UK, Germany (80 per cent higher), and France. The American record actually deteriorated, both relatively and absolutely, while the differential between the UK and Germany and France remained similar.[3] Belgian coalmines recorded the lowest incidence of all. British coalminers' occupational mortality rate, probably underestimated before 1870, was also relatively high. Drunkenness seems to have been higher in mining counties (and seaports) than in London or the manufacturing counties,[4] though alcoholism was well below the national average as a cause of miners' deaths. After about 1870 quite a sharp decline in miners' occupational mortality brought it below the average death rate for all occupied males, the combined result of a shift in age

[1] Anthony S. Wohl, *Endangered Lives: Public Health in Victorian Britain* (London, 1983), 224.
[2] Francis Crouzet, *The Victorian Economy* (London, 1982), 270.
[3] Buxton 1978.
[4] B. Harrison, *Drink and the Victorians* (London, 1971), 315.

structure and improvements in living standards. With the single exception of respiratory diseases, from the late nineteenth century miners were
less prone to tubercular and other diseases so commonly associated with
over-work and poor living conditions. Other illnesses peculiar to coalminers, however—pneumoconiosis, nystagmus, and in certain districts
silicosis, the most deadly of all lung diseases—presented special health
problems.

Before 1870 very high levels of migration had posed a threat to self-
containment and tendencies towards introversion within mining communities. Miners were as much open to influence on their behaviour
affecting fertility, female employment, and migration, by their
location—either in a rural or semi-rural mining community or in an
urban or mixed-economy coalfield where the influences were different—as they were by purely occupational factors. In the mixed industrial towns and cities where increasing numbers of miners worked or
dwelt they experienced those influences which affected the behaviour of
other industrial workers after the mid-century: improving living standards, educational provision and health, and the growth of commercial
entertainment.

Moreover, the cultural revolution, which some consider to have been
the secular manifestation of Nonconformity, in at least some instances
seems to have proved to be a powerful antidote against 'sensuality and
extravagance', vulgarity, disrespect, and a lack of restraint, the characteristics so often associated with the miners' public image. Both on practical and political grounds miners' leaders persistently advocated a
personal code of behaviour which was in key with the values proclaimed
by employers: sobriety, thrift, rational conduct, and moderation. Life
insurance, owner occupation (though limited), and other forms of postponed consumption in favour of prudent future provision were all on
the increase from the 1860s, and by the end of our period a greater proportion of coalminers belonged to superannuation schemes than any
other occupational groups. There is no doubt that in certain respects life
in the rural pit villages often displayed characteristics which have since
defined the image of mining communities, justifying (though not to the
degree common in labour history) the description of miners by H. S.
Jevons that they were 'to a great extent a class apart from the rest of the
community',[1] but there are reasons to suppose that the image as applied
to coalminers as a whole requires considerable qualification.

[1] H. S. Jevons 1915, 2.

The behaviour, or certainly the public posture, of mining trade-union leaders who represented the aspirations and attitudes of hewers, could hardly fail to correct the caricature, at least among those middle-class observers who had been responsible for projecting the image of the degraded collier that figured in the reports of the mid-nineteenth century: in 1874 two miners became the first working men to be elected to Parliament; of the eleven successful Lib-Lab candidates in the election of 1885, six were miners. This is indicative of the dominant labourist influence among mining trade-union leaders, which was also reflected in the mainly moderate approach by the unions to industrial relations, even after 1888 when the MFGB came into existence.

Before that time the structure, organization, and policies of the ephemeral county unions were so strongly affected by local differences and by conflicting economic interests arising from the mining of different types of coal and the markets which they supplied that even regional solidarity was rarely achieved. The same was true of the coalowners, for there is no justification whatever for the statement made by a historian of industrial relations, that 'the special features of the industry, particularly its regional groupings and relatively homogeneous output, led to the growth of employers' associations that were able to fix prices as well as present a united front to miners' demands'.[1] The same variations and conflicting interests which produced differences in strength, outlook, and policy of the county unions similarly affected the coalowners, whose associations flourished when trade-union membership was buoyant, but which even then contained divisions among members who managed concerted action only when they were challenged strongly by the trade unions.

The formation of the MFGB represented a shift towards a centralization of union policy which provoked the coalowners to adopt a similar strategy, the outcome being a series of major set-piece confrontations culminating in the national strike of 1912. However, the solidarity achieved then was not characteristic of the period since the formation of the MFGB, for one of the unexpected consequences of a greater degree of central co-ordination of policy and action was the emergence of a growing division between union leaders and rank-and-file miners, explicable partly by the changing political climate but also partly by variations in geological and economic conditions and geographical dispersion, as well as the close link (with or without sliding scales) between

---

[1] Burgess 1975, 188.

coal prices and miners' wages. For these reasons, therefore, except for the major confrontations, those issues, disputes, and actions which called for local initiatives and agreements continued to dominate industrial relations. This also explains why, despite the unusually high strike propensity of the miners, the most common method of settling disputes was through conciliation and pit-level negotiations. For the same reasons, strike frequency, which even before 1888 had earned the miners a reputation for unrivalled militancy, varied markedly between regions.

Hitherto, measured by days lost, the Edwardian years have been regarded as the most strike prone, but when the total number of colliery workers in the industry is taken into account the late Victorian period emerges as one of greater militancy; South Wales especially and Scotland recording the highest strike intensity, and on a different basis, Yorkshire, too. However, while the Edwardian years appear to have been less strike prone than the preceding decade, analysis of the major strike issues indicated a change in the character of strikes after 1900. Fewer were directed towards wages and wage-related improvements; more were concerened with solidarity issues. One possible interpretation is to see this as signifying a shift by the trade unions towards more radical objectives, and on that criterion, rather than strike intensity, to have represented a more militant posture.

The relatively high incidence of days lost due to stoppages should be seen in the context of simultaneous achievements in collective bargaining, outstanding in their extent before 1913 when compared with other industries. Collective bargaining developed as a consequence of the emergence of the MFGB, whose success from 1889 in strengthening trade-union organization and membership compelled coalowners in the inland coalfields to form a counter-organization. By 1910, agreements made between these two bodies covered half of all British coalminers, whereas agreements of this kind applied to no more than one-fifth of the entire British labour force.[1] Orderly wage bargaining was the positive outcome of collective organization, but at critical times, when negotiated agreements failed, gave rise to large-scale industrial battles between coalowners and miners. Representing one in four of all trade unionists, the coalminers succeeded in translating the special importance of their industry in the economic life of the nation into political terms.

The history of industrial relations between 1888 and 1913 commands

---

[1] Benson 1982, 200.

a special place in the historiography of labour history, which has
strongly influenced contemporary and modern views of the coalminers.
The sheer growth in the number of miners coupled with a high
trade-union density was accompanied, according to Raphael Samuel
summing up a widely held view, by the acquisition of 'a common political and trade union consciousness' in a period 'when the regional peculiarities of the individual coalfields . . . lost some of their original force'.
These were the elements, Samuel suggests, which help to explain why
coalminers—uniquely—have 'lodged themselves in the historian's consciousness'.[1] That the proportion of miners belonging to trade unions
was exceptionally high is indisputable (and in paying no unemployment
benefit miners' unions were also unique outside public authority
employees),[2] but just how complete that consciousness was which
accompanied trade-union membership is at least debateable. The affiliation of the MFGB to the Labour Party in 1909 was a major landmark in
British political history; but the miners were, it must be noted, the last
of the major unions to affiliate—nine years after its formation.

As for the diminution of regional differences, there is little doubt that
they continued to exert important influences upon miners' outlook,
attitudes, and behaviour. Commenting upon the persistence of regional
contrasts and the consequent difficulty of drawing general conclusions
concerning the industry's development in the early twentieth century,
the Samuel Commission noted that, 'the only generalization about it
that is safe is that no generalization is possible'.[3] Certainly there is no
reason to believe that the regional differences between economic structure, growth rates, and productivity levels were insignificant before
1914, and while such key features may not have determined the attitudes
and behaviour of miners, it would be surprising had regions exhibiting
disparate characteristics produced a common consciousness, whether
industrial or political. There is, indeed, abundant evidence to suggest
that inter-regional differences in outlook and behaviour were to be
found between miners, and that among colliery workers within regions
the signs of disharmony actually increased during this period, as witnessed by the pit-lad strikes and rank-and-file opposition to union
leaders identified with Lib-Lab philosophy.

Measured by the extent of support for the Labour Party, by counting
the distinct votes for affiliation in 1908 and for a political fund in 1913

---

[1] Raphael Samuel 1977, 3.
[2] R. Garside, *The Measurement of Unemployment* (Oxford, 1982), 14–15.
[3] *Samuel Commission* I, 44–5.

political militancy was greatest in Lancashire, Scotland, the North-east, and Cumberland, while in South Wales and Yorkshire progress was less pronounced, and was almost non-existent in the remaining areas of Derbyshire and Nottinghamshire, Staffordshire, and Warwickshire. Probably a majority of miners were in sympathy with the Labour Party and its objectives, yet the electoral performance of Labour candidates in mining constituencies was very poor in comparison with the Liberal candidates, not only in Derbyshire and Staffordshire which in 1908 had voted decisively against affiliation, but also in Yorkshire, Scotland, South Wales, and Durham.[1]

The reality behind the image is more complex than is often supposed. It cannot be denied, however, that coal and the miners have played a critical role in British social and political history. For the growth of the industry intensified, and geographically extended, enduring divisions. This is explicable neither by miners' solidarity, which was qualified, nor by especially radical convictions, which likewise found support among only some miners. But in one important respect miners were unique; unlike workers in other staple industries, miners were concentrated in their scattered locations throughout the industrial districts and formed a sizeable occupational stratum in each of the industrial areas. In effect, not only because of its size but also because of its geographical dispersion, potentially this occupational stratum was a consolidating influence upon working-class politics, from whose ranks parliamentary leadership formed the keystone of the Labour Party's emplacements established in the North and in South Wales. Thus, whereas since 1885 the Liberal Party had depended upon votes in the mining constituencies to deliver reliable majorities, the MFGB's affiliation to the Labour Party in 1909 presaged a shift in attitudes among a new generation of mining M.P.s; by 1929 the old Liberal fortresses had become Labour's bastions.[2]

While gaining momentum, the progress towards a transformation of British party politics was slow before 1913; it was in the field of industrial relations that miners made their greatest short-term impact. The intervention of government to settle the 1893 coal strike had been a major turning-point in the history of industrial relations in Britain. Stemming from the recognition of the potentially disruptive effects upon the national economy of a lengthy stoppage, government intervention in 1893 also helped to prepare the way for the first Conciliation

[1] Henry Pelling, *Social Geography of British Elections*, 1885–1910 (London, 1967), 235–6, 272–4, 306, 319, 333, 345, 359, 361–2, 370, 435; Gregory 1968, 184–9.

[2] Gregory 1968, 191.

(Trades Disputes) Act of 1896. This major confrontation between workers and employers revealed the persistence of deep sectional cleavages within the mining population, which leads to the conclusion that the compromise settlements reached as a result of government intervention might have secured more for the miners than would have been achieved in a fight to the finish—though it is also evident that employers' solidarity was by that time also under severe strain. Yet while solidarity was both fragile and ephemeral, between coalowners as well as among miners, it is possible to identify tendencies in the inter-relations between politics and industry which were symptomatic of a growing polarization of colliery workers and employers, the effects of which precipitated government intervention. The evolution of this process in the last twenty years before 1913 was signalled by several developments: mining trade-union membership achieved a density of 81 per cent across the coalfields; initiated by the Lanarkshire miners, the drive towards nationalization became the official policy of the MFGB in 1894, and in 1906 became the policy of the Labour Group in Parliament.

Presaging the seeming inseparability of industrial relations and the politics of labour, these developments assumed a heightened importance in 1912 when, so critical was coal to the economy's fuel supply that, even at the price of serious political embarrassment, the Liberal administration was forced to concede a minimum wage for the miners in order to avoid a general strike throughout the coalfields. The wider political significance of this episode is open to two inter-pretations, not mutually exclusive, stemming from ideological and elec-toral considerations. Agreement in principle to the minimum wage violated a tenet of Victorian liberalism, while the refusal to stipulate actual wage levels antagonized the miners and other trade unions shar-ing similar aspirations. Sir Edward Grey described the episode as mark-ing the beginning of a revolution, which heralded the transference of power from the House of Commons to the trade unions.[2] Lloyd George's verdict was less apocalyptic but none the less central to British political history, for he concluded that the outcome of the strike 'sounded the death knell of the Liberal Party in its old form'.[3]

[1] E. E. Barry, *Nationalisation in British Politics* (London, 1965), Chapt. 4.

[2] Peter Rowland, *The Last Liberal Governments, Unfinished Business 1911-14* (London, 1972), 154 fn.

[3] Lord Riddell, *More Pages from My Diary*, 1908-14 (London, 1934), 42-9; Peter Rowland, *Lloyd George* (London, 1975), 261; idem, *The Last Liberal Governments, Unfinished Business, 1911-14* (London, 1972), 148-54.

The fulcrum of Britain's economic pre-eminence throughout the nineteenth century, coal had reached a climax in British economic history, and the miners, who in numbers were at the peak of the long-term peacetime trend, were effectively organized to exert maximum industrial pressure. They were also on the verge of establishing a substantial parliamentary representation. The political divisions beginning to emerge out of the geographical position of the major coalfields, roughly north of a line between the Severn and the Wash, were reinforced by socio-economic divisions which later generations were to describe by the metaphor 'north and south'. Behind this image of implied contrasts in occupational characteristics, incomes, education, and social and political life, was the historic reality of the effects of coal in Victorian and Edwardian Britain. Where coal was the prime force behind the growth of employment, especially in certain areas which typified the 'North' (especially Durham, Northumberland, Central Scotland, Fife—but also Glamorgan and Monmouth), markedly inferior levels of service employment existed; beyond employment effects through income and expenditure, these districts also possessed a poor record in creating other forms of employment.[1] Even in areas not dominated by coal but where coalmining generated a sizeable proportion of employment none the less—Lancashire, the West Riding of Yorkshire, and Tayside—the service to population ratio was below the national average throughout the nineteenth century.

Major coalmining districts were vulnerable to any deterioration in the health of heavy industry, especially in Tayside, Tyneside, and South Wales, or to any weakening of the international predominance of British coal. The social and political ramifications of the great Victorian and Edwardian boom in coal production had as the sequel the events of 1925–6 and 1972–4, which were to demonstrate that the crumbling foundations of coal's pre-eminence had not yet diminished the historic role of the industry and its workers. The origins of the seeming inseparability between the industry, mining trade unions, and politics are to be found in the years between 1888 and 1912, when the growing political strength of the miners underlined the imperative for governments to begin to adopt an attitude, if not a policy, towards coal and towards the miners.

[1] C. H. Lee, 'Regional Growth and Structural Change in Victorian Britain', *EHR* 2nd ser. XXXIV (1981), 447–8.

Bibliography

A. *Manuscript sources*

The manuscript collections used in this study are listed below under the archives in which they are housed. Reference numbers for collections, where these have been allotted, are cited before the name of the collection.

University of Birmingham Archives
    Cannock Chase Colliery Company papers
British Library of Political and Economic Science (LSE), London
    Webb Collection
British Steel East Midland Region Records Centre, Irthlingborough
    Stanton and Staveley papers
British Steel Northern Regional Records Centre
    Bell Brothers papers
    Bolckow Vaughn papers
Brotherton Library, University of Leeds
    Henry Briggs Son and Co. papers
    West Yorkshire Coalowners' Association papers
County Library of South Glamorgan (Cardiff)
Clay Cross Company Ltd.
    Records
Companies Registration Office
    BT 31/   Returns to the Registrar of Joint Stock Companies, dissolved and undissolved
City of Coventry Record Office
    Wyken Colliery records
Library of the Department of Employment
    Rates of wages and hours of labour in various industries in the UK, 1850–1905
Derbyshire Record Office, Matlock
    NCB/503   Butterley Company records
Dudley Archives and Local History Department, Central Library
    Dudley Estate archive
Durham Record Office, Durham
    NCB First Deposit: NCB/1/JB Papers of John Buddle
                      NCB/1/SC Stella Coal Company papers
                      NCB/1/TH Thomas Young Hall papers
    D/Lo   Londonderry manuscripts
    NCB/I/Co   Durham Coal Owners' Association papers

NCB/I/Co   Statistical returns
University of Durham, Department of Paleography
  Local Necrology
Glamorgan Record Office
  D/DMC   The Main Colliery Company Ltd. papers
  D/DG   Dowlais Iron Company papers
University of Glasgow Archives
  UGD 161 Scottish Coalowners Association papers
Guildhall Library, London
  Records of the Coal Factors' Society
Lambton Estate Archives, Lambton Castle, County Durham
  Lambton Estate papers
Lancashire Record Office, Preston
  NCBw   Bridgewater Collieries papers
  DDX   Wigan Coal and Iron Company papers
               Clifton and Kearsley
               South West Lancashire Coalowners' Association records
Leeds City Archives Department
  MC   Middleton Colliery manuscripts
  NCB/A1   Henry Briggs Son and Co. records
Manchester Public Library Archives
  Bradford Colliery Company papers
Midland Bank
  Records of Managers' Interviews
National Library of Scotland, Edinburgh
  13300   Minto papers
               Register of Companies, active files
National Library of Wales, Aberystwyth
  South Wales Coalowners' Association records
Newton Chambers and Co. Ltd., Thorncliffe
  Records
North of England Institute of Mining and Mechanical Engineers, Newcastle-upon-Tyne
  Bell collection
  Bradford Collection
  Buddle Collection
  Buddle Atkinson Collection
  Forster Collection
  Johnson Collection
  Miscellaneous Deposits
  Weeks Collection
Northumberland Record Office, Newcastle-upon-Tyne
  725   Armstrong manuscripts

MBE   Benwell Manor manuscripts
                     Delavel manuscripts
NCB C1   Northumberland Coal Owners' Association
NCB/AS/ZMD   Ashington Coal Company and Colliery
NCB/BR   Broomhill Colliery Company
1439   Wallsend and Hepburn Coal Company
Miscellaneous Colliery Company records
1442   Northumberland and Durham Coalowners' Association, letters and accounts
1735   Coal Trade Reports and printed records
263   Joint Northumberland and Durham Coal Owners' Association
ZAN   Society of Antiquaries manuscripts

Nottinghamshire Record Office, Nottingham
NCB1   New Hucknall Colliery Company Ltd. papers
NCB   Wollaton Colliery Company Ltd. papers
NCB   Clifton Colliery, miscellaneous papers

University of Nottingham Archives
DrE   Drury Lowe MSS

Powell Duffryn Ltd., Stanhope Gate, London
Records

Public Record Office, London
BT 31/   The Register of Dissolved Companies

Rotherham Reference Library
Wath Main Collieries Company Ltd. papers

Scottish Record Office, Edinburgh
GD/224 Buccleuch MSS
CB2   Lochgelly Iron and Coal Company papers
CB3   Fife Coal Company Papers
CB4   William Baird and Co. papers
CB8   Lanarkshire Coalmasters' Association papers
CB24   Alloa Coal Company papers
GD40   Newbattle Colliery
                   Lothian MSS
BT 2/   The Register of Defunct Companies

Sheffield Central Library
NCB   United Steel Companies Ltd. papers
NCB   Mitchell Main Colliery Company Ltd. papers
NCB   Wharncliffe Silkstone Colliery Company papers
TR   Thorncliffe records
                   Newton Chambers and Company records
CR   Clarke records
                   Local Studies Department Collection

MD   South Yorkshire Coal Owners' Assurance Society papers
Somerset Record Office, Taunton
DD   Waldegrave MSS
Staffordshire County Record Office, Stafford
NCB D876   Hamstead Colliery Company papers
NCB D876   Walsall Wood Colliery Company papers
Wakefield Metropolitan District Library
John Goodchild loan manuscripts
Warwickshire County Record Office, Warwick
CR   Griff Colliery Company Ltd. papers
Wigan Record Office
D/D Lei   Leigh papers

B. *Contemporary printed material*

ASHLEY, W. J., *The Adjustment of Wages: A Study in the Coal and Iron Industries of Great Britain and America* (1903).

BAILES, W., *The Student's Guide to the Principles of Coal and Metal Mining* (Sunderland, 1879).

BAINBRIDGE, W., *A Practical Treatise on the Law of Mines and Minerals* (1841).

BIDDER, G. P., 'The Profits of Coal Pits', *The Nineteenth Century* 35 (1894).

BOWLEY, A. L., *Wages in the United Kingdom in the Nineteenth Century* (Cambridge, 1900).

BOYD, R. N., *Coal Mines Inspection: Its History and Results* (London, 1879).

BOYD, R. N., *Coal Pits and Pitmen: A Short History of the Coal Trade and the Legislation affecting it* (1892).

BREMNER, D., *The Industries of Scotland* (1869).

BROWN, T. F., 'On the South Wales Coalfield', *TSWIE* IX (1874-5).

BROWN, T. F. and ADAMS, G. F., 'Deep Winning of Coal in South Wales', *PICE* LXIV (1881) 75-91.

BULMAN, H. F., *The Cost of Producing Coal* (Newcastle, 1883).

BULMAN, H. F., 'Longwall Working . . .', *JBMS* X (1887-8).

BULMAN, H. F., 'The Cost of Producing Coal', *CG* XCLX (1910).

BULMAN, H. F., *Coal Mining and the Coal Miner* (1920).

BULMAN, H. F. and REDMAYNE, R. A. S., *Colliery Working and Management* (1896, 2nd ed. 1906).

BUNNING, T. W., *An Account of the Duties of Coal* (Newcastle, 1883).

COLLIERY GUARDIAN, *Digest of Evidence given before the Royal Commission on Coal Supplies* Vols. I–III (reprinted from the *Colliery Guardian* after revision by the witnesses, 1905).

COLLIERY MANAGER'S POCKET BOOK (1870 etc).

COLLIERY YEARBOOK AND TRADES DIRECTORY FOR 1927 (1923-64).

COURTNEY, L. H., 'Jevon's Coal Question Thirty Years After', *JRSS* 40 (1897).

COWAN, D., 'On the Valuation of Ironworks, Mines, etc.', *Transactions of the Mining Institute of Scotland* V (1883-4).

DALZIEL, W. G., *Records of the several Coal Owners' Associations in Monmouthshire and South Wales 1866 to 1895* (Cardiff, 1895).

DICKINSON, J., 'Statistics of the Collieries of Lancashire, Cheshire and North Wales', *Memoirs of the Literary and Philosophical Society of Manchester* XII (1853-4), 71-107.

DIGEST OF EVIDENCE, see COLLIERY GUARDIAN.

DONOHUE, O., 'The Valuation of Mineral Properties', *TFIME* XXXII (1906-7).

DUNN, M., *An Historical Geological and Descriptive View of the Coal Trade of the North of England ... Appended a Concise Notice of the Peculiarities of Certain Coal Fields in Great Britain and Ireland ...* (Newcastle, 1844).

DUNN, M., *A Treatise on the Winning and Working of Collieries* (Newcastle 1852).

FORDYCE, W., *A History of Coal and Coke, Coal Fields, Progress of Coal Mining ... Iron, its Ores and Processes of Manufacture* (London, 1860).

FOWLER, G., *Papers on the Theory and Practice of Coal Mining* (1870).

FOX-ALLIN, F., 'Mechanized Coal Cutting and Conveying: A Brief History of Early Developments in this Country', *Iron and Coal Trades Review* 159 (1949).

FYNES, R., *The Miners of Northumberland and Durham* (Sunderland, 1873).

GALLOWAY, R. L., *A History of Coal Mining in Great Britain* (1882).

GALLOWAY, R. L., *Annals of Coal Mining and the Coal Trade* 2 Vols. (1898).

GARFORTH, W. E., 'The Application of Coal-cutting Machines to Deep Mining', *TFIME* XXIII (1901-2).

GIBSON, Finlay, A. (ed.), *A Compilation of Statistics ... of the Coal Mining Industry of the United Kingdom and varous coalfields, and the Principal Foreign Countries of the World* (Cardiff, 1922).

GREEN, W., 'The Chronicles and Records of the Northern Coal Trade in the Counties of Durham and Northumberland', *TNEIME* XV (1865-6).

GREENWELL, G. C., *A Treatise on Mine Engineering* (1855, repr. 1869).

GREENWELL, G. C., *The Autobiography of George Clementson Greenwell* (1899).

HALL, T. Y., 'The extnet and probable duration of the Northern Coalfield; with remarks on the coal trade in Northumberland and Durham', *TNEIME* II (1853) 103-230.

HALL, T. Y., 'An abstract of the alphabet list of pits in Mr T. Y. Hall's Paper ...', *TNEIME* III (1854-5) Appendix.

HALL, T. Y., 'On the Rivers, Ports and Harbours of the Great Northern Coalfield', *TNEIME* X (1861) 41-89.

HEDLEY, J., *A Practical Treatise on the Working and Ventilation of Coalmines* (London and Wigan, 1851).

HEDLEY, T. F., 'On the Longwall System', *PSWIE* III (1861) 148-72.

HODGES, I., 'Increase of Working Costs in Coal Mines during the past Half Century, the Rate of Increase, and the Causes thereof', *TFIME* 40 (1910-11).

HOLLAND, J., *The History and Description of Fossil Fuel, the Collieries and Coal Trade of Great Britain* (1835, new impression 1968).

HOOKER, R. H., 'On the Relation between Wages and the Numbers Employed in the Coal Mining Industry', *JRSS* 57 (1894) 627–42.

HOOPER, W. E., *The London Coal Exchange: A Historical Survey with Sundry Engravings and Portraits* (1907).

HUGHES, H. W., *A Textbook of Coal Mining* (1904).

HULL, E., *The Coal-Fields of Great Britain: Their History, Structure, and Duration: With Notices of the Coal-fields of other Parts of the World* (1861).

HULL, E., *Our Coal Resources at the Close of the Nineteenth Century* (1897).

HUNT, R. (ed.), *Mineral Statistics of the United Kingdom of Great Britain and Ireland* (1854–82).

HYSLOP, J., *Colliery Management* (Wishaw, 1870).

JEVONS, H. S., *Foreign Trade in Coal* (1909).

JEVONS, W. S., *The Coal Question* (1865).

JOHNSON, H., 'South Staffordshire Coalfield: Method of Working, Ventilation, Extent and duration of coalfield', in TIMMINS, S. (ed.), *Birmingham and the Midland Hardware District* (1866).

JOHNSTON, J., *The Economy of a Coalfield* (1838).

JONES, J. H., 'The Present Position of the British Coal Trade', *JRSS* XCIII (1930) 1–63.

KERR, G. L., *Practical Coal Mining: A Manual for Managers, Under Managers, Colliery Engineers, and Others* (1904).

KIRKUP, J. P., 'Notes on the Housing of Miners', *Proceedings of the National Association of Colliery Managers* 2nd ser. III (1906) 284–7.

KNOWLES, J., 'The Coal Trade', *Transactions of the Manchester Geological Society* (1888).

LAIRD, W., *The Export Coal Trade of Liverpool: A Letter to Thomas Littledale, Chairman of the Liverpool Dock Trust* (1850).

LEIFCHILD, J. R., *Our Coal at Home and Abroad: With Relation to Consumption Cost, Demand and Supply... being Three Articles Contributed to the Edinburgh Review* (London, 1837).

LEIFCHILD, J. R., *Our Coal and Our Coal Pits: The People in them and the Scenes around them, by a Traveller Underground* (1854).

LUDLOW, J. M., 'An Account of the West Yorkshire Coal Strike and Lockout of 1858', *Trade Societies and Strikes* (1860) 11–51.

MACFARLANE, JAMES, 'Denaby Main: A South Yorkshire Mining Village', *BSLH* 25 (1972), 82–100.

MANN, J. and JUDD, C. A., *Colliery Accounts* (1909).

MEADE, R., *The Coal and Iron Industries of the United Kingdom Comprising a Description of the Coalfields... Occurrence of Iron Ores... History of Pig Iron Manufacture etc.* (1882).

MERIVALE, J. H., *Notes and Formulae for Mining Students* (3rd end., 1890).

MERIVALE, J. H., 'The Profits of Coalmining', in REDMAYNE 1903.

MILLER, A., *The Rise and Progress of Coatbridge* (Glasgow, 1864).

MINING ASSOCIATION OF GREAT BRITAIN, *Historical Review of Coal Mining* (1928).

MORRAH, D., 'A Historical Outline of Coal Mining Legislation' in *Historical Review of Coal Mining*, 301-20.

NATIONAL ASSOCIATION OF COLLIERY MANAGERS, *Transactions*.

PAMELY, C., *The Colliery Manager's Handbook: A Comprehensive Treatise on the Laying Out and Working of Collieries* (1904).

PARKINSON, G., *True Stories of Durham Pit Life* (1912).

PERCY, C. M., *The Mechanical Equipment of Collieries* (Manchester, 1905).

POTTER, E., 'On Murton Winning in the County of Durham', *TNEIME* 5 (1857).

REDMAYNE, R. A. S. (ed.), *The Colliery Manager's Pocket Book* (1903).

REDMAYNE, R. A. S., *Modern Practice in Mining*, 5 Vols. (1914).

RICHARDSON, T. and WALLBANK, J. A., *Profits and Wages in the British Coal Trade (1898-1910)* (Newcastle, 1911).

REGISTRAR GENERAL, *Annual Reports on Births, Deaths and Marriages*.

REPORT OF THE TAILROPE COMMITTEE, *TNEIME* XVIII (1967-8) 1-177.

SIMPSON, J. B., *Capital and Labour in Coal Mining* (Newcastle-upon-Tyne, 1900).

SKINNER, T., *The Stock Exchange Year-book*, 1876-1913.

SKINNER, T., *The Directory of Directors*, 1888-1913.

SILLIE, R., *My Life For Labour* (1924).

SMITH, A., *The 'Allowance' Coal Question* (Dudley, 1875).

SMITH, T., *The Miner's Guide, being a Description and Illustration of a Chart of Sections of the Principal Mines of Coal and Ironstone in the Counties of Stafford, Salop, Warwick and Durham* (1836).

SMYTH, W. W., *A Rudimentary Treatise on Coal and Coal Mining* (1900).

SOPWITH, A., 'Depreciation of Colliery Plant', *TSSEWIME* 9 (1883) 135-46, 156-62.

SORLEY, W. R., *Mining Royalties and their Effect on the Iron and Coal Trades: Report of an Inquiry made by the Toynbee Trustees* (1889).

STAMP, J. C., *British Incomes and Property: The Application of Official Statistics to Economic Problems* (1916).

STAMP, J. C., 'The Effect of Trade Fluctuation upon Profits', *JRSS* LXXXI (1918).

STEAVENSON, A. L., 'The Manufacture of Coke in the Newcastle and Durham Districts', *TNEIME* VIII (1859-60) 109-35 and *TNEIME* IX (1860-1) 35-57.

TAYLOR, T. J., *Observations, Addressed to the Coal Owners of Northumberland and Durham, on the Coal Trade of those Counties, more Especially with Regard to the Cause of Sand Remedy for its Present Depressed Condition* (Newcastle-upon-Tyne, 1846).

THOMAS, D. A., *Some Notes on the Present State of the Coal Trade in the United Kingdom* (Cardiff, 1896).

TRANSACTIONS AND RESULTS OF THE NATIONAL ASSOCIATION OF COAL, LIME, AND IRON-STONE MINERS OF GREAT BRITAIN, 1863.

TRURAN, W., *The Iron Manufacture of Great Britain Theoretically and Practically Considered* (1855).

WALKER, G. B., 'Coal Getting by Machinery', *TFIME* I (1889–90) 123–37.

WALKER, S. F., *Coal Cutting by Machinery in the United Kingdom* (1902).

WALKER, S. F., *Electricity in mining* (1907).

WEBB, S. and B., *The History of Trade Unionism* (1920).

WELTON, T. A., *England's Recent Progress* (1911).

WIGAN COAL AND IRON COMPANY LTD., *Historical, Statistical and General Particulars of the Company, and and Illustrated Handbook of Products* (Altrincham, 1908).

WILKINS, C., *The South Wales Coal Trade and its Allied Industries from the Earliest Days to the Present Time* (Cardiff, 1888).

WILLIAMS, R. P., 'The Coal Question', *JRSS* LII (1899) 1–46.

WILSON, T., *The Pitmen's Pay* (Gateshead, 1843).

WOOD, G. H., 'Real Wages and the Standard of Comfort since 1850', *JRSS* LXII (1909).

WOOD, N., 'On the Conveyance of Coals Underground in Pits', *TNEIME* V (1855) 239–318.

C. *Parliamentary papers*

Report of Select Committee (House of Lords) on the State of the Coal Trade, 1830 (9) VIII. 405.

Report of Select Committee on Accidents in Mines, 1835 (603) V. 1.

Report of Select Committee on State of the Coal Trade, 1836 (522) XI. 169.

Children's Employment Commission, 1842 (38) XV. 1; 1842 (381) XVI. 1; 1842 (382) XVII. 1.

Report of the Commissioners (Mr Tancred) on the Condition of the Mining Population of South Staffordshire Coalfield, 1843 (508) XIII. 1.

Report of Commissioners under Act 5 and 6 Vict C.98 to Inquire into the Operation of that Act and into the State of the Population in Mining Districts, 1844 (592) XVI. 1; 1845 (67) XXVII. 197; 1846 (737) XXIV. 383; 1847 (844) XVI. 401; 1848 (993) XXVI. 233; 1849 (1109) XXII. 395; 1850 (1248) XXIII. 571; 1851 (1406) XXSIII. 447; 1852 (1525) XXI. 425.

Report from Select Committee (House of Lords) on Dangerous Accidents in Coal Mines, 1849 (613) VII. 1.

Report from Select Committee on the Causes and Frequency of Explosions in Coal Mines, 1852 (509) V. 1.

Reports from the Select Committee on the Causes of the Numerous Accidents in Coal

Mines and the Best Means for their Prevention, 1852–3 (691) XX. 2, (740) XX. 179, (820) XX. 279.

Reports of the Select Committee on the Causes of the Numerous Accidents in Coal Mines and the Best Means for their Prevention, 1854 (169) IX. 1, (258) IX. 63, (277) IX. 219, (325) ibid.

Report of the Select Committee on the Bank Acts and Commercial Distress, 1857–8 V.

Report from the Select Committee on the Operation of the Act for the Regulation and Inspection of Mines, 1865 (398) XII. 605; 1867(496) XIII. 1, (496–1) XIII. 107.

Report of the Royal Commission on Trade Unions (1867–8) XXXIX. 1.

Report on the Truck Commission Act, 1871 C. 326 XXXVI. 1, C. 327 XXXVI. 281; 1872 C. 555–1 XXXV. 301.

Report of the Commissioners Appointed to Inquire into the Several Matters Relating to Coal in the United Kingdom, 1871, C. 435 XVIII. 1, 435–1 XVIII. 199, 435–2 XVIII. 815.

Copies of a Report, with Tabular Statements... 1872 LIV., no. 151.

Report from the Select Committee on the Present Dearness and Scarcity of Coal, 1873 (313) X. 1.

Reports of the Royal Commission on Accidents (from Explosions and other Causes) in Mines, 1881 C. 3036 XXVI. 1; 1886 C. 4699 XVI. 411.

Return Showing the Average Number of Hours and Days Daily and Weekly Worked ... 1890 (215) LXVIII.

Return Showing the Annual Average Prices of the Best Coals ... *in the Port of London*, 1886 (201) LX.

Report of the Royal Commission on the Depression of Trade and Industry, 1886 C. 4621 XXDI. 231, C. 4767 XXIII.

Return Showing the Annual Average Price per Ton ... *of the Best Coals* ... *in the Port of London*, 1890 (83) LXVIII.

Reports of the Royal Commission on Mining Royalties, 1890 C. 6195 XXII. 553; 1891 C. 653 XXIV. 583, C. 6529 XXIV. 817; 1893 C. 6979 XII. 1, C. 6980 XLI. 341.

Return of Rates of Wages in Mines and Quarries in the United Kingdom, 1890–1 LXXVIII. 569.

Reports to the Board of Trade on the Relation of Wages in Certain Industries to the Cost of Production, 1890–1 (1051) LXXVIII.

Reports of the Royal Commission Appointed to Inquire into the Subject of the Coal Resources of the United Kingdom, 1903 Cd. 1724 XVI. 1, Cd. 1725 XVI. 9, Cd. 1726 XVI. 381; 1905 Cd. 2353 XVI. 1, Cd. 2354 XVI. 45, Cd. 2355 XVI. 77, Cd. 2356 XVI. 101, Cd. 2357 XVI. 109, Cd. 2358 XVI. 119, Cd. 2359 XVI. 139, Cd. 2361 XVI. 171, Cd. 2362 XVI. 237, Cd. 2363 XVI. 659, Cd. 2364 XVI. 797.

Report of the Royal Commission on Labour, 1892 XXXIV. 313. II, XXXVI. 5. 111; 1893–4 XXXII. 5.

Tables Showing ... *the Quantity of Coal Produced and the Number and Average*

Wages of Coal Miners in the Years 1901 and 1902 Respectively etc., 1903 LXI. 783.

Report of the Departmental Committee on the Use of Electricity in Mines, 1904 Cd. 1916 XXIV. 1, Cd. 1917 XXIV. 31.

Report of the Departmental Committee Appointed to Inquire into the Probable Economic Effect of a Limit of Eight Hours to the Working Day of Coal Miners, 1907 Cd. 3426 XIV. 525, Cd. 3427 XIV. 529, Cd. 3428 XV. 1, Cd. 3505 XV. 261, Cd. 3506 XV. 349, Cd. 3495 XXXIV. 1045, Cd. 3496 XXXIV. 1075; 1908 Cd. 4386 XXXV. 1, Cd. 4387 XXXV. 7.

Report of the Royal Commission on Mines, 1907 Cd. 3548 XIV. 1; 1909 Cd. 4820 XXXIV. 599; 1911 Cd. 5561 XXXVI. 465; 1907 Cd. 3549 XIV. 65; 1908 Cd. 3873 XX. 1, Cd. 4349 XX. 425; 1909 Cd. 4667 XXXIV. 1; 1911 Cd. 5642 XXXVI. 487.

Report of the Departmental Committee on the Truck Acts, 1908 Cd. 442 LIX. 1; Cd. 4443 LIX. 147, Cd. 4444 LIX. 533; 1909 Cd. 4568 XLIX. 177.

Report of the Royal Commission on . . . the Causes and Means of Preventing Accidents . . . 1909 Cd. 4821 XXXIV. 1111.

Final Report of the First Census of Industrial Production, 1912–13 Cd. 6320 CIX. 1.

Report of the Departmental Committee on Conditions Prevailing in the Coal Mining Industry Due to the War, 1914–16 Cd. 7939 XXVIII. 1.

Report of the Coal Conservation Committee Sub-committee of the Ministry on Reconstruction and Electric Power in Great Britain, 1917–18 Cd. 8880 XII. 385, Cd. 9084 VII. 615.

Report of the Royal Commission on the Housing of the Industrial Population of Scotland, Rural and Urban, 1917–18 Cd. 8731 XIV. 345.

Report of the Acquisition and Valuation of Land Committee of the Ministry of Reconstruction, 1919 Cmd. 156 XXIX. 51.

Reports of the Royal Commission on the Coal Industry (Sankey Commission), 1919 Cmd. 156 XXIX. 51, Cmd. 84 XI. 263, Cmd. 85 XI. 277, Cmd. 876 XI. 297, Cmd. 210 XI. 305, Cmd. 359 XI. 373, Cmd. 360 XII. 1, Cmd. 361 XIII. 1.

Report of the Royal Commission on the Coal Industry (1925, Samuel), 1926 Cmd. 2600 XIV. 1; Vol II and III 1926 Mines Department, Board of Trade (non-parliamentary).

Annual Reports (on Mining Districts) to the Commissioner under 526 Vict., C. 99 (1842) 1844–59.

Annual Reports of Inspectors, 1851–1913.

Annual Reports of the Commissioners of . . . Inland Revenue (for years ending 5 April), 1843–1913.

Annual Returns of the Names, Objects, Places where Business is, or was, Conducted and Date of Registration of all Joint Stock Companies (limited), 1862–1919.

Mineral Statistics, 1882–1913.

D. *Theses*

BROOKS, E., 'Regional Functions of the Mineral Transport System in the south Wales Coalfield 1830–1851' (Cambridge University Ph.D. 1958).

BROWN, A. J. Youngson, 'The Scots Coal Industry 1854–1886' (Aberdeen University D.Litt. 1952–3).

BUNKER, R. C., 'Some Aspectsof Population Growth and Structure in the Warwickshire Coalfield since 1800' (Birmingham University MA 1952).

BYATT, I., 'The British Electrical Industry, 1875–1914' (Oxford University D.Phil. 1979).

BYRES, T. J., 'The Scottish Economy During the Great Depression 1873–1896, with Special Reference to the Heavy Industries of the South-West' (Glasgow University B.Litt. 1962).

CALVERT, R. H. B., 'An Examination of Education and Training in the Coal Mining Industry from 1840–1947, with Special Reference to the Work and Influence of the Mines Inspectorate' (Nottingham University M.Phil. 1970).

CASSELL, A. J.,'Her Majesty's Inspectors of Mines, 1848–1862' (Southampton University M.Sc. (Econ) 1962).

CHEETHAM, J. O., 'The History, Conditions and Prospects of the South Wales Coalfield, Considered Mainly from the Point of View of Markets and Industrial Organization' (Wales University MA 1921).

CORRINS, R. D., 'William Baird and Company, Coal and Iron Masters, 1830–1914' (Strathclyde University Ph.D. 1974).

CROMAR, P., 'Economic Power and Organisation: the Development of the Coal Industry of Tyneside, 1700–1828' (Cambridge University Ph.D. 1977).

DAVIES, J., 'Glamorgan and the Bute Estates, 1776–1947' (Wales University Ph.D. 1969).

DAVIES, P., 'Syndicalism in the Yorkshire Coalfields, 1910–1914' (Bradford University M.Sc. 1977).

DAVIES, J. F., 'The Forest of Dean and Bristol and Somerset Coalfields: A Comparative Study in Industrial Geography During the Nineteenth and Twentieth Centuries' (London University Ph.D. 1959).

DUFFY, A. E. F., 'The Growth of Trade Unions in England from 1867–1906' (London University Ph.D. 1956).

DUGGETT, M. J., 'A Comparative Study of the Operation of the Sliding Scale in the Durham and South Wales Coalfields' (Wales University Ph.D. 1977).

EEVISON, J., 'The Opening up of the "Central" Region of the South Yorkshire Coalfield and the Development of its Townships as Colliery Communities, 1875–1905' (Leeds University M.Phil. 1972).

FEREDAY, R. P., 'The Career of Richard Smith (1733–1868) Managers of Lord Dudley's Mines and Ironworks' (Keele University M.A. 1966).

FLIGHT, A. T., 'Legislation Relating to Mining in the 19th Century (1840–1876)' (London University Ph.D. 1937).

GILLAN, D. J., 'The Effect of Industrial Legislation on the Social and

Educational Condition of Children Employed in Coal Mines between 1840 and 1876, with Special Reference to Durham' (Durham University M.Ed. 1968).

GILLET, M., 'Le Bassin Houiller du Nord et du Pas-de-Calaid de 1815 à 1914: étude economique et sociale' (L'Universite de Paris IV, 1971).

GORDON, A., 'The Economic and Social Development of Ashington: A Study of a Coal Mining Community' (Newcastle University M.Com. 1954).

GRANT, E. J., 'The Spatial Development of the Warwickshire Coalfield' (Birmingham University Ph.D. 1977).

GREGORY, I., 'The East Shropshire Coalfield. The Great Depression 1873–96: The Effects of Depression' (Keele University MS 1978).

GRIFFIN, A. R., 'The Development of Industrial Relations in the Nottinghamshire Coalfield' (Nottingham University Ph.D. 1963).

GRIFFIN, C. P., 'The Economic and Social Development of the Leicestershire and South Derbyshire Coalfield 1550–1914', 3 Vols. (Nottingham University Ph.D. 1969).

GRIFFITHS, T. H., 'The Development of the South Wales Anthracite Coal Area, with Special Reference to its Industrial and Labour Organisations' (Wales University MA 1922).

HAIR, P. E. H., 'The Social History of the British Coal Miners, 1800–45' (Oxford University D.Phil. 1955).

HALL, A. A., 'Working Class Living Standards in Middlesbrough and Teeside 1870 to 1914' (Teeside Polytechnic PhD 1979).

HALL, V. G., 'The English Coal Mining Community, 1890 to 1914' (North Carolina University MA 1978).

HASSAN, J. A., 'The Development of the Coal Industry in Mid and West Lothian 1815–1873' (Strathclyde University Ph.D. 1976).

HEWITT, F. S., 'The Papers of John Buddle, Colliery Viewer in the Mining Institute, Newcastle-upon-Tyne: An Annotated List and Assessment of their Value to the Economic Historian' (Durham University MA 1961).

HISKEY, C. E., 'John Buddle 1773–1843, Agent and Entrepreneur in the Northeast Coal Trade' (Durham University M.Litt. 1978).

HOLBROOK-JONES, M. R., 'Work, Industrialization and Politics: 1850–1914 (Durham University Ph.D. 1979).

HOPKINSON, G. G., 'The Development of Lead Mining and of the Coal and Iron Industries in North Derbyshire and South Yorkshire 1700–1850' (Sheffield University Ph.D. 1958).

JOHN, D. G., 'An Economic and Historical Survey of the Development of the Anthracite Industry with Special Reference to the Swansea Valley' (Wales University MA 1923).

JOHNSON, W., 'The Development of the Kent Coalfield 1896–1946' (Kent University Ph.D. 1973).

JOHNSON, W. H., 'A North-east Miners' Union (Hepburn's Union) of 1831–2' (Durham University MA 1959).

JONES, M., 'Changes in Industry, Population and Settlement on the Exposed Coalfield of South Yorkshire, 1840–1908' (Nottingham University MA 1967).

KANEFSKY, J. W., 'The Diffusion of Power Technology in British Industry 1760–1870' (Exeter University Ph.D. 1979).

KENWOOD, A. G., 'Capital Investment in Northeastern England, 1800–1913' (LSE Ph.D. 1962–3).

McEWAN, A. M., 'The Shotts Iron Company 1800–1850' (Strathclyde University M.Sc. 1972).

MARSHALL, C. R., 'Levels of Industrial Militancy and the Political Radicalization of the Durham miners, 1885–1914' (Durham University MA 1977).

MEE, L. G., 'The Earls Fitzwilliam and the Management of the Collieries and other Industrial Enterprises on the Wentworth Estate, 1795–1857' (Nottingham Ph.D. 1973).

METCALFE, G. H., 'A History of the Durham Miners' Association, 1869–1915' (Durham University MS 1947).

MITCHELL, B. R., 'The Economic Development of the Inland Coalfields, 1870–1914' (Cambridge University Ph.D. 1955–6).

MOUNTFORD, C. E., 'The History of Johnd Bowes and Partners up to 1914' (Durham University MA 1967).

MUI, Hoh-Cheung, 'The Emergence of the Nationalisation Issue in the Coalmining Industry of Great Britain 1898–1919' (Columbia University Ph.D. 1950).

NEVILLE, R. G., The Yorkshire Miners 1881–1926: A Study in Labour and Social History' 2 Vols. (Leeds University Ph.D. 1974).

PAULL, C. A., 'Mechanisation in British and American Bituminous Coal Mines 1890–1939' (London University M.Phil. 1968).

PEDEN, J. A., 'The History of Kirkless Ironworks' (C. F. Mott Technical College 1965).

PETHERICK, F. R., 'The Movement for the Abolition of Child Labour in the Mines of England' (Boston University Ph.D. 1954).

RAYBOULD, T. J., 'The Dudley Estate: Its Rise and Decline between 1774 and 1947' (Kent University Ph.D. 1970).

RIMLINGER, G. V., 'Labor Protest in British, American and German Coal Mining Prior to 1914' (California University, Berkeley Ph.D. 1957).

SCOTT, H., 'The History of the Miners' Bond in Northumberland and Durham: With Special Reference to its Influence on Industrial Disputes' (Manchester University MA 1946).

SEELEY, J. Y. E., 'Coal Mining Villages of Northumberland and Durham: A Study of Sanitary Conditions and Social Facilities 1870–80' (Newcastle University MA 1974).

SLAVEN, A. G., 'Coal Mining in the West of Scotland in the Nineteenth Century: The Dixon Enterprises' (Glasgow University B.Litt. 1967).

SLIFER, W. L., 'The British Coal Miners and the Government, 1840–1860' (Pennsylvania University Ph.D. 1931).

SMITH, G. P., 'Social Control and Industrial Relations at the Dowlais Iron Company c.1850–1890' (University of Wales (Aberystwyth) M.Sc. 1982).

SPAVEN, P., 'The Historical Micro-comparative Study of Some Mining Communities in South Yorkshire, 1851–80' (Warwick University Ph.D. 1978).

STEPHENS, F. J., 'The Barnes of Ashgate: A Study of a Family of the Lesser Gentry in North-east Derbyshire' (Nottingham University M.Phil. 1980).

TAYLOR, E., 'The Working Class Movement in the Black Country 1867–1914' (Keele University Ph.D. 1974).

TELFORD, S. J., 'Ownership, Technology and Patterns of Coalmining Activity in Northumberland 1600–1850' (London University Ph.D. 1978).

VAMPLEW, W., 'Railways and the Transformation of the Scottish Economy' (Edinburgh University Ph.D. 1969).

WALTER, M. A., 'The Coal Miner this Century: Social and Economic Relationships in the Light of the Changing Labour Process' (Keele University MA 1981).

WEBSTER, F., 'Durham Miners and Unionism 1831–1916: a Sociological Interpretation' (Durham University MA 1973).

WEETCH, K. T., 'The Dowlais Ironworks and its Industrial Community 1760–1850' (London University M.Sc. 1963).

WILLIAMS, L. J., 'The Monmouthshire and South Wales Coal Owners' Association 1873–1914' (Wales University MA 1957).

WILSON, A. S., 'The Consett Iron Company Ltd: A Case Study in Victorian Business History' (Durham University M.Phil. 1973).

WILSON, G. M., 'The Miners of the West of Scotland and their Trade Unions, 1842–74' (Glasgow University Ph.D. 1977).

WOOD, O., 'The Development of the Coal, Iron and Shipbuilding Industries of West Cumberland' (London University Ph.D. 1952).

E. *Secondary printed works*

ALLEN, R. C., 'International Competition in Iron and Steel 1850–1913', *JEH* XXXIX (1979) 911–37.

ANDERSON, D., 'Blundell's Collieries: The Progress of the Business', *THSLandC* 116 (1965) 69–116.

ANDERSON, D., 'Blundell's Collieries: Wages, Disputes and Conditions of Work', *THSLandC* 117 (1966) 109–43.

ANDERSON, D., 'Blundell's Collieries: Technical Developments, 1766–1966', *THSLandC* 119 (1967).

ARNOT, R. P., *The Miners 1881–1910: A History of the Miners' Federation of Great Britain* (1949).

ARNOT, R. P., *The Miners: Years of Struggle from 1910 Onwards* (1953).

ARNOT, R. P., *A History of the Scottish Miners from the Earliest Times* (1955).

ATKINSON, F., *The Great Northern Coalfield 1700-1900* (Barnard Castle, 1966).

BAKER, D., *Coalville, the First Seventy-five Years, 1833-1908* (Anstey, 1983).

BARNSBY, G. J., 'Standards of Living in the Black Country during the Nineteenth Century', *EHR* 24 (2) (1971) 220–39.

BARNSBY, G. J., *The Working Class Movement in the Black Country 1750-1867* (Wolverhampton, 1977).

BARNSBY, G. J., *Social Conditions in the Black Country 1800-1900* (Walsall, 1980).

BELLAMY, J. M. and S. J. (eds.), *Dictionary of Labour Biography*, Vols. I, II, III, and IV (1972–7).

BENNY, M., *Charity Main: A Coalfield Chronicle* (1946).

BENSON, J., 'The Motives of 19th Century English Colliery Owners in Promoting Day Schools', *JEAH* 8 (1970) 15–18.

BENSON, J., 'Colliery Disaster Funds, 1860–1897', *IRSH* 19 (1) (1974) 73–85.

BENSON, J., 'English Coal-miners' Trade Union Accident Funds, 1850–1900' *EHR* 3 (1975) 401–12.

BENSON, J., 'The Thrift of English Coal-Miners, 1860–95', *EHR* 31 (3) (1978) 410–18.

BENSON, J., *British Coalminers in the Nineteenth Century: A Social History* (1980).

BENSON, J., 'Coalminings', in C. Wrigley (ed.), A History of British Industrial Relations 1875–1914 (1982).

BENSON, J. and NEVILLE, R. G. (eds.), *Studies in the Yorkshire Coal Industry* (Manchester, 1976).

BENSON, J., NEVILLE, R. G., and THOMPSON, C. H., *Bibliography of the British Coal Industry* (1981).

BENWELL COMMUNITY PROJECT, Final Report Series No. 6, *The Making of a Ruling Class* (Newcastle-upon-Tyne, 1979).

BIENFIELD, M. A., *Working Hours in British Industry: An Economic History* (1972).

BIRKS, J. A. and COXON, P., *An Account of Railway Development in the Nottinghamshire Coalfield* (Mansfield, 1950).

BROWN, A. J. Youngson, 'Trade Union Policy in the Scots Coalfield 1855–1885', *EHR* 6 (1953) 35–50.

BROWN, E. O. Forster, 'The History of Boring and Sinking', in Mining Association of Great Britain, *Historical Review of Coal Mining* (c.1924).

BULMER, M. I. A., 'Sociological Models of the Mining Community', *Sociological Review* 23 (1) (1975) 61–92.

BURGESS, K., *The Origins of British Industrial Relations* (1975).

BURT, T., *Thomas Burt, Pitman and Privy Councillor: An Autobiography* (1924).

BUXTON, N. K., *The Economic Development of the British Coal Industry* (1978).

BYATT, I., *The British Electrical Industry, 1875-1914: The Economic Problems of a New Technology* (Oxford, 1979).

CAIN, P. J., 'Traders Versus Railways: The Genesis of the Railway and Canal Traffic Act of 1894', *JTH* 8 (1973).

CAIRNCROSS, A. K., *Home and Foreign Investment* (Cambridge, 1953).

CAMPBELL, A. B., 'Honourable Men and Degraded Slaves: A Comparative Study of Trade Unionism in two Lanarkshire Mining Communites, *c.* 1830–1874' in Harrison 1978.

CAMPBELL, A. B., *The Lanarkshire Miners' A Social History of their Trade Unions, 1775-1874* (Edinburgh, 1979).

CAMPBELL, A. B. and REID, F., 'The Independent Collier in Scotland' in HARRISON 1978, 54–74.

CARVELL, J. L., *One Hundred Years in Coal: The History of the Alloa Coal Company* (Edinburgh, 1944).

CALLINOR, R. and RIPLEY, B., *The Miners' Association: A Trade Union in the Age of the Chartists* (1968).

CHALLINOR, R., *The Lancashire and Cheshire Miners* (Newcastle, 1972).

CHAPMAN, W. R. and MOTT, R. A., *The Cleaning of Coal* (1928).

CHAPLIN, S., 'Durham Mining Villages', in University of Durham Department of Sociology and Social Administration, *Working Papers in Sociology* No. 3, reprinted in M. Bulmer (ed.), *Mining and Social Change: Durham County in the Twentieth Century* (1977) 59–82.

CHAPMAN, S. D., *Stanton and Staveley: A Business History* (1981).

CHURCH, R. A., 'Profit Sharing and Labour Relations in England in the 19th Century', *IRSH* 16 (1971) 2–10.

CLAY CROSS COMPANY LTD., *A Hundred Years of Enterprise: Centenary of the Clay Cross Company Limited, 1837-1937* (Derby, 1937).

CLEGG, H. A., FOX, A., and THOMPSON, A. F., *A History of British Trade Unions Since 1889*, Vol. I (Oxford, 1964).

COATES, B. E., 'The Geography of the Industrialization and Urbanization of South Yorkshire, 18th Century to 20th Century', in S. Pollard and C. Holmes (eds.), *Essays in the Economic and Social History of South Yorkshire* (Barnsley, 1976) 14–27.

COLLS, R., '"Oh Happy English Children": Coal, Class and Education in the North-east', *PP* 73 (1976) 75–99.

COLLS, R., *The Collier's Rant: Song and Culture in the Industrial Village* (1977).

COTTRELL, P. L., *Industrial Finance 1830-1914* (1980).

CUNNINGHAM, A. S., *The Fife Coal Company Limited: The Jubilee Year 1872-1922 (Leven, 1954).*

DAUNTON, M. J., *Coal Metropolis, Cardiff, 1870-1914* (Leicester, 1977).

DAUNTON, M. J., 'Miners' Houses: South Wales and the Great Northern Coalfield, 1880–1914', *IRSH* XXV (1980).

DAUNTON, M. J., 'Down the Pit: Work in the Great Northern and South Wales Coalfields, 1870–1916', *EHR* 2nd ser. XXXIV (1981).

DAVIES, J., *Cardiff and the Marquesses of Bute* (Cardiff, 1981).

DOUGLASS, D., 'Pit Life in County Durham' (Oxford, Ruskin College), reprinted in R. Samuel (ed.), *Miners, Quarrymen and Saltworkers* (1977).

Down, C. G. and Warrington, A. J., *The History of the Somerset Coalfield* (Newton Abbott, 1971).

Dron, R. W., *The Economics of Coal Mining* (1928).

Edelstein, M., *Overseas Investment in the Age of High Imperialism: The United Kingdom 1850-1914* (New York, 1982).

Edwards, J. R., 'British Capital Accounting Practices and Business Finance 1852-1919: An Exemplification', *Accounting and Business Research* X (1980) 241-58.

Edwards, J. R. and Baber, C., 'The Dowlais Iron Company: Accounting Policies and Procedures for Profit Measurement and Reporting Purposes', *Accounting and Business Research* 9(1979) 139-51.

Edwards, N., *The South Wales Miners*

Feinstein, C. H., *National Income Expenditure and Output of the United Kingdom 1855-1965* (Cambridge, 1972).

Feinstein, C. H., 'Capital Formation in Great Britain', in Peter Mathias and M. M. Postan (eds.), *The Cambridge Economic History of Europe*, Vol. VIII (Cambridge, 1978).

Fine, B., *Landed Property and the British Coal Industry Prior to World War I*, Birkbeck College Discussion Paper No. 120, June 1982.

Fisher, C., 'The Little Buttymen in the Forest of Dean, 1870-86', *IRSH* XXV (1980) 53-76.

Fisher, C. and Smethurst, J., 'War on the Law of Supply and Demand: The Amalgamated Association of Miners and the Forest of Dean Colliers, 1869-75', in Harrison 1978, 114-55.

Fisher, C. and Smethurst, J., 'Alexander MacDonald and the Crisis of the Independent Collier, 1872-1874', in Harrison 1978, 156-78.

Fisher, C. and Spaven, P., 'Edward Rymer and the Moral Workman', in Harrison 1978, 232-71.

Fletcher, M., 'From Coal to Oil in British Shipping', *JTH1 3 (1975)* 1-19.

Flett, J. S., *First Hundred Years of the Geological Survey of Great Britain* (1937).

Flinn, M. W., *The History of the British Coal Industry, Vol. 1 1700-1830: The Industrial Revolution* (Oxford, 1984).

Fraser-Stephen, E., *Two Centuries in the London Coal Trade: The Story of Charringtons* (1952).

Friedlander, D., 'Demographic Patterns and Socioeconomic Characteristics of the Coal-mining Population in England and Wales in the 19th Century', *EDCC* 22 (1) (1973) 39-51.

Garside, W. R., 'Wage Determination and the 1892 Miners' Lockout', in *Essays in Tyneside labour history* (Newcastle, 1977).

Gayer, A. D., Rostow, W. W., and Schwartz, A. J., *The Growth and Fluctuations of the British Economy 1790-1850*, 2 Vols. (Oxford, 1953).

Gibson, F. A., *Coal Mining Industry of the United Kingdom ... and the Principal Foreign Countries* (1928).

GOODCHILD, J., *The Industrial and Social Development of South Yorkshire* (Doncaster, 1969).

GOODCHILD, J., 'Some Early Yorkshire Coal Masters' Associations', *South Yorkshire Journal of Economic and Social History* 2 (6) (1970) 5–7.

GOODCHILD, J., 'Some Notes on the Early History of Denaby Main Colliery', *South Yorkshire Journal of Economic and Social History* 4 (1973) 1–6.

GOODCHILD, J., *The Coal Kings of Yorkshire* (Wakefield, 1978).

GREASLEY, D., 'The Diffusion of Machine Cutting in the British Coal Industry, 1902–1938', *EEH* 19 (1982) 246–68.

GREEN, H., 'The Nottinghamshire and Derbyshire Coalfield before 1850', *Journal of the Derbyshire Archaeological and Natural History Society*, new ser. 9 (1935).

GREGORY, R., *The Miners and British Politics, 1906-14* (Oxford, 1968).

GRIFFIN, A. R., *Mining in the East Midlands, 1550-1947* (1971).

GRIFFIN, A. R., *The British Coalmining Industry, Retrospect and Prospect* (1977).

GRIFFIN, A. R. and GRIFFIN, C. P., 'The Role of Coal Owners' Associations in the East Midlands in the Nineteenth Century', *RMS* XVI (1972) 95–104.

GRIFFIN, A. R. and GRIFFIN, C. P., 'The Role of Coal Owners' Associations in the East Midlands in the Nineteenth Century', *RMS* 17 (1973) 95–121.

GRIFFIN, C. P., 'Three Generations of Miners' Housing at Moira, Leicestershire 1811–1934', *IAR* 1 (3) (1977) 276–82.

GRIFFIN, C. P., 'Technological Change in the Leicestershire and South Derbyshire Coalfield before 1850', IAR III (1) (1978).

GRIFFIN, C. P., 'Robert Harrison and the Barber Walker Co.: A Study in Colliery Management 1850-90', *TTS* LXXXII (1979).

GRIFFIN, C.P., 'Colliery Owners and Trade Unionism: The Case of South Derbyshire in the Mid-nineteenth Century', *MH* VI (1981).

GRIFFIN, C. P., *The Leicestershire and South Derbyshire Miners* Vol. I, 1840–1914 (Coalville, 1982).

HAINES, M. R., 'Fertility, Nuptiality and Occupation: A Study of British Midnineteenth Century Coal Mining Populations', *JIH* 8 (2) (1977) 245–80.

HAIR, P. E. H., 'Mortality from Violence in British Coalmines, 1800-50', *EHR* 21 (3) (1968) 545–61.

HALL, A. A., 'Wages, Earnings and Real Earnings in Teeside: A Reassessment of the Ameliorist Interpretation of Living Standards in Britain, 1870–1914', *IRSH* XXVI (1981) 202–19.

HANN, E. M., *Brief History of the Powell Duffryn Steamcoal Co., 1864-1921* (1922).

HARDY, S., 'The Development of Coal Mining in a North Derbyshire Village, 1635–1860', *UBHJ* 5 (1955–6).

HARRISON, R. (ed.), *Independent Collier: The Coal Miner as Archetypal Proletarian Reconsidered* (Hassocks, 1978).

HASSAN, J. A., 'The Supply of Coal to Edinburgh, 1790–1850', *TH* 5 (1972).

HASSAN, J. A., 'The Gas Market and the Coal Industry in the Lothians in the Nineteenth Century', *IA* 12 (1977).

HASSAN, J. A., 'The Landed Estate Paternalism and the Coal Industry in Mid-lothian, 1880–80' *SHR* 59 (1980).

HAUSMANN, W. J. and HIRSCH, B. T., 'Wages, Leisure and Productivity in the South Wales Coal Industry, 1874–1914: An Economic Approach', *Llafur* 3 (1982).

HAWKE, G. R., *Railways and Economic Growth in England and Wales, 1840-1870* (Oxford, 1970).

HEESOM, A. J., 'The Third Marquis of Londonderry as an Employer', *Bulletin of the North East Group for the Study of Labour History* (1972).

HEESOM, A. J., 'Entrepreneurial Paternalism: The Third Lord Londonderry (1778–1854) and the Coal Trade', *DUJ* 66 (3) (1974) 238–56.

HEESOM, A. J., 'The Northern Coalowners and the Opposition to the Coal Mines Act of 1842', *IRSH* XXV (1980) 236–71.

HEESOM, A. J., 'The Coal Mines Act of 1842: Social Reform, and Social Control', *HJ* 24 (1981) 69–88.

HILTON, G. W., *The Truck System* (Cambridge, 1960).

HINSLEY, F. B., 'The Development of Coal Mine Ventilation in Great Britain up to the End of the 19th Century', *TNS* 42 (1969–70) 25–39.

HINSLEY, F. B., 'The Development of Mechanical Ventilation in Collieries in the 19th Century', *University of Nottingham Mining Dept.* 21 (1969) 68–77.

HIRSCH, B. T. and HAUSMAN, W. J., 'Labour Productivity in the British and South Wales Coal Industry, 1870–1914', *Economica* 50 (1983) 145–57.

HISKEY, C. E., 'The Third Marquess of Londonderry and the Regulation of the Coal Trade: The Case Re-opened', *DUJ* LXXV (1983) 1–9.

HUNT, E. H., *Regional Wage Variations in Great Britain 1850-1914* (Oxford, 1973).

HYDE, C. K., 'The Adoption of the Hot Blast by the British Iron Industry: a Re-interpretation', *EEH* X (1972–3) 281–93.

JOHN, A. H., *The Industrial Development of South Wales* (Cardiff, 1950).

JOHN, A. V., *By the Sweat of their Brow: Women Workers at Victorian Coal Mines* (1980).

JONES, P. N., *Colliery Settlement in the South Wales Coalfield 1850-1926* (Hull, 1969: Hull University Occasional Papers in Geography No. 14).

JEVONS, H. S., *Foreign Trade in Coal* (1909).

JEVONS, H. S., *The British Coal Trade* (1915).

JONES, P. N., 'Workmen's Trains in the South Wales Coalfield 1870–1926', *TH* 3 (1) (1970) 21–35.

JOYCE, P., *Work, Society and Politics* (1980).

KANEFSKY, John W., 'Motive Power in British Industry and the Accuracy of the 1870 Factory Return', *EHR* 2nd series XXXII (1979), 360–75.

KENWOOD, A. G., 'Capital Investment in Docks, Harbours and River Improvement in North Eastern England 1825–50', *JTH* new ser. I (1971–2).

KIRBY, M. W., *The British Coalmining Industry 1870-1946* (1977).

KNOWLES, K. G. J. C., *Strikes: A Study in Industrial Conflict: With Special Reference to British Experience between 1911 and 1947* (Oxford, 1952).

LAMBERT, W. R., 'Drink and Work-discipline in Industrial South Wales, c.1800–1870', *Welsh History Review* 7 (3) (1975) 289–306.

LARGE, D., 'The Third Marquess of Londonderry and the End of the Regulation 1844–45', *DUJ* 51 (1) (1958) 1–9.

LEE, W. A., 'The Historyof Organisation in the Coal Industry' in Mining Association of Great Britain, *Historical Review of the Mining Industry* (c.1924).

LEWIS, E. D., 'Pioneers of the South Wales Coal Trade: Walter Coffin and George Insole', in Stewart Williams, *Glamorgan Historian* Vol. II (Barry, 1975).

McCLOSKEY, D., 'International Differences in Productivity? Coal and Steel in America and Britain before World War I' in D. McCloskey (ed.), *Essays on a Mature Economy: Britain after 1840* (Princeton, 1971).

McCORMICK, B. and WILLIAMS, J. E., 'The Miners and the Eight Hour Day 1863–1910', *EHR* XII (1959) 222–38.

McCORMICK, B. J., *Industrial Relations in the Coal Industry* (1979).

McCUTCHEON, J. E., *Troubled Seams: The Story of a Pit and its People etc.* (Seeham, 1955).

McCUTCHEON, J. E., *A Wearside Mining Story* (Seaham, 1960).

MACDONAGH, O. G. M., 'Coal Mines Regulation: The First Decade, 1842–1852' in Robson, R. (ed.), *Essays in honour of George Kitson Clark* (1967).

MACFARLANE, J., 'One Association—The Yorkshire Miners' Association: The Denaby Lockout of 1885', in Pollard, S. and Homes, C. (eds.), *Essays in the Economic and Social History of South Yorkshire* (Barnsley, 1976).

MACHIN, F., *The Yorkshire Miners: A History* (Barnsley, 1958).

MATHER, F. C., *After the Canal Duke: A Study of the Industrial Estates Administered by the Trustees of the Third Duke of Bridgewater in the Age of Railway Building* (Oxford, 1970).

MEE, G., *Aristocratic Enterprise: The Fitzwilliam Industrial Undertakings, 1795–1857* (Glasgow, 1975).

MEE, G., 'Employer: Employee Relationships in the Industrial Revolution: The Fitzwilliam Collieries', in Pollard, S. and Holmes, C. (eds.), *Essays in the Economic and Social History of South Yorkshire* (Barnsley, 1976).

MEIKLEJOHN, A., 'History of Lung Diseases of Coalminers in Great Britain: Part I, 1800–1875', *British Journal of Industrial Medicine* 8 (3) (1951) 127–37.

MEIKELJOHN, A., 'History of Lung Diseases of Coalminers in Great Britain: Part II, 1875–1920', *British Journal of Industrial Medicine* 9 (2) (1952) 93–8.

MELLING, J., 'Employers, Industrial Housing, and the Evolution of Company Welfare Policies in Britain's Heavy Industry: West Scotland, 1870–1920', *IRSH* XXVI (1981).

METCALF, B. L., 'A Century of Engineering Progress in British Coal Mines (1851–1951)', *Proceedings of the Joint Engineering Conference 1951 Arranged by the Institute of Civil Engineers, the Institute of Mechanical Engineers and the Institution of Electrical Engineers*.

MINING ASSOCIATION OF GREAT BRITAIN, *Historical Review of Coal Mining* (*c.*1924).

MITCHELL, B. R. and DEANE, P., *Abstract of British Historical Statistics* (Cambridge, 1962).

MOORE, R. S., *Pitmen, Preachers and Politics* (1974).

MORRIS, J. H. and WILLIAMS, L. J., 'The Discharge Note in the South Wales Coal Industry 1841–1898', *EHR* XI (1958) 286–93.

MORRIS, J. H. and WILLIAMS, L. J., 'The South Wales Sliding Scale 1876–79: An Experiment in Industrial Relations', *Manchester School and Social Studies* 28 (1960) 161–76; reprinted in Minchinton, W. E. (ed.), *Industrial South Wales 1750-1914: Essays in Welsh Economic History* (London, 1969).

MOTT, R. A. and GREENFIELD, G. J. (eds.), *The History of Coke Making and of the Coke Oven Managers' Association* (Cambridge, 1936).

MOTTRAM, R. H. and COOTE, C., *Through Five Generations, the History of the Butterley Company* (1950).

MUIR, A., *The Fife Coal Company Limited: A Short History* (Leven, 1952).

OWEN, Sir D. J., *The Ports of the United Kingdom* (1939).

OWEN, J. A., *The History of the Dowlais Ironworks 1759-1970* (Gwent, 1977).

PALLISTER, R., 'Educational Investment by Industrialists in the Early Part of the 19th Century in County Durham', *DUJ* 61 (1) (1968) 32–8.

PALMER, S., 'The British Coal Export Trade, 1850–1913', in Alexander, D. (ed.), *Voyages and Trade Routes in the North Atlantic* (Newfoundland, 1970).

PAMELY, C., *The Colliery Manager's Handbook* (5th edn., 1904).

PENCAVEL, J. H., 'The Distribution and Efficiency Effects of Trade Unions in Britain', *BJIR* 15 (2) (1977) 137–56.

PHELPS-BROWN, E. H., *The Growth of British Industrial Relations* (1959).

PHELPS-BROWN, E. H. and BROWNE, M., *A Century of Pay* (1968).

PHILLIPS, E., *A History of the Pioneers of the Welsh Coalfield* (Cardiff, 1925).

POLLARD, S., 'Trade Unions and the Labour Market 1870–1914', *YBESR* 17 (1965).

POLLARD, S., 'Labour in Great Britain', in Mathias, P. and Postan, M. M. (eds.), *The Cambridge Economic History of Europe* Vol. VII (Cambridge, 1978).

POLLARD, S., 'A New Estimate of British Coal Production, 1750–1850', *EHR* 2nd ser. XXXIII (1980).

PORTER, J. H., 'Wage Bargaining under Conciliation Agreements 1860–1914', *EHR* 23 (3) (1970) 460–75.

PORTER, J. H., 'Wage Determination by Selling Price Sliding Scales 1870–1914', *Manchester School of Economic and Social Studies* 39 (1) (1971) 13–21.

PORTER, J. H., 'Coal Miners and Conciliation', *BSSLH* 26 (1973) 27–8.

RICHARDS, E., 'The Industrial Face of a Great Estate: Trentham and Lilleshall, 1780–1860', *EHR* 2nd ser. 27 (1974).

RICHARDS, J. H. and LEWIS, J. P., 'House Building in the South Wales Coalfield 1851–1913', *Manchester School of Economics and Social Studies* 24 (3) (1956)

289–300, reprinted in Minchinton, W. E. (ed.), *Industrial South Wales 1750-1914: Essays in Welsh Economic History* (1969).

RICHARDSON, J. W. and BASS, J. M., 'The Profitability of the Consett Iron Company before 1914', *BH* VII (1965) 71–93.

RIDEN, P. J., 'The Output of the British Iron Industry before 1850', *EHR* 2nd ser. XXX (1977) 442–59.

RIDEN, P. J., 'The Iron Industry' in Church 1980, 63–87.

RIMMER, W. G., 'Middleton Colliery near Leeds, 1779–1830', *YBESR* VII (1955).

RODERICK, G. W. and STEPHENS, M. D., 'Mining Education 1850–1914', *Irish Journal of Education* 6 (1972).

ROGERS, E., 'The History of Trade Unionism in the Coalmining Industry of North Wales to 1914', *Denbighshire Historical Society Transactions* 12 (1963).

ROSEN, G., *The History of Miners' Diseases: A Medical and Social Interpretation* (New York, 1943).

ROSSINGTON, T. O., *The story of Treeton Colliery 1875-1975* (Rotherham, 1976).

ROWE, D. J., 'The Economy of the North-east in the Nineteenth Century: A Survey with a Bibliography of Works Published since 1945', *NH* VI (1971).

ROWE, J. W. F., *Wages in the Coal Industry* (1923).

SAMUELS, RAPHAEL, *Miners, Quarrymen, and Saltworkers* (London, 1977).

SANDERSON, M., *The Universities and British Industry 1850-1970* (1972).

SAVILLE, J., 'Some Notes on Ideology and the Miners before World War I', *BSSLH* 23 (1971) 25–7.

SCOTT, H., 'The Miners' Bond in Northumberland and Durham', *Proceedings of the Society of Antiquaries of Newcastle upon Tyne* 11 (2) (1947) 55–78, and (3) 87–98.

SLAVEN, A. G., 'Earnings and Productivity in the Scottish Coal-mining Industry during the Nineteenth Century: The Dixon Enterprises', in Payne, P. L. (ed.), *Studies in Scottish Business History* (1967).

SMAILES, A. E., 'Population Change in the Colliery Districts of Northumberland and Durham', *Geographical Journal* XCL (1938).

SMITH, R. A., *Sea Coal for London: History of the Coal Factors in the London Market* (1961).

SPAVEN, P. 'Main Gates of Protest: Contrast in Rank and File Activity among the South Yorkshire Miners, 1858–1894', in Harrison 1978, 201–31.

SPRING, D., 'The Earls of Durham and the Great Northern Coalfield, 1830–80', *Canadian Historical Review* XXXIII (1952).

SPRING, D., 'Agents to the Earl of Durham in the Nineteenth Century', *DUIJ* LIV (1962).

SPRING, D., 'English Landowners and Nineteenth Century Industrialism', in Ward, J. T. and Wilson, R. G. (eds.), *Land and Industry* (Newton Abbott, 1971).

STORM-CLARK, C., 'The Miners 1870–1970: A Test Case for Oral History', *Victorian Studies* 15 (1) (1971) 49–74.

STURGESS, R. W., 'Land Ownership, Mining and Urban Development in Nine-teenth Century Staffordshire', in Ward, J. T. and Wilson, R. G. (eds.), *Land and Industry (Newton Abbott, 1971)*.

STURGESS, R. W., *Aristocrat in Business: The Third Marquis of Londonderry as Coalowner and Port Builder* (Durham, 1975).

SWEEZEY, P. M., *Monopoly and Competition in the English Coal Trade, 1550-1850* (Cambridge, Mass., 1938).

TAYLOR, A. J., 'Combination in the Mid-nineteenth Century Coal Industry', *Transactions of the Royal Historical Society* 3 (1953) 232–39.

TAYLOR, A. J., 'The Miners' Association of Great Britain and Ireland 1842–48: A Study in the Problem of Integration', *Economica* 22 (1955) 45–60.

TAYLOR, A. J., 'The Wigan Coalfield in 1851', *THSLandC* 106 (1955) 117–26.

TAYLOR, A. J., 'The Third Marquis of Londonderry and the North Eastern Coal Trade', *DUJ* 48 (1) (1955) 21–7.

TAYLOR, A. J., 'The Sub-contract system in the British Coal Industry', in Press-nell, L. S. (ed.), *Studies in the Industrial Revolution Presented to T. S. Ashton* (London, 1960).

TAYLOR, A. J., 'Labour Productivity and Technological Innovation in the British Coal Industry, 1850–1914', *EHR* (1961–2) 48–70.

TAYLOR, A. J., 'Coal' in Greenslade, M. W. and Jenkins, J. G. (eds.), *Victoria County History of Stafford* Vol. 2 (Oxford, 1967).

TAYLOR, A. J., 'The Coal Industry', in Church (ed.), *The Dynamics of Victorian Business: Problems and Perspectives* (1980).

THOMAS, B., 'The migration of labour into the Glamorganshire Coalfield 1861–1911', *Economica* 10 (1930) 275–94, reprinted in Minchinton, W. E. (ed.), *Industrial South Wales, 1750-1914: Essays in Welsh Economic History* (1969).

THOMAS, D. A. 'The Growth and Direction of Our Foreign Trade in Coal during the last Half Century', *JRSS* 66 (1903) 439–522.

TUNZELMANN, G. N. von, *Steam Power and British Industrialization to 1860* (Oxford, 1978).

VICTORIA COUNTY HISTORIES OF CUMBERLAND, DERBYSHIRE, DURHAM, GLOUCESTERSHIRE, LANCASHIRE, LEICESTERSHIRE, SOMERSET, STAFFORD-SHIRE, WARWICKSHIRE, AND WORCESTERSHIRE.

WALTERS, R., 'Labour Productivity in the South Wales Steam-coal Industry, 1870–1914', *EHR* XXVIII (1975) 280–303.

WALTERS, R., *The Economic and Business History of the South Wales Steam Coal Industry* (New York, 1977).

WALTERS, R., 'Capital Formation in the South Wales Coal Industry, 1840–1914', *Welsh History Review* X (1980) 69–92.

WARD, J. T., 'West Riding Landowners and Mining in the Nineteenth Century', *YBESR*, 15 (1963) 61–74.

WARD, J. T., 'Landowners and Mining', in Ward, J. T. and Wilson, R. G. (eds), *Land and Industry* (Newton Abbott, 1971).

WARD, J. T., 'Some West Cumberland Landowners and Industry', *IA* 9 (1972) 341–62.

WELBOURNE, E., *The Miners' Unions of Northumberland and Durham* (Cambridge, 1923).

WILLIAMS, J. E., *The Derbyshire Miners: A Study in Industrial and Social History* (1962).

WILLIAMS, J. E., 'Militancy among the British Coalminers, 1890–1914', *BSSLH*, 13 (1966) 16.

WILLIAMS, J. E., 'The Miners' Lockout of 1893', *BSSLH* 24 (1972) 13–16.

WILLIAMS, L. J., 'The Coalowners of South Wales 1873–80: Problems of Unity', *Welsh Historical Review* 8 (1) (1976) 75–93.

WILLIAMS, L. J., 'The Coalowners' inSmith, D. (ed.), *A People and a Proletariat: Essays in the History of Wales 1780-1980* (1980).

WILLIAMSON, W., *Class, Community and Culture* (1982).

WOODS, D. C., 'The Operation of the Master and Servant Act in the Black Country, 1858–1875', *MH* 7 (1982) 93–115.

Index